THE ESSENTIAL WISDEN

THE ESSENTIAL WISDEN

An Anthology of 150 Years
of Wisden Cricketers' Almanack

Edited by
John Stern and Marcus Williams

BLOOMSBURY
LONDON · NEW DELHI · NEW YORK · SYDNEY

To Peter and Norman, whose paternal influence
inspired a love of cricket and yellow-covered books

First published in Great Britain 2013

Copyright © 2013 by John Wisden and Co

No part of this book may be used or reproduced in any manner whatsoever without written
permission from the publisher except in the case of brief quotations embodied in critical
articles or reviews

John Wisden and Co
An imprint of Bloomsbury Publishing Plc
50 Bedford Square
London
WC1B 3DP

www.wisden.com

Bloomsbury Publishing, London, New Delhi, New York and Sydney

A CIP catalogue record for this book is available from the British Library

ISBN 978 1 4081 7896 6

10 9 8 7 6 5 4 3 2 1

Typeset by Saxon Graphics Ltd, Derby
Printed and bound in Great Britain by CPI Group (UK) Ltd, Croydon CR0 4YY

Contents

LITTLE WONDERS (150, numbered and chronologically distributed throughout the book)

List of Illustrations

To the Reader

In offering our first edition of the CRICKETER'S ALMANACK to the patrons of the "Noble Game," we have taken great pains to collect a certain amount of information, which we trust will prove interesting to all those that take pleasure in this glorious pastime. Should the present work meet with but moderate success, it is intended next year to present our readers with a variety of other matches, which the confined nature of an Almanack precludes us from doing this year.

JOHN WISDEN & Co., 1864

From the 1993 Preface (Matthew Engel)

The most revered tradition of *Wisden* is its accuracy and I feel as bound to uphold that as if on oath. Inevitably, a volume of this size, produced under pressure, must contain some mistakes. All one can say is that the effort put into eliminating errors is as exhaustive (and exhausting) as the combination of the fallible human brain and the even more fallible computer can achieve.

There are other traditions that are just as sacred: *Wisden*'s continuity and its independence from cricket's ruling bodies so that it remains free to comment robustly on the issues the game faces. Whoever temporarily carries the torch has to maintain these.

x

Foreword

The Reduced Shakespeare Company are an American acting troupe who have been condensing literary and theatrical great works since 1981. One of their productions, in 1995, was entitled *The Bible: The Complete Word of God (abridged)*. Comedy, as well as brevity, is their stock in trade, and while *The Essential Wisden* is ploughing a more serious furrow – albeit with a sprinkling of light-heartedness – there have been many occasions during the book's lengthy construction when a sense of humour has been the best assistant in undertaking the monumental project of producing what might be termed *The Bible of Cricket (abridged)* in a single volume. *Wisden Cricketers' Almanack* has been mined before, but we hope to have unearthed a few gems previously untouched.

In its 150 years *Wisden* has published 133,491 pages. We have been able to extract less than one per cent of that content. Lack of space is, it seems, a perennial thorn in *Wisden*'s side. The report in the 1881 edition of the first Test match to be held in England begins: "The compiler much regrets that the limited space allotted to the Australians' matches in this book precludes the possibility of giving a lengthened account of this famous contest." As the game has expanded its horizons so has *Wisden*, and trying to keep the book's girth from reaching W. G. Grace-like proportions has been a major, oft-expressed headache for every editor.

The title of this book reflects that what we have produced is the essence of *Wisden*, the edited – and abridged – highlights of an annual which has moved from modest beginnings to become the foremost sporting publication of its type, filled with comment and good writing to accompany its primary task of recording the major cricketing happenings of the preceding year and the game's primary records. The founder declared coyly in 1864: "We of course make no comments upon the matches ... since a great many of our readers are at least equal, if not superior, to ourselves in arriving at a right judgment." In fact, *Wisden*'s readers have for many years since turned to it for informed opinion and for almost every cricket researcher it is the initial point of reference.

The first 112-page edition contained, alongside some cricket, information on the modern tea-table, the nobility of England, a list of Derby and other Classic race winners, the rules of bowls, and the dates of the Crusades. As one small sign of how far it has come in the meantime, its most recent 1,584-page incarnation – after 150 years of continuous publication, outlasting its many Victorian rivals and surviving German bombs in the Second World War – has an article by an England wicket-keeper coming out as gay, and another headlined "Headscarved heroines" about the female cricketers of Afghanistan. The breadth and depth of *Wisden* is breathtaking.

All cricket life is between its pages, as is plenty that has only a tangential relationship with the summer game. A look at the Obituaries section is testament to that.

Our book makes no claim to be a history of cricket. It would be impossible to do that even if we had the space to attempt it. Heretical though it might be to say, *Wisden*, for all its rigour, has omissions, inaccuracies and prejudices. These are easier to observe with hindsight, of course. For example, the first two Australia v England matches in 1877, subsequently acknowledged as the first Test matches, were unreported. Incidents of major significance, in or around a match, were sometimes ignored altogether or referred to with frustrating euphemism; as a result, our selection – or omission – of some material has been influenced by the lack of quality of the original reports or articles.

While *Wisden* might seem to the casual observer to represent an old guard, it is anything but. It has always had strong opinions and has used them to present an alternative future, rather than retrench a conservative position. In 1997, two years after making the initial proposal, Matthew Engel established the Wisden World Championship, which he believed "offers the chance to ignite interest in Test matches even among non-cricketers" and "could secure the future of the traditional game". It was the precursor to the ICC's Test rankings that are an accepted part of the five-day game's narrative today.

We have done our best to provide a fair representation of the span of time, the great players and the great moments in the game. The selected extracts are, of necessity, snapshots, of how *Wisden* saw an event, issue or individual in the year of publication. *Wisden* has always been unashamedly an Anglocentric publication, with the county game and the fortunes of the England team substantial planks on which each edition is built. Our structure reflects that emphasis. Cricket in all parts of the world has been given increased and deserved prominence in recent years, but *The Essential Wisden* presents an image of the book over its entire lifetime, not just as it is today.

Some universal themes emerge. The game is in perpetual crisis, and even the good times seem to be brief breaks in the cloud whereas the bad times are presented as impending Armageddon. Cricket's finances are a constant topic of discussion, whether the health of county clubs or the profitability of incoming tours to England. Every aspect of the game has been agonised over at some point. One striking concern emerges in the late 1950s as introspective, defensive attitudes infected county cricket and the regular Ashes contests. *Wisden* called for action via its Notes by the Editor and also a famous article by Denis Compton in 1968 entitled "Batsmen must hit the ball again". In these super-professional times where fear of failure is the demon on any cricketer's shoulder, one has increased admiration for the men, like Frank Worrell and Richie Benaud, who invested the game with attacking instincts and a sense of fun.

The structure of *The Essential Wisden* is broadly along the lines of the modern Almanack, with the key sections, such as Notes by the Editor, Cricketers of the Year, Obituaries, Test and county cricket, all represented. We have also included some of those quirky happenings on and around the cricket field which inspire a smile or even disbelief. *Wisden* has indexed them annually since 1996 but, as you will find, they go back to the earliest days of the book. They appear here in a dedicated section. In addition, scattered through the pages are a further 150 bite-sized extracts that we have called "Little Wonders" after the Almanack founder's soubriquet. Like the filler paragraphs that *Wisden* has used over the years they are intended to inform and entertain, without particular reference to the subject matter on the rest of the page. For simplicity's sake they are arranged in this book in chronological order.

Above all ours is a book of words, rather than numbers, and, though large, it has had to be kept within bounds. Apart from a few historic matches and the chapter on Records, we have therefore used summarised scores rather than full scorecards. To accommodate as many pieces as possible we have had to make cuts or take extracts, but the facts have not been altered and the words changed only where we have corrected (very rare) typographical errors, or for the sake of clarifying the sense or structure of a sentence; very occasionally a telling phrase has been moved for emphasis. Most of the headlines are ours, rather than those that appeared on the original articles; the authors of articles have been identified when their names accompanied those pieces in the original books. Over a century and a half *Wisden* has used a variety of styles for such things as match headings, numerals and cricket terms. For consistency we have adopted *Wisden*'s current style and have also dispensed with the italics and capital letters which, in the early days, were widely used in text for emphasis, and quotation marks which were used around words that might not have been as familiar at the time of publication as they are now.

In his Notes by the Editor in the 2013 edition Lawrence Booth wrote: "It's always struck me how many people think of it as a book of stats, when it contains so many interesting stories too." The context of his comment was *Wisden*'s changing relationship with the immediacy of the internet and the challenges and opportunities this brought. But his point is well-observed. All cricket-lovers, and many with only a passing knowledge of the game, have heard of *Wisden* but the perception of it as *just* a record of the game, or a reference book, is only a small part of its magnificence. Another is the rigour with which it checks its facts. As Matthew Engel put it in his Preface to the 1993 edition: "The most revered tradition of *Wisden* is its accuracy." Any book which has been listing its own Errata since 1870, and can publish a correction to a dinner menu (see page 61), cannot be faulted on those grounds.

We might know how many pages have been published since 1864, but we can only begin to guess at the exact word count. Suffice to say that there have been many million brilliant, fascinating and peculiar ones through the years. We have chosen some of the best of them – as one of our wives aptly suggested, the "150 Shades of Wisden". We must thank those wives, Clare and Wendy, for their patience and forbearance over the many months this book was in preparation. We must also offer thanks to Christopher Lane, *Wisden*'s consultant publisher and originator of this project, to Charlotte Atyeo and Nick Humphrey at Bloomsbury Publishing for their guidance and unstinting support, to the eagle eyes of Steven Lynch, deputy editor of *Wisden*, and Charles Barr, *Wisden*'s proofreader, for reading and checking the manuscript – and most of all to the writers, named and unnamed, whose contributions over the past 150 editions have turned John Wisden's "little work" into a not-so-little, wonder-ful publication. Through the words which follow that last group can now speak for themselves.

JOHN STERN and MARCUS WILLIAMS, August 2013

Notes By The Editor

They are, as Sir Tim Rice wrote in "A Century of Notes" in the 2000 edition, "the heartbeat of *Wisden*". He described them also as "permanently anxious, happy, innovative, conservative, serious, flippant, morose and triumphant". Notes by the Editor first appeared in 1901, though Sydney Pardon (editor 1891–1925) had been railing against illegal bowling actions in the Almanack for most of the decade since he replaced his late brother Charles in the editor's chair. Unlike the book itself, the Notes did not survive the two wars. In 1916 and 1917 they did not appear at all, and during the Second World War, when there was little cricket to report, they came from the pen of the acclaimed writer R. C. Robertson-Glasgow. He had been recruited to write the Notes in 1940 following the resignation of Wilfrid Brookes when Haddon Whitaker, the Almanack's publisher, took charge until the appointment of Hubert Preston for the 1944 edition.

Some years ago Malcolm Speed, then chief executive of the ICC, suggested (almost certainly in response to a kicking in the Notes) that it was about time people started to take less notice of *Wisden*. Nice try. Not everyone will agree with the opinions of a *Wisden* editor, least of all the targets of criticism, but the Notes never go unnoticed – in Manchester, Melbourne or Mumbai. There are, as this chapter hopefully shows, plenty of perennial issues that have occupied the minds of editors through the years.

Throwing, which exercised Pardon at the turn of the 20th century, resurfaced to infuriate Norman Preston (the longest-serving editor, 1952–80) in the late 1950s and 1960s. No sooner had the bent arms had been straightened than the Australians and West Indians were recreating the Bodyline series of 1932-33. John Woodcock (1981–86) was not amused, nor was he impressed by the increasing pressure being put on umpires by players. On-field behaviour is a staple of the Notes, as is the state and structure of county cricket. "A grave mistake has been made in not letting the game alone," thundered Pardon in 1919 about the switch to two-day county fixtures at the end of the First World War. In 1907 he had objected to the mooting of a two-division Championship, which came to pass 93 years later, much to the continual chagrin of Matthew Engel (1993–2000, 2005–07).

The over-arching tone of the Notes through the ages is conservative punctuated by shards of radicalism, such as the suggestion by Graeme Wright (1987–92, 2001–02) of a city-based competition to replace the County Championship. Engel effectively damned some of his predecessors when, in 1994, he wrote: "Nothing in cricket has disgraced the game over the years so much as its relationship with South Africa."

Engel and his successors have written powerfully on the over-commercialisation of the modern game, and they will doubtless continue to do so. *Wisden* editors never stop worrying, as Engel explains in our delightful opening extract from 1993. He also makes the point that the game "has always been in crisis", a situation that, as Lawrence Booth wrote in his Notes of 2012, "some of us, let's be honest, wouldn't have any other way".

The Editor's Worry
Matthew Engel, 1993

When you lie awake at four o'clock on a winter's morning, it is always the little things that are so damn bothersome. I sometimes wonder what would happen if, as is statistically probable some time soon, a cup final at Lord's ended with both teams having the same number of runs and wickets. Would they really give the trophy, as the rules insist, to the team with most runs after 30 overs? What on earth is the difference between a run scored off the last ball of the 30th over and the first ball of the 31st?

And why do they now announce Test teams any old day instead of on a Sunday morning, which was part of the warp and weft of an English summer? One would hear the England selectors' latest enormity and go out and vent one's frustrations by mowing the lawn or murdering the weeds. Has this tradition vanished because the few people in the know, so secretive when it suits them, cannot be trusted not to leak the names to their favourite Sunday newspaper? And why, if you ask in a sports store for a pair of cricket flannels, will the assistant only offer something resembling sandpaper but without the softness? If this is what professional crick-eters wear, does it explain why they are so keen to play as little as possible?

With luck, it is eventually possible to go back to sleep and worry about some-thing else the next night. But cricket does keep creeping back. There is something insidious about the game. Its glory is that it works on so many levels: well-briefed spectators will think they know what is going on even though the contest taking place in the middle may be full of all kinds of private subplots. It does not matter. Other spectators may be more detached, conscious only of white-clad (usually) figures in a summer's landscape; they might have found even the last over of the 1992 Lord's Test match [*Pakistan beat England by two wickets*] a restful backdrop to reading a book or doing their knitting.

Cricket can appeal to the athlete and the aesthete alike; it can veer between lyric poetry, differential calculus and Thai kick-boxing. No game has such range, such depth. But it is all extremely fragile. Editors of *Wisden* have been worrying about the game in these pages for most of the Almanack's existence. It has always been in crisis of one sort or another.

BODYLINE AND BOUNCERS

The English Would Not Stoop So Low
Stewart Caine, 1933

At the moment of writing these notes the Third Test match has just ended in a handsome victory for England but while followers of cricket in this country rejoice exceedingly over that success the public in Australia appear to be getting very excited about the fast bowling of some of the Englishmen and what is variously known as the leg theory, shock tactics and body-line methods. The ball to which such strong exception is being taken in Australia is not slow or slow-medium but fast. It is dropped short and is alleged in certain quarters to be aimed at the batsman rather than at the wicket. It may at once be said that, if the intention is to hit the batsman and so demoralise him, the practice is altogether wrong. That English bowlers, to dispose of their opponents, would of themselves pursue such methods or that Jardine would acquiesce in such a course is inconceivable.

PRESS WHIPPING UP A STORM
Sydney Southerton, 1935

No matter the angle from which it may be viewed it is next to impossible to regard the cricket season of 1934 as other than unpleasant. The whole atmosphere of cricket in England was utterly foreign to the great traditions of the game. As a journalist, born and bred in cricket and in mature years coming under the influence of that great lover and writer of the game, Sydney Pardon, I deplored the attitude of a certain section of the press in what seemed to me an insane desire constantly to stir up strife.

One can only assume that the modern idea of being always in search of a stunt – horrible word – was the dominating influence which caused them to see trouble where none existed and to magnify an incident into a dispute and subsequently into an international episode. All sense of proportion was lost and we constantly read during the Test matches, not so much how the game was going or how certain players acquitted themselves, but rather, tittle-tattle of a mischievous character which, in the long run, prompted the inevitable question: Are Test matches really worth while?

Royal Artillery v Gentlemen of MCC. At Lord's, June 3, 4, 1869. The attendance at this match was first-class, and so was the music played each day by one of the fine bands of the RA.

Little Wonder No. 1

SOMEONE WILL GET HURT
Norman Preston, 1952

The general form of the West Indies in Australia in 1951-52 fell a long way below expectations. My information is that "West Indies were bounced out of the Tests." More than likely they returned home in similar frame of mind to other teams who have faced Australia's fast bowlers since the war, believing that they cannot meet

Australia on level terms until they produce bowlers of like speed and method. That is, men capable of sustained attack of fast short-pitched bowling with the ball repeatedly flying around the batsman's head. In its origin cricket was never meant to be played that way. No matter what the issue involved, the game is greater than the individuals. It is a sad thought that sometimes this truth is submerged in the quest for victory and those with the interests of the game at heart regard the frequent use of the bumper as a menace. Action should be taken before someone is hurt, and hurt seriously.

BRUISED AND BATTERED
Norman Preston, 1975

Just as these final pages were going to press the news came that England had lost the Ashes. Australia, clearly the superior combination, made almost a complete sweep by going three up in four contests with two still to be played, though from many quarters came criticism of the manner of some of their bowling in achieving this end. Never in the 98 years of Test cricket have batsmen been so grievously bruised and battered by ferocious, hostile short-pitched balls as were those led conscientiously by Michael Denness until, owing to his own lack of form with the bat, he handed over the captaincy to John Edrich in the fourth match at Sydney.

CURSE OF THE MODERN GAME
John Woodcock, 1984

I am less in sympathy with umpires for the way they have allowed fast bowlers to resort ever more frequently to the thuggery of the bouncer. This has got so badly out of hand that for all but a few highly talented batsmen it is now madness not to have a helmet handy. The viciousness of much of today's fast bowling is changing the very nature of the game. The TCCB's decision to dispense with the agreement allowing only one bouncer an over in domestic English first-class cricket was a setback to those who see intimidatory bowling as a curse of the modern game. Already each season ends with more broken fingers and cracked ribs than the one before. One day, a white line may have to be drawn across the pitch, as a warning mark to bowlers.

QUICKS HAVE THEIR WINGS CLIPPED
Graeme Wright, 1992

It will be interesting to see how the West Indians react to the new ICC regulations concerning over-rates and short-pitched bowling, both of which have been integral to their game plan in their years at the top. They have not been so formidable in one-day cricket since the lawmakers clipped their wings. Personally, I do not like the restriction of one bouncer per over to one batsman. Not that I favour six an over, or even two. But this new limitation takes from the game a psychological element that made it intriguing. Now, as he wonders what the bowler will deliver after a bouncer, the batsman can be fairly sure that it won't be another bouncer, and I believe the game is poorer for that.

BALL-TAMPERING

LIFTING THE SEAM   Stewart Caine, 1926

Last summer in England, and later on in Australia, there arose two questions that caused considerable comment. Towards the end of our cricket season a statement appeared that a bowler had been reported to the MCC for having, in the Worcestershire and Middlesex match, lifted the seam of the ball. Whether this is correct or not is immaterial, but it is significant that the Marylebone Club subsequently issued to the first-class umpires a circular that contained, among other memoranda of importance, the following: "That the practice of lifting the seam by a bowler is illegal and comes within Law 43." If umpires had previously been in doubt, this ruling clearly pointed the way to them, as to the action they are to take in the future. Viewed from any angle the practice – happily, I think, very rare – is indefensible.

The other point did not come quite within the same category, but admitted of discussion. It cropped up over a statement by Mailey, the Australian googly bowler, that it was quite in order for a bowler to use resin on his fingers as a means of imparting additional spin to the ball. From enquiries made I found that resin had, in fact, been used at various times by some of our own bowlers. If not actually contrary to the laws, this is quite foreign to the spirit of cricket, and, for that reason alone, it should not be countenanced by the captain of a side.

ILLEGAL POLISHING   Norman Preston, 1964

The prevalence of seam bowling produced some words of wisdom from Mr S. C. Griffith, the MCC Secretary, in his speech to the county secretaries at their annual winter meeting at Lord's. He said that one could not blame the players for playing a game in the way most likely to pave the way for victory with conditions as they are; grassy pitches, lush outfields and expert ball-shining processes – some legal and some not so legal. Mr Griffith went on to say that he was sure we have got to consider the spin bowler and his needs in such a way as to ensure that he is at least as important to the side as the seam bowler. He felt that the practice of polishing the ball had gone too far and the time had come to add a word or two to Law 46 on fair and unfair play.

THROWING

UNITED ACTION   Sydney Pardon, 1901

I had intended to write at considerable length on the subject of unfair bowling and the no-balling of Mold and Tyler by James Phillips, but before I had started an agreement had been made to take united action in the season of 1901, for the purpose of ridding English cricket of all throwing and dubious bowling.

But I cannot help thinking what a number of scandals and an immense amount of grumbling would have been avoided if, in the middle of the 1880s, the county captains had taken concerted action. At that time, however, Lord Harris alone had the courage of his convictions, and really tried to grapple with an admitted evil. Things have never since been so bad as they were about that time, when on one occasion three unmistakable throwers took part in a Gentlemen v Players match at Lord's, but within the last few years there has unquestionably been great laxity. The mortifying fact was that the deplorable change was due entirely to our own weakness in not having the laws of the game carried out.

ENFORCE THE LAW
Norman Preston, 1952

Most reluctantly I feel compelled to draw the attention of MCC and other international cricket bodies to the problem of throwing by bowlers in the act of delivering the ball. I am told by some people who followed the MCC tour in Australia that they came across three bowlers whose actions were suspicious and two of these have played in Test matches. The problem cropped up in England last summer and nothing was done about it. In these days when the slightest incident on the cricket field may be magnified into an international affair it is no wonder that umpires are loath to take action, but I would remind umpires and all members of the Imperial Cricket Conference that Law 26 is perfectly clear as to the course that should be taken: For a delivery to be fair the ball must be bowled, not thrown or jerked; if either umpire be not entirely satisfied of the absolute fairness of a delivery in this respect, he shall call and signal "No Ball" instantly upon delivery. There is no question that the umpire must be positive that the man is throwing; he must call "No Ball" if there is any doubt in his mind about the delivery being absolutely fair.

DIGNITY MUST BE MAINTAINED
Norman Preston, 1966

The Australians, through their former captain, Richie Benaud, complained about the action of C. C. Griffith, the West Indies fast bowler, when he opposed them in the Caribbean, and K. F. Barrington and E. R. Dexter criticised Griffith in similar fashion following their experience of facing him in England three years ago. I certainly do not think that Griffith was a persistent thrower during that 1963 tour. In my opinion Griffith when really hostile does throw the odd ball; in fact he has been called in his country for this offence. He would have been most unwise to have bowled flat out in these friendly games when he knew West Indies would require him for their English tour in 1966, which I sincerely hope will go through without controversy or unpleasantness. Cricket will face immense competition from the World Soccer Cup tournament which will be the centre of attraction for the greater part of July. Whether or not tempers boil among the soccer players and/or spectators, here is a fine opportunity for cricket to maintain its dignity and sportsmanship.

THE LAST THROW?   Matthew Engel, 2000

If he [Sydney Pardon] were able to read this *Wisden*, he would probably be baffled by some of the contents, depressed by much of them, and would greet the fact that we are still wrestling with the problem of throwing with a sigh of intense weariness. The suspension of Shoaib Akhtar was handled in the usual clumsy ICC fashion – especially from the point of view of maintaining Shoaib's career, which is vital, because he is a huge asset to the game. It ended in a humiliating climbdown. But the principle employed was the right one: these decisions must in future be made rationally, using all the super-slo-mo technology now available, not on an umpire's whim. It is extremely rare these days to find a bowler in top-level cricket whose action is blatantly and consistently illegal. The problem, as it has been for the last 40 years, stems from those bowlers who throw the occasional ball, usually a faster ball or a bouncer, to gain the advantage of surprise. Such bowlers are never called by umpires. It is up to ICC to put a stop to them.

MATCH-FIXING

THE RUMOURS BEGIN   Matthew Engel, 1998

It might be healthier if cricket officials spent a little less time reaching for the sky and paid more attention to what was going on in the gutter. As 1998 began, the rumours that results in one-day internationals were being twisted to suit the interests of betting syndicates operating illegally, mainly in Mumbai and the Gulf, were moving from a murmur to something nearer a roar. Nobody now doubts that this gambling takes place, for large sums, and that cricketers are involved in the process.

ICC needs to set up a credible international investigation designed to discover the truth, not what everyone wants to hear. Anyone with experience of gambling will feel that the amount of smoke billowing out of this story is a pretty reliable indicator of fire. The international programme, particularly as played by India and Pakistan, is a guaranteed recipe for jiggery-pokery. The one-day tournaments of which these countries are so fond have no real meaning. No one remembers who wins them, so honour can never overcome profit.

The present system bears a resemblance to the one that was prevalent in tennis a decade or so ago. The top players would turn up in some hick town for what was billed as a showdown. They would split the profits amiably and put on a show for the locals. It was not that they didn't try, but no one except the poor saps watching cared who won. The difference is that the cricketers are not getting rich – not from cricket. A handful do manage to turn their fame to good commercial advantage, but that is not the same thing. It would be astonishing if some of the others had not been tempted by villainy.

HANSIE CRONJE
Graeme Wright, 2001

In Harvard Square in 1896, a man was knocked off his bike by a wagon and subsequently died. The wagon owners claimed that the accident "could not have been helped". "There are some things which must not happen," retorted Josiah Royce, professor of philosophy at Harvard. There are some things which can be avoided.

Royce's reply came back time and again as Hansie Cronje's reputation was peeled away, leaf by leaf, at the King Commission hearings last summer. Cronje's worst crime was not against cricket – accepting the bookies' bribes or trying to fix matches – but against morality and decency. It was in the way he ensnared the two most vulnerable members of his team, Herschelle Gibbs and Henry Williams. Cronje's white team-mates could afford to send him on his joking way with a rejection; he was just the captain, one of the boys. For Gibbs and Williams, however, even in the rarefied atmosphere of the new South Africa, Cronje was the white man in charge. It takes more than a rainbow for generations of social conditioning and economic deprivation to be washed away.

ETERNAL VIGILANCE
Scyld Berry, 2011

English cricket had largely been able to get away with thinking of match-fixing as a foreign concern, but last season this illusion was shattered. The current Pakistan captain, Salman Butt, and his two best pace bowlers, Mohammad Aamer and Mohammad Asif, were alleged to have been drawn into a plan by their agent, Mazhar Majeed, to bowl three no-balls at specific moments in the Fourth Test at Lord's against England

It would be comfortable to conclude that the episode was just an isolated incident – but wiser to observe how almost all inquiries lift the lid only so far as to find a transgressor or two, then close the lid again. It is, alas, not in officialdom's interest to probe more deeply, because "stakeholders" – especially sponsors and broadcasters – will be scared away. It is up to those of us who follow the game without vested interests to be eternally vigilant, and it would appear that we have not been sufficiently so.

SOUTH AFRICA AND ZIMBABWE

Basil D'Oliveira, the non-white, South African-born all-rounder, was initially omitted from England's tour of South Africa in 1968-69. But when Tom Cartwright withdrew, D'Oliveira replaced him and South Africa cancelled the tour. The consequence of the D'Oliveira Affair was South Africa's exclusion from official international cricket for a generation.

CRICKET THE LOSER
Norman Preston, 1969

Cricket has been the loser with its name tarnished and MCC thrown into divided camps. MCC has always fostered cricket wherever the game is played and for all their faults in this imperfect world I was pleased that the majority of the members rallied to their support when the matter was thrashed out at Church House, Westminster.

BRINGING PEOPLE TOGETHER
Norman Preston, 1970

As I write, with the cricket season only three months ahead, it is still uncertain whether the scheduled tour by the South Africans will be fulfilled either wholly or in part. Personally I have never condoned apartheid in sport. It was the British who took cricket to the ends of the earth. The game has brought all classes of people together, irrespective of colour or creed, except in South Africa. There the State maintains a barrier between white and black which it is not prepared to relax to meet overseas criticism.

POLITICAL PRESSURE
John Woodcock, 1982

More than in any previous year the question of the South African connections of first-class cricketers kept cropping up. When two countries wish to meet each other, it is no longer a simple matter of their respective boards of control arranging a tour and knowing that it will go ahead. Given half a chance the politicians will use it as a means of applying pressure on South Africa to renounce the system of apartheid.

There is no knowing where it will all end. In the autumn of 1981, while England's tour was in doubt, the world of cricket came close to being split into two halves, the dividing line being one of colour. The white and non-white countries are, in fact, so inter-dependent in a cricketing sense that for this to happen would be a setback from which the game might take generations to recover. When it comes to overturning racial prejudice, cricketers believe that the best contribution they can make is to compete together, whether in the same team or on opposite sides.

EXCESSIVE BANS
John Woodcock, 1983

It was ironic, some thought absurd, that [Allan] Lamb should be acceptable for England but not the 15 Englishmen, captained by Graham Gooch, who toured South Africa, Lamb's home country, in the spring of 1982 and were disqualified from Test cricket for three years for having done so.

The Prime Minister, on the other hand, refused to condemn them. Speaking in Parliament, Mrs Thatcher said: "We do not have the power to prevent any sportsmen or women from visiting South Africa or anywhere else. If we did we would no longer be a free country." Trapped in the maelstrom, the TCCB, by imposing a three-year ban – to preserve international multiracial cricket – bowed to political pressures, to the consternation not only of the players concerned but also of the average cricket follower.

I am sure that at all times the TCCB proceeded, as they thought, in good faith. They did all they could, once they had got wind of the tour, to dissuade the players from embarking on it. For all that, to act as they ultimately did, without doing anything for the cause of cricket in South Africa, smacked more of expediency than strength. A one-year suspension, with a future tightening of players' contracts, would have been ample. And knowing the West Indians as I do, and the importance they attach to playing cricket against England, quite apart from the joy they get from beating them, I believe that, come 1984, their politicians, like everyone else, would have accepted some reduction of the ban.

Little Wonder No. 2

A happier country. Projected visits from Australian, Indian, and American teams to play English Elevens all round our dear old country – the birthplace and home of the fine old game – bid fair, with fair weather, to keep the ball rolling in 1878 as it never rolled before. All right this; the more matches, the merrier season; and the more cricketers, the happier country.

SOUTH AFRICA'S FUTURE   Graeme Wright, 1989

What the member countries of the ICC have not said in recent years is what they want of South Africa. Perhaps they hope that, as it is no longer on the agenda, the question of South Africa will cease to exist. I wonder if an opportunity has been lost by ignoring what is being done by the South African Cricket Union in taking cricket into the black townships. South Africa has to change if justice is to prevail and each child, regardless of colour, is to begin life equal with the next. That change can come through bloodshed or through the political will of the South African electorate. The second way will take time and education. I know nothing of the work of the South African Cricket Union except for what I have read. It may be propaganda. But if black South African children are being taught a game which brings them into regular contact with white South African children, might not the latter come to acknowledge the rights of the former and grow to vote out a government which maintains apartheid?

Undue optimism? Probably, but I prefer subversion by the cricket bat to subversion by the Kalashnikov. If, however, the will of the voting class is not for change, no amount of cricket in the townships will destroy apartheid. And it is the ending of apartheid, not the number of black cricketers, which will influence world opinion.

The Gambling Of Goodwill
Graeme Wright, 1990

By playing as a team in South Africa, Mike Gatting's side become ineligible to play for England for at least five years under the ICC resolution of January 1989. Each claimed he was exercising his right to practise his trade as a professional cricketer. And we were told again of the short lifespan of the professional cricketer. Both are valid points in their own ways, but I am inclined to think the argument devalues the professional in this instance. I also feel that the South African Cricket Union has made a mistake – politically and tactically – in staging this tour. In recent years it has been improving its credentials, both as an opponent of apartheid and as a non-racial administration, through its cricket development programme in the black townships. Now it is gambling that goodwill on a venture that can be seen only as sanctions-busting by the country's black leaders.

Ineffectual And Half-Hearted
Matthew Engel, 1994

All being well, there will still be some wonderful moments when the South Africans finally arrive in England, 100 years after their first tour, and 29 after their last. Nothing in cricket has disgraced the game over the years so much as its relationship with South Africa. For two decades after the formal introduction of apartheid, administrators in the white countries did everything possible to avoid consideration of the ethical questions involved, although it was obvious at the time that South African cricket was rooted in a system that was fundamentally evil.

Cricket's attitude was ineffectual and half-hearted. The culture of the game was such that no odium attached to the players who were so well-rewarded for going on the seven rebel tours though, in their own small and moral-pygmyish way, they were acting as agents of apartheid. That war has now been won. The future of South Africa remains clouded with all kinds of terrible possibilities but this summer it will be possible to welcome their cricketers without reservation. Since the collapse of the last rebel tour in 1990, when South African administrators ceased their equivocation about their real intentions and merged into the United Cricket Board, they have done an enormous amount for the good of the game. No country is doing more to spread cricket to its own people; if only Lord's worked as hard in the deprived areas of English cities.

When Sport Meets Tyranny
Tim de Lisle, 2003

Months before the World Cup began it was clear that Zimbabwe was in a desperate state. Robert Mugabe's government, returned to power in a flagrantly fixed election, was running a vicious, thuggish police state, apparently indifferent at best to the famine afflicting millions of its people.

One poll after another suggested that three quarters of UK sports followers thought visiting teams should be allowed to switch their Zimbabwe games to South

African venues. Malcolm Speed [*ICC chief executive*] reacted to this idea like a new father who hears someone criticising his baby. He took umbrage and insisted, to the open-mouthed disbelief of those who had observed their machinations over the years, that the ICC were non-political.

When the ICC failed to give a lead over Zimbabwe, the England and Wales Cricket Board had the chance to fill the void. Instead, Tim Lamb [*ECB chief executive*] said: why us? Cricket, he argued, was part of the international leisure and entertainment industry. About 300 British companies were continuing to do business with Zimbabwe; why should cricket alone be expected to take a stand? The answer hardly needs spelling out. A national team has a symbolic dimension that a firm importing mangetouts does not. A cricket board is not a company: it may be businesslike, but it does not exist to make money. It exists to stage cricket, to promote it and protect its good name. Lamb's stance, like Speed's, brought the game into disrepute. How can they govern cricket, who only cricket know?

PICKING THE ENGLAND TEAM

THE CONFINES OF LUNACY   Sydney Pardon, 1910

Never, I should think, in the last five-and-twenty years have English cricketers felt more dissatisfied and disappointed with a season's play than in 1909. It was not merely that we lost the rubber. In the matches at Leeds and Manchester the selection committee made the best use of the material at their command, but at The Oval a fatal blunder was committed in leaving out Buckenham – a blunder for which it was generally understood that Archie MacLaren, the England captain, was responsible. Experts occasionally do strange things and this was one of the strangest. The idea of letting England go into the field in fine weather, on a typical Oval wicket, with no fast bowler except Sharp touched the confines of lunacy. The despised man in the street could not have been guilty of such folly.

NOT A PROPER TEAM   Sydney Pardon, 1922

England lost 5–0 in Australia in the winter of 1920-21 and then 3–0 at home to them the following summer.

During all the years I have edited *Wisden* there has never been a season so disheartening as that of 1921. The five defeats in Australia of the MCC's team showed us plainly enough what we should have to face, but the revelation came too late. Everything had been left to chance and we paid the penalty. The fact that 30 players appeared for England in the Test matches last summer is in itself proof that we had not a real eleven, but a series of scratch sides.

CLOSE BUT NO CIGAR
Hubert Preston, 1951

I thoroughly agree with the selection committee in their desire to introduce young men, but although many have been tried none has shown the ability expected of cricketers elevated to Test status. Yet for this tour of Australia the selectors gambled on five or six young men who had accomplished nothing in Test cricket. D. B. Close had spent the whole summer in the Army. Certainly he showed great promise in 1949, but constant match practice is necessary for youth to develop, and on the few occasions Close appeared in 1950 it was obvious he had gone back. His selection for Australia caused tremendous surprise.

SELECTION BY COMMITTEE LIVES ON
Matthew Engel, 1996

The TCCB's decision last March to sack Keith Fletcher and make Ray Illingworth manager as well as chairman of selectors was the only sensible response to the situation that had developed. Theoretically, Illingworth had more power than anyone has ever had over the national team. And he would regularly flex his muscles, laying down iron principles for the untrammelled exercise of his power and for selecting the team. Then, suddenly, those principles would prove unexpectedly changeable. Ultimately, it became clear that teams were being chosen much as they had been before, by a coalition in which the captain's voice was extremely important. To me, the biggest disappointment of Illingworth's reign so far is not that he has exercised too much power but the reverse: he would insist on citing form as a justification for selection instead of backing his judgment about a player's quality and then sticking with it, and facing the consequences. The style of leadership has changed dramatically; the sense that England selection policy will be blown around by the most fickle of winds has not.

CAPTAINING THE ENGLAND TEAM

NOT LEADERSHIP MATERIAL
Stewart Caine, 1932

There remains the big question who shall captain the side. A year ago everything pointed to the probability of the post being offered to Jardine. The old Oxonian not only possesses the experience born of a tour in Australia but can look back upon a series of fine performances accomplished out there and, if he was out of first-class cricket in 1930, he showed last year that he has lost nothing of his qualities as an exceptionally sound watchful batsman. On the other hand he does not seem to have impressed people with his ability as a leader on the field.

Douglas Jardine captained England to Australia in 1932-33 and presided over Bodyline, the most infamous Test series in history.

The Amateur Captain

Wilfrid Brookes, 1939

A very ticklish problem for the selection committee was solved when Walter Hammond announced that he intended to play in future as an amateur. At the time, I was among those who felt doubtful whether he should be saddled with the responsibility of the England captaincy. Fortunately, events proved that opinion wrong. Hammond last summer showed unmistakably that he was well fitted for the post; indeed he surprised his closest friends by his intelligent tactics. Undoubtedly Hammond proved himself a sagacious and inspiring captain. Directly he announced his intentions, there was only one possible choice for the leadership. It is common knowledge that the number of amateurs who can devote the necessary time to the game is not increasing. If this fact is disquieting to sticklers for tradition, the end of the convention which for so many years has directed that England's captain must be an amateur is by no means in sight.

Style Mistaken For Character

Graeme Wright, 1990

Ted Dexter said when announcing that Gower would captain England for the series, he was looking to him to set the tone and style for the team. It is the call for tone and style which interests me, for in the context of England performances in recent seasons, character and not style was the requirement. The two are not synonymous, though it has often seemed to me that in England style is mistaken for character. By character I mean mettle: a combination of ability, mental toughness and judgment. Style is apparent; and it has its place in, among other things, the arts, in the art of batting, in fashion and in good manners. Nevertheless, when inner reserves are required, it is character and not style which sees one through.

Gower has shown this in his batting; his leadership has never been so clear-cut. It has been said of him that the quality of life is important to him, but it has seemed sometimes that it is the quality of his own life which is important: his lifestyle. When defeat began to sour his life, Gower was not able to dig deep into his own character to make his players respond to the crisis. Instead, they were carried along by the air of despondency which enveloped him. It was not the tone and style Dexter had envisaged.

ALL BOWLED OUT

Lack Of Rest

Stewart Caine, 1927

There is one recent development of cricket life that may, I fear, militate against the prospects of England against Australia. That is the ever-increasing tendency to undertake winter tours in different parts of the world. These trips are obviously very agreeable or they would not prove so popular, and in so far as participation in them is confined to amateurs and to professionals outside the foremost rank, there can be no objection to them. It is a different matter when, as happens at the present moment, our leading bowlers, after a season's heavy work and that of another in front of them, are subjected to a further call upon their powers during the intervening months. For a time, no doubt, men at the height of their physical strength may appear to undergo this additional strain without any deterioration in skill, yet the lack of rest must tell in the long run, and so tend to shorten a brilliant career.

Ever Increasing Circles
Lawrence Booth, 2013

It remains to be seen how Australia's talented but injury-prone seamers cope with ten successive Ashes Tests, although Michael Clarke has done his best to portray rotation as a necessary evil. The Australian hierarchy have even come up with a condescending piece of jargon for their policy. All hail "informed player management". England, who are resigned to it as well, prefer the less slippery "rotation". You get the gist.

Yet you wonder about the point of it all if, fitness permitting, teams are disinclined to field their strongest side – a basic principle of international sport which, thanks to the schedule, has been made to look like a hopeless ideal. England's one-day defeat in India in January 2013 rang hollow without Trott, Anderson, Broad and Swann. Spectators wondering which star players they won't be seeing any time soon may sympathise with the French existentialist philosopher who once asked for a coffee without cream. "We're out of cream," said the waitress. "Would you like it without milk instead?"

Even Andy Flower admitted defeat in November, agreeing to hand England's limited-overs coaching duties to Ashley Giles. This was presented as a piece of forward thinking by the ECB. And in the circumstances it probably was: if an HGV needed to get from Portsmouth to Aberdeen and back in 24 hours, you'd hope for two drivers. But when cricket's talent has to job-share to stay awake at the wheel, you know something is wrong.

AN EXPENSIVE BUSINESS

Are These Tours Really Worth It?
Norman Preston, 1955

Test profits from tours of teams to England in the nine seasons since the war amount to roughly £746,000. Look at these figures:

		Profit to English Cricket	Profit to Tourists
1946	India	£12,500	£4,500
1947	South Africa	£30,000	£11,500
1948	Australia	£80,000	£75,000
1949	New Zealand	£31,700	£15,000
1950	West Indies	£45,500	£30,000
1951	South Africa	£58,800	£17,500
1952	India	£39,400	£12,000
1953	Australia	£130,000	£100,000
1954	Pakistan	£38,000	£15,100
		£465,900	£280,600

While the British public contribute freely to the coffers of visiting teams, MCC have received scant reward from many of their overseas tours; and when our men are subject to the treatment they received in the West Indies [*in 1953-54, a bad-tempered tour marred by crowd misbehaviour*], where there is no profit for the visitors, one begins to wonder whether some of these tours are worth while from an English cricket point of view.

ENGLAND: PLAYERS AND PERFORMANCE

COMPLACENCY   Norman Preston, 1959

The fight for the Ashes held the attention of the cricketing world in recent months and not for the first time it produced a good deal of controversy. England went to Australia with the unofficial title of "World Champions". At the time no one could deny that they ranked above all their rivals; yet when they went into action their standard of play bore no relation to their exalted position and they were toppled off their pedestal [*England lost 4–0 in Australia in 1958-59*]. Lately, the dice have been loaded far too heavily against the batsmen in England. Consequently the bowlers have not been compelled to toil for their wickets. No wonder things go wrong when our men go abroad. We have destroyed our breed of professional batsmen and at the same time extinguished the leg-spin and googly bowlers, besides producing a generation of fielders who show up poorly in the deep. Time and again over the past eight years I have drawn attention to the decline of professional batsmanship in England and now I wonder if some of the amateurs have not become too complacent.

Little Wonder No. 3

MCC and Ground (11) v 22 Colts of England. At Lord's, May 7, 8, 1877. This match was played out in as sunny, summerlike weather as cricketer could desire, but for all that, and notwithstanding Mr W. G. Grace played, the attendance was scant, the absence of the public pointedly proclaiming their distaste to those abominations, mistermed "matches", of Elevens v Twenty-twos, which ought never to find a home at Lord's.

BOYCOTT MUST COME TO TERMS WITH HIMSELF
Norman Preston, 1975

Frankly, I cannot believe that the presence of Geoff Boycott would have made any difference to England's fortunes [*they lost 4–1 in Australia in 1974-75*]. He is not at his best fending off the bouncer or in avoiding it. After being chosen among the 16 for the tour he withdrew some weeks later explaining that he had still not got over the pressures and tensions of international cricket and that he was not confident of being able to stand up to the rigours of a long Australian tour. He felt that it was in the best interests of the team that he should withdraw. There were no signs that he would have been in the right frame of mind to try to answer Thomson and Lillee.

Boycott, at 34, is not a young man with the years on his side in which to adjust. England's needs are immediate. It is high time the Yorkshire captain came to terms with himself and if the huge benefit of £20,639 which he reaped during 1974 helps to do that, then cricket generally might have cause to thank those schoolboys up and down the country who contributed their pence and those people inside the county who, still cherishing the memory of watching Herbert Sutcliffe, Percy Holmes, Maurice Leyland, Hedley Verity and Bill Bowes play their hearts out for the side, gave their pounds.

BREARLEY: A MASTER IN THE ART OF CRICKET   Norman Preston, 1978

In the first instance much of the credit for England's revival over the 18 months belonged to Tony Greig, but when as England's reigning captain he did his secret deal with Packer, the authorities at Lord's instructed Alec Bedser and his fellow selectors to choose another, although none of the Packer signatories was precluded as a candidate to play against Australia. The honour of leading the team went to Mike Brearley, the Middlesex captain, who had been the vice-captain on the tour to India, Sri Lanka and Australia. And Brearley followed in the footsteps of Percy Chapman and Sir Leonard Hutton in regaining the Ashes at home.

Brearley, a totally different captain from the volatile Greig, led his men with quiet efficiency. He is clearly a master in the art of cricket. He handled his bowlers skilfully and was ahead of Greig in field-placing. As a batsman, with his special headgear for protection against the bumper, he averaged only 27, but was nevertheless the obvious man to take England on a winter tour of Pakistan and New Zealand. Unfortunately a broken arm caused him to return home and miss what would have been his first visit to New Zealand.

TOO EASY   Graeme Wright, 1987

It is not only for Australia's sake that it should be a power in world cricket. While it may be good for England to beat Australia, it is not good for either country if Australian cricket is so weak that it ceases to be regarded as a major sport by its success-oriented citizens.

JUST ANOTHER WORKING DAY   Graeme Wright, 1990

Living in a country not one's own, one has a different perspective on it from that of the natives. Last season, as England were handsomely and decisively beaten by a well-prepared Australian team, I could see no reason, other than wounded nationalism, for the hollering and head-hunting that followed each Test defeat. What was new? In the four years I have been writing these Notes as editor of *Wisden*, England's cricketers have lost every home series, beaten by India, New Zealand, Pakistan, West Indies and now Australia. Only victory in a one-off Test against Sri Lanka interrupts the story tale of England's failure to win a Test match in England since 1985.

Nothing had changed to indicate it would be any different in 1989. All that happened was that the Australians were better than many had expected. And yet, man for man, were they that much better than England's cricketers at the start of the series? It was in their attitude and their approach that they were superior. They played with a purpose that was missing from England's players. As Allan Border once said of his own team, they had forgotten the reason for playing Test cricket: the feeling of national pride.

The news that Gatting would take a team to South Africa broke at the end of the Old Trafford Test in which England surrendered the Ashes to Australia. It left me, *l'étranger*, wondering what playing for England had meant to them. And, narrowing it further, what did England mean. Maybe this is an old-fashioned, not to say unfashionable, concept, but it seems to me that playing for one's country should be an honour – every time. Border spoke of national pride, and it was there for all to see in his team last year. They were playing for themselves, for each other and for their country. Watching some of the professional cricketers who have represented England in recent years, I can't help thinking that they regard a Test match as just another working day.

LIBERATION
Matthew Engel, 2006

There they were in Trafalgar Square, the boys of summer, the men of the moment. Under the noonday sun, they were wearing their blazers, dark glasses to hide their bloodshot eyes, and the broadest of grins. Thousands and thousands of people gazed up at them and hung on every syllable they spoke, however inane.

This was the England cricket team, for heaven's sake, being greeted on the streets of London as though they were pioneering astronauts getting a tickertape reception through New York. They were lauded on the front page of every newspaper. Alongside them were their counterparts, the England women's team who, by happy coincidence, had just won their own version of the Ashes. Stuffy old cricket suddenly looked inclusive: a game for everyone.

Around the country, kids who had never picked up cricket bats were suddenly pretending to be Freddie or Vaughany or Harmy or KP. And though autumn finally came, and jumper-goalposts inevitably replaced dustbin-wickets, there was evidence that the craze did not subside with the England team's sore heads, and that cricket had truly recaptured a slice of the nation's heart. For anyone who had lived through the dark years, it felt like a kind of liberation.

Journalists still tended to write that we had witnessed Probably The Greatest Test (Edgbaston), Probably The Greatest Series, and Probably The Greatest Crowd

To Greet A Victorious England Team. There is no need for the nervous adverb. This was The Greatest. The 2005 Ashes surpassed every previous series in cricket history on just about any indicator you choose. There had been close contests before, and turnarounds, and tension (1894-95, 1936-37, 1956, 1960-61 Australia v West Indies, 1981…), but never had cricket been so taut for so long. And certainly, previous players had never enjoyed adulation like this.

CLOSE TO PERFECTION Scyld Berry, 2011

It would be hard to think of a sizeable human organisation that has come closer to perfection for a couple of months than England's cricket team during the Ashes series in Australia. For those of us who have had to watch, for decades, the failure to translate the many resources of English cricket into achievement by the national side, England's performance over the last year – culminating in their retention of the Ashes – was especially satisfying.

The success flowed from the thorough and considerate planning of what I call the Andocracy, led by Andrew Strauss and Andy Flower. It would be wrong to say they conducted England's tour with military precision, because there was nothing regimented about it. The squad conveyed their enjoyment, whether doing their Sprinkler dance – a nice touch – or cavorting in Graeme Swann's video diaries or, most significantly, when playing.

England, I fear, will never be No. 1 for a sustained period until the ECB obey the two key recommendations of the Schofield Review that they themselves commissioned after the disastrous 2006-07 tour of Australia: to reduce the amount of England fixtures and of domestic fixtures.

THE PERFECT LENGTH (OF MATCHES)

THREE IS THE MAGIC NUMBER Sydney Pardon, 1903

There seems to be a strong feeling in favour of playing Test games in this country out to a finish. Personally, however, I am very doubtful of the wisdom of making cricket altogether independent of a time limit. Cricket has already suffered to some extent from the contrast to association football, with its hour and a half of concentrated excitement, and there is I think a danger in admitting the principle of devoting more than three days to any match. Time being of no consequence, the game would, I fear, lose its brilliant qualities and become little more than a matter of endurance.

LET THE GAME ALONE Sydney Pardon, 1919

The long nightmare of the War has come to an end, and in the coming summer first-class cricket will again be in full swing. I have a very strong opinion that a grave mistake has been made in not letting the game alone. The restriction of all county matches to two days strikes me as being a sad blunder. I can see most weighty objections to the scheme, little or nothing in its favour. Let no one in future repeat the stale old fable that the County Championship was only kept in existence for the benefit of the newspapers. By their recent action the advisory committee have made an absolute fetish of the Championship, risking on its behalf famous county matches that can boast a tradition of over 50 years. There was the less reason to take such a drastic step as county cricket in 1919, after a blank of four seasons, was bound to be a very speculative and experimental business. To my thinking it would have been far better to drop the Championship entirely for one year, allowing all the counties to make such arrangements as seemed best fitted to their own needs, while the game was being gradually brought back to its old footing. Most of the counties, however, were bent on having a systematic competition, no matter how imperfect it might be, and the final effort to save the three-day county match proved a dismal failure, the majority that on the fifth of February confirmed the original resolution of the advisory committee being, I believe, 11 to five.

Purposeless Draws

Wilfrid Brookes, 1938

A warning note is also sounded concerning the effect on the counties generally of any serious decline in the popularity of Test match cricket. Consequently the news that, for the Test matches of 1938 with Australia, agreement has been reached again to restrict the games to four days apiece and to reduce the hours of play by one and a half hours in each match, came as a surprise. Are we to have another run of purposeless drawn games with the possibility of one play-to-a-finish Test deciding the rubber?

How To Kill The Game

Norman Preston, 1960

The members of the Imperial Cricket Conference took another step in the right direction when they decided that 30 hours' playing time should not be a rigid rule for Test matches. Some years ago *Wisden* supported the plea for longer Tests, and indeed the five-day schedule, but experience has shown that the longer the time allowed, the less inclined are the players, and particularly the batsmen, to get on with the game. Much of the dull play which crept like a paralysis into three-day county cricket before the awakening of last summer was due to the example set mainly by Test players. Can anyone imagine anything more futile than some of England's stonewall batting, especially that of Bailey, in Australia two winters ago, or that by Worrell and Sobers for West Indies in the six-day Test at Bridgetown last January? Such tactics could in time kill first-class cricket.

FOUR DAYS – ARE YOU MAD? Norman Preston, 1971

For some time a programme of 16 four-day county matches in midweek has been a talking point, but I fancy that would lead to much defensive and purposeless cricket which the onlookers detest even if the players enjoy it.

FOUR DAYS – YOU *ARE* MAD Matthew Engel, 1993

This year the English three-day county game is replaced by the four-day game, much admired by those who sit in offices and planes, much despised by those who still go and watch it, especially at the Festival Weeks.

One pauses to speculate that the system chosen for 1993 will not last three years, as planned. Since 1989 they [*the TCCB*] have forced the counties to play their three-day games on four- or five-day pitches: any miscalculation in favour of result wickets has been punished by the threat of the 25-point deduction. Teams winning the toss this summer, aided by the four-day format, two runs for no-balls and the general climate in favour of batsmen, may well consider themselves failures if they are out before mid-afternoon on the second day for less than 450. The games may look neater in the 1994 *Wisden* than ever before. But if they contain any fun and entertainment for the spectator it is likely to happen only by accident; and no doubt someone at the Board will change the rules next winter to make sure that gets eliminated.

For the time being, everyone has to give the new system a chance, coloured clothing on Sunday and all. I have no profound objections to this gimmick – and the players should have had their names on their backs in all professional cricket years ago. If, however, the counties are planning to change their colours every year to exploit children and make them buy up-to-date gear at rip-off prices, which is what happens in football, then they are taking the road to hell.

THE COUNTY GAME: POINTS MAKE POINTLESSNESS

ENSLAVED BY DECIMAL FRACTIONS Sydney Pardon, 1911

Writing at the end of the year I am quite in the dark as to what the advisory committee will do with regard to Yorkshire's proposal to give points in county matches to sides leading on the first innings. Personally I hope the idea will not be entertained. I do not for a moment think that the salvation of county cricket will be found in a more complicated system of reckoning points. The end to aim at is to play every match on its own merits, let the final result be what it may. Repeating what I have said before in *Wisden*, I would like to see the Championship decided at the end of the season by the MCC on general play, without any slavish regard to decimal fractions.

FAIR ENOUGH BUT DISTRESSINGLY BUSINESSLIKE Stewart Caine, 1929

Yet a further plan for deciding the County Championship is to be tried this year, and, inasmuch as it does away with the necessity for percentages, it will give satisfaction to many worthy people, some of whom would have been still further pleased had the committee, drawing up the new scheme, seen their way to abolish first-innings points. Eight points are at issue in every match as under the previous system but whereas these, under the plan of 1927, lapsed when there was no play or no result on the first innings, each side in such circumstance will take four points. The big departure is the arrangement that, instead of the various counties playing whom they like, with of course, a minimum number of engagements required to qualify for participation in the competition, every county now plays 28 matches, with the committee deciding which two of the other 16 counties shall not be encountered. Likely enough the new plan will work out satisfactorily but it seems to be invested with distressingly businesslike regulations which have not hitherto invaded the great cricket competition.

HOW TO MAKE A COMPLEX GAME MORE COMPLICATED Matthew Engel, 2006

If there is one thought that I've tried to bang home most from this pulpit, it's this: a complex game needs simple structures. Yet administrators remain addicted to trying to achieve too many objectives at once. Thus, with all the bonus points and fractional over-rate penalties, the ECB has made the County Championship fairly incomprehensible. But that's nothing. Take a look, if you can face it, at our Cricket in South Africa section.

Bonus points awarded for the first 85 overs of each team's first innings: One bonus batting point was awarded for the first 100 runs and 0.02 of a point for every subsequent run... Gauteng 20.18 pts, Northerns 4.94. It gets worse. Consider Sri Lanka: ...0.1 pt for each wicket taken and 0.005 pt for each run scored up to 400... Galle 11.925 pts, Ragama 3.795.

The attendance for one Sri Lankan provincial match in early 2005 was reported as zero; I'm surprised they got that many. Under the circumstances, congratulations to Zimbabwe Cricket, who were unable to tell us, despite repeated requests, what points system, if any, was in operation for their domestic tournament. I was rather relieved, frankly.

THE COUNTY GAME: REFORMATION

SOMETHING (THAT MEANS NOTHING) MUST BE DONE Graeme Wright, 1992

Last summer the TCCB set up a working party, under the chairmanship of M. P. Murray, the Middlesex chairman, to investigate the state of the first-class game in England. This could be interpreted as recognition of the need for change in the game, were it not for the fact that, only six years ago, the counties chose not to implement the major recommendations of the Palmer Report into the Standards of Play of English Cricket in Test and First-class County Cricket. Establishing working parties and commissions is an easy way of persuading people that something is being done, even when nothing is done as result of them.

A TALE OF NEW CITIES

Graeme Wright, 2002

The time is approaching to reform the first-class county structure, as opposed to merely meddling with the cricket and the fixture list. What we have at the moment is a Victorian institution that resisted reform in the 20th century and struggled into the 21st on subsidies rather than public support. To be commercially viable, they have to satisfy their dual market needs. Because professional sport is essentially in the entertainment game, they should be able to attract and entertain an audience; and, such is the framework of English cricket, they must provide the right players for the national teams that generate much of the ECB's income. This is a well-rehearsed argument; it hardly requires repeating any more than the fact that many counties no longer seem capable of fulfilling these conditions. The system survives on a confederacy of mediocrity.

It would add interest to the debate to hear something more radical being discussed; something that would take into account England in the 21st century rather than the 19th. It has become an urban society, built on cities and conurbations. Why not a professional circuit based on these, rather than on shires and counties, however romantically their names resonate? The grounds are already firmly established in cities. The cricket club could incorporate civic identity, and benefit from the commercial and sponsorship opportunities such an association would provide. Yorkshire would doubtless claim to be an exception.

Assuming the globalisation of cricket continues apace, it will be only a matter of time before there is a television-driven demand for international inter-city tournaments. Cities are marketable commodities in a way that counties, states and provinces are not. This may seem fanciful now, but looking ahead often does. Cricket may never have the lion's share of the television sports market in England, but it has immense potential elsewhere. English cricket should not simply be aware of this potential but positioned to exploit it when the opportunity arises. Cricket has trundled along traditional lines for a long time, but the pace of change and growth is faster now than it has ever been.

Kent v Sussex. At Gravesend, June 22, 23, 24, 1882. This was the first county match played on the Bat and Ball Ground since 1806, and will be memorable for the extraordinary performance of Lords Harris and Throwley, who went in first for Kent, and, before they were parted, made the enormous score of 208.

Little Wonder No. 4

THE PICTURE IS GETTING FUZZY

Lawrence Booth, 2012

With impeccable timing, the County Championship reeled off its best storyline for years – and a last-minute twist to rival *Fever Pitch*. Only Warwickshire supporters and Yorkshiremen would have begrudged Lancashire their first title since 1950, when they shared it with Surrey, and their first outright triumph since 1934 (has any adjective more irked Lancastrians?).

And yet the story disguised a multitude of sins. The virtual absence of England players has robbed the County Championship of what remained of its glamour, and the days when top-drawer overseas stars returned time and again to the same club have fallen victim to the international treadmill and more lucrative offers elsewhere (this season, the Australian Marcus North was hoping to play for his sixth county). The ECB's performance-related fee payment scheme, which encourages counties to pick youth, is well intentioned but has further diluted the quality. Financial uncertainty is rife, not least among the Test-match counties.

The cause and effect between county cricket's structure and the success of the national side is forever exaggerated. But the two generally accepted aims of the domestic game – to exist in its own right and to supply players for England – are out of kilter. We can never go back to a time when England cricketers sped off down the motorway to join their counties as soon as a Test was over. But there is an uncomfortable feeling that England have prospered despite the domestic system and that the County Championship is now tolerated – to paraphrase David Cameron on Gordon Brown – as analogue cricket in a digital age. The picture is getting fuzzy.

THE COUNTY GAME: TWO DIVISIONS

FOOTBALL STYLE

Sydney Pardon, 1907

No season goes by without producing some discussion as to the County Championship, and 1906 was no exception to the rule. It was rather surprising, however, to find a proposal to arrange the Championship in two divisions, after the style of the Football League, emanating from W. G. Grace. I am, as everyone must be, quite conscious of the anomalies inevitable in a competition in which 16 counties play an unequal amount of matches, but for the two-division suggestion I have no liking whatever. I cannot bring myself to look with any favour on a scheme which might, as the result of one unlucky season, involve the most famous counties being put down into the second rank. The traditions of cricket are against such a system.

CHAOS AND CONFUSION

Matthew Engel, 1999

The entire country was opposed to the introduction of two divisions in the County Championship. Unfortunately, the country concerned was Wales. Glamorgan were against the idea in the vote at the First-Class Forum last December, but were swamped by the English. Durham and Essex abstained; all the other counties voted for the plan. Many did so not from conviction but from a weary certainty that this was an idea which would not go away. Thus the top nine counties of 1999 will form a First Division in 2000.

It was the culmination of a debate notable for its intellectual incoherence. Those who argued for two divisions did so for contradictory reasons; indeed some often contradicted themselves in the same breath. On the one hand, the reform was supposed to pep up the County Championship. On the other, reformers wanted the best players formally taken away from their counties and placed under the England selectors' control. What kind of championship is that?

The system, as introduced, makes no sense whatever. Six teams out of 18 will shift divisions each year. That will create confusion, not an elite. The whole scheme makes sense only for those who believe the counties should be heavily weeded, and reduced to a handful of big-city teams. It is a useful way-station on the road to that objective. I happen to think that would be a disaster, and that English cricket must be maintained and nurtured by 18 counties with full-time professional cricket. The counties have been bamboozled into a reform born of panic.

THE COUNTY GAME: STRAPPED FOR CASH

Going To The Wall
Sydney Pardon 1911

In the meantime many of the county clubs are undoubtedly finding it a hard matter to make both ends meet. Still it is a very hopeful sign that when things get to the worst the money required is always forthcoming. For example, there was a grave fear early in the autumn that Derbyshire as a first-class county club would cease to exist. The response to a special appeal, however, was so encouraging that, at a meeting on December 2, the committee resolved to go on as before, and at Lord's in the following week the usual fixtures were ratified. Of all the counties, Somerset could plead the best excuse for giving up the fight as hopeless, the supply of talent being so inadequate, but whatever may have been contemplated two years ago there is now no idea of winding up the club.

Appeal To Members: We Need Your Money
Norman Preston, 1975

Several counties found themselves in serious financial difficulties. Gloucestershire reckoned a loss of about £30,000 on the year, Hampshire £10,000, Middlesex £15,000, Nottinghamshire £9,000 and Yorkshire £7,000. Gloucestershire launched a fund to raise £25,000 to overcome the worst financial crisis in the county's history. An appeal was made to business firms suggesting that one hundred each donate an interest-free loan of £250, the proposed sale of the Bristol ground having been abandoned. The Middlesex president, G. C. Newman, wrote to the 7,000 members appealing for a minimum donation of £10 from each as the county would face bankruptcy by the end of this summer unless an additional £20,000 was forthcoming. Hampshire proposed increasing membership fees, but they will not play at Portsmouth because a stand at the United Services ground which screened the railway has been demolished.

LIVING ON BORROWED TIME Graeme Wright, 2002

In the same way that the board *[ECB]* chairman called the counties "academies", his chief executive Tim Lamb took to calling them "centres of excellence", which did nothing for the counties but made him sound like one of those well-spun politicians whose peculiar notion of excellence is applied in defence of failing institutions. Last year he took to describing the counties as "businesses". But, as the farming industry is currently debating, what happens to the business if the subsidy diminishes or disappears? Cricket may not be living on borrowed time; some counties clearly are. I suspect there is already a tendency to let the weakest go to the wall. Natural wastage, businessmen call it.

THE COUNTY GAME: COUNTER-ATTRACTIONS

THIS IS WHAT WE'RE UP AGAINST Norman Preston, 1952

The time has surely come when some counties should cut down the number of early finishes arranged for the third day. In one instance last season the home side and the umpires were staying at the same venue for the next match and the visiting team were travelling only 40 miles, yet long hours were played on the first two days and stumps were drawn early on the third. In another case only ten minutes' cricket took place after lunch on the third day when stumps were pulled up and the match left drawn. When lunch is included most cricketers think of a whole-day match, but not, apparently, some first-class county clubs. These things irritate the public. They do not always complain but do they come to cricket again when there are so many counter-attractions? I am indebted to Captain W. A. Powell, R. A. F. Staff College, Andover, for the following figures showing the growth of counter-attractions to cricket over the last 50 years:

	1900	1951
Baseball Teams	10	952
Lawn Tennis Clubs	320	5,300
Cinemas	12	5,700
Golf Clubs	120	2,100
Civil Flying Clubs and Schools	Nil	175
Dog-racing Courses	Nil	257
Ice-rinks	2	82
Sailing and Motor-boat Clubs	125	247
Private Cars licensed	4,300	5,200,000
Motor Cycles	3,000	681,000
Speedway Tracks	Nil	43

If first-class cricket is to survive, it must be able to challenge these formidable competitors.

THE COUNTY GAME: OVERSEAS PLAYERS

LIMIT THE IMPORTS
Sydney Pardon, 1906

No one I think wishes Australian or other Colonial players to be excluded absolutely from our county elevens but at the same time there is a very strong feeling that the free importation of ready-made players does not make for the good of county cricket. Counties like Yorkshire and Kent that do all they can to encourage and develop home-grown talent feel that they are exposed to unfair competition. Moreover, there is a conviction in many quarters that a healthy state of things can only be brought about by limiting the choice of players to those who have some real connection with the counties they represent.

WE WELCOME EXOTIC ENTERPRISE ...
Norman Preston, 1969

The innovation permitting each county to engage one overseas cricketer on immediate registration every three years without residential qualification, was, as I predicted, a great success. For too long county cricket had been stifled by dour, safety-first methods. The overseas players by their enterprise and natural approach brought a breath of life into the three-day match. Garfield Sobers, as befitted his reputation, was the outstanding personality.

... BUT NOW ENOUGH'S ENOUGH
Norman Preston, 1972

The flow of overseas cricketers has done much to improve the standard of county cricket, but when the presence of so many stifles the opportunities of home-bred talent it is imperative to take action and I am pleased that the Test and County Cricket Board have changed the registration rules. In future each county will be limited to two classified overseas players and, instead of five, it will take ten years for a cricketer from another country to be regarded in the same category as one born in England.

INTOLERABLE FRUSTRATION
John Woodcock, 1981

Yet even to some of their own supporters, Middlesex's victory [*winning the Championship*] meant less than if it had not owed so much to overseas assistance. The extent to which these cricketers from abroad are being allowed to hinder the progress of young English talent has become an intolerable frustration to the England selectors. Time after time in 1980, Alec Bedser, in his 19th season as a selector and his 11th as chairman, went, as he hoped, to see an England candidate in action, only to spend most of his day watching someone bat or bowl who was ineligible to play for England. At different times during the season ten West Indians, four South Africans, two Pakistanis, two Australians, a Zimbabwean and a New Zealander were to be found opening the bowling in English county cricket.

STRENGTH BECOMES WEAKNESS
Graeme Wright, 1989

It cannot be simply coincidence that a number of overseas players in county cricket have been critical of the commitment of their English colleagues. Career professionalism should be English cricket's strength, and yet it is arguable that it is its weakness. In that it gives cricketers of other countries the opportunity to develop their skills, and do so in English conditions, it might be said to be a double weakness. Yet I would be reluctant to advocate a total restriction on overseas players. They remain an attraction, which was a reason for having them initially, and county cricket generally is richer for their presence. On the other hand, a limit of one overseas player per county does seem sensible. Unfortunately, while paying lip-service to a restriction, the chairmen and their committees put county before country as success is seen in a local rather than a national light.

Little Wonder No. 5

Yorkshire v Kent. At Sheffield, June 14, 15, 16, 1886: The weather on Whit Monday in the North of England was extremely wet, and at Sheffield, cricket was only possible between a quarter to one and two o'clock. The rain prevented any more cricket, much to the irritation of the crowd, who most unreasonably broke into the ground, tearing up the stumps and trampling over the wicket.

OUT OF HAND
Matthew Engel, 2005

Club cricketers complain vociferously that the game is being run by the counties for their own benefit. "The ECB is not a national governing body," says Barrie Stuart-King of the Club Cricket Conference. "It's an 18-member private club." He sees no indications of improved grassroots funding as a result of the Sky deal, and claims that in 2005 counties are likely to spend an extra £4m flying in yet more overseas players. However, at almost every level, clubs share this addiction to imports. The former England manager Micky Stewart did a survey for the ECB a decade ago and estimated there were 10,000 overseas players (i.e. who have come over specifically to play cricket) every summer in the English game. "To my knowledge there is very little difference now," he says. Both these figures – four million, 10,000 – may be on the high side, but the general points seem valid. These players would range from fully fledged overseas professionals in the big leagues to Aussie and Kiwi lads who might play a bit, coach a bit, serve behind the club bar, and get a bit of cash in a brown envelope so they can backpack round Europe. It's all out of hand.

THE COUNTY GAME: ONE-DAYERS

SKILLS COMPROMISED   Norman Preston, 1965

The Knock-Out Cup Competition has proved a money-spinner in filling some grounds, but no one can pretend that the cricket, excepting a few instances, has been any better. In this one-day tournament most captains aim to bowl defensively to keep down the run-rate, for with the number of overs limited in each innings, there is no need to make a special effort to dismiss the opposition. Now, it is proposed that, on four Wednesdays and Thursdays in 1966, instead of the usual number of three-day county matches, two separate one-day matches be played to be incorporated in the Championship. How will this help to shape Test cricketers?

LIMITED IN EVERY WAY   Graeme Wright, 1990

Does limited-overs cricket have to be played so badly? Put another way, why can't it be played without the artificial restrictions which encourage bad technique, other than limiting the number of overs each team receives? Why limit the number of overs available to one bowler? There could be spin bowling as well as pace so that the over-rate is maintained, and captains would learn to do more than rotate five bowlers. In the Sunday League, additional points could be awarded for bowling sides out, rewarding attack rather than encouraging containment. With specialist bowlers employed, there would also be a need for specialist batsmen instead of the bits-and-pieces players currently best suited to the one-day game.

CONDENSATION   Matthew Engel, 2004

As some readers may know, I returned to edit *Wisden* having spent two years on the heathen shores of the United States. But cricket changes so fast these days that even after a short absence one comes back entirely disorientated. In a way, the arrival of Twenty20 cricket was the least of it. I am delighted by its success but also remember the initial ecstatic response to 65-over cricket (1963) and 40-over cricket (1969). Actually, Twenty20 went on a bit too long for my own taste. I shall try to hang on for Ten10 or maybe Five5.

THE COUNTY GAME

Marketing and Many Outgrounds Ousted

Matthew Engel, 1997

One of the minor sadnesses of modern county cricket is the way in which the game is being withdrawn from so many of the out-grounds, and moving closer towards the point when nearly all the matches will be played at the 18 county headquarters. Any argument against these changes is usually dismissed as soppy sentimentalism by county officials who like to present themselves as shrewd managers making sensible economic decisions in keeping with cricket's modern needs. The reverse is the case. Of all branches of the game, county cricket is the one that has most dismally failed to market itself – hence its appalling public image. The festival games have long been the one great exception, the time when county cricket comes alive, and draws in a wider public.

One Just Feels Sick

Matthew Engel, 1998

One always feels slightly uneasy at charity fundraisers when well-heeled people eat and drink to raise money for, say, the starving. But it is legitimate and effective charity. When they do this to raise money for sportsmen taking advantage of a tax anomaly, whose employers are simply too skinflint to pay them properly, one just feels sick. The benefit system, with its emphasis on time-serving and de-emphasis on excellence, is profoundly corrosive. While this goes on, argument about the format of the Championship is like those fierce debates between mediaeval scholars about how many angels can dance on a pinhead.

THE COUNTY GAME: PITCH COVERING

Sticky Dog Is Put Down

John Woodcock, 1981

As the year ended, and to the dismay of many traditionalists, the 17 first-class counties, through the Test and County Cricket Board, voted that in 1981 pitches should be fully covered in all Championship matches. Although groundsmen are to be asked to prepare drier pitches, which show earlier signs of wear, in order to compensate spin bowlers for being deprived of the occasional sticky dog to bowl on, this will be difficult to implement. At times, inevitably, the weather will prevent it; at others, broken pitches will be an embarrassment to the home authorities no less than to batsmen.

When pitches were last fully covered in Championship cricket, in 1959, the experiment was soon discontinued. Now that it is to be given another trial, it is as well to keep an open mind. I cannot forbear, even so, from lamenting even a temporary loss of a part of the very heritage of English cricket – a drying pitch and a sizzling sun. Some of the great feats of batsmanship have been performed under these conditions.

LOSS OF VARIETY   John Woodcock, 1985

Since full covering was introduced into county cricket in 1981 (it has come to stay in Test matches, in the interests, for better or worse, of uniformity and thrift) the game has lost in variety. There can be no doubt of that. One felt deprived last season of some absorbing cricket, wherein, but for the covers, batsmen could regularly have been seen using their defensive skills against a turning ball on a drying pitch. Instead, on a succession of plastic pitches, all the life taken out of them by constant covering, runs were as plentiful as they have ever been. All being well the covers will have been removed, if only partially, by the start of the 1986 season, or by 1987 at the latest, enabling the county game to regain some of its former diversity.

KILLING THE GOOSE ...

PLAYERS GET STALE   Sydney Pardon, 1904

First-class cricket has increased enormously since the promotion of various counties in 1894 and I am not alone in thinking that nowadays we have too many matches. In my opinion, bowling and fielding would be better if the leading players were not so constantly kept at full tension six days a week. Not many years ago the leading bowlers were able to vary their serious cricket with a holiday match now and then and the relief did them good. Now they are hard at it from the first week in May till the first week in September, and in fine summers are very apt to get stale.

SATURATION POINT   John Woodcock, 1981

The reason most often given for the decline in interest in the first-class game in Australia is that it has reached the point of saturation. The same applies to association football in England. There is too much of it, just as there is now, to my mind, too much Test cricket. Between the middle of July 1979 and the middle of February 1980, a matter of seven months, India played 17 Test matches. A series between them and West Indies, due to have taken place in March and April 1980, was cancelled simply because both countries were surfeited with Test cricket. Between December 1974 and the first week of September this year, England will have played Australia no fewer than 31 times. This is more than twice the rate at which they met until only a few years ago. In 1981, for the first time in England, Australia are playing six Test matches. We must be careful not to kill the goose that lays the golden egg.

TOO MUCH OF A GOOD THING   Lawrence Booth, 2013

In between their 2012 meeting with South Africa and the next, in 2015-16, England will have played 24 Tests against either Australia or India. By the end of the 2015 Ashes, the Australians will have visited this country for bilateral series five summers out of seven.

Part of the charm of the big series resides in its sense of occasion. But ten straight Ashes Tests from July to January will be less of an occasion, more of a routine. And if the cycle of two series against Australia every four years was disturbed to spare England winters containing both an Ashes and a World Cup, then no such excuse can be made for Australia's swift return here in 2015. Not since the start of the 20th century, when only three sides played Test cricket, have 15 Ashes matches been crammed into so short a span. Last year, we fretted about Twenty20 overkill. Now we face another extreme: over the next three years, one of the most durable encounters in all sport will be stretched to its limit. Administrators will point to full houses as proof that all is well. But a little of the magic will be lost.

THE POWER OF TELEVISION

TAIL WAGS DOG
Graeme Wright, 1992

Replying to a questionnaire sent out prior to the Special Meeting of TCCB in May last year, the majority of county members who replied gave an emphatic thumbs-down to coloured clothing. So did Refuge Assurance, the sponsors of the Sunday League. They chose not to renew their contract. But even worse, no one else wanted to sponsor the Board's colourful new package either.

This does raise a question. If members opposed coloured clothing, and sponsors didn't want it, for whom was it intended? Television? Only a small minority of potential viewers watch Sunday League cricket on television, now that the broadcasting rights reside with BSkyB, the satellite network. To realise how few of the game's supporters bother with BSkyB, one had only to hear the thunderous applause which greeted the announcement at Lord's during the Nat West Bank Trophy final, that the BBC would again cover the Benson and Hedges Cup, as well as continuing to screen the NatWest and all international matches in England. Money should not be the only determining factor when it comes to broadcasting rights. Cricket is not such a popular sport that audience figures can afford to be ignored, especially with cricket being played at fewer schools and young people being offered a whole range of alternative leisure activities.

Cricket needs maximum exposure more than ever. Thousands of viewers in Britain will have watched the World Cup, perhaps hundreds of thousands. The fact that it would have been millions had the World Cup been shown on the BBC or ITV should be of concern to the TCCB. One feels it is not.

POVERTY OF IDEAS
Matthew Engel, 1999

The BBC has lost its immemorial right to cover home Test matches, and deservedly so. For many years, its presentation of cricket has been (as with other sports) complacent and dreary. Many new techniques for broadcasting the game have been developed in the past two decades. So far as I am aware, not a single one has emanated from the BBC, though they cheerfully pinched the ideas from others.

The viewing figures will probably fall when Tests move to Channel 4 (and they will plummet for the one Test a year to be shown live only on Sky TV, which is unavailable in most homes), though I am not sure cricket will lose anyone who has really been watching. The coverage may or may not be an improvement. But it was a reasonable gamble by the ECB, which will enliven future bidding rounds without shunting too much of the game into the ghetto of satellite TV. The BBC lost out not because of its poverty, but because of its poverty of ideas.

POTENTIAL CATASTROPHE
Matthew Engel, 2005

Live cricket in England will cease to be shown on terrestrial television, starting from 2006, and instead move to the satellite network, Sky Sports. The pattern of TV viewing is indeed changing, though not in the way the deal's instigators claim. Giles Clarke, the board's chief negotiator, described terrestrial television as "a dying form". But though all TV is indeed scheduled to be digital by 2012, there will still be mainstream channels, available to all viewers, and specialist ones for paying customers only.

Sky's business model does not depend on drawing large audiences. It makes money by accreting minorities who want different aspects of their service. Sky Sports will indeed give a good service to cricket-lovers willing to pay the subscription. It will not, however, go beyond them. Cricket's post-war survival in Britain was driven by the BBC. Television and radio attracted not just the obvious audience, but drew in people who knew nothing about the game until they heard or glimpsed it by chance and were captivated. Sky will attract only the already committed. We are talking about a situation where the overwhelming majority of the British population will never come across a game of cricket in their daily lives. Never, never, never, never. There will be short-term consequences as sponsors drift away; the longer-term effects will take a generation to unfold. Some believe these could be serious. I think we're looking at a potential catastrophe.

GENTLEMEN AND PLAYERS

IN PRAISE OF THE AMATEUR
Norman Preston, 1963

To many people the abolition of the amateur status in first-class cricket provided yet another big surprise. We live in a changing world. Conditions are vastly different from the days of our grandparents; but is it wise to throw everything overboard? We have inherited the game of cricket. The story of its development during the last hundred years is appropriately given full treatment in this edition of *Wisden*. Right through these hundred years the amateur has played a very important part.

In the time of Dr W. G. Grace there was talk that the amateur received liberal expenses. Whether this was true or not, I do not believe cricket, as we know it today, would be such a popular attraction, or so remunerative to the professional, without the contribution which Dr Grace and his contemporaries made as amateurs. By doing away with the amateur, cricket is in danger of losing the spirit of freedom and gaiety which the best amateur players brought to the game.

THE COUNTY CRICKETER OF THE FUTURE
Graeme Wright, 1990

Another of the season's achievements was the Combined Universities' reaching the quarter-finals of the Benson and Hedges Cup. Perhaps this is an opportune moment to hope that the captaincy skills of John Stephenson, the Essex opening batsman, who led Durham to the UAU Championship in 1986, will not be neglected. Michael Atherton, able to captain in first-class cricket while at Cambridge, quickly attracted the attention of the media and the selectors, both with his cricket and his special leadership qualities. They are two of the cricketers to whom England will be looking in the coming years. More than that, they could represent the county cricketer of the future: coming into the game after university, equipped to make a career without depending on the game alone, playing to enjoy and to win instead of eking out his talent over the years of his possible playing career. He might not, however, want to play cricket every day of the week.

KEEPING THE GAME ALIVE

SAME OLD STUFF
Norman Preston, 1952

Fancy Jack Hobbs stating that he finds more pleasure in watching a village match than modern county cricket, which he says consists of the same old stuff served up time after time. He emphasised that he did not regard his generation as being better than any other, but in his opinion there are few personalities in the game today. Hobbs thinks that the game should be improving because the youngster gets more chances than in his day, but instead it is going back. He pinpointed one of the biggest faults for slow scoring when he remarked, "A good cricketer should be able to score off good bowling, instead of waiting for the loose ball."

RIGHTS AND WRONGS

UMPIRING ETIQUETTE
Sydney Southerton, 1935

It has been the custom – in my opinion a very bad one – for some years now for umpires when answering an appeal in the negative to turn their heads away: look towards the sightscreen and say nothing, or else tell the bowler or wicketkeeper to get on with it. In its simplest interpretation this gesture has always appeared to me to be of a contemptuous nature and unnecessary on the cricket field. I would urge the MCC to issue an instruction that when an answer to an appeal is in the negative the umpire must clearly and audibly say: Not out. There ought never to be any misunderstanding over the affirmative reply, which is the raising of the index finger above the head; equally there should be none when the answer to the appeal is in the batsman's favour.

HARDER THAN EVER
John Woodcock, 1981

One way and another it was a difficult year for umpires. With such large amounts of prize money at stake, and a levelling-out of standards in Test and other first-class cricket, the game is becoming ever more fiercely competitive and the umpire's job correspondingly more demanding. Not only that. Every decision a Test umpire makes is subjected to a slow-motion television replay. In the Jubilee Test match which England played in Bombay on their way home from Australia in February, an umpire was constrained to change a decision. Having shown his surprise at being given out to an appeal for a catch at the wicket, Taylor, the England wicketkeeper, was reprieved upon the request of the Indian captain. That this, however well intentioned, was a misguided gesture became more clear in England's second innings when the same umpire, having given Boycott out, leg before wicket, changed his own mind when the batsman stood his ground. An umpire without confidence is worse than no umpire at all.

I am opposed to the idea of neutral umpires for Test matches. By the very nature of their job all umpires are fallible, whoever they may be, and on the rare occasions that I have wondered about the integrity of an umpire it has usually been because one side or the other has been harassing him. Remember, too, that if ever neutral umpires are introduced into Test cricket, England will never again have the benefit of playing under those who by common consent are the best of all umpires – the two dozen or so, that is, who stand day in and day out in the English county game. By the John Langridges of the world, that is. After 52 years as player and umpire in first-class cricket, Langridge has gone into honourable retirement.

UMPIRE'S DECISION NOT SO FINAL
Matthew Engel, 1994

The new world order has brought changes, starting with the arrival of what they would prefer us not to call "neutral" umpires (all umpires are neutral, these are "third-country"), one in each Test for at least the next three years. However, 1993 was also the year when the system of umpiring by video spread to engulf the Test-playing world. I may be in a minority; I remain utterly convinced that this is a disaster. Umpires can now call for help from a third official watching the TV replay on run-outs, stumpings and, sometimes, boundary decisions; indeed, they can hardly not do so.

It is true that last year one or two players in Test matches may have been given in or out more accurately than would otherwise have been the case. What we also saw was very good umpires virtually giving up on their duties at square leg, knowing there was no point in even contemplating making a judgment: it could only get them into trouble; why take the risk?

Remember that it was a couple of outrageously wrong decisions that led to the demand for this system, not a lot of marginal ones. We saw players starting to pressurise umpires if they did not call for a replay. And we saw increasing demands (sometimes on the field) for the system to be extended to close catches as well. The heart of the game, the finality of the umpire's verdict, is being eaten away.

TARNISHED IMAGE
Norman Preston, 1966

There was a time when the phrase "It isn't cricket" was commonly used in criticising anything shady or unfair. It meant that cricketers would never stoop to do anything so low. In recent years the public image of the game has been tarnished by many petty squabbles and questionable tactics. The recent controversies over throwing, the use of the bumper to frighten and threaten the batsman with bodily harm, and the matter of a batsman "walking" when he knows he is out are cases in point. These unsavoury problems stem from Test cricket in which the leading players in the world should portray everything that is best in the game. Instead, the courtesies of cricket often disappear when two countries meet in Test "warfare".

WEAK GOVERNMENT IN AUSTRALIA
John Woodcock, 1982

Wisden 1981 carried a picture of Michael Holding kicking a stump out of the ground, during a Test match, to show his disapproval of an umpire's decision. This year, in the same disreputable category, is one of Trevor Chappell bowling a sneak in Melbourne, at his brother's behest, to prevent New Zealand from making the six runs they needed to tie a one-day match. Some say it is money that has caused this collapse in the ethics of the game, others that it is the reflection of a graceless age. In Australia, I am afraid, it is partly the result of weak government. For too long the Australian Cricket Board have been over-tolerant of indiscipline and actions of dubious intent. True cricket-lovers have been as sickened by Lillee's antics as they have been spellbound by his bowling. The latest precept, that Australian players shall penalise each other for misconduct, hardly seems a step in the right direction.

Kent 1887. The team suffered particularly from the loss of Lord Harris's leadership, official duties at the War Office preventing his lordship from assisting Kent on more than four occasions.

Little Wonder No. 6

WITHOUT AN INCH OF MORAL GROUND
Graeme Wright, 1988

Britain has good reason to be proud of a tradition of civilised behaviour. But in recent years the tradition and indeed the civilisation have been endangered by the unacceptable increase in violent attitudes. I am not referring to criminal violence such as physical assault; rather the ill-tempered outbursts one encounters from otherwise law-abiding citizens. This behaviour is manifest on our roads, on public transport, in restaurants and at sports grounds. Consideration towards those about us is in decline; tolerance has given way to a short-fused temper.

There are some, among whom are our politicians, for whom such attitudes of verbal aggression are a device, a professional posturing. But politicians have a duty to society. When they are heard on the radio and television bickering, shrilly dissenting and by no means behaving in a civil manner, who can throw up his hands when the average citizen emulates those who are regarded as the country's leaders? It was not without significance that Mike Gatting, when called upon by the TCCB to apologise for his behaviour towards the Pakistani umpire, Shakoor Rana, was reported to have said, "Does Maggie [Mrs Thatcher, the Prime Minister] back down when she's given no choice?" The implication was that he could see no difference between his own outburst against an umpire he felt was behaving unjustly and that of the Prime Minister against her opponents.

The refusal of Chris Broad, England's opening batsman, to leave the wicket when given out in the First Test in Pakistan cannot be condoned. Cited in mitigation were the frustrations of the England players which had been allowed to build up during the tour as a result of some bad umpiring. Sympathy was the prevailing sentiment. In the next Test match, at Faisalabad, Gatting lost his temper and indulged in an unedifying confrontation with Shakoor Rana. The nation was then held spellbound by the spectacle of two grown men standing on their dignity without a square inch of moral ground to support them. I doubt if there is a cricketer anywhere who has not been upset by an umpire's decision, especially when – as can happen in club and village matches – that umpire has affiliations with the other side. But without the unchallenged acceptance of the principle that the umpire's word is final, what chance does the game have?

THE GLOBAL GAME

THE BEST EVER?
John Woodcock, 1985

Such was the success of the West Indians in 1984 that it came to be wondered whether, perhaps, Clive Lloyd's team were the strongest ever to have taken the field. In 1882 three of the greatest contemporary judges – W. G. Grace, A. G. Steel and Alfred Shaw – had no doubt that the Australian side of that year, led by W. L. Murdoch, was the best to have visited England. Twenty years later similar claims were made on behalf of Joe Darling's Australians, as they were for Warwick Armstrong's in 1921 and Sir Donald Bradman's in 1948.

As Lloyd does now, Murdoch, Armstrong and Bradman each had at his disposal the leading fast bowlers of the day. It is this, more than anything, which makes the present West Indians so immensely formidable. Their presence has brought a new and, dare I say it, chilling dimension to the game. Batsmen, however heavily protected, face them at their peril, and, as on the infamous Bodyline tour of 1932-33, that is only partly to the bowlers' and their captain's credit. It should be a cause of real concern to cricket's administrators that the batsman himself has become as much a target for the fast bowlers of the world as the wicket he defends.

Miller and Lindwall, who played the game hard enough, would never have thought of bowling in the same way to Bedser when he acted as nightwatchman at Headingley in 1948; nor, I feel sure, would Gregory and McDonald, or the Demon Spofforth. Perhaps, when the International Cricket Conference do no more than pay lip service to the problem, it is not surprising that umpires are so compliant.

WORLD TEST CHAMPIONSHIP
Matthew Engel, 1995

The most immediate problem facing the game is little discussed: England remains the home of cricketing self-analysis, and the greatest triumph of English cricket (amidst its manifest failures) has been to maintain and enhance the status of Test cricket as the game's apogee. Full-length, i.e. five-match, Test series are extinct where neither England nor Australia are involved. And even West Indies v Australia this year is down to four matches.

It is hard to explain why a Test match between two mighty sides, Pakistan and Australia, should attract crowds barely touching four figures in Lahore, not a city famous for its range of competing leisure attractions. Tickets are often too expensive; it is cheaper and easier to watch one day rather than five; live TV coverage may be a hindrance. But Test cricket, crucially, depends on context. It needs a five-Test series (six is too long) for the personalities to emerge and the battle to capture the public imagination. These half-hearted one-off Tests rarely work.

There is a possible solution which would cost next to nothing, could bring in major sponsorship, and would give shape to the present mish-mash of world cricket, raise the game's profile and give it something it badly needs: a true world champion team to go alongside the one-day world champions, who are after all the winners of just one tournament. All the Test countries need do is undertake to play at least one Test home and away against all the others in a four-year cycle, which they are edging towards anyway. (In this context, it is worth saying that England's decision to play six Tests against West Indies in 1995 instead of inviting Zimbabwe is a rather churlish and unworthy exception.)

In an Ashes series, the World Championship would merely be a subplot and the whole series could count in the final table: two points, say, for the winner; one each if it were drawn. For countries which just played a single Test against each other, then the one game would count for everything. It would thus add particular pith to the matches that now seem least important. There is no reason why this Championship could not be instituted almost at once. It can do no harm and could be very good for the game.

WISDEN ACCEPTED   Matthew Engel, 1998

As is now well known, *Wisden* has a solution for the problems of Test cricket. The Wisden World Championship, devised in 1996, has now become widely accepted as the best – or at any rate the least worst – method of ranking the teams. The principle of an official Championship has now been agreed by ICC.

INDIA AND THE TWENTY20 REVOLUTION

THE PLATES SHIFT   Scyld Berry, 2008

Twenty-over cricket in India is shifting the tectonic plates of the professional game as never before. Leading cricketers can now earn more by representing an Indian city, whether in Zee TV's Indian Cricket League or the officially sanctioned Indian Premier League. City-based cricket has arrived and will surely spread, annulling the player's traditional relationship with his county, state or province. The day has lurched closer when England's best cricketers, in addition to representing England, will play for an English region in a first-class tournament at the start of each season; for an English city in the 20-over competition in mid-summer; and for an Indian city. County cricket will then become a relic at amateur level, like the county championship of English rugby.

Cricket administrators in Test-playing countries around the world should be prepared to ride this Indian tiger, to keep the 20-over game in proportion and not let it swamp all other forms. I am not convinced they are ready, because the standard of administrators is not high enough. For a start, they took ages to understand what baseball discovered in the United States several generations ago: that the majority of people want to watch their sport in a package of about three hours. Twenty20 cricket is making up for a lot of lost time.

YOUR SPORT NEEDS YOU   Lawrence Booth, 2012

India have ended up with a special gift: the clout to shape an entire sport. Some national boards would struggle to survive without an Indian visit. But too often their game appears driven by the self-interest of the few – officials unable to admit that injuries collected in, or aggravated by, the IPL damaged their side's chances in England; capable of suggesting disregard for the innings defeat at Sydney in January by responding with breathless news of the schedule for IPL5; and happy to whitewash the whitewashes with constant references to the World Cup. To judge by comments made in Australia, some of their players have become equally blasé.

Other countries run the game along self-serving lines too; cricket's boardrooms are not awash with altruism. But none wields the BCCI's power, nor shares their responsibility. The disintegration of India's feted batting line-up has coincided with the rise of a Twenty20-based nationalism, the growth of private marketeers and high-level conflicts of interest. It is a perfect storm. And the global game sits unsteadily in the eye. India, your sport needs you.

AND FINALLY…

FROM RUSSIA WITH A DROPPED CATCH
Hubert Preston, 1951

To Mr Harold Wilson fell the task of proposing the toast of "This Wonderful Century" [*at a lunch celebrating the centenary of John Wisden & Co.*]. He confessed that he was no cricketer himself, but he remarked: "I am a Yorkshireman, and cricket is never far from a Yorkshireman's thoughts." Then he amused us with an account of the last time he played cricket. He said it was in Moscow when he was there for trade talks with the Russians. "There was one Sunday afternoon, during a lull in the negotiations, when my delegation repaired to some woods not far from Moscow. A few weeks afterwards, following the breakdown of the discussions, the Moscow press, who seem to have observed our innocent pastime, came out with an account of the 'orgies and strange pirouettes by the lakeside of the English delegation.'" Continuing his reminiscence, Mr Wilson told this story: "My second over was interrupted by a gentleman from the NKVD or Ogpu, who was appointed to follow us around and see that we came to no harm. He stood in the middle of the pitch and remonstrated with us in a very long Russian speech which I understood came to this – that we could not do that there! He was supported by two men who came up on horseback with rifles. I persuaded him, after some negotiation, to take up his position at square leg, out of the way of even my bowling. The episode closed with the NKVD man's failure to make any attempt to catch a ball – and after that my opinion of the Russian secret police fell even lower." Mr Wilson suggested that the incident should be recorded in *Wisden* as the "only case of a catch being missed at square leg by a member of the NKVD off an off-spinner by a visiting British minister".

Cricketers

No element of the Almanack's content, apart from Notes by the Editor, epitomises *Wisden* quite like the Five Cricketers of the Year, an institution that was begun by Charles Pardon in 1889 and is thus the longest-running individual award of its kind in the game. It took a while to standardise into the award it is today. The first players honoured were "Six Great Bowlers of the Year", chosen "to signalise the extraordinary success that bowlers achieved in 1888", a comment which in itself indicates the generally condescending attitude towards bowlers in the late Victorian era. Some more modern bowlers would say that this attitude still prevails.

Other quirky labels of the winners include "Mr R. E. Foster and Four Yorkshiremen", redolent of Monty Python and their Yorkshiremen sketch, in 1901 and, in 1909, "Lord Hawke and Four Cricketers of the Year", suggesting his lordship's influence off the field to be rather greater than his capabilities on it. In 1918 and 1919 schoolboy cricketers were chosen because the county game had ceased during the First World War. In 1896 and 1926 only one eminent cricketer was chosen, W. G. Grace and Jack Hobbs respectively. In 2010 *Wisden* named only four Cricketers of the Year because of the spot-fixing scandal that had engulfed the intended fifth, generally thought to be the Pakistani pace bowler Mohammad Aamer. A year earlier Claire Taylor had become the first female Cricketer of the Year, at last fulfilling the apparently tongue-in-cheek suggestion made in the Preface to the 1970 edition by Norman Preston that Enid Bakewell, fresh from her exploits Down Under, should be a Cricketer of the Year.

In 2000 Five Cricketers of the Century – Sir Don Bradman, Sir Garfield Sobers, Sir Jack Hobbs, Sir Vivian Richards and Shane Warne – were chosen by an eminent electorate of 100. Bradman was the only unanimous selection. The regular Cricketers of the Year selection is made solely by the editor, and there are only two rules: the award is based "primarily but not exclusively, on the players' influence on the previous English season" and no one can be chosen more than once.

There are anomalies. Sir Pelham Warner was one of the Five in 1904 and then honoured alone with a "special portrait" in 1921 after leading Middlesex to the County Championship. Jack Hobbs had likewise been chosen in 1909, before being honoured alone in 1926 for overtaking Grace's record number of centuries. From 2001 to 2003 the award's scope was widened to include cricket all round the world rather than just in the English season. But in 2004 *Wisden* instituted the Leading Cricketer in the World honour, to allow a more global view of the game. In 2007 a panel of 16 writers and historians picked the world's top player for every year going back to 1900. Bradman was named on ten occasions and Sobers eight. There have been many fine players, such as Fred 'The Demon' Spofforth and Gubby Allen, who have never been Cricketers of the Year. Both these men, and many other greats who have been Cricketers of the Year, receive due treatment in the Obituaries chapter and elsewhere. In the 2008 edition Scyld Berry selected five who never received the accolade: Abdul Qadir, Bishan Bedi, Inzamam-ul-Haq, Wes Hall and Jeff Thomson. With the publication of the 2013 edition, the Cricketers of the Year pantheon had swelled to 570 players. We have selected 73 for our Cricketers chapter, all of whom have been a Cricketer of the Year. We are not saying these are the best 73 ever to play the game, though one could pick a few very satisfactory all-time XIs out of the list. They are chosen to represent a cross-section of cricket history.

In this section we have not restricted ourselves simply to players' Cricketer of the Year profiles, but allowed ourselves the luxury of other pieces written subsequently. We have not included Obituaries, though there are some posthumous articles, or extracts from Notes by the Editor. The players appear in chronological order by year of when they were a Cricketer of the Year.

1889–99

No Match Too Big Six Great Bowlers of the Year, 1889

GEORGE ALFRED LOHMANN was born at Kensington, June 5, 1865, and first played for Surrey in 1884. He is by general consent admitted to be one of the best bowlers and most accomplished all-round cricketers ever seen, and he fairly challenged comparison with the Australian, Charles Turner, by what he did during the season of 1888. Lohmann and Turner are, indeed, very much alike. They bowl with remarkable skill and judgment; their batting and fielding are invaluable to their side, and they both have that peculiar electrical quality of rising to a great occasion. It has often enough been said of cricketers of proved skill, when they have failed, that the match has been too big for them, but certainly no match was ever too big for George Lohmann or Charles Turner.

Surrey v Nottinghamshire. At Kennington Oval, August 1, 2, 3, 1887. Probably not expecting such a crowd as actually assembled, the Surrey Club had not secured a sufficient body of police, and during part of the opening day the boundaries were curtailed by quite 20 yards, a great deal of bottle-throwing and other playful eccentricities being indulged in by some of the holiday people.

Little Wonder No. 7

Second Only To Grace Nine Great Batsmen of the Year, 1890

ARTHUR SHREWSBURY, who may without the least reservation be described as the greatest professional batsman of the day, was born on April 11, 1856, and made his first appearance on Lord's ground for the Colts of England against the Marylebone Club on May 12, 1873, being then only a little more than 17 years old. Even at that early age his method of batting – obviously modelled on that of Richard Daft – was thoroughly formed, and it was at once made evident that Notts had discovered a colt of exceptional promise. At the start of his career, however, he was handicapped by ill-health, and did not come to the front quite so soon as he otherwise would have done. At the age of 19, however, he appeared in the Nottingham county eleven, and a year later he was chosen for Players against Gentlemen. Finely as he played on many occasions, it was not until after his visit to Australia in the winter of 1881-82 that he took his present position at the head of professional batsmen. Just before he went to the Colonies his health was so delicate as to cause considerable anxiety, but a winter in the warmer climate of Australia did wonders for him; and his batting during the last few years, as all cricket readers are well aware, has been some of the most remarkable in the history of the game. Indeed, on performances he can claim superiority over all English batsman save and except Mr W. G. Grace. In the season of 1887 his batting average in first-class matches was 78, which, curiously enough, just tied the highest average that Mr Grace had ever obtained. Certainly no batsman has ever equalled Shrewsbury in mastering the difficulties of slow wickets, and his supremacy in this direction is freely admitted by all cricketers. Subsequent to his first visit to Australia, Shrewsbury assisted in taking out cricket teams to the Colonies in the winters of 1884-85, 1886-87, and 1887-88, and as on this last occasion he remained behind to look after the interests of the English football team whose visit he had been largely instrumental in promoting, his services were lost to Nottingham during the summer of 1888. His return to England had no doubt a great deal to do with the wonderful improvement shown by the Notts eleven last season, and, though he was handicapped at different times by an injured hand and a sprained wrist, he yet came out second to Gunn in the county averages. We can only once remember having seen Shrewsbury bowl – in the famous England and Australia match at Kennington Oval in 1884 – but there is, perhaps, no better or safer field at point in the kingdom.

FROM BEATING CHURCHILL TO BEATING AUSTRALIA   Hubert Preston, 1948

F. S. Jackson was one of Five All-Round Cricketers in 1894.

The passing of Colonel The Honourable SIR FRANCIS STANLEY JACKSON, P.C., G.C.I.E., on March 9, in his 77th year, came as a shock, not only to all who knew him personally, but also to every lover of cricket who had watched and enjoyed his wonderful prowess on the field of play. From the time that F. S. Jackson at Lord's by his remarkable all-round success helped Harrow gain a victory over Eton by 156 runs in 1888, he went on from strength to strength, until he became one of the finest cricketers ever seen in England. Unfortunately he could not go on any tour to Australia owing to business reasons, and the presence of Lord Hawke in command of Yorkshire until 1910 prevented him from ever being the county captain, though occasionally in charge of the side. He reached the zenith of fame in 1905 when captain of England against Australia.

In all five Tests he won the toss; made 492 runs with an average of 70, among his scores being 144 not out at Leeds, 113 at Manchester, 82 not out at Nottingham, 76 and 31 at The Oval; took 13 wickets at 15.46 each, surpassing the efforts of all his colleagues and opponents. Of the five contests, England won that at Nottingham by 213 runs – after declaring with five men out – and that at Manchester by an innings and 80 runs, while they held much the stronger position in each of the three matches left unfinished. By a curious coincidence Stanley Jackson and Joseph Darling, then the Australian captain, were exactly the same age, both having been born on November 21, 1870. That was Darling's third visit as captain and his last tour in England.

Regarding his luck in winning the toss in those 1905 Tests and as captain of MCC, for whom he scored 85 in a rain-ruined match at Lord's, Jackson said that at Scarborough, when captain for the seventh time against the Australians: "I found Darling stripped to the waist. He said, 'Now we'll have a proper tossing, and he who gets on top wins the toss.' So I said to George Hirst, 'Georgie, you come and toss this time.' Darling then said, 'All right, we'll toss in the old-fashioned way!'" Again winning the toss, Jackson scored 123 and 31 not out, rain preventing a definite result.

Well-built and standing nearly six feet high, Stanley Jackson was equipped with special physical advantages for cricket; to these were added fine judgment, perseverance, and, above all, exceptional courage which amounted to belief in his own abilities. Free and stylish in method, he drove splendidly on either side of the wicket and was perhaps the finest forcing on-side batsman of his time. While essentially a forward player on hard wickets, he had at his command on sticky wickets a strength and science of back play to which few men have attained. His great stroke sent a good-length ball through the covers; he cut square or late and turned the ball cleverly on the leg side with similar precision. Nothing was better than the way he jumped in and drove the ball over the bowler's head, as shown in the lifelike picture at Lord's, and as I saw at Bradford, where he sent the ball high over the football stand.

In the South African War Jackson served with the Royal Lancaster Regiment of Militia, and in the first Great War, 1914-18, he was Lieutenant-Colonel of a West Yorkshire Regiment battalion which he raised and commanded. He entered Parliament in 1915 and remained Unionist member for Howdenshire Division of Yorkshire until 1926. One day in the House of Commons dining-room Mr Winston Churchill, who had been his fag at Harrow, said, "Let me introduce you to Mr Lloyd George." There came a quick exclamation: "I have been looking all my life for the man who gave Winston Churchill a hiding at school."

When he wanted to make his maiden speech the debate went unfavourably, and he received a note from the Speaker: "I have dropped you in the batting order; it's a sticky wicket." Then, at a better opportunity, he sent this hint: "Get your pads on; you're next in."

THE TRUE ALL-ROUNDER
Five Young Batsmen of the Season, 1895

MR CHARLES B. FRY was born on April 25, 1872. Since the days of C. J. Ottaway and the Hon. Alfred Lyttelton there has been no such Admirable Crichton in the way of outdoor sports at either university as Mr Fry, and if we had to deal with him as a long jumper, sprint runner, and football player, the demands upon our space would be extreme. We would not put Mr Fry as a batsman in the same class with such a player as Mr MacLaren, but he has any amount of pluck and resolution, and, inasmuch as he played three innings of over a hundred in first-class matches, he has a distinct claim to a place among the prominent batsmen of 1894. Mr Fry is a brilliant field, but for his bowling we cannot express admiration. In point of fairness of delivery it is by no means so bad now as it was when he first appeared in the Oxford eleven, but it still leaves a great deal to be desired.

As Good As He Ever Was
Sydney Pardon, 1896

In the 1896 edition there was only one Cricketer of the Year. Wisden published 13 pages of literary and statistical tribute to W. G. Grace, who turned 48 during the summer, as well as a "special photograph", which was trailed on the front cover.

It had for some years been intended to publish in *Wisden's Almanack* a portrait of W. G. GRACE, and it was felt before the season of 1895 had been many weeks in progress that the most suitable time had arrived. No one interested in cricket will need to be told that Mr Grace last summer played with all the brilliancy and success of his youth. In one respect, indeed, he surpassed all he had ever done before, scoring in the first month of the season a thousand runs in first-class matches – a feat quite without parallel in the history of English cricket. As everyone knows, in the course of the month of May he made, on the Gloucestershire county ground at Ashley Down, Bristol, his hundredth hundred in first-class matches, this special circumstance being the origin of the national testimonial which was afterwards taken up with such enthusiasm in all parts of the country, and in many places far beyond the limits of the United Kingdom. The details of Mr Grace's marvellous career are so familiar to all who have any love for cricket that I thought some favourable impressions of the great batsman, contributed by those who had played against him and on his side, would be far more interesting to the readers of *Wisden* than a formal biography.

Two Players In One
Lord Harris, 1896

There may arise a bat as good, and at point and to his own bowling a field as good, and, of course, there have been and will be bowlers as good, but I doubt one generation producing two such all-round cricketers. And remember, my young friends, that this super-excellence was not the result of eminent physical fitness only, it depended a good deal also on the careful life the old man led. He did not play brilliantly despite how he lived, as some, whose all too brief careers I can remember, did, but he regulated his habits of life with such care and moderation that his physical capacity was always at its best, and has lasted in the most marvellous manner. I shall always hold that WG was the best and pluckiest field to his own bowling I ever saw. The ground he used to cover to the off – and with the leg-break on of course the majority of straight balls went there – made him as good as a twelfth man. He used to have his mid-on nearly straight behind the bowler's arm so as to cover the balls hit straight back. I fancy I've noticed that he has not tried for long-leg catches so much since poor dear Fred Grace, the safest catch I ever saw, went home, but it may be only fancy. And then the hot'uns I've seen him put his hands to, half-volleys hit at ten yards distance, low down, with all the momentum of a jump in and a swinging bat, catches that looked like grinding his knuckles against the sole of his boot, but I never saw the old man flinch.

I always thought the old man depended rather too much on the umpire for leg-before, particularly when I was on the opposite side. He crossed the wicket so far to the off himself that he could not in many instances judge with any accuracy whether the ball pitched straight or not, and I don't think a bowler ought to ask for leg-before unless he is pretty sure as to the pitch. I remember one day at Canterbury, the wind was blowing pretty strongly across the ground, and WG was lobbing them up in the air to get all the advantage of the wind. I kept on fetching them round to sharp long leg – I never hit him square – or trying to, and every time the ball hit my leg he asked, and every time he asked Willsher shook his head, and the old man was getting almost savage, when, at last, I got my left leg too much to the off, and the ball went through my legs and bowled me. Of course, WG held that was proof positive that all the others would have hit the wicket too, whilst I held that that was possible, but that none of them had pitched straight.

BY HIS INITIALS ALONE YE SHALL KNOW HIM
Geoffrey Moorhouse, 1998

On July 18, it will be 150 years since W. G. Grace was born, but there are other ways of measuring how distant he is in time. For one thing, no one still alive, not even Jim Swanton, can remember seeing him play (although in *Sort of a Cricket Person*, EWS notes that "I am supposed to have watched [him] from my perambulator on the Forest Hill ground round 1910"). Eight decades have passed since Grace died, yet he dogs us still, demanding our attention at regular intervals.

The statistics of his career are alone enough to explain why – more than 54,000 first-class runs (there are at least two different versions of the precise figure, so let's leave it at that) spread across 44 seasons, including 839 in just eight days of 1876, when he hit a couple of triple-centuries, and only one other batsman managed to top a thousand runs in the entire season; a thousand in May in 1895, when he was nearly 47; and 2,800-odd wickets costing less than 18 runs apiece. I suppose we might wonder why his bowling average wasn't even more impressive, given the ropey pitches on which Dr Grace played. No modern cricketer would deign to turn out on them, which makes his batting all the more wondrous, and comparisons with Bradman or anyone since quite pointless.

But there was not that much to Grace apart from these skills and his devotion to his family. A hand of whist appears to have marked the limit of his capacity for celebration.

It was simply because the cricketing Grace totally dominated his own era that an exasperated C. L. R. James could not understand why standard history books of the period never mentioned him. This man, for heaven's sake, opened for England at the age of 50 – and at the age of 18 he had scored 224 not out for England against Surrey, in a match which he left halfway through in order to win a quarter-mile hurdles championship at the Crystal Palace! No wonder he was the best-known Englishman apart from Mr Gladstone, so much so that Evelyn Waugh's friend, Monsignor Ronnie Knox, waggishly suggested that Gladstone and Grace were really one and the same celebrity.

Athletic is not a word that obviously comes to mind when contemplating Grace in his prime, though a slim young man did precede the pot-bellied genius who in middle age was far too heavy for any horse to bear. I have often wondered how stylishly he played his strokes, ever since I saw some film in which he appeared to be brandishing his bat as though he was about to poke the fire with it. Something tells me that he never hit the ball as gracefully as Victor Trumper did in the famous photo of his straight drive; Grace, I suspect, was much more about power than aesthetics.

That, at any rate, would fit what we know of his character in general. Apart from tenderness to his relatives and a generous soft spot for children, he was not, I think, a particularly attractive man, though he could sometimes (and it is usually recorded as remarkable) encourage a young player on his own side with – as the saying went in his day – bluff good humour. After the Australians had experienced him for the first time, a commentator Down Under observed that, "For so big a man, he is surprisingly tenacious on very small points." He was notorious for employing, in order to pursue victory or personal achievement, a variety of wiles and tricks that may be thought of as, well, hardly cricket. He was also, throughout his career, quite breathtakingly grasping when his eye caught the glint of hard cash.

The astonishing thing about the mercenary Grace, of course, is that he was classified, and has ever since been glorified, as an amateur. Nothing more exposed the humbug that used to smother the entire topic of Gents v Players than an examination of Grace's financial rewards from the game; and nothing more reveals the intellectual dishonesty at the heart of the humbug than something Grace once said when trying to argue the Gloucestershire committee into playing more amateurs than professionals.

He declared his fear for the future of cricket if it became wholly professional. "Betting and all kindred evils will follow in its wake, and instead of the game being followed up for love, it will simply be a matter of £ s d." Prophetic words, perhaps; but it ill became W. G. Grace to mouth them.

It will be gathered from the above that he has never been a hero of mine, not since the day in adolescence when I discovered that he was sometimes a shameless cheat in a game that, I was being asked to believe, was wholly honourable. I shall nevertheless drink to his memory on July 18 because his tremendous gifts, especially his phenomenal batting, were largely responsible for the elevation of cricket from just another 19th-century game, which had become popular partly because it lent itself to gambling.

Grace's towering presence, more than any other single factor, transformed it into the unrivalled spectator sport of summer, first of all in England, subsequently in other lands spread widely across the world. I would even suggest that a true measurement of WG's unique stature is that he is instantly identifiable, even by some who are uninterested in his vocation, by his initials alone. I cannot think of another human being in any sphere, not even W. C. Fields, of whom this is also true.

GENIUS UNDERESTIMATED Five Cricketers of the Season, 1897

KUMAR SHRI RANJITSINHJI, the young Indian batsman who has in the course of four seasons risen to the highest point of success and popular favour, was born on September 10, 1872. When he first began to be talked about, the statement gained currency that he knew nothing whatever of cricket before coming to England to complete his education, but on this point Ranjitsinhji has himself put the world right. It is true that when he went up to Cambridge he had nearly every-thing of the real science to learn, but he had played the game in his schooldays in India, and was by no means such an entire novice as has sometimes been repre-sented. It was in 1892 that the English public first heard his name, and there is little doubt that he ought that year to have been included in the Cambridge eleven. He made lots of runs in college matches, and was already a brilliant field. The author-ities at Cambridge perhaps found it hard to believe that an Indian could be a first-rate cricketer, and at the complimentary dinner given to Ranjitsinhji at Cambridge on September 29 – when his health was proposed by the Master of Trinity – Mr F. S. Jackson frankly acknowledged he had never made so great a mistake in his life as when he under-estimated the young batsman's powers. However, Ranjitsinhji's opportunity came in 1893 when, in his last year at the University, he, to his great delight, gained a place in the Cambridge eleven. It was not his good fortune to do much against Oxford at Lord's – getting out for nine in the first innings, and without a run in the second – but on the whole he batted very well, scoring 386 runs with an average of 29 and coming out third in the Cambridge averages. Moreover he had the honour of being chosen for the South of England against the Australians at The Oval, and though his real greatness as a batsman was as yet scarcely suspected, he made himself a very popular figure in the cricket world, his free finished batting and brilliant work in the field earning him recognition wherever he went. Having left Cambridge, and not being yet qualified for Sussex, his opportunities in 1894 were very limited, and in first-class matches he only played 16 innings. Still he did well, averaging 32 with an aggregate of 387 runs. For the immense advance he showed in 1895, it is safe to say that very few people were prepared. Qualified by this time for Sussex, he made a truly sensational first appearance for the county against the MCC at Lord's, scoring 77 not out, and 150, and almost winning a match in which Sussex had to get 405 in the last innings. From this time forward, he went on from success to success, proving beyond all question that he was now one of the finest of living batsmen. In the first-class averages for the year, he ran a desperately close race with A. C. MacLaren and W. G. Grace, scoring 1775 runs with the splendid average of 49. As a batsman Ranjitsinhji is himself alone, being quite individual and distinctive in his style of play. He can scarcely be pointed to as a safe model for young and aspiring batsmen, his peculiar and almost unique skill depending in large measure on extreme keenness of eye, combined with great power and flexibility of wrist. For any ordinary player to attempt to turn good-length balls off the middle stump as he does, would be futile and disastrous. To Ranjitsinhji on a fast wicket, however, everything seems possible, and if the somewhat too-freely-used word genius can with any propriety be employed in connection with cricket, it surely applies to the young Indian's batting.

Batting genius: Ranji was a familiar and popular figure on every cricket field

Eton v Harrow. At Lord's, July 14, 15, 1893. Uncertain weather and the strong counter-attraction of the meeting of Orme and La Flêche in the Eclipse Stakes at Sandown considerably affected the attendance on the opening day, the company scarcely numbering more than 12,000, of whom 4,500 paid for admission at the gates.

Little Wonder No. 8

PACY AND POPULAR

Five Cricketers of the Season, 1897

THOMAS RICHARDSON – beyond all question the most famous of contemporary bowlers – was born at Byfleet, in Surrey, on August 11, 1870. After making a considerable reputation at Mitcham, he first found a place in the Surrey eleven in 1892, the year in which Surrey, after seeming certain to only take second place, wound up by beating Notts for the Championship. It was not at first realised that Surrey had discovered the most deadly fast bowler since Freeman, but Richardson did enough in 1892 to make his future position in the county eleven pretty secure. No great opportunity was afforded him in the chief county matches, but against the counties then treated as below first-class rank, he proved extremely destructive, and his record for Surrey for the whole season came out at 101 wickets for just over 13½ runs each. It cannot do Richardson any harm now, to say that when he first came into important cricket, his delivery was, to say the least of it, dubious. Indeed – our views being confirmed at the time by the opinions of many famous batsmen – we have no doubt that he threw a great deal. The fact that he went through the tour of Mr Stoddart's Team in Australia, in the winter of 1894-95, without, so far as we have heard, his action being even questioned, is the best proof of the alteration in his style. The season of 1893 took him at once to the top of the tree and he has from that time to the present moment been the first of English bowlers. Lohmann's enforced absence from England through illness gave him in 1893 a great opportunity, and he emphatically made the most of it, taking in the County Championship matches for Surrey 99 wickets for something over 14 runs each, and coming out in the first-class averages of the year with a record of 174 wickets, at an average cost of 15.70. Since then he has never looked back, his greatest season being that of 1895, when in first-class matches he took the almost unprecedented number of 290 wickets for less than 14½ runs each. Nearly all his work was done for Surrey, no fewer than 237 wickets falling to him in county matches alone. Out in Australia Richardson at first found the exceptionally fast and easy grounds very trying, and we believe it is a fact that his first three wickets in the Colonies cost him about a hundred runs each. So far from being disheartened by early failures, however, he persevered with the utmost pluck, and had the satisfaction, through a splendid piece of work, of rendering possible the victory in the conquering Test match at Melbourne, which was gained in the end by the wonderful batting of Brown and Albert Ward. Last season Richardson did not equal his record of 1895, but on the dry wickets of May, June and July, he was as much as ever the best bowler in the country. When the rain came, however, he seemed a little overdone, and on some occasions – notably in Surrey's two matches against the Australians – he was less effective than might have been expected. His greatest feats last summer were certainly performed in the England matches at Lord's and Manchester. On the last day at Old Trafford, he bowled unchanged for three hours, and nearly won a match in which England had followed on against a majority of 181 runs. The characteristics of Richardson's bowling are too well known to require detailed description. It is generally agreed that no bowler with the same tremendous speed, has ever possessed such a break from the off. Personally no professional cricketer in England enjoys greater popularity with the general public and among his brother players.

FEARLESS GAME-CHANGER Five Cricketers of the Year, 1898

MR GILBERT L. JESSOP was born on May 19, 1874. It is perfectly safe to say that there are few more popular figures on the cricket field at the present time than the young amateur who has during the last few seasons done so much to restore the fortunes of the Gloucestershire eleven. The public dearly love a fearless hitter, and in days like these, when there is a tendency in many directions to make cricket a little too steady and methodical, a batsman of Mr Jessop's delightful qualities is sure of an enthusiastic welcome wherever he goes. We have never before produced a batsman of quite the same stamp. We have had harder hitters, but perhaps never one who could, in 20 minutes or half an hour, so entirely change the fortunes of a game. Those who during the past season saw Mr Jessop in the Oxford and Cambridge, and Gentlemen v Players matches, witnessed some hitting that in its way could not have been surpassed. The manner in which, on a somewhat worn wicket, he literally flogged the best professional bowling in England in the Gentlemen's second innings was simply astonishing. Of course he had a little luck – daring hitters are proverbially fortunate – but we could name on the fingers of one hand the batsmen now before the public, to whom such an innings would have been possible. Not less remarkable was the brilliant bit of hitting with which, at The Oval in June, he went so far toward securing the Gloucestershire eleven their victory over Surrey. It was very happily said of him on that occasion, that he treated Richardson as though the Surrey crack had been an ordinary medium-pace bowler. As a batsman Mr Jessop is individual to a degree. No one could be taught to play his game, inasmuch as the power to hit fast bowling as he hits it is scarcely given to half a dozen batsmen in a generation. When he fails to come off he is sometimes advised to be more careful, but the criticism always strikes one as being beside the mark. If he modified his method and played like other people, half his value would be gone. Where he sometimes makes a mistake, however, is in trying to hit directly he goes in without having first got a sight of the ball or judged the pace of the ground. He is a keen judge of his own capabilities and we have heard him say that, with bowling that keeps at all low, he is apt to be very soon out. Taking such liberties as he does and trying to score so continually from good-length balls, this can be readily understood. Having regard to all he has done, no good judge of cricket would wish him to be other than he is. A batsman who can in half an hour win an apparently lost game is a prize for any eleven. As everyone knows, however, Mr Jessop is a great deal more than a mere batsman. Even if he lost his power to get runs his bowling and fielding would ensure him a prominent place in first-class cricket. There is scarcely another amateur fast bowler who can keep up an end so long without tiring, and at cover point he can hold his own with almost anyone. He is altogether a most brilliant and remarkable cricketer.

INSTANTLY IRRESISTIBLE   Five Great Players of the Season, 1899

WILFRED RHODES's appearance for Yorkshire last season illustrated in a most striking way the truth of the proverb that the hour brings forth the man. Robert Peel's long and honourable connection with Yorkshire having terminated under rather painful circumstances in 1897, the county's one pressing need was a left-handed slow bowler to take his place, and in young Rhodes exactly the bowler required was forthcoming. Whatever he may do in the future, there can be no doubt as to the greatness of his achievements last summer. Quite unknown at the beginning of May outside the limits of local cricket in Yorkshire, he sprang at once into fame, bowling in match after match for Yorkshire with astounding success. His sudden rise to the front rank recalled the doings of Mr A. G. Steel in 1878, there being a close parallel between the performances of the two bowlers. In one respect, however, Rhodes's record was the more remarkable, for whereas he was an unknown quantity, Mr Steel before appearing in first-class matches had earned for himself a reputation at Marlborough as a first-rate school bowler. It may without unfairness be said that Rhodes was fortunate in coming out when bad weather was day after day making the wickets slow and difficult, but one must not on this account do him less than justice. He made the fullest use of his opportunities and even if his gifts as a bowler had been backed up by experience he could scarcely have proved more effective. Naturally when the dry weather set in he was less successful than before but, as we have had occasion to point out in dealing with Yorkshire cricket, the occasions were very few on which he was fairly collared. His qualities as a slow bowler struck everyone as being exceptional. He bowls with a high, easy action, his pitch is wonderfully accurate, and whenever the ground gives him assistance he can get a lot of spin on the ball. On some days, notably when Yorkshire beat Surrey in a single innings at Bradford, he was irresistible, combining so much break with a perfect length that the batsmen could do nothing against him. His value as a cricketer is by no means restricted to his bowling, as he has already proved himself a dangerous run-getter. Only 21 years old, and with a position already established, it will be disappointing indeed if he does not enjoy a brilliant career in the Yorkshire eleven.

1901–19

HERCULEAN PROMISE   Mr R. E. Foster and Four Yorkshiremen, 1901

GEORGE HERBERT HIRST was born at Kirkheaton, on September 7, 1871. He joined the village club about 1885 and remained connected with it until 1889, in which year the eleven carried off the Lumb Challenge Cup. In the cup ties Hirst did very well as a bowler, and made so good an impression that late in the season he was given a trial for Yorkshire at Huddersfield against Cheshire.

It was in 1892 that Hirst became known to the general public, his first match being for Yorkshire against the MCC at Lord's. Without doing anything sensational he yet showed such capital form, both as bowler and batsman, that no good judge who saw the game could doubt that an all-round player of far more than ordinary promise had come forward. He was then less than 21 years of age, but in appearance a small Hercules, and it was quite certain that whether or not his skill as a cricketer developed, he would never fail for want of strength or stamina.

KING OF SWING

Major R. O. Edwards, OBE, 1922

In purely county cricket Hirst was perhaps the greatest match-winning professional cricketer yet produced. His best work was done for Yorkshire, and, with a few notable exceptions, he was singularly unsuccessful in Test match cricket. For his county he generally came off in a crisis either with bat or ball or both, and during his long and wonderful career, by sheer grit and determination, he constantly carried his county to victory when defeat had seemed certain. Fourteen seasons (11 in succession) Hirst performed the double feat of scoring over 1,000 runs and capturing more than 100 wickets – easily a record. Twice he passed the 2,000-runs mark in addition to taking 100 wickets, whilst in 1906 he actually had 2,385 runs and 208 wickets to his credit – a distinction without parallel in first-class cricket. Hirst was a cricketing genius, and a personality in any assemblage of famous sportsmen. Originally a fast-medium left-hand bowler, Hirst later developed the swerve, which he cultivated to an extent never previously approached even by Barton King, the Philadelphian. His deceptive flight when combined with a cross-wind made him quite unplayable at times, even when the pitch was perfect. Some of his outstanding performances were at the expense of Gloucestershire, yet curiously enough he never secured the wicket of W. G. Grace. Hirst admitted the correctness of this tragedy to me one day, hastily adding, with a mischievous twinkle, "but the Old Man never got mine either".

SIMPLY THE BEST

Five Cricketers of the Year, 1903

VICTOR TRUMPER, at the present time, by general consent, the best batsman in the world, was born on November 2, 1877. He came out in Australia in the same season as Clement Hill – 1894-95 – but his powers ripened far more slowly than those of the great left-handed batsman, and for a year or two he did little to foreshadow the career that was in store for him. Against Mr Stoddart's team in the season of 1897-98, he was not picked for any of the Test matches, his appearances against the Englishmen being limited to the two engagements with New South Wales. In these he did very little, being out for 5 and 0 in the first match, and 4 and 23 in the second. In the following season he showed marked improvement, and with a score of 292 not out against Tasmania convinced good judges of the game in Sydney that a new star had risen. Still it was only as 14th man that he was picked to come to England in 1899, and not until the tour had been some little time in progress, and his success assured, was he placed on the same financial footing as the other members of the team. The season of 1899 was a triumph for him. He played a magnificent innings of 135 not out against England, at Lord's; at Brighton against Sussex he made 300 not out – the highest score ever obtained by an Australian batsman in this country. The whole team were delighted with him, and it is said that Noble predicted then that he would become a greater batsman than Ranjitsinhji. On getting home again he added to his reputation in the Inter-State matches, helping New South Wales to win the Sheffield Shield. In the Australian season of 1900-01, he did still greater things, playing an innings of 230 against Victoria, at Sydney, and scoring, in all, in the Inter-State matches, 458 runs with an average of 65. Against MacLaren's team in the Australian season of 1901-02, however, he did not do himself justice, his cricket being affected by the fact that he was engaged a great deal in office work at night time. His performances in this country during the past season put into the shade everything that had ever before been done in England by Australian batsmen, scoring, despite the bad weather and wet wickets, 2,570 runs. Apart from his batting, Trumper is one of the finest of outfields, and a very serviceable change bowler. Success has not in any way spoilt him, and alike on English and Australian cricket fields he is deservedly one of the most popular of players.

DEVOTED TO THE GAME Sydney Pardon, 1921

Pelham Warner was one of the Five Cricketers of the Year in 1904. This special portrait appeared in 1921 when no other Cricketers of the Year were selected.

There have been many greater cricketers than PELHAM WARNER but none more devoted to the game. Nothing has ever damped his enthusiasm. Whether winning or losing he has always been the same. When, having made up his mind to finish with county cricket last season, he had the extreme satisfaction of leading Middlesex to victory in the Championship it was suggested that though he had already found a place in the *Wisden* portrait gallery there could be no more appropriate picture for this year's issue of the Almanack than a special photograph of him at the end of his career. The previous portrait appeared in 1904, Middlesex then, as now, having gained first place among the counties. Mr Warner has had a long and varied experience of the cricket field. He has played in Australia, South Africa and the West Indies. From his earliest days in the Rugby eleven he was marked out for distinction, but it was not till he played regularly for Middlesex that he became famous as a batsman. He was only in the Oxford eleven in the last two of his four years, and though he scored fairly well he did nothing out of the common. A wonderful innings of 150 at Lord's for Middlesex against Yorkshire in 1899 gave him an assured position, and from that year right on to the time of his dangerous illness in Australia in 1911 he met with little but success. It is no secret that when during the War his illness recurred he almost despaired of playing cricket any more, but happily he made a good recovery and did much to keep the game going in the two dreary summers that preceded the Armistice. When cricket came to its own again he was not the batsman he had been, but even in 1919, when the long hours of two-day matches did not suit him at all, he managed to add one to his splendid list of hundreds at Lord's, and last summer he was something like his old self. Still it was not his batting but his skill as a captain that made his final season memorable. But for his leadership Middlesex would never have gained in August the wonderful series of victories that culminated with the triumph over Surrey. His great asset as a captain in that month of strenuous matches, counting for even more than his judgment in changing the bowling and placing the field, was his sanguine spirit. He was full of encouragement and got the very best out of his men by making them believe in themselves.

Little Wonder No. 9

***Wisden* 1894**. Instructions to umpires: Umpires should not allow themselves to be unduly influenced by appeals from such of the field who were not in a position to form a judgment on the point appealed upon, or by tricks – such as throwing up the ball, and appealing for a catch at the wicket, without waiting for the decision. Such devices are obviously unfair, and are not in accordance with the spirit in which cricket should be played. By order of the committee of the MCC.

YORKSHIRE'S GUIDING HAND

Lord Hawke and Four Cricketers of the Year – Sydney Pardon, 1909

The presentation to LORD HAWKE at Leeds last July in celebration of the fact of his having in the previous summer completed 25 years' service as captain of the Yorkshire eleven, afforded a happy opportunity of giving his portrait in *Wisden*. Lord Hawke has made many a good score, but it is as captain of Yorkshire for more than a quarter of a century that he will live in cricket history. His unique work in managing for such a length of time a team composed almost entirely of professional players, has to a large extent overshadowed his doings as a batsman. He was intended for the Army, and it was only by chance that he was able to give so much of his time to cricket. He has said himself that his acceptance of the Yorkshire captaincy was the happiest event of his life. The well-being of Yorkshire cricket has since 1882 been his abiding interest, and today, when as a cricketer he must be regarded as something of a veteran, he is just as keen and enthusiastic as in his early manhood. It was no small responsibility that he took upon his shoulders. The Yorkshire team in the early eighties was full of genius, but the results obtained were not, taking one year with another, commensurate with the individual gifts of the player. There is no unkindness in saying that some of the brilliant cricketers who fought Yorkshire's battles in those days lived their lives rather carelessly and were lost to the game much sooner than they should have been. The full result of his work has been seen in recent years, Yorkshire, beginning with 1893, having come out first among the counties eight times in 16 seasons. The players who carried off the Championship three years in succession, 1900–01–02, were not more gifted than their predecessors but they were far more consistent. Thanks to discipline and careful living they were able to do their best every day in the season, and in the fact of being always in form could be found the secret of their success. In every respect, both on and off the field, he has been the Yorkshire professionals' best friend. To him, I imagine, is due the wise provision that nowadays the great bulk of the money derived from benefit matches in Yorkshire is soundly invested so that the players concerned may have something substantial to fall back upon when their cricket days are over. During his captaincy the system of winter pay has been adopted, and he has devised his own plan of rewarding special excellence in batting, bowling, and fielding. It so happened he was born – on August 16, 1860 – in Lincolnshire, but by family ties and all associations he is a Yorkshireman.

A CHILL WIND BEYOND THE BOUNDARY   Peter Gibbs, 2012

S. F. Barnes was one of the Five Cricketers of the Year in 1910

Jack Ikin stood on the footplate of the team bus scanning the road ahead. Once of Lancashire and England, now – in the summer of 1964 – captain of Staffordshire, he seemed unusually agitated as we drew alongside a tall, lean figure waiting at the kerb. The morning had begun damp and murky, and the man wore a black Homburg and a dark overcoat more suited to a February funeral than a day in late summer.

As a small boy I had seen S. F. BARNES once before, when he bowled the honorary first ball in the match between the 1953 Australians and a Minor Counties XI at the Michelin Works Ground in Stoke. He was 80 at the time, but declined the new ball in case he induced a collapse. My only previous recollection of him had been a photograph in *The Book of Cricket*, written in grandiloquent style by Denzil Batchelor. I would guess he was in his seventies when the photo was taken, and judging by his expression he found the experience sorely trying. That he was demanding company was something I was about to discover at first hand.

"Sydney's come for a day out," said the skipper. "I'd like you to look after him. It's not every day you get a chance to impress one of the greats." Being the junior member of the team might have had its advantages, but I sensed this was not one of them.

On our arrival at Walsall, where we were due to play Bedfordshire, Ikin introduced me to SF as an "opening batsman and recently dubbed Oxford Blue". The old boy reacted as if he had been asked to accommodate a scorpion in his pants. Observing his response, the skipper added that I also played for Norton in the more prosaic surroundings of the North Staffordshire League.

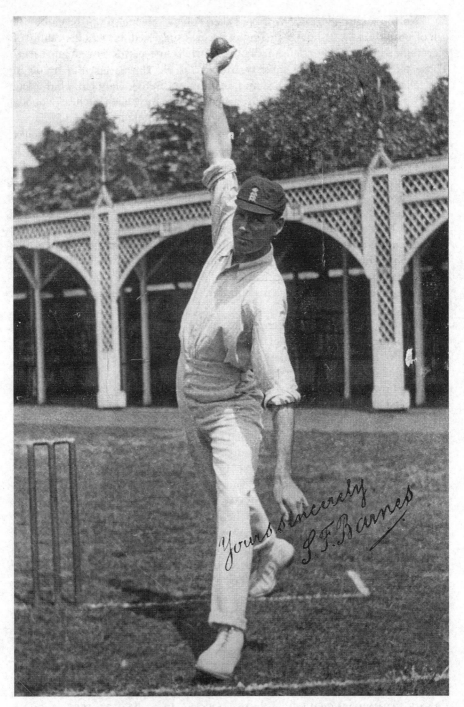

S. F. Barnes: a demanding bowler – and demanding company

"Norton?" said SF. "Yes." "Worrell, Laker, Sobers." He reeled off the club's roll call of professionals. A slight softening in his eyes suggested this was the calibre of players he could readily relate to. "Frank Worrell, fine player. Fine man. Laker? Those pitches in '56 were a travesty. Money for old rope. What did he do in Australia?" His gimlet eyes searched my face for the answer. "Not much?" I hazarded. Of SF's 106 Ashes victims, 77 had been bagged on plum Australian pitches. "Nobody got all ten when I was bowling at the other end," he chuntered.

I could hear the clink of cups and saucers inside the pavilion. "Would you like a coffee, Mr Barnes?" But he was lost in deliberation. "Sobers I like. Batting or bowling, he attacks. That's the thing – attack, attack. A gamble, of course, for a left-hander against someone like me." Holding an imaginary ball, SF sketched three deliveries with a flick of his long fingers – the first two pitching and beating the outside edge, the last breaking the other way through the gate.

I was handed a bunch of scorecards by our No. 4. He was playing on his home ground and had been asked by kids in the club's junior section to get them the autograph of the "famous old bloke". He would have asked himself, he claimed, but he was next man in. Given SF's prickly reputation, I folded the scorecards inside a newspaper in order first to gauge his humour. He had always been quick to rebuke and just as swift to take offence.

"Would you mind signing these scorecards for some of the junior members?" SF frowned at me, then at the batch of cards. "Have you a pen?" Encouraged, I produced one. "A biro? Never touch them. An Oxford man should have a fountain pen." Even into his nineties, SF's skill as an inscriber of legal documents was still in demand.

"The bowlers might like to roll this pitch up and take it with them?" I ventured. "They need all the help they can get. Cricket's a batters' game. Always has been." Anyone perusing SF's figures might think otherwise. His 719 first-class wickets (189 in Tests) were captured at an average of 17.09. His 1,441 wickets for Staffordshire cost less than half that, and his 4,069 league victims barely six runs apiece.

"Even so, an ideal pitch for cutters?" I persisted. "Possibly. I was a spinner, not a cutter." His expression had clouded again at my apparent confusion.

There was no classification in my MCC coaching manual for a fast-medium spin bowler, though I had heard how he made the ball swerve in the air before bouncing and breaking sharply either way. The patented Barnes Ball was the leg-break delivered at pace and without rotation of the wrist. It was at its most potent on the matting tracks of South Africa when, at the age of 40, he took 49 wickets in four games, still a record for a Test series. Fielders at mid-off and mid-on reported hearing the snap of his fingers as he bowled, the batsmen unable to read which way the ball would break. In that respect he was the Ramadhin or Muralitharan of his day.

KENT'S CLEAN DRIVER Five Cricketers of the Year – Sydney Pardon, 1911

FRANK EDWARD WOOLLEY was born at Tonbridge on May 27, 1887, and thus has the best of qualifications to play for Kent. As a small boy he was always to be found on the Tonbridge Cricket Ground, and his natural ability both as batsman and bowler attracted so much attention that in 1903 he was engaged to take part in the morning practice and play in a match or two if required. In the following year he became a regular member of the Tonbridge Ground staff, and those behind the scenes knew when he was given his chance in the county eleven in 1906 that Kent possessed a colt of exceptional promise. To the general public, however, he was almost unknown and his all-round form against Surrey at The Oval in his third county match came as nothing less than a revelation. To begin with he took three Surrey wickets, clean-bowling Hayward, Hayes, and Goatly. He then played an innings of 72 and when Surrey went in again he obtained five wickets for 80 runs. Finally he scored 23 not out, winning a wonderful game for Kent by one wicket. The match established his reputation. Thenceforward he was regarded on all hands as one of England's coming cricketers. He followed up his score at The Oval with an innings of 116 against Hampshire at Tonbridge. In 1906 it will be remembered Kent first carried off the Championship. From that year onwards Woolley has been a regular member of the Kent eleven. In the last four seasons he has done many brilliant things, but he has not, as his friends hoped, gone right ahead of all other left-handed batsmen in this country. He is today a first-rate county cricketer – one of the most valuable members of the strongest team – but he has yet to assert himself in representative elevens. As a set-off against these disappointments, however, he can show a fine record for Kent. As a batsman Woolley, when well set, is one of the most attractive of left-handers – the cleanest driver since F. G. J. Ford – but he often starts badly and there is something wanting in his defence. His natural powers are great, but it ought to be a harder matter than it is to bowl him out. However, though he can look back upon five seasons of first-class cricket he is quite young enough to overcome his weakness. If his defence were equal to his hitting he would be at the top of the tree. As a bowler he began by modelling his style closely upon that of Blythe, but of late he has gained much in individuality. He makes good use of his height – he must be well over 6ft – and bowls with an easy swing.

1920-35

THE MASTER
Five Cricketers of the Century – Matthew Engel, 2000

Jack Hobbs was a Cricketer of the Year in 1909 and then honoured again in 1926 with a "special portrait", a reward for scoring 3,024 first-class runs at 70.32 in the previous season.

Every December 16, a special club meets at The Oval for a lunch party to celebrate the anniversary of the birth of one man. The menu, by tradition, is that man's favourite meal – tomato soup, roast lamb, apple pie – though it is now nearly 40 years since he himself was able to attend. At this lunch, there is just one toast. It is, quite simply, to "The Master". This is the Master's Club. Note the position of the apostrophe. There is only one Master: Jack Hobbs.

The vast majority of the guests now never even saw him play. But the tradition thrives. It is a telling tribute, not simply to Hobbs the cricketer, but to Hobbs the human being.

Jack Hobbs scored more runs than anyone else in the history of first-class cricket: 61,237. He scored more centuries than anyone else, 197. Most astonishingly from a modern perspective, the last 98 came after his 40th birthday. However, his career batting average is 50.65, which does not even put him in *Wisden*'s top 50.

Only 16 of those hundreds were double-hundreds. One says only with trepidation, because just four men have surpassed that. But the figure does not remotely compare with Bradman's 37 or Walter Hammond's 36. Hobbs was not primarily interested in scoring runs for their own sake. For much of his career he would go in at the top of a strong Surrey batting order on good Oval pitches. His job was to get the innings started. He would frequently be out for a-hundred-and-few, and was content enough himself with 60 or 70, though he liked to please his friends who took such things more seriously. But there were other times, when wickets had fallen and the ball was flying: "That was the time you had to earn your living," he said.

More than that, it was when he earned his undying reputation, his knighthood and his place as a Cricketer of the Century. He was never as dominant as Bradman; he never wanted to be. But his contemporaries were in awe of his ability to play supremely and at whim, whatever the conditions.

Hobbs set the standard for 20th-century batsmanship. As he attained his peak in the years before the First World War, he switched the emphasis away from gentlemanly Victorian off-side play to a more pragmatic approach, with an emphasis on the businesslike pull, plus an acute judgment of length, footwork and, where necessary, pad play to counter the googly bowlers of his youth. He was not an artist, like some of his predecessors, nor yet a scientist, like some of the moderns; he was perhaps the supreme craftsman.

Sir John Berry Hobbs was born in 1882 in Cambridge, then a place of strict hierarchies. His father was a net bowler at Fenner's and later a college groundsman. Jack was the oldest of 12 children, and the family teetered on the brink of outright poverty. Nothing came easy except the art of batting. When his father began to bowl to him, he said later, "I could sense the spin."

But there was another aspect to his mastery. There seems no record of any unkindness in his make-up. Perhaps the least creditable episode in his life was his failure to condemn Bodyline when, with the help of a ghost writer, he was covering the 1932-33 Australian tour as a journalist. But the England captain, Douglas Jardine, was his county captain, and there were loyalties that could not be breached. In old age, he was never even heard to utter a word deprecating modern cricketers. He would always say, if the subject were broached, that he made his runs when the "lbw law was framed more kindly to the batsman".

This graceful modesty characterised everything in his life. He was deferential but quietly determined, on the field and off it; unlike his contemporary Sydney Barnes, he shied away from confronting authority, not because it was wrong but because his way worked better. He was neat and correct and moral, yet never humourless (indeed, he was a renowned dressing-room joker). He shied away from the limelight without ever resenting it. Into old age, he could be sought out by all-comers at his sports shop in Fleet Street.

More than anyone else, he lifted the status and dignity of the English professional cricketer. If some of that has vanished in an age of chancers and graspers and slackers and hustlers, the enduring glow of Hobbs's life gives us hope that the golden flame could yet be rekindled.

> **ERRATA – WISDEN, 2000** [2001]: The traditional starter at the annual Master's Club dinner in memory of Sir Jack Hobbs is game pâté, not tomato soup.

Setting the standard: Jack Hobbs completes his 126th century at Taunton in 1925 to equal the record held by W. G. Grace. Hobbs scored another century to beat the record in the second innings (match report, p. 756)

FROM MINER TO MAJOR
Five Cricketers of the Year, 1927

HAROLD LARWOOD, than whom few fast bowlers have jumped to the top of the tree more quickly, was born on November 19, 1904, at Nuncargate, a Notts colliery village. Practically unknown in 1924 – he appeared once for Notts in that season – he received only two years later the honour of playing twice for England against Australia. Larwood became a member of the Trent Bridge groundstaff when 18, and for Notts Second Eleven against Lancashire Second Eleven at Kirkby in 1925 he obtained eight wickets for 44 runs. That performance secured him a place in the county eleven almost immediately afterwards, and he soon became the leading bowler of the side. He did not come into the team until the middle of June yet he took 73 wickets – 11 of them for 41 runs against Worcestershire. Last season in all matches his record was 137 wickets.

England's resources in the matter of fast bowlers of real class being so limited, it was obvious that if Larwood kept his form in 1926 he was bound to be seriously considered for the Test teams, and he played at Lord's and The Oval. Bowling splendidly in the second innings of the last Test match, he began Australia's collapse, getting Woodfull caught in the slips before a run had been scored, dismissing Macartney in similar fashion at 31, and Andrews at 63. In addition he caught Ponsford low down in the slips. Standing only 5ft 7½in high, and weighing 10st 8lb, Larwood – who began life as a miner – is, despite a somewhat frail appearance, very strong physically. He gets great pace off the ground, probably because he has a perfect run-up to the wicket, and at times makes the ball come back so much that he is almost unplayable. Except that he drags his right foot and is inclined to stoop slightly at the moment of delivery, his action is all that a fast bowler's should be. Under the tuition of James Iremonger, now coach at Trent Bridge, his powers have developed amazingly. Only 22 years of age, he should have a big future.

SELF-TAUGHT STYLIST

Five Cricketers of the Year, 1928

WALTER REGINALD HAMMOND, than whom no one of recent years has more abundantly fulfilled his early promise, was born at Dover on June 19, 1903.

Hammond may with justification be termed a self-taught cricketer. Until he went to school he received no serious training, but while there he gave clear indication of his ability by hitting up a score of 365 in a boarders' match. Even at Cirencester there was no systematic coaching, but the headmaster gave him such advice as lay in his power, and after his advent in first-class cricket he received many invaluable hints from George Dennett, the old Gloucestershire slow bowler.

Beautifully built and loose-limbed with strong and pliant wrists, Hammond is essentially a stylist in method, and moreover, a firm believer in making the bat hit the ball. For the most part he is a forward player, and even in making a defensive stroke in this way he comes down harder on the ball than does the average man. He employs all the modern means of scoring, and can cut and turn the ball to leg with equal skill, but, above everything else, his driving is superb. With a new ball he can be most deceptive with his medium-pace bowling, obtaining swerve in flight, and imparting spin to get life off the pitch. A beautiful fielder, he is particularly brilliant in the slips or anywhere on the off side.

Beautifully balanced physique: Wally Hammond walks out to bat
in the first Ashes Test of 1930 at Trent Bridge

CRICKET IN EXCELSIS   Neville Cardus, 1966

When the news came in early July of the death of W. R. Hammond, cricketers everywhere mourned a loss and adornment to the game. He had just passed his 62nd birthday and had not played in the public eye for nearly a couple of decades, yet with his end a light and a glow on cricket seemed to go out. Boys who had never seen him said, "Poor Wally"; they had heard of his prowess and personality and, for once in a while, youth of the present was not sceptical of the doings of a past master.

"Wally" indeed was cricket *in excelsis*. You had merely to see him walk from the pavilion on the way to the wicket to bat, a blue handkerchief peeping out of his right hip pocket. Square of shoulder, arms of obvious strength, a beautifully balanced physique, though often he looked so weighty that his sudden agility in the slips always stirred onlookers and the batsmen to surprise. At Lord's in 1938, England won the toss v Australia. In next to no time the fierce fast bowling of McCormick overwhelmed Hutton, Barnett and Edrich for 31. Then we saw the most memorable of all Wally's walks from the pavilion to the crease, a calm unhurried progress, with his jaw so firmly set that somebody in the Long Room whispered, "My God, he's going to score a century."

Hammond at once took royal charge of McCormick, bouncers and all. He hammered the fast attack at will. One cover drive, off the back foot, hit the palings under the Grand Stand so powerfully that the ball rebounded halfway back. His punches, levered by the right forearm, were strong, leonine and irresistible, yet there was no palpable effort, no undignified outbursts of violence. It was a majestic innings, all the red-carpeted way to 240 in six hours, punctuated by 32 fours.

His career as a batsman can be divided into two contrasted periods. To begin with, when he was in his twenties, he was an audacious strokeplayer, as daring and unorthodox as Trumper or Compton. Round about 1924 I recommended Hammond to an England selector as a likely investment. "Too much of a 'dasher'," was the reply.

As the years went by, he became the successor to Hobbs as the Monument and Foundation of an England innings. Under the leadership of D. R. Jardine he put romance behind him "for the cause", to bring into force the Jardinian theory of the Survival of the Most Durable.

As a slip fieldsman his easy, lithe omnipresence has not often been equalled. He would stand at first slip erect as the bowler began to run, his legs slightly turned in at the knees. He gave the impression of relaxed carelessness. At the first sight, or hint of, a snick off the edge, his energy swiftly concentrated in him, apparently electrifying every nerve and muscle in him. He became light, boneless, airborne. He would take a catch as the ball was travelling away from him, leaping to it as gracefully as a trapeze artist to the flying trapeze.

Illness contracted in the West Indies not only kept him out of cricket in 1926; his young life was almost despaired of. His return to health a year later was a glorious renewal. He scored a thousand runs in May 1927, the season of his marvellous innings against McDonald at Whitsuntide at Old Trafford. I am gratified that after watching this innings I wrote of him in this language: "The possibilities of this boy Hammond are beyond the scope of estimation; I tremble to think of the grandeur he will spread over our cricket fields when he has arrived at maturity. He is, in his own way, another Trumper in the making."

NO LIMIT TO HIS POSSIBILITIES   Five Cricketers of the Year – Sydney Southerton, 1931

DONALD GEORGE BRADMAN, who, coming to England for the first time, met with greater success as a batsman than any other Australian cricketer who has visited this country, was born at Cootamundra, a small up-country township in New South Wales on August 27, 1908. While still a child he accompanied his parents when they moved to Bowral, some 50 miles from Sydney. Although not his birthplace, therefore, Bowral enjoys the distinction of giving the first insight into the game to a young man who, at the present moment is one of the most remarkable personalities in cricket. When it is considered that Bradman made his first appearance in a big match only just over three years ago – to be exact it was at Adelaide in December, 1927 – his rise to the very top of the tree has been phenomenal. Yet in that particular encounter, his first for New South Wales in the Sheffield Shield series of engagements, he showed clearly he was someone out of the common by scoring 118 and 33.

Just as they did during the last tour of the Englishmen in Australia, so, at the present time, opinions differ as to the merit of Bradman's abilities, judged purely from the standpoint of the highest batsmanship. Certain good judges aver that his footwork is correct; others contend the reverse is the case. Both are right. For a fast, true wicket his footwork, if not on quite such a high plane as that of Charles Macartney, is wonderfully good. When the ball is turning, however, there are limitations to Bradman's skill. As was observed by those who saw him on a turning wicket at Brisbane and on one nothing like so vicious at Old Trafford last summer, this young batsman still has something to learn in the matter of playing a correct offensive or defensive stroke with the conditions in favour of the bowler.

Still, as a run-getter, he stands alone. He does not favour the forward method of defence, much preferring to go halfway or entirely back. His scoring strokes are many and varied. He can turn to leg and cut with delightful accuracy but above all he is a superb driver. One very pronounced feature of his batting is that he rarely lifts the ball, and as he showed English spectators so frequently last season, and particularly against England at Lord's, he will send two consecutive and similar deliveries in different directions. In grace of style he may not be a Trumper or a Macartney but his performances speak for themselves. Over and above his batting he is a magnificent field and, like all Australians, a beautiful thrower. Occasionally he has met with success as a bowler, but while his powers as a run-getter remain with him there is no need for him to cultivate the other side of the game.

Not yet 23, Bradman should have years of cricket in front of him and, judging by what he has already accomplished, there would seem to be no limit to his possibilities.

HIS FAME WILL NEVER FADE   Five Cricketers of the Century – John Woodcock, 2000

"He's out!" – to the thousands who read them, whether they were interested in cricket or not, the two words blazoned across the London evening newspaper placards could have meant only one thing: somewhere, someone had managed to dismiss Don Bradman, of itself a lifelong claim to fame.

Sir Donald George Bradman was, without any question, the greatest phenomenon in the history of cricket, indeed in the history of all ball games. To start with, he had a deep and undying love of cricket, as well, of course, as exceptional natural ability. It was always said he could have become a champion at squash or tennis or golf or billiards, had he preferred them to cricket. The fact that, as a boy, he sharpened his reflexes and developed his strokes by hitting a golf ball with a cricket stump as it rebounded off a water tank attests to his eye, fleetness of foot and, even when young, his rare powers of concentration.

Bradman himself was of the opinion that there were other batsmen, contemporaries of his, who had the talent to be just as prolific as he was but lacked the concentration. Stan McCabe, who needed a particular challenge to bring the best out of him, was no doubt one of them. "I wish I could bat like that," Bradman's assessment of McCabe's 232 in the Trent Bridge Test of 1938, must stand with WG's "Give me Arthur" [Shrewsbury], when asked to name the best batsman he had played with, as the grandest tribute ever paid by one great cricketer to another.

By his own unique standards, Bradman was discomfited by Bodyline, the shameless method of attack which Douglas Jardine employed to depose him in Australia in 1932-33. Discomfited, yes – but he still averaged 56.57 in the Test series. If there really is a blemish on his amazing record it is, I suppose, the absence of a significant innings on one of those "sticky dogs" of old, when the ball was hissing and cavorting under a hot sun following heavy rain. This is not to say he couldn't have played one, but that on the big occasion, when the chance arose, he never did.

His dominance on all other occasions was absolute. R. C. Robertson-Glasgow called the Don "that rarest of Nature's creatures, a genius with an eye for business." He could be 250 not out and yet still scampering the first run to third man or long leg with a view to inducing a fielding error. Batsmen of today would be amazed had they seen it, and better cricketers for having done so. It may be apocryphal, but if, to a well-wisher, he did describe his 309 not out on the first day of the Headingley Test of 1930 as a nice bit of practice for tomorrow, he could easily have meant it.

He knows as well as anyone, though, that with so much more emphasis being placed on containment and so many fewer overs being bowled, his 309 of 70 years ago would be nearer 209 today. Which makes it all the more fortuitous that he played when he did, and, by doing so, he had the chance to renew a nation and reinvent a game. His fame, like WG's, will never fade.

A PERSONAL RECOLLECTION   E. W. Swanton, 2002

Jim Swanton followed Don Bradman's progression from his first appearance at Worcester in April 1930 through his four tours of England and MCC's first post-war tour of Australia. After Bradman's retirement in 1948 they developed a friendship and maintained a correspondence that lasted until Swanton's death in January 2000. Written in 1996, this recollection was commissioned to appear in Wisden *after Sir Donald Bradman's death.*

In estimating Don Bradman's cricket and his personality, one is confronted by a dichotomy between public acclaim and private qualification. Whereas his batting in the English summer of 1930 lifted him swiftly to a pinnacle of achievement beyond compare, he was simultaneously imprisoned by fame to a degree he could not readily accept. His own country, a young nation in search of home-grown idols, found in him something of a reluctant hero.

His 309 not out on the first day of the Third Test at Headingley not only beat R. E. Foster's 287 at Sydney, hitherto the highest in England–Australia Tests, but also was 95 runs more than anyone (Foster, again) had scored in a day's Test cricket. It commenced with a hundred before lunch. By chance, I shared a cab back to the Queen's Hotel in Leeds that evening with two or three of the Australians and so had an insight into Don's relationship with the rest of the team. "Now we'll be good for a drink from the little beggar," was the comment, but no such luck. At the hotel desk there he was, asking that a pot of tea be brought to his room. I cannot claim to have known him then, but it is well established that he showed no inclination for the company off the field of his colleagues. He was teetotal, a young country boy in a touring party most of whom were not only older but came from the more sophisticated background of the city. Yet, while he did not put his hand in his pocket or in any way court popularity with them, he was alive from the first to the financial opportunities that fame was bringing. Depression was deep in Australia. His ambition was to achieve a degree of security that would enable him to marry his childhood friend, Jessie Menzies.

What turned the coolness of most of his fellow-players to indignation and worse was the decision of his employers, the Sydney sports-goods firm of Mick Simmons, to transport their celebrity from Perth to Sydney by rail and air, ahead of the team who continued their homeward journey by ship. Australia had found a hero beyond all imagination, and his arrival in turn at Adelaide, Melbourne and Sydney brought scenes of utmost hysteria. Don found himself enveloped in mayoral welcomes, presentations and dinners that had been arranged to greet the team, whose feelings, as they trailed unheralded in his wake, can be easily imagined. It meant nothing to them that in every impromptu speech Don paid warm tribute to his captain, Billy Woodfull, and to the team. He has always stressed in his writings how embarrassing he found this triumphal cavalcade; apart from the embarrassment, the episode permanently damaged relationships with his contemporaries.

When Don was promoted to the captaincy, for the 1936-37 tour of G. O. Allen's side, he knew that several under his command would have preferred playing for the popular, outgoing Vic Richardson. This element, headed by Bill O'Reilly and Jack Fingleton, was still with him in the side he brought to England in 1938. The bowling in support of O'Reilly was too weak for Australia to do better than halve the rubber, but with 13 hundreds in 26 innings – one every other! – the captain could well be said to have led by example, until he broke his ankle at The Oval. What richer irony could be imagined than that, after congratulating Len Hutton on surpassing his record 334, Bradman should turn his ankle over in the deep bowling-mark dug by O'Reilly? My belief is that he did not have an Australian side solidly behind him until after those two Irish-Australians retired.

When at The Oval [in 1948], needing just four runs to average 100 in Test cricket, he was bowled by Eric Hollies for a duck, there were two Australians in the press box who nearly died laughing. They were, of course, O'Reilly and Fingleton.

IN HIS BLOOD   Five Cricketers of the Year – Sydney Southerton, 1932

HEDLEY VERITY, the Yorkshire left-handed slow bowler, who, if yet lacking the phenomenal skill of Wilfred Rhodes, is rightly regarded as the natural successor to that famous player, ought by reason of his birthplace to have cricket in his blood. He was born on May 18, 1905, at Headingley, within a mile of the ground where so many great matches have taken place.

Verity has jumped to the front in his own class of bowling very quickly indeed, his career in first-class cricket having lasted so far less than two seasons. He played first towards the end of May in 1930, at Huddersfield in the friendly match against Sussex and while, owing to another engagement, he could not secure a regular place in the eleven, he met with such success that he finished at the top of the Yorkshire bowling figures, taking 52 wickets for less than 11 and a half runs apiece.

In that year he accomplished some notable performances, obtaining nine wickets for 60 runs in the second innings against Glamorgan at Swansea, while against Hampshire at Bournemouth he dismissed 13 batsmen for 83 runs, and in the return with Sussex at Brighton had nine wickets for 104 runs.

Such good work clearly demonstrated that Yorkshire, just as when Rhodes followed Peel, had at once found a fine left-handed bowler, and last season Verity went right ahead. Again he was really top of the bowling figures with 138 wickets at an average of less than 12 and a half runs per wicket. Admittedly circumstances were in his favour because of the number of rain-affected wickets on which he had to bowl, but he took full advantage of the opportunities that came his way.

His outstanding performance during the season was at Leeds when, after taking three wickets for 61 runs in Warwickshire's first innings, he obtained all ten in the second for 36 runs. By a happy coincidence this success came to him on his birthday. He played for the Players against the Gentlemen at Lord's and The Oval, and later in the season enjoyed the distinction of being in the England team against New Zealand at The Oval and at Old Trafford.

There is no doubt that in once again carrying off the Championship, Yorkshire owed a great deal to the fine work accomplished by their left-hand bowler. Verity does not yet suggest the ability to flight the ball which was such a marked characteristic of Rhodes's bowling, but he has fine finger-spin and accuracy of length, while now and again he sends down a faster ball which goes with his arm.

It is greatly in his favour that, unspoilt by success, he realises that he still has a good deal to learn, particularly in the subtle variation of his pace and flight which can only come by continuous practice. Happily he has avoided the fetish of the swerve.

Verity is the first to acknowledge the debt he owes to Wilfred Rhodes for much valuable advice given at a time when it was most likely to be of the greatest service in helping him indeed to become one of the best left-hand slow bowlers of the day.

Nottinghamshire 1899. In August a trial was given to Mr G. J. Groves. In each case the result was satisfactory, Mr Groves, who from his boyhood has been engaged in reporting cricket, playing admirably against Surrey at The Oval and Middlesex at Trent Bridge. Short in stature and with no advantage of reach, he plays a watchful game, and has plenty of strokes all round the wicket.

Little Wonder No. 11

CARIBBEAN'S FINEST Five Cricketers of the Year – Sydney Southerton, 1934

GEORGE ALPHONSO HEADLEY, born at Panama on May 30, 1909, is beyond all question the best batsman the West Indies have ever produced. Paying his first visit to England with the West Indies team last summer, he landed on these shores with a name already established. That the reputation which preceded him was in every way justified he quickly proceeded to demonstrate, and returned home with his fame considerably increased. Learning his cricket at school in Jamaica, Headley, in common with the other boys, had largely to fend for himself. There was nobody who could give the lads any coaching or mould their style, so that of Headley it can truly be said he is a self-made batsman. In January 1930, Headley made his first appearance in the highest company, and against the MCC team scored 21 and 176, thus enjoying the distinction of making a century in his first match for his own country. He was not successful in the next big match, but in February, at Georgetown, British Guiana, he put together scores of 114 and 112, so joining an extremely select band of cricketers who have made two separate hundreds in a Test match. Good scores for Jamaica followed, and then in the succeeding representative encounter Headley, dismissed for 10 in the first innings, hit up 223 in the second. His batting average during that tour was over 87 for eight innings and his aggregate 703.

During the winter of 1930-31, Headley toured Australia. In the course of the tour he made four hundreds, two of them in Test matches and the other two against Victoria. All the critics in the Commonwealth were agreed that he stood out by himself as a batsman. Returning home, Headley in March of 1932 accomplished a series of great performances against Lord Tennyson's team in Jamaica, by scoring in four innings 344 not out, 84, 155 not out and 140. The innings of 344 is, it is hardly necessary to state, the highest ever made by a West Indies cricketer.

It will thus be seen that in the course of a very short career, this wonderful young batsman has achieved a measure of success usually spread over the lifetime of other famous cricketers. Last summer in England he headed the batting averages for his team both in Test matches and in first-class games. During the season he scored seven hundreds, with a highest of 224 not out against Somerset, and in 38 innings averaged over 66. Among the landmarks of what for him was almost a triumphant march could be numbered the fact that on the occasion of his first appearance at Lord's he scored 129 against MCC. A blow on the chest from a rising ball kept him out of the next three matches, but resuming he made 129 at Cardiff, this being followed by his big innings at Taunton.

Built on small lines, Headley yet had power in hitting, his timing of the ball being, for the most part, perfect. Happily for him, he had a fine hot summer with hard wickets for his first experience of batting under English conditions, so that it was not in the least surprising he did so well. It was the considered opinion of most good judges that few men in present-day cricket watched the ball so far on to the bat. This, of course, made him a very difficult man to dismiss. He drove, cut and hit to leg with equal certainty and power, but the outstanding feature of his batting – the one by which he will be longest remembered – was his facility for going back to his right foot to drive to the on, and the manner in which he placed the ball almost exactly where he wanted. Altogether, with his smart fielding and at times, useful slow bowling, a very remarkable cricketer.

1936–49

INSPIRED BY HOBBS
Five Cricketers of the Year, 1938

LEONARD HUTTON, of Yorkshire, was born on June 23, 1916, at Fulneck, one mile from Pudsey. As his father was a good club cricketer and his three elder brothers were also real enthusiasts, cricket was the topic of the home and Leonard, from an early age, studied all the available books on the game. He says that one book by Jack Hobbs fired his imagination so much that he set his mind upon becoming proficient at cricket. When, at the age of 12, he joined Pudsey St. Lawrence, a club which provided Yorkshire with such stalwarts as John Tunnicliffe, Major Booth and Herbert Sutcliffe, he did not attempt to model his style upon that of any famous cricketer but soon developed and got into the first team. The club president in those days – the late Mr R. Ingram, a member of the Yorkshire committee – placed Hutton's name before the county officials, and Hutton was watched at the nets by George Hirst. From that day, Yorkshire kept him under observation. He was only 16 years old when he appeared for the Minor Counties side, and immediately those connected with the county realised they had found a batsman of undoubted talents. That season, Hutton scored 699 runs.

The following summer (1934) Hutton, when 17, made his début in a first-class match, and a supremely confident innings of 196 against Worcestershire drew the attention of the cricket world to the rising Yorkshireman. Sutcliffe also caused a stir by predicting that Hutton would play for England. In 1935, because of illness, little was seen of Hutton in the cricket field, and although he completed his 1,000 runs in 1936 this was not considered anything remarkable for a player whose praises had been so loudly sung two years before. Last season, however, Hutton attracted wide-spread notice by his wonderful batting feats. He hit eight hundreds for Yorkshire, another in the Test Trial match and one for England against New Zealand. A part-nership with Sutcliffe of 315 for Yorkshire's first wicket and an individual score of 153 against Leicestershire on his 21st birthday followed an innings of 271 not out against Derbyshire in the previous match.

Blessed with the right temperament for the big occasion, Hutton, given good health, should for many years serve Yorkshire as nobly as did Brown, Tunnicliffe, Holmes and Sutcliffe. In addition, he should furnish England with one of the opening batsmen so badly needed since the breaking of the Hobbs–Sutcliffe part-nership. Eminently sound in defence, he plays the new ball extremely well and prefers to wear down the bowling rather than take risks. It must be said that he often carries caution to an extreme, and yet when inclined he brings into play all the strokes. His off-drive is beautifully made. Hutton, besides being a batsman of high merit, is a useful leg-break bowler and his fielding is first-rate.

WONDERFUL EYE　　　　　　　　　　　　　　　　Five Cricketers of the Year, 1939

DENIS CHARLES SCOTT COMPTON, of Middlesex, one of the youngest crick-eters ever to play for England against Australia, was born at Hendon on May 23, 1918. His activities in sport date back almost as far as he can remember. At the age of 10, he played in his school eleven, and showed form far above that of most lads of the same age. His outstanding ability did not long escape recognition. He was selected to play for the London Elementary Schools against Mr C. F. Tufnell's XI at Lord's, and his brilliant batting in scoring 112 so impressed those who saw it, among them Sir Pelham Warner, that Compton was induced to join the Lord's staff as soon as he left school. His achievements were not solely confined to cricket, for in the same year (1932) he joined Arsenal football club.

An adaptable player with a touch of genius, Compton possesses a sound defence, a wonderful eye and the right stroke for every ball. Among the young batsmen of the day, there is no one better worth watching. He is particularly strong on the leg side, and his confidence, coolness and resource are remarkable for so young a player.

PRECIOUS GIFTS OF NATURE   Neville Cardus, 1958

Denis Compton counts amongst those cricketers who changed a game of competitive and technical interest to sportsmen into a highly individual art that appealed to and fascinated thousands of men and women and boys and girls, none of whom possessed a specialist clue, none of whom could enter into the fine points of expert skill. He lifted cricket into an atmosphere of freedom of personal expression. The scoreboard seldom told you more than half the truth about what he was doing on the field of play. In an age increasingly becoming standardised, with efficiency the aim at the expense of impulse – for impulse is always a risk – Compton went his unburdened way, a law to himself.

At his greatest – which is really to say most days in a season – he made batting look as easy and as much a natural part of him as the way he walked or talked. Versatility of strokeplay; swift yet, paradoxically, leisurely footwork; drives that were given a lovely lightness of touch by wristy flexion at the last second; strokes that were born almost before the bowler himself had seen the ball's length.

His batting was founded on sound first principles – nose on the ball, the body near to the line. But he was perpetually rendering acquired science and logic more and more flexible. He was a born improviser. Once a beautiful spinner from Douglas Wright baffled him all the way. He anticipated a leg-break, but it was a googly when it pitched. To adjust his future physical system at the prompting of instinct working swift as lightning, Compton had to perform a contortion of muscles which sent him sprawling chest-flat on the wicket. But he was in time to sweep the ball to the long-leg boundary.

It is not enough to remember his brilliance only, his winged victories, his moments of animation and fluent effortless control. He has, in the face of dire need, played defensively with as tenaciously and as severely a principled skill as Hutton commanded at his dourest. Compton's 184 for England at Trent Bridge in 1948 must go down in history among the most heroically Spartan innings ever played.

In a dreadful light Compton defended with terrific self-restraint against Miller at his fiercest. It is possible the match might have been snatched by him from the burning. Alas, at the crisis, a vicious bumper from Miller rose shoulder high. Compton instinctively hooked, thought better of it too late, slipped on the greasy turf, and fell on his wicket. For six hours and 50 minutes he mingled defence and offence in proportion. He did not, merely because his back was to the wall, spare the occasional loose ball. At Manchester, in the same rubber of 1948, Compton again showed us that there was stern stuff about him, the Ironside breastplate as well as the Cavalier plume. He was knocked out by Lindwall. Stitches were sewn into his skull and, after a rest, he came back when England's score was 119 for five. He scored 145 not out in five hours 20 minutes.

In his 40th year he is as young at heart and as richly endowed in batsmanship as at any time of his life. There are ample fruits in his cornucopia yet – if it were not for that knee! Still, we mustn't be greedy. He has shared the fruits of the full and refreshing cornucopia generously with us. He will never be forgotten for his precious gifts of nature and skill, which statistics have no power to indicate let alone voice. Whatever his future, our hearts won't let him go. Thank you, Denis!

THE SPONTANEOUS CRICKETER
John Arlott, 1972

Learie Constantine was one of the Five Cricketers of the Year in 1940.

LORD CONSTANTINE, MBE, died in London on July 1, 1971. The parents of the child born in Diego Martin, Trinidad, almost 70 years before, may in their highest ambitions have hoped that he would play cricket for the West Indies. They cannot have dreamt that he would take a major share in lifting his people to a new level of respect within the British Commonwealth; that along the way he would become the finest fieldsman and one of the most exciting all-rounders the game of cricket has known; and that he would die Baron Constantine, of Maraval in Trinidad and Tobago, and of Nelson, in the County Palatine of Lancaster, a former Cabinet Minister and High Commissioner of his native Trinidad.

Learie – or "Connie" to 40 years of cricketers – came upon his historic cue as a man of his age, reflecting and helping to shape it. He made his mark in the only way a poor West Indian boy of his time could do, by playing cricket of ability and character. He went on to argue the rights of the coloured peoples with such an effect as only a man who had won public affection by games-playing could have done in the Britain of that period.

As C. L. R. James has written, "he revolted against the revolting contrast between his first-class status as a cricketer and his third-class status as a man". That, almost equally with his enthusiasm for the game, prompted the five years of unremitting practice after which, in 1928, he came to England under Karl Nunes on West Indies' first Test tour as an extremely lively fast bowler, hard-hitting batsman and outstanding fieldsman in any position.

Muscular but lithe, stocky but long-armed, he bowled with a bounding run, a high, smooth action and considerable pace. His batting, which depended considerably upon eye, was sometimes unorthodox to the point of spontaneous invention: but on his day it was virtually impossible to bowl at him. In the deep he picked up while going like a sprinter and threw with explosive accuracy; close to the wicket he was fearless and quick; wherever he was posted he amazed everyone by his speed and certainty in making catches which seemed far beyond reach. His movement was so joyously fluid and, at need, acrobatic that he might have been made of springs and rubber.

Crowds recognised and enjoyed him as a cricketer of adventure: but the reports alone of a single match established him in the imagination of thousands who had never seen him play. At Lord's, in June *[1928]*, Middlesex made 352 for six and West Indies, for whom only Constantine, with 86, made more than 30, were 122 behind on the first innings. When Middlesex batted again, Constantine took seven for 57 – six for 11 in his second spell. West Indies, wanting 259 to win, were 121 for five when Constantine came in to score 103 out of 133 – with two sixes, 12 fours and a return drive that broke Jack Hearne's finger so badly that he did not play again that season – in an hour, to win the match by three wickets. Lord's erupted: and next day all cricketing England accepted a new major figure.

That performance confirmed the obvious, that Constantine was, as he knew he needed to be, the ideal league professional – surely the finest of all. He wanted a part-time living adequate for him to study law. England was the only place, and cricket his only means, of doing both. No man ever played cricket for a living – as Constantine needed to do more desperately than most professional cricketers – with greater gusto. Any club in the Lancashire leagues would have been grateful to sign him. Nelson did so, with immense satisfaction on both sides. Constantine drew and delighted crowds – and won matches: Nelson won the Lancashire League eight times in his ten seasons there – an unparalleled sequence – and broke the ground attendance record at every ground in the competition. Less spectacularly, he coached and guided the younger players with true sympathy. Among the people of Nelson, many of whom had never seen a black man before, "Connie" and his wife, Norma, settled to a happy existence which they remembered with nostalgia to the end. In 1963 the Freedom of the Borough of Nelson was bestowed on the man who then was Sir Learie Constantine.

A NOD OF SATISFACTION   John Woodcock, 2011

Alec Bedser was one of the Five Cricketers of the Year in 1947.

ALEC BEDSER was one of the great bowlers, and someone to whom commitment was the first commandment. That he remained wedded to cricket until his dying day, and got out and about until into his nineties, made him a national treasure, chunter though he would at an open-chested bowling action, the absence of a third man or for want of a pint of bitter.

Through having served six years in the Second World War, by the time his career started in earnest he already had something of the veteran about him. His bowling was essentially a product of the English game as it was played for the first two-thirds of the last century. Still being uncovered, the pitches encouraged lateral movement at medium-pace to an extent seldom found elsewhere, and that was Bedser's stock-in-trade.

He followed in the correspondingly imposing footsteps of Maurice Tate, of whom R. C. Robertson-Glasgow wrote, as he might have done of Bedser, that "he had many imitators but no equals". They were both supreme in their day, and, as if to quell all argument, each had his triumphs in Australia as well as England, Bedser's 30 wickets there in 1950-51 being heroic in the same way as Tate's 38 had been in 1924-25, also in a losing cause.

Such is the emphasis placed now on fitness, agility and bowling speed that it is perfectly possible they would both be left on the rack today. More with regret than rancour, Bedser would say so himself. But to his contemporaries he was the champion, and you can ask no more than that. One could but marvel and despair at the frequency with which he beat the bat on the first morning of the Second Test at Melbourne on that tour of 1950-51, a spell of bowling which prompted those who had seen or played against the legendary Sydney Barnes to compare the two. Neil Harvey, already a very fine player, was as utterly confounded as Warren Bardsley, Clem Hill and Victor Trumper must have been by Barnes on the same ground 39 years earlier.

Bedser's chief pride and joy was his bowling action, the culmination of a methodical yet rhythmical run-up of no more than six full strides. On average he took two and a half minutes to bowl an over. He had the frame for the job, the heart to go with it, and big hands. The ball with which he bowled Don Bradman for nought in the Fourth Test at Adelaide in February 1947, a fillip like no other, had a lot to do with the size of his hands.

Often referred to as the perfect leg-cutter, and by Bradman as being as good a ball as ever got him out, Bedser always insisted that he didn't cut it but that he spun it, which he was able to do because his hands were so large. His natural movement in the air was into the right-handed batsman, and that, when followed by what amounted to a fast leg-break, was some combination. He spurned the outswinger, mainly in the interests of accuracy.

Bowling was Bedser's abiding interest, the theory of it as much as the practice. No one ever went to him without coming away the wiser. This was particularly so during his days on the county circuit, and the younger players loved him for it. He enjoyed playing the part of the guru. When James Anderson was starting to make a name for himself, Bedser, by then in his mid eighties, wrote him a long letter in his own hand with what he hoped would be helpful suggestions.

When he was managing the England side in Australia in 1974-75, I can see him now laying out a page of Melbourne's *Age*, then a broadsheet, on a net pitch as he set about drilling Mike Hendrick in the adjustment he would need to make to his English length on Australia's faster, bouncier pitches. And when I said to him one day that I had a great-nephew who was showing a bit of form as a right-arm spinner, his message was typically brief and to the point: "Tell him to bowl over his left shoulder," as Bedser himself had done so inveterately and for so long.

Bedser finished playing in 1961, the end of his Test career precipitated, unhappily, by a bout of shingles on the 1954-55 tour to Australia, barely a year after his having taken a record 39 wickets in the Ashes series of 1953 in England. As a manager and selector of England teams for 23 years after his retirement, he cared almost to a fault. Nothing was too much trouble to him, other than coming to terms with all the changing proprieties of a sportsman's life.

Once, when paying his customary visit to the England dressing-room after a day's play at The Oval, either as chairman of selectors or manager of the side, he heard a strange whirring noise. "What's that?" he asked Tony Greig, the England captain. "Bob Woolmer's hair-dryer," came the reply. "Hair-dryer," said Alec, "what's wrong with a bloody towel?" As Woolmer had just made a hundred and England were playing Australia, Bedser needed to be careful not to seem to be ridiculing him – but, to the old-timer, hair-dryers were for women and always would be. Just as "strength and conditioning courses for bowlers", to use the current term, were best spent not in the gymnasium but out in the middle, bowling, or even digging the garden.

Not even Sir Pelham Warner and Lord Hawke between them can have helped to pick more Test sides than Bedser, and he had a remarkable memory for all the whys and wherefores of the different eras. More than anything, selectors need genuine all-rounders to help them out, and for his last few years Bedser was fortunate in having Ian Botham round whom to build a side. The successful decisions to bring back Mike Brearley as captain in 1981 in place of Botham, and to plump for Ray Illingworth ahead of Colin Cowdrey to lead the side in Australia in 1970-71, were not quite as straightforward as they may seem now. Bedser was not, I think, given to agonising over things, but he always wanted to see justice done. The irony was certainly not lost on him when, 36 years after the selectors, under Bedser's chairmanship, had felt obliged to suspend Tom Graveney for three Test matches for "a serious breach of discipline", the villain became president of MCC!

From the days when, as a member of the groundstaff at The Oval, he had to do what he was told by Mr Holmes and Mr Garland-Wells, until he was assured of a right royal reception at Lord's and knighted by the Queen, Bedser's career has nothing in cricket quite to match it. It would make a good film if twins of the right shape could be found to play Alec and his identical and inseparable brother, Eric, who predeceased him by four years. They would be seen getting away together from Dunkirk, and their mother would be heard to say "But that's what he's paid for, isn't it?" when asked what she thought of Alec taking 11 wickets in his first Test match.

Alec must have taken after his mother. I wasn't there to see him bowl Bradman at Adelaide in 1947, the most famous of his 236 Test wickets, but I saw most of the others and each one brought no more than a nod of satisfaction. The hugging and mauling which go on today, and that he would have so detested, had yet to come in. There was a native dignity about Alec, besides a becoming unselfconsciousness and gentle homespun humour, a candour, an incumbent melancholy and a liking for the old ways, which all went towards making him the institution he was – along with his indomitable bowling.

1950–59

| THE MAN FOR EVERY CRISIS | Christopher Martin-Jenkins, 2011 |

Trevor Bailey was one of the Five Cricketers of the Year in 1950.

Environment, talent, unshakable self-confidence and an astute, pragmatic mind combined to make TREVOR BAILEY one of England's greatest all-rounders. Happy to face any challenge, he took the new ball, held brilliant close catches, shored up the middle order, and even opened the batting in 14 of his 61 Tests for his country, doing everything but captain them. Traces of cynicism and iconoclasm prevented that happening, but he was at the right hand of both Len Hutton and Peter May.

He was a pillar of Essex cricket from the late 1940s to his last year as captain in 1966. As a swift and incisive soccer forward, despite having played only rugby at school, he won an FA Amateur Cup winner's medal in 1952. As a writer and broadcaster, his analytical mind got to the heart of things, maintaining his popularity through a second period of fame as a pundit on BBC's *Test Match Special*. As a husband and father, he was as steadfast as his famous forward defensive.

With other household names of the early 1950s like Alec Bedser, Bailey first helped the national team's post-war recovery and then joined emerging talents such as Cowdrey, May, Trueman, Tyson and Statham to become the resolute pivot of the best side in the world. His death at 87 in sad circumstances on February 10, 2011, after a fire in his retirement flat, left alive only Tom Graveney, Reg Simpson and Roy Tattersall of the England players who had shared in the series victory over Australia in the Coronation Year of 1953. That the Ashes were regained amid national rejoicing after 19 years owed much to Bailey's verve, intelligence and bottomless determination. At Lord's, he shared with Willie Watson the fifth-wicket stand on the last day that lasted from 12.42 until 5.50pm, saving England from defeat. At Headingley, Australia needed only 66 runs in 45 minutes with seven wickets left when he persuaded Len Hutton to change tactics, taking the initiative and bowling outside the leg stump to a heavily protected on-side field. Graeme Hole, who had put on 57 with Neil Harvey in half an hour, was caught on the boundary, Bailey conceded only nine runs from six overs, and England survived again. At The Oval, his solid 64 ensured the first-innings lead that paved the way for Jim Laker and Tony Lock to spin through Australia.

Over the next three years Bailey took a leading part in two more winning series against Australia. His impassable forward-defensive stroke, played well ahead of his front pad, had become a symbol of British defiance. It made him a folk hero and earned him his soubriquet "Barnacle".

He was a familiar voice on radio from 1966 to 1999. His penchant at the microphone was the succinct summary of a player or an incident, the pithier the better. No one assessed players better. It was Trevor who immediately spotted, on the first Test appearance in England of the tearaway Richard Hadlee, the seeds of a great bowler.

Perceptive as he was, he could be vague about names and in his life generally. He took his wife Greta to the spa town of Harrogate on the rest day of his first Test in Leeds, under the firm impression that they were about to enjoy a day on the beach. In 1993, conducting England supporters around India, he arrived at Bombay airport with a party of 30 but no tickets. They had been thrown away in the hotel waste-paper basket. But Trevor's charm, and his calmness, averted every crisis.

Gentlemen v Players. At Kennington Oval, July 9, 10, 11, 1900. W. G. Grace, who took part in his first Gentlemen v Players match at The Oval in 1865, batted admirably for his 58, and would have made more runs if he could have run faster between the wickets.

Little Wonder No. 12

Even those who bemoan the lack of personalities in modern cricket agree that THOMAS GODFREY EVANS of Kent provides at least one exception. In an age in which possibly too much first-class cricket has caused some of the English game to look routine in character, Evans remains the embodiment of energy and enthusiasm. To play with him is as much a tonic to the jaded cricketer as to watch him is a source of delight to the spectator, and of no man could it more truthfully be said that he has an ideal big-match temperament. Whether batting or keeping wicket, he brims over with unshakable self-confidence. In other spheres of life he is the same – tireless and aggressive, revelling in the action of the moment. To appreciate to the full his vitality it is best to see him abroad, chasing a ball to the boundary or sprinting to the dressing-room at the end of an exhausting day under a burning sun which has sapped the strength of the majority of his colleagues. His constitution provides a source of wonderment even to his friends, and his hardiness is such that he was not kept out of the game through injury until he broke a finger towards the end of the 1950 season, by which time he had played in 30 Test matches. In fact, previously his hands showed no sign of his calling.

Evans now belongs to Kent, but this was not always so. He was born on August 18, 1920, at Finchley, and even when his parents moved to Faversham, in Kent, the link with Middlesex was not severed completely. The house to which the Evans family moved bore the imposing title of Lord's. From a boarding school at Deal, Evans moved to Kent College, Canterbury, where he quickly won colours for hockey, cricket and football and became captain of all three sports.

After leaving school, Evans for a time worked with his brother in the motor trade, but an ambition to become a professional cricketer so fired him that he spent many hours during the winter of 1936-37 at an indoor school in Acton. Next spring he attended the nets at Canterbury for a trial, as a result of which he joined the Kent staff as a wicketkeeper-batsman.

In his first full season of county cricket Evans won his England cap for the last Test with India, and that winter, as a member of W. R. Hammond's side to Australia, he took part in the first of four successive MCC tours. He missed the First Test in Australia but came in at Sydney for the Second, which began a run of 22 consecutive Test appearances. In the Australian series Evans created another two world records. He did not concede a bye until 1,024 runs had been scored – 659 in the second and 365 in the Third Test – and in the Fourth, at Adelaide, he stayed longer, 95 minutes, than any batsman in Test cricket before opening his score. Playing a game foreign to his normal adventurous style, Evans batted two hours and a quarter in an unforgettable stand with Denis Compton which helped England to save the match. They made 85 together without being parted, Evans scoring his 10 off seven of the 98 balls bowled to him.

On his 1950 displays Evans is without an equal in the world as a wicketkeeper. His performance in the Test Trial on a sticky pitch at Bradford deserved the description of classic. Not only is he safe in catching and lightning in stumping, but he has the additional virtues of inspiring the bowler and worrying the batsman. Evans helps bowlers to take wickets which normally they would not expect, and few batsmen can dispel from their minds the nagging feeling that he is after them, tensed to pounce upon the least lapse of concentration or hesitation.

The happy disposition which characterises Evans on the field does not disappear when the day's play is over. He laughs his way through life, and those who are his friends laugh with him. Evans is married and has one son. He and his family live near Maidstone in a house appropriately called "The Wickets."

DESTROYER OF MYTH
Sir Learie Constantine, 1968

Frank Worrell was one of the Five Cricketers of the Year in 1951.

Sir Frank Worrell once wrote that the island of Barbados, his birthplace, lacked a hero. As usual, he was underplaying himself. FRANK MAGLINNE WORRELL was the first hero of the new nation of Barbados, and anyone who doubted that had only to be in the island when his body was brought home in mid-March of 1967. Or in Westminster Abbey when West Indians of all backgrounds and shades of opinion paid their last respects to a man who had done more than any other of their countrymen to bind together the new nations of the Caribbean and establish a reputation for fair play throughout the world. Never before had a cricketer been honoured with a memorial service in Westminster Abbey.

Sir Frank was a man of strong convictions, a brave man and, it goes without saying, a great cricketer. Though he made his name as a player his greatest contribution was to destroy for ever the myth that a coloured cricketer was not fit to lead a team. Once appointed, he ended the cliques and rivalries between the players of various islands to weld together a team which in the space of five years became the champions of the world. He was a man of true political sense and feeling, a federalist who surely would have made even greater contributions to the history of the West Indies had he not died so tragically in hospital of leukaemia at the early age of 42, a month after returning from India.

People in England can have little idea of the problems of West Indian cricket. It is not a question of a few countries bordering each other coming together in a joint team. Jamaica is 1,296 flying miles from Barbados and Georgetown in Guyana 462 miles from Bridgetown in Barbados. Before that wonderful tour of Australia in 1960-61, Barbadians would tend to stick together and so would the Trinidadians, Jamaicans and Guyanese. Worrell cut across all that. Soon there were no groups. Just one team.

He told his batsmen to walk if they were given out. When Garry Sobers appeared to show his dissent with a decision, he reprimanded him. After that, everyone walked as soon as the umpire's finger went up. So when half a million Australians lined the streets of Melbourne in their tickertape farewell to Worrell and his men, they were not only paying a final tribute to the team's great achievements, they were recognising the capacity and potential of equals both on and off the turf.

Sir Frank started life in Barbados, worked and lived in Trinidad, and died in Jamaica after doing much useful work at the University of the West Indies there. He incurred enmity by leaving his birthplace but he did not care much for insularity, cant and humbug. He saw the many diverse elements of the West Indies as a whole, a common culture and outlook separated only by the Caribbean Sea. This is why he upset certain people in Barbados when he wrote to a newspaper there criticising the island for having the cheek to challenge the rest of the world to celebrate independence.

Worrell was strongly criticised for this action, bitterly in fact in some quarters. But being attacked did not worry him. He always had the courage to say what he felt about every issue he thought vital to the well-being of the islands. Sadly, the news that he was dying came through as Barbados played the Rest of the World XI. But Worrell held no rancour against his homeland. He had bought a piece of land there and had intended to retire there eventually.

Throughout his life, Sir Frank never lost his sense of humour or his sense of dignity. Some nasty things were said and written during that 1965 tour [*a difficult West Indies tour to Australia, which he managed*] but Sir Frank was ever the diplomat. He lost no friends, made no enemies yet won more respect. West Indians really laugh their laughs. And Sir Frank laughed louder than most of us. He was a happy man, a good man and a great man. The really tragic thing about his death at the age of 42 was that it cut him off from life when he still had plenty to offer the islands he loved. He was only at the beginning. Or was it that the opportunity came to him a bit too late?

HONORARY SOUTHERNER Five Cricketers of the Year – Norman Preston, 1952

Among the many off-break bowlers who enjoyed considerable success in the English season of 1951 none looked superior to JAMES CHARLES LAKER, of Surrey and England. Born at Shipley on February 9, 1922, Laker is a product of Yorkshire, and that he slipped through the hands of his native county can be ascribed to the twists of fortune brought about by war.

Laker intended to take up banking as a career and spent two years at Barclays, Bradford, before joining R. A. O. C. in 1941. That meant goodbye to cricket for two years. Returning from overseas, Laker still had six months to serve; he was posted to the War Office, being billeted with a friend at Catford. He joined Catford CC whose president, a prominent Surrey member, introduced him to the Kennington Oval officials. After a trial Surrey asked Laker to sign as a professional, but he doubted whether he was good enough for first-class cricket and instead asked the bank to transfer him to London. Six months passed, and then Laker decided to take his chance with Surrey for whom he made his first appearance against Combined Services at The Oval in 1946.

In 1947, Laker made his debut in the County Championship and soon his promise was noted beyond The Oval. He headed the Surrey bowling that season and finished seventh in the first-class averages with 79 wickets. Next came an invitation to go with G. O. Allen's team to the West Indies.

He continued to shine for Surrey, and though in 1949 he appeared in one Test against New Zealand he seemed to be almost forgotten by the selectors until at the end of May 1950 he ruined the Test Trial staged at Bradford Park Avenue, only five miles from his birthplace. England sent in The Rest and in 110 minutes they were all out for 27, the lowest total for a match of representative class. In 14 overs (12 maidens) Laker took eight wickets for two runs.

Laker reckons that was his best performance, but it was not enough for the selectors. They chose him for the First Test at Manchester against West Indies – the only one of the four that England won – but he took only one wicket and was passed over until 12 months later he was again selected for Manchester, where he bowled extremely well against South Africa. Yet again he was dropped for the following Test at Leeds, only to be recalled for the last at The Oval when he bowled England to victory with ten wickets for 119 runs.

Laker deservedly has the reputation of being a splendid fielder, particularly in the gully where he holds the hottest of catches. As he is no more than 30 he should have several seasons left as a player, and with five English seasons behind him, besides visits to West Indies, India and New Zealand, he has had the necessary time to settle down in the best company and learn the essential secrets of how to become a top-class bowler.

BORN WITH BAT IN HAND

Five Cricketers of the Year – Reg Hayter, 1952

Schoolboy prodigies do not always justify predictions but, by the end of the 1951 season, PETER BARKER HOWARD MAY at 21 had achieved sufficient to prove the judgment of those who several years before proclaimed him as the most promising batting prospect of English post-war cricket. Selection for the last two Tests against South Africa came as early recognition of May's talents but, given the time to play regularly and with, at the least, normal maintenance of skill, he then looked to have touched only the fringe of the honours which might be his.

May, born at Reading on December 31, 1929, and also of Surrey allegiance, headed the first-class batting last season with 2,339, average 68.79, performances of special distinction being centuries on his first appearances for England and in the Gentlemen v Players match at Lord's. He easily topped the poll in the Cricket Writers' Club vote for the best young cricketer of the year.

The story of May's cricket ascent is that of a boy reared, as it were, with a ball in his hand or at his feet. The urge to kick or hit a ball came to him strongly at a very early age and, with youthful zest, he spent many hours doing so in the garden and on the hard tennis court at the back of his parents' Reading house. He made no attempt at specialisation. All games provided enjoyment. Thus he acquired a ball-sense which became the foundation of all-round sporting ability. At 15 he first played for Public Schools at Lord's, and during holidays that year and the next received experience of bigger cricket in a few games for Berkshire. When 17 and in his last season at Charterhouse he played an innings of 146 against Combined Services at Lord's about which those who saw him spoke in the most glowing phrases.

For the next two years May served in the Royal Navy. At first, few cricket opportunities came to him but, on being moved to Chatham in 1949, he was picked regularly both for the Navy and for the Combined Services. With service finished, May moved to Cambridge where next year, as a 20-year-old freshman, he hit 227 against Hampshire. After the Varsity Match, in which he achieved nothing notable, May played for Surrey for whom he had been specially registered. He finished second in their averages and received his county cap.

Runs flowed from May's bat still more freely in 1951 when he scored nine centuries, five in one peak period of nine innings which brought him 871 runs from July 18 to August 14. May subsequently lost some of his touch but there could never be any doubt about his class. The century at Leeds with which May announced his Test entry could be cited as the embodiment of all his batting attributes. From first to last he treated every ball on merit and he was as composed at the start and on completion of 100 as at any time in his innings. His progress through the nineties typified May's imperturbable temperament and he went from 98 to 106 with two glorious straight-drives which sizzled to the boundary.

Surrey v London County. At Kennington Oval, April 28, 29, 30, 1902. Fry, who only two days previously had taken part in the Final Tie for the Football Association Cup, showed surprisingly good form, assisting Grace to put on 130 for the first wicket.

Little Wonder No. 13

THE GREATEST FAST BOWLER OF ALL TIME? Bill Bowes, 1970

Fred Trueman was one of the Five Cricketers of the Year in 1953.

Greatness is a relative term, but anyone making a study of the career figures of FRED TRUEMAN could be forgiven if they claimed he was the greatest fast bowler of all time. He has more victims in Test cricket than any other bowler. In a career which began in 1949 and ended with his retirement at the end of the 1968 season he took over 2,300 wickets at 18.3 each, and apart from obtaining all ten wickets in an innings he claimed almost every honour in the game.

He performed the hat-trick on four occasions, claimed five wickets or more in an innings 126 times, and was credited with ten wickets or more in the match 25 times. As a hard-hitting batsman he hit three centuries. From the boundary edge he could throw low and accurately into the gloves of the wicketkeeper with either hand. He was a very good fieldsman at short leg, and mainly in that position he took 438 catches.

The crowds loved Trueman. Not only had he an ability which they could enjoy; the newspaper men, television commentators and publicity men projected an image they liked. Freddie was a tremendous talker. In this department he was the greatest. He was never silent – except during his actual run up to bowl and in the delivery action; it would have been a pity if anything had marred this beautiful, sometimes awe-inspiring, sight. He ran the length of another cricket pitch to bowl. Some critics said he ran much too far, but Trueman himself said he felt better that way.

With a sweet gathering of momentum Freddie, black hair waving, came hurtling to the bowling crease. With no change of rhythm there came the change from forward to sideways motion, the powerful gathering of muscles for the delivery itself, and then the explosive release. A perfect cartwheel action, with every spoke of arms and legs pointing where the ball was to go – the batsman seeing nothing but left shoulder prior to the moment of delivery – gave the ball its 90mph propulsion. There was the full-bodied follow-through to the action, a run through while he braked, which worried umpires if he got too near the line of the stumps, and then, a hundred to one, more talk. Sometimes it was to tell the batsman how lucky he had been. Sometimes it was to indicate to all and sundry how unlucky he, Trueman, had been; to congratulate a fieldsman on a good stop; to tell the skipper where he wanted the fieldsman to go; or to mutter darkly to himself under his breath. But he talked. He talked in the field to anybody who would listen. He talked in the dressing-room to such an extent that his Yorkshire team-mates seldom answered back because this was encouragement, and as a result half an hour before the start of play in any match Trueman could invariably be found still talking in the dressing-room of the opposing team, where the audience was more polite.

One can only guess the innermost thoughts of opposing batsmen when Trueman, after holding court in their dressing-room, got to his feet about 15 minutes before the start of play. "So you're batting, eh? George" (looking at the number one batsman), "I shall get you wi't'new ball. Charlie, I've no need to worry about you." Then looking round the whole room he would add, "I've got a few candidates today," and his parting shot would be, "I only want a bit of luck with you, skipper, and I've got another six or seven wickets."

The pressmen found plenty of sensational copy in his willingness to talk. His antagonism got him into trouble with umpires and at times the crowd, too. He had to be reminded that the England captain, Len Hutton, was now no longer a Yorkshire colleague but The Boss. If any cricketer did or said anything mean on this controversial tour [*to West Indies in 1953-54*] Freddie got the blame. He was, to many people, a bother-causer. The England captain and selectors somewhat understandably turned to Typhoon Tyson as their fast-bowling partner for Statham. Despite 134 wickets in 1954 Trueman missed the tour to Australia, and did not play in another Test match until Tyson blistered his heel and had to withdraw from the Lord's Test of 1955 against South Africa.

All these things made Trueman a character the game and the public enjoyed, and yet, while giving this impression that he knew it all, there was that extreme and opposite side to him which responded to confidence, and was ready to listen to a helping voice. Then he could charm more than dominate. Towards the end of his career when seniority earned him the right to lead Yorkshire whenever D. B. Close was absent, he proved himself a capable and knowledgeable captain and had the high distinction of leading Yorkshire to victory over the touring Australian team. The honour put another yard of pace into his bowling. He wanted to prove he was still good.

Leading the field: Fred Trueman at The Oval in 1964
after becoming the first bowler to take 300 Test wickets

HE MAKES IT LOOK EASY

Neville Cardus, 1965

Tom Graveney was one of the Five Cricketers of the Year in 1953.

THOMAS WILLIAM GRAVENEY, who in the summer of 1964 made his hundredth hundred in first-class cricket, is one of the few batsmen today worth while our inspection if it is style and fluent strokes we are wishing to see, irrespective of the scoreboard's estimate of an innings by him.

His accumulated runs, up to the moment I write this article, amount to no fewer than 38,094, averaging a little above 45. Yet he has seldom been regarded as a permanent member of the England XI; he has been for more than a decade on trial. Nobody in his senses with half a notion of what constitutes a thoroughbred batsman would deny Graveney's class, his pedigree.

He came out of the Gloucestershire stable following the glamorous period of Hammond and Barnett, while their influence still pervaded the atmosphere of the county. Since Hammond's glorious reign the character and economy have become tougher and tighter. Cricket everywhere, reflecting character and economy in the world at large, has tended to change from a sport and artistic spectacle to a competitive materialistic encounter, each contestant mainly setting his teeth not to lose.

Batsmen not fit to tie Graveney's bootlaces, considered from the point of view of handsome stroke-embedded play, have been encouraged to oust Graveney from Test matches stern and generally unbeautiful. Style has become a corny word everywhere, so it is natural enough that we have lived to see and extol an honest artisan such as Boycott building his brick wall of an innings, while Graveney must-content himself scoring felicitous runs for his adopted county (incidentally going far towards winning the Championship for Worcestershire). No batsman not truly accomplished is able to play a characteristic Graveney innings. Today he has no equal as a complete and stylish strokeplayer. Dexter can outshine him in rhetoric, so to say; Marshall in virtuosity of execution. But neither Dexter nor Marshall is Graveney's superior in point of effortless balance.

When he is in form Graveney makes batsmanship look the easiest and most natural thing in the world. I have no rational explanation to account for his in-and-out form in Test matches. I decline to keep out of the highest class a fine batsman simply on the evidence of his half-success in Test matches. Indeed I'm not too sure nowadays that success in Test cricket most times is not an indication of dreary effi-ciency. It is a modern notion that anybody's talents need be measured by utility value in the top places of publicity. Graveney is one of the few batsmen today orna-menting the game, who not out at lunch, pack a ground in the afternoon. Bloggs of Blankshire sometimes empties it or keeps people away – the truth of his perfor-mances may copiously be found out from the subsequent published statistics.

Critics who think of Test matches as though they were of dire consequence to the nation politically, economically and what have you, have maintained that Graveney has on occasion let England down. But nobody has claimed that Tom Graveney has ever let cricket down. In form or out of form he has rendered tribute to the graces of cricket.

FUN COMES FIRST

Five Cricketers of the Year – Reg Hayter, 1954

Even the Golden Age of cricket would have been enriched by a character so colourful as KEITH ROSS MILLER, proclaimed by many as Australia's finest all-rounder since the retirement of M. A. Noble some 40 years ago. In the 1953 Test series with England, Miller emulated the hitherto unique achievement of Wilfred Rhodes with 2,000 runs and 100 wickets in international cricket. Yet figures are the last thing by which this unpredictable personality, a man with the instinctive flair for turning a crowd's annoyance into instant delight, should be assessed. Miller has always placed the fun of the game above every consideration. No doubt, had he consistently applied himself to all situations with the determination he has produced at moments of crisis, his batting and bowling averages would have been higher and, in his 40 Tests, he would already have exceeded the 2,325 runs and 127 wickets of Rhodes. Maybe so, but that would not have been Miller, of the few personal cricket ambitions, who thrives on incentive but takes scant pleasure in cheap runs or wickets. A true guide to the estimation of his fellow cricketers is that nearly every captain of a country defeated by Australia in her magnificent post-war run believed that, with Miller on his side, the issue would have been far closer, or have gone the other way.

The place and circumstance of Miller's birth were not without coincidence. He, the youngest of four children, was born at Sunshine, Melbourne, on November 28, 1919, at a time when Sir Keith Smith and Sir Ross Smith were creating world history with the first flight from England to Australia. It took 27 days 20 hours. His parents gave him the Christian names of the two famous airmen. Years later his own exploits in the air, as a night fighter pilot, earned for him a reputation as a dashing, devil-may-care fellow which his subsequent approach to big cricket confirmed.

As a boy Miller, now 6ft 1in, was below average size, and his first attempts at hitting a hard ball on rough paddock pitches resulted in so many painful knocks that he changed to a soft ball. In this way he learned to play his strokes without fear of physical injury. Miller, who lived near the Caulfield Racecourse, was so tiny that he hoped to become a jockey, but between 16 and 17 he grew more than a foot and any such idea had to be abandoned. Even so, Miller has retained his love of horses and horse racing. Most of his free days on tour are spent at the racecourse.

SOMETIMES HE BOWLED TOO WELL
Neville Cardus, 1969

Brian Statham was one of the Five Cricketers of the Year in 1955.

Two Lancastrian fast bowlers satisfied the severest tests of breeding and deportment, Brearley and BRIAN STATHAM; but only one fast bowler playing for my native county could stand comparison, in point of classic poise and action, against Statham, and he was an Australian, E. A. McDonald. I make a great compliment both to Statham and to the ghost of Ted McDonald by coupling their names. McDonald's action was as easy and as rhythmical as music, and so was Statham's.

Purist critics, during Statham's first seasons, suggested that as his right arm swung over, the batsman was able to see too much of his chest; the left shoulder didn't point the way of the flight down the wicket. The truth about Statham's action is that it was so elastic and balanced (and double-jointed) that there was no forward shoulder rigidity possible; his movement, from the beginning of his run to deliver, to the final accumulated propulsion, had not an awkward angle in it at all.

The whole man of him, from his first swinging steps of approach to the launching of the ball from the right foot, was the effortless and natural dynamo and life-force of his attack. He wasn't called "The Whippet" for nothing.

Fast bowlers, as a rule, are aggressive by nature, rough-hewn and physically overbearing. Statham, like McDonald, was unruffled of temper, almost deceptively pacific. I have seen McDonald lose control and let fly a fusillade of unbeautiful bouncers, wasting fuel, or petrol, like a perfectly engineered car backfiring going uphill. Never have I seen the equanimity of Statham's temperament or technique rendered out of harmony for a minute.

At the age of 20, Statham provoked some sensation in the Lancashire v Yorkshire match at Old Trafford, 1950, by taking five wickets for 52, in the ancient enemy's first innings. On the strength, maybe, of this performance he was flown out, with Tattersall, as reinforcement for F. R. Brown's gallant team in Australia, 1950-51.

These two Lancashire lads arrived in what must have seemed to them then a truly foreign climate; for they had been rushed out of an English winter, still unnourished in a post-rationed environment, to a land of plenty. They came to Sydney looking as though each had escaped from a Lowry canvas, lean and hungry.

Statham did not play in a Test match during this rubber; in fact he found the Australian air rather a strain on his breathing apparatus. Nonetheless, he took 11 wickets at 20 runs each against State and Country XI's and in New Zealand.

Back in England he began to foretell the quality soon to come; he had 90 Championship wickets for Lancashire, average 14.65; and in two Test matches v South Africa his contribution as a bowler was four wickets for 78.

The Statham–Trueman collaboration of speed is recent history. Trueman in Test matches took 307 wickets, average 21.57. Statham in Tests took 252, average 24.84. It is useless to measure one against the other. As well we might try to assess Wagner and Mozart on the same level. Trueman, on occasion, nearly lost a big match by loss of technical (and temperamental) control; Statham never.

I particularly like Frank Tyson's story of the West Indies bowler who hit Jim Laker over the eye. When subsequently the West Indies bouncer came in to bat and reluctantly took guard, somebody asked Statham to retaliate in kind and explosive kick. "No," said Statham, "I think I'll just bowl him out." Here, in a phrase, is the essence of Statham's character. Gentleman "George".* Sometimes he bowled too superbly to tail-end batsmen, they were not good enough to get a touch.

In his first-class seasons of the game, Statham overthrew no fewer than 2,259 batsmen, and each of them were glad to call him a friend. He has been an adornment to the game, as a fast bowler of the classic mould, and as a man and character of the rarest breed and likeableness.

* To his friends he has been George through his cricketing career.

CAPTAIN COURTEOUS   John Arlott, 1969

Colin Cowdrey was one of the Five Cricketers of the Year in 1956.

When England met Australia on June 12, 1968, at Edgbaston, COLIN COWDREY became the first man to play in 100 Test matches. He was captain of England in that match and, appropriately enough, he scored a century. Characteristically, too, he reached 95 overnight and appeared much less anxious than his friends while he made the next five runs on the following morning.

One by one the records have gone down before him. As this tribute is written he has scored more runs in Test cricket than any other batsman except Hammond. By the time it is printed he will almost certainly have passed that figure: and half a dozen years of play at the highest level should still lie ahead of him.

Among the batsmen we have seen, only Sobers, who is four years younger, can be expected to pass his ultimate total in representative play, while Graveney alone among cricketers still active has scored more runs in all first-class cricket. His once-promising leg-spin bowling is no longer regarded seriously, but he is arguably the finest slip fieldsman in the world at present.

Colin Cowdrey's cricket and his behaviour are both characterised by unruf-flable rectitude. His batting is correct, splendid in its controlled rhythms but never in unorthodoxy or violence. Similarly, his bearing in face of treatment which has often been at least tactless, and which would have roused most normally quiet men to indignation, has been impeccably courteous.

Yet it would miss his quality completely to think him insensitive: his almost boyish jump of glee in the field when an important wicket falls or his gaily quick recognition of a joke are those of a responsive and lively-witted person. His family life is ample indication of the depth and warmth of his feelings. His entire upbringing, however, conspired to make him self-contained, a man who thinks before he speaks – and then, often, does not speak.

His father, the cricket enthusiast (top-scorer for the Europeans against Arthur Gilligan's 1926-27 touring team in India) who christened his son Michael Colin Cowdrey to give him the initials of the unique cricket club, was a tea-planter in India. His only child was born in Bangalore and, at the age of five, was sent to England, a boarding-school education and the homes of different relatives during vacations. After 1938 Colin Cowdrey did not see his parents until 1945 and subsequently only during their four-yearly leave periods until 1954.

The father who was so delighted by his success, whom he had missed, and whom he so much desired to please, had retired and returned to England at the beginning of that summer. Sadly enough he watched his son as captain of Oxford have a relatively indifferent playing season on a series of wet pitches, so that it was for his unmistakable ability rather than current form that he was chosen for Hutton's 1954-55 team to Australia.

While he was on the voyage out, his father died. Once more Colin Cowdrey contained his emotions and went on to the success that was, we may suspect, his tribute to the father he had so briefly known.

He batted capably in the first two Tests, and then at Melbourne, with the rubber even and England reduced by Miller to 41 for four, he made his first Test century and tilted the match which turned the series. From that innings he has remained one of the world's outstanding batsmen. He was dropped from the team against Australia in 1964 and West Indies in 1966 by selectors torn by the old tug between class and current form.

The mark of greatness is clear in the air of time to spare about his stroke-making. He never appears to have to hurry and he is remarkably sure of the ball. The nicety of his timing and assessment of line and length are such that, with perhaps the exception of Garfield Sobers, he middles the ball more consistently than any other batsman of this time.

1960–69

THE ACCUMULATOR   John Woodcock, 1970

Ken Barrington was one of the Five Cricketers of the Year in 1960.

The illness which ended KEN BARRINGTON's career at the age of 38 revealed the extent to which a rugged physique had been undermined by the anxieties of representative cricket. It also deprived England of a remarkable batsman.

Between 1959 and 1968 Barrington amassed runs, for Surrey and more particularly for England, with implacable intensity. It was his ambition to surpass every

Test match aggregate, and he was well on the way to doing so when the effort caught up with him. Playing in Melbourne, in a double-wicket tournament, he suffered a thrombosis which led to his announcing his retirement in April, 1969. Now, as the father of a new-born son, a writer on the game, the co-owner of a sports-clothing business and a keen golfer, he is leading a relaxed and happy life.

To say that Barrington had a unique appetite for runs would be to go too far. Bradman and Ponsford, Hutton and Hanif Mohammad, to mention only four, were no less insatiable. But as a percentage player I doubt whether there has ever been anyone to equal Barrington. He joined Surrey, from the Reading club, in 1948, when he was 17. During National Service from 1949 to 1951 he was still looked upon mainly as a bowler. But on his return to Surrey it was as a batsman that he established himself in the county side. By 1955 he was making enough runs to be chosen for England against South Africa. In his two Test matches that year he made 0, 34 and 18, and when, peremptorily, the selectors dropped him, he pledged himself to compile such a stack of runs that sooner or later they would be obliged to bring him back. Regardless of the rate at which he scored, he set his course, eliminating, along the way, those attacking strokes which contained an element of risk.

To make a success of such a scheme Barrington needed, and possessed, immense determination and considerable talent, as well as a stubborn streak. On the occasions when he let himself go, as against Australia at Melbourne in 1966 when he scored 102 in two and a half hours, he displayed every shot in the book. There was none that he lacked. And when, sometimes, he decided to act the fool, his improvisation and impersonation were equally brilliant. But the Barrington we got to know, and came to stand by, was first and foremost an accumulator. He remained faithful to the cut, in all its varieties, and was a wonderfully deft placer of the ball on the on-side. By adopting an extravagantly open stance, to counter the predominance of in-swing bowling, he restricted the range of his driving. To hit a half-volley between cover point and extra cover he needed to swivel his left shoulder from the direction of wide midwicket to a line outside the off stump. Not surprisingly, this was something which he was prepared to attempt only when he was well set, and even then his bottom hand remained the master.

On a day when he was not in the mood Barrington would walk to the wicket as though delaying, for as long as possible, the dreaded moment when he took his guard. For a long time he might survive only by using his front leg as a second bat and by shuffling his back leg across the stumps as a further line of defence. Anything intended for mid-off would go to mid-on; anything beating the bat would prompt a long and anxious examination of the pitch. To batsmen whose turn was yet to come it must have been an unnerving sight. Yet, remembering his resolution that it was only runs that mattered, he would resist the temptations of despair. As the hours passed he might offer his bat to the barrackers, but to each ball he would apply himself with every corner of his mind.

Off the field Barrington was a most amusing companion. Gone was the introspection of his batting, if not the determination which was so much a part of it.

His sense of humour extended to his reaching no fewer than four Test hundreds with a six – at Melbourne, Adelaide, Durban and Trinidad. The stroke he used for the purpose was a violent pull which took everyone completely by surprise and invariably ended a protracted period of defence. He was a splendid mimic, the Australian, Ken Mackay, being among those he took off with great skill. Nor does anything go on under the bonnet of a motor car which mystifies him. Sometimes, to hear him talk, you might suppose he looked upon slow bats-manship as one of the deadly sins. But it is a trait of captains and batsmen that they cast off their inhibitions when they retire. And Barrington, by the time he did so, had made for himself an extraordinary collection of batting records. Of these his own personal favourites are shared with no one. He alone has made a Test hundred on every Test match ground in England and in every Test-playing country of the world.

Little Wonder No. 14

Oxford v Cambridge. At Lord's, July 2, 3, 4, 1903. Raphael, only given his "Blue" two days prior to the contest, was ninth man out at 259, after being at the wickets rather more than three hours and a half. His 130 included 13 fours, eight threes and 12 twos. Raphael had not only represented his University at rugby football but in the previous winter acted as one of the England threequarters in all three international engagements. No doubt this experience of big encounters served him in good stead on such an anxious occasion.

ENNOBLED BY BRADMAN

Five Cricketers of the Century – Ian Wooldridge, 2000

Garry Sobers was one of the Five Cricketers of the Year in 1964.

Born to frugality and early tragedy in a one-storey wooden house on July 28, 1936, Garry Sobers seemed an unlikely candidate to become an icon at anything outside the parish of St Michael in Barbados. He was one of seven children, one of whom died in an accident with a kerosene lamp. Then, when he was five, a telegram arrived saying his father, a merchant seaman, had drowned with all hands when his ship was torpedoed by a U-Boat in the Atlantic. His mother, a strong Christian woman, heroically kept the family intact. Her pension was insulting. At 14, hardly an academic, he was a gopher in a furniture factory.

In February 1975, already celebrated as a face on Barbadian postage stamps, Sir GARFIELD ST AUBRUN SOBERS was knighted by the Queen at the Barbados Garrison Racecourse, barely a mile down the road from where he was born in Walcott Avenue. It was not quite the ultimate accolade. In 1988, Sir Donald Bradman conferred on Sobers the title of the greatest all-round cricketer he had ever seen. Bradman's judgment in these matters is regarded as Holy Writ.

None would contest it. Across two decades Sobers brought to a cricket world as diverse as the Caribbean, the Test arena, English county cricket with Nottinghamshire, Sheffield Shield cricket with South Australia, and even North Staffs and South

Cheshire League cricket with Norton, plus hundreds of charity games, a vibrancy, nobility of spirit and versatility of accomplishment that transcended all statistics.

These were remarkable enough: 8,032 runs, 235 wickets and 109 catches in 93 Test matches for West Indies. More significantly, he could turn the tide of a Test within an hour, and it was on these occasions that partisanship was suspended. You simply sat back and marvelled at the occasion. From the direst situation his only thought was to attack. He was physically fearless. He never wore a thigh-pad, never mind a helmet, and, from his boyhood days with the Barbados Police team until his retirement, he was only seriously hit twice. Such was his adaptability that he could bowl left-arm very fast, swinging it both ways, left-arm finger-spin and left-arm wrist-spin. By his own recollection, he was no-balled fewer than half a dozen times during his entire career.

Perhaps the most fundamental argument against the modern idiom of cricket is that Sobers was never coached. He mistrusted coaches. He learned the game playing all spare hours in the street with his brothers and friends and then, after the early Barbados sunset, playing on with miniature implements, much to the detriment of the furniture, in his despairing mother's house.

His real apprenticeship started at the age of 12 when, as the kid next door, he started bowling in the nets to members of the fashionable Wanderers Club, earning a 50-cent piece every time he knocked it off the centre stump. It made him more money than he earned at the furniture factory down the road. At 16, he was playing for Barbados against the touring Indians and taking seven wickets. At 17, he played his first Test for West Indies. At 21, against Pakistan in Jamaica, he broke Len Hutton's Test record with 365 not out.

By now the world was acquainted with the kid from Walcott Avenue. He was an instinctive back-foot player, attacking with the lightest of bats (2lb 4oz) which frequently slapped his buttocks on the follow-through. Then he would bowl, crouched for wrist-spin, back arched for finger-spin, lithe as a panther when bowling fast. There was never a moment on a cricket field when you could take your eyes off him.

In 1971-72, Sobers led a World XI to Australia. Watching him in Melbourne, Bradman saw him play a straight-drive against Dennis Lillee which smashed into the sightscreen almost before Lillee had straightened up from his follow-through. Sobers scored 254 (after a first-innings duck). Bradman, no soft touch when it came to criticism, rated it the greatest innings he had ever seen on Australian soil.

There was a fourth dimension to Sobers. In fact there were several others, since he was not averse to a drink or a gamble, and had a pretty complicated domestic life. But on the Test cricket field, when he succeeded Frank Worrell as captain, he was the last Corinthian of a dying breed. He walked when he had nicked a catch to slip, without even bothering the umpire. He would not abide sledging. And, once to his own detriment, he would risk the result to entertain a crowd.

In Trinidad in 1967-68, against Colin Cowdrey's England team, he became so frustrated by their go-slow tactics that he declared, setting England 215 to win at 78 an hour. His bowlers sent down 19 overs an hour. England won. I met him that evening in a bar down by the port. He was all alone, and next day the Caribbean press rated him alongside a war criminal. It was never war to him, which was part of his greatness.

SELFISH OR SINGLE-MINDED: THE PUBLIC DECIDE   Terry Brindle, 1978

Geoffrey Boycott was one of the Five Cricketers of the Year in 1965.

GEOFFREY BOYCOTT's place in cricket folklore was assured long before that warm Headingley evening last summer when he succeeded where only would-be bombers and the infernal weather had succeeded before and stopped an English Test match in its tracks for almost ten minutes.

Boycott's 100th century – in a Test match, before his Yorkshire public – was indeed the stuff that dreams are made of. There was hardly a dry contact lens in the house. But the abiding significance of his 100th century was not simply statistical; Boycott himself conceded that one century on record was much the same as the one before or the one to follow. It was the realisation, vitally important to Boycott himself, that the public were prepared to accept his peace offering after a controversial absence from Test cricket.

Boycott and controversy have shared the longest opening partnership in the game. The owlish, introverted young man who broke into county cricket with Yorkshire in 1962 and who was regarded as a dedicated technician rather than a talented strokemaker developed his skills to prove the unbelievers wrong, and neglected his personality to convince his critics they were right.

The trauma of Trent Bridge [*where he ran out local hero Derek Randall*] and the Headingley homecoming which followed combined, as never before, Boycott the public man with Boycott the private person. To his unconcealed delight, the public showed themselves ready to accept both.

Cricket tends to traditionalise its heroes, seeking to find in them all the qualities of unselfishness and character which lend an amateur's zeal to a highly professional game. Boycott, complex and warted, refused to fit the pattern and was not easily forgiven.

Yet Boycott the technician has rarely been doubted. He is compact, beautifully balanced, professionally expert, arguably the most adroit player of the ball off the wicket in the modern game. The very soundness of his technique tends to detract from the drama of his innings, even of centuries carved with fastidious determination.

Others have created their own legends more extrovertly, more gloriously, more entertainingly. Boycott builds an innings brick by brick, cementing each stroke to the next with that extraordinary power of concentration which frustrates good bowling and intimidates poor. His centuries are an act of will.

That single-mindedness has exposed Boycott to accusations of selfishness which are bound to be levelled from a distance; easier to challenge with an insight into the man and the situation thrust on him as captain of a young and inexperienced Yorkshire side.

Boycott's responsibilities weigh heavily and the proven frailty of Yorkshire's batting has led him to believe he cannot, must not fail. The conviction that his runs are indispensable – and Yorkshire without them would have struggled fearfully in the recent past – feeds an already characteristic strain of stubbornness. Boycott in or out of form cannot contemplate giving his wicket away; the very idea is anathema, an admission of failure. If his single-mindedness is a flaw, England were glad enough of it at Trent Bridge and again at Headingley.

It is ironic and perhaps unfortunate that Boycott's moment of historic achievement should lend itself to discussion of his character, of his weaknesses as much as his strengths. Yet Boycott's character and performance are indivisible; more than any modern player he has been judged in terms of personality.

Boycott, knowing it and sometimes wounded by it, withdrew into the security of the art he knew best and resolved that if he could not be the most popular of players he would be the most effective. A century of centuries insists that he did not fail.

His welcome back into Test cricket and the warmth of his reception at Trent Bridge and Headingley tapped a fund of popular sympathy and admiration which Boycott never knew existed. Rather like a clip from an old film in which a recluse Queen Victoria returns from a triumphal jubilee procession and confides with some surprise, "Y'know. I really think they like me after all" … Corny, perhaps, but Boycott was never more sincere.

A SQUARE-CUT ABOVE   Five Cricketers of the Year – Louis Duffus, 1966

Among the memories of the South African tour of 1965 none will linger longer into posterity than the prodigious performances of the two Pollocks, the brothers who left an indelible imprint on public perception wherever they played. Yet to those familiar with their background the impact they made in England was not surprising

The younger brother ROBERT GRAEME POLLOCK was born in Durban on February 27, 1944. His father, a native of Scotland, had played in provincial cricket as a wicketkeeper for the Orange Free State. They are a sport-loving family. The two sons entered into all games with relish and skill, and it soon became obvious that Graeme was destined to become a prodigy. He was only three when his mother tried in vain to prevent his taking stance as a left-hander. Heredity had asserted itself. Like his father, Graeme does everything except batting with his right hand predominant.

The first evidence of his precocious gifts for cricket came when he was nine and accompanied the Grey Junior School XI to play in the nearby town of Graaff Reinet. He scored his first century (117 not out) and took ten wickets for 25 runs. Until he was 12 he was a fast bowler like his brother, but was persuaded to change to leg-spin. At Grey High School he excelled in every sport in which he played. On leaving school he shot up from 5ft 10in to his present height of 6ft 2in.

All his career has been distinguished by the early age of his achievements. On his 13th birthday he played for the school XI and continued for an unprecedented four years – the last year as captain. He made a record number of runs, and on being chosen for Eastern Province in the Nuffield Schools Week established the highest score of 152.

When he was 16 years and 335 days old he became the youngest cricketer to score a century in the Currie Cup tournament, and at 19 the youngest South African to hit a double-century in a first-class match. At the same age of unsurpassed youthfulness he recorded the first of his four Test centuries – 122 against Australia in Sydney in 1963-64.

Both Pollocks owed much to their school coach George Cox, of Sussex. While on a visit to Britain with his parents in 1961 Graeme played in six games for the county second eleven. The genius of his cricket burst into full flower on his first tour – to Australia. In his second first-class match against a Combined XI, including five Test cricketers, at Perth he scored 127 not out. The reaching of his hundred in 88 minutes prompted Sir Donald Bradman to remark to him, "If you ever score a century like that again I hope I'm there to see it." In the Fourth Test at Adelaide he played an exhilarating innings of 175, including two sixes, two fours and a two off an over from Bobby Simpson. With E. J. Barlow he put on a record 341 for the third wicket. His tour aggregate was 1,018 with a third-place average of 53.57, and he was fourth in the Test figures with 57.00.

In England last summer, the summit of his achievements was his chanceless 125, out of 269, scored in the Second Test at Trent Bridge. He went in to bat when two wickets had fallen for 16 and gave full rein to his elegant off-side strokes, studded with square and cover drives. When he had scored 28 he became the youngest player to pass 1,000 runs in Test cricket.

Although his Test innings at Trent Bridge endured while five wickets fell for 80 and paved the way for South Africa's only victory and the winning of the rubber, his greatest satisfaction was derived from his 137 and 77 not out in the Fifth Test against England in 1964-65 before his home crowd at Port Elizabeth. He left England at the top of both the Test (48.50) and tour (57.35) averages. With only two wickets he was also head of the Test bowling. At an age when many have not yet started their Test careers he is already regarded as one of the most accomplished batsmen in contemporary cricket. It is a comforting thought for his host of admirers that probably the best of Graeme Pollock is still to come.

Pollock played only eight more Tests, all against Australia, before South Africa's exclusion from international cricket in 1970.

HE SHALL OVERCOME   Five Cricketers of the Year – J. E. Godfrey, 1967

The story of Basil D'Oliveira is a fairytale come true; the story of a nonentity in the country of his birth who because of the colour of his skin was confined to cricket on crude mudheaps until he was 25, yet after only one season in the County Championship played for England. No Test player has had to overcome such tremendous disadvantages along the road to success as the Cape Coloured D'Oliveira. Admirable though his achievements were against the West Indies in 1966, undoubtedly his triumph in ever attaining Test status was more commendable.

That he did not fall by the wayside of the stony path he was compelled to tread is a tribute to the courage and skill of this player from the land of apartheid. To say that he never contemplated giving up the game before reaching the hour of glory was hardly the case. The hazards he encountered were very nearly too great even for the stout-hearted D'Oliveira. Suffice to say that of the 25,000 South African coloured cricketers who would dearly love to make the county grade over here D'Oliveira is the first to have done so. Hundreds of others are doomed to spend their lives in a class of cricket far beneath their skill. They will stay because no one ever sees them in this unfashionable outpost of the game.

Born in Cape Town on October 4, 1934, BASIL LEWIS D'OLIVEIRA inherited his father's love for the game, but until he was 15 practically the only cricket he played was in the street. There were no facilities at either of his schools, St Joseph's Catholic or Zonnebloem Training College, as money for the promotion of school sport was non-existent. His schooldays over, he joined St Augustine's, the club for which his father, Lewis D'Oliveira, played as an all-rounder for something like 40 years. There, in one of the South African leagues for non-Europeans, young Dolly began to blossom under the guidance of his father, as a right-handed batsman and medium-paced bowler.

His team-mates would walk miles to a suitable strip of grassless earth, sand or gravel over which to lay a mat after first preparing their pitch with a spade and wheelbarrow. D'Oliveira thought nothing of walking ten miles to his home ground. The alternative was a four-mile stroll to the nearest bus stop. His club shared the ground with other teams, and it was not uncommon for square leg in one match find himself standing near third slip in the next. Yet these primitive conditions served only to imbue D'Oliveira with a zest and enthusiasm for the game. He was deeply impressed on his visits to first-class matches in Cape Town, in particular to see Compton, Harvey and May.

He never missed an opportunity to study closely the manner in which these and other great batsmen moved about the crease and into their strokes. He reasoned for himself why any particular stroke was made, and soon reports of his own phenomenal scoring feats began to trickle through. D'Oliveira scored 80 centuries in the Cape and once hit 225 in 70 minutes. In a federation tournament he thrashed 168 in 98 minutes and in another innings made 46 in an eight-ball over. English professionals who went to South Africa coaching during the winter spoke of him as a natural player who moved well and struck the ball hard.

Yet, it seemed, it was not easy to convince anyone that he could be a top-class player against top-class opposition. He played, however, in one or two testimonial matches in South Africa against white teams, then against the Kenya Asians, and went on an all-coloured team's tour of East Africa. For a couple of years, John Arlott, the broadcaster and cricket writer, tried to get people in England to take an interest in D'Oliveira, and eventually, with the aid of the urgings of two other journalists, Middleton, of the Central Lancashire League, after failing to get several better-known players, offered him a contract at £450 for the 1960 season. He was then 25.

Raffles, fêtes and matches were organised in the locality of his tenement home in the coloured quarter of Cape Town to raise his fare to England. As an £8 10s a week machine-minder for a printing firm there was little scope for savings of his own with a wife and baby to support. For an unproved player with the Manchester suburban club he was little or no better off to begin with. He had just enough to live frugally during the summer and pay his return fare home to bring back his wife. At Middleton, D'Oliveira's competitors included Garry Sobers, Cecil Pepper, John McMahon and Salim Durani. So that with only 25 or so runs and three or four wickets to show for his endeavours after five matches in the League he was all set to pack his bags. He felt he was clearly out of his depth. Then, almost suddenly as the weather warmed up and pitches became faster, runs began to flow from D'Oliveira's bat as in his native South Africa. By the end of his first summer he had made 930 runs, average 48.95, which was slightly better than Sobers and the best of the league. For good measure he gained 71 wickets at 11.72 each. Middleton's gamble had paid off. The coloured cricketer from the Cape stayed for four years.

When he first arrived in England in April 1960 the extremely modest and well-behaved D'Oliveira was quite stunned at being treated as an ordinary human being unaffected by any colour bar. He would have been perfectly content to have spent the rest of his life in Middleton, where he established himself with more than 3,600 runs for an average of over 48, and 238 wickets at under 17 each. It was Tom Graveney who persuaded Dolly that he was good enough to be a success at county level. They were on a private Commonwealth tour together, and in the face of competition from Gloucestershire (after Lancashire had turned him down) D'Oliveira joined Worcestershire.

And so to 1965, his first year of Championship cricket. If there were any lingering doubts that at the age of 30 his weaknesses would be exposed, these were soon dispelled. He made five centuries, totalling 1,523 runs (average 43.51), and he and Graveney were the only batsmen in the Championship to exceed 1,500 that season. D'Oliveira also took 35 wickets, proved himself in the top flight as a slip fielder and gained the distinction in his first county season of helping Worcestershire in no small measure to retain the Championship pennant. As his captain, Don Kenyon, remarked at the end of a memorable summer, "D'Oliveira did everything we hoped he might do and a lot more ... all the predictions that a turning ball might find him out proved utterly false."

Undoubtedly the most memorable year of his life was 1966, by which time he had become a British citizen. Although he had shown every promise in MCC matches at Lord's, to be selected for England against the West Indies was beyond his wildest dreams. It was D'Oliveira himself who said after his Test debut at Lord's, "This is a fairytale come true. Six years ago I was playing on mudheaps. Now I have played for England and met the Queen; what more could I possibly ask?" People who have delighted in the manner in which he has savaged county bowling in Worcestershire's cause consider that his best days for England are still to come. As he grows in confidence and experience in the Test sphere England could find themselves with one of the finest all-rounders in post-war cricket.

The D'Oliveira Affair is covered in the England chapter on page 264.

Little Wonder No. 15

Essex v Surrey. At Leyton, June 1, 2, 3, 1905. On Essex going in a second time, McGahey and Turner scored 95 together, and Gillingham and Reeves 112 in just over an hour. Gillingham was brilliantly caught by Inns, the Essex cricketer, who died suddenly about a fortnight later. [Inns was acting as substitute.]

TEST CRICKET'S YOUNGEST CAPTAIN   Five Cricketers of the Year – Dicky Rutnagur, 1968

It is debatable whether it is an asset or otherwise to be born the son of a famous man, especially if one has aspirations in the same sphere in which the father made his mark. Comparisons are inevitable, and comparisons can be so unnerving and oppressive to the one being compared.

MANSUR ALI, THE NAWAB OF PATAUDI, who captained India in England last summer, inherited more than a princely title when he was born at Bhopal on January 5, 1941. Also handed down to him was a talent for cricket which made his father an outstanding batsman during one of cricket's most prosperous eras.

The younger Nawab has followed gloriously in his father's footsteps, and that in spite of the severe handicap of losing the use of his right eye as the result of a motor car accident, in 1961. Pataudi came to greatness without the guiding influence of his father, although anyone who knows him has no doubt that he has always been inspired by his memory. He was only 11 – in fact it was on his birthday – that the former Nawab died of heart failure while playing polo in New Delhi.

Not many months after his father died, in 1952, Pataudi came to England. The passenger list of the ship on which he travelled included many illustrious cricket names. There was Vinoo Mankad, making his annual trip to play in the Lancashire League; then there were the Three Ws and Ramadhin, returning from Australia at the end of the West Indies tour. Pataudi played deck games with them, and their constant company further stoked his cricketing ambitions.

Hardly could Frank Worrell have imagined then that in ten years, almost to the month, his young shipmate would be walking out with him to toss for innings in a Test match. This happened in Barbados, when Pataudi took over the Indian captaincy. Pataudi then had played in only three Test matches and, at 21, became the youngest captain ever in international cricket.

LEARNING SPIN THE FAST WAY   Five Cricketers of the Year – Norman Preston, 1969

Few young cricketers have made such a direct impact on their entry to first-class cricket as DEREK LESLIE UNDERWOOD, hero of England's victory over Australia in the final Test at The Oval last season. At the age of 23 this left-arm slow-medium-paced bowler of Kent may be said to be on the threshold of a great career in world cricket.

In six years he has taken 744 wickets, no doubt a record for one so young, and he bids fair to follow in the wake of such renowned England left-arm slow bowlers as Bobby Peel, John Briggs, Wilfred Rhodes, Hedley Verity and Tony Lock.

From the lean youth who first played for Kent, Underwood has developed physically, having grown to nearly six feet and having also acquired quite broad shoulders. His fastest ball is as fast as was Doug Wright's, and given the slightest help from the pitch he can be truly devastating.

He always bowls at the stumps; he has natural orthodox leg-spin, not too much, and after rain he can make the ball stand up. In fact, in that Oval Test the ball seemed to stop and check on pitching, leaving the Australians helpless – they were committed too soon to play their strokes.

Born at Bromley in north-west Kent, on June 8, 1945, Underwood developed naturally as a cricketer. He owes much to his father, Leslie Underwood, a capable right-arm medium-fast bowler who played village cricket for Farnborough, Kent and was so keen for his two sons to play the game that he set up a net in his garden with concrete pitch and matting on top. That was where Derek and his elder brother, Keith, learned the vital essentials of accurate length and direction.

Like so many youngsters he had always bowled as fast as he could, but when he played for Beckenham CC in 1961 he realised he was not really fast and would have to evolve something different. He tried reducing his pace and the spin came naturally.

Underwood never saw Kent play until he played for the county. Kent could not have chosen a more difficult assignment for his introduction to first-class cricket in 1963. They took him to Hull to face the champions, and on a drying pitch he demonstrated his possibilities by taking four for 40 in the Yorkshire first innings.

He stayed in the Kent team for the remainder of the season and he has been there ever since. Indeed, that year he headed the county averages, and at 17 he was the youngest player ever to take 100 wickets, a feat he has repeated regularly.

Until 1964 Underwood says he had always bowled round the wicket. It was necessary to learn to bowl over the wicket. This did not come easily, but the effort proved its worth, for in 1966 he claimed 68 more victims compared with the previous season at little more than half the cost.

That year he became the first Kent cricketer to head the national bowling averages since Colin Blythe in 1914. His 144 wickets for Kent was their highest for 21 years since the days of Tich Freeman.

Of quiet, pleasant disposition, Underwood lives for cricket. He has a file of all his performances, carefully pasted in books at the end of each season besides albums of press photographs in which those of the final Test of 1968 figure prominently. He hoped to get the ball with which he took seven for 50 and brought England victory, but it was swallowed up when the crowd engulfed the arena.

1970–79

VOLUME NOT VERVE   Norman Harris, 1983

Glenn Turner was one of the Five Cricketers of the Year in 1971.

In retrospect, it almost seems that Glenn Turner was destined to score his 100th hundred on May 29. One would hardly say he had tried *not* to reach the milestone on some other day on some other ground. But, after a run of low scores, a gloriously fine Saturday at Worcester suddenly seemed the obvious setting.

It was also clear that Turner would not want to just score 100 in adding his name to the 18 players who had previously registered the feat. He would surely want to do so in particularly glittering fashion. Securing 100 before lunch was the most obvious way. Almost inevitably, he achieved it.

The occasion seemed even more appropriate, with Billy Ibadulla on hand to come out to the middle with a celebratory gin and tonic. It was Ibadulla, once a coach in Dunedin, New Zealand, who had encouraged Turner to go to England and arrange a trial with Warwickshire. It was Warwickshire who had not been able to offer him a contract, and against whom Turner has always scored particularly heavily. And it was Warwickshire's bowlers who were now suffering again. With

Turner 128 at lunch, the afternoon offered a further challenge; as the runs mounted up it became clear that he was after his 300. He reached it at 5.36 and at the declaration, six minutes later, was 311 not out.

The performance brought to mind other famous scorers of many runs, notably Bradman. Certainly the great Australian run-maker scored centuries far more often than Turner or anyone else, especially in Test matches. But it is difficult to think of any batsman, Bradman included, who could respond to particular challenges with more certainty and flair. There was another celebrated example of this in 1973 when Turner, touring England with the New Zealanders, achieved the rare feat (only six others have done it) of scoring 1,000 runs before the end of May. He needed 93 in his last possible innings, at Northampton; the wet wicket was, by his own judgment, dangerous, and the opposition bowlers included Bishan Bedi.

There have also been six occasions when Turner has scored two hundreds in a match, most notably when New Zealand gained their first victory against Australia at Christchurch in 1974. The fall of wickets around him has seemed to provide extra stimulus, for he has twice carried his bat in Test matches, and when he did it in a 1981 county match against Glamorgan his unbeaten 141 out of 169 constituted a record 83.4% of the total.

His initial season in first-class cricket, as a schoolboy in New Zealand, might not have promised such an abundance of runs. But it did indicate the character and the technique: once he scored just three runs in an entire morning session, and he recalls wryly that his defensive technique was so sound that he didn't even get any runs from snicks. Further evidence of character was to be found in his giving up his job as an insurance clerk and working in a bakery for ten months in order to save the money for his trip to England.

Several seasons were to pass before, quite suddenly, he shed his reputation for slow scoring. Having established himself with Worcestershire, he decided to try to gain – and give – some pleasure with his batting. He drove the ball with great power for one who, even in his mid-twenties, looked unusually slender and boyish.

An independent streak, and his belief in his monetary worth as a leading professional, caused him to fall out with the New Zealand cricket authorities and, sadly, to withdraw for some years from Test cricket. In 1978 he opted to continue playing for Worcestershire and help organise his benefit rather than tour with the visiting New Zealanders.

Since then, while at the height of his powers, he has covered Test series in New Zealand as a television commentator instead of playing in them. This has deprived him of the opportunity of playing against the best Test teams, with the fastest bowlers of his time, a fact which has had to be entered as a caveat by critics ranking him among the greats. Nor, when scoring all the runs he did against West Indies in 1971-72 and against Australia in New Zealand in 1973-74, did he, other than very rarely, dominate the bowling.

Perhaps circumstances will still allow him to prove this point. If not, how will history assess him? A remarkable record-breaker? That seems a little unfair, as it ignores his match-winning efforts at all levels of cricket and, most particularly, it fails to recognise the aesthetic element in his batting. Yet, however unsatisfactory, that at the moment is as it may be.

Few cricketers in recent years have captured the public imagination in the manner of Clive Lloyd. This tall, bespectacled all-rounder, short-sighted but by no means handicapped by the affliction, joined Lancashire two years ago and has played a leading part in the revival of cricket at Old Trafford where crowds are now big again and enthusiasm is ever growing. Born in Georgetown, British Guiana, on August 31, 1944, and christened CLIVE HUBERT, LLOYD would be the last to proclaim that his signing from the Lancashire League club, Haslingden, had anything more than a passing significance. He would, of course, be wrong. No cricketer has made a greater impact on his county than has Lloyd on Lancashire. He has set an example with the bat, with the ball, and in the field, that has inspired every other member of the team and the staff at Old Trafford to strive for similar perfection.

Lloyd is a cricketer who does things by instinct. He learned the game as so many West Indies cricketers do – in the streets and backyards of his native Georgetown, with the help of his one brother and four sisters who were roped in to help retrieve the many balls Clive dispatched into other backyards and streets farther afield. A man of some 6ft 5in with a reach that enables him to dictate a length to every bowler, Lloyd won a place in the Demerara School team as a ten-year-old and at once made it apparent that here was a boy with tremendous cricketing potential. Lloyd harnesses his ability to cover a deal of ground with his long, loping stride, with a tremendous reach and a powerful throw. His hands are big enough to make catches a formality. Little escapes him in the air or on the ground and he does it all with the casual ease of a man born to thrill the cricketing crowds all over the world.

After making his first-class debut with Guyana in 1963-64 he was blooded in Test cricket in India in 1966-67, making a century against England at Port-of-Spain and also hitting 129 on his Australian debut at Brisbane a year later. He was ambitious as well as talented, and when Wes Hall suggested to Lloyd that he would benefit from a spell in league cricket in Lancashire it was an easy task to find him a club. Haslingden signed him in readiness for the 1967 season.

Lancashire, outpriced in their bid for Sobers, turned their attention to Lloyd when the new overseas registration rule came into being, and because he had settled down so well and got to know the people of Lancashire at Haslingden, he signed for the county and has no regrets.

He still has one or two cricketing ambitions to fulfil. He would like, eventually, to captain the West Indies and to be a member of a Lancashire side that wins the County Championship. Neither of these targets is beyond his realisation, for at 26 Clive Lloyd still has the cricketing world at his feet. Averages mean little to him. He reads now and again that he needs so many runs for a special target or so many catches to create a new record, but these things never worry him. A career record of over 6,000 first-class runs means nothing to him as yet. His selection for all five Rest of the World matches against England last summer pleased him immensely but caused him to reflect that he had to miss several Lancashire games to do so. It is not of great importance to Lloyd for whom or where he plays his cricket. It is how he plays that matters most, and although well aware of his great pulling power with the crowds he modestly insists that they come to see the team and not him alone.

The Haslingden club in the Lancashire League has a lot to answer for in the emergence of Dennis Lillee as Australia's trump card in the 1972 tour of England. Lillee, who is not yet at his peak, should be in even better bowling form when the England side comes to Australia next year, and he gives full credit to the season he had in Lancashire League cricket.

Not too many English spectators will hold it against the Lancashire League club that they had a hand in the emergence of Lillee as a fine fast bowler on that tour. He definitely added excitement to the game of cricket, if one can excuse the problem of perhaps too long a run to the crease. But, in keeping with other great fast bowlers like Lindwall, Tyson and Hall, the long run is inclined to add to the excitement.

DENNIS KEITH LILLEE was born at Subiaco, Perth, on July 18, 1949, and he began playing with the Perth Cricket Club when 15 years of age. Four years later, he made his debut against Queensland at Brisbane, capturing the wicket of the opening batsman, Sam Trimble, as his first victim in first-class cricket. It was a moderate debut by the then slimly built West Australian, for he took two for 60 in the first innings and one for 16 in the second. But, from that point on, he could do nothing wrong.

This was the fast and furious Lillee, who paid scant regard in those days to accuracy and the finer points of bowling, but concentrated only on getting the ball from his end to the batsman's end in the shortest possible time. The following season in Australia he had the unnerving experience of bowling when Barry Richards hit that astonishing 356 off the Western Australian attack at Perth. Lillee's share was 18 overs, no wicket for 117, and he still marvels at the strokeplay of Richards on that day. That season, 1970-71, was the Australian year of fast bowlers – for England anyway. Snow, Willis and Lever gave the Australians a torrid time and, with the Fourth Test at Sydney going to England by a mammoth 299 runs and the Fifth in Melbourne being drawn, the Australian selectors decided to make changes for the Sixth Test at Adelaide. They put in Lillee and he repaid them by taking five wickets in the first innings and going on to take another three wickets in the final Test match played at Sydney, a game also won by England.

When the South African tour of Australia was cancelled in 1971, a series against the Rest of the World XI was put on in its place and, when the second representative game came along in Perth on December 10, 1971, Australians, for the first time since Davidson, were able to welcome a new fast-bowling star.

The match was scheduled for five days but lasted only three. The World XI made just 59 in their first innings, Lillee taking eight for 29, and then he chipped in with four for 63 in the second, allowing Australia to win by an innings and 11 runs.

In the 1972 Test series, Lillee did a magnificent job for his skipper, Ian Chappell, bowling 250 overs and breaking the Australian wicket-taking record for a series against England with 31 victims. His long hair flying and his features adorned with a moustache in the best tradition of old-time cricketers, such as Spofforth, he always posed a problem, even for the best of England's batsmen.

With Massie at the other end, he was the speed partner in a combination in the very best traditions of fast-bowling pairs over the years. Though he looks flamboyant in action on the field, Lillee is essentially a man of simple character, preferring a king-size steak to the more spicy continental dishes, and the occasional glass of beer to a magnum of champagne.

On the field a man who shows an obvious dislike to batsmen, he is of equable temperament once the day's play is over, and the only thing he is prepared to dislike in cricket at the moment is the type of field set for him in one-day cricket fixtures on the England tour. "There was one occasion where they even wanted to take my slip away," he said. "When that happens, it's almost time to give the game away."

Lancashire v Nottinghamshire. At Manchester, June 29, 30, July 1, 1908. Whitehead, taking part in his first county match, had a curious experience as he put together an innings of 131 and on the same day was no-balled for throwing. He batted with fine skill and judgment.

Little Wonder No. 16

NORDIC SUPERMAN
Five Cricketers of the Year – Basil Easterbrook, 1975

Standing nearly 6ft 8in, his head capped by blond hair that gleams like a golden helmet in the sun, Tony Greig, on all counts, possesses what Noel Coward described simply as star quality. Here is the Nordic superman in the flesh, but although he has the fiercely competitive quality on the field, Greig is a friendly, gentle soul off it. His impact upon the English cricket scene matched his striking physical presence, and it is astonishing in the light of all that has followed that his début was as recent as May 1967.

When he walked out to bat for Sussex at Hove for the first time the scoreboard showed 34 for three, and waiting to give him his baptism of fire was the formidable Lancashire trio, Brian Statham, Ken Higgs and Peter Lever. On his own admission he forgot all about the first principles of batting; having made up his mind to hit out before the ball left the bowler's hand, he took no care over his shots. Head up, feet in the wrong position, no idea of the correct line. "You name the mistake, I made it."

All terribly reprehensible, but no one could take from this unknown 20-year-old South African the fact that he made 156 in ten minutes under four hours and Sussex recovered to a total of 324. Three days later at Fenner's he was gated first ball by the Cambridge off-spinner, David Acfield. When he came in Alan Oakman demanded 22 shillings and handed him in exchange a Primary Club tie dotted liberally with shattered stumps and flying bails. "It didn't take me long to join the first-ballers club," says a rueful Greig.

Against Lancashire in his very first game Greig showed his potential as a future international batsman. When Gloucestershire came to Hove later that same season he showed that here was something even more valuable, a genuine all-rounder who could well fill the gap left by Trevor Bailey's retirement. Greig rolled over Gloucestershire with fast-medium seam bowling that brought him figures of eight for 25.

He was elected Best Young Cricketer of the Year by the Cricket Writers' Club in 1967, the year Sussex capped him. He transferred from Border to Eastern Province in 1970-71 and Sussex made him their captain in 1973. Between 1972 and 1973 he appeared in no fewer than 19 Tests. He did the hat-trick for Eastern Province against Natal at Port Elizabeth in 1971-72 and also took three wickets in four balls against Hampshire at Hove in 1967. He has been named Man of the Match four times in Gillette Cup ties.

Although his accent conjures up thought associations like Table Mountain, the Transvaal and Sari Marais, Greig is proud of his British stock. His father is a Scot from Edinburgh, the son of a family businessman with shops in towns like Falkirk and Bathgate. Dad was more interested in adventure than baubees, however, as his life pattern proclaims: he emigrated to South Africa where he married, and worked at the vastly differing callings of fighter pilot, insurance man and sports writer.

ANTHONY WILLIAM GREIG was born on October 6, 1946 at Queenstown in the Eastern Cape in Border Province. He was educated at Queen's College, Cape Town, and the choice of this particular seat of South African learning was to decide his cricket destiny. Queen's College has always looked to Sussex to supply their coaches, and during Tony Greig's time there, Jack Oakes, Alan Oakman, Ian Thomson, Ron Bell, Richard Langridge and Mike Buss all came out for a winter of work in the sunshine. All returned to the South Coast and sang the praises of a boy called Greig. Sussex decided, naturally, that they could not all be wrong and when Border Province blooded him in the Currie Cup at the age of 19, the club offered him a trial. His father had to decide whether his son should go on to University to work for his BA or accept the Sussex offer. "He used to slam into me for not reading enough, for being generally immature. He would look at me some-times and say 'Boy, when I was your age I was fighting a war', but in the end he grinned and said: 'Go over to England for one year – one year mind – and see what you can do.'"

After the taste of that first innings against Lancashire Tony wrote a short note to his father which said: "Goodbye to that university career." Quixotic, like that maiden century? Undoubtedly, but again, handsome is as handsome does, for over 30 appearances for England crammed into four years still all criticism.

Tony has never set much store on security since at the age of seven he had an experience which reads like something from the pages of an Alistair MacLean novel. He was bathing with his mother off the coast near East London when a shark seized his mother by the leg and started to drag her out to sea. In a frenzy of fear Mrs Greig struck at the shark's snout with her hands and, incredibly, it not only released her but turned and swam away. Mother and son managed to get ashore, but only the use of a special serum flown into East London saved Mrs Greig's leg from amputation. She will bear the scars of that terrible moment all her life and she has never been near the sea again. It took Tony years to fight down his own aversion to salt water.

The great thing about him is his approach to the game and his unfailing ability to make a valuable contribution, one way or another, in nearly every match he plays in. It is a quality which by the time he leaves the first-class game may have admitted him to the highest company of the true all-rounders of history.

CAPPED CRUSADER   Five Cricketers of the Century – Vic Marks, 2000

Viv Richards was one of the Five Cricketers of the Year in 1977 after scoring 829 runs at 118.42 in four Tests in England and a then-record 1,710 Test runs in a calendar year.

Fast bowlers, usually West Indian, have caused countless sleepless nights and/or some nasty nightmares over the years, but Vivian Richards was the one batsman I've encountered who could intimidate his opponents – even before he had received a ball.

His journey to the crease was a declaration of intent. It was usually delayed a fraction to enable the outgoing batsman to disappear from view. Richards did not want any distractions from his entry. He glided slowly to the crease in his own time, checking the light on the way; there was a hint of a swagger, which became more marked as the years rolled by. And there was the cap, the most obvious symbol of his superiority. In a decade when the fast bowler's stock ball whizzed past the batsman's nostrils, Richards was the last hold-out who shunned the helmet. The cap was the reminder that no bowler, however fast, would threaten his domination.

For Richards was never content with mere survival. Bowlers had to be subjugated, to recognise that he was the master. There were occasions when he might sleepily tap back some medium-pacers from a novice who had just graduated from the second team – for Richards was not primarily an avaricious gleaner of runs. But he would always launch a fearsome assault upon anyone with an international reputation. In England, this meant that Derek Underwood and Bob Willis, England's two world-class bowlers of the 1970s, had to be destroyed rather than blunted. Richards's pride demanded nothing less. In fact, it was a compliment to be on the receiving end of an onslaught from him, though the bowlers in question rarely appreciated it at that time.

Richards was capable of technical excellence. His forward-defensive stroke, which he sometimes played with exaggerated, ironic care, just to inform the bowler that he could have smashed a boundary but had chosen not to, could be as impenetrable as Boycott's. But he didn't use it that often. More frequently, he ignored the coaching manuals and, relying on the keenest pair of eyes and phenomenal reflexes, just trusted his instincts.

He reckoned that, if he played an on-drive in classical style, the ball would simply speed into the hands of mid-on. So instead he continued to turn the wrists and play the ball squarer – through the gaps. His front foot was planted down the wicket and his bat swung across his pad. All wrong, yet Richards made it seem the safest shot in the world. We tried to copy him and were plumb lbw. Despite the lunge of that front foot, his hook shot was the one that astounded his new county colleagues in 1974. No one hooked his fellow Antiguan Andy Roberts, who was terrorising county batsmen for Hampshire, except Richards. We couldn't work out how he did that.

Sir ISAAC VIVIAN ALEXANDER RICHARDS (he was knighted by the Antiguan government in 1999) separated himself from his rivals by his ability to perform at his peak on the grand occasion. He adored Lord's in a way that is peculiar to overseas players, who first pictured the ground while listening to crackling radios in the old colonies. He played in eight Lord's finals, five for Somerset and three for West Indies, and failed – by normal standards – only once. Even that day, the inaugural World Cup final against Australia in 1975, his fielding altered the course of the match. "When I was batting at Lord's," he said, "I wanted to make sure that no one else was going to come in. It was my stage."

If the cap fits: Viv Richards, who never wore a helmet,
hooks his friend Ian Botham to the Oval boundary
during the fifth England v West Indies Test of 1984

When it really mattered, he might proceed a little more cautiously at the start of his innings; he would sweat even more profusely, and then he would set about tinkering with fate as only the great players can. Take two innings at another of his favourite spots, the Recreation Ground at St John's, Antigua. West Indies played their first Test there in 1981 – mostly thanks to the prominence Richards himself had given the island. He willed himself to a hundred, edgy by his standards. Five years later, against England again, his mission was to entertain those who had seen him grow up. One hundred came from 56 balls, the swiftest Test century recorded. Sixes disappeared down the high street. Richards could destroy both clinically and ferociously, provided he had a cause to play for. He usually did.

BRAVE, BULLISH AND BRILLIANT Five Cricketers of the Year – Eric Hill, 1978

IAN TERENCE BOTHAM, aged 21, took five Australian wickets on his first day of Test match cricket. By an apposite twist of chance, that day brought Brian Close's announcement of his retirement 28 years after his first England appearance at 19 years of age.

Botham has tremendous respect for Close, his county captain, with whom he has much in common. He says "he kept me in order" and avers stridently, "we were always a better side with him there." They share a fierce determination to succeed, besides outstanding courage. Within weeks of coming into the first-class game Botham, then 18, displayed all his qualities in an unforgettable performance at Taunton on June 12, 1974. The occasion was the Benson and Hedges quarter-final against Hampshire. Botham had bowled his medium-paced outswingers, successfully, and had fielded – in any position – with his normal brilliance. However, shortly after arriving at the crease when Somerset at 113 for eight, needing 183, seemed doomed, Botham was hit full in the mouth by a bouncer from Roberts, then the quickest bowler in the game. Fiercely declining to leave the field, bleeding profusely, and eventually losing four teeth, he carried on, and hit two marvellous sixes while making 45 not out. He really won the match and the Gold Award in glory. Here indeed was a player to watch. In retrospect Botham thinks he should have come off the field, but still his abiding memories are of his two tail-end partners, Moseley and Clapp, who assisted him manfully.

Sport runs deeply in the family. His father, a regular in the Fleet Air Arm for 20 years spanning the war, played most sports, including cricket and soccer. His mother played cricket, too, and she remembers a match at Sherborne for the VAD nursing service as captain in 1946 as one of her big days. Botham was born at Heswall in Cheshire in November 24, 1955, and the family moved to Yeovil before his third birthday.

His abundant talent and unquenchable enthusiasm for cricket and soccer took him into the school teams at Milford School and Buckler's Mead. A sports master, Mr Hibbert, gave him a sound start, while the Boys' Brigade at Yeovil – always keen to help young sportsmen – provided plenty of chances. It was a common sight to see Botham, about nine years old, haunting the Mudford Road Recreation Ground, kit at the ready, eager to get a game for any side that was short. He got into the various county youth teams and, having worked his way to the MCC groundstaff at Lord's largely by his own efforts, began to attract much wider attention with some startling performances for the Somerset Second Eleven. Already he had been a regular attender of Somerset's coaching sessions and acknowledges with much appreciation the excellent help and advice received from the Somerset players Peter Robinson, Graham Burgess and Ken Palmer.

Two John Player matches in 1973 gave him his first taste of county cricket and the next year – a highly successful one for Somerset – brought his wonderful effort against Hampshire plus 441 runs and 30 wickets in first-class cricket. The development continued with 584 runs and 62 wickets in 1975, while, as his knowledge and application grew, 1976 brought his first superb century, 1,000 runs for the first time and 66 wickets. He was learning to harness his glorious straight hitting and square-cutting, and beginning to vary his bowling techniques under the guidance of that doyen of medium pacers, Tom Cartwright. Bouncers of different paces, and a brisk inswinging yorker added spice and batting danger to his outswinger.

The 1977 season was marred only by a week's cricket idleness carrying the drinks at the Prudential matches, and a foot injury which ruined for him the end of the season and probably robbed him of a rare double. He finished with 88 wickets and 738 runs. He found the England team spirit magnificent, with everyone working for each other as he took five wickets in the first innings of each of his first two Tests, and the birth of his son in August crowned a marvellous year.

Selection for the major winter tour was largely taken as a formality and Botham (pronounced as in both by the family, although colleagues sound it as in moth) was on his way. A determined, straightforward, pleasant character, who knows where he is aiming, and who, in the best old-fashioned sense, has a good conceit of himself, Ian will, quite naturally and fiercely, be addressing himself to an interesting view, held by several knowledgeable cricketers. It is that before his Test match triumphs he was under-rated but that after them he was over-rated. Botham has the tenacity, courage and exciting ability to prove them wrong. After all, when he joined the Lord's groundstaff his father gave him two aims: "Play for your county at 18 and your country before 25." He achieved one and handsomely surpassed the other – a remarkable start to a very stiff programme.

"IT COULD HAVE GONE ANYWHERE"   Five Cricketers of the Year – Michael Carey, 1979

The sun scarcely graced the English cricket scene with its presence in 1978, but when it did it seemed to adorn the blond head of DAVID IVON GOWER. The young Leicestershire left-hander could do little wrong. He typified a new, precocious breed of strokeplayers, imperious and exciting, who added colour and glamour to an otherwise bedraggled English summer. Plucked, to his astonishment, from Grace Road to play for MCC in their early-season showcase for maturing talent, Gower went on to make runs in one-day internationals and Tests almost as of right, becoming the youngest batsman to make a hundred for England since Peter May.

Had all this been combined with helping Kent to cut a controversial swathe through the land as they lifted two trophies, the image would have been complete, for Gower was born in that county, in Tunbridge Wells, on April 1, 1957. Leicestershire's secretary-manager Michael Turner has never disguised his astonishment and delight that when he wrote to Kent for permission to offer terms to Gower, it was unhesitatingly granted.

Gower spent his early years in Tanganyika, as it then was, where his father was in the Colonial Service. He came home at the age of six to attend Marlborough House preparatory school at Hawkhurst, Kent. The Leicestershire connection began two years later when his father, after turning down a post in Eastbourne (thus are the fortunes of the counties affected), became registrar of Loughborough Colleges, and young Gower was educated for a time in Quorn before moving to King's School, Canterbury. It was there that his cricketing skills began to emerge, although he is not aware that at that stage he was singled out for special coaching or in any way earmarked for a cricketing career. He played for the first eleven for three years, making two centuries in his last season, and it was hereabouts that a perspicacious opponent, who he thinks was playing for Stragglers of Asia, noted his ability and wrote to Leicestershire.

In the holidays he played a handful of second-team and under-25 matches for the county, but when he left school he had no clear idea of what lay ahead. Oxford University turned him down but he was able to gain a place at University College, London, where he read law. In 1975, three Championship appearances and six John Player League games made his name just a little more familiar to the Grace Road public.

Even then, he made no conscious decision to make a career out of cricket. "I think I just drifted into it," he recalls. "People were advising me to go to university and get some kind of a career behind me, but I was bored by a lot of the law course. At the back of my mind I always felt I could go back to it if I failed as a cricketer, and this no doubt made it a bit easier for me when I joined Leicestershire. Certainly I was never conscious of being under any pressure to succeed." Tours of South Africa with the English Schools and West Indies with the England Young Cricketers eased his transition from second eleven to Championship cricket.

Now, of course, the mantle of cricket's golden boy slips easily over Gower's lithe shoulders. One can imagine many gnarled old professionals who would like to be restarting their careers in this age of sponsorship and handsome pay cheques. Outwardly, and especially as he strides to the middle in a Test match, Gower appears to take it all with a calm beyond his years. But he admits that there is quite a lot more going on underneath. "Oh, yes, there is bit of tension and a bit of self-doubt, just like anyone else," he says. "You always wonder what the first ball will bring. I remember making a century in the Prudential Trophy against Pakistan and not really being conscious of the occasion, but it suddenly hit me when I was due to go in in the Edgbaston Test match. I suddenly said to myself, 'Hang on, this is a Test match. You must get the old feet moving... you don't want to freeze out there.' So I hooked the first ball for four and thought 'Heavens, what have I done? It could have gone anywhere. Suppose I had been caught?' Surprisingly, you may think, I do not regard that as the ideal way to start an innings. I much prefer to begin slowly. That way I think I'm more likely to make runs."

Gower is something of a cerebral cricketer. Away from the game he likes to relax with crossword puzzles or to listen to classical music. He plays squash to maintain his fitness. He may be the envy of hundreds of young players throughout the country, but his rise to fame has not affected his polite, level-headed, and easy-to-approach attitude to life. The world of cricket may, in the next few years, lie at his feet, but at the moment those feet are planted firmly on the ground.

Little Wonder No. 17

Essex v Derbyshire. At Leyton, July 23, 24, 25, 1908. The outstanding feature of this match was the scoring of two separate hundreds by Ernest Needham, the famous Sheffield United and international football player. He carried his bat through the first innings, being in for three hours and a half, and on the second occasion he was in for three hours and a quarter.

1980–89

THE METICULOUS CRAFTSMAN   Five Cricketers of the Year – Dicky Rutnagur, 1980

SUNIL MANOHAR GAVASKAR was born in Bombay on July 10, 1949, with the scent of bat oil in his nostrils, for his father was still a very active club cricketer and his uncle from his mother's side, M. K. Mantri, was Bombay's and India's wicket-keeper. In the circumstances, it was no surprise that a toy cricket bat was among his earliest possessions, and that the infant Gavaskar's afternoon naps were followed by practice against the bowling of a doting mother and the houseboy.

The most prolific Indian batsman ever in Test cricket says that he learnt to read numbers from scoreboards. While children of his age went to bed listening to tales of Red Riding Hood and Goldilocks, Gavaskar had his little ears trained to the radio and the voices of John Arlott and Rex Alston describing the Test matches of 1952, in which uncle Madhav was engaged. For him, the big bad wolf was F. S. Trueman.

When Gavaskar went visiting his uncle, he would ask him to unlock his wardrobe and display his various caps, sweaters and blazers, the colours of Bombay University, Bombay and India. The child that stared at them with awe was to win all those colours himself before he was 20 and to wear them with great distinction.

Gavaskar has made and broken records at all levels of the game. Flip through the statistical section of *Wisden*'s Indian counterpart and his name figures on almost every page. During the recent 1979-80 series against Australia, he became the first Indian to complete 5,000 runs in Test cricket. At the end of it, with 22 hundreds, he stood third (jointly with Walter Hammond and Colin Cowdrey) in the international list of Test century-makers. The only two in front were Sir Donald Bradman (29) and Sir Garfield Sobers (26). The diminutive Indian has also established himself as the most successful opening batsman in Test history, having made three more centuries than any other (Sir Leonard Hutton made 19).

As is obvious from Gavaskar's Test record, he is capable of intense concentration and discipline. But he summons these virtues only when India are in trouble or when he senses the chance of a win. He is not one for making big scores just for the sake of records. When he sets his sights high, he builds his innings with meticulous craftsmanship, limiting himself to the strokes he plays best – drives through the covers, past the bowler, and between mid-on and midwicket. But when he lets his hair down, his range of shots and the power behind them are quite astonishing. He can lay claims to a six at the Melbourne Cricket Ground. As an exhibition of brilliant batsmanship in a Test match, his 205 against West Indies at Bombay two winters ago was outstanding.

An executive with a textile firm, Gavaskar, educated at St Xavier's School and St Xavier's College, is married and has a son, named after his boyhood hero and one-time West Indian adversary, Rohan Kanhai. Gavaskar's sister Kavita (meaning poetry) is married to the other Indian batting genius, Gundappa Viswanath. It is mind-boggling to contemplate the talent of their offspring – when he arrives.

THE NO. 1 RUN MACHINE
Christopher Martin-Jenkins, 1998

Graham Gooch was one of the Five Cricketers of the Year in 1980.

The golfer Joyce Wethered was once playing a crucial shot in a major championship when an express train suddenly thundered past. "Didn't the train put you off?" she was asked later. "What train?" she replied. The ability to forget the clutter of everything else and concentrate this completely is surprisingly rare, even among great performers in sport. But Graham Gooch had it in full measure.

And this skill, more the result of mental steel than any natural gift, was the single most important reason for the fact that, by the time he started his final match for Essex on July 23, 1997, GRAHAM ALAN GOOCH, born at Whipps Cross in Leytonstone exactly 44 years before, had become the most prolific player in history.

One had sensed that he must be somewhere near, when all his limited-overs runs had been added to his final tally of 44,841 in first-class games at an average of 49.11, but it took the computations of Robert Brooke to confirm for *Wisden* this stupendous fact. No single batsman, not Grace, nor Hobbs, nor Woolley, nor Boycott, nor any of his contemporaries in an age of proliferating fixtures, had made so many runs in top-class cricket as the pink-faced, heavy-limbed yeoman of Essex. He had, in fact, unnoticed, overtaken Jack Hobbs's total of 61,237 runs when he reached 67 in a Benson and Hedges Cup game between Essex and Gloucestershire at Chelmsford on May 9, 1995. He finished with 65,928 at 45.81. It is hard to imagine who might ever overtake him.

Gooch, unfortunately, chose to release the news of his retirement through a Sunday newspaper whose chief business is scandal-mongering, but he was always acutely aware of his own worth and the need to make the most of that. In cricketing terms that made him the dedicated professional *par excellence*: steady, sound, sober, solid. It is still a revelation to know that he was not just the latest, perhaps the last, in a long line of that sort of English professional batsman, but, by numerical proof, the hungriest and most acquisitive of them all. He surpassed men like Sutcliffe, Hutton and Boycott from the north; Grace, Hayward, Hobbs and Mead from the south.

It seems natural to exclude Woolley, Hendren, Hammond and Graveney of the other leading batsmen, because they were somehow different in their nature and approach: more artists than accountants. Yet Gooch himself – and this makes his achievement all the more remarkable – belongs more truly with the entertainers: he was a magnificent sight in full sail. This was no dabber of singles, no delicate leg-glancer or specialist in the smooth caress of a half-volley through extra cover. On the contrary, he was a bold, imposing player: a mighty driver and fierce square-cutter, who looked at the crease to be taller and bulkier than be actually was, with a bat apparently broader than the law permits.

When I first saw him, for MCC against the Australians in 1975, he was still only 21 but he pull-drove Jeff Thomson into the Lord's Grand Stand for six, before repeating the treatment on Gary Gilmour. Six years later at Sabina Park, in the final Test of England's 1980-81 tour of the West Indies, he temporarily obliterated a ferocious attack of Holding, Marshall, Croft and Garner. Croft, hitherto bullyingly successful, was savaged for 56 runs in eight overs on a pitch which was hard and bouncy. Gooch cut him over third man for one six and hooked Marshall for another. He had made 103 out of 155 for two in the 40th over and 153 out of 249 when he was fifth out.

His greatest innings was one run higher and also against West Indies, at Headingley in grey weather on a tricky pitch in June 1991. It took him seven and a half hours. The forces arrayed against him were no less fierce: Ambrose, Patterson, Walsh and Marshall. Gooch was captain and more than just the backbone of his side. Throughout England's second innings, he virtually was the side. He carried his bat for 154 out of 252 and England went on to win. So they had, too, of course, when he made his 333 and 123 in a single Test at Lord's against India in 1990. These, however, constituted easier pickings.

All this does not, of course, make Graham Gooch the greatest player of his time but, even if we judge him only by the timeless yardstick of first-class cricket, ignoring the mind-wearying, sinew-stretching demands of the limited-overs game, his stature is clear. After the reduction in Championship matches in 1969, he alone scored above 2,000 runs in more than three seasons. He did so in five: 1984, 1985, 1988, 1990 and 1993; another 56 runs in his last full season, 1996, would have made it six. He made eight first-class hundreds that year and, had he not promised his dying father that he would play one more year, it would have been the right note on which to finish.

It was one of the few occasions when he allowed emotion to supersede his cricketing judgment. What made him special was his capacity for hard work and rigid self-discipline. He earned every run.

FEWER PACES, MORE WICKETS　　　Five Cricketers of the Year – Graeme Wright, 1982

One of the top five fast bowlers in the world was how his captain, Clive Rice, described Richard Hadlee as Nottinghamshire prepared for their final fixture of the 1981 Schweppes Championship. And the following day Rice invited Glamorgan to face the best fast-bowling attack at Trent Bridge since the unforgotten summers of

Larwood and Voce. By lunch the Welsh county were fielding, Richard Hadlee, with four for 18 off 12 overs, had become the first, and only, bowler in 1981 to reach 100 wickets, and Nottinghamshire were on course for the victory that took the County Championship title to Trent Bridge for the first time since 1929.

Yet RICHARD JOHN HADLEE, born in Christchurch, New Zealand, on July 3, 1951, might not have participated in the celebrations that followed – in the unlikely event, that is, of Nottinghamshire winning the title without his all-round contribution of 105 wickets and 745 runs. Unhappy with a disastrous 1980 season, when fitness problems limited him to seven Championship games, he was hesitant of renewing his contract in 1981. "I'm not happy playing my cricket on the sidelines," he said in his forthright way. "But the club asked me to rethink." It says much for their opinion of his ability: in his three seasons with them he had played only 23 games for his 96 wickets (from 641 overs) and 549 runs, though he missed half of his first season by joining the 1978 New Zealand touring party. Many ordinary professionals play that number of games in a season.

Richard Hadlee, however, is no ordinary performer, and he set out to prove to the English public that he was what his Test record states: a world-class fast bowler whose aggressive left-handed batting entitles him to all-rounder status.

Usually operating off a shorter run – 15 paces as against 23 – he bowled to telling effect: a lean, hard six-footer, with his Lillee-smooth approach to the delivery stride of a textbook high action, he was still too sharp and too uncomfortable for most batsmen, still able to stick him on his backside or beat the bat. And he could make the ball do more; as his great rival and idol, Dennis Lillee, had shown. In 1981 he bowled 708.4 overs. No seam bowler delivered more, and only five others exceeded 600. The more overs you get through, the better your chances was his philosophy, and certainly his striking-rate was evenly distributed: 31 wickets in May and June, 35 in July, and 33 in August and September. His best innings return was seven for 25 against Lancashire at Liverpool: he never once took ten wickets in a match.

Fourth son of Walter Hadlee, who captained New Zealand in the post-war years and later became chairman and then president of the country's governing body, Richard Hadlee did not suffer from the expectations that accompany the sons of famous fathers. Those pressures had fallen on his elder brother Barry, a batsman like his father, and had been further absorbed by another older brother, Dayle, a fast-medium bowler who first played for New Zealand in 1969. The three brothers were in the New Zealand party for the 1975 World Cup.

Wisden's headmasterly assessment after his first tour of England, in 1973, was that his best bowling came late in the tour, but he had considerable prospects ahead. Those words were not yet wet ink when he helped bowl New Zealand to a moral victory in Sydney and, a few months later in Christchurch, with returns of three for 59 and four for 75, to their first-ever victory over Australia. Still his place was not secure, and even he did not expect to play when he was included in the 12 for the third Test against the visiting Indians in 1976. However, New Zealand excluded the spinner, Hedley Howarth, and Hadlee, coming on initially as fourth seamer, finished with a match return of 11 for 58, Test record figures by a New Zealander.

Later that year he led the New Zealand attack in India and Pakistan, bowling with pace and hostility in conditions that have tested the heart and stamina of more experienced fast bowlers. "Richard Hadlee has come of age," said the New Zealand captain, Glenn Turner, after the tour, and England's batsmen were to taste the fire of the new Hadlee when, with match figures of ten for 100 at Wellington in February 1978, he bowled New Zealand to their first Test victory over England. Another double-figure haul, 11 for 102, was responsible for New Zealand's dramatic win over West Indies two years later, as well as making him New Zealand's leading wicket-taker. In addition, he is the only New Zealander to have taken 100 wickets and scored 1,000 runs in Tests. For his services to cricket, he was awarded the MBE in the 1980 Queen's Birthday Honours.

UNROMANTIC, UNCOMPLICATED, UNCOMPROMISING   Mike Coward, 1995

Allan Border was one of the Five Cricketers of the Year in 1982.

Allan Border, who retired in May 1994 as Test cricket's highest run-scorer, committed the greater part of a long and distinguished career to re-establishing the credibility and image of Australian cricket. A self-effacing man of simple tastes and pleasures, Border served at the most tempestuous time in cricket history, and came to represent the indomitable spirit of the Australian game. As it grappled with two schisms, the first over World Series Cricket, the second over the provocative actions of the mercenaries in South Africa, it was debilitated and destabilised as never before and cried out for a figure of Bradmanesque dimensions to return it to its rightful and influential position on the world stage.

Into the breach strode earnest ALLAN ROBERT BORDER, a working-class boy, born at Cremorne on the north shore of Sydney Harbour, who grew up over the road from the Mosman Oval that now bears his name. At one time he was a beach bum, who was cajoled from his indolence and indifference by the noted coach and former England Test player, Barry Knight. But Border, standing just 5ft 9in, bestrode the Test match arena like a colossus for more than 15 years.

When he retired 11 weeks before his 39th birthday, after fulfilling his ambition to lead Australia in South Africa, Border was entitled to be ranked alongside Sir Donald Bradman as the greatest of Australian cricketers. Certainly no one since Sir Donald has done more to advance Australian cricket throughout the world – particularly in developing countries.

Border's batting cannot really stand comparison with Bradman, but many of his achievements go far beyond the Bradmanesque – 156 Test matches, 153 of them consecutive, on 36 grounds in eight different Test-playing countries (Sir Donald played 52 Tests on ten grounds, all in Australia and England); 11,174 runs at 50.56 with 27 centuries and 63 fifties; 93 consecutive Test matches as captain; 156 catches; 273 limited-overs appearances, 178 as captain, including Australia's victory in the 1987 World Cup final. All of these accomplishments are in a league of their own and some may remain so.

Yet only in the twilight of his career did Border become even faintly interested in his statistical achievements. Essentially he was an unromantic, uncomplicated but uncompromising workman-cricketer. It is problematical whether Border, unlike

Bradman, has ever understood his place in history. He reinvigorated Australian cricket and provided it with stability, direction and enthusiasm; this was the most significant of his many contributions and the one which gave him the greatest satisfaction. There is a remarkable set of figures to underscore the extent of the stability Border provided. From the time he succeeded his fragile friend Kim Hughes on December 7, 1984 until his captaincy ended on March 29, 1994, opposing countries commissioned 38 captains – 21 of them against Australia. From his first Test, at Melbourne, on December 29, 1978, he played with and against 361 different players.

To gain a true appreciation of Border, it is necessary to examine his formative years in the leadership when his team was scorned and he was disturbingly close to a breakdown. In 1985 when Australian cricket reached its nadir and a collection of leading players defected to South Africa, Border, the least political of men, was dragged into a black hole of depression. He was barely four months into his term of office – while he forgave them, he never forgot the hurt caused by those team-mates who pursued the dollar rather than the dream, and opted to play in South Africa. For a man who placed such store in team loyalty, it was a cruel lesson.

Many of his attitudes were formed and much of his philosophy as a captain formulated at this time when Australia were not expected to win and, in the main, did not. The dire circumstances of the day compelled him to think defensively, and it was not until 1989, when he engineered a memorable 4–0 eclipse of a dispirited England, that there was a measure of optimism and aggression about his leadership. But while his entitlement to the job was hardly ever questioned, the negativism of his captaincy was the area that most occupied the attention of his critics. In mitigation, he insisted that the circumstances of his time had made it impossible for him to develop a totally positive philosophy. He evolved into an enterprising captain when he was finally in charge of able and ambitious men, as was evidenced by his thoughtful and often bold use of the leg-spinner Shane Warne. In this period, some English critics felt that Australia's approach was getting too hard; that might say more about them than about Border.

With customary candour, he often pleaded guilty to periods of moodiness and regretted that, at least in the dressing-room, his instinct was to internalise his deepest thoughts and feelings. Paradoxically, he was an expansive and articulate spokesman, and was much admired by the media for being accessible, courteous and forthright. So he had good reason to resent the Captain Grumpy tag foisted upon him by the tabloids.

SMALL BUT PERFECTLY FAST   Five Cricketers of the Year – Alan Lee, 1983

Cricketers seldom agree on the relative merits of fast bowlers. Debates about the fastest, bounciest or most difficult to play will invariably rage unresolved through a tour or a season. But not in 1982. Then, almost without exception, the batsmen on the county circuit nominated MALCOLM DENZIL MARSHALL, born in St Michael, Barbados, on April 18, 1958, as the quickest they encountered.

This accolade was remarkable enough for its unanimity, but there was more. Fast bowlers as a race are often treated with suspicion, if not outright resentment, by the men they attack day by day. But Marshall somehow earned an element of admiration, for his ability, his work-rate – if one can apply such a clichéd soccer word to him – and his cheerful Barbadian humour.

He has shown much resourcefulness since the May day in 1979 on which he made his Hampshire début, and his sense of humour has been needed. Not long off the plane from the sand, surf and sun of his homeland, Marshall found himself running in to bowl against Glamorgan while the English climate played one of its more eccentric tricks – snow fell on the Southampton ground. Undeterred, though maybe mystified, he took nine wickets in the match, figures which he never quite lived up to during the rest of that summer. He finished with 47 wickets and less than 200 runs, missed virtually all the following season owing to the West Indians' tour, and then, in 1981, made his first significant impact on county cricket, taking 68 wickets despite missing one-third of Hampshire's matches.

The improvement accelerated dramatically in 1982. Suddenly, this man with the wispy beard, searching eyes and infectious grin was no longer just one in the pack of West Indian bowlers in the English game; he was looking like the best. He had learnt how to bowl in English conditions and he could do it for as long as he was allowed. His total of 134 wickets was 44 more than his closest challenger, Nick Cook, who also happened to be the only other leading bowler to get through more than 800 overs in the season. Marshall's total output of 822 was startling for a strike bowler; the traditional county workhorses were well behind.

Marshall had a great deal to live up to when he arrived with Hampshire. For the previous five years, Andy Roberts had been taking the new ball, and with his loss of enthusiasm and subsequent departure, the county's followers quite naturally feared the worst. Who could possibly fill such boots?

Incentive was another motivator. West Indies' quartet of pace bowlers was well established, and Marshall was just one of a cluster trying hard to break in. He had time on his side, maybe, but there was a degree of impatience in him. He wanted to play Test cricket and he saw the county game as a showcase. It is said he put on a yard of pace to impress Clive Lloyd whenever the West Indies captain happened to be at the receiving end. His persistence paid off, at least to the extent that he became the regular fifth seamer in the squad.

Marshall has many of the traits of the typical West Indian. But if the popular conception of the Barbadian remains dominated by *mañana*, then Marshall is a misfit. Tomorrow, for him, will never be good enough. He wants to be the best today and is prepared to work to achieve his aims.

He is a great believer in training, particularly the specific muscle exercises for quick bowlers, and he completes his own routine of them religiously before play each day. He sees bowling as a business but, like most high-fliers in that branch of industry, remains convinced he is very nearly as good a batsman. He made runs, too, in 1982, and a first-class century against Lancashire – yes, Clive Lloyd's county again.

Twelve times during the season, Marshall took five wickets in an innings, and a huge proportion of his wickets were "bowler's victims" – 27 bowled, 37 lbw and a further 25 caught by wicketkeeper Parks. His eight for 71 against Worcestershire was a career-best, but the performances which may live longer in the memory came at The Oval and Bournemouth. Against Surrey, he took seven for 38, dismissing the home side for 100 and securing an extraordinary three-run win; and on an unpleasant pitch at Dean Park his five wickets hurried out Somerset for 74 when they needed only 85 to win.

Marshall is below six feet, small for a fast bowler, and at 12st he is no heavy-weight either. But on that sprinting, low-slung approach, his balance invariably seems perfect, the delivery merely a flowing continuation. His tally of wickets in 1982 was the highest by any individual since the Championship was reduced in matches.

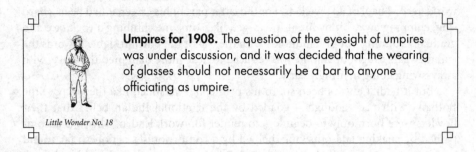

Umpires for 1908. The question of the eyesight of umpires was under discussion, and it was decided that the wearing of glasses should not necessarily be a bar to anyone officiating as umpire.

Little Wonder No. 18

CHARMING BUT DEADLY
Mike Selvey, 1995

Kapil Dev was one of the Five Cricketers of the Year in 1983.

Perhaps the hardest thing to appreciate about KAPIL DEV finally exchanging his cricket box for the TV commentary box is the fact that he was only 35 years old when he did so. Well, give or take a bit maybe: he might be a touch more geriatric than that; it is often suggested that at the time he was born, whenever that was, it was not necessarily the custom in northern India to register the year of birth. But that misses the point: however old he was, he seemed to have been around for a lot longer, prancing in to shore up the Indian attack and joyfully retrieving an innings with uninhibited squeaky-clean hitting. An Indian team without him will never seem quite the same.

With his departure comes the end of an era that has been blessed with a quartet of all-rounders unmatched in the history of the game, beginning in the early 1970s with Richard – later Sir Richard – Hadlee and Imran Khan, progressing to the laddo Botham, and finally, with his Test debut in October 1978, to the man who became known to his countrymen as the Haryana Hurricane.

What deeds from these four! Between them, they took 1,610 Test wickets and scored 17,379 runs. With the possible exception of Hadlee, each was equipped tech-nically to play international cricket as a specialist in either role. But what a contrast: Hadlee the Inquisitor, with a surgeon's touch and an accountant's brain; Imran, the haughty, proud Pathan; Botham, the bull elephant who lived cricket and life on the edge; and Kapil, flamboyant and cavalier, charming but deadly. Today, Wasim Akram alone is left to carry a torch for the standards set by these four.

Kapil has perhaps been regarded as the most lightweight of the group. But with 434 wickets and 5,248 runs, he is the one who proved, in the end, to be the most prolific with both ball and bat. That has much to do with the fact that he played 131 Tests compared with Hadlee's 86, Imran's 88 and Botham's 102. And, as the last to survive, he was in a position to make sure that he finished top of the heap. But he laid out his credentials as soon as he entered Test cricket. His teeth may have flashed a disarming smile but this was a formidable competitor worthy of his fierce Punjabi ancestors.

Kapil has always regarded bowling as his primary role. And on February 8, 1994 he took the wicket of the Sri Lankan, Hashan Tillekeratne, to go past Hadlee's world-record haul of 431 wickets. For the latter part of his career, it had been a hard slog, chipping away bit by bit at the target, like someone climbing a rock face and gradually running out of handholds with the top of the pitch in sight. Towards the end the years caught up and he was reduced to little more than medium-pace, with away-swing going invitingly early.

But it hadn't always been so. In his prime, he was much like the young, lithe Botham, with pace enough – goaded by the irrational Indian belief that their bowlers were born only to beguile – to render footwork leaden. This was accompanied by snaking late outswing, helped by a contortionist's action so far round that it presented his left shoulderblade to the batsman, and a wicked break-back that struck with the speed of a cobra. Superficially, his bowling may have lacked Hadlee's relentlessly searching examination, or Imran's leaping, muscular pace, or Botham's bludgeon and willpower, but it was deceptively effective for all that.

Yet in the fullness of time, he may be remembered more for his carefree, hawk-eyed batting. He was helped by the fact that he was an all-rounder and so had the freedom to play as he did: one discipline fuelled the other. The rate at which he was capable of scoring was phenomenal. At Lord's in 1982, he brought the England bowling to its knees, hitting 13 fours and three sixes, an innings of 89 that came from just 55 balls, well on course then for what would have been the fastest Test century in history. And in his last Lord's Test, in 1990 – Gooch's match – he scored the 24 India required to save the follow-on by hitting Eddie Hemmings for four successive straight sixes while the last man, Hirwani, blinked myopically at the other end and got out next ball.

And yet perhaps his finest moment came not in a Test but in a limited-overs international against Zimbabwe, not even a Test-playing nation then, at, improbably enough, Tunbridge Wells. In 1983, it was Kapil's lot to lead India in the World Cup, and he found himself at the crease on a damp pitch, with the scoreboard reading 17 for five. He was to play what he has described as the innings of a lifetime, scoring an unbeaten 175 as India reached 266 for eight and went on to win the game.

Eventually, they progressed to the final at Lord's where, against all the odds, they beat West Indies, then arguably the most potent cricket force ever to set foot on the ground. Kapil and India showed they could be taken, and an illusion was shattered: West Indies have not won the World Cup since.

CAPTAINCY CHANGED THE CAVALIER   Five Cricketers of the Year – Scyld Berry, 1983

In the early part of last season, before he had turned into the glamorous public figure he was soon to become, Imran Khan was playing as usual for Sussex in the

County Championship. During their game at Edgbaston, Imran hooked a ball from one of Warwickshire's pace bowlers down to the fine-leg fielder, who caught it but then carried it over the boundary: not out. Nothing daunted, Imran tried another hook shot at the very next ball, and gave a simple catch to square leg. On seeing this indiscretion, a Sussex colleague commented: "He would be a great player if only he used his head."

By the end of the season Imran *had* combined thoughtfulness with a natural ability which had always been outstanding. What brought about this transformation, as Imran readily admits, was his appointment to the captaincy of his native Pakistan. This sense of responsibility turned a fine cavalier into a great cricketer.

Whether the newly transformed Imran had become the equal of Ian Botham as an all-rounder made one of the liveliest debates of the summer. On the one hand, Imran did not have the batting record in Test cricket which Botham had; on the other, Imran as a pace bowler probably had the edge over Botham as he then was. Indeed some critics, Mike Brearley amongst them, rated Imran as the best of all contemporary bowlers even at the relatively advanced age of 29.

IMRAN KHAN NIAZI was born in Lahore on November 25, 1952. His father was a Pathan landowner in the region to the north of Baluchistan. His mother was one of three sisters of the Burki tribal family: one sister gave birth to Javed Burki, who became an Oxford Blue and captain of Pakistan; the other gave birth to Majid Khan, a Cambridge Blue and captain of Pakistan. Like his cousins, Imran was born to affluent circumstances in which he could devote as much time as he wished to the development of his cricket. During his schooldays he also slipped while climbing a tree, and broke his left arm when trying to cling on to a branch. The arm was set badly in hospital and has given Imran trouble ever since – not in his bowling, but he has to practise constantly at holding his bat, otherwise his grip stiffens up.

His feat against England last season, of taking 21 wickets in three Tests, was nothing extraordinary by his recent standards, which have been of the highest. His run-up made a most exhilarating spectacle as he charged in, leaning forward from the waist, and leapt at the crease; so did the end-product of some extremely fast, indipping yorkers and virtually unplayable outswingers.

This much, however, was expected of Imran Khan. The surprise was his common-sensical approach to batting now that he had the captaincy. It had been given to him as a compromise candidate in the dispute between Javed Miandad and Pakistan's senior players, but he was more tactically astute than a mere novice.

Imran's own batting, meanwhile, was progressing so rapidly that his No. 7 position, and record of only one Test century, had become false labels by the time of Headingley. There he scored more runs in the match that anyone else, and he was dismissed only once, when hitting out with the last man in. The maturity with which he chose his strokes was astonishing to those who had known him only as a Sussex player.

Having won belated fame in his 30th year, Imran's private life became a regular subject of discussion in certain newspapers. As he was not married at the time, and handsome of face and build, the matter of his future wife was widely speculated upon. Imran himself, however, said that he did not intend marriage so long as he was playing full-time cricket, which could keep the females amongst his admirers in suspense for the next two or three years at least.

WE ALREADY KNEW HE COULD BAT Peter Roebuck, 1989

Graeme Hick was one of the Five Cricketers of the Year in 1987.

In 1895 one Archie MacLaren arrived in Taunton to meet a Somerset eleven led by Sammy Woods, a local legend. Archie hadn't faced any bowler over 14 years of age for five weeks, but his dad was in the crowd so he wanted to do well. Only by a squeak did he survive his first ball. A day and a half later he lobbed a catch and walked off. He'd scored 424. Gamlin was the bowler, one of nine tried. Gamlin wasn't much of a cricketer. Sam told his chums at the Clarke's Tap that he was playing "on account of being good at rugby". Sam was that sort of bloke. Somerset was that sort of county. And he was very good – at rugby.

MacLaren's score sat in the record books, speaking of the time as might a snuff-box in a museum. In a changed world it reminded us of a past of Free Foresters and Devon Dumplings. It could not be done again, could it? Golly, even Somerset rarely fielded total incompetents these days. Besides, the fielding had improved, the ball had shrunk (1927) and the stumps had grown (1931). Big scores were still possible. Gimblett had hit 310 in 1948 and Viv Richards 322 in 1985, but no one had approached 400 in county cricket since the old Queen died.

Had Worcestershire not declared at tea (there were no tea intervals in Archie's day) on May 6, 1988, MacLaren's record would have been broken. It is not for this writer to decide if Somerset's tactics were quite as sound as those of Mr Woods, but it can be taken that our selection was rather more conservative. Moreover our fielding was good and the bowling did not flag until the second afternoon when the captain, seeing that the horse had bolted and emptied the yard besides, served up some atrocious swingers to which a tiring and expansive batsman nearly fell. Nothing was given away easily. Yet GRAEME HICK scored 405 not out.

One thing had changed in 1988. Four-day cricket was being tried. Batsmen could bat for two days. Some were doing so. Already Gooch had plundered 275 off Kent; and that was just in the first innings. Hick was in form too, taking 212 off Lancashire bowlers at Old Trafford. Around the counties, cricketers were staggered by the new scale of things. These scores were beyond contemplation. As it turned out, Hick was only warming up.

At Taunton, he was nearly out first ball, clipping a drive inches off the ground in front of square leg. Our man was patrolling behind square. I'd considered moving him for Hick but had let it be for a minute, a fatal delay. Only by a narrow squeak did he avoid playing on a few minutes later. On 148 he was dropped in the gully where, ironically, he was to be caught twice in the return game a fortnight later. He never really gave Somerset a ghost of a chance until he'd passed 300. I never thought 300 could be written as if it were a staging-post. It takes me a month to score 300 runs.

Once or twice his leg shots were lifted, but they were hit with a power that was efficient rather than savage and they thundered through or over the field. Standing erect and immense yet never imperious, Hick boomed drives to mid-off or through extra cover – "not a man move shots" – and he late-cut delicately. Throughout he ran fast between the wickets, throughout he used a bat so broad that bowlers felt as if they were trying to knock down a tank with a pea-shooter.

Yet there was never any sense of awesome personality in this awesome batting. Hick did not impose himself save as a batsman. From slip I saw a simple, straight-forward fellow with a simple technique founded upon straight lines, power and fitness. Whenever possible he put his foot down the wicket and hit the ball hard. He was never as menacing as Viv Richards, whose saunter to the crease can have the effect upon a bowler that a bugle has upon a stag. Nor did Hick coil himself into an intensity of idea, execution and will as might Martin Crowe. No, he strode to the wicket as soon as Gordon Lord was out, took guard and began hitting the ball in order to score runs. He did not say much, and yet he was neither distant nor aloof. I never saw Walter Hammond bat, but I imagine he was something like this – authoritative, commanding, civil and durable.

At the crease Hick avoided flamboyance, eschewed the macho. Discipline was at the core of his game. If he was bowled a good ball he blocked it. Bad balls were hit. Unlike Richards or Botham he does not try to destroy a bowler's length. Unlike lesser batsmen he never gives his wicket away, whatever his score. Watching him, you cannot tell if he is on 10 or 210. He simply carries on. His game is as pure as a punched hole. It is this that frightens bowlers.

Most impressive of all, his 405 was a deeply unselfish innings. On a good pitch and in good weather his team had subsided to 132 for five. One mistake from Hick and they'd have been all out for a poor score. Yet after some hours of run-making Hick ran a fast three off the last ball of an over to give Newport an extra run and the strike. It was this sense of being in a team that caught our eye because it said so much about the man. We already knew he could bat.

Test cricket awaits Hick. Imran Khan has said that Hick might not be so effective at Test level because, like Zaheer Abbas, he is fundamentally a front-foot player. Yet maybe Zaheer disappointed for other reasons as well. Hick is a tough, strong character, a man with the courage to meet every challenge. He will, I believe, be a major force in Test cricket. After his final innings of the 1988 season, one Glamorgan player said he was "Unbelievable. I'd never seen anything like it. He played and missed only three or four times. He didn't seem to get the balls others were getting."

I don't think he ever will.

MELTING THE ICEMAN
Nasser Hussain, 2004

Steve Waugh was one of the Five Cricketers of the Year in 1989.

At the beginning of this year, the cricketing world witnessed a remarkable week in which the people of Sydney poured out their affection towards their beloved son Stephen Waugh.

STEVE WAUGH was not a cricketing god or a genius, like Tendulkar or Lara, nor even technically brilliant like Rahul Dravid. Like the rest of us, he was human. But a previously unremarkable household in suburban Sydney was definitely given more than its fair share of talent when the Waugh twins, Stephen and Mark, arrived on the scene nearly 39 years ago. Their little games of backyard cricket eventually led to the pair of them playing nearly 300 Tests and scoring nearly 20,000 runs between them. Some would argue that one was given a little bit more talent than the other. As one member of the Barmy Army once said, as he dared to sledge the greatest sledger of them all, "Oy, Stephen, best batsman in the world? You ain't even the best batsman in your family!"

Well, for over a decade Stephen Waugh made himself into the best batsman in the world. He was given two useful cricketing skills at birth: incredible hand–eye co-ordination and the fastest pair of hands of any cricketer I have played against. The rest he has had to work for. He has proved one cricketing cliché during his career: that the higher the level you play, the more it is played in your head. And he was, mentally, the strongest player of his era. He didn't deal with the short ball particularly well and he moved around the crease a lot as the bowler delivered, staying back and not really transferring all his weight on to the front foot when the ball was pitched up. But, hey, that is the game. Every batsman has weaknesses, and it is up to the player to overcome them and the opposition to exploit them. Waugh overcame his deficiencies because his hand–eye co-ordination meant he could keep the good ones out and put the bad ones away – and because his mental toughness helped him through every situation batting can throw up.

Many a pre-Ashes Test meeting stopped when S. Waugh's name hit the projector screen. Half the team got animated and said "Look, skip, just put in a leg gully and a short leg and we'll pepper him with the short stuff. It's only a matter of time." The other less-emotional half, usually the batters and the coach, said "No, pitch it up and try to hit off stump early, because he has a tendency to get his head off-side of the ball a bit, and then there's a chance of him being bowled or lbw." The final thing always said was that, when he first came in, everyone must be on their toes as he loved to push a single and get off strike. Meeting finished. Everyone happy.

Next day, if we were doing really well and had reduced Australia to 300 for three, we would be pleased with ourselves. In comes Waugh, red handkerchief hanging out of pocket, pushes the ball (usually to someone like dopey Gough standing at mid-on) and scampers a single, smiles and stays off strike for a while. This would be followed by a few short balls (which Waugh finds uncomfortable, but never gets out to), and the bowlers begin thinking that they had better start pitching it up. They over-correct and these incredible hands start to caress the ball through the covers. Before you know it, you look up at the scoreboard and he's 30 not out, off and running. Groundhog Day! You've seen it all before, but there seems nothing you can do to stop it happening all over again.

As a player, Waugh was always at his most dangerous when confronted by a real challenge. All his great innings came in the face of adversity. Whether it was a poor wicket, or a poor calf, or a poor press hinting at the waning of his power, he felt most at home in difficult situations. It was as if he believed in his own reputation as the "iceman" and was keen to enhance it. Nothing would give him more pleasure than reading the next day about another gutsy Steve Waugh innings.

As a captain, Waugh used the same principles that he did as a player: he made the most of what he was given. Luckily for him, he was given a remarkable collection of batsmen plus three all-time-great bowlers in McGrath, Warne and Gillespie. His side played in such a way that they basically took the draw out of the equation.

Richie Benaud, a man who should know, believes Waugh's team has produced in the last four or five years the most exhilarating cricket in the history of the game.

I can't say I have ever got to know Steve Waugh well. He never let his guard slip for fear of letting anything penetrate his veneer of inscrutability. The nearest I came to cracking it was in a bar in Adelaide after we had failed to regain the Ashes in 1998-99, when I picked Steve's brain over his attitude to batting. How did he make himself so good? He told me that the most important aspect to him was body language. He liked to almost sprint to the crease to emphasise that he was relishing the battle ahead; he liked to give off an aura of aggression.

Throughout his career, Waugh, almost on purpose, maximised the challenge – whether it be a sore calf, a last-chance-saloon innings, or a fired-up Ambrose – to bring the best out of himself. Basically, for over 20 years he has been playing mind games with himself and the opposition. The crowds did not turn up at Sydney to thank him for his statistics. They came to thank him for his character.

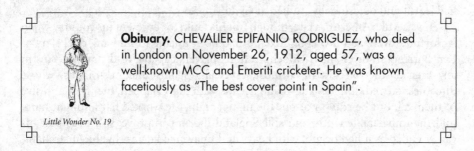

Obituary. CHEVALIER EPIFANIO RODRIGUEZ, who died in London on November 26, 1912, aged 57, was a well-known MCC and Emeriti cricketer. He was known facetiously as "The best cover point in Spain".

Little Wonder No. 19

1990–99

UNTOUCHED BY FORTUNE   Peter Roebuck, 2002

Mike Atherton was one of the Five Cricketers of the Year in 1991.

Throughout the 1990s MICHAEL ATHERTON was the face of English cricket. Head still, eyes wary, left elbow high and feet moving neatly into position, he dedicated himself to the tasks of scoring runs, resisting bowlers and protecting his team's position. For beneath his pale, youthful and sometimes defiantly stubbled exterior could be found a wilful man blessed with skill and determination. What was wanting were the particular abilities needed by the hour; he lacked the sparkle and drive required to rouse a team from its slumbers, and if ever a team needed rousing during his years as Test cricketer and captain, it was England. But it was not his way to intone "Awake, arise, or be for ever fallen!" He was more inclined to say, in his suburban way, "Come on, lads, let's get stuck in."

In every respect Atherton remained untouched by the vicissitudes of fortune and the ravages of time. Stoicism was his most obvious quality – he played for a decade on constant medication for an inflammatory condition affecting his spine – and there was a dryness of outlook that made him as much an observer as a participant. He was tough, though, and did not flinch in the face of furious bowling or allow his spirit to wilt in adversity. Indeed he was in his element in these circumstances, as the ingredients of his Lancastrian character came together to produce a towering effort.

Just as he did not strive to appease his opponents, nor did he seek to impress the baying public, even if in time the public took him to its heart and claimed him intimately as "Athers". Not that this affected him; proud and private, he performed his duties on the field and then withdrew. Atherton enjoyed the community of the dressing-room and the fellowship of the football crowd, but otherwise he was content to be alone, reading, fishing or looking for a pair of socks in a bulging drawer.

He was a tidy cricketer, and yet also expressive, for he did not depend entirely on the regimented. There was a touch of subcontinental subtlety in a manly Anglo-Saxon game, a thinness of the arm, a hint of wrist as he stroked the ball through point off back or front foot, sending it skimming to the boundary. None the less he regarded himself as a craftsman, not an entertainer, and he did not listen to the whispers of indulgence. His northern common sense outweighed the delicacies he had learnt and occasionally studied at Cambridge.

It was Mike Atherton's fate, though not his fault, to represent his country when its fortunes were at a low ebb. England had been unable to find any cricketers of Ken Barrington or Graham Gooch's calibre, players capable of dictating terms in any arena. Atherton did his utmost, especially against the Australians, whose directness stirred him: he later made friends with Ian Chappell, the most abrasive of them all. But he could not put the matter right. He worked hard, fought hard, told the unpalatable truth, and still England did not improve; so it was that his career ended as it had begun, with heavy and unavenged defeat by the Australians. Perhaps he lacked a clarity of character needed to provoke change. He was a wanderer and not a man of action.

It was also his fate that his generation threw up some of the great bowlers of any age. There wasn't much relief. Whereas batsmen of previous generations could hope to take advantage of humdrum attacks fielded by weaker nations, Atherton was confronted by Marshall, Ambrose and Walsh, Waqar and Wasim, Donald and Pollock, McGrath and Warne. No wonder he soon lost the carefree approach sometimes seen in his early days.

Better than most thoughtful men, Atherton could withdraw into a cocoon of concentration, an asset as a batsman but not necessarily as a captain. He was intelligent rather than intellectual and made his decisions easily, at the crease anyhow. A purposeful man with strong opinions and principles, he did not allow his career to fritter away; instead, after last summer's Oval Test, he cut it short in the belief that his battles had been lost and won, and it is for the defiant innings he played in his country's colours that he will be remembered. His duels with Allan Donald and Glenn McGrath were cricket played at its highest pitch. These bowlers strove for his wicket because they knew it was resourcefully protected. Atherton did not give in, his wicket had to be taken from him. He had the heart for the fight regardless of conditions and obstacles.

Donald sometimes prevailed, whereupon he wore a surprised and delighted look. Sometimes the batsman had the better of him, most notably in his unbeaten 185 at Johannesburg in 1995-96, an innings spanning three weeks, or so it seemed, an effort of mind and body that saved a Test match. It was the innings that secured for Atherton the respect and national affection he had not sought through any artificial means.

Atherton was the finest English batsman of his generation, and captain in 54 Tests, a record for England. He was an even-tempered cricketer, a fierce patriot and a man prepared to fight his corner, popular with team-mates and, eventually, with distant observers. Yet he could seem aloof, even arrogant, to those who occasionally crossed his path. His retirement was well timed and he'll be able to relax now, writing books and articles, voicing his concerns, telling amusing stories and generally confirming that he is better company than he sometimes cared to show. He made an outstanding contribution to his country's cricket and his only regret must be that greatness did not bestow its largesse upon him.

MANIPULATOR OF BATSMEN'S MINDS   Five Cricketers of the Year – Stephen Thorpe, 1992

The spectre of the gangling Curtly Ambrose will undoubtedly haunt those batsmen unfortunate enough to confront him in England last season, when the 27-year-old Antiguan carried all before him, and single-handedly almost stilled the nascent Test career of Graeme Hick, a figure so thoroughly disenchanted before the series was complete that the selectors were forced to drop him. Ambrose has the ability to exert a debilitating psychological influence which so often precipitates a cluster of wickets after the initial breach has been made. It is no fun waiting in the wings, knowing your time is nigh. Hick, as an obvious example, often looked a sentenced man on his way to the crease, and this from a player who usually raced down the pavilion steps in expectation of the plunder to come.

No other explanation exists, either, for that telling passage off the first ball of the Fourth Test at Edgbaston, when Graham Gooch sparred at a widish loosener from Ambrose, only for Carl Hooper, uncharacteristically, to put the chance to grass. Surely no other bowler could have provoked such an involuntary response from the England captain. Ambrose accounted for Hick six times out of seven before England's new recruit was relieved of duty to undergo a very necessary period of recuperation outside the demanding environment of Test cricket. But in that he was not alone. Others before had had their profile reduced by the 6ft 7in marauder who was born on September 21, 1963, in Swetes, a village in the parched interior of Antigua.

CURTLY ELCONN LYNWALL AMBROSE grew up as a natural basketballer and considered migrating to the United States before starting cricket at 17, graduating from beach cricket and umpiring to the parish team. Andy Roberts was an early mentor, emphasising the psychological aspect of bowling and instilling a belief in Ambrose that he could join countrymen Baptiste, Ferris and Benjamin at the highest level.

In 1986, at Viv Richards's instigation, Ambrose had summered in England, playing for Chester Boughton Hall in the Liverpool Competition, where he is remembered as "an inveterate late arriver, though he only lived across the road". The following year he moved to Heywood in the Central Lancashire League, in which he garnered 115 cheap wickets, and in 1988 he was back again, but this time as a member of the West Indian touring team. Extremely shy and retiring, and sometimes lugubrious in his formative years as a cricketer, he never enjoyed the tag of "pro" and has tended towards reclusiveness beneath the ubiquitous "Walkman".

If, as his name suggests, he is not quite a Lindwall in terms of the range of his bowling, he does have outright pace and he generates a disconcerting, steepling bounce from fuller-length deliveries. But while he was once no-balled for throwing, by the Trinidadian umpire, Clyde Cumberbatch, in the Leewards' first match of the 1987-88 Red Stripe Cup, against Trinidad & Tobago at Guaracara Park, Ambrose's action is unequivocally legal. His height and a slender, sinewy wrist contribute greatly to the final velocity, the wrist snapping forward at the instant of release to impart extra thrust to the ball's downward trajectory. Michael Holding had this vital asset, and Courtney Walsh's wrist action, too, has given rise to notions of illegal delivery. Never a great swinger of the ball, he compensates with a smooth, leggy run-up, fast arm action and accuracy. Like Joel Garner, he possesses a lethal yorker and a nasty bouncer, but his career-best eight for 45 against hapless England at Bridgetown in 1990 owed everything to the virtues of speed and straightness. Five victims were lbw, pinned to their stumps as Ambrose squared a series England had waged so gallantly until then.

Jeffrey Dujon's station has allowed him a unique insight into the relative merits of the phalanx of West Indies quicks over the years, and in his assessment Holding was undeniably the fastest, while Roberts, an introvert and a deep thinker, was capable of delivering two different bouncers with no discernible change in action. "Wonderful control was the essence, and the faster one shocked some very good batsmen," Dujon affirms. He reserves special affection, too, for the relatively inexperienced Ambrose, who he reckons has the credentials to take his place among the greats. "He is mature beyond his years, has pace, accuracy, heart and determination, plus, importantly, real pride in economical figures."

LEFT OUT ON HIS OWN
Five Cricketers of the Year – Derek Hodgson, 1993

Whatever the controversy surrounding their methods there is no question that in 1992 Wasim Akram and Waqar Younis were the most successful cricketers in the world. Opening the bowling for Pakistan, they had a variety and aggression that made them as potent a pair as the game has seen.

In the Test series in England, Wasim took 21 wickets in four Tests. In the other tour matches he was even more devastating and finished with 82 first-class wickets in all at 16.21 each. He had already made his name as a batsman of sometimes astonishing power. In January 1993 he was suddenly appointed to succeed Javed Miandad as Pakistan's captain, with Waqar as his deputy. Few cricketers were so obviously destined for the game's aristocracy, but his elevation came even sooner than his admirers had expected. As captain he will be recognised more clearly and more widely as head of state than whichever general or politician holds the nominal office in Islamabad.

None of this was obvious in his boyhood. WASIM AKRAM was born in Lahore on June 3, 1966, to a moderately affluent middle-class family, in which his father was mostly concerned with his son's happiness rather than his success. His mother was the more ambitious for him, but her thoughts hardly embraced professional sport. They sent him to the fee-paying Cathedral School in Lahore, where all the lessons, other than Urdu, were conducted in English. In the tradition of the English public school, the Cathedral's scholars were expected to play games. Wasim, dreaming of the feats of Zaheer Abbas, Asif Iqbal and Mushtaq Mohammad, needed no urging to play cricket.

At 12 he was opening the bowling and batting for the school team. At 15 he was captain, his whole life consumed by cricket, at school, in nets at home, in the garage with his brother, and in street games played with a tennis ball. At 18 his big inswing and formidable hitting attracted attention. He won further nomination to the Pakistan Under-19 camp in Karachi. There the sight of this tall, lively left-armer offering so much promise delighted Pakistan's former fast bowler, Khan Mohammad, who soon taught him to lift his arm in the delivery stride, adding pace.

By sheer chance Javed Miandad, seeking practice, took a turn in the Under-19 net. He was so impressed by the youngster's ability to move the ball at speed, while retaining control, that he insisted Wasim be included in a squad of 14 for a three-day Patron's XI match against the New Zealanders at Rawalpindi. Wasim, again at Miandad's insistence, displaced the better-known Tahir Naqqash in the final selection, and fewer first-class débuts have been more impressive: seven for 50 in the first innings, two more wickets in the second. His scalps included John Wright, Bruce Edgar and John Reid. In such circumstances a Pakistani newspaper's description of Wasim as a sensation was restrained.

His reputation soon reached England and Lancashire began tracking him almost immediately. Wasim signed an unparalleled six-year contract for Lancashire, in secret, on the first night of the 1987 tour. He burst on English cricket the following summer with a maiden first-class century in his second Championship match, against Somerset, and a performance of Sobers-like proportions against Surrey at Southport. There he took five for 15 including a hat-trick, made a half-century in the first innings and then, with Lancashire struggling, scored 98 off 78 balls. The scores were level when he was last man out, caught on the boundary.

Meanwhile, his reputation as a Test cricketer was growing all the time. At Adelaide in 1989-90, he had a partnership with Imran Khan that saved Pakistan from what looked like imminent defeat and took them to the edge of victory. Wasim's driving to the long, straight boundary of the Adelaide Oval was as powerful as anything ever seen on the ground. Imran was the junior partner. For some time Imran had been saying that Wasim was the world's greatest all-rounder. Here was the evidence.

After 1992, it is possible to say more than that. He stands at the moment as perhaps the fastest and most destructive left-arm bowler the world has seen.

PRECISION PERFORMANCE   Five Cricketers of the Century – Greg Baum, 2000

There are three elements to Shane Warne's greatness – skill, novelty and drama – and all were manifest in the one great delivery that made his name, at Old Trafford in 1993.

The delivery was exceptionally skilful. It began its flight innocently so as to lull Mike Gatting, drifted to leg, pitched in the batsman's blind spot, then rounded on him fiercely and bent back off stump. It was at once pinpoint in its accuracy and prodigious in its spin, qualities that had always been thought to be irreconcilable.

The delivery was something different. West Indies and their battery of pace bowlers had set the agenda for 20 years; spin, particularly wrist-spin, had become nearly defunct, but suddenly here it was again in more irresistible form than ever before.

Most of all, the Gatting ball was not just early in his spell, but his very first delivery – in the match, in the series, in Ashes cricket. That gave the ball a sense of theatre, and Warne a name for showmanship, that has grown at each new threshold of his startling career, and at its peak made him nearly mystical. In the modern era, only Ian Botham could compare.

The triumph of SHANE KEITH WARNE is of the rarest kind, of both substance and style together. At his best, he has the ruthlessness of a clinician and the flourish of a performer, and his bowling is simultaneously a technical and dramatic master-piece. It was not enough for him to take a hat-trick; it had to be in an Ashes Test on the MCG. It was not enough for him to take 300 wickets; the 300th had to be accompanied by lightning and apocalyptic thunderclaps at the climax of another consummate and match-winning performance against South Africa at the SCG.

Thus in 1993 a theme was established for Warne's career: extraordinary perfor-mances, extraordinary production values. He was the cricketer of and for his times. Australia's finest moments, but also their worst, their most controversial, most splendid, most dramatic, most sordid, have all revolved around Warne. From the wretchedness of the bookmakers' scandal to the glory of the World Cup triumph, from the agony of a one-wicket defeat in Pakistan in 1994-95 to the ecstasy of a come-from-behind Ashes win in 1997, he was always the central character.

By cold statistics, Warne had not had such a profound influence on Australian cricket in his time as Dennis Lillee in his. Australia were already on the rise when Warne joined the team and, when they had their crowning moment, in the Caribbean in 1994-95, he was good, but not dominant. He takes fewer wickets per match than Lillee at a more profligate average. Moreover, Australia can and do win matches without him. But Warne's impact can never be understated. When he was first picked, cricket was under the tyranny of fast bowling and aching for another dimension. Soon enough, the world came to know that a man could take Test wickets, by seduction as well as extortion.

And the legend grew, moment by moment, coup by coup, performance by performance. He made fools of good players, short work of fools. Australia's method was indestructibly simple: bat first, bowl last, win quickly. Always it was the stage that invigorated him as much as the challenge. For Australia, he has taken more than 350 wickets, and he is already by some margin the most successful spinner in Test history.

At length, intimations came of Warne's mortality. Wear, tear and public glare took a toll. Variously, the fitness of his finger, shoulder, stomach, ethics and manners for Test cricket were called into question, but not until recently, when he returned too hastily from shoulder surgery, was his capability doubted.

Physically, undoubtedly, his powers have declined, but not his hold on oppo-nents. So it was that on the biggest stage of all, at the climax of the World Cup, at a moment when Australia looked impossibly behind, he came again. The only caveat on making him one of the cricketers of the 20th century is that he may yet figure in deliberations for the 21st.

Wisden 1922. Board of Control of "Test" Matches at Home: regulation 17. No player on the fielding side shall leave the field for the purpose of having a rub-down or shower whilst a match is actually in progress.

Little Wonder No. 20

"DID I ENTERTAIN YOU?"

Mike Atherton, 2008

Brian Lara was one of the Five Cricketers of the Year in 1995.

You don't really want to remember great players like this: BRIAN LARA filling his boots, not with runs but dollars, in the fledgling Indian Cricket League at a far-flung cricketing outpost on the outskirts of Chandigarh, the surroundings of Panchkula more scrub than stadium.

Puffy-cheeked and short of inspiration is no way to remember the most instinctive, attractive batsman of his era, so it was slightly appropriate that he made a match-winning century for Trinidad & Tobago in an attempted comeback a few weeks later. In any event, he was denied the grand farewell to his international career that two other modern-day greats, Shane Warne and Glenn McGrath, were accorded last year in Sydney, with the Ashes in the bag and the public paying full homage. At the magnificently revamped Kensington Oval, Lara had the setting all right, but not the script to match.

Responding in turns to Marlon Samuels's confused calls for a single, Lara shuffled forwards, backwards and then finally towards the pavilion for the last time. For once, he was at the mercy of events, rather than controlling them. Even now, at the end of his career, Lara could not escape the intrigue and controversy that accompanied his cricket from the moment in Antigua in 1994 that he broke Sir Garfield Sobers's world record for the highest score in Tests. For some said Samuels had been disillusioned about the way Lara as captain had treated him, and this was the ultimate payback. Others said the cock-up confirmed the deep malaise within the West Indies team, that not even the basics could be executed competently – a malaise, moreover, in which Lara was deeply complicit. All this was a pity.

Quite how Lara could have come to evoke such visceral and conflicting opinions, at a time when West Indies were not exactly flush with talent, is one for West Indian cricket historians. For some in the Caribbean, those two developments – Lara's ascent to greatness and the decline of the West Indies team – are inter-woven; for others, he was simply unlucky with his timing, and the fact that he was a great player in an undeniably shabby side merely added lustre to his reputation. Some day, someone from inside the West Indies dressing-room will write the defin-itive tale. It should be quite a read, failure being more interesting than success.

Lara's quixotic impact within the four walls of the West Indies dressing-room is, anyhow, beyond the scope of this appreciation. Lara the batsman can be assessed objectively on what we saw, rather than what we did not see. And any fair-minded assessment could only conclude that he must be one of the finest entertainers to have played in this or any other era.

For entertainment was the creed by which he lived as a batsman. Many talk the talk but Lara, undeniably, walked the walk. Records and statistics must have been important to him – how else does a batsman galvanise himself to score 501 in a county match against Durham? – but the means were never sacrificed to the ends. "Did I entertain you?" he bellowed to the spectators in the newly minted Kensington stand at the end of his last match. They cheered, but not loudly enough. "Did I entertain you?" he asked again. And even those in the anti-Lara camp could not deny it.

This unrestricted repertoire, the widest of arcs being open to him, and the ability to hit good balls to the boundary made him uniquely feared by opposing captains. You might worry about Adam Gilchrist, say, butchering an attack and smashing a bowler to smithereens, but Lara made captains, not bowlers, look silly. If you knew you were going to die, you'd prefer a single bludgeoning blow to the head, or a quick bullet to the brain, rather than death by a thousand ever-so-precise cuts. Eleven fielders were never enough; there were always gaps to plug. When he scored his 375 against my England team, I remember moving first slip out when Lara had scored 291. He edged the very next ball right where first slip had been. I'd love to know whether it was deliberate; I always doubted it, simply on the basis that such a level of genius was beyond my comprehension.

Lara was undoubtedly the best player of spin in his era, an era that did not lack for world-class spinners. It was no coincidence, perhaps, that it was against Lara's West Indies in 1999 that Warne was dropped for the first and last time in his Test career. That series saw Lara at the peak of his powers, and his unbeaten 153 to win the Barbados Test is the fourth reason he stood out. Great batsmen play great innings, and on that day Lara created, I believe, the best innings I have seen either as player or observer of the game. England were watching in Lahore, where we were preparing for the 1999 World Cup, and no other contemporary batsman would have had the effect of keeping a bunch of professional cricketers glued to the screen until the small hours of the morning. It was a stunning innings. "Christ," one of the team said to me, "I wish you'd get as excited by some of our players." Well, honesty always was my downfall.

Only one reason prevents this observer from placing Lara at the apex of modern West Indian batsmen. Against extreme pace he got hit too often, and he could seem extraordinarily jumpy at the crease. I've often wondered what kind of effect removing helmets would have on modern-day players, a hypothetical that doesn't apply to Vivian Richards.

A NATION WALKS WITH HIM   Leading Cricketer in the World – Ramachandra Guha, 2011

Sachin Tendulkar was one of the Five Cricketers of the Year in 1997.

From the middle of October to the middle of December 2010, the Republic of India was beset by a series of corruption scandals. The amount stolen by politicians (of all parties) ran into hundreds of billions of rupees. The scandals dominated the headlines for weeks until they were temporarily set aside to make way for SACHIN TENDULKAR's 50th Test hundred. This was met with relief, but also with wonder and admiration – indeed, it revived calls for the batsman to be awarded the Bharat Ratna, India's highest honour, previously reserved for politicians, scientists and musicians.

For Tendulkar to be viewed as a balm for the nation's (mostly self-inflicted) wounds was not new. As long ago as 1998, the Bombay poet C. P. Surendran wrote: "Batsmen walk out into the middle alone. Not Tendulkar. Every time Tendulkar walks to the crease, a whole nation, tatters and all, marches with him to the battle arena. A pauper people pleading for relief, remission from the lifelong anxiety of being Indian, by joining in spirit their visored saviour."

Over the next decade, the social anxieties of Indians abated. Economic liberalisation created a class of successful entrepreneurs, who in turn generated a growing middle class. Hindu–Muslim riots became less frequent. Meanwhile, Rahul Dravid, Sourav Ganguly, V. V. S. Laxman and Virender Sehwag arrived to take some of the burden of making runs (and relieving fans) off Tendulkar. It became possible once more to appreciate him in purely cricketing terms, rather than as the Saviour of the Nation.

Viewed thus, there appear to have been three distinct stages in Tendulkar's career as an international cricketer. For a full decade following his debut as a 16-year-old in 1989, he was a purely attacking batsman. Coming in at (say) ten for two, he would seek not to stabilise an innings but to wrest the game away from the opposition. There was no shot he would not play, no form of bowling that in any way intimidated or even contained him.

Then Tendulkar began to slow down. He now ducked the short ball (previously he would have hooked it), and played spin bowlers from the crease. The back-foot force through cover that was his trademark became scarce. He still scored runs regularly, but mostly through the on side, via dabs, sweeps, drives and the occasional pull.

We now know that this transformation in Tendulkar's game was due to a sore elbow. But while it lasted it appeared to be permanent. On the advice of a Mumbai doctor, he rested his left hand completely – he would not even, I am told, lift a coffee mug with it. The treatment worked, for as his elbow healed he recovered his fluency. The hook shot and the lofted drive were used sparingly, but his mastery of the off side was once more revealed in all its splendour.

It is commonplace to juxtapose Tendulkar with Don Bradman, but a more relevant comparison might be with the great Surrey and England opening batsman Jack Hobbs. There was a pre-war and a post-war Hobbs, and there has been a pre-tennis elbow and post-tennis elbow Tendulkar. Like Hobbs, in his late thirties he no longer so wholly dominates the bowling, but he is still pleasing to watch, and remains the batsman whose wicket the opposition prizes most highly.

Young Sachin enjoyed several truly fabulous years, but 2010 was the annus mirabilis of the Late Tendulkar. Last year he scored more Test runs (1,562, at an average of 78) than anybody else. In February he scored the first double-century in one-day internationals; in December, he became the first man to score 50 Test hundreds, both landmarks achieved against the best pace attack in world cricket, South Africa.

Hanif Mohammad once said of Garfield Sobers that he "had been sent by God to Earth to play cricket". It is not only Indians who think that way about Tendulkar.

Like Hobbs, he is equally admired by fans and players, by team-mate and adversary alike. His off-field conduct has been exemplary (with one trifling exception – when he asked for a tariff waiver on the import of a fancy foreign car). Australians venerate him; they do not even sledge him.

What might mean even more to him is the frank adoration and love of his team-mates. Indian cricket was long marked by personal rivalries and parochial jealousies; if that seems now to be behind us, this is the handiwork of a generation of gifted and selfless cricketers, among them Dravid, Laxman, Ganguly and Anil Kumble, but perhaps Tendulkar most. One image captures it all. A cake was being cut to mark victory in a hard-fought one-day series in Pakistan several years ago. The first piece was offered to the player of the tournament, Yuvraj Singh, who immediately turned the plate towards his hero and said, "*Pehlé Sachin bhai ko*": the first one is for our elder brother, Sachin.

RELENTLESS PURSUER OF PREY   Five Cricketers of the Year – Bruce Wilson, 1998

Friends who were there recall a day last year, deep in the Queensland bush "out the back of Longreach", on a pig-shooting weekend with the man they call "Pigeon" and the cricketing world knows as Glenn McGrath. The tall fast bowler had spotted a large boar, and he disappeared into the bush in hot pursuit. Three shots were heard, and McGrath came loping back into view, reached into the four-wheel drive, said "Out of ammo," and loped off again, all, at the same relentless, steady pace. He got the pig. It is a story many who have played against him will recognise uneasily; wild boar or batsman, Glenn McGrath tends to get what he is hunting.

He was demonstrably the best quick bowler on either side in the Ashes series of 1997 and, but for the presence of one Shane Warne, could claim to be the best bowler of all; indeed, it is a claim he might make anyway, if he were a different kind of man. To do so, though would be big-noting and, where McGrath comes from, there are few greater sins.

GLENN DONALD McGRATH was born on February 9, 1970, in Dubbo, New South Wales, first of three children of Kevin and Beverly. He carries on the great Australian bush cricketing litany, most famously represented by Sir Donald Bradman, and movingly depicted in Sir Russell Drysdale's painting of two bush kids playing against a stone wall in the sombre ochre of the Australian outback. Dubbo is a wheat and sheep farming centre a couple of hundred miles north-west of Sydney, not quite the real bush, but McGrath's father farmed in a succession of tiny settlements outside Dubbo with names smelling of gum-leaves: Eumungerie, Galgandra, Narromine. It was at the last that the young Glenn went to primary and high school, and where he started to play cricket.

McGrath recalls that there was only one turf wicket available; concrete was more usual. He was on the fringe of the game, and says that he only started to take the sport seriously when he was about 15. His captain in the local club side "thought I couldn't bowl". The captain's name is Shane Horsborough and, says McGrath, "he still reckons I can't bowl". You get very little chance to become big-headed in the Australian bush. Still, someone thought he could bowl because, at 17, he was picked in the NSW Country Cup. It was then he was spotted by various good judges, above all Doug Walters. At 19, at Walters's instigation, McGrath moved to Sydney and the Sutherland club. Odd jobs and living in a caravan followed, and four seasons of weekend cricket, until, in January 1993, he was selected for New South Wales against Tasmania. He took 5 for 79, and was away. By November, he was playing his first Test, against New Zealand at Perth: three wickets for quite a lot.

Since then, he has become Australia's strike bowler, with Warne. At the end of 1997, McGrath had 164 wickets at the remarkable average of 23.43 from 36 Tests. He arrived in May with a huge reputation, especially after his feats against West Indies, when he had considerably better figures than Ambrose, Walsh and Bishop. Yet, after the First Test at Edgbaston and England's famous win, people were asking what all the fuss was about. McGrath's match figures of 2 for 149 were a fair indication of how he bowled. He failed to understand the nature of that wicket and what needed to be done on it. But he learned, as all the good ones do, very quickly.

On a wicket made for line-and-length fast bowling at Lord's, McGrath had 8 for 38 in England's humiliating first innings. The question "Who is this Glenn McGrath anyway?" had been roundly answered. He was integral to Australia's wins in the Third and Fifth Tests, and took 7 for 76 in the first innings of a losing cause at The Oval. He was the only Australian quick to play in all six Tests. He had Mike Atherton's number, in particular, dismissing him seven times. Atherton, in fact, was McGrath's 150th Test wicket, at The Oval.

There is a thousand-dollar bet in the Australian dressing-room about whether McGrath will make a first-class fifty – ever. Yet he practises his batting with the same purpose he puts into dismissing batsmen or killing wild boars. So far his best attempt is 24. But if determination is going to count, the wise money would be on McGrath. He is a fine outfielder and, if he has a flaw, it is his apparently unstoppable habit of sledging opponents. It is odd, really, because off the field he is a quiet, modest man. He has the odd extravagance: he recently purchased 30,000 acres of wild bush in western New South Wales where he can go to be alone with his mates. Good news for them; tough on the pigs.

McGrath won his bet by scoring 61 against New Zealand in Brisbane in November 2004 – the highest score by an Australian number 11 until Ashton Agar's 98 against England at Trent Bridge in July 2013.

WONDERS – AND WHISPERS – NEVER CEASE
Five Cricketers of the Year – Jim Holden, 1999

Maybe the whispers and rumours will never cease; maybe Muttiah Muralitharan will forever have to lure international batsmen to their doom with a murky cloud of suspicion over his twirling arm. It would be a shame, though – for cricket in general, and for the off-spin assassin who bewitched players and spectators alike at The Oval last summer when taking 16 for 220 to give Sri Lanka their first Test victory in England.

These remarkable figures were the fifth-best of all time in Test cricket, yet Murali's cunning strategies, his marathon patience and his sporting instincts were overshadowed by controversy. David Lloyd, the England coach, made remarks on television that implicitly suggested a problem with his bowling action. It was another day, another victory, tainted. Murali's response to the doubters is emphatic. "I don't care what anyone says now," he protests, the insistence in his gentle voice as sharp as the spin he imparts on a cricket ball. "I know I am not a cheat. It has been medically proved that I am not chucking." The 16 wickets at The Oval took Murali past 200 in Test matches. His new target is 300. A sense of history and a sense of injustice have now become powerful twin motivating factors to his career.

The eternal problem for Murali is that his action does look distinctly odd. First impressions are that he must be a chucker. The arm is bent, the wrist action is generous, to say the least. But that is nature, not nurture. The deformity in his right arm was there at birth. His three brothers have exactly the same "bend". His wrist is also especially flexible, which means extra leverage on the ball. Yes, it may give him an advantage over other slow bowlers, but it is not an unfair one, according to ICC, which commissioned many hours of analysis into Muralitharan's action and found that it conformed to Law 24 because his arm does not straighten.

MUTTIAH MURALITHARAN was born on April 17, 1972, in Kandy, Sri Lanka, the first of four sons for Sinnasami and Laxmi Muttiah, who still run the Lucky Land biscuit and confectionery firm in the city. His progress through the Sri Lankan A team to the full international side was rapid, and he made his Test debut against Australia in August 1992. After one wicket in the first innings, he dismissed Tom Moody and Mark Waugh with successive deliveries in the second. Seven months later, Murali had his first bittersweet taste of triumph and trauma. He took five wickets in the match as Sri Lanka decisively defeated England in Colombo. However, as *Wisden* noted, there were murmurings about his action.

England's players were privately scathing, but refused to go public. Various umpires and match referees subsequently kept their suspicions out of the public domain too, until the dam burst on Boxing Day 1995, in the Melbourne Test against Australia. After 22 Tests, Murali was suddenly called for throwing seven times by umpire Darrell Hair. Ten days later, he was again repeatedly no-balled by umpire Ross Emerson in a one-day international.

His world fell apart. "It affected everything, my friends and family, all those who believed in me," he says. "It was very cruel. Everyone was watching me for all the wrong reasons, thinking I was cheating. I wasn't." For a short time he considered quitting cricket and retreating to the family business, a life of selling candy to Kandy. Instead, with support from the Sri Lankan board, Murali decided to fight back.

Medical experts gave evidence about his bent arm, the bowling action was filmed from 27 different angles, and ICC eventually sided with the Sri Lankan view that the problem was an optical illusion. The murmurings never ceased, but no umpire called him again until Emerson reappeared at Adelaide in January 1999. The general opinion was that the umpire discredited himself more than the bowler. What the whole process has done is give Murali an enviable mental toughness to complement his fiendish array of deliveries: the prodigious off-breaks, the occasional leg-break, the startling top-spinner that goes on yet bounces high at the batsman. It has made him an even more formidable cricketer.

Consistent success has flowed since, including the 1996 World Cup triumph, culminating in the waterfall of wickets at The Oval last summer. England captain Alec Stewart gave a gracious tribute afterwards, saying: "It was a very special performance, and clearly here is a bowler of great quality." Whatever the arguments, no one can deny that.

Class distinction. For the Test matches the following scale of payments, per match, for 1924, was approved: Players, £27 plus the cost of 3rd-class railway fare. Umpires, £15 plus the cost of 3rd-class railway fare. Amateurs, expenses not exceeding £2 a day for not more than five days plus the cost of 1st-class railway fare.

Little Wonder No. 21

2000–13

"HE WAS GOOD EVERYWHERE"
Ian Healy, 2008

Adam Gilchrist was one of the Five Cricketers of the Year in 2002.

ADAM GILCHRIST is a player who should be remembered as being even better than his statistics suggest – a big statement, but a true one.

Given that he made more dismissals (416) than anyone else in Tests, and had a batting average of 47.60, the stats say a lot about his greatness. But they don't quite reveal the full story of the comfort and confidence he gave his team-mates. "Leave it to Gilly," is the phrase that keeps coming into my head. Many times Australia did. Hardly ever did he let them down. Of his 96 Tests, Australia won 73 and lost just 11. It is no coincidence that in the only two series he played that Australia lost – in India in 2000-01, and in England in 2005 – he struggled as a batsman.

He was a remarkable performer because, for all his greatness, he did not create the constant fuss that surrounds champion specialists such as Brian Lara or Sachin Tendulkar or Ricky Ponting, who always seem to be generating headlines and massive expectations as the danger-men of the day. People rarely concentrated on Gilchrist in such a way – but everyone knew he was there, and everyone knew he was dangerous.

Gilchrist had an unusual batting technique, brutally crude and brash, and unconventionally brilliant. It first made my jaw drop even before he had played international cricket. The Queensland side I was playing in came up with a plan to bowl yorkers to him, but he was thrashing our best efforts down the ground. He had a big, high, sloppy backlift you would back yourself to get the ball under. But suddenly that ball would disappear.

His ability to hit to all parts made him extremely difficult to bowl to. There was no black hole in his scoring range, and Matthew Hayden once admitted that, while the area behind point was something of a personal blind spot, Gilchrist was "good everywhere… which is what makes him so great".

I remain staggered by his durability. He didn't miss a Test match – he played 96 straight – and barely ever missed a one-dayer through injury either, which will be a source of satisfaction to him. He never had to do major rehabilitations, and was rarely injured, which showed how professional he was with things like diet (his wife Mel is a dietician) and treatment of his knees. When I first saw how much he had to do to keep his kneecaps in order as a youngster, I felt there was no way he could go the long journey and do what he has done. His raw endurance was, to me, as impressive as any part of this great cricketing package.

Gilchrist maintained a long tradition among Australian wicketkeepers of celebrating wins with a decent night's drinking. A consolatory drink was often as valuable as the celebratory one: he was the champ there too. A "none or a gutful" man, but one who knew how to drink – never in a moment's trouble after any of Australia's Test wins, three World Cups, and plenty more.

An Australian batsman who walked was a new breed in the modern era and, ironically, to my knowledge he never had to walk again after his initial World Cup gesture against Sri Lanka at Port Elizabeth in 2003. Gilly was in an extremely strong position to begin walking – he was averaging superbly with the bat, with glovework to match. He took on a tough position, though, as the wicketkeeper who walked. There are always times when keepers appeal without full knowledge of whether something is out, and this was the dilemma he took on – to leave it to the umpire in the field but not while batting.

Another facet of his play which was rarely talked about was gamesmanship. A turn of phrase, delivered succinctly at appropriate moments and disguised with humour, became extremely effective. His blood boiled over at times, and he was spoken to more than once by match referees. While he was Mr Natural, he loved to get shirty and dirty, which further enhanced his image among his peers.

Incredible talent unsurpassed in the game's history, in a style never before seen; a team man who provided confidence to all around him, allowing them to perform naturally without fear of losing; someone who would scrap with you in tough times. What more could you ask for? The answer is nothing. Adam Gilchrist had the lot, and was able to show us it all.

CELEBRITY BY CHOICE   Five Cricketers of the Year – Paul Hayward, 2006

When talent announces itself these days we rush to buy tickets for the burnout. This modern scepticism attached itself to Kevin Pietersen long before his bludgeoning and decisive innings of 158 on the final day of the Ashes. The genre for Pietersen's rise as cricketer and celebrity is one known to David Beckham, Jenson Button of Formula 1 and the self-basting Gavin Henson, Welsh rugby's icon for the iPod generation. With all these ubiquitous idols we observe the billboard competing with the scoreboard. It's a truism of modern sport that many young athletes have the party before they have fully done the work. In fact, there are those who worry that sport now exists as a fame academy – a factory for the making of deals – with the game itself an incidental part of the manufacturing process.

Pietersen certainly did the work at The Oval, and he sure as hell had the party afterwards. But when Pietersen stopped the victory bus to dive into Starbucks to relieve himself, cynics expected him to come out clutching a deal establishing him as the new face of the caramel macchiato.

The talent is the thing. Always the talent. If the gift is authentic it's easier to ignore the peripheral ringing of tills and vacuous celebrity chatter. On that front, Pietersen struck 473 runs in five Tests against Australia. This, after "KP" had recorded an average in 23 one-day internationals of 73.09. These are the figures of a resoundingly good cricketer. The ICC anointed him both Emerging Player and One-Day Player of the Year. His belligerent and fearless innings at The Oval lit the imagination's touchpaper way beyond cricket. His team-mate Ashley Giles observed: "It was real grandchildren stuff. 'Gather round and I'll tell you about that innings I played with Pietersen, with the white stripes and the earrings.'" In the ensuing tide of English euphoria it was swiftly forgotten that KP had been dropped three times, most calamitously by Shane Warne, his Hampshire colleague and friend. That simple error turned Pietersen into a household name and millionaire. Sport's soundtrack is the music of chance.

The 158 may be a landmark Pietersen will never surpass. "Yes, I do think about that sometimes," he says. "But nothing I did that day was more important than us winning the Ashes. It was all about us winning the Ashes."

Though he might fail one of the government's citizenship quizzes, KEVIN PETER PIETERSEN, born in Pietermaritzburg on June 27, 1980, has worked hard to establish himself as a John Bull Englishman – ever since he walked out, aged 19, on his native South Africa to play for Nottinghamshire, citing the injustice of a quota system that was hampering his progress with KwaZulu-Natal. Summoned to meet Dr Ali Bacher, then head of the United Cricket Board, Pietersen restated his belief that quotas were the enemy of merit. "He tried to change my mind," Pietersen said. And failed. Thus he acquired the twin roles of crusader and opportunist, according to which ethical continent you happened to be standing on.

In South Africa, the unforgiving accuse him of fleeing to the UK under a mother of convenience. Mrs Pietersen is English. An equally persistent whisper is that over-confidence made him a pariah among his new county colleagues. Not so, he says: "I was treading water. I left Nottinghamshire for cricketing reasons. I needed to get to Hampshire to improve my game." Under the psychological tutelage of Warne, that Mephistopheles of spin, he convinced the England selectors that he could transfer to the Test arena the instinctive athletic brilliance of his one-day cricket. His elevation at the expense of Graham Thorpe was, of course, a seminal example of ambivalence and age being usurped by youth and eagerness.

Excitability might seem a more apt word, because Pietersen's six dropped catches in the series put gunpowder in the muskets of his critics, who detected a dilettante streak. Geoff Boycott received no thanks from Camp KP for reminding the new hero that greatness is achieved over years, not hours, and that frivolity has destroyed many promising careers.

Boycott, and others, will cite the skunk hairdo, the £50,000 earrings, the Three Lions tattoo, the dates with Caprice and a former Big Brother contestant, and the Los Angeles celebrity party to which Pietersen gained access with help from the dissolute actor Mickey Rourke. There he was romantically linked with Paris Hilton – an heiress, incidentally, not somewhere nice to stay in France. The game has never seen anything like this. Pietersen is surely the first man in flannels who chose to be famous – who set out to be world-renowned – just as Beckham and Henson have in their chosen fields. So now we stand back to find out whether he will be remembered as the cricketer who ate himself or a legend of the willow. Take your eyes off him if you can.

BEARING THE BURDEN   Five Cricketers of the Year – Bruce Wilson, 2006

After that most delirious of summers, now destined to bore countless thousands of unborn grandchildren, it might seem perverse-to-absurd to include in this annual salute to excellence a batsman whose Test average dipped, who made arguably the worst decision by an Australian captain in 30 years, who was fined for what might be called excessive surliness and lost the Ashes.

Yet Ricky Ponting joins this unique roll-call for any number of reasons, some of which approach the abstract; not least, for example, is the one that it takes two to tango. Without Ponting's own particular persona combating Michael Vaughan's very different one, the chemical formulae that exploded into the 2005 Ashes would not have reacted as spectacularly as they did. Ponting's flaws and strengths were all part of the magic mix.

His strengths included one of the great match-saving innings – by far the most consequential batting performance by an Australian all summer: the 156 at Old Trafford, when he stood between Australia and total Ashes meltdown. It was his 23rd Test century, made in circumstances far rougher than most of the others.

Ponting's greatness as a batsman has never been in dispute, nor his place in the *Wisden* pantheon. In 2004, he was the first recipient, by acclamation rather than vote, of the Almanack's newest award, the Leading Cricketer in the World. That came after a 2003 when he led Australia to victory in the World Cup, scored 11 international centuries in the calendar year and unleashed two successive double-centuries against India, the series that until last year stood as Australia's most eventful and competitive of recent times. In 2005, there was a strong argument that, as commanding officer, he was responsible for the warship losing its teeth. The questions over his tactical captaincy, the nuts-and-bolts everyday stuff of field placings and just when to turn the screw, persisted until the last day of the Fifth Test. But Ponting's defenders went to The Oval noting that with just a couple of drops of luck Australia could have been leading the series 3–0. And the failure of so many of his team-mates to reach their normal heights was not his fault.

The background noise to all this, though, was the stark fact that Ponting sent England in to bat at Edgbaston having just seen his main strike bowler, Glenn McGrath, taken to hospital. The ubiquitous "team sources" were quick to say that the decision had been made inflexibly by committee. Ponting, typically, would have none of that, and shouldered the blame.

RICKY THOMAS PONTING was born on December 19, 1974, in Launceston, Tasmania's second city, in the north of that beautiful if eccentric island. His aston-ishing and quite natural talent has never been in doubt. At 20, he was already in the Test team. He lost his place at 21. At 22, he returned to the team to score a chanceless maiden century at Headingley.

It was still not all smooth after that. But the bumps in his career, apart from a chastening against spin in India, were largely self-induced and off the field, until he settled down, gave up the beefsteak'n'bourbon life, and got married. He main-tained, though, his love for what Australians call the dishlickers – well-bred grey-hounds. His nickname remains "Punter". Marriage somehow enabled him to make runs even more regularly, and helped harden the selectors' view that he, rather than the *très méchant* Warne, was Steve Waugh's natural successor in both forms of the game. And until the Ashes series, Ponting's captaincy had kept Australia at an unfaltering position at the top of the world. But by Old Trafford last summer, a lesser man might have buckled, if from nothing else but the sheer weight of cutlery in his back. Instead, he played the defensive innings of his life to scramble the draw.

In the next Test we had the Pratt Affair, when substitute fieldsman Gary Pratt ran Ponting out and the stuff that had been rumbling away erupted in a fiery cascade of expletives. Ponting was admonished, heavily fined, and he apologised. The epilogue to this went almost unnoticed.

With the Ashes just lost at The Oval, the teams were drinking together (and Ponting's personality surely played a part in that kind of fraternising) when a nervous Pratt asked if a photograph might be signed. Jokes ensued and Ponting, instead, handed the young Durham man two pairs of his initialled boots. "I think he was pleased," Ponting said. Astoundedly delighted, said an eye-witness. It was seen as a typical gesture from this understated man.

PILLAR AND ROCK   Five Cricketers of the Year – Christopher Martin-Jenkins, 2013

The best, most classical and most durable all-rounder of his generation, and arguably of all time, was the mighty difference between South Africa and England in the summer of 2012.

Kallis's implacable alliance with Hashim Amla made possible England's humiliation at The Oval, where his unbeaten 182 was as easy to miss as any such score could be. He also bowled with shrewdness and calculated venom, undermining England's first innings with the vital wickets of Kevin Pietersen and Ian Bell, and swallowed fast, flying catches at second slip.

Overall, he was for South Africa what he had been for at least 15 years: a pillar and a rock. At last, the claim in 2012 that he had never quite received the credit he deserved felt wrong; but the comparisons with Garfield Sobers did not.

Born in Cape Town on October 16, 1975, JACQUES HENRY KALLIS was quickly recognised as a special talent at his school, Wynberg Boys' High, a couple of miles from Newlands, his spiritual home. Indeed, the school's cricket field was renamed "The Jacques Kallis Oval" in 2009. He first played for his country, against England in the Durban Test of 1995-96, at the age of 20. That Oval hundred was the 43rd of his Test career (only Sachin Tendulkar has more), to go with 17 in one-day internationals. Injuries have been rare, perhaps because of a bowling action reminiscent of Alec Bedser: sideways on, with the left arm leading, a full turn of a strong frame, and a surging follow-through.

Like Jack Nicklaus, the greatest of golfers, he has kept extraordinary command of his emotions, his expression inscrutable until he takes another wicket or reaches another century. Then a wide smile lights his even wider face. Massive strength and a temperament as cool as an igloo have made him the most consistently formidable all-round cricketer since the era of Botham, Imran, Hadlee and Kapil – and, like them, Kallis has done things his own way. He ascribes his longevity to managing his fitness: "I've always tried to listen to my body and pick up early warning signs. In the early days I trained all day and bowled in the nets. I was in my mid-twenties when I realised I had to change."

As a batsman he quickly learned to switch off between deliveries; a monumental calm has always pervaded his cricket. Once set, often from the first ball, he looks unmovable, as he confirmed during his unbroken stand of 377 with Amla. Impressive rather than exciting, and utterly orthodox, he rarely looks hurried; his bat appears broader than the Laws allow. Only his strike-rate has drawn criticism: just occasionally, he has seemed wrapped up in personal battles, and once or twice in mid-career he failed to produce the gear-change his team needed.

To select from his achievements feels invidious, but a few feats capture him best. In 2001-02, he went 1,241 minutes – nearly 21 hours – between Test dismissals. Two years later, he made centuries in five successive Tests, one short of Don Bradman's record. Depicted by some, at times fairly, as a reluctant bowler, he finished the England tour with 555 international wickets, to say nothing of 319 catches.

Short but intensive preparation has been vital to these insatiable performances. "The key," he explains, "is to treat every ball you bowl or face as if it's the real thing. With that intensity you can do your preparation in 20 balls rather than an hour or two. I learned a long time ago that physical preparation for international cricket takes place a long time before the match. It's mental preparation that counts on the eve of the match.

ANGLES AND CALCULATIONS   Five Cricketers of the Year – Scyld Berry, 2009

It is one of sport's axioms that you can defeat only the opposition in front of you; and one of cricket's that defeating Australia in Australia is the ultimate achievement. In February 2008, England Women beat Australia Women in a one-off Test at Bowral – only their fourth Test victory in Australia (and two of those had come on their inaugural 1934-35 tour). They were steered home by the single-minded determination of Claire Taylor, who followed a first-innings 79 with 64 not out when set 142 to win. In men's Ashes cricket, only half a dozen England batsmen have dictated the course of a deciding Test with the same mental strength.

Last summer, as England Women won all nine of the one-day internationals that rain allowed to conclude, Taylor was dismissed only twice by a bowler, and twice run out. In May, she was named England Women's Cricketer of the Year. In October, she was installed at No. 1 when the ICC launched its one-day international rankings for women. In an era when run-scoring has been neither so high nor so fast as in men's cricket, she has averaged 43 in Tests, 39 in one-day internationals, and 30 in Twenty20 internationals – and in her early career she was a batsman-wicketkeeper rather than a specialist batsman.

SAMANTHA CLAIRE TAYLOR was born in Amersham on September 25, 1975, to a father who played rugby and a mother who had played hockey for Northumbria. The nearest she came to cricket was softball, as the only girl in the Dolphin School team, until she was spotted, aged 13, at a summer sports camp by Carol Bosley, captain of Ridgeway (which then merged with Reading). Hockey was more her game in her teens – she was in the England Under-17 and Under-19

Excellence personified: Claire Taylor in the Long Room at Lord's
after becoming the first female Cricketer of the Year in 2009

squads as a centre-forward – but, being agile and energetic, Claire also kept wicket from 16, firstly for Thames Valley (starting before women switched to trousers), then for Queen's College First XI when she went to Oxford to read maths. In the men's college team she learned to play off the back foot, whereas women's cricket is more of a front-foot game. She also played alongside Iain Sutcliffe, who went on to represent Leicestershire and Lancashire. She won three hockey Blues, and three Half Blues for cricket: in a 50-over game against Cambridge, she hit 158 at No. 3.

"Her game is based on doggedness and determination, but it's her ability to think several overs ahead and work the field around which makes her the world No. 1," says the England women's coach Mark Lane.

Whether her mathematical training helps is a matter for conjecture. "I don't know if other people do it, but when I'm batting at my best I have a 3D awareness of the shape of the field and where the spaces are – I used to play chess at Montessori school. Maths, I think, has given me more control and confidence when I'm calculating the runs per over we have to score."

Taylor has the unblinking gaze and fast metabolism of most international batsmen. She writes a key message or two on her left arm before she bats. Younger team-mates, including her promising namesake (but no relation) Sarah Taylor, have learned from her about gears. "When you go in, it's a passive–reactive phase and the game flows around you – it's information-collecting really," says Claire Taylor. "As soon as I can, I move into the next gear, controlled aggression."

At this stage of its evolution, women's Test cricket is similar to that of men's in the 19th century when it was becoming professionalised: when most players were amateur, and used light bats, and the normal run-rate was around two runs an over, against medium-pace or spin.

There was no money for retaining the Ashes, not even a tour fee; just the intangible rewards of honour, pride and satisfaction. However, thanks to Sport England funding through the ECB, Taylor has been compensated for the time she spends training (she is the kind who goes for a four-mile run before she has a net), and combines cricket with the projects she undertakes as a part-time management consultant. In addition, eight members of the women's squad combine training with 25 hours a week as coaches for Chance to Shine. Since taking over women's cricket in 1998, the ECB have organised it excellently, giving England Women the best chance of succeeding at international level (if only, some might add, the same applied to the men). And Taylor, in her batting, has personified this excellence.

Little Wonder No. 22

Gentlemen v Players. At Scarborough, September 6, 8, 9, 1924. Rhodes in the course of the afternoon completed for the 15th time in his career the double feat of scoring 1,000 runs and taking 100 wickets in a season. In doing this he beat the record he had previously equalled of George Hirst, who, as it happened, was standing umpire.

It is an innings Alastair Cook regards with "a tinge of disappointment". That it brought him 294 career-best runs speaks volumes. Even after grinding down India at Edgbaston, he wanted more. He always wants more. It is the sign of a batsman of the highest calibre and discipline.

His year had begun with 189 at Sydney and the winning of the Ashes series. But fatalism stalks most batsmen. He made a staggering 766 runs in those five Tests; only Wally Hammond, with 905 in 1928-29, had compiled more for England in a series against Australia. It had to end some time, didn't it? Cook was determined to scupper that assumption. In his next three Test innings, against Sri Lanka, he made 133, then 96, then 106. And so it went on. In 2011 alone, he scored 927 Test runs at an average of 84.

He clearly disliked the taste of failure that had visited his plate in the summer of 2010, when he had made only 106 runs in eight Test innings against Bangladesh and Pakistan. He was close to being dropped for the first time in his Test career. For almost a year, he had been wandering, attempting to use a different technique. His batting had never been the easiest on the eye – slightly at odds with his good looks – but now he was cricket's equivalent of a gorgon, with a stiff and unnatural backlift he kept fussily glancing at, and so many trigger movements he could have been tap-dancing.

It was then that Cook made a huge decision. Before the Oval Test against Pakistan in August 2010, he told coach Andy Flower: "I'm going back to how I was." He would revert to his old technique, with a double backlift and back-and-across feet movement, that had first brought international recognition and nine Test centuries, even if he had made three more (one against South Africa, two against Bangladesh) during his period of tinkering. He failed in the first innings at The Oval and, on the second evening, he and Andrew Strauss had to face three uncomfortable overs. Strauss did not survive, but Cook did, negotiating two balls without scoring. The first delivery he faced the next morning from Mohammad Aamer was full and on off stump. Cook hit it wide of mid-on for four. "I was away," he says. He certainly was – to his 13th Test century. His life has never been the same since.

ALASTAIR NATHAN COOK was born on Christmas Day, 1984, in Gloucester, the son of Graham, a British Telecom engineer, and Elizabeth, a teacher from Swansea. They lived in Essex, but were planning to visit their families – Graham's in Cam, Gloucestershire, and Elizabeth's in Wales – over the festive period, when Alastair, the second of three boys, arrived two months early at Gloucestershire Royal Hospital.

Cook grew up in Wickham Bishops, a village near Maldon, and at the age of eight was offered a place in the St Paul's Cathedral Choir School. By the age of 13 he had decided a life in music was not for him, but it had not been time wasted. For a start, he was able to get a music scholarship to Bedford School. And the dedication required at St Paul's had inculcated a lasting rigour. "It enabled me to learn about concentration. We simply could not make any mistakes. It definitely helped my cricket."

At Bedford, now aged 14, Cook was sitting through double physics, miffed he had not been selected for the first eleven against MCC. But MCC were one short. He rushed to his boarding house for his kit, and arrived at the ground to be told he was batting at No. 3. By the time he was padded up a wicket had fallen. He hurried to the middle. And scored a century. He proved rather good at making stunning and often immediate statements. Take the two-day match in 2005 for Essex against the Australians, when Cook scored 214. Six months later, he was making his England debut. Summoned to India from an A-team tour of the West Indies, he was batting only two days after arriving in Nagpur. He made 60, then, gloriously, 104 not out in the second innings. "The pressure was off," he says. "You're not supposed to be able to fly halfway round the world and make runs straight away in Indian conditions." But it helps if you don't sweat: during that remorseless 294 at Edgbaston, all 773 minutes of it, he did not once change his gloves.

England cannot have produced too many more amiable and self-deprecating cricketers. In time, it will probably be confirmed that England never produced a more prolific Test batsman either. By the end of the 2011-12 series against Pakistan, aged only 27 and now a married man, Cook had 6,027 Test runs with 19 centuries; only Sachin Tendulkar had reached 6,000 at a younger age. His mentor and coach Graham Gooch's national record of 8,900 runs stands little chance. And neither do the 22 centuries made by Hammond, Colin Cowdrey and Geoffrey Boycott. The struggles of 2010 feel like another lifetime.

THE LOST CRICKETER OF THE YEAR   1995

In 1918, in the absence of any first-class cricket, *Wisden* named five public-school bowlers as its Cricketers of the Year. Among them was H. L. CALDER, for his feats the previous summer as a 16-year-old spin bowler at Cranleigh School.

The years passed. In 1994, we tried to track down the oldest surviving Cricketers of the Year to invite them to the annual *Wisden* dinner – indeed R. E. S. Wyatt, then almost 93 and thought to be the oldest survivor, was present. But there was a small mystery. There was no record of Harry Calder's death. Indeed, there was no record of his life. Cranleigh had no knowledge of what became of him; nor did cricket's best-known Old Cranleighan, E. W. Swanton.

However, Robert Brooke, perhaps cricket's most assiduous researcher, had a hint that he had been heard of in Port Elizabeth, South Africa in the 1930s. On the off-chance, Brooke wrote to a newspaper there; a friend read the article and Calder wrote to us from a rest home in Cape Town, not as well as he had been before a stroke in 1992 but, at 93, three months older than Wyatt, very much alive.

Calder's father, Henry, had played for Hampshire in the 1880s and later captained Western Province. The family went back to South Africa in 1921. Henry Calder wanted his son to join the Wanderers Club, but all Harry saw was "a sea of gravel", so he decided to play tennis and golf instead, while he made his living in banking and industry. He never played serious cricket again and, until Brooke got in touch with him, never even knew he was a member of the game's elite. But he was "delighted" to hear the news, 76 years late.

Feature Articles

Wisden's first feature article, three pages titled "Individual innings of 200 or more runs" by the editor W. H. Knight, appeared in 1869. It followed a high-scoring season and in order that readers should have a ready and authoritative listing of those big scores, Knight put them together with an accompanying tabulated list which he hoped "will be found interesting to the readers of *The Cricketers' Almanack*". But it was not until 1888 that articles of comment and analysis, as opposed to reports, became a regular part of the book. In the Preface to that year's edition, *Wisden's* 25th, the editor Charles Pardon wrote: "A few articles on cricket have been introduced, the subjects of leg before wicket and the classification of counties has been dealt with." And dealt with they were by Lord Harris and the umpire Robert Thoms, who also contributed an article the following year entitled "A few jottings".

Feature articles range from technical analyses by the leading players of the day – and what an XI they would make, with some very handy reserves – through coruscating criticism of the game's major issues to whimsical reminiscence or observation. A commission to contribute to *Wisden* is highly prized whether the writer be a professional cricket journalist, player or notable public figure. In the contemporary Almanack the articles form the meaty Comment section, a richly flavoured part of the book that defines its unique place on the *Wisden* shelf as much as the Notes by the Editor. The 1946 piece by Jim Swanton, "Cricket under the Japs", is one of the most famous of all *Wisden* articles and Swanton's copy of the 1939 edition is probably the most famous single Almanack. It survived his period as a prisoner of war where it became, for many of the inmates, a much-loved, much-read distraction from the horrors of the situation. On Swanton's death in 2000, it was bequeathed to the Lord's museum.

THE GAME: SKILLS AND TECHNIQUE

THE ART OF VARIATION   George Lohmann, 1890

The chief characteristics of an effective bowler are good length, break, a tendency to rear up quickly from the pitch, and a deceptive delivery. This last is perhaps more important than any of the others, as, for instance, a ball which a batsman imagines is coming faster or slower than it really is very often proves fatal through his failing to time his stroke. I think this is the reason why so many men are bowled by "yorkers", while some return the ball tamely to the bowler or poke it up by playing too soon. A good-length ball loses half its terrors if bowled over after over on a good wicket, as a batsman becomes accustomed to it, and soon begins to punish this orthodox ball. But if the bowler is able to put one in now and then which is, from the style of his delivery, apparently a fast ball, but really a slow or medium one, the batsman will not dare to take any liberties, and will probably feel a little abroad. Some batsmen are rather puzzled by a ball which pitches on the off and breaks away from the wicket, and which consequently is only half hit, and then there may be a catch on the off side. The same rule applies to this ball as to any other – its frequency will lessen its destructiveness; therefore it should be varied by a break from the off to the wicket, one with nothing on at all, or a fast "yorker", and the batsman, not knowing what is coming next, does not feel so confident or determined as he would do if he had the same ball sent down continually. Care should be taken to make the delivery of these different balls as much alike as possible.

I think it is necessary for a bowler to understand at least the theory of batting, as he is then able to find out the batsman's weak points, and bowl accordingly. You cannot lay down any hard and fast rule to break through all defences, for what one man has great difficulty in playing another will score from. The wickets are in such good order nowadays that in dry weather it is no easy matter to get really first-class batsmen out, and you must rely upon some little artifice such as I have tried to explain. The ball that takes by surprise is usually the fatal one, and it is the unexpected that batsmen have most reason to dread.

Why Posh Boys Can't Bowl

F. R. Spofforth, 1904

Meeting the editor of this interesting Almanack at Lord's during the cricket season he asked how it was the professionals were so much better bowlers than the gentlemen, adding that the latter rarely produced a really first-class bowler; and in a moment of "mental aberration" I consented to write him a short article on this subject.

Now in comparing amateurs with professionals from their early start in life all the advantages appear with the former. As children, they are better looked after, clothed and fed (or they ought to be) and have all the advantages of a higher education, are sent to schools and colleges where cricket is taught, and if they show aptitude for a particular department of the game special attention is paid to them. They also have the apparent advantage of playing on good pitches which are looked after by competent caretakers. In my opinion no one can ever think of being a first-class bowler without he really works hard and often and starts early, for this is the great secret, because it gives elasticity to the muscles without which it is almost impossible to excel, and this elasticity cannot be got without one starts quite young, and certainly not after 21 years of age. This is where the professional has the advantage. He has no one to instruct him, bowls just as he likes on some village green where the pitches are bad and the ground does the breaking for him, and probably the faster he bowls the greater his success. Furthermore he has no one to prevent him practising every day as much as his school hours will allow.

This is not so with the amateur. He is to a certain extent taught but he is not allowed to bowl to his full extent as long as he likes, because others are waiting for their turn, and above all he is taught to spin a ball which in my opinion is just like trying to teach a child to run before it can walk, because directly you start spinning a ball you check pace and therefore development of elasticity which cannot be gained afterwards. How often one hears of splendid boy bowlers but never hears anything of them afterwards, or only for a short time. As they grow older the work is too hard for them but had they bowled harder and longer when quite young and stretched their arms to the full extent they never would find the work too laborious. In conclusion, I consider the real reason why the sons of gentlemen don't succeed as bowlers is that they don't do the necessary work when young. Their scholastic duties, together with games such as tennis, squash rackets, etc, etc, which they can play at high-class schools, colleges and universities take away a great amount of time which the young professional devotes to the practice of bowling.

BOWL AT THE STUMPS
Charles Kortright (in an interview), 1948

One of the questions my friends most frequently ask me is why there are so few fast bowlers today compared with the start of the century, and why the few there are attain comparatively small success. They seem to think there was some sort of magic about the old-time men of pace, and that I may be able to explain how it was obtained. Let me disillusion them at once. There is no magic in fast bowling; but, on the contrary, much hard work, coupled with intelligent methods, is the key to success.

I have little patience with modern bowlers who condemn "these shirt-front wickets" and ask how can they be expected to get men out when the pitch will not help. There were many such pitches in my playing days, the sort on which if we could bounce the ball bail-high we thought ourselves pretty clever. A basic principle of cricket which I feel is sometimes overlooked is that the prime object of a bowler is to get batsmen out. For this reason I do not favour the modern craze for such expressions as "inswingers", "outswingers", all sorts of "spins" and "swerves". Some bowlers seem to concentrate on these dubious achievements so much that they forget to keep a length and to bowl at the stumps.

If England can find a real fast bowler who is willing to take a bit of advice from an old-timer, here is a wrinkle he might well remember. He should never forget to try bowling a fast yorker on the leg stump to a newly arrived batsman. It can be a deadly ball to face early in an innings; I have dismissed many top-class batsmen with it. I frequently used to advise the late Kenneth Farnes to pitch the ball farther up to the batsmen, because I considered that he wasted too much energy on pointless short deliveries, like many other modern pace bowlers. One of the clearest recollections of my early days is the "little cricket" we played at Brentwood School. This involved creeping out through a window at four in the morning, with any sort of makeshift gear, to play against the chapel wall until seven o'clock, the official time for rising. If discovered, we were in trouble, but I thought the game well worth the risk, and I was always ready for two and a half hours of compulsory cricket practice when school was over for the day.

My favourite story is rather hard to believe, but I vouch for its truth. Playing in a club match at Wallingford on a very small ground with a pitch perhaps best described as sporty, I bowled a ball which rose almost straight and went out of the ground, without a second bounce. I suggest that this made me the first man to bowl a six in byes! The ball was pitched right up to the batsman and on the wicket, so that it was undoubtedly within the striker's reach, and there was no question of wides being awarded.

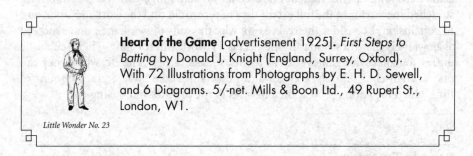

Heart of the Game [advertisement 1925]. *First Steps to Batting* by Donald J. Knight (England, Surrey, Oxford). With 72 Illustrations from Photographs by E. H. D. Sewell, and 6 Diagrams. 5/-net. Mills & Boon Ltd., 49 Rupert St., London, W1.

Little Wonder No. 23

THE GOOGLY – THE SCAPEGOAT OF CRICKET

B. J. T. Bosanquet, 1925

The visit of the South African team has revived interest in the googly. Poor old googly! It has been subjected to ridicule, abuse, contempt, incredulity, and survived them all. Nowadays one cannot read an article on cricket without finding that any deficiencies existing at the present day are attributed to the influence of the googly. If the standard of bowling falls off, it is because too many cricketers devote their time to trying to master it, instead of carrying on with the recognised and hallowed methods of bowling. If batsmen display a marked inability to hit the ball on the off side, or anywhere in front of the wicket, and stand in apologetic attitudes before their wicket, it is said that the googly has made it impossible for them to adopt the old aggressive attitude and make the old scoring strokes.

But, after all, what is the googly? It is merely a ball with an ordinary break produced by an extraordinary method. It is quite possible and, in fact, not difficult, to detect, and, once detected, there is no reason why it should not be treated as an ordinary "break-back". However, it is not for me to defend it. Other and more capable hands have taken it up and exploited it, and, if blame is to be allotted, let it be on their shoulders. For me is the task of the historian, and if I appear too much in the role of the "proud parent", I ask forgiveness.

Somewhere about the year 1897 I was playing a game with a tennis ball, known as "Twisti-Twosti". The object was to bounce the ball on a table so that your opponent sitting opposite could not catch it. It soon occurred to me that if one could pitch a ball which broke in a certain direction and with more or less the same delivery make the next ball go in the opposite direction, one would mystify one's opponent. After a little experimenting I managed to do this, and it was so successful that I practised the same thing with a soft ball at "Stump-cricket". From this I progressed to a cricket ball, and about 1899 I had become a "star turn" for the luncheon interval during our matches at Oxford. That is, the most famous batsman on the opposing side was enticed into a net and I was brought up to bowl him two or three leg-breaks. These were followed by an "off-break" with more or less the same action. If this pitched on the right place it probably hit him on the knee, everyone shrieked with laughter, and I was led away and locked up for the day.

During this and the following year I devoted a great deal of time to practising the googly at the nets, and occasionally bowled it in unimportant matches. The first public recognition we obtained was in July, 1900, for Middlesex v Leicestershire at Lord's. An unfortunate individual (I believe it was Coe) had made 98 when he was clean bowled by a fine specimen which bounced four times. The incident was rightly treated as a joke, and was the subject of ribald comment, but this small beginning marked the start of what came to be termed a revolution in bowling.

SUCCESSFUL SPIN: STUDY THE BATSMAN   A. P. Freeman (in an interview), 1938

The best piece of advice which I offer to the young bowler is: watch and experiment. To my mind, too many bowlers in modern cricket neglect to use their intelligence; their efforts are little more than mechanical. It is absolutely essential that a bowler should study the batsman, not in a casual sort of way, but with proper concentration. I am convinced that I learned most because I spent so much time all through my career in watching both batsmen and other bowlers. Never having received a day's coaching in my life, I am very sure that bowlers are born and not made. If the ability is there, it can, of course, be brought out and developed, but without natural gifts no one can hope to attain real eminence as a bowler.

If the art of studying the batsman and watching for his weak spots was cultivated more both in county and club cricket, we should not hear so many lamentations about the scarcity of good spin bowlers. It is important to study the batsman right up to the moment of releasing the ball. A movement by him before the ball has left my hand has prompted me to pitch the ball a little wide and often to get him stumped. It may take you half an hour to find out his weakness but it is worth while. Never mind giving a batsman 20 runs or so. Four wickets for 100 at The Oval always pleased me more than, say, eight for 20 on a bad wicket against a poor side. Humour the batsman if he has a particular hit but be sure you have safe fieldsmen in the position where a catch may be put up. A good captain will always consult the bowler before altering the placing of the field; otherwise he is likely to ruin the bowler's best-laid plans.

I always enjoyed pitting my brains against the top-class batsmen. I preferred to bowl to Jack Hobbs more than anybody. He played every ball on its merits, took no liberties and if you got his wicket you earned it. I always knew he would play every ball as it deserved. During the later years of my career in Kent cricket I believe I knew every batsman's weakness. That knowledge, carefully memorised, I was always ready and willing to pass on to younger bowlers in the team. When Warwickshire were playing Kent at Gravesend in the first year Douglas Wright turned out for us, I got a wicket with the last ball of an over and Bates came in to take the next ball from Wright. I suggested to Wright he should bowl a googly first ball; he did and

Bates's leg peg went down. Bates said to me afterwards: "You told him, Tich, didn't you, to bowl a googly?" and I admitted the little strategy.

Always be ready to experiment is a good motto for bowlers. If you cannot get a man out, try anything. Never be afraid of being hit. If a batsman starts hitting, keep him at it; a little more flight and the batsman may make a mistake. It is when the wicket is "dead" that you need to experiment most. At such times bowl a bit faster but not forgetting to slip in an occasional slow one with the same action. Whenever I am asked to give advice on bowling, I always urge the prime importance of these points of studying the batsman and experimenting.

FIELDING: LETHARGY AND LAZINESS
D. L. A. Jephson, 1901

Much has been written with regard to the batting of the past season, and much has been written with regard to the bowling; much praise, and rightly too has been bestowed on the one, and on the other a modicum of commendation. To write in the same congratulatory vein of the fielding necessitates the pen of a ready writer, the pen of a Defoe. As these are not numbered among my possessions, it is a difficult task. To write well of the fielding in 1900 is but to forge a romance that exists nowhere, save in the writer's brain.

Taken as a whole the fielding has been bad, thoroughly bad. Men stand in the field to day like so many "little mounds of earth"*, or waxen figures in a third-rate tailor's shop. The energy, the life, the ever-watchfulness of ten years ago is gone, and in their place are lethargy, laziness, and a wonderful yearning for rest. Today a ball is driven through two so-called fieldsmen, and instead of a simultaneous rush to gather it, to hurl it to one end or the other, the two "little mounds of earth" stand facing each other with a lingering hope in their eyes that they will not be compelled to fetch it. There are, unfortunately, but a few counties, regarded as sides, to which the above censure does not apply. The two northern counties, the two best elevens of the year, fielded well, perhaps as well as any teams it has been my pleasure to play against, but the majority of the rest are absolutely outclassed by many a local club throughout the country.

Another feature that presents itself is that the lethargy, the laziness, the wonderful yearning for rest, are more noticeable in our great batsmen than in our great bowlers. A great batsman having produced a colossal score seems content with his performance, he loafs in the field, and when not loafing he peacefully slumbers. Sometimes, fortunately for the side on which he plays, he drifts into the slips and sustains a rude awakening when the rising ball is faintly touched and he receives it on the wrist or on the ankle, as the case may be. Naturally for a while, so long as the pain is acute, he is awake, and perhaps during this lucid interval he makes a catch or two, but then again the yearning for rest is felt, and peacefully he dozes. It were a good thing for cricket if many a great batsman could be confined to the slips, for there is always this chance of a sudden shock, a sudden realisation that he is in the field to do some work.

* A timid, though euphonious paraphrase of "Clods of Dirt"; a definition given by an old cricketer, of many latter-day fieldsmen.

THE SECRET OF INJURY-FREE WICKETKEEPING

D. L. A. Jephson, 1920

To many, who like myself were at Lord's last year during the Varsity Match and saw and chatted with Gregor MacGregor, the news of his sudden death in a nursing home came almost with the force of a physical blow.

I have known MacGregor and played cricket with him for more years than the average man cares to count. I have played with him in games which men label "first class" – in games of the country house, or "brown sherry" variety, as they are often derisively called, and I have played against him in college and county cricket, and whether with him or against him or under him, he was always the same – even-tempered – imperturbable – at times perhaps bordering on the cynical; rarely if ever depressed by fear of disaster, or over-elated with the joy of success.

Some men behind the "sticks" led away by the excitement of a close finish – the rapid advance of defeat or the approach of victory – snatch at an appeal – but MacGregor never did – he was a grand *clean* stumper – clean in every sense of the word – a stumper, absolutely "frill-less". He never gesticulated – he never jumped about like a jack-in-the-box or as a badly regulated monkey on a stick – he was the personification of quietude.

One of the most wonderful things connected with MacGregor's wicketkeeping is the fact that he never hurt his fingers. Now, I have looked with keen interest at the hands of many of our great stumpers, and some of them are as the gnarled roots of trees – twisted – curved – battered joints protrude everywhere. I looked at MacGregor's hands – and they were untouched – unmarked. "Why?" I asked him one day at The Oval – and this was his answer: "As a boy I learnt to bend my wrist backwards, so that I take the ball with my fingers pointing down – the result being that if I do not take it clean, my fingers are simply bent backwards – not driven in at the tips." In other words the front of his hand faced the ball – not his finger-tips, and this is the reason why he never broke down.

BATTING INNOVATION: DIFFERENT STROKES FOR DIFFERENT TIMES

Simon Briggs, 2003

According to the MCC Coaching Manual of 1952, the art of batting is a very simple one. This central text, which acquired an almost religious status within the game, has at its core the argument that every shot is really an adaptation of either the forward or back defence. It proceeds to list five major species – drives, cuts, pulls, hooks and leg glances – with all the fussiness of a lepidopterist.

Out on the field, even in 1952, things were a little more flexible. Denis Compton, the book's principal model, was a master of the sweep – a shot MCC appeared not to recognise. Yet the dominance of Test cricket, with the draw common and timeless Tests not consigned to history, fostered an essential conservatism among batsmen. For most of them, the first concern was to minimise risk; run-scoring came a long way down the agenda.

Fifty years on, the world's bowlers find themselves facing a quite different challenge. One-day cricket, with its improvised twists and pre-emptive strikes, is the paymaster now, and its values have spread. Something has happened to the players' inbuilt coaching manuals since 1952, something that Charles Darwin might have recognised. And even as this addendum to the batting handbook was being compiled, the pace of change kept rising, driven on by the sheer volume of top-level cricket.

The reverse sweep

There is evidence that the reverse sweep dates back at least to the 1920s, when K. S. Duleepsinhji played a wide off-side ball "backwards towards third man with his bat turned and facing the wicketkeeper". This contemporary account, written by the non-striker L. P. Jai, adds that "there was an appeal for unfair play but the umpire ruled it out". Duleepsinhji's opponents may never have seen the shot before, but they instinctively knew it was a transgressive stroke. In its most common form, it combines a right-hander's body position – left foot forward, right knee on ground, right hand below left on the handle – with a left-hander's horizontal swing of the bat, which moves clockwise from three o'clock to nine, sweeping the ball to third man: cricket's equivalent of cross-dressing.

This flagrant disregard for the first rule of Fred Trueman – cricket is a sideways-on game – explains why the reverse sweep has been treated with suspicion. The stroke's most famous moment came when the England captain Mike Gatting bungled it cata-strophically during the 1987 World Cup final. But it was rehabilitated in the early 1990s thanks to Warwickshire's captain–coach team, Dermot Reeve and Bob Woolmer. Their tactics were a response to the challenges thrown up by off-spinners in one-day cricket. If a bowler could sustain a good length, he could wheel away to a 3–6 on-side field with no one behind square on the off side. Woolmer and Reeve reckoned the reverse sweep could be more than just a run-getter in itself. By forcing the fielding side to cover third man, it would open up gaps for more orthodox strokeplay to exploit.

With respect to Duleepsinhji, the reverse sweep is basically a creature of the last two decades. Having successfully percolated down to club level, it can now claim to be the most important batting innovation since the arrival of helmets. Most contro-versially, New Zealand's Craig McMillan has started switching his hands as well as his intended scoring area, so transforming himself from right-hander to left-hander as the ball comes down. This has implications for the lbw law, among other things. The ploy has already forced an amendment to the Laws, defining off and leg stumps according to the batsman's stance "at the moment the ball comes into play for that delivery". The reverse-sweep taboo has been well and truly broken.

The scoop

This is another new twist on an old standard. In the early 20th century, an Australian undertaker-cum-wicketkeeper by the name of Hanson Carter developed a novel alternative to the leg glance. As Christopher Martin-Jenkins writes in his biographical dictionary of Test cricketers, Carter's "chief delight was a stroke by which he lifted the ball over his left shoulder just as a labourer shovels the dirt out of a drain he is digging".

We could call it the shovel, in Carter's honour, but that term has become asso-ciated with a subspecies of on-side deflections, so let's settle for the scoop. Pakistan's Moin Khan was a prime exponent of the stroke, using it to fine effect against Glenn McGrath in the 1999 World Cup. But while Moin's scoop was usually played off a good-length ball, with the aim of lofting it over the fine-leg boundary, the shot can also be a useful counter to the yorkers and low full tosses that dominate the final overs. To make this play, the batsman attenuates the stroke, bending his front knee and cocking his wrists like a tennis player punching a low forehand volley.

The cross-court flick

How do you score off a straight ball that is what the professionals call "back of a length"? A full-blooded pull is too risky unless the pitch is a belter or your name is Aravinda de Silva. But Tendulkar and Hayden have worked out a higher-percentage option: you offer a straight bat, as if to force down the ground, then turn the wrists at the last second. The ball tends to be heading just over the top of off stump, so the result looks like a waist-high tennis forehand, whipped cross-court with top-spin. It is hard to imagine this stroke being coached; it is best left to the elite, and even the world's top players have spent years developing their own takes on it. Tendulkar and his disciple, Sehwag, like to hang right back in the crease. Hayden, with his extra height, tends to step into the ball slightly. And then there is Vaughan, who has a technique all his own. Less wristy than the others, Vaughan uses a kind of straight-batted pull to hit back-of-a-length balls wide of mid-on. Because he shuffles across the stumps as the bowler releases, he can get his back foot outside off stump and swivel his hips to face midwicket. The bat comes down like a straight forcing shot, with Vaughan's body position providing the angle.

PITCHES TOO PERFECT   A. C. MacLaren, 1905

Until five years ago, any batsman who could make his century in a county match was, in my humble opinion, a good player, but owing to the too-perfect wickets of the last few seasons, making it impossible for good bowlers to hold their own against only moderate batsmen who lay themselves out for runs, my appreciation of certain centuries of late years has been considerably less. More runs are made today, not because the batting has improved, but owing to the fact that the wickets have been over-prepared – result, there have been fewer good bowlers annually, with a corresponding increase of good batsmen, enabling the good player to knock the ball about with such demoralising effect that, when the fair batsman comes along, the bowler has no reserve power left, resulting in this player today making far more runs than he would have done ten years or so back.

The greatest mischief caused by these too-perfect wickets is the compulsory cricket on the third day of the match without the remotest chance of a finish. This is the time, above all others, when our bowlers get ruined, having to bowl for some four or five hours without that enthusiasm so necessary if one is to be successful. This gruelling work, with no fitting reward at the end of it, is quite as fatiguing as the work meted out, at times, to some of our good bowlers who have to bowl so many hours at the nets to whatever duffer comes along. The after-effects of these performances are so telling that it is not long before some of these bowlers acquire a mechanical sort of style with no variation whatsoever, making it impossible for them to become bowlers in the true sense of the word.

PITCH PREPARATION UNCOVERED   David Green, 2001

Writing as one who first played county cricket 42 seasons ago, and has remained close to the game in one capacity or another, I cannot recall a time when English pitches have caused such dissatisfaction. Despite much-trumpeted advances in knowledge of soils and grasses, and the development of more sophisticated equipment for groundsmen, squares are widely considered unsatisfactory and attract blame when England's Test side performs poorly.

In 2000, former players such as Tony Brown, David Hughes and Phil Sharpe, operating under the leadership of former England captain Mike Denness, became what were euphemistically called "pitch liaison officers". Their brief was to check that pitches were only lightly grassed, so as not to favour seam bowlers, hard and dry to provide pace and carry for the quicker bowlers, and wearing sufficiently towards the end of the match to help spinners.

Monitoring should eliminate deliberate "fixing" of pitches. Of more concern to David Bridle, head groundsman at Bristol for 35 years, has been the tendency towards central control of pitches, which he feels has increased over the past 20 years. "There seems to be more and more pressure towards a uniform type of pitch. First Surrey loam was pushed, then Ongar loam. Also, the coarser rye-grasses were recommended ahead of the fine fescue grass favoured in the past." Rye-grass, if not cut close, offers greater movement off the seam. "The problem is that Ongar loam doesn't bond with all soils, and when there's no bond the surface cracks like crazy paving. We have too many different types of soil in this country for standardisation to work." Denness, however, rejected the idea that standardisation was being imposed, insisting that a menu of treatments had been set out from which groundsmen could make their choice.

Such doubts about the long-term value of covering pitches are shared by many who played or watched cricket on fully uncovered pitches. Yet the case for covering is a strong one. Prior to 1970, county pitches remained uncovered after the start of midweek games, though for matches beginning on Saturday the pitch was covered from Saturday evening to start of play on Monday morning. (This was in that blissful age when county matches were all of three days, started on Wednesday or Saturday, and cricket followers knew where they stood.)

Those who have not experienced fully uncovered pitches should realise that they were only rarely physically threatening to a batsman. Fast bowlers, because they could not keep their feet, generally could not operate on wet pitches. For slow bowlers, however, and particularly for finger-spinners, such a pitch, as it dried, would form a slight crust from which the ball would "pop" towards the splice of the bat or the glove.

In these circumstances, good footwork and judgment of length were essential for survival. The bowler, meanwhile, needed the strictest control because, with four or more close catchers, there were big spaces to thump the bad ball into. True, a hard pitch might "fly" for a few overs after a shower, but the odd smack in the ribs has always been part of the game. In good weather, there was little difference from today except, vitally, that pitches left open to wind, dew and early sun had a good deal more life in them. Moreover, they generally started as true as the groundsman could make them. There was little point in making "result" pitches when there was a good chance of the elements making them awkward anyway.

English cricket, then, seems likely to remain dominated by bowlers who rely on swing, seam or a combination of both. In fairness, there were signs last year that, on pitches starting absolutely dry, there can be sufficient encouragement for spin on the fourth day. Even so, with England scratching about for one spin bowler of Test quality, it bears recalling that there were times when they picked three in the same side.

Such days are not likely to return under present pitch-covering regulations. Because we miss the contrast and the technical challenge that spin provides, and because batsmen in today's domestic game are plainly missing it, too, this is a matter of regret for many of my generation.

Lancashire v Rest of England. At Kennington Oval, September 11, 13, 14, 1926. Lancashire, after the tremendous "towelling" their bowlers had met with, proceeded to bat so wretchedly, that they were all out in two hours for 134.

Little Wonder No. 24

CAPTAINCY: TYRANNY OR COLLABORATION?   Mike Brearley, 1982

The captain of a county cricket team is, all at once, managing director, union leader, and pit-face worker. He has almost total charge of the daily running of the concern; he is the main, if not the only, representative of the workforce in the boardroom (i.e. on the committee); and he has to field, bat and maybe bowl. He conducts the orchestra and he performs: perhaps on the front deck of the violins or as second tambourine. (It varies; I've been both.) Consequently it is hard to play God, to read the Riot Act about carelessness or incompetence, when one throws one's own wicket away or plays ineptly – if not today, tomorrow or yesterday. Any conscience on this score can inhibit one's own play: the captain oscillates between pawkiness – being over-anxious about carelessness – and, aware of the tendency to criticise others for slow scoring, an inappropriate desperation for quick runs.

Social changes, together with the related changes in cricket's arrangements, have over the past 15 or 20 years made the captain's job more, rather than less, difficult. Social hierarchies have become flatter: authority figures are taken for granted less and criticised more. A leader has to earn the respect of the led. Doctors are sued more frequently for alleged incompetence: I await the day when a captain is sued for negligence by an injured close fielder. The aristocratic tyrant has given way to the collaborative foreman, although some older players still yearn for the old-style discipline and for the voice accustomed to command. There are, moreover, county sides in which over half the players believe that they themselves should, or could, be captain. Twenty years ago, such ambitions would have been much more circumscribed. Envy, today, is less limited, and criticism from within the team less inhibited.

Similarly, criticism from outside is more vociferous. Today's press are more demanding and inquisitive. They expect answers, quotes, and cooperation. Kim Hughes, speaking at a dinner shortly before last summer's final Test, agreed that his team had not batted well and deserved criticism. But, he went on, some of the things said about them were such that, if you were walking along the street and a fellow said that to you, if you had any go about you at all, you'd deck him!

Last summer, I found an England team more embittered by the press than I'd ever known. Ian Botham refused to speak to them after his century at Leeds, and Bob Willis was outspoken on television immediately after that match. I myself felt that rows were planted, cultivated and encouraged out of the most arid, unpromising soil by certain sections of the media. Of course there always has been some meanness in the relations between performer and critic, but the type of writing fostered by the modern craving for excitement and sensation puts today's public figures under a type of pressure unknown to their pre-war predecessors.

CAPTAINCY: LOSING THE X-FACTOR
Michael Vaughan, 2009

A lot of captaincy is about acting: you want your team-mates to play naturally and be themselves, but the captain has to act. Your job is to lead with a calm authority. On that Sunday morning at Edgbaston in 2005 when we won the Second Test against Australia by two runs, I was unbelievably stressed. I was flapping like hell inside, but couldn't show it.

I always tried to put myself in the position of the players and think about what they wanted to hear. Sometimes it has to be harsh words; sometimes you have to pick them up. But whatever it is, you have to speak naturally and be consistent. You have to make them feel comfortable and wanted, especially a new player. No way can you arrive in the breakfast room or dressing-room and show the team that you are feeling bad. If you get nought, they don't want to see you sulking for three or four hours; you have got to go and sit on the balcony and front up. The players in my last year as captain didn't know I was struggling – and that is one of the things I will always be proudest of.

Cricket is all about decision-making. As a batsman you have to make a decision every ball you face, and a captain has to make decisions all the time. Do you bat or bowl first? What's the batting order? Which bowlers do you put on and what about the field-placings? Do you change something so you are three or four overs ahead of the game, or do you let it go and perhaps allow the game to drift? For three-quarters of the time I was England captain I was 100% confident in my decision-making and didn't give a monkey's about what anybody thought.

I wasn't very good at switching off. I thought about the captaincy 24/7 and that is why it took its toll. There is always going to be some negative stuff, like whether you are going to tour Zimbabwe or not, and how you cope decides how long you can captain for. Even in the year out with my knee injury I was still thinking about how to make us a great team. Even when playing golf, after two or three holes I'd get back to strategies for beating Australia and what sort of cricket we had to play.

Dealing with the media was one of the best parts of the job. It got me down in the end, but in general I liked going to press conferences, and talking to TV when doing the toss and putting on a positive spin, or doing interviews after the game. I would love to do that part of the job again. In a strange way I found it more difficult to explain the good times and the victories than the defeats. I said that for three-quarters of my time I didn't worry about my decision-making. Towards the end, especially in the last series against South Africa, I started to question myself – and in sport, the more you start to think, the more you have a problem. I didn't want to go on as captain for a year too long.

Generally it is down to luck: you move a fielder wider at slip and the ball goes to him. Then something changes, and the ball goes between the fielders, and the sparkle goes and the X-factor disappears. In my last Test at Edgbaston, Graeme Smith was given not out when the TV replays showed he might have gloved Monty Panesar. In the first half of my captaincy that sort of decision had gone my way. When Mike Kasprowicz gloved one down the leg side off Steve Harmison on that Sunday at Edgbaston in 2005, Billy Bowden gave him out. Or if Ricky Ponting had chosen to bat first in that Test, that would have been luck again and the result could have been different. We would have gone 2–0 down and I would never have been installed as a great captain. There is an egg-timer out there, and my time had run out.

CHEATING AND CHUCKING

A GAME IN SHAME
Mihir Bose, 2001

Cricket corruption, like taxes and poverty, may always be with us. But after cricket's *annus horribilis* of 2000 we can, for the first time, understand how a combination of players' greed, dreadful impotence and infighting by cricket administrators, and a radical shift in cricketing power from England to the Indian subcontinent helped create cricket's darkest chapter.

Two incidents illustrate this, and both occurred in India. The first was in 1984, some months after India's unexpected victory in the 1983 World Cup. One evening a Delhi bank clerk, Mukesh Kumar Gupta, was walking near his home in the grimy bylanes of old Delhi when he saw some people betting small amounts on a cricket match. This, as he would later tell the Central Bureau of Investigation, India's top police investigators, caught his imagination. Having ascertained that the betters were neither well educated nor well informed about cricket, Gupta began to hone his cricket knowledge by listening to the BBC. And over the next decade he would travel the world, following cricket and meeting many of the world's top cricketers. Meeting and bribing.

Meanwhile, as Gupta was transforming himself from a lowly bank clerk to cricket's most notorious match-fixer, and enriching himself in the process, cricket was also being reinvented and enriched. By the mid-1990s, even the Ashes Tests, the bedrock of the international game for more than 100 years, had been – away from the insular focus of England – sidelined in favour of one-day internationals.

By 1996, and the heyday of Gupta the match-fixer, there had been an enormous spread of such matches, the greatest expansion in the history of the game, with series in "non-cricketing" venues such as Sharjah, Singapore and Toronto. Sharjah had started by staging benefit matches for Indian and Pakistani cricketers, who had no recourse to an English-style system. Toronto provided a North American haven for India versus Pakistan, not always possible in the subcontinent for political reasons, while Singapore, and similar tournaments, represented the commercial opportunities that limited-overs cricket provided to businessmen seeking to reach the emerging Indian middle classes.

Ironically, it was a Delhi crime-branch detective, Ishwar Singh Redhu, who, on April 7, 2000, forced everyone to come clean. Asked to investigate complaints by Delhi businessmen of extortion with menace, he was listening to telephone taps on two suspects when Cronje's name – and the fixing of one-day games in the current series between India and South Africa – cropped up. Then Cronje himself was heard discussing the fixing of matches with a London-based Indian businessman called Sanjeev (also known as Sanjay) Chawla.

Before that moment, five and a half years after Shane Warne, Mark Waugh and Tim May had made allegations of match-fixing against the Pakistan captain, Salim Malik, there had been inquiries in India, Pakistan and Sri Lanka, as well as media investigations led by the Indian magazine *Outlook*. But apart from the fines on Waugh and Warne for receiving $A6,000 and $A5,000 respectively from an Indian book-maker in return for information, which the Australian board and ICC had covered up, nothing had been done. It would subsequently emerge that Justice Qayyum had recommended a life ban on Salim Malik, but his report was still to be published.

The immediate reactions to the Delhi police's charges of match-fixing and betting against Cronje and the team-mates he had mentioned to Chawla – Nicky Boje, Herschelle Gibbs, Pieter Strydom and Henry Williams – were of utter disbelief that a born-again Christian like Cronje could be involved. Cronje denied every-thing – "Absolute rubbish." Ali Bacher, managing director of South African cricket, backed him – "unquestionable integrity and honesty" – and the South Africans denounced the tactics of the Delhi police.

In June, two weeks after the Qayyum report was published, a South African judicial commission under retired judge Edwin King began to hear devastating evidence from South African players. The entire South African team had considered an offer to throw a one-day match in 1996 and, in yet another confession, Cronje admitted he could have taken as much as $US140,000 from Gupta and other book-makers between 1996 and 2000.

Gupta's first cricket contact was Ajay Sharma, very much a bit-player in inter-national cricket – one Test and 31 one-day internationals for India – but a useful conduit to other cricketers. They first met at a club tournament in Delhi in 1988 when Gupta, impressed by the way Sharma batted, gave him 2,000 rupees (£100 at the current rate of exchange) as a token of his appreciation. Gupta saw this as an investment for the future, and it was to prove a shrewd one. A fortnight later Sharma contacted him and soon the two men had formed a bond which, as the CBI report made clear, "was to prove beneficial to both". When Sharma toured New Zealand with India in 1990, Gupta claimed he provided him with information about the pitch, weather and the team which he used to make "a good amount of money". Sharma denies he provided any information, but he did later introduce Gupta to Manoj Prabhakar, who was keen to get a new car: "A Maruti Gypsy with wide tyres." On the 1990 tour of England, said Gupta, Prabhakar gave him information about the team and "underperformed" in one of the drawn Tests. Prabhakar got his

Maruti Gypsy – he told the CBI he paid for it himself – and Gupta got to know yet more cricketers. The picture Gupta painted for the CBI, which was often backed in testimony from Sharma, Prabhakar, Azharuddin, Ajay Jadeja and even Cronje, shows how frighteningly casual the whole thing was.

The age of Gupta the match-fixer ended in May 1998, and there is some evidence to suggest that the high tide of cricket match-fixing ended then, although Majid Khan, former chief executive of the Pakistan board, remains convinced that Pakistan's two World Cup losses to India and Bangladesh in 1999 were fixed. However, no player or bookie has come forward to provide any details, and the World Cup did not fall within the compass of Justice Qayyum's inquiry.

Since its initial report, the CBI has begun looking into links between cricketers, bookmakers and the Indian underworld, and could discover more secrets. The King Commission wants to go back to the beginning of 1992, when South Africa re-emerged into international cricket. It has high hopes of unlocking more secrets, but others in South Africa would prefer to see a line drawn under the whole sorry business. This would be a mistake. The high tide of match-fixing in cricket may have ebbed, but the full story of what happened throughout the 1990s has not yet been told.

BENT: A HISTORY OF CHUCKING
David Frith, 2005

Across the ages, apart from match-fixing and political interference from outside its walls, cricket has wrestled with no more contentious issue than suspect bowling actions. The complaints against Arthur Mold which W. G. Grace piped through his whiskers in the 1890s were paraphrased and purpled up more than a century later by Nasser Hussain and directed at Muttiah Muralitharan. The 1998 edition of the *Wisden Book of Cricket Records* has a disconcerting four-page list of bowlers who have been no-balled for throwing.

The pioneers of overarm bowling, before its legalisation in 1864, were dubbed "throwers" simply because they raised their arms above the permitted level. Earlier still, curious underhand deliveries, as purveyed by the Hambledon ace David Harris, involved kinky elbow movement, but nobody complained. It was the turn of the century before cricket began to catch up with those who threw in the modern sense. Sydney Pardon, *Wisden* editor from 1891 to 1925, played a key role in eliminating the scourge of throwing when it first became rampant. He condemned the actions of Ernie Jones and Tom McKibbin after Australia's 1896 tour of England (adding a dollop of diplomacy by stating that it was all England's fault: the Australians were merely copying).

A big, fearless, itinerant Australian umpire, Jim Phillips, finished the job. Having called Jones once in a state match and once in a Melbourne Test during 1897-98, Phillips came over to England and dealt with somebody at the other end of the social scale, the eminent Mr C. B. Fry, whose action had been widely condemned. Encouraged, other umpires then called Fry. Editor Pardon was ecstatic. "A case of long-delayed justice," he called it. Fry thereafter concentrated on his batting.

But Phillips returned and dealt with a far more significant threat, the Lancashire and England fast bowler Arthur Mold, called by Phillips at Trent Bridge in 1900 and then again, 16 times in ten overs, at Old Trafford against Somerset the next year. Between the two seasons, the county captains had agreed not to use 14 bowlers regarded as suspect; Mold's captain, Archie MacLaren, was the one dissenter, so more direct action had become essential. Film of Mold, recently discovered, reveals a bowling action seemingly without blemish. It was shot at Old Trafford in 1901, the day after Phillips had called him the last time. Mold was now conscious of being filmed, and was probably not only on his best behaviour but below his lethal top speed. Still, he vanished from first-class cricket, and thereafter reckoned that his career (1,673 low-cost wickets) amounted to nothing. The game was cleansed – for the time being.

The outbreak of chucking more than half a century later was eventually put down just as dramatically and symbolically in 1963 by the no-balling of Ian Meckiff, the Australian left-armer, four times in an over by Col Egar in the Brisbane Test against South Africa. This was another intervention carried out by an umpire of strong character who knew he was backed by the administrators. Umpires have often looked in vain for the backing of the authorities who appointed them. The great Frank Chester was not alone in being convinced that South Africa's 1951 tourist Cuan McCarthy was a thrower, but the influential and incurable appeaser P. F. "Plum" Warner urged him to hold his fire, pleading: "These people are our guests." Chester thereafter gazed ostentatiously into the distance while standing at square leg whenever McCarthy bowled.

In the atmosphere of the time, almost everyone who did not have Alec Bedser's perfect action gave rise to suspicion, even Fred Trueman and Brian Statham. This was cricket's McCarthyite period. But realisation was now dawning that some bowlers were endowed with what was termed "hyper-extension" of the elbow – an ability to drop the extended forearm below the horizontal. The whippy Statham, who took 252 wickets for England, had this abnormality. Harold Rhodes had a similar arm formation, played in only two Tests, was called several times while playing for Derbyshire in the 1960s, and wrote an understandably bitter book.

Ernie Jones was no-balled only twice, which suggests he might have thrown only his extra-fast ball. These occasional throwers are hardest to sort out. England's Peter Loader was thought by many to throw his bouncer and his slower ball. Similarly with Charlie Griffith. He lumbered to the crease and bowled unexceptional medium-fast – until something almost invisible came down on the batsman. Brian Close later reflected that "you could almost put one hand in your pocket and play him... then one would come at you four yards quicker!"

In an age when freedom of speech was in much better health than subsequently, several major batsmen, Ken Barrington and Norm O'Neill among them, aired their anguish over Griffith's action, and Richie Benaud, recently retired as a player, was not exactly fêted in the Caribbean when he produced incriminating photographs. In the match in which a Griffith bouncer almost killed the Indian captain Nari Contractor at Bridgetown, he was called for throwing, but not until an all-but-unnoticed one-off by Arthur Fagg in the West Indians' match against Lancashire in 1966 did it happen again.

Once more it was timid officialdom that had blocked potential action by conscientious umpires. Cec Pepper, a formidable Australian cricketer who settled in England and might have become the Jim Phillips of his day, was convinced that

Griffith threw but, to his disgust, he was quietly asked by the rulers of the English game to do nothing.

Bowlers tend to protest their innocence to the grave. One exception comes to mind. In 1999 the former West Indies spinner Sonny Ramadhin, in an interview with Peter Johnson in the *Daily Mail*, confessed that his faster ball was thrown: "Nowadays, the television cameras would have picked it up immediately... But I got away with it in every grade of cricket for 30 years." Ramadhin, who bowled with sleeves buttoned at the wrist, expressed doubts about Muralitharan's action, and marvelled that he had taken so many Test wickets.

After decades of muddled attempts to defenestrate erring bowlers, the ICC procedure has seemed to be close to perfection, apart from the clause permitting reported bowlers to continue playing while still undergoing remedial work. The ICC pursues a progressive scientific charter, though the precise effect remains unpredictable, especially with this increased licence for all to flex the bowling arm as much as 15 degrees. Over a century ago, Spofforth surprisingly suggested that bowlers should be allowed to throw, and the matter would soon sort itself out. Perhaps even the Demon himself did not quite know what he meant by that. Maybe we are about to see all manner of dart throwers and baseball pitchers entering the bowling ranks. It does feel as if something precious and fundamental is being torn from the heart of the game.

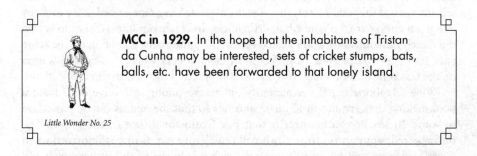

MCC in 1929. In the hope that the inhabitants of Tristan da Cunha may be interested, sets of cricket stumps, bats, balls, etc. have been forwarded to that lonely island.

Little Wonder No. 25

ASIA'S ILLICIT GAMBLING DENS

Rob Crilly, 2011

Business is good for Goshi and his small band of bookmakers, tucked away in a smoky front room overlooking the slums of Lahore. And it's about to get better. "I'm going to buy a Prado after the World Cup – you know, one of the big 4×4s with the alloys and the fancy stuff," he says, throwing back his head and laughing. It is not an idle boast. His makeshift gambling operation rakes in millions of rupees with every one-day international – even in a conservative Muslim country where betting is illegal.

The den was in full swing barely a day after Salman Butt, Mohammad Aamer and Mohammad Asif had received lengthy bans for their role in the spot-fixing scandal. Yet nobody thought the punishments would help clean up Pakistani cricket. "The bans aren't as heavy as they could have been. No one has been banned for life," says Goshi. "So when you look at how much players can earn from working with bookies – and many of these players come from very poor homes – I don't think this will put people off getting involved in fixing." A flat-screen television on one wall shows the action as James Anderson fires a delivery at Brad Haddin in the seventh one-day international between Australia and England. Five bookies keep one eye on the TV as they answer phones, shout odds and note down wagers in neat Urdu script. It does not matter to them that, in Doha, three of Pakistan's leading players have just been sanctioned for corruption. A scattering of cushions on the floor is the only concession to comfort. The bookies sit cross-legged as they concentrate on their calculators, pausing only for a drag on marijuana-laced cigarettes. Illicit dens just like this are thriving across Pakistan, and in India, where bookmakers run tiny businesses from bedrooms, empty offices and half-built houses – almost anywhere with a television and a mobile-phone signal.

One of the eight wireless phones spread in a semi-circle on the floor suddenly belts out a lively Bollywood tune. Even at 8.30am there are punters ready to place bets on a match taking place on the other side of the world. "This is nothing," says Goshi, who asks that his full name is not used. "It's early. Everyone spent yesterday watching the Pakistan match [a one-day international in New Zealand]. They are only getting up now. It will get busier." He notes down a bet of 20,000 rupees (£160) on an England win. The minimum stake is set at Rs5,000, a considerable amount of money in a country where one third of the population survives on less than a pound a day. "Our clients are businessmen. No one else can really afford it," says Goshi in Urdu, as he sits leaning against the wall. The phones – each connected to a tape recorder to avoid any disagreements over who paid what – ring incessantly when punters dial in to bet on the match outcome, or a complicated series of "figure" bets, gambling on the score after 10- or 20-over periods. Goshi's crew shun fancy bets, where gamblers lay wagers on the outcome of individual balls, as too complex and too easy to fix.

One telephone is left permanently on speakerphone to receive odds from a bookmaking mastermind in Karachi; another so that the figures can be passed on to some 20 smaller outfits nearby that pay Goshi for a slice of the action. The business relies in part on trust. Cash will not change hands until tomorrow, when Goshi's runners will fan out through the richer suburbs to collect payments and deliver winnings. The figures soon mount up. A day earlier Goshi's small team took Rs2m (£16,000) during the match between Pakistan and New Zealand. During the World Cup, he reckons they will earn Rs10m (£80,000) in profit alone. And with as many as 1,000 illegal dens operating in Lahore – according to police estimates – millions of pounds change hands each match.

But with that comes the darker side of Pakistan's illegal industry. Allegations of match-fixing and spot-fixing have dogged the national team for years. "It stands to reason. You see how big this is," says Goshi. "If Australia are the favourites and loads of money is being put on them, then people could make a lot of money by getting them to lose." On another afternoon, in another den – this one set up in a squalid bedroom, a temporary home while police raided properties close to the normal office – another bookie, PK, said he had no doubt fixing was rife during the England–Pakistan series of 2010. "When we set our own odds we always lose. But when we take the odds from bookmakers in Karachi then we stay in profit. So we think they must have inside information on what is going on," he says. "We knew Pakistan would win last week. The odds we were given didn't make sense."

He has little in the way of evidence, other than a hunch and some painful losses. At the same time, though, these Lahore bookmakers say their operation sits at the bottom of a web connected by telephone to Karachi, the teeming, chaotic commercial capital of Pakistan, and from there on to Mumbai. The money, they say, ends up in Dubai and England. Many believe Dawood Ibrahim, the notorious Indian crime lord, sits at the top. As well as suspecting him of racketeering and drug-running, the US believes he has links to al-Qaeda and has funded terrorist attacks in India. "Nothing this big, and crossing so many borders, could run without his say-so," according to a police officer speaking on condition of anonymity.

The phones ring all morning, as the narrow room gradually fills with smoke, dimming the sunshine flooding through a single window. Only when England's fifth wicket falls for 64 in the early afternoon, and Australia look certain to end up winning the series 6–1, does the betting stop. "It's difficult to judge when Australia are batting because you never know what they might do," says Goshi. "But I think it's obvious the match is over. The book is closed." Not for long.

THE SPOT-FIXING TRIAL   R. D. J. Edwards, 2012

From the moment proceedings started on October 5, this was like nothing I had seen in a decade of court reporting – not least because it was one of the first trials in which journalists could tweet live. Salman Butt and Mohammad Asif, two Pakistanis in a foreign country, two sportsmen in a courtroom, should have felt out of place in this functional, sterile London building bedecked with cheap wooden panelling. Lawyers with a shaky grip on cricketing parlance tried to explain the seemingly irrelevant minutiae of the game to a bewildered jury of 12 self-professed laymen. Butt had to be interrupted by his lawyer as he started to define a doosra, while Asif, whose run-up was helpfully described by his lawyer as 1,058 inches long, uproariously called for a new ball so he could explain his art. Mr Justice Cooke, the affable high court judge, stopped him and said with a smile: "You don't have to give away all your secrets, you know."

Long afternoons of a trial which ate up 132 court hours were spent watching cricket on television. For expert opinion, the prosecution turned to David Kendix, the Lord's scorer, ICC ratings guru and trained actuary, who was more clinical than a pathologist in a murder trial. In surely the greatest statistical examination of the no-ball, Kendix revealed they represented 1.08% of all deliveries from the previous 240 Tests; that one in 130 of Aamer's deliveries was a no-ball; and one in 90 of Asif's. In total, said Kendix, there was a one in 1.5m chance that anyone could have correctly predicted the timing of three no-balls.

The cricket fanatic had plenty more to revel in, and it was extraordinary to watch Butt being asked, on oath, to justify his mediocre Test average of 30. He admitted the figure was unacceptable, but partly blamed Pakistan's lack of home matches. He also apportioned his side's fielding woes at Lord's to the difficulty of seeing the ball "because of the ties the members wear", and described how, in Pakistan, a nightwatchman is known as a "sacrificial goat".

The evidence lurched from bizarre insights into how younger Pakistan players all dine out at the sandwich chain Subway, via sublime moments of bitchiness (the resentment at having to "kiss the arse" of former Test captain Shahid Afridi "every day"), to the ridiculous boasts of *[the agent Mazhar]* Majeed, who even the judge agreed was a "bullshitter" after he claimed to be close friends with Hollywood star Brad Pitt. When Asif later turned on his captain, claiming Butt deliberately took up an unorthodox fielding position to pressure him into bowling his no-ball, 20 minutes of argument were devoted to the definition of silly mid-off. Butt's barrister, Ali Bajwa, QC, a cricket fan, even argued that Butt's position, straight and on the drive, came with an impeccable precedent: Michael Vaughan used it to stifle Matthew Hayden during the 2005 Ashes.

There was no longer any doubt: the debate was going over the jury's head. Aftab Jafferjee, QC, prosecuting, appeared to have an open-and-shut case. But despite a groaning weight of circumstantial evidence, the outcome still felt in the balance when he wrapped up his arguments at the end of the trial's eighth day. Some of the jury appeared sniffy about the testimony of Mazher Mahmood, the *News of the World*'s so-called Fake Sheikh, who – by dint of carrying out the sting – had proved himself a brilliant liar and undercover operator (the hiding of secret microphones in his underpants became known in court as the "crotch recording"). The defence inevitably accused Mahmood of the phone hacking which had closed down his paper three months earlier; they were, he snapped, "barking down the wrong tree".

Jafferjee himself admitted he was no cricket expert, despite his Sri Lankan heritage. But he came into his own as a brilliant interrogator when Butt and Asif took the stand. In some of the most dramatic moments of the trial, the façade of the likeable cricketers with their matey anecdotes came crashing down as every word of their defence was scrutinised under cross-examination. Butt had crafted an image of a man too honourable, too intelligent and, frankly, too rich to get involved in corruption. Then, he came unstuck. Early on, Butt had taken against Jafferjee, shaking his head haughtily when the prosecutor claimed he lacked the skill to play out a maiden over against the new ball during the Oval Test. Now he tried to get too cute – and spectacularly misjudged the moment.

Asked if he agreed that fixing could "destroy" the game, Butt murmured: "It depends." Jafferjee's ears pricked up and he went for the kill. Butt stumbled into an extraordinary analogy, claiming American wrestling proved fans watched the sport even when it was known to be rigged. It was a turning point and, as Jafferjee tore into him, Butt went on the defensive, his voice frequently rising with anger. He stood with his arms crossed and nostrils flaring, attempting to stare down his interrogator from five yards, like a batsman in the prime of battle.

IN MY DAY – PLAYERS REMEMBER

THE IDEAL REMINISCENCE
A. G. Steel, 1891

I was sitting in the smoking-room of a country house one night last autumn, thoroughly tired out after a long day's shooting. I felt perfectly comfortable in my large armchair watching the smoke slowly ascend from my "briar". My companions, of whom there were several, were all lazily inclined, and beyond an occasional remark about some shooting incident of the day none seemed inclined to do much talking. I was dreamily thinking of some old Cambridge friends now scattered over various quarters of the globe, and as their names flashed through my mind each one brought happy recollections of well-fought matches at Fenner's, Lord's, and The Oval. I was far away, oblivious almost to the presence of others, and my thoughts in their hazy wanderings had fixed on one particular hit – never by me to be forgotten. Charley Bannerman was the striker, P. H. Morton the bowler, and the match Cambridge v Australians at Lord's, 1878. Half-asleep I seemed to see again that sturdy striker raise his massive shoulders and hit the ball a warrior's knock; the ball flew low, over the bowler's head, struck the iron-bound ground 20 yards in front of the outfield, and bounded right over the awning of Lord Londesborough's drag and struck the wall behind. Truly a mighty hit. I could almost hear the cheers and shouts that greeted it.

NO ONE TO MATCH WALLY
Frank Woolley, 1939

The time has come for me to say farewell to cricket as a player, and I readily acquiesce to the invitation of the Editor of *Wisden* to record some of the greatest moments of my career. It is a severe wrench leaving the game which I have enjoyed so much. Even my last season in first-class cricket brought me memorable days when I touched my best form, but I do think it is best to say goodbye before I fail to satisfy my admirers. I believe I could have gone on for another season or two, but I might have struck a bad patch and then many people would have said, "Why doesn't he retire?"

I do not think there are so many good players in the game now as before the *[1914–18]* War. In the old days we were probably educated in cricket in a far more serious way than now. For the purpose of giving the younger people my idea of the difference I will put up Walter Hammond, England's captain, as an example. Before 1914 there were something like 30 players up to his standard and he would have been in the England team only if at the top of his form. I make these remarks without casting the slightest reflection on Hammond. He is a grand player and one of the greatest all-round cricketers since the War – in fact, the greatest.

I doubt whether English cricket has really recovered from the effects of the War. You see, we missed half a generation, and since then young men have found many other ways of occupying their leisure hours. Still, I believe it is only a passing phase and cricket will one day produce an abundance of great players.

Touching on another personal subject I have been asked if I can explain why I was dismissed so many times in the nineties. I can honestly say that with me it was never a question of the nervous nineties. Lots of times I was out through forcing the game. We were never allowed to play for averages in the Kent side or take half an hour or more to get the last ten runs under normal conditions. We always had to play the game and play for the team. It is a Kent tradition.

TOO MUCH CRICKET
Sir Pelham Warner, 1955

The late Lord Harris once said that "the more cricket played the better for everyone", but I think this great increase has brought some disadvantages. The Australians and others of our opponents across the seas play far less than we do, yet often are more than our equals. From May 1 to the middle of September our cricketers have a heavy strain put upon them and tend to regard some of their fixtures not as an event, but as a sort of routine.

In 1903, however, a departure was made from precedent and the MCC undertook the management, financing and selection of teams abroad and have continued to do so ever since. By the way, in that year, when I went to Australia, there was not a single cricket correspondent from an English newspaper accompanying the team, and this continued until, I think, 1932, when two or three made the voyage. Before 1932, descriptions of the matches were done by *Reuters* and *Central News* representatives in Australia, and very excellent and accurate were their criticisms.

In September last, 30 correspondents left England in the *Orsova* and on arrival in Australia were joined by representatives of the Australian press. They form an army in themselves. Many of them are very good indeed and help us through the winters of our discontent, but others indulge over-much in personalities and are not always accurate. They tend to cheapen the game. A terrific amount of lime-light beats on the cricketers of today and their private lives are invaded; this may, and in fact does, lead to irritations and misunderstandings. In the world as it is today, any individual who happens for the moment, however briefly, to be in the public eye, has about as much privacy as a goldfish. The newspapers and the BBC wield great influence, and in all matters the greater the responsibility the greater the care.

Recently there has been a move to cover the whole length of the pitch and, under pressure from the Australians, the MCC agreed to accept this during the recent tour as an experiment. At the time of writing it is not known whether the experiment is likely to win favour, but many cricketers of experience and repute in both countries have expressed strong opposition to it. They argue that it would make cricket a mechanical and plumb-wicket game and create nothing but dullness and tedium. Many indeed are the instances of tense and dramatic moments and hours produced by rain and sticky wickets; they live in the history of the game. And surely the real test of a batsman is his ability to make runs under difficult conditions. Moreover, variety is the very essence of cricket. If we are not careful, we might eventually come to a type of indoor game with a glass roof over the whole of the ground. I fear that £ s. d. is at the bottom of these ideas, and when finance – too much of it – comes in at the door, the best interests of cricket may well fly out of the window. To my mind it is not cricket as it was intended to be played.

FROM DR GRACE TO PETER MAY · Herbert Strudwick, 1959

I feel that I owe a debt to a lady, a Miss Wilson, daughter of the Vicar of Mitcham, where I was born on January 28, 1880. She used to supervise the choirboys' cricket matches in which, when I was about ten years old, I took part. It was my habit to run in from cover to the wicket to take returns from the field and I apparently did this well enough to prompt her to say one day: "You ought to be a wicketkeeper." From that time I became a stumper, and I was sufficiently good at the job to play for Surrey for 25 years and to keep for England 28 times at a period when Australia and South Africa were our only Test opponents.

I have known nearly all the famous cricketers of the 20th century, from Dr W. G. Grace to Peter May, the present Surrey and England captain. One recollection I have of Grace was when I played for Surrey against London County at the Old Crystal Palace ground in 1902. On the day that WG bowled me for my second duck of the match, Southampton and Sheffield United were fighting out the FA Cup final, also at the Crystal Palace. As I passed the Doctor on my way out, he said to me: "Why didn't you tell me you got a duck in the first innings, youngster? I would have given you one to get off the mark." "Never mind, sir," I said. "I want to see the second half of that Cup final." And away I scampered.

The young professional of today has a much easier time than when I began, of that I am sure. First of all, he has a fixed wage guaranteed all the year round, differing, I presume, according to the ability of the player. My first wage was £1 per week – no match fees – for four months during the summer, expenses, train-fare and 2s 6d a day for lunch. Tea was free, and how we enjoyed it. If we could not get lunch on the ground, we went to a pub, for there was always one close by. There we had either arrowroot biscuit and cheese or a large piece of bread and cheese. That cost 9d or 1s 0d, so we made 1s 6d on our lunch allowance – which was then quite a lot of money.

In my younger days cricket was the only summer sport, except for golf and lawn tennis, which were too expensive for the average chap. So most people played cricket, and the majority of spectators understood the finer points of the game and appreciated good bowling besides good batting and fielding. For that reason crowds of that time showed more patience than those of to-day. They were content to watch and enjoy cricket, knowing full well that the bowler was doing his best to get the batsmen out and not to give him runs. Another thing, cricket received more space in the newspapers, and it was given to good news and not to how many fours a batsman hit and how long he batted. I wish that reporters would be more free with praise instead of finding so much to criticise in the best game in the world.

More amateurs played 60 years ago than now. In 1899 Surrey had seven at different times, Gloucestershire seven, Somerset eight, Middlesex seven, Kent eight, Essex six, Hampshire five and so on. Now the amateurs cannot spare the time and so have taken up golf. As long as I can remember, Surrey have had an amateur captain, and I hope they will always find one good enough to take over. They are lucky to have such a fine player as Mr May to lead them and to captain England.

I was naturally delighted when I got my first game with Surrey's first team, against the West Indies in 1900, though I had the feeling that a better man in Fred Stedman was standing down. Wicketkeepers used to have to put up with a good deal of knocking about then, for it was not always possible to gauge how the ball would come to you and our equipment was not what it is now. Stedman used to protect his chest with a copy of the South Western Railway timetable, and on one occasion, after receiving a specially heavy blow, he remarked to a team-mate: "I shall have to catch a later train tonight. That one knocked off the 7.30!"

Middlesex v Worcestershire. At Lord's, May 22, 23, 1929. Although Gilbert, the Old Oxonian, afterwards met with pronounced success, taking five of the eight remaining wickets, the home county won very easily on Thursday by an innings and 190 runs. Some exception was taken to the condition of the pitch, Gilbert, indeed, addressing a letter on the subject to *The Times*.

Little Wonder No. 26

STEALING SINGLES WITH JACK HOBBS

Andy Sandham, 1972

I was given a game in 1911 for the county eleven against Cambridge University and, in my very first first-class match, I scored 53. There was at that time a public house with a flat roof over on the gasworks side of The Oval, with six or seven tiered seats for customers who could see cricket for nothing. As the pubs were then open all day long and the beer was both cheaper and stronger, the customers by the afternoon got a bit under the influence and frequently gave us "the bird". I got it on my first appearance and I thought it rather hard, for I naturally wanted to do well and took only two hours for my 53. All this, too, from people who were not in the ground!

We lesser lights had to put in our own practice with the coach at 10am and then wait for any visiting players and our own first-eleven players who came out for a knock and bowl to them. I remember rushing to bowl against G. L. Jessop, but after he played "forward" and the ball narrowly missed my head, I had sense enough to bowl at his legs.

Soon after my "baptism" against Cambridge, I was as usual bowling at the nets when, ten minutes before the start of a match with Lancashire, I was told that I was playing, Tom Hayward having dropped out. This was such a shock that I nearly dropped, too. In those days there was a telegraph office on the ground and, having seen the batting order, I sent my father a wire telling him the news. My father, who was a Lancashire man, had taken a few hours off from work and come to The Oval, so that he missed my telegram. He told me that he was sitting in the crowd, but had not got a scorecard. So he turned to the man next to him and asked: "Who is this lad coming in to bat?" He was shaken when he was told: "It's a second-eleven lad named Sandham." I scored 60 and my father said that after I was out he left for home.

I remember being nearly run out at 49 by that splendid batsman, R. H. Spooner. Come to think of it, it seems rather silly to risk a run-out at 49 or 99. In this connection, I have often been asked how Jack Hobbs and I managed to steal so many sharp runs. I guess I must have run hundreds for him, for I never called him for one! As a matter of fact, he used not to call, for I knew from his push-stroke to the off that he wanted to run. I was always a yard or so down the pitch after the ball had been delivered and as I was rather fast between wickets, he knew I would make it. I remember Herbert Sutcliffe talking to me after being in with Jack for the first time about these short runs. I said: "Well, I know when he wants a quick run without calling, so I run." Herbie said something to the effect that he was not going to run any; they had got to stop; but I noticed that he found that he had to when coupled with Jack in Tests – and a jolly good job they made of it, too.

Many people have asked if any particular person taught me. The fact is that I must have had a natural aptitude for batting and I always watched the established players. I was always on the players' balcony to see Tom Hayward and Jack Hobbs open the innings for Surrey. Tom was my idol then, though later on he frightened me, for when I was twelfth man away from home and he had made a good score, he would bark at me to get him a whisky and soda. I would say "Yes, sir," but was afraid to ask him for the money. My own fault, I suppose, but Tom had many a whisky and soda on me! He was the senior professional and well in with the various captains Surrey had had, and what he said went.

Fielding, I think, may be better than in my time – maybe because we played till later in life and were not termed veterans at 39 or 40. It must, however, be remembered that we had to chase the ball to the far-distant boundaries, for the 75-yards boundary was not then the vogue. I remember before the 1914 war, when I was in and out of the county side, I played in a game against Oxford University at The Oval. In those days three or four of the eleven were rested for such matches and the likes of me given the chance. Tom Rushby had asked for a rest but was refused and, no doubt fed up, did not try too hard when put on to bowl. I was at mid-on when he bowled from the Vauxhall end of a pitch well over on the gasometer side. The other boundary was a very long way away and when Tom was hit to the deep I chased the ball, thinking: "I wonder how many these lively young men have run?" In fact they ran six! I had scarcely regained my position at mid-on than I was off again next ball to the same place, and again they ran six. Slightly annoyed with Tom and also out of breath, I had to pursue the next ball in the same direction though they only ran five that time! It was on my third journey that the secretary, Mr Findlay, looked out of his office window. Next morning he sent for me and said chidingly that he was surprised to see me not running very fast – though he did apologise when I pointed out that I had chased the two previous balls while 12 runs were scored!

VIEW FROM THE PAVILION

MANAGING TOURS TO AUSTRALIA	Sir Frederick Toone, 1930

So far as I am personally concerned, I have from the very outset regarded these tours primarily as imperial enterprises, tending to cement friendship between the Mother Country and her Dominions. Players, therefore, selected to take part in them – and this has always been borne in mind by the MCC – should not be chosen for their cricket qualities alone. They must be men of good character, high principle, easy of address, and in every personal sense worthy of representing their country, in all circumstances, irrespective of their work on the field.

The travelling arrangements for these tours, including the selection of the hotels at which the team will stay, are made on the other side but they have to be ratified by the MCC. The carrying out of these arrangements, of course, devolves upon the manager, who makes it his first duty to see that the comfort of the players is properly provided for. This, indeed, is the constant consideration of the manager, and it necessarily involves some degree of tact and not a little patience. No trouble must be spared; no little detail overlooked. The health of the players, too, must be a special managerial care. No illness, or mishap however slight, can be neglected. An expert masseur always accompanies the team, and is constant in his attentions. The need of such services can be judged when it is said that, apart from the strains of continuous match play, we had on the last tour to spend between 20 and 30 nights in the train, the longest journeys being from Perth to Adelaide which occupied about four days – i.e. three nights on the train – and, after the last Test, from Melbourne to Perth. The whole tour means a round journey of between 40,000 and 50,000 miles.

Though one does not like to stress it, managing an Australian cricket tour is hard work. An avalanche of letters has to be dealt with, a mountain of data about plans and itinerary removed. Not the least of this work has reference to the social side of the tour. A very great deal of tact is required in this connection for the offers of hospitality are innumerable, and one has to be very careful that the comfort, the convenience and personal wishes and health of the players are properly considered without giving the least cause to any host to feel slighted.

During the last tour I was asked to give my definition of cricket, and as it roused considerable interest, and I believe was received with approval, I may be forgiven for including it in this, I fear somewhat sketchy, contribution to *Wisden*'s immortal pages.

"It is a science, the study of a lifetime, in which you may exhaust yourself, but never your subject. It is a contest, a duel or melee, calling for courage, skill, strategy and self-control. It is a contest of temper, a trial of honour, a revealer of character. It affords a chance to play the man and act the gentleman. It mean going into God's out-of-doors, getting close to nature, fresh air, exercise, a sweeping away of mental cobwebs, genuine recreation of the tired tissues. It is a cure for care, an antidote to worry. It includes companionship with friends, social intercourse, opportunities for courtesy, kindliness, and generosity to an opponent. It promotes not only physical health but mental force."

TRIALS OF A COUNTY SECRETARY – 40 YEARS OF CRICKET MANAGEMENT

R. V. Ryder, 1936

I am attempting to give the reader an insight into county cricket organisation from the management point of view, together with impressions of change during the past 40 years, the period I have acted as secretary to Warwickshire.

Fixture-making, for one thing, was an unhurried business, commencing in September, through the agency of the penny post, and culminating in a visit to Lord's in December where the silk hat and frock coat were *de rigueur*. Most matches started on Monday, and I may say many of my Sundays were far from days of rest.

In the days when Monday starts were the rule our groundstaff was smaller, so we frequently had to scout round for the occasional player engaged perhaps with a local club, and persuasion was often needed to get a business man or a schoolmaster to fill a gap. The need of persuasion many times found me spending Sunday in a hansom cab trying first this man and then another. The telephone had no place then in team collection. I imagine my committee regarded it as a luxury!

The days of the horse

And apropos of the changes cricket has undergone in the past 40 years let us turn to the following account of the scene outside the ground during that memorable Test. [*England v Australia, 1902 – the first Test ever played at Edgbaston*].

"At the corner of the road it was amusing to come across an imposing but obviously excited coachman (with a pair of restive horses) trying to ascertain from a humble pedestrian the whereabouts of the county cricket ground, the while a lady, cool, composed and statuesque reclined in a tandem. Every minute a hansom dashed up, carriages and pairs were as common as blackberries in autumn, and bicycles crept in and out everywhere."

Yes, I remember it all very well. Not a single motor vehicle reached the scene of *that* cricket encounter. Horse transport was the thing in those days. What quaint reading is afforded now by the perusal of this extract from the Warwickshire committee minutes of April 26, 1897: – A member wrote suggesting that accommodation should be provided for horses as many members had to travel long distances.

Warwickshire lost Wilfred Rhodes

And while my thoughts are on those old minutes, let me quote another recorded in 1897, one which will probably bring a sigh of regret as well as a smile to Warwickshire members whose eyes may fall upon it. This entry, dated October 4, reads: "It was decided that on account of the heavy expenses already incurred in connection with next year's groundstaff an engagement could not be offered W. Rhodes of Huddersfield." If we had only known!

CRICKET'S MASONIC BOND

The Rt Hon. Sir Robert Menzies, Prime Minister of Australia, 1963

And, like all great institutions which are part of our inheritance, it [cricket] gets into the blood, and can even invade the seats of judgment. I will illustrate this by an experience I had in my earlier days at the Victorian Bar. The story will be thought scandalous by some, and perhaps it is. But it is true, and it makes my point.

I had been appearing a good deal before an elderly judge who was not a great lawyer but who had for a brief period been a better than average cricketer. He was somewhat pernickety and abhorred slang expressions, but he was always approachable through his three special hobbies: roses, poultry and cricket. I suppose that purists will say that no advocate should play upon the weaknesses or foibles of a judge. My reply is that any advocate who does not study and know his judge or judges is going to lose many cases, most needlessly.

Anyhow, my story is this. I was for the defendant in a civil action which arose out of events in the neighbourhood of Ballarat, the famous old gold-mining city. My client, as I discovered after a conference with him and his solicitor, was a very decent and honest, but dull, man, quite incapable of stating the facts in any coherent or consecutive fashion. Right through the first day of the hearing, the plaintiff and his witnesses were heard. I cross-examined with no particular success. Yet I had a feeling that my bucolic client was right, if he could only register himself with the judge. The plaintiff's case closed just on the adjournment.

The judge looked at me, kindly enough (he approved of me because he thought I spoke good English!), and said: "Mr Menzies, I think I should tell you that I find the plaintiff's case and witnesses most impressive." With my usual air of confidence, I replied: "I would ask Your Honour to suspend judgment until you have heard my client, who will, I am sure impress you very much!"

After the adjournment, I led the solicitor and client (we had no other witness) down to my chambers. All efforts to extract coherence from the client failed. I then produced my cards.

M. "Mr X, have you ever grown roses?"
X. "I think the wife has some in the garden."
M. "But can you distinguish a La Belle France from a Frau Carl Drushki?"
X. "Not a hope!"
M. "Do you keep fowls?"
X. "The wife has a few."
M. "Can you distinguish between a White Leghorn and an Orpington?"
X. "Not for the life of me!"
M. "Have you ever played cricket?"
X. "Ah! Now you're talking. I played for Ballarat and District against Ivo Bligh's Eleven!"
M. "Good. Conference ended!"

The next morning I opened my case and called the defendant. He was quite dreadful as a witness. At one stage it became necessary to ask him about a date. Before he could reply I said, in the most helpful manner: "Take your time, witness. I know that dates are not always easy to remember. Now, if I were to ask you about the date when you played cricket for Ballarat and District against Ivo Bligh's eleven, that would be much easier!"

The judge, beaming with excitement and delight, switched round in his chair and said "Is that so? Tell me about the match. Were you a batsman or a bowler?" And at once they were into it. Who was the fast bowler? How many runs did the defendant get? For half an hour we had cricket reminiscences galore. By the time my client, completely relaxed, had returned to and concluded his evidence, the judge turned to the plaintiff's astonished counsel and said: "Of course, Mr Y., you may cross-examine if you like. You have a perfect right to do so. But I think I should tell you that in all my years on the bench I have never been more favourably impressed by any witness."

It is hardly necessary to add that the defendant won and, I think, rightly, on the merits. But it was cricket that did it!

STATE OF THE GAME

QUESTIONABLE QUALITY
Jack Hobbs, 1935

Efforts have been made more than once, because of the heavy programmes and constant play day after day, to limit first-class matches to two days. I am not altogether opposed to this; in fact I would ask: why not two-day matches of one innings each? That would give a lot of our professionals a much-needed rest and, as far as I can see, the main argument against this would come from professionals themselves because they would not be able to earn quite as much as they do now. Possibly, however, that is a question which time will solve.

I think the development of the County Championship in regard to the number of counties now competing is rather to be regretted. There are too many counties – some of them, I am afraid, not quite up to the best standard – and we in England have got a false opinion of the strength of our cricket. The trouble is that, against the weaker counties, players get plenty of runs and wickets and they are thought at once to be Test match cricketers. It is much harder now to pick a team for a Test match than it was 30 years ago. The field of choice is so much wider and the all-round standard consequently more on a level – especially in the county averages.

The past 30 years have brought with them a remarkable increase in tours to this country and visits abroad of English teams. As the Mother Country of cricket, England, as represented by the MCC, have naturally considered it politic to foster the game overseas, but I am of opinion that, on the question of elevating countries like South Africa, West Indies, New Zealand and India to the same rank as Australia in the matter of Test matches, we have been premature. The vast host of cricket followers throughout the world know in their own minds that there are only two really top-class cricketing countries – England and Australia. The honour of wearing the England cap with the three silver lions on it has, I am afraid, become rather cheap since its inception. These caps should have been awarded only to cricketers who have appeared in England against Australia.

During my years of first-class cricket I do not think captaincy has improved. With one or two exceptions there has been too much chopping and changing about but, of course, other considerations have to be remembered, for amateurs do not find it so easy to spare the time for first-class cricket as their predecessors did. I have often thought that it was a mistake for counties to put an amateur into the team merely to act as captain when he has had little or no experience of county cricket. We had an example last season in Maurice Tate, of how well a professional could acquit himself as leader of a side, but I definitely always prefer to see an amateur rather than a professional captaining England if his cricket ability entitles him to a place in the eleven.

Cricket At The Crossroads   •   Donald Bradman, 1939

No matter how much we love cricket and desire to regard it as a friendly pastime we cannot possibly disassociate its future, at least in the first-class category, from the cold, hard facts of finance. Nor can we blind ourselves to the fact that at this very moment public support for cricket (possibly excepting Test cricket, around which there is special glamour) suggests either that cricket is becoming less attractive or other forms of entertainment are gaining ground. It is a state of affairs calling for very serious consideration from player and legislator alike.

I am all in favour of "hastening slowly" and have admired the peaceful but purposeful way in which cricket has for so long been administered in England.

Nevertheless, I cannot help feeling that with the quickening of modern tempo, the more Americanised trend which is demanding speed, action and entertainment value, it behoves all of us to realise we are the custodians of the welfare of cricket and must guard its future even more zealously than its present.

No matter what we may desire individually, we cannot arrest nor impede the tenor of everyday life whether it be in business or sport. With such thoughts uppermost in my mind, my reflections are intended to convey the impressions gleaned by an Australian who will naturally view things from a slightly different angle to the average Englishman. Also my opinions are based upon experience in the middle allied to contact with administrative officers and the public.

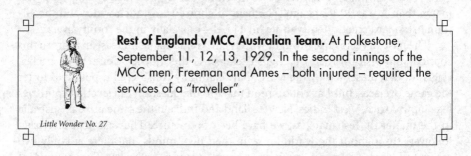

Rest of England v MCC Australian Team. At Folkestone, September 11, 12, 13, 1929. In the second innings of the MCC men, Freeman and Ames – both injured – required the services of a "traveller".

Little Wonder No. 27

GRASSROOTS MORE IMPORTANT THAN "BIG CRICKET"

H. S. Altham, MCC president, 1961

Cricket today certainly does not lack its Jeremiahs. The ever-mounting overheads and the diminishing gates of the first-class game, even though somewhat offset by the substantial increase of county club membership, present a serious financial picture: indeed I believe it is no exaggeration to say that, but for supporters' clubs, the Championship as we know it would be standing today with at least one foot on the scaffold.

Against the background of the Welfare State, with its increasing tempo, its television, its greater mobility and the ever-growing variety of entertainment and relaxation competing for its patronage, county and Test cricket face a formidable challenge. But beneath these clouds there is surely a wide and much brighter landscape. However important may be the stimulus provided by the publicity and panache of "big cricket", what matters, surely, is the healthy survival of the game as a whole as something integral to and reflecting the English way of life, a recreation in the truest and widest sense of the word for body, mind and spirit.

That health is, I believe, to be assessed not so much in the attendance at a Test match, still less in the destiny of a rubber, but in the number of cricketers who will go on playing the game because they love it, on club grounds, on village greens, in the public parks, wherever, in fact, there is room to bowl and to hit a ball: and that total will in each successive generation be determined by the number of boys whose loyalty to the game can be cemented by their being helped to play it as well as they can and so enjoy it to the full.

Finally, I would like to say a word in answer to the constant criticism of our whole approach, that "group coaching", which is inevitably its basic medium, is defensive in concept and stultifying to individual initiative, that it turns out "robots", stifles genius and drains the game of that instinctive enjoyment that it should always provide. To such critics I would say – let them come to Lilleshall and spend just one day with a course there, and if at the end if it they are still of the same mind, if they have not enjoyed it and do not feel it has something to offer any cricketer, young or old, club or county, I would gladly stand them the refreshment.

THE PUBLIC MUST BE ENTERTAINED
Sir Donald Bradman, 1986

At the request of the Editor I wrote a short piece for the 1939 *Wisden*. My main theme then was a plea for cricket to adapt itself to the quickening tempo of modern life, for administrators to consider ways of speeding up the game, to face up to financial problems, and so on. Little did I appreciate at the time what a revolution would engulf cricket before another 50 years had passed.

The great stadiums of Sydney and Melbourne now display huge electronic scoreboards costing millions of dollars and giving a wealth of information to the spectators. The enormous electric-light towers turn night into day at the flick of a switch. That, in turn, demands the use of a white ball, and to satisfy the television and marketing moguls the players turn out in a variety of coloured outfits.

The whole scene stirs up human emotions ranging from those of a largely new and young audience (more liberally sprinkled with females than of yore), who yell and scream their support, to those of the dyed-in-the wool lovers of Test cricket, who yearn for more peaceful, bygone days. As with so many things, it becomes well-nigh impossible to bring about a reconciliation between the opposing attitudes.

But where does the truth lie and what about the future?

Despite my deep feeling for the traditional game, and my conviction that a vast majority of players and the public still regard Test cricket as the supreme contest, we must accept that we live in a new era. If Sir Neville Cardus were alive today, I can well imagine how eloquently he would bemoan the huge attendances at pop concerts compared with the lack of support for opera or a Beethoven evening. But I am sure he would also admit that, irrespective of the quality of the music or the musicians, the public are primarily interested in entertainment. Perhaps he would throw in his well-known reference to an eagle, no matter how beautiful in flight, being no match for the Concorde. I am satisfied that one-day cricket, especially day/night cricket, is here to stay. If there is a threat to the survival of the game of cricket, that threat lies in the first-class arena, and it behoves the administrators to understand the challenge and face up to it.

I confess to a love for both types of game. Nothing can match the continuous cut and thrust of a Test match, where the advantage see-saws and the result is unpredictable to the last ball. It starkly revealed the Achilles heel of the limited-overs match, namely the premium placed on defensive bowling and negative and defensive field-placing. One can get bored to death watching countless singles being taken when even the world's fastest bowler may be operating with no slips and five men on the boundary.

But let me turn to the good thing about one-day cricket. It rids the game of the unutterable bore who thinks occupancy of the crease and his own personal aggrandisement are all that matter. It demands fieldsmen of great speed and agility with good throwing arms. The standard of fielding at all levels of cricket has undoubtedly been lifted. Running between the wickets, too, has taken on a new dimension. Risks must be taken to maintain the essential run-rate. Umpires are put under enormous pressure, having to adjudicate frequently on split-second issues: to their credit, I believe they have responded in a very positive manner and improved their standards.

Lovers of cricket will find in the pages of *Wisden* plenty of evidence that cricket has had its problems for a century past. Things have not changed much. Problems are still there – they are just different. It remains for players and administrators to accept the challenge to keep cricket alive and vibrant, and not to shrink from the decisions needed to ensure that end.

Why We Beat The Poms
Ian Chappell, 1994

Why do Australia beat England? In general, because Australia play an aggressive brand of cricket and, when the talent is there, they get in position to seek victory more often.

Notwithstanding that, Australia couldn't have lost the last three Ashes series even if they had bet heavily on the opposition. England played badly, often. In particular, the bowling was abysmal. England's ability to over-theorise and complicate the game of cricket is legendary. Ever since I became involved in Ashes battles, I've felt that Australia could rely on some assistance from the England selectors.

When Australia hit rock bottom through the 1984–87 period, the standard of Sheffield Shield cricket was low. The problem was addressed because talented and gutsy young players were encouraged. Now it is a vibrant competition and an excellent breeding ground. England are on the right track with four-day first-class games, but it will take time for the benefits to accrue. I think they should go a step further and reduce the number of teams to make it more competitive, as there are players in the county structure who are not up to first-class standard. Any system that protects incompetence needs changing. If this means having a first and second division then that could be the way to accommodate part-time players who want to combine business and cricket.

These changes could be part of a package to convince the counties that they must put England's needs at the top of their list, rather than on a level with deciding which colour to paint the pavilion roof. Any move to improve the structure should be aimed at increasing pride in playing for the national team. Lack of pride manifests itself in a number of ways, and in England's case the most serious has been to capitulate in a Test when trouble loomed. Their players used to be the best in the world at extricating themselves from trouble. This generation needs to rediscover that urge. The inability to save Tests must also have something to do with technique and mental strength. In an age where we have more coaches than ever throughout the cricket world, I query how much good they are doing. I believe in good coaching, but I think players are better to have none (i.e. work it out for themselves) than to have bad coaching.

Like so many things, the English invented one-day cricket and other countries have improved on their system, leaving them languishing. There are some signs of modern thinking in the marketing of English cricket but it has taken an inordinate amount of time to occur. In the end, though, the marketing men need a strong England side. So does the whole of cricket.

ENGLISH CRICKET: A MANIFESTO Lord MacLaurin, 1997

Where is cricket going to be in 20 or 30 years? We're under pressure from a host of activities – passive and active. My belief is that the prime task of the new Board is to ensure that, by the time we get to the 2020s, cricket in England and Wales is at least as healthy as it is at the moment. And that it remains the national summer sport. That may sound unadventurous. Obviously we want to grow, to get more and more people playing and watching the game. But we're in an increasingly competitive market-place – something I've had to cope with in the retail trade – with new leisure activities coming in all the time. Just to stay where we are will be a very sizeable achievement.

How do we ensure that? The main message that Tim Lamb, the new chief executive, and I have been taking to the counties is that the top priority has to be a successful national side. That's the key to our cricket and to our business. I remember when my own son was nine or ten: it is so much easier to capture kids' attention if they've got heroes they can look up to, and try to emulate.

Yet it's been so rare for England to win Test matches that people can almost remember where they were when it happened. We need more results like last year's soccer – England 4 Holland 1 – which will capture the public imagination. Tetley's announcement of their withdrawal from England team sponsorship was depressing. There were all kinds of reasons involving corporate restructuring that were behind that decision, but it can't have been coincidental that England had been so unsuccessful for so long. There are some amber lights flashing over our game, and we have to respond.

In so many ways we have so much going for us. There are as many people playing cricket as have ever played it. Although there is less school cricket, there are now 4,000 clubs with colts' sections. And our finances have never been in better shape. But to maintain the support of TV, sponsors and the public, the flagship – the England team – has to be successful. People want to be associated with winners. This doesn't mean the whole of our game is going to be sacrificed on the altar of national success. County cricket is an important, integral part of the game, of the fabric of the country. So is village cricket. And we wouldn't dream of changing that. But now the whole of cricket is run under one roof, we can give the game a strategic plan and a framework that will move us forward.

Tim Lamb and I are a new team, and we have a blank sheet of paper. We're prepared to talk to the counties about issues that in the past might have been filed under "too hard": the amount of one-day cricket, uncovered wickets, two divisions, anything. Perhaps we will have a more radical agenda than people expect. But, clearly, we've got to get it right at the top level, so all the other levels can thrive.

SEEING TWENTY20: A VIEW FROM THE OLD DEAR Clement Freud, 2006

There was so much I did not know: that it was called Twenty20 not 20-20 like my eyesight used to be; that they played in differing coloured pyjamas; that there were rules about who could field where for however many overs; nor that it happened at Old Dear Park. I had thought this would be a location peopled by elderly, cardiganed Newberry Fruit-eating pensioners. Turned out to be Old Deer Park; I resent ageism of all kinds.

The occasion – where they were kind and welcoming and let me drive almost into the pavilion because of my lameness – was an evening fixture: Middlesex v Hampshire but for the fact that each county has an added name like Crusaders and Hedgeclippers (I might have got that last one wrong), and they start when you rather expect cricket matches to finish. The evening was fine and, as the pavilion is situated on the east side of the park and the sun has this habit of setting in the west, you don't see a lot, unless you have brought dark glasses.

The crowd was around 3,000, mostly men arriving from work, with a few marauding gangs of teenage girls whose movements from one side of the ground to the other had less to do with the cricket than the male spectators. Middlesex batted first; one could not see a great deal, but whenever there was a boundary or a wicket, a disc jockey-ette played a snatch of loud music: a couple of bars from Oklahoma, a burst of the Trumpet Voluntary, a roll of drums accompanying a band I did not know… but then there are not too many bands I do know. Lew Stone was one I remember fondly.

I lived as a child in St John's Wood, spent my summer Saturdays at Lord's with a bottle of amber-coloured Tizer and applauded good shots, quite often shouting "Good shot, sir!" as my hands met. Middlesex were my team in as much as Surrey were not. Nothing south of the River Thames had much going for it – though Middlesex seem to be playing there now – and brown caps were sartorially poor. I collected cigarette cards and wished my parents smoked. Price kept wicket for Middlesex; I was a wicketkeeper at school and very much admired the fact that Price kept without a long-stop. My long-stop won the fielding cup.

I digress. At Old Deer Park the crowd chatted and queued for beer; when there were significant bursts of music they came out to see whether it was a boundary or a wicket. But what surprised me was the fact that there was little in the way of partisanship. No breathless hush in the close tonight, let alone ten to make and a match to win.

Middlesex lost wickets at a rate of knots. When the requisite 20 overs had been bowled in the prescribed hour and a quarter, there came a blast of "Love is All Around" and I went and queued in the bar where they served light meals: burgers and chips, sausages and chips, pizza and chips. When I was still 15 people back, the woman behind the counter called "Anyone who doesn't want chips come to the front." So I did. "No chips?" I was going to ask for "a lobster cocktail, easy on the tabasco" but my courage failed and I had pasta. It was all right, though I wouldn't have gone to Richmond for it.

We had friendly announcements such as one doesn't get at Lord's. "Please help the stewards by using the large red bins for your rubbish." "Please watch out for flying balls, especially if you have children." I chatted to a nice woman behind the Middlesex shop counter, seriously considered buying a picture of Mr Shah, and talked to a man who explained what a "free hit" was. Hampshire (the Hawks, I have just remembered) batted competently, kept the music flowing and were always going to win... which they did almost in time for there to be a beer match. Hardly anyone applauded, everyone looked content and there was still time to do all sorts of other things before it got dark, like have another beer and thank the stewards for their kindness and hospitality and mutter "bad luck" to people wearing the MCC tie. "Where have you been?" asked my wife when I came home just after 9pm. I told her I had been watching cricket and listening to music. She said don't be silly.

WAR-TIME

CRICKET UNDER THE JAPS   Major E. W. Swanton, RA, 1946

It is strange, perhaps, but true, how many of us agreed on this: That we were never so thankful for having been cricketers as we were when we were guests of the Japanese. There were periods when we could play "cricket", if our antics do not desecrate the word. There were occasions when we could lecture, and be lectured to, about it. It was a subject that filled countless hours in pitch-dark huts between sundown and the moment that continued to be euphemistically known as lights-out. And it inspired many a daydream, contrived often in the most gruesome setting, whereby one combated the present by living either in the future or the past.

In the days that followed shortly on the fall of Singapore, before work for prisoners had become widely organised, there was a certain amount of play on the padangs of Changi camp that really deserved the name of cricket. It is true that one never seemed able to hit the ball very far, a fact probably attributable about equally to the sudden change to a particularly sparse diet of rice, and the conscientious labours of generations of corporals in charge of sports gear, for whom a daily oiling of the bats had clearly been a solemn, unvarying rite. These Changi bats must have reached saturation point in the early thirties, and I never found one that came up lighter than W. H. Ponsford's three pounder. However, the pitches were true – matting over concrete – and there were even such refinements as pads and gloves.

Cricket at Nakom Patom reached its climax on New Year's Day, 1945, when a fresh, and certainly hitherto unrecorded, page was written in the saga of England v. Australia. The scene is not easy to put before you, but I must try. The playing area is small, perhaps 60 yards by 30, and the batsman's crease is right up against the spectators, with the pitch longways on. There are no runs behind the wicket, where many men squat in the shade of tall trees. The sides are flanked by long huts, with parallel ditches – one into the ditch, two over the hut. In fact all runs by boundaries, 1, 2, 4 or 6. An additional hazard is washing hung on bamboo lines. Over the bowler's head are more trees, squaring the thing off, and in the distance a thick, high, mud wall – the camp bund – on which stands a bored and sulky Korean sentry. (Over the bund no runs and out, for balls are precious.) In effect, the spectators are the boundaries, many hundreds of them taking every inch of room. The dress is fairly uniform, wooden clogs, and a scanty triangular piece of loin-cloth known (why?) as a "Jap-Happy". Only the swells wear patched and tattered shorts. The mound at long-on is an Australian preserve, their "Hill". The sun beats down, as tropical suns do, on the flat beaten earth which is the wicket. At the bowler's end is a single bamboo stump, at the other five – yes, five – high ones. There is the hum of anticipation that you get on the first morning at Old Trafford or Trent Bridge, though there are no scorecards, and no "Three penn'orth" of comfort to be bought from our old friend "Cushions".

KEEP CALM AND FOLLOW ON
Stephen Chalke, 2010

The news on Thursday August 24, 1939 was ominous: German threats against the Polish city of Danzig, a treaty between Hitler and Stalin, an Emergency Powers Act passing through parliament. Yet county cricket was playing on: in the words of Neville Cardus, "a haven of peace in an unruly world". Some saw cricket as a distraction – Surrey's Errol Holmes said it felt "rather like going on a picnic when your home was on fire" – but many recognised its potential to raise morale. As *The Cricketer* put it, "It takes people out of themselves, and if we are a fortress let us have some fun inside the fortress so long as it does not conflict with military exigencies."

In August 1940, while the Battle of Britain raged in the skies over south-east England, cricket continued at Lord's. Playing for Sir Pelham Warner's XI, Essex's Reg Taylor, freshly decorated with the Distinguished Flying Cross, was cheered all the way to the wicket, bowled for nought and cheered all the way back again. "It is hard," Warner wrote, "to remember any cricketer receiving a greater reception." On Saturday September 7, with the German blitzkrieg intensifying, air-raid sirens seemed to have ended the day's play at Lord's. Then an all-clear brought the players back, and the last four wickets fell in seven balls. In the evening, Warner stood at the top of the pavilion, watching the fires blazing in the London docks. Sirens, gunfire, shell-splinters, smoke: there would be no more cricket that summer. *Wisden* called it "a strange and dramatic end", though – with its offices suffering extensive damage – the Almanack did not appear till December 1941, 15 months later. Less than half the size of its predecessor, it nevertheless followed tradition and listed the fixtures for 1941.

In July 1943 Hedley Verity, a professional cricketer who had risen to the rank of captain in the Green Howards, was shot while leading his men against German fire in Sicily. At Lord's, on the Saturday following the announcement of his death, his Yorkshire captain Brian Sellers stepped out to toss for the Army against the National Police. In his blazer pocket he found a note from 1939, from the scorer at Hove: "6–1– 9–7" – Verity's last bowling figures.

The war in Europe ended in May 1945, and five three-day Victory Tests between England and Australia were staged. They were not official Tests – too many cricketers were still elsewhere – but the cricket was dynamic, and a total of 367,000 people watched the 15 days. It was the first first-class cricket in England since 1939. Three of the Tests were played at Lord's, the others at the war-ravaged grounds of Bramall Lane and Old Trafford. For the Manchester game, Lancashire employed German prisoners of war at three farthings an hour to repair and paint the ground.

The fifth Test at Old Trafford took place the week after Victory in Japan. The sight of packed Manchester omnibuses labelled "Cricket Ground" and gates closed at midday added to the general euphoria. When Bill Edrich hit the winning runs, levelling the series at 2–2, *The Times* declared it "as good a game of cricket as the heart of man could throb for".

Many cricketers had had easy wars as physical training instructors, but others – such as Trevor Bailey driving past lines of emaciated prisoners at Belsen – had seen sights that would never leave them. They had lost important cricket years but, as Alec Bedser says, "The war made men of us. It toughened us up. After that I was never nervous when I played cricket." Sir Home Gordon in *The Cricketer* noticed a greater acceptance of umpires' decisions: "I have seen a few shocking verdicts, but none of the pre-war disgruntlement on returning to the pavilion." He attributed this to "the widespread inoculation of obedience and discipline". "You had a better attitude," Bedser says. "You learned just to get on with things. You didn't ask questions."

The war did raise questions, however, not least in social attitudes. In 1943 Learie Constantine booked into the Imperial Hotel, Russell Square, but on arrival he was called "a nigger" and told that his presence would be unacceptable to their American guests. He took the hotel to the High Court and won his case. Then in August 1945, the only black man in the side, he captained the Dominions against England at Lord's. It could not have happened in 1939.

Little Wonder No. 28

Somerset v Sussex (A. Young's Benefit). At Bath, July 26, 28, 29, 1930. Young experienced exceptionally bad luck. Rain on Saturday delayed the start for half an hour and prolonged the luncheon interval by an hour and a half. On Monday showers prevented the game being proceeded with until 2.45 and on Tuesday, with a saturated pitch subjected to a heavy storm, no play could be attempted. The gate receipts amounted to £62.

THE MEDIA

ART AND CRAFT   John Arlott, 1950

One might have expected a small output of cricket books in 1949 after the spate which greeted the Australians in 1948. More than 70 books dated 1949, however, stand before me.

The major problem facing the critic in his assessment of these books lies in their being directed to different sections of the public and, hence, having no common denominator of style, aim or method. This rules out all but the most limited comparative criticism and, simultaneously, demands a statement of the critical standard to be applied. *Wisden* is largely published for those interested in cricket and who, we may assume, will be to some extent sympathetic to almost *any* book on the game. For these readers, a cricket book must be accurate in its technical and statistical content. Indeed, such accuracy is an obvious prerequisite of the records and reports which every game has – as its original chronicles. But cricket has more: it has produced a body of minor but genuine art which is a vital ingredient in the unique character of the game.

It is this cultural and imaginative characteristic which gives cricket its high standing even in the eyes of those who do not value the game as such. Therefore, those of us who are jealous for the reputation of cricket must be concerned for the preservation of its creative quality in its books, the medium where it has most often manifested itself. On the other hand, to demand of every book on cricket – or, indeed, on any other subject – that it should be a work of art in its own right, is absurd. Moreover, any balanced cricket library must contain a considerable body of works whose main bias is technical, statistical or documentary.

It seems a first requirement of a book on cricket that it should be accurate and should be presented in an orderly and literate manner. However, those few great books on cricket entitled to the name of literature have gone further: although they may have aimed no higher than our basic requirement, the vital fusion between craftsmanship and experience which is called "art" has taken place within them. The books which achieve this fusion must be given recognition, for, not only do they win respect for their subject, but their quality will outlive their subject-matter.

NOVELTY AND IMPACT
John Arlott, 1965

The Birthday Honours List of 1964 included the award of the CBE to Mr Neville Cardus "for services to music and cricket". It was the first – and, some may feel, belated – official recognition of the modest man who, for almost 50 years, has written with sympathy and integrity about the two chief interests – indeed, enthusiasms – of his life. Throughout that time his work has never become jaded, but has unfailingly reflected the happiness of one who always felt privileged, even grateful, to earn his living from his pleasures.

Few are qualified to compare his writings on the two subjects: in any case, the comparison would be pointless. It may be said, however, that while his standing in the world of music is high, in the field of cricket it is unique. The form of musical criticism had already been shaped before Mr Cardus came to it. On the other hand, by innovation and influence, he virtually created modern cricket-writing. In doing so, he led thousands of people to greater enjoyment of the game.

Today he may be regarded as just one of a number of imaginative cricket writers; but he appears so only to those who do not recall the immense novelty and impact of his writing when it first reached the public in the 1920s. Before then there had been much competent cricket-reporting, informed, sound in judgment, pleasant in manner. But the Cardus of the years shortly after the First World War first brought to it the qualities of personalisation, literary allusion and imagery. By such methods as presenting the contest between bowler and batsmen as a clash not only of skills but of characters, he created something near to a mythology of the game.

His early writing has been described, not always with complimentary intent, as romantic. That is the essence of his appeal. To the enthusiast, cricket *is* romantic: and in Mr Cardus's reports, the ordinary spectator saw his romantic and heroic feelings put into words for the first time.

Every modern cricket writer with any pretensions to style owes half that he is to Neville Cardus, if only in the stern realism of making such an approach acceptable to editors. The consciously literary method can lead to lush and imprecise writing and in the cases of some of Mr Cardus's imitators, that has happened. His own work, however, always has a ballast of practicality, humanity and humour.

It may be true that cricket was always an art, but no one until Neville Cardus presented it as an art with all an artist's perception. Because of him, thousands of people enjoy watching the game more than they would have done if he had not lived and written. He has said that his recipe was laid down by C. E. Montague: "To bring to the day's diet of sights and sounds the wine of your own temperament."

A MARRIAGE IS ANNOUNCED Alastair McLellan, 2003

The internet could have been invented for cricket. A game taking place in discrete moments – a wicket, a boundary, a bouncer – but spreading over a whole day is perfect for a medium that can capture those instants in real time, review them within minutes, and then allow them to be debated by fans and experts alike. Throw in a white-collar audience with computers on their desks and a packed international schedule taking place in many time zones, and the internet's ability to keep followers in touch with the game is unparalleled.

When 2002 began, it was still early days for the boldest experiment yet by a cricket website – the decision by Wisden.com to launch a subscription service. For most of the year, an intriguing talking point was whether Wisden.com would merge with CricInfo. The biggest cricket website was talking to the one with the most purchasing power; the two most famous names in cricket publishing were thinking about becoming one.

CricInfo was born in 1993, the brainchild of a young British scientist, Dr Simon King. Stranded at the University of Minnesota, King used the fledgling internet to cure his homesickness by creating a site which allowed him to follow Middlesex and England from afar. His ferocious determination attracted others who shared his obsessive commitment to making CricInfo the online home of the game. The world's cricket fans, especially expatriate Indians, flocked to the site. In 2000, CricInfo launched as a commercial operation on the back of a US$37.5million investment which valued it at US$150million. It was, in the words of the *Financial Times*, "one of the biggest, sexiest dotcoms".

A year of craziness followed in which CricInfo spent money like water and even ended up sponsoring the County Championship. But the internet bubble had burst and CricInfo's investors were getting nervous. In 2001, in a foreshadowing of Wisden.com's sudden switch of strategy, the backers demanded that costs were cut and more money made. Simon King, who had fallen out with his fellow directors, found himself sidelined, and a few months later he resigned.

CricInfo's battle-scarred team struggled on, constantly searching for ways to make their huge traffic pay. In 2002, they added four different betting services to the site, upgraded the online equipment and video shop, and introduced a "global" mobile-phone score update service. They also introduced a subscription of their own, CricInfo Plus, which did not rope off an area of the site (a labour-intensive business, requiring a restructuring) but charged $12 a year for faster access to pages that could be clogged by their own popularity, especially when India were playing. About 5,000 users paid up, but the company was still only just breaking even: not much use if you have debts of more than £1.5million.

It is video and audio content which the punter is most used to being asked to pay for. And it is here that the internet may finally deliver fully on its promise to provide truly interactive coverage of the game. Cricket coverage on the internet is about to enter a new age of interactivity. Video offers the most exciting opportunity (for those with broadband), but there are others. During the Ashes and the World Cup you could see a cult in the making in the over-by-over text commentaries provided by the Guardian Sport site, which incorporated edited emails from users to create a kind of global banter – *Test Match Special* meets a chatroom.

It's becoming clear that there is often little to stop internet sites offering unofficial audio coverage, with the commentators following the game on television as Wisden.com did during the World Cup. As with video, the technology now makes this kind of service much more cost-effective and feasible. What price a dozen internet commentary services all following the same match but reflecting the tastes, biases and languages of their audiences?

The TV Executive's Decision Is Final: The Power Of Babel   Mihir Bose, 2005

In 1977, when the last major revolution in cricket took place, led by the Australian magnate Kerry Packer, India had barely entered the television age. There were fewer than 700,000 sets in a country whose population was already over 600 million: barely one per thousand. All that was on offer was the state channel, Doordarshan, showing programmes about as professional and entertaining as those available in the Soviet bloc. Not a single ball of cricket had ever been televised in India.

Today there are still remote villages where people will gather to watch the one communal TV set: a flickering screen powered by an unreliable generator. But the pan shops, offering betel nuts and crackly radio commentary, now have competition from smart restaurants, often with large screens. And 80 million homes, containing maybe a third of the population, have their own sets. The 1977 schism came about because the Australian Cricket Board refused to consider Packer's offer of $US3.25m to show five years of cricket in Australia. In the autumn of 2004 Zee TV offered $308m for four years of cricket in India: a hundred times as much. Inflation cannot entirely explain this away.

Various factors came together to produce this explosion. By coincidence, they reached a critical mass together. The turning-point was 1991, when changes in cricket were matched by changes in society. That year, under pressure from the World Bank, India was forced to open up its economy and allow foreign investment into what had been one of the most protected markets on the planet. It was the year of the first Gulf War; suddenly Indians learned it was possible to follow world events on television rather than just through newspapers and cinema newsreels.

And that was also when cricket at last became one family: South Africa, having shed its apartheid past, was readmitted into the game and finally played a non-white country, launching its rebirth with a one-day series in India. That historic tour made the Indian board realise it had television rights, which it could sell. Doordarshan had by now started to televise big games within India but, far from paying anything, it had often demanded fees from the board to cover the cost of production.

Now two South African channels wanted to show the games. Amrit Mathur, an official who worked for then Indian board president Madhavrao Scindia, recalls: "We had to find out first who owned the rights and then how much they were worth." Mathur discovered that they belonged to the Indian board, and that they were surprisingly valuable. So as South Africa realised what it is to play against someone outside the white commonwealth, the Indians realised that they were sitting on a goldmine.

They might never have dug for it but for the intervention of one man. Mark Mascarenhas, a Bangalore boy who went to live in Connecticut, was convinced cricket could make big money. He bought the rights for the 1996 World Cup held in the subcontinent, and guaranteed $10m to the host countries; he delivered $30m. At the time seasoned broadcasters thought Mascarenhas was mad. Hardly – he also became Sachin Tendulkar's agent and a big power in the game before his death in a car crash in 2002. And the Indian board's profits, as they ruthlessly commercialised the World Cup, enabled every major cricket ground in the country to be equipped with floodlights.

This was the turning-point for TV rights in general, and in India in particular. By 1996 India had also gone from two channels to 50, provided by more than 60,000 cable operators. Now there are 200 channels, and this Babel makes it easier to watch cricket, and even English football, than it is in England; I have watched Tottenham play Manchester City, a fixture not shown live at home, on a Saturday night in Darjeeling.

Not So Much A Programme, More A Way Of Life   Gillian Reynolds, 2007

The history of *TMS* is a backstairs chronicle of the BBC itself, its journey an adroit passage through the corporation's internal tides and political reefs. Listeners follow favourite programmes. Executives use this loyalty to shore up sagging schedules and hang on to territory. The programme is still there because it speaks to significant people, not just significant numbers.

So, to begin at the beginning, do you remember when you heard it first? For me it was in the 1960s, with John Arlott, Rex Alston and E. W. Swanton. Mark Damazer, Radio 4's controller, thinks he was about ten when he started listening. He wasn't good at games – indeed he found it almost impossible to play cricket – but loved the voices. Roger Wright, Radio 3's controller, remembers tuning in under the bedclothes at night to hear winter Tests from abroad. Listening to such games now, he says, shoots him immediately back to childhood and "the feeling of being let into a secret world, the world of radio opening up to me".

Radio coverage of English Test cricket dates back to the early days of radio. The big change 50 years ago was the introduction of ball-by-ball. Robert Hudson, then a senior outside broadcasts producer (later a *TMS* commentator himself), realised how frustrating it was for cricket followers to get only bits of each day's play. So for the Edgbaston Test of 1957 (otherwise remembered for May and Cowdrey's huge stand), the BBC were able to boast complete coverage under the slogan: "Don't miss a ball. We broadcast them all." And the Third Programme, as well as the cricket audience, was the beneficiary: it covered play up to 5.15 on medium wave, when it switched to the Light Programme, the forerunner of Radio 2.

The Third, offering a very highbrow diet of music and arts, had been under fierce attack for being too expensive and unpopular. The addition of *TMS* deflected opposition, and instantly pushed up the listening figures. By 1965 the BBC officially admitted that "audiences for ball-by-ball were anything from five to 50 times as great" as they would be for classical music. When rain stopped play in those days music was played but, for those apprehensive of the Third's fearsome reputation, it was of a "family-fare nature".

Peter Baxter, who first worked on *TMS* in 1966, became its producer in 1973, and has nurtured the programme ever since – he retires in June after the West Indies series. He still remembers his days as an apprentice and the storms inside the commentary box. Michael Tuke-Hastings, his only predecessor as producer, would be back in the studio at Broadcasting House, giving Baxter messages to relay: "Tell Arlott he's talking rubbish," for instance. The feud between Tuke-Hastings and Arlott was such that, though both men retired to tiny Alderney, they never spoke. Arlott believed, says Baxter, that Tuke-Hastings had kept him unsure of his future and had destroyed the tapes of some of his best commentaries.

There have always been tensions in the commentary box, but somehow they rarely convey themselves to the listeners, many of them with no cricket background, for whom *TMS* has always evoked a perfect idyll of English summer and calm. In 1970, a further element was added when Brian Johnston, having been dropped by television, aged 58, came in and became the joker in the pack. Though the ruminative poet Arlott would continue for another ten years and Swanton was still giving his magisterial after-match summaries, the lighter Johnston style became increasingly dominant. He would continue into his eighties, and his influence lives on.

Baxter must have possessed the patience of Job and the diplomacy of Solomon to have moulded such a team, to provide the defining combination of expertise, observation and good humour. Yet the *TMS* commentary team has been extremely stable over the years. "We don't do a lot of recruiting," says Baxter. "The audience seems to like that – knowing the commentators." This listener wonders whether the circle has seemed occasionally a little too cosy but, out of respect for Baxter's magnificent achievement in holding it all together for so long, refrains from pushing it. And in 2006, two newcomers – Mark Saggers and Arlo White – made their home debuts.

I remember the old commentary box at Lord's. To get there you had to go through the Long Room, where women were then not normally allowed. But I was with the BBC's Head of Sport and Outside Broadcasts, the remarkable Patricia

Ewing, so we were ushered, eyes down, across the hallowed floors and up the sacred steps into the rickety attic into which were squeezed the *TMS* team – Miss Ewing's employees – who welcomed us with hushed dignity while duly attending to the job.

The new commentary box lies opposite, at the Nursery end, within the huge glittering envelope which also houses the world's press. Baxter isn't keen. "It's too high. All around the world, it's the same. Up and up and up. Identification of players gets harder." When the commentary team is this far away from the field, he thinks, it makes it much harder to convey the essential *TMS* feeling of being at a game with a couple of friends.

Which is, of course, why we listen. These friends have to know we are there. If they sound as if they are talking only to each other it gets dull. A little grit helps, which is where Geoff Boycott can come in handy. I miss the wider world view of Arlott and Johnston, but then I miss that in a lot of sports journalism nowadays. I am heartily sick of the cakes, the bacon rolls, the pork pies and what everyone had last night for dinner.

Perhaps I am not typical. Last summer I noted a coming attraction at the Chichester Festival Theatre. *Rain Stops Play*, it promised for October. The Stars of *Test Match Special...* a "unique opportunity for cricket fans to share a hilarious and memorable evening... There will be a question and answer session and the famous *Test Match Special* cake competition! Take your cake to the stage door on the evening of the show to enter." Between three and four million people listen to *TMS*, and the evidence is that cricket is audience Viagra: when cricket takes over from normal programmes on Radio 4's long-wave frequency, the figures jump by 300,000.

Yet there are always Radio 4 devotees who complain that it belongs on Radio 5 Live. Some BBC executives are thought to want the programme to imitate 5's matier style, and that may come in the post-Baxter era. Already *TMS* is part of radio's digital future through 5 Live Sports Extra. Could it go digital altogether? Were the BBC, in that fully digital future, to offer some services on subscription, wouldn't it be logical to make *TMS* earn a living? Logical, definitely. Practical? Not exactly. Mark Damazer insists the programme is a natural part of Radio 4. "Good cricket coverage, free at the point of delivery. I can't see anyone in their right mind saying 'that's not value'. There's a huge market out there."

"The BBC would be in huge trouble if they tried to close down *TMS*," said Sir David Hatch, former head of BBC Network Radio. "It would be political suicide. Completely. Think about all those MPs, all those members of the House of Lords, the MCC, cricket clubs all over the country. Think of the national rejoicing when we won the Ashes."

I see what he means. If cricket is more than a game, *Test Match Special* is definitely more than a programme.

Yorkshire v Middlesex. At Sheffield, June 25, 27, 28, 1932. Leyland, handicapped by lameness, had to ask for a "traveller"; nevertheless he drove magnificently, sending the ball to the boundary 28 times.

Little Wonder No. 29

AESTHETICS AND ATTITUDE

BATSMEN MUST HIT THE BALL AGAIN   Denis Compton, 1968

In my opinion there is nothing wrong with cricket; it is the attitude of so many first-class players that has gone awry. Cricket is still a wonderful game as played in the schools and at club level, but so much big cricket is no longer the spectacle it used to be, and, in particular, the County Championship, which provided me with so much fun, no longer attracts huge crowds. Modern trends, like the family car and the thirst for excitement the whole time, now challenge cricket probably more than any other spectator sport. The safety-first outlook has bedevilled professional cricket far too long and like our traffic in the big cities the three-day game has come almost to a full stop.

Naturally, it must be difficult to work up enthusiasm playing in front of deserted stands and terraces for six days a week. The right atmosphere can make all the difference. I was lucky playing soon after the war before enthusiastic onlookers who had been starved of sporting entertainment. Because of the absence of crowds at county games in the past few seasons, some cricketers advance the argument that it is difficult to provide entertaining play in such an unreal atmosphere. What they fail to realise is that nobody can be drawn back to the game unless the players – and, in effect, committees – change their attitude.

I was encouraged last season when I heard that Stuart Surridge, in his first season as chairman of Surrey's cricket committee, made his own stand during a second eleven match at The Oval when he saw a Surrey batsman who has had considerable first-team experience playing without any sign of aggression. Surridge squirmed in his seat until he could stand it no longer and asked the Surrey coach, Arthur McIntyre, to go out to the middle and instruct the batsman to play the game the right way or get out! Too much of the modern game seems to be complicated by theory and the shutting out of natural talent by coaches who insist that all players should be of the same mould as laid down in the coaching manuals. The younger of the overseas cricketers who have been signed up by the counties during the winter will undoubtedly find some of their methods frowned upon by coaches when they first enter county cricket. I very much hope they will have enough strength of character to resist the attempts to turn them into the factory models filling our county sides.

Last summer I was surprised when one of our leading batsmen, with many overseas tours behind him, told me he was not happy with the way he was holding the bat. He asked how I held mine. "I've not the slightest idea," I replied. "I never paid any attention to any special grip. I held it the way it felt most comfortable." So I should have thought, would any batsman.

CAMOUFLAGED BY VISORS   Trevor Bailey, 1981

One of cricket's many charms used to be the way it was possible to walk into a ground and instantly recognise the batsman at the crease. Apart from his style, he was unmistakable because of his build, features, headgear or hair. Who could have failed to pick out Cyril Washbrook with his cap at a jaunty angle, or Jack Robertson, who wore his with the precision of a guardsman? Then again, there was the hair-style of Herbert Sutcliffe, black patent-leather glinting in the sun, complete with the straightest of partings, the blonde waves of Joe Hardstaff, Reg Simpson's dark curls, and Denis Compton's, so unlike those Brylcreem advertisements, forever unruly. Today, as often as not, it is impossible to tell who is batting without first consulting a scorecard, so many players being encrusted in helmets and camouflaged by visors. This gives them a space-age image, devoid of individuality and as dull as dirty denims.

Obviously a helmet makes batting, which personally I never considered as even a vaguely dangerous occupation, less dangerous; just at wearing one in a car, or on a bicycle in traffic, would reduce the risk of injury following a road accident. However, assuming the player obeys the fundamental principle of batsmanship and keeps his eye on the ball, he should not be hit on the head by a fast bowler – provided the pitch is reasonable and the batsman competent. He is, in fact, safer than a fieldsman in any of the more suicidal bat-and-pad positions or a wicketkeeper standing up to fast-medium bowling. It is interesting that keepers, who have the riskiest job in cricket, have so far rejected the helmet, perhaps because increased safety fails to compensate for lack of comfort. No batsman with reasonably quick reflexes should be struck on the head, though there is always the risk of his edging a hook into his face. The latter fate is most likely to occur against very fast bowling, especially when the stroke has been attempted against a ball that is too fully pitched for hooking safely.

A fascinating, somewhat ironic outcome of the helmet has been the marked increase in the number of batsmen hit on the head and in the face. This can't be put down solely to the increase in fast and medium-paced bowling. What, then, is the reason? My view is that the extra protection has meant that batsmen have become less worried and apprehensive. As a result, they are attempting to play, or hook, deliveries which previously they would have been thankful to have avoided. The outcome is that they are not moving quite so quickly, and are being hit.

INTIMIDATORY BATTING

Simon Barnes, 2003

Never has a cricketer had so appropriate a surname. But let us understand that aright. Steve Waugh's cricketing warfare has never been a matter of hatred, jingoism and senseless aggression, any more than a matter of chivalry, romance and the search for personal glory.

No. Waugh's wars have been about the most efficient possible means of despatching the enemy. They are about a clear understanding of the opposition's strengths and weaknesses, and an equally uncluttered understanding of the strengths and weaknesses of his own side. Sometimes the results are spectacular, but that is by the way. Spectacle is a by-product of a hard head, clear vision, an analytical mind and an impersonal lust for victory.

Waugh wants to defeat you personally – but nothing personal, if you see what I mean. He has that air possessed by very few, even at the highest level of sport: that sense of vocation, that urge to beat not the opposition but the limitations of your self, your game, your world. There was something of that unearthly quality in Ayrton Senna, the Brazilian racing driver. Ellen MacArthur, the British sailor, has it too.

Waugh has the gift of reducing complex matters to simple ones: he sees without prejudice how best to exploit the opposition's weakness, how best to deploy his own strengths. The approach, cold-blooded, scientific, is that of a general, rather than a character in Sir Thomas Malory.

Waugh has conducted his cricketing campaigns in a mood of dispassionate ferocity. He famously remarked that sledging was "mental disintegration"; but that is not so much the aim of Waugh's sledging as of Waugh's cricket. The batting, bowling and fielding of his teams have all had the aim of causing mental disintegration: a moment of uncertainty that leads to self-doubt that leads to defeat. Waugh always wants defeat to be personal and complete, the better to prey on the opposition mind.

And in the process, he has transformed Test cricket. Over the past four years, his Australians played in a manner that was once unthinkable. A captain is usually assessed on the way he operates his bowlers and sets his field, for it is supposed to be the fielding captain who controls the tempo of a match. Waugh is, of course, spectacularly good at all that. But it is the way he manages his batting line-up that is revolutionary.

We traditionally think of fast scoring as something dashing and devil-may-care: Jessop, Milburn, Botham. It was merry and jaunty and beery, the way you batted if you were a bit of a lad. Fast scoring was not altogether serious – it came in the drive-for-show category. Waugh's Australians have put it into the putt-for-dough department. For them, fast scoring is not a bonnets-over-the-windmill slogfest: it is deadly serious. It is done first to undermine the opposing bowlers, and with them the rest of the fielding side. And then it gives Australia extra time in the quest for 20 wickets: a free session for your bowlers every innings.

It is not so much a tactic as an emphasis: when in doubt, attack. Not for fun – as a thought-out ploy. As a team policy. Speed is not self-indulgence but duty. The idea is to win every session of every Test match, and mostly that is what Australia have been doing. If things go amiss, there is always the captain to come in later in the order. The only disappointment in Waugh's later career is that there have been so few occasions when he has been required to do his one-man rescue act.

The tactic of speed has been enthralling, but Waugh did not do it to enthral. He did it to enslave. There was an awful lot of guff talked about "brighter cricket" in the 1960s: if that was brighter cricket, what would audiences of 40 years back have made of the Australian speed machine? Waugh doesn't employ the tactic to make cricket brighter. But – and it is an aspect of his greatness – he didn't allow his prejudice against mere entertainment to muddle his thinking. In its intention, the Australian strokemaking is as flamboyant as an atom bomb.

ART AND GRAFT   Mike Atherton, 2013

Talent. We have a curious relationship with it in English cricket. If it is generally defined as possessing either a natural gift, or a capacity for success, then our game invariably tags as talented those who enjoy the gift, but not necessarily the success. Many England cricketers who have struggled to establish themselves in the international game – Chris Lewis, Mark Lathwell, Owais Shah and Ravi Bopara, to name four recent examples – are routinely described as being among the most talented players of their time.

The notion of a natural gift has taken a battering in recent years, thanks in particular to the work of one scientist. The Swedish psychologist K. Anders Ericsson has gone a long way towards deconstructing the myths of talent by showing that elite performance is almost always the result of ferocious hard work, relentless self-improvement and specific, rigorous practice – all within a cultural context in which the appetite for self-improvement can flourish. In other words, few have reached the top without putting in the hours.

In looking for examples of talent, we nearly always exaggerate the importance of an eye-catching moment, or a graceful style. Aesthetics outweigh almost everything else. Mark Ramprakash's feats were far from modest, but it was his elegance – the ease with which he appeared to play, the extra time he appeared to enjoy – that encouraged the notion he was unusually talented.

Most of us are prone to this weakness of falling for the kind of talent that a moment of brilliance implies: a breathtaking stroke, a scintillating piece of fielding. As a result, we underestimate the gifts given to those who achieve consistently, if not spectacularly. After watching a young Dwayne Smith, the West Indian all-rounder who had made a rapid century on Test debut, smash a length ball from Steve Harmison over midwicket and out of the ground in Trinidad some years ago, I turned to my companion and said: "I've just seen the next great West Indian batsman." One shot was enough to fool me. All through the disappointing years that followed, I kept expecting what I thought was exceptional talent to blossom. It never did.

We are apt to hold too narrow a definition of what constitutes talent. One of Ramprakash's contemporaries was Graham Thorpe. More than a decade ago in Colombo, I watched him score a hundred against Sri Lanka's spinners in conditions that could not have been more testing, with the sun beating down and the pitch disintegrating into dust. His strokeplay was not eye-catching; in fact, the innings was devoid of any flowing shots at all. But what an innings it was – one of the finest I ever saw from an England player.

That day, Thorpe revealed so many different aspects of his talent. He played the ball off the pitch later than any of his team-mates. It takes a particular gift to let the ball keep coming and coming until the bowler is almost yelping with success, but he adopted a kind of French-cricket technique, keeping his backlift low, and turning the blade with his wrists at the last moment to pierce gaps that most others would have needed satellite navigation to find. His talent was to adapt to his surroundings.

As for my own career, I take an innings of 99 at Headingley against South Africa in 1994 as one that revealed my own special – for want of another word – talent. It was after the dirt-in-the-pocket match at Lord's and, in the intervening week, I had to cope with an unusual degree of public interest, with a tabloid tracking my every movement. Between Tests, I had not been able to practise, and there had been no county match for Lancashire.

The attention was not on my batting, but on my captaincy and character. I had been forced to sit through two torturous televised press conferences, and to listen to a range of critics, from the comedian Jimmy Tarbuck to the chairman of the Headmasters' Conference, who sought my resignation. It was an uncomfortable time, and before I walked out to bat, I had not given a moment's thought to the innings. I scratched around for a couple of hours before lunch, and forced myself into some kind of rhythm by dint of nothing more than pure bloody-mindedness. But what I had managed to do, between walking to the middle and facing the first ball, was to put the events of the previous fortnight to the back of my mind.

The ability to shut out the noise and the clamour is something I see now – to a far greater degree – in Alastair Cook. It is not an aptitude that stands out, is easily recognised, or regarded as exceptional. Hidden from view it may be but, set against the requirements for success at international level, with all its pressures, it is a talent as important as the ability to play a good-looking cover-drive. It is only now, after over 7,000 Test runs and more hundreds than any other England player, that observers (I have been more guilty than most) are starting to think of him as gifted.

THE CORRIDORS OF POWER

A WHOLE NEW WORLD
Jack Bailey, 1994

On February 2, 1993, what was almost certainly the most acrimonious and shambolic meeting in the history of ICC broke up amid signs of lasting anguish. The central debating point had been the venue for the next World Cup. So strongly had feelings run on all sides that a one-day meeting had gone on well into the night. The issue of the World Cup was finally resolved on the morning of the second day. It would be played in India, Pakistan and Sri Lanka – this in spite of a decision in favour of England at a previous ICC meeting.

The announcement of the World Cup decision was followed *sotto voce* – as an afterthought, almost – by a statement to the effect that David Richards, chief executive of the Australian Cricket Board, had been appointed chief executive of the International Cricket Council. He would take up his duties, at Lord's, five months later.

The meeting focused on the World Cup marked an alarming departure from the way business had been conducted within ICC from its foundation as the Imperial Cricket Conference in 1909. Since then, the name had changed to the International Cricket Conference and then to the International Cricket Council, and ICC had seen some contentious times. But that 1993 meeting was something different. It was the outward and visible sign, if one were needed, that the playing of cricket as a game, so long the chief preoccupation of those gathered round the tables of the MCC committee room at Lord's, and pursued invariably with an attitude of quiet and civilised deference, had been overtaken.

The meeting had been prolonged, almost beyond endurance, by a series of legal quibbles concerning an interpretation of ICC rules. There were frequent adjournments so that India's two chief representatives (of the nine apparently present at various times) could seek the support of India's Lord Chief Justice for their contention that a simple majority of those voting was all that was necessary to determine the destination of the next World Cup.

This had been the case with the allocation of previous World Cups. By rule, the 19 Associate Members had one vote; the Test-playing countries, with two votes each, mustered 18 between them. But because this put the Associate Members in a position of strength, unwarranted in the eyes of Full Members, the voting had been changed. A binding resolution now required a simple majority of those present. But that would apply only if support were given by two-thirds of the Full Members, of whom at least one had to be a Foundation Member (England or Australia).

Complicated perhaps; but, since this rule change had been made with the backing of India and the other Full Members, not, one would have thought, questionable. The new voting system applied to all decisions categorised as binding. From all accounts, the position of India and her supporters was to question that the World Cup vote should fall into the category of a binding decision. Here the mind boggles. If a decision as to where the World Cup would be staged, at a meeting called specifically to decide the issue, was not considered binding, then what was?

Madhavrao Scindia, the president of the Indian Board and one-time Minister of Civil Aviation and Tourism, was supported by representatives of Pakistan and Sri Lanka in a determined and prolonged attempt to win the day. The intrusion of legalistic arguments into the game had already become familiar to Sir Colin Cowdrey, chairman of the meeting. The Pakistan tour of England, with its ball-tampering row and the swift interventions by lawyers employed by Pakistan, had surely prepared him and the MCC secretariat, or should have done. The obduracy of India and others in the face of ICC's own lawyers must have come as a shock, however, and the meeting degenerated. All that cricket used to stand for was thrown out of the committee-room window.

Politicking and favour-seeking among member countries by those from the subcontinent had apparently begun well before the meeting. Those representing the Associate Members were aware that substantial funds would be made available. India had supported Zimbabwe's elevation to full membership; talk was rife of favours being called in.

After the ICC meeting, an unprecedented press conference was called by the chief executive of the British Test and County Cricket Board, A. C. Smith. Never one to volunteer information ("no comment but don't quote me" has often been put forward as one of his more adventurous remarks), Smith went to town. "We endured a fractious and unpleasant meeting beset by procedural wrangling," he said. "There was no talk of anything like cricket. It was, by a long way, the worst meeting I have ever attended." He confirmed that although his board felt that a previous minute nominating England as the next host country for the World Cup was still valid, they had finally succumbed in the best and wider interests of the world game. Smith also confirmed that a price for his Board's compliance had been that they would definitely host the World Cup after next, currently scheduled for the English summer of 1998. As part of the deal, they also ensured that the profits of the tournament supposed to be held in 1995 (which is actually now scheduled for early 1996) would fund the new ICC secretariat.

BEHIND THE SCENES AT THE ICC – FEAR AND LOATHING IN DUBAI

Gideon Haigh, 2012

The jurisdiction the ICC exert over their pennywise junior membership tends to show up the limited authority they have over their frequently pound-foolish Full

Members, who split threequarters of the ICC's annual distributions ten ways
without having to provide so much as a receipt. Since January 2009, Associate
Members have in return for their distribution been expected to provide the ICC
with a budget and a business plan signed off by their regional development
manager; they are also retrospectively assessed by one of five support and
compliance officers according to a metric known as "the scorecard", based not only
on results but numbers of coaches, umpires, grounds, and levels of non-ICC
income. Attempts in Lorgat's time to strengthen the ICC's supervision of how the
Full Members spend their money, by contrast, have been largely fruitless. "They
hate giving us their financial information," says one ICC officer. "They give us
certain information but it's a constant struggle. In fact, we need to know. We're an
international federation and custodians of the game. If a Full Member is in financial
trouble, it impacts the health of cricket generally."

It is the ten Test nations, rather, who keep the ICC on short rations. The organisation is funded by a quaint system of member subscriptions, based on annual
costs, currently $25-30m, threequarters paid for by Full Members, a quarter by the
rest; they accumulate reserves, which are capped at one and a half times annual
expenses, basically by coming in under budget, although some would like the ICC
to dispense with reserves altogether. Directors also bellyache constantly about the
costs of operating in the Emirates. Just months after the ICC moved into their new
headquarters, some on the executive board began lobbying for them to relocate
either back to London or to Mumbai – at least until the potential tax impost was
disclosed. Their own privileges, of course, remain untouchable. The ICC executive
board spent more on their own entertainment at the 2,000th Test than was at the
time on offer as annual prize money for the world's No. 1 Test nation.

The BCCI in particular are a law unto themselves. It is commonly said in Dubai
that every dealing with India "starts with a no". It can improve from there, and
ground has sometimes been given with unanticipated grace. In general, however,
their representatives are said to arrive at meetings ill-prepared and disdainful,
having done their deals ahead of any formal discussion, rendering that discussion
pointless; Lalit Modi is recalled as acting as BCCI representative at one meeting
with two laptops and four mobile phones in front of him, which he continued
using throughout; Lorgat's attempts to stimulate debate in the general absence of it
merely earned him India's ire. With their huge financial heft, the BCCI can also
exert influence simply by absence of approval. Although they were not chief among
the refuseniks two years ago, it was essentially the BCCI's preference for the less
effectual Australian Jack Clarke over the potentially hard-headed John Howard that
prevented Howard's nomination to the ICC vice-presidency – resulting in the
promotion instead of the beige New Zealander Alan Isaac.

It was once fondly thought that an Indian president would improve relations
between the ICC and the BCCI; in fact, it has probably worsened them. For all his
political prestige as India's agriculture minister, Sharad Pawar had been too obviously an ally of Modi's when the IPL came unglued in May 2010, and thereby
courted the distrust of the BCCI's incoming president, Narayanaswami Srinivasan.
With Srinivasan's nomination to the executive board last year, in fact, the ICC
inherited a new director who embodies many of their problems, already running a
state association, a national board and an IPL franchise, in apparent adherence to

Kerry Packer's old dictum about conflict of interest: "If yer don't have a conflict, yer don't have an interest." He also holds the ICC in contempt. After one acrimonious debate at Srinivasan's first executive board meeting, New Zealand Cricket's Justin Vaughan said sympathetically to Lorgat: "I don't know how you put up with it."

Little Wonder No. 30

Surrey 1933. Hobbs had previously announced his intention of dropping quietly out of the team and, having become more or less a free agent, he played only when the weather was warm and genial and when he felt he was sufficiently fit to be able to stand the strain of a three-day match. In his 51st year he showed clearly that he had lost little if any of his great skill, scoring nearly 800 runs in 16 innings with an average of over 47.

MODERN WAYS

THE APPLIANCE OF SCIENCE: A VIEW FROM THE DRESSING ROOM

Derek Pringle, 1998

Until recently, cricket's ties with science had gone little beyond a basic understanding of the aerodynamics of swing. And the use of daring technology peaked with the bowling machine and the cat's cradle – a contraption used for practising slip catching but doubling, far more usefully, as a place for tired bowlers to catch some shut-eye.

What has science now brought to the sport? The answer is probably not much. Surrounding the players with psychologists, nutritionists and fitness gurus may seem a thoroughly professional move but, in a game that is still dominated by skill, their effectiveness is hard to measure. And, as even the most inattentive schoolchild knows, science has to be measured by results. In cricket, with its myriad variables and imponderables, this is impossible, and even the converted must see there can be little point in measuring Shane Warne's fitness levels or body-fat content, unless he intends swapping wrist-spin for steeplechasing.

The progressives – among them England coach David Lloyd, South African coach Bob Woolmer and former England captain Bob Willis – have embraced science with enthusiasm. And the change of attitude in the England dressing-room has been dramatic. Actual change has been a bit slower. Tea and coffee (now considered bad for hand–eye co-ordination and the healing of injuries) and a post-match beer (bad for recovering muscles) are out of favour; even Jack Russell is now only a ten-cup-a-day man. Fruit juice and pizza are the latest to be dispensed with science's blessing.

Yet if the theory behind the rehydration and carbo-loading makes perfect sense to those spending their working lives cooped up with laboratory rats, the comfort zone for those who regard cricket as a sport with a social dimension is visibly shrinking on and off the field. As the economic pariahs of professional sport, crick-eters have never found it easy to sacrifice their lifestyle; many regard the difference between fitness and fatness as nothing more than a changed vowel.

Where does this no-stone-unturned pact with science leave the game? English cricket has found itself wanting as big money has rolled in from television: an amateurish blot on a sporting landscape paved with gold. Science could be seen as the game's response to its guilty conscience. It will not guarantee better results, but at least it shows that the game is willing to respond to external pressures. However, science can only try to create ever-efficient machines out of players. This is a game whose appeal relies on its unpredictability. They may be able to clone sheep. Eleven Ian Bothams would keep the bar well and truly propped up after play, but they would not make the game any more intoxicating.

THE RISE OF THE BACKROOM BOYS
Gideon Haigh, 2006

The formative trends in cricket, as in the world in general, are often understood only in retrospect. So it is with coaching. Twenty years ago, after an unsuccessful tour of New Zealand, the Australian Cricket Board appointed Bob Simpson as the first full-time coach of the national team. Today, the role in every country is crucial, controversial and rather precarious.

However, the first cause for wonder is not the 20 years in which coaches have been a phenomenon, but the preceding century in which they were not. Every other sport knelt at the altar of the coach, manager or guru; in cricket, despite a technical rigour and complexity that begat so many instructional books, the captain remained all-powerful. The game, as it were, was learned without formally being taught. There have been figures called coaches in first-class cricket for many years, but they tended in olden times to be sinecured former players responsible for duties like managing net practice or taking care of the team's equipment. W. T. Grayburn was "coach" at Surrey when Jack Hobbs joined a century ago, for example, but Hobbs learned nothing from him. "As a matter of fact, I have never had one hour's coaching from anybody in my life," he recalled, "and the reason why I emphasise this point here is that I am a natural batsman, entirely self-taught."

There was certainly no question of a Test team having a formal, full-time coach. If players had something to learn, they did so from each other. When Neil Harvey struggled to come to terms with English conditions on his first tour in 1948, he sought advice from Bradman via his room-mate Sam Loxton, and received back the oracular counsel: "Hit the ball on the ground and you can't be caught."

The situation changed, almost by chance, in the late 1970s when Ken Barrington began to carve out a role separate from that of the ambassadorial tour manager, a post which was considered as much an honour as a job. Barrington had two turns as manager, struggling with the political fallout from the Packer breakaway, but excelling so much as an adviser and paterfamilias that Lord's agreed to take him to Australia as an assistant in 1978-79. Two years later, he was initially excluded and then reinstated on the players' insistence for the tour of the West Indies, on which he suddenly died.

Australia's decision to name a full-time coach in 1986 met with considerable scepticism. The first man offered the job, Ian Chappell, declined because he doubted the role was necessary; the second, Simpson, said he regarded it as finite, and foresaw making himself redundant; when England appointed Micky Stewart to a similar role later the same year, he was designated not "coach" but "team manager". The impetus for the appointments of Simpson and Stewart was simple: failure, and resultant dislocation in leadership. Australia had had four captains in five years, England six, and the latest appointments, Allan Border and Mike Gatting, were bearing their burdens uneasily. The creation of the roles also reflected the trend to specialisation in numerous occupations: how could a captain be responsible for technical supervision and physical conditioning as well as pre-match strategy and on-field tactics? Cricket was not pioneering anything, so much as catching up with other sports.

The other factor in the rise of the coach, generally ignored, was television. Instant, then slow-motion, video replays made it possible to study technique up close over and over again. Brian Booth, who captained Australia in the 1960s, recalled that in his entire career he saw himself bat for only one delivery: by chance, he once saw himself being bowled on a newsreel. Ricky Ponting, the present incumbent, can now watch every ball of his international career as often as he wants, on TV or his laptop. It is one thing to tell a player he is doing the wrong thing; it is quite another to show him. The role of replays has expanded from the analytical to the motivational, for Test cricketers today routinely prepare for playing by watching footage of their earlier successes: a means of reminding themselves of what they are capable.

Simpson was a coach of a conservative disposition, but conservatism in his time was a form of revolution. He stressed basics like fielding and running between wickets, and preached the gospel of hard work to a team, at first, averse to it: "In many cases, the work ethic was non-existent. What was worse, they did not seem to want to match up. Instead, they treated the whole training exercise as a bit of a joke, in order, I believe, to disguise the fact that they couldn't hack it." When Australia won the 1987 World Cup as rank outsiders, their strength was perceived as a dedication to detail, and a vindication of the idea of an off-field task master.

Cricket is a game that measures almost everything. But how was the coach to measure the value he was adding to his team by anything other than the banal ledger of wins and losses, or the subjective gauge of observation and anecdote? After all, when Yogi Berra was once asked what made a great baseball coach, he replied simply: "A great ball team". The 1990s became, accordingly, a period of considerable experimentation. The experiences of Kapil Dev with India and Vivian Richards with West Indies suggested that getting the right coach was not as easy as appointing a great player, but nor did astute captains like England's Keith Fletcher and New Zealand's Geoff Howarth make off-field masterminds. The reign of Ray Illingworth did little for the cause of a single supremo with selection as well as training responsibilities; in fact, apprehension about the consolidation of too much power in one individual saw Simpson lose his role in selection. Meanwhile, the ambit of other coaches, particularly in Pakistan, was too restricted for them to make much difference.

Two men in particular were perceived to have moved the game onwards. Bob Woolmer ran South Africa's team innovatively with help from sports scientist Tim

Noakes from the University of Cape Town. And eventually Australia turned to John Buchanan, who has a degree in "human movements" from the University of Queensland and a first-class batting average of 12. Not all Woolmer's innovations, however, occasioned admiration, particularly the earpiece with which he fitted captain Hansie Cronje at the 1999 World Cup; the later revelation that his players consorted with match-fixers without telling him also suggested communication between them was less than constant. And Buchanan, with his affinity for management-consultancy jargon, has never convinced, for instance, Ian Chappell: "If I had a son, the last bloke in the world I would take him to for cricket coaching would be John Buchanan."

But the individuals most closely identified with significant improvement have been three hard-working sweats who made the most of sometimes limited abilities in their playing days, and who are likewise capable as coaches of wringing extra from talent at their disposal: Dav Whatmore in Sri Lanka, John Wright in India and Duncan Fletcher in England. All came from outside their respective cricket systems. All won reputations for meticulous preparation and close relationships with their captains.

The deadpan Fletcher, a former skipper of Zimbabwe whose coaching spurs were won at unfashionable Western Province and Glamorgan, has been the most surprising. His former captain Nasser Hussain has admitted nothing but surprises in the early stages of their partnership: "I thought I would be starting off as the senior partner with the perceived upper hand in our relationship because I was the one who had played a lot of Test cricket. I thought he would be coming to me saying 'What's he like?', 'What's that one like?' How wrong could I have been! I soon realised that Duncan knew everything about everyone!"

THE LONELINESS OF THE LONG-DISTANCE CRICKETER

DON'T MARRY A CRICKETER   Derek Pringle, 2003

Cricket and family life have never been easy bedfellows. A relationship which was at odds long before women were given the vote appears to have reached a crisis of late. Within the game, there has been a spate of well-publicised marital break-ups; outside it, the world is adapting to new rules of engagement between the sexes. The leading players are finding that cricket is making greater demands on them than ever before – and so are their wives.

Even though a successful Test career is now shorter than it used to be, at six to ten years, wives and girlfriends are no longer tolerating their lot as cricket widows and virtual single parents. A high-profile husband may have his allure but, once the cachet fades, many are swapping them for men who spend their weekends at home washing the car and mowing the lawn – or even cooking the lunch and bathing the kids.

The sheer time taken by the game, especially at weekends, has rarely been popular with families: up to ten hours a day, often seven days a week, if you include journeys and preparation time. Normal folk who receive an invitation to a christening from a professional cricketer have to look at it twice because it tends to be during the week. Add lengthy tours of three or four months to the load and it amounts to a huge strain, particularly on those who have come to expect more of husbands and fathers than previous generations.

The absenteeism is felt far more in England, where little more than a few weeks separate the hectic six-month home season and the moment wives wave their husbands off on tour in October. It would not be sanctioned now, but on the 1982-83 tour of Australia and New Zealand, Chris Tavaré, who had recently married, brought his wife Vanessa along for the entire 148-day trip. What none of the team knew at the time was that Vanessa had phobias about flying and heights, both of which required heavy sedation. With 23 flights and most of the hotels set in downtown skyscrapers, a lot of sedative was needed. If Tavaré was unhappy he never showed it. It wasn't until the Fourth Test in Melbourne that he played his first shot in anger.

Once a relationship becomes strained, cricket rarely seems able to offer a compromise. Recently, Darren Gough, Graham Thorpe, Mark Butcher and Dominic Cork have all seen their marriages break up while on England duty. In Thorpe's case, the public saw it too: he flew home from India at the beginning of a Test match in an attempt to save his marriage, appeared on his doorstep in Surrey to talk frankly about it, and later played for England at Lord's when clearly not himself during a custody battle over his two small children.

There is a distinct generation gap. Sue Fletcher, a stoic by nature, recalls the England wives of the late 1960s and early '70s being a close-knit group that was more like a self-help collective than a bunch of disillusioned housewives. "We knew what the form was about looking after the kids; our husbands made that clear from day one," she says. "When they were on tour, and they were long tours in those days, the wives used to visit each other back in England. It helped that we all got on well and had children roughly the same age. But we rallied round and got on with it because that's how it was."

In those days, families were allowed to tour but were not encouraged. "I remember going to visit Keith on tour and being allowed to spend 21 nights with him," Sue Fletcher says. "We had to pay every penny and often it took up the entire tour fee so you'd make nothing. Because of those financial constraints, wives on tour, especially with kids in tow, were the exception rather than the rule."

These days, there are still limits, but they are less strict. Providing a player is abroad for more than 60 days, the England and Wales Cricket Board allow 30 days' family provision for players who are in both the Test and one-day sides and 16 for those in one or the other. The board also pay for return flights (in economy) for wives and children under 18, all accommodation, some internal travel and a modest daily meal allowance.

Family visits, even when the cost to players is minimal, are often fraught. Denise Fraser, wife of Angus, was one of the generation of England wives after Sue Fletcher. Denise had mixed feelings about her times on tour. "Before the children were born, trips to the West Indies were great fun, especially when players like David Gower and Allan Lamb were about. But in my experience, we were not always made to feel welcome and, although the wives and kids often lifted morale when we arrived, we also added to the stress."

Denise Fraser remembers the 1995-96 tour of South Africa as particularly blighted. England's tour party grew from 20 to over 70 as families arrived for

Christmas in Port Elizabeth and Cape Town. The team manager, Illingworth, was so incensed by the chaos that he blamed it for England's defeat in the series – the Fifth Test, at Newlands, was the only one with a result.

"It was disastrous," Denise Fraser says. "We stayed in a city-centre hotel that had no facilities for the kids, and players had to give up their seats for us on the team bus. We felt unwelcome, especially when Illingworth blamed us for the defeat, which was unfair. I remember England winning in both Barbados and Melbourne just after the wives had come out."

The paradox of all the time away from home is that the problems can start when it finishes. A player comes off an arduous tour, expecting to be greeted like a conquering king (or a defeated one), and may find that he no longer fits into the rhythms of home life. "You become so used to their absence," Denise Fraser says, "that Angus would upset my routines when he got back. Suddenly there is another body in the equation and you have to get used to living together again.

"Let's face it, most players are a selfish breed who, if not too tired to help out around the house, bring their problems home with them. They are used to getting everything put on a plate and there were times when I couldn't wait to get him on his way again."

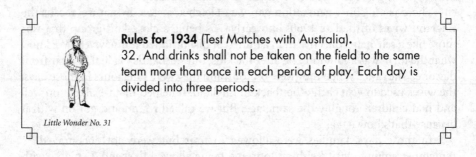

Rules for 1934 (Test Matches with Australia).
32. And drinks shall not be taken on the field to the same team more than once in each period of play. Each day is divided into three periods.

Little Wonder No. 31

CRICKET AND DEPRESSION: AN INSIDER'S TALE — Mike Yardy, 2012

The irony was that 2010 had been the most successful period of my career. I had helped England win the World Twenty20, established myself in the one-day side and, that summer, played in three series wins. But deep down, I knew I was in a bad place: I was not enjoying what should have been a fantastic experience. I was very tense and living on an increasingly short fuse – both with myself and others.

I had always had high expectations, but things were getting out of hand. I could never please myself, was constantly striving for more and setting unrealistic goals, which just increased the pressure I was putting on myself. Because of the self-doubt, I would take things people said to me and twist them beyond all context. I would be looking for any comment to latch on to. "There you go, Mike, told you so," I would think. "You're no good, you can't do it."

I was supposed to be living my dream. Instead, I felt angry with myself: here, after all, was a scenario most people would love. I remember coming back to Sussex after playing for England in a one-day international in July 2010 and having a couple of arguments with the umpire during a Twenty20 game against Essex. We then played Hampshire and I was run out for nought. I walked past my batting partner and good friend Murray Goodwin and subjected him to a tirade of abuse, which I had never done before. I felt terrible afterwards.

A lot of things were happening that were out of character. I have always liked my own space, but now the very act of being around other people became an effort. My mind was saying: "They don't like you, anyway. Why would they? You're a loser." Everyone has negative thoughts, but I was letting mine rule my life. I joined up with the one-day squad early in September to play Pakistan, and – though it hurts to say so now – I wasn't really looking forward to it. I started the series well, but my performances deteriorated – inevitable, perhaps, given my state of mind.

I had learned to put on a brave face, but I woke up on the morning of the last one-dayer at Southampton and couldn't carry on. I didn't want to get out of bed. I just wanted to go home. I spoke to my wife Karin, who knew I had been struggling. She was in a difficult position because she knew how hard I had worked to follow my dream, but she was also aware, to a certain extent, of how I was feeling. I went to see Andy Flower, who was unbelievably supportive. It was a huge relief just to tell him. My place in that game went to my county colleague Luke Wright.

Over the coming months, I received great support from Brett Morrissey, a clinical psychologist recommended by Andy. I felt comfortable playing Twenty20 cricket for Central Districts in New Zealand before joining up with the one-day squad after the Ashes in January 2011. I was very anxious, but knew I was better able to deal with things – even though my support network was on the other side of the world. I really started enjoying the experience of playing for England. I took the good and bad days for what they were, and was looking forward to the World Cup on the subcontinent. I had been there before and knew that, because of security, it would be difficult to get about. But I thought I could handle it.

After a few weeks there, however, my mind started to win the battle, and negative thoughts took over. Because I was not playing very well, it had something to grip hold of. Once more, I was fighting myself and rarely stopped to think I was taking part in a great tournament. At night, I would lie for hours battling with my mind. It became a vicious circle: I was missing my family, I was performing badly, and my self-belief was low. The harder I tried, the more I just kept hitting a brick wall. In many ways, all that time spent thinking was worse than the sleep deprivation.

When we arrived in Sri Lanka for our quarter-final, I was struggling. I was out of the team and remember operating at a training session in a daze. Our spin-bowling coach Mushtaq Ahmed, a great friend and former Sussex team-mate, insisted I needed to think of my health. At this point I knew I had to go home and spoke to Andy, who again was very understanding. I was desperate not to be a distraction before such a big game, but I had been fighting this for so long. I just didn't have any fight left.

England

Twice in the recent past – 1982 and 2006 – an edition of *Wisden* has had to be reprinted because of popular demand. The only reason on both occasions was the level of interest in stunning, heart-stopping Ashes series, won with varying degrees of improbability by England. The fortunes of the England team – the agonies and occasional ecstasies – have formed a central plank of *Wisden* since the 1890s when the concept of international competition became formalised. The 1899 edition reported a significant moment in the early history of the England Test side: "Early in May Lord Hawke expressed the opinion that the time had come for the Test matches in the country between England and Australia to be placed under the control of a specially constituted body, and such strong support did he receive from the various counties that after an interval of a few months he found practically all his ideas carried into effect." So the "Board of Control for 'Test' Matches at Home" came into being, chaired by the president of MCC and containing five other members of its committee and a representative each from the ten most successful counties from the previous season. MCC effectively ran the England team until 1969 when the Test and County Cricket Board was formed. England's touring sides carried the MCC name until the mid-1970s and the club's colours until 1997.

As early as 1866 *Wisden* published results of the All-England Eleven matches, which were private enterprises rather than official representative sides, and mostly against 22-man club teams. The preface ("To the Reader") said: "J. W. and Co. have this year published the matches of the three All England Elevens, feeling certain, from the great favour with which these celebrated elevens are received in all parts of the country, their doings will be read with interest." Touring sides to England received coverage, whether they be the Aboriginal side of 1868, or the Americans who received this notice in the 1875 edition: "The Twenty-two comprised 11 members of the Boston (*red stockings*), and 11 of the Philadelphia Athletes (*blue stockings*)." The Americans won all their matches (against weak sides) including a defeat of Gentlemen of MCC at Lord's. American touring sides were regular visitors in the late 19th century. *Wisden* 1898 alerted readers to the phenomenon of Bart King, the father of swing bowling who caused a sensation by "making the ball swerve in the air in the manner of the baseball pitchers".

In 1878 the Australians arrived for the first time. The tour was arranged by James Lillywhite, who had taken a side to Australia in 1876-77 for what became regarded as the first Test matches. The 1879 edition reported: "When at the back end of 1876 rumour was busy about a probable visit of an Australian cricketing team to the old country, it quickly became evident that such a visit would be received with pleasure, and the team warmly welcomed by English cricketers of all ranks; and however incredulous most of us then were as to the chances of success the Colonials would have, all heartily applauded the pluck of young Australia in coming so far to play the game, level-handed, against the well-seasoned skilled cricketers of old England." Not for the last time, English complacency would prove their undoing, and the performances of "young Australia" duly impressed *Wisden*, which was particularly taken with their fielding: "practically demonstrating how a well placed thoroughly disciplined eleven, working with a will *all round*, could at times win matches by their splendid abilities in *saving runs*." Fred "The Demon" Spofforth, Australia's first great fast bowler, took 123 wickets on the tour.

It was not until 1884 that *Wisden* carried full reviews of tours to England, though they had started to carry lengthy match reports. As much as the quality of the play or the results, *Wisden* concerned itself with the profitability or otherwise of tours to England. In 1895: "The tour of the South African team in England satisfied, in a cricket sense, all reasonable expectations, but there is no getting away from the fact that the eleven were entirely unsuccessful in attracting the English public." Money was a thorny issue, particularly in relation to the remuneration of the professional players, which often prevented England from getting their best eleven on the field. Another concern was that Test matches were becoming too popular. "More and more in these days the interest of an Australian visit centres in the matches with England, all the other fixtures being strictly subservient to the great games," wrote Sydney Pardon in his review of the 1909 Australians' tour. Goodness knows what Pardon would have made of the modern tour, where matches against counties are glorified net sessions in which the counties themselves generally look to rest their best players.

Or indeed what he would have made of our almost exclusive focus on Test matches in this chapter and the following one on the other Test-playing nations. We have retained the *Wisden* tradition (broken in 2013) of placing reports of tours to England in one section and matches in overseas territories in other sections. So, for example, the 2005 Ashes is in this chapter but the 2010-11 series is in the Australia section. For the first time the 2013 Almanack placed all of England's internationals played in 2012, whether they be home or away, in one section. *Wisden* has never had a consistent style regarding how touring teams were described – even, in some years, in the same book. For extracts of tour reports we have adopted the style of, for example, Australians in England. There have been many changes to the presentation of international cricket, most significantly the expansion of coverage to reflect both the vast increase of matches played in all forms of the game in the past 20 years but also to give a more equal place in the book to cricket that does not involve England. In 2003 Tim de Lisle, editing the Almanack for a single year, introduced a World View section early in the book, which summarised each of the Test nations' years. The 2013 edition contains more than 500 pages of international cricket.

1878–89

Anglo-Australian rivalry had already been ignited by a series of tours Down Under, but the Australians' tour to England in 1878 was greeted with wonderment and fascination. The first Test in England in 1880 was not labelled as such by Wisden, but they happily got caught up in the excitement. Two years later England lost at The Oval, a defeat that spawned the Ashes though the urn itself received scant recognition in Wisden. The first mention was in a piece by Bernard Bosanquet looking back on the 1903-04 tour of Australia. Its next appearance was not until 1926.

1878 – NOTTINGHAMSHIRE v AUSTRALIANS: GREAT ANTICIPATION · 1879

At Nottingham, May 20, 21, 22, 1878. The Australians' first match in England was looked forward to with much interest by the cricketers of the old country, and the fact that the Notts authorities had obtained the favour of that first match being played on their ground, naturally caused the interest of cricketing England to be centred on Nottingham on that 20th of May, and the enquiries that day on other grounds of "Do you know how the Australians are getting on," were earnest and frequent. Arriving at Nottingham on the 14th, the Colonials were met at the Midland by various members of the Notts CCC, who as heartily as courteously welcomed them to Notts and old England. The Australians had then but four clear days to find their land legs and take a bit of practice, and although from that practice different men formed different opinions, those who practically know the effects of a 16,000-miles' voyage, and the contrast in pace between Australian and English wickets, foretold the best form of the Colonials could not possibly be displayed until they had become more acclimatised to the air, light, and wickets of England; nevertheless there were many good judges of the game who thought highly of their cricket, and one of the most famous of the famous Notts eleven wrote to the compiler of this little book "The Australians are a splendid team," an opinion given before they had commenced match playing, that was verified to the letter long before they had concluded match playing in England.

Australians 63 (A. Shaw 5-20, F. Morley 4-42) and 76 (Shaw 6-35, Morley 4-30); Nottinghamshire 153 (J. Selby 66; T. P. Horan 5-30).

1878 – MCC AND GROUND v AUSTRALIANS: DEMON BOWLING · 1879

At Lord's, May 27, 1878. This, one of the most remarkable matches ever played at Lord's, was commenced at three minutes past 12, and concluded at 20 minutes past six the same day. Only 128 overs and two balls were bowled, and but 101 runs, from the bat, scored in the match. One Australian bowler (Allan) got the crack bat of England caught out from the second ball in the match. Another Australian bowler (Spofforth) clean-bowled the said crack for nought in the second innings. The aforesaid Australian bowler (Spofforth) made a distinct mark in the bowling of the match by delivering six overs (less one ball) for 14 runs and six wickets – three bowled. *[In the second innings of MCC]* a ball bowled by Spofforth painfully hurt and prostrated Hornby, compelling him to retire. The decisive victory of the Australians was earnestly applauded by the members of MCC, and tumultuously so by the thousands of other Englishman present, whose bones will have moulded to dust long, long before the cricketers of the future – Colonial and English – ceased to gossip about the marvellous short-time match played by the Australians at Lord's on May 27, 1878.

MCC and Ground 33 (F. R. Spofforth 6-4) **and 19** (Spofforth 5-16);
Australians 41 (A. Shaw 5-10, F. Morley 5-31) **and 12-1**.

Trailblazers: the 1878 Australian touring team, (back row, from left)
J. McC. Blackham, T. Horan, G. H. Bailey, J. Conway (manager),
A. C. Bannerman, C. Bannerman, W. L. Murdoch; (seated) D. W. Gregory;
(on ground) F. R. Spofforth, F. E. Allan, W. E Midwinter, T. W. Garrett, H. F. Boyle.

1878 – MIDDLESEX v AUSTRALIANS: Grace gets his man 1879

At Lord's, June 20, 21, 22, 1878. Midwinter was to have played for the Australians, and just before noon on the first day he was duly flannelled and practising at Lord's ready for play, but shortly after, W. G. Grace arrived in hot haste from Kennington, claiming and obtaining Midwinter to play for Gloucestershire v Surrey, which match was commenced that day on The Oval. It was rumoured W. G. Grace acted on a prior made agreement; be that as it may Midwinter played that day for Gloucestershire, and never again played for the Australians.

Australians 165 (R. Henderson 4-60) **and 240** (F. R. Spofforth 56; Henderson 5-96);
Middlesex 122 (Mr A. J. Webbe 50; T. W. Garrett 7-38) **and 185** (Hon. E. Lyttelton 113; F. E. Allan 6-76).

1880 – ENGLAND v AUSTRALIA: WORLDWIDE INTEREST   1881

At The Oval, September 6, 7, 8, 1880. The compiler much regrets that the limited space allotted to the Australians' matches in this book precludes the possibility of giving a lengthened account of this famous contest. He must therefore rest content to put on record the following facts anent the match: That in the history of the game no contest has created such worldwide interest; that the attendances on the first and second days were the largest ever seen at a cricket match; that 20,814 persons passed through the turnstiles on Monday, 19,863 on the Tuesday, and 3,751 on the Wednesday; that fine weather favoured the match from start to finish; that the wickets were faultless; that Mr Murdoch's magnificent innings of 153 not out was made without a chance; that Mr W. G. Grace's equally grand innings was made with only one hard chance; that superb batting was also shown by Mr Lucas, Lord Harris, Mr McDonnell, and Mr Steel; that the fielding and wicketkeeping on both sides was splendid; that a marvellous change in the aspect of the game was effected on the last day; that universal regret was felt at the unavoidable absence of Mr Spofforth; and that England won the match by five wickets.

England 420 (Dr W. G. Grace 152, Mr A. P. Lucas 55, Lord Harris 52) **and 57-5;**
Australia 149 (F. Morley 5-56) **and 327** (W. L. Murdoch 153*).

1882 – ENGLAND v AUSTRALIA: BIRTH OF THE ASHES   1883

At The Oval, August 28, 29, 1882. It will be observed that in every instance the batting average of each member of the Australian team is lower than that of the English batsman placed opposite him, and that the bowling averages of the two men who had the largest share of the trundling for England are both better than either of those of the two bowlers who sent down the largest number of overs for Australia.

A perusal of these statistics must in the first place create a feeling of surprise that when the two elevens met there was the slightest probability of the English one being defeated. Secondly, no sensation but one of the highest admiration of the achievement of the Australian team can be felt when the result of the match is considered; and thirdly the figures prove, if figures prove anything, that the inevitable result of a series of encounters between the two elevens would be victory for the Englishmen in a very large proportion of the matches; and they further offer the strongest protest to the oft-raised cry of the decadence of English cricket.

With these few remarks the compiler proceeds to give a short account of the contest, leaving the reader to attribute the Australian victory to the fact that the Colonists won the toss and thereby had the best of the cricket; to the fact that the English had to play the last innings; to the brilliant batting of Massie; to the superb bowling of Spofforth; to the nervousness of some of the England side; to "the glorious uncertainty of the noble game"; or to whatever he or she thinks the true reason.

England, wanting 85 runs to win, commenced their second innings at 3.45 with Grace and Hornby. Spofforth bowled Hornby's off stump at 15, made in about as many minutes. Barlow joined Grace, but was bowled first ball at the same total. Ulyett came in, and some brilliant hitting by both batsmen brought the score to 51, when a very fine catch at the wicket dismissed Ulyett. 34 runs were then wanted, with seven wickets to fall. Lucas joined Grace, but when the latter had scored a two he was easily taken at mid-off. Lyttelton became Lucas's partner, and the former did all the hitting. Then the game was slow for a time, and 12 successive maiden overs were bowled, both batsmen playing carefully and coolly. Lyttelton scored a single, and then four maiden overs were followed by the dismissal of that batsman – bowled, the score being 66. Only 19 runs were then wanted to win, and there were five wickets to fall. Steel came in, and when Lucas had scored a four, Steel was easily caught and bowled. Read joined Lucas, but amid intense excitement he was clean-bowled without a run being added. Barnes took Read's place and scored a two, and three byes made the total 75, or ten to win. After being in a long time for five Lucas played the next ball into his wicket, and directly Studd joined Barnes the latter was easily caught off his glove without the total being altered. Peate, the last man, came in, but after hitting Boyle to square leg for two he was bowled, and Australia had defeated England by seven runs.

Australia 63 (R. G. Barlow 5-19, E. Peate 4-31) **and 122** (H. H. Massie 55; Peate 4-40);
England 101 (F. R. Spofforth 7-46) **and 77** (Spofforth 7-44).

Leicestershire 1934. During the season a suggestion was made that Leicestershire should amalgamate with Lincolnshire, but naturally nothing came of the proposal and the Leicestershire authorities decided to carry on in the hope of better support in the future.

Little Wonder No. 32

1886 – ENGLAND v AUSTRALIA (SECOND TEST):
SHREWSBURY SUPREME
1887

At Lord's, July 19, 20, 21, 1886. The meeting of England and Australia at Lord's is by almost common consent reckoned to be the most important match of a Colonial tour in this country, and the immense superiority of the best eleven in England over Australia, as represented by the Melbourne Club team of 1886, was clearly and unmistakably proved.

Shrewsbury, who had gone in first wicket down with the score at 27, was the last man out, and too much praise cannot be afforded him for his most extraordinary performance. He was at the wickets for six hours and 50 minutes, and though he gave a couple of difficult chances, there was scarcely any fault to be found with his batting. It should be stated that the wicket on this morning was rapidly improving, but Shrewsbury had thoroughly mastered all the varying conditions of the ground. Up to this time his 164 was the largest score ever made against Australian bowling in England. The Australians had always had such a reputation for playing an uphill game, that many people naturally expected great things from them, more especially as when they went in the wicket afforded bowlers little assistance. As it turned out, however, the batting was of a most disappointing character. The chief cause of this remarkable breakdown was the superb bowling of the Lancashire professional, Briggs, who was put on as first change, and took five wickets at a cost of only 29 runs. Going in a second time against the formidable majority of 232, the Australians lost one wicket, that of Garrett, for 12 runs, before the call of time.

When the score was 76 for two wickets, however, Briggs was put on at the pavilion end in place of Steel, a change which proved to be the turning-point of the innings. From this pavilion end Briggs bowled with even greater success than he had met with on the previous day when he was bowling from the nursery wicket, and one after another the Australians went down before him. Briggs, who was immensely cheered all round the ground, took six wickets at a cost of only 45 runs, so that in the whole match he obtained 11 wickets for 74 runs.

England 353 (A. Shrewsbury 164, W. Barnes 58; F. R. Spofforth 4-73);
Australia 121 (J. Briggs 5-29) and **126** (Briggs 6-45).

1886 – ENGLAND v AUSTRALIA (THIRD TEST): WG'S FIVE LIVES   1887

At The Oval, August 12, 13, 14, 1886. The third and last meeting between England and Australia had been robbed of a large amount of its interest by the poor form shown by the Australians, who had suffered defeat on each of the two previous occasions.

Although Mr W. G. Grace made the highest innings he had ever scored against Australian bowling, it was pretty generally admitted that his cricket was more faulty than usual. He gave an easy chance to Scott at short slip when he had made six, when his score was 23 he hit a ball very hard back to Giffen, which was a possible chance to that bowler's left hand; when he had scored 60 he might perhaps have been caught in the long field, had Bruce started earlier for the ball, and when his total was 93 McIlwraith had a difficult one-handed chance of catching him at slip. Moreover, just before getting out, when his total was 169 he hit a ball straight back to Garrett, who failed to hold it. Still, these blemishes notwithstanding, the innings was a very fine one. He made the enormous proportion of 170 out of 216 during his stay.

Being assisted by the condition of the ground, Lohmann and Briggs bowled magnificently and carried all before them. All ideas as to the ability of the 1886 Australian eleven to meet the full strength of England were totally dispelled by this crushing defeat. In fairness to the Colonials it must be stated that, at The Oval at any rate, they had all the worst of the wicket; but they played throughout with a lack of the life and energy that have usually characterised Australian cricket.

England 434 (Mr W. G. Grace 170, Mr W. W. Read 94, J. Briggs 53; F. R. Spofforth 4-65);
Australia 68 (G. A. Lohmann 7-36) and 149 (Lohmann 5-68).

1890–99

Australia remained the only major touring side to England, though English teams were undertaking tours to South Africa by this point. The 1896 Ashes was a spicy affair (England won a three-match series 2-1), with Wisden *exercised by the dubious bowling actions of the Australians, Jones and McKibbin, as well as a controversy over whether W. G. Grace, notionally an amateur, was being paid.*

1890 – ENGLAND v AUSTRALIA (SECOND TEST): OVERTHROW THRILLER 1891

At The Oval, August 11, 12, 1890. The committee of the Surrey Club, through no fault of their own, were unable to secure for the second of the representative matches the England team they would have wished to put into the field, a variety of circumstances occurring to thwart them. Yorkshire retained Ulyett and Peel to play against Middlesex at Bradford, Mr Stoddart preferred to assist the latter county, while Briggs and Attewell were suffering from injuries, and did not feel justified in taking part in so important an engagement.

Under ordinary circumstances the task of getting 95 runs would have been an easy matter for the England team, but with the wicket as it was it was impossible to feel over-confident. Mr Grace ought for the second time in the match to have been caught from the first ball that he received, but Trott at point dropped a ball that was cut straight into his hands. Despite this lucky let-off, however, the four best England wickets fell for 32 runs, the interest then reaching a very acute point.

The score had been taken to 83 – only 12 to win with six wickets to fall – when Maurice Read was caught at long-on for an invaluable 35. On his dismissal there came a collapse that recalled the great match in 1882, Mr Cranston, Lohmann and Barnes being dismissed in such quick succession that with eight men out two runs were still wanted to win. Amid indescribable excitement Sharpe became Mr MacGregor's partner, and five maiden overs were bowled in succession, Sharpe being beaten time after time by balls from Ferris that broke back and missed the wicket. Then at last the Surrey player hit a ball to cover point, but Barrett, who had a chance of running out either batsman, overthrew the ball in his anxiety, and a wonderful match ended in a victory for England by two wickets.

Australia 92 (F. Martin 6-50) and 102 (Martin 6-52);
England 100 (J. J. Ferris 4-25) and 95-8 (Ferris 5-49).

1893 – ENGLAND v AUSTRALIA (Second Test): Jackson's feat   1894

At The Oval, August 14, 15, 16, 1893. The game, which was the only one of the three Test matches brought to a definite issue, proved a great triumph for English cricket, the Australians being beaten by an innings and 43 runs. There was a most exciting over bowled by Giffen to Jackson, the batsman being in sad difficulties with one or two balls, but at length he lifted one right on to the covered seats, and so achieved the great distinction of making a hundred for England against Australia.

England 483 (Hon. F. S. Jackson 103, Mr A. E. Stoddart 83, Mr W. G. Grace 68, A. Shrewsbury 66, A. Ward 55, W. W. Read 52; G. Giffen 7-128); Australians 91 (W. H. Lockwood 4-37) and 349 (G. H. S. Trott 92, A. C. Bannerman 55, Giffen 53; J. Briggs 5-114, Lockwood 4-96).

1896 – Australians In England: bent arms   1897

There is one thing left to be said and that unfortunately is not of a pleasant nature. Up to last season one of the special virtues of Australian bowling was its unimpeachable fairness. Despite the evil example set by many English throwers, team after team came over to this country without a bowler to whose delivery exception could have been taken, but unhappily things are no longer as they once were. We have not the least hesitation in saying that a fast bowler with the action of Jones, or a slow bowler with a delivery so open to question as McKibbin, would have found no place in the earlier elevens that came to England. Jones's bowling is, to our mind, radically unfair, as we cannot conceive a ball being fairly bowled at the pace of an express train with a bent arm. Now that the evil effects of our own laxity with regard to unfair bowling have spread to Australia, it is to be hoped that the MCC will at last be moved to action in the matter.

1896 – ENGLAND v AUSTRALIA (Third Test): players' strike   1897

At The Oval, August 10, 11, 12, 1896. The third and conquering Test match [*England won by 66 runs*] was preceded by a regrettable incident which for a time caused intense excitement in the cricket world. The Surrey committee, after much deliberation, chose nine cricketers as certainties for the England eleven, and four others amongst whom the last two places were to be filled. Early in the week previous to the match, however – indeed almost as soon as the selection had been known – they received a letter signed by Lohmann, Gunn, Abel, Richardson and Hayward, in which those players demanded £20 each for their services in the match. Ten pounds per man had been paid to the professionals in the Test matches at Lord's and Manchester, and the Surrey committee, without going into the question of whether £20 was an excessive fee on an occasion of such importance, declined point blank to be dictated to.

Friendly counsels, however were soon at work, and on the evening of Saturday August 8, a communication was received at The Oval from Abel, Hayward, and Richardson to the effect that they withdrew from the position they had taken up, and placed themselves without reserve in the hands of the Surrey committee. However, the match committee were by no means at the end of their difficulties. Statements in certain newspapers as to the allowance made for expenses to amateurs caused great irritation, and for a time there was much uncertainty as to how the England eleven would be finally constituted. In the end matters were smoothed over, but not until a definite statement had been made public as to the financial relations between Mr W. G. Grace and the Surrey Club.

England 145 (H. Trumble 6-59) **and 84** (Trumble 6-30);
Australia 119 (J. T. Hearne 6-41) **and 44** (Hearne 4-19).

1896 – GRACE AND FAVOUR   Notes by the Editor, 1897

Nothing in connection with cricket has for some years past caused so much excitement as the so-called strike of the professionals, on the eve of the England and Australia match at The Oval.

The earnings of the players have certainly not risen in proportion to the immensely increased popularity of cricket during the last 20 years, but to represent the average professional as an ill-treated or down-trodden individual is, I think, a gross exaggeration. There is plenty of room for further improvement, but, taken all round, things are certainly far better than they were. Into the thorny question of amateurs' expenses I do not propose to enter, for the good and suffi-cient reason that I do not possess the necessary information. No doubt there are some abuses, but as a famous cricketer – a county captain and quite behind the scenes – has assured me that he does not know more than half a dozen men, playing as amateurs, who make anything out of the game, the evil would not seem to be very widespread. Mr W. G. Grace's position has for years, as everyone knows, been an anomalous one, but "nice customs curtsey to great kings" and the work he has done in popularising cricket outweighs a hundredfold every other consideration.

1896 – MR W. G. GRACE AND THE SURREY CLUB   1897

Various rumours having gained currency as to the amount of money allowed to Mr Grace for expenses when playing for England at The Oval, the following official statement was made public on August 10 – the opening day of the third Test match.

"The Committee of the Surrey County Cricket Club have observed paragraphs in the press respecting amounts alleged to be paid, or promised to, Dr W. G. Grace for playing in the match England v Australia. The Committee desire to give the statements contained in the paragraphs the most unqualified contradiction. During many years, on the occasions of Dr W. G. Grace playing at The Oval at the request of the Surrey County Committee, in the matches Gentlemen v Players and England v Australia, Dr Grace has received the sum of £10 a match to cover his expenses in coming to and remaining in London during the three days. Beyond this amount Dr Grace has not received, directly or indirectly, one farthing for playing in a match at The Oval.

Signed on behalf of the Committee,
August 10, 1896.   C. W. ALCOCK.

1900–19

England lost their third successive Ashes series in 1902, flayed by the great Victor Trumper among others. But it was an epic, matched only for excitement and tension by 1981 and 2005. Gilbert Jessop's hitting in the final Test, albeit with the rubber lost, would be invoked 79 years later in Wisden's *report of the Old Trafford Test when Ian Botham smashed 118. The South Africans arrived in 1907 with a fleet of leg-spinners that raised eyebrows and earned approval. They returned in 1912 for an experimental triangular tournament also involving Australia. The weather was dreadful and the idea has yet to repeated, though in 2013 the ICC announced that England would host the inaugural four-team Test Championship in 2017. The sun had better shine.*

1902 – ENGLAND v AUSTRALIA (THIRD TEST): TATE'S MATCH   1903

At Manchester, July 24, 25, 26, 1902. The fourth of the Test games produced one of the most memorable matches in the whole history of cricket, the Australians, after some extraordinary fluctuations of fortune, winning by three runs. At the end of the first day they looked to have the game in their hands, and at the end of the second it seemed equally certain that they would be beaten. Nothing that English cricketers did against the Australians last summer – not even the victory at The Oval in the final Test match – was more brilliant than the way in which they recovered themselves on the second day, turning an apparently hopeless position into one that suggested an easy win.

The Australians derived great advantage from winning the toss as up to lunchtime the ball did nothing at all on the soft turf. By magnificent hitting Trumper and Duff scored 135 in an hour and 20 minutes for the first wicket and when lunchtime came the total without further loss had reached 173, the Australians seeming already on the high road to victory. Duff, Hill and Darling all played fine cricket, but the chief batting honours rested with Trumper, who scored his 104 without making a mistake of any kind. His pulling was a marvel of ease and certainty.

Excitement was at its highest point when the Australians entered upon their second innings, everyone feeling that the result of the match might depend on the next hour's play. The fourth wicket would have fallen at 16 if Darling had not been missed at square leg off Braund's bowling by Tate. If the catch had been held it is quite likely, as Lockwood was bowling in such wonderful form, that the Australians would have been out for a total of 50 or 60. As it was, Darling and Gregory stayed together for an hour, their partnership producing 54 runs. England [were] left with 124 to get to win. For Lockwood, as a bowler, the match was nothing less than a triumph, his analysis for the two innings coming out at 11 wickets for 76 runs. Finer bowling than his on Friday afternoon can rarely have been seen.

As no one could tell how the wicket would play, the Englishmen entered upon their task under very anxious circumstances. With six wickets in hand and only 32 runs wanted, England still seemed sure of victory, but from this point everything changed, Trumble and Saunders, backed up by superb fielding, bowling so finely that in 50 minutes five more wickets went down for 24 runs. With 15 runs required, Rhodes joined Lilley and in three hits, one of them a big drive over the ring by Rhodes the score was carried to 116, or only eight to win. At this point, Lilley, from a fine hit, was splendidly caught by Hill at square leg, the fieldsman just reaching the ball when running at full speed. Heavy rain then drove the players from the field and there was a delay of threequarters of an hour before the match could be finished. Tate got a four on the leg side from the first ball he received from Saunders, but the fourth, which came a little with the bowler's arm and kept low, hit the wicket and the match was over, Australia winning by three runs.

Australia 299 (V. T. Trumper 104, C. Hill 65, R. A. Duff 54; W. H. Lockwood 6-48, W. Rhodes 4-104)
and 86 (Lockwood 5-28); **England 262** (Hon. F. S. Jackson 128; H. Trumble 4-75)
and 120 (Trumble 6-53, J. V. Saunders 4-52).

Fred Tate, whose selection for his debut on the morning of the match was described by Wisden as a "blunder", never played for England again. But his son Maurice would do so, 39 times.

Deaths in 1934. Correction: Mr E. L. Bartlett, West Indies, of whom an obituary notice appeared in last year's issue of the Almanack, wrote from Bridgetown in March with the assurance "that I am very much alive and fit". It is a pleasure to publish this message.

Little Wonder No. 33

1902 – ENGLAND v AUSTRALIA (FIFTH TEST): THE JOY OF JESSOP   1903

At The Oval, August 11, 12, 13, 1902. Australia having already won the rubber, the fifth and last of the Test matches had not at starting the same importance that would under other circumstances have attached to it, but it produced a never-to-be-forgotten struggle and a more exciting finish, if that were possible, than the one at Manchester. In face of great difficulties and disadvantages England won by one wicket after the odds had been 50 to one on Australia. Some truly wonderful hitting by Jessop made victory possible after all hope had seemed gone.

England went in with 263 wanted to win the match. Half the side were out for 48 and the match looked all over. At this point Jackson, who had gone in third wicket down, was joined by Jessop and a stand was made which completely altered the game. At first, however, Jessop's cricket was far from suggesting the wonderful form he afterwards showed. When he had made 22 Kelly missed stumping him and at 27 he gave a rather awkward chance to Trumper at long-off. After the interval Jessop settled down at once, and hit as he only can. At one point he scored four fours and a single off successive balls from Saunders. The partnership had added 109 runs in 65 minutes when Jackson was easily caught and bowled. Jessop went on hitting for some little time longer, but at 187 he closed his extraordinary innings by placing a ball gently into short leg's hands. He scored, in just over an hour and a quarter, 104 runs out of 139. All things considered a more astonishing display has never been seen. What he did would have been scarcely possible under the same circumstances to any other living batsmen. The rest of the match was simply one crescendo of excitement.

Australia 324 (H. Trumble 64*, M. A. Noble 52; G. H. Hirst 5-77) **and** 121 (W. H. Lockwood 5-45); **England** 183 (Trumble 8-65) **and** 263-9 (Mr. G. L. Jessop 104; J. V. Saunders 4-105, Trumble 4-108).

1905 – AUSTRALIANS IN ENGLAND: JACKSON THE LUCKY GENERAL   1906

There is no need to go over familiar ground and insist upon Jackson's extraordinary luck in winning the toss upon all five occasions. Even making the most liberal allowance for this good fortune, the play pointed to the superiority of England, and this, I believe, the Australians themselves admitted, though they naturally thought they would have got on far better if they had once or twice had the advantage of batting first. It so happened that the English batsmen, with Jackson easily first [*scoring successive hundreds in the Third and Fourth Tests*], did themselves full justice on these all-important occasions, whereas the best of the Australians, though capable of getting any number of runs in ordinary matches, were for the most part curiously unsuccessful.

1905 – ENGLAND v AUSTRALIA (FIRST TEST): **BOWLED OVER BY BOSIE**   1906

At Nottingham, May 29, 30, 31, 1905. In the end England won by 213 runs, but only after some truly sensational cricket was this result arrived at. Standing in a far better position than they could possibly have expected after their paltry first innings, the Englishmen went in for the second time before half-past 12, and at the drawing of stumps they had scored 318 for five wickets. Under ordinary circumstances they would in the same space of time have made a bigger score, but at about three o'clock Armstrong was put on to keep down the runs. It was something quite new to see the Australians on the second afternoon of a Test match playing for a draw rather than a win, and the innovation gave rise to endless discussion. Armstrong's method of keeping the ball wide of the leg stump for over after over irritated the crowd who, quite forgetting their manners, became rather noisy. MacLaren was out second at 222, being finely caught low down at mid-off from a hard drive. His innings of 140, which lasted three hours and 40 minutes, was for the most part magnificent.

The Australians wanted 402 to win. It was not to be supposed, especially with Trumper disabled, that the runs could be obtained, and the only question was whether the Australians would be able to avoid defeat. In the end, as everyone knows, Bosanquet beat them. Hill was out to a remarkable catch. He hit a ball back to Bosanquet so high that only a man standing fully six feet could have got near it. Bosanquet jumped up, got the ball with one hand and kept his hold of it, though he stumbled backwards and fell to the ground. It was a great change from 62 for no wicket to 93 for four, and a little later Armstrong was easily caught at cover point, the Englishmen then looking to have the match in their hands. Bosanquet had taken all the five wickets. The Englishmen owed everything to Bosanquet. He took eight of the nine wickets that fell, completely demoralising the batsmen with his leg-breaks. He gained nothing from the condition of the ground, the pitch remaining firm and true to the end. In the first flush of his triumph his place in the England team seemed secure for the whole season, but he never reproduced his form, and dropped out of the eleven after the match at Leeds.

England 196 (J. T. Tyldesley 56; F. Laver 7-64) and 426-5 dec. (Mr A. C. MacLaren 140, Hon. F. S. Jackson 82*, Tyldesley 61); **Australia 221** (C. Hill 54, M. A. Noble 50; Jackson 5-52) and 188 (S. E. Gregory 51; Mr B. J. T. Bosanquet 8-107).

1907 – SOUTH AFRICANS IN ENGLAND: REVELATORY BOWLING 1908

The South Africans had abundant reason to feel satisfied with the general result of their English tour. No one in this country, except the members of the team sent out to Cape Town by the MCC the year before last, realised their strength or thought they would do well. There was, indeed, a widespread feeling that in asking to be placed on the same footing as the Australians and given Test matches with England they were courting failure. At Leeds, in the only match of the three that was played out, England, with the best of luck, had to work desperately hard to win, and the drawn games were stoutly contested. For the success of the tour the South Africans had chiefly to thank their remarkable bowlers. Not since the days of the early Australian elevens, when Spofforth and Palmer astonished us by their improvements on old methods, has there been such a revelation.

A LEGION OF LEGGIES R. E. Foster, 1908

The interest in the attack of the South Africans is centred round four men – Schwarz, Vogler, Faulkner, and White. These men all bowled with a leg-break action, and could make the ball come in from the off. Though England can claim the "proud originator" of this style of bowling in Bosanquet, it has been left to South Africa to improve it – I will not say perfect – as I am convinced that this style is capable of still further improvement, which in time will be brought nearly to perfection. Bosanquet taught Schwarz, and Schwarz taught the others, and the others are better than their mentors, as Bosanquet has practically given up bowling in this way, and Schwarz, possibly because he finds he can get as many people out as he wishes, only breaks the ball from the off, but always with a leg-break action. His has been a great achievement this year, of which he and the South Africans may justly be proud, for he is top of the bowling averages, having taken 143 wickets with an average of 11.51 apiece, a perfor- mance that speak for itself. It is rather hard to explain his great success, as, though his bowling is the most difficult to hit of the four bowlers mentioned, it is much the easiest to play, because he only breaks one way, and the batsmen have never got to think of the possibility of the ball breaking the other way. The ball comes very slow through the air, and having hit the ground goes off at the most extraordinary pace. There is nothing very deceptive in the flight, but the break varies from six inches to 18 inches, and on sticky wickets he is quite capable of breaking a yard.

1909 – AUSTRALIANS IN ENGLAND: TOO MANY TESTS

Sydney Pardon, 1910

Inasmuch as they beat England in decisive fashion – not only winning two of the three Test matches that were played out, but having all the best of the drawn games at Manchester at The Oval – the Australians can look back on the tour of 1909 with keen satisfaction. They achieved their main object, and in comparison with that nothing else mattered. More and more in these days the interest of an Australian visit centres in the matches with England, all the other fixtures being strictly subser- vient to the great games. The Australians have become more or less indifferent to the ordinary matches on their list, their one object being to have their best eleven fit and well, and at the top of their form on the five big occasions. There is no like- lihood of a return to the old system, but looking at the matter from a sporting point of view, and ignoring financial considerations, I cannot help thinking that it would be better to have only three Test matches, with an extra allowance of time to admit of their being played out. Looking back on the season of 1909 there is no getting away from the fact that at many grounds the presence of the Australians was not the event that it used to be. Even at Scarborough in September there was a marked falling-off from the public support of previous years. The Test matches themselves, especially those at Lord's and The Oval, were as attractive as ever, but they dwarfed the other fixtures to an extent that was certainly not the case in earlier tours.

1912 – ILL-FATED EXPERIMENT

Sydney Pardon, Notes by the Editor, 1913

The Fates fought against the Triangular Tournament. Such a combination of adverse conditions could hardly have been imagined. To begin with, the Australians, who had been allowed to have everything their own way in choosing the time for the first trial of Sir Abe Bailey's ambitious scheme, quarrelled so bitterly among themselves that half their best players were left at home. In the second place the South Africans, so far from improving, fell a good way below their form of 1907 and, to crown everything, we had one of the most appalling summers ever known, even in England. In the circumstances it was not surprising that the tournament, as a public attraction, failed to realise the expectations of its supporters. The result is that the experiment is not likely to be repeated for many years to come – perhaps not in this generation.

1920–29

The resumption of Tests after the First World War was a grim experience for England, who were whitewashed in Australia in 1920-21 and then lost heavily again at home the following summer. While acknowledging the brilliance of Warwick Armstrong's Australia, Sydney Pardon was at his wits' end in his Notes and criticised England's selectors, saying they "lacked a settled policy". England beat South Africa at home in 1924 but they lost in Australia again, and his Notes in 1925 talked of a "shadow of inferiority to Australia". Sounds familiar. The Ashes were regained in 1926 when Wisden actually referred to the "mythical Ashes" for the first time. It was an epithet they would return to, though it couldn't be decided whether it should be Ashes or ashes or indeed "ashes". We have settled on Ashes. West Indies joined the Test-match family, and New Zealand toured for the first time in 1927.

1921 – AUSTRALIANS IN ENGLAND: TOURISTS WITHOUT WEAKNESS
Sydney Pardon, 1922

The Australians had a wonderful tour, and narrowly missed setting up a record that might have stood for all time. When on the 27th of August they stepped on to the field at Eastbourne to play the England eleven A. C. MacLaren had got together, it seemed any odds that, surpassing the doings of all previous teams in this country, they would go home unbeaten. As every one knows, they met with an outstanding reverse, and after that, in their last match, they were defeated for a second time. No doubt they were much disappointed at the change that came over their fortunes, but they had done more than enough for fame. One need not hesitate to say that Armstrong had a great side. Their record speaks for itself [P38, W22], but the statistics on the printed page give a poor idea of the consummate ease with which for four months they crumpled up nearly all the teams that opposed them.

Given fine weather the Australians as a side had not a weak point of any kind. They could all get runs, even the last man being capable on occasion of hitting up 20 or 30; their fielding was magnificent; and above all they possessed in Gregory and McDonald two very fast bowlers of the highest class. To back up McDonald and Gregory the Australians had in Armstrong himself and Mailey two right-handed slow bowlers so strongly contrasted in method as two men could be. Armstrong had an almost miraculous accuracy of pitch, combined at times with enough break to beat the bat, whereas Mailey, varying very much in length and constantly asking to be hit to the ring, relied to an enormous extent on his finger-spin.

Bardsley hit up nine hundreds and Macartney eight, the latter's 345 against Nottingham being the highest score of the season and the highest ever obtained by an Australian batsman in this country. Macartney was a law to himself – an individual genius but not in any way a model to be copied. He constantly did things that would be quite wrong for an ordinary batsman, but by success justified his audacities. Except Victor Trumper at his best, no Australian batsman has ever demoralised our bowlers to the same extent.

1921 – ENGLAND v AUSTRALIA (THIRD TEST): INJURY AND ILLNESS   1922

At Leeds, July 2, 4, 5, 1921. The Third Test ended in defeat for England, and so Australia won the rubber straightaway. It is not at all likely that in any circumstances the Australians would have been beaten, but England had horrible luck. Hobbs had sufficiently recovered from his leg troubles to take his place in the team, but he felt unwell before the match and after fielding for the greater part of the first afternoon he had to retire. He was found to be suffering from appendicitis. As if this misfortune were not enough, Tennyson, who had been made captain, split his hand badly while fielding, and though he scored 63 and 36, he batted under great difficulties. Nor did the trouble end here, as Brown was more or less disabled by the recurrence of an old injury, and was obliged to have a man run for him in the second innings. On the third day Douglas could not field owing to the serious illness of his wife – suddenly attacked, like Hobbs, by appendicitis.

Australia 407 (C. G. Macartney 115, W. W. Armstrong 77, C. E. Pellew 52, J. M. Taylor 50; C. H. Parkin 4-106) and 273-7 dec. (T. J. E. Andrews 92); England 259 (Mr. J. W. H. T. Douglas 75, Hon. L. H. Tennyson 63, G. Brown 57, E. A. McDonald 4-105) and 202.

FEARLESS AND RESOURCEFUL   Obituary, 1952

TENNYSON, THE THIRD BARON (LIONEL HALLAM TENNYSON), who died at Bexhill-on-Sea on June 6, aged 61, was a grandson of the poet and succeeded his father in the title in 1928. Intimately identified with Hampshire cricket from 1913 to 1936, he captained the county team for 14 years from 1919 onwards. He knew no fear, and the more desperate the position the more likely was he to accomplish something brilliant. Gregory and McDonald, the famous Australian fast bowlers who frightened so many of our professional batsmen in 1921, held no terrors for him. At Leeds, while fielding, he damaged his hand badly enough to have justified him in forgoing his innings. That course made no appeal to him. Wearing a basket guard, he duly went in to bat and, though suffering great pain with every contact of bat and ball, faced Gregory and McDonald in such plucky and resourceful fashion that he made 63 and 36.

1921 – AN ENGLAND XI v AUSTRALIANS: ASTONISHING COMEBACK   1922

At Eastbourne, August 27, 29, 30, 1921. This was the match that produced the sensation of the season. Unbeaten up to the closing days of August, it seemed certain that the Australians, surpassing the records of all the previous teams, would go through their tour without suffering defeat, but, as events turned out, the side selected by MacLaren won the game after a tremendous struggle by 28 runs. MacLaren all through the summer had maintained that he could pick a side good enough to overcome the Australians, but all hope of victory seemed gone when on winning the toss, and taking first innings on a perfect wicket, the Englishmen went down in an hour and a quarter for a score of 43. The Australians were left with only 196 to get, and most people took it for granted that they would win readily enough. At 73 a fine ball clean-bowled Macartney, this being perhaps the turning-point of the game. Mailey, the last man, joined McDonald with 42 runs still wanted. Thirteen runs were added, and then Gibson clean-bowled Mailey and won the match. When it was all over there was a scene of wild enthusiasm, MacLaren, in particular, coming in for endless congratulations.

An England XI 43 (W. W. Armstrong 5-15, E. A. McDonald 5-21)
and 326 (Mr G. A. Faulkner 153; McDonald 6-98);
Australians 174 (W. Bardsley 70; Mr M. Falcon 6-67) and 167 (Mr C. H. Gibson 6-64).

1923 – WEST INDIES TOUR: BLEAK AND BITTER   1924

Those who promoted the tour of the West Indies team in this country last summer were well advised, but fortune proved unkind. Our quaint climate was in a mood little calculated to bring out the best qualities of cricketers accustomed to a semi-tropical temperature. The bleak and bitter days of May and early June were a sore handicap. All the more credit to the team for doing so well in face of adverse circumstances. Playing 26 matches – 20 of them first-class – they won 12, lost seven and left seven unfinished.

1924 – ENGLAND v SOUTH AFRICA (First Test): 30 ALL OUT   1925

At Birmingham, June 14, 16, 17, 1924. The first of the Test matches, taken in conjunction with the startling failure against Lancashire at Old Trafford, went far to prove that the South Africans had no chance of beating England. It is true that, when in a hopeless position, they made a great effort to save a lost game but the fact that, with nothing in the condition of the wicket to excuse such a heavy collapse, they went down before Arthur Gilligan and Tate for a score of 30 told heavily against them in public estimation. The half-crown charge for admission kept many people away, the full attendance numbering scarcely more than 10,000. The sensation of the match came on the second day. England's innings soon ended for 438 and then in three-quarters of an hour Gilligan and Tate rattled the South Africans out for 30 – the lowest total in any Test match in England. The lowest before this match – also, curiously enough, on the Edgbaston ground – was 36 by Australia in 1902. There was another record, Gilligan's figures of six wickets for seven runs never having been equalled. He bowled very fast and with any amount of fire.

England 438 (J. B. Hobbs 76, E. H. Hendren 74, H. Sutcliffe 64, F. E. Woolley 64; G. M. Parker 6-152);

South Africa 30 (Mr A. E. R. Gilligan 6-7, M. W. Tate 4-12)

and 390 (R. H. Catterall 120, J. M. Blanckenberg 56, M. J. Susskind 51; Gilligan 5-83, Tate 4-103).

Unfair bowling. Before the 1933-34 season the inter-state conference decided to adopt the Australian Board of Control's "anti-bodyline" law for the Sheffield Shield competition. The law reads: "Any ball delivered which, in the opinion of the umpire at the bowler's end, is bowled at the batsman with intent to intimidate or injure him, shall be considered unfair and 'no-ball' shall be called."

Little Wonder No. 34

1926 – ENGLAND v AUSTRALIA (THIRD TEST): HUNDRED BEFORE LUNCH

1927

At Leeds, July 10, 12, 13, 1926. Played upon a different pitch from that originally intended, the game had a truly dramatic opening, Bardsley being caught at slip off the first ball sent down and Macartney off the fifth ball of Tate's over giving a chance in the slips to Carr. Thus the second wicket ought to have gone down with only two runs on the board. It did not fall until nearly two hours and 50 minutes later, and by that time the score had been raised to 235. The occasion was seized upon by Macartney to give one of the most glorious displays of his great career. The fact of having narrowly escaped disturbed the famous batsman not at all. Going for the bowling at once, he was soon complete master of the situation. Driving, cutting and placing to leg superbly, he accomplished the remarkable feat of scoring a hundred before lunch – a performance previously achieved in a Test match only by Victor Trumper. His footwork was perfect and his off-driving magnificent. To such an extent did he overshadow Woodfull that he made 51 out of 64 and 100 out of 131 with never a false stroke – bar that at the start – until he skyed a short-pitched ball to mid-off. Included in his 151 – an innings it was a privilege to witness – were 21 fours.

Australia 494 (C. G. Macartney 151, W. M. Woodfull 141, A. J. Richardson 100; M. W. Tate 4-99);

England 294 (G. G. Macaulay 76; C. V. Grimmett 5-88)

and 254-3 (J. B. Hobbs 88, H. Sutcliffe 94).

1926 – ENGLAND v AUSTRALIA (Fifth Test): Ashes regained   1927

At The Oval, August 14, 16, 17, 18, 1926. After a wonderfully interesting struggle, the Fifth Test match – arranged, however long it might last, to be played to a finish – ended shortly after six o'clock on the fourth day in a splendid victory for England by 289 runs. Winning in this handsome fashion, the only one of the five Test games in which a definite issue was reached, the old country regained possession of the mythical Ashes that Australia had held since the wholesale triumph over the English team led by John Douglas in the Commonwealth during the winter of 1920-21. Looked forward to with extraordinary interest, the contest underwent some truly dramatic changes. England, on the opening day, appeared to have jeopardised their chances by some strangely reckless batting, and yet left off on the first evening in distinctly the stronger position. On Monday, Australia played an uphill game to such good purpose, that they gained a slight lead. Tuesday brought with it some superb batting on a difficult wicket by Hobbs and Sutcliffe, and to wind up, came the collapse of Australia, who, when set 415 to win, failed so completely that they were all out for 125 – their second-lowest total during the whole tour.

England's eleven underwent no fewer than four changes from that which had met Australia three weeks earlier at Manchester. Chapman succeeded Carr in the captaincy of the side, and Geary, Larwood and Rhodes displaced Ernest Tyldesley, Kilner and Root. The inclusion of Rhodes, a man nearly 49 years of age, naturally occasioned a good deal of surprise, but it was crowned with complete success, the bowling of the veteran Yorkshireman proving no small factor in determining the issue of the struggle. Chapman, too, despite lack of experience in leading a first-class team in the field, turned out a very happy nomination for the post of captain, the young amateur, for the most part, managing his bowling with excellent judgment, and in two or three things he did, showing distinct imagination.

Under the conditions which obtained, there never existed the slightest likelihood of Australia making the 415 runs required for victory, but no one could have been prepared to see a famous batting side collapse so badly. As matters went, an easy win for England was assured in 50 minutes, the first four wickets falling for 35 runs. The heavy roller brought up little moisture but Larwood made the ball fly, and Rhodes, directly he was tried, made it turn. Moreover, not a catch was missed nor was a run given away, the whole England side rising gallantly to the occasion. Naturally a scene of tremendous enthusiasm occurred at the end, the crowd swarming in thousands in front of the pavilion, and loudly cheering the players, both English and Australian.

England 280 (H. Sutcliffe 76; A. A. Mailey 6-138)
and 436 (Sutcliffe 161, J. B. Hobbs 100; C. V. Grimmett 3-108, Mailey 3-128);
Australia 302 (J. M. Gregory 73, H. L. Collins 61) and 125 (W. Rhodes 4-44).

1928 – WEST INDIANS IN ENGLAND: A MISTAKE   1929

Considering what the West Indies team of 1923 had accomplished, the performance of the side which visited England last summer proved extremely disappointing.

Tours of English cricketers in the West Indies since that time suggested such progress that the programme arranged for the men led by R. K. Nunes included three encounters with the full strength of England. Unhappily expectations were rudely shattered. So far from improving upon the form of their predecessors, the team of 1928 fell so much below it that everybody was compelled to realise that the playing of Test matches between England and West Indies was a mistake. Whatever the future may have in store, the time is certainly not yet when the West Indies can hope to challenge England with a reasonable hope of success.

1930–49

No sooner had England recovered their self-respect (with a 4–1 Ashes victory in 1928-29) than they walked into the brick wall that was Don Bradman. He dominated the period in a way unlike anyone before – except Grace – or since. In between his phenomenal summers of 1930 and 1934 came India's first Test tour of England and a visit from West Indies, who offered a portent of their late 20th-century pace dominance by roughing up the England captain, Douglas Jardine. Their batting was dominated by George Headley. England's fortunes improved in 1938 when Len Hutton batted his way into the record books. The following year's West Indies tour was, according to Wisden, *"begun in miserable weather and ended prematurely by the anticipation of war". As before, war sapped English cricket of its strength, as well as depriving a number of players of their best years, and Bradman's farewell series in 1948 was an unalloyed triumph for the Australians despite his own failure in his final Test innings at The Oval. The end of the Second World War was marked by the Victory Tests against Australia, which were played in an understandable – and very welcome – spirit of adventure and bonhomie.*

1930 – Australians In England: The Don has landed   Sydney Southerton, 1931

This particular tour will always be remembered by reason of the amazing batting successes which attended the efforts of Bradman. It is not too much to say that he took both England and the whole cricket world by storm. Those who, like myself, had seen him play in Australia against the team captained by A. P. F. Chapman were fully prepared for something out of the common but little did we dream that his progress would be of such a triumphal nature. Nothing like his series of colossal innings in the Test matches had ever before been witnessed.

He lost no time in demonstrating to the English public that he was a most remarkable young cricketer, leading off with 236 in the opening fixture against Worcestershire. For Test matches alone, without a not-out to help him, he had an average of rather more than 139 with an aggregate of 974 runs in seven innings. In all games he scored 3,170 runs and averaged over 99.

In the course of the tour he demonstrated that he could play two entirely different games and that while he could be brilliant to a degree, he could also bat with a patience and restraint second only to that of Woodfull himself. There were several features about his batting with which one could not fail to be struck. To an eye almost uncanny in its power to gauge the length of a ball was allied really beautiful footwork. Bradman seldom played forward as a means of defence; he nearly always stepped back to meet the ball with a vertical bat. A glorious driver, he hit the ball very hard, while his placing was almost invariably perfect. He scored most of his runs by driving but he could cut, hook, or turn the ball to leg with nearly the same certainty. And only on rare occasions did he lift it.

1930 – ENGLAND v AUSTRALIA (Second Test): FLOGGED BY BRADMAN

1931

At Lord's, June 27, 28, 30, July 1, 1930. Beating England, after a memorable struggle, by seven wickets Australia took an ample revenge for their overthrow a fortnight previously at Trent Bridge. The batting, particularly that of Bradman, will assuredly live long in the minds of those who saw it. The Australians batted to a set plan, Woodfull and Ponsford steadily wearing down the bowling for Bradman later on to flog it. In obtaining his 254, the famous Australian gave nothing approaching a chance. He nearly played on at 111 and, at 191, in trying to turn the ball to leg he edged it deep into the slips but, apart from those trifling errors, no real fault could be found with his display. Like Woodfull, he scarcely ever lifted the ball and, while his defence generally was perfect, he hit very hard in front of the wicket.

England 425 (K. S. Duleepsinhji 173, M. W. Tate 54; A. G. Fairfax 4-101)
and 375 (Mr A. P. F. Chapman 121, Mr G. O. Allen 57; C. V. Grimmett 6-167);
Australia 729-6 dec. (D. G. Bradman 254, W. M. Woodfull 155, A. F. Kippax 83,
W. H. Ponsford 81) and 72-3.

1930 – ENGLAND v AUSTRALIA (Third Test): TOIL AND TRIPLE

1931

At Leeds, July 11, 12, 14, 15, 1930. Drawn. The Third Test, while it afforded that remarkable young batsman, Bradman, the opportunity of leaving all individual batting records in representative matches far behind, was in many respects an unsatisfactory affair. The game will go down to history on account of the wonderful batting performance accomplished by Bradman who, with an innings of 334, beat the previous highest – 287 by R. E. Foster for England at Sydney – which had stood since December 1903. Bradman achieved fame in other directions. Like C. G. Macartney on the same ground four years previously, he reached three figures before lunchtime on the first day. Not out 309 at the close, he had then exceeded a total of a thousand runs in Test cricket and reached an aggregate of exactly 2,000 for the season. Truly could it be called Bradman's Match. Bigger though it was and characterised by splendid strokeplay, Bradman's innings did not quite approach his 254 at Lord's in freedom from fault, but as to its extraordinary merit there could be no two opinions. As usual, he rarely lifted the ball and when making two or more consecutive scoring strokes seldom sent it in the same direction. His footwork was admirable as was the manner in which he played his defensive strokes to balls just short of a length.

Australia 566 (D. G. Bradman 334, A. F. Kippax 77, W. M. Woodfull 50; M. W. Tate 5-124);
England 391 (W. R. Hammond 113; C. V. Grimmett 5-135) **and 95-3**.

1930 – ENGLAND v AUSTRALIA (FIFTH TEST): WOODFULL'S PRESENT · 1931

At The Oval, August 16, 18, 19, 20, 21, 22, 1930. Beating England in an innings with 39 runs to spare, Australia won the rubber and so regained possession of the Ashes they had lost four years previously on the same ground. Once more Australia owed a great deal to Bradman. As usual he scored well in front of the wicket but he obtained a large number of runs on the leg side, while from start to finish his defence was altogether remarkable. All the same he did not play in anything like the attractive style he had shown at Lord's; indeed, there were periods when he became monotonous. Scoring so heavily as he did, Bradman again overshadowed everyone else, but his task was made the easier by the good work accomplished, before he went in, by Ponsford and Woodfull, who once more wore the bowling down by their workmanlike and steady cricket. Very appropriately, the day on which Australia regained the Ashes with this victory coincided with the birthday of Woodfull, their captain, who was then 33.

England 405 (H. Sutcliffe 161, Mr R. E. S. Wyatt 64, K. S. Duleepsinhji 50; C. V. Grimmett 4-135)
and 251 (W. R. Hammond 60, Sutcliffe 54; P. M. Hornibrook 7-92);
Australia 695 (D. G. Bradman 232, W. H. Ponsford 110, A. Jackson 73, W. M. Woodfull 54,
S. J. McCabe 54, A. G. Fairfax 53*; Mr I. A. R. Peebles 6-204).

1932 – INDIANS IN ENGLAND: IF THE CAP DOESN'T FIT · 1933

Although they suffered defeat in their one representative match against the full strength of England, the team of Indian cricketers acquitted themselves on the whole, if not with marked distinction, at any rate with great credit. Some little difficulty was experienced with regard to the captaincy, and after one or two disappointments the choice fell upon the Maharajah of Porbandar. For reasons apart from cricket the necessity existed of having a person of distinction and importance in India at the head of affairs, and it was almost entirely because of this that Porbandar led the team. No injustice is being done to him, therefore, by saying that admirably fitted as he was in many respects for the task, his abilities as a cricketer were not commensurate with the position he occupied. Wherever they went the tourists made friends, not only by the fine regard they had for the traditions of the game, but by their modest and correct demeanour at all times.

1933 – ENGLAND v WEST INDIES (SECOND TEST): OWN MEDICINE   1934

At Manchester, July 22, 24, 25, 1933. The second of the three Test matches was left drawn, but West Indies enjoyed the satisfaction of putting together their highest total in a Test in England, while to Headley and Barrow fell the distinction of being the first two West Indies batsmen to make hundreds in a Test in this country. Their batting success after so many previous disappointments being quite welcome and affording probably just as much enjoyment to English people as it did gratification to the tourists themselves.

No account would be complete without reference to the method of attack adopted by Martindale and Constantine for the West Indies and Clark for England. Jardine himself had to bear the greatest brunt of this form of bowling. Both Martindale and Constantine directed it at him with unflagging zeal, and it was to the great credit of the English captain that he played it probably better than any other man in the world was capable of doing, while putting together his first three-figure innings in a Test match. The fact that Jardine showed that it was possible to meet it without suffering physical injury or losing his wicket through any impatient or wild strike, did not, however, make the sight of it any more welcome, and most of those who were watching it for the first time must have come to the conclusion that, while strictly within the law, it was not nice.

Far more conducive is it to write about the magnificent batting of Headley, who cut, drove and forced the ball off his legs to the on with a ready adaptability and perfection of timing which enabled him to resist the England bowling for six and a quarter hours without giving a single chance. Hitting 18 fours, he had a magnificent reception when the innings ended.

West Indies 375 (G. A. Headley 169, I. Barrow 105; E. W. Clark 4-99)
and 225 (C. A. Roach 64, L. N. Constantine 64; J. Langridge 7-56);
England 374 (Mr. D. R. Jardine 127; E. A. Martindale 5-73).

1934 – AUSTRALIANS IN ENGLAND: FELLED BY GRIMMETT   Sydney Southerton, 1935

The Australian team of 1934 arrived in this country with the knowledge that during the previous series of Test matches in Australia they had been beaten four times and successful only once, and to the majority of people at home the idea of England losing the rubber was as remote as it had been in 1930. Australia, however, won two Test matches to England's one – the struggles at Manchester and Leeds being left drawn – and, by a remarkable coincidence, Woodfull, again as in 1930, led his side at The Oval to the victory which regained the Ashes, on the anniversary of his birthday – August 22.

Australia, when the wickets were hard, bowled better, batted better and fielded better than England. Both Grimmett and O'Reilly were, above all, masters of length and finger-spin and they seldom looked other than first-class. In his [Grimmett's] flighting of the ball he was as skilful as ever; he made it turn just as effectively and brought into action a particular delivery at which he had practised assiduously before he left Australia. This ball, the effect of which was either a googly or one which sped off the pitch at pace with top-spin, came from his hand in a slightly different manner from that usually associated with the googly or top-spinner. Instead of coming over the little finger, it left the hand via the forefinger, but with the action used in the ordinary googly, and as Grimmett very soon discovered it was exceedingly difficult of detection by the batsman. Naturally he kept this a very well-guarded secret and dismissed many men lbw with it and it is a matter of considerable doubt if any of our cricketers ever really found it out.

1934 – ENGLAND v AUSTRALIA (Second Test): Verity's victory   1935

At Lord's, June 22, 23, 25, 1934. For their defeat at Trent Bridge, England took an ample revenge at Lord's, winning the match in three days in an innings with 38 runs to spare. This was England's first success in a Test match against Australia at Lord's since 1896 [*and their last until 2009*]. While everyone in England naturally was jubilant over the triumph it could not be denied that they were helped by the weather.

Winning the toss, England put together a total of 440, but before the end of the second day Australia had 192 runs on the board with only two men out. There existed no sound reason why they should not have closely approached, if not even have passed, the England total, but they suffered the cruellest luck, rain falling during the weekend and rendering their chances almost hopeless. Fortunately England had in the team a bowler capable of taking full advantage of the conditions that prevailed, and Verity, obtaining seven wickets in the first innings for 61 runs, followed this up with eight in the second for 43. Verity's length was impeccable and he made the ball come back and lift so abruptly that most of the Australians were helpless. The majority of them had had no experience in England of such a pitch, and they showed no ability or skill in dealing with bowling like that of Verity under these conditions. Those who tried to play forward did not get far enough, and their efforts at playing back were, to say the least, immature.

England 440 (L. E. G. Ames 120, M. Leyland 109, Mr C. F. Walters 82; T. W. Wall 4-108);
Australia 284 (W. A. Brown 105; H. Verity 7-61) and 118 (Verity 8-43).

Little Wonder No. 35

Essex v Lancashire. At Chelmsford, June 22, 24, 25, 1935. An heroic innings by Pearce, whose wife during the day underwent an operation in the local hospital, and irresistible bowling by Nichols enabled Essex completely to turn the tables. At the crease four hours, Pearce well deserved the honour of being the first Essex player to reach three figures [in the season].

1934 – NOTTINGHAMSHIRE v AUSTRALIANS: Bodyline returns 1935

At Trent Bridge, August 11, 13, 14, 1934. A match rendered unpleasant by the antagonistic attitude of the spectators towards the visitors ended in a draw. The Australians, encountering "direct attack" bowling for the first time during the tour, fared none too well. During Voce's various spells of bowling, the Australian batsmen were obviously uncomfortable with short-pitched deliveries, and found themselves subjected to considerable barracking. Voce placed five men on the leg side, four of them close to the batsman, and of his eight victims, five fell to catches in this "leg trap". The absence of Voce – stated to be suffering from sore shins – on Tuesday began a series of rumours, the crowd apparently attributing his withdrawal from the match to an Australian protest. Consequently, the atmosphere grew increasingly hostile, and when the Australians took the field for the last innings, they were greeted by a storm of booing.

Australians 237 (W. M. Woodfull 81, A. G. Chipperfield 57; W. Voce 8-66)
and 230-2 dec. (W. A. Brown 100*); Nottinghamshire **183** (C. V. Grimmett 4-70) **and 128-6.**

1934 – ENGLAND v AUSTRALIA (Fifth Test): 451 partnership 1935

At The Oval, August 18, 20, 21, 22, 1934. Four days proved sufficient for Australia to win by 562 runs. Being successful in the rubber by two victories to one, they brought their number of wins in the whole series of encounters between the two countries to 52 as against 51 by England. Under conditions which favoured neither side unduly the result was a fitting tribute to the superior all-round skill of Australia.

Between them Ponsford and Bradman gave another glorious display of batting, engaging in a partnership which left Leeds far behind and produced 451 runs in five hours and a quarter. It would be hard to speak in too high terms of praise of the magnificent displays of batting given by Ponsford and Bradman. Before Bradman joined him Ponsford had shown an inclination to draw away from the bowling of Bowes but he received inspiration afterwards from the example of his partner, who from the very moment he reached the centre and took up his stance was coolness and mastery personified.

The pitch did not help bowlers at all. Clark tried leg-theory with a packed leg-side field but, even if he now and again dropped the ball short, scarcely came under the category of what is known as Bodyline. Incidentally Clark and the others tried all sort of theories but they had no effect on Bradman who, as the afternoon wore on, invested his batting with increasing daring. He drove and cut with the utmost certainty and power and when the ball did bounce he just stepped back and hooked it. Ponsford was not quite so sure as Bradman and he frequently turned his back to the ball to receive blows on the thigh. All the same, he drove with great power and was clever in getting the ball away between the fieldsmen placed close in. This great partnership meant that in consecutive representative encounters Bradman and Ponsford in two stands scored 839 runs in ten hours and three-quarters. Ponsford offered three very difficult chances and one when 115 comparatively easy; Bradman's batting, as far as was seen, was flawless.

Australia 701 (W. H. Ponsford 266, D. G. Bradman 244; W. E. Bowes 4-164, Mr G. O. Allen 4-170)
and 327 (Bradman 77, S. J. McCabe 70; Bowes 5-55, E. W. Clark 5-98);
England 321 (M. Leyland 110, Mr C. F. Walters 64) and 145 (C. V. Grimmett 5-64).

1935 – ENGLAND v SOUTH AFRICA (Second Test): FIRST WIN   1936

At Lord's, June 29, July 1, 2, 1935. Beating England by 157 runs, South Africa, after striving for 28 years, won a Test in England for the first time. Although undoubtedly fortunate in winning the toss, they richly deserved their victory. In batting and bowling they were definitely superior, and brilliant fielding, notably by Wade, the captain, in the silly mid-off position, also played a conspicuous part in the success. Bruce Mitchell, very strong in back play, watching the ball right on to the bat, and making the off-drive perfectly, batted from the start of South Africa's second innings until Wade declared without a palpable mistake. Some neglect to force the pace a little during the latter part of his innings prevented him surpassing H. W. Taylor's 176 at Johannesburg in 1923 – the highest innings for a South African against England. Wade left his opponents four and three-quarter hours to score 309 runs to win. Balaskas bowled unchanged and was always a source of trouble to England's batsmen, one or two of whom appeared overawed by the occasion.

South Africa 228 (H. B. Cameron 90) and 278-7 dec. (B. Mitchell 164*);
England 198 (Mr R. E. S. Wyatt 53; X. C. Balaskas 5-49) and 151 (A. C. B. Langton 4-31, Balaskas 4-54).

1936 – INDIANS IN ENGLAND: DISCIPLINARY PROBLEMS   Wilfrid Brookes, 1937

Most unfortunately, dissension developed among members of the party and although much of the gossip was exaggerated many of those who watched the Indians last season formed the impression that there was a want of harmony on the field. If a tour of India cricketers to be successful, differences of creed will have to be forgotten. Another blow to the prospects of the team came a week before the first of the Test matches when it was announced that Amarnath had been sent back to India as a disciplinary measure. This drastic action – unparalleled in the history of modern cricket – deprived the team of their most successful all-round player.

The leadership of the Indian team was no sinecure, and the Maharaj Sir Vijaya Vizianagram – he received a knighthood during his visit here – carried far more cares and worries than are usually the lot of the captain of a touring team. He did not accomplish anything out of the common in batting but could not alone be held responsible for the limited success of the side. Cricket is essentially a team game, and in a band of players divided amongst themselves the will to pull together was not often apparent.

1938 – ENGLAND v AUSTRALIA (First Test): McCabe runs riot   1939

At Nottingham, June 10, 11, 13, 14, 1938. Drawn. England, in a match memorable for the setting-up of many new records including seven individual hundreds, put together the highest innings total ever hit against Australia. Not until half past three on the second day did Australia have an opportunity of batting, and with 151 scored half their wickets had fallen. McCabe then played an innings the equal of which has probably never been seen in the history of Test cricket; for the best part of four hours he maintained a merciless punishment of the bowling. Although his phenomenal effort did not save his side from the indignity of having to follow on, it broke the control of the play which England had held from the outset, and by concentrating upon defence in their second innings Australia saved the game.

The amazing batting from McCabe gave such an epic turn to the game. Six wickets were down for 194 and then McCabe altered the whole aspect of affairs. In a little less than four hours, McCabe scored 232 out of 300 – his highest score in a Test match. His driving was tremendously hard, he hooked short balls with certainty and power, one off Farnes yielding a six, and he showed real genius in combatting Hammond's efforts to keep him away from the bowling. While McCabe was running riot, the England captain delayed calling for the new ball and took other measures in the hope of keeping down runs, but the Australian, having completed his first hundred in two hours, 20 minutes, proceeded to score fours much more readily. Wright was hit for 44 runs off three successive overs. Although he travelled so fast, McCabe did not offer a real chance, but once Edrich made a plucky effort to hold a ball hooked with terrific power. In the last ten overs bowled to him, McCabe took the strike in eight and hit 16 of his 34 fours, and in a last-wicket stand of 77 with Fleetwood-Smith he scored 72 in 28 minutes. His glorious innings ended in a fitting way, for in attempting a big hit off Verity he skied the ball to cover. Brown and Fingleton adopted stonewalling tactics which called forth mild barracking from some of the spectators, and Fingleton followed the extraordinary procedure of stepping away form his wicket, taking off his gloves and laying down his bat.

England 658-8 dec. (E. Paynter 216*, C. J. Barnett 126, D. C. S. Compton 102, L. Hutton 100; L. O'B. Fleetwood-Smith 4-153);
Australia 411 (S. J. McCabe 232, D. G. Bradman 51; Mr K. Farnes 4-106, D. V. P. Wright 4-153) and 427 (Bradman 144*, W. A. Brown 133).

1938 – ENGLAND v AUSTRALIA (Second Test): short boundaries   1939

At Lord's, June 24, 25, 27, 28, 1938. Drawn. A match of many fluctuations and fine personal achievements ended with Australia needing 111 runs to win and with four wickets to fall. In the Nottingham game, the scoring of a double-hundred on each side had been unprecedented, and yet in the very next Test match the same thing was done again. Hammond, who with able assistance from Paynter and Ames rescued England from a deplorable start, played an innings of 240 – the highest in England against Australia. Brown batted through the whole of Australia's first innings, scoring 206 not out and equalling the performances of Dr J. E. Barrett, Warren Bardsley and W. M. Woodfull by carrying his bat through a Test innings against England.

Hammond went to his hundred after two hours and 25 minutes' masterly batting and gradually Paynter, bringing into play the off-drive, cut and hit to leg, scored more freely. So large was the crowd that the gates were closed before noon. Part of the record partnership between Hammond and Paynter was watched by His Majesty the King. On Saturday, the cricket was seen by the largest crowd ever to assemble at headquarters – the attendance was officially returned as 33,800. The gates were closed before the start and, after hurried consultations between officials, spectators were permitted to retain positions they had taken up on the grass, the boundary ropes being moved forward a few yards, thus reducing the playing area.

England 494 (Mr W. R. Hammond 240, E. Paynter 99, L. E. G. Ames 83; W. J. O'Reilly 4-93, E. L. McCormick 4-101) **and 242-8 dec.** (D. C. S. Compton 76*); **Australia 422** (W. A. Brown 206*, A. L. Hassett 56; H. Verity 4-103).

1938 – ENGLAND v AUSTRALIA (FIFTH TEST): LEN BECOMES A LEGEND   1939

At The Oval, August 20, 22, 23, 24, 1938. No more remarkable exhibition of concentration and endurance has ever been seen on the cricket field than that of Leonard Hutton, the Yorkshire opening batsman, in a match which culminated in the defeat of Australia by a margin more substantial than any associated with the series of matches between the two countries. Record after record went by the board as Hutton mastered the bowling for the best part of two and a half days. At the end of an innings which extended over 13 hours, 20 minutes, this batsman of only 22 years had placed the highest score in Test cricket to his name, and shared in two partnerships which surpassed previous figures. As a boy of 14, Hutton at Leeds in 1930 had seen Bradman hit 334 – the record individual score in Test matches between England and Australia. Now on his third appearance in the series the Yorkshireman left that figure behind by playing an innings of 364.

This Test will always be remembered as Hutton's Match, and also for the calamity which befell Australia while their opponents were putting together a mammoth total of 903. First of all Fingleton strained a muscle and Bradman injured his ankle so badly that he retired from the match and did not play again during the tour. Before this accident, England had established a supremacy which left little doubt about the result; indeed, Hammond probably would not have closed the innings during the tea interval on the third day but for the mishap to the opposing captain. The moral effect of the loss of Bradman and Fingleton upon the other Australians was, of course, very great.

England at the end of two days had put together a total of 634 and only half their wickets had fallen. Hutton claimed exactly 300 of the runs scored at this point and the 30,000 people who assembled at The Oval on Tuesday saw fresh cricket history made. The bowling and fielding of Australia looked more formidable than at any other time in the game and as Hutton carried his score nearer to the record Test innings, Bradman, the holder of it, brought several fieldsmen close in to the wicket for O'Reilly bowling. Every run had to be fought for. As might be supposed, Hutton showed an occasional sign of strain and he completely missed the ball when with his total 331 he had an opportunity of beating the record by hitting a no-ball from O'Reilly. However, with a perfect cut off Fleetwood-Smith, Hutton duly reached his objective and the scene at the ground, with the whole assembly rising to its feet, and every Australian player, as well as Hardstaff, congratulating Hutton, will be remembered for a long time by those who saw it. It was said that O'Reilly, who bowled 85 overs, wore the skin off a finger in imparting spin to the ball.

Before Australia scored a run, Badcock fell to a catch at short leg, and McCabe left at 19. An unusual incident happened during the eighth and last stand, in which Fleetwood-Smith participated. When Brown cut the last ball of an over, intending to run a single Hutton, with the idea of trying to give the less-experienced batsman the strike, kicked the ball to the boundary. Instructions to umpires, however, provide for four runs to be added to the runs already made should a fieldsman wilfully cause the ball to reach the boundary, and as this meant the award to Brown of five runs he kept the bowling. On the fourth day, the proceedings were so one-sided as to be almost farcical. The fact that Australia batted only nine men removed some of the honour and glory from England's triumph, but there was nothing in the condition of the wickets to excuse the poor resistance of so many Test batsmen.

ENGLAND _First innings_

L. Hutton c Hassett b O'Reilly	364
W. J. Edrich c Hassett b O'Reilly	12
M. Leyland run out	187
*Mr W. R. Hammond lbw b Fleetwood-Smith	59
E. Paynter lbw b O'Reilly	0
D. C. S. Compton b Waite.	1
J. Hardstaff not out	169
†A. Wood c and b Barnes	53
H. Verity not out.	8
B 22, l-b 19, w 1, n-b 8	50

1-29 2-411 3-546 4-547   (7 wkts. dec) 903
5-555 6-770 7-876

Mr K. Farnes and W. E. Bowes did not bat.

Waite 72–16–150–1; McCabe 38–8–85–0; O'Reilly 85–26–178–3; Fleetwood-Smith 87–11–298–1; Barnes 38–3–84–1; Hassett 13–2–52–0; Bradman 3–2–6–0.

AUSTRALIA	*First innings*		*Second innings*	
C. L. Badcock c Hardstaff b Bowes		0	– b Bowes	9
W. A. Brown c Hammond b Leyland		69	– c Edrich b Farnes	15
S. J. McCabe c Edrich b Farnes		14	– c Wood b Farnes	2
A. L. Hassett c Compton b Edrich		42	– lbw b Bowes	10
S. G. Barnes b Bowes		41	– lbw b Verity	33
†B. A. Barnett c Wood b Bowes		2	– b Farnes	46
M. G. Waite b Bowes		8	– c Edrich b Verity	0
W. J. O'Reilly c Wood b Bowes		0	– not out	7
L. O'B. Fleetwood-Smith not out		16	– c Leyland b Farnes	0
*D. G. Bradman absent hurt		–	– absent hurt	–
J. H. Fingleton absent hurt		–	– absent hurt	–
B 4, l-b 2, n-b 3		9	B 1	1

1-0 2-19 3-70 4-145 5-147 6-160 7-160   201   1-15 2-18 3-35 4-41 5-115 6-115 7-117   123
8-201   8-123

First Innings – Farnes 13–2–54–1; Bowes 19–3–49–5; Edrich 10–2–55–1; Verity 5–1–15–0;
Leyland 3.1–0–11–1; Hammond 2–0–8–0.
Second Innings – Farnes 12.1–1–63–4; Bowes 10–3–25–2; Verity 7–3–15–2; Leyland 5–0–19–0.

Umpires: F. Chester and F. Walden.

Sweeping all before him: Len Hutton on his way to a world-record Test score,
364 against Australia at The Oval in 1938

1939 – WEST INDIANS IN ENGLAND: BY GEORGE

Hubert Preston, 1940

Begun in miserable weather and ended prematurely by the anticipation of war, the tour of the West Indies, despite these handicaps, brought considerable distinction to the team admirably captained by R. S. Grant. Defeat in the first match at Worcester and other reverses from Surrey and Glamorgan might have discouraged a less happy set of players, but the cheerful control of a leader well accustomed to the vagaries of the English climate kept all the team ready for more favourable surroundings.

If West Indies could not retain the Test honours wrested from England four years before, one individual record was established. In 1930 at Georgetown, Headley scored 114 and 112. He repeated this performance with 106 and 107 at Lord's, and additional credit belongs to him as a member of the losing side.

With a highest score of 234 not out made at Trent Bridge, besides 227 against Middlesex, Headley built up an aggregate of 1,745 runs, and his average, 72.70, was the best of the season. He beat Hammond, foremost of England batsmen, by over nine runs an innings, but was far behind Hutton in the Tests.

Constantine, approaching 37, repeated all the amazing energy that made him one of the most dazzling cover points when first he came to England in 1923 and on his next two visits. No matter where placed he performed wonders in getting to the ball. In bowling Constantine stood out by himself just as Headley did in batting. By relying on varied spin and mixed pace, from quite slow to a very fast ball sparsely used, Constantine altered his attack completely from the fast-medium swingers which he employed formerly.

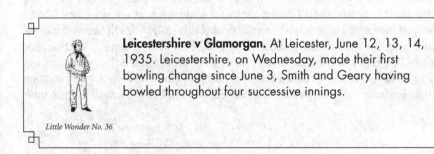

Leicestershire v Glamorgan. At Leicester, June 12, 13, 14, 1935. Leicestershire, on Wednesday, made their first bowling change since June 3, Smith and Geary having bowled throughout four successive innings.

Little Wonder No. 36

1939 – ENGLAND v WEST INDIES (SECOND TEST): DENIS'S DELIGHT

Norman Preston, 1940

At Lord's, June 24, 26, 27, 1939. England won by eight wickets. While England were unquestionably the better side and deservedly gained the victory, the match provided a personal triumph for Headley who had the distinction of being the first cricketer to make two separate hundreds in a Test at headquarters. Moreover he became the first player to hit two hundreds against England twice. The West Indies bowled and fielded keenly, but in batting too much responsibility devolved upon Headley. While he stayed the resistance was stubborn, but the side collapsed twice.

In the first innings the last five wickets fell for 32 runs, and when the side batted again the last five fell for 35.

The [second] day's cricket was memorable for the glorious batting of the two youngsters, Hutton and Compton, who in a feast of run-making put on 248 for the fourth wicket in two hours 20 minutes. With only a single to his credit Compton offered a hard chance off Martindale to second slip, and from the next ball the Middlesex man gave one on the leg side to the wicketkeeper, who threw himself to the left, but could not hold the ball. In the following over from Cameron, Hutton, too, might have been taken at slip, but, like the two chances given by Compton, this catch was very difficult. In this way the initiative passed to England, for Compton, appreciating his luck, immediately proceeded to attack the bowling. He refused to be curbed and delighted everyone with his easy strokeplay. Compton excelled with strokes all round the wicket, his pulling and driving being specially noteworthy.

West Indies 277 (G. A. Headley 106, J. B. Stollmeyer 59; W. H. Copson 5-85)
and 225 (Headley 107; Copson 4-67);
England 404-5 dec. (L. Hutton 196, D. C. S. Compton 120) and 100-2.

1945 – ENGLAND v AUSTRALIA (First Victory Match): SPIRIT OF THE AGE

Norman Preston, 1946

At Lord's, May 19, 21, 22, 1945. Australia won by six wickets. In a dynamic finish, true to the exhortation expressed in the post-war cricket plans, Pepper made the winning hit off the fourth ball of the last possible over just at seven o'clock. To the majority of the 18,000 people who saw the cricket this really fine climax gave intense pleasure and the Australian batsmen reached the pavilion amidst enthusiastic applause. The England team deserved equal praise for the splendid sportsmanship in doing their part in the speediest manner, changing positions quickly and starting each over without delay when the waste of seconds might have meant a drab draw.

England 267 (Sq. Ldr L. E. G. Ames 57, Capt. J. D. B. Robertson 53)
and 294 (Robertson 84, Sq. Ldr W. J. Edrich 50; Sgt C. G. Pepper 4-80);
Australia 455 (P/O K. R. Miller 105; Lt Col J. W. A. Stephenson 5-116) and 107-4 (Pepper 54*).

1945 – ENGLAND v THE DOMINIONS: MILLER HITS HEIGHTS   1946

At Lord's, August 25, 27, 28, 1945. The Dominions won by 45 runs with eight minutes to spare. One of the finest games ever seen produced 1,241 runs, including 16 sixes, a century in each England innings by Hammond, and grand hundreds for the Dominions by Donnelly, the New Zealand left-hander, and Miller, of Australia. In addition, the result was a triumph for Constantine, who, in the absence of Hassett through illness, was chosen captain by the Dominions players just before the match began.

The final stage will be remembered chiefly for the glorious driving of Miller. He outshone everyone by his dazzling hitting. In 90 minutes he raised his overnight 61 to 185, and in threequarters of an hour of superb cricket he and Constantine put on 117. Though travelling at such a pace, Miller played faultlessly. One of his seven sixes set the whole crowd talking. It was a terrific on-drive off Hollies, and the ball lodged in the small roof of the broadcasting box above the England players' dressing-room.

The Dominions 307 (M. P. Donnelly 133, H. S. Craig 56, C. G. Pepper 51; D. V. P. Wright 5-90)

and 336 (K. R. Miller 185; Wright 5-105);

England 287 (W. R. Hammond 121, W. J. Edrich 78; Pepper 4-57)

and 311 (Hammond 102, J. G. W. Davies 56).

1946 – INDIANS IN ENGLAND: MODESTY, MANKAD AND MERCHANT   Reg Hayter, 1947

In one important particular India's 16 cricketers who visited England in 1946 accomplished more towards raising the status and dignity of their country's sport than was achieved by either of the two previous touring sides. While the politicians at home argued the rights of independence, the cricketers abroad showed to the world that they could put aside differences of race and creed and join together on and off the field as a single unit, working as one for the same cause. These young men came as their country's ambassadors. By their cricket they won the hearts of the English public; by their modesty and bearing they earned the respect and admiration of everyone with whom they came into close contact. In anything like reasonable weather crowds everywhere flocked to India's matches.

No praise could be too high for Merchant, who, on any reckoning, must be accounted one of the world's greatest batsmen. The first Indian to score 2,000 runs on a tour, Merchant gave of his best in every situation, showing a degree of concentration and determination, especially on a big occasion such as a Test, more developed and controlled than any batting of some of his team-mates. He exceeded 50 in 20 out of his 41 innings. Yet figures do him less than justice. His cutting, both square and late, touched the heights of brilliance; he hooked, drove and played the ball off his legs with masterly certainty, and, with all his triumphs, remained a charming, unassuming man and a studious captain whenever Pataudi was absent. His 128 at The Oval in the Third Test was the highest ever played for his country against England.

Few men have accomplished finer deeds on their first cricket tour to England than did Vinoo Mankad, India's left-arm slow bowler and right-hand batsman, who set the seal on consistently good work by becoming the first Indian ever to perform the double event of 1,000 runs and 100 wickets in a season. Mankad was called upon for a tremendous amount of work, but he was seldom collared, and he mixed with considerable guile flight and pace, a finger-spun leg-break, and a faster ball which accounted for a big proportion of his wickets, even though he lacked devil on sticky wickets.

1946 – ENGLAND v INDIA (First Test): Alec's arrival   Hubert Preston, 1947

At Lord's, June 22, 24, 25, 1946. The seventh consecutive single brought the match to an emphatic success for England just at half past one on the third day. This concluding fight for runs typified the cricket from first to last and, though defeated so severely, India deserved high credit for the way they put the utmost keenness and effort into all their doings. Alec Bedser, one of the Surrey twins, accomplished probably the finest performance ever recorded by a bowler in his first Test match. Using his height, six feet two inches, to the full extent and putting his weight behind every ball, Bedser maintained an admirable length at fast-medium pace, with swerve or spin which often turned the ball appreciably from the sodden turf. For each of the four bowlers considered necessary Hammond placed an attacking field with three short legs and a silly point usually on duty; sometimes even more men stood very close to the bat.

India 200 (R. S. Modi 57*; A. V. Bedser 7-49)
and 275 (M. H. Mankad 63, L. Amarnath 50; Bedser 4-96);
England 428 (J. Hardstaff 205*, P. A. Gibb 60; Amarnath 5-118) **and 48-0.**

1947 – South Africans In England: Terrible Twins   Reg Hayter, 1948

For the first time in England, South Africa took part in four-day Tests and, although a record of three defeats and two draws was the worst since 1924, any team meeting Compton and Edrich in such tremendous form could be regarded as unfortunate. The influence which these two men bore on the tour was so great that, in the hypothetical case of one being allotted to each country, the rubber might well have gone to South Africa. Altogether during the summer the South Africans conceded over 2,000 runs to this remarkable pair (Compton 1,187; Edrich 869), but the number of runs alone did not reveal the full effect of the Terrible Twins, as they became known to the South Africans. An even more important factor was that the touring team's bowlers lost much of their previous sting after the hammering they received when Compton made 745 and Edrich 708 in seven consecutive innings against them, for Middlesex and in the first three Tests. So masterful was Compton that he hit six centuries against the South Africans, three of his four in the Tests coming in successive innings.

1947 – ENGLAND v SOUTH AFRICA (Second Test): unbreakable
Reg Hayter, 1948

At Lord's, June 21, 23, 24, 25, 1947. England won by ten wickets. From first to last this was a delightful match. South Africa put up a brave fight and were by no means as inferior as the result would suggest. Their bowlers again provided an object lesson in length, direction and bowling to a field, and their fielding remained at a superlatively high standard. Yet these factors were outweighed by the advantage England gained in winning the toss, the greatness of Edrich and Compton, who established a new world record in Test matches with a third-wicket stand of 370, the shock bowling and slip catching of Edrich, and the consistently fine work of Wright on his first appearance of the season against the touring side.

In view of the obviously long tail, no little responsibility rested on Edrich and Compton, and an enthralling struggle developed between them and a determined attack, splendidly supported in the field, before the two Middlesex batsmen assumed mastery. Then followed a sparkling exhibition of fluent strokeplay, and South Africa conceded 370 runs before the partnership ended. Compton used everything in his complete repertoire, including the brilliant leg-sweep off a slow bowler, and Edrich specially excelled in on-side play. He hooked Rowan for one glorious six and frequently brought off a powerful lofted pulled-drive. In three hours ten minutes to the close the stand produced 216 runs, Edrich reaching his first Test century in England and Compton his second in successive Test innings against South Africa. The day was marred by an unfortunate accident to Melville. Shortly before the close a throw-in from the deep struck him over the right eye. Melville sank to the ground, but, after attention, was able to resume, though during the weekend his eye turned black and became almost completely closed.

England 554-8 dec. (D. C. S. Compton 208, W. J. Edrich 189, C. Washbrook 65; L. Tuckett 5-115) **and 26-0**; **South Africa 327** (A. Melville 117, A. D. Nourse 61; D. V. P. Wright 5-95) **and 252** (B. Mitchell 80, Nourse 58; Wright 5-80).

1948 – AUSTRALIANS IN ENGLAND: THE INVINCIBLES   Reg Hayter, 1949

When, announcing his retirement from first-class cricket, D. G. Bradman claimed that the 1948 side bore comparison with any of its predecessors, he accurately reflected the majority of opinion on the 19th Australian team visiting England. In retaining the Ashes held by Australia since 1934, these Australians enjoyed almost uninterrupted success, while becoming the first side to go unbeaten through an English tour: certainly they achieved all that could be expected of a combination entitled to the description great.

A summary of their achievements proved the might of probably the most united Australian party sent to England. Not only did they win exactly half their 34 matches with an innings to spare, two by ten wickets, one by nine wickets, two by eight wickets and one by 409 runs, but 11 batsmen between them hit 50 centuries, and in first-class games seven of their 17 players completed 1,000 runs, with Loxton only 27 short when he broke his nose while batting at Scarborough. Comparisons of totals reveal even more. The Australians made 350 or more in 24 innings whereas, apart from the Tests, the highest total against them was Nottinghamshire's 299 for 8. Twice the Australians failed to reach 200, but they dismissed opponents for less than that figure no fewer than 37 times, and in seven innings for under 100.

1948 – ESSEX v AUSTRALIANS: 700 IN A DAY   1949

At Southend, May 15, 17, 1948. Australians won by an innings and 451 runs. In light-hearted vein, they made history by putting together the highest total scored in a day of six hours in first-class cricket. Bradman led the run-getting revel on the Saturday. Complete master of the Essex bowlers on a fast pitch, he scored 187 in two hours five minutes and by a wide variety of orthodox and unorthodox strokes hit 32 fours and a five. The biggest partnerships were 219 in 90 minutes between Brown and Bradman for the second wicket, 166 in 65 minutes by Loxton and Saggers for the sixth, and 145 in 95 minutes between Barnes and Brown for the first. Bailey dismissed Brown and Miller with successive balls, but generally the bowlers failed to stem the scoring. Because of injury Bailey did not bat in either innings. Essex, dismissed twice on Monday, first failed against the pace of Miller and the cleverly varied left-arm deliveries of Toshack; then in the follow-on – apart from Pearce and P. Smith, who made a stand of 133 – they broke down in face of Johnson's off-spinners, The attendance and receipts – 32,000 and £3,482 – were ground records.

Australians 721 (D. G. Bradman 187, W. A. Brown 153, S. J. E. Loxton 120,
R. A. Saggers 104*, S. G. Barnes 79; T. P. B. Smith 4-193);
Essex 83 (E. R. H. Toshack 5-31) and 187 (T. N. Pearce 71, Smith 54; I. W. Johnson 6-37).

1948 – ENGLAND v AUSTRALIA (FIRST TEST): MILLER BARRACKED
Reg Hayter, 1949

At Nottingham, June 10, 11, 12, 14, 15, 1948. Bravely as England fought back, the result became nearly a foregone conclusion by the end of the first day after their disastrous batting against a fast attack of exceptionally high standard. A dazzling slip catch by Miller set the keynote on Australia's excellent fielding, but Australia suffered a handicap when Lindwall pulled a groin muscle midway through the innings and could not bowl again in the match.

Seldom had Bradman been so subdued in a big innings as he was over the 28th Test century of his career. He did not welcome Yardley's tactics in asking his bowlers to work to a packed leg-side field, and he spent over three hours and a half in reaching his 100, the last 29 runs taking 70 minutes. A last-wicket partnership of 33 emphasised England's difficulties, which were increased immediately they began the second innings, 344 behind. Once more Australia gained the incentive of a fine start, when in Miller's second over Washbrook attempted to hook a bumper and edged a catch to the wicketkeeper. At this period Miller bowled medium-paced off-breaks, but he turned again to fast deliveries and incurred the noisy displeasure of sections of the crowd when he bowled five bumpers to Hutton in his last eight balls, one of which struck the batsman high on the left arm. Before play began on Monday the Nottinghamshire secretary, Mr H. A. Brown, broadcast an appeal to the crowd to leave the conduct of the game to the umpires, and he deplored the barracking of Miller on Saturday.

Compton batted in masterly fashion when continuing his third century in successive Tests at Trent Bridge. England faced an almost hopeless task at the beginning of the last day when they stood only one run ahead with four wickets left, but hope remained as long as Compton was undefeated. He held out till ten minutes before lunch, when Miller released a lightning bumper. The ball reared shoulder-high, Compton shaped to hook then changed his mind and tried to get his head out of the way. As he ducked Compton lost his balance on the muddy turf and tumbled into his wicket. This tragic end to one of the best innings of Compton's career and his highest in Test cricket against Australia sealed England's fate. No praise could be too high for the manner in which Compton carried the side's responsibilities and defied a first-class attack in such trying circumstances.

The match ended humorously. After making a boundary stroke Barnes thought the game was over when the scores were level, and he snatched a stump before racing towards the pavilion. Barnes was halfway up the pavilion steps when the shouts of the crowd made him realise the error and he returned to the crease. When Hassett did make the winning hit, another scramble for souvenirs took place; and in this Barnes was unlucky.

England 165 (J. C. Laker 63; W. A. Johnston 5-36)
and 441 (D. C. S. Compton 184, L. Hutton 74, T. G. Evans 50; K. R. Miller 4-125, Johnston 4-147);
Australia 509 (D. G. Bradman 138, A. L. Hassett 137, S. G. Barnes 62; Laker 4-138) **and 98-2** (Barnes 64*).

Gloucestershire v Nottinghamshire. At Gloucester, August 29, 31, September 1, 1936. Hammond was in really wonderful form and putting together an innings of 317 beat his previous-best score in England and surpassed the aggregate of 1,278 runs in August set up by W. G. Grace.

Little Wonder No. 37

1948 – ENGLAND v AUSTRALIA (FOURTH TEST): RECORD RUN-CHASE

Leslie Smith, 1949

At Headingley, July 22, 23, 24, 26, 27, 1948. Australia won by seven wickets. By the astonishing feat of scoring 404 for three wickets on the fifth day of the match when the pitch took spin, Australia won the rubber. Until that fatal last stage England were on top, but a succession of blunders prevented them gaining full reward for good work on the first four days.

The biggest mistake occurred before the game started, for the selectors decided to leave out Young, the slow left-arm bowler who had been invited to Leeds as one of the original party. Consequently England took the field with an unbalanced attack. Having only one slow bowler available, Yardley did not know what to do for the best on the last day, and he was forced to make Compton the spearhead and to employ Hutton, who to that point had bowled no more than 22 overs in the season. Even then England should have won. Evans, behind the wicket, fell a long way below his best form, and three catches were dropped in the field.

At the close of the fourth day England led by 400 with two wickets left. To most people Yardley's decision to continue batting for five minutes next day came as a surprise, and the reason for it aroused plenty of comment. The main idea was to break up the pitch by the use of the heavy roller. Three runs were added in two overs, and then Yardley declared, leaving Australia to score 404 in 345 minutes. The pitch took spin and the ball lifted and turned sharply. Unfortunately, Laker was erratic in length. Compton, bowling his left-hand off-breaks and googlies, baffled the batsmen several times, but without luck. Evans should have stumped Morris when 32, and Compton only gained reward when he held a return catch from Hassett at 57, but he ought to have dismissed Bradman, Crapp dropping a catch at first slip. When 59 Bradman had another escape off Compton, and Yardley, in despair, called for the new ball even though the pitch favoured spin. Evans should have stumped Bradman when 108, and Laker at square leg dropped Morris when 126. Not until 301 had been put on did England break the stand, and by that time the match was as good as won. Morris batted four hours 50 minutes for 182. Miller did not last long, but Harvey made the winning stroke within 15 minutes of time. No fewer than 66 fours were hit in the innings, 33 by Morris and 29 by Bradman. The attendance figures of 158,000 created a record for any match in England.

England 496 (C. Washbrook 143, W. J. Edrich 111, L. Hutton 81, A. V. Bedser 79)
and 365-8 dec. (D. C. S. Compton 66, Washbrook 65, Hutton 57, Edrich 54; W. A. Johnston 4-95)
Australian 458 (R. N. Harvey 112, S. J. E. Loxton 93, R. R. Lindwall 77, K. R. Miller 58)
and 404-3 (A. R. Morris 182, D. G. Bradman 173*).

1948 – ENGLAND v AUSTRALIA (FIFTH TEST): THE DON DEPARTS
Hubert Preston, 1949

At The Oval, August 14, 15, 16, 17, 18, 1948. Australia won by an innings and 149 runs, so completing their triumph in the rubber with four victories and one draw. England having been placed in a humiliating position already, the selectors tried further experiments which aroused strong condemnation.

Extraordinary cricket marked the opening day. So saturated was the ground by copious rain during the week that the groundsmen could not get the pitch into a reasonable state for a punctual start. The captains agreed that play should begin at 12 o'clock, and Yardley, having won the toss, chose to bat – an inevitable decision with the conditions uncertain and the possibility of more rain. As it happened, apart from local showers early on Sunday morning, the weather proved fine until England fared badly for the second time. All things considered, the Australians found everything favourable for them. This does not explain the lamentable collapse of England for the lowest score by either side in a Test at The Oval, apart from the 44 for which Australia fell in 1896. The reasons for such a meagre score were the splendid attack maintained by Lindwall, Miller and Johnston in humid atmosphere against batsmen whose first error proved fatal. Lindwall, with his varied pace and occasional very fast ball, excelled. Always bowling at the stumps, he made the ball rise at different heights. Four times he clean bowled a hesitant opponent.

Everything became different when Australia batted. Barnes and Morris, with controlled assurance and perfect stroke play, made 117, and shortly before six o'clock Bradman walked to the wicket amidst continued applause from the standing crowd. Yardley shook hands with Bradman and called on the England team for three cheers, in which the crowd joined. Evidently deeply touched by the enthusiastic reception, Bradman survived one ball, but, playing forward to the next, was clean bowled by a sharply turning break-back – possibly a googly.

The usual scramble for the stumps and bails as Morris held a lofted catch from Hollies marked the close; but much happened subsequently. Mr H. D..G. Leveson Gower on the players' balcony called for three cheers for Bradman and the victorious Australians. Responses over the microphone came in due course, the crowd of about 5,000 enthusiasts coming up to the pavilion to hear and see all that happened as a curtain to this series of Test matches in which Australia completely outplayed and conquered England.

England 52 (R. R. Lindwall 6-20) **and 188** (L. Hutton 64; W. A. Johnston 4-40);
Australia 389 (A. R. Morris 196, S. G. Barnes 61; W. E. Hollies 5-131).

Last look back: Don Bradman, in his final Test innings,
is bowled for a duck by Eric Hollies at The Oval in 1948

1949 –ENGLAND v NEW ZEALAND (Second Test): Mann's mistake

Leslie Smith, 1950

At Lord's, June 25, 27, 28, 1949. On a pitch which seemed to improve, there appeared little hope of a definite result, but the game was made memorable by an incorrect declaration on the part of F. G. Mann, the England captain, and a brilliant innings of 206 by M. P. Donnelly, the New Zealand left-hander. Shortly after six o'clock on Saturday, with England's total 313 for nine wickets, Mann closed the innings and New Zealand in 15 minutes scored 20 without loss. At the time he did not realise his mistake, but on Sunday he issued the following statement:

"When I declared the England innings closed on Saturday evening I thought that the experimental rule which allows a declaration to be made on the first day of a three-day match applied to the present series of Test matches. I regret very much that I was wrong in this respect, but I am very glad indeed that we did not in fact gain any advantage from the declaration."

On Monday, with the New Zealand total 160 for four, the game stood in an even position. Then Donnelly took complete control of the attack and the game swung round in New Zealand's favour. Donnelly was quite content to wait for the loose ball and batted much more cautiously than usual. He took three and a half hours to complete his first hundred, but on Tuesday he changed his style completely and in under an hour and a half he obtained 80 out of 112. His innings was the highest for New Zealand in any Test. Powerful pulls and neat late cuts brought him a large number of his runs and he made no mistake until, after passing 200, he hit out at every ball.

England 313-9 dec. (D. C. S. Compton 116, T. E. Bailey 93; T. B. Burtt 4-102)
and 306-5 (J. D. B. Robertson 121, L. Hutton 66);
New Zealand 484 (M. P. Donnelly 206, B. Sutcliffe 57; W. E. Hollies 5-133).

1950–59

Shocked initially by the emergence as a genuine Test force of West Indies, England enjoyed the 1950s. They regained the Ashes in the Queen's Coronation year (and retained them against the odds in 1954-55). With a well-balanced side containing some of the game's best-known players – Hutton, May, Compton, Trueman and Laker – England could genuinely lay claim to being the best side in the world. There were blips, such as the series-levelling defeat by Pakistan on their first Test tour of England. There were signs, though, as the decade wore on that the cricket played, by England and others, was becoming ultra-defensive. Wisden was not happy.

1950 – WEST INDIANS IN ENGLAND: BE AFRAID, BE VERY AFRAID

Jack Anderson, 1950

We in the Caribbean are told that our too rare visits are likened unto a welcome western zephyr that passes too quickly. It carries nothing of the tempestuous ferocity of the south wind that more often than not – in fact as late as 1948 – blows everything before it. But the western zephyr wafts along good, unadulterated, light-hearted and honest-to-goodness cricket. I can assure the English that the team this year will in this respect be no exception to their predecessors. I warn you that the zephyr has developed velocity, and the Englishman who keeps abreast of overseas cricket will realise this is no idle boast.

1950 – WEST INDIANS IN ENGLAND: FULLY GROWN
Norman Preston, 1951

In the summer of 1950 West Indies cricket firmly established itself. Actually it was 22 years since they were given Test status in 1928, but whereas some cricket bodies take a long time to grow up, there was no question that the representatives of the Caribbean reached maturity on their seventh visit to the cradle of cricket.

Those of us who saw them overwhelm G. O. Allen's MCC team on their own fields in the early months of 1948 were prepared for surprises, but I do not think any of us expected they would go from one triumph to another and outplay England in three of the four Tests.

Certainly their path to success took a vastly different course to anything envisaged. It was anticipated that if the West Indies gained the ascendancy it would be achieved through their pace bowlers, Johnson, Jones and Pierre. As it was, these three took no more than 91 wickets in the 31 first-class matches, while two 20-year-old slow bowlers, Ramadhin and Valentine, who were unknown in first-class cricket even in the West Indies at the beginning of the year, shared 258 wickets.

1950 – ENGLAND v WEST INDIES (SECOND TEST): SPIN TWINS
Reg Hayter, 1951

At Lord's, June 24, 26, 27, 28, 29, 1950. West Indies won by 326 runs. They fully merited their first Test victory in England, which, to their undisguised delight, was gained at the headquarters of cricket. In batting, bowling and fielding they were clearly the superior side, with Ramadhin this time the more successful of the two 20-year-old spin bowlers who during the 1950 summer wrought such destruction among English batsmen. In the match Ramadhin took 11 and Valentine seven wickets.

No blame could be attached to the pitch. It gave slow bowlers a little help, but only to those who used real finger spin as did Ramadhin and Valentine. Ramadhin bowled with the guile of a veteran. He pitched a tantalising length, bowled straight at the wicket and spun enough to beat the bat. No English batsman showed evidence of having mastered the problems of deciding which way Ramadhin would spin, and he was too quick through the air for any but the most nimble-footed to go down to meet him on the half-volley with any consistency. Valentine lent able support, but the English batsmen might, with profit, have tackled him more boldly. England's score was their lowest for a completed innings in a home Test against West Indies.

England started the last day with six wickets left and 383 runs required to win, but when Ramadhin yorked Washbrook, who did not add to his score, the end was in sight and nothing happened to check the inevitable defeat. Ramadhin and Valentine were again the chief executioners.

West Indies 326 (A. F. Rae 106, E. D. Weekes 63, F. M. M. Worrell 52; R. O. Jenkins 5-116)
and 425-6 dec. (C. L. Walcott 168*, G. E. Gomez 70, Weekes 63; Jenkins 4-174);
England 151 (S. Ramadhin 5-66, A. L. Valentine 4-48,) and 274 (C. Washbrook 114; Ramadhin 6-86).

1950 – ENGLAND v WEST INDIES (THIRD TEST): WORRELL ... WEEKES ... WIN
Leslie Smith, 1951

At Nottingham, July 20, 21, 22, 24, 25, 1950. West Indies won by ten wickets. A gallant attempt by England to fight themselves out of an almost hopeless position failed, and good bowling on the first day, supported by a wonderful innings by Worrell, gave West Indies an easy victory.

More bad luck dogged England in the matter of team selection. On the eve of the match Hutton was found to be suffering from a recurrence of lumbago and Gimblett was troubled by a boil on his neck. The selectors, at 10pm on Wednesday, made a hurried telephone call for Dewes of Middlesex to join the team. From the side beaten at Lord's, England were without Hutton, Edrich, Doggart and Wardle.

The English bowling was trounced, particularly during a fourth-wicket stand between Worrell and Weekes. Worrell batted in scintillating style, and the bowlers and fieldsmen were unable to check a wonderful array of fluent strokes. Weekes, usually a quicker scorer, was overshadowed until Worrell tired near the end of the day. At the close West Indies were 479 for three, with Worrell 239 and Weekes 108. They had put on 241, and so easily did he play the bowling that there were many people who considered that Worrell stood a good chance of beating Hutton's record Test score of 364.

England 223 and 436 (C. Washbrook 102, R. T. Simpson 94, W. G. A. Parkhouse 69,
J. G. Dewes 67, T. G. Evans 63; S. Ramadhin 5-135);
West Indies 558 (F. M. M. Worrell 261, E. D. Weekes 129, A. F. Rae 68; A. V. Bedser 5-127) and 103-0.

1951 – ENGLAND v SOUTH AFRICA (FIRST TEST): NOURSE EASES PAIN
Norman Preston, 1952

At Nottingham, June 7, 8, 9, 11, 12, 1951. South Africa won by 71 runs. A most remarkable match ended with South Africa gaining their first Test victory for 16 years and their second in England. Between those two successes they had failed to lower the colours of England and Australia in a total of 28 Tests. Undoubtedly the hero was Nourse, the South African captain. He carried his side with a lionhearted not out 208. Mere figures cannot convey the magnitude of Nourse's performance. His innings occupied nine and a quarter hours, and during the whole of that time he batted under a great handicap. The left thumb which he had broken at Bristol three weeks previously gave him severe pain, particularly when he tried to impart any power into his strokes, and the longer he stayed the more it swelled. Nourse declined to have an injection to relieve the pain because he feared that it might numb his hand and affect his grip.

When his long innings was over, he followed medical advice and took no further part in the match, so that South Africa were reduced to ten men in the second innings. The captaincy devolved on Eric Rowan, who enjoyed the honour of leading the team to victory in the field. Nourse's 208 was the highest individual score for South Africa in the 75 matches between the two countries – seven weeks later Eric Rowan beat it with 236 in the Leeds Test.

South Africa 483-9 dec. (A. D. Nourse 208, J. H. B. Waite 76, G. M. Fullerton 54)
and 121 (A. V. Bedser 6-37); **England 419-9 dec.** (R. T. Simpson 137, D. C. S. Compton 112,
L. Hutton 63, W. Watson 57; C. N. McCarthy 4-104, G. W. A. Chubb 4-146)
and 114 (A. M. B. Rowan 5-68, N. B. F. Mann 4-24).

1951 – ENGLAND v SOUTH AFRICA (Fifth Test): Obstructing the field

Norman Preston, 1952

At The Oval, August 16, 17, 18, 1951. England won by four wickets. This was the best match of the whole five. The only thing new to Test cricket was the dismissal of Hutton for obstructing the field, a decision that had been given only four times previously in first-class cricket.

From England's point of view, the hero was Laker, the Surrey off-break bowler. Unafraid to pitch the ball well up to the batsmen, he attacked them persistently. Bowling round the wicket, he gave the ball plenty of air and his finger-spin whipped off the pitch across the bat towards his leg-trap of Hutton, Brown and Tattersall.

England wanted 163 and the two Yorkshiremen, Hutton and Lowson, batted with such ease and confidence that an easy victory seemed certain. In 50 minutes they took the score to 53, and then came the Hutton sensation and calamity. A ball from Athol Rowan lifted abruptly and struck Hutton on the glove. It ran up his arm and, when he looked round, it appeared to him, as he afterwards explained, to be falling on to his wicket. In that split-second Hutton never thought about the wicketkeeper making a catch. He flicked at the ball with his bat and missed it, but it fell neither on to his stumps nor into Endean's gloves. The wicketkeeper had been obstructed and the South Africans rightly appealed. Just as rightly, Dai Davies signalled Hutton out. Hutton did not wilfully obstruct the wicketkeeper, but he wilfully waved his bat, an action which prevented the wicketkeeper from getting to the ball. From his point of view it was a most unsatisfactory ending to his 100th innings in Test cricket. On Hutton's departure the issue again became open. One moment England were on top; the next South Africa were in the fight with a good chance of success. Appropriately Laker made the winning hit by turning Rowan to long leg for three. So England won the rubber by three victories to one, but only those present that day know how close South Africa came to sharing the honours. It was England's first win at The Oval since they beat Australia in 1938.

South Africa 202 (E. A. B. Rowan 55; J. C. Laker 4-64) **and 154** (Laker 6-55);
England 194 (D. C. S. Compton 73; M. G. Melle 10–6–9–4) **and 164-6**.

1952 – INDIANS IN ENGLAND: FEAR OF FAILURE   Leslie Smith, 1953

India returned home at the end of the 1952 tour of England well satisfied with a profit of over £11,000, but far from happy about their performances on the field. Frankly, they were a big disappointment and few countries have finished with such a poor record. Admittedly they lost only five matches, but they won no more than four of their first-class games and offered little opposition in the Tests. No fewer than 20 of the 29 games were drawn – a fact that showed the biggest failing of the team. From the moment the Indians arrived there seemed to be an attitude of defensive caution in their play, and the longer the tour progressed and the failures continued the more pronounced it became. Defeat was the horrid ogre in their path, and to ward it off they retired into a cave, pulled a massive rock over the entrance and attempted to defy all efforts to dislodge them.

Little Wonder No. 38

Wisden 1938. County secretaries meeting: In a tribute to umpires in first- and second-class cricket, the MCC secretary emphasised that the umpires were on the ground for six hours, and concentrating for long hours was a tiring and arduous job. Yet the number of criticisms, he said, was remarkably few compared with those about referees and umpires in other games.

1952 – ENGLAND v INDIA (FIRST TEST): FIERY FRED   Leslie Smith, 1953

At Leeds, June 5, 6, 7, 9, 1952. England won by seven wickets. History was made in the match which, if not reaching the high standard expected from Test cricketers, was crammed with exciting incidents, remarkable collapses and gallant recoveries. But, above all, were the events which occurred at the commencement of India's second innings. They went in facing a first-innings deficit of 41, and within a few minutes the match seemed almost over. India lost their first four wickets without a run scored, and the crowd were stunned into silence as the drama unfolded before them. No Test side had ever before made such a bad start to an innings. India possessed a reasonable chance of victory before this disaster overtook them, and although they tried hard to make up for it the blow was too severe. In the end England won comfortably enough, but the margin does not show how hard they had to fight. Success by India might well have given them the confidence they so badly needed and which never came throughout the tour.

For Hutton the match was a personal triumph. Tradition had been broken with his appointment as a professional captain of England and he must have known that the eyes of the world were upon him. He did not falter and his astute leadership earned him many admirers and, perhaps, guided future policy. The cricket, already exciting, became even tenser before the large Saturday crowd. Graveney, whose fine innings of the previous day helped to save his side, did not last much longer, but the audacious batting of Evans placed England on top. Then came that astonishing Indian breakdown that virtually settled the issue. In the course of the first 14 balls Trueman [*on his Test debut*] claimed three wickets and Bedser one. Only the dismissal of Gaekwad by Bedser was the result of the ball doing the unexpected. Trueman upset Roy, Manjrekar and Mantri by his fiery pace and hostility.

India 293 (V. L. Manjrekar 133, V. S. Hazare 89; J. C. Laker 4-39)
and 165 (F. S. Trueman 4-27; R. O. Jenkins 4-50); **England 334** (T. W. Graveney 71, T. G. Evans 66; Ghulam Ahmed 5-100) **and 128-3** (R. T. Simpson 51).

1953 – AUSTRALIANS IN ENGLAND: ASHES RECLAIMED   Norman Preston, 1954

After having held the Ashes for 19 years, the longest period on record, Australia surrendered them at The Oval where, after four drawn Tests, England won the last in convincing fashion. If the winning of Test matches were the only thing that mattered, then Lindsay Hassett's team did not carry out its mission. But rarely has any series of matches produced such interesting and exciting cricket. Day after day and sometimes hour after hour the pendulum swung first towards Australia and then towards England. Time and again it seemed that one side had established absolute mastery only for it to be taken away. No other series of Tests captured such public attention. What with day-by-day front-page newspaper articles and radio and television broadcasts there were times when industry almost stood still while the man in the street followed the tense battle. Above everything else was the true spirit of cricket which existed between the England and Australian players both on and off the field. The main difference between the sides was in batting. Since 1926 until the last tour all Australian sides in England had enjoyed the services of Bradman, who broke almost every individual batting record. The gap his retirement left can be seen in the batting figures: for the first time in 50 years not a single Australian batsman could show an average of 40 in the Tests.

1953 – ENGLAND v AUSTRALIA (FIRST TEST): BEDSER'S RECORD
Reg Hayter, 1954

At Nottingham, June 11, 12, 13, 15, 16, 1953. So stirring was the cricket of the first three days that the anti-climax brought about by prolonged bad weather aroused bitter disappointment. Chiefly through the magnificent bowling of A. V. Bedser, England finished on Saturday needing 187 to win with nine second-innings wickets left. The position promised a tremendous struggle, but heavy rain washed out any hopes of play on Monday and a resumption was impossible until half past four on the last day. The consequences of the weather break must have been particularly galling to Bedser. He was England's hero, with a match analysis of 14 wickets for 99 runs. Only the Yorkshiremen, Wilfred Rhodes and Hedley Verity, who took 15 wickets apiece, had dismissed more batsmen in any of the previous 159 Tests between England and Australia. Bedser deserved to join them, but, as it was, he made the match memorable for himself by passing the English Test record of 189 wickets held by S. F. Barnes, who, at 80 years of age, saw his own figures overtaken. Barnes was among the first to congratulate the new record-holder.

Australia 249 (A. L. Hassett 115, A. R. Morris 67, K. R. Miller 55; A. V. Bedser 7-55) and 123 (Morris 60; Bedser 7-44); England 144 (R. R. Lindwall 5-57) and 120-1 (L. Hutton 60*).

1953 – ENGLAND v AUSTRALIA (Second Test): Barnacle Bailey
Reg Hayter, 1954

At Lord's, June 25, 26, 27, 29, 30, 1953. In its swift changes of fortune the cricket followed a pattern similar to that of the Nottingham Test, except that here the suspense continued to the last over of the fifth day. First one side, then the other, built up an apparently commanding position, only for a series of dramatic incidents to swing the balance again. Yet everything in the first four days paled before England's last-ditch stand which brought them a draw as stirring as the majority of victories.

One hour remained for play on the fourth day when England began the last innings, needing 343 to win. That was an hour to make Australia happy and England miserable. Lindwall struck two shattering blows at once, getting Kenyon caught at mid-on and Hutton at slip, and when Langley made a thrilling diving catch off Graveney three men were out for 12. Although Watson stayed with Compton to the close, he might have been caught off Ring at short leg in the last over. The costliness of that miss was to be seen on the last day.

The general view of England's prospects of saving the game was shown by the size of the crowd which gathered for the final stages. In contrast to thousands having to be turned away, the crowd numbered only 14,000. Few of those could have imagined they would witness anything approaching the gallant resistance by which England escaped defeat. First came the not-out batsmen, Watson and Compton. Compton held out for 95 minutes before being leg-before to a ball that kept low. This brought in Bailey, the last of the recognised batsmen. Nearly five hours remained for play. The odds on Australia winning were high. At first Australia did not appear unduly worried, but, as Bailey settled down to his sternest defence, the bowlers produced all they knew. Still Bailey went on playing a dead-bat pendulum stroke to every ball on his wicket. His batting was far from attractive to the eye but it was thoroughly efficient and founded in first principles. Watson, too, met the ball with the full face of the bat. The most testing period came midway through the afternoon when Lindwall and Miller took the new ball. Three times

246

Bailey was struck on the hand by a bouncer, but after each he paused only to wring his hand. The batsmen, unmoved and seemingly immovable, pursued their determined course. Their mood so infected spectators that often cheers broke out for purely defensive strokes.

At the end of five and threequarter hours Watson's vigil came to an end. Soon afterwards Bailey, who stood in the breach for four and a quarter hours, shook off his self-imposed shackles and essayed a cover-drive which resulted in a fairly easy catch. His annoyance was plain for all to see. At the fall of the sixth wicket 35 minutes were left for play, and the way the ball turned to Brown and Evans gave rise to thoughts that, after all, Australia might finish England's resistance in time, but, riding his luck, Brown struck out boldly. Even so, feelings were such that when Brown was out in the last over the prospects of Benaud taking three wickets in the last four balls to win the match were discussed seriously. Wardle soon brought speculation to an end. So finished a Test of wonderful character.

Australia 346 (A. L. Hassett 104, A. K. Davidson 76, R. N. Harvey 59; A. V. Bedser 5-105)
and 368 (K. R. Miller 109, A. R. Morris 89; F. R. Brown 4-82);
England 372 (L. Hutton 145, T. W. Graveney 78, D. C. S. Compton 57; R. R. Lindwall 5-66)
and 282-7 (W. Watson 109, T. E. Bailey 71).

1953 – ENGLAND v AUSTRALIA (FIFTH TEST): HUTTON WEARS THE CROWN
Norman Preston, 1954

At The Oval, August 15, 17, 18, 19, 1953. England won by eight wickets and so won the Ashes for the first time since 1932-33. It was a most welcome victory in Coronation year and a triumph for Len Hutton, the first modern professional to be entrusted with the captaincy of England. There was something unique in the victory of Hutton's men as far as England and Australia were concerned. Hutton was the only captain who had lost the toss in all five Tests and yet won the series.

The absence of a genuine spin bowler proved a severe handicap to Australia. The issue was virtually decided on the third afternoon when Australia, 31 behind on the first innings, lost half their side to Laker and Lock for 61. In one astonishing spell of 14 minutes four wickets fell while only two runs were scored. England needed 132 to win with ample time at their disposal. Fifty minutes remained on Tuesday when Hutton and Edrich began England's final task. Both produced some excellent strokes, but at 24 Hutton brought about his own dismissal. He hit Miller firmly to square leg and took the obvious single, but when De Courcy fumbled he tried to steal a second run and failed to get home. Hutton looked terribly disappointed as he walked slowly back to the pavilion. They now needed 94, and only rain and a sticky pitch were likely to deprive them of the victory so near their grasp. How those Australians fought to hold the Ashes! Slowly the score crept to 88, and then Miller, having dispensed with his slips – five men were on the leg side for his off-spin – got May caught at short fine leg. The stand produced 64 in one hour 50 minutes.

Earlier Edrich magnificently hooked two successive bumpers from Lindwall. Now he was joined by his Middlesex colleague, Compton, and they took England to victory. Compton made the winning hit at seven minutes to three when he swept Morris to the boundary. At once the crowd swarmed across the ground while Edrich fought his way to the pavilion with Compton and the Australian team. In a memorable scene both captains addressed the crowd, stressing the excellent spirit in which all the matches had been contested both on and off the field.

Australia 275 (R. R. Lindwall 62, A. L. Hassett 53; F. S. Trueman 4-86)
and 162 (G. A. R. Lock 5-45, J. C. Laker 4-75);
England 306 (L. Hutton 82, T. E. Bailey 64; Lindwall 4-70) **and 132-2** (W. J. Edrich 55*).

1954 – ENGLAND v PAKISTAN (Fourth Test): MAGICAL MAHMOOD

Leslie Smith, 1955

At The Oval, August 12, 13, 14, 16, 17, 1954. Pakistan won by 24 runs. Just before half-past 12 on the fifth day of the final Test, Pakistan achieved the greatest moment of their short career as a cricket country by beating England and so sharing the rubber. Their success was well deserved, for they showed great fighting spirit when victory seemed beyond their grasp. To Fazal Mahmood, the medium-paced bowler, went chief credit, his six wickets in each innings causing the batting failures of England.

England did not field their full strength, the selectors deciding that the opportunity of Test match experience should be given to some of the players chosen to tour Australia a few weeks later. Thus two stalwarts, Alec Bedser and Trevor Bailey, were omitted. Tyson and Loader, both fast bowlers, replaced them and they in no way let down the side; but it can fairly be said that the determined batting of Bailey was badly missed and that Bedser might have turned the match on a pitch ideally suited to a bowler of his type. The England tail proved far too long for a Test match and at the vital stage this weakness almost certainly meant the difference between victory and defeat.

England needed 168 to win and appeared keen to get the runs in the two hours 35 minutes available that [fourth] evening. Simpson and May put on 51 in 40 minutes for the second wicket. May batted beautifully for 53 and when he left victory for England seemed near, only 59 runs being needed with seven wickets to fall. Then came a surprising decision, Evans being sent in, presumably to attempt to force a win in the half an hour which remained. Evans failed and so did Graveney, and when Compton fell just before the close, Pakistan were on top. With all the recognised batsmen gone and McConnon having to bat with a dislocated finger – the result of a fielding accident – England began the last day needing 43 to win with four wickets left. In 55 minutes the match was over, the cautious methods of the remaining England batsmen proving of no avail. Fazal, who this time took six wickets for 46, was helped considerably by the safe wicketkeeping of Imtiaz, who held seven catches in the match.

This was the first defeat for England in a home match since South Africa won at Nottingham in June 1951 On the Saturday 16,800 people paid for admission, the second-highest number since the war.

Pakistan 133 (F. H. Tyson 4-35) and 164 (J. H. Wardle 7-56);
England 130 (D. C. S. Compton 53; Fazal Mahmood 6-53, Mahmood Hussain 4-58)
and 143 (P. B. H. May 53; Fazal Mahmood 6-46).

1956 – AUSTRALIANS IN ENGLAND: POST-BRADMAN DISORDER   Norman Preston, 1956

The gradual decline in Australia's cricketing strength since the retirement of Sir Donald Bradman at the end of his triumphant tour of England in 1948 was not halted by the team of 17 players led by Ian Johnson in 1956. Although they lost the rubber by the bare margin of two wins against one, they were more or less outplayed in four of the five Tests and gave a disappointing display against the majority of the counties.

1956 – ENGLAND v AUSTRALIA (FOURTH TEST): LAKER'S MATCH
Leslie Smith, 1957

At Manchester, July 26, 27, 28, 30, 31, 1956. England won by an innings and 170 runs with just over an hour to spare and so retained the Ashes. This memorable game will always be known as Laker's Match because of the remarkable performance by the Surrey off-break bowler in taking nine wickets for 37 runs in the first innings and ten wickets for 53 in the second. Laker broke all the more important bowling records in the history of cricket.

Those are bare facts, interesting in themselves, but they fail to capture the drama of one of the most exciting and controversial matches for a long time. The excitement came towards the last day, first when England were trying hard to make up for the time lost by rain to gain the victory which would settle the destination of the Ashes, and later as Laker drew nearer and nearer his ten wickets in the innings. The controversy arose over the preparation of the pitch, and for days cricketers, officials, critics and the general public could talk of little else.

May won the toss for the third time in the series and he gave England a big advantage. The pitch was completely useless to fast and fast-medium bowlers and Richardson and Cowdrey, as at Nottingham, gave delightful displays. Mutterings about the pitch could be heard that evening, but they rose to full fury next day. The Australians still could not get the ball to bite as much as they ought to have done and England went gaily on. England made their 459 runs in 491 minutes, an unusually rapid rate for Test cricket in recent years.

Australia began their reply just after half past two and before play ended on the second day they had lost 11 wickets. Laker did not start his devastating work until switched to the Stretford end, from where he took each of his 19 wickets. Lock took his only wicket with the first ball after the *[tea]* interval and Laker did the rest, his after-tea spell being seven wickets for eight runs in 22 balls. While admitting that Laker spun his off-breaks appreciably, the Australian batsmen gave a sorry display and appeared to give up too easily.

Following on 375 behind, Australia finished the day with one wicket down for 51 and the controversial storm broke that night. Accusations were made that the pitch had been prepared specially for England's spin bowlers, and these were denied by the Lancashire authorities. The Australians were said to be extremely bitter over the condition of the pitch, but their captain, Johnson, declined to comment. The arguments continued over the weekend, and not until Laker's wonderful bowling on the last day overshadowed everything did they abate.

England looked like being robbed of victory by the weather, but it improved considerably on the last day and play began only ten minutes late. The soaking the pitch received left it slow and easy-paced, and by fighting, determined cricket, McDonald and Craig remained together until lunchtime when the score was 112 for two with four hours left. Shortly before the interval the sun appeared and almost immediately the ball began to spin quickly. Afterwards Laker began another devastating spell, sending back Craig, Mackay, Miller and Archer in nine overs for three runs. With an hour and 55 minutes left, England needed to capture four wickets.

The tension mounted as Laker captured his eighth and ninth wickets. There was never a question of giving Laker his tenth wicket for England's only thought was victory. Lock repeatedly beat the bat, but it was not his match and at 27 minutes past five a great cheer went up as Laker successfully appealed to the umpire, Lee, for lbw against Maddocks. The match was over and Laker had taken all ten wickets. He earned his triumph by remarkable control of length and spin and it is doubtful whether he bowled more than six bad-length balls throughout the match. As Johnson said afterwards: "When the controversy and side issues of the match are forgotten, Laker's wonderful bowling will remain." That night the rain returned and the following day not a ball could be bowled in any of the first-class matches, so it can be seen how close was England's time margin, and how the greatest bowling feat of all time nearly did not happen.

England 459 (Rev. D. S. Sheppard 113, P. E. Richardson 104, M. C. Cowdrey 80; I. W. Johnson 4-151);

Australia 84 (J. C. Laker 9-37)

and 205 (C. C. McDonald 89; Laker 10-53).

Little Wonder No. 39

MCC v Yorkshire. At Lord's, April 30, May 2, 3, 1938. A strange incident, probably without parallel, caused lively discussion at Headquarters on the opening day of the season. The announcements board bore a notice that MCC would bat, but this was contradicted, and an official statement explained that "The delay in starting the match was due to a disagreement regarding the validity of the first toss won by the MCC. As a result the captains agreed to toss again, on which occasion Yorkshire won." The first toss was made in the dressing-room, the second in front of the pavilion.

1957 – WEST INDIANS IN ENGLAND: MORE CARE, LESS CALYPSO   Norman Preston, 1958

The change in the balance of cricket power during the last seven years was reflected in the outcome of the five Tests played by West Indies in England last summer. Far from repeating their success of 1950, when they won the rubber by three matches to one, they were thrice beaten by an innings in less than three days and escaped only narrowly in the other two matches that were drawn. To Sobers, a tall left-handed all-rounder, fell the distinction of hitting the highest score of the tour – 219 not out against Nottinghamshire at Trent Bridge. Sobers undoubtedly was a very fine strokeplayer who should go far. Rohan Kanhai, 21 years old and the youngest member of the party, came primarily as a batsman and he too could make a name for himself. When things were going right for them, this West Indies team, like their predecessors, provided rare entertainment. Hailed on arrival as the gay Calypso cricketers from the Caribbean, they possibly became careless in their efforts to play attractive cricket. More determination was necessary, but for many of the youngsters the experience gained on such a long and arduous tour, which produced so many pitches of very different character, should be invaluable.

1957 – ENGLAND v WEST INDIES (FIRST TEST): RECORD DEFIANCE
Norman Preston, 1958

At Birmingham, May 30, 31, June 1, 3, 4, 1957. Drawn. The return of Test cricket to Edgbaston after 28 years produced one of the most remarkable matches of all time. The contest was notable for some excellent personal performances and a wonderful recovery by England who seemed on the brink of defeat when they began their second innings 288 behind. In the end, West Indies had their backs to the wall and had to fight strenuously to ward off disaster.

Among the records set, the following were most notable:

1. May and Cowdrey put on 411 together, a Test record for the fourth wicket: the highest stand ever made for England and the third-highest for any side in the history of Test cricket.
2. May's 285 not out was the best score by an England captain, surpassing Hammond's 240 against Australia at Lord's in 1938.
3. Ramadhin, in his marathon performance, bowled 774 balls, the most delivered by a bowler in a Test, beating Verity's 766 against South Africa at Durban in 1939. He also bowled the most balls (588) in any single first-class innings, including Tests.

Monday was memorable for the feat of May in batting all day and, excepting the first 20 minutes, Cowdrey was with him the whole time. It was a tremendous struggle. Both found the answer to Ramadhin by playing forward to him. As the wonderful partnership ripened on the last day many new records were established. After their gruelling time in the field, West Indies, set to make 296 in two hours 20 minutes, lost Kanhai and Pairaudeau to Trueman for only nine runs. Then with the fielders clustered round the batsmen, Laker and Lock ran riot, seven wickets going for 68 runs, but Goddard, the captain, defended solidly for 40 minutes, constantly putting his pads to the ball, and Atkinson was there for the final seven minutes. No doubt May could have declared when Cowdrey left, but having seen his side out of trouble he was not prepared to give West Indies the slightest chance of success.

England 186 (S. Ramadhin 7-49)
and 583-4 dec. (P. B. H. May 285*, M. C. Cowdrey 154);
West Indies 474 (O. G. Smith 161, C. L. Walcott 90, F. M. M. Worrell 81, G. S. Sobers 53;
J. C. Laker 4-119) and 72-7.

1958 – ENGLAND v NEW ZEALAND (Second Test): OVER TOO QUICKLY
Norman Preston, 1959

At Lord's, June 19, 20, 21, 1958. New Zealand had the ill luck to be trapped twice on a wet pitch after England, with May winning the toss, had batted on a true surface, and they were dismissed for 47, the lowest total in the long history of Tests at Lord's and the fourth-lowest in England. Again the Surrey spinners, Lock, nine wickets for 29, and Laker, five for 37, proved almost unplayable.

The match began in sad circumstances with the announcement that news had just been received of the death of Douglas Jardine in a Swiss nursing home. Jardine captained England at Lord's in 1931 when New Zealand played their first Test match. The MCC and New Zealand flags were lowered to half-mast.

It was one of the shortest Tests for many years, being completed in 11 and a half hours. With 25,000 people present, the captains arranged an exhibition match of 20 overs each which, played in a light-hearted way, caused plenty of fun. Richardson kept wicket for England while Evans bowled.

England 269 (M. C. Cowdrey 65; J. A. Hayes 4-36, A. R. MacGibbon 4-86);
New Zealand 47 (G. A. R. Lock 5-17, J. C. Laker 4-13) and 74 (Lock 4-12).

1960–69

The Sixties were not so much swinging as soporific. Book-ended by controversies of very different kinds relating to South Africa, there was an epic drawn Test at Lord's against West Indies in 1963 and some imaginative and attacking captaincy from the Australian Richie Benaud. But there was also the deathly batting of Ken Barrington and Geoff Boycott, who were both dropped for slow scoring two seasons apart, and the Australian captain Bob Simpson in the Old Trafford Test of 1964 which, with no weather interruptions, only just managed to get into its third innings. West Indies returned in 1966 to retain the Wisden Trophy, initiated in 1963 to celebrate the Almanack's 100th edition, in a series dominated by Garry Sobers.

1960 – SOUTH AFRICANS IN ENGLAND: CHUCKING ROW — Norman Preston, 1961

From nearly every point of view, the ninth South African tour of England proved disappointing. England soon settled the rubber by winning the first three Tests and, though the last two were drawn and showed the visitors in a more favourable light, the team returned home with almost nothing to reveal for their efforts.

Several factors told against the side of 15 players who had two experienced leaders in D. J. McGlew, the captain, and Dudley Nourse, the manager. The tour began under a cloud with the Apartheid troubles in South Africa and antagonistic feelings over the same question in Great Britain. Indeed, at one stage it was suggested that the tour should be cancelled, and MCC gave the South Africa board the option of doing so, but they decided to come and, all things considered, this proved a wise decision. Unfortunately, it was a wet summer. There were demonstrations of a minor character outside the majority of the grounds where the South Africans played as well as on their arrival at London airport.

On top of all this, the South Africans soon found themselves embroiled in a throwing controversy regarding the legitimacy of the action of Griffin, one of their two genuine fast bowlers. To add to their troubles the two opening batsmen, McGlew and Goddard, failed to come up to expectations in the Tests and none of the young players really did themselves justice.

Not for the first time South Africa gambled on a fast bowler with a doubtful action. In 1951, McCarthy escaped official disapproval on the part of the umpires. Indeed, until 1960, no visiting cricketer to England had been called for throwing. History was made at Lord's during the match against MCC in May when F. S. Lee and John Langridge no-balled Griffin three times for throwing. A week later at Trent Bridge two more umpires, Bartley and Copson, called him eight times for the same offence in the Nottinghamshire match.

After that Griffin went to A.R. Gover, the former Surrey and England fast bowler, for an intensive three-day coaching course which took place on the ground of the Spencer Cricket Club, Wandsworth. He came through the Whitsun match against Glamorgan and the First Test without being faulted, but the trouble recurred when he was bowling against Hampshire at Southampton, both umpires, Parks and Elliott, calling him six times in all for throwing.

Matters finally came to a head in the second Test at Lord's. In England's only innings, Lee called Griffin 11 times for the same offence. Buller, the other umpire, had no opportunity during the Test to pass judgment on his action, but he was at square leg in the exhibition which followed when McGlew put on Griffin. Buller looked at him from that position, then crossed to point, and on returning to square leg called him four times, the bowler completing the over under-arm.

Altogether seven first-class umpires condemned Griffin's action as unfair, and he was no-balled for throwing 28 times in four first-class matches apart from the exhibition game. At the conclusion of the First Test, when Griffin bowled without venom, Mr Foster Bowley, vice-president of the South African Cricket Association, who was present at Edgbaston, telephoned his board, after a discussion with members of the team (McGlew, Goddard and Waite), suggesting that another player should be sent, but this was turned down. Then, following the controversy which raged at the end of the second Test, Mr Geoffrey Chubb, the president of the South

African Cricket Association who had recently arrived in England, announced that it had been decided that Griffin would continue as a member of the touring team, but for reasons obvious to all he would not bowl any more while in this country.

1961 – AUSTRALIANS IN ENGLAND: BENAUD THE CAREFREE CAPTAIN
Norman Preston, 1962

Adapting an almost carefree policy throughout their five months' stay, the 23rd Australian team to visit this country returned home with their main object achieved. They retained the Ashes which they regained during P.B.H. May's MCC tour of the Antipodes in 1958-59. Thirteen years had passed since Australia previously proved victorious in a Test series in England.

The tour was a personal triumph for Richie Benaud, possibly the most popular captain of any overseas team to come to Great Britain. As soon as he arrived Benaud emphasised that he and his men wanted to play attractive cricket wherever they went. They never deliberately set themselves to play for a draw. Benaud preferred to challenge the clock in the three-day matches and, consequently, there were a number of exciting finishes in which the Australians sometimes only narrowly escaped defeat.

Prior to this tour a controversy raged over the problems of throw and drag. Only the previous year the South African visit had been marred by the case of Griffin. In order to avoid a possible repetition the cricket administrators of England and Australia agreed on a throwing truce during the first five weeks of the 1961 season – up to the First Test. During that period if any umpire considered a bowler guilty of throwing (in an Australian match) he did not call no-ball, but sent a report to MCC. In the event H. Rhodes, the Derbyshire bowler, alone was reported and that when appearing for MCC against the Australians at Lord's.

For various reasons – mainly loss of form – the Australians left behind the controversial bowlers, and this move no doubt contributed to the goodwill that prevailed everywhere. Indeed, the tour which marked the passage of 100 years since the first English party visited Australia went through without adverse incident and was most pleasant and entertaining for everyone. Encouraged by Benaud, the Australians never queried an umpire's decision and at times, when they knew they had touched a ball and been caught, did not wait to be given out, but went their way as, indeed, did the England players.

1961 – ENGLAND v AUSTRALIA (THIRD TEST): TRUEMAN TOO HOT
Norman Preston, 1962

At Leeds, July 6, 7, 8, 1961. England won by eight wickets with two days to spare. This will be remembered as Trueman's Match. Two devastating spells by him caused Australia to collapse. The first occurred immediately after tea on the first day when Australia had reached 183 for two. Then, in the course of six overs, he dismissed five men for 16 runs. His figures were even more remarkable when he came on at 3.40pm on Saturday with Australia 98 for two. At once he conceded a single to O'Neill before he again claimed five wickets, this time in 24 deliveries, for 0. Trueman finished the match with 11 wickets for 88 runs, easily his best in Test cricket.

The game will also be remembered for the controversy over the state of the pitch. In the previous Test the Lord's ridge loaded the dice in favour of the bowlers. This time the batsmen were at the mercy of the bowlers on a whitish-green piebald surface. It had been chemically treated only a few weeks before the contest and never played true, although it did not carry the same physical danger to the batsmen as the one at Lord's. The main trouble was that no one could judge how the ball would behave. Sometimes it came through fast and low; at other times it would check in the broken soft places and stand up so that the batsmen had almost completed their strokes before establishing contact. It favoured all types of bowlers, and Trueman came out triumphant. Consequently, England inflicted the first defeat of the tour on the Australians and made the series all square with two Tests to play.

> **Australia 237** (R. N. Harvey 73, C. C. McDonald 54; F. S. Trueman 5-58)
> **and 120** (Harvey 53; Trueman 6-30);
> **England 299** (G. Pullar 53, M. C. Cowdrey 93; A. K. Davidson 5-63) **and 62-2.**

1961 – ENGLAND v AUSTRALIA (FOURTH TEST): TRIPLE FIGHT BACK
Leslie Smith, 1962

At Manchester, July 27, 28, 29, 31, August 1, 1961. Australia won by 54 runs and made certain of retaining the Ashes. They deserved great credit for fighting back three times when in difficulties, but England, on top for a large part of the match, disappointed, particularly on the last day. Dropped catches proved costly to England and had an important bearing on the result. The game was intensely keen throughout and was the best of the series.

> **Australia 190** (W. M. Lawry 74; J. B. Statham 5-53)
> **and 432** (Lawry 102, A. K. Davidson 77, N. C. O'Neill 67, R. B. Simpson 51; D. A. Allen 4-58);
> **England 367** (P. B. H. May 95, K. F. Barrington 78, G. Pullar 63; Simpson 4-23)
> **and 201** (E. R. Dexter 76; R. Benaud 6-70).

1961 – BENAUD'S MANCHESTER MASTERSTROKE
Jack Fingleton, 1962

It was a famous victory for Australia; on the evidence, it was an infamous defeat for England. Twice, on that last day, England had merely to close its collective fingers on victory. England wanted 256 runs in 230 minutes. In mid-afternoon, the game was as good as over. England, 150 for one, needed only 106 runs in as many minutes. Back in Australia, with the hour around midnight, most turned off their radios and went to bed, accepting the seemingly inevitable.

Come weal, come woe, no Test side in such a position should ever have lost this game. Dexter, in one of the great attacking innings of the century, was 76. Benaud didn't seem to have a card to play. Benaud played absolutely his last card in the pack. He came around the stumps to pitch on Trueman's marks at the other end. He had to bowl around the stumps to hit the marks at such an angle that the batsmen were forced to play at the ball. Had he bowled over the stumps, the batsmen need not have played with the bat the ball off the roughage.

Benaud had discussed the possibilities of this move the night before with Ray Lindwall, the old Australian bowling fox. Lindwall thought there was merit in it although I doubt whether either thought there was victory in it. Had Benaud thought so, surely he would have tried it sooner. So, then, did Trueman's footprints on the Old Trafford pitch leave their imprint on the sands of cricket time. Thus is history made. A little but an important thing with a man like Benaud about.

1963 – WEST INDIANS IN ENGLAND: KINGS OF THE CARIBBEAN

George Duckworth, 1964

The West Indies team of 1963 was the sixth to visit England since 1928 and play an official Test series. No more popular side has ever toured the old country, and with so many thousands of the coloured population from the Caribbean having emigrated to the big cities of Great Britain the cricketers received plenty of support from their own people. They flocked to the grounds and their good humour and incessant banter helped to keep the game alive.

It was recognised that England's invincibility at home against the majority of countries would face a most serious challenge when Frank Worrell and his men arrived in London in the early days of April. Already they had won fame two years earlier by their deeds in Australia which included the memorable tie in the Test at Brisbane. They revitalised interest in cricket in Australia. Now they came to England and again by their sparkling batting, bowling and fielding they caused the whole nation to follow the progress of the Tests.

That this combination of players, assembled from all quarters of the globe through the professional engagements of Sobers, Hall and King, should take the field within a few days of their arrival as a perfectly balanced cricketing unit had to be seen to be believed.

Little Wonder No. 40

England v Australia (Fifth Victory Match). At Old Trafford, August 20, 21, 22, 1945. As at Sheffield, this match outside London was staged by the Inter-Services Sports Committee, and German prisoners were paid three farthings an hour for painting the buildings (outside) and putting certain parts of the bomb-scarred ground in a safe condition.

1963 – ENGLAND v WEST INDIES (SECOND TEST): COWDREY CAST AS HERO

Leslie Smith, 1964

At Lord's, June 20, 21, 22, 24, 25 June, 1963. Drawn. One of the most dramatic Test matches ever to be played in England attracted large crowds and aroused tremendous interest throughout the country. All through the cricket had been keen and thrilling, but the climax was remarkable, Cowdrey having to go in with a broken bone in his arm. About 300 people rushed the ground at the end of the match seeking souvenirs and patting the players on the back. The West Indies supporters called for Worrell and Hall, who appeared on the balcony, sending them home happy. When the final over arrived any one of four results could have occurred – a win for England, victory for West Indies, a tie or a draw. The match was drawn with England six runs short of success and West Indies needing one more wicket. Most people felt happy about the result, for it would have been a pity if either side had lost after playing so well.

England went in to get 234 to win. Their hopes sank when Edrich, Stewart and Dexter were out for 31, but Barrington again rose to the occasion. He and Cowdrey had to withstand some fierce bowling from Hall, who often pitched short and struck the batsmen on the body and fingers. Eventually Cowdrey received such a blow that a bone just above the left wrist was broken and he had to retire, having shown his best form of the series and helping to carry the score to 72. Close and Parks took the score to 158, and Titmus also fought well. At tea, it was still anyone's game with England 171 for five, Cowdrey injured and 63 needed in 85 minutes. With West Indies averaging only 14 overs an hour, this was a harder task than it looked on paper.

The game moved back in West Indies' favour when Titmus and Trueman fell to successive balls. Close, who had defended with rare courage despite being hit often on the body and finishing with a mass of bruises, decided the time had come to change his methods. He began moving down the pitch to Hall and Griffith to upset their length. He succeeded for a time, but eventually he just touched the ball when trying a big swing and was caught at the wicket. Worrell said afterwards that while not wishing to detract from a very fine innings, he thought Close's changed tactics were wrong. Others paid high tribute to what they termed a magnificent and courageous innings which lasted three hours, 50 minutes. He made 70, easily his highest score for England. Shackleton joined Allen with 19 minutes left and 15 runs required. They fell further behind the clock and when Hall began his last dramatic over eight were needed. Singles came off the second and third balls, but Shackleton was run out off the fourth when Worrell raced from short leg with the ball and beat the batsman to the bowler's end. That meant Cowdrey had to come in with two balls left and six wanted. He did not have to face a ball, Allen playing out the last two. If he had to shape up, Cowdrey intended to turn round and bat left-handed to protect his left arm. Hall, in particular, and Griffith, showed remarkable stamina. Hall bowled throughout the three hours and 20 minutes that play was in progress on the last day, never losing his speed and always being menacing. Griffith bowled all but five overs on the last day. The game, which attracted 110,287 paying spectators and approximately 125,000 all told, gave cricket a fine boost. It was a game to remember.

West Indies 301 (R. B. Kanhai 73, J. S. Solomon 56; F. S. Trueman 6-100)

and 229 (B. F. Butcher 133; Trueman 5-52);

England 297 (K. F. Barrington 80, E. R. Dexter 70; C. C. Griffith 5-91)

and 228-9 (D. B. Close 70, Barrington 60; W. W. Hall 4-93).

1963 – ENGLAND v WEST INDIES (Fifth Test): home from home

Norman Preston, 1964

At The Oval, August 22, 23, 24, 26, 1963. West Indies won by eight wickets with a day to spare and therefore carried off the rubber and the Wisden Trophy. There was no question that they were the superior side in all phases given decent weather and a firm pitch, but at the end of three days in this match honours were even. Indeed, England held a first-innings lead of 29 and West Indies, batting last, found themselves wanting 253 to win on Saturday evening when they knocked off five without loss.

Trueman was England's key man but he damaged his left ankle on Saturday morning. The injury, diagnosed as a bruised bone, did not respond to treatment over the weekend and as Trueman sent down only one over in the West Indies second innings they found little to trouble them and coasted home comfortably to the delight of hordes of exuberant supporters who filled The Oval all four days.

Those who were present will never forget the fantastic final scene. Early in the day the gates had been closed with 25,350 present. About two-thirds of the attendance were West Indies people now resident in London. They were jubilant, excited and well-behaved, but as Hunte and Butcher got nearer to the target so those in the front crept nearer to the boundary. Then on the stroke of 25 minutes past five, Butcher made the winning hit off Statham – an on-drive – and the ball was never seen again as the hundreds of coloured supporters invaded the field running towards the pavilion. There they stayed for some time cheering their heroes as each appeared on the balcony.

The game was also memorable for the action of Buller, the umpire, in taking a firm stand over the problem of dangerous and short-pitch intimidatory bouncers delivered by Hall and Griffith. Early on the first day after Edrich had been struck by Hall and the same bowler, in his sixth over, sent down two successive bouncers at Bolus, Buller walked over to Worrell and said: "We don't want this sort of bowling to get out of hand otherwise I will have to speak to the bowler."

Later, just before the close of play, Buller warned Griffith direct about his short-pitched bowling in accordance with the procedure laid down in Law 46 (Fair and Unfair Play) and he also told Worrell that he had spoken to the bowler, saying: "Look, this can't go on. You will have to stop it skipper." Griffith then remarked, "I am allowed two every over," and Buller replied, "No. You are not allowed any." Happily, Worrell abided with Buller's action and after play he closed the incident, saying: "As far as I am concerned the umpires are the sole judges of fair and unfair play."

England 275 (P. J. Sharpe 63; C. C. Griffith 6-71) and 223 (Sharpe 83; W. W. Hall 4-39);

West Indies 246 (C. C. Hunte 80, B. F. Butcher 53) and 255-2 (Hunte 108*, R. B. Kanhai 77).

1964 – ENGLAND v AUSTRALIA (Fourth Test): METHODICAL MADNESS

Harry Gee, 1965

At Manchester, July 23, 24, 25, 27, 28, 1964. Drawn. For all the remarkable personal achievements in the match, a bad taste was left in the mouth of the cricket enthusiasts who saw Australia retain the Ashes. Simpson's strategy, with his team one up and two to play, was to make certain that Australia did not lose. Dexter, with England kept in the field until the third morning was well advanced, had no hope of winning and so a boring situation resulted in which 28 and a quarter hours of play were needed to produce a decision on the first innings!

Both sides were to blame for frequent periods of needlessly tiresome batting on a perfectly made closely cut, firm pitch of placid pace which gave neither quick nor spin bowlers the slightest help. The intention to win was never once apparent after Simpson, for the first time in the series, won the toss, and only rarely were the justifiable expectations of the spectators for entertainment realised. Methodically, the batsmen wore down the toiling bowlers in sunshine. On the second day, Simpson and his colleagues maintained their dominance yet seldom became free-scoring. Simpson again batted in subdued, if almost faultless, fashion and was barracked before displaying some of his characteristic cuts and drives.

The crowd, having overlooked the dull spells of his batting, generously gave him an ovation for his score of 311 out of 646 for six. He defied England for three minutes under 12 and threequarter hours. The Australians had to bat a second time for the closing five minutes, and it was a suitable ending, seeing what indecisive cricket had gone before, that Simpson and Lawry were bowled to by Barrington and Titmus using an old ball. Simpson, who square-cut Barrington for the four runs obtained, was on the field for all but a quarter of an hour of the match.

Australia 656-8 dec (R. B. Simpson 311, W. M. Lawry 106, B. C. Booth 98) **and 4-0**;
England 611 (K. F. Barrington 256, E. R. Dexter 174, J. M. Parks 60, G. Boycott 58; G. D. McKenzie 7-153).

1965 – ENGLAND v NEW ZEALAND (First Test): FROZEN FARE

Norman Preston, 1966

At Birmingham, May 27, 28, 29, 31, June 1, 1965. Seldom in England has a Test been contested in such cold cheerless weather. It never differed throughout the five days and the total attendance during that period numbered no more than 21,000. Only 107 paid at the turnstiles on the final day when England won by a quarter to one.

Everything else on the second day was overshadowed by Barrington's tedious exhibition. Adopting the most exaggerated two-eyed stance ever seen he occupied the crease altogether for seven and a quarter hours for 137. Barrington stayed at 85 for 62 minutes without scoring while 20 overs were delivered. That the bowling, generally, was not so difficult as Barrington suggested was revealed as soon as he completed his hundred in six and a quarter hours. He promptly celebrated by punishing the off-spinner, Pollard, for 14 in one over, including a mighty drive for six.

Smith, the England captain, arrived when the conditions were most cheerless; twice they served hot coffee on this second day, and he had the misfortune of being leg-before during Barrington's barren hour. It was Smith's fourth duck in his last six innings and his tenth in Test cricket.

England 435 (K. F. Barrington 137, M. C. Cowdrey 85, E. R. Dexter 57; R. C. Motz 5-108) and 96-1;

New Zealand 116 (F. J. Titmus 4-18)

and 413 (V. Pollard 81*, B. Sutcliffe 53; R. W. Barber 4-132).

1965 – ENGLAND v NEW ZEALAND (THIRD TEST): EDRICH'S TRIPLE

Norman Preston, 1966

At Leeds, July 8, 9, 10, 12, 13, 1965. England won by an innings and 187 runs. This match was a triumph for Surrey in the persons of Edrich and Barrington. Both men made a glorious return to the England team. The left-handed Edrich, after hitting a century on his debut against Australia at Lord's the previous summer, was left out of the Oval Test and the tour to South Africa. Barrington reappeared after being dropped for his negative attitude during the First Test a month earlier.

Edrich, 310 not out, gained the distinction of being only the eighth batsman in the history of Test cricket to score a triple-century. Batting for eight minutes short of nine hours, Edrich hit five sixes and 52 fours. He scored more runs in boundaries than any other Test player.

With such a feast of runs the feat of Titmus on the fourth day when he took four wickets in six balls scarcely received the acclaim it deserved. Apart from a bitterly cold north wind, the conditions were perfect for the batsmen. Edrich excelled with the cover drive which he placed with perfect precision. He celebrated his 150 by driving Pollard for his second six and soon came his third, also from Pollard – a mighty on-drive into the corner of the cricket–football stand. Edrich had the unusual experience of being on the field throughout the match.

England 546-4 dec. (J. H. Edrich 310*, K. F. Barrington 163);

New Zealand 193 (J. R. Reid 54; R. Illingworth 4-42, J. D. F. Larter 4-66)

and 166 (V. Pollard 53; F. J. Titmus 5-19).

1966 – ENGLAND v WEST INDIES (FOURTH TEST): ELLIOTT v GRIFFITH

Norman Preston, 1967

At Leeds, August 4, 5, 6, 8, 1966. West Indies won by an innings and 55 runs with a day to spare. So they completed three wonderful years in which they twice won the rubber convincingly in England and for the first time beat Australia in a series. They achieved their ambition like world champions and, while they excelled as a team, standing high above the rest of them was their captain, Sobers. In the four

Tests Sobers had then scored 641 runs, average 128.20 and taken 17 wickets, as well as holding ten catches close to the bat.

Sobers had the rare experience of hitting a hundred between lunch and tea [on the second day]. During the course of his great display, in which he square-cut, hooked, pulled and drove as he pleased, he became the first cricketer to attain a Test aggregate of 5,000 runs and also 100 wickets. In addition, in this, his 18th innings of the tour, he completed his 1,000 for the summer. Sobers declared at 500, West Indies' highest total of the tour, and Barber and Boycott scored four from the four overs delivered by Hall and Griffith before the end of the day. An opening spell of 80 minutes by Hall at his fastest and best destroyed England on Saturday when he sent back Boycott, Cowdrey and Graveney. Sheer speed led each batsman into error, and Milburn also suffered through not offering a stroke to a ball that struck him such a painful blow on the left elbow that he had to retire. When Milburn returned three and a half hours later he could only defend, as he lacked power in that arm to hit with his usual freedom.

When the England total stood at 18 for two, just before midday, Griffith was cautioned against throwing by umpire Elliott after he had delivered a vicious bouncer to Graveney. Both umpires conferred and later Elliott said: "I told Syd Buller that in my opinion that delivery was illegal. We agreed that I should speak to Griffith about it. I then said to him: 'You can bowl, Charlie. Any more like that and I will have to call you. That delivery to Graveney was illegal.'" Following the incident, much of Griffith's pace disappeared and he took only one more wicket in the match. when D'Oliveira skied a loose ball to cover.

West Indies 500-9 dec. (G. S. Sobers 174, S. M. Nurse 137; K. Higgs 4-94);
England 240 (B. L. D'Oliveira 88; Sobers 5-41) **and 205** (R. W. Barber 55; L. R. Gibbs 6-39).

1967 – ENGLAND v INDIA (First Test): Geoffrey's go-slow
Norman Preston, 1968

At Leeds, June 8, 9, 10, 12, 13, 1967. England won by six wickets with two and three-quarter hours to spare. On Friday, England treated the depleted Indian attack mercilessly and in three and a half hours put on 269 before Close declared. Boycott finished with 246 not out, the highest individual innings for any Test between England and India, as well as his own highest in first-class cricket. He hit one six and 29 fours and did not make a false stroke, but his lack of enterprise met with much disapproval and the selectors dropped him for the next Test. D'Oliveira hit his first Test century, and his stand of 252 with Boycott was the second-highest in the series, falling only 14 behind that by W. R. Hammond and T. S. Worthington at The Oval in 1936.

England 550-4 dec. (G. Boycott 246*, B. L. D'Oliveira 109, K. F. Barrington 93,
T. W. Graveney 59) **and 126-4**;
India 164 (Nawab of Pataudi 64) **and 510** (Pataudi 148, A. L. Wadekar 91,
F. M. Engineer 87, Hanumant Singh 73; R. Illingworth 4-100).

1968 – AUSTRALIANS IN ENGLAND: GRIM BALANCE SHEET Norman Preston, 1969

Of all the 25 Australian teams that have visited the United Kingdom the latest combination under W. M. Lawry was perhaps one of the most disappointing. Nevertheless, they succeeded in their main objective to retain the Ashes, which Australia have now held for ten years.

At Worcester, for the first time in history the opening match of an Australian tour was completely ruined by rain and as the dismal story continued, 100 hours were lost altogether. When the first day of the fourth match, against MCC at Lord's, was blank the touring side had lost 49 hours' playing time out of their first possible 60.

The following Monday was miserably cold but it did at least allow the Australians their first full day's cricket in 11 attempts. Whereas in 1964 at a similar stage in the tour the four matches had yielded the visitors £6,085, the Australians arrived at the Sunday of their match with MCC with only £1,858, a loss of £4,227. The financial situation caused so much concern that the Australian manager asked all the counties with whom the side had fixtures from the beginning of June to play on Sundays. Only Kent were able to fall in with his suggestion, and so for the first time in England the Australians played on a Sunday at Canterbury.

Glamorgan v Indians. At Cardiff, June 8, 10, 11, 1946. Glamorgan lost their seven remaining wickets for 76, and the last two batsmen, Clay and Judge, batted straight on for the start of the second innings 227 behind. To Judge occurred the extraordinary experience of being out first ball to successive deliveries – bowled in each innings by Sarwate.

Little Wonder No. 41

1968 – ENGLAND v AUSTRALIA (FIFTH TEST): CROWD MOP UP
Norman Preston, 1969

At The Oval, August 22, 23, 24, 26, 27, 1968. England won by 226 runs with six minutes to spare and squared the rubber with one victory to each country and three matches drawn, but the Ashes stayed with Australia. Down the years Kennington has generally proved a good place for England and now, after rain had robbed Cowdrey's men at Lord's and Edgbaston, even a storm that flooded the ground at lunchtime on the last day could not save Australia.

Just before the interval England's final task appeared to be a mere formality with Australia toiling at 85 for five. In half an hour the ground was under water, but the sun reappeared at 2.15pm and the groundsman, Ted Warn, ably assisted by volunteers from the crowd, armed with brooms and blankets, mopped up to such purpose that by 4.45pm the struggle was resumed. Only 75 minutes remained and even then the deadened pitch gave the England bowlers no encouragement.

Inverarity and Jarman stood up nobly to Brown, Snow, Illingworth and Underwood, no matter how Cowdrey switched his attack with a cordon of ten men close to the bat.

Finally, Cowdrey turned to D'Oliveira, who did the trick with the last ball of his second over; it moved from the off and hit the top of the off stump as Jarman reached forward. Now 35 minutes were left for England to capture the four remaining wickets. Cowdrey promptly whisked D'Oliveira from the Pavilion end and recalled Underwood, who finished the contest by taking those four wickets in 27 deliveries for six runs.

The Kent left-arm bowler found the drying pitch ideal for this purpose. He received just enough help to be well-nigh unplayable. The ball almost stopped on pitching and lifted to the consternation of the helpless Australians. Underwood had Mallett and McKenzie held by Brown in the leg trap in the first over of his new spell; Gleeson stayed 12 minutes until his off stump was disturbed, and to everyone's surprise Inverarity, having defied England for four hours with rare skill, offered no stroke at a straight ball and was leg-before. So Underwood, with seven wickets for 50 runs, achieved his best bowling analysis in Test cricket. No praise could be too high for the way he seized his opportunity on this unforgettable day.

England 494 (J. H. Edrich 164, B. L. D'Oliveira 158, T. W. Graveney 63) and 181;
Australia 324 (W. M. Lawry 135, I. R. Redpath 67) and 125 (D. L. Underwood 7-50).

Cleaned up: Derek Underwood has Australian batsman John Inverarity leg before
to complete an improbable England victory at The Oval in 1968
after spectators helped dry the rain-sodden playing area

1968 – THE D'OLIVEIRA AFFAIR
Michael Melford, 1969

The bitterness engendered by the sequence of events leading up to the cancellation of MCC's proposed tour of South Africa only six weeks before the scheduled starting date made a sad end to the 1968 English season. Almost from the moment that England walked off the field at The Oval with a rare victory over Australia to their credit, English cricket was caught up in a whirlpool of acrimony and political argument such as it can seldom have known before. The culmination, on September 17, was the refusal by the South African prime minister, Mr John Vorster, to accept Basil D'Oliveira, a Cape Coloured, as a member of the MCC team, and the MCC committee's consequent cancellation of the tour.

Since D'Oliveira came successfully into English cricket, and even before he first played for England in 1966, it had been evident that a delicate situation might arise if he were selected for this tour of his native country. However, what appeared to be a relatively simple problem of whether he was acceptable or not had been greatly complicated when the time came, especially by his original omission from the team and the outcry which greeted it. Not until December, when, at a special general meeting of MCC the committee defeated three resolutions put forward by dissident members, was relief in sight from a period of unpleasantness which must have been a nightmare to the ordinary sensitive lover of cricket.

D'Oliveira had toured West Indies with Colin Cowdrey's team but without success. He had played in the First Test against Australia at Old Trafford in June and had made 87 not out in the second innings, but he had been left out at Lord's in favour of a third fast bowler. England almost won at Lord's and as their fortunes improved without him, D'Oliveira lost form for Worcestershire with the bat. Though he took plenty of wickets later in the season, they were mostly on imperfect pitches and were not obvious recommendations for a Test place. However, after the team for the Fifth Test had been chosen on August 18, R.M. Prideaux, one of the opening batsmen in the prolonged absence through injury of G. Boycott, dropped out through bronchitis. He was replaced by D'Oliveira, an unexpected choice, made partly to help the side's balance and partly, perhaps, on a hunch.

The hunch came off. D'Oliveira, though little used as a bowler, made 158. England won and that night, August 27, the selectors sat down to pick the team for South Africa. When it was announced next day that this did not include D'Oliveira, the chairman of the selectors, D. J. Insole, explained that the selectors regarded him "from an overseas tour point of view as a batsman rather than an all-rounder. We put him beside the seven batsmen that we had, along with Colin Milburn whom we also had to leave out with regret." This explanation of a selection was no new departure and followed the selectors' practice over the last 15 years.

To the non-cricketing public, however, D'Oliveira's omission immediately after his innings at The Oval was largely incomprehensible. It was easy for many to assume political motives behind it and a bowing to South Africa's racial policies. More knowledgeable cricketers were split between those who agreed that on technical grounds D'Oliveira was far from an automatic choice and who were doubtful if he would be any more effective in South Africa than he had been in West Indies, and those who thought that after his successful comeback to Test cricket, it was inhuman not to pick him.

Some holding the latter opinion were also ready to see non-cricketing reasons for the omission, refusing to believe Mr Insole and Mr Griffith [secretary of MCC], who publicly stated that none existed. Much was said which was regretted later – four out of 19 members of MCC who resigned in protest applied for reinstatement within a few days – and Lord Fisher of Lambeth, the former Archbishop of Canterbury, was prompted to write to the *Daily Telegraph* condemning a leader which appeared to cast doubt on the word of the selectors. A group of 20 MCC members, the number required to call a special meeting of the club, asserted this right, co-opting the Rev. D. S. Sheppard as their main spokesman. For three weeks the affair simmered like an angry volcano.

1970–79

England saw plenty of the Australians because of South Africa's exclusion following the D'Oliveira Affair, although the decade began with a series against the Rest of the World as a last-minute replacement for the planned tour by South Africa. Under Ian Chappell, Australia were initially vibrant and challenging opponents, though by the late 1970s, having been bled dry by Packer defections, they were weak and "colourless". Their place as the world's pre-eminent side was taken by West Indies, who were welcomed in 1976 by Henry Blofeld as "gay, excitable and flamboyant". After being brutalised with bat and ball, England may have chosen other adjectives. Editor Norman Preston spotted a talented 19-year-old all-rounder in his Notes of 1975. He urged the selectors to give him a chance while he was "young and enthusiastic". His name was Ian Botham.

1970 – THE 1970 TEST MATCHES: WORTHY OPPONENTS   Norman Preston, 1971

When England were forced by the Government to cancel the tour arranged for South Africa to the United Kingdom the authorities at Lord's devised a series of five matches against The Rest of the World. At the same time it was announced that England caps would be given to the home team and that the matches would be accorded the dignity of unofficial Test status. [*This was later rescinded, Glamorgan's Alan Jones losing his solitary Test cap.*]

The series was sponsored by Guinness who put up a handsome silver trophy and £20,000. The Rest won four matches and so carried off the main spoils, a curious feature being that in all the five matches victory went to the side that fielded first. For the most part attendances at the matches were disappointing. Nevertheless, the cricket reached a very high standard; possibly only the Australian sides of 1921 and 1948 could have risen to the heights attained by The Rest, yet England, after a frightful start on the first day of the opening match, proved worthy opponents. They won at Trent Bridge and in two other games – at Headingley and The Oval – the issue remained in the balance until the closing stages.

1970 – ENGLAND v REST OF THE WORLD (Fifth Test): Pollock and Sobers

Geoffrey Wheeler, 1971

At The Oval, August 13, 14, 15, 17, 18, 1970. Rest of the World won by four wickets. There were four notable individual performances in a match which brought a magnificent series to a distinguished close. The quality of the cricket was such that 53,000 spectators watched play over the five days. Graeme Pollock re-established his reputation as one of the world's great batsmen with a graceful century. His partnership of 165 with Sobers was a batting spectacle which will live long in the minds of those privileged to see it. Everything else on the second day was overshadowed by the artistry of Pollock and Sobers, who put on 135 in the last two hours. Pollock, with only 108 runs from his previous six innings, made England pay dearly for a missed slip catch when he was 18. There was one six and 16 fours in his 114, which took just over two and a half hours.

England 294 (M. C. Cowdrey 73, R. Illingworth 52, A. P. E. Knott 51*; G. D. McKenzie 4-51)

and 344 (G. Boycott 157);

Rest of the World 355 (R. G. Pollock 114, G. S. Sobers 79, M. J. Procter 51; P. Lever 7-83)

and 287-6 (R. B. Kanhai 100; J. A. Snow 4-81).

1970 – Record Revisionism

Norman Preston, Notes by the Editor, 1980

Much against my will, it has been decided by the publishers of Wisden to delete from the Records the five unofficial Tests played in England against the Rest of the World in 1970. I would emphasise that ten years ago these matches were broadcast by the BBC and ITV, published by the newspapers throughout Great Britain, and sold to the public as Test matches, as advised by the Test and County Cricket Board. The International Cricket Conference at their meeting at Lord's in 1972 reaffirmed that matches played between England and the Rest of the World in 1970 were not official Tests and should not be included in the Test match records. The two countries which dug their toes in on this issue were Australia and West Indies, although I have always understood that Sir Garfield Sobers, who captained the Rest, accepted that office only because the matches would be played as Test matches.

The cricket played that year by the two teams was some of the finest ever seen in England. It had all the fervour of a Test occasion. Considering how much money all their Test opponents have taken back from England over the years, how inter-dependent both financially and in other ways, it was strange that they should be so mean and narrow-minded on this unique occasion. There is no copyright on the term "Test match". The first known use of the words occurred in Australia in W. J. Hammersley's Victorian Cricketer's Guide 1861-62 when referring to five matches played on the first visit of an English team under H. H. Stephenson against Victoria, New South Wales, and Combined Victoria and NSW.

1971 – INDIANS IN ENGLAND: DANCING IN THE STREETS   Dicky Rutnagur, 1972

In Bombay, the birthplace of Indian cricket, unprecedented scenes were witnessed on the night of August 24, the day India beat England in the Third Test match at The Oval. There was dancing in the streets. Revellers stopped and boarded buses to convey the news to commuters. In the homes, children garlanded wireless sets over which the cheery voice of Brian Johnston had proclaimed the glad tidings of India's first Test victory in England, a victory which also gave them the rubber.

As in the West Indies, the spin attack was the cornerstone of India's success. The inclusion of Chandrasekhar gave it a sharper edge and its effectiveness was enhanced no less by the vast improvement in fielding standards. For this, credit goes mainly to the manager, Lt. Col. H. R. Adhikari, who, to borrow from football parlance, was a "track-suit" manager.

Chandrasekhar, Bedi, Venkataraghavan and Prasanna comprised one of the most versatile spin combinations that any country has ever sent on tour. Of the 244 wickets that fell to bowlers on the whole tour, these four captured 197, and in the Tests Chandrasekhar, Bedi and Venkataraghavan accounted for 37 as against 11 by the two seamers, Abid Ali and Solkar. Masters of their craft, the spinners bowled well even under unfavourable conditions and at Lord's and The Oval, where the pitches assisted them, they were quite menacing. Bedi bowled tirelessly, and in the challenging manner of the classical left-arm spinner. He must rank amongst the finest bowlers of his type to have toured this country. Prasanna, whom many (Garry Sobers included) consider the world's best off-spinner today, failed to gain a Test place.

1971 – ENGLAND v INDIA (THIRD TEST)**: HISTORIC WIN**   Geoffrey Wheeler, 1972

At The Oval, August 19, 20, 21, 23, 24, 1971. India won by four wickets. India made cricket history by winning a Test match on English soil for the first time. In doing so, they brought to an end England's record run of 26 official Tests without defeat. The Indian match-winner was the wrist-spinner Chandrasekhar who took six for 38 as England were dismissed in their second innings for 101, their lowest score against India and their third-lowest total since the war.

The Indians were left 173 to make in the fourth innings and by consistent batting on a slow, turning pitch gained a victory which gave them the series. It was an unexpected win, for until Chandrasekhar's inspired spell on the fourth day England seemed to have the match well in hand. India finished the fourth day with 76 for two. Gavaskar was lbw to Snow without scoring, but Mankad played his longest innings of the series and then Wadekar and Sardesai denied England a breakthrough. Next morning, Wadekar was run out attempting a quick single to D'Oliveira before a run had been added.

The tension was high and the Indians, avoiding all risks, took three hours to make the last 97 runs. Illingworth, in his own way, again bowled beautifully, but without luck; and his field placings were masterly, as was his handling of the attack. Underwood was dangerous when operating in a slower style, but was not as consistently taxing as his captain. Sardesai and Viswanath batted in dedicated fashion and when they were out Engineer struck some telling blows. Abid Ali cut the winning boundary to bring the jubilant Indian supporters racing on to the field to acclaim their heroes, who had shown that their success in the West Indies was well merited and in no way a fluke. So India won in England for the first time in 39 years.

England 355 (A. P. E. Knott 90, J. A. Jameson 82, R. A. Hutton 81) and 101 (B. S. Chandrasekhar 6-38); India 284 (F. M. Engineer 59, D. N. Sardesai 54; R. Illingworth 5-70) and 174-6.

1971 – ENGLAND v PAKISTAN (First Test): Zaheer's record   1972

At Birmingham, June 3, 4, 5, 7, 8, 1971. Drawn. Pakistan took all the honours. They had a wonderful chance of winning when rain intervened on the last day. On an easy-paced pitch five centuries were made and the most remarkable was that by Zaheer Abbas, whose 274 was the highest individual score made by a Pakistan batsman against England. Zaheer and Mushtaq Mohammad enjoyed a record second-wicket stand of 291, while Asif Iqbal with 104 not out emphasised Pakistan's immense batting strength. Ward's third delivery struck Aftab Gul on the head and he had to retire to have the wound stitched. This brought in Zaheer and one soon appreciated that he was a batsman out of the ordinary. He was particularly strong on the leg side, piercing the field with ease. Zaheer stayed for nine hours ten minutes, hitting 38 fours before a sweep at Illingworth brought his downfall. When he reached 261, Zaheer became the first batsman to complete 1,000 runs in the English season. He said afterwards that he had not felt too tired and was thinking in terms of the world Test record just before he was dismissed.

Pakistan 608-7 dec. (Zaheer Abbas 274, Asif Iqbal 104*, Mushtaq Mohammad 100); England 353 (A. P. E. Knott 116, B. L. D'Oliveira 73; Asif Masood 5-111) and 229-5 (B. W. Luckhurst 108*; Masood 4-49).

1972 – An Unreasonable Dislike Of Australians   Ted Dexter, 1972

I have on occasions taken a quite unreasonable dislike to Australians. Sorry, but it is the truth. And if I blush at the thought, let alone the telling of it publicly, I derive a certain amount of comfort from the knowledge that I am not alone amongst England's cricketers in my feelings, highly reprehensible though they of course are.

Entirely irrational I know. But I take further comfort from having long ago learned that this barbaric level of response is not entirely directed from us to them. Under provocation no greater, certainly, than is needed to stimulate our own aggression Australians can, and do, quite readily and often in my experience, throw off all their 180 years of civilised nationhood; they gaily revive every prejudice they ever knew, whether to do with accent, class consciousness or even the original convict complex, and sally forth into battle with a dedication which would not disgrace the most committed of the world's political agitators.

To try to give adequate reasons for this intensity of reaction, as quick, positive and predictable a process as when photographic paper is first exposed to light, would be to attempt the arduous, if not the impossible. Psychology, history, politics, sport, religion and many factors besides would need thorough investigation. However, I cannot help feeling that an almost complete lack of guilt on both sides is a primary cause. Like puppies from the same litter we feel perfectly entitled to knock hell out of one another for as long as we like, until passions burn themselves low and we continue once more, for a limited period, to display outward signs of peaceful co-existence.

The indisputable fact is that we come from the same stock and can therefore indulge ourselves rather splendidly in an orgy of superficial hate which neither our consciences nor *Panorama* (whichever of them it was that came first) can possibly allow in relation to any of the other cricketing nations with whom we consort. However much we may be infuriated by Indians: annoyed by Pakistanis: get angry with West Indians: niggle New Zealanders (who are just too much like our better selves for us to care about them so strongly): or get upset by South Africans (South Africans more than any): we are honour-bound to maintain a more formal diplomatic front. Not so with the Diggers. Little, if anything, is sacrosanct in the feuding, and no point remains too small or insignificant not to be turned to advantage if humanly possible.

1972 – AUSTRALIANS IN ENGLAND: LILLEE LET LOOSE   Norman Preston, 1973

In many respects the Australian team surpassed themselves even if they did not regain the Ashes. Dennis Lillee was the real find of the tour. He established a record for an Australian bowler in England by capturing 31 wickets in the Test series, beating 29 by C. V. Grimmett in 1930 and by G. D. McKenzie in 1964.

1972 – ENGLAND v AUSTRALIA (SECOND TEST): MASSIE'S MATCH
Norman Preston, 1973

At Lord's, June 22, 23, 24, 26, 1972. Australia won by eight wickets. So Australia soon avenged their defeat at Manchester in a contest which will be remembered as Massie's Match. The 25-year-old fast bowler from Western Australia surpassed all Australian Test bowling records by taking 16 wickets for 137; in all Tests only J. C. Laker, 19 for 90 for England against Australia in 1956 and S. F. Barnes, 17 for 179 for England against South Africa in 1913-14, stand above him. Moreover, Massie performed this wonderful feat on his Test debut, the previous-best by a bowler on his first appearance for his country being as far back as 1890 when at The Oval Frederick Martin, a left-arm slow-medium-pacer from Kent, took 12 for 102.

Not for the first time, particularly in recent years, England were badly let down by their specialist batsmen, who failed lamentably in all respects. From the start they allowed the Australian bowlers to take the initiative, and their excessive caution met with fatal results. Illingworth won the toss for the seventh consecutive time and one must admit that the hard fast pitch was ideal for men of pace. During the first three days, too, the atmosphere was heavy and ideally suited to swing. Massie maintained excellent length and direction and his late swing either way always troubled the England batsmen.

One must also stress the important part Lillee played in Australia's victory. He had tidied his long fast approach of 22 strides, he was truly fast and he sent down far fewer loose deliveries. Massie capitalised on the hostility of his partner. Only the most optimistic Australian could have anticipated the success which so soon attended the efforts of Lillee and Massie. The England [second-innings] collapse – half the side were out for 31 – began when a fast shortish ball from Lillee lifted and Boycott, instead of dodging, preferred to let it strike his body while his bat was lifted high. It bounced off his padded front left ribs over his shoulder and dropped behind him on to the off bail. It was most unlucky for Boycott as well as England. Obviously the Australians, having captured so valuable wicket so cheaply, now bowled and fielded like men inspired.

England 272 (A. W. Greig 54; R. A. L. Massie 8-84) and 116 (Massie 8-53);
Australia 308 (G. S. Chappell 131, R. W. Marsh 50; J. A. Snow 5-57) and 81-2 (K. R. Stackpole 57*).

Middlesex v Somerset. At Lord's, May 10, 12, 13, 1947. Somerset won by one wicket. Lunch was taken with 16 wanted. Despite a close-set field, defence still prevailed until Tremlett lifted an almost straight drive into the members' stand and, with two threes to the on, he finished the match. The Middlesex team lined up and cheered as their successful opponents went to the pavilion.

Little Wonder No. 42

1972 – ENGLAND v AUSTRALIA (FOURTH TEST): DEADLY DEREK

Bill Bowes, 1973

At Leeds, July 27, 28, 29, 1972. England won by nine wickets to take a 2–1 lead in the series and so retain the Ashes no matter what happened in the Fifth Test at The Oval. A pitch that afforded considerable help to the spin bowlers found batsmen in both teams unable to cope and the Australian cricketers – the less practised against a turning ball – as they were on the same ground in 1956 and again in 1961, were completely outplayed.

Not for a moment would one suggest that conditions had been deliberately engineered to produce such a result, but the fact remained that they were conditions least likely to help the tourists; and one recalled that when the Headingley ground was granted regular Test match status alongside Lord's and The Oval, the Yorkshire club, through their chairman, Mr A. B. Sellers, had to give an assurance that the pitch would be up to Test match standard. That cannot be claimed for the pitch prepared for this game, even allowing for the fact that Underwood is the most skilful bowler in the world when there is help for finger-spin. It was without pace, took spin from the first day and grew progressively helpful. [*The Headingley pitch had been attacked by the fusarium fungus following a freak storm the weekend before the Test.*]

Illingworth came on to bowl and, after he had delivered three overs, Underwood bowled. Spin bowlers on the first morning of a Test match? Illingworth had obviously read the signs aright. Although there was no indication of the havoc to be caused by spin when Australia came in to lunch with a score of 79 for one wicket, things began to happen immediately after the interval. Underwood was brought into immediate attack. Sensationally, Australia had slumped to 98 for seven, and the crowd of 19,000 almost ironically applauded the 100 in the 62nd over.

On the second day the off-spinner Mallett bowled at Underwood's pace and the left-arm slow Inverarity at Illingworth's pace. They returned some of the spin-bowling problems to England. By lunchtime England had lost six wickets for 112 runs. Illingworth played a real captain's part by scoring 54 not out in England's total of 252 for nine by Friday evening. In the context of the game Illingworth played superbly. In terms of Test cricket as an exhibition of all that is best in the game it need only be said that his innings occupied four and a half hours. It would be poor watching if this was always the only successful method.

As expected, the Australian second innings disintegrated before the bowling of Underwood. Underwood took five wickets for 18 runs in 13 overs and ripped through the heart of Australia's batting. Underwood, perhaps the world's best bowler on a helpful pitch, snatched ten wickets for 82 runs in the match. Batting on both sides was flimsy.

Australia 146 (K. R. Stackpole 52; D. L. Underwood 4-37) **and 136** (Underwood 6-45); **England 263** (R. Illingworth 57; A. A. Mallett 5-114) **and 21-1**.

1973 – NEW ZEALANDERS IN ENGLAND: HADLEE HOPE   R. T. Brittenden, 1974

New Zealand's determined efforts to improve their Test status very nearly won a rich reward. No New Zealand team, at home or abroad, has been so near an anxiously awaited first victory over England. The New Zealand bowling lacked hostile pace or penetrative spin, but the most promising of the faster bowlers, R. J. Hadlee, played in only one Test. His best bowling came late in the tour, but he has considerable prospects of success ahead.

1973 – ENGLAND v WEST INDIES (SECOND TEST): UMPIRE WITHDRAWS
Norman Preston, 1974

At Birmingham, August 9, 10, 11, 13, 14, 1973. Drawn. Kanhai and his West Indies team made sure of not losing the three-match rubber by holding England to a draw, but the methods adopted caused much unpleasantness. While the cricket itself may soon be forgotten, the match will be remembered for the unprecedented action of the umpire Arthur Fagg, who at the end of the second day threatened to withdraw from the match; indeed Alan Oakman, the Warwickshire coach and a former first-class umpire and Test player, stood for the first over on Saturday morning before Fagg resumed his duties following talks with Mr Esmond Kentish, the West Indies manager, and Mr A. V. Bedser, chairman of the England selectors.

The trouble began early in the England innings when several of the West Indian team confidently appealed against Boycott for a catch at the wicket off Boyce. It was turned down by Fagg, and for the next two hours or more Kanhai openly showed his annoyance. Fagg requested an apology from the West Indies and although this was not forthcoming at the time Mr Kentish stated that the West Indies team "are fully satisfied with Mr Fagg's umpiring".

The match was also notable for the fact that for the first time a touring Test team contained 11 English county players. It should be emphasised that following the scenes at The Oval, where the crowd frequently raced over the boundary into the middle, the officials at Edgbaston marked no boundary, which went to the actual fences behind which the crowd remained throughout the five days; so there were no interruptions through invasions, but runs were harder to come by. The first session before lunch on Saturday, when 20,000 people were present, was most unpleasant. Indeed during the interval the umpires warned against the slow over-rate of 26 in the two hours, but Boyce and Julien also constantly flung down short bouncers and ran down the pitch.

West Indies 327 (R. C. Fredericks 150, B. D. Julien 54)
and **302** (C. H. Lloyd 94, G. S. Sobers 74; G. G. Arnold 4-43);
England 305 (G. Boycott 56, D. L. Amiss 56, K. W. R. Fletcher 52) **and 182-2** (Boycott 82*).

1973 – CAPTAINS MUST TAKE CHARGE   Norman Preston, Notes by the Editor, 1974

The reaction of Fagg while at boiling point met with much criticism, and it would certainly have been better had he grappled with the situation through the Test and County Cricket Board representative who was on hand for just such an occurrence, rather than in the press, but at least it brought the matter to a head. For too long, and not only in this country, players from junior to senior standing have been reflecting their dislike at umpire's decisions almost with disdain. Now the TCCB have taken a firm stand by declaring at their December meeting that umpires will receive full support in reporting, as is their duty, any pressurising on the field. Captains more than anyone hold the key to clearing up a bad habit which has no place in the game of cricket.

1973 – ENGLAND v WEST INDIES (THIRD TEST): ENGLAND BOMBED OUT
Geoffrey Wheeler, 1974

At Lord's, August 23, 24, 25, 27, 1973. West Indies won by an innings and 226 runs. This match will assuredly be known in cricket history as The Bomb Scare Test. There was drama on the Saturday afternoon when 28,000 people were ordered to leave the ground following a telephone warning that a bomb had been planted. The call proved to be a hoax, but no chances could be taken with the safety of players and spectators because an IRA bomb campaign was in full swing in London at the time.

The incident caused the loss of 85 minutes' playing time, and it was agreed that half an hour would be added to the day's play after further extra time provided for on Monday and Tuesday. But the triumphant West Indies had no need of it and they won with a day and a half to spare. They swept aside a demoralised England side whose margin of defeat had been exceeded once only, at Brisbane on the 1946-47 tour of Australia.

As Illingworth said afterwards, "We were outbatted, outbowled and outfielded. There are no excuses." It was a sad end to the Illingworth era, for England's cricketers, with a few doughty exceptions, played without spirit or fight. The crowd behaviour was once more unsatisfactory. Despite the lessons of The Oval the ground authorities decided to allow spectators to sit on the grass. As West Indies gained the upper hand the unruly elements became more and more uncontrollable, and when Boycott was leaving the field on the Saturday evening he was buffeted by a group of them. As a result the crowd were confined to the stands on the Monday, a Bank Holiday, when soon after lunch thousands of West Indians were dancing around the outfield to celebrate victory after a match that was embarrassingly one-sided.

On a fine Saturday the ground was packed to capacity. Although Amiss was soon accounted for, England made a useful recovery as the confident Fletcher and a rather fortunate Greig added 79 for the fifth wicket. The loss of Fletcher and Illingworth to successive balls just before lunch sent the innings into its final decline.

Half an hour after the interval, as Willis came out to join Arnold, the secretary of MCC announced over the loudspeakers that the ground would have to be cleared. For some time the players stayed in the middle surrounded by curious spectators. Eventually the West Indies went back to their hotel in Maida Vale and the England players to a tent behind the pavilion while police searched the empty stands. Thousands stayed on the playing area, refusing to leave.

West Indies 652-8 dec. (R. B. Kanhai 157, G. S. Sobers 150*, B. D. Julien 121; R. G. D. Willis 4-118); **England 233** (K. W. R. Fletcher 68; K. D. Boyce 4-50, V. A. Holder 4-56) **and 193** (Fletcher 86*; Boyce 4-49).

1974 – ENGLAND v INDIA (SECOND TEST): TOURISTS' NEW LOW

Norman Preston, 1975

At Lord's, June 20, 21, 22, 24, 1974. This was an extraordinarily one-sided contest, yet for three days India, handicapped because Chandrasekhar injured a thumb on the first day, put up gallant resistance; but, compelled to follow on late on Saturday evening 327 runs behind, they capitulated in 77 minutes on Monday morning for 42, their lowest Test total and the lowest ever in a Test at Lord's. The match was notable for several other milestones. England's total of 629 was their highest at Lord's and their best since making 654 for five against South Africa at Durban, 1938-39. They had also only once surpassed the margin of victory, an innings and 579 runs against Australia at The Oval, 1938. It was also England's first win at Lord's for five years. When India batted a second time in a heavy atmosphere Arnold revelled in swinging the ball either way. He made the breakthrough and Old completed the debacle, Hendrick, who might have done just as well, being merely a spectator.

England 629 (D. L. Amiss 188, A. W. Greig 106, J. H. Edrich 96; B. S. Bedi 6-226);

India 302 (F. M. Engineer 86, G. R. Viswanath 5; C. M. Old 4-67) and 42 (G. G. Arnold 4-19, Old 5-21).

1975 – AUSTRALIANS IN ENGLAND: FIRE AND HEAT

Norman Preston, 1976

The Australians rendered a great service to English cricket by staying in the country after the World Cup and playing four Test matches, for the tour was not in the original calendar. The presence of the two controversial and hostile fast bowlers Lillee and Thomson ensured the attendance of large crowds, and as the summer was one of the hottest for many years the gates were closed on several occasions.

I doubt whether any previous Australian side has brought together such a galaxy of genuine pace bowlers, for besides Lillee and Thomson there were Walker, Gilmour and Hurst. Many other captains would have envied Ian Chappell's problem of whom to leave out. Little was seen of the capable but unfortunate Hurst, who never got into the Test side, and even such a superb all-rounder as the left-handed Gilmour appeared in only one Test.

1975 – ENGLAND v AUSTRALIA (SECOND TEST): MAN OF STEELE

Norman Preston, 1976

At Lord's, July 31, August 1, 2, 4, 5, 1975. Drawn. Graced on the first day by the presence of The Queen, to whom the players and officials were introduced in front of the pavilion during the tea interval, and before play began by The Duke of Edinburgh, president of MCC, who inspected the pitch and chatted with Jim Fairbrother and his groundstaff, this match produced much splendid cricket while the fortunes of both sides ebbed and flowed. As Denness had informed the selectors during England's unhappy time in the First Test that he was willing to resign the captaincy, the leadership now passed to Greig, and after another disastrous start he lifted England's morale with a dashing innings of 96 in just over two and a half hours, including nine boundaries. A surprise choice by England was David Steele, the bespectacled grey-haired 33-year-old Northamptonshire batsman. He entered when Wood was the first of five men leg-before during the innings. Three times Steele hooked Lillee's short ball and he also cut effectively, but above all he showed the value of playing forward in a calm and calculated manner.

England 315 (A. W. Greig 96, A. P. E. Knott 69, D. S. Steele 50; D. K. Lillee 4-84)

and 436-7 dec. (J. H. Edrich 175, B. Wood 52); Australia 268 (R. Edwards 99, Lillee 73*; J. A. Snow 4-66)

and 329-3 (R. B. McCosker 79, I. M. Chappell 86, G. S. Chappell 73*, Edwards 52*).

1975 – ENGLAND v AUSTRALIA (THIRD TEST): PITCH VANDALISED

Norman Preston, 1976

At Leeds, August 14, 15, 16, 18, 19, 1975. Abandoned as a draw after vandals had sabotaged the pitch in the early hours of the fifth day. The perpetrators [*protesting against the conviction for armed robbery of George Davis*] got under the covers at the pavilion end and dug out holes with knives near the popping crease and poured a gallon of crude oil in the region where a good-length ball would have pitched. They made certain that millions of people in England and in Australia would be deprived of the enjoyment of what promised to be a truly great day's cricket. As it happened, rain set in at midday and would have washed out the proceedings in any case. There had been a night-guard of one solitary policeman, and following this outrage it was obvious that in future much greater vigilance would be necessary to ensure that cricket grounds, and particularly pitches, should receive better protection. The captains, Tony Greig and Ian Chappell, looked at other parts of the square but could not find a suitable alternative pitch on which to continue the match, nor could the authorities find any way to arrange another match so late in the season and when most of the Australians were committed to return home immediately after The Oval Test.

England 288 (D. S. Steele 73, J. H. Edrich 62, A. W. Greig 51; G. J. Gilmour 6-85)

and 291 (Steele 92);

Australia 135 (P. H. Edmonds 5-28) and 220-3.

1976 – WEST INDIES: EXCITABLE AND FLAMBOYANT

Henry Blofeld, 1976

The West Indies may not have made much of an impact on Test cricket until after the Second War, but their cricket and their cricketers have always been as full of character and individuality as any in the world. The West Indians are a people with volatile temperaments and they have always tended to play their cricket in the same way that they live their lives. Because they are by nature gay, excitable and flamboyant, their approach to cricket has captured the imagination in a way which the cricket of no other country has done.

To be fully understood and appreciated West Indian cricket ought really to be seen in its own indigenous surroundings in the Caribbean. There, the game and the crowd are one and indivisible, and there is total participation not only by the players and the spectators, but also by the entire population of each island or territory. When West Indies teams have played abroad in recent years, particularly in England, the expatriate West Indians have done their best to recreate the atmosphere which is found at, say, the Queen's Park Oval in Port-of-Spain. Great fun it has been too, but West Indian gaiety and frivolity and exuberance do not always lie easily on the more staid and unbending atmospheres of Lord's or The Oval. An impromptu calypso is splendid, but it is not the same as an impromptu calypso under a palm tree on the popular side of a West Indian ground. How could it be?

1976 – ENGLAND v WEST INDIES (FIRST TEST): VIV'S BLAZE OF GLORY

Norman Preston, 1977

At Nottingham, June 3, 4, 5, 7, 8, 1976. Drawn. A marvellous innings of 232 by the 24-year-old Vivian Richards overshadowed everything else in this match. Although there were moments when Richards played and missed, his display was more notable for brilliant strokes all round the wicket and particularly his stylish and powerful driving off the front foot. Kallicharran concentrated more on defence, and at the close on Thursday Richards (143) had completed his ninth hundred since January; Kallicharran was 52. Next day, the pair remained together until 2.30pm, their stand producing 303, of which Kallicharran's share was 97. Richards finished in a blaze of glory, for he hit 36 runs off the last 13 balls he received before Greig on the long-off boundary held a steepling catch. From England's point of view it had been a disappointing performance.

West Indies 494 (I. V. A. Richards 232, A. I. Kallicharran 97; D. L. Underwood 4-82)
and 176-5 dec. (Richards 63; J. A. Snow 4-53);
England 332 (D. S. Steele 106, R. A. Woolmer 82; W. W. Daniel 4-53).

Surrey v Old England. At The Oval, June 12, 1947.
Field-Marshal Lord Montgomery, born at St. Mark's vicarage overlooking the ground, the guest of honour, shook hands with both teams on the field.

Little Wonder No. 43

1976 – ENGLAND v WEST INDIES (THIRD TEST): "WE GOT CARRIED AWAY"

Geoffrey Wheeler, 1977

At Manchester, July 8, 9, 10, 12, 13, 1976. West Indies won by 425 runs. After holding the world's fastest bowlers at bay in the previous five Tests England finally bowed the knee to pace on a cracked, often unpredictable pitch at Old Trafford. The England batsmen were overwhelmed by Roberts and Holding, with Daniel a dangerous accomplice. Only Australia has dismissed England for fewer than the first-innings total of 71 – on seven occasions. The match was not only a triumph for West Indies fast bowlers, because Greenidge became the first batsman to make a century in each innings of a Manchester Test. George Headley alone among West Indies cricketers had previously hit two hundreds in one match against England.

Holding, who took five for nine in 7.5 overs, was the leader of a fearsome trio. Some balls lifted at frightening speed, and Greig and Underwood both had narrow escapes from what could have been a serious injury. Woolmer and Hayes received balls which were all but unplayable and even the greatest of batting sides would have been severely taxed. England went in needing 552 in 13 and a quarter hours, a forlorn prospect. The period before the close of the third day brought disquieting cricket as Edrich and Close grimly defended their wickets and themselves against fast bowling which was frequently too wild and too hostile to be acceptable. Holding was finally warned for intimidation by umpire Alley after an excess of bouncers. Lloyd admitted after the match: "Our fellows got carried away. They knew they had only 80 minutes that night to make an impression and they went flat out, sacrificing accuracy for speed. They knew afterwards they had bowled badly."

West Indies 211 (C. G. Greenidge 134; M. W. W. Selvey 4-41)

and 411-5 dec. (I. V. A. Richards 135, Greenidge 101, R. C. Fredericks 50);

England 71 (M. A. Holding 5-17) **and 126** (A. M. E. Roberts 6-37).

1976 – ENGLAND v WEST INDIES (FIFTH TEST): SUPREME SPEED
Norman Preston, 1977

At The Oval, August 12, 13, 14, 16, 17, 1976. West Indies won by 231 runs. The previous time England went down by a similar margin in a home series was in 1948 against Bradman's Australia side. West Indies, moreover, recorded their fifth victory in the last eight Tests in England, many by wide margins.

This contest produced many splendid personal performances. Holding achieved two bowling records for West Indies by taking eight first-innings wickets for 92, and with six for 57 on the fifth day his full analysis was 14 for 149 – a great triumph for one of the world's fastest bowlers of all time. After Lloyd had won the toss for the fourth time in the five Tests, Richards gave yet another glorious display with the bat. Making 291 out of 519, he hit 38 fours in a stay of eight minutes short of eight hours.

For England, Amiss made a memorable return to the Test match scene. He looked the only class batsman in the side as he held the England first innings together by scoring 203 out of 342 before being seventh to leave, bowled behind his legs. He played nobly for seven hours, 23 minutes.

Richards passed Sir Frank Worrell's 261 at Trent Bridge in 1950, the previous-best for West Indies in England. One imagined that he would challenge Sir Garry Sobers's 365, the highest for all Tests, but having driven Greig high towards the Vauxhall end he went to repeat the stroke next ball only to touch it into his stumps.

With the pitch slow and dusty, West Indies' decision to rely on the pacemen to the exclusion of any recognised spinner caused a good deal of comment, but Holding's speed through the air provided the answer, particularly as his side had so many runs on the board. [On day three] Greig raised hopes of a long stay with two grand cover-drives off Holding, but trying again he was bowled off his pads. A disgraceful scene followed. A huge section of the crowd, mainly West Indians, swept over the ground and trampled on the pitch with the departure of the England captain. The umpires led the players off the field at about 6.10pm. When peace was restored Amiss and Underwood played out the last seven minutes.

West Indies 687-8 dec. (I. V. A. Richards 291, C. H. Lloyd 84, R. C. Fredericks 71, L. G. Rowe 70,

C. L. King 63) and 182-0 dec. (Fredericks 86*, C. G. Greenidge 85*);

England 435 (D. L. Amiss 203, A. P. E. Knott 50; M. A. Holding 8-92)

and 203 (Knott 57; Holding 6-57).

1977 – AUSTRALIANS IN ENGLAND: A GREY SHADE OF GREEN   Harold Abel, 1978

Although the day should never come when an Australian cricket team is described as colourless, the 1977 party to England took on a very light shade of grey. The players had none of the air of their predecessors, and the longer the tour went on the more one's mind drifted back to the billowing green caps which had fallen out of fashion. They always seemed to set the Australians apart from the opposition, and goodness knows this party could have done with some distinguishing mark. Left behind was one of the worst records of any Australian team making a comparable tour. A side no more than a good average had been allowed to beat them, with some comfort, in three Tests in England for the first time since 1886, so winning back the Ashes at home for only the third time this century.

1977 – ENGLAND v AUSTRALIA (THIRD TEST): A STAR IS BORN
Norman Preston, 1978

At Nottingham, July 28, 29, 30, August 1, 2, 1977. England won by seven wickets ten minutes after tea on the last day. It was England's first victory against Australia at Trent Bridge since 1930. Blessed with fine weather, the ground was packed on the first four days and made a wonderful sight. Moreover, The Queen was in the Midlands for the Silver Jubilee celebrations and visited the ground on the first day. Play was interrupted briefly at 5.30pm when the players and officials were presented to Her Majesty in front of the pavilion.

Memorable mostly from a cricket point of view was the return of Boycott to the England team after three years of self-imposed absence. He had the singular experience of batting on all five days of the match. Among several other splendid personal achievements, Botham distinguished his Test debut by taking five wickets for 74. He moved the ball each way and at one time took four for 13 in 34 balls. It was this feat which put England in the ascendancy on the first day.

With the gates closed before lunch for the first time at Trent Bridge since 1948, McCosker and Davis gave Australia a sound start. For a time Chappell and Hookes looked safe, but after an hour drinks were taken and then came Botham's devastating spell. His first ball was short and Chappell, intending a fierce drive, played on, and with Walters, Marsh and Walker also falling to Botham's varied swing, Australia were reduced to 155 for eight.

Australia fought back on the second day and had England reeling at 82 for five thanks to some splendid pace bowling by Pascoe and Thomson. Randall began in great style but he was run out when Boycott went for an impossible single after stroking the ball down the pitch where Randall was backing up. In the end Randall sacrificed his wicket to save Boycott, who stood dejected covering his face with his hands. Boycott freely admitted that he was to blame, and he continued to defend with the utmost resolution. With Australia now on top, Knott rose to the occasion in his own impudent style. Knott went on to make the highest score by an England wicketkeeper against Australia, beating 120 by Ames at Lord's, 1934.

Australia 243 (R. B. McCosker 51; I. T. Botham 5-74)
and 309 (McCosker 107; R. G. D. Willis 5-88);
England 364 (A. P. E. Knott 135, G. Boycott 107; L. S. Pascoe 4-80)
and 189-3 (J. M. Brearley 81, Boycott 80*).

1977 – ENGLAND v AUSTRALIA (Fourth Test): Boycott's perfect script

Geoffrey Wheeler, 1978

At Leeds, August 11, 12, 13, 15, 1977. England won by an innings and 85 runs, to regain the Ashes. The completeness of their triumph left no room for doubt as to which was the superior side. It was the first year since 1886 that England had won three Tests in a home series against Australia.

A historic game was made more memorable by Boycott who, on the opening day, became the first player to score his 100th century in a Test. The Yorkshire crowd seemed to regard the achievement of this landmark as inevitable, and Boycott batted with such ease and assurance that he gave his loyal supporters few qualms and the Australian bowlers scant hope. His was a remarkable feat, for he was only the 18th cricketer to reach this goal. Two of the others, Herbert Sutcliffe and Sir Leonard Hutton, were present for at least part of the match. By the time Boycott was finally out for 191, Australia had lost any hope of saving the series.

A strong local conviction that cricket history was about to be made helped to fill the ground close to overflowing on the first two days, when the gates were shut well before the start. Although Brearley was caught at the wicket off Thomson's third ball, Boycott soon took the measure of the attack and apart from one edged stroke off Walker, which nearly carried to Marsh, looked well-nigh invincible. Partners came and went, while Boycott proceeded as his own measured pace. He had been in for five hours, 20 minutes when a full-throated roar from the crowd told those for miles around that the local hero had done it. An on-driven boundary off Chappell took the Yorkshire captain to three figures and brought the inevitable invasion of the middle. Happily this did not cause a lengthy hold-up in play or cost Boycott his cap, which was sheepishly returned by a would-be souvenir hunter.

England 436 (G. Boycott 191, A. P. E. Knott 57; L. S. Pascoe 4-91, J. R. Thomson 4-113);
Australia 103 (I. T. Botham 5-21, M. Hendrick 4-41)
and 248 (R. W. Marsh 63; Hendrick 4-54).

1978 – ENGLAND v PAKISTAN (First Test): IMMEDIATE IMPACT

Norman Preston, 1979

At Birmingham, June 1, 2, 3, 5, 1978. England won by an innings and 57 runs. This convincing victory was accomplished in only 20 hours, four minutes playing time, and contained notable displays from Old, Radley, Gower, and Botham. Gower's 58 was one of the most auspicious beginnings in recent years. The satisfaction at these achievements was overshadowed, though, by a distressing incident on the fourth and last morning.

Pakistan had used Iqbal Qasim as a nightwatchman on Saturday evening, and when play resumed on the Monday, Willis, with a stiff breeze behind him, gave Qasim at least three lifting balls, including one in his first over which flew narrowly over the batsman's head. These failed to unsettle the defiant left-hander and, at 12.10, Willis went round the wicket. From this new angle he immediately hurled in another bumper which leapt from the pitch, forced its way between Qasim's hands, and struck him in the mouth. Fortunately he was not severely hurt, but he was led from the pitch bleeding freely and needed two stitches in his lip. The ramifications of this ball continued into the Second Test.

[Earlier, on day two] the quality of the batting was immediately raised when Gower nonchalantly pulled his first ball in Tests – a long-hop from Liaqat Ali – for four. Though badly missed when 15 by Liaqat at mid-on off Mudassar, Gower played with the assurance of a Test veteran, hitting the ball off his legs and past cover with cultured, firm strokes for the bulk of his nine fours.

After the game, Pakistan's manager, Mahmood Hussain, described Willis's tactics when bowling at Qasim as "unfair". Brearley defended his policy by observing: "Anyone who takes a bat in his hand accepts a certain amount of risk, and a night-watchman expects to be treated like a batsman." Between the first two Tests the controversy was debated at all levels of cricket. The TCCB issued two statements the core of which was that they "bitterly regretted" the incident, reminded Brearley of his responsibilities, and encouraged the captains to exchange lists of non-recognised batsmen.

Pakistan 164 (C. M. Old 7-50) and 231 (Sadiq Mohammad 79; P. H. Edmonds 4-44); England 452-8 dec. (C. T. Radley 106, I. T. Botham 100, D. I. Gower 58; Sikander Bakht 4-132).

1978 – ENGLAND v PAKISTAN (Second Test): ALL-ROUND BRILLIANCE

Norman Preston, 1979

At Lord's, June 15, 16, 17, 19, 1978. England won by an innings and 120 runs. The win was a triumph for Botham, who hit a dazzling century – his second in successive Test innings – and finished the match by taking eight wickets for 34 runs. These were the best figures by an England bowler in an innings since Jim Laker's at Old Trafford in 1956. There had never been an all-round performance like Botham's in a Test match. In his seven Test matches to date, Botham now claimed three hundreds besides five wickets or more in an innings five times.

The fall of the last eight wickets for 43 on Monday morning came as a complete surprise when, on a cloudless day, Botham swung the ball in astounding fashion. He beat the bat with three or four outswingers an over. The ball was a substitute for one that went out of shape on Saturday evening, after which the spinners, Edmonds and Miller, had gone into action. Brearley expected to have to rely on them on this Monday morning. Instead, Botham seized his opportunity when he went on at the Nursery End so that Willis, with the wind having veered, could change ends.

England 364 (I. T. Botham 108, G. R. J. Roope 69, D. I. Gower 56, G. A. Gooch 54);
Pakistan 105 (R. G. D. Willis 5-47, P. H. Edmonds 4-6) **and 139** (Botham 8-34).

1979 – ENGLAND v INDIA (FOURTH TEST): GRIPPED BY GAVASKAR
Terry Cooper, 1980

At The Oval, August 30, 31, September 1, 3, 4, 1979. The match was drawn after the most gripping closing overs in a home Test since the draw at Lord's against West Indies in 1963, a match it closely resembled as all four results were possible with three balls left. Gavaskar's inspiring and technically flawless 221 earned him the Man of the Match award and brought that rarity in recent Tests in England – a final day charged with interest. Botham played the major part in preventing an Indian victory and confirmed his status as Man of the Series. As the teams fought each other to a standstill, there were many Englishmen in the crowd who would not have displayed their customary dejection at a Test defeat.

Gavaskar's innings was the highest by an Indian against England, overtaking the unbeaten 203 by the younger Nawab of Pataudi at Delhi in 1963-64. India's 429 for eight – they were set 438 in 500 minutes – was the fourth-highest score in the fourth innings of a Test. To reach their target they would have needed to set a new mark for a side batting fourth and winning, but this generation of Indian batsmen have some notable performances in that department and the job did not frighten them.

Gavaskar masterminded the show, doing all the thinking and playing most of the shots. Tea came at 304 for one and, after a mere six overs between the interval and five o'clock – England ruthlessly slowed down the game – the last 20 overs began at 328 for one with 110 wanted, and India favourites.

At 365 Botham uncharacteristically dropped Vengsarkar on the boundary – an error for which he swiftly compensated by transforming the match with three wickets, a catch and a run-out in the remaining 12 overs. Yashpal Sharma and Gavaskar rattled the score along to 389, when Botham returned with eight overs left. It was a gamble by Brearley, for Botham had looked innocuous during the day. But he struck with the key wicket, Gavaskar drilling a catch to mid-on shortly after England had taken a drinks break – a rare move, tactically based, with the end so near. A target of 15 from the last over was too much, and the climax came with fielders encircling the bat.

England 305 (G. A. Gooch 79, P. Willey 52) **and 334-8 dec.** (G. Boycott 125);
India 202 (G. R. Viswanath 62; I. T. Botham 4-65); **429-8** (S. M. Gavaskar 221).

1980–89

Spectacular Botham-inspired victories over Australia, who were riven by disharmony and later rebel-tour exclusions, masked a malaise that brought series defeats by India and New Zealand (their first in England) in 1986 and successive beatings (5–0 and 4–0) by West Indies in 1984 and 1988. In his 1989 Notes, following the latest defeat by West Indies in which England had had four different captains, Graeme Wright mused: "There is no reason why, in a country where it is often impossible to have building work done or a motor car serviced properly, its sporting tradesmen should perform any better." In the same year the Australians were welcomed by a piece from Matthew Engel which wondered whether an Ashes series was "such a big deal any more?" England maybe agreed. They lost 4–0 and would not hold the Ashes for another 16 years.

1980 – ENGLAND v WEST INDIES (FIRST TEST): HOSTS LET IT SLIP

Peter Smith, 1981

At Nottingham, June 5, 6, 7, 9, 10. West Indies won by two wickets. Barely 1,000 spectators made the effort to turn up for the final morning with West Indies requiring only 99 runs for victory with eight second-innings wickets in hand. But those who saw the ending were rewarded by a gripping and courageous fightback, by England's bowlers in general and Willis in particular, that went close to presenting Botham with a startling victory in his first Test as captain.

Throughout the previous four days the bowlers on both sides had held the upper hand on a wicket that offered extravagant movement off the seam and in conditions conducive to swing bowling. On the final morning even putting bat against ball proved difficult, and only Haynes batted with any degree of authority during his 305-minute match-winning vigil. Willis's heroic bowling was rewarded with nine wickets in the match, and if one of two vital catches on the final day had been taken England might easily have won. The bitter split in English cricket caused by the Packer Affair was officially healed with Knott and Woolmer being welcomed back into the England side for the first time since they rejected their country in 1977. In making his half-century Botham demonstrated he could cope with the responsibility of leading a Test side without losing his belligerence.

West Indies were left with a target of 208 in just over eight hours, one that was never going to be easy, especially after Greenidge was caught behind with only 11 on the board. There followed, however, probably the decisive innings of the match as Richards ripped into England's bowling. In 56 minutes he scored 48 runs, striking eight boundaries with supreme arrogance, before Botham produced a leg-cutter to get him lbw shortly before the close.

Although Richards's innings eased the pressure on the rest of the batsmen, the tension returned immediately next morning when West Indies started the final day only 99 runs from victory with eight wickets in hand. With Willis showing the stamina many believed he had lost, West Indies suffered casualties regularly. That they were still inching their way towards the target owed much to the resolute Haynes, who might have fallen to Willis at slip when he was 23.

Roberts, too, was dropped off Willis when West Indies needed just 13 to win. Even then their anxiety showed as Haynes, after five hours five minutes at the crease, was run out by a direct throw from Willey after being sent back. Haynes raced from the field in tears, believing he had thrown away a victory by his rashness, even though only three runs were required with two wickets left. Two balls later it was all over when Roberts, chancing his arm again, lifted Botham over long-on to secure victory for his side and the Man of the Match award for himself. West Indies' victory, achieved half an hour after lunch, was one of the closest winning margins in Tests between the two countries, and put them one ahead in the series.

England 263 (I. T. Botham 57; A. M. E. Roberts 5-72) and 252 (G. Boycott 75; J. Garner 4-30);
West Indies 308 (I. V. A. Richards 64, D. L. Murray 64; R. G. D. Willis 4-82)
and 209-8 (D. L. Haynes 62; Willis 5-65).

Eton v Harrow. At Lord's, July 11, 12, 1947. On Friday the King and Queen, Princess Elizabeth, Princess Margaret and Lieutenant Philip Mountbatten, RN, watched the play from one of the Clock Tower boxes.

Little Wonder No. 44

1980 – ENGLAND v AUSTRALIA (CENTENARY TEST): UMPIRES GET THE BIRD
Crawford White, 1981

At Lord's, August 28, 29, 30, August, September 1, 2, 1980. Drawn. It had been hoped that England's Centenary Test, to mark the centenary of the first Test played in England – at The Oval in 1880 – might be played in late-summer sunshine with many a nostalgic reunion, some splendid fighting cricket and a finish to savour. Over 200 former England and Australian players assembled from all over the world; it was impossible to move anywhere at Lord's without meeting the heroes of yesteryear. The welcoming parties, the dinners and the takeover by Cornhill Insurance of a London theatre for a night were all hugely successful. Sadly, however, the party in the middle was markedly less so.

After almost ten hours had been lost to rain in the first three days, the match ended in a tepid draw. As much as for the cricket, though, the game will be remembered for a regrettable incident, seen by millions on television on the Saturday afternoon, in which angry MCC members were involved in a momentary scuffle with umpire Constant as the umpires and captains moved into the Long Room after their fifth pitch inspection of the day.

Two MCC members, identified by Chappell, were questioned by the secretary, Mr J. A. Bailey, after the incident on Saturday afternoon. This was followed, on the Monday, by the following statement: "Enquiries instituted today into the behaviour of certain MCC members towards the umpires and captains on Saturday leave no doubt that their conduct was inexcusable in any circumstances. Investigations are continuing and will be rigorously pursued with a view to identifying and disciplining the culprits. Meanwhile the club is sending to the umpires and to the captains of both sides their profound apologies that such an unhappy incident should have occurred at the headquarters of the game and on an occasion of such importance."

Fifty minutes had been lost to rain on the first day, and all but an hour and a quarter on the second. On the third, the Saturday, 90 minutes' rain in the early morning left a soft area around two old uncovered pitches on the Tavern side of the ground. The groundstaff, however, thought play could have started by lunch, as did a crowd of some 20,000 who were growing increasingly impatient in sunshine and breeze. Umpires Bird and Constant were the sole judges of when play should start, with one captain noticeably keener to play than the other; Australia being in the stronger position, Chappell was the more eager of the two. They conducted inspection after inspection, seemingly insensitive to the crowd's rising anger and the need for flexibility on such a special occasion. By the time the president of MCC, Mr S. C. Griffith, exerted pressure on the umpires to get the game started, the pavilion fracas had occurred.

On the field Australia were much the more convincing side. Hughes graced the occasion and played the most spectacular stroke of the match when he danced down the pitch to hit the lively Old on to the top deck of the pavilion.

Australia 385-5 dec. (K. J. Hughes 117, G. M. Wood 112)
and 189-4 dec. (Hughes 84, G. S. Chappell 59)
England 205 (G. Boycott 62; L. S. Pascoe 5-59, D. K. Lillee 4-43) **and 244-3** (Boycott 128*).

1981 – ENGLAND v AUSTRALIA (SECOND TEST): MORBID TREND

Terry Cooper, 1982

At Lord's, July 2, 3, 4, 6, 7, 1981. Drawn. Lord's and Test-match time in recent years have become synonymous with bad weather, controversy and abysmal public relations, redeemed only partially by isolated individual performances. The second Test followed this morbid trend. At the end of a personally disappointing match [*he made nought in both innings*], which concluded a fruitless year as captain, Botham resigned as leader. Controversy came when the umpires took the players off for bad light during the extra hour of this second day. The sun reappeared, but Messrs Oslear and Palmer were under the false impression that no resumption could be allowed once play had stopped in the extra period. In protest at what happened the crowd jeered and threw their cushions on to the ground, and next day the TCCB issued a statement regretting the misunderstanding.

England 311 (P. Willey 82, M. W. Gatting 59; G. F. Lawson 7-81)
and 265-8 dec. (D. I. Gower 89, G. Boycott 60);
Australia 345 (A. R. Border 64) **and 90-4.**

1981 – ENGLAND v AUSTRALIA (THIRD TEST): BEYOND BELIEF   Alan Lee, 1982

At Leeds, July 16, 17, 18, 20, 21, 1981. England won by 18 runs. A match which had initially produced all the wet and tedious traits of recent Leeds Tests finally ended in a way to stretch the bounds of logic and belief. England's victory, achieved under the gaze of a spellbound nation, was the first this century by a team following on, and only the second such result in the history of Test cricket.

The transformation occurred in less than 24 hours, after England had appeared likely to suffer their second four-day defeat of the series. Wherever one looked, there were personal dramas: Brearley, returning as captain like England's saviour; Botham, who was named Man of the Match, brilliant once more in his first game back in the ranks; Willis, whose career has so often heard the distant drums, producing the most staggering bowling of his life when his place again seemed threatened.

It will come as a surprise when, in future years, people look back on a Test of such apparently outrageous drama, to know that the second day was pedestrian in the extreme. Botham, to some degree, salvaged English pride by taking five more wickets. Despite his efforts, Australia extended their score to 401 for nine. At this stage, the odds seemed in favour of a draw. An England win was on offer generously, though by no means as extravagantly as 24 hours later when Ladbrokes, from their tent on the ground, posted it at 500 to 1. The reason for their estimate was a truncated day on which England were dismissed for 174 and, following on 227 behind, lost Gooch without addition.

On the Monday England were then 135 for seven, still 92 behind, and the distant objective of avoiding an innings defeat surely their only available prize. The England players' decision to check out of their hotel seemed a sound move. Three hours later, the registration desks around Leeds were coping with a flood of re-bookings, Botham having destroyed the game's apparently set course with an astonishing, unbeaten 145, ably and forcefully aided by Dilley. Together, they added 117 in 80 minutes for the eighth wicket, only seven short of an England record against Australia. Both struck the ball so cleanly and vigorously that Hughes's men were temporarily in disarray.

Botham advanced his unforgettable innings to 149 not out before losing Willis the next morning, but Australia, needing 130, still remained clear favourites. Then, at 56 for one, Willis, having changed ends to bowl with the wind, dismissed Chappell with a rearing delivery and the staggering turnabout was under way. Willis bowled as if inspired. It is not uncommon to see him perform for England as if his very life depended on it, but this was something unique. In all, he took eight wickets for 43, the best of his career, as Australia's last nine wickets tumbled for 55 runs. Old bowled straight and aggressively and England rose to the need to produce an outstanding show in the field. Yet this was Willis's hour, watched or listened to by a vast invisible audience. At the end, the crowd gathered to wave their Union Jacks and chant patriotically, eight days in advance of the Royal Wedding.

Australia 401-9 dec. (J. Dyson 102, K. J. Hughes 89, G. N. Yallop 58; I. T. Botham 6-95)
and 111 (R. G. D. Willis 8-43);
England 174 (Botham 50; D. K. Lillee 4-49)
and 356 (Botham 149*, G. R. Dilley 56; T. M. Alderman 6-135).

On the up: Ian Botham attacks Terry Alderman during his unbeaten 149 at Headingley in 1981, the innings that transformed the Test and the Ashes

1981 – ENGLAND v AUSTRALIA (FOURTH TEST): HISTORY REPEATS ITSELF
Derek Hodgson, 1982

At Birmingham, July 30, 31, August 1, 2, 1981. England won by 29 runs. A startling spell of bowling by Botham, which brought him five wickets for one run in 28 deliveries, ended an extraordinary Test match at 4.30pm on a glorious Sunday afternoon. And so, for a second successive Test, England contrived to win after appearing badly beaten. As at Leeds, a large crowd helped give the match an exciting and emotional finish and once again critics, commentators and writers were left looking foolish, a fact that the players of both teams were quick to point out afterwards.

Miracles, wrote a distinguished correspondent, like lightning, do not strike twice. Border was his resolute self and at 105 for four, with only 46 more needed, Australia seemed to have the match won. However, Border was then desperately unlucky to be caught off his gloves, a ball from Emburey suddenly lifting prodigiously. Brearley, who had ordered Willey to loosen up with the idea of using spin at both ends, in a last gamble, changed his mind and called on a reluctant Botham. Somerset's giant bowled quicker than for some time, was straight and pitched the ball up, and one after another five Australian batsmen walked into the point of the lance. The crowd, dotted with green and gold, were beside themselves with agony and ecstasy as, only 12 days after Headingley, history amazingly repeated itself.

England 189 (T. M. Alderman 5-42) and 219 (R. J. Bright 5-68);
Australia 258 (J. E. Emburey 4-43) and 121 (I. T. Botham 5-11).

1981 – ENGLAND v AUSTRALIA (FIFTH TEST): DAZZLING POWER

John Thicknesse, 1982

At Manchester, August 13, 14, 15, 16, 17, 1981. England won by 103 runs, retaining the Ashes by going 3–1 up in the series. Like its two predecessors, the Fifth Test was a game of extraordinary fluctuations and drama, made wholly unforgettable by yet another *tour de force* by Man of the Match Botham, who, with the pendulum starting to swing Australia's way in England's second innings, launched an attack on Lillee and Alderman which, for its ferocious yet effortless power and dazzling cleanness of stroke, can surely never have been bettered in a Test match, even by the legendary Jessop.

Striding in to join Tavaré in front of 20,000 spectators on the Saturday afternoon when England, 101 ahead on first innings, had surrendered the initiative so totally that in 69 overs they had collapsed to 104 for five, Botham plundered 118 in 123 minutes. His innings included six sixes – a record for Anglo-Australian Tests – and 13 fours, all but one of which, an inside edge that narrowly missed the off stump on its way to fine leg, exploded off as near the middle of the bat as makes no odds. Of the 102 balls he faced (86 to reach the hundred), 53 were used up in reconnaissance in his first 28 runs. Then Alderman and Lillee took the second new ball and Botham erupted, smashing 66 off eight overs by tea with three sixes off Lillee, all hooked, and one off Alderman, a huge pull far back in the crowd to the left of the pavilion. He completed his hundred with his fifth six, a sweep, added the sixth with an immense and perfectly struck blow over the sightscreen, also off Bright, and was caught at the wicket a few moments later off 22-year-old Mike Whitney.

Unkindly, it was to the greenhorn Whitney, running back from deep mid-off, that Botham, at 32, offered the first of two chances – nearer quarter than half – a high, swirling mishit over Alderman's head. Of the 149 Botham and Tavaré added for the sixth wicket – after a morning in which England had lost three for 29 off 28 overs – Tavaré's share was 28. But his seven-hour 78, embodying the third-slowest fifty in Test cricket (304 minutes) was the rock on which Knott and Emburey sustained the recovery as the last four wickets added 151.

England 231 (C. J. Tavaré 69, P. J. W. Allott 52*; D. K. Lillee 4-55, T. M. Alderman 4-88) and 404 (I. T. Botham 118, Tavaré 78; Alderman 5-109); Australia 130 (M. F. Kent 52; R. G. D. Willis 4-63) and 402 (A. R. Border 123*, G. N. Yallop 114).

1982 – PAKISTANIS IN ENGLAND: COMING OF AGE

John Woodcock, 1983

The Pakistanis, paying their seventh visit to England, were a strong and experienced side, led for the first time by Imran Khan. England, who did well to beat them, were helped by an unsteadiness of temperament which tended at vital moments to be Pakistan's undoing. In terms of pure cricketing ability, Pakistan, man for man, were at least as good a side.

From the start, it was clear that Pakistan could expect a lot of rowdily vocal, expatriate support. This added to the somewhat disputatious nature of an exciting Test series. The days have long gone when Pakistan came meekly to the slaughter.

Imran is one of the world's outstanding all-rounders. He led a fine, if volatile, batting side, and in Abdul Qadir he had the best leg-spinner in the game.

Imran was the commanding figure of the tour. If he had a failing, other than picking out the umpires for criticism, it was in trying to do too much of the Test bowling himself. Being so much the most dangerous of the faster bowlers, the temptation was obvious. He led from the front, never sparing himself in any of his bowling spells, batting with more application than those higher in the order, and handling his side with authority.

1982 – ENGLAND v PAKISTAN (Second Test): Sunday best

Graeme Wright, 1983

At Lord's, August 12, 13, 14, 15, 16, 1982. Pakistan won by ten wickets, a margin which reflected their superiority but failed to record the tension of the closing stages as the Pakistanis sought only their second-ever victory over England. It in no way detracts from Pakistan's win to say that England were handicapped by the limitations of their attack once Willis pronounced himself unfit, ironically as a result of a neck injury incurred avoiding Imran's bouncers at Birmingham. Gower, with little experience at the job, assumed the captaincy.

Both the quality of England's bowling and the nature of the pitch were shown in true perspective when Mohsin drove back Botham's first ball for four. Before lunch the batsmen had disdained wearing helmets, and these did not reappear until the 89th over. Mohsin, whose delightful batting was resplendent with cover-drives and forceful strokes off his legs, [became] only the second post-war batsman to score 200 in a Lord's Test. Imran's overnight declaration brought early reward. In the evening session, England's later batsmen were severely embarrassed by Qadir's mixture of leg-spin, googlies and top-spin. Only Gatting looked confident, and he had guided England to within three runs of the follow-on figure when, with Jackman just in, he accepted the umpires' offer of bad light. Perhaps he should have batted on, for next morning, after pushing Imran's third ball for a single, he saw Jackman adjudged lbw to the last.

So Sunday's play, the first such at Lord's, began with high drama before many of the 11,200 spectators had gathered. (It was to end in cheap farce after most of them had gone home.) The drama was heightened by an amazing spell of bowling by Mudassar who, coming on for the tenth over, accounted for Randall, Lamb and Gower in six balls for no runs. Lamb apart, his victims fell as much to their own imperfections as to his medium-pace seam and swing.

Tavaré and Botham, however, dug in, Tavaré remaining on 0 for 67 minutes. When Mudassar was brought back for the first time since his morning spell of 5–2–11–3, the umpires conferred and went off for bad light. It was then seven o'clock. They reappeared 37 minutes later, allowed Mudassar one maiden over in the pleasant sunshine, looked at their light-meters, and brought the day to a somewhat banal close.

Monday began darker and cloudier than the previous evening, precipitating an early stoppage and increasing the possibility of England being saved by the weather. Soon after midday Mudassar made the vital breakthrough, getting one to lift and having Botham well caught at backward point, and persuading Gatting to flash fatally at a long-hop. Tavaré, however, went on, venturing a selection of fine strokes, and just after three o'clock he saw England past an innings defeat. His 50, off 236 balls, had absorbed 352 minutes and was second only to T. E. Bailey's at Brisbane in 1958-59 as the slowest on record. When, finally, he succumbed outside off stump to Imran's persistent hostility, he had batted for six hours, 47 minutes.

Pakistan 428-8 dec. (Mohsin Khan 200, Zaheer Abbas 75, Mansoor Akhtar 57; R. D. Jackman 4-110)
and 77-0; England 227 (Abdul Qadir 4-39)
and 276 (C. J. Tavaré 82, I. T. Botham 69; Mudassar Nazar 6-32).

Somerset v Middlesex. At Taunton, July 16, 17, 18, 1947. Middlesex were further handicapped by a mishap to Hever, who split a finger when fielding on the first day and bowled no more in the match. Because of this, Leslie Compton kept wicket to Gray and bowled alternate overs with the new ball at the start of Somerset's second innings.

Little Wonder No. 45

1983 – ENGLAND v NEW ZEALAND (SECOND TEST): KIWI HISTORY MAKERS

John Thicknesse, 1984

At Leeds, July 28, 29, 30, August 1, 1983. New Zealand won by five wickets. New Zealand's first victory in a Test in England, following 17 defeats and 11 draws, arrived shortly after tea on the fourth day when Coney completed their task of scoring 101 with a leg-side four off Botham – the first ball of the only over Willis permitted Botham, so unintelligently had he bowled in New Zealand's first innings.

For England, only Willis, who took the nine wickets he needed to become the fourth man to reach 300 in Test cricket, and Gower, with a handsome but unavailing 112 not out in the second innings, had reason to remember [the match] with satisfaction. The toss was admittedly important, enabling Howarth to give his bowlers first use of a pitch that started damp to make it last; but in matters of skill, not excluding team selection, they proved themselves the better side.

It was happy, too, that the man who made the winning hit should have a sense of history: with Willis charging down the slope at the end from which he took his eight for 43 against Australia in 1981, New Zealand hearts were fluttering when the lanky Coney walked in to bat at 61 for four. Nerves had let them down before in similar positions. A fifth wicket fell, all five to Willis, at 83. But Coney kept a steady head and with Hadlee, watched by father Walter, steered New Zealand home. Later, asked what was in his mind as Willis imperilled what had looked a fairly simple victory, Coney modestly tipped his cap to history by saying: "The main feeling was thinking of all the New Zealand players who have been coming here for 52 years, better players than myself, and making sure that their sweat and effort had not been in vain."

England 225 (C. J. Tavaré 69, A. J. Lamb 58; B. L. Cairns 7-74)
and 252 (D. I. Gower 112*; E. J. Chatfield 5-95);
New Zealand 377 (J. G. Wright 93, B. A. Edgar 84, R. J. Hadlee 75; R. G. D. Willis 4-57)
and 103-5 (Willis 5-35).

1984 – WEST INDIANS IN ENGLAND: ONE OF THE GREAT TEAMS
Christopher Martin-Jenkins, 1985

As far as the records are concerned, the 1984 West Indians, under the captaincy of Clive Lloyd, were unique. No country had hitherto achieved a 100% record in a full Test series in England. Apart from one limited-overs international, at Trent Bridge early in their tour, not a game was lost. Only four other rubbers of five games or more in the history of Test cricket have finished with a similar whitewash for one of the competing teams, and Lloyd's West Indians must rank as the equals at least of the others on this very short list: Australia against England in 1920-21 and South Africa in 1931-32, England against India in 1959, and West Indies, under another of their elder statesmen, Frank Worrell, against India in 1961-62.

Blessed by a dry summer, maturely led, strong and adaptable in batting, possessing in Roger Harper the best West Indian off-spinner since Lance Gibbs, and basing their attack on a formidably fit and hostile band of fast bowlers, Lloyd's was a team of almost all the talents. Whatever may have appeared to be the case on paper, they relied on no special individuals. There was a man for every moment.

The invincibility of the West Indians was based again upon their relentless fast bowling. Joel Garner, towering above the batsmen, was the most consistently dangerous; Malcolm Marshall, wiry as a whippet, was the fastest. Michael Holding, graceful but intelligently menacing, bowled mainly off a shorter run than of old but was still capable of taking vital wickets with near-unplayable balls; and Baptiste bowled with admirable stamina and accuracy, if not with quite as much ferocity as the others.

Such praise, however, must be tempered by two reservations. Before the tour began, the West Indies Cricket Board refused to agree to the Test and County Cricket Board's idea of insisting on a reasonable minimum number of overs in a day, an expedient which had worked well in England in 1982 and 1983. As a result both sides bowled their overs in the Test matches at a rate which was unacceptably low. Over the series, England averaged 13.4 overs an hour, West Indies 13.5. Only at Old Trafford, when Pocock, Cook and Harper bowled long spells, did either side maintain a rate of more than 15 overs an hour.

Equally typical of contemporary cricket, for which West Indies, being the best team in the world, have set the trend, the bouncer was used by their fast bowlers to such an extent that batting against them became as much an exercise in self-defence as in defence of the wicket. Andy Lloyd and Paul Terry both sustained serious injury while playing for England. Several others were hit on the helmet. Uneven pitches and poor batting techniques partially explained this, but so, too, did the West Indian strategy (aped by other teams but most effectively carried out by themselves) of digging the ball in short and watching the hapless batsmen dance to their tune.

1984 – ENGLAND v WEST INDIES (First Texaco Trophy match):
DARING AND POWER   1985

At Manchester, May 31, 1984. West Indies won by 104 runs. A magnificent innings by Richards, which he himself considered to be one of the best he had ever played, dwarfed all else. Almost single-handed he won the match for West Indies after they had been in deep trouble. Having won the toss and chosen to bat, they were 102 for seven in the 26th over, on a pitch which was of little help to the faster bowlers but allowed Miller generous turn with his off-breaks. In a memorable display Richards received 170 balls and hit 21 fours and five sixes, one of these, a straight-drive, going out of the ground at the Warwick Road end. In 14 overs for the last wicket Richards and Holding added 106, Richards's share being 93. He batted with daring and immense power, giving only one technical chance, a leg-side stumping off Miller when he was 44.

West Indies 272-9 (55 overs) (I. V. A. Richards 189*; G. Miller 3-32);
England 168 (50 overs) (A. J. Lamb 75; J. Garner 3-18).

1984 – ENGLAND v WEST INDIES (Second Test): CHASE BECOMES A STROLL
Terry Cooper, 1985

At Lord's, June 28, 29, 30, July 2, 3, 1984. West Indies won by nine wickets. England were either level or on top until the last four hours of the match. West Indies then strolled nonchalantly to victory, making the fifth-highest score to win a Test. Only Bradman and Hammond have made higher scores in a Lord's Test than Greenidge's 214 not out in West Indies' second innings. Yet despite their overwhelming defeat, England managed several skilful and brave performances. Gower, however, might not have relished the occasion. It was his second defeat as captain at headquarters and he became the first England captain since Yardley in 1948 to declare in the second innings and lose.

West Indies [had to chase] 342 to win in five and a half hours. The swing and movement that had been there all match seemed to have vanished, England's change bowlers looking second-rate and nobody but Willis bowling the right line or setting the right field to the powerful and phlegmatic Greenidge. Although England finally blocked his square cut, the midwicket and long-on boundaries saw plenty of Greenidge's 29 fours. It was Greenidge's day, the innings of his life, and his ruthless batting probably made the bowling look worse that it was. He was dropped by an inattentive Botham, the sole slip, off Willis, when he was 110, but by then a

West Indies win was certain. Gomes was missed as soon as he arrived, but these were the only real hints that the two great batsmen padded up, Richards and Lloyd, might be required. Gomes, as at Birmingham, provided the perfect partner to a batsman in control. Their unbroken stand of 287 was a second-wicket record for West Indies against England, overtaking Rowe and Kallicharran's 249 at Bridgetown in 1973-74, and West Indies won with 11.5 of the last 20 overs to spare. Botham's tireless bowling in West Indies' first innings enabled him to share the Man of the Match award with Greenidge, the first time such an award had been split.

England 286 (G. Fowler 106, B. C. Broad 55; M. D. Marshall 6-85) **and 300-9 dec.** (D. I. Gower 110);
West Indies 245 (I. V. A. Richards 72; I. T. Botham 8-103)
and 344-1 (C. G. Greenidge 214*, H. A. Gomes 92*).

1984 – ENGLAND v SRI LANKA (ONLY TEST): STAKING THEIR CLAIM
Michael Carey, 1985

At Lord's, August 23, 24, 25, 27, 28, 1984. Drawn. Sri Lanka marked their inaugural appearance at Lord's with a splendid performance, especially with the bat, which won them a host of new admirers and in only their 12th match at this level left few in any doubt about their right to Test status. None of them had played at Lord's before, yet three of their batsmen, Wettimuny, Silva and Mendis, all made centuries. Indeed, Mendis, the captain, was only six short of a second rapid century when he fell to a Botham off-break as the game was drifting to a draw on the final day.

England, by contrast, had many dreadfully inept moments, with both bat and ball, and Gower's leadership was short of imagination. Wettimuny's tremendous effort ended after ten hours 42 minutes, the longest innings in a Test match at Lord's. His 190 was the highest score by any batsman on his first appearance in a Test in England. The only surprise was that, with three bowlers carrying injuries and an attack which on their tour had bowled out only one county side in 11 innings, Sri Lanka did not go beyond 491 for seven, which was their highest Test total.

But it scarcely mattered, for England continued with the bat as modestly as they had performed in the field. From 27 overs between lunch and tea, the focal point of a Saturday at Lord's, Tavaré and Broad scored only 49 runs. The ground now rang with shouts of derision after the cheers for Sri Lanka, and Gower even apologised to spectators at his Saturday-evening press conference, saying: "That kind of cricket is no fun to watch and it is certainly worse to play like it."

England avoided the follow-on with five wickets down on the fourth day, although Lamb's escape and two near things for Ellison, before he had scored, illustrated how hard they found the going against bowling that was no more than workmanlike on a pitch which remained good. The draw meant that England had gone 12 Test matches without a win, equalling the two most barren spells in their history.

Sri Lanka 491-7 dec. (S. Wettimuny 190, L. R. D. Mendis 111, A. Ranatunga 84)
and 294-7 dec. (S. A. R. Silva 102, L. R. D. Mendis 94; I. T. Botham 6-90);
England 370 (A. J. Lamb 107, B. C. Broad 86, D. I. Gower 55; A. L. F. de Mel 4-110, V. B. John 4-98).

1985 – AUSTRALIANS IN ENGLAND: SAGGY GREENS

David Frith, 1986

The 1985 Australian touring team, the 30th to play Test cricket in England, disappointed its supporters. After four matches in the Cornhill Test series, England and Australia had a victory apiece, and one further success by Australia in the remaining two Test matches would have ensured their retention of the Ashes. At this point, while England were felt to be the better side, it was beyond most objective pundits to foresee England's two crushing victories, each by an innings, that unveiled a conclusive superiority.

That so many of Australia's shortcomings remained only half-revealed for so long was attributable to the determined and often daring batsmanship of Allan Border, the captain. The selection of this touring party was hampered by the unavailability of those who chose to sign contracts for the disapproved tour of South Africa, though Kim Hughes and Graham Yallop signed only after their surprising omission from the team bound for England.

1985 – ENGLAND v AUSTRALIA (FIFTH TEST): GOWER AT THE DOUBLE

David Field, 1985

At Birmingham, August 15, 16, 17, 19, 20, 1985. England won by an innings and 118 runs. Rain, rivalling Australia as England's greatest adversary, rolled away on the final afternoon to allow just enough time for Gower's side to force a thoroughly warranted victory. There was, however, a dark cloud of controversy waiting to shed its gloom. Australia's captain asserted that the crucial, quite freak dismissal of Phillips should not have been allowed, claiming that enough doubt existed for the umpires to have judged in the batsman's favour. Border insisted that the incident cost Australia the match. Phillips hit a ball from Edmonds hard on to the instep of Lamb, who was taking swift evasive action at silly point. The rebound gently stood up for Gower, a couple of yards away, to catch, and 48 minutes later England won when it had seemed that the weather-induced frustrations which prevailed at Manchester would deny them again.

It was a pity Border blamed defeat on this one incident, especially as England had forged their supremacy with a succession of outstanding individual performances, none more so than Ellison's. The Kent swing bowler fought off the debilitating effects of a heavy cold to capture ten for 79 in the match, be named as Man of the Match, and announce his coming of age as a Test bowler. Gower, in addition to savouring the fruits of victory and being appointed ahead of schedule for England's winter tour to the West Indies, exquisitely unveiled his strokemaking talents with a career-best 215 on the ground where he had scored his previous double-hundred for England, against India in 1979. Helped by some badly directed bowling, the England captain remorselessly punished Australia in a sumptuous, high-speed partnership of 331 with Robinson. It was the seventh alliance of over 300 by an England pair and the best in England since John Edrich and Ken Barrington added 369 against New Zealand at Headingley in 1965. Gower, by that time, had gone past Denis Compton's record aggregate of 562 in a home series against Australia.

Australia 335 (K. C. Wessels 83, G. F. Lawson 53; R. M. Ellison 6-77)
and 142 (W. B. Phillips 59; Ellison 4-27);
England 595-5 dec. (D. I. Gower 215, R. T. Robinson 148, M. W. Gatting 100*).

1985 – ENGLAND v AUSTRALIA (SIXTH TEST): GOOCH CASHES IN
John Thicknesse, 1986

At The Oval, August 29, 30, 31, September 2, 1985. England won by an innings and 94 runs. Australia's modest chance of salvaging the Ashes effectively vanished on the opening morning when Gower won an exceptionally good toss and was then blessed by a good deal of luck in the first hour of what blossomed into a match-winning second-wicket stand of 351 with Gooch. The Essex opener, who had been rather overshadowed in the first five Tests by Robinson, his opening partner, made a chanceless 196 but though Gower, too, went on to play brilliantly in scoring 157, he had started loosely, lobbing the slips at two while attempting to kill a rising ball from McDermott, and surviving further narrow escapes at 31 and 35 during an over from Lawson. Given extra help by ill-directed bowling, much of it over-pitched and leg-side, England had sped to 100 for one off 25 overs by lunch, from which point Australia played like a losing side. As in 1926 and 1953, when the Ashes were also regained at The Oval, several thousand spectators massed in front of the pavilion when the match was over, to hail the England captain and his team and to give Allan Border a heartfelt cheer.

England 464 (G. A. Gooch 196, D. I. Gower 157; G. F. Lawson 4-101, C. J. McDermott 4-108);
Australia 241 (G. M. Ritchie 64*) and 129 (A. R. Border 58; R. M. Ellison 5-46).

1986 – ENGLAND v INDIA (FIRST TEST): THE CAP DOESN'T FIT
Graeme Wright, 1987

At Lord's, June 5, 6, 7, 9, 10, 1986. India won by five wickets. India's first Test victory at Lord's was only their second in 33 Tests in England. It was, in addition, England's sixth successive defeat since regaining the Ashes so comprehensively the previous season, and at the end of the match Gower was informed by the chairman of selectors, Mr P. B. H. May, that he had been relieved of the captaincy. Gatting, the vice-captain, was promoted to lead England in the next two Tests.

Gower's tenure began to look insecure on the third afternoon when, with Vengsarkar suffering from cramp in his left arm, India's last two wickets put on 77 runs in 25 overs. So ebbed England's prospects of victory. And when India's bowlers, Kapil Dev and Maninder Singh especially, exposed all manner of deficiencies in England's batting on the fourth day, Gower's fate was sealed. England could not even rely on the weather: when they batted, the cloud came down to encourage movement through the air and off the seam; when India batted, the cloud was high and the sun shone in approval of their batsmen's technique.

Vengsarkar became the first overseas batsman to score three hundreds in Test matches at Lord's – G. Boycott, D. C. S. Compton, J. H. Edrich, J. B. Hobbs and L. Hutton had done so for England. Off 170 balls in 266 minutes, his tenth Test century was one of classical elegance, charm and responsibility.

England 294 (G. A. Gooch 114, D. R. Pringle 63; C. Sharma 5-64) and 180 (Kapil Dev 4-52);
India 341 (D. B. Vengsarkar 126*, M. Amarnath 69; G. R. Dilley 4-146) and 136-5.

1986 – ENGLAND v INDIA (Second Test): COMING APART AT THE SEAMS
Derek Hodgson, 1987

At Leeds, June 19, 20, 21, 23, 1986. India won by 279 runs. Hammonds Sauce Works Band, playing in front of the Football Stand, was the indisputable success for England during a match which India won by a resounding margin in under three and a half days. This victory, their first in England outside London, gave them a decisive 2–0 lead in the three-match series. Summing up England's performance, their chairman of selectors said: "We were outplayed in every department."

It could be argued that there were extenuating circumstances. For the first time since 1978, England took the field without either Botham, who was suspended, or Gower, who, after practising on the Wednesday, withdrew to nurse a shoulder injury. Furthermore, Gooch, England's third player with pretensions to world class, had an unlucky but poor match. Whatever the reason, England, a summer tapestry in 1985, were ragged around the edges and coming apart at the seams one year later. It was an unhappy start to Gatting's term as captain.

India 272 (D. B. Vengsarkar 61) and 237 (Vengsarkar 102*);
England 102 (R. M. H. Binny 5-40) and 128 (Maninder Singh 4-26).

1986 – ENGLAND v NEW ZEALAND (First Test): COMINGS AND GOINGS
Terry Cooper, 1987

At Lord's, July 24, 25, 26, 28, 29, 1986. Drawn. It would hardly be a drawn Lord's Test without rain and bad light plus a much-discussed, if short-lived controversy. This came on the second day when French, England's injured wicketkeeper, was replaced by the former England wicketkeeper, R. W. Taylor. French had been struck on the back of the helmet when he turned away from a Hadlee bouncer, the resulting cut requiring three stitches and the blow leaving him groggy until after the weekend. Athey deputised for two overs at the start of the New Zealand innings until Taylor could hurry round the ground – from his duties as a host for Cornhill, the match's sponsor – and equip himself with an assortment of borrowed kit, although he did, far-sightedly, have his own gloves in his car. Despite having retired from first-class cricket two years earlier, Taylor, at the age of 45, kept almost without a blemish. He did his old job until the 76th over, near the lunch interval on Saturday, after which

R. J. Parks of Hampshire, following his father and grandfather, appeared in a Test match. However, Parks, a more authentic substitute, should have been on standby at the start of play because recovery from such a head wound is seldom immediate. French finally resumed his appointed role for one ball on Monday morning. All these switches were made with the generous permission of New Zealand's captain, Coney. With substitutes also needed for Willey and Foster and for Coney and Jeff Crowe, 29 players took the field at various times.

England 307 (M. D. Moxon 74, D. I. Gower 62; R. J. Hadlee 6-80) **and 295-6 dec.** (G. A. Gooch 183);
New Zealand 342 (M. D. Crowe 106, B. A. Edgar 83, J. V. Coney 51; G. R. Dilley 4-82,
P. H. Edmonds 4-97) **and 41-2.**

Little Wonder No. 46

First-class match defined: The six countries represented at the Imperial Cricket Conference on May 19, 1947, reached agreement in regard to the definition of a first-class match. This will not have retrospective effect. A match of three or more days' duration between two sides of 11 players officially adjudged first-class, shall be regarded as a first-class fixture. Matches in which either team have more than 11 players or which are scheduled for less than three days shall not be regarded as first-class. The governing body in each country shall decide the status of teams.

1986 – ENGLAND v NEW ZEALAND (SECOND TEST): HADLEE AT HOME
Matthew Engel, 1987

At Nottingham, August 7, 8, 9, 11, 12, 1986. New Zealand won by eight wickets. New Zealand's victory was their fourth Test win over England since the 48-year drought broke in 1978. It was a thoroughly deserved and comprehensive win too, dominated by Hadlee, who reacted to the challenge of facing England on his adopted home ground in his customarily combative manner. He took ten wickets in a Test for the seventh time (a feat achieved before only by Barnes, Grimmett and Lillee) and played an important role in New Zealand's first-innings batting recovery, which in the end marked the difference between the teams. When New Zealand were 144 for five, chasing England's 256, the game was nicely balanced. But on the Saturday England's bowlers were outwitted by the capable set of batsmen masquerading as the New Zealand tail, and Bracewell went on to make 110 from 200 deliveries, only the third century of his life.

For New Zealand, this was further confirmation of their new high standing in world cricket; a triumph for Hadlee's exceptional qualities and the whole team's professionalism, resilience and adaptability. For England, it was yet another dismal game, the eighth defeat in ten Tests, and one that was heavily laden with off-the-field murmurings. Gooch was under pressure to announce his availability or otherwise for the tour of Australia (he said no three days after the game); Gower's inclusion had become a matter for debate because his form and spirits had understandably declined after he had lost the England captaincy; and then, on the rest day, 50 miles away at Wellingborough, Botham [*serving a drugs ban*] broke the Sunday League six-hitting record. It was like a distant thunderclap.

England 256 (D. I. Gower 71, C. W. J. Athey 55; R. J. Hadlee 6-80)

and 230 (J. E. Emburey 75; Hadlee 4-60);

New Zealand 413 (J. G. Bracewell 110, Hadlee 68, J. G. Wright 58, E. J. Gray 50) **and 77-2**.

1986 – ENGLAND v NEW ZEALAND (THIRD TEST): BOTHAM'S RETURN
Graeme Wright, 1987

At The Oval, August 21, 22, 23, 25, 26. Drawn. England's attempts to square the series were frustrated first by Wright's grim resolve for seven hours, seven minutes and finally by rain and bad light, which accounted for 15 hours, 40 minutes. Botham's return to Test cricket was a dramatic one: a wicket with his first ball when Edgar dabbed a lifting delivery to Gooch at second slip. Thus he equalled D. K. Lillee's record of 355 Test wickets. The next ball Jeff Crowe edged low past the left hand of Emburey at third slip, but it was a short-lived reprieve. The last ball of Botham's second over cut back at Crowe and Botham had become the leading wicket-taker in Test cricket.

New Zealand 287 (J. G. Wright 119; G. R. Dilley 4-92) **and 7-0**;

England 388-5 dec. (D. I. Gower 131, M. W. Gatting 121, I. T. Botham 59*).

1987 – PAKISTANIS IN ENGLAND: SWEET AND SOUR
Graeme Wright, 1988

Having, earlier in the year, fulfilled one ambition by leading Pakistan to their first series victory in India, Imran Khan achieved another when, under his captaincy, Pakistan won their first series in England. For the 34-year-old all-rounder, in his benefit year and nearing the end of his international career, it was a memorable double. It would not be doing an injustice to his team-mates to say that, without Imran's leadership, or his ability as a player, such triumphs would not have been celebrated.

Victory over England, by an innings at Headingley with the other four Tests drawn, provided compensation for defeat by two Tests to one in 1982, Pakistan's previous tour to England. At the time Imran, rankled, had expressed his dissatisfaction with some of the umpiring; five years older, he was more circumspect. His team's manager, Haseeb Ahsan, who had come to England with the 1962 Pakistan team, was less so. He had, in 1962, suffered foot trouble in the first match and had returned home early. By way of coincidence, if somewhat surprisingly, this was Pakistan's first full tour of England since then.

The tour was not without its less salutary moments. Accusations of cheating were levelled against some of the Pakistan players following incidents in the one-day international at The Oval and the Test match at Headingley. At Old Trafford, time-wasting was the charge when, with Imran off the field for an X-ray of his thumb, only 11 overs were bowled in an hour after tea on the second day. This is a practice by no means unique to Pakistan, but the situation was exacerbated by statements to the press from both the England and Pakistan managements. In addition, Pakistan's grievance over the selection of D. J. Constant and K. E. Palmer to the Test match umpires' panel, and the TCCB's subsequent refusal to replace them, was allowed into the public domain. A less loquacious manager might have stilled some of the off-the-field controversies. Unfortunately, Haseeb, albeit a charming man, served only to fuel them.

1988 – WEST INDIANS IN ENGLAND: FOUR CAPTAINS, NO CLUE   Tony Cozier, 1989

The morale and reputation of English cricket has seldom been as severely bruised as it was during the 1988 Cornhill Insurance Test series against West Indies. Another resounding loss, with four consecutive and heavy defeats after a drawn First Test, was not unusual – the margins in the previous series between the countries, in 1984 and 1985-86, had been complete; 5–0 to West Indies each time. England even had the satisfaction, brief and illusory though it might have been, of winning all three one-day internationals for the Texaco Trophy. The euphoria ended there and the season was quickly transformed into a sequence of traumatic events, on and off the field.

It began with the dismissal after the First Test of Mike Gatting, the captain since 1986, on the evidence of obscene allegations in the tabloid press of his nocturnal relationship with a young barmaid during the match. The affair, filled with sordid controversy, shook the foundations of English cricket, undermined the confidence of the team, and opened the selectors, under the continued chairmanship of Peter May, to harsh and widespread criticism.

England's selectors did not seem to know where to turn, either for a new captain or for a settled team. Their confusion was evident even in the dismissal of Gatting. While accepting his assertion that nothing improper had taken place with the young woman, they removed him all the same for improper behaviour. After that, they appointed John Emburey for the Second and Third Tests, even though Emburey's place in the team was increasingly tenuous. When they decided that Emburey was not their man, they chose Christopher Cowdrey on the basis of his influence in Kent's current success in the County Championship. Cowdrey, son of a great batsman and former England captain, as well as May's godson, came with well-founded doubts over his ability as a player of Test quality. It was generally taken almost as a blessing in disguise when, after England had lost heavily under him at Headingley, he injured his foot in a county match and was ruled out of the final Test at The Oval. With most of their major candidates exhausted, the selectors made Graham Gooch their fourth captain of the summer. Gooch, a cricketer of vast experience, had relinquished the captaincy of Essex at the end of the previous season in order to concentrate on his batting.

England did somewhat better under him but lost nevertheless, by eight wickets. He confirmed that he remained one of the finest batsmen in the game and was the only Englishman to play in all five Tests, although Allan Lamb, along with him the only century-maker, and Graham Dilley, the leading wicket-taker, were prevented from doing so only by injury. Even David Gower was dropped after reaching the rare landmark of 7,000 runs in his 100th Test, at Headingley. In all, 23 players were chosen for the five Tests, which was a manifesto for failure, especially against opponents quick to spot and exploit the slightest weakness. At the end, England were without either an obvious captain or a single player who had established himself during the series.

1989 – AUSTRALIANS IN ENGLAND: EXTRAORDINARY TRANSFORMATION

John Thicknesse, 1990

Allan Border could hardly have dared hope for a more triumphant fourth tour of England, and second as captain, that the one that unfolded in 1989. Arriving with a record which, though markedly better than England's since the 1985 tour, was still far from satisfactory for one of the co-founders of the Test game, Australia gained such confidence from winning the First Test that when the series ended they had a right to consideration as the next-strongest to West Indies in the world.

It was an extraordinary transformation which stemmed from a variety of factors. Among them was the Australians' remarkable freedom from injuries, and the hottest, driest English summer since 1976, which at times not only encouraged the illusion they were playing in Adelaide or Perth but also provided constant match-play. There was no doubt, however, that the biggest factor, by a distance, was the single-minded hunger for success implanted by the leadership.

Border had had neither a successful nor conspicuously happy time as captain since the job was thrust on him by the resignation of Kim Hughes in 1984-85. But his commitment was undiminished, and in the coach, 53-year-old former captain R. B. Simpson, he had a kindred spirit. Like Border, Bob Simpson had been a batsman of enviable natural ability who by determination and application had become one of the most feared and prolific of his day. Relieving England of the Ashes would have been high on both men's lists of life's priorities; and when the chance was there they grabbed it. They were a highly impressive and effective partnership and, unobtrusively supported by Lawrie Sawle, the manager, they produced the best-motivated Australian team in England since 1972, the first of Ian Chappell's. In training and coaching, Simpson concentrated on the game's basics. If a team has ever run better between wickets – more brilliantly would be the fairer comparison in the cases of Dean Jones and Stephen Waugh – I have not seen it.

1989 – ENGLAND v AUSTRALIA (FIRST TEST): WAUGH ZONE

John Callaghan, 1990

At Leeds, June 8, 9, 10, 12, 13, 1989. Australia won by 210 runs. England's first match under the new management team headed by E. R. Dexter, and with Gower restored as captain, fell sadly into the sorry pattern of so much that had gone before in that they contributed significantly to their own downfall. It was their fourth successive defeat at Headingley, where the Australians had not won since 1964, and the outcome extended to nine the sequence of positive Test results on the ground.

Australia, very much the outsiders at the start, outplayed England to an embarrassing extent. England's plans were thrown into confusion by injuries to Botham and Gatting, for whom Smith and Barnett were the replacements, but it could not be argued realistically that this misfortune had a serious influence on the outcome. More important were two major errors of judgment by Gower and his advisers. In the first place they left out the spinner, Emburey, so that the attack was desperately short of variety; and, ignoring the groundsman's advice, they then elected to give Australia first use of an excellent pitch. The decision to field first was apparently based on the theory that a build-up of cloud might allow movement through the air. In fact it was much too cold and the ball behaved predictably in every way.

All the England seamers persistently bowled short and wide, offering easy runs, and no matter how he juggled his resources, Gower could not change the bowling. Wearing a cap instead of the familiar helmet, Waugh reminded many spectators of a bygone age, despatching the ball stylishly through the gaps and timing his forcing strokes so well that he brought an effortless quality to the proceedings. His unbeaten 177 came in 309 minutes from 242 deliveries and included 24 fours, many of them driven gloriously off the back foot through the off side in the textbook manner.

Border was able to declare on the final morning and set England a remote target of 402 for victory. The more interesting part of the equation, though, related to the minimum 83 overs which were available for the Australian bowlers to dismiss England. In theory, their prospects of success should have been no brighter than the England batsmen's of surviving, but so feeble was England's response to this challenge that Australia had 27 overs to spare in completing their task. Only Gooch, battling through 176 minutes to make 68 from 118 balls, caused Border to worry. Barnett shared in a partnership worth 50 and Gower in one which added 57, both in 12 overs, but England for the most part found the straight ball unplayable.

Australia 601-7 dec. (S. R. Waugh 177*, M. A. Taylor 136, D. M. Jones 79, A. R. Border 66)
and 230-3 dec. (Border 60*, Taylor 60);
England 430 (A. J. Lamb 125, K. J. Barnett 80, R. A. Smith 66; T. M. Alderman 5-107)
and 191 (G. A. Gooch 68; Alderman 5-44).

1989 – ENGLAND v AUSTRALIA (Fourth Test): SINKING SHIP

Don Mosey, 1990

At Manchester, July 27, 28, 29, 31, August 1, 1989. Australia won by nine wickets. Australia's win at Old Trafford gave them the series and the Ashes, and Border thus became the first captain since W. M. Woodfull in 1934 to win back the trophy in England. It was a success which was all the more noteworthy because few people in this country gave the tourists much chance of victory when their party was first announced.

It was a game played not only beneath the familiar Manchester clouds but also others of an even more threatening nature hovering over Gower, the England captain. He had been the object of an increasingly virulent campaign in some newspapers since the first defeat of the series, and even the more sober and responsible journals had expressed disquiet at what seemed to be a lack of positive leadership. Gower's resignation after four Tests appeared to be unavoidable when salvation came from an unexpected quarter. On the final morning of the Test came formal confirmation that a party of 16 players would go to South Africa to play between January and March, thus effectively debarring themselves from playing international cricket for England for the next seven years.

Three of the players named were currently involved in the Fourth Test – Robinson, Emburey and Foster; a fourth, Dilley, had been selected to play but was unfit on the first morning. Five of the others – Gatting, Broad, Jarvis, DeFreitas and Barnett – had already played in the earlier Tests of 1989, and of the remaining seven, six were former internationals. Only Graveney, the Gloucestershire slow left-arm bowler, who was named as player-manager, had not won an England cap.

England 260 (R. A. Smith 143; G. F. Lawson 6-72)
and 264 (R. C. Russell 128*, J. E. Emburey 64; T. M. Alderman 5-66);
Australia 447 (S. R. Waugh 92, M. A. Taylor 85, A. R. Border 80, D. M. Jones 69) **and 81-1.**

1989 – ENGLAND v AUSTRALIA (FIFTH TEST): 300 OPENING STAND
Martin Johnson, 1990

At Nottingham, August 10, 11, 12, 14, 1989. Australia won by an innings and 180 runs. The bad luck which seems to accompany a side guilty of bad play (or should it be the other way round?) struck again for England when Small withdrew on the eve of the match, thus preserving their 100% record of being unable to choose from the originally selected squad in every Test in 1989.

On a flat, grassless pitch expected to assist the spinners as the match wore on, England named both Cook and Hemmings in their final eleven, and Cook it was who took the first Australian wicket. As it arrived at 12 minutes past 12 on the second day, this was not a matter for great rejoicing. Border, having won an important toss, had then spent the best part of four sessions joining in the applause as Marsh and Taylor went past numerous records in their opening partnership of 329.

The milestones began just after lunch on the first day with the comparatively modest figure of 89 – Australia's previous-highest opening partnership at Trent Bridge – and ended at 323, the highest by two openers in Ashes history, a record that had stood to Hobbs and Rhodes since 1911-12. As for individual landmarks, Marsh made his first century in 22 Tests since the 1986-87 Ashes encounter in Brisbane, while Taylor continued his remarkable summer with a career-best 219 to take his aggregate for the series to 720 runs at an average of 90. Only three Australian totals in Ashes history remained above that, all of them compiled by D. G. Bradman.

Following on 347 in arrears on Monday morning, England were bowled out for 167 soon after tea. Atherton, batting almost three hours (127 balls) for his 47, was the one batsman to make a half-decent fist of it. Only once before, to Bradman's 1948 side, had England lost four home Tests in an Ashes series, and the final ignominy for them in the statistical avalanche was the fact that an innings and 180 runs represented their heaviest defeat in England by Australia.

Australia 602-6 dec. (M. A. Taylor 219, G. R. Marsh 138, D. C. Boon 73, A. R. Border 65*);
England 255 (R. A. Smith 101; T. M. Alderman 5-69) **and 167.**

1989 – NETHERLANDS XI v ENGLAND XI: Dutch courage
Dave Hardy, 1990

At Amstelveen, August 16, 1989. Netherlands XI won by three runs. Although it was not England's Test team, it was in effect an England Second Eleven, containing many of the best young players, and it travelled under the England Test and tour management of Micky Stewart and Peter Lush. Moreover, it was the first meeting between a representative team from England and the Netherlands, even though over the years the Dutch had entertained every other Test-playing country; and in 1964 they beat the Australians. The historic occasion was made even more memorable by the exceptional performance of the Dutch team, especially in the field as they prevented England from overtaking their modest total of 176.

Netherlands XI 176-7 (40 overs) (N. E. Clarke 77);
England XI 173-7 (40 overs) (R. J. Bailey 68*, J. P. Stephenson 43).

1990–99

The millennium edition of Wisden *did not have glad tidings to report as England, after defeat by New Zealand, sank to the bottom of the rankings table that the Almanack itself had so vociferously promoted. "With the match-fixing crisis temporarily swept under various carpets, the English crisis is now the greatest crisis in world cricket." For all that the 1990s produced memorable series, particularly against the reintegrated South Africans, and glimmers of hope against the previously indomitable West Indies. The Australians remained untouchable, despite a gloriously false dawn in 1997, and English spectators had their first sighting of a leg-spinner whose "reputation before the tour was more that of a beach-boy than a budding Test-winner".*

1990 – NEW ZEALANDERS IN ENGLAND: SIR RICHARD
David Leggatt, 1991

The Birmingham Test brought down the curtain on Hadlee's remarkable career. With his impeccable sense of occasion, he took his 431st and final wicket with his last ball in a Test. Although past his finest days, he showed he could still severely embarrass the world's top batsmen. Before the Lord's Test Hadlee had been awarded a knighthood for his services to the game, the first New Zealander so honoured, and if there was criticism of the timing of the announcement, there was precious little doubt about the worthiness of the recipient. Hadlee's knighthood also made the Lord's Test scorecard a unique modern-day sporting document.

1990 – ENGLAND v INDIA (First Test): Gooch's 333 — John Thicknesse, 1991

At Lord's, July 26, 27, 28, 30, 31, 1990. England won by 247 runs. The Indians, and especially their captain, Mohammad Azharuddin, had small reason to think so by the end, but the First Test was as brilliant a match as the players could hope to take part in, or spectators to watch. England's winning margin made it look one-sided; and no one would dispute that, from lunch on the first day, when they were 82 for one after being put in, England were in control until the end. Certainly England's win, inspired by Gooch's historic innings of 333 and 123, which broke all kinds of records, was the result of a powerful performance by his team, and following the victory over New Zealand in the last Test of the previous series, it provided the first instance of England winning successive Tests since 1985.

Yet it would not have been the match it was without the vibrant batting of the tourists. Shastri and Azharuddin made splendid hundreds of contrasting styles, and Kapil Dev struck a high-velocity 77 not out, jauntily rounded off with four successive sixes to limit England's lead to 199 and thus save the follow-on. Each was straight-driven off Hemmings's offspin into the building works that throughout the season masqueraded as the Nursery end.

At close of play on the first day, when England were 359 for two, Azharuddin tried to justify his decision to field by pointing out that had More, the wicketkeeper, held a routine chance when Gooch was 36, the score would have been 61 for two after 90 minutes' play. But 653 for four declared, with hundreds also from Lamb and Smith, painted the picture truly. Azharuddin had made a bad misjudgment, and England made the most of it.

England 653-4 dec. (G. A. Gooch 333, A. J. Lamb 139, R. A. Smith 100*)
and 272-4 dec. (Gooch 123, M. A. Atherton 72);
India 454 (M. Azharuddin 121, R. J. Shastri 100, Kapil Dev 77*,
D. B. Vengsarkar 52; A. R. C. Fraser 5-104) and 224.

Glamorgan v Somerset. At Neath, June 11, 13, 1949.
On a very difficult pitch batsmen nearly always groped for the ball. It moved at such strange paces and angles that normal strokes were practically useless.

Little Wonder No. 47

1990 – ENGLAND v INDIA (SECOND TEST): TENDULKAR'S ENTRANCE

Graham Otway, 1991

At Manchester, August 9, 10, 11, 13, 14, 1990. Drawn. Of the six individual centuries scored in this fascinating contest, none was more outstanding than Tendulkar's, which rescued India on the final afternoon. At 17 years and 112 days, he was only 30 days older than Mushtaq Mohammad was when, against India at Delhi in 1960-61, he became the youngest player to score a Test hundred. More significantly, after several of his colleagues had fallen to reckless strokes, Tendulkar held the England attack at bay with a disciplined display of immense maturity.

Tendulkar remained undefeated on 119, having batted for 224 minutes and hit 17 fours. He looked the embodiment of India's famous opener, Gavaskar, and indeed was wearing a pair of his pads. While he displayed a full repertoire of strokes in compiling his maiden Test hundred, most remarkable were his off-side shots from the back foot. Though only 5ft 5in tall, he was still able to control without difficulty short deliveries from the English pacemen.

England 519 (M. A. Atherton 131, R. A. Smith 121*, G. A. Gooch 116; N. D. Hirwani 4-174)
and 320-4 dec. (A. J. Lamb 109, Atherton 74, Smith 61*);
India 432 (M. Azharuddin 179, S. V. Manjrekar 93, S. R. Tendulkar 68; A. R. C. Fraser 5-124)
and 343-6 (Tendulkar 119*, M. Prabhakar 67*, Manjrekar 50).

1991 – ENGLAND v WEST INDIES (FIRST TEST): GOOCH UNYIELDING

John Callaghan, 1992

At Leeds, June 6, 7, 8, 9, 10, 1991. England won by 115 runs. England gained their first home victory over West Indies since 1969, when Illingworth's team also won at Headingley. In addition to Gooch, the outstanding batsman, and DeFreitas, the most successful bowler, they possessed a greater discipline in testing conditions, and this eventually enabled them to outplay their opponents, in their 100th encounter.

Gooch gloriously confirmed his standing on the international stage. His decisive, unbeaten 154 in the second innings was the product of seven and a half hours of careful application. Unyielding concentration carried him through three interruptions for rain on the fourth day, and mental toughness enabled him to survive a series of disasters at the other end. In 331 deliveries, England's captain collected 18 fours and scored two-thirds of his side's runs from the bat as they built on a lead of 25; and he became the first England opener to carry his bat through a completed innings since G. Boycott finished with 99 not out, in a total of 215, against Australia at Perth in 1979-80. Three other England batsmen had achieved the feat, among them Sir Leonard Hutton, the only one previously to do so in England.

England 198 (R. A. Smith 54) and 252 (G. A. Gooch 154*; C. E. L. Ambrose 6-52);
West Indies 173 (P. A. J. DeFreitas 4-34)
and 162 (R. B. Richardson 68, DeFreitas 4-59).

1991 – ENGLAND v WEST INDIES (FIFTH TEST): THE WHEEL TURNS

David Field, 1992

At The Oval, August 8, 9, 10, 11, 12, 1991. England won by five wickets. As if by calculation, Botham struck his only delivery of England's second innings to Compton's corner to complete the victory which secured a drawn series against West Indies for the first time since 1973-74. Compton's famous sweep for the Ashes triumph of 1953 had finished in the same spot, and in many ways this match was just as memorable in Oval Test history. Certainly it could hardly have had a more popular final scene to gladden English hearts, Botham, with his Comptonesque flair for the big occasion, sealing the win in his first Test appearance for two years. It was, moreover, his first taste of victory in 20 Tests against West Indies.

This was the *coup de grâce*, but notwithstanding Smith's hundred, it was the left-arm spinner, Tufnell, who played the key role in a result many thought beyond England, against opposition nearing their formidable best after wins at Nottingham and Birmingham. His six for 25 on a hot Saturday afternoon obliged West Indies to follow on for the first time against England in 22 years and 48 Tests, and presented his captain, Gooch, with a priceless equation of runs and time.

Richards, in his 121st Test and his 50th as captain, was leading West Indies for the last time. The third day belonged to Tufnell, when Richards might have been expected to take command on his farewell stage. From 158 for three, West Indies declined rapidly to 176 all out as Tufnell spun the ball generously in a devastating spell of six for four in 33 deliveries either side of lunch. It has to be said, though, that a rash of reckless strokes contributed to this collapse.

There were no easy pickings for Tufnell on the fourth day, however. Twice Hooper struck him for six during a magnificent display of strokemaking which illuminated the first hour. Then Richards, given a standing ovation to the wicket, put on 97 for the fifth wicket with Richardson to put his side ahead for the first time in the game. Richards began needing 20 runs to guarantee an average of 50 in Tests, and he had gone well past that when he drove Lawrence to mid-on. He left the Test arena to rapturous applause, stopping on the way to raise his bat and maroon cap to both sides of the ground in gracious acknowledgment.

England 419 (R. A. Smith 109, G. A. Gooch 60) **and 146-5;**
West Indies 176 (D. L. Haynes 75*; P. C. R. Tufnell 6-25)
and 385 (R. B. Richardson 121, I. V. A. Richards 60, C. L. Hooper 54; D. V. Lawrence 5-106).

1992 – ENGLAND v PAKISTAN (SECOND TEST): LIKE A ONE-DAY FINAL

David Norrie, 1993

At Lord's, June 18, 19, 20, 21, 1992. Pakistan won by two wickets. Wasim Akram drove Salisbury through the covers at 6.40 on Sunday evening to give Pakistan a one-match lead in the series and conclude an astonishing day of Test cricket. Seventeen wickets tumbled and the close-to-capacity crowd could be forgiven for thinking this was a one-day final. Pakistan saw near-certain victory evaporate into near-certain defeat before Wasim and Waqar Younis – as a batting partnership for once – defied England's depleted and tiring attack for the final nerve-wracking hour. That last boundary ended England's brave fightback, and provoked some of the most emotional scenes ever seen at Lord's as the Pakistan touring party raced on to the playing surface in celebration.

Wasim's elegant drive also saved the Test and County Cricket Board from facing the wrath of a frustrated crowd for the second successive Test. Had Salisbury bowled a maiden, proceedings for the day would have been concluded. The battle would have resumed on Monday morning with England needing two wickets to tie the Test and Pakistan wanting one run to win. In fact, it would not have been the TCCB's fault: the Pakistanis had rejected the customary provision for an extra half-hour before the tour began. It was not a great Test match, but Sunday was a great Test day, and it would have been dreadful if this ding-dong battle had not been resolved there and then because of a technicality.

England 255 (G. A. Gooch 69, A. J. Stewart 74; Waqar Younis 5-91)
and 175 (Stewart 69*; Wasim Akram 4-66);
Pakistan 293 (Aamir Sohail 73, Asif Mujtaba 59, Salim Malik 55; D. E. Malcolm 4-70) and 141-8.

1992 – ENGLAND v PAKISTAN (Third Test): TENSIONS BOIL OVER
Ted Corbett, 1993

At Manchester, July 2, 3, 4, 6, 7, 1992. Drawn. This Test had moments of pure pleasure – Aamir Sohail's batting, Wasim Akram's bowling, David Gower's record aggregate – yet it will be remembered best for the incident between Aqib Javed, umpire Roy Palmer and Pakistan captain Javed Miandad that soiled the end of the England innings on the evening of the fourth day. Palmer warned Aqib for intimidatory bowling against Malcolm, and the situation became inflamed when Palmer returned Aqib's sweater with more emphasis than usual, probably because it was caught in his belt. That set off an exchange orchestrated by Miandad, as a Pakistan supporter ran on waving a rolled-up newspaper and chased by two security men. It was all too reminiscent of the confrontation between Mike Gatting and Shakoor Rana at Faisalabad in 1987-88, except that Shakoor shouted back, while Palmer retained the dignity of a patient policeman watching a family squabble.

Conrad Hunte, deputising for match referee Clyde Walcott who had left early for an ICC meeting in London, fined Aqib half his match fee, approximately £300. He also severely reprimanded team manager Intikhab Alam for telling the press, while Hunte was holding his inquiry, that Palmer had insulted his players by throwing the sweater at Aqib. Hunte urged Miandad and Gooch to tell their men to play according to the spirit of the game, which infuriated Gooch, who had not been involved. Intikhab was censured again – this time by ICC – when he repeated his remarks, and declined to apologise, after the match. The Pakistan players were also fined 40% of their match fees for their slow over-rate.

Pakistan 505-9 dec. (Aamir Sohail 205, Javed Miandad 88, Asif Mujtaba 57, Ramiz Raja 54)

and 239-5 dec. (Ramiz 88);

England 390 (G. A. Gooch 78, C. C. Lewis 55, I. D. K. Salisbury 50;

Wasim Akram 5-128, Aqib Javed 4-100).

1992 – ENGLAND v PAKISTAN (Fourth Texaco Trophy match):
BALL-TAMPERING CLAIMS   1993

At Lord's, August 22, 23. Pakistan won by three runs. An enthralling contest, spread across two days, was decided in Pakistan's favour when Waqar Younis bowled out last man Illingworth with the second delivery of the final over. Unhappily, the match will be remembered primarily for what followed off the field. Within minutes of the close, it was revealed that umpires Palmer and Hampshire had found it necessary, during the second-day lunch interval, to change the ball being used by Pakistan's bowlers. They had consulted with match referee Deryck Murray, who refused to make public comment. The implication was "ball-tampering", though Pakistan argued that the ball was merely out of shape. Five days later – with allegations, counter-claims and threats to sue for libel still coming thick and fast – the International Cricket Council ruled the matter closed without either clearing or convicting Pakistan. What was undeniable was that the tourists had bowled brilliantly to win a match against the odds and end England's hopes of a clean sweep. Botham, deputising as opener for the injured Gooch, launched England's pursuit by hitting Wasim Akram's first three deliveries to the boundary before a halt was called after just two overs. Conditions were far better for batting on Sunday, and England looked set for victory when they reached 172 for five shortly after lunch. Lamb, however, was caught behind, and Wasim and Waqar cleaned up the tail with some magnificent fast bowling – and the replacement ball.

Pakistan 204-5 (50 overs) (Javed Miandad 50*, Salim Malik 48);

England 201 (49.2 overs) (A. J. Lamb 55, I. T. Botham 40; Waqar Younis 3-36).

1993 – AUSTRALIANS IN ENGLAND: THE MOST FAMOUS BALL EVER BOWLED
John Thicknesse, 1994

Australia's third overwhelming Ashes victory in succession was as well merited as its predecessors in a series that ended Graham Gooch's reign as England captain and Ted Dexter's as chairman of the England committee. The course of the series – Allan Border leading his team to victory at Old Trafford, Lord's, Headingley and Edgbaston before The Oval brought England the consolation of their first win in 19 Tests against Australia – stemmed even more than usual from confidence. In England's case, it was the lack of it, following a tour of India and Sri Lanka on which they lost all four Tests and five one-day internationals out of eight. It was no surprise, then, that when Mike Atherton, taking over the captaincy from Gooch, led

England to a big win at The Oval in his second match in charge, the change of fortune aroused relief as much as joy.

Twenty-three-year-old leg-spinner Shane Warne played the starring role. Although Warne had two startling analyses to his credit in his 11 previous Tests, his reputation before the tour was more that of a beach-boy than a budding Test-winner. His shock of dyed blond hair, earring and blobs of white sun-block on the tip of his nose and lower lip lent his appearance a deceptive air of amiability, which an expression of wide-eyed innocence enhanced. However, his incessant niggling of umpires and truculent questioning of unfavourable decisions made it obvious that the sunny exterior hid a graceless streak, which stopped him earning the unqualified respect of his opponents. In his hitherto unexplored method of attack, founded on ferociously spun leg-breaks, as often as not angled a foot or more outside the leg stump from round the wicket, he left no doubt that Australia had uncovered not only a match-winner of singular inventiveness but a cricketer crowds would flock to see.

Thanks to TV, Warne's first ball in Ashes cricket, which bowled Mike Gatting, may become the most famous ever bowled. It was flighted down the line of middle and leg, the fierceness of the spin causing it to swerve almost a foot in its last split-seconds in the air, so that it pitched six inches outside the leg stump. From there, it spun viciously past Gatting's half-formed forward stroke to hit the off stump within two inches of the top. Had Gatting been in half an hour longer, or ever faced Warne before, he might have got a pad to it. As it was the ball was unplayable and, by impressing the bowler's capacities on England, it had a profound impact on the series. Of Warne's subsequent 33 wickets, only two came from deliveries that seemed to turn as far – 18 inches or more – and in each case the spin was accentuated by the ball being delivered round the wicket. Gooch was the victim on both occasions, caught at slip for 120 in the second innings of the Third Test, and bowled behind his legs for 48 in the second innings of the Fifth. Nothing better illustrated England's problems than the fact that one of the most experienced batsmen in the world could be bowled in this way when all he was attempting was to block the ball's progress with his pads.

Warne bowled half as many overs again as any other bowler, without showing signs of tiring, even in his frequent two-hour spells. Of leg-spinners, only Arthur Mailey, with 36 in 1920-21 (in five Tests) has taken more wickets in an Ashes series than Warne's 34.

1994 – ENGLAND v SOUTH AFRICA (First Test): DUST TO DUST

Matthew Engel, 1995

At Lord's, July 21, 22, 23, 24, 1994. South Africa won by 356 runs. The first Test between the countries for 29 years began with the word historic being used to the point of monotony but ended with controversy engulfing the England captain, Mike Atherton, and threatening his future. The Atherton Affair took over all discussion of the match and the genuinely historic outcome – a devastating South African victory – was all but forgotten amid the fuss.

Normally, England being bowled out for 99 on a sound wicket might have caused a great deal of anguish. However, everyone was preoccupied by the fact that Atherton, fielding on Saturday afternoon, was seen by the TV cameras taking his hand out of his pocket and rubbing it across the ball before passing it back to the bowler. He was called before the referee, Peter Burge, to explain what the official statement called his unfamiliar action and answer suspicions that he had broken Law 42.5 by using an artificial substance to alter the condition of the ball. Burge said he had accepted Atherton's explanation without saying what it was. But the following day, after further TV pictures were shown that looked even more sinister and England's batsmen had crumpled to a humiliating four-day defeat, Atherton admitted publicly that he had not told Burge the truth by saying that he had nothing in his pocket. In fact, he said, he had some dirt there that he picked up to keep his hands dry and prevent moisture getting on the ball while Darren Gough was trying to reverse-swing it; the second set of pictures clearly showed some of the dirt falling off it.

Ray Illingworth, the chairman of selectors, immediately fined Atherton £2,000 – half for using the dirt, though that was not a breach of any Law, and half for the lie. He hoped that would close the matter. But over the next 48 hours, there was a tidal wave of public emotion in which almost everyone from the cricket corre-spondent of the BBC to people who had never seen a match in their lives demanded Atherton's resignation. Illingworth and the TCCB remained staunch in their support, though. The umpires said the condition of the ball had not been changed and the South Africans made no complaint, except to grumble that their triumph had been ignored. Five days after the game ended, Atherton relieved the pressure by emerging from something close to hiding and calling a press conference at which he did not entirely explain away the pictures but stressed repeatedly that he had never cheated at cricket. If Atherton was a cheat, he was not a very successful one. England's bowlers mostly failed, though not quite as humiliatingly as their batsmen.

The formalities included the officials being presented to Thabo Mbeki, the recently appointed deputy president of South Africa, and reports of the almost as ritualised refusal-of-admission-to-the-pavilion: the victim was the Archbishop of Cape Town, Desmond Tutu, who was out of uniform and not wearing a jacket. The new South African flag did flutter in the closing stages, despite MCC's earlier request to the team to obey their regulations banning all flags. The match throughout was played in extreme heat and some humidity, which helped the swing bowlers and, according to Atherton, explained why he needed the dirt to dry his hands. It may also have contributed to the air of frenzy that took over when the cricket finished.

South Africa 357 (K. C. Wessels 105, G. Kirsten 72; D. Gough 4-76) **and 278-8 dec.** (Gough 4-46); **England 180** (A. A. Donald 5-74) **and 99.**

Cambridge University v Yorkshire. At Cambridge, May 11, 12, 13, 1949. Yorkshire gave a trial to three young players, Lowson, an opening batsman, Close, an all-rounder, and Trueman, a spin bowler [*sic*]. All gave the county much assistance during the season, and Close, aged 18, played for England.

Little Wonder No. 48

1994 – ENGLAND v SOUTH AFRICA (Third Test): "you guys are history"

Ted Corbett, 1995

At The Oval, August 18, 19, 20, 21, 1994. England won by eight wickets. It will always be Malcolm's Match, but there was so much more to this astonishing Test than Devon Malcolm's nine for 57 in South Africa's second innings. Jonty Rhodes went to hospital after being struck on the helmet by Malcolm; Atherton and de Villiers were fined for dissent and both teams for their slow over-rates; and Malcolm delivered himself of a threat so graphic when he was hit in his turn that it has already become part of cricket folklore. The content, excitement and drama were at the level of a *Superman* film; value for money, even at TCCB ticket prices.

England made a traumatic start when Atherton was given lbw to his first ball, looked at his bat and shook his head repeatedly as he left: that evening he was summoned before the match referee, Peter Burge, fined half his match fee – £1,250 – and reprimanded. England were only 28 behind when the innings finished next morning. That was after Gooch had called the team together in Atherton's absence and urged them to rally behind the captain. It was also after Malcolm was hit on the helmet, straight between the eyes, first ball by de Villiers. He was not hurt, only angry. He stared back at the fielders who gathered round. "You guys are going to pay for this," he was reported to have said. "You guys are history."

Malcolm turned his words into action in 99 balls, the most devastating spell by an England bowler since Jim Laker wiped out the Australians in 1956. It was the sixth-best Test analysis ever and, until Cullinan was caught off Gough, it looked as if Malcolm might join Laker by taking all ten. The Kirstens and Cronje had gone for one run and the last six wickets fell for 38, with only Cullinan, who made 94, standing firm for long. Malcolm produced a series of classic deliveries: five catches to slip and wicketkeeper from lifting balls, a bouncer hooked to long leg, a desperately determined caught and bowled and two sets of stumps sent clattering by yorkers. He answered every question save one. Why did the selectors make him wait so long to bowl against a team who appeared alarmed by fast bowling?

South Africa's performance was wretched compared with their win at Lord's, but England saw the victory as a rebirth, not for the first time.

South Africa 332 (B. M. McMillan 93, D. J. Richardson 58; P. A. J. DeFreitas 4-93, J. E. Benjamin 4-42)
and 175 (D. J. Cullinan 94; D. E. Malcolm 9-57);
England 304 (G. P. Thorpe 79, A. J. Stewart 62; P. S. de Villiers 4-62)
and 205-2 (G. A. Hick 81*, M. A. Atherton 63).

1995 – WEST INDIANS IN ENGLAND: ATHERTON LEADS FROM THE FRONT

Tony Cozier, 1996

England and West Indies contested a fascinating, fluctuating series watched by packed houses in a gloriously hot summer. For a variety of reasons, they were more evenly matched than for some time and, fittingly, they shared it 2–2.

If West Indies enjoyed the better of the last two drawn, high-scoring Tests, and had the satisfaction of retaining the Wisden Trophy they have held through 22 years and 12 series, captain Richie Richardson's assessment that they performed below their potential was self-evident. In every department their cricket was inconsistent. England showed great spirit to recover from heavy defeats at Headingley and, especially, Edgbaston (where they were routed for 147 and 89) to draw level twice and then bat through difficult last days to safety at Trent Bridge and The Oval when West Indies held the upper hand. The home team overcame injuries that were mainly responsible for the use of 21 players in the six Tests – the longest series ever scheduled between the two teams – and could take considerable comfort from the authoritative leadership of Mike Atherton.

Only a year earlier, the England captain's position was under a cloud following the ball-tampering controversy in the Lord's Test against South Africa. He had returned from a disappointing Ashes campaign in Australia despondent and with his relationship with team manager and chief selector Ray Illingworth unsettled. Now West Indies manager Wes Hall reflected general opinion when, in choosing Atherton as England's Man of the Series, he identified him as the defining difference to the result of this series. Atherton had, observed Hall, led from the front, taking the fire of the West Indies pace bowlers unflinchingly.

1995 – ENGLAND v WEST INDIES (SECOND TEST): CORKING DEBUT

John Etheridge, 1996

At Lord's, June 22, 23, 24, 25, 26, 1995. England won by 72 runs. A match of startling fluctuations and compelling cricket was finally settled by a historic bowling performance. Dominic Cork, the 23-year-old Derbyshire bowler, returned an analysis of seven for 43, the best by an England player on Test debut and fifth on the list for any country. England levelled the series with the sort of aggression, determination and plain good sense that were so woefully lacking in the First Test. For West Indies, it was their third defeat in six Tests – a sequence of failure unknown during their two decades of world dominance – and their first at Lord's since 1957.

The game's balance of power shifted so frequently that all three results were quoted by bookmakers at four to one or longer at various times. Requiring 296 to win, West Indies lost Hooper early, but Lara tore into the bowling. He played and missed and struck boundaries in equal quantity as he raced to 38 not out, with eight fours, from 44 balls on the fourth evening. The destiny of the match rested in his hands of genius. But, after two more fours the next day, he was superbly caught by Stewart, plunging to his left, off Gough. This was the crucial dismissal of the game. Campbell hung on for over five hours, until he was eighth out for 93, but no other batsman passed 14. Most of them fell to Cork, from the Nursery end, bowling wicket-to-wicket with enough outswing to cause problems. His virtues were old-fashioned – line, length and movement – coupled with a fierce and demonstrable will.

England 283 (R. A. Smith 61) **and 336** (Smith 90, G. A. Hick 67; C. E. L. Ambrose 4-70);
West Indies 324 (K. L. T. Arthurton 75, J. C. Adams 54; A. R. C. Fraser 5-66)
and 223 (S. L. Campbell 93, B. C. Lara 54; D. G. Cork 7-43).

1996 – ENGLAND v INDIA (SECOND TEST): DICKIE'S FINAL DECISION
R. Mohan, 1997

At Lord's, June 20, 21, 22, 23, 24, 1996. Drawn. The chances of India taking the honours in this Test seemed minimal. They had just been beaten in a little over two days by Derbyshire, and a downbeat Azharuddin viewed the Lord's pitch with a great deal of suspicion. But they were able to place England under severe pressure in the closing stages after being put in a strong position by two debutants introduced because of injuries at Edgbaston. Sourav Ganguly made a century and Rahul Dravid fell short of his hundred by just one scoring stroke. Had Dravid succeeded, it would have been the first instance of two debutant centurions in the same team in Test history. Only two Test newcomers (Harry Graham of Australia in 1893 and John Hampshire of England in 1969) had previously attained this distinction at the game's HQ.

But the match will probably be best remembered as the final Test appearance of celebrated umpire Dickie Bird. He had made an emotional entrance through a guard of honour formed by both teams on the opening morning, ruled the England captain out lbw in the very first over, and made his last decision, in his 66th Test, when he gave Russell – the Man of the Match – out leg-before in the final session. He left the Test arena with the same authority and reliable impartiality that distinguished him as one of the greatest umpires in history, while his idiosyncrasies had also made him the most recognisable official of them all.

On the Saturday afternoon, play was stopped by the cheering when England's soccer team won a penalty shootout to end their European Championship quarter-final against Spain at Wembley; this tournament completely overshadowed the Test for the domestic audience.

England 344 (R. C. Russell 124, G. P. Thorpe 89; B. K. V. Prasad 5-76) **and 278-9 dec.** (A. J. Stewart 66); **India 429** (S. C. Ganguly 131, R. Dravid 95).

1996 – ENGLAND v PAKISTAN (THIRD TEST): PUNCTURED WHEELS COME OFF
David Norrie, 1997

At The Oval, August 22, 23, 24, 25, 26, 1996. Pakistan won by nine wickets. In a predictable repeat of the Lord's Test, England's batting sank to the leg-spin of Mushtaq Ahmed on the final afternoon after they appeared to be in sight of land at lunchtime. This collapse left Pakistan comfortable winners of their fifth successive series over England. While Mushtaq collected his fifth five-wicket haul in his last six Tests and Pakistan captain Wasim Akram celebrated his 300th Test wicket, retiring chairman of selectors Ray Illingworth suffered his first home series defeat after three years in charge.

The ingredients of Sunday's principal drama were a puncture on a Mercedes convertible and the late arrival of the most naturally talented and irritating England cricketer of recent times. Lewis's only appearance at The Oval at the correct time was on Illingworth's list for the one-day squad, announced an hour before the start.

The man himself appeared 25 minutes later. After a meeting with Atherton, who then discussed the matter with Illingworth and Lloyd, Lewis was replaced in the one-day squad by Kent's Dean Headley. The big crime for the England management was his failure to ring in, even though all the players had been given mobile phones by a sponsor, for just such an eventuality. Lewis's brilliant run-out of Asif Mujtaba later in the day served only to emphasise general bewilderment at his unfulfilled talent and irresponsibility.

Wasim declared 195 ahead; Atherton and Stewart had to survive the 23 overs remaining on the fourth day. They were still together at the close, which came at 7.18pm, because of rain, after a hostile barrage from the Pakistan fast bowlers. Mushtaq had come on to deliver the tenth over, from the Vauxhall end, and he bowled unchanged until 4.20pm on the final afternoon when the innings ended. England had reached 158 for two at lunch – reminiscent of Lord's, where they were 152 for one. This time, they seemed to be in a stronger position, just 37 runs away from making the tourists bat again. But Mushtaq was already bowling round the wicket and Atherton had already gone. England's last eight wickets went down for 76 in 27 overs. Hussain received no benefit of the doubt from Sri Lankan umpire B. C. Cooray, and Crawley's concentration was disturbed by two streakers, but, generally, it was a sorry display.

England 326 (J. P. Crawley 106, G. P. Thorpe 54; Waqar Younis 4-95)
and 242 (A. J. Stewart 54, N. Hussain 51; Mushtaq Ahmed 6-78);
Pakistan 521-8 dec. (Saeed Anwar 176, Salim Malik 100*, Ijaz Ahmed 61) **and 48-1.**

1997 – AUSTRALIANS IN ENGLAND: BACK DOWN TO EARTH   Tim de Lisle, 1998

The best skyline in English cricket is the one you see from the top of The Oval pavilion, encompassing the gasometer, Big Ben, the incongruous gaudiness of the M15 headquarters, and, on a clear day, half of London. In 1997, there was an extra attraction: "The World's First Tethered Balloon Ride", in the Harleyford Road. Every so often, a hot-air balloon would rise behind the sightscreen at the Vauxhall end, dangle for a few minutes, and return to earth.

It could have been put there to represent England's summer. They started so commandingly, in the one-day internationals and the First Test, that the nation became more excited about the team's performance than it had been at any time since Kingston 1989-90, arguably since Headingley 1981. But the Australians, undisputed world champions for the first time in many years, dug deep into their reserves of skill and willpower. After having the better of a rainy stalemate at Lord's, they needed only three Test matches to draw level, pull ahead, and then secure both the Ashes and the series. At The Oval, England finished as they had begun, with a pulsating victory. It was too late. The balloon had been tethered all along.

Of all the possible scorelines, 3–2 was the one most likely to satisfy both sides. For Australia, it was a third major victory in nine months, following the series against West Indies and South Africa, and a fifth consecutive series win over England – a sequence they had never achieved in 115 years of the Ashes.

1997 – ENGLAND v AUSTRALIA (THIRD ONE-DAY INTERNATIONAL):
19-YEAR-OLD STEALS SHOW   1998

At Lord's, May 25, 1997. England won by six wickets. England made a clean sweep of the series with their third consecutive six-wicket victory. Every match began with Atherton winning the toss and ended with a stroke from Adam Hollioake. But it was Adam's 19-year-old brother Ben who stole the show here, on his debut, as he thrilled Lord's with an audacious half-century. Australia, captained by Steve Waugh because Taylor had dropped himself, had set England 270, their most demanding target yet, despite a five-wicket haul by Gough. Hollioake junior made his entrance when the reply stood at 21 for one, and drove his third ball back past McGrath for four. He lasted just 45 more balls, but some glorious strokes – including a swept six off Warne – and some streaky edges had already taken him to 63, with another ten fours. England still needed 157 when he fell, but the run-rate was down to five an over. Stewart, Crawley and Thorpe cruised along with few alarms.

Australia 269 (49.2 overs) (M. E. Waugh 95; D. Gough 5-44);
England 270-4 (49 overs) (A. J. Stewart 79, B. C. Hollioake 63, J. P. Crawley 52).

1997 – ENGLAND v AUSTRALIA (FIRST TEST): ASHES COMING HOME?
John Etheridge, 1998

At Birmingham, June 5, 6, 7, 8, 1997. England won by nine wickets. The ripples of patriotic optimism which followed England's 3–0 victory in the one-day internationals had become a tidal wave of emotion and euphoria by the end of this extraordinary match. There were reasons to think England might perform well – their growing confidence in New Zealand, the whitewash in the one-day internationals, Taylor's personal purgatory, Australia's injuries and general lack of form – but nothing had prepared a disbelieving public for what actually happened.

The game had everything as far as England were concerned: Australia's collapse to 54 for eight on the opening morning, magnificent innings by Hussain and Thorpe, a heroic century by Taylor and a suitably dramatic finale. England won at 6.52pm on Sunday evening, when Stewart cracked Warne to the extra-cover boundary. They passed their target of 118 in just 21.3 overs and the crowd, close to a fourth successive full house, engulfed the field. "They're coming home, they're coming home, Ashes coming home," they sang, to the tune made famous in the Euro 96 soccer championships. Not even the most hard-bitten realists dared argue: the electric, jingoistic atmosphere was a feature of the grand occasion.

Australia 118 (A. R. Caddick 5-50)
and 477 (M. A. Taylor 129, G. S. Blewett 125, M. T. G. Elliott 66);
England 478-9 dec (N. Hussain 207, G. P. Thorpe 138; M. S. Kasprowicz 4-113)
and 119-1 (M. A. Atherton 57*).

1997 – ENGLAND v AUSTRALIA (SIXTH TEST): TUFNELL'S TRIUMPH

Matthew Engel, 1998

At The Oval, August 21, 22, 23, 1997. England won by 19 runs. Too late to rescue the Ashes, but not too late to rescue their self-respect, England won a sensational victory after a contest fit to rank with the great games of Ashes history. The match was over at 5.24pm on the third day, but the cricket that did take place was amazing, and the climax utterly riveting. Australia, needing only 124 to win, were bowled out for just 104. The Oval crowd celebrated England's triumph in a manner not seen at least since the Edgbaston win, 11 weeks earlier – but that seemed like an awfully long time ago.

Australia's collapse maintained their reputation for vulnerability in a run-chase, and for flunking the Tests that matter least. It was the third time in 1997 they had lost the last match of a series they had already won. It did not much dent their reputation as one of the great Ashes teams. Like so many great matches, this came about thanks to what is conventionally known as a bad pitch. It was too dry, and by the second day it was crumbling. This came as a surprise to just about everyone. When England were all out on the first day, it was assumed to be yet another pathetic batting failure, and perhaps a terminal one for Atherton's captaincy. The first assumption was correct, because the pitch was still mild and there was no excuse at all for their collapse from 128 for three to 132 for seven.

Australia needed just 124 to win. But there was a sense that the situation was not hopeless. The crowd roared Malcolm in as he took the new ball, and he responded by straightening his fourth delivery to dismiss Elliott.

Tufnell bowled over the wicket to turn the ball from the crumbling pitch rather than the footmarks, and applied enough pressure to help the bowler at the other end. The beneficiary was Caddick, who removed Taylor and Blewett, given out caught behind, though TV replays suggested this was a quaint decision – by no means his first – by umpire Barker. The Waughs soon followed. Australia were 54 for five and suddenly all England was agog, even if it was the first day of the league football season.

Ponting and Healy battled back, with a stand of 34. But Tufnell finally trapped Ponting on the back pad, and Caddick took a return catch from Healy, juggled with it one-handed twice, and then clung on. Warne, batting with a runner, tried to lash out again. This time Martin got underneath his first big hit. Since Martin's fielding is willing rather than athletic, and he had dropped Warne badly 24 hours earlier, he seemed a plausible candidate to be the modern answer to Fred Tate. But he took it easily. England were confident now. The last act was Thorpe catching McGrath at mid-off – Tufnell's 11th victim – and his sunglasses falling off as he did so.

This was the first three-day Test at The Oval since 1957. On the Saturday evening Mark Taylor received a replica Ashes urn from the master of ceremonies David Gower, who had waved around a similar copy 12 years earlier. But this was greeted with only casual applause. It was a moment for England, and not just for the team. For the administrators, desperate to keep the game alive in the hearts of the public in difficult times, it was a priceless victory.

England 180 (G. D. McGrath 7-76)

and 163 (G. P. Thorpe 62; M. S. Kasprowicz 7-36);

Australia 220 (P. C. R. Tufnell 7-66) **and 104** (Tufnell 4-27).

1998 – SOUTH AFRICANS IN ENGLAND: BACK FROM THE BRINK   Tim de Lisle, 1999

It is a requirement of thriller writing that the hero should be taken almost to the point of no return. At the end of the second act, he (or she) will ideally be clinging to a precipice, in a hurricane, by one finger, while the baddie takes leisurely aim, from a sheltered vantage point, with an automatic weapon. This is precisely the position in which the England cricket team found themselves on July 5-6, 1998.

They had followed one follow-on, at Lord's, with another, graver, one at Old Trafford: in reply to South Africa's 552 for five declared, they had scraped 185 all out – a third of the runs, for twice as many wickets. Sent in again by Hansie Cronje, England were soon 11 for two. In terms of competing, chairman of selectors David Graveney admitted, we're just not there. The players were not the only ones who were not there: Old Trafford was nowhere near full. The football World Cup was still raging and, even with England knocked out, the back pages belonged to men in shorts. It wasn't just the cricket team that appeared to be in mortal danger, but English cricket. An SOS went out: Save our Summer, perhaps even Save our Sport.

Cometh the three hours, cometh the man. Robert Croft, wicketless all summer and virtually runless for a year, chose this moment to stand up and be counted, to fend off the straight ones and dig out the yorkers, to punch the wide ones through the covers and waft only at anything that was too good for him to get a touch. When Ramprakash was out, there were still nearly two hours to go, but Darren Gough, Croft's soulmate and fellow under-achiever with the bat, also rose to the occasion. At 20 to six, Gough fell to Allan Donald, and the precipice beckoned again: England were still two runs behind. Donald thudded a yorker into Angus Fraser's lower shin. If umpire Cowie's finger had gone up, England could not have won the series. The finger stayed down. Fraser survived 13 balls, and even laid a bat on one of them. Stewart, who had apparently started the recovery with a dressing-room speech on Sunday morning, reserved his most stirring rhetoric for the media: "I'd rather be one down than two down."

1998 – ENGLAND v SOUTH AFRICA (FOURTH TEST): ATHERTON v DONALD

Hugh Chevallier, 1999

At Nottingham, July 23, 24, 25, 26, 27, 1998. England won by eight wickets. This was the match English cricket desperately needed. In a summer of endless televised sport, previous Tests had been heavily overshadowed by the football World Cup, fuelling talk of a game in crisis. Now, though, a window in the sporting calendar gave Test cricket the chance to hog the limelight. It grabbed the opportunity, producing a spectacle that, for passion and controversy, was every bit the equal of a penalty shoot-out. The drama mounted steadily until the fourth afternoon when, with England chasing 247 for victory, Atherton and Donald, two giants of the modern game, fought out a titanic battle. One of the largest fifth-day crowds for many years, 11,000, then saw Stewart exuberantly lead his team to an emphatic victory – his first as Test captain. The win set the series alight: one-all with one to play. As Atherton hit the winning runs, the Headingley switchboard was besieged by requests for tickets for the final Test. Amid the euphoria, talk of a crisis evaporated.

England's target was 247 in a day and a half, a total which, amazingly, they had not reached in the fourth innings to win a home Test since The Oval in 1902. Donald began at a furious pace, frequently registering 88mph or more. But only Butcher got out. Atherton and Hussain fought on, punishing the rare loose ball. Then came a passage of play to rank with the greatest cricketing duels. Cronje, desperate for a wicket, brought back Donald. With England 82 for one, Atherton, on 27, gloved the umpteenth vicious short delivery to Boucher. The celebrations were loud, but short-lived. The batsman stood his ground; umpire Dunne was similarly unmoved. Donald was first incredulous, then livid. The next ball shot off the inside edge to the boundary. The bowler, now incandescent, snarled at Atherton, who stared impassively back. Channelling all his fury into an unremittingly hostile spell, Donald refused to let the pressure drop. Physically bruised but mentally resilient, Atherton was relishing the battle. Hussain, when 23, having weathered much of the same storm, was eventually beaten; but to Donald's utter disbelief, Boucher dropped the catch. At the close, England, on 108 for one, were within sight of victory.

Soon after the end of the game, the two teams, Donald and Atherton included, were sharing a beer.

South Africa 374 (W. J. Cronje 126, S. M. Pollock 50; A. R. C. Fraser 5-60, D. Gough 4-116)
and 208 (Cronje 67, D. J. Cullinan 56; Fraser 5-62);
England 336 (M. A. Butcher 75, M. R. Ramprakash 67*, M. A. Atherton 58; A. A. Donald 5-109)
and 247-2 (Atherton 98*, N. Hussain 58).

1998 – ENGLAND v SOUTH AFRICA (FIFTH TEST): DRUNK ON SUCCESS

Peter Johnson, 1999

At Leeds, August 6, 7, 8, 9, 10, 1998. England won by 23 runs. At the end of an epic Test, the hardest-to-please audience in the cricketing world gathered, thousands strong, beneath Headingley's balcony to watch the England players dousing themselves with champagne. The game's rulers, pausing in their planning for an uncertain future, could be forgiven for joining the faintly delirious rejoicing. On the way to winning their first major series for nearly 12 years, England had, it seemed, conquered the public cynicism bred during an era in which humiliation followed hope as routinely as day turned into night.

South Africa [were left] to aim for 219. On another day and another ground, it would have been well within their scope. Here, though, the crowd was hostile and the opposition rampant. Within 15 overs, they were 27 for five. Gough, so often unbalanced by Headingley's adulation, was this time inspired. He got three of those five for only ten. It took the bouncy Rhodes and the bear-like McMillan to cool the temperature. They reached 144 for five before McMillan, who made 54 in two and a half hours, top-edged his swing at Cork and lobbed a catch to Stewart. Minutes later, Rhodes's superb 85 was over and Gough was celebrating his 100th Test wicket, as were the zealots on the Western Terrace. With their alcohol rationed by an anti-hooligan campaign, they had got steadily drunk on success.

Many of them were there next morning when Gough finished off South Africa to collect his best Test analysis, six for 42. Stewart, having led England positively and sometimes adventurously in his first series as captain, was not slow to realise that this new, precious rapport with the public had to be preserved. The presentation ceremony was droning on when he cut it short, demanded the Cornhill Trophy and brandished it, Cup-final fashion, before the crowd. They had waited long enough.

England 230 (M. A. Butcher 116; M. Ntini 4-72)
and 240 (N. Hussain 94; S. M. Pollock 5-53);
South Africa 252 (W. J. Cronje 57; A. R. C. Fraser 5-42)
and 195 (J. N. Rhodes 85, B. M. McMillan 54; D. Gough 6-42).

1998 – ENGLAND v SRI LANKA (ONLY TEST): BITTER SIXTEEN

David Hopps, 1999

At The Oval, August 27, 28, 29, 30, 31, 1998. Sri Lanka won by ten wickets. Only three weeks after a Test series victory against South Africa had encouraged talk that English cricket was embarking upon a more successful era, the unique bowling talents of the Sri Lankan off-spinner, Muralitharan, brought England back down to earth in the final Test of the summer. Muralitharan, the hill-country Tamil and son of a biscuit manufacturer, born with a deformity of the elbow joint and a highly manoeuvrable wrist, produced one of the most phenomenal bowling displays in Test history as Sri Lanka won by ten wickets inside the final hour. Muralitharan's 16 for 220 was the fifth-best match analysis in Test history; his nine for 65 in England's second innings was seventh on the all-time list. On the way, he passed 200 Test wickets in his 42nd Test. Among spinners, only Clarrie Grimmett had reached 200 in fewer Tests; another Australian, Shane Warne, also took 42. Many who observed Muralitharan's prodigious performance wondered whether, given continued fitness, he could become the greatest Test wicket-taker in history.

England had long identified Muralitharan as Sri Lanka's prime bowling threat (indeed, Sri Lanka's captain, Ranatunga, had no compunction in referring to him as his only real asset), and the nature of the Oval surface strengthened that conviction. Slow and largely unresponsive to the seamers, the pitch negated the England trio of Gough, Fraser and Cork that had been central to the defeat of South Africa. Salisbury's leg-spin, seemingly fraught with anxiety, also failed to impress. That left the only battle between Muralitharan, his own exhaustion and the tortuous resistance of the England batsmen. Muralitharan's unorthodox action, angled in from wide of the crease, achieved turn and dip from the outset, and provided an engrossing spectacle, even against batsmen largely committed to survival. As long as ICC remains satisfied by its legitimacy, it is an unorthodox action that we are privileged to witness. Evidence suggested that only a small minority of spectators at The Oval had much sympathy with England's coach, David Lloyd, when he hinted at his unhappiness with Muralitharan's methods on the fourth evening. Lloyd's remark that "I have my opinions that I have made known to the authorities" brought an official protest to the ECB from the Board of Control for Cricket in Sri Lanka, and led to Lloyd receiving a severe reprimand.

Rarely has a Test innings encouraged more misleading conclusions than England's first. England took not far short of two days to make 445 and were assumed, at the very least, to be safe from defeat: they weren't. Hick's computerised, indeed colourless, century on the first day had been greeted as making his selection for the winter's Ashes series inevitable; thanks to Crawley's subsequent 156, a crisper, more appealing affair, it didn't. And, thirdly, the widespread condemnation of Ranatunga, for putting England in to bat, had to be gradually re-addressed. Ranatunga later crowed that he had wanted Muralitharan to have a rest in between innings, a point-scoring explanation which required us to believe that, had Sri Lanka batted first, they would have automatically made England follow on.

England 445 (J. P. Crawley 156*, G. A. Hick 107, M. R. Ramprakash 53; M. Muralitharan 7-155) and 181 (Muralitharan 9-65); Sri Lanka 591 (S. T. Jayasuriya 213, P. A. de Silva 152) and 37-0.

1999 – ENGLAND v NEW ZEALAND (Fourth Test): ROCK BOTTOM
Hugh Chevallier, 2000

At The Oval, August 19, 20, 21, 22, 1999. New Zealand won by 83 runs. Ten minutes after lunch on the fourth day, Roger Twose, an English emigrant, held a steepling catch at mid-on that gave victory in the match – and the series – to a young and self-confident New Zealand side. The ignominy of a home defeat by the team previously considered the weakest in Test cricket unleashed a hail of criticism on the England players and – after the departure during the summer of the coach and two selectors – what remained of the management. This was no ordinary failure. As almost everyone noticed, the defeat meant that for the first time since the Wisden World Championship was launched in 1996, England were at the bottom of the heap.

In truth, England's performance was not wholly inept. Hussain's captaincy was inventive, the bowling thoughtful and the fielding near-faultless. The batting, though was execrable. Atherton held the second innings together for a while but, the moment he was out, the familiar, gaping deficiencies were cruelly exposed. The end, as it usually is with England, was swift, painful and rather embarrassing.

With both teams able to win the series, the stakes were high. On the first morning, they were raised again. Cornhill, who had pumped almost £25million into English Test cricket since 1978, let it be known they were reviewing the sponsorship deal. The implication was that, if results did not improve, it would not be renewed in 2000.

England were left needing 246, the highest score of the match. They lost two wickets cheaply but, by the close, sensible batting from Atherton and Thorpe saw them to 91. This switchback of a Test promised an intriguing climax. England needed an overdue hundred from a top-order batsman or, failing that, a century partnership. But, for the first time ever in a home series of more than two Tests, they could produce neither. Once Atherton was fourth out for a positive 64 – the 50th time he had reached 50 in Tests – the batting descended into farce, the remaining six wickets adding 19 runs. Over their two innings, England's last three wickets fell for a total of two runs; New Zealand's 92. Chairman of selectors David Graveney belatedly promised that England would never again pick what amounted to three No. 11s – Mullally, Tufnell and Giddins – in the same Test. Graveney was not in the best of moods even before the defeat; he had only recently discovered that Thorpe had opted out of the winter tour and was furious at not being told earlier. The crowd jeered as Hussain collected the loser's cheque.

New Zealand 236 (S. P. Fleming 66*, D. L. Vettori 51) and 162 (C. L. Cairns 80);
England 153 (Cairns 5-31) and 162 (M. A. Atherton 64; D. J. Nash 4-39).

2000–12

England's new captain Nasser Hussain forged an alliance with their previously unknown (except to followers of Glamorgan) coach Duncan Fletcher that would take the side back in the direction of the promised land. Firstly the West Indies giant was finally slain before Michael Vaughan took over the reins for the next stage of the journey that would culminate in the 2005 Ashes series, possibly the greatest Test rubber of all time. Andrew Strauss, now in cahoots with Andy Flower, took England on yet further to the top of the world Test rankings following a remarkable thrashing of India in 2011. The crash to earth the following summer was considerable – battered into submission by a granite-hard South African side and Hashim Amla's relentless run-scoring. Yet in among the thrilling cricket were two Pakistan-shaped stains: the 2006 ball-tampering dispute that caused them to forfeit the Oval Test, and the more serious, shocking revelation of two of their bowlers in 2010 delivering no-balls to order in a spot-fixing sting.

2000 – ENGLAND v WEST INDIES (SECOND TEST): VALUE FOR MONEY
Derek Pringle, 2001

At Lord's, June 29, 30, July 1, 2000. England won by two wickets. The 100th Test match played at Lord's also proved to be one of the most exciting, with England winning a low-scoring encounter to level the series. Many talk about the Lord's Test of 1963 as being the apogee between these two sides: for sheer drama and sustained excitement, this one may have usurped it.

The uncertainty was contagious and, right up until Cork struck the winning boundary just after 7pm on Saturday, it was a match that defied prediction. Momentum in Test cricket is usually a gradual, shifting force, but here it changed hands quicker than a spare ticket among the touts, who, sensing something special, thronged the pavements surrounding the ground. On Friday, when 21 wickets fell in 75 overs, including West Indies' second innings for just 54, value for money was given ten times over. In fact, the day saw at least one ball of all four innings, an instance unique in more than 1,500 Tests.

Chasing 188 did not sound much, but on a bouncy seaming pitch, against two of the world's best new-ball bowlers, the task was stern. If most realists made West Indies favourites, they hadn't reckoned on Atherton and his heir apparent, Vaughan (playing only because of Hussain's injury).

With the job only half done, both fell in the forties to Walsh, who took the first six wickets to fall and improved his best figures against England for the second Test running, completing ten in the match for the first time against them. At 140 for six the pendulum, having creaked England's way, was back in West Indies' territory. When Knight, nursing a cracked finger, fell to Rose for a two that had spanned a courageous hour, their second victory looked assured.

However, Cork, dripping adrenalin and with a decisive glint in his eye, had entered the fray at the fall of the sixth wicket. Unfazed by the tension, he set about getting the runs. A lofted drive for four off the tiring Walsh, a pull for six off Rose and sundry stolen singles were all executed with his usual sense of theatre. As Gough kept him company with an admirably straight bat, Cork chipped away at both the total and the heartstrings of the public. Only when he had forced Walsh through the covers for the winning runs was the tension finally released, amid euphoria and ecstasy.

West Indies 267 (S. L. Campbell 82, W. W. Hinds 59; D. G. Cork 4-39, D. Gough 4-72)
and 54 (A. R. Caddick 5-16); **England 134** (C. E. L. Ambrose 4-30, C. A. Walsh 4-43)
and 191-8 (Walsh 6-74).

2000 – ENGLAND v WEST INDIES (FOURTH TEST): TWO-DAY FINISH

David Hopps, 2001

At Leeds, August 17, 18, 2000. England won by an innings and 39 runs. The first two-day Test win for 54 years – and England's first since crushing South Africa at Old Trafford in 1912 – ensured that the 2000 Headingley Test would claim a prominent place in cricket folklore. Inspirational English pace bowling, a mediocre surface and West Indies' continued fallibility against the seaming or swinging ball combined to bring England victory with astonishing haste. It was their first innings win over West Indies since 1966.

The worldwide trend for shorter Test matches – out of kilter with the game's reputation as an imperceptible battle for supremacy over five long and contemplative days – had already been noted with some disquiet. But nowhere had the pace been so unremittingly frenetic as at Headingley. West Indies were routed just as they had been at Lord's, dismissed in their second innings for only 61 in 26.2 overs, in seven minutes over two hours.

On the second morning, the match swung England's way. Vaughan, on his home midden and batting in the scholarly, slightly formal manner of a country parson, made a Test-best 76. When Walsh claimed Gough's wicket, the unimagined bounty of another 167 runs, at four an over, had put England exactly 100 ahead.

What followed rivalled even the drama of Headingley 1981. The bounce had been awkward for batsmen facing bowling from the Rugby Stand end, but West Indies' collapse was primarily brought about by high-quality swing bowling at speed. Gough, twice overshadowed by Yorkshire colleagues, now delivered for the faithful, dismissing a trio of left-handers with in-duckers in his first three overs. After tea, Caddick was finally allowed to switch to the Rugby Stand end, where he produced the most devastating over of his Test career. Jacobs was lbw to the first ball, then the stumps were shattered three times – dismissing McLean, Ambrose and King – in four legitimate deliveries to leave this impassive cricketer wheeling around the outfield in disbelief. It took him another eight balls to complete the job. Five batsmen had departed for ducks in the lowest Test total recorded at Headingley. England took a 2–1 lead and Saturday's sell-out crowd had to make other arrangements.

West Indies 172 (R. R. Sarwan 59*, C. White 5-57) **and 61** (D. Gough 4-30, A. R. Caddick 5-14);
England 272 (M. P. Vaughan 76, G. A. Hick 59; C. E. L. Ambrose 4-42, C. A. Walsh 4-51).

Yorkshire 1950. The batting of Watson in the few matches in which he played was a revelation. Because he toured South America with England's World Cup football party, Watson did not join the side until August. In his first innings he made 122, and hit two other centuries in his eight matches. He finished top of the English first-class batting averages, but more important was the increased confidence and power he showed in his stroke-play.

Little Wonder No. 50

2000 – ENGLAND v WEST INDIES (FIFTH TEST): JEERS TO CHEERS

Richard Hobson, 2001

At The Oval, August 31, September 1, 2, 3, 4, 2000. England won by 158 runs. Earlier in the season, a critic of the sport had described cricket as "a grey game played by grey people". The misguided journalist should have been at The Oval on the final day to see the conclusion of a momentous contest, itself the culmination of a memorable series. This was sport at its vibrant, colourful best, and it rekindled the public's love affair with cricket. Some 18,500 spectators crammed into the ground; thousands more were turned away, left to wander the Harleyford Road, hearing the roar that urged England on to triumph. In a show of admirable common sense, the Surrey club – who also admitted children at no cost – gave several hundred luckier fans access to the executive boxes.

Consensus suggested it was the first sell-out on a final day in England since Hutton, Compton, et al. recovered the Ashes here in 1953. Now, as then, England needed merely to hold their nerve. When Cork trapped Walsh 12 minutes after tea to complete the 3–1 win, the jubilant crowd packed in front of the pavilion and stretched back as far as the square to witness the presentation ceremony. Some of them, a year previously, had booed Hussain, the England captain, after a miserable defeat by New Zealand, but such churlishness was long forgotten as England celebrated a first series win against West Indies in 31 years. There could be no doubting the choice of Man of the Match. Atherton, who hinted during the game at retirement after the 2001 Ashes series, top-scored in both innings, in all batting for more than 12 hours on a pitch that showed enough life to keep the bowlers interested throughout.

England formed guards of honour for Ambrose, playing his final Test, and Walsh, his last in England, as they strode to the crease, but there was nothing either man could do to reverse the result.

England 281 (M. A. Atherton 83, M. E. Trescothick 78)
and 237 (Atherton 108; C. A. Walsh 4-73);
West Indies 125 (C. White 5-32) **and 215** (A. R. Caddick 4-54).

2001 – AUSTRALIANS IN ENGLAND: OVER IN 11 DAYS   David Frith, 2002

Seldom has such high expectation before an Ashes series ended in such summary demolition. Peter May's 1958-59 England team, which had a truly formidable look about it, was crushed 4–0 by Richie Benaud's eager combination, yet it was 63 days into the series before the Ashes were relinquished. In 2001, with its compressed schedule (five Tests within 54 days), Steve Waugh's Australians made sure of retention in only 31, framing a mere 11 days of combat; Benaud's needed 22. After emphatic defeat in seven successive Ashes series, will deflated England ever be equipped to challenge the Baggy Green brigade seriously? Contrariwise, will Australia be capable of introducing reliable talent after the likes of the Waughs, Glenn McGrath and even Shane Warne (whom Heaven protect) are gone? This side's average age was 30, Australia's ripest since 1948.

They arrived in England as outstanding favourites, notwithstanding their reversals at Kolkata and Chennai and the revival in England's performances under Nasser Hussain and coach Duncan Fletcher. England had crushed Zimbabwe and West Indies the previous summer, and their winter tour had returned notable successes in Pakistan and Sri Lanka. They had then won at Lord's against Pakistan, before slipping up at Old Trafford. At the outset, Steve Waugh knew England were stronger than in recent years, and acknowledged that forecasting was fraught with difficulties. But he did add ominously, "If we can get on top early, we can open up some old scars."

It remained for us to try to assess whether we had been watching the best cricket team of all time. Wasted though the exercise may be, the man in the traffic jam or the halted railway carriage was eager for debate about the relative qualities of the 1902, 1921, 1948 and 1975 Australians, the 1950s England sides, South Africa 1969-70, the West Indies combination of 1984.

2001 – ENGLAND v AUSTRALIA (FOURTH TEST): BUTCHERED

Jim Holden, 2002

At Leeds, August 16, 17, 18, 19, 20, 2001. England won by six wickets. Few cricketers play a Test innings that will become an Ashes legend. Mark Butcher joined this elite when he struck an exhilarating 173 not out to ensure single-handedly that there would be no "greenwash", and show that, for a day at least, McGrath, Gillespie and Warne could be tamed.

Butcher's score matched that of Don Bradman in 1948, when Australia made 404 for three here on the last day to win against the odds. But the immediate comparison was with Ian Botham's 149 not out in 1981, when his hitting transformed not only a match but a whole summer, and a whole sport. Butcher's knock was not as important as that. A fairer parallel would be the fabled 1902 innings of Gilbert Jessop, whose attacking shots and endless verve inspired a remarkable Test victory no one thought possible. As here, it was England's only win of the series.

Butcher's innings, entirely out of character with the rest of a one-sided Ashes contest, was Jessopian in vein: he cut anything short of a length with exquisite power and timing, stepped forward to drive McGrath through the covers, and clipped sweet boundaries off his legs when the bowlers erred in line. The Australians could not contain him and, though it was the only such day of the summer, his innings will never be forgotten.

Australia's stand-in captain, Gilchrist, had not thought anything like it possible when he closed his team's second innings on the fourth evening with a lead of 314 runs and 110 overs still to play. Rain had seriously disrupted his game plan, taking maybe two sessions of Australian batting time. But Gilchrist's decision spoke volumes for the tourists' aura of invincibility, and their desire to win the series 5–0. Few in England gave the home side hope of victory either: only once, at Melbourne in 1928-29, had England scored as many in the fourth innings to win.

Gilchrist and all the Australian players shook the English hero's hand. Their sportsmanship was welcome, and genuine. Even though they had dominated the first four days and were superior in class and attitude, their smiles were not forced.

Australia 447 (R. T. Ponting 144, D. R. Martyn 118, M. E. Waugh 72; D. Gough 5-103)
and 176-4 dec. (Ponting 72); **England 309** (A. J. Stewart 76*; G. D. McGrath 7-76)
and 315-4 (M. A. Butcher 173*, N. Hussain 55).

2002 – INDIANS IN ENGLAND: VAUGHAN'S PRINCELY HUNDREDS

Rahul Bhattacharya, 2003

A series of more than three Tests is a rare thing these days. Its shifting dynamics embrace such abstractions as momentum, luck, form, intensity – karma, even – as if it were a universe in itself. India's tour of England in 2002 captured the ebb and flow, the up and down, of this strange and enchanting realm.

The scoreline, 1–1, was frustrating but fair. Michael Vaughan, who came of age with three princely hundreds, did not deserve to be on the losing side; nor did Rahul Dravid, who matched him for excellence if not for excitement. The series was India's first of more than three Tests in England since 1979, and in those 23 years Indian ready-meals had sprung up in Marks & Spencer, chicken tikka masala had overtaken fish and chips as the national dish and Britain had become more multi-cultural, or more comfortable in its multiculturalism. On hoardings and TV screens, the summer was branded as Indian: there were more Indian movie festivals than anyone could possibly attend, plus the opening season of Andrew Lloyd Webber's musical *Bombay Dreams*. And the lasting flavour of the cricket was Indian.

2002 – ENGLAND v INDIA (NatWest Series final): THE GREATEST DAY

Lawrence Booth, 2003

At Lord's, July 13, 2002. India won by two wickets. This game wasn't merely a case of saving the best until last: it was one of the most thrillingly topsy-turvy limited-overs internationals ever played. At 146 for five in pursuit of 326 – more than they had ever scored batting second – India were down and out.

Their four senior batsmen were all back in the pavilion, and only Yuvraj Singh, aged 20, and Mohammad Kaif, 21, stood between England's bowlers and the tail. But Yuvraj played some punishing strokes off the back foot, Kaif was all wrists through midwicket, and the pair added 121 in less than 18 overs. When Yuvraj top-edged a sweep to short fine leg, Harbhajan helped add a quick 47 with Kaif to take India to the brink, but Flintoff tilted the balance once more with two wickets in the 48th over.

Even so, India needed just 11 runs off 12 balls. Kaif thick-edged Gough to the third-man boundary to reduce the target to two off six, and Zaheer Khan stole the winning runs with three balls remaining courtesy of an overthrow. As England's players wandered off in a daze, the Indians celebrated in style. In an echo of Flintoff's antics at Mumbai five months earlier, Ganguly whipped off his shirt and whirled it round his head on the players' balcony, before running through the Long Room to kiss the Lord's turf and embrace Kaif. The capacity crowd, many of them Indians, stood and cheered. After nine consecutive defeats in one-day finals, India had made it tenth time lucky.

England 325-5 (50 overs) (N. Hussain 115, M. E. Trescothick 109);
India 326-8 (49.3 overs) (M. Kaif 87*, Yuvraj Singh 69, S. C. Ganguly 60).

2003 – ZIMBABWEANS IN ENGLAND: POLITICAL HOT POTATO

Simon Briggs, 2004

Less than three months after England's failure to fulfil their World Cup fixture in Harare, a party of Zimbabwean cricketers arrived at Gatwick. As their visit represented something of a political hot potato, the England and Wales Cricket Board shared a common aim with its team: to get through this awkward little tour without suffering too much embarrassment.

Though the mandarins came under far more pressure than the players, both would emerge largely unscathed. The Zimbabwean captain, Heath Streak, was leading a painfully inexperienced squad: only Grant Flower had scored a Test hundred. Streak thus had rather less ammunition than Kate Hoey, the Labour MP and former Minister for Sport.

"The Zimbabwe Cricket Union have [President] Mugabe as their patron," Hoey wrote in the *Daily Telegraph* on April 19. "Yet on May 22 at Lord's, the most famous ground in the world, England will play against a country soaked in the blood of men, women and children who have done nothing other than stand up for the freedoms and rights that we in this country take for granted."

Hoey's invective served as a rallying cry for the Stop The Tour campaign, which was soon claiming the support of around 100 MPs. Yet only a handful of them attended the first day's demonstrations outside the Grace Gates, where the most recognisable figure was the serial agitator Peter Tatchell. The game suffered two low-key interruptions in the afternoon, when a couple of Tatchell's comrades wandered on to the pitch with placards. And that was about as rough as things got for the ECB.

Crucially, the Stop The Tour movement went unsupported by the two political parties who could have given it legitimacy. One was the ruling British Labour Party, whose cabinet minister Tessa Jowell approved the tour in a letter to the ECB. The other was the Zimbabwean opposition party, the Movement for Democratic Change (MDC), who seemed to view cricket as a useful tool for redirecting the British media's attention towards Mugabe's outrages. The US-led war against Iraq, which preceded the tour, meant that the plight of millions of Zimbabweans facing food shortages had gone largely unreported.

Without Andy Flower in particular, Zimbabwe proved to be a soft touch on the field. England cashed in on Zimbabwe's naivety. For the first time in 25 years, they won every Test in a series – even if the series was only two games long.

2003 – SOUTH AFRICANS IN ENGLAND: NON-STOP EXCITEMENT John Etheridge, 2004

Five unpredictable and action-laden Test matches, all squeezed into less than seven weeks, gave South Africa's third series in England since readmission an almost non-stop rush of excitement. The buzz started when South Africa scorched to 398 for one on the opening day of the First Test, and finished with England completing a staggering comeback in the Fifth. There was scarcely time to pause for breath.

Although South Africa dominated large chunks of the series they will ultimately judge their tour as one of frustration and lack of fulfilment, if not exactly failure. Undoubtedly they played the more consistent cricket, and the final result – a 2–2 draw – gave little clue as to how the matches actually unfolded. Graeme Smith, at the age of 22 and on his first major tour as captain, was left to ponder how his side failed to win the rubber by a convincing margin.

Rain probably deprived them of a win in the First Test, although they achieved a victory of sorts when the opposition captain, Nasser Hussain, decided to resign immediately afterwards. They won the Second overwhelmingly, but England drew level after winning a crucial toss in the Third. In the Fourth, at Headingley, South Africa hauled themselves to an unlikely victory after England surrendered at least three positions of superiority. Going into the last match, South Africa could easily have been leading 4–0 rather than 2–1.

2003 – ENGLAND v SOUTH AFRICA (Fifth Test): EPIC CLIMB

Hugh Chevallier, 2004

At The Oval, September 4, 5, 6, 7, 8, 2003. England won by nine wickets. At the start of the second day, bookies were offering 40 to one against an England win – not quite the 500 to one that tempted Rod Marsh and Dennis Lillee at Headingley in 1981, but an indication of the mountain England climbed to claim this epic. South Africa had lost a wicket to the last ball of the first day but, even at 362 for four, a huge score beckoned, and with it victory in the series. That wicket turned out to be the fulcrum on which the match pivoted. From then on, England produced far the sharper cricket. On this sublime pitch, South Africa's 484 simply wasn't enough. Only once before in a Test in England, when Arthur Morris and Don Bradman triumphed at Headingley in 1948, had a first-innings total of 450 or more led to defeat.

It was not just the delicious reversal of fortune that made this a classic: there were myriad subplots to intrigue and absorb a packed house for five days. Alec Stewart, at the age of 40 and in his record 133rd and avowedly final Test appearance for England, wrapped himself in the cross of St George for the last time, at least on a cricket pitch. Thorpe, back from the wilderness only because another of Nasser Hussain's brittle bones was broken, achieved redemption with a beautiful hundred. And Bicknell, strutting his stuff on the big stage, hinted at what he might have done as a regular Test cricketer. Huge roars from the crowd regularly filled the air at the exploits of these three, Surrey stalwarts all.

A deafening cheer greeted Stewart, collar up, as he strode through the South Africans' generous guard of honour. Several bat twiddles and knee squats later, he was slotting the ball between the fielders – though not for as long as the crowd wanted. On 38, he played across a straight ball, and a career totalling 8,463 runs at a shade under 40 was almost over. Cue more rapturous applause.

Shortly before lunch, Vaughan declared 120 ahead. England had bowled decently on the first day, but without fire. Now the South Africans wilted in the heat. Harmison subtly honed his "They don't like it up 'em" technique and deservedly reaped dividends. Bicknell slanted two awayswingers across Rudolph, then bowled a majestic inswinger, unwisely ignored. By the close – and still no rain to speak of – South Africa, effectively 65 for six, had nowhere to hide.

South Africa **484** (H. H. Gibbs 183, G. Kirsten 90, S. M. Pollock 66*, J. H. Kallis 66)
and **229** (M. P. Bicknell 4-84, S. J. Harmison 4-33);
England **604-9 dec.** (M. E. Trescothick 219, G. P. Thorpe 124, A. Flintoff 95) and **110-1** (Trescothick 69*).

Wild scenes. The Australian Cricket Board of Control at a meeting in September discussed the current practice at the end of Test matches of scrambling for souvenirs such as stumps, bails and balls. They considered it to be most undesirable and felt that some steps should be taken to stop it. There were some particularly wild scenes after the final Test between Australia and England at Melbourne in February 1951.

Little Wonder No. 51

2004 – ENGLAND v NEW ZEALAND (FIRST TEST): CHANGING OF THE GUARD

Mike Walters, 2005

At Lord's, May 20, 21, 22, 23, 24, 2004. England won by seven wickets. Rarely has Lord's witnessed a surge of affection for one of English cricket's grandees to match the final flourish of Nasser Hussain's career, which concluded an extraordinary sequence of events. The theory that a butterfly flapping its wings in Casablanca can lead to a hurricane in Cuba found powerful supporting evidence in this compelling match. It was a wonderful setting for anyone's farewell.

The first twist came three days before a ball had been bowled in anger. Vaughan, the England captain, attempted an innocuous sweep at a 19-year-old net bowler, left-arm spinner Zac Taylor, collapsed in a heap and was carted from the Nursery practice ground with a twisted right knee. The repercussions were momentous: Trescothick stood in as captain for the first time in Tests and the Middlesex captain Andrew Strauss, not named in the original 13-man squad, became only the fourth player to launch his Test career with a century at Headquarters.

Without their fastest bowler, Bond, New Zealand's attack could hardly raise a gallop, and it was England's openers who made all the running with a fluent stand of 190 in 54 overs. Trescothick, punching 13 fours with the assurance of an immigration officer stamping passports, was finally beaten down the slope by Oram, 14 short of becoming only the third man to score a hundred in his first Test as England captain. But Strauss, batting on his home ground and serenaded by the crowd warbling the "Blue Danube" in his honour, was not to be denied.

On 91, he enjoyed a miraculous slither of good fortune when his inside edge off Martin brushed off stump firmly enough to make the timber wobble but somehow failed to dislodge the bails. Another trail of scorched earth through the covers soon confirmed England's first centurion on debut since Graham Thorpe in 1993, and their superiority. But the applause was accompanied by a sense of wonder: Vaughan would have to come back, and Strauss could hardly be dropped. So who would make way? No one was considering the implications more clearly than a 36-year-old ex-captain already known to be close to retirement. England eventually needed 282 from 95 overs to win – 64 more than they had ever managed in the fourth innings to win in 105 previous Lord's Tests.

At 35 for two, the chase began to look forlorn until Hussain – who had already decided, unknown to his team-mates, that this would be his final Test innings

– marched out to join Strauss for his last hurrah. Strauss was the dominant partner in a 108-run stand and was on course for a century in each innings. Then he sacrificed himself in a Keystone Kops mix-up with Hussain. While the crestfallen Strauss would soon be mollified by the match award, Hussain was distraught after "doing a Boycott on the local lad" – a reference to Geoff Boycott running out Derek Randall against Australia at Trent Bridge 27 years earlier.

Only leading England to victory from the wreckage of Strauss's heartbreak would atone for Hussain's part in the catastrophe, and they were still 139 away. But few men are blessed with such willpower. Fortified by a succinct pep-talk from fellow warhorse Thorpe – "Stop whingeing and get on with it" – Hussain scrambled to his fifty in 158 deliveries before he was carried to glorious redemption, and the final curtain, on one last rush of adrenalin. He reached his 14th Test hundred with a lofted on-drive and signature extra-cover drive off successive deliveries to level the scores, and the ovation had not subsided before he collared Martin through the covers again and swayed triumphantly into the sunset. Forgiveness rained down and, less than three days later, he confirmed what everybody had suspected from his nostalgic body language: after 96 Tests spanning 14 years, he was giving up the game in a blaze of glory.

New Zealand 386 (C. L. Cairns 82, J. D. P. Oram 67, M. H. Richardson 93, N. J. Astle 64;
S. J. Harmison 4-126) and 336 (Richardson 101, B. B. McCullum 96; Harmison 4-76);
England 441 (A. J. Strauss 112, M. E. Trescothick 86, A. Flintoff 63)
and 282-3 (N. Hussain 103*, Strauss 83).

2004 – WEST INDIANS IN ENGLAND: STARTING TO BELIEVE   Stephen Fay, 2005

Two decades after the successive "blackwash" series that marked the high tide of Caribbean cricketing dominance, England completed a double rout of their own over West Indies so easily that English cricket-lovers who had grown stoical in defeat started to take winning for granted. Having won a four-Test away series 3–0 earlier in the year, England swept the four at home, with Michael Vaughan's leadership of a relatively young team growing in skill and conviction all the time. Though he still lacked experience against hardened opposition from Australia and India, his team was beginning to expect to win even when the going was toughest.

2005 – AUSTRALIANS IN ENGLAND: THE GREATEST SERIES   Stephen Brenkley, 2006

If there has been a more compelling series, history forgot to record it. If there is a better one in the future, you would beg to be there. England regained the Ashes after a gap of 16 years and 42 days, when bad light brought a formal end to the Fifth Test: a series full of extraordinary climaxes and reversals, in the end, just dwindling away in the more usual cricketing fashion to the point where an Australian victory became impossible, even in this summer.

Australia needed 338 runs to win from the 17.2 overs remaining to draw level at 2–2 and retain the Ashes. So 2–1 to England it was, though but for a run here, a wicket there or a catch almost anywhere it could conceivably have been either 4–1 or 0–4. It is somehow soothing to relate the bare facts and the strangely prosaic conclusion. The contest was gripping from the beginning. As it reached the end, not just regular English cricket-followers, but the whole country and the rest of the cricketing world were in its thrall. It was so intense and played with such purpose that it supplanted football on the back pages and much else on the front pages. Television viewing figures went through the roof.

When the series outcome was finally confirmed, after an audacious maiden Test century by Kevin Pietersen prevented Australia from having a decent tilt at the victory they required, there was an outpouring of relief and jubilation. The scenes at The Oval, splendidly refurbished and packed with 23,000 spectators on five successive days, were astonishing enough. There were countless renditions of "Jerusalem" which, like it or not, had become accepted as the team anthem, as well as "Land of Hope and Glory" and "There'll Always Be An England". The little scene when England's captain, Michael Vaughan, planted a kiss on the replica of the Ashes urn brought the house down, in the way that the hoisting of the FA Cup by the winning captain once did. And it was done with the judgment and delicacy of touch that had been apparent in his leadership throughout.

The following day, anything between 100,000 and quarter of a million people lined the streets of London as the triumphant squad and support staff, wives and in some cases children paraded on an open-topped double-decker bus. Crowd estimates are invariably as trustworthy as a dodgy builder's, but there were decidedly more than the two men and a dog Matthew Hoggard said he was expecting. The procession ended in Trafalgar Square, where roughly 25,000 paid homage to the victors – before they went to Downing Street to meet the prime minister. Had the players known how many would turn up, they might have postponed the all-night bender that led many of them (not least the player of the series, Flintoff) to report for this extra day of duty somewhere below the level of fitness that sustained them through the series. If English cricket had seen the like before, nobody was alive who could remember.

2005 – AUSTRALIA v BANGLADESH (NatWest Series): Goliath, bowled David
Julian Guyer, 2006

At Cardiff, June 18, 2005. Bangladesh won by five wickets. Two days after being humbled by England, Bangladesh produced the greatest upset in 2,250 one-day internationals to outclass world champions Australia. This match looked like David and Goliath in more ways than one. Mohammad Ashraful's mother had worried about her slightly-built son taking on the physically imposing Australians, but he emerged a hero, striking 11 fours in a dazzling, run-a-ball innings. He kissed the pitch after reaching a maiden one-day hundred with a single off McGrath. Bangladesh, chasing 250 to win, now needed just 23 off three overs with six wickets left. Ashraful fell next ball, caught at long-on off Gillespie. But Aftab Ahmed, little taller than Ashraful, and Mohammad Rafique held their nerve, bringing it down to seven off six balls. The murmur of anticipation was now a barely suppressed roar. Aftab struck the first ball of Gillespie's final over for six wide of long-on to level the scores. A scrambled single completed the miracle, only Bangladesh's tenth victory in 108 one-day internationals. Attempts to keep joyful fans off the field were no more successful than Australia's to hold back Bangladesh's batsmen.

Australia's day was awkward from the start. They dropped Symonds after an alcohol-fuelled night in Cardiff, and Lee was injured.

"This is probably one of the biggest upsets in the history of cricket, and my worst defeat as captain," said Ponting. Dav Whatmore, the Bangladesh coach and former Australian Test batsman, showed a Kipling-like approach to victory and defeat, but admitted the whole team were "jumping up and down when that six was hit". They were not alone. The reaction of anyone who took the pre-match odds offered by some London bookmakers of 500-1 *on* Australia would have been somewhat different.

Australia 249-5 (50 overs) (D. R. Martyn 77, M. J. Clarke 54; Tapash Baisya 3-69);
Bangladesh 250-5 (49.2 overs) (Mohammad Ashraful 100, Habibul Bashar 47).

2005 – ENGLAND v AUSTRALIA (SECOND TEST): THE GREATEST TEST
Steven Lynch, 2006

At Birmingham, August 4, 5, 6, 7, 2005. England won by two runs. If Australia had been rolled over in a couple of balls on the fourth morning, which was wholly possible, this would still be remembered as a great Test match: it produced exciting, fluctuating, often brilliant cricket from day one. But the crowd that turned up and filled Edgbaston on the Sunday seemed to sense they would be seeing something more worthwhile than three minutes' cricket and a victory singsong.

They still got the win they desperately wanted and expected, but in a manner that will never be forgotten. When the Old Trafford Test began four days later, *The Greatest Test* DVD was on sale. And no one was arguing with the description. On that sunlit fourth morning, England strode out on to the field with Australia 175 for eight, chasing 282. The main batsmen were all gone, and so was the swaggering confidence that had characterised Australia's Test performances for almost the whole of the previous 16 years.

But sometimes there is nothing quite as invigorating as a hopeless situation. Warne started brightly, Lee jumped solidly behind the ball, collecting bruises as well as runs, and the target ticked down. Warne trod on his stumps with 62 wanted, but still it wasn't over. The bowlers dug the ball in too short and too straight, aiming for catches off the splice rather than in the well-stocked slip cordon. England's confidence turned to concern to alarm to panic. And the last pair, Lee and Kasprowicz – with plenty of help from Extras – whittled the target down towards single figures.

With 15 required, Kasprowicz flicked Flintoff uppishly to third man, where Simon Jones failed to hold on to a difficult catch as he dived forward. England's last chance appeared to have gone. But finally, with just three wanted, Harmison banged one into the left glove of Kasprowicz, who hunched down horrified as the ball looped down the leg side and Geraint Jones plunged for the winning catch, the signal for tumultuous celebrations. A mournful Kasprowicz said afterwards. "It just got big quick, and I didn't see too much of it." Nor did umpire Bowden.

After umpteen TV replays, it was possible to conclude that Kasprowicz's left hand was off the bat at the moment of impact and, technically, he was not out. Bowden, however, would have needed superhuman vision to see this, and an armed escort involving several regiments to escape the crowd had he actually refused to give it out. It was also the right decision for cricket: 2–0 to Australia would have been the signal for the football season to begin; 1–1 lit the blue touchpaper. The Greatest Test became the Greatest Series, and the pyrotechnics illuminated the summer. The final margin was the closest in England-Australia Tests, edging the three-run thrillers at Old Trafford 1902 and Melbourne 1982-83 – and neither of those could match this one in its relentless unmissability.

England 407 (M. E. Trescothick 90, K. P. Pietersen 71, A. Flintoff 68; S. K. Warne 4-116)
and 182 (Flintoff 73; B. Lee 4-82);
Australia 308 (J. L. Langer 82, R. T. Ponting 61)
and 279 (Flintoff 4-79).

2005 – ENGLAND v AUSTRALIA (THIRD TEST): PONTING'S DEFIANCE

Chloe Saltau, 2006

At Manchester, August 11, 12, 13, 14, 15, 2005. Drawn. Cricket had hardly caught its breath after Edgbaston; the superlatives had not even settled. But now 2005 had something else to give. A draw, of all things: the first in 17 Ashes Tests. Yes, five days passed and nobody won. But an estimated 10,000 had to be turned away from Old Trafford on the final morning, and thousands more were turned back before they could get close. Roads were clogged for miles around.

This reflected the mounting enthusiasm for the series, but also the decision to offer last-day tickets for only £10 to adults and £5 for juniors; the black market put their value at around £80. Those who failed to join the 22,000 in the ground had to join the estimated 7.7million who watched the conclusion on TV. This involved Australia's last pair, Lee and McGrath, keeping out the last 24 balls to save the game, something this Australian team has hardly ever had to contemplate. Two nations held their collective breath yet again. The end was only made possible by an inspirational innings from Ponting – the man who got the blame for Edgbaston this time deserving the credit. He batted nearly seven hours for 156 after England had kindly set Australia 423 to win. It was the loneliest of hands on a wearing pitch: no one else even got close to 50; no one else could ease his misery if, as now seemed possible, he lost the Ashes. When he was ninth out, with four overs still left, he thought he had blown it. Ponting left the field, not with the satisfaction of having played a great innings, but in a fury. He went into the dressing-room and threw a private tantrum while his tailenders in the middle kept their cool.

England 444 (M. P. Vaughan 166, M. E. Trescothick 63, I. R. Bell 59; B. Lee 4-100)
and 280-6 dec. (A. J. Strauss 106, Bell 65; G. D. McGrath 5-115);
Australia 302 (S. K. Warne 90; S. P. Jones 6-53) **and 371-9** (R. T. Ponting 156; A. Flintoff 4-71).

2005 – ENGLAND v AUSTRALIA (FOURTH TEST): NATIONAL ANXIETY

Lawrence Booth, 2006

At Nottingham, August 25, 26, 27, 28, 2005. England won by three wickets. The law of averages demanded a dull draw after the showstoppers at Edgbaston and Old Trafford, but this was a series in which the usual laws did not apply. By the time Giles and Hoggard scampered the winning runs on a sun-kissed Sunday, both teams – both nations – had been put through the wringer once more.

But now England were ahead, a point not lost on the home supporters. "What's the score, Glenn McGrath, what's the score?" they chanted at the 5–0 predictor on the Australian balcony. He responded with another forecast, holding up two fingers on each hand, but the gesture seemed poignant. Not only was a 2–2 draw the best Australia could still hope for; McGrath himself had now missed two Tests in the series, both lost. This time, it was down to wear and tear to his right elbow.

England were eventually left needing an awkward 129. At 32 without loss after five overs, they were coasting. But cricket has never had a scene-stealer – not even Ian Botham – who could match Warne. He removed Trescothick and Vaughan with the opening deliveries of his first two overs, then snared Strauss at leg slip in his fifth to make it 57 for three. When Bell hooked Lee to long leg without addition, the talk was of Australian revenge for Headingley 1981. As on the Sunday morning at Edgbaston and Monday afternoon at Old Trafford, news from Trent Bridge began to savage the peace of a warm August English Sunday. Then Pietersen and Flintoff, against type, calmed everyone's nerves by adding 46, but Lee had Pietersen caught behind with the first ball of a new spell and in his next over bowled an incredulous Flintoff with a beauty that proved Australia could produce reverse swing, to tremendous effect. With 13 still needed, Geraint Jones spooned Warne to deep extra cover. England were down to the bowlers.

The anxiety was not confined to the spectators. As Hoggard trooped to the crease, Giles provided a cheerless assessment of Lee's bowling: "He's reversing it at 95 miles an hour." Somehow, though, the runs came in dribs and drabs: Giles kept out Warne, Hoggard handled Lee. Catharsis arrived when Hoggard drove a Lee full toss to the cover fence to take England within four runs of their target, and victory was secured in the next over when Giles clipped Warne through midwicket.

With more support for Lee and Warne – Kasprowicz and Tait bowled six wicketless overs for 43 between them – Australia might have won. Instead, it was England who celebrated a result which ensured that, for the first time in nine Ashes series, they would not be on the losing side. Could they now take the one last step towards the Ashes?

England 477 (A. Flintoff 102, G. O. Jones 85, M. E. Trescothick 65, M. P. Vaughan 58; S. K. Warne 4-102)
and 129-7 (Warne 4-31); **Australia 218** (S. P. Jones 5-44)
and 387 (J. L. Langer 61, S. M. Katich 59, M. J. Clarke 56).

Leap of faith: Andrew Strauss catches Adam Gilchrist at Trent Bridge,
one of the many remarkable moments in the epic 2005 Ashes

2006 – ENGLAND v SRI LANKA (SECOND TEST): KP'S NAUGHTY SHOT

Jim Holden, 2007

At Birmingham, May 25, 26, 27, 28, 2006. England won by six wickets. One moment of genius lifted this otherwise moderate Test above the norm. One bravura batting stroke gave the game its own little place in history. One individual contest – the heart of cricket – made everyone who watched smile with joy and gasp in astonishment.

All along, the personal battle between Kevin Pietersen and Muttiah Muralitharan was a sheer delight. Pietersen relied on his unique combination of power, panache, instinct and thoughtful unorthodoxy. Muralitharan countered with all his wit and guile, persistence and unique double-jointed blend of variations. And there was no doubting that Pietersen was the victor, even though Murali twice had the final word.

But the real triumph came in England's first innings. Pietersen had already scored 136 from 154 balls, while no other batsman topped 30. As Muralitharan danced towards the wicket, Pietersen did his own pirouette at the crease, changing his feet and his grip to turn himself into a left-hander. He then unleashed the ball into the crowd for six. It was more than just a reverse sweep, and the word "sweep" hardly conveys the lethal power of the stroke, still less its awesome inventiveness. Murali could no more believe it than anyone else. He said afterwards that Pietersen was now "on top of the world" as a batsman. The official ICC rankings merely lifted him to No. 10.

Pietersen called it "a naughty shot", an admission that it was reckless as well as revolutionary. Some said it was too naughty. He fell attempting an orthodox sweep two balls later, and perhaps he had become over-confident. But most spectators revelled in the moment: to see one of the world's most baffling bowlers looking so baffled himself was a treat. In the endless duel between batsman and bowler, Pietersen had given us an entirely new variation, and few cricketers can say that. He was rightly named man of a match that England – unchanged from Lord's, despite all the criticism – again dominated. But this time they pressed home their superiority.

Sri Lanka 141 and 231 (M. G. Vandort 105, T. M. Dilshan 59); **England 295** (K. P. Pietersen 142; M. Muralitharan 6-86) **and 81-4.**

Nottinghamshire v Glamorgan. At Nottingham, June 30, July 2, 3, 1951. Drawn. So slowly did Glamorgan score on the first day that Simpson, the Nottinghamshire captain, bowled an over of lobs as a protest and, following this incident Glamorgan lost four wickets for 11 runs.

Little Wonder No. 52

2006 – ENGLAND v SRI LANKA (Third Test): DEATH BY DOOSRA
Sa'adi Thawfeeq, 2007

At Nottingham, June 2, 3, 4, 5, 2006. Sri Lanka won by 134 runs. England came into the final Test expected to complete a 2–0 series win. Instead, they stumbled to a four-day defeat as Sri Lanka levelled the series. The reasons for England's downfall were two-fold. At last, a dry pitch and bright, sunny weather made Sri Lanka feel at home. And then there was Muralitharan.

Eight years after demolishing England at The Oval with 16 for 220 – the fifth-best match analysis in Test history – there came another act of smiling assassination. Armed now with the *doosra*, cleverly mixed in with his off-breaks, Muralitharan wreaked havoc. He took 11 for 132, including eight for 70 in the second innings, the best figures in a Trent Bridge Test, beating eight for 107 by B. J. T. Bosanquet 101 years before. When he snaffled the first seven wickets on the fourth afternoon, Muralitharan was within tantalising reach of perhaps the greatest of all statistical bowling feats.

Watching the destruction from square leg was umpire Darrell Hair, who tainted Muralitharan's career by calling him for throwing at Melbourne in 1995-96. But since the ICC's ruling that bowlers could straighten their arms by 15 degrees during delivery – nothing less being visible to the naked eye – Muralitharan had been free to use his *doosra*, so Hair looked on, whether in despair or wonderment. Some one-time critics had been won over. Former England captain Nasser Hussain, now a television commentator, declared that "There is no shame in being bowled out by a genius." And the current Sri Lankan captain, Jayawardene, urged everyone to enjoy Muralitharan while they could; already 34, he might not tour England again.

England's target was 325 – more than they had ever made in a winning run-chase at home. Even so, Trescothick and Strauss started with such momentum that Sri Lanka had a nervy look about them. Their opening stand mounted to 84 before Trescothick failed to pick the *doosra* and was bowled. That began a sequence in which Muralitharan took eight for 26 in 105 balls.

Sri Lanka 231 and 322 (K. C. Sangakkara 66, C. K. Kapugedera 50; M. S. Panesar 5-78); **England 229 and 190** (A. J. Strauss 55; M. Muralitharan 8-70).

2006 – ENGLAND v PAKISTAN (FOURTH TEST): THE MURKY DEPTHS
Hugh Chevallier, 2007

At The Oval, August 17, 18, 19, 20, 2006. England were awarded the match when Pakistan refused to play. One day before the scheduled end of a Test series previously remarkable for a lack of serious controversy, cricket made up for lost time and plunged into crisis – and the water turned out to be deep, cold and very murky. Outraged at being punished for ball-tampering, the Pakistan team refused to take the field after tea and, in front of a full and voluble house, Darrell Hair, the senior of the two umpires, melodramatically removed the bails. The gesture brought a symbolic and actual end to the game, the first ever forfeited in 1,814 Tests and 129 years. It also unleashed a media frenzy that splashed cricket over the front pages for days.

The first signs of the impending turmoil came shortly after 2.30 on the fourth afternoon, when Trevor Jesty, the fourth umpire, brought out a box of balls. It was assumed that the current ball, 56 overs old, had gone out of shape through wear and tear. However, the choice of its replacement fell not to the umpires, but to the batsmen – an indication that the officials believed the ball had been doctored. Umpire Hair then slowly tapped his left shoulder with his right hand: five penalty runs were awarded to England's total. Without warning, without opportunity to defend themselves and without apparent thought to the ramifications, Pakistan were very publicly found guilty of cheating. Though visibly shocked, the Pakistan captain, Inzamam-ul-Haq, did not seem to dwell on the incident, and play continued until bad light forced the players off at 3.47. Several observers commended Inzamam for his restraint. Matters were about to change.

Almost an hour later, under brighter skies, the umpires took the field for the resumption. The England batsmen, Collingwood and Bell, appeared on the balcony, but the Pakistan players did not. A couple of minutes later, as umpires Hair and Doctrove returned to the pavilion, Inzamam briefly emerged from the dressing-room, shrugged his shoulders and went back in. At 4.55, the umpires, now joined by the batsmen, walked back to the middle. The Pakistan dressing-room door remained resolutely shut, and the umpires decided they had ceded the game.

Behind that closed door fervent diplomatic activity was taking place involving, among others, the ECB chairman David Morgan and Shaharyar Khan, his PCB counterpart. The Pakistan team, livid at what they saw as national humiliation, were eventually persuaded to abandon their protest and, at 5.23, Inzamam led his players on to the field. They spent a minute or two standing around then, in the absence of umpires, traipsed off. These various tableaux were acted out to a soundtrack of boos and jeers from spectators – most of them baffled as to what was actually happening – and a resounding silence from the Tannoy. Some in the crowd amused themselves by creating 40ft snakes of stacked plastic beer glasses before, at 6.13, the announcement came that play was called off for the day.

Not until four hours later was it confirmed that the Test really was over, and that England had won. The two boards, both teams and the referee, Mike Procter, had wanted to resume next morning, but the umpires objected. The ECB promised 40% refunds for the 20,000 spectators attending on Sunday, and full refunds for the 11,000 with tickets for Monday.

Hair, who had a track record of embracing controversy, was now accused of a heavy-handed approach on the field – why had he not had a quiet word with Inzamam about the ball? – and intransigence off it. He and Doctrove argued that, by not resuming after tea, the Pakistanis had irrevocably forfeited the match. The cricket may have stopped, but the revelations, recriminations and repercussions were just starting.

One crucial revelation was missing, however: the perpetrator of the crime. Not one of the 26 TV cameras at The Oval had captured any sign of ball-tampering. When charges were brought, they were against Inzamam as captain, rather than any individual, suggesting the umpires, too, had little evidence other than the state of the quarter-seam. But Inzamam was also charged with bringing the game into disrepute. Word leaked out that, if their captain were banned from the forthcoming one-day series, Pakistan might abandon the tour.

The biggest shock of the lot came five days later. ICC chief executive Malcolm Speed flew to London to release emails from Hair, who had gone to ground amid accusations that he was a racist. He had offered to resign from the elite panel of umpires – in return for $500,000. The Pakistan camp claimed vindication; others saw it as a huge error of judgment on Hair's part, though an even bigger act of betrayal by the ICC.

England 173 (Umar Gul 4-46, Mohammad Asif 4-56)
and 298-4 (K. P. Pietersen 96, A. N. Cook 83, A. J. Strauss 54);
Pakistan 504 (Mohammad Yousuf 128, Mohammad Hafeez 95, Imran Farhat 91; S. J. Harmison 4-125).

2008 – WHAT DUNCAN DID FOR US
Andrew Strauss, 2008

Following England's disastrous Ashes tour of 2006-07, Duncan Fletcher resigned as coach after almost eight years in the job.

To those who played under him there will always be a legacy, regardless of whether they got on with him personally or not. His ideas became so much of a blueprint for England cricket over the time he was in charge that I defy any recent player to stand up and say he didn't learn anything off Duncan Fletcher, whether he played one Test or a hundred.

His method was taken from business. He believed strongly in having a management group of senior players who would report problems to him and the captain, while feeding information back to team-mates from those in charge. At the same time he strongly believed in players learning to think for themselves, using him and other coaches more as consultants to their game, rather than being told what to do. He was particularly keen on analysis, but wasn't about to shove it down throats. It was very new and very different to a crop of players used to a coach occasionally telling them that their foot was getting too far across or their elbow wasn't high enough.

What Fletcher mainly did, however, was confront problems. Those who he felt did not buy into the team environment, or were unwilling to change their ways, found that they were surplus to requirements pretty quickly. In their place came the likes of Trescothick and Michael Vaughan. These were players who were picked out of county obscurity by a coach who believed they had the technique and temperament to succeed at the highest level.

More importantly they added to the team. Both brought bags of enthusiasm, were willing to train harder, and bought into the idea of taking the England team forward. Fletcher, meanwhile, was willing to stick his neck on the line for them. He was to be loyal to the death. In return he expected the absolute loyalty of those around him.

Over the years that Duncan was in charge huge changes were made to the set-up in terms of support personnel. He believed strongly that a world-class team needed to have a world-class support network behind it. Doctors, analysts, bowling coaches, psychologists, fitness gurus, physios and masseurs travelled with us everywhere by the time of his departure. How much effort it took for him to get all those positions in place with his employers is anyone's guess, but I suspect that there were some battles fought which the players were not privy to.

2007 – ENGLAND v INDIA (Second Test): Zaheer full of (jelly) beans
Ravi Shastri, 2008

At Nottingham, July 27, 28, 29, 30, 31, 2007. India won by seven wickets. This was one of India's finest away wins: only their 29th in all, in their 200th Test abroad. They bounced back after Lord's, without any cricket in between, and played as a team, aggressively when needed. Traditionally, India are slow starters and have often lost their opening Test in England. But whenever they have avoided defeat in that first game, they have gone on to win the series. Learning quickly, India were much tighter in their bowling, batting techniques and general application than at Lord's; only one catch was dropped, a chance offered by Tremlett to Tendulkar at first slip.

The behaviour of both sides came under the microscope as tempers frayed and it became clear that this would be a "result Test" which would probably decide the series. When tailender Zaheer Khan walked out to bat on the third evening, he found a couple of jelly beans in the batting crease. Incensed at this breach of manners – putting sweets and rubbish on the pitch was known in the county game but not international cricket – Zaheer brandished his bat at Pietersen, who denied any wrongdoing, and suspicion fell on Bell, who was fielding closer to the bat. It seems to have been a childish prank which got out of hand; newspapers called it

"Jellybeangate". Although England's coach, Peter Moores, did not condemn it during the game, Vaughan expressed regrets afterwards. "If we offended Zaheer in any way, we apologise, but there were no jelly beans thrown from the slip cordon," he said. From short leg, then? What is certain is that the incident fired up Zaheer to bowl his best in England's second innings, and his aggression rubbed off on his team-mates. England lost their final seven for 68 as the second new ball caused mayhem. Zaheer never had a better or more valuable day in Test cricket. India chased down their target of 73 on the final morning [and] went on to record only their fifth win in 47 Tests and 75 years of visiting England.

England 198 (Zaheer Khan 4-59) and 355 (M. P. Vaughan 124, P. D. Collingwood 63,

A. J. Strauss 55; Zaheer 5-75); India 481 (S. R. Tendulkar 91, S. C. Ganguly 79,

K. D. Karthik 77, W. Jaffer 62, V. V. S. Laxman 54; M. S. Panesar 4-101) and 73-3.

2008 – NEW ZEALANDERS IN ENGLAND: DUBIOUS PRIORITIES   Stephen Brenkley, 2009

The start of the tour epitomised the grim truth that there are haves and have-nots in world cricket and that New Zealand, because of their small population, their geographical isolation and the fact that rugby rules all, are firmly in the have-not category. Five of their players, including the captain Daniel Vettori, arrived a week late because New Zealand Cricket had given them permission to play in the opening rounds of the Indian Premier League. Vettori and the other four – Brendon McCullum, Jacob Oram, Kyle Mills and Ross Taylor – earned money in the glittering new Twenty20 competition that NZC could not hope to match. If it was odd for a third of the squad to miss the tour's first two matches because they were fulfilling other duties, it was a necessary compromise, regardless of the effect it might have on the rest of the dressing-room.

2008 – ENGLAND v SOUTH AFRICA (SECOND TEST): "ILLOGICAL, PATHETIC"
Chris Waters, 2009

At Leeds, July 18, 19, 20, 21, 2008. South Africa won by ten wickets. From the moment on the first morning when Yorkshire hastily withdrew scorecards that billed it as England v West Indies this was a remarkable Test even by Headingley's standards. No sooner had that mistake been corrected than another was committed; in one of the biggest bombshells in Test history, England handed a debut to Darren Pattinson, a 28-year-old former roof-tiler born in Grimsby, raised in Australia, and a veteran of only 11 first-class appearances, five of them for Victoria. What followed was England's worst performance since the 2006-07 Ashes, amid much condemnation for the selection of a player who admitted he had never aspired to represent them. Sir Ian Botham – looking on with Truemanesque indignation from the commentary box – described Pattinson's call-up as "the most illogical, pathetic and diabolical piece of selecting I've ever seen". Others were less charitable.

England 203 (D. W. Steyn 4-76) **and 327** (S. C. J. Broad 67*, A. N. Cook 60);
South Africa 522 (A. B. de Villiers 174, A. G. Prince 149) **and 9-0**.

2008 – ENGLAND v SOUTH AFRICA (THIRD TEST): SKIPPER-SLAYER SMITH
Scyld Berry, 2009

At Birmingham, July 30, 31, August 1, 2. South Africa won by five wickets. Graeme
Smith staged one of the all-time captain's innings to drive South Africa home on
the fourth evening and give his country their first series win in England since 1965.
It was a Test match of ever-increasing drama – a heroic duel between Kallis and
Flintoff, controversy over the sightscreen behind Flintoff's arm, a century by
Collingwood when his Test career was on the brink, and below-average umpiring
which compared unfavourably with the referrals system being trialled simultane-
ously in Sri Lanka. But in the end everything was dominated by Smith, who single-
mindedly and almost single-handedly led South Africa to the highest fourth-innings
Test total at Edgbaston, let alone the highest to win.

Five years before on this ground, Smith's 277 had precipitated the resignation
of Nasser Hussain in favour of Michael Vaughan. This time, his series-winning 154
precipitated the resignation of Vaughan. At lunchtime on what had been scheduled
as the fifth day, in an emotional press conference at Loughborough, Vaughan said:
"It is a fairytale to captain your country, but it hasn't had a fairytale ending. I know
it is the right time because my mind told me it was." The following day, Kevin
Pietersen was made England's captain in both Test and limited-overs cricket;
Collingwood had also decided to step down.

When England reduced South Africa to 93 for four, a target of 281 and the
highest fourth-innings total at Edgbaston seemed impossibly far away – except to
Smith. He had two advantages: the pitch remained easy-paced, and Sidebottom was
unfit again, operating at 80 not mid-80s mph. Panesar became overexcited at the
rough outside the left-hander's off stump, appealed too much and clearly received
a warning to calm down, so that when he appeared to have Smith caught off a glove
on 85 (and, earlier, Prince), the appeals were muted, and dismissed. He was also
called twice in an over for back-foot no-balls.

Smith was unperturbed by the rough, reaching forward to work Panesar
through the leg side and hitting the other danger man, Flintoff, mainly with front-
foot off-drives, for seven of his 17 fours. After Boucher had settled in, the fight
drained out of England with alarming speed, which no doubt convinced Vaughan
that he could take this team no further. The tourists, having silenced another
patriotic crowd, took the extra half hour. When Smith hit the winning four, off the
next England captain, he had scored his 154 from only 246 balls. Vaughan's end as
captain was as his beginning: defeat by South Africa.

England 231 (A. N. Cook 76, I. R. Bell 50)
and 363 (P. D. Collingwood 135, K. P. Pietersen 94; M. Morkel 4-97);
South Africa 314 (N. D. McKenzie 72, J. H. Kallis 64; A. Flintoff 4-89)
and 283-5 (G. C. Smith 154*).

2009 – AUSTRALIANS IN ENGLAND: JUST GOOD ENOUGH

Christopher Martin-Jenkins, 2010

The 2005 Ashes, with its high-octane cricket, sustained tension and vivid, unpredictable action, had been truly an unforgettable epic; four years later it was followed by an intriguing whodunnit, with as many twists and misleading clues as an Agatha Christie. The final oddity was that the losing team was the one with the stronger and more effective batting, especially once Kevin Pietersen had limped out after two Tests to have an operation on a damaged Achilles tendon. For the first time in more than 130 years of Test cricket, a side scoring six more individual hundreds than its opponents managed to lose the series. How do you explain that, Miss Marple? "If we've had a bad session we've had a really bad session," said Ponting. "When we were bad we were very bad, but when we were good we were just good enough," said Strauss.

2009 – ENGLAND v AUSTRALIA (FIRST TEST): SOUTHPAW HEROES

Steve James, 2010

At Cardiff, July 8, 9, 10, 11, 12. Drawn. Wales's first Test match was a triumph in every respect bar the provision of an England victory. But a thrilling draw, with England's last pair surviving 11.3 nerve-shredding overs, was more than ample consolation, another mini-epic to add to a lengthy list in Ashes history. The throbbing atmosphere lost little in comparison with even the greatest of rugby days at the nearby Millennium Stadium. But never before had English defiance been so fanatically cheered by the Welsh. Panesar lasted 35 balls, his partner Anderson 53; two southpaw heroes whose stumps were seldom threatened by the Australians bowlers. There was controversy, too. Twice in the closing stages England sent twelfth man Bilal Shafayat on to the field. On the second occasion he was accompanied by the stand-in physiotherapist Steve McCaig, an Australian. Even Anderson, obviously unhurt, looked embarrassed. The visitors accused England of time-wasting.

England 435 (K. P. Pietersen 69, P. D. Collingwood 64, M. J. Prior 56) and 252-9 (Collingwood 74); Australia 674-6 dec. (R. T. Ponting 150, M. J. North 125*, S. M. Katich 122, M. J. Clarke 83).

Little Wonder No. 53

Wisden 1953. Pennant for county champions: The Advisory County Cricket Committee adopted a resolution by Warwickshire that a Championship pennant be introduced to the competition. The pennant to be of triangular design and to show the crest of the champions on a white background. It could be flown the following season at all matches in which they were engaged.

2009 – ENGLAND v AUSTRALIA (Second Test): the 75-year itch
Hugh Chevallier, 2010

At Lord's, July 16, 17, 18, 19, 20, 2009. England won by 115 runs. Shortly before lunch on the last day Swann, who had been giving his off-breaks a tempting flight, saw Johnson advancing and darted an arm-ball in faster. It beat the bat, crashed into middle, and, as Lord's went up in ecstasy, the Australian fortress came down in ruins. For the first time since June 1934, when Hedley Verity crafted 15 wickets with his left-arm spin on a wet pitch, Australia had lost an Ashes Test at HQ – an event as rare as a sighting of Halley's Comet, which also comes once every 75 years.

It was just one match, one victory, with three Tests left, but it felt danger-ously as though the Ashes were reclaimed already. Even in the heady days of 2005, England came a cropper here. Now they had won, and won handsomely. England's cricketers, none more prominently than Flintoff, appeared on almost every front page.

Beforehand, Flintoff was also the talk of the back pages. On the eve of the match, he announced that his creaking body (especially the right knee he had injured during the IPL in April) had told him the Ashes would be his Test swansong. Ponting, ever on the watch for a psychological stick with which to beat his oppo-nents, said a four-Test farewell could only distract England. From the available evidence, he could not have been more wrong.

A galvanised Flintoff, driven by his last chance of glory at Lord's, produced one of the most relentlessly hostile spells by an England bowler for a generation. For someone with just one serviceable knee, it was astonishing. Flintoff, who pitched too short in the first innings, was deadliest on the last morning. Thanks to an iron-willed fightback by Clarke and Haddin, Australia had recovered from 128 for five to begin the day at 313, still five down. The sun was shining, the pitch true, and condi-tions for batting the best Australia enjoyed all match. Their target was the small matter of 522 (nine more than the highest winning fourth-innings total in all first-class cricket), but the unbeaten stand of 185 had instilled doubts – Strauss admitted to a poor night's sleep. Flintoff, sporting aggression made flesh, thundered in; not once in his first over of the day did he fall below 90mph. Unsure whether the ball would move down the slope, Haddin edged low to Collingwood at second slip. Flintoff then told his captain he was staying on until the last wicket fell. "It seemed a good plan to me," said Strauss.

The session belonged to Flintoff, who bowled all ten overs from the Pavilion end at a ferocious pace, honouring his word to his captain but horrifying the medical staff. Twice he demolished the stumps with unplayable balls that swung in and jagged down the slope. Siddle's wicket gave Flintoff a coveted Lord's five-for, only his third in any Test.

England 425 (A. J. Strauss 161, A. N. Cook 95; B. W. Hilfenhaus 4-103)
and 311-6 dec. (M. J. Prior 61, P. D. Collingwood 54);
Australia 215 (M. E. K. Hussey 51; J. M. Anderson 4-55)
and 406 (M. J. Clarke 136; B. J. Haddin 80, M. G. Johnson 63; A. Flintoff 5-92, G. P. Swann 4-87).

2010 – ENGLAND v BANGLADESH (SECOND ONE-DAY INTERNATIONAL):
UNSPOILT JOY   Julian Guyer, 2011

At Bristol, July 10. Bangladesh won by five runs. As Strauss pointed out later, it was inevitable that Bangladesh would one day defeat England. But, after Nottingham, few would have foreseen a victory that ended a run of 24 losses in all formats since they beat Zimbabwe in November. Bell was unable to bat at No. 3 after breaking his left foot in a forlorn attempt at a leaping catch. But England had picked an extra batsman in Trott, and a target of 237 should not have been difficult. This time, though, they not only lost early wickets but continued to lose them as the ball did not quite come on to the bat. Only Trott held firm, but he seemed unable to change gear against accurate bowling. Most of the impetus in the final powerplay came from Broad, until he was caught by a leaping Shakib Al Hasan off Mashrafe bin Mortaza, who then caught and bowled Anderson. Some Bangladesh players began celebrating but had to be calmed down; Bell, wearing a surgical boot and with Morgan as his runner, limped out with England needing ten off the last over and Trott on strike. Two twos followed before Trott, whose 94 took 130 balls, was caught behind off Shafiul Islam, sparking scenes of unspoilt joy in a Bangladesh side well worth this win.

Bangladesh 236-7 (50 overs) (Imrul Kayes 76; A. Shahzad 3-41);
England 231 (49.3 overs) (I. J. L. Trott 94).

2010 – PAKISTANIS IN ENGLAND: SUMMER OF SHAME   Stephen Brenkley, 2011

The storm broke on the eve of the fourth day of the Fourth Test. It was never to recede. Until that moment, it had all been going so well – or as well as could have been expected, considering the deeply unpromising beginnings.

After assuming the Pakistan captaincy upon Shahid Afridi's sudden resignation in July, Salman Butt had helped to engineer a Test win against Australia. Following two heavy defeats by England in the next couple of weeks, he had overseen another unexpected victory to make it 2–1 with one Test remaining. So there was all to play for at Lord's in the final match. It began wonderfully for Pakistan, with their 18-year-old fast bowler Mohammad Aamer initially irresistible, putting the seal on a summer he had illuminated and which augured a golden future.

All that changed overnight. The rest of the season – and indeed what had gone before – was overshadowed by a startling report in the *News of the World* which emerged on Saturday night accusing Pakistan of bowling no-balls to order during England's first innings. The newspaper named Aamer and his new-ball colleague Mohammad Asif, and claimed they had acted with the collusion of their captain, Butt. It alleged that undercover reporters, posing as businessmen who wished to be involved in a purported scam taking advantage of illegal Asian betting markets, paid a middleman £150,000 to ensure that the deliveries were bowled at pre-arranged moments.

The allegations provoked a furore. There were immediate fears that the match itself would be unfinished and the tour cancelled there and then. Both went ahead. In an eerie, sepulchral atmosphere on Sunday morning, England duly completed an innings victory to win the series 3–1. Celebrations were muted and the mood sombre. The presentation ceremony was transferred from the Lord's outfield to the privacy of the Long Room. It supplied an enduring image which embodied the turn of events. Giles Clarke, the ECB chairman handing out the gongs, could not bring himself to shake the hand of Aamer, who had entranced audiences throughout the summer, as he stepped forward to receive his Man of the Series award.

Such a calculated snub was a measure not only of Clarke's response to the newspaper allegations but also of deep personal hurt. Clarke had long championed Pakistan's cause and had been instrumental in their being invited to England to play their series against Australia, which could not be staged at home because of fears of terrorism. As head of the ICC task force established to help cricket in Pakistan, he took his duties seriously. The tour limped on, though nobody's heart was in it. Open season was declared on the game in general and Pakistan in particular. The issue of corruption, always lurking on the undercard, was back at the top of the bill. Speculation, most of it without compelling evidence, mounted that it was rife. Both Ijaz Butt, the chairman of the Pakistan Cricket Board, and Wajid Shamsul Hasan, the country's High Commissioner in London, attempted to defend their players.

Later in the week Salman Butt, Asif and Aamer withdrew from the squad, citing mental torture. They made their decision just in time; it was clear that England were reluctant to continue with them present. All three were then provisionally suspended by the ICC pending the outcome of both the criminal investigation by the Metropolitan Police, to which the *News of the World* had handed its dossier, and the ICC's own inquiry. The trio were charged with various breaches of its anti-corruption code and warned that, if found guilty, life bans could ensue. (In the event, on February 5, 2011, the three were given five-year bans, while Butt was given another five years suspended, and Asif two years suspended.) No matter the outcome of the eventual hearings, it seemed to be an example of the governing body wishing to be seen governing.

2010 – ENGLAND v PAKISTAN (Fourth Test): OVER THE LIMIT
Scyld Berry, 2011

At Lord's, August 26, 27, 28, 29, 2010. England won by an innings and 225 runs. The last Test of England's previous home series against Pakistan had ended in the first forfeiture in the history of Test cricket. The last Test of this England series against Pakistan was even more controversial.

The first two alleged transgressions, later to be proven in the eyes of the ICC's independent tribunal, occurred on the rain-interrupted opening day when play was limited to 12.3 overs in the afternoon. At 1.56pm Aamer delivered a no-ball as the first ball of his second over from the Pavilion end – the third over of England's innings – as predicted. The left-armer was a foot beyond the line of the popping crease, a remarkable distance. Moreover, the fact that he no-balled at all was unusual: in the three previous Tests of the series Aamer had bowled only three no-balls in total. Aamer spent time examining the spikes of his right boot, and scraping some mud off them, but the amount was minimal: the fine Lord's drainage system had done its work. His captain Salman Butt brought some sawdust in his cupped hands from the pile near the start of Aamer's run-up. But the ground did not appear to have been slippery, and Aamer's front foot had landed firmly. From the Nursery end, Asif delivered a no-ball for what would have been the last ball of his fifth over, although only by a small margin later to be measured as two inches. After Strauss had pushed the ball to point for a single, Butt again brought up sawdust for the bowler to spread around the crease. Asif was later reported to have said he was making an extra effort: the illegal delivery was timed at 80.2mph, 0.8mph faster than his average speed in this opening spell.

On the second morning, dry and cloudy, Aamer began with a superlative spell of swing bowling in which, for the first time in England's history, their Nos 4, 5 and 6 all made nought. However, after Butt had walked up to Aamer at the start of his run and talked, without any change being made in the field, Aamer's third ball of his third full over of the day – the 19th of England's innings – was a no-ball. Again he was about a foot past the popping crease, and prompted the Sky TV commentator Michael Holding to say: "How far over was that? Wow!"

Aamer's second no-ball was a bouncer at Trott – and all the more threatening for being delivered well over the line and that much closer to the batsman. Trott only just managed to fend it away for a single. He could have been injured. Part of Butt's subsequent defence was that he and Aamer wanted to stop Trott pushing forward to reduce the swing.

These controversial no-balls overshadowed some of the finest cricket played at Lord's in recent times. Trott found a partner in Broad, who joined him in what became a Test-record partnership of 332 for the eighth wicket. By the close of the second day, the stand between Trott and Broad was only two short of England's previous record of 246, by Les Ames and Gubby Allen against New Zealand in 1931, and Lord's was almost intoxicated with delight at this fighting spirit being shown in the last Test before the Ashes. Broad had also joined two Middlesex players, Allen and John Murray, in becoming only the third No. 9 to score a Test century for England. Such was his calmness, there was no guessing that Broad's hundred was his first in Test or county cricket, and only the second of his life.

England 446 (I. J. L. Trott 184, S. C. J. Broad 169; Mohammad Aamer 6-84); **Pakistan 74** (G. P. Swann 4-12) **and 147** (Umar Akmal 79*; Swann 5-62).

2011 – INDIANS IN ENGLAND: THE PINNACLE
Andrew Miller, 2012

In 134 years of Test history, it is doubtful whether any contest between two apparently well-matched teams has turned out to be so spectacularly one-sided. India arrived as the world's No. 1 Test team and recently crowned 50-over champions. They left, two months later, without a single international victory in ten attempts across three formats, and – following a 4–0 whitewash – with the ICC Test mace now in the hands of their opponents. It was India's heaviest beating since 1991-92, when they lost by the same margin in Australia, though in a five-match series.

The overwhelming story of the summer ought to have been England's ascent to the top of the Test rankings. In 31 matches since Andrew Strauss and Andy Flower were confirmed as a partnership in April 2009, they had racked up 20 wins, the same number England had managed in the whole of the 1980s. And yet the tale of India's decline was just as compelling. They competed gamely, but unevenly, for the first seven days of the series, only for England's superior fitness and resolve to muscle them out of the big moments. By the third evening of the Second Test, the rout was well and truly on. When Alastair Cook batted almost 13 hours for 294 in the Third, at Edgbaston, he was only six runs short of India's highest total of the series.

Dravid's aggregate of 461 runs at 76 included one of the most heroically futile performances of all time. By carrying his bat for 146 in the first innings at The Oval, he enabled India to reach 300 for the only time in the four Tests. Ten minutes later, he was marching out again in the follow-on. His magnificence was India's only saving grace. But once again he found himself playing second fiddle in the public's affections to Tendulkar, whose continuing quest for his 100th international hundred was perhaps the most poignant expression of India's struggles.

Tendulkar was also 38, and his fifth tour of England was widely presumed to be his last. Each of his eight innings was accompanied by two standing ovations: the first full of expectation, the second tinged invariably with regret. He managed only 273 runs at 34, with a best of 91 at The Oval, where the crowd's ardour was dampened by an lbw decision from Rod Tucker – tight, but fair, according to the DRS technology that India had refused to endorse. Tendulkar slipped silently out of the country a fortnight later, when the recurrence of an old toe injury ruled him out of the limited-overs games.

India's lone stance on umpiring technology – essentially, they distrusted the predictive element of Hawk-Eye – cast a shadow over the series, and appeared to conform to the old playground truism that the boy who brings the bat sets the rules.

2011 – ENGLAND v INDIA (First Test): WAITING FOR SACHIN

Steven Lynch, 2012

At Lord's, July 21, 22, 23, 24, 25, 2011. England won by 196 runs. This was a match full of outstanding figures, as befitted the 2,000th Test and the 100th between England and India. But an even more magical number never happened: Tendulkar went into the game with 99 international centuries and left with his highest score from five Tests at Lord's still only 37. England, who dominated after a hesitant start, closed in on another important figure: India's No. 1 Test ranking. And they did so in front of a last-day crowd of 27,728 – perhaps the most vivid number of the lot.

The early exchanges went India's way. But Zaheer's third spell brought a summer-changing moment: in his 14th over, he grimaced, felt the back of his right leg, and trudged out of the match – and, it transpired, the series – with hamstring trouble. The release of tension was palpable. When bad light and rain ended play soon afterwards, England had lost only two wickets in testing conditions.

India's problems meant Dhoni became the first wicketkeeper in 123 Lord's Tests to take off his pads and bowl. Kapil Dev, India's other World Cup-winning captain, grumbled that Dhoni was "demeaning Test cricket", but he bowled at a respectable medium-pace, had a good lbw shout against Pietersen first ball, and actually had him given out caught behind by his stand-in, Dravid, for 73 in his next over, only for the decision to be overturned on review when Hot Spot failed to show an edge.

India were left 458 to win in what became 125 overs. The final morning saw huge queues around the ground. Many did not make it in, but the majority of those who did were Indian supporters and youngsters (under-16s were admitted free), which created an unusual atmosphere at cricket's headquarters – mainly of the party variety, although England were booed by a section of the crowd during their warm-up.

Tendulkar had been absent for much of the fourth day, nursing a viral infection and spending so much time off the field that he was not permitted to bat until around 12.30. Right on cue, Laxman short-armed a long-hop to midwicket, and Tendulkar received another huge ovation. He almost went straight back, Anderson's first ball snaking between bat and pad, before a flick to the square-leg boundary eased the tension slightly. But Gambhir fell in the next over, another left-handed lbw victim for Swann, and Tendulkar ground to a halt after lunch. He was stuck on 11 for 38 balls and 47 minutes, during which he was lbw to Broad but – to the bowler's evident exasperation – given not out by umpire Bowden (unchallenged, because it had been agreed not to use the DRS for lbws). Then, after Tendulkar broke the stalemate with a single to fine leg, the crowd gasped when Strauss dropped him at first slip off Anderson. It was not expensive: two balls later he was struck right in front again, this time playing no stroke, as Anderson zipped one back in. It was the only wicket of the afternoon session, but a vital one.

The last four wickets tumbled in 29 balls. England's win – with nearly 30 overs to spare – was their 35th in 100 Tests against India, but their 11th in 16 meetings at Lord's, where India have won only once. Dhoni was philosophical: "Most of the things that could have gone wrong in the game went wrong."

England 474 (K. P. Pietersen 202*, M. J. Prior 71, I. J. L. Trott 70)
and 269-6 dec. (Prior 103*, S. C. J. Broad 74*); India 286 (R. Dravid 103*; Broad 4-37)
and 261 (S. K. Raina 78, V. V. S. Laxman 56; J. M. Anderson 5-65).

2011 – ENGLAND v INDIA (Second Test): GRAND GESTURE Dean Wilson, 2012

At Nottingham, July 29, 30, 31, August 1, 2011. England won by 319 runs. India's act of sportsmanship in recalling Bell, who had been legitimately – if controversially – run out from the last ball before tea on the third day, was as generous as it was diplomatic. And though the debate it reignited about the spirit of cricket contained its usual dose of idealism, the gesture undoubtedly avoided souring everything that followed.

As the players re-emerged after the break, the boos from a crowd that had unfairly discerned Indian skulduggery quickly turned to cheers once it was clear Bell had been reinstated. Dhoni later explained the dismissal "did not feel right". And while his change of heart had little impact on a game won with ease by an England side that went from resilient to rampant in claiming a 2–0 lead, it ensured him a place in cricket's pantheon of sporting gestures. Even the hat-trick taken by Broad the previous day was forgotten amid the drama. But that may have been little consolation for Dhoni, who for the first time in 29 Tests as captain had presided over successive defeats, and twice watched his side squander strong positions.

The unvarnished truth was that Bell did not necessarily deserve his Sunday-afternoon let-off. Having played exquisitely for his 15th Test century, he switched off after completing a third run following Morgan's flick to long leg. Wrongly assuming Kumar had failed to prevent the ball from touching the boundary, Bell wandered up the pitch to congratulate his team-mate and head off for tea. Kumar, apparently unsure himself whether he had saved the four, casually threw the ball to Dhoni, who underarmed it to Mukund, standing over the stumps at the striker's end. Mukund removed the bails and quietly appealed.

It had been so different on the opening day, when India – after winning another good toss – took control in conditions tailor-made for swing and seam. But from 124 for eight, Broad and Swann – both of Nottinghamshire – counter-attacked, adding 73 in 70 balls, before Broad and Anderson took the total to an almost-respectable 221.

Gambhir's replacement Yuvraj – badly dropped by Pietersen in the gully on four – helped Dravid take the score to 267 for four after tea. Enter Broad, this time to change the game for good. Armed with the second new ball, he produced a spell of five wickets for no run in 16 balls, including a hat-trick – the 12th in Tests by an England bowler, the first on home soil for 16 years and the first by any side against India. Criticised during the Sri Lanka series for pitching too short, Broad had rediscovered the virtue of getting the ball up to the bat.

England 221 (S. C. J. Broad 64) **and 544** (I. R. Bell 159, T. T. Bresnan 90, M. J. Prior 73, E. J. G. Morgan 70, K. P. Pietersen 63; P. Kumar 4-124); **India 288** (R. Dravid 117, Yuvraj Singh 62, V. V. S. Laxman 54; Broad 6-46) **and 158** (S. R. Tendulkar 56; Bresnan 5-48).

Wisden **1954.** County secretaries' meeting: Mr R. Aird, secretary of MCC, said: "While being a supporter of television I am very conscious of its great danger to counties who play matches at the same time as Test matches which are being televised, and for that reason those of us who have considered this question believe that hours of transmission must still be limited on all but the third days of such county matches. The fees at present received for television are nothing like big enough to compensate counties for the loss of gate-money."

Little Wonder No. 54

2012 – ENGLAND v SOUTH AFRICA (First Test): ANNIHILATION

Hugh Chevallier, 2013

At The Oval, July 19, 20, 21, 22, 23, 2012. South Africa won by an innings and 12 runs. On a warm Sunday evening, a beery roar spread across the ground: four blokes in yellow jerseys and fake sideburns were basking in vicarious glory after news arrived from Paris that the real Bradley Wiggins – also sporting a yellow jersey, but more authentic facial hair – had been officially crowned as the first Briton to win the Tour de France.

Spectators were in the mood for applause, since they had seen a tour de force themselves. There are few clearer proofs of a batsman's mental strength or physical adaptability than a Test triple-century, and minutes earlier Hashim Amla had become the first South African to breathe such rarefied air. For at least four reasons it was a genuinely great achievement: with Petersen gone for nought, it was born in adversity; it came away from home against the team rated best in the world; it was an innings of real beauty, with shots played all round the wicket, off front foot and back; and, like only nine of the previous 25 Test triples, it would lead to victory. In fact it led to more than that: it led to annihilation. No one was sure when England had been so utterly outflanked, though Hastings in 1066 was a possibility. In losing by an innings, Strauss's team scraped just two wickets, and one of those – Smith bowled via bat and pad – was a touch fluky.

England 385 (A. N. Cook 115, I. J. L. Trott 71, M. J. Prior 60; M. Morkel 4-72)
and 240 (I. R. Bell 55; D. W. Steyn 5-56);
South Africa 637-2 dec. (H. M. Amla 311*, J. H. Kallis 182*, G. C. Smith 131).

2012 – ENGLAND v SOUTH AFRICA (SECOND TEST): CRYPTIC SELF-PITY

Lawrence Booth, 2013

At Leeds, August 2, 3, 4, 5, 6, 2012. Drawn. An absorbing Test was played out against the weird and not-so-wonderful backdrop of the Kevin Pietersen saga. Or was it the other way round? By the end – as Pietersen followed a typically dazzling 149 on Saturday afternoon with a Monday-evening press conference full of cryptic self-pity – it was hard to say: the distinction between plot and subplot had become hopelessly blurred. And with the Olympic athletes down in joyful London resembling one big happy family, the dysfunctional England dressing-room felt depressingly out of kilter.

The facts, though, were these: needing victory to stand a chance of extending their sequence of Test series wins at home to a record eight, England could manage only a draw, despite briefly threatening something extraordinary on the final day, the fifth in succession to be interrupted by rain or bad light. Pietersen then announced that the Third Test at Lord's – on which England's No. 1 ranking now depended – could well be his last, following a breakdown in relations with his team-mates. When it emerged later in the week that he had sent text messages to the South Africans for which he subsequently felt the need to apologise, he was dropped anyway. Really, you couldn't make it up.

South Africa 419 (A. N. Petersen 182, G. C. Smith 52)
and 258-9 dec. (J. A. Rudolph 69, Smith 52; S. C. J. Broad 5-69);
England 425 (K. P. Pietersen 149, M. J. Prior 68) and 130-4.

Other Countries

AUSTRALIA

Wisden's relationship with Australia is as old as the book itself. The first edition contained scores of The English Eleven against The Victoria Eighteen. The second edition, in 1865, contained the results of George Parr's tour of Australia and New Zealand in 1863-64 and praised "his great judgment in match-making, always choosing the best men that can be procured, and invariably doing the best he can to add fresh laurels to his renowned Eleven". But they missed the big story. Despite publishing a valedictory note in the 1877 edition to James Lillywhite's touring side, which appeared at the bottom of a page listing "The four English twelves who have visited Australia", there were no reports of the games which would become recognised as the first Test matches. It was left to Gordon Ross in the 1976 edition, which celebrated the forthcoming Centenary Test between Australia and England at Melbourne in March 1977, to reprise the early history.

Wisden has always cared primarily about how English sides perform overseas, particularly in Australia, and there are rarely grey areas in Ashes tour reports. The 1920-21 whitewash by Warwick Armstrong's side was a "disaster"; the 1954-55 come-from-behind victory was a triumph for the "skilful and zealous captaincy of Len Hutton"; England's 3–1 series defeat in 1998-99, their sixth successive Ashes loss, "could have been 5–0"; similarly, in 2010-11 when England won their first series in Australia for 24 years, Mark Nicholas wrote that the scoreline "barely did justice to England's superiority and certainly flattered Australia".

The only thing that Wisden has cared about more than whether England were any good was the spirit of fair play. Pages were devoted to an umpiring row at Sydney in 1878-79 during a match between Lord Harris's English Eleven and New South Wales. Letters were exchanged – and leaked to the British papers – and all printed in full in Wisden. Bodyline, of course, was the biggest Anglo-Australian rumpus, and one that threatened the very essence of the international relationship. The cables between MCC and the Australian board were published at length. While acknowledging the Adelaide Test "as probably the most unpleasant ever played", Wisden suspected that the Australians were exaggerating the gravity of the situation. But in his analysis of "the bowling controversy", the editor Sydney Southerton concluded that, judging by the number of Australian complaints, "they cannot all be wrong". In the 2013 edition Murray Hedgcock's story of the Cricket Reporting Agency, which provided so much of Wisden's content between 1887 and 1965, explains how Southerton was making his judgments "sight unseen", from Britain rather than

Australia, while the CRA's man on the ground "kept strictly to his brief to refrain from comment".

The greatness of the modern Australian teams has been covered with relish and reverence in *Wisden*, but their aggression was not to everyone's taste. Scyld Berry wrote of the 2002-03 Ashes: "Throughout the series some of the sledging, led by Hayden and Justin Langer, was all too obvious. If Waugh's team generated the same admiration as the Invincibles, they did not prompt quite the same public affection." That affection was tested to the limit in 2007-08 following the racism allegations involving Andrew Symonds and the Indian spinner Harbhajan Singh. "Up and down the country, there was an outpouring of anger at the disposition of the Australian side," Greg Baum wrote. When it came to the controversy of Kerry Packer's World Series Cricket, the editor Norman Preston was open-minded enough to write "the public will pronounce the verdict".

Australian players have been filling the pages of *Wisden* through word and deed since the beginning. The quick bowlers J. J. Ferris and Charlie "Terror" Turner were among Six Great Bowlers of the Year chosen in 1889, the inauguration of what became the annual Cricketers of the Year award. In all 71 players have been chosen following their achievements for Australia; the next most-represented country is South Africa, with 29. In the 2013 edition the recently retired Ricky Ponting's career was celebrated by Gideon Haigh. But Australian cricketers have also been great contributors to the book itself, not least Don Bradman, a great Wisdenphile, who wrote two articles, both of which are extracted earlier in this anthology.

1876-77 ANTIPODEAN ADVENTURE   1877

This [James Lillywhite's] team left England on the 21st of September, 1876. They steamed away from Southampton on calm water and under a sunny summer-like sky, roars of good hearty English cheers from shore wishing them "God speed". The Compiler of this book hopes they have had a pleasant voyage out; wishes them a successful career in Australia, and trusts they will have a safe return home to Old England.

1876-77 – AUSTRALIA v ENGLAND (FIRST TEST): BRILLIANT BANNERMAN
Gordon Ross, 1976

At Melbourne, March 15, 16, 17, 19, 1877. Charles Bannerman did not commit his name to history purely because he scored the first run in a Test match – he happened to make 165. Both sides were very much below full strength. W. G. Grace was missing to begin with. These early Australian tours were organised by private individuals, and until MCC took over the management of official touring teams in 1903-04, the sides were never fully representative. But the same can be said of Australia. Evans, Allen and Spofforth all declined to play, the latter stating categorically that the absence of Murdoch to keep wicket was his reason for refusing to take part.

Bannerman's was a truly remarkable performance. He scored 165 before retiring hurt after receiving a blow on the hand; the next-highest score by an Australian was 18 – and this by Garrett, the No. 9. A collection was taken to mark Bannerman's feat, and it raised one pound a run. England needed 154 to win and were favourites to get them, but they were shattered by the bowling of Kendall. England's first four batsmen totalled 79 between them; the other seven contributed only 24. Australia had won by 45 runs.

Australia 245 (C. Bannerman 165*) and 104 (A. Shaw 5-38);
England 196 (H. Jupp 63, W. E. Midwinter 5-78) and 108 (T. K. Kendall 7-55).

1876-77 – AUSTRALIA v ENGLAND (Second Test): English revenge
Gordon Ross, 1976

At Melbourne, March 31, April 2, 3, 4, 1877. So nettled were the English party that they were anxious to arrange another match on level terms (11 players each side) and this was done. On Saturday, March 31, 1877, and the Monday, Tuesday and Wednesday following, England met the Combined Australians on the Melbourne Ground. This time, Mr Spofforth sank his differences, and was in the Australian team, and with his presence in their side the local public predicted a second victory. But England won by four wickets, due principally to the splendid batting of George Ulyett, who scored 52 in the first innings and 63 in the next. This time the Australian public accused England of kidding in the first match in order to obtain another game and another gate. On a previous occasion when Spofforth and Evans had bowled the side out for 35, and in the next innings Armitage scored 38, a critic asked: "How can they be playing square, when they make only 35 one day between all of them, and on another day one man makes more than the whole of the team put together?"

Australia 122 (A. Hill 4-27) and 259 (J. Lillywhite 4-70, J. Southerton 4-46);
England 261 (G. Ulyett 52; T. K. Kendall 4-82) and 122-6 (Ulyett 63).

1878-79 –NEW SOUTH WALES XI v ENGLISH XI: THE DISTURBANCE   1880

At Sydney, February 7, 8, 10, 1879. Being in a minority of 90 runs, the NSW men, in due course, "followed on". Nineteen runs had been made, 10 of them by Murdoch, when an appeal to Coulthard, the umpire, resulted in Murdoch being run out, then arose The Disturbance that *The Australasian* remarked would "for ever make the match memorable in the annals of New South Wales cricket". It appears that on the decision being given Murdoch (like a true cricketer) retired; whereupon arose cries of "Not Out!" – "Go back, Murdoch!" – "Another Umpire!" and so on. The crowd rushed to the wickets, and, stated *The Australasian*, "rowdyism became rampant for the rest of the afternoon". The eleven Englishmen were surrounded by a rough and excited mob, who prevented further cricket being played that day.

English XI 267 (A. N. Hornby 67, G. Ulyett 55, A. P. Lucas 51; E. Evans 5-62, F. R. Spofforth 5-93);
New South Wales XI 177 (W. L. Murdoch 82; T. Emmett 8-47) and 49 (Emmett 6-21).

1882-83 – AUSTRALIA v ENGLAND (Third Test): Series secured   1884

At Sydney, January 26, 27, 29, 30, 1883. The first match having resulted in a win for the Australian eleven by nine wickets, and the second in a victory for the Englishmen by an innings and 27 runs, the third contest was invested with extraordinary interest, and on the opening day the attendance was the largest ever witnessed on the Moore Park ground, it being computed that from 20,000 to 23,000 spectators were present.

Murdoch's team was set the task of scoring 123 to win, and in the little time left for play before stumps were drawn for the day Morley bowled four overs and Barlow three, without a run being scored or a wicket lost. At 11.10 on the Tuesday the game was resumed in splendid weather. Giffen was clean-bowled at 11, and Bannerman, the other overnight not-out, caught at point at 12. Murdoch was caught at 18, and without any runs being added, McDonnell fell to a splendid catch at point. Horan was run out at 30 and Massie was caught at 33. Blackham hit with great vigour. He lost the company of Bonnor – clean bowled – at 59, and Spofforth – caught – at 72, and then played a ball on to his wicket at 80. Garrett, the last man, came in, and when two leg-byes and a wide had been scored, Barlow bowled him, and the innings terminated for 83, the Englishmen thus winning the match by 69 runs.

England (Hon. Ivo Bligh's Team) 247 (W. W. Read 66, E. F. S. Tylecote 66; F. R. Spofforth 4-73)
and 123 (Spofforth 7-44);
Australia (Mr Murdoch's XI) 218 (A. C. Bannerman 94; F. Morley 4-47) and 83 (R. G. Barlow 7-40).

Bligh's team won the series and the Ashes – the concept of which had been born at The Oval in 1882 – 2–1, before a fourth match was played at Sydney, which the Australians won.

1884-85 – SHAW'S TEAM IN AUSTRALIA: all about money   1886

From the moment the members of Murdoch's team landed from the "Mirzapore", prior to the commencement of the third match, it became evident they were animated by a feeling of bitter hostility towards Shaw and his party. As a commencement, the Victoria contingent of the team declined to play for their Colony against the Englishmen, urging as an excuse their want of practice, while it afterwards transpired that Murdoch's eleven had endeavoured to arrange a match with New South Wales on the same days as those fixed for the contest between Shaw's team and Victoria. Next, Murdoch and A. Bannerman refused to take part in the match New South Wales v Shaw's Eleven, and after the South Australian Cricket Association had succeeded in bringing about a meeting between Shaw's team and Murdoch's eleven at Adelaide, each side receiving £450, the climax of the quarrel was reached when Murdoch's men declined to play for Combined Australia against the Englishmen on New Year's Day. This unpatriotic conduct was severely condemned by the public and press of Australia, as the following will show:

"At a luncheon given at Adelaide during a cricket match on New Year's Day the Attorney-General of South Australia (the Hon. C. C. Kingston) said that he could not let the occasion pass, as a lover of the game for itself, without referring to the conduct of the Australian eleven, who appeared to sink everything for monetary considerations. If the cricketing public of Australia were to allow the game to be sacrificed for money it would be a national calamity from a cricket point of view. (Applause.)"

1886-87 – AUSTRALIA v ENGLAND (First Test): IMPROBABLE
COMEBACK   1888

At Sydney, January 28, 29, 31, 1887. The great match, and also the most conspicuous triumph of the tour, the Englishmen winning by 13 runs, after being dismissed in their first innings for a total of 45. When stumps were drawn on the Saturday they did not seem to have even a remote chance of success, being only some 20-odd runs to the good with three wickets to fall in their second innings. On the Monday, however, they played up in splendid style, and gained a victory that might fairly be compared to the seven-runs win of Australia over England at Kennington Oval in 1882. Briggs, Flowers, and Sherwin batted so well that Australia had to go in with 111 to get to win. With the wicket in very fair order this seemed an easy task, and defeat was not thought of, but Barnes bowled so finely, and was so ably supported by Lohmann, that the total only reached 97. Barring one mistake the English fielding was magnificent.

England (Shaw's Team) 45 (G. A. Lohmann 17; C. T. B. Turner 6-15, J. J. Ferris 4-27)
and 184 (J. Briggs 33, W. Barnes 32; Ferris 5-76);
Australia 119 (H. Moses 31, S. P. Jones 31) and 97 (Moses 24; Barnes 6-28)

England's first-innings total of 45 remains their lowest in Test cricket.

Gloucestershire v Derbyshire. At Cheltenham, August 11, 12, 1954. Derbyshire achieved the rare feat of gaining first-innings lead before lunch on the opening day. On a drying pitch, Jackson, Gladwin and Morgan routed Gloucestershire [*43 all out*] in 70 minutes.

Little Wonder No. 55

1891-92 – AUSTRALIA v ENGLAND (SECOND TEST): UPHILL TRIUMPH   1893

At Sydney, January 29, 30, February 1, 2, 3, 1892. The second of the three big matches produced one of the finest performances in the history of Australian cricket, a performance, indeed, fully comparable to the seven-runs victory at The Oval in 1882, or the great, but unsuccessful fight on the same ground in 1880.

The Australians proved victorious by 72 runs, and it can safely be said that the records of first-class cricket furnish few instances of a finer uphill game. Up to the end of the second day everything went in favour of the Englishmen. Thanks to Lohmann's bowling and Abel's batting, they gained indeed so commanding an advantage that the match seemed as good as over. The close of an innings on each side had left them with a lead of 163, and the Australians, on going in for the second time, lost Trott's wicket for a single run. Abel's superb innings of 132 not out lasted five hours. Only once before had anyone taken his bat right through the innings in an England and Australia match.

On the third day, there came an extraordinary change in the cricket, Lyons, Bannerman, and George Giffen batting with such success that it took the Englishmen all the afternoon to obtain two wickets. On the fourth day the weather was unsettled and rain considerably affected the wicket. Everything went wrong with the Englishmen, who made several bad mistakes in the field. The Australians' innings closed for 391, and the Englishmen, wanting 229 to win, had to go in when the ground was in a very treacherous state. The innings was finished off for 156, Australia winning the game by 72 runs, and so gaining the rubber in the Test matches. Bannerman's innings of 91 had much to do with the victory. At the finish of the game, there was a scene of almost indescribable enthusiasm.

Australia 144 (G. A. Lohmann 8-58)
and 391 (J. J. Lyons 134, A. C. Bannerman 91, W. Bruce 72; J. Briggs 4-69);
England (Lord Sheffield's team) 307 (R. Abel 132*; G. Giffen 4-88)
and 156 (A. E. Stoddart 69; Giffen 6-72, C. T. B. Turner 4-46).

1894-95 – AUSTRALIA v ENGLAND (FIRST TEST): MOST SENSATIONAL   1896

At Sydney, December 14, 15, 17, 18, 19, 20, 1894. This was probably the most sensational match ever played either in Australia or in England. Going in first, the Australians made a poor start, losing three wickets – all bowled down by Richardson – for 21 runs. Iredale and Giffen, however, put on 171 for the fourth wicket, and Giffen and Gregory 139 for the fifth. Giffen's splendidly played 161 lasted a little over four hours and a quarter.

At the close of the first day the score stood at 346 for five wickets, and in the end the total reached 586, Gregory and Blackham scoring 154 together for the ninth wicket. In recognition of his wonderful innings of 201 a collection was made for Gregory, the sum subscribed on the ground amounting to £103. In face of a score of 586 the Englishmen had a dismal prospect, but they set to work with the utmost resolution and kept the Australians in the field from Saturday afternoon till the following Wednesday. Still, though they ran up totals of 325 and 437 – Albert Ward taking the chief honours in each innings – they only set Australia 177 to get. At the close of the fifth day 113 had been scored for two wickets, and the match looked all over. Drenching rain in the night, however, followed by bright sunshine, completely altered the condition of the ground, and Peel – well backed up by Briggs – proved so irresistible that the Englishmen gained an astonishing victory by ten runs.

Australia 586 (G. Giffen 161, F. A. Iredale 81, S. E. Gregory 201; T. Richardson 5-181)
and 166 (J. Darling 53; R. Peel 6-67);
England 325 (A. Ward 75, J. Briggs 57; Giffen 4-75)
and 437 (Ward 117, J. T. Brown 53; Giffen 4-164).

1894-95 – AUSTRALIA v ENGLAND (Fifth Test): Brown's match 1896

At Melbourne, March 1, 2, 4, 5, 6, 1895. As was only natural, with the record standing at two victories each, the fifth and last of the Test matches excited enormous interest. Indeed, it may be questioned whether any previous game in the Colonies had ever aroused such intense and widespread excitement. Numbers of people journeyed thousands of miles in order to be in Melbourne on the all-important occasion. As everyone knows, Mr Stoddart's team gained a brilliant and remarkable victory for England by six wickets. It was only, however, after a desperate and protracted struggle that this result was arrived at, the game lasting well into the fifth day. From first to last the match was played on a perfectly true wicket, which gave no advantage to one side over the other.

Mr Stoddart's team [were left] 297 to win, and it was anybody's match. At the call of time the score stood at 28 for one wicket, and to the dismay of the Englishmen, Mr Stoddart was out lbw from the first ball bowled next morning. The position was desperate, but at this point Albert Ward and Brown made the stand which, if they are never to do anything more, will suffice to keep their names famous in the history of English and Australian cricket. By wonderful batting – Ward's patient defence being scarcely less remarkable than Brown's brilliant hitting – they put on 210 runs together, their partnership practically ensuring the success of their side. After the fourth wicket had fallen, the end soon came, MacLaren and Peel being in at the finish. Though the crowds of spectators were, of course, greatly disappointed, they cheered the Englishmen most heartily.

Australia 414 (J. Darling 74, S. E. Gregory 70, G. Giffen 57, J. J. Lyons 55; R. Peel 4-114)
and 267 (Giffen 51, Darling 50; T. Richardson 6-104);
England 385 (Mr A. C. MacLaren 120, Peel 73, Mr A. E. Stoddart 68; Giffen 4-130, G. H. S. Trott 4-71)
and 298-4 (J. T. Brown 140, A. Ward 93).

Jack Brown's first 50 was scored in 28 minutes and remained the fastest Test half-century in terms of time until 2007.

Warwickshire v Glamorgan. At Birmingham, August 25, 26, 27, 1954. During Warwickshire's second innings Wooller completed the cricketers' double for the first time in his career. To mark the feat the Warwickshire chairman, Mr C. A. F. Hastilow, took out a glass of wine to the Glamorgan captain, who drank it at the wicket.

Little Wonder No. 56

1903-04 – AUSTRALIA v ENGLAND (FIRST TEST): FOSTER'S RECORDS   1905

At Sydney, December 11, 12, 14, 15, 16, 17, 1903. The first of the five Test matches was in many ways the best of the series. Indeed a finer game has rarely been seen in Australia. It lasted into the sixth day, and attracted in all about 95,000 people.

The third day was marked by the most brilliant and sensational cricket seen during the tour, R. E. Foster, with a magnificent innings of 287, beating all records in Test matches. Altogether he was batting for seven hours, among his hits being 38 fours. The latter part of his innings was described on all hands as something never surpassed. Foster and Braund added 192 runs together, Braund playing an admirable innings, but with eight men out the Englishmen were only 47 ahead.

Then came the startling play, Relf and Rhodes helping Foster to put on respectively 115 and 130 runs for the ninth and tenth wickets. The last-wicket partnership set up a new record in Test games. Foster's triumph was the more remarkable as he had never before played in an England and Australia match. Going in against a balance of 292 runs, Australia had scored 17 without loss when stumps were pulled up.

Next day they did great things, carrying their score to 367 and only losing five wickets. There was a very regrettable and indeed disgraceful demonstration on the part of a large section of the crowd when Hill was given run out, a storm of hooting and booing going on for a long time. On the fifth day the Australian innings ended for 485, Trumper carrying out his bat for a faultless 185.

England wanted 194 to win, and found the task a very heavy one. They won on the sixth day by five wickets, but they would very probably have been beaten if, after four wickets had fallen for 83, Laver at short leg had not missed Hirst before that batsman had scored a run. As it was Hayward and Hirst made a great stand, and almost won the game together. Hayward was batting just over four hours for his beautifully played 91.

Australia 285 (M. A. Noble 133; E. G. Arnold 4-76)
and 485 (V. T. Trumper 185*, R. A. Duff 84, C. Hill 51; W. Rhodes 5-94);
England 577 (Mr. R. E. Foster 287, L. C. Braund 102, J. T. Tyldesley 53)
and 194-5 (T. W. Hayward 91, G. H. Hirst 60*).

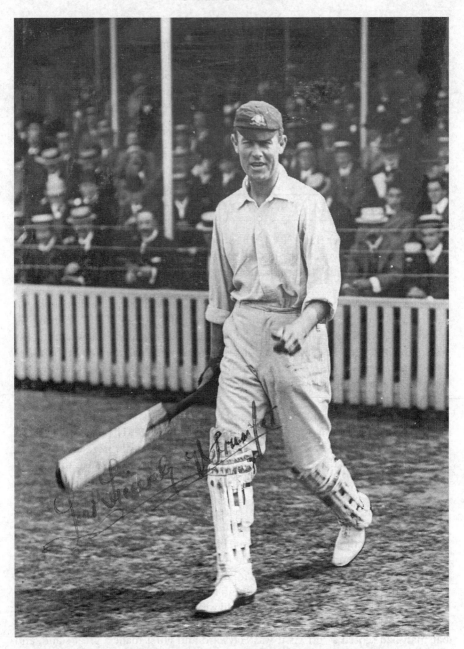

Trumped: Victor Trumper carried his bat for a faultless 185 in the Sydney Test but was overshadowed by Foster

1907-08 – AUSTRALIA v ENGLAND (SECOND TEST): HEART-STOPPING DEBUT

1909

At Melbourne, January 1, 2, 3, 4, 6, 7, 1908. In England's first innings Hobbs and Hutchings were seen at their best. Hobbs, who had never before taken part in a Test match, scored 83 out of 160 in a trifle over three hours, his defence being very strong. England wanted 282 to win. On the sixth and last day the Englishmen began badly and when their eighth wicket fell with 73 runs still required, the match looked all over. However, Humphries and Barnes put on 34 together and then, to the astonishment of everyone concerned, Barnes and Fielder hit off the remaining 39 runs, and won the match. The last run was a desperately short one and if Hazlitt, throwing in from cover point, had managed to hit the wicket, the result would have been a tie.

Australia 266 (M. A. Noble 61; J. N. Crawford 5-79) and 397 (W. W. Armstrong 77, Noble 64,
V. T. Trumper 63, C. G. Macartney 54, H. Carter 53; S. F. Barnes 5-72);
England 382 (Mr. K. L. Hutchings 126, J. B. Hobbs 83; A. Cotter 5-142) and 282-9 (F. L. Fane 50).

1910-11 – AUSTRALIA v SOUTH AFRICA (SECOND TEST): SHOCK COLLAPSE

1912

At Melbourne, December 31, 1910, January 2, 3, 4, 1911. This was the sensational match of the tour, the South Africans suffering defeat by 89 runs when everyone thought they had the game in their hands. In the second innings of Australia Trumper played superbly, scoring 159 out of 237 in less than three hours, but no one else gained any real mastery over Schwarz and Llewellyn. South Africa only required 170 to win, but the occasion proved too much for them. They were soon in a losing position, half the wickets being down for 46, and the innings ended for 80, Australia winning the match by 89 runs. Whitty's bowling was described as beyond praise. No excuse could be offered for the failure but it was thought that Faulkner flattered the bowlers by his extreme caution. Zulch left a sick bed in order to take his innings.

Australia 348 (W. Bardsley 85, W. W. Armstrong 75, V. S. Ransford 58,)
and 327 (V. T. Trumper 159; C. B. Llewellyn 4-81, R. O. Schwarz 4-76);
South Africa 506 (G. A. Faulkner 204, S. J. Snooke 77, J. H. Sinclair 58*; Armstrong 4-134)
and 80 (W. J. Whitty 6-17, A. Cotter 4-47).

1911-12 – MCC IN AUSTRALIA: PLUM JOB
Sydney Pardon, 1913

The tour of the MCC's team in Australia was, in a cricket sense, a triumphant success. The Englishmen won the rubber of five Test matches by four to one. Mr P. F. Warner was chosen to captain the side, but after scoring 151 in the opening match against South Australia he had a serious illness, and could take no further part in the tour, the leadership devolving on Mr Douglas, who, after the first Test match, proved himself an excellent captain.

1911-12 – AUSTRALIA v ENGLAND (SECOND TEST): JACK'S ALL RIGHT 1913

At Melbourne, December 30, 1910, January 1, 2, 3, 1911. It was in the second Test match that the Englishmen, with a victory by eight wickets, first revealed their full strength. Up to this point they had not impressed the critics that they were anything more than an ordinarily good side, and few people in Australia thought they were at all likely to win the rubber. The match was won at the start, some marvellous bowling by Barnes giving England an advantage which, though seriously discounted at one point by weak batting, was never wholly lost. On Australia winning the toss and going in, Barnes led off by bowling five overs, four maidens, for one run and four wickets. With six men out for 38, the Australians were in a desperate plight. On Monday there was a big attendance, over 31,000 people being present. Before play began, Mr Warner, who was getting better after his illness, went out to inspect the wicket, and had a great reception when the crowd recognised him. The Englishmen were batting all day. Out fifth at 224, Hearne made his 114 without a mistake of any kind. Going in on Tuesday against a balance of 81, the Australians made a very bad start, losing four wickets for 38 runs. Armstrong, however, played finely, and received such good support that, at the end of the day, the total, with eight wickets down, had reached 269. On the fourth day England won the match in most brilliant style. The Australians added 30 runs, leaving England 219 to get. Rhodes left at 57, and then Hobbs and Gunn practically won the match, carrying the score to 169 before Gunn was caught by the wicketkeeper. Hobbs played one of the finest innings of his life. He scored his 126 not out in just under three hours and a half, and did not give a chance of any kind.

Australia 184 (S. F. Barnes 5-44) and 299 (W. W. Armstrong 90; Mr F. R. Foster 6-91);
England 265 (J. W. Hearne 114, W. Rhodes 61; H. V. Hordern 4-66, A. Cotter 4-73)
and 219-2 (J. B. Hobbs 126*).

1920-21 – MCC IN AUSTRALIA: 5-0 WHITEWASH 1922

The tour of the MCC's team in the winter of 1920-21 resulted in disaster, all the Test matches being easily won by Australia. Never before in the history of English or Australian trips since Test matches were first played had one side shown such an overwhelming superiority.

As the news came to hand of defeat after defeat, people thought the Englishmen must be playing very badly. Not till the Australians came here in the summer and beat us three times in succession on our own grounds did we fully realise the strength of the combination that had set up such a record. The MCC were very doubtful as to the wisdom of renewing the interchange of visits so soon, feeling that

English cricket had not had time to regain its pre-war standard, and it will be remembered that they declined a pressing invitation to send out a team in the winter of 1919-20. However, in face of Australia's keen desire, they could not insist on further delay. That the Australian authorities had judged the situation rightly was proved by results. In a financial sense the tour was an immense success, the Test matches attracting bigger crowds than ever.

1920-21 – AUSTRALIA v ENGLAND (First Test): STRONG-ARMED   1922

At Sydney, December 17, 18, 20, 21, 22, 1920. Though the first Test match ended in disaster for them, the Englishmen started uncommonly well, bowling and fielding so finely that the Australians took the whole of the first afternoon to score 250 for eight wickets. The great chance for England came the next day, but it was hopelessly missed. In facing a modest total of 267 the team were in a far better position than they could have expected, and when 140 went up with only three men out the prospect was very hopeful. So dismally did the batting collapse, however, that the innings was all over for 190. Going in for the second time with a lead of 77 the Australians carried their total to 332 for five wickets. Following up his 70 in the first innings Collins gave a splendid display, completing his hundred in just over three hours and a half. Macartney, after a curiously slow start, was very brilliant. The most remarkable cricket of the match came on the fourth day, Armstrong playing a magnificent innings. Getting runs at the rate of 45 an hour, he scored 158 in less than three hours and a half out of the 246 put on while he was in. His hits included 17 fours, most of them splendid drives. For their huge total of 581 the Australians were at the wickets just upon nine hours. The Englishmen were left with the impossible task of getting 659 to win and, considering their hopeless position, they did not do badly to score 281.

Australia 267 (H. L. Collins 70) **and** 581 (W. W. Armstrong 158, Collins 104, C. Kelleway 78, C. G. Macartney 69, W. Bardsley 57, J. M. Taylor 51); **England** 190 (F. E. Woolley 52) **and** 281 (J. B. Hobbs 59, J. W. Hearne 57, E. H. Hendren 56).

1924-25 – MCC In Australia: Hobbs and Sutcliffe the bright spot   1926

Setting forth in September, 1924, with great hopes of recovering the mythical "Ashes", the MCC team, under the leadership of Arthur Gilligan, failed in their quest, Australia winning the first three games of the rubber and altogether four out of the series of five matches. The disappointment to everybody in this country was, of course, very great but, in these depressing days, some consolation could be found in the fact that the reputation of English cricket suffered no such damaging blow as on the occasion of the tour of 1920-21.

Finer and more consistent batting than that of Hobbs and Sutcliffe in the first four Test matches could not well be conceived. The two men, going in at Sydney against a total of 450, put on 157 before they were separated, and in the second innings when England had 605 to make to win, they raised the score to 110. An even greater achievement than either of these two followed immediately at Melbourne where, after an innings of 600 by Australia, they started the England batting with a partnership of 283. At Melbourne in the Fourth Test they were associated in a stand that realised 126. Thus four times they participated in a first-wicket partnership of over a hundred runs.

1928-29 – MCC IN AUSTRALIA: RARE TRIUMPH DOWN UNDER Sydney Southerton, 1930

Opinions may differ as to the exact place in the relative table of merit of visiting teams occupied by the combination which, for the first time since the war, won in Australia the rubber for England. Having had the good fortune to see all their matches, I have no hesitation in allotting to them a very high position. There may have been teams which included players more brilliant and skilful individually but rarely has a side gone to Australia and played from beginning to end of a strenuous and in many respects tiring tour with the team spirit so admirably maintained in every engagement.

1928-29 – AUSTRALIA v ENGLAND (FIRST TEST): RECORD VICTORY 1930

At Brisbane, November 30, December 1, 3, 4, 5, 1928. Having by now run into first-rate all-round form, England entered upon the opening Test match with feelings of confidence, but not even the most sanguine member of the team could have anticipated that they would gain a victory by such an astounding margin as that of 675 runs – easily the most pronounced success by runs in the history of Test matches.

England triumphed in such a startling manner as to cause real consternation in Australian cricket circles. Australia were set the tremendous task of getting 742 runs to win. Australia's wretched position was made hopeless by heavy rain during the night followed in the morning by bright sunshine. Kippax left at 33 and then, White going on at 43 and Tate changing ends, the issue was quickly settled. The last six wickets – the two invalids [*Gregory injured and Kelleway ill*] being still unable to bat – went down in 50 minutes, Australia being all out for 66. Woodfull, batting splendidly, received no support at all, nearly everyone who joined him hitting out wildly immediately on going in. The English fielding was again magnificent, and White had the astounding record of four wickets for seven runs.

England 521 (E. H. Hendren 169, H. Larwood 70, Mr A. P. F. Chapman 50)
and 342-8 dec. (C. P. Mead 73, Mr D. R. Jardine 65*; C. V. Grimmett 6-131);
Australia 122 (H. Larwood 6-32) and 66 (Mr J. C. White 4-7).

1928-29 – AUSTRALIA v ENGLAND (SECOND TEST): HAMMOND'S HEROICS
1930

At Sydney, December 14, 15, 17, 18, 19, 20, 1928. England won the second Test match by eight wickets and, even if three good scores were hit against them in the second innings, they were, to all intents and purposes, definitely on top the whole way through. Australia were now in rather a desperate position and found themselves handicapped by having to go into the field without a fast bowler. The match proved a great triumph for English batting, every man on the side reaching double figures while Hammond carried off chief honours by playing the second-highest individual innings ever hit in Test matches between England and Australia. When within reasonable distance of equalling or beating R. E. Foster's 287 on the same ground almost to a day 23 years before, Hammond got his feet mixed up and was bowled in playing back. His greatest innings was, over and above the skill shown, a wonderful test of his physical condition. He went in at 20 minutes past two on the second afternoon and was not dismissed until after one o'clock on the fourth, being at the wickets for seven hours and a half, or exactly half an hour longer than the time occupied by Foster. When 19, he was nearly run out; at 148, he gave a tremendously hard right-handed return chance to Ryder, and at 185, walked right in to Blackie but had the good fortune to deflect the ball with his leg – too wide for Oldfield to get at it. These were the only errors of judgment or execution during the whole of a very remarkable display characterised by watchful defence and extraordinarily fine hitting on the off side.

Australia 253 (W. M. Woodfull 68; G. Geary 5-35)

and 397 (H. L. Hendry 112, Woodfull 111, J. Ryder 79; M. W. Tate 4-99);

England 636 (W. R. Hammond 251; E. H. Hendren 74, Geary 66; D. D. Blackie 4-148) **and 16-2**.

1928-29 – AUSTRALIA v ENGLAND (FOURTH TEST): TEEN SPIRIT
1930

At Adelaide, February 1, 2, 4, 5, 6, 7, 8, 1929. The rubber having been won, the English team had no cause for anxiety beyond the desire to preserve their unbeaten record. Still, they did not exhibit any lack of keenness in the Fourth Test match which, characterised by very even scoring throughout, had a most exciting finish, England gaining a victory by 12 runs. England had no reason for changing their eleven, but Australia brought in Jackson for Richardson, the young New South Wales batsman enjoying the distinction of playing a three-figure innings in his first Test match. [*Archie Jackson was 19 years and 152 days old. He died from tuberculosis aged 23.*] Before going further, it is only right to pay a great tribute to his performance. Accomplished in circumstances calculated to daunt a player of mature experience, it was, in point of style and beauty of execution and strokeplay, the best innings played against the Englishmen during the whole tour. Going in on the second day just before half past three, Australia made a deplorable start, three wickets falling for 19 runs. It was then that Jackson revealed his great powers. The position did not seem to trouble him in the slightest, and he drove, cut and hit to leg with the utmost certainty and confidence.

England 334 (W. R. Hammond 119*, J. B. Hobbs 74, H. Sutcliffe 64; C. V. Grimmett 5-102)
and 383 (Hammond 177, Mr D. R. Jardine 98; R. K. Oxenham 4-67);
Australia 369 (A. Jackson 164, J. Ryder 63; Mr J. C. White 5-130)
and 336 (Ryder 87, D. G. Bradman 58, A. F. Kippax 51; Mr White 8-126).

1931-32 – SOUTH AFRICANS IN AUSTRALIA: BRADMANIA   1933

These particular five matches served to emphasise the wonderful ability of Bradman, [who] scored a hundred in every Test match except the last when he was injured. Leading off with 226 in the First Test at Brisbane, he followed with 112 at Sydney, 167 at Melbourne, and 299 not out at Adelaide. In addition to these huge scores he also made 219 and 135 for New South Wales. As the outcome of all this he headed the batting figures against the tourists with the extraordinary average of 201.50.

1932-33 – MCC IN AUSTRALIA: WINNING AT ALL COSTS   Sydney Southerton, 1934

While in some of the early tours to Australia strong differences of opinion on various points arose to cause trouble, it is very doubtful if ever a team from England travelled through the Commonwealth and met with such openly expressed hostility as that visiting Australia in the winter of 1932-33. The members of it were successful in their mission, and, winning four of the five Test matches, recovered the Ashes which had been lost in 1930. The chief cause of the disagreement which came very near to causing a termination of the tour and, indeed, almost brought about a complete breach in the friendly relations between England and Australia [was] a method of bowling – mainly with the idea of curbing the scoring propensities of Bradman – which met with almost general condemnation among Australian crick-eters and spectators and which, when something of the real truth was ultimately known in this country, caused people at home – many of them famous in the game – to wonder if the winning of the rubber was, after all, worth this strife.

1932-33 – AUSTRALIA v ENGLAND (FIRST TEST): McCABE MANS
BURNING DECK   1934

At Sydney, December 2, 3, 5, 6, 7, 1932. Leading off in fine style in the series of Test matches, England won this, the first, early on the fifth day by ten wickets. The bowling of Larwood, who in the two innings dismissed ten men at a cost of 124 runs – five of them in the second innings for less than six runs apiece – and the batting of Sutcliffe, Hammond and Pataudi stood out as the prominent successes of the match from the English point of view.

At the same time the encounter brought great fame to McCabe, the young Australian cricketer, who, with an innings of 187, obtained his first century in Test matches and scored off Larwood's bowling in a style which for daring and brilliance was not approached by any other Australian during the tour. Sutcliffe gave a typical exhibition, being wonderfully sure in defence and certain in his off-driving; Hammond, if not quite so dashing as a little time previously at Melbourne, was eminently good, but Pataudi – like two other famous Indians, Ranjitsinhji and Duleepsinhji, reaching three figures in his first Test match – was, for the most part, plodding and rather wearisome to watch.

Going in a second time, Australia collapsed badly. Larwood, again bowling at a great pace, and well backed up by Voce, carried everything before him and when play ceased [on the fourth day] Australia had lost nine wickets for 164 runs. Thus they had exactly cleared off the arrears. Larwood's speed was tremendous and nobody faced him with any confidence. Reference to the fact that Bradman, owing to illness, was unable to play in the match must not be omitted, although in view of subsequent events it is, to say the least, questionable, if his presence would have staved off disaster.

Australia 360 (S. J. McCabe 187*; H. Larwood 5-96, W. Voce 4-110) **and 164** (Larwood 5-28); **England 524** (H. Sutcliffe 194, W. R. Hammond 112, Nawab of Pataudi 102) **and 1-0.**

1932-33 – AUSTRALIA v ENGLAND (THIRD TEST): PANDEMONIUM   1934

At Adelaide, January 13, 14, 16, 17, 18, 19, 1933. The Third Test of the tour, in which England – well on top when an innings had been completed on each side – were victorious by no fewer than 338 runs, will go down to history as probably the most unpleasant ever played.

So hostile was the feeling of the Australian public against Jardine that on the days before the game started people were excluded from the ground when the Englishmen were practising. As Jardine won the toss and England batted first, nothing out of the common occurred to begin with, but later on, when Australia went in and Woodfull was hit over the heart again while Oldfield had to retire owing to a blow he received on the head, the majority of the spectators completely lost all hold on their feelings. Insulting remarks were hurled at Jardine, and when Larwood started to bowl his leg-theory he came in for his share of the storm of abuse. Not to put too fine a point on it, pandemonium reigned.

A passage of words between Pelham Warner [*England's joint manager*] and Woodfull in the dressing-room increased the bitter feeling prevalent in the crowd, and the despatch of the cablegram protesting against body-line bowling served no purpose in whatever endeavours were made to appease tempers already badly frayed by the various happenings. Altogether the whole atmosphere was a disgrace to cricket. One must pay a tribute to Jardine. He did not shrink from the line of action he had taken up; he showed great pluck in often fielding near to the boundary where he became an easy target for offensive and sometimes filthy remarks; and above all he captained his team in this particular match like a genius. Much as they disliked the method of attack he controlled, all the leading Australian critics were unanimous in their praise of his skill as a leader.

England 341 (M. Leyland 83, Mr R. E. S. Wyatt 78, E. Paynter 77; T. W. Wall 5-72)
and 412 (W. R. Hammond 85, L. E. G. Ames 69, Mr D. R. Jardine 56; W. J. O'Reilly 4-79);
Australia 222 (W. H. Ponsford 85, Mr G. O. Allen 4-71)
and 193 (W. M. Woodfull 75*, D. G. Bradman 66; Mr Allen 4-50, H. Larwood 4-71).

1932-33 – AUSTRALIA v ENGLAND (FOURTH TEST): PAYNTER'S PLUCK   1934

At Brisbane, February 10, 11, 13, 14, 15, 16, 1933. England won the fourth Test match by six wickets, so being successful in the rubber and regaining the Ashes. The Australians at times seemed to have more than a reasonable chance, but they failed to drive home a temporary advantage, and generally speaking they did not appear to be a well-balanced side, while there is no doubt that nearly all of them were overawed by Larwood. The match will always be memorable for the great part played in the victory of England by Paynter. Suffering from an affection of the throat, he left a sickbed to bat, and put together a splendid innings of 83, while he enjoyed the additional satisfaction later on of making the winning hit with a six.

At Adelaide, Paynter and Verity put on 96 at a critical period; at Brisbane they added 92 runs in about two hours and 35 minutes. Paynter's display of patient and skilful batting was certainly one of the greatest examples of pluck and fortitude in the history of Test cricket. He was in for nearly four hours, and sent the ball ten times to the boundary.

Australia 340 (V. Y. Richardson 83, D. G. Bradman 76, W. M. Woodfull 67; H. Larwood 4-101) and 175;
England 356 (H. Sutcliffe 86, E. Paynter 83, W. J. O'Reilly 4-120) and 162-4 (M. Leyland 86).

Leg theory: a great example of the Bodyline field setting as Bill Woodfull,
the Australian captain, ducks a bouncer from Harold Larwood at Brisbane in 1932-33

Cheltenham v Haileybury and ISC. At Lord's, July 29, 30, 1954. After fairly sound Haileybury batting, Ghods, a Persian boy, unsettled Cheltenham with tantalising deliveries.

Little Wonder No. 57

1932-33 – BODYLINE: THE CAPTAINS' RESPONSIBILITY   Sydney Southerton, 1934

Cricketers can gather from the various cables between MCC and the Australian board the whole course of the disturbance over the question of fast leg-theory bowling. I have purposely omitted to use the expression "Bodyline bowling". It may have conveyed to those to whom it was presented at the outset the meaning the inventor of it wished to infer, but to my mind it was an objectionable term, utterly foreign to cricket, and calculated to stir up strife.

Animosity existed and was fanned into flame largely by the use of the term "Bodyline" when Larwood and others met with such success. The despatch of a petulant cablegram by the Australian board even put the completion of the tour in jeopardy. Saner counsels prevailed, and MCC never lost their grip of the situation and, what was more important, refused to be stampeded into any panic legislation.

What of this fast leg-theory method of bowling to which not only the Australian players themselves but the vast majority of the Australian public took grave exception? Jardine stated in his book that the bowling against which the Australians demurred was not of this description, and Larwood, the chief exponent of it, said with equal directness that he had never bowled at a man. On the other hand, there are numerous statements by responsible Australians to the effect that the bowling was calculated to intimidate, pitched as the ball was so short as to cause it to fly shoulder and head high and make batsmen, with the leg side studded with fieldsmen, use the bat as protection rather than in defence of the wicket or to make a scoring stroke.

Victor Richardson has said that when he took his ordinary stance he found the ball coming in to his body; when he took guard slightly more to the leg side he still had the ball coming at him; and with a still wider guard the ball continued to follow him. I hold no brief either for Jardine or Larwood or for Richardson, Woodfull or Bradman; but while some of the Australians may have exaggerated the supposed danger of this form of bowling I cling to the opinion that they cannot all be wrong. When the first mutterings of the storm were heard many people in this country were inclined to the belief that the Australians, seeing themselves in danger of losing the rubber, were not taking defeat in the proper spirit. I will confess that I thought they did not relish what seemed to me at that stage to be a continuous good-length bombardment by our fast bowlers on to their leg stump. This idea I afterwards found was not quite correct.

For myself, I hope that we never see fast leg-theory bowling exploited in this country. Mainly because it makes cricket a battle instead of a game, I deplore its introduction and pray for its abolition, not by any legislative measures, but by the influence which our captains can bring to bear.

1936-37 – MCC IN AUSTRALIA: 2–0 LEAD SQUANDERED   1938

Although the MCC team failed in their quest to regain the mythical "Ashes", it is probable that they would have achieved their object had not some wonderful batting feats by Bradman for Australia turned the scale. After winning two Tests, England were beaten in the remaining three and so for the first time *(and only, so far)* a side which lost the first two games of a series came out on top. Australia must be heartily congratulated on the success. In each of the five games the captain who won the toss led the winning eleven. The fluctuating nature of the Test struggles gripped the Australian public, and financially the tour broke all records. The total number of people who watched the five games was over 900,000 and the receipts amounted to £90,909.

1946-47 – MCC IN AUSTRALIA: TOO MUCH TOO SOON   Norman Preston, 1948

The MCC tour to Australia in 1946-47 resembled that of 1920-21, not a Test being won by England. In both cases English cricket had not recovered from the effects of world war. Weakness in bowling was the main cause of the team's failure, coupled with poor catching which affected the side in spasms. The inability of Hammond to make any large scores in the first four Tests in which he played, and the time taken by Hutton and Compton to produce their true form in the Tests, were contributory factors.

We found the Australians much stronger than we anticipated. By the time we arrived at Brisbane for the First Test we realised they were much better equipped in bowling. Hammond nursed Bedser and Wright carefully in the early months of the tour. Yet these bowlers, through sheer necessity, were called upon to do far too much work in the gruelling heat. Special Army leave was given to Voce and Pollard for the tour, but neither had sufficient pace to be really troublesome in the clear Australian atmosphere. The change from English rations to the excellent Australian food, coupled with the benefit gained from a sea trip and glorious Australian sunshine, caused all the party to put on weight, and none more so than Voce and Pollard.

1946-47 – AUSTRALIA v ENGLAND (FIRST TEST): CLEAN CATCH CONTROVERSY
1948

At Brisbane, November 29, 30, December 2, 3, 4, 5, 1946. Australia won by an innings and 332 runs. Whereas in past tours England enjoyed the good fortune of twice catching Australia on a sticky wicket at Brisbane, this time the tables were turned and England in each innings batted after a violent thunderstorm. From the England team's point of view the whole course of the match balanced on an incident when Bradman was 28 and the total 74 for two wickets. Facing Voce, the Australian captain chopped the ball to second slip, where Ikin thought he made a perfectly good catch. Bradman survived the appeal, and not only went on to hit his first Test century against England at Brisbane but, with Hassett, he added 276 and established a new third-wicket record stand for these matches. Bradman and Hassett gradually wore down the bowling in the relentless heat. Bedser bowled nobly for long spells, but could not return after tea owing to stomach trouble – a legacy of his war service in Italy. Hassett always remained subdued, but Bradman found his true form, and the first day ended with Australia 292 for two – Bradman 162, Hassett 81.

Australia 645 (D. G. Bradman 187, A. L. Hassett 128, C. L. McCool 95, K. R. Miller 79;
D. V. P. Wright 5-167);
England 141 (Miller 7-60) **and 172** (E. R. H. Toshack 6-82).

1946-47 – AUSTRALIA v ENGLAND (Second Test): Barnes-Bradman   1948

At Sydney, December 13, 14, 16, 17, 18, 19, 1946. Australia won by an innings and 33 runs. Brilliant sunshine on Sunday transformed the pitch, which rolled out perfectly on Monday when cricket took place in glorious weather. The biggest crowd of the match, 51,459, saw Barnes bat all day. Only three wickets fell this day, all to Edrich, as after Miller left at ten minutes to four, Bradman, without a runner, stayed with Barnes until the stumps were drawn with the total 252 for four wickets. Not before 20 minutes to six the following day did England break the Barnes–Bradman stand. Then, in successive overs, Bradman, who batted superbly despite a pronounced limp which must have been very painful, and Barnes were dismissed at the same total. Each hit 234, and they established a new fifth-wicket Test partnership record of 405.

England 255 (W. J. Edrich 71, J. T. Ikin 60; I. W. Johnson 6-42)
and 371 (Edrich 119, D. C. S. Compton 54);
Australia 659-8 dec. (S. G. Barnes 234, D. G. Bradman 234).

1950-51 – AUSTRALIA v ENGLAND (First Test): Hutton's sticky wicket
1952

At Brisbane, December 1, 2, 4, 5, 1950. Australia won by 70 runs. Most Australians agreed with the general view that the intervention of a typical Brisbane storm brought in its train defeat for the side which batted better, bowled better and fielded better than the winners. Virtually the game was won and lost at the toss of the coin.

When Brown called incorrectly to Hassett, he allowed Australia first use of a good pitch more suited to batting, even though its slow pace did not encourage forcing strokes. Yet the first day belonged to England. They surprised everybody by dismissing Australia for such a meagre total in the conditions.

To the end of the Australian innings the cricket was exciting enough. It became more so. A successful appeal against the light by England's new opening pair, Washbrook and Simpson – Brown decided to put Hutton at No. 5 to give strength to the middle – was the final act on that dramatic Friday. Inside a few hours the storm broke, and cricket could not be resumed until half an hour before lunch on Monday. For 30 minutes Washbrook and Simpson provided skill and courage so far unsurpassed in the match. In that time they scored 28 runs together on a pitch just as treacherous as it played through the remainder of the day, in which 20 wickets went down for 102.

True to tradition, the pitch was the game's villain. Medium-paced bowling of good length presented a well-nigh insoluble problem. Sometimes the ball reared head high, at other times it kept horribly low. Both captains placed nearly all their fieldsmen in a circle a few yards from the bat, and 12 of the wickets resulted from catches close to the wicket. When the back of England's innings had been broken, Brown declared. His one hope was to force Australia in again as soon as possible. Moroney, who experienced the disaster of a pair on his Test debut, Morris and Loxton were out before a run was scored, and wickets continued to go down so quickly that Hassett retaliated by a declaration which gave England an hour and ten minutes to bat before the close. They required 193 to win. If only two or three men had been lost then their prospects might have been bright. It was not to be.

Australia were within sight of victory, but it was not theirs until Hutton had given yet another exhibition of his wonderful batsmanship on tricky turf. Aided first by Brown and then by Wright, Hutton thrashed the fast bowlers majestically and played the turning or lifting ball with the ease of a master craftsman. When assisted by Wright in a last-wicket stand of 45, Hutton even looked capable of carrying England through, but Wright succumbed to temptation to hook the last ball before lunch. Hutton's was an innings to remember.

Australia 228 (R. N. Harvey 74; A. V. Bedser 4-45) **and 32-7 dec.** (T. E. Bailey 4-22);
England 68-7 dec. (W. A. Johnston 5-35) **and 122** (L. Hutton 62*; J. B. Iverson 4-43).

1950-51 – MCC IN AUSTRALIA: AUSTRALIANS DEFEATED AT LAST   Reg Hayter, 1952

On Wednesday, February 28, 1951, at Melbourne, Australia's record of 26 post-war Tests without defeat came to an end. That was a day for F. R. Brown and his England colleagues to rejoice. Australia had not been beaten since the Oval Test of 1938, and rightly the victory was acclaimed as a fillip to English cricket. In a match played under equal conditions to both, the better side triumphed and Australia, as a whole, applauded the victors generously. Most Australians, in fact, were as delighted at England's success as were the players.

Australia won the five-Test series 4–1.

1952-53 – SOUTH AFRICANS IN AUSTRALIA: BIGGEST SHOCK 1954

Rarely in the history of international cricket has a team so thoroughly routed the prophets as did the young and markedly inexperienced side, led by J. E. Cheetham, which made South Africa's third visit to the Antipodes so momentous. The atmosphere in which the South Africans sailed could scarcely have been more gloomy. Many, acknowledged as sound and dispassionate judges, had suggested that the tour should be cancelled rather than allow South Africa's cricket, admittedly at a low ebb, to suffer a sequence of seemingly inevitable crushing defeats which could cause long-standing damage.

The five-Test series was drawn 2–2.

1952-53 – AUSTRALIA v SOUTH AFRICA (SECOND TEST): TAYFIELD'S TIME
1954

At Melbourne, December 24, 26, 27, 29, 30, 1952. South Africa won by 82 runs. Their first victory over Australia for 42 years came as reward for superior all-round cricket. Endean and Tayfield played specially notable roles, but the whole side deserved praise for two fielding performances which drew favourable comparison with some of the best teams of the past. Little indication of the events which were to lead to Australia's third defeat in 33 post-war Tests – all in the last eight matches – was contained in the early play. South Africa ran into immediate trouble against Miller and Lindwall, and the total only became respectable through solid rescue work by Murray, top scorer, Mansell and Tayfield.

Throughout the series South Africa gave no finer display of out-cricket than on the second day. Apart from the hard-driving Miller, the middle batsmen failed against the off-breaks of Tayfield and the leg-spin of Mansell. By steady length and bowling to his field, Tayfield gave nothing away in an unchanged spell of nearly four hours, at one stage of which he took the wickets of Ring, Miller and Johnston for one run.

The spectacular catch which dismissed Morris set South Africa's standard for the innings. A drive hit Cheetham's upflung hands close to the wicket but bounced away from him. Tayfield spun round, raced after the ball, and caught it in a full-length dive. Cheetham and McGlew made other excellent catches, and Endean, with his back to the iron fence, held a drive by Miller above his head.

Poor light did not help Australia when they started the last innings, but more high-class bowling by Tayfield was the chief reason for their failure to score the 373 required to win. In one period of nine maiden overs he sent back Miller, Langley and Hole, and he richly merited his match record of 13 wickets for 165. A ninth-wicket stand of 61 by Benaud and the hard-hitting Ring temporarily raised Australia's hopes, but Tayfield split the stand and, when he also brought Ring's brave innings to a close, he fittingly clinched South Africa's triumph.

South Africa 227 (A. R. A. Murray 51; K. R. Miller 4-62) **and 388** (W. R. Endean 162*, J. H. B. Waite 62);
Australia 243 (C. C. McDonald 82, Miller 52; H. J. Tayfield 6-84)
and 290 (R. N. Harvey 60, D. T. Ring 53; Tayfield 7-81).

Northamptonshire v Kent. At Northampton, August 20, 22, 23, 1955. Extras contributed no fewer than 73 [b 48, lb 23, w 2] – more than any single batsman – to Northamptonshire's first-innings lead. Sunburn seriously impeded Catt's movements, and he found difficulty in taking Wright, who spun the ball sharply.

Little Wonder No. 58

1954-55 – MCC IN AUSTRALIA: AGAINST THE ODDS

Reg Hayter, 1956

Under the zealous and skilful captaincy of Len Hutton, England won the rubber in Australia for the first time for 22 years and so retained the Ashes. On paper the success gained by the players who sailed from Tilbury in September appears most convincing and rather suggests a comfortable tour against indifferent opposition. That was far from the case. It was a hard tour with its days of triumph and days of regret, but in the end superb fast bowling by Tyson and Statham turned the scales so that finally the Australian batsmen were completely humbled.

1954-55 – AUSTRALIA v ENGLAND (SECOND TEST): TYSON A KNOCKOUT

Reg Hayter, 1956

At Sydney, December 17, 18, 20, 21, 22, 1954. England won by 38 runs at 12 minutes past three on the fifth day with one day in hand. Such a victory seemed beyond any possibility when England lost eight wickets for 88, but among a crop of batting failures in both teams the tailenders made their presence felt.

The match was a triumph for pace bowlers and in particular for Tyson and Statham. Many people feared that Tyson had been seriously hurt when, batting just before lunch on the fourth day, he turned his back on a bouncer from Lindwall and it struck him on the back of the head. Temporarily, Tyson was knocked out, but not only did he resume his innings but the next day he knocked out Australia.

Tyson won the match for England because he kept his head. After his painful experience he might well have been tempted to hurl down bouncers, particularly at Lindwall, but he never did so. Possibly Lindwall expected retaliation, for Tyson yorked him as he did Burke and Hole in the same innings. The cricket at this vital stage emphasised that, above everything else in bowling, perfect length and direction win matches.

Australia wanted 223 for victory, not an unreasonable task, but at once Statham and Tyson, with more pace than Lindwall, made the ball fly nastily. Harvey remained unbeaten, having played one of his finest innings for Australia. While justice must be done to Tyson who bowled without relief for over 90 minutes down wind in that vital spell, England could not have won without the valuable work Statham accomplished bowling into the wind for 85 minutes. The whole of Hutton's party faced Christmas and the New Year in a new frame of mind – optimistic that their luck had changed and that the rubber could be won.

England 154 and 296 (P. B. H. May 104, M. C. Cowdrey 54);
Australia 228 (F. H. Tyson 4-45, T. E. Bailey 4-59)
and 184 (R. N. Harvey 92*; Tyson 6-85).

1954-55 – AUSTRALIA v ENGLAND (THIRD TEST): "BLAZED LIKE A BUSH FIRE"

Reg Hayter, 1956

At Melbourne, December 31, January 1, 3, 4, 5, 1954. England won by 128 runs with a day to spare. As in the previous Test, the combined speed of Tyson and Statham proved too much for Australia and again the two young amateur batsmen, Cowdrey and May, carried the England batting on a sporting pitch which was said to have been doctored on the Sunday. Certainly large cracks were evident on Saturday yet on Monday these had closed and for a time the surface behaved more kindly to batsmen. The Victorian Cricket Association and the Melbourne Cricket Club held an inquiry into a report published in *The Age* alleging watering and issued the following statement: "After a searching inquiry it is emphatically denied that the pitch or any part of the cricket ground has been watered since the commencement of the Third Test." Australia were left 240 to win. The pitch was worn and the experts predicted that England must look to Appleyard, pointing out that the conditions were made for his off-spin, but Tyson and Statham saw England home. Sheer speed through the air coupled with the chance of a shooter at any moment left the Australian batsmen nonplussed. Tyson blazed through them like a bush fire. In 79 minutes the match was all over, the eight remaining wickets crashing for 36 runs.

England 191 (M. C. Cowdrey 102; R. G. Archer 4-33) **and 279** (P. B. H. May 91; W. A. Johnston 5-85);
Australia 231 (J. B. Statham 5-60) **and 111** (F. H. Tyson 7-27).

1958-59 – MCC IN AUSTRALIA: NOT GOOD ENOUGH

Harry Gee, 1960

England certainly had a number of injuries, but neither this factor nor complaints about umpiring and the doubtful actions of several bowlers could gainsay the fact that the tourists were not good enough. This was the basic reason for their disappointing displays against an Australian side which, though excellent as a team, was far from brilliant in individual achievement.

On paper, established players seemed to have justified selection, but long before this tour was over it became apparent that several had turned the corner. Tyson could not produce his bewildering speed; Bailey was not a match-winning quantity either as batsman or bowler, and Lock rarely constituted a danger. Evans gave evidence of a decline in power, but the shortcomings of Richardson, who so frequently failed as opening bat, were the most serious for the side.

May, as a player – probably the finest batsman in the world – ranked as high as his rival [Benaud], but there the comparison ended. Whether or not his policies were decided by others – his tour selection committee consisted of himself, Cowdrey, Evans,

Bailey and Brown, the manager – the fact remained that May never seemed to communicate to his team the driving force which Benaud gave to Australia. May's field-settings were stereotyped, especially in the placings for his fast bowlers with the new ball.

On this very controversial tour, perhaps the most vexed question was related to the delivery action of some Australian bowlers. Not once in Tests or in other first-class matches did the umpires no-ball a man for throwing or jerking.

The actions of the bowlers concerned varied from a bent elbow or a poised upright arm to a bent wrist – movements difficult to analyse even with the help of a film camera – but all had in common a look admitted to be doubtful even by a good proportion of Australian cricket enthusiasts. As the Law stipulated that umpires should call no-ball if they were not entirely satisfied of the absolute fairness of a delivery, there seemed to be something radically wrong.

The Australian Board of Control denied the existence of a throwing problem. At home and when the visit to Australia had concluded, MCC, the English ruling body, were bolder in admitting that they had for some time entertained misgivings about the doubtful actions of certain bowlers in England and instructed umpires and county officials to take the necessary remedial steps. Lock, whose action was often questioned by Australians, changed his style on returning home to one embracing a smoother delivery at slower pace.

1960-61 – AUSTRALIA v WEST INDIES (First Test): the Tied Test
E. M. Wellings, 1961

At Brisbane, December 9, 10, 12, 13, 1960. I was there. I saw it all. That is something that countless thousands would give much to be able to say. For it was The Greatest Test Match, The Greatest Cricket Match and surely The Greatest Game ever played with a ball. Australia v West Indies at Brisbane was already a great match before it bounded explosively to its amazing climax to produce the only tie in the history of Test cricket.

Some time has elapsed since the remarkable events of Hall's last over, in which the final three Australian wickets fell, five runs were made to bring the scores level and one catch dropped. But the picture of those events is more vivid now than it was at the time. Then all was confusion, for so much happened and thrill followed thrill so rapidly that everything became an exciting jumble. Even Meckiff, the last man out, was confused and thought West Indies had won by a run.

The Final Over
Six runs were wanted by Australia when Hall began what had to be the final over. The first ball hit Grout high on the leg, dropped at his feet, and he and Benaud scampered a single. Now the odds were heavily on Australia for Benaud was 52 and batting in match-winning vein.

But immediately the odds were levelled. The next ball was a bouncer and Benaud aimed to hook it, as Davidson a few minutes earlier had superbly hooked a similar ball. He merely nicked it, and every West Indian leapt for joy as Alexander took the catch. So Meckiff arrived to play his first ball quietly back to Hall, and Australia needed a run off each ball.

A bye was run, and Grout skied the fifth ball just out on the leg side. Fielders converged from all directions, but Hall was the tallest and most determined, and he alone put his hands to it as the batsmen were running a single. It bounced out, and the fielders drooped in despair.

The next delivery almost completed their despair, for Meckiff courageously clouted it loftily away to leg. He and Grout ran one, then another, and staked all on a third to win the match as Hunte was preparing to throw from the square-leg boundary. It was a glorious low throw, fast and true, and though Grout hurled himself at the line and skidded home on severely grazed forearms he could not counter the speed of the ball.

Umpire Hoy flung his right arm high to announce the decision immediately to everyone anxiously looking towards him, and again the West Indies leapt and flung their arms in triumph. A minute or so later umpire and fielders repeated their actions, only more so. At the fall of the last wicket the joy of the West Indies was so expressed in leaps and bounds and running about that the scene might have served for a ballet of ultramodern abandon.

The man who sent them into transports of delight and tied the match was little Solomon, when Kline smoothly played the seventh ball of that fateful last over towards square leg. Meckiff at the other end was well launched on a run, but he never made it. With little more than one stump's width to aim at, Solomon threw the wicket down, as he had done some dozen minutes earlier from farther away to run out Davidson and give his side the chance to save themselves.

That final over lasted nine minutes and ended four minutes after the appointed time. Not so long ago it would have been cut short at the dismissal of Grout. But for a comparatively recent law amendment, which provided for the last over being played out whatever the time, we lucky spectators would not have palpitated to the last tremendous thrill of that last tremendous over. Nor perhaps would spectators, bounding with excitement no less than the fielders, have raced across the ground to cheer and call for the heroes of the day, and repeat their cheers again and again in front of the players' pavilion.

They were not so numerous as those gathered rapturously in front of The Oval pavilion in 1953, when Hutton's team at last recovered the Ashes from Australia, but the Queenslanders made up for their relative lack of numbers by their enthusiasm. We all recognised that this was more than a tied match. It was tied by teams playing in Homeric manner.

WEST INDIES	*First innings*		*Second innings*	
C. C. Hunte c Benaud b Davidson		24	c Simpson b Mackay	39
C. W. Smith c Grout b Davidson		7	c O'Neill b Davidson	6
R. B. Kanhai c Grout b Davidson		15	c Grout b Davidson	54
G. S. Sobers c Kline b Meckiff		132	b Davidson	14
*F. M. M. Worrell c Grout b Davidson		65	c Grout b Davidson	65
J. S. Solomon hit wkt b Simpson		65	lbw b Simpson	47
P. D. Lashley c Grout b Kline		19	b Davidson	0
†F. C. M. Alexander c Davidson b Kline		60	b Benaud	5
S. Ramadhin c Harvey b Davidson		12	c Harvey b Simpson	6
W. W. Hall st Grout b Kline		50	b Davidson	18
A. L. Valentine not out		0	not out	7
L-b 3, w 1		4	B 14, l-b 7, w 2	23

1-23 2-42 3-65 4-239 5-243 6-283 7-347   453   1-53 2-88 3-114 4-127 5-210   284
8-366 9-452   6-210 7-241 8-250 9-253

First Innings – Davidson 30–2–135–5; Meckiff 18–0–129–1; Mackay 3–0–15–0; Benaud 24–3–93–0; Simpson 8–0–25–1; Kline 17.6–6–52–3; *Second Innings* – Davidson 24.6–4–87–6; Meckiff 4–1–19–0; Mackay 21–7–52–1; Benaud 31–6–69–1; Simpson 7–2–18–2; Kline 4–0–14–0; O'Neill 1–0–2–0.

AUSTRALIA	First innings		Second innings
C. C. McDonald c Hunte b Sobers	57	– b Worrell.	16
R. B. Simpson b Ramadhin	92	– c sub (L. R. Gibbs) b Hall.	0
R. N. Harvey b Valentine	15	– c Sobers b Hall.	5
N. C. O'Neill c Valentine b Hall	181	– c Alexander b Hall.	26
L. E. Favell run out	45	– c Solomon b Hall	7
K. D. Mackay b Sobers	35	– b Ramadhin	28
A. K. Davidson c Alexander b Hall	44	– run out.	80
*R. Benaud lbw b Hall	10	– c Alexander b Hall.	52
†A. T. W. Grout lbw b Hall	4	– run out.	2
I. Meckiff run out	4	– run out.	2
L. F. Kline not out	3	– not out.	0
B 2, l-b 8, w 1, n-b 4	15	B 2, l-b 9, n-b 3	14
1-84 2-138 3-194 4-278 5-381 6-469 7-484	505	1-1 2-7 3-49 4-49 5-57 6-92 7-226	232
8-489 9-496		8-228 9-232	

First Innings – Hall 29.3–1–140–4; Worrell 30–0–93–0; Sobers 32–0–115–2; Valentine 24–6–82–1; Ramadhin 15–1–60–1; *Second Innings* – Hall 17.7–3–63–5; Worrell 16–3–41–1; Sobers 8–0–30–0; Valentine 10–4–27–0; Ramadhin 17–3–57–1.

Umpires: C. J. Egar and C. Hoy.

1960-61 – WEST INDIANS IN AUSTRALIA: THE GAME SMILES AGAIN   1962

Never has it been more apparent that the game is greater than the result than in Melbourne on February 17, 1961. Commerce in this Australian city stood almost still as the smiling cricketers from the West Indies, the vanquished not the victors, were given a send-off the like of which is normally reserved for Royalty and national heroes. Open cars paraded the happy players from the Caribbean among hundreds of thousands of Australians who had been sentimentalised through the medium of cricket as it should be played.

Worrell, the handsome West Indies captain, Hall, a bowler big in heart as well as stature, Kanhai, a fleet-footed batsman in the best tradition, and the suave Ramadhin, who had come a long way since he was introduced to cricket at the Canadian Mission School in Trinidad, were among those who it was said, were moved to tears by the enthusiasm of the farewell. Four months earlier these same players had arrived almost unsung but vowing, through their captain, that they were going to re-instil some lost adventure into cricket, which for several years had in the main been a dull, lifeless pastime to watch internationally.

The forthright Australian captain, Benaud, supported him. Cynics, and the not so cynical, who had witnessed so much drab play over the last decade or so, thought they had heard it all before. Too much was at stake nationally, they argued, for any lightness of heart to prevail. Worrell and Benaud and their associates happily proved them wrong. The opening match between the countries produced grand cricket and the first tie in a Test; Australia won the second, West Indies the third and the fourth was drawn.

So the series built up to a magnificent climax at the vast Melbourne stadium. The struggle intensified and support grew and grew. A world-record crowd of 90,800 saw play on the Saturday of this vital match, watched in all by 274,404 people who paid £A48,749, the highest receipts for any Australian match. Over 40,000 were present on a drama-charged final day. A fair percentage of that crowd became allies of the opposition when a debatable decision at the vital moment went against West Indies and, as Australia finally squeezed victory and the rubber by a mere margin of two wickets, the batsmen had the crowd surging towards them as they went through for the winning single – a bye. Such was the intensity of the occasion. Summer's glorious pastime had returned as a spectacle of some consequence, and faith in the game was restored among the all-important younger fraternity on whom its popularity, and indeed its very existence, depends. That Worrell and Benaud were the leaders cannot be stressed too much. Upon their insistence on attractive, sensible cricket was laid the foundations of a true demonstration of this great game.

The report on the Tied Test appeared in the 1961 Almanack. The rest of the tour was covered in 1962.

1963-64 – AUSTRALIA v SOUTH AFRICA (First Test): Meckiff no-balled
1965

At Brisbane, December 6, 7, 9, 10, 11, 1963. Drawn. There was never much hope of a definite result with one day lost through rain, but the match was made memorable by the no-balling of Meckiff for throwing and his subsequent retirement from first-class cricket. Australia made a shaky start but Booth rallied them, going on to make 169, and the innings closed for 435. Then came the dramatic over by Meckiff who was no-balled by Egar on his second, third, fifth and ninth deliveries. That was his only over. Egar was booed and Meckiff was carried shoulder-high by a section of the crowd at the close. On the fourth day extra police were sent to the ground because of fears that the umpires, selectors and Benaud might be molested because of the Meckiff incident. There were no scenes.

Australia 435 (B. C. Booth 169, N. C. O'Neill 82; P. M. Pollock 6-95) **and 144-1 dec.** (W. M. Lawry 87*);
South Africa 346 (E. J. Barlow 114, J. H. B. Waite 66, T. L. Goddard 52) **and 13-1.**

1965-66 – MCC In Australia: wives are a liability
E. M. Wellings, 1967

M.J. K. Smith in Australia had more than a team to lead. Shortly before Christmas he was joined by his wife and two small children. He had to think about them as well as his team and escort them round the country. Skippering on tour is a job on its own big enough for anyone. The addition of the cares of a family in a strange country, which Smith himself had not previously visited, is a crippling additional burden. Wide experience of touring during the past 20 years has firmly persuaded me that wives accompanying cricketers are a liability, however well they behave and aim to keep themselves in the background, as those in Australia did on this occasion. The husbands cannot leave them to fend for themselves. They must accordingly be a distraction to the cricketers. In the case of the skipper, whose responsibilities are greater, the distraction is more serious.

MCC should also give some thought to travel. For the first time the team flew by fast jet aircraft all the way to Australia – and in the cramping discomfort of economy class – and numerous players suffered stomach disorders and odd indispositions, which were grandly called virus diseases. Even the common cold was thus termed. The complaint was just the same but with a vital difference. Called a cold, it was too insignificant to keep a cricketer from playing. Described in hifalutin fashion as a virus infection, it became grand enough to keep him out of action.

1968-69 – WEST INDIANS IN AUSTRALIA: ON THE RISE   Henry Blofeld, 1970

The tour saw a major shift in the balance of power in world cricket. The famous West Indies side of the previous decade finally disintegrated against the young and highly efficient Australian team which itself was nearing greatness by the end of the series. The West Indies won the First Test at Brisbane mostly as a result of winning the toss on a wicket which broke up, but from then on they were systematically destroyed by a side which outplayed them at all points and went on to win the series 3–1.

The Australians went from strength to strength after the First Test as they collectively revealed the qualities of application and concentration which the West Indies so badly lacked. The tour will be remembered for the batting of Walters, Ian Chappell and Lawry, who between them scored 1,915 runs in the series. In six Test innings – injury kept him out of the First Test – Walters's lowest score was 50 and his aggregate was 699. In all matches Chappell made over 1,000 runs against the West Indies, and he has developed into one of the outstanding batsmen of this generation. This Australian side will take a lot of beating over the next six years.

1970-71 – MCC IN AUSTRALIA: INSPIRATIONAL ILLY   E. M. Wellings, 1972

No captain of a touring team since D. R. Jardine nearly 40 years ago has had such a difficult task as Raymond Illingworth, leader of MCC in Australia in 1970-71. Some English critics, who had championed the cause of M. C. Cowdrey, were against the skipper. The attitude of numerous Australians has never in my experience been so hostile to an English captain in advance of the tour. Before a ball was bowled Sir Donald Bradman, leader of Australian cricket, was critical of Illingworth as a man who overdid leg-side field-placing. Few, if any, of those critics had ever seen him lead a side, and for a country possessing W. M. Lawry as their captain to cavil at leg-side field-placings was to tread on dangerous ground.

Strangely, the many difficulties which Illingworth had to overcome could be held as being partly responsible for the team's success. They produced a brand of team spirit which has been equalled during the post-war years only by sides led by M. J. K. Smith.

Even before the change of programme the fixture list was bad. There were nine one-day games of no consequence, which cost the touring team several injuries, and the last four Tests were due to be played with only one other first-class match intervening in which to exercise the reserves. An international side should consistently meet worthy opposition, and not be asked to frolic with up-country teams of club standard. One-day games in future should be restricted to over-limited games such as the one in Melbourne which attracted 46,000 spectators.

The first one-day international, staged because the Third Test was washed out, on which Wisden *published only summarised scores.*

1970-71 – AUSTRALIA v ENGLAND (FOURTH TEST): SNOW STORM

E. M. Wellings, 1972

At Sydney, January 9, 10, 11, 13, 14, 1971. England won by 299 runs. Great batting by Boycott and superb fast bowling by Snow on a pitch taking spin, which was too slow for other pace bowlers, were too much for Australia. In the second innings England lost their first three wickets for 48, during which time Boycott ran out Edrich. He made amends during stands of 133 with D'Oliveira and 95 with Illingworth. Both partners played excellently while Boycott ruthlessly broke the Australian attack. He played to a schedule which allowed Illingworth to leave over nine hours for Australia's second innings. The England bowlers needed less than half that time, and only Lawry, who stayed throughout an innings of four hours and a quarter of stern defence, could live against Snow. And he faced few of Snow's deliveries on the final day, when Snow took five for 20 in eight overs. His seven for 40 was his finest Test performance. The pitch was without pace, but on occasions Snow made the ball kick viciously from a worn patch and had his opponents apprehensive from first to last.

England 332 (G. Boycott 77, J. H. Edrich 55; J. W. Gleeson 4-83)

and 319-5 dec. (Boycott 142*, B. L. D'Oliveira 56, R. Illingworth 53);

Australia 236 (I. R. Redpath 64, K. D. Walters 55; D. L. Underwood 4-66)

and 116 (W. M. Lawry 60*; J. A. Snow 7-40).

Surrey v Yorkshire. At The Oval, June 4, 6, 7, 1955. The match provided something unique in the appearance of the two current England captains, May and Hutton, serving under their two official county captains, Surridge and Yardley.

Little Wonder No. 59

1970-71 – AUSTRALIA v ENGLAND (SEVENTH TEST): ROWDY CONCLUSION

E. M. Wellings, 1972

At Sydney, February 12, 13, 14, 16, 17, 1971. On the first day 12 wickets fell. Ian Chappell, Australia's new captain, sent England in first and the batsmen fell to spin, despite another fine, resolute innings by Illingworth. Australia slumped to 66 for four, but England let their strong position slip, largely because Walters was missed three times. During the closing stages of the innings Jenner ducked into a ball from Snow and was hit on the face. Snow was warned by umpire Rowan against the use of persistent bumpers, which led to a protest by Illingworth. The crowd demonstrated against Snow, and Illingworth led his side off the field, but returned after being warned by the umpires that the match would otherwise be awarded to Australia.

Edrich and Luckhurst more than countered Australia's lead with an opening stand of 94, and a series of useful scores finally set Australia to make 223. Snow bowled Eastwood with his sixth ball, but in the fifth over, going for a high hit to long leg off Lever, he broke his right hand on the boundary fencing and was put out of action. On the final day Greg Chappell was Australia's last hope, and he was winkled out by Illingworth, who pulled out his best to compensate for Underwood being disappointing in conditions expected to make him the match-winner. For England to win without Boycott, their top batsman, and then without Snow at the climax of the game was a great achievement.

England 184 and 302 (B. W. Luckhurst 59, J. H. Edrich 57);
Australia 264 (G. S. Chappell 65, I. R. Redpath 59) and 160 (K. R. Stackpole 67).

1974-75 – MCC IN AUSTRALIA: TAKEN TO PIECES

John Thicknesse, 1976

An unpleasant surprise was in store for MCC on their eighth post-war tour of Australia. Having been selected on the assumption that as a consequence of Dennis Lillee's back injury early in 1973, Australia were unlikely to call upon a genuinely fast bowler, Denness's side in fact found themselves confronting two – Lillee and a youngster from Sydney, Jeff Thomson, who up to that time had made a bigger name for himself by what he had said in a magazine about hurting batsmen than by anything he had done on the cricket field.

Thomson, 6ft tall, 24 years old, and equipped with the extremely powerful V-shaped back that characterises many fast bowlers, took 33 wickets in four and a half Tests and looked sure to break Arthur Mailey's longstanding record, 36 in 1920-21, when he hurt himself playing tennis on the rest day of the Adelaide Test and was unable to bowl again in the series.

Lillee, within himself at Brisbane, bowled with a hostility that bordered on savagery throughout the series. Watching the two in action, it was easy to believe they were the fastest pair ever to have coincided in a cricket team. The umpires, Brooks and Bailhache, gave Thomson and Lillee considerable freedom in respect of short-pitched bowling. Thomson's tremendous strength – or perhaps some feature of his perfectly fair but "hurling" action – enabled him to get the ball up from a fuller length than any fast bowler I had seen. But even from him, there were often two unmistakable bouncers an over, while Lillee sometimes bowled three or even four.

Thomson's steep lift was by no means the only factor that made it so hard for the umpires to apply Law 46 to everyone's satisfaction. Another was the size of the crowds and the extent to which they identified themselves with the two fast bowlers. Not since 1958-59 had Australians been able to see England taken to pieces, and it wasn't a chance they were about to miss. More than a quarter of a million watched the Third Test, at Melbourne, including 77,000 on Boxing Day.

When Thomson and Lillee were bowling, the atmosphere was more like that of a soccer ground than of a cricket match, especially at Sydney, where England's batsmen must have experienced the same sort of emotion as they waited for the next ball as early Christians felt as they waited in the Colosseum for the lions.

England's batting, arguably their weakest in Australia since the war, had little experience against fast bowling and was painfully at sea against it, broadly because of an inability or reluctance to get in line. They were without Boycott, who withdrew a month before the team left England because "he couldn't do justice to himself"; saw their other linchpin, Amiss, reduced to mediocrity; and to cap everything ran into a sequence of injuries and illness of which Alec Bedser, the manager, could not remember the like in all his years in cricket.

1974-75 – AUSTRALIA v ENGLAND (Second Test): Cowdrey's comeback

John Thicknesse, 1976

At Perth, December 13, 14, 15, 17, 1974. Australia won by nine wickets. The match was virtually decided on the first day when England, put in, collapsed in two and threequarter hours from 99 for one to 208 all out. Thomson added seven wickets to his nine at Brisbane, generating great speed on a pitch that gained pace after the first day, and Lillee again had four – a bag that would have been bigger if the luck had run for him. England's troubles were accentuated by Australia's brilliant catching in the slips and gully, 13 being taken out of 14 offered. Greg Chappell established a Test record with seven catches in the match, all but two of them at second slip.

Thomson needed only five balls to inflict his first injury, hitting Luckhurst on the top hand off a good length. Luckhurst was able to bat on, but the hand swelled overnight, preventing him from fielding, and in the second innings he batted No. 7. Cowdrey stepped out for his 188th Test innings (and first for 3½ years) to as warm an ovation as he is accustomed to at Canterbury, and having narrowly survived his first three balls gave a demonstration of defensive technique against fast bowling that was subsequently equalled only by Knott, in the first innings, and Titmus, who was playing his first Test since February 1968. Only these three consistently observed the principle of moving their bodies into line against Thomson and Lillee. Just before the Test's halfway point Lloyd and Cowdrey opened England's second innings. Thomson ended a staunch partnership of 52 when a good-length ball cut back to hit Lloyd in the abdomen, causing him to retire hurt.

England 208 (A. P. E. Knott 51) **and 293** (F. J. Titmus 61; J. R. Thomson 5-93);
Australia 481 (R. Edwards 115, K. D. Walters 103, G. S. Chappell 62) **and 23-1**.

Welcome back: Colin Cowdrey, days from his 42nd birthday and playing his first Test
for three and a half years, is bounced by Dennis Lillee at Perth
during England's 4–1 Ashes defeat in 1974-75

1975-76 – WEST INDIANS IN AUSTRALIA: FIRE AGAINST FIRE   Henry Blofeld, 1977

When Australia's intended tour to South Africa was cancelled, the West Indies Board of Control agreed to send a side to Australia to play six Test matches, two years before their next scheduled visit. With Thomson and Lillee on one side and Roberts and several other fast bowlers on the other, it was obviously going to be a trial of strength between the two best international sides of the time. When the West Indies beat Australia in the Prudential Cup final, the anticipation of this series was heightened considerably. As it happened, in spite of the best possible start, for Australia and the West Indies each won one of the first two Tests, it turned out to be a sad anticlimax.

Temperamentally, West Indian sides have always been suspect, and it was probably only the discipline, the example and the sympathetic understanding of Frank Worrell which enabled their formidable side of the early 1960s to be successful for so long, first under his own captaincy and then under Sobers's. Man for man the West Indies side in Australia was at least as talented as Australia's. The difference lay in their response to pressure and in their respective abilities to work out what was required of them if they were to win an extremely exacting series.

Australia won easily because they were better led, they were tougher opponents when the pressure was on, they were admirably single-minded about the job of winning and their cricket was far more disciplined. The West Indies have never won a series in Australia and, before it started, it looked as if this tour would give them a wonderful chance. Although Australia won and convincingly so, one came away with the over-riding impression that this had been a series which the West Indies had, if anything, done more to lose than Australia had to win.

From the very start of the tour it was obvious that the West Indies' chances were going to be severely handicapped if their batsmen were not going to be able to check their desire to play their strokes regardless. By the time the First Test came round in Brisbane, their main batsmen had all played beautiful innings of thirties and forties and fifties, but hardly any had gone on to make hundreds.

In many ways the progress of these West Indies players round Australia was summed up by the first morning of the series. Lloyd won the toss and batted, and the West Indies played as if they were involved in a one-day knockout game. Eighteen overs were bowled before lunch, every conceivable stroke was played, and at the interval they were an incredible 125 for six.

In the context of Test cricket it made no sense whatever – and the first seven West Indies batsmen had all had the experience of playing county cricket and therefore understood the discipline that was required. It also revealed Lloyd's tactical weaknesses as a captain. When in the field, he was slow to appreciate situations and to read the game.

1976-77 – AUSTRALIA v ENGLAND (CENTENARY TEST): UNFORGETTABLE
Reg Hayter, 1978

At Melbourne, March 12, 13, 14, 16, 17, 1977. Australia won by 45 runs. An occasion of warmest reunion and nostalgia, the cricket continuously compelling, a result straining credulity. A masterpiece of organisation resulted in an event which none fortunate enough to be present could forget. Unlucky were those who missed it. Invitations were sent to the 244 living cricketers who had played for Australia or England in the series. All but 26 of these were able to accept for an event unique in history.

The oldest Australian Test player present was the 87-year-old Jack Ryder. Even though suffering from near-blindness, the 84-year-old Percy Fender made the enervating air journey from Britain as the oldest English representative. He was accomplished by his grandson, Jeremy, who became his cricketing eyes.

Of those who went to Melbourne many told unusual stories. Colin McCool was marooned in his Queensland home by floods and had to be hauled up from his front lawn by helicopter for the airport. Jack Rutherford's train broke down and he finished the journey to the airport by taxi. Denis Compton – who else? – left his passport in a Cardiff hotel and, but for the early start to the pre-flight champagne party at London airport which enabled a good friend to test the speed limits on the M4, would have missed the plane. The gradual gathering of all at the Hilton Hotel, 200 yards across the Jolimont Park from the Melbourne Oval, brought meetings and greetings of unabated happiness. Not a hitch, not one.

Fittingly, this was also Melbourne's Mardi Gras, a week called Moomba, the Aboriginal word for "let's get together and have fun". After a champagne (much was drunk between London and Melbourne and back) breakfast and an opening ceremony in which ex-Test captains accompanied the teams on to the field, the crowd were also given the opportunity of a special welcome to all the former Test players.

Australia, handicapped by the early departure of McCosker, who fractured his jaw when a ball from Willis flew off his hand into his face, were always on the defensive. England's batting buckled even more swiftly against Lillee, at the zenith of his form and speed, and Walker. That was the last of the bowling mastery. On the second, third and fourth days Australia increased their first-innings lead of 43 so much that their declaration left England 463 to win at 40 an hour.

And, in the presence of the Queen and the Duke of Edinburgh – during an interval they drove round the ground and were hugely acclaimed – royally did they apply themselves. The innings to remember was played by Randall, a jaunty, restless, bubbling character, whose 174 took England to the doorstep of victory. The Australian spectators enjoyed his approach as much as Indian crowds had done on the tour just finished.

Once, when Lillee tested him with a bouncer, he tennis-batted it to the midwicket fence with a speed and power that made many a rheumy eye turn to the master of the stroke, the watching Sir Donald Bradman. Words cannot recapture the joy of that moment. Another time, when Lillee bowled short, Randall ducked, rose, drew himself to his full five feet eight, doffed his cap and bowed politely. Then, felled by another bouncer, he gaily performed a reverse roll. This helped to maintain a friendly atmosphere in what, at all times, was a serious and fully competitive match.

Some time after it was over someone discovered that the result of the 226th Test between the two countries – victory by 45 runs – was identical, to the same side and to the very run, with that of the 1877 Test on the same ground.

Australia 138 and 419 (R. W. Marsh 110*, I. C. Davis 68, K. D. Walters 66, D. W. Hookes 56; C. M. Old 4-104);

England 95 (D. K. Lillee 6-26, M. H. N. Walker 4-54)

and 417 (D. W. Randall 174, D. L. Amiss 64; Lillee 5-139).

First news of what was to become, virtually, "The Packer Explosion" came from South Africa towards the end of April 1977 when South Africa's *Sunday Times* broke the news that four South African cricketers had signed lucrative contracts to play an eight-week series of matches throughout the world.

In the middle of May, *The Bulletin*, Australia's 97-year-old magazine owned by The Australian Consolidated Press Limited (chairman: Kerry Packer) announced the completion of a huge sporting deal in which 35 top cricketers had been signed for three years to play specially arranged matches, beginning with a series of six five-day Test matches, six one-day games, and six three-day round-robin tournaments in Australia in 1977-78. Prize money would be $100,000. The deal had been put together by JP Sports and Television Corporation Limited, proprietors of Channel 9 in Sydney (chairman: Kerry Packer).

On May 13, The Cricket Council issued a statement at the end of an emergency meeting to the effect that Greig was not to be considered as England's captain in the forthcoming series against Australia. The statement went on: "His action has inevitably impaired the trust which existed between the cricket authorities and the captain of the England side." F. R. Brown, chairman of the Council, added: "The captaincy of the England team involves close liaison with the selectors in the management, selection and development of England players for the future and clearly Greig is unlikely to be able to do this as his stated intention is to be contracted elsewhere during the next three winters."

At the end of May, Packer arrived in England, and at a press conference said: "It is not a pirate series but a Super-Test series. I have sent telegrams to all the cricketing bodies but they don't reply. I am willing to compromise but time is running out." He referred to cricket as the easiest sport in the world to take over, as nobody had bothered to pay the players what they were worth.

At this point the only cricket subject being discussed, from the highest committee room in the land to the saloon bar of the tiniest inn, was "Packer", and from all the multifarious points raised, one was likely to be proved the dominant factor in the end. In this age of extreme partisanship, had non-partisanship cricket any future? Could a collection of players, however great, stimulate public interest, when there was nothing on the end of it, except a considerable amount of money for the participants? And moreover, the whole crux of this matter was linked to big business – the business of television, and not so much to the furtherance of cricket or cricketers.

Mr Packer, as chairman of Channel 9 of Australia, was bitterly disappointed that an offer he had made to the Australian Board of Control for television rights for conventional Test cricket had not been given the due consideration which he felt the offer had merited. Out of this frustration, his scheme was born and nurtured.

The judgment

Mr Justice Slade granted three English cricketers who had contracted to play for Mr Kerry Packer's World Series Cricket Pty Ltd. declarations that all the changes of the rules of the International Cricket Conference and all their resolutions banning them from Test cricket are ultra vires and void as being in unreasonable restraint of trade.

So, too, are the Test and County Cricket Board's proposed rules governing qualification and registration of cricketers in Test and competitive and county cricket.

Wisden 1979 carried scorecards but no reports of the WSC "Supertests".

THE PUBLIC WILL DECIDE Notes by the Editor, Norman Preston, 1978

The summer of 1977 will be remembered by most people for the Queen's Silver Jubilee. For lovers of cricket there were two other important topics. First, England won back the Ashes and secondly, there came the announcement in May that Kerry Packer, the Australian newspaper and television magnate, had secretly signed up at fabulous fees 35 Test stars from England, Australia, the West Indies, South Africa and Pakistan.

No one can be positive for the time being about the success or failure of Mr Packer's venture. It is said that he would be willing to spend as much as nine million Australian dollars to put his World Series Cricket firmly on the map, but in the end it will be the public who will pronounce the verdict, mainly by their attendance at his matches and the time they devote to his TV presentations.

As things stand no solution would appear to be in sight and the cricket authorities, particularly those in England, who spend thousands of pounds raising young talent to the top level, run the risk of losing players to any rich entrepreneur, for Packer could only be the first in the line. I feel that those who signed for Packer were placed in a dilemma – loyalty to those that nurtured them or the attraction of financial reward for playing another kind of cricket that excludes them from first-class recognition.

AN OUTSIDER TO THE END Obituaries, 2013

Greig had never disguised his intention to become "the first millionaire cricketer". Catching the militant mood of the 1970s, he once stood up at a Professional Cricketers' Association meeting and suggested a work-to-rule on Sundays. But it was Packer who provided his route to those riches, and the pair strode down the Strand shoulder to shoulder when the WSC players took the authorities to the High Court after they had been banned from the first-class game; the players won.

When a peace deal was brokered after two disrupted Australian summers, Packer's offer of a job for life came good. For the next three decades, Greig was integral to Channel Nine's coverage. His excitable style did not please everyone, but his voice became almost as familiar as Richie Benaud's.

In October 2012 it was revealed Greig was suffering from lung cancer; two months later, he died in a Sydney hospital after suffering a heart attack at home. On the Saturday morning when Britain awoke to the news, the honours list was published. Mike Denness had been awarded an OBE. It left Greig as the only England captain without such recognition – an outsider to the end.

E. W. Swanton's Team in West Indies, 1956. Stewart, who batted well in both Barbados matches, left the party immediately after the match against the West Indies XI and flew to Britain in order to assist his soccer club, Corinthian-Casuals, in the replayed final of the FA Amateur Cup against Bishop Auckland, but delays to his planes owing to the weather thwarted him and he arrived at the ground in Middlesbrough five minutes after the match had started.

Little Wonder No. 60

1977-78 – INDIANS IN AUSTRALIA: SIMPSON TO THE RESCUE   Dicky Rutnagur, 1979

Both Australia and India responded magnificently to the challenge of World Series Cricket and to the enthusiasm of those who watched and followed the Test matches. The tourists kindled the flame of public interest by winning every State game leading up to the first Test.

In what turned out to be a fascinating series, Australia won the first two Tests, but both in desperately close finishes. Then India won the Third and Fourth Tests, both more decisively than Australia had won the two preceding encounters. The two-all situation set up the series for a glorious finish, and the finale was indeed dramatic and exciting. Australia won the six-day final Test on the last day after India, in an heroic second-innings recovery, had made a record losing score of 445.

Even before it was dismembered by Packer, the Australian side had looked a poor collection during the tour of England in the summer of 1977. Obviously, the hurriedly rebuilt teams that Australia fielded were of moderate class, and much credit for Australia winning the series under these circumstances is due to the inspiring leadership and personal achievement of Bobby Simpson who, at 41, came out of a ten-year retirement to aid Australian cricket in its worst crisis ever.

1977-78 – AUSTRALIA v INDIA (SECOND TEST): MANN ENOUGH
Dicky Rutnagur, 1979

At Perth, December 16, 17, 18, 20, 21, 1977. Australia won by two wickets. The pulsating finish, with 22 balls remaining, was a fitting climax to a match in which fortunes fluctuated with almost every session. Both sides approached the match with commendable enterprise and, in view of the fact that 1,468 runs were scored, the achievement of a decisive finish was remarkable.

The Australian victory was largely owed to their veteran captain, Bobby Simpson. Coming in at 65 for three in the first innings, and that only after a brief rest following a long stint in the field, Simpson rallied Australia with a dogged 176, lasting six hours 41 minutes.

Australia were left six hours and 40 minutes to score 339 runs for victory. The one wicket India captured before the close on the penultimate day proved a mixed blessing, for Tony Mann, who came in as nightwatchman, stayed on next day to play a match-winning innings of 105 in just over three hours. Only 58 runs were wanted at the start of the mandatory 15 overs of the last hour. However, in the second of these overs, with the margin now cut down to 44, a brilliant piece of fielding by Madan Lal, the bowler, ran out Simpson. In the same over, he produced a beautiful ball which nipped back and trapped Hughes lbw. Then, with only nine runs wanted and almost six overs left, Toohey, who had batted with discipline and in a most accomplished manner to make 83, had a rush of blood and played a fatal, lofted drive off Bedi. There was a suggestion of panic as Rixon, in the same over, played across the line and fell lbw to Bedi, but Australia had come too near winning to be foiled.

India 402 (M. Amarnath 90, C. P. S. Chauhan 88; J. R. Thomson 4-101)
and 330-9 dec. (S. M. Gavaskar 127, Amarnath 100; J. B. Gannon 4-77);
Australia 394 (R. B. Simpson 176, J. Dyson 53, S. J. Rixon 50; B. S. Bedi 5-89)
and 342-8 (A. L. Mann 105, P. M. Toohey 83; Bedi 5-105).

1978-79 –AUSTRALIA v PAKISTAN (First Test): super Sarfraz

Brian Osborne, 1980

At Melbourne, March 10, 11, 12, 14, 15, 1979. Pakistan won by 71 runs. At 4.30pm on the fifth and last day, Australia, with seven wickets in hand and only 77 runs needed for victory, appeared to have gained a decisive hold over an entertaining Test of changing fortunes. But then the vastly experienced Sarfraz Nawaz took charge and the match was at an end within an hour – or 65 balls and five runs later. Sarfraz's personal contribution of seven wickets for one run from 33 deliveries represented one of the greatest bowling feats in the history of Test cricket.

Pakistan 196 (R. M. Hogg 4-49) **and 353-9 dec.** (Majid Khan 108, Zaheer Abbas 59);
Australia 168 (Imran Khan 4-26)
and 310 (A. R. Border 105, K. J. Hughes 84, A. M. J. Hilditch 62; Sarfraz Nawaz 9-86).

1978-79 – England In Australia: unequal struggle

Alex Bannister, 1980

A lone trumpeter on the sparsely filled Hill at Sydney grimly symbolised Australia's embarrassing defeats, domestic confusions and divided loyalties, by sounding the Last Post as England won the Sixth Test inside four days and the series by five to one.

For Brearley, a comfortable victor over Greg Chappell in the home summer of 1977, it was a continuation of his triumphant progress since he took over the captaincy from Greig. In the space of 20 months he defeated Australia eight times in 11 Tests, and it is not uncharitable to say that his one defeat at Melbourne might have been avoided if he had not lost an important toss.

No England captain, or for that matter any captain, had won five Tests in a series in Australia. Brearley's critics will no doubt argue that Australia, drained by defections to World Series Cricket, have never been weaker in the 102 years of struggle between the two countries.

The competition from World Series Cricket put heavy demands on the Australian authorities, and the game at large suffered from an over-heavy programme and too much exposure on television. The well-oiled and professional WSC publicity machine often distracted attention from the Ashes series, and the public grew tired of supporting a losing team. The public longed for better results and new heroes. One emerged in Rodney Hogg, the 27-year-old fast bowler, whose 41 wickets passed the record 36 taken by Arthur Mailey in the five-Test series against England in 1920-21. Fittingly Hogg broke the old record in front of his home crowd at Adelaide in the Fifth Test.

Just before the party left England Botham injured a wrist; yet no cricketer was more impatient to get into action. Once in the thick of the fight Botham, a brave, combative and highly skilled competitor, was never out of it. His batting carried the dash of a cavalier, his bowling had the spice of aggression and experiment, and his fielding was inspired in any position. As if their task was not difficult enough, Australia created a bizarre record by having one of their openers run out in every Test.

1979-80 – ENGLAND IN AUSTRALIA: CRICKET, BUT NOT AS WE KNOW IT

Peter Smith, 1981

Forty-eight hours before England's cricketers flew out of Melbourne for the last time, Alec Bedser was asked his considered view of the experimental twin-tour programme, the first product of the marriage between the Australian Cricket Board and World Series Cricket which had taken place some nine months earlier. He gave it a definite thumbs-down.

Privately, at least, the Australian players agreed with Bedser. With a programme of six Test matches – three each against England and West Indies – plus the trian-gular one-day competition, the Australian players became very much a touring side inside their own country. So anxious was their captain Greg Chappell to rejoin a family he had hardly seen for two months that he was flying home to Brisbane within an hour of bringing the final Test against England in Melbourne to a swift and victorious conclusion.

England's cricketers were just as unhappy with the complicated programme of matches that brought a constant switch from one-day to five-day cricket. It could be claimed that England's verdict was coloured by their 3–0 series defeat in the Tests [*because it was only a three-match rubber, the Ashes were not at stake*], but Clive Lloyd, West Indies' captain, was just as critical.

It was not only the match programme but the whole atmosphere that the England players found disagreeable. Their captain, Brearley, was the subject of a disgraceful campaign wherever he went, and a large section of the Melbourne crowd was so abusive that the Australian team manager, John Edwards, was moved to issue a statement in which he said they made him ashamed to be an Australian.

The show-business style presentation of the one-day matches succeeded in appealing to a new public, but the loutish, drunken behaviour of many of the newcomers posed additional headaches for the ground authorities. Both in Melbourne and Sydney costly extra security measures were taken, along with a restriction on the amount of alcohol sold inside the grounds or taken in. This improved the behaviour but not the language.

1979-80 – AUSTRALIA v ENGLAND (First Test): TEST OF METAL

Peter Smith, 1981

At Perth, December 14, 15, 16, 18, 19, 1979. Australia won by 138 runs. It was unfortunate that Australia's victory at the end of an enthralling match was soured by Lillee's unsavoury behaviour in seeking to use an aluminium bat in the first innings despite objections from Brearley, the umpires and his own captain. He caused play to be held up for ten minutes before being persuaded by Chappell to exchange it for the traditional willow. The incident served only to blacken Lillee's reputation and damage the image of the game as well as, eventually, the reputation of the Australian authorities because of their reluctance to take effective disciplinary action. Lillee's behaviour also partly overshadowed other individual performances more in keeping with the spirit of the game, notably the bowling of Botham and Dymock, the batting of Hughes and Border, and Boycott's gallant attempt to save England on the final day.

Australia 244 (K. J. Hughes 99; I. T. Botham 6-78)
and 337 (A. R. Border 115, J. M. Wiener 58; Botham 5-98);
England 228 (J. M. Brearley 64; D. K. Lillee 4-73) and 215 (G. Boycott 99*; G. Dymock 6-34).

1980-81 – AUSTRALIA v NEW ZEALAND (World Series Cup, Third Final): UNDERHAND

1982

At Melbourne, February 1, 1981. Australia won by six runs. With New Zealand needing six runs to tie the match off the last ball, Trevor Chappell, instructed to do so by his brother and captain, Greg, bowled McKechnie an underarm ball [*rolled along the ground*], which caused a furore that could haunt Australia–New Zealand cricket for a long time. Edgar, with a splendid hundred to his name, was not out at the end. After some good blows by Parker, Trevor Chappell came on to bowl the last over with 15 still needed and four wickets left. Hadlee straight-drove the first ball for four and was lbw to the second. Smith then hit two twos before being bowled, swinging at the fifth ball, leaving New Zealand with six to tie off the now infamous underarm delivery.

Australia 235-4 (50 overs) (G. S. Chappell 90, G. M. Wood 72);
New Zealand 229-8 (50 overs) (B. A. Edgar 102; G. S. Chappell 3-43).

1980-81 – AUSTRALIA v INDIA (THIRD TEST): DISAGREEMENT

Dicky Rutnagur, 1982

At Melbourne, February 7, 8, 9, 10, 11, 1981. India won by 59 runs. This was a sensational match, not only for Australia's astonishing collapse in the second innings against an Indian attack that was badly handicapped by injuries. India had come near to forfeiting the match on the previous day when their captain, Gavaskar, so sharply disagreed with an lbw decision against himself that he wanted to call off the contest. When Gavaskar was given out by umpire Whitehead, he first indicated that he had edged the ball on to his pad, and then, as he walked past Chauhan he urged him to leave the field with him. Fortunately the manager of the Indian team, Wing Commander S. K. Durrani, intervened, meeting the incoming pair at the gate and ordering Chauhan to continue his innings. With this controversial dismissal of Gavaskar, Lillee put himself level with Richie Benaud as Australia's highest wicket-taker in Test cricket, and he surpassed Benaud's record of 248 wickets a quarter of an hour later when Chauhan square-cut him to cover point.

When Australia batted again, with just over an hour left to the end of the fourth day, they needed 143 to win and India were without the bowling of Kapil Dev, who had strained a thigh muscle, and Yadav, whose foot injury had worsened from his efforts in the first innings. Doshi, too, was in great distress, but soldiered on. Nevertheless, the weakened attack made major inroads before the day was out, with Dyson, Wood and Chappell (out first ball, bowled behind his legs) all back in the dressing-room and only 24 runs on the board. Kapil Dev, who had batted with a runner and had not appeared on the field on the previous day, joined the fray on the final morning and bowled unchanged to take five of the seven remaining Australian wickets that fell in just over two and a quarter hours. Following Lillee's lead, Kapil Dev bowled straight and to a length and let the pitch do the rest.

India 237 (G. R. Viswanath 114; D. K. Lillee 4-65)

and 324 (C. P. S. Chauhan 85, S. M. Gavaskar 70; Lillee 4-104);

Australia 419 (A. R. Border 124, K. D. Walters 78, G. S. Chappell 76) and 83 (Kapil Dev 5-28).

1981-82 – PAKISTANIS IN AUSTRALIA: UGLY CONFRONTATION   Brian Osborne, 1983

Javed Miandad led the side and batted well throughout, although his confrontation with Lillee during the Perth Test was a wretched affair and he did not appear to have the full support of his whole team at all times. He was also involved in strong but unsuccessful requests by the Pakistani management to have the umpires replaced for the Second Test.

The confrontation between Miandad and Lillee was one of the most undignified incidents in Test history. Miandad, batting to Lillee, had turned a ball to the on side and was in the course of completing a comfortable single when he was obstructed by Lillee. In the ensuing fracas Lillee kicked Miandad, who responded by shaping to strike him with his bat. The Australian team imposed a $200 fine (£120 approx.) on Lillee and sought an apology from Miandad for his part in the affair. However, the umpires, who had assisted in quelling the incident, objected to the penalty as being too lenient, and the matter was dealt with at a Melbourne hearing before Mr R. Merriman, the co-ordinator of the Australian Cricket Board's cricket sub-committee. His ruling was that Lillee's penalty, set by the players, was not sufficient and he imposed a suspension from Australia's two ensuing one-day internationals – against Pakistan and West Indies. No apology was forthcoming from Miandad, whose participation in the incident was also referred to in the umpires' report.

1981-82 – AUSTRALIA v WEST INDIES (FIRST TEST): HUGHES'S HOT STREAK

Henry Blofeld, 1983

At Melbourne, December 26, 27, 28, 29, 30, 1981. Australia won by 58 runs. Soon Australia were 26 for four, and it needed a superb innings by Hughes to effect some sort of recovery. Holding, in particular, was extremely fast. Yet Hughes was determined not just to concentrate on passive defence. When the ninth wicket fell at 155 Hughes had reached 71, but Alderman kept his head down and his bat straight while his partner played some marvellous strokes, reaching his hundred with a thrilling square-cut for four off Garner. West Indies were left with 35 minutes' batting on the first evening, which produced most dramatic cricket as Alderman and Lillee took four wickets for ten runs. Alderman had Bacchus, opening in place of Greenidge whose knee injury had not mended, caught at fourth slip; Lillee, who began the match needing five wickets to beat Lance Gibbs's record of 309 Test wickets, then had Haynes splendidly caught by Border above his head at second slip. Croft, the nightwatchman, was leg-before, shuffling across his stumps in the same over. And with the last ball of the day Lillee bowled Richards off the inside edge as he tried to drive. Lillee thus began the second day needing two more wickets for his record. Dujon, having batted excitingly well, was the first, being caught at deep backward square leg off a hook that would have been a big six on many grounds. Lillee got his record when Gomes was caught by Chappell at first slip.

Australia 198 (K. J. Hughes 100*; M. A. Holding 5-45)

and 222 (B. M. Laird 64, G. M. Wood 46, A. R. Border 66; Holding 6-62);

West Indies 201 (H. A. Gomes 55; D. K. Lillee 7-83) **and 161** (B. Yardley 4-38).

Rain deters crowds. The total of paying spectators in 1956 for all first-class matches was 2,003,618 compared with 2,708,670 in 1953 when the Australians were previously in Great Britain. The County Championship attendances in 1956 were 1,174,079, the lowest figure since the war. The wet summer undoubtedly helped to keep the crowds away.

Little Wonder No. 61

1982-83 – AUSTRALIA v ENGLAND (FOURTH TEST): ONE OF THE BEST

John Woodcock, 1984

At Melbourne, December 26, 27, 28, 29, 30, 1982. England won by three runs. A magnificent Test match, to be ranked among the best ever played, produced a finish of such protracted excitement that it had the whole of Australia by the ears. Needing 292 to win, Australia were 218 for nine when Border and Thomson embarked on a last-wicket partnership of epic proportions. At close of play on the fourth day they had taken the score to 255 for nine, leaving another 37 runs to be found on the last morning for Australia, there and then, to regain the Ashes.

Although, on this last day, the match could have been over within moments, 18,000 spectators, admitted free of charge, went to the Melbourne Cricket Ground in the hope of seeing Border and Thomson achieve their improbable goal. All things considered, among them a new ball taken at 259 for nine, Thomson was rarely in trouble; Border never was. By the time Botham began the 18th over of the morning Australia were within four runs of victory. His first ball was short of a length and wide of the off stump. Thomson, sparring at it, edged a none-too-difficult catch to Tavaré, the second of Botham's two slips. Tavaré managed only to parry it, the ball bouncing away behind him but within reach of Miller, fielding at first slip, deeper than Tavaré. With a couple of quick strides Miller reached the catch and completed it, the ball still some 18 inches off the ground.

For the first time in a Test match, Melbourne's huge video scoreboard was in operation, the screen being used to show action replays and advertisements as well as the score and other sundry details. It was, on the whole, well received, although Willis remarked after the match that there had been occasions when, needing to know the score, he found himself looking instead at a picture of a motor car or a meat pie.

England 284 (C. J. Tavaré 89, A. J. Lamb 83; R. M. Hogg 4-69, B. Yardley 4-89)
and 294 (G. Fowler 65; G. F. Lawson 4-66);
Australia 287 (K. J. Hughes 66, D. W. Hookes 53, R. W. Marsh 53)
and 288 (Hookes 68, A. R. Border 62*; N. G. Cowans 6-77).

1984-85 – AUSTRALIA v WEST INDIES (SECOND TEST): TEARFUL RESIGNATION

Tony Cozier, 1986

At Brisbane, November 23, 24, 25, 26, 1984. West Indies won by eight wickets. Another shattering defeat in four days for Australia led immediately to the resignation of their captain, Hughes, emotionally announced at a post-match press conference. Trying unsuccessfully to hold back his tears, Hughes, in a prepared statement, said: "The constant criticism, speculation and innuendo by former players and a section of the media over the past four or five years have finally taken their toll." Australia were again betrayed by their batting. Garner bowled Wessels with the last ball of the first over after Lloyd had chosen to field, and Australia never recovered from this psychological setback. For the second time in successive Tests Hughes was caught at long leg hooking, and it needed Phillips's aggression to carry

Australia past 150. Garner became the fifth West Indies bowler to take 200 Test wickets when he bowled Lawson.

Australia 175 (J. Garner 4-67)
and 271 (K. C. Wessels 61, W. B. Phillips 54, D. C. Boon 51; M. D. Marshall 5-82, M. A. Holding 4-92);
West Indies 424 (R. B. Richardson 138, C. H. Lloyd 114, Marshall 57; G. F. Lawson 5-116) **and 26-2.**

1985-86 – New Zealanders In Australia: out of the shadows
Don Cameron, 1987

Perhaps because New Zealand cricket had existed in the shade of Australia for so many decades – one Test was played in 1946, and regular Test exchanges did not start until 1973-74 – Australian cricket loomed over New Zealand. So it was with a sense of wonderment, and delight, that New Zealanders greeted the success of Jeremy Coney's team as they took, by two Tests to one, their first-ever series against Australia. With a little more luck it might have been 3–0, for between New Zealand's innings victory in the first Test at the Gabba and the six-wicket win at Perth, New Zealand narrowly missed victory in the nip-and-tuck struggle at Sydney.

1985-86 – AUSTRALIA v NEW ZEALAND (First Test): Hadlee delivers
Don Cameron, 1987

At Brisbane, November 8, 9, 10, 11, 12, 1985. New Zealand won by an innings and 41 runs. When Coney sent Australia in to bat on a pitch which seemed to have some moisture in it, and with cloudy, humid weather aiding the faster bowlers, there was no early indication of the drama that this Test would provide. Wessels, 38 not out, led Australia uncertainly to lunch at 72 for two, and he had 69 not out, and Australia 146 for four, when bad light cut short the first day. Hadlee's 15 overs had brought him four wickets for 35, and early on the second, humid morning he dismissed Wessels for 70. He then demolished the Australian innings with one of the outstanding pieces of contemporary Test match bowling, having taken all eight by the time Australia were 175 for eight. He missed the chance of all ten wickets by taking a well-judged catch in the deep from Lawson to give Brown his first wicket in Test cricket, whereupon Brown returned the favour by catching Holland and Australia were all out for 179, with Hadlee returning figures of 23.4–4–52–9. Only J. C. Laker (twice in 1956 at Manchester) and G. A. Lohmann (in 1895-96 in Johannesburg) had recorded better analyses in Test cricket.

Australia 179 (K. C. Wessels 70; R. J. Hadlee 9-52)
and 333 (A. R. Border 152*, G. R. J. Matthews 115; Hadlee 6-71);
New Zealand 553-7 dec. (M. D. Crowe 188, J. F. Reid 108).

1986-87 – AUSTRALIA v ENGLAND (FIRST TEST): BOTHAM ROLLS BACK YEARS

John Thicknesse, 1988

At Brisbane, November 14, 15, 16, 18, 19, 1986. England won by seven wickets. Following England's poor performance in their preceding match at Perth and the development of several of their own players on the recent tour of India, Australia were widely fancied to achieve what would have been their seventh victory in 11 post-war Tests against England at Woolloongabba.

England's emphatic victory was a salutary reminder of the dangers of reading too much into omens and too little into experience, especially in the first match of a series when nerves – and nerve – play such a part. The opening session was to have a decisive bearing on how the match developed. Though Reid moved one away to have Broad caught at the wicket after 35 minutes, Australia's attack lacked the accuracy to put England under pressure.

Australia, ill served by their fast bowlers, at no stage promised to recover. England at 198 for two were nicely placed. On the second morning, however, the game changed rapidly. Lamb was out first ball, Athey three overs later with the score unaltered, and still at 198 Gower was missed off Hughes by C. D. Matthews at third slip, a sharp chance off a slash two-handed to his right. The match turned in that instant. While Gower took half an hour to settle, Botham played with much authority; he dominated their stand of 118. Botham's 138, which included an assault on Hughes which brought 22 in the over of his century, was comparable to his 118 at Old Trafford in 1981 for power and control. He batted 249 minutes (174 balls) and hit four sixes – straight-drives – and 13 fours before Hughes sprinted in to catch him at long leg.

England 456 (I. T. Botham 138, C. W. J. Athey 76, M. W. Gatting 61, D. I. Gower 51) and 77-3;

Australia 248 (G. R. J. Matthews 56*, G. R. Marsh 56; G. R. Dilley 5-68)

and 282 (Marsh 110; J. E. Emburey 5-80).

1986-87 – AUSTRALIA v ENGLAND (FOURTH TEST): SMALL MERCIES

John Thicknesse, 1988

At Melbourne, December 26, 27, 28, 1986. England won by an innings and 14 runs. A combination of excellent outswing bowling by Small, playing in his first Test of the series, and an inept appraisal by Australia of their best means of success, effectively decided the match, and the destination of the Ashes, by tea on the first day. Australia, put in on a pitch not fully dry, were bowled out for 141 in 235 minutes, Small maintaining a high degree of accuracy to take five for 48 in 22.4 overs. A last-minute replacement for Dilley, who failed a fitness test on a jarred knee on the morning of the match, Small amply justified his preference to Foster by dismissing five of the first seven batsmen in the order. With two more wickets in the second innings, including that of Border when with Marsh the captain was showing signs of keeping Australia in the match, a valuable 21 not out at No. 11, and a good catch in the deep to finish the game, Small was a deserving winner of the Man of the Match award in only his third Test. Well as Small bowled, however, both he and more especially

Botham were helped by Australia's ill-conceived approach. Botham, bowling off the shortened run he had used three days earlier in Canberra, took five for 41, a disproportionate reward for 16 overs at medium-pace with faster variations.

Australia 141 (D. M. Jones 59; G. C. Small 5-48, I. T. Botham 5-41) **and 194** (G. R. Marsh 60);
England 349 (B. C. Broad 112; B. A. Reid 4-78, C. J. McDermott 4-83).

1986-87 – AUSTRALIA v ENGLAND (WORLD SERIES CUP): LAMB'S LATE SHOW

1988

At Sydney, January 22, 1987. Lamb struck Reid for 2, 4, 6, 2, 4 in the final over to blast England to a tremendous win with a ball to spare. Although the pitch lacked pace, Australia, who chose to bat first, should have scored more than 233 for eight after passing 150 in the 33rd over. England's innings followed a similar pattern, Broad's 45 coming off 58 balls and Gower and Lamb adding 86 off 20 overs. However, a clever spell by Matthews, supported by good fielding, left England needing 32 off three, 25 off two and 18 off the final over. Lamb, who until then had been at loggerheads with his timing and had not hit a boundary, was equal to the task, hauling Reid twice to square leg and once over deep midwicket.

Australia 233-8 (50 overs) (D. M. Wellham 97; J. E. Emburey 3-42);
England 234-7 (49.5 overs) (A. J. Lamb 77*, D. I. Gower 50, B. C. Broad 45; S. P. O'Donnell 3-39).

1988-89 – AUSTRALIA v WEST INDIES (FOURTH TEST): ALL ABOUT BORDER

John Woodcock, 1990

At Sydney, January 26, 27, 28, 29, 30, 1989. Australia won by seven wickets. As had happened in 1984-85, on West Indies' last full visit to Australia, a bare and slow Sydney pitch, on which the ball turned from the start, gave Australia the chance to attack West Indies at their weakest point and inflict on them a rare defeat, their first for 11 Tests. West Indies departed from their usual formula by bringing in a spinner, Harper, in place of a fourth fast bowler, Patterson, and against every current trend the match produced 279.3 overs of spin, the most in a Test match in Australia for 57 years. To take advantage of the conditions, Australia chose Hohns, the Queensland leg-spinner.

When Richards won the toss and West Indies reached 144 before losing their second wicket, the match looked to be slipping away from Australia at an early stage. But Border then embarked on an all-round performance seldom surpassed by a captain in Test cricket. Having bowled only two overs in the first three Tests, he now destroyed West Indies' first innings, with some co-operation from the batsmen, by taking seven for 46 with the orthodox left-arm slows he had never thought worth taking seriously.

West Indies' second innings followed much the same course as their first. Although they had wiped out Australia's lead of 177 with seven wickets in hand, they finished by leaving Australia with only 80 to win. Border took his tally for the match to 11 for 96. He had never taken more than four wickets in a first-class match before. Fittingly enough, Border hit the winning runs.

West Indies 224 (C. G. Greenidge 56, D. L. Haynes 75; A. R. Border 7-46) **256** (Haynes 143; Border 4-50); **Australia 401** (D. C. Boon 149, Border 75, S. R. Waugh 55*; M. D. Marshall 5-29) **and 82-3**.

1992-93 – AUSTRALIA v WEST INDIES (THIRD TEST): BREATHTAKING BRIAN
Tony Cozier, 1994

At Sydney, January 2, 3, 4, 5, 6, 1992. Drawn. An innings of breathtaking quality by Brian Lara towered over everything else in a high-scoring match. It drastically altered the course of a series that was slipping away from his team when he joined Richardson in the second over of the third day.

In between breaks for rain Lara unleashed a dazzling array of strokes. He needed only 125 balls to reach his maiden Test century in his fifth match. By the end of the day, he was 121, Richardson 94 and their partnership of 217 was already the highest for West Indies' third wicket in a Test in Australia. "I can hardly remember my hundred," Richardson said afterwards. "It was difficult playing and being a spectator at the same time."

By this time Lara was scoring at will in all directions, dominating another partnership, of 124, with Arthurton. Australia were powerless to stop him until he committed himself to a single to cover off Matthews and could not beat Martyn's return to the wicketkeeper when Hooper sent him back. His 277 was the third-highest individual Test score against Australia (behind L. Hutton and R. E. Foster) and the highest for either side in Tests between Australia and West Indies. He struck 38 fours off 372 balls in seven hours 54 minutes. Lara's pre-eminence on the rain-shortened fourth day was such that he added 156 and struck 23 fours, outscoring his three partners by more than two to one. His solitary chance, low to Steve Waugh at gully off Hughes, was when he was 172.

Australia 503 (S. R. Waugh 100, G. R. J. Matthews 79, D. C. Boon 76, A. R. Border 74, M. E. Waugh 57) **and 117-0; West Indies 606** (B. C. Lara 277, R. B. Richardson 109, J. C. Adams 77*).

1992-93 – AUSTRALIA v WEST INDIES (FOURTH TEST): BOX OFFICE
Tony Cozier, 1994

At Adelaide, January 23, 24, 25, 26, 1993. West Indies won by one run. Adelaide 1992-93 took its place as one of the greatest of all Test matches when Craig McDermott failed to get out of the way of a lifter from Courtney Walsh and gloved a catch to give West Indies victory by one run, the narrowest victory anyone has achieved in 116 years of Test cricket.

But it had been a game of fluctuating fortunes throughout. When Australia, needing 186 to win, lost their eighth second-innings wicket for 102, it appeared to have made its decisive shift. But then the 22-year-old debutant Justin Langer, who came in only when Martyn was injured at pre-match practice, added 42 with the No. 10 Tim May, who was playing his first Test in four years. After that May and the last man McDermott put on another 40 to get Australia within two of their target.

The unfolding drama lifted the TV cricket ratings in Australia to a new record. And, with the Adelaide Oval within walking distance of the city centre, new spectators rushed to the ground. Finally, a short ball from Walsh, pitched on off stump, lifted to brush McDermott's hand on its way through to Murray. Umpire Hair upheld the appeal. The West Indians on the field celebrated emotionally. The crowd who had been singing Waltzing Matilda as Australia inched towards their goal were stunned into silence.

The Australian captain Border did not dispute Hair's decision, though he said that, like the result, it was a very close one. "What can you say – one run? I was very confident of getting 186 at the start of the day." His opposite number Richardson said: "I knew Walshy would get a wicket with that very ball. I never lost hope." Both leaders paid tribute to the man who made the result possible: Ambrose consolidated his reputation as the world's leading fast bowler with ten wickets in the match and a burst of three wickets in 19 balls after lunch to dismiss Steve Waugh, Border and Hughes. "I have never seen a bowler like him," said Richardson.

West Indies 252 (B. C. Lara 52; M. G. Hughes 5-64) **and 146** (R. B. Richardson 72; T. B. A. May 5-9); **Australia 213** (C. E. L. Ambrose 6-74) **and 184** (J. L. Langer 54; Ambrose 4-46).

1993-94 – AUSTRALIA v SOUTH AFRICA (SECOND TEST): LEEDS REVISITED
Steven Lynch, 1995

At Sydney, January 2, 3, 4, 5, 6, 1994. South Africa won by five runs. An Australian collapse reminiscent of Botham's Test at Headingley in 1981 – the eventual total of 111 was exactly the same – allowed South Africa to take an unexpected lead in the series after the home side had made most of the running. South Africa's unlikely hero was de Villiers, in only his second Test: he took ten wickets, and his second-innings six for 43 included the first four as Australia slumped to 56 for four before the end of the fourth day. By then they might well have been celebrating victory but for some late-order South African resistance organised by Rhodes, who came in at 107 for four and saw 132 added.

The last part of South Africa's stunning success was presided over by Cronje after Wessels broke a finger attempting a slip catch. The young deputy marshalled his troops well on the tense final morning, and his turn, throw and direct hit to run out Warne from wide mid-off was a devastating blow for Australia.

Needing only 117 to win, Australia looked to have shrugged off the early loss of Slater, reaching 51 before de Villiers rocked them with three wickets in five balls. South Africa felt victory depended on the quick removal of Border. They got their wish in the first over of the final day, when he played no shot at one from Donald which cut back and clipped his off bail. Waugh – leg-before to Donald's Waqar-like yorker – and Healy soon followed, as did Warne, needlessly run out. In came McDermott, a veteran of a similarly pulsating situation at Adelaide the previous season. He spanked four quick fours on his way to 29, the top score of the innings, but his partner Martyn's nerve failed after 106 minutes and six singles. He holed out to cover, and McGrath soon followed, sparking off emotional scenes in the South African dressing-room. UCBSA managing director Ali Bacher – who led his country to the 4–0 thrashing of Australia when the two last met in 1969-70 – called it "our finest achievement ever."

South Africa 169 (G. Kirsten 67; S. K. Warne 7-56)
and 239 (J. N. Rhodes 76*; C. J. McDermott 4-62, Warne 5-72);
Australia 292 (M. J. Slater 92, D. R. Martyn 59; A. A. Donald 4-83, P. S. de Villiers 4-80)
and 111 (de Villiers 6-43).

1994-95 – ENGLAND IN AUSTRALIA: HUMILIATION — John Thicknesse, 1996

England's misfortune with illness and injuries was so uniformly foul that six replacements were required. Granted Australia's known superiority, especially in bowling through Shane Warne's devastating leg-spin and Craig McDermott's fire and pace, it was no disgrace that, after being two down with three to play, England held the margin to 3–1. The executive committee of the Test and County Cricket Board took a different view, however. Within a month of the tour ending, Keith Fletcher was told by A. C. Smith, the TCCB's chief executive, that his contract as team manager had been terminated midway through its five-year course. Two days later, Smith announced that Ray Illingworth, the chairman of selectors, was in addition to take on Fletcher's duties. The longer the tour lasted, the more obvious it became that in the small print of the game – fielding, running between wickets, practice techniques, plus attitude to practice – England were running second not only to Australia, but to state and colts teams too: successive defeats by Cricket Academy XIs at North Sydney Oval on a weekend in December ranked among their worst humiliations.

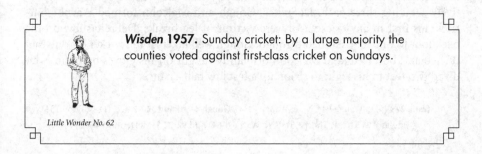

Wisden 1957. Sunday cricket: By a large majority the counties voted against first-class cricket on Sundays.

Little Wonder No. 62

1994-95 – AUSTRALIA v ENGLAND (First Test): FAMILIAR WARNE-ING

1996

At Brisbane, November 25, 26, 27, 28, 29, 1994. Australia won by 184 runs. Yet another display of exceptional all-round cricket took Australia to victory by the now-familiar crushing margin. Warne, who had held England's batsmen spell-bound from the moment he bowled Gatting at Old Trafford in 1993, was again the executioner, taking three for 39 and eight for 71 – his best analysis in first-class cricket. It was not until the final innings, though, that he commandeered the spotlight. On the last day, Warne was irresistible. In action from the start with May and – in contrast to the fourth day – bowling mainly round the wicket, he pinned Thorpe to defence for half an hour before beating him with a yorker. The 160 Thorpe added with Hick in 275 minutes was England's highest stand in eight Ashes Tests. Gooch hit ten fours in scoring 56, but he became the last of Healy's nine victims (equalling the Australian Test record) and the first wicket of Warne's final spell, in which he captured the last four wickets to bring his figures on the final day to six for 27 off 25.2 overs. They truly told the story of Warne's brilliance.

Australia 426 (M. J. Slater 176, M. E. Waugh 140, M. A. Taylor 59; D. Gough 4-107)
and 248-8 dec. (Taylor 58; P. C. R. Tufnell 4-79);
England 167 (M. A. Atherton 54; C. J. McDermott 6-53)
and 323 (G. A. Hick 80, G. P. Thorpe 67, G. A. Gooch 56; S. K. Warne 8-71).

1994-95 – AUSTRALIA v ENGLAND (SECOND TEST): HAT-TRICK   1996

At Melbourne, December 24, 26, 27, 28, 29, 1994. Australia won by 295 runs. England's remote chance of holding out for 120 overs vanished when Fleming, playing his second Test, had Gooch caught behind and Hick bowled with textbook outswingers in his first two overs. When Thorpe succumbed to a loose stroke and Atherton received a second dubious decision from umpire Bucknor, England closed at 79 for four. The remaining batsmen fell in 12.5 overs on the final day, McDermott and Warne – who had passed the milestones of 250 and 150 Test wickets respectively – taking three each. DeFreitas, Gough and Malcolm formed Warne's hat-trick, his first in any cricket. All were victims of leg-breaks, DeFreitas lbw on the back foot to one that skidded through, Gough well taken at the wicket off one that turned and bounced, and Malcolm brilliantly caught off his gloves by Boon, who dived two feet to his right to scoop up a fast low half-chance.

Australia 279 (S. R. Waugh 94*, M. E. Waugh 71; D. Gough 4-60) **and 320-7 dec.** (D. C. Boon 131);
England 212 (G. P. Thorpe 51; S. K. Warne 6-64) **and 92** (C. J. McDermott 5-42).

1995-96 – SRI LANKANS IN AUSTRALIA: MURALI GETS THE ELBOW   Trent Bouts, 1997

Sri Lanka arrived to provide the second and, according to most forecasts, the subsidiary act of the Australian summer. On their departure ten weeks later, Arjuna Ranatunga's men were so much the main event that the two countries' political leaders were forced to take note. Sadly, government interest had less to do with the cricket than with the drama it generated. The three Tests barely qualified as contests. Mark Taylor's Australians were both professional and ruthless.

When Muttiah Muralitharan was called for throwing by Australian umpire Darrell Hair on the first day of the Melbourne Test, both had a right to ask why the bowler had been able to negotiate 22 Tests, indeed his entire first-class career, in safety until then. Either Hair was wrong or some, if not all, of those who had not called Muralitharan in the past six years were. ICC divulged that umpires, via match referees, had expressed doubts about his legitimacy for more than two years. But Sri Lanka produced an array of doctors and biomechanists who declared the off-spinner in the clear. None said Muralitharan could not throw, but they argued that the elbow he had been unable to straighten completely since birth could create the visual illusion of a throw, a contention lost on most observers. It was certainly lost on Ross Emerson who, umpiring his first international ten days later, also no-balled Muralitharan repeatedly, even after the distraught bowler resorted to leg-spin. Instead of the intended celebration of the 25th anniversary of one-day internationals, the first such match under lights in Brisbane provided one of the short game's darkest hours. The umpires were booed from the field under police escort and Muralitharan did not play again on tour.

1995-96 – AUSTRALIA v SRI LANKA (Second Test): Hair raising   1997

At Melbourne, December 26, 27, 28, 29, 30, 1995. Australia won by ten wickets. Ranatunga gambled by sending Australia in on a fine pitch. But that soon paled against the drama on the first afternoon, when umpire Hair called Muralitharan seven times in three overs for throwing. Unusually, he made his judgment from the bowler's end, and several minutes passed before the crowd realised that Muralitharan's elbow, rather than his foot, was at fault. Many were unimpressed. Ian Meckiff, who retired after being called in Brisbane in 1963, was so affected that he went home. Muralitharan switched ends and bowled until tea on the second day. Then Hair told the Sri Lankans he was ready to call him from square leg.

Australia 500-6 dec. (S. R. Waugh 131*, D. C. Boon 110, R. T. Ponting 71, M. J. Slater 62, M. E. Waugh 61) **and 41-0; Sri Lanka 233** (A. Ranatunga 51, R. S. Kaluwitharana 50; G. D. McGrath 5-40) **and 307** (A. P. Gurusinha 143; S. K. Warne 4-71).

1997-98 – South Africans In Australia: Dr Who v Daleks   Steven Lynch, 1999

It seemed almost as if, when pitted against Australia, the South Africans had an inferiority complex – not something they exhibit against other countries nor, indeed, in many other sports. Captaincy came into it too: sometimes, when comparing the thoughtful Mark Taylor with the rather mechanical Hansie Cronje, one was reminded of Dr Who outwitting the Daleks.

1997-98 – AUSTRALIA v SOUTH AFRICA (THIRD TEST): CHANCE BLOWN

1999

At Adelaide, January 30, 31, February 1, 2, 3, 1998. Drawn. Dropped catches – at least ten of them – scuppered South Africa's chances of the victory they needed to square the series. Their failure was felt most keenly by their captain, Cronje, who speared a stump through the door of the umpires' room. Some pundits suggested Cronje should be banned: in the end, a letter of apology seemed to settle the matter.

Kirsten's sixth Test century set up a declaration which left Australia 361 in 109 overs. Elliott went early and Taylor soon followed, after nearly 24 hours on the field, but Pollock was unable to repeat his earlier heroics, and a century from Mark Waugh took Australia to safety. He batted 404 minutes but was the centre of controversy late on: he received a Pollock lifter which hit him on the arm, and walked away as if in disgust; as he did so, his bat brushed the stumps and dislodged a bail. The South Africans appealed vehemently, even though he had clearly finished his stroke and could not therefore have been given out hit wicket under Law 35. The umpires prolonged the agony, consulting the third umpire, Steve Davis. South Africa's misery was compounded when Bacher, at short leg, dropped Waugh next ball. In fact, Waugh was dropped four times, three of them by Bacher.

South Africa 517 (B. M. McMillan 87*, G. Kirsten 77, W. J. Cronje 73, A. M. Bacher 64, P. L. Symcox 54) **and 193-6 dec.** (Kirsten 108*); **Australia 350** (M. A. Taylor 169*, M. E. Waugh 63; S. M. Pollock 7-87) **and 227-7** (M. E. Waugh 115*; L. Klusener 4-67).

1998-99 – ENGLAND IN AUSTRALIA: ONE-WAY TRAFFIC — John Etheridge, 2000

England were once more overwhelmed by Australia, who won their sixth successive Ashes series. More than a century earlier, England won eight on the trot, but only one was a five-Test rubber; and the haphazard tours of the 1880s are hardly comparable to the intensity of modern Test cricket. To be realistic, Australia's success in 1998-99 continued a period of unrivalled dominance in Test cricket's most enduring conflict. Since 1989, they had won 20 Tests to England's five. It could have been 5–0.

1998-99 – AUSTRALIA v ENGLAND: OUT OF THE BLUE — Simon Briggs, 2000

At Melbourne, December 26, 27, 28, 29, 1998. England won by 12 runs. After their limp showing at Adelaide, and outright humiliation in the tour match at Hobart, England flew to Melbourne in low spirits. "They just can't seem to take a trick on this tour," said the man on the Channel Nine news, trying – and failing – to look sympathetic. But English players are at their most dangerous when their pride and places are threatened, and at Melbourne they responded with the latest in a series of overseas wins against the run of play.

The [fourth] day was believed to be the longest in Test history. First, Stewart, Hussain and Hick all reached 50 without being able to go much further. It took some heaves from Mullally to lift the target to 175, theoretically simple but the sort that has often turned Australia shaky. At 103 for two, those shakes were hardly visible. But a remarkable piece of fielding from Ramprakash, who plucked a scorching pull from Langer out of the air, lifted England's spirits. Headley soon forced Mark Waugh to edge to second slip, then followed up brilliantly in a mini-spell of four for four in 13 balls. Even with Steve Waugh still hanging on grimly, at 140 for seven Australia were suddenly in danger.

Nicholson ratcheted the tension still higher, showing an assurance out of all proportion to his experience as he and Waugh took the score to 161 – 14 short of victory. At 7.22pm, Waugh claimed the extra half-hour, despite Stewart's appeals to the umpires to use their discretion. Because of an early tea, and the attempts to make up for lost time, England had already been on the field for three hours and 50 minutes.

Headley and Gough had more reason to object than anyone, having bowled the previous six overs in tandem. But, as shadows stretched across the ground, they just kept coming. Headley found Nicholson's edge, then Waugh took a single off the first ball of Gough's next over. Stewart, whose captaincy had clearly benefited from his lightened workload, was sticking to his policy of attacking the tailenders, and this time it came off: Gough fired his trademark inswinging yorker through MacGill's defences, and hit McGrath on the toe two balls later. Umpire Harper raised his finger, ending the day, after eight hours three minutes, and the match. England had won a superb Test, and the series was not merely vibrant again, but set for a tumultuous finale at Sydney.

England 270 (A. J. Stewart 107, M. R. Ramprakash 63; S. C. G. MacGill 4-61)
and 244 (G. A. Hick 60, Stewart 52, N. Hussain 50);
Australia 340 (S. R. Waugh 122*; D. Gough 5-96) **and 162** (D. W. Headley 6-60).

1998-99 – CARLTON & UNITED SERIES: REPEAT OFFENCE   Robert Craddock, 2000

Australia won their home one-day international series for the 12th time in 20 years. But long after the result fades into cricket's "who cares?" file, people will be talking about other aspects of the tournament. Cricket has featured more than 1,400 one-day internationals over the past 30 years, but rarely one as dramatic as England v Sri Lanka at Adelaide in January 1999, when Muttiah Muralitharan was called for throwing. Umpire Ross Emerson, who had called him for the same offence three years earlier, watched his action from square leg, decided nothing had changed and no-balled him in his second over.

Pandemonium broke out. Sri Lankan captain Arjuna Ranatunga led his side towards the boundary where they milled about for nearly 15 minutes as he spoke to Sri Lankan officials in Colombo via a mobile phone. The game resumed, but later in the night there was a series of spats between Sri Lankan and England players.

Ranatunga was charged with breaking five terms of the International Cricket Council's Code of Conduct. But he arrived at the disciplinary hearing accompanied

by lawyers who argued that suspension would be restraint of trade. They managed
to prevent the inquiry from hearing the evidence. ICC referee Peter van der Merwe,
close to tears, was reduced to imposing a suspended six-match ban and a small fine.
Sri Lanka were accused of changing the face of cricket by using the law to tie the
hands of officials responsible for the conduct of the game. In a further bizarre twist,
Emerson was stood down by the Australian board for the rest of the tournament. It
was announced that he had been officiating at Adelaide while on sick leave from his
regular employment for a stress-related condition.

Even before the Adelaide showdown, the tournament prompted embarrassing
headlines when Tasmanian batsman Ricky Ponting was knocked senseless in a
Sydney nightclub. Suspended for three games, he later gave a press conference
confessing that he had a drink problem and promising to seek help.

1999-2000 – AUSTRALIA v PAKISTAN (Second Test): BACK-YARD BATTING

2001

At Hobart, November 18, 19, 20, 21, 22, 1999. Australia won by four wickets.
Australia achieved an extraordinary victory to secure the series, registering the
third-highest fourth-innings total to win a Test match. They had been on the ropes
at 126 for five, but Langer and Gilchrist put on 238 in 59 overs, a sixth-wicket
record by any country against Pakistan, to take their side to within five runs of their
goal. The win was not without controversy. Umpire Parker's refusal to judge Langer
caught at the wicket in the first hour of the final morning left Wasim Akram,
Pakistan's captain and also the unlucky bowler, almost incandescent with rage.
Wasim's curiously negative approach to the first hour's play on the final day allowed
Langer and Gilchrist to gain the ascendancy. Gilchrist's attitude to batting was so
relaxed that his captain said of him, "He could be playing in his own back yard." His
unbeaten 149 came off only 163 balls in four and a half hours. Langer, on the other
hand, took more than seven hours. When it was all over, Waugh described the Test
as one of the "great wins" of his career. Wasim was so distraught that he could not
face the press and sent a messenger to say he was feeling unwell.

Pakistan 222 (Mohammad Wasim 91)
and 392 (Inzamam-ul-Haq 118, Ijaz Ahmed 82, Saeed Anwar 78; S. K. Warne 5-110);
Australia 246 (M. J. Slater 97, J. L. Langer 59; Saqlain Mushtaq 6-46)
and 369-6 (A. C. Gilchrist 149*, Langer 127).

2000 – AUSTRALIA v SOUTH AFRICA (Super Challenge One-Day Series): RAZZMATAZZ UNDER THE ROOF

Neil Manthorp, 2001

Steve Waugh wondered if August 16, 2000, might be remembered as the day when
cricket changed for ever – and just in case it was, he hit a hundred to be remembered
by. Four days later, when South Africa squared the first official one-day international

series played indoors, Australia's captain might have been quite content for cricket's latest innovation to be little more than a footnote in the game's history.

Played beneath the roof of Melbourne's Colonial Stadium, and accompanied by the kind of razzmatazz that appears compulsory on such occasions, the Super Challenge formed the second leg of a six-match home-and-away programme. The Australians saw the indoor experiment as a novel way of bringing cricket to the people in winter – and people to cricket. The overall attendance was 94,278, which was in line with expectations if some way short of the stadium's potential: the capacity for a cricket game was 48,000.

That batsmen did not ultimately dominate the series was no reflection on the high-quality drop-in pitches prepared by Les Burdett. The outfield, having hosted Australian Rules football and rugby union games, was a little damp and soft, but the short square boundaries swung the balance back towards the batsmen – as well as bringing out the best in two athletic fielding sides. The umpires had been told to declare the ball "dead" if it hit the roof, but there was never a likelihood of that.

Kent v Essex. At Canterbury, August 7, 8, 9, 1957. During the Essex first innings, the band of the Buffs stopped playing after lunch on the second day at the request of Taylor and Insole, who complained that the music disturbed them.

Little Wonder No. 63

2002-03 – AUSTRALIA v ZIMBABWE (FIRST TEST): HAYDEN'S 380   2004

At Perth, October 9, 10, 11, 12, 13, 2003. Australia won by an innings and 175 runs. Matthew Hayden went to work with a sore back. He wore a heavy vest to keep it warm, and hardly indulged in the sweep shots that have served him so well in the past. Instead he played blissfully, ruthlessly straight. He went to work on a wicket friendlier to batsmen than WACA pitches prepared at the height of summer, after Streak won the toss and invited Australia to bat ... and bat. At the end of it Hayden, this muscle-bound, sun-loving Queenslander, sat in the dressing-room gripping a bottle of beer, wearing whites, baggy green cap and flip-flops; he also sat comfortably in the company of his era's other master batsmen, Sachin Tendulkar and Brian Lara.

Hayden played within himself at first. He gave the impression of being on the brink of destroying Zimbabwe's attack, but didn't. Not yet. The cyclonic period before stumps on the first day produced three sixes. By then, Australia were 368 for three and Hayden was 183 not out, his sights firmly trained on the 203 that breathed fresh life into his career at Chennai in 2001, but the records were not in focus yet.

That happened early on day two. Hayden dispensed with the vest, as if to show that he had limbered up now, and in due course replaced his helmet with the emblematic olive cap. On his way from 200 to 300, he unleashed five enormous sixes, mistiming some of them, an incredulous Streak noted later. By now a curious calm had come over Hayden. His concentration did not waver until after he had passed the revered Australian number of 334, set by Don Bradman and equalled by Mark Taylor, by sending a floating full toss to the boundary.

At 335, he faltered, but so too did the hapless Gripper, who fumbled a catch at deep midwicket and allowed Hayden to cruise on towards Lara's record. After driving to long-off three balls before tea on the second day, Hayden celebrated lustily as he ambled through a single and into territory never before explored by a Test cricketer. He wheeled his bat in celebration and embraced his batting partner Gilchrist. There was also something reverent about his reaction – especially when he touched the black band wound around his biceps in remembrance of the 88 Australians killed in the Bali terrorist attacks a year earlier.

Australia 735-6 dec. (M. L. Hayden 380, A. C. Gilchrist 113*, S. R. Waugh 78, D. R. Martyn 53; S. M. Ervine 4-146); Zimbabwe 239 (T. R. Gripper 53) and 321 (H. H. Streak 71*, M. A. Vermeulen 63, Ervine 53; A. J. Bichel 4-63).

2002-03 – ENGLAND IN AUSTRALIA: SWIFT DESPATCH   Scyld Berry, 2004

As in 1989 and the six subsequent Ashes series, so it was in 2002-03. The standard of Australia's cricket was so superior that England never came close, and lost for the eighth time running. When the series was alive, in the first three Tests, Australia won by mountainous margins – once by 384 runs, twice by an innings – and so swift was their despatch of England that only 11 days of play were necessary for the destiny of the Ashes to be decided.

2002-03 – AUSTRALIA v ENGLAND (First Test): WORST NIGHTMARE
Trevor Marshallsea, 2004

At Brisbane, November 7, 8, 9, 10, 2002. Australia won by 384 runs. It will go down as one of the costliest decisions in Test history. England captain Nasser Hussain had forecast in his last pre-Ashes newspaper column that "the worst nightmare" would be working out what to do if he won the toss. Despite the fact opening batsmen Vaughan and Trescothick were clearly his side's most potent weapons, Hussain sent Australia in. At stumps on day one, Australia were 364 for two. There went the match and the momentum. Hussain's choice will rank up there with David Gower's invitation to the 1989 Australians to bat at Headingley, a gesture repaid by a first-innings score of 601 for seven declared. Australia went on to win that Ashes series 4–0, and have been winning them ever since.

Australia 492 (M. L. Hayden 197, R. T. Ponting 123, S. K. Warne 57; A. F. Giles 4-101) and 296-5 dec. (Hayden 103, D. R. Martyn 64, A. C. Gilchrist 60*); England 325 (M. E. Trescothick 72, J. P. Crawley 69*, M. A. Butcher 54, N. Hussain 51; G. D. McGrath 4-87) and 79 (McGrath 4-36).

2002-03 – AUSTRALIA v ENGLAND (FIFTH TEST): FIRST CRACKS?

Christian Ryan, 2004

At Sydney, January 2, 3, 4, 5, 6, 2003. England won by 225 runs. England carried over their Melbourne momentum to inflict Australia's first home defeat in four years. It was tempting to blame it on dead-rubber syndrome, but this was a hard-fought, fair-dinkum English victory. Their two previous Test wins against Australia hinged on a miraculous spell by Dean Headley and an even more miraculous innings by Mark Butcher. This time, they played grinding cricket for five days. They did it under a hot sun and an unflinching leader. And maybe, just maybe, they exposed the first crack in a mighty empire.

The match was witnessed by the second-biggest Sydney crowd in history. A further 2.1million TV viewers – one in nine Australians – tuned in for the gripping second evening. And yet, for all of them, this was about one man. Steve Waugh's 102 was not, contrary to local hyperbole, the greatest century in Ashes folklore; next day, Gilchrist and Vaughan produced a couple every bit as good. But few, if any, have hit hundreds with such a sense of inevitability.

The looming US invasion of Iraq dominated the New Year, but Australians were preoccupied with a different Waugh. Should he stay or should he go? Waugh entered the Test – his 156th, matching Allan Border's record – knowing it could be his last. He entered the final over of the second day needing five runs for 100. Then came the magical bit. Dawson's first three balls were dead-batted down the pitch. Waugh square-drove his fourth for three, but Gilchrist did the right thing and pushed a single. One ball left, two runs needed. Unflustered, Waugh leaned back and drilled a flattish delivery through extra cover for four, sparking a roar that the writer David Frith reckoned was the loudest he had heard in 52 years' watching at the SCG. Pink-skinned revellers at the nearby Captain Cook Hotel were still chanting Waugh's name two hours later.

For the first time since November 1992, Australia started with neither McGrath (side strain) nor Warne (shoulder). Without those two, as many had long suspected, they were half the side. Vaughan's seventh hundred in eight months was his best yet. He erupted in the third over of the innings, swinging Gillespie for a glorious six off his hips, before settling into an almost flawless rhythm.

Australia [were set] 452. Fat chance turned swiftly to no chance. Banging the ball in purposefully, Caddick made the most of some uneven bounce and undisciplined batting to collect ten wickets in a Test for the first time. Hussain, long-sleeved white shirt buttoned to his throat and wrists, was his usual gloomy self at the post-match press conference. But he had glimpsed a new world, a brighter world, a world without McGrath and Warne. It was hard to shake the feeling that, after 14 years of ritual Ashes humiliation, the worst for England might finally be over.

England 362 (M. A. Butcher 124, N. Hussain 75, A. J. Stewart 71)
and 452-9 dec. (M. P. Vaughan 183, Hussain 72);
Australia 363 (A. C. Gilchrist 133, S. R. Waugh 102; M. J. Hoggard 4-92)
and 226 (A. R. Caddick 7-94).

2003-04 – INDIANS IN AUSTRALIA: ONE ERA ENDS, ANOTHER BEGINS   Sambit Bal, 2005

Every once in a while comes a special sporting contest that leaves behind a whiff of glory and magic. Australia and India played one such Test series in 2000-01; Kolkata was a match for the ages and Chennai not far behind. But ever so rarely comes a series that marks a turning point in history. It may be years or decades before the significance of India's tour of Australia in 2003-04 can be truly assessed, but in this series they announced themselves as a force in Test cricket, after years of living on promise and vain dazzle. They didn't quite end Australia's reign, but how close they came.

The 1–1 scoreline did not fully reveal India's gains. These have to be viewed through the prism of their wretched past. The last time they had won a Test series outside the subcontinent was in England in 1986, and not since 1980-81 had they won a Test in Australia (where they had lost seven of their last eight). Meanwhile, under Steve Waugh, Australia had won 21 out of 25 Tests at home.

For Australia, the series meant a great deal more than the chance to keep their impressive home record intact. A legacy was at stake. Waugh, one of the most innovative of all Test captains, revealed beforehand that he would retire at the end of the series – an announcement whose timing would be questioned repeatedly.

It was ironic that Waugh, whose legacy to Test cricket was the virtual elimination of the draw, ended his career with one. But if India denied Waugh the captain a fitting end, they set the stage for one last scrap from Waugh the warrior batsman. A record fifth-day crowd watched as he made his way in for the final time, with Australia not yet out of danger at 170 for three. He began with a shovel-drive that could have got him out and minutes later the crowd gasped as a sweep flew off the edge to fall a few feet short of a fielder running in from deep square leg. But Waugh soon found his nerve, to hit a string of rasping boundaries, and a child held up a banner on Yabba's Hill: WAUGH RULES, OK.

He didn't rule his last series, but he played his part in saving it. After an emotional parade around the ground on the shoulders of his team-mates, Waugh walked off, with two of his children in his arms, doting wife beside him, to applause heard around the cricket world. A glorious era had ended, and the promise of another was on the horizon. It was one hell of a series.

2003-04 – AUSTRALIA v INDIA (SECOND TEST): WAUGH v THE WALL
Sambit Bal, 2005

At Adelaide, December 12, 13, 14, 15, 16, 2003. India won by four wickets. After five breathless days it was difficult to decide what was more confounding. Just how had Australia managed to lose after scoring 556 by the second afternoon? Or how had India managed to win after being 85 for four in reply? Only once had a team scored more runs in the first innings of a Test and yet lost, and that 109-year-old record too belonged to Australia: they made 586 at Sydney in the Ashes opener of 1894-95, enforced the follow-on, and fell 11 short of the 177 needed to win.

The victory was all the more incredible because India had not won a Test in Australia in 23 years, and Australia had not lost a home Test of consequence in five

– and because Australia had scored 400 runs on the first day, a record for any day on this ground.

India slumped from 66 without loss to 85 for four when Ganguly was run out. Laxman joined Dravid. It took Australia 94 overs to separate them. It was not quite Kolkata; there, they had added 376 for the fifth wicket, here it was a mere 303. That made them only the third pair to share two triple-century stands in Tests, after Bradman and Ponsford and, more recently, the South Africans Gibbs and Smith.

The Test took a decisive turn on the fourth day when a combination of weariness, tight bowling and a fatal urge to dominate the bowlers caused a dramatic Australian collapse. India were left to make 230 in 100 overs; Dravid redeemed a pledge to himself by being there to score the winning runs. There was a minor scare when India lost their fourth wicket on 170, but Dravid sealed a historic victory by cutting MacGill to the cover boundary. Waugh chased the ball all the way, retrieved it from the gutter, handed it over to Dravid and said "Well played." Indeed.

Australia 556 (R. T. Ponting 242, S. M. Katich 75, J. L. Langer 58; A. Kumble 5-154)

and 196 (A. B. Agarkar 6-41);

India 523 (R. Dravid 233, V. V. S. Laxman 148; A. J. Bichel 4-118) **and 233-6** (Dravid 72*).

2005-06 – AUSTRALIA v ICC WORLD XI (ICC SUPER SERIES)
Richard Hobson, 2006

The idea of pitting the leading team in the world against the best of the rest sounded wonderful in theory but, in practice, "Super Series" proved a highly inappropriate description of four one-sided games. Within an hour of the World XI losing the Test match by 210 runs more than two days ahead of schedule, the ICC's chief executive Malcolm Speed told a press conference that there were no plans to repeat the exercise in this form, even though the governing body's own website proclaimed that it was "expected to become a regular feature played every fourth year". Flaws in the concept soon became evident, and the ICC, having cynically bestowed full Test and one-day international status on the matches, seemed keener than anybody to move on. They received a tepid greeting from the Australian public. With the MCG undergoing redevelopment before the 2006 Commonwealth Games, the Telstra Dome in Melbourne's docklands was a cold, soulless substitute, never more than 60% full during the three one-day games. Apart from the visit of Zimbabwe in 2003-04, the crowd for the first three days of the Test was the lowest aggregate at the SCG since 1996-97.

2005-06 – AUSTRALIA v SOUTH AFRICA (THIRD TEST): NOT TRICKY FOR RICKY
Neil Manthorp, 2006

At Sydney, January 2, 3, 4, 5, 6, 2006. Australia won by eight wickets. Ricky Ponting became the first man to score centuries in both innings of his 100th Test match to set up a stunning final-day victory following a brave declaration by his opposite number. Australia were asked to score 287 in 76 overs, but Ponting's fierce counter-attack made a mockery of the equation. He thundered his way to 143 from only 159 balls, and Australia won with 15.3 overs to spare. Such was Ponting's form and confidence after his first-innings 120 that he ignored the traditional playing-in period, flicking straight deliveries off his pads through midwicket and then cutting with the certainty of a guillotine when the bowlers overcompensated outside off. Graeme Smith became only the second captain to lose a Test after declaring twice – Garry Sobers was the other, for West Indies against England at Port-of-Spain in 1967-68.

South Africa 451-9 dec. (A. G. Prince 119, J. H. Kallis 111) **and 194-6 dec.** (H. H. Gibbs 67, Kallis 50*);
Australia 359 (R. T. Ponting 120, A. C. Gilchrist 86; A. Nel 4-81)
and 288-2 (Ponting 143*, M. L. Hayden 90).

2006-07 – ENGLAND IN AUSTRALIA: REVENGE SERVED HOT   Simon Briggs, 2007

For just over 14 months, since England seized the Ashes from Australia at The Oval, two great cricketing nations had been keyed up for a humdinger of a return contest – an epic page-turner, it was assumed, with all the plot twists and somersaults of 2005. But from the moment Steve Harmison opened the series with a wild embarrassing wide that went straight into the hands of Andrew Flintoff at second slip, reality took hold. This time there were to be no twists, at least not during the Test series. The story of the first ball would essentially be the story right through to the last. If England won the 2005 series by a nose, they lost the rematch by the length of the Nullarbor Plain. They were defeated in every one of the five Tests – a fate previously reserved for one team in Ashes history. And J. W. H. T. Douglas's 1920-21 side represented a country still devastated by the effects of the Great War. Andrew Flintoff's 2006-07 team had no such excuse.

2006-07 – AUSTRALIA v ENGLAND (SECOND TEST): THE GREAT MAN
Matthew Engel, 2007

At Adelaide, December 1, 2, 3, 4, 5, 2006. Australia won by six wickets. Great Man theory, originally associated with the philosopher Thomas Carlyle, holds that the whole of human history has been determined by a handful of people. In cricketing terms, it has always been hard to dispute, especially when you're sitting at Don Bradman's home ground.

For four days and 43 minutes of this Test match, there was plenty of time to think about such matters, and also whether it might be more amusing to spend the final afternoon hiring a pedalo on the River Torrens instead of watching this turgid contest dribble away to its inevitable draw. Then came the Great Man. Shane Warne conjured up perhaps the most astounding victory of even his career. Here was a pitch that, all along, had offered the possibility to a batsman with sufficient stamina and perseverance of staying at the crease until the 2010-11 Ashes. Suddenly the placid earth began to crack and crumble and boil and bubble, as if the San Andreas Fault had opened directly underneath. But the fault was all England's. In the first innings, they had convinced themselves the Wizard of Oz was no great magician but just a cunning illusionist. Now they thought he could make the earth move. And so he did. From 69 for one, England withered to 129 all out. Australia's task – 168 in 36 overs – was no certainty. But the force was with them, and they won with 19 balls to spare. You could replay the final day a hundred times, and the game might be drawn every time. But it won't be replayed. Such a day could never happen quite like this again.

From the start, England's cricket seemed suddenly tentative. After Bucknor gave out Strauss (even the appeal sounded only threequarter-hearted), the doubts turned into blind panic. Collingwood stood firm but was completely constricted and, though the tail did better than the body, England were gone by 3.42. The gates were thrown open, and spectators began to arrive as they used to do when they heard Bradman was batting.

England 551-6 dec. (P. D. Collingwood 206, K. P. Pietersen 158, I. R. Bell 60) **and 129** (S. K. Warne 4-49);

Australia 513 (R. T. Ponting 142, M. J. Clarke 124, M. E. K. Hussey 91, A. C. Gilchrist 64;

M. J. Hoggard 7-109) **and 168-4** (Hussey 61*).

2006-07 – AUSTRALIA v ENGLAND (FOURTH TEST): WARNE'S 700TH

Greg Baum, 2007

At Melbourne, December 26, 27, 28, 2006. Australia won by an innings and 99 runs. Shane Warne stole his own show. From the moment he announced his retirement a few days beforehand, this Test was always going to be about Melbourne's farewell to its favourite cricketing son. Glenn McGrath's decision to quit, too, sharpened the sense of a grand occasion. Already, record crowds had been forecast to flock to the spectacularly refurbished MCG. Now the match would surely be five festive days of farewell.

Two forces of nature intervened. One was rain over Christmas – much needed in a parched state, but not here, not now. It was a cold rain too, and trimmed the crowd figure on Boxing Day to a mere 89,155 (an Ashes record, but 1,645 below the 46-year-old record for any properly audited day's Test cricket).

The other force was Warne himself. His five wickets on the opening day thrilled the crowd, but put an end to the match before it had properly begun. It took Australia just two more days to complete victory, forcing Cricket Victoria not only to refund $A2.3m (more than £900,000) worth of tickets for day four, but to wring its hands at the thought of the takings lost on day five. Melbourne might not have been gasping for more, but the administrators were. Flintoff won the toss, prompting roars from both sets of fans: the English because they would bat first, the Australians because Warne would bowl on Boxing Day, needing one wicket to become the first Test bowler to claim 700.

Another chapter: Shane Warne sets off on a lap of the MCG after bowling
Andrew Strauss, his 700th Test victim

Warne's introduction had the effect of a detonator. Extra security appeared inside the fence. Soon, Collingwood fell to Lee, then Strauss, so watchful for three and a half hours that he managed just one four, suddenly hit over and around a conventional Warne leg-break and was bowled. Warne had his milestone wicket, the crowd its keepsake moment. England's resistance thereafter was minimal. Pietersen, again left with the tail, hit out and got out, and they finished up with 159. Warne took five in an innings for the 37th time in Tests, again transfixing England in conditions that should have put him at their mercy.

England 159 (A. J. Strauss 50; S. K. Warne 5-39) **and 161** (B. Lee 4-47);
Australia 419 (A. Symonds 156, M. L. Hayden 153; S. I. Mahmood 4-100).

Leicestershire 1957. Palmer frequently resorted to "donkey-drops". The strange, high-tossed deliveries often surprised the opposition, and in the West Indies match accounted for Kanhai, Asgarali and Worrell.

Little Wonder No. 64

2007-08 – INDIANS IN AUSTRALIA: DEEPENING TENSIONS   Greg Baum, 2008

"Bollyline" in Sydney will go down in history as a kind of cricketing six-day war. It was all too real and nasty while it was happening, but it was over almost as soon as it had begun. By the start of the next Test in Perth ten days later, there was such peace and harmony on the surface it was as if nothing had ever happened.

As in real wars, circumstances conspired fatefully. Questionable sportsmanship, poor umpiring and alleged racism set the Second Test at Sydney on a daily more precipitous edge, and tipped it over as Australia pursued a record-equalling 16th successive win on the last day in typically relentless fashion. They did snatch improbable victory from the jaws of stalemate, but it seemed to be made Pyrrhic in its moment by the engulfing firestorm.

There were casualties, not least among them the game's dignity. Harbhajan Singh was given a three-Test ban (later rescinded). Posturing Indian authorities threatened to abandon the tour. Commentator Peter Roebuck called for the sacking of Ricky Ponting. Steve Bucknor lost his umpiring commission, and seemed unlikely ever to regain it. India's captain Anil Kumble dramatically invoked the spirit of a previous cricket war when he declared that "Only one team was playing in the spirit of the game."

But the least-expected damage was collateral. Up and down the country, there was an outpouring of anger at the disposition of the Australian side. Roebuck's controversial call for the captain's head polarised the public in a way that shocked the team. More broadly, this war deepened unresolved tensions between Australia and India, cricket's on-field superpower and its financial powerhouse. Their scramble for the high moral ground made for an unedifying spectacle.

2008-09 – AUSTRALIA v SOUTH AFRICA (FIRST TEST): HUGE CHASE 2009

At Perth, December 17, 18, 19, 20, 21, 2008. South Africa won by six wickets. The first great irony was that in a match seemingly destined to be a tale of two tails, South Africa didn't need theirs to achieve the second-biggest successful run-chase in Test history. The second irony was that Australia, after recovering from the perilous position of 15 for three on the first morning, controlled the game for the best part of four days, but lost.

Jean-Paul Duminy was a last-minute replacement for Ashwell Prince, whose thumb was broken by Ntini in the nets on the eve of the Test. Duminy wore a diamond earring like his hero Herschelle Gibbs, but there was nothing too flashy about his batting, which was composed and confident. De Villiers was a bundle of energy whose brilliant catching helped tame Australia's batsmen, and who returned to his hotel room with 11 not out on the penultimate evening feeling tense. "I was really nervous and shaking, and I thought, I've got a massive mountain to climb tomorrow." Smith, meanwhile, went to bed feeling satisfied and relieved. Satisfied that he had scaled his own mountain, reaching his first century in nine Tests against Australia, and relieved that his dismissal to Johnson for 108 had not precipitated a repeat of the wreckage wrought by the left-armer in the first innings. Still, there were 242 runs still to be made when he was out, and the captain dared not dream of victory. As South Africa celebrated their finest win of the post-apartheid era, one Australian newspaper dubbed Ponting "Captain Pout".

Australia 375 (S. M. Katich 83, M. J. Clarke 62, A. Symonds 57; M. Ntini 4-72) **and 319** (B. J. Haddin 94);
South Africa 281 (J. H. Kallis 63, A. B. de Villiers 63; M. G. Johnson 8-61)
and 414-4 (G. C. Smith 108, de Villiers 106*, Kallis 57, H. M. Amla 53, J-P. Duminy 50*).

2008-09 – AUSTRALIA v SOUTH AFRICA (SECOND TEST): STEYNED 2009

At Melbourne, December 26, 27, 28, 29, 30, 2008. South Africa won by nine wickets. The empire had already crumbled by the time Hashim Amla stroked the winning runs off his pads to seal South Africa's first-ever series victory in Australia. For the home side it was not so much the scale of the defeat but the manner that was so shocking, and at the end Ponting stood amid the rubble with nothing to show for his determined knocks of 101 and 99 but the stigma of being the first Australian captain since Allan Border against West Indies in 1992-93 to preside over a home series defeat.

Few Australians could recall a more dispiriting day's cricket in those 16 years than the third at Melbourne, when Duminy and Steyn – a remarkable rookie and a genuine tailender – humiliated the undermanned and inexperienced bowling attack.

They orchestrated a stunning, series-defining turnaround, batting for 238 minutes and 382 deliveries for a partnership of 180, the third-highest ninth-wicket stand in Test history – and Steyn was not done. While the Australians laboured to prise out 11 wickets in the match, Steyn captured ten on his own with high-class pace and swing.

For the second time in a fortnight, Australia gave up a winning position. Before dusk settled on the MCG, and after some celebratory beers, the history-making captain led his team back to the middle of the arena, pointed to the empty grand-stands and bellowed several renditions of "You're not singing any more". They weren't singing in the Australian dressing-room, either.

Australia 394 (R. T. Ponting 101, M. J. Clarke 88*, S. M. Katich 54; D. W. Steyn 5-87)
and 247 (Ponting 99; Steyn 5-67);
South Africa 459 (J-P. Duminy 166, Steyn 76, G. C. Smith 62; P. M. Siddle 4-81)
and 183-1 (Smith 75, N. D. McKenzie 59*).

2010-11 – ENGLAND IN AUSTRALIA: INTO THE HISTORY BOOKS Mark Nicholas, 2011

In Barack Obama-speak, the Ashes of 2010-11 was a shellacking. Indeed, the 3–1 scoreline barely did justice to England's superiority and certainly flattered Australia. In each discipline of the game Andrew Strauss's team were stronger, more consistent, just better than their opponents. Never before in a celebrated history had the Australians suffered three innings defeats in a series. Unlikely as it might seem, the question now was how long might it be before Australia were a superpower again?

In those three matches out of five – Adelaide, Melbourne and Sydney – England appeared to be playing on a different pitch. Alastair Cook and Jonathan Trott batted their team into impregnable positions before Kevin Pietersen and Ian Bell led the crushing of Australian minds. Pietersen's double-hundred at Adelaide was an innings of spectacular enterprise. Bell's first hundred against Australia came at Sydney, and confirmed the image of a complete batsman.

On all three occasions England passed 500 with extraordinary ease before the bowlers took on the role of executioner. Suddenly these flat tracks spat venom at batsmen whose footwork was found wanting, and whose "previous" counted for nothing. Ricky Ponting, the greatest Australian batsman of the modern era and, some say, the second-greatest of all Australians, averaged 16 in the series.

Strauss led his team into the history books and joined an illustrious group of men who have won Ashes series away from home. Among them, Ray Illingworth may have been a smarter tactician, Len Hutton a finer batsman and Douglas Jardine a more ruthless autocrat, but the sum of this captain's parts was greater than the whole, and it was right that Strauss now joined such rarefied company.

2010-11 – AUSTRALIA v ENGLAND (FOURTH TEST): PERFECT PLUS

Gideon Haigh, 2011

At Melbourne, December 26, 27, 28, 29, 2010. England won by an innings and 157 runs. Having played what their coach called a "perfect" game at Adelaide, England went close to improving on perfection in the Boxing Day Test, rebounding from their setback at the WACA to lead all the way, ensuring the retention of the Ashes just before noon on the fourth day. It was a victory for preparation, discipline but also fun: the players celebrated in front of their fans in the Great Southern Stand by performing the Sprinkler dance popularised through the video diaries posted on the ECB website by their incurably game off-spinner Graeme Swann. Victory, of course, begets enjoyment; here, one fancied, was a case of enjoyment begetting victory.

Bresnan, despite bowling only 69 first-class overs in almost two months, claimed six for 75 in two innings. The first difference was that England's pace attack enjoyed initial use of the pitch and overhead conditions; the second was that they were clearly superior, taking only two sessions to demoralise their hosts on the first day for Australia's lowest score in an MCG Ashes Test.

The only interruption to England's progress was a rain-break which banished the players from the field in the middle of the day for an hour and a half. It gave England the chance to savour the dismissal of their stalwart rival, Hussey, who nicked the penultimate ball of the session to provide Prior with the first of his eventual six catches. All ten batsmen eventually offered chances behind the wicket; all were accepted. Clarke eked out 20 in 89 minutes; nobody else lasted an hour. Ponting received an excellent delivery from Tremlett that lifted and left him; otherwise a succession of batsmen fell going hard at the ball, as though they had never seen swing so wicked. On only 17 occasions in the previous century had Australia been dismissed for double figures in Test cricket; not since falling for 78 at Lord's in 1968 had they collapsed for fewer against England.

Australia 98 (C. T. Tremlett 4-26, J. M. Anderson 4-44)
and 258 (B. J. Haddin 55*, S. R. Watson 54; T. T. Bresnan 4-50);
England 513 (I. J. L. Trott 168*, M. J. Prior 85, A. N. Cook 82, A. J. Strauss 69; P. M. Siddle 6-75).

2011-12 – AUSTRALIA v NEW ZEALAND (SECOND TEST): 26-YEAR ITCH

2012

At Hobart, December 9, 10, 11, 12, 2011. New Zealand won by seven runs. Australia had seven sessions to score 241, and the seesaw swung their way again as they cruised to 72 without loss. On the fourth day, the pitch still offered variable bounce, and there was also a breeze to aid outswing. Hughes's miserable series ended in the second over, caught for the fourth time running by the same fielder (Guptill) off the same bowler (Martin), a unique occurrence in Tests. In the ABC Radio commentary box, the former Test leg-spinner Kerry O'Keeffe observed that "if Hughes is shaving tomorrow and gets a nick, Guptill will appear from the medicine cabinet with a band-aid". Still, Australia had moved to 122 for one – needing only 119 more

– before Boult had Khawaja held by Taylor, one of six slip catches during the day. After New Zealand's woeful display at Brisbane, their coach John Wright had staged several lengthy slip-catching sessions: in Hobart, his charges didn't shell one.

Suddenly, New Zealand seized control; Australia lost eight wickets for 77, seemingly in the blink of an eye. When Bracewell shattered Starc's stumps, second ball, it looked all over at 199 for nine. But the drama had hardly begun. Warner celebrated his first Test century, off 145 balls, with a leap and punch of the air. He and last man Lyon needed to score 42, and Warner had faith. He didn't farm the strike, and Lyon got bat on ball. Taylor and his team tensed up.

The target dwindled to single figures, and the small crowd found their voice. Taylor set the field back to Warner, and had a final charge at Lyon. In his 16th over of the day, Bracewell summoned one last effort and seamed one back through the gate to knock back middle stump. Lyon, who had survived for 43 minutes and 27 balls, was desolate, and dropped to his haunches. The New Zealanders could finally rejoice in victory. It was their first over Australia since Wellington in March 1993, but their first in Australia since Perth in December 1985. Warner, who offered a consoling arm to his partner, had carried his bat for 123 in 317 minutes – enough, controversially, to win him the match award ahead of Bracewell after a vote by the Australian public via text message. Following an outcry in New Zealand, the system was immediately scrapped. For Australia – spectators and players – it had been a bad couple of days.

New Zealand 150 (D. G. Brownlie 56; J. L. Pattinson 5-51) **and 226** (L. R. P. L. Taylor 56); **Australia 136 and 233** (D. A. Warner 123*; D. A. J. Bracewell 6-40).

Little Wonder No. 65

Obituary 1957. Mr F. L. FANE. Owing to an unfortunate error, the 1956 *Wisden* reported the death of Mr F. L. Fane, the former Essex and England cricketer. The error occurred because of a similarity of initials. The Mr F. L. Fane who died in December 1954, was Mr Francis L. Fane, a cousin of the cricketer, Mr Frederick L. Fane. By a coincidence, Mr Fane informs us, his father also once read his own obituary!

2011-12 – AUSTRALIA v INDIA (SECOND TEST): APPROVAL RATING

Greg Baum, 2012

At Sydney, January 3, 4, 5, 6, 2012. Australia won by an innings and 68 runs. This was the 100th Test match played at the SCG, and it duly became a carnival of centuries. In all, nine were made or conceded, 11 if you count each of Clarke's three-in-one that will define the game for future generations. At the other end of the scale, Ishant Sharma, India's best bowler, maintained humour enough to doff his cap to the crowd's mocking applause when a century off his bowling was raised. It at least made for a more convivial meeting than the last one here between these teams.

Clarke declared with 329 to his name – Sydney's highest Test score, beating Tip Foster's 287 for England on debut in 1903-04, but within a lusty blow of Don Bradman's Test-best of 334. Arguably, the declaration was needlessly selfless, for the match was only half-played and, as it happened, Australia would win with a day to spare.

That led some to wonder if Clarke was trying too hard to gain the approval of Australian cricket fans who had read his apparent love of the high-profile high life as a lack of commitment and somehow un-Australian; who, in the course of Australia's decline, had made him (with Ponting) their favourite scapegoat; and who, only the previous summer, had hooted him at the same venue. It typified the ambiguity that has characterised Clarke's reception as an Australian player that even about this, his finest hour, there was debate. There could, though, be no misinterpretation about the outcome. Australia were still at best a team in transition, but yet again India, away from home, were meek and ineffectual.

At the end, Clarke was walking on air, but footsore nonetheless: in four days, he had been off the field for barely 50 minutes. If this massive win did not herald a new era, at least it evinced a new aura: surely now, Clarke had the legitimacy he craved.

India 191 (M. S. Dhoni 57*; J. L. Pattinson 4-43)
and 400 (G. Gambhir 83, S. R. Tendulkar 80, V. V. S. Laxman 66, R. Ashwin 62; B. W. Hilfenhaus 5-106);
Australia 659-4 dec. (M. J. Clarke 329*, M. E. K. Hussey 150*, R. T. Ponting 134).

SOUTH AFRICA

An English team played two Tests (only recognised as such much later) on their first tour of South Africa in 1888-89. They were captained by two different men, Monty Bowden and Aubrey Smith, who both decided to stay in South Africa after the end of the tour and set up in business together. They would not be the last English cricketers to maintain a close professional relationship with the country. For decades South Africa was a haven for many players to coach and play regardless of the government's racist apartheid policy, instigated in 1948, or of any moral objections raised from their own country or elsewhere. Broadly speaking *Wisden* had a conciliatory attitude towards South Africa as the sporting world woke up to the inequities of its society during the 1960s. The prevailing view was that sport and politics should not, and did not need to, mix. South Africa's absence from the early World Cup tournaments was bemoaned. In 1983 Graham Johnson, the Kent all-rounder, wrote a piece for *Wisden* defending his periods working as a coach in South Africa and also the English rebel tour of 1981-82. "Tours such as that, provided they are handled correctly, can do a great deal to further changes within South Africa," he said. "The idea of a cricket world split in two, comprising those with and without contacts with South Africa, is disastrous."

In 1993 the ICC declared that matches on that rebel tour, and the subsequent others, were no longer deemed first-class. Editor Matthew Engel "concluded that this whimsical and belated anti-apartheid gesture was too pathetic to obey". Those words appeared in a 2006 article entitled "Setting the records straight" in which he and the statistician Andrew Samson amended the official *Wisden* records to incorporate 223 matches between non-white teams from the apartheid era now considered first-class. The quality of South African cricket, and cricketers, has never been in doubt, whatever their colour. Peter Sichel sounded glib in the 1981 domestic cricket report but he was not wrong: "Many would agree that, given the opportunity, South Africa would perform with distinction against any of the Test-playing countries of the world." When they finally got their chance again in 1991 they did not disappoint, and remarkably they seem to have come through the trauma of the Hansie Cronje match-fixing scandal. The racial mix of the side has continued to be a controversial subject but their all-round quality, under their long-serving captain Graeme Smith, was impressive. Recent teams have proved to be worthy successors to the team of Graeme Pollock and Barry Richards, who demolished Australia 4-0 in 1969-70 but were cut off in their prime by the subsequent isolation.

1888-89 – THE ENGLISH TEAM IN SOUTH AFRICA: CAPE JAPES   1890

It has been stated on the best authority that the tour – arranged by Major Warton, and carried out under his direction – did not pay its expenses, but in every other sense than the financial one it was eminently successful. The cricketers were enthusiastically welcomed, and, though some of their early engagements ended unexpectedly in defeat, they repaid the welcome by playing remarkably well. All the beatings were sustained in the early part of the trip, and it is no libel to say that for a time generous hospitality had a bad effect upon the cricket.

However, as soon as the men settled down to the serious business of their tour they did even better than might have been expected from the composition of the side, and went on from victory to victory. It was never intended, or considered necessary, to take out a representative English team for a first trip to the Cape, and certain laments which were indulged in at home when the news of the early defeats came to hand were found to be quite uncalled for. The heroes of the trip were undoubtedly Abel and Briggs, the former with the bat and Briggs with the ball literally doing marvels. Three times Abel exceeded the hundred, and his play all through was some of the best ever shown for a travelling side.

1888-89 – SOUTH AFRICA v ENGLAND (FIRST TEST):
GRATIFYING RESULT   1890

At Port Elizabeth, March 12, 13, 1889. The first of the two 11-a-side matches that were played, and a victory for the Englishmen by eight wickets. Good all-round cricket, rather than any specially noteworthy individual achievement, brought around this gratifying result. Mr Smith, however had a capital bowling average in the first innings of South Africa. Abel, as on many other occasions, made the best score for his side.

South Africa 84 (Mr C. A. Smith 5-19, J. Briggs 4-39) and 129 (A. J. Fothergill 4-19);
England 148 (Mr A. R. Innes 5-43) and 67-2.

1888-89 – SOUTH AFRICA v ENGLAND (Second Test): BRILLIANT BRIGGS
1890

At Cape Town, March 25, 26, 1889. The last match of the tour was a complete triumph for the Englishmen who out-played their opponents at every point, and won in an innings with 202 runs to spare. The South African team could do nothing against Briggs. The Lancashire bowler met with wonderful success, taking in all 15 wickets for 28 runs.

England 292 (R. Abel 120, H. Wood 59; W. H. Ashley 7-95);
South Africa 47 (J. Briggs 7-17) **and 43** (Briggs 8-11).

1895-96 – LORD HAWKE'S TEAM IN SOUTH AFRICA: LAVISH LOHMANN
1897

The success of the eleven was mainly was mainly brought about by the effective bowling of George Lohmann, who had the splendid record of 157 wickets for less than seven runs each. The Surrey professional accomplished his best work in the 11-a-side games with South Africa, taking in the three matches no fewer than 35 wickets. At one time it was feared that the disturbances in the Transvaal [*the Jameson Raid*] would seriously affect the tour, but such happily was not the case.

1905-06 – MCC IN SOUTH AFRICA: SAD FAILURE
1907

The tour was, as regards first-class cricket, a sad failure. Everything else in the tour was naturally subordinate to the five Test matches with South Africa, and of these the Englishmen won the Fourth and lost the other four. Of course nothing that was done could compensate for these defeats, and the team left the Cape somewhat crestfallen. As to the merit of the play that brought about the South African triumphs there was little difference of opinion. Indeed several of the Englishmen were loud in their praise, and did not hesitate to say that, at any rate on the Johannesburg ground, the South Africans were a great side.

1905-06 – SOUTH AFRICA v ENGLAND (First Test): NAIL-BITER SETS THE TONE
1907

At Johannesburg, January 2, 3, 4, 1906. The first of the five Test matches was the most remarkable of the series, the Englishmen being beaten by one wicket [*South Africa's first Test victory*] after they had seemed to have the game in their hands. South Africa had 284 to get in the last innings, and when the sixth wicket fell before lunch the score was only 134. White played wonderfully well, resisting the bowling for four hours and ten minutes, but despite all his efforts – he was out eighth at 226

– 45 runs were still required when Sherwell, the last man, joined Nourse. Amid ever increasing excitement the runs were hit off, South Africa thus winning by one wicket. Nourse was batting three hours and 40 minutes for his 93 not out – in every way a splendid innings. There was nothing exceptional in the cricket of the English team, but Crawford played two good innings, and Lees bowled finely.

England 184 and 190 (Mr. P. F. Warner 51; G. A. Faulkner 4-26);

South Africa 91 (W. S. Lees 5-34)

and 287-9 (G. C. White 81, A. W. Nourse 93*).

1922-23 – MCC In South Africa: no compensation
1924

Inasmuch as the English team in South Africa during the winter of 1922-23 won the rubber and, in a programme of 22 matches, suffered only one defeat, the tour on the face of it was a complete success – one might almost say a triumph. Examined in detail, however, the trip, though in many ways highly satisfactory, did little to restore the damaged prestige of English cricket and afforded no real compensation for the crushing defeats so recently inflicted by Australia. As in all similar tours in these days the Test matches meant everything, the other games being quite subsidiary – many of them in this particular case insignificant.

1922-23 – SOUTH AFRICA v ENGLAND (Second Test):
MISSED CHANCES
1924

At Cape Town, January 1, 2, 3, 4, 1923. The Englishmen won the Second Test match, but they only just scrambled home by one wicket after a desperate finish. The Englishmen required only 173 to win, but Sandham and Mead alone played Hall's bowling with any confidence and things looked very bad indeed when, at the end of the afternoon, the score stood at 86 with six wickets down. The finish on Thursday was exciting to a degree. Mann, not out 12 overnight, made a great effort, and was so well backed up by Jupp that the seventh wicket put on 68 runs. At lunchtime, with three wickets to fall, only 19 runs were wanted. However, Mann fell to a splendid catch in the slips at 167, and with a single added, Brown was run out, the wicket being thrown down from deep point. With five runs still required, Macaulay, the last man, joined Kennedy. The latter brought off a boundary hit on the leg side and a single by Macaulay finished the match. The result might easily have been different, Mann and Jupp being both let off during their invaluable partnership. Hall, whose bowling so nearly won the game for South Africa, was carried off the field shoulder-high.

South Africa 113 (Mr P. G. H. Fender 4-29)

and 242 (R. H. Catterall 76, H. W. Taylor 68; G. G. Macaulay 5-64, A. S. Kennedy 4-58);

England 183 (J. M. Blanckenberg 5-61, A. E. Hall 4-49)

and 173-9 (Hall 7-63).

Suffering defeat in the one Test match brought to a definite issue and so losing the rubber, the team that toured South Africa in the winter of 1930-31 experienced considerable misfortune. Captained by A. P. F. Chapman, the side included of those who had made a similar tour four years before only R. E. S. Wyatt, I. A. R. Peebles and Hammond, and again the MCC did not get together the full strength of England. Sutcliffe, Woolley and Larwood, in particular, would have added much power to the side for the Test matches. The absence of the famous Yorkshireman became a very serious matter when Sandham, after scoring 72 and six in the opening games, met with a motor accident which prevented him from playing any more during the whole course of the tour. To accentuate the trouble thus caused, Chapman, Allom, Hammond, Hendren, Duckworth and Tate, at different times, were all overtaken by illness, the shortage of players becoming so acute at one period that permission was obtained to enlist the services of H. W. Lee, who happened to be at the Cape fulfilling a coaching engagement.

The contest which, as it happened, decided the rubber took a somewhat remarkable course. Chapman showed such sound judgment that South Africa, sent in to bat, scored no more than 126, but a lead of 67 did not mean a big advantage and England, having to play the last innings, suffered defeat by 28 runs. All the other four matches were left drawn so this one victory gave South Africa, for the third time, the honours over England.

The last match of the series began with an unprecedented incident. Bails requisite to fit the large stumps were not available and, the fact not being discovered until Chapman had decided that South Africa should bat, an appreciable delay occurred in commencing the game. The loss of time necessarily meant that the England bowlers had their opportunity of showing what they could do on a drying pitch materially reduced. As it happened rain soon intervened but, had there been no delay, the game might well have taken so different a course that England, with victory attending their efforts, would have saved the rubber.

1938-39 – SOUTH AFRICA v ENGLAND (Fifth Test): BOLT FOR THE BOAT
Norman Preston, 1940

At Durban, March 3, 4, 6, 7, 8, 9, 10, 11, 13, 14, 1939. Unparalleled in the history of the game this was in many ways an extraordinary match, emphasising that there are no limits to the possibilities of what may occur in cricket; but it ended farcically, for insufficient time remained to finish the "timeless" Test. Although undecided, the final Test left the rubber with England after a magnificent and unequalled performance by W. R. Hammond and his men. Stopped by rain on the tenth day, the longest match ever played produced amazing records and brought personal triumph to Edrich who, after most heartbreaking experiences in Test cricket, established his reputation by hitting a double-century at a time when England needed an almost superhuman effort to avoid disaster.

South Africa set England to make 696 to win and few people imagined the team had a ghost of a chance of averting defeat, much less of scoring such a colossal total. Instead of going in with their tails down the batsmen set about their task in a magnificent manner and proved what can be done when the wicket remains unimpaired. It was an astonishing achievement to get within 42 runs of their objective with five wickets in hand, but, like the Oval Test between England and Australia the previous August, the game developed into a test of endurance. For one thing the pitch was much too good, and many batsmen discarded their natural methods and adopted unnecessary caution.

When heavy rain prevented any more cricket after tea on the tenth day the South African Board of Control and the two captains went into conference before issuing a statement that the game had been abandoned because the England team had to catch the 8.05pm train that night from Durban in order to reach Cape Town in time to make the necessary arrangements for their departure on the *Athlone Castle* on Friday. The date of sailing for England could not be postponed.

South Africa 530 (P. G. V. van der Bijl 125, A. D. Nourse 103, A. Melville 78, R. E. Grieveson 75, E. L. Dalton 57; R. T. D. Perks 5-100)

and 481 (Melville 103, van der Bijl 97, B. Mitchell 89, K. G. Viljoen 74; Mr K. Farnes 4-74);

England 316 (L. E. G. Ames 84, E. Paynter 62; Dalton 4-59)

and 654-5 (W. J. Edrich 219, Mr W. R. Hammond 140, Mr P. A. Gibb 120, Paynter 75, L. Hutton 55).

1948-49 – SOUTH AFRICA v ENGLAND (FIRST TEST): UNBEATABLE DRAMA
1950

At Durban, December 16, 17, 18, 20, 1948. England won by two wickets. No greater support could have been given to the contention that an exciting cricket match can provide as intense a thrill as anything else in sport than by the drama of the final stages. With three balls left any one of four results remained possible. Before Bedser brought the scores level with a single from Tuckett off the sixth delivery of the last over, a draw or a tie could be visualised as easily as a victory for either side.

Gladwin hit at but missed the seventh ball. Then in a mid-wicket conference about the last ball he and Bedser decided to run in any event except the wicket being hit. Few of their England colleagues in the pavilion could bear the strain of watching as Tuckett began his run-up. As he did so the fieldsmen started to run in like sprinters towards the wicket to prevent the single which would win the match. Gladwin went into his stumps, swung his bat, but again missed his stroke. The ball struck his thigh and bounced a yard or two in front of him. From short leg Mann pounced on the ball, but both batsmen galloped to safety. With Bedser and Gladwin executing a jubilation one-step, hundreds of people invading the pitch and some chairing off their varying heroes, there ended a Test which will provide a rich memory for everyone fortunate enough to have participated or to have watched.

South Africa 161 (A. V. Bedser 4-39) **and 219** (W. W. Wade 63; D. V. P. Wright 4-72);
England 253 (L. Hutton 83, D. C. S. Compton 72; A. M. B. Rowan 4-108, N. B. F. Mann 6-59)
and 128-8 (C. N. McCarthy 6-43)

1949-50 – SOUTH AFRICA v AUSTRALIA (THIRD TEST):
HERO HARVEY   1951

At Durban, January 20, 21, 23, 24, 1950. After at one time looking almost certain to be defeated, Australia staged a dramatic recovery and gained a glorious victory with only 25 minutes to spare. This success gave them the rubber, the first two Tests having been won by convincing margins. South Africa reached a respectable total, and no one could have anticipated the remarkable cricket which followed. Yet when the second day was over South Africa had established a lead of 236, Australia having been dismissed for 75 – their lowest total in a Test match against South Africa. The player largely responsible for this astonishing collapse was Tayfield, a newcomer to Test cricket this season. This Natal off-break bowler worried all the batsmen and took seven for 23 in 8.4 overs. Nourse was left with the weekend in which to decide whether to enforce the follow-on. Probably influenced by the threat of rain, he decided to bat a second time, and though the turf now aided spin the failure of the South African batsmen was difficult to understand. The side were all out for 99, and Australia began the final day needing 256 to win with seven wickets in hand.

The odds still favoured South Africa, but Harvey refused to be deterred by the immensity of the task. Helped by Loxton and McCool, he adopted a dogged style quite out of keeping with his normal game and stayed five hours 30 minutes without making a mistake. This innings of extraordinary patience and skill, which enabled Australia to record their remarkable victory, left a lasting impression upon all who witnessed it. The history of Test cricket provides few comparable feats.

South Africa 311 (E. A. B. Rowan 143, A. D. Nourse 66; W. A. Johnston 4-75)

and 99 (Johnston 4-39, I. W. Johnson 5-34);

Australia 75 (H. J. Tayfield 7-23) and 336-5 (R. N. Harvey 151*, S. J. E. Loxton 54).

1956-57 – SOUTH AFRICA v ENGLAND (FOURTH TEST): FRATERNAL FAVOUR
1958

At Johannesburg, February 15, 16, 18, 19, 20, 1957. South Africa won by 17 runs and gained their first victory over England in their own country for 26 years. Never before had they beaten England in South Africa on a turf pitch. The match proved a personal triumph for Tayfield, although both sides deserve credit for making the game so exciting. The cricket followed the usual pattern of slow, cautious batting, but there was plenty of interest throughout. Tayfield established a new record for a South African bowler in taking nine wickets in an innings of a Test. He also became the first South African to take 13 wickets in a Test against England.

England started the last day requiring 213 [*with nine wickets in hand*] at a rate of 34 an hour. This was the most exciting day of the series. England for a long time looked almost certain victors before finally collapsing. South Africa's chief hope was Tayfield. He spun the ball just enough to be difficult and, as in previous Tests, bowled most accurately to a well-placed field. England decided on a bold policy which nearly succeeded. At tea the game was still open, England wanting 46 with four wickets left, but the end came 50 minutes later with Arthur Tayfield, fielding substitute for Funston, who hurt a leg, catching Loader on the long-on boundary off his brother's bowling.

Hugh Tayfield was deservedly chaired off the field. He bowled throughout the four hours 50 minutes on the final day, sending down 35 overs, and although heavily punished by the early batsmen he always looked menacing. Cowdrey, finding himself running out of partners, tried attacking him, but when he gave a return catch, the end was in sight. After a closely fought and keen struggle South Africa went into the last Test with a chance of sharing the rubber – an excellent effort considering they were two down after two matches.

South Africa 340 (R. A. McLean 93, T. L. Goddard 67, J. H. B. Waite 61) **and 142**;
England 251 (P. B. H. May 61; H. J. Tayfield 4-79)
and 214 (D. J. Insole 68, M. C. Cowdrey 55; Tayfield 9-113).

South Africa did win the final Test to square the series 2–2 on a pitch that aroused plenty of controversy and on which, according to Wisden, *"the ball kept exceptionally low from the end of the first day onwards and the number of shooters was more than one sees in a full season".*

Sussex v Yorkshire. At Hove, July 31, August 1, 2, 1957. Watson, leading Yorkshire, spent an hour over his first 12 runs and while he and Close were together the Sussex captain and off-spin bowler, Marlar, ended a long spell by sending down one ball – a wide – left-arm.

Little Wonder No. 66

1957-58 – AUSTRALIANS IN SOUTH AFRICA: WRECKER RICHIE   1959

The Australians restored their sagging prestige with a highly successful tour and their splendid form raised their hopes that they would recover the Ashes when England toured their country a year later. Under the youthful captaincy of Ian Craig, the Australians developed into a powerful, confident side and they went through the tour unbeaten. The outstanding personality was R. Benaud, who, in bowling and batting, enjoyed a tour of unbroken success. Adding the googly to his leg-break and top-spinner, Benaud once more revealed the South African's dislike of flighted spin, bowled out of the back of the hand. Thirty of his wickets came in the Test matches and four times he took five wickets in an innings. Only in the First Test did Benaud fail to cause chaos with the ball, but he scored 122 in that match. He also hit another century in the Fourth Test. Benaud's aggressive batting made him a great favourite with the crowds and his all-round skill was a major factor in the Australian success.

THE BEGINNING OF THE END   Norman Preston, Notes by the Editor, 1962

The automatic disappearance of South Africa from the Imperial Cricket Conference when the country ceased to be a member of the British Commonwealth has left a complex problem. South Africa's matches against other countries can no longer be classified as Tests. They come second to Australia as England's oldest opponents, the first match having taken place at Port Elizabeth in March, 1889. Efforts are being made to find a means of restoring South Africa to membership of the Conference. This move may receive support from England, Australia and New Zealand, whom South Africa meet on the field, but it is likely to be vehemently opposed by the West Indies, India and Pakistan, who because of the colour question, have never met the Springboks at cricket. The matter will come up for discussion again when the Imperial Cricket Conference next meet at Lord's in July. Pakistan, I understand, are putting forward a novel suggestion to form a kind of "second division" to incorporate all the cricket-playing countries which are not Conference members, such as Ceylon, Malaya, Kenya, East and West Africa, Hong Kong, Singapore, Canada, the United States of America, Denmark and Holland. In the end, everything may depend upon whether or not South Africa will agree to change their ideas and consent to play against the "coloured" countries.

1961-62 – NEW ZEALANDERS IN SOUTH AFRICA: RIPPING REID   1963

John Reid's pre-tour prediction that he was leading the best team ever to represent New Zealand abroad was in the light of subsequent events fully justified. To share the rubber deservedly with South Africa was a magnificent achievement; in fact, never before in the history of cricket had New Zealand won a representative match outside their own country.

The tour of 24 matches must go down in history as belonging almost exclusively to Reid. This quiet, unassuming master of bat and ball smashed most of the records open to him. In the five Test matches he scored more runs than any two of his colleagues. His tour aggregate of 1,915 runs eclipsed Compton's 13-year-old record. He topped the century seven times, including a glorious 203 on his favourite Newlands and easily headed the fielding statistics with 22 catches.

Apart from Reid, the batting was far too brittle, with the possible exception of the Third Test when several of the players ran into form simultaneously. The bowlers never let up and although Reid held pride of place with four wickets for 44 runs in a marathon spell of 45 overs when he won the all-important final match almost single-handed, Cameron, Motz and Alabaster deserved the plaudits for their tenacity and refusal to admit defeat in every match. In Alabaster we were privileged to meet the finest leg-spinner – a genuine finger worker – seen in this country for many years.

1964-65 – MCC IN SOUTH AFRICA: HEARTS AND MINDS   Basil Easterbrook, 1966

For the first time for five years England won an overseas Test series, a welcome and somewhat unexpected success which assured the tour its niche in cricket history. When the side left London it attracted little attention, for its departure coincided with the general election. The events were not entirely unrelated for the political situation played a part in change of leadership on the cricket field.

E. R. Dexter, who had captained England the previous summer, was adopted as Conservative candidate for a Cardiff constituency, and while he was engaged on the hustings the task of putting some needed hustle into English representative cricket was given to a tried and proven skipper, Michael John Knight Smith, who had taken Warwickshire near to the head of the County Championship.

Knowledgeable cricket enthusiasts gave him hardly much chance, for the bowling available to him looked decidedly limited, while South Africa had confirmed the rise of several new stars in Australia. Yet Smith and his men went through their entire programme of 19 matches undefeated. Cricket is a game played in the hearts and minds of men as well as with the hands and feet, and from first day to last the choice of Carr and Smith as executives proved as near ideal as anything can be in this imperfect world.

MCC have sent more powerful teams from Lord's than this one, but never one superior in terms of corporate effort on the playing pitch and harmony in the pavilion. Of the young, comparatively untried players, none was able to force his way irresistibly to the fore as Boycott of Yorkshire had done in a matter of two years.

1966-67 – AUSTRALIANS IN SOUTH AFRICA: POLLOCK'S PRESENCE
Geoffrey A. Chettle, 1968

Graeme Pollock had forced his way to the top flight of international stars on a solid foundation as the youngest century and double-century maker in the country's history. At the same time Colin Bland, the tall athletic Rhodesian, had acquired a public and TV image as one of the world's greatest fieldsmen.

Denis Lindsay, successor to Waite, who so ably represented South Africa in 50 Tests and gained distinction as a wicketkeeper-batsman of world class, blossomed as an aggressive attacking force, scoring three centuries and an aggregate of 606 runs to register the highest individual contribution by any wicketkeeper in a series of international cricket.

The left-hander Pollock confirmed his standing as the best 23-year-old batsman in Test cricket. The impact he made in Australia and the United Kingdom was re-emphasised during a fantastic innings of 209 at Newlands, where he virtually carried his side for six hours. His 90 in the First Test was, however, acclaimed the real masterpiece, and the young maestro concluded the series at Port Elizabeth, as he began it, with another century.

1966-67 – SOUTH AFRICA v AUSTRALIA (First Test): TOPPLED AT LAST
Geoffrey A. Chettle 1968

At Johannesburg, December 23, 24, 26, 27, 28, 1966. South Africa won by 233 runs. The match will go down as one of the most memorable in the history of South African cricket. Australia's proud record of 64 years without defeat in Test matches in South Africa was smashed after even the most sanguine supporter had written off the Springboks' chances within an hour of play commencing.

On a ground saturated by days of rain, which only ceased 48 hours before the start, the margin and quality of victory were unbelievable. Five wickets down for 41 was the sequel to van der Merwe's decision to bat first. Lance and Lindsay stopped the rot and added 110 for the sixth wicket, but South Africa totalled only 199, of which Simpson and Lawry erased 118 before being separated. At that stage Australia were in complete command. They passed the South African total with nine wickets intact and then a dramatic collapse occurred and the lead was restricted to 126.

The Springboks wiped off this deficit and, taking full advantage of some amazing dropped catches, they soared to incredible heights while achieving the highest South African total in Test cricket. Lindsay hit his maiden Test century yet the gem of the innings was Pollock's 90. On this display the young left-hander looked without peer and his timing, placing and wristwork were an object lesson for the purist.

South Africa 199 (D. T. Lindsay 69; G. D. McKenzie 5-46)
and 620 (Lindsay 182, R. G. Pollock 90, P. L. van der Merwe 76, H. R. Lance 70, A. Bacher 63, E. J. Barlow 50);
Australia 325 (W. M. Lawry 98, R. B. Simpson 65) **and 261** (T. R. Veivers 55; T. L. Goddard 6-53).

1969-70 – AUSTRALIANS IN SOUTH AFRICA: THE MIDAS TOUCH
Geoffrey A. Chettle, 1971

The visit of the seventh Australian team to tour South Africa lasted only 12 weeks, but will always be remembered by cricket enthusiasts because of the willingness of W. M. Lawry and his team to tackle the Springboks immediately following a strenuous and disturbing Test series in India. Thus ended an unpleasant and totally unnecessary three-year period of isolation imposed on our cricketers – and spectators.

The South African Test-starved players were raring to go, confident of their ability to consolidate the 3–1 victory over R. B. Simpson's side. This was indeed South Africa's year. From the moment the new Springbok captain, Dr Ali Bacher, won the toss at Newlands and elected to bat in the First Test, the series followed an almost stereotyped pattern. Bacher wins the toss; South Africa takes first knock; the visitors' reply is characterised by the abject failure of the majority of the top six batsmen.

The Australians' immaculate ground fielding was always a feature, but the spate of dropped catches, some of which granted reprieves to Graeme Pollock and Richards, attained such alarming proportions that more than 70 chances went begging in the 12 matches. By way of contrast the Springboks held almost everything that came their way. As a team they bore a charmed life and everything they attempted turned to gold.

1969-70 – SOUTH AFRICA v AUSTRALIA (SECOND TEST):
POLLOCK'S TECHNICAL PERFECTION   1971

At Durban, February 5, 6, 7, 9, 10, 1970. South Africa won by an innings and 129 runs. The match produced a host of new records, pride of place going to Graeme Pollock for his mammoth 274 which gave him the individual record for a South African in Test matches. His concentration never wavered, and he attacked continuously and with merciless efficiency.

Another highlight of the match was Richards's maiden hundred in only his second Test. In an exhibition of technical perfection the 24-year-old Natal and Hampshire batsman scored 140 of the 229 runs on the board. He reached his hundred off 116 deliveries and his only false stroke in a three-hour innings was his last one. He had Pollock as a partner for the last hour and the spectators were treated to a superb display as the pair added 103 runs for the third wicket. Between them they scored 414 runs of South Africa's gigantic total.

South Africa 622-9 dec. (R. G. Pollock 274, B. A. Richards 140, H. R. Lance 61);
Australia 157 (A. P. Sheahan 62) **and 336** (K. D. Walters 74, I. R. Redpath 74*, K. R. Stackpole 71).

South Africa won the four-Test series 4–0. It was their last official international competition for almost 22 years.

1981-82 – SAB ENGLISH TEAM IN SOUTH AFRICA: THE REBELS   John Woodcock, 1983

On February 27, 1982, a party of English cricketers slipped out of London, having taken every precaution to keep their departure a secret, to play a series of matches in South Africa. Before their first fixture, less than a week later, strenuous efforts were made to dissuade them from their venture. From the Test and County Cricket Board went a cable urging them, if it was not too late, to think again. Implicit in this was a warning that they were hazarding their cricketing futures, a threat which was duly implemented when, on March 9, a three-year ban from Test cricket was imposed on them.

There were six subsequent unofficial tours of South Africa by teams from Australia, West Indies and Sri Lanka. The last in January 1990, by an England team led by Mike Gatting, was met by violent protests and demonstrations at every turn. Nelson Mandela was released from prison only a few weeks later.

1992-93 – INDIANS IN SOUTH AFRICA: DIPLOMACY AND HISTORY

Richard Streeton, 1994

A great deal of humdrum cricket failed to detract from the diplomatic and sporting history made when India embarked on a tour of Zimbabwe and South Africa late in 1992. Slow scoring and negative captaincy, coupled with moribund pitches, marred both Zimbabwe's inaugural Test and the first series staged in South Africa for 23 years. The visit had the active support of the African National Congress and was almost entirely free from political rancour. More than £650,000 of the profits made by the United Cricket Board of South Africa (UCBSA) went into their development programme for black cricketers. The Indians undertook a heavy schedule of duties off the field, in townships and elsewhere, and proved fine ambassadors.

1992-93 – SOUTH AFRICA v INDIA (THIRD TEST): DONALD, DUCK

Richard Streeton, 1994

At Port Elizabeth, December 26, 27, 28, 29, 1992. South Africa won by nine wickets. Hostile fast bowling by Donald, who took 12 wickets, and a solid century by Cronje were the decisive performances as South Africa completed victory with a day to spare. It was their first Test win since they were readmitted to ICC; their last had been over Australia on the same ground in March 1970. Donald's figures were the fourth-best for South Africa, and Richardson was the first South African wicketkeeper to take nine catches in a Test. A flamboyant hundred by Kapil Dev, coming in when India were 27 for five in their second innings, prolonged the game, but otherwise India were badly let down by their batsmen. South Africa never lost the initiative after taking eight wickets on the opening day, when Wessels surprised most people by asking India to bat in good conditions. Donald extracted plenty of life from a slow pitch, but several Indians got out playing loose strokes.

India 212 (M. Azharuddin 60; A. A. Donald 5-55) and 215 (Kapil Dev 129; Donald 7-84); South Africa 275 (W. J. Cronje 135, A. C. Hudson 52) and 155-1 (K. C. Wessels 95*).

Sussex v Glamorgan. At Hastings, July 24, 25, 26, 1957. At the end of the second day the Glamorgan captain, Wooller, dissatisfied at the slow scoring-rate, bowled five underarm deliveries to his rival captain, Marlar.

Little Wonder No. 67

1995-96 – ENGLAND IN SOUTH AFRICA: MALCOLM V MANAGEMENT   Scyld Berry, 1997

Unfortunately for England, when Russell was promoted to No. 6 for the deciding Test, and for once five bowlers were selected, it was the one time he and Atherton failed with the bat in both innings – and another South African last-wicket stand prospered. Although Devon Malcolm was made the scapegoat for bowling too gently at Adams, England's other bowlers – and the fielders – also wilted at the crucial moment. None the less, this marked the terminal breakdown in relations between Malcolm, who believed he was being treated unfairly, and the England management, who believed he had been carrying an injury when the party was selected, and would not listen to technical advice. The slanging between Malcolm and the manager, Ray Illingworth, continued in print and led to both being hauled up before the TCCB: Malcolm was reprimanded and Illingworth fined £2,000, later rescinded. The whole business apparently hastened the departure from Test cricket of both of them.

1995-96 – SOUTH AFRICA V ENGLAND (SECOND TEST):
ATHERTON'S FINEST HOURS   Scyld Berry, 1997

At Johannesburg, November 30, December 1, 2, 3, 4, 1995. Drawn. "One of the great innings of all time," in the opinion of Ray Illingworth, saved England from going 1–0 down. Others acclaimed Atherton's innings as the finest by any England captain, as he had no particular partner until Russell joined him for the last 277 minutes, whereas Peter May had Colin Cowdrey to help repulse Sonny Ramadhin at Edgbaston in 1957. Possibly only the 262 not out by Dennis Amiss at Kingston in 1973-74 was a greater match-saving innings for England.

Atherton, resolutely single-minded in any event, became even more so when he saw his decision to play four fast bowlers and send South Africa in fail badly. This was his bowlers' fault as much as his. South Africa were so cautious that they came off for light that was not unplayably bad when 428 ahead. Next morning, they went on for 92 more minutes to add 50 superfluous runs.

England therefore had to survive for four overs and five sessions, not two whole days, or more. They had drawn their three previous Tests, but only after batting first and banking large totals. Atherton and Stewart, in his 50th Test, were aspiring to new heights when they set out to save the game – a target of 479 was theoretical. Only a shower was forecast, and that did not materialise. What did help was that the one lively pitch of the series went to sleep once it had fully dried, and its numerous cracks never became influential. A full house of 30,000 on the fourth day waited for England to capitulate, and by the close Atherton had lost four partners. Twice in three balls, McMillan hit the stumps with yorkers – Ramprakash beaten in an uncontrolled drive for the second time – and yet they were not scathed again in the next nine hours.

On the fifth morning Atherton took a while to return to his groove, until his feet began moving again. On 99, he forced off his body into Kirsten's hands at short leg, and straight out again. He hooked his next ball from Donald to bring up his ninth hundred and 4,000 runs in Tests, and celebrated with rare animation, exchanging hugs with Smith. Soon after, Smith's slash was caught at third man and Russell offered a return catch to Pringle when five, which was missed. A draw was still only the faintest of hopes.

Gradually that hope grew stronger. Back home, England's supporters hung on to television and radio commentaries, if not quite as grimly as Atherton and Russell. The captain's tempo was perfect, as he did not try an uncontrolled shot, and restricted his scoring arc to his favourite areas square of the wicket, yet he put away the bad ball to the boundary 28 times to stop the bowlers getting on top. Russell took more than his share of the strike and kept reminding his captain of England's collapse in the Barbados Test of 1989-90.

Cronje made little effort to disturb the batsmen's rhythm by varying his bowlers and fields. Donald had nothing left when the third ball was taken – and certainly no time to exploit it, owing to the timing of the delayed declaration. Atherton batted for 643 minutes in all – the fourth-longest innings for England – and 492 balls, Russell for 277 minutes and 235 balls.

South Africa 332 (G. Kirsten 110, D. J. Cullinan 69; D. G. Cork 5-84, D. E. Malcolm 4-62)
and 346-9 dec. (B. M. McMillan 100*, Cullinan 61; Cork 4-78);
England 200 (R. A. Smith 52) **and 351-5** (M. A. Atherton 185*).

1996-97 – SOUTH AFRICA v AUSTRALIA (Second Test):
WINNING WAUGH   Jack Bannister, 1998

At Port Elizabeth, March 14, 15, 16, 17. Australia won by two wickets. Mark Waugh's magnificent fourth-innings 116 clinched a wildly fluctuating Test and, with it, the series – South Africa's first home defeat in six series since resuming Test cricket in 1992. Australia began and finished strongly, but for much of the match South Africa seemed bound to square the series. The key was the pitch, which had such a thick mat of grass that it looked like an Essex ground of the 1950s, Westcliff or Clacton maybe. It was automatic that Taylor would bowl.

Australia needed 270. Though two and a half days remained, another 40 or 50 might have defeated them. But the chance was there and Mark Waugh took it. He later described it as his best innings in any cricket: it lasted nearly five and a half hours and included a six and 17 fours. Stern defence was twinned with innate elegance after he arrived in a crisis – 30 for two. Taylor failed again, and Hayden was comically run out when he and Elliott lunged for the same crease as Cronje burst between them to knock down the other wicket.

Waugh reached his fifty by the close, when Australia were an encouraging 145 for three, with his brother Steve digging in at the other end. But Kallis had Steve caught in the covers and when Adams bowled Blewett, at 192 for five, South Africa were back in the match. The crowd, though disappointingly small, was close to delirium. Bevan came in to help Waugh to the brink of victory but, with 12 still wanted, Kallis dismissed Waugh and Cronje had Bevan caught at slip. Warne soon followed. Two wickets were left, five needed. But not for Healy the

Hirst–Rhodes tactic of getting them in singles – he swung Cronje high over long leg for six.

South Africa 209 (B. M. McMillan 55; J. N. Gillespie 5-54) **and 168**;
Australia 108 and 271-8 (M. E. Waugh 116).

1997-98 – PAKISTANIS IN SOUTH AFRICA: FACT OR FICTION? Paul Weaver, 1999

A series between Pakistan, the world's most gifted side, and the heroically resilient South Africans always promised momentous cricket. Some saw the series as deciding the silver medal position in world cricket.

It was certainly a memorable series, fairly drawn 1–1. But, although there was some outstanding cricket, the mood and shape of the contest was directed by incidents off the field. Not for the first time, a Pakistan tour mixed enthralling cricket with mayhem.

The First Test was delayed for 24 hours (Pakistan asked for longer) after fast bowler Mohammad Akram and off-spinner Saqlain Mushtaq claimed they had been mugged outside the team hotel. Later reports said they had been seen at two exotically named nightspots, Club 69 and Blue Orchid, and that the injuries had actually been sustained there. The players could not describe their assailants or agree on the time of the attack.

The seeds of mistrust were sown and poisoned the entire series. Ali Bacher, managing director of the United Cricket Board of South Africa, worked and wheedled frantically to keep the tour on course. "I could have written a best-seller to describe what happened on this tour," he said at the end. The mugging issue was never resolved. South African officials felt they had been hoodwinked, and the players were in danger of being charged with wasting police time. Even on the day of their departure to Zimbabwe there was trouble: coach Haroon Rashid declared that Shoaib Akhtar and Fazl-e-Akbar were to be sent home for late-night partying, but the decision was reversed.

1997-98 – SOUTH AFRICA v SRI LANKA (FIRST TEST): SIGNIFICANT DEBUT
1999

At Cape Town, March 19, 20, 21, 22, 23, 1998. South Africa won by 70 runs. The selection of Makhaya Ntini was a significant event for South African cricket. The 20-year-old son of a domestic servant from a small village in the Eastern Cape, he was the first product of South Africa's development programme to make the Test team. He had been weaned on mini-cricket, a soft-ball game for children, and attended Dale College, a strong sporting school, on a cricket scholarship. Ntini's own debut performance was patchy, but he slotted well into a successful team as, for the second season in succession, Newlands hosted the most entertaining Test match of the South African summer.

South Africa 418 (D. J. Cullinan 113, S. M. Pollock 92, G. Kirsten 62; M. Muralitharan 4-135)

and 264 (W. J. Cronje 74, Cullinan 68; Muralitharan 4-108);

Sri Lanka 306 (P. A. de Silva 77, M. S. Atapattu 60; S. M. Pollock 4-83)

and 306 (Atapattu 71, G. P. Wickremasinghe 51).

1998-99 – WEST INDIANS IN SOUTH AFRICA: UNTHINKABLE   Geoffrey Dean, 2000

Even though they had been defeated 3–0 in Pakistan a year earlier, the notion that West Indies would suffer a 5–0 series whitewash on their first Test tour of South Africa was inconceivable. On paper, there was little between the two sides.

The pay dispute with the West Indies board, which culminated in crisis talks in London, unsettled the team before the tour even began. Only half the West Indies party arrived in South Africa at the scheduled start of the tour. The rest, including captain Brian Lara and vice-captain Carl Hooper, stayed in London after the Mini World Cup in Bangladesh. The remainder of the squad then flew into Heathrow from South Africa to present a united front to the board, who initially sacked Lara and Hooper, then sought reconciliation. How united that front really was is open to question: the junior players found themselves dragged into a dispute in which the seniors were largely seeking a pay increase for themselves. Certainly, there was a divided air about the West Indies party for much of the tour. Lara admitted after the Fifth Test that "we are not together as a team". That appeared an understatement, and, for that lack of unity, Lara had to bear some responsibility. His public criticism of two of his bowlers, Nixon McLean and Mervyn Dillon, after the Second-Test capitulation, seemed to sap their confidence, and neither bowled consistently all tour. Lara failed to get the best not only from them but also several other unproven Test players.

Lara himself continued to underachieve with the bat, extending his sequence of matches without a Test hundred to 14. While Jonty Rhodes excelled at No. 6 for South Africa, that position remained highly problematic for the visitors throughout. Jimmy Adams, who would have filled it, was badly missed, having to return home after suffering a mysterious hand injury – reportedly caused by a butter-knife – on the flight to Johannesburg.

1999-2000 – ENGLAND IN SOUTH AFRICA: GATHERING STORM   Colin Bateman, 2001

The tour took place against a background of political unrest in South African cricket, which was promoting a policy of "affirmative action". The political brouhaha did not improve the demeanour of South Africa's captain, Hansie Cronje, often a brooding figure, unhappy with his masters and his own form. Already disgruntled at starting the series with a short-term appointment for two Tests only, subsequently extended to cover the remaining Tests and the one-day games against England and Zimbabwe, he reportedly offered to drop himself before the Third at Durban because he strongly opposed the selectors' decision to leave out Jonty

Rhodes. Throughout, Cronje was widely criticised for being too cautious tactically, yet at the end he was again a national champion, hailed both for the series victory and for his initiative on the last day at Centurion Park. Within months, however, his career, possibly his life, was in ruins.

1999-2000 – SOUTH AFRICA v ENGLAND (First Test): OVER BEFORE IT BEGAN

Colin Bateman, 2001

At Johannesburg, November 25, 26, 27, 28, 1999. South Africa won by an innings and 21 runs. South Africa overpowered a new-look England side who went to the Wanderers full of optimism and left realising the scale of the task ahead. It was South Africa's tenth consecutive home Test win. The match was dominated by South Africa's peerless new-ball pairing of Donald and Pollock, who exploited perfect conditions for fast bowling to claim 19 wickets between them. Poor England. They turned up on the first morning to find a damp, spongy pitch underfoot and heavy, low clouds overhead. Then Cronje won the toss. It took just 17 deliveries to put all England's plans and preparation through a shredder as they lost four wickets for two runs, their worst start to a Test match.

Donald did the principal damage, bowling Atherton second ball with a late inswinger. Donald's devastating first two overs also accounted for Butcher and Stewart, out first ball, so that Chris Adams, coming in at No. 6, found himself batting to prevent a hat-trick within 15 minutes of his debut. With Hussain out third ball to an almost unplayable lifter from Pollock in between, any contest was as good as over. That England achieved 122 owed much to Vaughan, who impressed on his first outing, and some controlled hitting by Flintoff, back in Test cricket after 15 months' absence. But with the ball swinging through the air and seaming off the pitch, batting was a lottery. Or it appeared that way until England had the ball in their hands. Gough, Caddick and Mullally lacked the potency of South Africa's fast men and, when Hussain turned to his support bowlers, the home team plundered runs at will on the second day as the sun shone and the pitch dried out.

England 122 (A. A. Donald 6-53, S. M. Pollock 4-16) **and 260** (A. J. Stewart 86; Donald 5-74, Pollock 4-64); **South Africa 403-9 dec.** (D. J. Cullinan 108, H. H. Gibbs 85, L. Klusener 72; D. Gough 5-70).

1999-2000 – SOUTH AFRICA v ENGLAND (Fifth Test): THE GAME, THE SHAME

Neil Manthorp, 2001

At Centurion, January 14, 15, 16, 17, 18, 2000. England won by two wickets. History was made on the final day when a match apparently reduced to the deadliest of finishes, following three consecutive playless days, was brought back to life by the captains. For the first time in Test cricket, innings were forfeited and this produced a memorable, entertaining climax. When play resumed, with South Africa still in the first innings, the many hundreds of travelling English supporters and a few hundred hardy locals had every reason to expect the worst. What they were treated to was a gripping finale that saw England win with five balls and two wickets remaining.

Five months after the match, however, came the bitterness of deceit when Cronje, South Africa's captain, admitted receiving 53,000 rand (around £5,000) and a leather jacket from a bookmaker, who had urged him to initiate a positive result, rather than let the match peter out as a draw. At the King Commission inquiry into match-fixing, which opened in Cape Town in June, he insisted that his motives were "for the good of cricket", but the fact that financial reward formed a part of his motivation tainted the match for ever. History would also record that it was the first Test in which "fixing" was proven.

Inevitably, some wondered whether Test cricket had been compromised, even belittled, by the contrived result. Cronje was adamant that, should the game's administrators at the ICC be among those showing disapproval, he "wouldn't want to be a part of cricket any more. What is wrong with trying to make a game of it?" he said afterwards. But his previous dealings with bookmakers, as revealed at the King Commission, had forced him into that position. It was the first, albeit oblique, evidence of what had become a sadly corrupted outlook on the game and his responsibilities. "Test cricket needs to do everything it can to advertise itself and be competitive in a busy sporting market," he went on. "It hurts to lose – we lost a 14-match unbeaten run because of this – but it was a fabulous game in the end and people deserve to be entertained."

Hussain, understandably delighted, paid special tribute to Cronje at the time. "It was a very special thing that Hansie did and I hope he gets the credit he deserves. It certainly was a great finish to be a part of." But later, when it emerged that corruption had played its regrettable part in the shaping of the final day, he would write in his newspaper column that England's win had been ruined. "We can't get away from that," he said. "It will always be remembered as a Test that was fixed."

Yet the cricket was played as hard as both teams were able, and that is some consolation. Cronje's goal was to achieve a positive result and, while a captain without thought of personal gain might have opted for defence and the safety of a draw when the match was slipping away, South Africa did almost pull off a remarkable win.

South Africa 248-8 dec. (L. Klusener 61*) **and second innings forfeited;**
England 0-0 dec. and 251-8 (A. J. Stewart 73).

2001-02 – INDIANS IN SOUTH AFRICA: UNDESIRABLE   Dicky Rutnagur, 2003

This tour made history of a thoroughly undesirable sort. The final Test, to be played at Centurion from November 23 to 27, was stripped of its official status by the International Cricket Council when India refused to play under the supervision of Mike Denness, the appointed referee. Denness, an England captain of the 1970s, had imposed penalties on six Indian players he had found in breach of the ICC Code of Conduct during the Second Test, which ended in Port Elizabeth on November 20. The list included the captain, Sourav Ganguly, and the people's favourite, Sachin Tendulkar.

When the ICC rejected India's demand for Denness to be replaced, the Indian board threatened to cut short the tour. The tourists were mere bystanders while war was waged on their behalf by Jagmohan Dalmiya, newly elected president of the Indian board and also a former president of the ICC.

At the eye of the storm, however, was the allegation against Tendulkar that he too had brought the game into disrepute through "interference with the match ball, thus changing its condition". This statement could only mean that Tendulkar had tampered with the ball and, by implication, he was a cheat. At first, Denness refused to comment on his verdicts or penalties, but he later issued a vague explanation of the Tendulkar case: it suggested he had not tampered with the ball, but had failed to observe the technicality of asking the umpires to supervise removal of mud from the ball. Denness added that there had been no complaint from the umpires; he had acted on his own initiative after scrutiny of video footage. Tendulkar, who hitherto had an unblemished disciplinary record, was fined 75% of his match fee, with a suspended ban for one Test.

The Indian public were outraged at the slight against the character of their idol. There were street protests in towns and cities throughout the country, and scenes of uproar even in parliament. It did not escape notice that Denness had overlooked a highly aggressive appeal by the South African captain, Shaun Pollock; the omission reinforced the general view held in the subcontinent that ICC referees are racially biased. Therefore, Dalmiya had to take a stand – not that he needed much provocation to adopt a bellicose posture. He was presented with an ideal opportunity to settle scores with his old ICC adversaries.

2001-02 – SOUTH AFRICA v AUSTRALIA (First Test): POT SHOT

Neil Manthorp, 2003

At Johannesburg, February 22, 23, 24, 2002. Australia won by an innings and 360 runs. After three savage beatings in Australia, South Africa came home to something worse – the second-heaviest defeat in Test history. A single moment summed up the crushing superiority of Australia and the brilliance of their star, Adam Gilchrist. It came when he took a pot shot at an advertising hoarding offering a bar of gold, worth 1.3million rand (over £80,000), for a direct hit. The sponsor, a local gold-mine, hardly seemed in danger: the billboard was 30 feet in the air and well behind the deep midwicket boundary, a carry of at least 100 yards.

Gilchrist was 169, and had butchered the entire frontline attack, which badly missed the injured Pollock. With McKenzie bowling gentle medium-pace, he could resist no longer. Like a golfer hitting a wedge approach shot, he scooped a length delivery towards the target – and started to jump up and down as he realised how close it would be. He missed by a couple of feet, but what remained of South Africa's spirit was broken. Gilchrist was playing with them like a cat keeping a half-dead mouse alive for entertainment. And it was only the second day of the series.

Australia 652-7 dec. (A. C. Gilchrist 204*, D. R. Martyn 133, M. L. Hayden 122, M. E. Waugh 53);
South Africa 159 and 133 (G. D. McGrath 5-21, S. K. Warne 4-44).

Little Wonder No. 68

Wisden 1959. Shortened MCC tours: "The leading cricketers in this country play virtually six days a week throughout the home season, including, in many cases, five Test matches, and are called upon to tour abroad two out of three winters. They are thus subjected to considerable strain and are separated from their families for long periods. The county clubs unreservedly support MCC's view that, both in the personal interests of their players and for the maintenance of the standard of play in county and international cricket, the duration of the longer MCC tours must be curtailed."

2004-05 – ENGLAND IN SOUTH AFRICA: VAUGHAN AGAIN
John Etheridge, 2005

England, under the calm yet increasingly bold captaincy of Michael Vaughan, won an often thrilling Test series 2–1 and secured their first victory in South Africa for 40 years. Admittedly, it was only their third Test tour to the country since M. J. K. Smith's team won in 1964-65, but that should not diminish their achievement. Only Australia, twice, had previously won a series in South Africa since their return from sporting isolation in 1991-92. It is a very tough country in which to win.

2004-05 – SOUTH AFRICA v ENGLAND (FOURTH TEST): HOGGARD'S SHOULDERS
Matthew Engel, 2005

At Johannesburg, January 13, 14, 15, 16, 17, 2005. England won by 77 runs. Most of the time, this Test resembled a well-run sightseeing tour (probably to a safari park, since this was definitely Big Game): it was always so varied and interesting no one objected that it seemed certain to lead them back exactly where they started. Then, just after lunch on the final day, the bus was hijacked by Hoggard, with a classical display of swing bowling. The draw all the shrewdies expected never happened, and England managed what eluded them in Durban. Once again, they found the onset of darkness harder to beat than South Africa, but this time they just managed it, and went 2–1 up.

It was their 12th Test win in ten months, and the most improbable of the lot. Vaughan's final-day declaration was a touch conservative, understandably so since his attack was in tatters: the spearhead Harmison had fallen so far that mid-match speculation suggested he might fly home; Flintoff seemed both wounded and distracted; Anderson had not played a first-class match since August, and it showed; even the spinner Giles was hurt. So Hoggard carried the team on his shoulders like Atlas. He bowled them to victory with seven for 61 and match figures of 12 for 205, England's best in 25 years.

England declared overnight, setting South Africa 325 in what seemed a notional 68 overs, because of the likelihood of bad light. This was Hoggard's moment. He found the perfect length, swing in both directions and growing cracks in both the pitch and the batsmen's composure. England were anxiously scanning the clouds, and even sent out their spare players (most of whom had not set foot on a field in weeks) to act as ballboys in the absence of a last-day crowd. Twice the sun went in, and England groaned. Twice it came out again. At seven minutes to six, Hoggard induced a nick from last man Steyn. England had their first Test win at the Wanderers in 48 years, and one to rank among their most remarkable anywhere.

England 411-8 dec (A. J. Strauss 147, R. W. T. Key 83, M. P. Vaughan 82*; M. Ntini 4-111)
and 332-9 dec. (M. E. Trescothick 180, Vaughan 54);
South Africa 419 (H. H. Gibbs 161, M. V. Boucher 64; M. J. Hoggard 5-144)
and 247 (Gibbs 98, G. C. Smith 67*; Hoggard 7-61).

2005-06 – SOUTH AFRICA v AUSTRALIA (FIFTH ONE-DAY INTERNATIONAL):
UNSURPASSED   Neil Manthorp, 2007

At Johannesburg, March 12, 2006. South Africa won by one wicket. The 2,349th one-day international was, quite simply, a match that surpassed all the other 2,348. On perhaps the best batting surface ever prepared in South Africa, Australia became the first team to sail past 400. And lost. With a ball to spare, Mark Boucher hit Brett Lee to the long-on boundary, giving South Africa the match and the series. This took the match aggregate to 872, increasing the old record of 693 by a quarter.

There were extraordinary innings from both No. 3s, Ponting and Gibbs. In a blur of outrageous shots, neither needed more than 100 balls to reach 150. Records cascaded almost as fast as runs: highest (and second-highest) total; fastest (and second-fastest) international 150; most expensive bowling figures; most runs in boundaries, and many more.

Oddly, the scale of the South Africans' task set them free. In the interval, Kallis had broken the ice in a sombre dressing-room with the words "Come on, guys: it's a 450 wicket. They're 15 short!" As Smith and Gibbs admitted afterwards, it allowed the team to have a "little chuckle" before the reply, and the pair played with an abandon inspired by their sense of the absurd. The coach, Mickey Arthur, remained pragmatic, setting an initial target of 185 from 25 overs. The score was actually 229 for two.

Swinging his bat like a battleaxe, Smith zoomed to 90 from only 55 balls, including 13 fours and two sixes, even outscoring the flying Gibbs. South Africa's most serious wobble came in the 43rd over when, still needing 80, they lost their sixth wicket. But van der Wath launched three sixes in five balls to keep the fantasy alive. With the last pair in and two needed from three balls, Lee bowled a near-perfect yorker to Ntini. However, instead of his usual swish, he calmly steered the ball to third man for a single. Scores level. And then Boucher hit the next ball for four, completing one of his finest fifties – and the most phenomenal of games. South Africa had won the series. And how.

Australia 434-4 (50 overs) (R. T. Ponting 164, M. E. K. Hussey 81, S. M. Katich 79, A. C. Gilchrist 55);
South Africa 438-9 (49.5 overs) (H. H. Gibbs 175, G. C. Smith 90, M. V. Boucher 50*; N. W. Bracken 5-67).

Thrill of the chase: Makhaya Ntini, left, and Mark Boucher embrace
after South Africa's astonishing one-wicket victory at Johannesburg in 2005-06
when they chased down Australia's world-record total of 434

An Australian tour of South Africa is about so much more than the cricket. It crackles with a tension that reaches tipping point when siblings of a similar psyche face each other 22 yards apart. Thousands of South Africans have chosen Australia over their own country as a place to live, and the suspicion is buried deep among South Africans that, whatever they think, say and do, Australians will always be able to think, say and do it better.

In other respects, the series was a radical and unwelcome departure from the norm. Why the additional Twenty20? Why only two Tests? And, while we're at it, what exactly were they thinking giving a Test to Newlands in November, a wet month in the Cape? The detractors were fully armed after a Test series that enthralled and entertained. The first match was done and dusted in a little over two days. Australia did something quite extraordinary: in a game where only 663 runs were scored, their captain Michael Clarke made 151 in one visit; they bowled South Africa out for 96 to take a first-innings lead of 188 – and then lost by eight wickets.

The Second Test belonged to the new 18-year-old fast bowler Pat Cummins, Australia's youngest Test debutant since Ian Craig in 1952-53. Cummins looked a cut above Australia's other bowlers: his six wickets in the second innings kept the fourth-innings target down to 310, which he polished off himself. But no bowler profited more from the helpful pitches than the relentlessly accurate Vernon Philander, who banished memories of his first crack at international cricket four years earlier to take 14 wickets.

On what would have been the fourth night of the Cape Town Test, Peter Roebuck, a renowned cricket writer, ended his life by jumping from the window of his hotel room. The precise reasons for his death were unknown but, for a few days, Roebuck was the only story in town.

WEST INDIES

The trophy for which England and West Indies have competed since 1963 may bear the Wisden name, but the Almanack has had a love-hate relationship with Caribbean cricket. It has celebrated and revered the exceptional talent and the imposing personalities – Constantine, Headley, Worrell, Sobers, Lloyd, Richards, Lara et al – but been riled by what it, and many others, perceived as excessive and dangerous use of short-pitched bowling. MCC's tours of the West Indies in the decade or so after the Second World War were, in *Wisden*'s eyes, routinely dogged by unruly crowds, weak or biased umpiring, and bouncers. In his review of the 1967-68 tour, E. M. Wellings, whose pen was one of the Almanack's most acidic, questioned whether touring sides could continue to visit to the Caribbean if things didn't change. As Tony Cozier, the veteran Barbadian broadcaster and *Wisden* correspondent, wrote in "The ride of a lifetime" in the 2013 edition: "There has never been a dull moment."

The 1896 edition reported: "The tour of the amateurs under Mr R. S. Lucas's captaincy, in the West Indies during the early months of the year, was very interesting, inasmuch as it opened up new ground to English cricketers." Four years later, following the 1899 West Indies tour of England, Pelham Warner wrote: "Prior to the visit of Mr R. S. Lucas's team, the West Indies as a field for cricket – despite the performances of Mr Jingle [*a character from Dickens's* Pickwick Papers] – were quite unknown to the majority of English sportsmen. The results of that tour showed, however, that there is was plenty of good cricket scattered over the islands which only needed encouragement and development to become first-class." Warner toured the West Indies in 1896-97 and scored heavily for Lord Hawke's team. There were in fact two English teams there at the same time because of a "misunderstanding". In our first extract Warner, from 1898, encourages the selection of black players in the Caribbean, a discussion that might seem utterly bizarre on contemporary viewing but less so when one considers that West Indies did not have a regular black captain until the appointment of Frank Worrell in 1960.

West Indies bestrode the cricket world for parts of the 1960s and then for almost two decades from the mid-1970s until 1995, when they lost at home to Australia. "The great wall crashed at last," *Wisden* reported. It has been more or less downhill since then. "The transformation has been abrupt and complete," Cozier wrote mournfully in 2013. In 2004 England won a series in the West Indies for the first time since 1967-68. The largesse of Texan financier Allen Stanford promised much for the region and briefly delivered, but ended in "a fraud of shocking magnitude". Contractual disputes between players, whose heads have been turned by IPL riches, and the West Indies board have dogged recent years. In 2009 Bangladesh, Test cricket's whipping boys, won both Tests in the Caribbean following the withdrawal of 13 West Indies players just before the series.

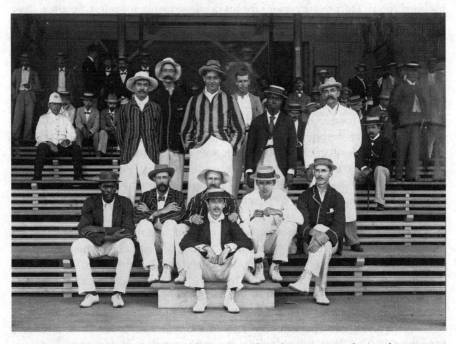

Inclusive: a team from the West Indian inter-colonial tournament during the 1890s

1898 – BLACK MEN MUST BE SELECTED

P. F. Warner, 1898

In estimating the respective merits of Trinidad, Barbados and Demerara, it must not be forgotten that Trinidad played black professional bowlers, while Barbados and Demerara did not. For the Inter-Colonial Cup which is played for every other year between these teams, black men are excluded; and Trinidad, thus deprived of its bowling, is by no means so good as either of its opponents. In the smaller islands, such as Grenada, St Vincent, Antigua, St Kitts, and St Lucia black men are always played (and as a matter of fact, it would be impossible in these islands to raise a side without them), but Barbados and Demerara have strenuously set themselves against this policy. With the attitude taken up by Barbados and Demerara I cannot altogether agree. These black men had considerably to the strength of a side, while the inclusion makes the game more popular locally, and tends to instil a great and universal enthusiasm amongst all classes of the population.

1929-30 – WEST INDIES v MCC (THIRD REPRESENTATIVE MATCH):
FIRST VICTORY

1931

Played at Georgetown, February 21, 22, 23, 24, 25, 26, 1930. The third meeting with the full strength of the West Indies ended in defeat for MCC by 289 runs. In achieving a noteworthy victory [*their first in Tests*], West Indies owed a great deal to the batting of Headley – who created a record by scoring a hundred in each innings in a representative engagement – and to that of Roach, and also to some effective fast bowling by Constantine and Francis. MCC's fielding was badly at fault when West Indies opened their first innings with a stand of 144, Hunte being missed four times. Roach, however, played brilliantly for rather less than five hours and in partnership with Headley he added 196. Slow methods at their second attempt almost deprived the home team of success for MCC, when facing the task of getting 617 runs, set themselves to save the game and held out until within a quarter of an hour of time.

> West Indies 471 (C. A. Roach 209, G. A. Headley 114, E. A. C. Hunte 53)
> and 290 (Headley 112, C. R. Browne 70*; W. E. Astill 4-70);
> England 145 (E. H. Hendren 56; G. N. Francis 4-40, L. N. Constantine 4-35)
> and 327 (Hendren 123; Constantine 5-87).

1929-30 – WEST INDIES v MCC (FOURTH REPRESENTATIVE MATCH):
SANDHAM SUPREME

1931

At Kingston, April 3, 4, 5, 7, 8, 9, 10, 11, 12, 1930. Each side having won once and one game having been drawn, it was decided to play to a finish the fourth representative match, but rain prevented cricket on the eighth and ninth days. By that time the MCC team were due to return home so no result could be reached. While the run-getting was very consistent and Ames registered a capital hundred, Sandham carried off the honours with an innings of 325 which, occupying ten hours, included a seven, a five and 27 fours. Headley made a great effort for his side, staying six hours and a half and hitting 28 fours.

England 849 (A. Sandham 325, L. E. G. Ames 149, G. Gunn 85, E. H. Hendren 61,
Mr R. E. S. Wyatt 58, J. O'Connor 51; O. C. Scott 5-266)
and 272-9 dec. (Hendren 55, Sandham 50; Scott 4-108);
West Indies 286 (R. K. Nunes 66)
and 408-5 (G. A. Headley 223, Nunes 92).

George Headley became the youngest to score a Test double-century until Javed Miandad in 1976-77. He was the only batsman to score four Test hundreds before his 21st birthday until Sachin Tendulkar surpassed him in 1992-93.

1934-35 – MCC IN WEST INDIES: HEADLEY AND SHOULDERS ABOVE THE REST 1936

The MCC tour of the West Indies during the winter of 1934-35 was rendered note-worthy by the fact that it supplied the opportunity for West Indies to win the Test match rubber and so accomplish a triumph that had hitherto been beyond their powers. The MCC party could scarcely be regarded as representative of the full strength of England. At the same time, the team, before the events of the tour, were considered sufficient for the occasion. How erroneous this impression proved was shown by the results of the Test matches.

The fact remained, however, that our batting was generally at fault, breaking down badly against the concentrated attack of fast bowling represented by Martindale, Constantine and Hylton, a combination described by Wyatt himself as the best of its kind in the world. While the West Indies never resorted to the packed leg side, some of the England players complained of occasional attempts at intimidation in the matter of short-pitched deliveries and full-tosses directed at the batsmen.

The West Indies, in addition, possessed in George Headley the best batsman for the prevailing conditions. In the Test matches, Headley scored 485 runs for an average of 97, and his 270 not out in the Fourth Test created a new record for his country in matches with England.

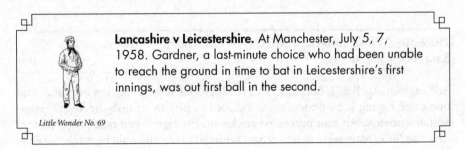

Lancashire v Leicestershire. At Manchester, July 5, 7, 1958. Gardner, a last-minute choice who had been unable to reach the ground in time to bat in Leicestershire's first innings, was out first ball in the second.

Little Wonder No. 69

1934-35 – WEST INDIES v ENGLAND (FIRST TEST): WET-WICKET THRILLER
1936

At Bridgetown, January 8, 9, 10, 1935. The first Test match ended in a remarkable victory for England by four wickets. The ball, on a pitch affected by rain, nearly always mastered the bat. Sensations began at the start, for Wyatt, upon winning the toss, sent his opponents in to bat. Thanks to begin with to the fast bowling of Farnes, and later to the slow deliveries of Paine and Hollies, considerable success attended the venture. Farnes, making the ball lift awkwardly, dismissed four West Indies batsmen at a personal cost of 15 runs, and half the side were out for 31. Headley alone offered real resistance. England fared no better and, although Hammond saved the side from complete collapse, half the wickets were down for 81 when the first day ended. Wyatt, realising the treacherous state of the wicket, declared with his side still 21 runs in arrear. G. C. Grant, in turn, adopted the bold policy of declaring, leaving England 73 runs to get for victory. With a view to knocking the bowlers off their length, Wyatt sent in Farnes and Smith to open the innings, but England met with a series of reverses, six wickets falling – five of them to Martindale, who bowled at a tremendous pace – for 49 runs. Fortunately for England, Hammond, at a critical period, revealed his best form. Hammond steadily gained something of a mastery over the bowling and, Wyatt defending stoutly, the end came without further success to bowlers. Hammond enjoyed the satisfaction of bringing off the winning hit – a huge drive for six at the expense of Martindale.

West Indies 102 (G. A. Headley 44; Mr K. Farnes 4-40) **and 51-6 dec.** (C. I. J. Smith 5-15); **England 81-7 dec.** (W. R. Hammond 43) **and 75-6** (Hammond 29*; E. A. Martindale 5-22).

1947-48 – MCC IN WEST INDIES: TIME TO TAKE IT SERIOUSLY   Norman Preston, 1949

For the first time in history MCC went through an overseas tour without a single victory. The prestige of English cricket suffered severely through this complete failure of G. O. Allen's 1947-48 team. Several factors contributed to MCC's depressing record. In the first place the strongest combination was not available, while L. Hutton only joined the party midway through the tour following urgent cables by Allen imploring MCC to send out someone immediately to reinforce the side.

The request for Hutton was caused mainly through so many players meeting with illness or injury. The first casualty was Allen, [who] pulled a calf muscle while skipping on the ship deck on the way out. In fact, at the age of 45, Allen was too old. Much was expected from Butler but he pulled a leg muscle in the opening match, developed a serious attack of malaria during the second Trinidad match, and broke down again in Jamaica. Almost throughout the tour Laker fought bravely against pain caused by strained stomach muscles; Ikin spent several days in hospital with carbuncle trouble which left him weak; Tremlett complained of strained ribs; Brookes chipped a finger bone while fielding in the First Test and took no further part in the tour; Hardstaff missed several matches through tearing a leg muscle while fielding in the first match at Trinidad; and Place bruised a knuckle in the First

Test and ruptured a groin muscle while hitting a century in the second Trinidad match. After these experiences it is essential that MCC treat a West Indies tour as seriously as one to Australia.

1952-53 – WEST INDIES v INDIA (Fifth Test): THREE W HUNDREDS   1954

At Kingston, March 28, 30, 31, April 1, 2, 4, 1953. Drawn. The match was notable for the double-hundred by Worrell and five other centuries. In the finish the West Indies, already one victory to the good, did not attempt the task of making 181 to win in 135 minutes. It was the first time the Three Ws had each hit a hundred in the same innings. West Indies, 103 for one at the close, raced to 400 for three on the third day, thanks to Worrell, who batted brilliantly for 171 not out, and Weekes, who helped him put on 197. Both were in entertaining form. On the fourth day Worrell and Walcott, by more careful methods, increased their fourth-wicket partnership to 213. Gupte, bowling his leg-breaks skilfully, and Mankad sent the last six wickets tumbling for 33, but West Indies reached their highest score in a home Test. Weekes passed Headley's 1929-30 record of 703 runs in a Test series in the West Indies.

India 312 (P. R. Umrigar 117, P. Roy 85; A. L. Valentine 5-64)

and 444 (Roy 150, V. L. Manjrekar 118; Valentine 4-149);

West Indies 576 (F. M. M. Worrell 237, C. L. Walcott 118, E. D. Weekes 109, B. H. Pairaudeau 58; S. P. Gupte 5-180, M. H. Mankad 5-228) and 92-4.

1953-54 – MCC IN WEST INDIES: TOO FIERY   Reg Hayter, 1955

In the arrangement of tours Marylebone Cricket Club always has set the furtherance of friendship between man and man, country and country, as one of its main hopes and objectives. Such an attitude should be encouraged rather than criticised as out-dated and unrealistic. This made it all the more regrettable that the visit to the West Indies aroused such controversy and uneasiness. Certainly the early insistence of so many people that the cricket championship of the world was at stake did nothing to ease the situation. Nor did the constant emphasis upon victory which the MCC players found to be stressed by English residents in the West Indies.

A certain amount of tension was thus created before a ball had been bowled. This quickly became heightened through crowds whose intense noise, coupled with almost ceaseless torrid heat, provided a background in which tempers too easily became frayed. At times some crowds were demonstrative and twice they became menacing. Convinced by the happenings on the field that the general standard of umpiring in the West Indies was not adequate for Test cricket, the touring team felt that the crowd atmosphere made the work of the men in the middle even harder than it should have been. To a man the MCC team recognised their responsibilities as ambassadors of sport, but, being human, the less phlegmatic did not always hide their annoyance and displeasure.

Only one or two of Hutton's team deserved this censure, but even the slightest sign of disagreement became public property, as must be accepted in times when Test matches are given increasing prominence in newspaper, radio and newsreel, self-control should have been regarded as essential. Earlier and firmer handling of the most recalcitrant member, the fiery Trueman, might have avoided several situations, but, anxious not to dim the spark of Trueman's hostility and aggressiveness, Hutton probably waited too long before calling his lively colt to heel.

From first to last no batsman compared with Hutton. His performance in leading the Test averages on either side, with 96.71, was overshadowed by the mastery he showed of every bowler in every innings of any length. In concentration and certainty he stood alone and, when inclined, he produced his most majestic attacking strokes, without ever allowing the wine of them to course to his head. In the last three Tests Hutton's average was a shade under 150, and throughout he was the bulwark of England's batting.

1957-58 – WEST INDIES v PAKISTAN (Third Test): Sobers's monument

1959

At Kingston, February 26, 27, 28, March 1, 3, 4, 1958. West Indies won by an innings and 174 runs. All else in this crushing defeat for Pakistan was overshadowed by the feat of Garfield Sobers, the West Indies 21-year-old left-hander, in beating the Test record individual score, 364 by Sir Leonard Hutton, made for England against Australia at The Oval nearly 20 years previously. Sobers passed that by one run and was still unbeaten when West Indies declared at the vast total of 790 for three. So elated were the crowd of 20,000 at Sabina Park that they swarmed over the field and the pitch became so damaged that the umpires ordered repairs and the last 55 minutes of the fourth day could not be played. Sobers's monumental innings was his first century in Test cricket. On a perfect pitch he made strokes freely throughout.

Pakistan 328 (Imtiaz Ahmed 122, W. Mathias 77, Saeed Ahmed 52; E. S. Atkinson 5-42)
and 288 (Wazir Mohammad 106, A. H. Kardar 57);
West Indies 790 (G. S. Sobers 365*, C. C. Hunte 260, C. L. Walcott 88*).

West Indies won the five-Test series 3–1. In the first Test Pakistan's Hanif Mohammad scored 337 in 970 minutes, which was the longest first-class innings.

1959-60 – WEST INDIES v ENGLAND (Second Test): bouncer war   1961

At Port-of-Spain, January 28, 29, 30, February 1, 2, 3, 1960. England won by 256 runs after one of the most dramatic Test matches for many years. Excitement was intense throughout and it led to an unfortunate and remarkable scene on the third day. A crowd of almost 30,000, a record for any sporting event in the West Indies, became so inflamed that soon after tea tempers boiled over and a few hooligans began throwing bottles on to the outfield. This started an orgy of bottle-throwing, and a large part of the crowd wandered on to the playing area. Things became so bad that a riot developed. The England players were escorted from the field, though no animosity was being shown to them. No further play was possible that day.

May won the toss again on a pitch faster than at Bridgetown, but England were soon in trouble. After doing little for half an hour, Hall and Watson changed ends and unleashed a blistering attack of bumpers and short-pitched balls which sent England reeling to 57 for three. At one point Hall was cautioned by the umpire, Lloyd, for excessive use of the short-pitched ball. Barrington batted five hours 50 minutes for his second successive Test century in his only two innings against West Indies. Hunte and Solomon were also subjected to bouncers from Trueman and Statham when they batted for the last 26 minutes on the second day. On the dynamic third day West Indies broke down badly in face of England's deadly accurate fast attack. Eight wickets were down for 98 when the bottle-throwing began. The atmosphere on the last three days was calm and peaceful. England steadily built a powerful position.

England 382 (K. F. Barrington 121, M. J. K. Smith 108, E. R. Dexter 77) **and 230-9 dec.;**
West Indies 112 (F. S. Trueman 5-35) **and 244** (R. B. Kanhai 110).

1961-62 – INDIANS IN WEST INDIES: WORLD-BEATER GIBBS   Dicky Rutnagur, 1963

India, after their triumph against England in 1961-62, had reason to embark on their tour of the West Indies with hope and great heart, if not with glowing optimism, but they returned home vanquished in all five Tests and the colony game against Barbados. To look at the other side of the coin, there were few chinks in the West Indies' armour, and these were not fully exposed because of the limitation of the opposition. In the spin attack, Gibbs looked a world-beater. So masterly was his variation of flight that he appeared capable of succeeding on the truest pitches [*in the final session of the Third Test at Bridgetown his figures were 15.3–14–6–8*]. Sobers again proved his versatility with the ball. As a purveyor of the chinaman and the left-hander's googly, he looked a vastly improved bowler than when he toured India in 1958-59.

1961-62 – BARBADOS v INDIANS: CONTRACTOR'S FIGHT FOR LIFE

At Bridgetown, March 16, 17, 19, 1962. Barbados won by an innings and 95 runs. This was a sordid and unhappy section of the tour. Overshadowing all else was the injury to Contractor, who was hit over the right ear by a ball from the fast bowler, Griffith, at the start of the first innings. This bowler was later no-balled for "throwing", but while this occurred, Contractor was fighting for his life. He had been rushed to hospital with a fractured skull and immediately underwent an emergency brain operation, which undoubtedly saved his life. A specialist brain surgeon was flown from Trinidad and another operation followed. A blood clot had formed from the fracture and pressed on the brain. Three of his team, Borde, Nadkarni and Umrigar, gave blood for Contractor, as did the West Indies captain, Worrell. Manjrekar, too, was injured in the first innings. He was hit on the nose and retired hurt but courageously batted a second time and scored 100 not out.

Barbados 394 (A. S. King 89, W. W. Hall 88, C. W. Smith 61; E. A. S. Prasanna 4-158);
Indians 86 and 213 (V. L. Manjrekar 100*).

1964-65 – AUSTRALIANS IN WEST INDIES: LOGIC A STRANGER   Alex Bannister, 1966

The West Indies defeated Australia for the first time by two Tests to one in the series for the unofficial championship of the world. For the most part they were worthy of their new status, although the sharp edge of triumph was frayed by the controversy surrounding the bowling action of Charlie Griffith.

The rich and varied talents at his disposal were skilfully used by the new captain, Garfield Sobers, and after three Tests the West Indies led two victories to nothing. By all logic, Australia, twice well beaten and seemingly without luck or hope, should have been close to the point of surrender. Logic, however, mercifully remains a total stranger to cricket in the West Indies, and, in the face of form and predictions, Australia made the bold running in the drawn Fourth Test, and handsomely won the last on an unpredictable pitch at Port-of-Spain with three days to spare. Australia's finest hours were in the shadow of defeat.

The one cloud on the West Indies horizon, which darkened the sunny relations between the two countries, was the argument caused by Griffith's action. Australia's complaints, though never officially voiced, were often directed at Griffith's most dangerous deliveries, his yorker and short-pitcher. At the end of the tour the simmering bitterness came to the boil in articles published under O'Neill's name. They, in turn, provoked an official protest from the president of the Board of Control for Cricket in the West Indies.

1964-65 – WEST INDIES v AUSTRALIA (FOURTH TEST): RACE TO THE FINISH
1966

At Bridgetown, May 5, 6, 7, 8, 10, 11, 1965. Drawn. Simpson and Lawry mastered the bowling with such purpose that they batted throughout the first day for 263, and, on the next, became the first opening pair in Test history to score double-centuries in the same innings. Their stand of 382, only 31 short of the world Test record, represented a complete transformation of all that had gone before in the series.

Griffith was cautioned for his excessive use of bumpers by umpire Kippins, restored after the troubles at Georgetown, and the West Indies' discomfort was complete when Cowper added his century with almost disdainful ease.

With time running out, Simpson had no alternative but to gamble and declare early in the second innings. West Indies had to get 253 in four and a half hours.

Hunte and Davis made 145 in ten minutes under three hours, a West Indies first-wicket record against Australia, but when Kanhai was out 106 were needed in 90 minutes then 70 in 55 and down to 28 in 16. By then Simpson had eight defending the boundary, and despite a gallant effort by Sobers, the West Indies fell 11 runs short with five wickets left in as thrilling a finish as any could wish to see. The result meant the rubber for the West Indies.

Australia 650-6 dec. (W. M. Lawry 210, R. B. Simpson 201, R. M. Cowper 102, N. C. O'Neill 51)

and 175-4 dec. (O'Neill 74*, Lawry 58 retired hurt);

West Indies 573 (S. M. Nurse 201, R. B. Kanhai 129, C. C. Hunte 75,

G. S. Sobers 55; G. D. McKenzie 4-114)

and 242-5 (Hunte 81, B. A. Davis 68).

Pakistan v Australia. An historic day for cricket was December 8, 1959, when Mr Dwight Eisenhower, president of the United States of America, graced the third Test of the series between Pakistan and Australia at the National Stadium, Karachi. It was the first occasion that the head of the United States has witnessed a Test match, and he was seen in a very happy mood applauding attractive strokes by the batsmen and good work by the fielders.

Little Wonder No. 70

1967-68 – MCC IN WEST INDIES: CARIBBEAN CALAMITY   E. M. Wellings, 1969

From the English viewpoint the tour was a conspicuous success. From the West Indies point of view the events were anything but satisfying. The tour focused a spotlight on unpleasant aspects of West Indies cricket. Chief among these were the clearly substandard umpiring and unruly crowds. Such is the pressure from supporters desiring success for the home side that even an efficient umpire is apt to be influenced.

Umpiring and crowd behaviour are, therefore, closely associated. Quite the most professional of the umpires was Sang Hue, but he was never so efficient after as before his correct decision against Butcher in the second Test [*a diving leg-side catch by Jim Parks*], which sparked a bottle-throwing riot by his fellow Jamaicans. That riot, the third serious one of its kind in recent West Indies Test history, came when England were winning the match. That was the worst crowd incident of the tour. Some would prefer that no mention should be made of such matters. Correction can never be achieved by concealment. For the future of big cricket in the West Indies it is essential that those things patently wrong should be put right. The islands, rich in cricketing talent, have much to contribute to world cricket. It would be a loss to the game if the conditions of their play compelled other countries to cease sending them touring teams.

It was against this background that MCC triumphed. It was necessary for Cowdrey's team to be quite 30 per cent better than the opposition in order to come out on top. They did come out on top by winning one Test and drawing the other four. For the first time England became holders of the Wisden Trophy. That had not been expected four months earlier. The West Indies were then generally regarded as the unofficial world champions, and the MCC team had been chosen in the midst of controversy. The selectors made public the fact that they wanted Close as captain, although he had been censured for his conduct of the Yorkshire team in their match against Warwickshire. Cowdrey in fact was third choice, psychologically handicapped by the vote of no-confidence, which was implied when Insole, chairman of the selectors, announced that they had opposed his selection. In the event Cowdrey did a splendid job.

Titmus suffered a boating accident shortly before the Third Test. He lost four toes when his left foot was caught in the screw of a small boat, placed in the middle of the craft and, contrary to regulations, without a guard.

1970-71 – INDIANS IN WEST INDIES: INDIA'S NEW CHAPTER · Dicky Rutnagur, 1972

The tour was India's most successful cricket venture abroad. West Indies, the only country they had not so far beaten, were mastered in the Second Test. Victory in the series opened a new chapter in the history of Indian cricket. Gavaskar's achievements equalled, surpassed or approached several important records. No Indian batsman had hitherto made 700 runs or more in a single series. Only K. D. Walters before him had scored a century and a double-century in the same Test. Gavaskar also established a new record for the highest aggregate in a maiden Test series (703 by G. A. Headley in 1929-30 was the previous-highest). Only one other batsman can pride himself on a higher average for a series than Gavaskar – Sir Donald Bradman (201.50 v South Africa in 1931-32, and 178.75 v India in 1947-48). Although Chandrasekhar, later the scourge of England, was left at home, the Indian bowlers excelled themselves, the three main spinners, Prasanna, Bedi and Venkataraghavan, between them taking 48 of the 68 Test wickets that fell to the bowlers. All of them were remarkably accurate and even if the pitches tended to aid them, there is no doubt that their mastery in flighting the ball gave them a great advantage.

1973-74 – MCC IN WEST INDIES: TOP JOB FOR TONY? · Clive Taylor, 1975

For England to have drawn the series in the West Indies was a surprise, a pleasant one, but not an altogether just one. The West Indies had first-innings leads in excess of 200 in each of the first three Tests, yet were defied in the end by dogged and courageous batting performances by England's players, who seemed repentant for their earlier failings, and the extreme docility of the pitches which consistently refused to give the bowlers the help they were entitled to on the fifth day.

The final performance by Greig set the accolade on his tour. He emerged from it as a giant among all-rounders with Test figures of 430 runs – second only to

Amiss – and 24 wickets, 15 more than the next English bowler. Not surprisingly his success gave rise to conjecture about his future as England's captain, especially as Denness's performances, both as captain and as player, were less convincing. Yet there remained about Greig the doubt caused by his explosiveness when the desire to succeed seemed to overwhelm his judgment.

Undoubtedly Greig could end up as England's captain, but there were moments on this tour when it would have been embarrassing had he been the current leader. The Kallicharran incident was the most important and the most publicised of these. Briefly it occurred when Greig, within the laws if not the spirit of the game, fielded the ball off the last ball of the day during the First Test and ran out Kallicharran who, in the ill-advised belief that play was over, had left the bowler's crease on his way to the pavilion as Knott pulled up the stumps before the ball was dead. There was never any suggestion that Greig's action had been anything but spontaneous. Malice was not one of the ingredients. Whatever the causes, the effect was devastating.

After a long meeting between members of the West Indies Board of Control and representatives of MCC, it was agreed as a compromise that the appeal should be withdrawn – thus taking the onus off the umpires – and that Kallicharran should be allowed to resume his innings.

1973-74 – WEST INDIES v ENGLAND (Fifth Test): PRESSURE TELLS   1975

At Port-of-Spain, March 30, 31, April 2, 3, 4, 5, 1974. England won by 26 runs. The final Test was well and deservedly won by England on the strength of two outstanding personal performances – by Greig, who, bowling almost entirely in his new style as an off-spinner, took 13 wickets for 156, and by Boycott, who in each innings played more convincingly that at any time since the First Test on the same ground.

The West Indies had been set a target of 226 to win. Greig, significantly, had opened the England bowling with off-spinners. Perhaps in the end the most decisive factor in the result was the tension that built up during the day. The England players withstood it better than those of West Indies, among whom some of the most experienced seemed to be the most vulnerable.

Greig again took charge for England, dismissing Kanhai and Lloyd, both of whom were clear victims of tension. Then the match swung again as Sobers, playing even in these circumstances with a charm that marked his pedigree, put on 50 for the sixth wicket with Murray, another player of good temperament. Sobers suddenly hit over a ball from Underwood and was bowled, Murray was caught driving at Greig, and at 166 for eight West Indies seemed doomed.

Even then they came close to winning, for Inshan Ali, batting with a composure not apparent in some of his betters, was not dismissed until only 29 were needed and Denness in desperation had taken the new ball.

England 267 (G. Boycott 99) and 263 (Boycott 112);
West Indies 305 (L. G. Rowe 123, R. C. Fredericks 67, G. S. Sobers 52; A. W. Greig 8-86)
and 199 (Greig 5-70).

452

1975-76 – INDIANS IN WEST INDIES: BATTERED AND BRUISED   Dicky Rutnagur, 1977

As at the end of the tour, the Indian team trudged along the tarmac towards their homebound aeroplane at Kingston's Norman Manley Airport, they resembled Napoleon's troops on the retreat from Moscow. They were battle-weary and a lot of them were enveloped in plasters and bandages. The bandages were the campaign ribbons of a controversial and somewhat violent final Test which the West Indies won to prevail 2–1. Following an overwhelming win for the West Indies in the opening contest in Barbados, the second in Trinidad was drawn, with India very much on top. At the same venue, India won the third in a blaze of glory, their triumph being achieved by scoring over 400 runs in the final innings – a feat that had only one precedent in the history of Test cricket.

1975-76 – WEST INDIES v INDIA (FOURTH TEST): INTIMIDATION   1977

At Kingston, April 21, 22, 24, 25, 1976. West Indies won by ten wickets. This was a stormy Test, with accusations from the Indians of persistent intimidatory bowling after three of their batsmen were put out of action in their first innings. The virgin pitch had an immense bearing on the tactics of the West Indies, as also on the result. It was the unpredictability of bounce that contributed to the unsafe manner in which the Indian batsmen took evasive action and, consequently, suffered nasty injuries.

This is not to say that there was no short-pitched bowling. There was a surfeit of it – overdone, in fact, to the extent where the umpires should have intervened. The first day, shortened by bad light, belonged to India. India's problems set in the following morning. Viswanath was caught off the glove, the impact leaving a finger both fractured and dislocated. The fall of the fourth wicket at 280 would suggest that the West Indies offensive had been checked. But, in fact, two batsmen, Patel and Gaekwad, had meanwhile retired with injuries that put them out of the match. Patel, facing Holder, took his eye off the ball and edged it on to his mouth. Gaekwad was struck just above the left ear, having ducked into a ball that was not too short, but the bounce of which bore no relation to its length. India declared 15 minutes before tea, at 306 for six, not because they considered themselves strongly placed but because Bedi wished to protect himself and Chandrasekhar, both key bowlers, from the risk of injury.

When [*in India's second innings*] Holding had Gavaskar caught at short leg in the third over, India's spirit was broken. They slid to 97 for five in less than three hours, and at that point, the innings closed as five batsmen in all absented themselves because of injury. At first it was thought that Bedi had declared again – with India only 12 runs in front – and it was only after West Indies had won that a statement was issued by Bedi that the Indian innings should be recorded as completed.

India 306-6 dec. (A. D. Gaekwad 81 retired hurt, S. M. Gavaskar 66; M. A. Holding 4-82) **and 97** (M. Amarnath 60); **West Indies 391** (R. C. Fredericks 82, D. L. Murray 71, I. V. A. Richards 64, M. A. Holding 55; B. S. Chandrasekhar 5-153) **and 13-0.**

1977-78 – AUSTRALIANS IN WEST INDIES: PACKER PALAVER   Tony Cozier, 1979

Australia's fourth tour of the West Indies was depressingly dominated more by events off the field than on them. The inauguration of Kerry Packer's World Series Cricket, which had created such chaos throughout the cricket world, had considerable influence over the series.

The Australian Cricket Board of Control adamantly refused to select any of the Packer players. The West Indies board, on the other hand, decided they would choose players contracted to WSC on the grounds that they had never refused to play for their country and had now made themselves available.

With the two teams thus constituted, West Indies proved far superior in the first two Tests, which they won by large margins inside three days. By the end of the Second Test, however, it was clear that relations between the board and the Packer players were becoming strained.

The board was "to say the least, extremely disappointed" when three young players – Austin, Croft and Haynes – signed contracts with WSC despite an earlier verbal assurance not to do so. The players were irritated by the decision to relieve Deryck Murray, their spokesman, of the vice-captaincy in mysterious circumstances on the opening day of the series. Clive Lloyd made an almost immediate protest, announcing his resignation from the captaincy. Within two days, other West Indian players contracted to WSC also withdrew from the team in solidarity with Lloyd.

The impasse caused an emotional explosion throughout the Caribbean with heated arguments raging everywhere. Kerry Packer himself flew to the West Indies to meet with his players and state his case.

With the teams more evenly matched as a result of the dispute, the final three Tests produced far keener cricket. Australia won the Third narrowly, and West Indies the Fourth to regain the Sir Frank Worrell Trophy they had last held in 1965. Australia were on the verge of victory in the Fifth when the crowd, reacting violently against an umpiring decision, halted play by throwing stones, bottles, and debris on the field. When an attempt was made to restart the match on an unscheduled sixth day to make up lost time, it did not meet the approval of one of the umpires and the match had to be left abandoned as a draw – the final bizarre twist in a series bedevilled throughout by acrimony and confusion.

1980-81 – ENGLAND IN WEST INDIES: ILL FORTUNE   Michael Melford, 1982

In playing terms England's three-month tour of West Indies went no better and no worse than expected. Two-nil was not a massive defeat considering the known difference in the strength of the two sides. Moreover, not many touring sides have been as beset by ill fortune as was this one in the first half of the tour.

When practice on good pitches was urgently required, the England party were handicapped by bad weather, turning pitches untypical of what was to come, and the withdrawal for political reasons from Guyana. When normality was about to be restored, the death of their assistant manager, coach and friend, Ken Barrington, during the Barbados Test match came as a shattering blow. It was a shock to his countless friends throughout the world. To those who had been working away at the nets with him through the previous, mostly dispiriting, two months, it was more poignant, and they went through the next day's play almost in a daze.

The team had been in Guyana for two days when, early on February 23, they were joined by Jackman, the replacement for Willis who had returned home after breaking down in Trinidad. No attempt was made to conceal the fact that Jackman, like others in the party, had spent winters playing in South Africa.

Three days before the Second Test was due to start, it was known that a radio commentator in Jamaica had suggested that the Guyana government, by admitting Jackman with his South African connections, was in contravention of the Gleneagles agreement. It was also learnt that the Guyana government was taking the matter seriously. The next day the British government stated clearly through the Minister for Sport, Hector Monro, that the Gleneagles Declaration was irrelevant in this case as it made no reference to actions by one country against the nationals of another.

However, the British High Commissioner in Georgetown was informed by the Guyanese Minister of Foreign Affairs that Jackman's visitor's permit had been withdrawn and that he must leave the country. A statement was issued simultaneously by the England manager, Alan Smith, in Georgetown and by the Cricket Council meeting at Lord's, saying that England would not play the Second Test as it was no longer possible for the Test team to be chosen without restrictions being imposed. In fact, it had not been envisaged that Jackman, newly arrived from an English winter, would play at all in Guyana, but injuries to Dilley and Old would probably have forced his inclusion if the match had taken place.

Alan Smith, in collaboration with the High Commissioner and with sympathy and support from other Caribbean countries, at once set in motion plans to withdraw the England party which, with press, radio and television representatives, was now over 40 strong. This was done next morning and, after a long wait at Georgetown airport, the team arrived that night in Barbados to a warm welcome.

1982-83 – WEST INDIES v INDIA (FIRST TEST): NO ONE'S SAFE   1984

At Kingston, February 23, 24, 26, 27, 28, 1983. West Indies won by four wickets. West Indies won in a frenzied finish with four balls of the final 20 overs remaining. At tea on the final day, after the first heavy rain in Kingston for two years had washed out the fourth day, a draw appeared inevitable as India, 168 for six, were 165 in the lead with four wickets standing. Roberts then dramatically changed the course of the match by dismissing Kirmani, Sandhu and Venkataraghavan in his first over on resumption and completing the rout with the last man, Maninder, in his fourth over.

Even then, West Indies needed to score 172 off what turned out to be 26 overs to secure the lead in the series. Haynes set them on their way with a delightful 34 off 21 deliveries, but it required batting of exceptional brilliance from Richards for the target to be reached. His appearance delayed to one position below his accustomed No. 3 because of a painful shoulder, Richards's first scoring stroke was the first of four huge sixes, and, off 35 deliveries, he attacked mercilessly for 61. When he was out at 156 for five, West Indies required 16 off two and a half overs and, with sixes from Logie – off his first ball – and Dujon, over square leg off Amarnath, West Indies won amidst scenes of great excitement.

India 251 (B. S. Sandhu 68, Yashpal Sharma 63; A. M. E. Roberts 4-61) and 174 (Roberts 5-39);
West Indies 254 (C. G. Greenidge 70; Kapil Dev 4-45, R. J. Shastri 4-43)
and 173-6 (I. V. A. Richards 61; Kapil Dev 4-73).

1985-86 – ENGLAND IN WEST INDIES: BLACKWASH II   John Thicknesse, 1987

It would be less than fair to David Gower and the team he captained in the West Indies to label the tour simply a disaster. Their record, true enough, was all of that – another blackwash in the Test series and only two wins, compared to ten defeats, in 14 matches. Much went wrong, too, that with firmer captaincy and management might not have.

But there were many mitigating circumstances, of which the brilliance of the opposition, captained by Viv Richards, and the poor quality of too many of the pitches were the most decisive. In cold fact, England never had a hope. That they could and should have done better, few who saw them would dispute. Their lack of commitment was reflected in their attitude to practice, a department in which West Indies showed them up as amateurs. However, any chance England had of competing in the series – slender at the best of times on the record of West Indies since the middle 1970s – vanished to all practical purposes when the batsmen reached the First Test in Jamaica without having met, in four matches, one pitch on which to find their confidence. On top of that, they had been deprived by injury of Mike Gatting, who had been in better form than anyone. Gatting, the vice-captain, had his nose broken by Malcolm Marshall in the first one-day international, misjudging the ball to hook, and the consequences were long-lasting both in playing terms and psychologically.

1985-86 – WEST INDIES v ENGLAND (Fifth Test): HISTORY-MAKER   1987

At St John's, Antigua, April 11, 12, 13, 15, 16, 1986. West Indies won by 240 runs. Richards's 110 not out in West Indies' second innings, the fastest Test hundred ever in terms of balls received (56 to reach three figures, 58 in all), made the final Test historic on two counts. The other was West Indies' achievement in emulating Australia, previously the only country to win all five home Tests on more than one occasion.

Richards's display, making him the obvious candidate for the match award, would have been staggering at any level of cricket. What made it unforgettable for the 5,000 or so lucky enough to see it was that he scored it without blemish at a time when England's sole aim was to make run-scoring as difficult as possible to delay a declaration. Botham and Emburey never had fewer than six men on the boundary and sometimes nine, yet whatever length or line they bowled, Richards had a stroke for it. His control and touch were as much features of the innings as the tremendous power of his driving. Plundered in 83 minutes out of 146 while he was at the wicket, it had to be, by any yardstick, among the most wonderful innings ever played.

West Indies 474 (D. L. Haynes 131, M. D. Marshall 76, M. A. Holding 73, R. A. Harper 60)
and 246-2 dec. (I. V. A. Richards 110*, Haynes 70);
England 310 (D. I. Gower 90, W. N. Slack 52, G. A. Gooch 51; J. Garner 4-67) **and 170** (Gooch 51).

1987-88 – WEST INDIES v PAKISTAN (THIRD TEST): OFF THE HOOK   1989

At Bridgetown, April 22, 23, 24, 26, 27, 1988. West Indies won by two wickets. Pakistan's hope of becoming the first team from their country to win a series in the West Indies was dashed at the last by a match-winning stand of 61 between Dujon and Benjamin, who came together at 207 for eight with West Indies needing another 59 to win and defeat in sight. Their unbeaten ninth-wicket stand enabled West Indies to square the series half an hour after lunch on the final day, Benjamin finally hitting the winning boundary off Abdul Qadir. It had not been a happy day for the Pakistani leg-spinner. Denied two confident appeals for lbw and a catch off Dujon, he had allowed himself to get involved with a heckler on the boundary. A punch was thrown, the heckler was hit, and $US1,000 was paid to the offended party in an out-of-court settlement so that Qadir would not have to remain in Barbados to face charges.

Pakistan 309 (Ramiz Raja 54, Shoaib Mohammad 54; M. D. Marshall 4-79)
and 262 (Shoaib 64; Marshall 5-65);
West Indies 306 (I. V. A. Richards 67, C. L. Hooper 54)
and 268-8 (R. B. Richardson 64; Wasim Akram 4-73).

West Indies' victory levelled the three-Test series at 1–1 and prevented them losing a home series for the first time since 1972-73.

1989-90 – ENGLAND IN WEST INDIES: THE INJUSTICE OF IT ALL   Alan Lee, 1991

The essential weakness of any statistical record is that it can reflect neither circumstance nor injustice. A potted summary of England's Test series in the Caribbean, early in 1990, indicates merely that they lost 2–1, with one match drawn and the other abandoned. In years to come, that stark scoreline may be read to mean that England did slightly better than anticipated. The truth of the matter is that at worst they merited a shared series, and at best an unimaginable upset of the world champions of Test cricket.

England's nine-wicket victory in the First Test, at Kingston, unarguably qualified to be one of the most outlandish results in Test history. West Indies were thoroughly outplayed. Georgetown, venue for the Second Test, was struck by atrocious weather which prevented a ball being bowled, but those who maintained that the Jamaica Test result had been an unrepeatable freak were silenced in Trinidad.

England, with the benefit of winning an important toss, set up a second victory, which was cruelly denied them by a persistent downpour on the final afternoon. This, if you like, was a real freak.

The tour was never the same after that. With their strongest side, England might have withstood the travesty and risen again. But for the two remaining Tests they were without Gooch, whose captaincy had become even more crucial than his batting, and Angus Fraser, the most dependable member of a startlingly influential four-man seam attack. It was too much to bear. In Barbados England battled ferociously, losing a dramatic and controversial match with half an hour's daylight remaining on the final evening. In Antigua, for the finale, they had nothing left to offer and were beaten, by an innings, before tea on the fourth day.

Umpiring was at the centre of an explosive situation during the Barbados Test. Rob Bailey, who suffered a wretched tour, was given out on the fourth evening, caught behind down the leg side off Curtly Ambrose. The ball had appeared to make contact only with his hip, but a debatable decision became a major incident owing to interpretations of Richards's startling, finger-flapping rush at the umpire, Lloyd Barker, in the moments before and during the raising of his finger. Some construed this as intimidating the official, and a remark to that effect by the BBC cricket correspondent, Christopher Martin-Jenkins, broadcast on the World Service, prompted a quite hysterical counter-reaction. The implied suggestion was that all such comments were basically racist.

Richards, still troubled by illness, had a generally unhappy time. He offended Caribbean Asians with comments about his African team, and subsequent to the scene involving umpire Barker, he responded so irrationally to criticism by an English journalist that he chose to confront the writer in the Antigua press box instead of leading his players on to the field.

Kent v Hampshire (A. H. Phebey's Benefit). At Canterbury, July 30, August 1, 2, 1960. For Phebey the match was not a success from a playing standpoint. He lost the toss, dropped a vital catch, and made only 16 runs.

Little Wonder No. 71

1990-91 – AUSTRALIANS IN WEST INDIES: LOSS OF HONOUR   Tony Cozier, 1992

Australia's sixth tour of the West Indies began with exalted expectations of an epic contest between arguably the two strongest teams in the game. Above all else, what should have been a compelling advertisement for cricket was ruined by the obvious acrimony between the teams. At the final presentation ceremony, the president of the West Indies board, Clyde Walcott, a great player in his time, referred to the soured relations, and it seemed appropriate that the Frank Worrell Trophy was nowhere to be found. It transpired that it had been lost since the West Indians' tour of Australia in 1984-85. Given that it was inaugurated to honour the late West Indies captain of the unforgettable 1960-61 series in Australia, its presence in such circumstances would have been incongruous.

1991-92 – WEST INDIES v SOUTH AFRICA (ONLY TEST): DRAMATIC COLLAPSE
Geoffrey Dean, 1993

At Bridgetown, April 18, 19, 20, 22, 23, 1992. West Indies won by 52 runs. An epic inaugural Test between the two countries ended in West Indies' 11th consecutive victory at the Kensington Oval. But South Africa were on top for the first four days, until a dramatic collapse preserved their hosts' 57-year-old unbeaten record in Barbados. Needing only 201 to win, the South Africans were well placed at 122 for two at the start of the fifth day. Quality fast bowling from Ambrose and Walsh removed their last eight wickets while another 26 runs were scored, and they were bowled out for 148, 20 minutes before lunch. Attendances throughout the game were minimal because Barbadians stayed away in protest against West Indian selection policy. The total attendance was only 6,500 and there were fewer than 500 spectators on the ground to witness one of West Indies' finest fightbacks, but scores of them charged ecstatically after their team on its lap of honour.

On a pitch that was now uneven, the South Africans quickly lost both openers. But they were manoeuvred into a winning position by Wessels and Kirsten, the senior members of the side. They had added 95 in 42 overs by the close, but were swept away next morning by Walsh, in an inspired spell of four for eight in 11 overs. Cutting the ball both ways, he finally found the form that eluded him earlier. Ambrose mopped up the tail to finish with match figures of 60.4–26–81–8.

West Indies 262 (K. L. T. Arthurton 59, D. L. Haynes 58; R. P. Snell 4-83)
and 283 (J. C. Adams 79*, B. C. Lara 64);
South Africa 345 (A. C. Hudson 163, K. C. Wessels 59; Adams 4-43)
and 148 (Wessels 74, P. N. Kirsten 52; C. E. L. Ambrose 6-34. C. A. Walsh 4-31).

1993-94 – WEST INDIES v ENGLAND (THIRD TEST): 46 ALL OUT
1995

At Port-of-Spain, March 25, 26, 27, 29, 30 1994. West Indies won by 147 runs. The fourth day of this match witnessed an astonishing transformation: when it began England were enviably placed for a victory which would have kept the series alive; by the end they were threatened by their lowest score in history. Eventually, by a single run, they avoided the ultimate indignity of equalling the 45 all out recorded at Sydney, 107 years earlier, but the England side of 1887 actually won. The 1994 side lost both match and series during a staggering collapse to fast bowling of the highest calibre from Ambrose, who finished with six for 24 in the innings and 11 for 84 in the match.

England were facing a target at least 70 runs bigger than it should have been. Furthermore, a rain-break meant that only 15 overs of the day remained. This was crucial, because Ambrose was able to give his all and England knew they would have to face him again next morning. He supplied one of the most devastating spells of even his career. Atherton, half forward, was leg-before to the first ball of the innings and Ramprakash, nervily calling a second run to long leg, run out off the fifth. Smith and Hick, confidence low, were swept aside and when Stewart, the one batsman to get a start, lost his off stump, it was 26 for five. Walsh, almost the Lock to Ambrose's Laker, took a wicket at last when Salisbury was caught at slip. But Ambrose, rampaging in as if on springs, added Russell and Thorpe to his collection before play ended with England a mortifying 40 for eight, all hope lost. The game lasted only 17 minutes on the final morning, Walsh claiming the last two wickets. As Ambrose was carried shoulder-high from the ground, the great calypsonian Lord Kitchener serenaded his success outside the dressing-room. For England, a match which had promised much for three days had ended in utter humiliation.

West Indies 252 (R. B. Richardson 63; A. R. C. Fraser 4-49, C. C. Lewis 4-61)
and 269 (S. Chanderpaul 50; A. R. Caddick 6-65);
England 328 (G. P. Thorpe 86; C. E. L. Ambrose 5-60) **and 46** (Ambrose 6-24).

1993-94 – WEST INDIES v ENGLAND (FIFTH TEST): LARA RAISES BAR — 1995

At St John's, Antigua, April 16, 17, 18, 20, 21, 1994. Drawn. A contest which scarcely progressed beyond its first innings, tied at 593 runs each, nevertheless earned an eternal place in cricket history by dint of an innings of 375 by Brian Lara, beating by ten runs the record individual score in Test cricket, created 36 years earlier by Sir Garfield Sobers. Lara broke the record from the 530th ball he faced, having batted for the equivalent of more than two days. He had not given a single chance and, until tension and fatigue almost overcame him in the home straight, scarcely made a mistake. Sobers himself came onto the field to shake Lara's hand in the chaotic moments which followed an exultantly pulled four from a short ball by Lewis. It was only Lara's third Test century, but the previous two had been 277 and 167, confirming his appetite for the long innings. After the 277 he said he had been thinking of the record.

Lara had never looked likely to get out but, as the remaining milestones to the record were ticked off and the enormity of it all combined with his natural weariness, he needed shepherding through the final stages by the impressively mature Chanderpaul. He reached 365, the famed Sobers figure, with a cover-driven four off Caddick which had the capacity crowd on its feet, then composed himself once again for the historic pull off Lewis and the inevitable pitch invasion ensued. When Lara fell to a tired drive, with the declaration due, he had batted 766 minutes, faced 538 balls and hit 45 fours.

West Indies 593-5 dec. (B. C. Lara 375, S. Chanderpaul 75*, J. C. Adams 59);
England 593 (R. A. Smith 175, M. A. Atherton 135, C. C. Lewis 75*, R. C. Russell 62;
K. C. G. Benjamin 4-110).

Record collectors: Garry Sobers, left, with Brian Lara at Antigua in 1993-94
after Lara had set a new Test highest score. His 375 against England
beat Sobers' 365 not out made in 1957-58

1994-95 – AUSTRALIANS IN WEST INDIES: END OF EMPIRE   Robert Craddock, 1996

On May 3, 1995, the great wall crashed at last. After 15 years and 29 series, world
cricket's longest-lasting dynasty was overthrown by the relentless, underestimated
Australians – the most distinguished run of triumphant success gone with the
Windies. The last time West Indies lost a series was in March 1980, when Clive
Lloyd's tourists lost to Geoff Howarth's New Zealanders. Mark Taylor led Australia
to victory by 2–1, despite losing all four tosses. They had other problems: two
leading pace bowlers, Craig McDermott and Damien Fleming, missed the series
after injuries; and during the First Test, Australian coach Bob Simpson developed a
blood clot in his left leg and was admitted to hospital.

Against all expectations, ball dominated bat in the Tests, despite under-strength
or outdated attacks. The cricket was like arm-wrestling, with white knuckles tilted
back and forth until the strain told, the weaker man snapped and his arm was
crunched into the table. Two Tests were completed within three days and the winning
margins were all landslides – ten wickets, nine wickets and an innings and 53 runs.

How did Australia do it? All discussion must start and finish with Steve Waugh,
whose 429 runs at 107.25 represented the most courageous, passionate and decisive
batting of his life. With his low-risk, keep-the-ball-along-the-ground game, Waugh
scored 189 more than the next Australian – his brother, Mark – and 121 more than
West Indies' most prolific batsman, Brian Lara. But his tour was laced with drama

from the first day of the First Test, when he claimed a catch off Lara which, seemingly unbeknown to him, had touched the ground as he tumbled. As an unsavoury consequence, he was heckled every time he came to the crease, branded a cheat by local crowds, publicly chastised by Viv Richards, and subjected to intimidatory phone calls in the small hours. In Trinidad, he had a verbal clash with Curtly Ambrose, who had to be restrained by captain Richie Richardson. During the final Test, he woke up to discover a security guard in search of some unsanctioned souvenirs. Weary but undeterred, he went in next morning to conjure one of the best innings by an Australian in decades, batting nearly ten hours for a maiden Test double-century. Every media critic in Australia had, at some stage, branded Steve Waugh gun-shy against short-pitched bowling. Yet at Kingston he took more than six blows on the hands, arms and body; over the series, he absorbed more than 500 rib-rattlers by ducking or offering a straight defensive bat, sometimes with both feet six inches off the ground. Nineteen Australian wickets fell to the hook, but he refused to play the stroke, arguing it was too risky.

1997-98 – ENGLAND IN WEST INDIES: ATHERTON QUITS   Scyld Berry, 1999

Their captain, Mike Atherton, thought that beating West Indies was a realistic objective, and hinted that he would resign if England did not win. And resign he did – at the very moment Lara, who displaced Walsh as captain before the series, was parading the Wisden Trophy round the ground in Antigua, the 13th successive occasion the West Indies captain had received it. West Indies won the Test series 3–1 (and the one-day series 4–1), but it was only at the end – after a series of continual drama which lived up to its billing – that their superiority was definitively established. Along the way, the pendulum swung from side to side with each Test. West Indies had the stronger team, if only because they had Curtly Ambrose back to something near his peak form, but the final margin was unjustly wide.

1997-98 – WEST INDIES v ENGLAND (FIRST TEST): CALL IT OFF
Matthew Engel, 1999

At Kingston, January 29, 1998. Drawn. After the third ball of the match flew off a length past the England captain's nose, one alleged sage turned to his neighbour in the press box and whispered: "Well, we can rule out a draw, that's for sure." This was proved wrong with astonishing rapidity. After just 56 minutes' cricket, the contest – which enthusiasts had been looking forward to with relish for months – was called off in sensational and, at this level, unprecedented circumstances because the umpires considered the pitch to be dangerous.

Sixty-one balls (and a no-ball) were bowled in that time, and the England physio Wayne Morton came on to the field six times to attend batsmen who had suffered direct hits from Ambrose and Walsh. Neither bowled exceptionally well, by their standards. It was unnecessary; almost anyone could have propelled a hard ball lethally off such a surface.

It rapidly became clear that the batsmen were suffering more than the normal terrors England players expect when confronted with a fired-up West Indies attack. They lost three wickets quickly: Butcher for a golden duck. But observers quickly sensed these might be trivial details. The ball was moving so unpredictably that a serious injury looked a near-certainty.

After Stewart was hit for the third time and Thorpe for the second, the end was in sight. Atherton, the England captain, came on to the field and got agreement from his opposite number, Lara, that the game could not go on. After ten minutes' discussion, the umpires led the players off and the final decision to abandon came nearly an hour later. Stewart was left on what was widely agreed to be the most heroic nine not out in history.

1998-99 – AUSTRALIANS IN WEST INDIES: EXHAUSTING INTENSITY Mike Coward, 2000

Any series for the Frank Worrell Trophy is something to savour, but in advance it was impossible to foresee quite how fascinating this one would be. In the months preceding the series, West Indies had been humiliated 5–0 in South Africa, while Australia could have defeated England 5–0 but for a tropical storm in Brisbane and arrogant complacency in Melbourne. Rather than a contest for a prize many Australians now treasure as much as the Ashes, this seemed a mismatch with potentially serious consequences for the game. But these series have developed such importance and proud traditions over three decades that both teams played with an intensity which exhausted all who competed and observed.

1998-99 – WEST INDIES v AUSTRALIA (THIRD TEST): HAND OF GENIUS

2000

At Bridgetown, March 26, 27, 28, 29, 30, 1999. West Indies won by one wicket. Another transcendent innings by Lara saw West Indies touch the heights of glory just 22 days after they had hit rock bottom in Trinidad. Irrefutably, his undefeated 153 was the hand of a genius. Exhibiting the new awareness and maturity he discovered in Jamaica, he brilliantly orchestrated the conclusion to an unforgettable match. He guided his men to victory as though leading the infirm through a maze.

Two days earlier, West Indies had been 98 for six in response to Australia's imposing 490, and seemed destined to follow on. But they turned the game round so successfully that they found themselves needing 308 to take the lead in the series. It seemed improbable, but it was within Lara's reach.

No one else scored more than 38, and the eighth wicket fell with 60 still wanted for victory. But Ambrose obdurately occupied the crease for 82 minutes to be followed by Walsh, who survived five balls, helped by a wide and a no-ball, before Lara crashed Gillespie to the cover boundary to complete a victory even more astonishing than the last one, giving West Indies a 2–1 lead in the series.

It was only the fourth time West Indies had scored more than 300 to win a Test, the last occasion being at Lord's in 1984. Despite the result, Steve Waugh, who survived some extraordinary pace bowling from Ambrose to score a priceless 199, said he had never played in a better match – a telling observation, given that he had appeared in the tied Test against India in 1986-87.

Australia 490 (S. R. Waugh 199, R. T. Ponting 104, J. L. Langer 51) **and 146** (C. A. Walsh 5-39);
West Indies 329 (S. L. Campbell 105, R. D. Jacobs 68; G. D. McGrath 4-128)
and 311-9 (B. C. Lara 153*; McGrath 5-92).

Australia won the Fourth Test by 176 runs to square the series.

Gates drop but membership up. Attendances at Championship matches in 1961 dropped by 76,722 to 969,382, the lowest aggregate since the war. It was pointed out that every county showed an increased membership, with a total of 110,000 more than double that of 1939.
Little Wonder No. 72 Crowds at weekend games dropped, whereas those for matches starting on Wednesdays increased.

1999-2000 – WEST INDIES v ZIMBABWE (SECOND TEST): TOP OF THE LIST

2001

At Kingston, March 24, 25, 26, 27, 28, 2000. West Indies won by ten wickets. Jamaica's favourite cricketer became Test cricket's leading wicket-taker in front of several thousand ecstatic countrymen. In his 16th international season and 114th Test, Courtney Walsh reached the magical mark of 435 at 5.12pm on the fourth day when Zimbabwe's last man, Olonga, pushed a lifting ball to short leg, where Hinds pouched it left-handed. The catch took Walsh past India's Kapil Dev, who took 434 wickets in 131 Tests.

The crowd sensed history, but they, and Walsh, were kept waiting until the end as Zimbabwe's middle order was swept away by Walsh's colleagues. When he returned for his third spell, at 98 for seven with Streak unable to bat, the tension grew – and became electric when Rose accounted for Strang. But the fifth ball of Walsh's 16th over was short of a length, jagging back into Olonga's rib cage, and produced the desired result. It was the signal for wild celebrations. Walsh started with high fives, then kissed the pitch where he had taken 42 wickets in ten Tests. There were hugs and kisses from his mother, Joan Wollaston, and 13-year-old son Courtney Junior, a lap of honour after the day's play, and special tributes from Kapil (live from Sharjah, where he was coaching India) and Jamaica's prime minister. The next night, Walsh was honoured by the government and presented with a plot of land.

Zimbabwe 308 (M. W. Goodwin 113, A. Flower 66; R. D. King 5-51) **and 102;**
West Indies 339 (J. C. Adams 101*, F. A. Rose 69; N. C. Johnson 4-77) **and 75-0.**

2002-03 – WEST INDIES v AUSTRALIA (FOURTH TEST): THRILL OF
THE CHASE   2004

At St John's, May 9, 10, 11, 12, 13, 2003. West Indies won by three wickets. Many expected the final Test to bring a disappointing series to a historic conclusion with Australia's first Caribbean clean sweep. Few, though, could have imagined the controversies that the game would bring and still less that West Indies would etch their names in the record books by achieving the largest successful run-chase in 1,645 Tests.

Lawson, fast and furious, pocketed career-best figures. But by the end of the day the word was spreading around the Recreation Ground: to many, Lawson's action, which had first drawn the attention of the series referee, Mike Procter, during the First Test in Guyana, looked dubious. By the fourth day, Procter confirmed that Lawson had been reported to the ICC for a suspect action.

By restricting Australia to 417, about 150 fewer than Waugh had envisaged, West Indies had left themselves a target which, though unlikely, was not impossible now that the pitch had lost its juice if not its bounce. With more than two days available, time at least was on their side. Hope was all but extinguished when Lara was fourth out at 165, trying to belt MacGill for a fourth huge six down the ground. But Sarwan and Chanderpaul, who was nursing a broken finger, got on with the task – and under the skin of the Australians, especially McGrath. As Sarwan approached a mature hundred, there were signs that Australia were losing the plot. McGrath, who started the verbal war, became utterly incensed at Sarwan's riposte – he apparently referred to McGrath's wife.

When Sarwan had taken his score to 105 and his stand with Chanderpaul to 123, he mishooked Lee to leave the game perfectly poised: at 288 for five, either 130 runs or five wickets would settle it. The first-ball dismissal of Jacobs, caught behind though he was struck on the elbow, initially tilted things Australia's way. The crowd were furious, and disrupted play by throwing bottles on to the outfield. Through all this – and a rain delay – Chanderpaul kept his concentration to reach a magnificent hundred. By the close, Australia needed four wickets for the clean sweep; West Indies 47 runs to prevent it.

Australia 240 (J. J. C. Lawson 7-78) **and 417** (M. L. Hayden 177, J. L. Langer 111; M. Dillon 4-112); **West Indies 240** (B. C. Lara 68) **and 418-7** (R. R. Sarwan 105, S. Chanderpaul 104, Lara 60; B. Lee 4-63).

2003-04 – WEST INDIES v ENGLAND (FIRST TEST): HURRICANE HARMY
Rob Smyth, 2005

At Kingston, March 11, 12, 13, 14, 2004. England won by ten wickets. The denouement came like a bolt from the clear blue Kingston skies. For three days this was a gritty arm-wrestle of a match; then, on the fourth morning, West Indies collapsed for 47, their lowest total ever. Steve Harmison, bowling with cold-eyed purpose, finally came of age, taking the cheapest seven-wicket haul in Test history in a performance described by his captain Vaughan as "one of the greatest spells by an England bowler".

This was an exaggeration: only one batsman, Jacobs, got a real snorter. And Harmison himself felt he was to bowl better in Port-of-Spain five days later. Harmison's success, though spectacular, was a reward for getting the fundamentals right rather than sudden inspiration. After getting carried away and underpitching in the first innings, he simply increased his length, cut his pace a fraction, and concentrated on the basics. It worked, probably beyond his wildest dreams. Only two bowlers in Test history have taken more wickets in an innings more cheaply: George Lohmann and Johnny Briggs, both for England in South Africa in the 19th century. Soon after the game had finished, though, some of the West Indies players were dancing giddily in the stands, partying with their supporters as though ten-wicket defeats by England were all in a day's work.

West Indies 311 (D. S. Smith 108, R. O. Hinds 84) and 47 (S. J. Harmison 7-12);
England 339 (M. A. Butcher 58, N. Hussain 58) and 20-0.

2003-04 – WEST INDIES v ENGLAND (FOURTH TEST): RECLAIMED

Tony Cozier, 2005

At St John's, April 10, 11, 12, 13, 14, 2004. Drawn. One hundred and eighty--five days after losing his position as scorer of Test cricket's highest innings, Brian Lara reclaimed the record from Matthew Hayden and became the first man to reach 400 in a Test.

Twenty-five minutes before lunch on the third day, he danced down the pitch to hoist Batty's invitingly flighted off-break into the stand at long-on for the six that lifted him past his own 375 and level with Hayden at 380. He then swept the next ball, flatter and ill-directed, to fine leg for four, to secure once more the record he had taken from another celebrated West Indian left-hander, Garry Sobers, on the same ground against the same opposition ten years earlier. It was the tenth time the record had changed hands; no one else had ever recovered it.

The reception this time was joyful enough, but less frenetic than first time round. There was no spectator invasion, as in 1994, except for an inappropriate appearance by a government entourage headed by the new prime minister of Antigua and Barbuda, Baldwin Spencer. As in Bridgetown, travelling England supporters formed the majority of the estimated 10,000 in the stands. They politely rejoiced that they were there to see history. Over in the popular, open section adjoining Independence Avenue, where hardly a pale face was to be seen, the celebrations were understandably more boisterous.

After handshakes from weary opponents, Lara again stooped to kiss the pitch – prepared under the supervision of Andy Roberts, the formidable fast bowler of an earlier era – that had once more favoured him. He was so composed, so concentrated, so invincible that he surely could have carried on to 500, or 600 if he had been so minded. Geraint Jones, who had replaced Read as England wicketkeeper and thus had the closest vantage point, observed how fresh Lara looked throughout, hardly raising a sweat.

Two other men were on the field during both record innings: England's Graham Thorpe, and Australian umpire Darrell Hair. Indeed, Hair had also officiated when Lara scored the first of his 25 Test hundreds – and the first of his seven doubles – 277 in Sydney in 1992-93. Yet, had Hair been persuaded by a convincing appeal for a catch at the wicket, Lara would not have scored a run. Hair shook his head, and television replays indicated he was correct.

West Indies 751-5 dec. (B. C. Lara 400*, R. D. Jacobs 107*, R. R. Sarwan 90, C. H. Gayle 69);
England 285 (A. Flintoff 102*, M. A. Butcher 52; P. T. Collins 4-76)
and 422-5 (M. P. Vaughan 140, M. E. Trescothick 88, Butcher 61, N. Hussain 56).

2008-09 – THE STANFORD SUPER SERIES
Scyld Berry, 2009

In the middle of February 2009, while England were playing the second of their two Test matches in Antigua, Sir Allen Stanford was charged by the Securities and Exchange Commission of the United States with an alleged $9.2billion investment fraud. The ECB immediately suspended negotiations with Stanford but, by then, they had suffered enormous embarrassment from their close links to the Texan who claimed to be a billionaire.

Much wisdom was expressed after Stanford was charged; and the images of the ECB's top brass virtually throwing themselves at Stanford's feet when he landed at Lord's in a helicopter will be indelible. But the essential fact was that the ECB, during the summer of 2008, did not have much alternative to getting into bed with him.

Kevin Pietersen, at least before he was appointed England's captain in August, was loud in his determination to become a million-dollar cricketer in the IPL, and Andrew Flintoff made similar noises. Cricketers were now freer agents than they had ever been before. The ECB had to find them some major dollars, and quickly; and Stanford, for all the doubts about him, was the one available option.

Before the big game on November 1, many expressed concerns about the details of the hasty arrangements, especially the use of the England name; and Collier arrived in Antigua only during the week of the Super Series tournament to try to sort them out. There was, nevertheless, a prevailing belief that the most lucrative ever cricket match should be played, if only as a one-off; and that the Lord's quadrangular (for England, the Stanford Superstars, New Zealand and Sri Lanka) should go ahead. It was also mooted that the Superstars would be one of two overseas teams in the English Premier League of 2010.

A public-relations disaster followed during the second warm-up game. Stanford, as he owned the place, liked to mingle with anybody he fancied, with a cameraman in tow. So he went into the England players' dressing-room, oblivious to the tradition that it is sacrosanct – while the England players were oblivious to the tradition of American sport that owners can go anywhere. Then Stanford went and talked to some women in a stand, and sat one of them on his knee: it was Matt Prior's wife, Emily, and she was pregnant. Stanford had to ring the England team hotel next day and apologise to Pietersen and Prior. The British press had a field day; the ECB, rapidly getting cold feet, suggested the Stanford tournament might be a one-off, not the first of five annual matches as originally announced.

2008-09 – ENGLAND IN WEST INDIES: 51 ALL OUT — John Etheridge, 2010

England were engulfed in turmoil before they left for the West Indies in early 2009, and the team's performances were not good enough to allow the pre-tour conflict to be forgotten completely. Under a new captain, Andrew Strauss, and a makeshift coach, Andy Flower, England lost the Test series 1–0. The defining passage of play came on the fourth day of the First Test in Jamaica, when Jerome Taylor produced a high-quality, high-velocity spell of swing bowling and England were blitzed for 51, the third-lowest total in their history.

After England contrived to lose their head coach and captain – Peter Moores and Kevin Pietersen were sacked a fortnight before the squad departed – the first task of Strauss and Flower, who had been batting coach under Moores, was to restore harmony. By and large, this was achieved. Strauss was imperious with the bat, and his captaincy and public pronouncements grew in stature. He was articulate and clean-cut, and even those who believed he left his declarations in Antigua and Trinidad too late could not seriously doubt he was the right man for the job.

2009 – BANGLADESHIS IN WEST INDIES: SIMMERING — Tony Cozier, 2010

On their second tour of the Caribbean, Bangladesh were inadvertently provided with all the circumstances to transform their habitual Test agony into historic success. They arrived to find the perennial row between the West Indies Cricket Board and the West Indies Players' Association simmering ominously; it came to the boil a couple of days before the First Test when, under advice from the WIPA, all 13 players selected declared themselves unavailable, as did several others who would have qualified as their replacements.

2010-11 – WEST INDIES v PAKISTAN (FIRST TEST): SEVEN UP

Tony Cozier, 2012

At Providence, Guyana, May 12, 13, 14, 15, 2011. West Indies won by 40 runs. West Indies' first Test win since February 2009 was especially satisfying. It came against the background of familiar controversy: Chris Gayle was left out after an incendiary radio interview, while Chanderpaul was grudgingly selected after being just as vocal about his exclusion from the preceding one-day series. Victory was particularly fulfilling for Sammy, who responded to widespread questioning of his place in the side with a performance that won him the match award: his spot-on medium-pace was ideally suited to the conditions, and produced match figures of 29–13–45–7.

In this case, statistics did not lie: they revealed the defects of a pitch as hard and dry as a board, which led to a record 20 lbw dismissals, allowed just a solitary individual half-century and kept the overall run-rate to 2.4 an over. Pakistan's spinners capitalised on some generous turn, claiming 17 wickets, with Saeed Ajmal's off-breaks and doosras bringing him 11 for 111. For West Indies, Sammy and Rampaul shared 14 wickets, mainly by adhering to the stump-to-stump line that made the most of the inconsistent bounce.

West Indies 226 (Saeed Ajmal 5-69) **and 152** (Ajmal 6-42);
Pakistan 160 (D. Bishoo 4-68) **and 178** (Misbah-ul-Haq 52; D. J. G. Sammy 5-29).

NEW ZEALAND

❝ New Zealand's balloon floats only when the gases are mixed just right and everyone is fresh, willing and ambitious," according to the 1984 Cricketer of the Year profile for Jeremy Coney, who had been part of the team that won a Test in England for the first time in 1983 and three years later captained the side to their first series victory in England. That team contained two of New Zealand's greatest players, Sir Richard Hadlee and Martin Crowe, but the gases are not often mixed just right, at least in the five-day game. New Zealand's first Test victory came in their 45th match, 26 years after their debut. Against their nearest neighbours Australia they played a single Test in 1945-46, which was not recognised as such until 1948, but were not granted another until 1973-74. Referring to the deposing of captain Ross Taylor and the subsequent fall-out, *Wisden* 2013 reported: "New Zealand are no strangers to cricketing drama, but Hollywood's finest scriptwriters would have marvelled at the turmoil packed into 2012. Fluctuating performances, leadership conflicts and vehement protests from fans and former players made for a compelling but destructive soap opera." Six World Cup semi-final appearances point to a greater proficiency in the shorter forms of the game.

1929-30 – NEW ZEALAND v ENGLAND (First Test): MAIDEN TEST   1931

At Christchurch, January 10, 11, 13, 1930. Despite some delay on the first day and the complete loss of Saturday owing to rain, the MCC, in the course of two days' cricket, won the First Test match by eight wickets with 55 minutes to spare – a remarkable occurrence in these times of prolonged struggles. New Zealand failed to recover from a disastrous start on a firm pitch. Blunt, very steady, Lowry, more restrained than usual, Dempster and Page – all well-known in England – were their only batsmen to show much skill. At the start Nichols took three wickets and then four men fell to Allom in five balls of one over, Lowry, James and Badcock being the victims in a hat-trick. Nichols bowled very fast and Allom, in making the ball swerve either way, also received help from a strong wind. Allom in the whole match took eight wickets for 55 runs and Nichols six for 51. These two bowlers received good support from their colleagues, but New Zealand did not field well.

New Zealand 112 (M. S. Nichols 4-28, M. J. C. Allom 5-38) **and 131**;
England 181 and 66-2.

1932-33 – NEW ZEALAND v ENGLAND (SECOND TEST):
HAMMOND OVERTAKES BRADMAN
1934

At Auckland, March 31, April 1, 3, 1933. Drawn, like the other Test, because of the weather, the second match against New Zealand was made memorable by the record score of Hammond, whose 336 not out surpassed Bradman's 334 obtained at Leeds in 1930. The great performance was the more remarkable as it came after a poor batting display by New Zealand. Hammond went in when Sutcliffe left at 56 and got his runs out of 492 – a wonderful proportion. Hitting freely from the start, Hammond completed 50 in 72 minutes, and his hundred came less than an hour later. His third fifty occupied only 38 minutes and, after reaching 200 in four hours, he actually added a hundred in 47 minutes while when Wyatt declared he had been at the wickets no more than five hours and a quarter. Hammond when 134 gave the one real chance in his great innings, but Dempster was hurt in trying to make a catch that he found too hot to hold. Showing to the utmost advantage in driving, pulling and cutting, Hammond placed strokes with astonishing accuracy no matter how the bowlers positioned their fieldsmen. Throughout he treated the moderate attack with unflagging freedom. By clever footwork he took the bowling at the length he desired and aroused the spectators to enthusiasm. Of ten sixes, three were off successive deliveries from Newman.

New Zealand 158 (C. S. Dempster 83*; W. E. Bowes 6-34) and 16-0;
England 548-7 dec. (W. R. Hammond 336*, Mr R. E. S. Wyatt 60).

Overseas Cricket, 1960-61. A 30-year-old Sydney junior cricketer, Jim Clissold, performed three hat-tricks in one day. Clissold, a medium-paced left-hander, playing for Sutherland against Ryde, at Ryde Oval, in the Municipal and Shires competition, took six for 50, including a hat-trick in the first innings, and seven for 15, including two separate hat-tricks, in the second.

Little Wonder No. 73

1954-55 – NEW ZEALAND v ENGLAND (SECOND TEST): LOWEST OF
THE LOW
1956

At Auckland, March 25, 26, 28, 1955. Len Hutton's team finished their triumphant tour by setting up a world record. They dismissed New Zealand in the second innings for 26, the lowest total in the history of Test cricket. The previous-lowest score was 30, made twice by South Africa against England.

Actually the issue appeared to be evenly balanced, but in one hour and 44 minutes the game and the tour were completed. As in Australia, Tyson and Statham were mainly responsible for the collapse by getting rid of the early batsmen.

It was exactly three o'clock on a glorious summer's day when New Zealand began their task. The pitch was dry and not particularly fast, but the ball went through at varying heights and took spin. In 40 minutes before tea New Zealand lost Leggat, Poore and Reid for 13 runs. By clever strategy Hutton brought on Wardle, left-arm slow, to tackle Sutcliffe, New Zealand's talented left-handed batsman. That move made the record lowest score possible as Wardle tempted Sutcliffe into a big hit against his chinaman and he was completely deceived and bowled.

With four men out for 14, Appleyard entered the attack, relieving Tyson, and he removed McGregor, Cave, MacGibbon and Colquhoun, who went first ball in each innings. In fact Appleyard claimed three wickets in four balls but Moir again prevented a hat-trick, the ball falling only just short of Graveney who was in great form in the leg trap. Hutton decided to give Statham and Tyson the chance of making the kill, but one over from Statham sufficed. First he got Rabone leg-before with his fourth delivery and finally established the new world record by sending Hayes's middle stump flying.

New Zealand 200 (J. R. Reid 73; J. B. Statham 4-28) and 26 (R. Appleyard 4-7);
England 246 (L. Hutton 53; A. M. Moir 5-62).

1955-56 – NEW ZEALAND v WEST INDIES (FOURTH TEST):
26 YEARS OF HURT   1957

At Auckland, March 9, 10, 12, 13, 1956. New Zealand won by 190 runs. Local offices closed and excited crowds streamed to the Eden Park ground on the last afternoon as Cave and Beard bowled New Zealand to their first victory in 26 years of Test cricket. New Zealand owed much to the example of Reid, their captain. Until his arrival at the crease on the opening day nothing about New Zealand's cricket suggested their eventual triumph. Miller and MacGibbon struggled unconvincingly against a keen attack, following the early dismissal of McGregor, and Reid brought the first touch of mastery to the batting.

Reid set West Indies the formidable task of scoring 268 in four hours. Against the hostile swing bowling of Cave and Beard, West Indies collapsed so completely on a good batting pitch that the board soon showed 22 for six. Weekes and Binns rallied their team briefly but, after Alabaster dismissed both in an economical spell of leg-breaks, Cave and Beard completed West Indies' rout for their lowest score in Test cricket.

New Zealand 255 (J. R. Reid 84; D. T. Dewdney 5-21) and 157-9 dec. (D. S. Atkinson 7-53);
West Indies 145 (H. A. Furlonge 64; H. B. Cave 4-22, A. R. MacGibbon 4-44) and 77 (Cave 4-21).

1973-74 – AUSTRALIANS IN NEW ZEALAND: BIG BROTHER BEATEN   1975

New Zealand cricket has known no greater occasion than March 13, 1974, when a Test against Australia was won for the first time at the sixth time of asking.

It was particularly gratifying for the New Zealanders for two reasons. They had fought out a drawn series with the West Indies in 1972, had twice come very close to victory against England in 1973, and at Sydney, only a few weeks earlier, had been robbed by rain of an almost certain and substantial success. So the win at Lancaster Park was the fruit of long endeavour.

The second cause for pride was that New Zealand won at Christchurch absolutely on their merits. It was a game of sustained excitement, played on a pitch which scarcely varied throughout the five days; in almost every session, the initiative changed hands dramatically.

New Zealand owed their five-wicket victory largely to G. M. Turner, who became the first New Zealander to score separate centuries in a Test. There was also some good, aggressive bowling by the New Zealand seamers on a strip which always yielded some movement and a brisk but even bounce.

This was New Zealand's first Test win since Pakistan were defeated at Lahore in 1969 – a success which led to New Zealand's only Test rubber victory. It underlined the progress New Zealand cricket has made. In their first 44 Tests, over 26 years there was not a single success. In the last 18 years there have been eight wins in 70 matches – a modest record, but clearly an improving one. The defeat of Australia left only England who have not yet been beaten by New Zealand.

The three-Test series was drawn 1–1. Immediately prior to this series, New Zealand had conducted their first full Test tour of Australia, described by Wisden as "a most belated act of recognition by the Australian authorities". Their first Test against Australia in 1945-46 at Wellington was not officially recognised as such until 1948.

1974-75 – NEW ZEALAND v ENGLAND (FIRST TEST): LUCKY TO BE ALIVE
1976

At Auckland, February 20, 21, 22, 23, 25, 1975. England won by an innings and 83 runs. An accident to Ewen Chatfield, the New Zealand No. 11 batsman, from what proved to be the very last ball of this match, cast an ugly shadow on all the splendid cricket that took place during the first four days. Chatfield narrowly escaped death on his Test debut after he had deflected a bouncer from Lever into his face. It caused a hairline fracture of the skull from the blow that struck him on the left temple.

Bernard Thomas, the MCC physiotherapist and John May, an ambulanceman, rushed to the pitch and Mr Thomas gave the stricken batsman heart massage and mouth-to-mouth resuscitation before Chatfield could be removed to the ambulance. Thomas said that Chatfield's heart had stopped beating for several seconds, adding: "It was the worst case I have seen and I never want to see another."

Lever left the field behind the stretcher weeping and would not be consoled, though his team-mates tried to convince him that he was not to blame. That day he made two visits to the hospital to see Chatfield. The first time Chatfield was still unconscious, but he was much recovered when Lever returned and he assured the distraught Lever that the accident was his own fault.

England 593-6 dec. (K. W. R. Fletcher 216, M. H. Denness 181, J. H. Edrich 64, A. W. Greig 51);

New Zealand 326 (J. M. Parker 121, J. F. M. Morrison 58, K. J. Wadsworth 58; Greig 5-98)

and 184 (Morrison 58, G. P. Howarth 51*; Greig 5-51).

1977-78 – NEW ZEALAND v ENGLAND (First Test): WIND OF CHANGE

1979

At Wellington, February 10, 11, 12, 14, 15, 1978. New Zealand won by 27 runs. After 48 years and in the 48th Test between the two countries, New Zealand beat England for the first time.

Though England's form and fortune struck rock-bottom in the crucial final innings, it was a great and deserved triumph for New Zealand and for Richard Hadlee, the fast-bowling son of Walter Hadlee, the former Test captain and much-respected chairman of the NZ Cricket Council. Success was all the sweeter, and more exciting, because of the remarkable turnaround of the match. At tea on the fourth day the air was loaded with foreboding for New Zealand; the portents were all for the pattern of history to continue.

Willis, supported by superb catching, had caused a collapse of nine for 41 in two hours and England, with time of no concern, had to score a moderate 137 to win. Only two hours later, New Zealand gloom was transformed into joy as England, with Rose retired with a bruised right arm, tottered on the brink of defeat with eight down for 53. England, in turn, had been routed by Richard Hadlee and Collinge. The next morning, after a frustrating delay of 40 minutes for rain, New Zealand took 49 minutes to complete a famous victory in an understandably emotional atmosphere. The crowd gathered in front of the pavilion and sang, "For they are jolly good fellows," followed by three cheers.

Hadlee fittingly took the last two wickets. In the first innings he had four for 74, and in the second six for 26. Apart from one over by Dayle Hadlee, Richard Hadlee and Collinge bowled unchanged as England were dismissed for 64. England's previous-lowest total against New Zealand was 181 at Christchurch in 1929-30 – the first series between the countries. In some ways it was a bizarre game, with a gale-force wind blowing directly down the pitch on the first day, and changing direction several times during the next four playing days.

New Zealand 228 (J. G. Wright 55; C. M. Old 6-54)

and 123 (R. G. D. Willis 5-32);

England 215 (G. Boycott 77; R. J. Hadlee 4-74)

and 64 (R. J. Hadlee 6-26).

1979-80 – WEST INDIANS IN NEW ZEALAND: LOSING FACE   R. T. Brittenden, 1981

New Zealand's first victory in a Test rubber at home should have been a happy occasion, but the New Zealand cricket public, which had looked forward keenly to the West Indians' visit, was glad to see the back of them. New Zealand won the First Test by the narrowest of margins, and drew the remaining two. Yet the West Indians lost more than a Test series. Their reputation for sportsmanship went too. There were several extremely unsavoury incidents on the field in the first two Tests, and the situation was not improved by the extravagant statements made by their harassed manager, Willie Rodriguez.

Their main complaint in New Zealand was about the umpiring, and in retrospect there is little doubt that if both sides suffered from difficult, debatable decisions, more went against West Indies than against New Zealand. Mr Rodriguez, after stating that he did not think the umpiring was biased, only incompetent, claimed after his departure that the West Indians had had to get batsmen out nine times before getting a decision. And his allegations went well beyond the bounds of acceptable comment when he claimed the West Indians were "set up; that there was no way we could win a Test"; that New Zealand were celebrating 50 years in Tests and were determined to do something about it. This thinly veiled suggestion that there had been collaboration between the New Zealand administration and its umpires was highly insulting to men of integrity.

On the field, the West Indian players behaved in an extraordinary fashion. In the First Test Holding, having had an appeal disallowed, kicked the stumps out of the ground at the batsmen's end. When West Indies lost the match, Greenidge showed similar ill-temper as he left the field. At Christchurch in the Second Test, Croft, after being no balled, flicked off the bails as he walked back, and a little later ran in very close to the umpire, F. R. Goodall – so close that the batsman could not see him – and shouldered Goodall heavily. It was the height of discourtesy when Goodall, wishing on two occasions to speak to Lloyd about Croft's behaviour, had to walk all the way to the West Indian captain, standing deep in the slips. Lloyd took not a step to meet him.

It was in this match that the West Indians refused to take the field after tea on the third day, saying they would not continue unless umpire Goodall was removed. They were finally persuaded to continue 12 minutes late. That evening they emptied their dressing-room and there was a distinct prospect that the tour would end there and then. Following protracted negotiations with the New Zealand board it was agreed to continue the match and the rest of the tour. The board made clear its feeling that Croft, after his attack on Goodall, should not be considered for the Auckland Test, but in the event he did play.

The Auckland Test, the last of the series, produced yet another extraordinary situation. Four senior members of the West Indian team booked flights home which would have required their leaving the ground soon after lunch on the last day of the Test. However, they were dissuaded from this dramatic action after representations from the New Zealand board.

The West Indians, being badly led and managed, were the author of their own misfortunes. For a side described as the best in the world, and the strongest since the 1948 Australians, this was singularly disappointing. It was extraordinary that New Zealand, held in scant regard by the West Indians and everyone else, actually deserved their narrow victory, for they played better cricket and played as a team, whereas the West Indians sulked or stormed in turn.

1979-80 – NEW ZEALAND v WEST INDIES (FIRST TEST): ORDER OF
THE BOOT 1981

At Dunedin, February 8, 9, 10, 12, 13, 1980. New Zealand won by one wicket. Clear evidence of an inability to adjust to New Zealand conditions was given by West Indies' batting on the first day. The West Indian bowlers were as much at fault as their batsmen as New Zealand built up a lead of 109. They bowled much too short, unlike the New Zealanders who had made the most of the conditions by keeping the ball up. The New Zealand batsmen took a physical hammering, but they showed considerable determination in grafting for their runs.

New Zealand were left needing only 104 to win. By lunch, under intense pressure, they had fought to 33 for two. About 20 minutes before lunch, Parker was given not out when Holding appealed for a catch by the wicketkeeper, which prompted Holding to demolish the stumps at the batsman's end with a full swing of the right foot. In the afternoon West Indies seemed to have the game won. At tea it was 95 for eight.

Only one run had been added after tea when Holding beat Cairns, but the ball touched the off stump without dislodging a bail. When Cairns was out at 100, Boock, whose best Test score was eight, saw out the last five balls of Holding's over. Garner bowled the final over. The first ball produced a bye. Boock, the non-striker, tried to

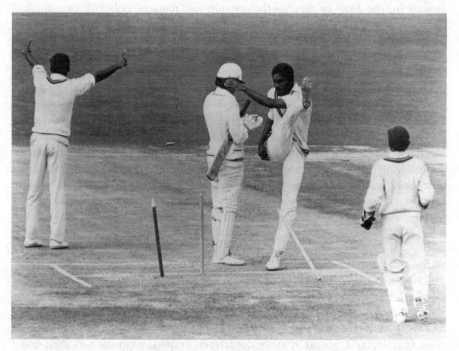

Own goal: West Indies fast bowler Michael Holding unleashes his anger at an
umpiring decision during the first Test against New Zealand at Dunedin in 1979-80.
West Indies, frustrated by the umpiring throughout, lost the series
but were not defeated in another Test rubber until 1994-95

make it two runs and turning back was almost run out. Second ball, he survived an appeal for lbw. He kept the next two out and then squeezed two runs backward of point to level the scores. The last ball went from his pads to backward square and the batsmen ran the leg-bye, Parry's return to the non-striker's end going wildly astray. It was the narrowest of victories, but well-earned. Hadlee, with 11 wickets for the match and a Test record of seven leg-before decisions, took his Test tally to 118, two ahead of New Zealand's previous record-holder, Richard Collinge.

West Indies 140 (D. L. Haynes 55; R. J. Hadlee 5-34) **and 212** (Haynes 105; Hadlee 6-68);
New Zealand 249 (B. A. Edgar 65, Hadlee 51; C. E. H. Croft 4-64) **and 104-9** (J. Garner 4-36).

1983-84 – ENGLAND IN NEW ZEALAND: UNWANTED RECORDS   John Thicknesse, 1985

England's tour of 1983-84 has claims to rank among the unhappiest they have ever undertaken. Ineptly selected, burdened with a bad itinerary and losing three out of 15 players through injury or illness (including the captain), they became the first English team to be beaten in a Test series by New Zealand and Pakistan – and to fill their cup to overflowing they were publicly accused of taking drugs. Following allegations in *The Mail on Sunday* that certain members of Bob Willis's team had smoked pot in New Zealand, the Test and County Cricket Board held an inquiry, which resulted in the party being cleared of having done anything off the field which might have affected their playing performance.

Because of injuries to Neil Foster and Graham Dilley, England had taken the uncommon step of going outside the touring party to complete their team, calling up the 25-year-old Sussex opening bowler, Tony Pigott, who was playing for Wellington in New Zealand's domestic first-class competition. It was a mixed experience for him, the satisfaction of becoming the first Harrovian to win a cap since M. C. Bird, in 1913, being outweighed, one would presume, by involvement in such a mortifying display. An ironic footnote was that to make himself available, Pigott postponed his wedding, little thinking that by the Monday of a match begun on Friday there would be time to have started a honeymoon in South America and got married as well.

1983–84 – NEW ZEALAND v ENGLAND (SECOND TEST):
CHRISTCHURCH CRUSH   1985

At Christchurch, February 3, 4, 5, 1984. New Zealand won by an innings and 132 runs. Outplaying England in every department, especially in the way their faster bowlers used a suspect pitch, New Zealand achieved their largest-ever victory in 12 hours' playing time.

On the first day, abysmal England bowling, later condemned by Willis as some of the worst he had seen in Tests, enabled New Zealand to score at 4.2 per over after winning the toss. Hadlee, coming in with the innings in the balance, struck 99 in 81 balls, taking heavy toll of a surfeit of long-hops from Botham and half-volleys from a tiring Pigott, in his first Test.

Willis bowled a hostile and unlucky opening spell, but the inadequacy of England's bowling on the first day was reflected by the concession of 42 fours, although the ball both swung and moved off the seam. Fowler, deceived by Boock, the slow left-armer, was bowled in the last over of the opening day, whereupon England dived headlong to defeat.

England's hopes of saving the embarrassment of having to follow on for first time against New Zealand vanished on the third morning when Pigott was beaten by Cairns's slower ball, and 40 minutes before lunch their second innings started. They were 225 runs behind. Tavaŕé and Fowler hung on till the interval, but 65 minutes afterwards the score was 33 for six and the only question was whether England could surpass their previous-lowest score against New Zealand, 64 at Wellington in 1977-78. Randall and Taylor achieved that by adding 39; but Taylor's run-out, when Randall rejected a sharp single to Edgar in the covers, ended the resistance.

New Zealand 307 (R. J. Hadlee 99; R. G. D. Willis 4-51); **England 82 and 93** (Hadlee 5-28).

Northamptonshire v Gloucestershire. At Kettering, June 2, 4, 5, 1962. Northamptonshire were so sluggish on the last day that all the Gloucestershire team except Milton and the wicketkeeper bowled, in an attempt to produce scoring strokes; Jarman sent down three balls of one over with his right arm and the other three with his left.

Little Wonder No. 74

1992-93 – PAKISTANIS IN NEW ZEALAND: LANDMARK BAN

1994

The tour may be most clearly remembered for a regrettable landmark in cricket history. After Pakistan's limited-overs defeat at Napier, Aqib Javed became the first international cricketer to be suspended for his behaviour on the field. Australian referee Peter Burge banned him from the deciding fixture of the series for obscene abuse of an umpire who had no-balled him. Aqib already had the unfortunate distinction of having been the first player to be fined under the same ICC rules, during the Old Trafford Test six months earlier.

1998-99 – NEW ZEALAND v SOUTH AFRICA (FIRST TEST): STICKING POINT

Don Cameron, 2000

At Auckland, February 27, 28, March 1, 2, 3, 1999. Drawn. Seven days before the first ball of this bizarre Test was bowled, it was clear that all was not well with the pitch. A fungal disease had ruined much of the grass cover. Ross Dykes, chairman of the New Zealand selectors, claimed the pitch was so poor that the teams should decamp to Hamilton, 75 miles south, but lost the argument.

However, on the first morning, the teams were surprised to see an apparently grassless, but very firm and true surface; the groundstaff had applied litres of PVA glue and then rolled in grass clippings to give a healthy tinge. So began the long, unequal struggle between feasting batsmen and subservient bowlers. An hour into the third day, Cullinan passed the previous-highest Test innings for South Africa: Graeme Pollock's 274 against Australia at Durban in 1969-70. Cullinan hit 27 fours and two sixes, faced 490 balls and batted two minutes short of 11 hours, longer than any other South African in Tests.

There was another batting record, though this was no more than a monument to the turgidity of the Test. Allott, a genuine No. 11, joined Harris with the follow-on target still over a hundred runs off. For 101 minutes, he toiled away, eventually establishing a record for the longest Test nought. "It was the best duck I'll ever make," said Allott. The sparse crowd gave more generous applause to his non-batting than to Cullinan's patient accumulation.

South Africa 621-5 dec. (D. J. Cullinan 275*, G. Kirsten 128, S. M. Pollock 69*, J. N. Rhodes 63);
New Zealand 352 (M. J. Horne 93, C. Z. Harris 68*)
and 244-3 (N. J. Astle 69*, R. G. Twose 65, Horne 60).

2000-01 – NEW ZEALAND v PAKISTAN (THIRD TEST): 26 OFF AN OVER
Kip Brook, 2002

At Hamilton, March 27, 28, 29, 30, 2001. New Zealand won by an innings and 185 runs. New Zealand achieved their largest Test victory to level the series, while the unpredictable Pakistanis went down to their heaviest defeat. On the fourth day, McMillan inspired his team-mates by thumping a single over for 26 runs, a Test record, after which the young Kiwi pace attack cleaned Pakistan out. With the second day and half the third washed out, the entire match lasted less than 190 overs, barely two days' play.

Richardson fell to the third delivery of the fourth day, clearing the way for McMillan's scorching 98 off 97 balls. He hit Younis Khan's single over for 444464 – three of the fours from reverse sweeps and the six a hefty off-drive out of the ground. McMillan pulled ahead of five players who had scored 24 off a Test over, and went on to a record seventh consecutive boundary when he hit his next ball, from Saqlain Mushtaq, for another six, his third. Having taken 80 deliveries for his fifty, he advanced to 98 off another 16 before, trying to reach three figures, he was caught at deep third man.

Pakistan 104 (D. R. Tuffey 4-39, C. S. Martin 4-52)
and 118 (J. E. C. Franklin 4-26);
New Zealand 407-4 dec. (M. H. Richardson 106, M. D. Bell 105,
C. D. McMillan 98, S. P. Fleming 51*).

2001-02 – NEW ZEALAND v ENGLAND (First Test): AT THE DOUBLE

Lawrence Booth, 2003

At Christchurch, March 13, 14, 15, 16, 2002. England won by 98 runs. This game will be remembered for perhaps the most glorious failure in the history of Test cricket. When an injured Cairns walked out to join Astle late on the fourth afternoon, New Zealand were 333 for nine, still 217 short of a wildly improbable victory. What happened next had to be seen to be believed. Astle, 134 at the fall of the ninth wicket, proceeded to treat England's attack as if they had been drafted in from the local kindergarten. He smashed his way to by far the fastest double-century in Tests and briefly raised hopes of a jaw-dropping, eye-popping win. In the end, England, thanks to their earlier all-round efforts, prevailed. But this was, and will always be, Astle's Match.

A cricket ball had perhaps never been hit so cleanly, so often. Astle's first hundred had come from a brisk 114 deliveries, but he was merely playing himself in. The carnage began in earnest when Hussain took the second new ball: the next four overs, even though they included a wicket maiden from Caddick, yielded 61 runs. Hoggard, unplayable on the second day, was smashed for 41 in two overs – and out of the attack. So Astle turned his attention to Caddick, steaming in with the confidence of a man who had already grabbed six wickets in the innings. But in seven balls spread across two overs, Astle sprayed graffiti all over Caddick's figures by smacking him for 38. One six flew over third man, another landed on the roof of the stand at extra cover, and three more – over cover, midwicket, and straight down the ground – came in successive deliveries as the home sections of the crowd began to sing and dance in disbelief. England's supporters, so raucous moments before, were stunned into silence.

Another six off Flintoff, a gentle sweep for a single off Giles, and Astle had raced from 101 to 200 in a scarcely believable 39 balls. He reached his maiden Test double-century in 153, smashing the record – set by Adam Gilchrist at Johannesburg just three weeks earlier – by 59 deliveries. He had taken 217 minutes, three more than Don Bradman at Leeds in 1930, when the balls were not totted up (but over-rates were generally higher). It was as though Astle had taken two seconds off the 100 metres record.

Two more sixes off Hoggard followed, bringing the deficit down to double figures. England were seriously worried, and Astle later admitted he would have started to look for ones and twos had New Zealand come within 70 runs of victory. So the relief England felt when Astle drove at Hoggard and was caught behind for 222 was palpable.

England 228 (N. Hussain 106)

and 468-6 dec. (G. P. Thorpe 200*, A. Flintoff 137);

New Zealand 147 (M. J. Hoggard 7-63)

and 451 (N. J. Astle 222, M. H. Richardson 76; A. R. Caddick 6-122).

New Zealand squared the series in the Third Test at Auckland after a draw at Wellington which was overshadowed by news of the death, in a car crash in Western Australia, of England's 24-year-old all-rounder Ben Hollioake.

2004–05 NEW ZEALAND v AUSTRALIA (INAUGURAL TWENTY20 INTERNATIONAL): TRIPLE TRIUMPH

2006

At Auckland, February 17, 2005. Australia won by 44 runs. Australia made it a historic three out of three by easing to victory in the very first Twenty20 international. They had triumphed in both the inaugural Test (against England at Melbourne in 1877) and the inaugural one-day international (same ground, same opponents, 94 years later). Now they beat New Zealand at Auckland's Eden Park, an apt name for what some saw as a new beginning for international cricket – although New Zealand's women had already defeated England's in a Twenty20 international at Hove in August 2004. However, neither side took the game especially seriously, and the sizeable crowd might have been excused for thinking they had been transported back in time. Both teams wore garish body-hugging kits last seen in the 1980s, while the New Zealanders went one stage further and sported all manner of outmoded facial hair, creating a cabaret feel that helped camouflage the fact that – with no senior 20-over competitions in either country – few players had experience of the new format. Australia began unsteadily, losing three wickets in four overs before Ponting and Katich decided authentic strokes rather than baseball swipes represented the prudent approach. Ponting came within one stroke of the first 20-over international century, his unbeaten 98 coming from just 55 balls. It soon became clear that a total of 214 was beyond the New Zealanders. Despite his success, Ponting was underwhelmed: "I think it is difficult to play seriously," he said. But he added: "If it does become an international game then I'm sure the novelty won't be there all the time."

Australia 214-5 (20 overs) (R. T. Ponting 98*; K. D. Mills 3-44);
New Zealand 170 (S. B. Styris 66; M. S. Kasprowicz 4-29).

2010 – INEPTITUDE

Lynn McConnell, 2011

Twelve wasted months: that has to be the verdict on one of the most lamentable periods of New Zealand's inconsistent cricket history. After the sacking of coach Andy Moles in November 2009, the nation's cricket was placed under the control of captain Daniel Vettori. Admirable as Vettori's acceptance of this responsibility may have been – and he did win the first Test of his regime, against Pakistan at Dunedin – the problem he faced was apparent as early as the Second Test, which resulted in a heavy loss. New Zealand's age-old inability to string two good performances together exposed the obvious shortcomings of asking the side's best player to take control of preparation: in the modern world it was never going to last.

The former Test batsman Mark Greatbatch, now an experienced coach, joined the side – ostensibly as a batting coach who would be a mentor for Vettori, but the lines of responsibility became blurred. After a year of predictable confusion, successive one-day whitewashes by Bangladesh (4–0; one game was rained off) and India (5–0) precipitated an internal review by New Zealand Cricket.

There was more administrative ineptitude when New Zealand were party to the controversial decision to nominate former Australian Prime Minister John

Howard as the region's candidate for the ICC vice-presidency, supposedly for his diplomatic qualities. New Zealand had initially wanted past NZC chairman Sir John Anderson, who enjoyed respect at ICC level. A special committee, weighted in Australia's favour, eventually broke the deadlock between the two countries, but Howard was rejected by ICC members. New Zealand went back to Anderson, who declined the role, and it fell to Alan Isaac, almost by default.

2012 – BREAKDOWN IN RELATIONS
Andrew Alderson, 2013

Worse, the goodwill engendered from New Zealand's first Test win in Sri Lanka for more than 14 years evaporated immediately, when – at the instigation of coach Mike Hesson – Ross Taylor was removed from all forms of captaincy, and replaced by Brendon McCullum. A public-relations shambles ensued. "I knew [working with Hesson] would be tough from the outset," said Taylor. "I gave him as much support as I could, but it wasn't reciprocated." Taylor had batted New Zealand to a series-levelling victory in Colombo with 142 and 74, knowing Hesson would recommend his demotion as captain regardless. Hesson maintained that his intention, articulated in hotel-room meetings the day after the 50-over series defeat earlier on the tour, was to push for a split leadership, in which Taylor would keep the Test captaincy but pass on limited-overs duties to McCullum. Taylor claimed this plan was not made clear at the time, and interpreted it as a move to get rid of him altogether. In his last match in charge, he saved his side from the ignominy of equalling New Zealand's worst losing streak of six Tests, set in the dark days of the mid-1950s. But it did not stop him pulling out of the end-of-year visit to South Africa, saying: "I don't believe I can give 100% to the game at this time."

INDIA

The first mention of Indian cricket in *Wisden* was in the 1887 edition, damning the 1886 tour of England by the Parsees as a "failure, and we have not thought it worthwhile to print any of the scores". Four years later *Wisden* reported George Vernon's tour of India in 1889-90, the first by an English side. Surprise was expressed that more cricketing progress had not been made in India, though the one defeat for the English side, by the Parsees, "aroused the greatest interest". Overall "the trip was of the most pleasant description" even though "one or two members of the side were somewhat affected by the climate". This would not be the last heard of cricketers struggling to acclimatise to India. Arthur Gilligan's MCC side found "extreme heat very trying at times", according to the 1928 edition. And it was observed that during Shane Warne's 1997-98 showdown with Sachin Tendulkar he "could not manage the cuisine and had cans of baked beans and spaghetti flown out".

Wisden 1894 carried full scorecards of Lord Hawke's team in India, and two years later the Almanack began to get excited by the batting of Ranjitsinhji for Sussex. Public interest in the game never failed to impress, even if standards on the field were mixed. India achieved Test status in 1932, but they did not win a match for 20 years. The 1950s were notable for two hand-wringing articles by Vijay Merchant, one of India's finest batsmen. The first, in 1952, criticised, among other things, the custom of selecting aristocratic captains who did not merit a place in the side, and discussed the effect of Partition on the quality of the Indian side. Seven years later he wrote that Indian cricket "is at the crossroads", and lamented how "party politics and personal prejudices have affected our organisation". In 1967 Dicky Rutnagur, the Indian journalist, was concerned about the inability of Indian cricket to move beyond urban boundaries: "This handicap must be overcome if the enthusiasm for the game is to be reflected truly in playing standards at the highest level." This hurdle has only recently been overcome, with Mahendra Singh Dhoni, India's 2011 World Cup-winning captain, the flag-bearer for rural recruitment.

The last 30 years, since India's nation-changing World Cup win at Lord's in 1983, has brought increased quantity and quality of coverage in *Wisden*. India now boasts some of the finest writers on cricket in the world, many mentored by Sambit Bal, the global editor of ESPNcricinfo, and they have all been showcased in the pages of the Almanack. In 2013 *Wisden* launched an Indian edition.

India's wealth of playing talent has been celebrated, its financial wealth agonised over. "India, your sport needs you," was the message from editor Lawrence Booth in 2012, articulating the concern of many outside India's boundaries that its cricket authorities exercise power without responsibility. They might argue that after decades of rule from Lord's, now it is their turn.

1933-34 – MCC IN INDIA: GREAT IMPROVEMENT   Hubert Preston, 1935

Decisive wins came in two of the Tests, and England held a big advantage in the drawn game at Calcutta until the loss of two wickets spoiled the final position, but, unlike the previous side which went through a heavy programme without a reverse, Jardine's team suffered defeat from Vizianagram by 14 runs.

This break in the regular run of defeats or drawn matches must give encouragement to the further development of the game in India. A marked advance was noticeable already throughout the tour in the great improvement in the condition of the grounds, the accommodation provided and the increased attendances. All these important points meant real progress, but cricket itself had not risen to the same degree as the authorities had shown in their preparations for the visit. The public interest taken in every engagement helped to make the trip very enjoyable.

Members of the [MCC] team on their return said they rarely met such stern opposition or saw so much skilful play as expected after what the Indians did when in England. Of the Indian team the captain [C. K. Nayudu] himself was no doubt the best all-round cricketer in the country. Amarnath, who played a great innings in the First Test [*the first Indian to score a Test hundred*], The Yuvraj of Patiala and Merchant stood out prominently as batsmen. Nissar, the fast bowler, looked scarcely so good as when over here, but Amar Singh fully upheld his reputation for length and spin, notably when bowling round the wicket. Mushtaq Ali, a slow left-hand bowler and good right-hand batsman, should make a name.

1951-52 – INDIA v ENGLAND (FIFTH TEST): FIRST VICTORY 1953

At Madras, February 6, 8, 9, 10, 1952. India made history by recording their first Test victory, and they did it in emphatic style. Undoubtedly India were the superior all-round side, and they went all out for success from the first ball. Their hero was Mankad, who bowled superbly in each innings, taking 12 wickets for 108. His performance of eight for 55 in the first innings has seldom been bettered in Test cricket when it is considered that the pitch gave him little assistance. Mankad's bowling inspired the whole side, the fielding being far better than in previous matches and the batting possessed a more adventurous spirit, necessary for the occasion.

During the afternoon the death of King George VI was announced and arrangements were changed, the second day being made the rest day. Subsequently India batted consistently, with Roy again in fine form. Fourth out at 191, he scored his second century of the series.

England, 191 behind, survived the last quarter of an hour on the third day, but with the pitch wearing they were soon struggling next day. The scenes at the finish were surprisingly subdued, but the Indian officials and players were delighted at the first victory by their country at the 25th attempt to win a Test match.

England 266 (J. D. B. Robertson 77, R. T. Spooner 66; M. H. Mankad 8-55)
and 183 (Robertson 56; Mankad 4-53, Ghulam Ahmed 4-77);
India 457-9 dec. (P. R. Umrigar 130*, P. Roy 111, D. G. Phadkar 61).

Leicestershire v Somerset. At Ashby-de-la-Zouch, June 30, July 2, 3, 1962. The pitch, which had been found to be a yard too long, proved ideal for Alley's medium-paced swing and he captured six wickets for 42.

Little Wonder No. 75

1952 – THE EFFECT OF PARTITION Vijay Merchant, 1952

The Partition of India has deprived Indian cricket of some outstanding cricketers. Above all, it has deprived India of future fast bowlers. In the past, India often relied for fast bowling on the Northern India people who, because of their height and sturdy physique, are better equipped for this kind of bowling than the cricketers of Central India or the South. Now this source of supply has ceased and the gap has not yet been filled. Some time may elapse before India possesses a fast bowler of the calibre of Mahomed Nissar, who hailed from the Punjab.

This year India come to England. I sincerely trust we shall show that we have overcome many of the weaknesses which have persisted with Indian cricket in recent years. I am writing several months before the team will be chosen and I hope that Vijay Hazare, who should be an admirable captain, will be given a large proportion of young cricketers. In India too much premium has always been placed on experience and too little faith in youth. A stage has been reached when it would be better to gamble with youth than to retain faith in older players. Indian cricket needs an injection of youth and I hope that injection will be administered for the 1952 visit to England.

1952-53 – PAKISTANIS IN INDIA: MANKAD MASTERY   1954

Pakistan's performance on their entry into official Test cricket was not without encouragement for the future. They gained only one victory in 12 first-class fixtures, but individual achievements suggested they possessed the youthful talent on which to build for subsequent engagements. The superiority in spin bowling gave India mastery. That was mainly because India could call upon Mankad. The Pakistan batsmen were never comfortable against his cleverly varied left-arm slows.

1955-56 – INDIA v NEW ZEALAND (FIFTH TEST): BATTING BIG   1957

At Madras, January 6, 7, 8, 10, 11, 1956. India wound up the high-scoring series by breaking more records and gaining an overwhelming victory. Mankad and Roy, the Indian opening batsmen, mastered the New Zealand bowlers on an easy-paced pitch, and they were not parted until after lunch on the second day. They made 413, a record for Test cricket [*which stood until 2007-08*]. Mankad scored 231, and passed the Indian individual Test record of 223 which he and Umrigar each made earlier in the series. India's 537 for three set up a new record total for that country. The first-wicket partnership was also the best by an Indian pair in first-class cricket, exceeding 293 by V. M. Merchant and Mankad for the Indians against Sussex at Hove in 1946. New Zealand, by steady bowling and keen fielding, managed to restrict the scoring rate for long spells, and the opening stand lasted for nearly eight hours. Gupte, with leg-breaks, and Jasu Patel, an off-break bowler playing his first Test of the series, worried New Zealand, who despite cautious batting followed on 328 behind. Again spin upset them, this time Mankad, with left-arm slows, proving an effective partner to Gupte.

India 537-3 dec. (M. H. Mankad 231, P. Roy 173, P. R. Umrigar 79*);
New Zealand 209 (S. P. Gupte 5-72) **and 219** (J. G. Leggat 61, J. R. Reid 63; Gupte 4-73).

1959 – DEFENSIVE MINDSET   Vijay Merchant, 1959

Indian cricket is at the crossroads. After 27 years in the international sphere we seem to have got nowhere and have only five victories to our credit in Test matches.

Indian cricketers of today are not inclined to put in the same effort that marked the determination of our players of a previous generation. The outlook on the game has completely changed. There is a greater tendency than ever before to play more scientific and defensive cricket. We play now not so much to win matches as not to lose them. During the last five years our rate of scoring has gone down so considerably that except against weaker sides we have not been able to register victories.

India has no fast bowlers and for many years no effort has been made to find one. Our selectors are waiting for someone ready-made. There must be a five-year plan to pick very young well-built cricketers who have a flair for fast bowling and are prepared for hard work. As a necessary step we shall have to change the nature of our pitches and make them fast enough to give real encouragement to fast bowling.

Finally, party politics and personal prejudices have affected our organisation and consequently our cricket. I do not know how much cricket there is in our politics but there is a lot of politics in our cricket. Sport in India has become sufficiently important now for people with high ambitions to intervene by getting the necessary votes to gain a majority on the board.

1959-60 – INDIA v AUSTRALIA (SECOND TEST): PATEL PERFORMS   1961

At Kanpur, December 19, 20, 21, 23, 24, 1959. The chief architect of India's first Test victory over Australia since the two countries first met in 1947 was Patel, the Ahmedabad off-spin bowler, who took 14 wickets for 124 runs. In the Australian first innings Patel exploited newly laid turf and achieved an analysis of nine for 69 – India's finest Test bowling performance. Then on the last day, amid scenes of great excitement, he routed Australia a second time and took five more wickets for 55 runs.

India 152 (A. K. Davidson 5-31, Benaud 4-63) and 291 (N. J. Contractor 74, R. B. Kenny 51; Davidson 7-93); Australia 219 (C. C. McDonald 53, R. N. Harvey 51; J. M. Patel 9-69) and 105 (Patel 5-55, P. R. Umrigar 4-27).

1961-62 – MCC IN PAKISTAN AND INDIA: DON'T PICK AND CHOOSE
Leslie Smith, 1963

Between October 8, 1961 and February 20, 1962, the MCC cricketers took part in one of the most strenuous tours undertaken by any side. They played 24 matches in India, Pakistan and Ceylon, including eight five-day Tests, three in Pakistan and five in India.

The original tour plans had to be changed because India subsequently arranged a trip to West Indies in the February. This meant a strange programme, with three games, including one Test, being played in Pakistan, followed by the complete Indian part of the tour and then a return to Pakistan to finish the programme.

A solitary success in eight Tests could scarcely be regarded as satisfactory from England's point of view, even though there were extenuating circumstances. In the first place England were not represented by their full-scale side. Players like Cowdrey, Statham and Trueman would almost certainly have made a big difference and, perhaps, tipped the balance in England's favour, for there was never much between the Test teams.

This business of leading players declining certain tours needs consideration by the authorities. India rightly point out that they have never seen a full-strength MCC side and resent the fact that the star players make a habit of turning down the trip.

Admittedly English players find the tour harder and less comfortable than any other, but this scarcely justifies players, once they are established, picking and choosing which tour they want to make. It is no secret that in general the men who go to India, Pakistan and Ceylon regard themselves as a second eleven, often play like it and are caustic about the stars who stay at home.

India and Pakistan, for their parts, deserve the best, for the enthusiasm there has grown remarkably in a few years. Close on two million people watched the MCC, with approximately 1,200,000 at the eight Tests.

1964-65 – INDIA v AUSTRALIA (SECOND TEST): PATAUDI TO THE FORE   1965

At Bombay, October 10, 11, 12, 13, 14, 15, 1964. India won by two wickets and drew level in the series after a close fight. The issue might well have been different had O'Neill been fit. He went down with stomach pains just after the start and could not bat in either innings. Needing 254 to win, India were 74 for three overnight, but on the last day, before a crowd of 42,000, they gained a victory with half an hour to spare. At 122 for six they looked beaten, but Pataudi and Manjrekar turned the tide with a partnership of 93.

Australia 320 (P. J. P. Burge 80, B. N. Jarman 78, T. R. Veivers 67; B. S. Chandrasekhar 4-50) and 274 (R. M. Cowper 81, B. C. Booth 74, W. M. Lawry 68; R. G. Nadkarni 4-33, Chandrasekhar 4-73); India 341 (Nawab of Pataudi 86, M. L. Jaisimha 66, V. L. Manjrekar 59; Veivers 4-68) and 256-8 (D. N. Sardesai 56, Pataudi 53).

1966-67 – INDIA v WEST INDIES (SECOND TEST): BATON CHARGE
Dicky Rutnagur, 1968

At Calcutta, December 31, January 1, 3, 4, 5, 1967. West Indies won by an innings and 45 runs. This match will find a place in history not because of the cricket it produced, but because of the horrible riot that broke out on the second day. The authorities had sold more tickets than there were seats and inevitably the surplus spectators tried to find accommodation on the grass round the boundaries. The constabulary mounted a baton charge, the crowd launched a counter-attack and when the outnumbered police force fled, the crowd burnt down the stands and the furniture. It was indeed a frightening scene and the players, worried about their own safety, were reluctant to continue the match, which came pretty close to being abandoned till assurances were received from high governmental quarters that there would be no further incidents.

West Indies 390 (R. B. Kanhai 90, G. S. Sobers 70, S. M. Nurse 56,);
India 167 (L. R. Gibbs 5-51) **and 178** (Sobers 4-56).

1969-70 – AUSTRALIANS IN INDIA: SAGA OF SPIN
P. N. Sundaresan, 1971

The two-month Australian tour provided keen cricket and stirred tremendous public interest. While big crowds watched every match, those for the five Tests far exceeded the gatherings that turned up to see the West Indies in 1966-67. The daily attendance for the Tests ranged from 35,000 to 50,000, only the limitation on accommodation keeping out many more.

The 3–1 triumph in the series, however, was not as clear or comfortable as the margin suggested. India had a great opportunity to win the final Test at Madras when their spin attack took a firm grip on the game, but vital fielding lapses in both innings enabled Australia to come out on top. If India had won they would have squared the rubber, which would have been a truer indication of the form of the series.

The Tests resolved into a tremendous battle between the Australian batsmen and the Indian spinners, the left-arm Bedi, and the two off-spinners Prasanna and Venkataraghavan. Bedi and Prasanna, especially, struck as penetrative a combination as Lock and Laker, the Englishmen, or Valentine and Ramadhin, the West Indians. The trio shared 726.3 of the total 929.1 overs delivered in the Tests and claimed 59 of the 70 wickets that fell to bowlers. Their domination of the Test scene (with the off-spinner Mallett's performance of 28 wickets for Australia) really made the series a saga of the spinners. Prasanna (26) and Bedi (21) shared 47 of the 59 wickets.

1972-73 – INDIA v ENGLAND (SECOND TEST): GREAT GREIG NOT ENOUGH
Clive Taylor, 1974

At Calcutta, December 30, 31, 1972, January 1, 3, 4, 1973. India won by 28 runs. This was a memorable match in many ways. Eden Gardens, with about 70,000 spectators basking in the open stands every day, provided a spectacular setting for the match while the fascinating changes of fortune, with the outcome unpredictable till the last ball, kept the fans on their toes. The victory enabled India to draw level with England, who had won the First Test.

Greig was the cock of the walk on the [fourth] day. He demolished the Indian innings by claiming four wickets for four runs in 33 balls. Keeping a fine length and varying his cutters with the straight ball, he took five for 24, his best in Tests. Greig followed this effort by halting a batting collapse when England, mesmerised by Bedi, lost four wickets for 17 runs. He and Denness batted till the close to raise the total to 105 for four, and to raise hopes of victory.

Chandrasekhar, however, dashed these when he trapped Greig lbw with a top-spinner and then had Knott caught by Durani at midwicket off a pull. Picking up Denness in the next over Chandrasekhar showed figures of 4.3–2–5–3. Bedi dismissed Pocock and Underwood, and it seemed all was over when Cottam put up a simple return catch, but Bedi floored this. Cottam had another escape off Chandrasekhar and, profiting by these, he and Old took the score to 160 by lunch. The break proved a blessing for India as in his first over after it Chandrasekhar had Cottam lbw, to bring his side an exciting victory.

India 210 (F. M. Engineer 75) and 155 (S. A. Durani 53; A. W. Greig 5-24, C. M. Old 4-43); England 174 (B. S. Chandrasekhar 5-65) and 163 (Greig 67; B. S. Bedi 5-63, Chandrasekhar 4-42).

1974-75 – WEST INDIANS IN INDIA: ENTER RICHARDS AND ROBERTS
Dicky Rutnagur, 1976

The fourth tour undertaken by the West Indies of the Indian subcontinent was remarkable. For the first time, every Test match of a series in India produced a definite result, and the Fifth Test started against the dramatic background of India having levelled the rubber after being overwhelmed in the first two Tests. Despite India's gallant rally, West Indies deserved to win the final Test and the series, as there was never any question of their all-round superiority.

West Indies decided on a strategy of attack against the Indian spinners. Lloyd himself showed the way, using his reach, eye and tremendous weight of shot to over-power the Indian bowling. Such a method carried risks, but luck rode with Lloyd more often than not and he easily topped the averages as well as aggregates for both the whole tour, during which he accumulated 1,363 runs, and the Test matches. He exceeded the four-figure mark on the Indian leg alone, averaging 103.50.

Rowe's withdrawal from the tour opened new possibilities for Richards, and he used his opportunity to the fullest. After two failures in the First Test, he played a match-winning innings of 192 in the Second. Even during this innings, one noticed that Richards matured in temperament and improved his technique against high-class spin.

Roberts, making his first tour, was the outstanding bowler. He took 63 wickets on the tour, 23 more than Holder, the next most successful bowler. What was so admirable about Roberts' performance was that his enthusiasm remained undampened by slow pitches and he bowled as fast as any contemporary bowler.

1976-77 – MCC IN INDIA: AT THEIR WEAKEST
Dicky Rutnagur, 1978

After severe and depressing losses to Australia and the West Indies in successive home summers, the tide turned for English cricket during the 1976-77 tour of India and Sri Lanka. For the first time in five ventures since the Second World War, England beat India on their own soil. The margin of England's victory in the series was decisive. And the extent of England's superiority in achieving these three wins was no less convincing – an innings and 25 runs, ten wickets and 200 runs. They were inspired by their flamboyant and articulate captain, Tony Greig, and team management, under Ken Barrington, must also take credit for the excellent spirit and discipline that prevailed. It must be pointed out that India looked as weak as they have ever done in their 42 years in international cricket. What slight potential they had as a team they did not realise until after the series was decided.

1976-77 INDIA v ENGLAND (THIRD TEST): GAUZE AND EFFECT

Dicky Rutnagur, 1978

At Madras, January 14, 15, 16, 18, 19, 1977. England won by 200 runs. The unfortunate Vaseline incident took place just before the innings subsided. Lever, who took five for 59 in the innings (two of them on the previous day) was reported by umpire Reuben to be carrying on his person a strip of surgical gauze impregnated with Vaseline. He considered it to be a breach of Law 46.

The MCC authorities did not deny the presence of the offending strip of gauze, but offered an explanation: "During the morning session, both Lever and Willis had suffered from smarting eyes because of sweat running into them from the forehead. So, on the advice of the team's physiotherapist, Mr Bernard Thomas, they went out wearing these gauze strips which were intended to divert the trickle of perspiration away from their eyes."

Ken Barrington, the MCC manager, said that while there had been a technical breach of the law governing fair and unfair play, the offence was totally unintentional. At a press conference the following day, the rest day, the captain and manager emphasised in further defence of Lever that the gauze strips were not worn until after lunch, and that by then England had made such large inroads into the Indian innings that such unfair methods were quite unnecessary.

Fuel had been added to the fire by Bedi, the Indian captain, stating after the incident that even at Delhi, during the First Test, he had suspicions that a polishing agent of some kind had been used. The remnants of the Indian innings folded up on the final morning. Underwood soon added Viswanath to his bag, and Willis (three for 18) and Lever hastened the end, which came well before lunch. India were all out for 83, their lowest total in a home Test.

England 262 (J. M. Brearley 59, A. W. Greig 54; B. S. Bedi 4-72)
and 185 (B. S. Chandrasekhar 5-50; E. A. S. Prasanna 4-55);
India 164 (J. K. Lever 5-59) and 83 (D. L. Underwood 4-38).

1979-80 – PAKISTANIS IN INDIA: PASSIONS SPILL OVER

1981

Much the same Pakistan side that had totally outplayed India at home a year earlier, and won the series 2–0, went down by the same margin in a tense, controversial rubber of six Tests [*India's first series victory over Pakistan*]. There was a very apparent division of loyalties within the [Pakistan] party. Discipline was low, with the players distracted by commercial and social interests. They alleged bias on the part of the umpires and in Bombay, during the Third Test, they accused the ground authorities of doctoring the pitch after the match had started. After a stormy Fourth Test, in which Sikander Bakht kicked down the stumps after having an appeal disallowed, Asif Iqbal talked of calling off the rest of the tour. The atmosphere on the field had been soured and standards of conduct had dropped to deplorable levels.

1979-80 – INDIA v PAKISTAN (FIFTH TEST): KING KAPIL   1981

At Madras, January 15, 16, 17, 19, 20, 1980. India won by ten wickets. Two men shaped this decisive Indian victory – Gavaskar, with an innings of 166, the longest played in a Test match by an Indian (593 minutes), and Kapil Dev, with an outstanding all-round performance. He took 11 wickets in the match, including seven for 56 (the best figures of his Test career) in the second innings, and contributed a boisterous 84 to India's total of 430. The great-hearted bowling of Kapil Dev minimised India's self-imposed disadvantage of going into the match with only four bowlers, off-spinner Yadav having been left out.

Pakistan 272 (Majid Khan 56; Kapil Dev 4-90)
and 233 (Wasim Raja 57, Javed Miandad 52; Kapil Dev 7-56);
India 430 (S. M. Gavaskar 166, Kapil Dev 84; Imran Khan 5-114) and 78-0.

1979-80 – INDIA v ENGLAND (GOLDEN JUBILEE TEST): BOTHAM EXTRA
Dicky Rutnagur, 1981

At Bombay, February 15, 17, 18, 19, February, 1980. England won by ten wickets. With the rival sides fatigued, both mentally and physically, at the end of an arduous season, the Test match to celebrate the Golden Jubilee of the Board of Control for Cricket in India produced poor cricket. But it was redeemed by an extraordinary all-round performance by Botham, whose versatility was in full bloom. There was hardly a session on which he did not bring his influence to bear, performing the unprecedented feat of scoring a century and capturing 13 wickets in a Test. Taylor, the England wicketkeeper, also established a new world Test record by taking ten catches in the match. Batting as indifferently as they did in Australia, England at 58 for five looked most unlikely to match India's score. But they were only 13 runs behind when they lost their next wicket two hours 20 minutes later. Botham, batting for 206 minutes and hitting 17 fours, scored 114 in an innings which was responsible and yet not lacking in enterprise.

India 242 (I. T. Botham 6-58) and 149 (Botham 7-48);
England 296 (Botham 114; K. D. Ghavri 5-52) and 98-0.

1984-85 – ROTHMANS TROPHY IN SHARJAH Tony Lewis, 1986

A four-nations tournament of one-day matches, played in Sharjah at the end of March, was won by India. Australia were runners-up and Pakistan beat England in the play-off for third place.

Although cricket in Sharjah began in 1981 and has been enthusiastically supported by many of the 700,000 Indians and Pakistanis who live in the United Arab Emirates, this was the first time that the Test match Boards of Control had chosen the sides and attended the competition. The representatives were delighted with what they saw – a well-organised contest, a new stadium for 12,000 spectators set like a mirage in the desert just outside the town, a field of real soil which had been hauled hundreds of miles by lorry before being heaped into a gaping hole in the sands, and a pitch on which the ball turned a lot, but which was level and fair.

The introduction of cricket to this particular part of the Emirates was the inspiration of the Arab businessman, Mr Abdulrahman Bukhatir. He grew to love cricket when he was a student in Pakistan and raised £2million to build the stadium. His cricket manager is Asif Iqbal, the former Pakistan and Kent all-rounder. They organise matches without profit in mind, except to make contributions to the benefits of players past or present.

1984-85 – ENGLAND IN INDIA: CHARACTER AND STATURE John Thicknesse, 1986

England got more than they bargained for on their tour of India, and it was much to their credit that they became the first team from any country to win a series there coming from behind. Within a few hours of their arrival in New Delhi, in the early morning of Wednesday, October 31, they were awoken with the news of the assassination of Mrs Gandhi, the Indian Prime Minister. The memory of this was still fresh when, on the eve of the First Test, less than four weeks later, the British Deputy High Commissioner, Mr Percy Norris, a cricket-lover who had entertained the touring party at a reception in his home the previous evening, was shot dead as he was being driven to his Bombay office. Both outrages took place within a mile or two of where the team were staying.

Mr Norris's murder affected them more personally, and with a Test due to start next day they felt under threat themselves. Had the decision been left to the team, or more particularly to a majority of the representatives of the British press, there is little doubt they would have taken the first available flight home. But as in Delhi, Tony Brown, the England manager, retained his sense of perspective, took advice from all relevant bodies, including the Foreign Office, and after consultation with the Test and County Cricket Board at Lord's, decided the best course was to stay and play.

England started the series disastrously, losing the First Test by eight wickets despite Mike Gatting's long-awaited maiden Test hundred. Laxman Sivaramakrishnan, still 18 at that stage and playing his first home Test, took 12 for 181 with leg-breaks and googlies. It all looked depressingly familiar to those who had been on Fletcher's tour three years before, and it was tempting to write off England's chances there and then. However, the expected sequence of dull draws on soul-destroying pitches did not follow. The Second Test, in Delhi, where Tim Robinson scored 160, was snatched by England's spinners, Phil Edmonds and Pat Pocock, when India succumbed to the pressure of relentless accuracy on the final afternoon; and a month later the series was decided by an exceptional display in the Fourth Test in Madras.

England, losing the toss, were in charge within an hour of the start of the Madras match when Neil Foster and Norman Cowans shared three wickets. Foster, playing his first Test of the series, took six for 104 (his match figures were 11 for 163) to bowl India out for 272, and then Graeme Fowler and Gatting thrust home the advantage by becoming the first pair of England batsmen to score 200 in the same Test.

Leadership did not seem to come naturally to David Gower. However, he developed a good team spirit and it was an advantage for him that Gatting, his vice-captain, and Edmonds, another forceful character, had the self-confidence and drive to influence matters on the field, their stature bolstered by personal success.

1986-87 – INDIA v AUSTRALIA (FIRST TEST): DEAD HEAT   R. Mohan, 1988

At Madras, September 18, 19, 20, 21, 22, 1986. Tied. On a hot and humid Monday, one of the most memorable Test match finishes was witnessed by some 30,000 spectators at Chepauk. For the second time in 1,052 Tests, the result was a tie, and coincidentally Australia had been involved each time. Yet there had been little hint of such a climax on the first four days; indeed, as India were being outplayed on the first three days, the thoughts of some Australians were possibly inclined to an innings victory. Only an inspired century against the odds by the Indian captain, Kapil Dev, precluded the possibility of India having to follow on after Australia had amassed their highest total in India – 574 in 742 minutes.

Jones cemented the solid start, first reaching his maiden Test hundred and then extending it to Australia's first double-hundred in a Test in India. Batting in all for eight hours 23 minutes, Jones had to overcome bouts of nausea and leg cramps.

Border declared first thing on the final morning, setting India 348 to win in a minimum of 87 overs. When they went in to tea at 190 for two, a last-session chase (158 off 30 overs) against an Australian side reduced to defence was on the cards, and when the final 20 overs began, India were suitably placed with 118 needed and seven wickets in hand.

With 18 needed off the last 30 balls, the match seemed to be India's, but when Chetan Sharma, caught on the boundary, and More were dismissed in one over by Bright, a third possible result – an Australian victory – was sighted for the first time that day. Yadav, who had struck Matthews for six to take India within seven runs of victory, was next out, bowled off his pads by Bright, leaving India 344 for nine with eight balls remaining. Maninder Singh defended the last two balls from Bright, which gave Shastri the strike for the last over, from Matthews. He blocked the first ball and, scenting victory off the second, hit a shade too eagerly: the ball went in front of deep square leg off a thick inside edge and a misfield enabled two runs to be taken safely. The next ball he placed calmly towards midwicket for the single which eliminated the possibility of an Australian win. Maninder defended the fourth ball, with some difficulty, and at 5.18pm was leg-before to Matthews's penultimate delivery. The Australians were jubilant, none more so than a tiring Matthews, who had been bowling since the ninth over and had taken his second five-wicket return, giving him ten in a match for the first time. With Bright also taking five wickets, all ten wickets in India's second innings had fallen to spin.

AUSTRALIA	First innings		Second innings
D. C. Boon c Kapil Dev b Sharma	122	– lbw b Maninder Singh	49
G. R. Marsh c Kapil Dev b Yadav	22	– b Shastri	11
D. M. Jones b Yadav	210	– c Azharuddin b Maninder Singh	24
R. J. Bright c Shastri b Yadav	30		
*A. R. Border c Gavaskar b Shastri	106	– b Maninder Singh	27
G. M. Ritchie run out	13	– c Pandit b Shastri	28
G. R. J. Matthews c Pandit b Yadav	44	– not out	27
S. R. Waugh not out	12	– not out	2
B 1, l-b 7, w 1, n-b 6	15	L-b 1, n-b 1	2

1-48 2-206 3-282 4-460   (7 wkts dec.) 574   1-31 2-81 3-94 4-125 5-165   (5 wkts dec.) 170
5-481 6-544 7-573

†T. J. Zoehrer, C. J. McDermott and B. A. Reid did not bat.

First Innings – Kapil Dev 18–5–52–0; Sharma 16–1–70–1; Maninder Singh 39–8–135–0; Yadav 49.5–9–142–4; Shastri 47–8–161–1; Srikkanth 1–0–6–0.
Second Innings – Kapil Dev 1–0–5–0; Sharma 6–0–19–0; Maninder Singh 19–2–60–3; Yadav 9–0–35–0; Shastri 14–2–50–2.

INDIA	First innings		Second innings
S. M. Gavaskar c and b Matthews	8	– c Jones b Bright	90
K. Srikkanth c Ritchie b Matthews	53	– c Waugh b Matthews	39
M. Amarnath run out	1	– c Boon b Matthews	51
M. Azharuddin c and b Bright	50	– c Ritchie b Bright	42
R. J. Shastri c Zoehrer b Matthews	62	– not out	48
C. S. Pandit c Waugh b Matthews	35	– b Matthews	39
*Kapil Dev c Border b Matthews	119	– c Bright b Matthews	1
†K. S. More c Zoehrer b Waugh	4	– lbw b Bright	0
C. Sharma c Zoehrer b Reid	30	– c McDermott b Bright	23
N. S. Yadav c Border b Bright	19	– b Bright	8
Maninder Singh not out	0	– lbw b Matthews	0
B 1, l-b 9, n-b 6	16	B 1, l-b 3, n-b 2	6

1-62 2-65 3-65 4-142 5-206 6-220 7-245   397   1-55 2-158 3-204 4-251 5-253 6-291   347
8-330 9-387   7-331 8-334 9-344

First Innings – McDermott 14–2–59–0; Reid 18–4–93–1; Matthews 28.2–3–103–5; Bright 23–3–88–2; Waugh 11–2–44–1.
Second Innings – McDermott 5–0–27–0; Reid 10–2–48–0; Matthews 39.5–7–146–5; Bright 25–3–94–5; Waugh 4–1–16–0; Border 3–0–12–0.

Umpires: D. N. Dotiwalla and V. Vikramraju.

Yorkshire v Northamptonshire. At Sheffield, July 14, 16, 17, 1962. After Yorkshire gained the lead Andrew, the Northamptonshire wicketkeeper, went on to bowl and took the first two wickets of his career. Binks, the Yorkshire wicketkeeper, also bowled, when Northamptonshire went in again.

Little Wonder No. 76

1986-87 – INDIA v PAKISTAN (FOURTH TEST): SUNNY DELIGHT

R. Mohan, 1988

At Ahmedabad, March 4, 5, 7, 8, 9, 1987. Drawn. Gavaskar brought a sense of occasion to the 11th consecutive draw between these two countries when, with a delectable late cut off Ijaz Faqih, he scored the 58th run needed for his 10,000 runs in Test cricket. The first to scale this summit, he achieved it in his 124th Test and 212th innings. The fourth day was marred by crowd disturbances in a city with a history of communal trouble. In the afternoon, the Pakistan outfielders were pelted with stones and, having with the umpires' consent taken his players off, Imran was reluctant to continue. Kapil Dev and Gavaskar appealed for calm over the public-address system, and when play resumed after tea, some 50 minutes having been lost, the Pakistanis injected a dose of ironic humour as six of them took the field wearing helmets.

Pakistan 395 (Ijaz Faqih 105, Imran Khan 72, Manzoor Elahi 52; N. S. Yadav 4-109)

and 135-2 (Rizwan-uz-Zaman 58);

India 323 (D. B. Vengsarkar 109, S. M. Gavaskar 63, Kapil Dev 50*; Wasim Akram 4-60).

1986-87 – INDIA v PAKISTAN (FIFTH TEST): RIVETING THEATRE

R. Mohan, 1988

At Bangalore, March 13, 14, 15, 17, 1987. Pakistan won by 16 runs to record their first series win in India and only their third victory in any series outside Pakistan. The behaviour of the pitch, so encouraging to spin bowling, provided a match of riveting theatre, although both captains had anticipated seaming conditions. India's cause [*chasing 221*] was not helped when they lost Srikkanth and Amarnath to successive balls and Vengsarkar was bowled on the eve of the rest day. But on the fourth day, on a pitch which allowed even an off-spinner to bowl bouncers, Gavaskar gave a masterly exhibition of technique and judgment. Only when he was out, having batted five hours 23 minutes and faced 266 balls for his 96, caught at slip off a ball that kicked off a good length, could Pakistan assume victory. A late chancey charge by Binny cut the margin to 16, leaving India to consider what might have been had Kapil Dev and Shastri been able to resist the rush of blood that cost them their wickets.

Pakistan 116 (Maninder Singh 7-27) and 249 (R. J. Shastri 4-69);
India 145 (D. B. Vengsarkar 50; Iqbal Qasim 5-48, Tauseef Ahmed 5-54)
and 204 (S. M. Gavaskar 96; Qasim 4-73, Tauseef 4-85).

Pakistan thus won the five-Test series 1–0 to complete their first series victory in India. The Bangalore result ended a sequence of 11 successive draws between the two countries.

1987-88 – INDIA v WEST INDIES (Fourth Test): TRUE SPECTACLE

Dicky Rutnagur, 1989

At Madras, January 11, 12, 14, 15, 1988. India won by 255 runs. India's winning margin of 255 runs was the most decisive of their six victories against West Indies. Its main author was a new cap in Hirwani, a bespectacled, 19-year-old leg-spinner, who had the assistance of an underprepared pitch which afforded turn from the opening day. In the circumstances, the scales were tipped heavily in India's favour when Shastri, captaining for the first time in a Test match, won the toss. Hirwani captured eight wickets in each innings to equal the Australian R. A. L. Massie's feat of taking 16 wickets on his debut, against England at Lord's in 1972. If Hirwani was able to give the ball air, as he did, and challenge the batsmen to counter-attack, it was because of India's first-innings total of 382, which was owed principally to a dashing 109 by Kapil Dev, scored off only 119 balls and including 17 fours.

The pitch, if a nightmare for the batsmen, made equally high demands on the wicketkeepers, and More deserved much credit for stumping six batsmen in the match, five of them in the second innings. Both figures were a record for stumpings in a Test.

India 382 (Kapil Dev 109, Arun Lal 69; W. W. Davis 4-76)
and 217-8 dec. (W. V. Raman 83; C. A. Walsh 4-55);
West Indies 184 (I. V. A. Richards 68; N. D. Hirwani 8-61) and 160 (A. L. Logie 67; Hirwani 8-75).

1991-92 – SOUTH AFRICANS IN INDIA: WELCOME BOK

Matthew Engel, 1993

Twenty-one years and eight months after Ali Bacher took a catch at mid-off to dismiss Alan Connolly in a Test at Port Elizabeth, the cricketers of South Africa – isolated ever since because of global opposition to the apartheid policy – rejoined the world by playing three one-day internationals in India. In the intervening years people had often wondered how, when or even whether South Africa's isolation might end: no one could have dared invent an ending quite so ironic and incongruous as this.

The South Africans arrived in Calcutta, four months after rejoining the International Cricket Council, at the insistence of the Board of Control for Cricket in India after Pakistan had called off a scheduled tour because of worsening Hindu–Moslem tensions. The visit was arranged almost as hurriedly as some of the rebel tours in which South Africa had lately specialised. But it was organised with the special blessing of the Marxist government of West Bengal. Thousands of people lined the route from the airport to the hotel to welcome the team, carrying banners with slogans that only a few months would have been politically unthinkable: "South Africa–India friendship long live". The tourists' plane was said to be the first from South Africa ever to land in India.

Another banner at the hotel welcomed "the Springboks", but this was hurriedly torn down at the insistence of the United Cricket Board of South Africa, which was anxious not to use a nickname associated with the days of exclusively white sport. The 14-man squad – captained by Clive Rice and managed by Bacher, South Africa's last Test captain before isolation – was all white, but the party included four youngsters, two white and two black, brought along for the experience and to make a political and diplomatic point.

1991-92 – INDIA v SOUTH AFRICA (FIRST ONE-DAY INTERNATIONAL)

Matthew Engel, 1993

At Calcutta, November 10, 1991. India won by three wickets. South Africa's first officially blessed representative match in almost 22 years, first one-day international and first-ever game against India attracted a crowd widely claimed as beating the world record for a day's cricket of 90,800. The cricket was a disappointment and India's victory was easier than the margin suggested. Even in defeat, the South Africans were still overwhelmed by the occasion: "I know how Neil Armstrong felt when he stood on the moon," said their captain Clive Rice.

South Africa 177-8 (47 overs) (K. C. Wessels 50);
India 178-7 (40.4 overs) (S. R. Tendulkar 62, P. K. Amre 55; A. A. Donald 5-29).

1992-93 – ENGLAND IN INDIA: STUBBLE TROUBLE

Peter Hayter, 1994

While England were going down to a terrible defeat in a one-day international in Sri Lanka, the Test and County Cricket Board met at Lord's to discuss the England team's spectacular failure on the three-month tour of the subcontinent.

A. C. Smith, the chief executive, insisted that the debate on England matters had been lengthy, wide-ranging and, above all, constructive. Unfortunately, this was not what came through in the newspapers. The main item of news to emerge from this meeting was nothing to do with the cricket. There is a modern fashion for designer stubble, Dexter was quoted as saying, and some people believe it to be very attractive. But it is aggravating to others and we will be looking at the whole question of people's facial hair.

Thousands of miles away, even the tour manager Bob Bennett had been criticised after he was pictured wearing a T-shirt and ill-fitting shorts at a press conference. He had already written to the board to say the players had been made aware of their responsibilities concerning their appearance. One of the players expressed relief: "At least now we know we didn't lose because we played terribly," he said.

It was in their specific technical preparation that England were badly let down. After having returned from a costly spying mission to watch India's Test in Johannesburg, Fletcher [Keith, team manager] announced the following verdict on [Anil Kumble], the bespectacled leg-spinner: "I didn't see him turn a single ball from leg to off. I don't believe we will have much problem with him." Fortunately for Fletcher, on a tour like this, such a statement seemed merely a routine misjudgment.

1992-93 – INDIA v ENGLAND (THIRD TEST): HOME-TOWN DELIGHT   1994

At Bombay, February 19, 20, 21, 22, 23, 1993. India won by an innings and 15 runs. England became the first side to lose every game of a Test series in India, despite the commanding century from Hick for which he and the England selectors had been waiting since his debut in 1991. Hick knew that his performances on this tour might make or break his career after the disappointment of his baffling failure to bridge the gap between county and Test cricket. Pressure on him to live up to his undoubted but unproven potential was even greater because of the controversy over the omission of Gower.

Once again, the Indian batsmen capitalised on some woeful bowling and fielding. Sidhu and Prabhakar put on 109 for the first wicket. On 174, Sidhu was picked up at silly point off Tufnell. In the next over, Kambli skied a simple catch to long-off and DeFreitas made a hash of it. The spill instantly drained the England players of their last dregs of optimism. Kambli went on to make 224 on his home ground, his first Test century in only his third match. Only 11 men have scored more in their maiden Test century, and it was the highest score ever for India against England. The third-wicket partnership with his Bombay schoolfriend Tendulkar produced 194 runs, a partnership that produced special home-town delight for the crowd. Kambli's was an innings of rare quality, full of daring strokeplay executed with a joyfulness that rippled round the ground. He batted nearly ten hours, faced 411 balls and hit 23 fours. It enabled his team to reach 591 and leave their opponents completely demoralised.

England 347 (G. A. Hick 178) and 229 (R. A. Smith 62, M. W. Gatting 61; A. Kumble 4-70);
India 591 (V. G. Kambli 224, N. S. Sidhu 79, S. R. Tendulkar 78, P. K. Amre 57; P. C. R. Tufnell 4-142).

Counties abolish amateur-pro status. At the Advisory County Cricket Committee at Lord's on November 26, 1962, the first-class counties decided by a clear majority to abolish amateur and professional status and call all players cricketers.

Little Wonder No. 77

1998-99 – INDIA v PAKISTAN (FIRST TEST): POLITICS PARKED

Qamar Ahmed, 2000

At Chennai, January 28, 29, 30, 31, 1999. Pakistan won by 12 runs. The first Test between India and Pakistan for nine years began amid massive security, after vandalism by Hindu extremists had forced the Indian board to transfer the match from Delhi to Chennai. The Chidambaram Stadium was guarded by 3,000 police and military officials. Well before the end of the game, though, the talk was not of politics but of thrilling cricket.

A nailbiting finish on the fourth day saw India, chasing 271, slump to 82 for five – two of the wickets controversially given out by umpire Dunne. When Tendulkar and Mongia combined to add 136 for the sixth wicket, however, they seemed to be on their way to victory. Then Mongia was caught for 52. Still Tendulkar kept going, despite a back strain, and India were only 17 from their target when he holed out at mid-off, trying to hit Saqlain Mushtaq out of the ground. He had batted 405 minutes and scored 136, his 18th Test hundred, including 18 fours. But India's last three wickets added only four more runs; Saqlain finished them off with five for 93, giving him ten for 187 in the match. The Pakistanis bowed to the ground in prayer and embarked on a lap of honour, to a standing ovation from the Chennai crowd, whose sporting behaviour won much praise.

Pakistan 238 (Moin Khan 60, Yousuf Youhana 53; A. Kumble 6-70)
and 286 (Shahid Afridi 141, Inzamam-ul-Haq 51; B. K. V. Prasad 6-33);
India 254 (S. C. Ganguly 54, R. Dravid 53; Saqlain Mushtaq 5-94)
and 258 (S. R. Tendulkar 136, N. R. Mongia 52; Saqlain 5-93).

1998-99 – INDIA v PAKISTAN (SECOND TEST): IMPOSSIBLE TO DREAM

Qamar Ahmed, 2000

At Delhi, February 4, 5, 6, 7, 1999. India won by 212 runs. India won a massive victory, their first over Pakistan since 1979-80, to draw the series. But the headlines belonged to leg-spinner Anil Kumble. He claimed all ten wickets in Pakistan's second innings, becoming only the second man in history to take ten in a Test innings, following English off-spinner Jim Laker in 1956. Kumble's match figures of 14 for 149 were the third-best by an Indian in Tests.

Pakistan had little hope of winning after being set a formidable target of 420, but needed only a draw to take the series, and had seemed well placed at 101 without loss. After lunch, Kumble operated from the Pavilion end: he bowled 20.3 overs and claimed ten for 47, aided by some brilliant fielding and a substandard pitch – hastily repaired after the fundamentalists' vandalism a month earlier.

Kumble started the slide when Shahid Afridi was given out caught behind dabbing outside off stump. With his next ball, Kumble had Ijaz Ahmed lbw as he stretched forward. Inzamam-ul-Haq averted the hat-trick, but played on off an inside edge minutes later. Pakistan slumped to 128 for six, and Kumble had taken six for 15 in 44 balls. "That was the moment when I thought all ten could be mine," he said afterwards.

But he had to wait until after tea for No. 7, as Salim Malik and Wasim Akram held firm in a stand of 58. Then Kumble resumed the demolition. He bowled Malik, trying to pull; Mushtaq Ahmed was caught at gully off an awkward bounce; and the next ball hit Saqlain Mushtaq on the toe and trapped him lbw. That ended Kumble's 26th over, with one wicket remaining. Azharuddin privately instructed Srinath to bowl a wayward line in his next over. Wasim, who had resisted for an hour and a half, then kept out the hat-trick ball, and the next one, but top-edged Kumble's third ball to Laxman at short leg.

Kumble was carried back to the pavilion on his colleagues' shoulders as the crowd rejoiced. "My first reaction is that we have won," he said. "No one dreams of taking ten wickets in an innings, because you can't. The pitch was of variable bounce, and cutting and pulling was not easy. All I had to do was pitch in the right area, mix up my pace and spin, and trap the batsmen. The first wicket was the hardest to get – the openers were cruising."

The rest was history, for Kumble, and for Richard Stokes, a 53-year-old English businessman. As a schoolboy, he had seen Jim Laker take some of his ten wickets at Old Trafford in 1956, and he arrived at Feroz Shah Kotla – on his birthday – just in time to see Kumble repeat the feat.

India 252 (M. Azharuddin 67, S. Ramesh 60; Saqlain Mushtaq 5-94)

and 339 (Ramesh 96, S. C. Ganguly 62*; Saqlain 5-122);

Pakistan 172 (A. Kumble 4-75)

and 207 (Saeed Anwar 69; Kumble 10-74).

1999-2000 – SOUTH AFRICANS IN INDIA: WHIFF OF FIXING   Dicky Rutnagur, 2001

By beating India 2–0 in a two-match rubber, South Africa ended India's sequence of 14 unbeaten home series since Pakistan won there in March 1987. Consequently, victory also gave them the distinction of becoming the only country in that 13-year period to win series in all three countries of the subcontinent. Sadly, South Africa's achievement would be first undermined by accusations of match-fixing against their captain, Hansie Cronje, and four team-mates, then overshadowed by Cronje's admission to the King Commission in June that he had accepted money from bookmakers since South Africa's tour of India in 1996. Cronje continued to deny all allegations of match-fixing, but the integrity of his captaincy, along with his team's record, had been seriously besmirched. For the Pepsi Cup one-day tournament that followed, India's captaincy passed to Sourav Ganguly, who immediately led them to victory in the first two games and went on to win the series 3–2. But the sweet smell of success did not last long. Within three weeks, Delhi police investigations into match-fixing, following intercepted phone calls between Indian bookmakers and between Cronje and a bookmaker, cast doubt on the games at Kochi, Faridabad and Nagpur.

2000-01 – AUSTRALIANS IN INDIA: FINAL FRONTIER Dicky Rutnagur, 2002

Although the Australians began the tour with the awesome achievement of 15 consecutive Test wins, they deemed victory in the series against India as absolutely essential if they were to stand comparison with the greatest teams Australia had fielded. Winning in India was, in their eyes, a conquest of the "final frontier", not least because 31 years and four tours had passed since Australia last left there triumphant. Steve Waugh's team seemed to be on the point of emulating Bill Lawry's when they won the First Test at Mumbai, by ten wickets in three days, and then made India follow on 274 behind in the Second at Kolkata (formerly Calcutta).

2000-01 – INDIA v AUSTRALIA (SECOND TEST): VERY VERY SPECIAL
Dicky Rutnagur, 2002

At Kolkata, March 11, 12, 13, 14, 15, 2001. India won by 171 runs. An astonishing Indian recovery provided several records and culminated in only the third victory in Test history for a side who had followed on. Australia were the victims in the previous instances also, losing to England at Sydney in 1894-95 and Leeds in 1981. Laxman amassed 281, the highest Test score for India, while his partnership of 376 with Dravid was an Indian fifth-wicket record. Their feats almost overshadowed the outstanding performance of off-spinner Harbhajan Singh, who claimed India's first Test hat-trick while capturing a career-best seven wickets in the first innings, and followed up with a match-winning six in the second.

India lost four wickets before the first-innings deficit of 274 was cleared, but as Dravid's batting recovered its sparkle in Laxman's company, the game was transformed. They batted together for 104 overs, including the whole of the fourth day, when they added 335 in 90 overs. Their efforts not only dispelled India's troubles, but opened up an avenue to a momentous victory. Dravid was eventually run out for a chanceless 180 from 353 balls in seven hours 24 minutes, with 21 fours.

When Ganguly declared with a lead of 383, India had equalled the second-highest Test total by a side batting second. It meant Australia had to bat out 75 overs for a draw, on a pitch affording turn without being devilish. Their prospects looked good when Hayden, given an early life, and Slater stayed together for 23 overs. But once they were separated, wickets fell at regular intervals. Australia were all out in the 69th over, and their record run of Test wins had come to an abrupt and spectacular halt.

Australia 445 (S. R. Waugh 110, M. L. Hayden 97, J. L. Langer 58; Harbhajan Singh 7-123)
and 212 (Hayden 67; Harbhajan 6-73);
India 171 (V. V. S. Laxman 59; G. D. McGrath 4-18)
and 657-7 dec. (Laxman 281, R. Dravid 180).

India won the series 2–1. Australia had to wait until 2004-05 to breach their "final frontier" and win a Test series in India for the first time since 1969-70.

2004-05 – INDIA v PAKISTAN (SECOND ONE-DAY INTERNATIONAL)

Osman Samiuddin, 2006

At Visakhapatnam, April 5, 2005. India won by 58 runs. A maiden international century of unyielding brutality by wicketkeeper Mahendra Singh Dhoni lit up a sleepy seaside town, overshadowed a stellar batting line-up, ensured overnight messianic status and enabled India to go 2–0 up. Dhoni, sporting red-tinted hair and the strut of rock royalty, unleashed a bewildering array of orthodox and impudent strokes, including four sixes, in his 148 off 123 balls, an Indian record against Pakistan. He began with a slapped straight-drive for four first ball, then grew irreverent, never more than when he played a ramped shot against Abdul Razzaq that flew over the keeper's head.

India 356-9 (50 overs) (M. S. Dhoni 148, V. Sehwag 74, R. Dravid 52; Naved-ul-Hasan 3-54);
Pakistan 298 (44.1 overs) (Abdul Razzaq 88, Yousuf Youhana 71; A. Nehra 4-72, Yuvraj Singh 3-55).

2004-05 – THE DHONI FAMILY AND THEIR STRUGGLE AGAINST THE EUNUCHS

2006

The morning after Dhoni's triumph, his parents had a set of unwelcome visitors at their home when a group of eunuchs barged in, showered them with traditional blessings and demanded 50,000 rupees (about £600) for doing so. Dhoni's father, Pan Singh, slipped away to a neighbour's house and phoned for help. His mother plied the eunuchs with sweets until the police arrived. It is customary in India to give money to eunuchs on auspicious occasions – but of late their demands have become regarded as a nuisance, and the police are regularly called.

2005-06 – INDIA v ENGLAND (THIRD TEST): COMEBACK KIDS

Rahul Bhattacharya, 2007

At Mumbai, March 18, 19, 20, 21, 22, 2006. England won by 212 runs. Andrew Flintoff asked for a "monumental effort" from his team before this match, and they delivered a monumental victory – England's first Test win in India in 21 years, and their biggest by runs on Indian soil. It squared the series 1–1, a fine achievement for any party touring here, but a marvellous one for a side missing half their first-choice players. This was the complete performance from England: debutants, comeback kids and ancient journeymen were galvanised in the liquid heat of Mumbai by Flintoff. While an estimated 3,000 visiting English fans celebrated with uncontained joy at the Wankhede Stadium and in the bars of South Mumbai, home supporters were mutinous.

The final day will linger in the memory as one of the most frenetic and dramatic bouts of Test cricket between these nations. From 75 for three at lunch, India crumbled to 100 all out in another 15 overs. Flintoff, hurling thunderbolts, finished with the remarkable analysis of three for 14 from 11 overs; Udal, whose off-spin had brought him three wickets at 92.33 in his three previous Tests, went one better than his captain with four for 14. Dravid later described the collapse as "a collective lapse of reasoning". That lapse was illustrated vividly when Dhoni made a madman's swipe off Udal to Panesar at mid-off – just three balls after Panesar had somehow failed to get his hands around an identical chance.

Flintoff said afterwards that the team had roused themselves during the lunch interval by singing along and thumping their feet to Johnny Cash's "Ring of Fire", and not even the drenching humidity could douse the flames around India thereafter.

England 400 (A. J. Strauss 128, O. A. Shah 88, A. Flintoff 50; S. Sreesanth 4-70) **and 191** (Flintoff 50); **India 279** (M. S. Dhoni 64, R. Dravid 52; J. M. Anderson 4-40) **and 100** (S. D. Udal 4-14).

2008 – INDIAN PREMIER LEAGUE: FLIGHT TWENTY20 TAKES OFF

Lawrence Booth, 2009

Such was the impact of the Indian Premier League on world cricket that it created major headlines two months before the second tournament was due to start. When Andrew Flintoff and Kevin Pietersen were both sold for $1.55m (well over £1m) in Goa's Hermitage Hall on February 6, 2009, they became "Cricket's Most Expensive Players" and "Richest Cricketers Ever".

Much to their chagrin, England players had missed out on the inaugural IPL, apart from Dimitri Mascarenhas. While most of the most famous names in the contemporary game flocked to India in April 2008 – drawn by unprecedented sums of money and, also, by unprecedented glamour for a cricket event – England's Test players had to represent their counties and play against New Zealand. Never again: such was the collective determination of Flintoff, Pietersen and several others to go east, and fulfil the wishes of the IPL chief commissioner Lalit Modi, that they forced major concessions out of the England and Wales Cricket Board. A three-week window, from the start of the second IPL tournament on April 10, 2009, until May 1, only five days before the Lord's Test against West Indies, was eventually agreed. For the first time English cricketers were going to play outside England during the English season other than on national service. Such was the shift in the game's balance of power.

Some had tried to argue after the inaugural IPL that it was little more than a glorified domestic league. After the signings of Flintoff and Pietersen, this argument ran out of its remaining legs. The IPL was established as the place to be for any young cricketers, and for older ones who were not old-fashioned specialists.

The IPL's second auction appeared able to defy the worldwide recession thanks to the success of its inaugural tournament, which at times suggested a soap opera on fast forward. In the space of just over seven weeks, there were petty rows and even physical ones, dolled-up women in short skirts, gratuitous sackings, walk-on parts for celebrities, the occasional cliffhanger and an implausible main storyline – all of it underpinned by the bottom line.

But it was hard to escape the conclusion that much of the sporting drama was pretty good too – from the moment Brendon McCullum spectacularly raised the curtain on a heady night in Bangalore, to Rajasthan Royals' last-ball victory over Chennai Super Kings in the final in Mumbai 44 evenings later. The subsequent rush by rival national boards to establish their own Twenty20 leagues spoke volumes for a tournament which some had feared would drown in a sea of hype.

Even the potentially tricky moments were somehow turned to the competition's advantage. When Harbhajan Singh slapped Sreesanth, the IPL's chairman and commissioner, Lalit Modi, emerged smelling of roses by taking swift and decisive action against the off-spinner; when Charu Sharma, CEO of struggling Bangalore Royal Challengers, was sacked, comparisons were made with the unforgiving but glamorous world of English football, a sporting world regarded with envy by IPL insiders; and when Shane Warne publicly denounced Sourav Ganguly following a disputed catch in a game in Jaipur, the debate made headlines for days. It all meant a greater degree of IPL-consciousness for the average Indian.

More fortunate for the tournament organisers was the identity of the eventual winners. Warne's Rajasthan Royals charmed through their sheer improbability. None of the other seven franchises had spent as little at the first auction, in Mumbai, and none had been so written off in advance. But Warne's ability to get the best out of a motley crew of Indian youngsters and overseas imports was the story of the tournament. And by embodying one of sport's most enduring themes – the triumph of the underdog – it reminded observers that the IPL really could be about more than just money.

2008-09 – ENGLAND IN INDIA: THE SHOW MUST GO ON   David Hopps, 2009

England's 2008 tour of India was one of the most politically significant in cricket history. From the moment that the vibrant Indian city of Mumbai fell prey to Islamist extremism, and a shaken touring party flew home without playing the last two one-day matches because of safety fears, arguments resounded about whether they should return to fulfil the two Tests before Christmas. That they did go back was a decision that did them great credit. The prime minister, Gordon Brown, called them "brave and courageous".

The stock of Kevin Pietersen, an undaunted and self-confident captain, had never been higher; his influence never more apparent. But Pietersen's ambitions went beyond the bounds of ordinary mortals. Even before the Tests concluded, he was pressing the ECB to sack the coach, Peter Moores, who he felt was not up to the job. A "him or me" ultimatum became public knowledge (through no fault of his own); Moores was sacked shortly after the tour, but Pietersen, whose ego was perceived to be out of control, was forced to relinquish the captaincy.

2008-09 – INDIA v ENGLAND (First Test): for all Indians

Scyld Berry, 2009

At Chennai, December 11, 12, 13, 14, 15, 2008. India won by six wickets. A historic occasion, and a magnificent match, culminated in the highest fourth-innings run-chase ever to succeed in an Asian Test, enabling India to win with about an hour to spare. The start came only two weeks after the terrorist attack on Mumbai, and the Test was staged amid "presidential-style" security, but by the end the most famous of all Mumbaikars had gone some way to erasing the memories. In a century he dedicated to all Indians, Sachin Tendulkar masterminded the run-chase after Virender Sehwag had snatched the initiative from England's grasp with batting of equal brilliance.

Requiring a further 256 on the final day, India were always ahead of the rate. Scoring a hundred in a successful fourth-innings run-chase was, according to Tendulkar, something he had wanted, the one achievement missing from his CV: in consequence, he rated his hundred as "up there" and "one of the best". It was a masterclass in its conception – of what shots to play, and how often – and in its execution, especially of the sweep in all its forms. Pietersen changed his bowlers with the greatest frequency but never found a pair to stem the flow.

England 316 (A. J. Strauss 123, M. J. Prior 53*, A. N. Cook 52)
and 311-9 dec. (Strauss 108, P. D. Collingwood 108);
India 241 (M. S. Dhoni 53)
and 387-4 (S. R. Tendulkar 103*, Yuvraj Singh 85*, V. Sehwag 83, G. Gambhir 66).

2009 – View From The Summit

Anand Vasu, 2010

For years – no, decades – the complaint India's players endured from their overseas peers was that the country produced brilliant individuals but few world-beating teams. In the meantime, Indian cricket administrators were traditionally never accused of brilliance, but it was said they were worried only about votes or money. Against this backdrop, 2009 was a crucial year for Indian cricket. The team rose to the top of the ICC's Test rankings for the first time – yet this only sharpened the criticism of administrators.

If cricket's biggest challenge is asserting the primacy of Test matches, three specific areas require addressing: the need for a careful balance between bat and ball, only ensured by sporting pitches; thoughtful scheduling of matches in all formats; and a quality experience at grounds for the paying public. On all these counts, the Board of Control for Cricket in India abdicated its substantial responsibility.

Getting a lift: Yuvraj Singh picks up Sachin Tendulkar, who finished on 103 not out, after the pair had led India to a six-wicket victory over England at Chennai in 2008-09. The Test came two weeks after the Mumbai terrorist attacks

2009-10 – INDIA v SOUTH AFRICA (SECOND ONE-DAY INTERNATIONAL)

Ken Borland, 2011

At Gwalior, February 24, 2010. India won by 153 runs. Sachin Tendulkar produced a dazzling display of top-class strokeplay to become the first man to score a double-century in a one-day international, and sealed India's series victory. He needed just 147 balls, having reached his 46th one-day hundred (to go with 47 in Tests) in 90, and he collected 25 fours and three sixes. From the outset, Tendulkar looked on course for something special. After the early loss of Sehwag, he raced to his fifty in 37 balls, driving superbly square of the wicket; with Karthik ensuring his senior partner had plenty of strike, India breezed to 219 for two in the 34th over. Tendulkar had 124 at that stage, and he forged on remorselessly, his placement so perfect, his timing so precise that South Africa were simply blown away. Dhoni's pyrotechnics – seven fours and four sixes off 35 balls – ensured the innings ended in a blur, even though cramp meant Tendulkar was running out of puff towards the end. He passed the previous one-day international record of 194 (shared by Saeed Anwar of Pakistan and Zimbabwe's Charles Coventry) in the 46th over, before being briefly becalmed as Dhoni flailed away. But a single steered behind point off the third ball of the final over brought up the historic 200, amid a tremendous hullabaloo from the capacity crowd.

India 401-3 (50 overs) (S. R. Tendulkar 200*, K. D. Karthik 79, M. S. Dhoni 68*);
South Africa 248 (42.5 overs) (A. B. de Villiers 114*; S. Sreesanth 3-49).

Little Wonder No. 78

Wisden 1963. The Gillette trophy: The Advisory Committee accepted a block grant of £6,500 from Gillette, who will sponsor the new knockout competition. This grant, together with television and broadcasting fees, to be divided equally among the 17 first-class counties. A trophy, to be known as the Gillette trophy, would also be awarded to the winners. Meritorious performances in each of the 16 games involved would warrant awards, to the man or men of the match, such awards to be made at the conclusion of each tie on the ground.

2010-11 – INDIA v AUSTRALIA (FIRST TEST): YES, NO, WAIT

Daniel Brettig, 2011

At Mohali, October 1, 2, 3, 4, 5, 2010. India won by one wicket. India scrambled to the narrowest of their 106 Test victories despite requiring 92 runs at the time the eighth wicket went down. That they did so was thanks to yet another miraculous performance by V. V. S. Laxman, a man who produces the impossible on a regular basis against Australia. This time he managed it with the impediment of back spasms so serious that he had been unable to bat until No. 10 in the first innings.

Laxman would still have fallen short without an ally, and he found a perfect foil on the final day in Ishant Sharma, who took on the air of no less a tail-end tormentor than Test double-centurion Jason Gillespie. Johnson did shake Sharma up with short balls, but only 11 runs were needed when Hilfenhaus finally dismissed him, lbw to an off-cutter that would have missed leg stump (once again, the Decision Review System was not in use as the ICC and the Indian board bickered over who should pay for it).

Ojha has few pretensions as a batsman and even fewer as a sprinter, and Laxman lost his characteristic cool, wildly urging his partner to run harder, even threatening to use his bat as punishment. These comedic gesticulations did little to ease the tension, and what turned out to be the final over of the match began with six required and last man Ojha on strike. Johnson whirred one at middle stump, Ojha was struck on the pad and the Australians went up as one. Their shock at umpire Bowden's refusal – he was to argue forcefully for an inside edge – quickly turned to grief when the substitute Steve Smith at point threw for the run-out and screamed in exasperation when no one on the leg side was around to back up. The resultant four overthrows left only two runs to win, and two leg-byes a couple of balls later did the trick.

The game – only the 12th Test to end in victory by a single wicket – was rightly celebrated as one of the greatest of the modern era, at a time when it was most needed.

Australia 428 (S. R. Watson 126, T. D. Paine 92, R. T. Ponting 71; Zaheer Khan 5-94) **and 192** (Watson 56);
India 405 (S. R. Tendulkar 98, S. K. Raina 86, R. Dravid 77, V. Sehwag 59; M. G. Johnson 5-64)
and 216-9 (V. V. S. Laxman 73*; B. W. Hilfenhaus 4-57).

2012-13 – INDIA v ENGLAND: HISTORY MEN George Dobell, 2013

England left India celebrating a victory for the history books. And yet, in the aftermath of their nine-wicket defeat in the First Test at Ahmedabad, it had been hard to avoid a sense of gloomy inevitability. Ranged against them, apparently, were all their old failings – and some recent ones too: scars from the 3–0 defeat in the UAE by Pakistan and their slow bowlers were still raw. They had not won a series in Asia, Bangladesh excepted, for 12 years; and they had not won in India since 1984-85, when David Gower's side had become the first – and, until now, only – visiting team to beat them in a Test series after falling behind.

2012-13 – INDIA v ENGLAND (SECOND TEST): SPIN TWINS
Gideon Brooks, 2013

At Mumbai (Wankhede Stadium), November 23, 24, 25, 26, 2012. England won by ten wickets. When Cook lost what looked like a crucial toss, he gazed heavenwards in frustration. And well he might have looked away from the source of his expected chagrin – the roughened red Mumbai soil and a pitch, used for a Ranji Trophy match three weeks earlier, that Dhoni had demanded should spin like a waltzer from ball one. Less than ten sessions later, Cook could have been forgiven for falling jubilantly into the Wankhede's dusty embrace after England had completed a scarcely believable ten-wicket win. It not only dragged them level in the series, but was arguably one of their finest away victories in the 79 years since they had first played Test cricket on the subcontinent, a mile or so away along Marine Drive at the Bombay Gymkhana.

Instead, Cook wrapped his arms round fellow opener Compton, before whipping out three stumps and handing two of them on the dressing-room steps to the pair who had done most to make victory possible – Pietersen, the Man of the Match, and Panesar, a close runner-up. For India, it was only a second home defeat in 24 Tests. Gallingly, they had been trumped in conditions thought to be ideally suited to a three-pronged spin attack, with Harbhajan Singh replacing the injured fast bowler Umesh Yadav; not since India themselves hosted South Africa at Kanpur in 2004-05 had a team entered a Test with only one specialist seamer.

Cook's was a nice touch after his first victory as full-time captain, which arrested an alarming slide in fortunes since the turn of the year. The personal milestones were a bonus: both Cook and Pietersen equalled England's Test record of 22 centuries, while Panesar – who finished with a career-best 11 for 210 – shared 19 wickets with Swann, the best performance by English spinners in a Test since Tony Lock and Jim Laker, who also took 19, against New Zealand at Headingley in 1958.

India 327 (C. A. Pujara 135, R. Ashwin 68; M. S. Panesar 5-129, G. P. Swann 4-70)
and 142 (G. Gambhir 65; Panesar 6-81, Swann 4-43);
England 413 (K. P. Pietersen 186, A. N. Cook 122; P. P. Ojha 5-143) **and 58-0.**

PAKISTAN

No Test-playing nation has contrived to include so much that is brilliant, bad or bizarre into such a short time span as Pakistan. "Cricket and life have for so long been one and the same thing in Pakistan, wrapped in such an embrace of love, disgust, hate and ecstasy," Osman Samiuddin wrote in *Wisden* 2010 about the "morbid inevitability" of the Lahore terrorist attacks on the Sri Lankan team in March 2009. In 60 years at international cricket's top table Pakistan they have produced fast bowlers who combined searing pace and athletic beauty, spinners of geometric genius and batsmen with finesse and fight. There have also been ball-biters and spot-fixers, aggressors and diplomats. Pakistan cricket is a non-stop page-turner. Pakistan's Test debut in India in 1952-53 "was not without encouragement for the future", according to *Wisden*, which was particularly interested in the "youthful talent" of the 17-year-old Hanif Mohammad, a member of Pakistan's great cricketing dynasty. But their first home Test series in 1954-55, also against India, was a dour affair. The two countries, in political and then military conflict, would meet only once more (in India) until 1978-79. The emergence of Imran Khan brought an attacking intent to Pakistan's cricket. His fast-bowling successors, Wasim Akram and Waqar Younis, brought the art of reverse swing to the world's notice, and famous victories – particularly in England – to Pakistan. The fraternal harmony of India's tour to Pakistan in 2003-04, their first full tour of the country for 14 years, now seems a lifetime away after the terror threats – and attacks – that forced Pakistan's cricketers to set up home in the United Arab Emirates, and the subsequent spot-fixing scandal of 2010. Their 3–0 drubbing of England in 2011-12 was an unexpected, welcome relief.

1954-55 – INDIANS IN PAKISTAN: FEAR OF FAILURE   1956

The first official Test series to be played in Pakistan did little credit to cricket generally. Pakistan and India faced each other like two boxers tentatively sparring for an opening, but being afraid to strike the first blow in case some unexpected counter might be forthcoming. With neither side prepared to take the initiative the series ended in stalemate, all five Tests being drawn for the first time in history. Fear of defeat remained uppermost in the minds of the two teams, and it does appear that until the two countries realise that the loss of a Test match is not the shattering tragedy they seem to imagine, games between them are likely to remain dull and practically devoid of interest.

Sussex v Middlesex. At Hove, August 3, 5, 6, 1963.
Russell gave a dour display lasting four hours 20 minutes – a performance which led to four spectators demanding and receiving the return of their admission fees.

Little Wonder No. 79

1955–56 – MCC A TEAM IN PAKISTAN: CULTURE CLASH   1957

The first MCC A team to undertake a tour abroad returned from Pakistan amid a storm of controversy. For most of the tour all went well, but the difficulties arose during the third representative match against Pakistan at Peshawar. An incident, which began as a joke on the part of some of the MCC players, was magnified to such alarming proportions that a few days later it led to an offer from the MCC president, Lord Alexander of Tunis, to call off the rest of the tour.

The incident involved the ragging of one of the umpires, Idris Begh, when what was known as "the water treatment" took place. One of the standing jokes on the tour between the MCC players themselves had involved the use of cold water much in the same way as students might do in a rag. Unfortunately, some of the players did not realise that the type of humour generally accepted by most people in Britain, might not be understood in other parts of the world.

More important was the unhappy timing of the affair, for it occurred during the course of a match in which some comments had been made about umpiring decisions. The MCC players and manager made it quite clear when they returned home that the umpiring had nothing to do with their rag. They thought that Begh was a willing "victim" and, indeed, all might have passed off without comment had not other Pakistanis happened to witness the tail-end of the incident.

1958-59 – PAKISTAN v WEST INDIES (THIRD TEST): MUSHTAQ, AGED 15

1960

At Lahore, March 26, 28, 29, 30, 31, 1959. West Indies won by an innings and 156 runs after an eventful match, this being Pakistan's first Test defeat at home. West Indies again started unpromisingly, but this time their recovery was complete and massive. Kanhai and Sobers, who was dropped first ball, shared an attractive stand of 162, and Kanhai went on to dominate the innings.

Pakistan had the worst of the conditions, for rain interfered in both their innings. They made a bright start, but Ijaz Butt retired after being struck by a bumper from Hall. Taking advantage of conditions, Hall brought the innings to an abrupt end on the third morning when his five wickets included a hat-trick. Pakistan followed on 260 behind, and on a sticky pitch broke down against spin bowling. Mushtaq Mohammad, who made his debut for Pakistan at the age of 14 years and 125 days*, became the youngest cricketer to play in a Test match.

West Indies 469 (R. B. Kanhai 217, G. S. Sobers 72, J. S. Solomon 56);
Pakistan 209 (W. W. Hall 5-87) **and 104** (S. Ramadhin 4-25).

The match report was at odds with the tour review which had his age at 15 years, 125 days. Wisden now records his age as 15 years, 124 days. Mushtaq's Cricketer of the Year profile in 1963 contained more than 250 words devoted to the confusion about his age.

1968-69 – MCC IN PAKISTAN: WINTER OF DISCONTENT

E. M. Wellings, 1970

With one exception nothing went right with England's 1968-69 touring plans. Cricket was unhappily caught between two bigoted groups exploiting an opportunity to further their political aims, and the proposed tour of South Africa had to be abandoned. It was then planned to visit India and Pakistan, but finance caused the Indian half to be abandoned, and the Pakistan tour was a fiasco. The one exception was a 12-day visit to Ceylon, which opened up new prospects for touring there.

From excellent organisation by considerate Ceylonese officials MCC moved to the chaos of Pakistan. The country was in political upheaval, students and others rioting, law and order breaking down, bloodshed and destruction. Again cricket became a pawn in an unsavoury political game. When trouble erupted throughout the country before MCC arrived in Karachi, the tour should have been called off. That it was kept going from crisis to crisis was due to the ruling politicians of Pakistan and the diplomats of Britain. They seemed anxious for the cricket to be played regardless of the safety of the players. If they hoped the games would exert a calming influence, their calculations were sadly awry. The Test matches rather served as rallying points for the agitators. The tour programme was changed when MCC arrived. It was further changed to restore Dacca to the fixture list after days of political manoeuvring.

Rioting broke out on the first day of the Test in Lahore, and the match was never free from disorder. In Dacca, law and order had broken down completely. The police and military had been withdrawn, and left-wing students claimed to be in control. The Second Test was understandably disturbed by rowdiness. Finally the trouble reached breaking point, even for the politicians and diplomats who were so long-suffering at the expense of others, during the Karachi Test. The match was abandoned before the first innings had been completed and the tour abruptly ended, an outcome which had long appeared inevitable.

1976-77 – PAKISTAN v NEW ZEALAND (THIRD TEST): MAJESTIC MAJID
1978

At Karachi, October 30, 31, November 1, 3, 4, 1976. Drawn. An enforced change in captaincy [*Glenn Turner was injured*] brought about no alteration in New Zealand's luck with the toss. Mushtaq won it again and Pakistan amassed a total of 565 for nine declared. The innings was notable for Majid Khan becoming the first Pakistani, and the first from anywhere in 46 years, to score a Test century before lunch. His innings was packed with imperious hooks and fluent, effortless cover-drives. Javed scored 206 and Mushtaq registered his second century in successive Tests.

Pakistan 565-9 dec. (Javed Miandad 206, Majid Khan 112, Mushtaq Mohammad 107, Imran Khan 59; R. J. Hadlee 4-138) **and 290-5 dec.** (Miandad 85, Mushtaq 67*, Majid 50); **New Zealand 468** (W. K. Lees 152, Hadlee 87, B. L. Cairns 52*) **and 262-7.**

1977-78 – PAKISTAN v ENGLAND (FIRST TEST): BRICKS AND STONES
Alex Bannister, 1979

At Lahore, December 14, 15, 16, 18, 19, 1977. Drawn. A tedious five days was marred by two serious crowd disturbances and over-cautious batting on a slow pitch. The first stoppage, on the second afternoon, was caused by a premature celebration of Mudassar Nazar's century, which was the longest in Test history. When he was 99 some spectators invaded the pitch.

After one had been belaboured by police, running fights began. Police were chased across the ground, and four found refuge in the England dressing-room. Bricks and stones were hurled in the direction of the dressing-rooms and the VIP enclosure. Tea was taken during the trouble, and only 25 minutes of actual playing time were lost. Incredibly, the rioters voluntarily cleared the ground of debris.

Mudassar, the 21-year-old son of former Test opener Nazar Mohammad, now Pakistan national coach, completed his century in nine hours 17 minutes – 12 minutes slower than the previous record by D. J. McGlew for South Africa against Australia in the 1957-58 series. His record might not have lasted long if Boycott had not been beaten by a brilliant delivery which pitched middle and took the off stump when he was 63. Boycott's 50 in four hours 50 minutes was 20 minutes slower than Mudassar's 50.

The second and more serious riot, clearly with a political motivation, caused play to be abandoned 55 minutes before the scheduled ending on the third evening. Police fired tear-gas to disperse a section of a crowd estimated at between 30,000 and 35,000. Fortunately, the next day was a rest day, but the rest of the Test suffered from a lack of atmosphere. Attendances dwindled to a few thousand and there was a considerable show of police and military strength. It was hard to concentrate in such a tense situation.

Pakistan 407-9 dec. (Haroon Rashid 122, Mudassar Nazar 114, Javed Miandad 71) **and 106-3**;
England 288 (G. Miller 98*, G. Boycott 63; Sarfraz Nawaz 4-68).

1978-79 – INDIANS IN PAKISTAN: HAPPIER DAYS   Dicky Rutnagur, 1980

Pakistan and India, who had confronted each other twice on battlefields since they last played a Test match, resumed cricket contact after almost 18 years when India undertook an eight-week tour of Pakistan which included three Test matches. Pakistan, distinctly the stronger side, won the Second and Third Tests [*their first series victory over India*]. The First was drawn. The warmth and enthusiasm with which the Indians were received, plus the cordial relations between the players, made it plain enough that the renewal of cricketing rivalry between the two neighbouring countries was long overdue. The tour would have been happier without the notorious Sahiwal incident, on the occasion of the last of three one-day internationals. As the Indians, with plenty of wickets in hand, approached their target, Sarfraz Nawaz indulged in an excess of bumpers which were obviously out of the batsmen's reach. There was no intervention from the umpires and Bedi, the Indian captain, conceded the match in protest. His action raised controversies both in Pakistan and at home. The significant feature – and a very happy one – of the Test series was the positive approach of both sides, in bold contrast to the attitudes struck in past series between the two countries.

1980-81 – WEST INDIANS IN PAKISTAN: RETALIATION Ghulam Mustafa Khan, 1982

On the second day of the Fourth Test [at Multan] occurred a shameful incident. [Sylvester] Clarke, fielding on the boundary, reacted to a barrage of oranges being thrown at him by hurling a brick into the crowd and knocking out a spectator – the president of one of the students' unions – who was carried off the field, his head bleeding profusely. Mr Jack Bailey, the neutral observer for the match and Secretary of the International Cricket Conference, submitted a report of the incident to that body. Jackie Hendriks, the West Indian team manager, expressed his regret, Clarke apologised, and both men later visited the injured student in hospital.

1985-86 – INDIA v PAKISTAN (AUSTRAL-ASIA CUP FINAL): SIX TO WIN
Qamar Ahmed, 1987

At Sharjah, April 18, 1986. Pakistan won by one wicket. With four runs needed to win, Javed Miandad struck Chetan Sharma's final delivery for his third six. Pakistan's requirement of just under five an over drifted to nine with ten overs remaining, but Miandad and Abdul Qadir picked up the rate in their fifth-wicket stand of 71, and Miandad kept the impetus going with exciting running between the wickets. His 100, as he faced the final ball from Chetan Sharma, contained only two sixes and two fours, but with India's field set to prevent a third four, he won the match in the most dramatic fashion.

> India 245-7 (50 overs) (S. M. Gavaskar 92, D. B. Vengsarkar 50; Wasim Akram 3-42);
> Pakistan 248-9 (50 overs) (Javed Miandad 116*; Chetan Sharma 3-51).

1986-87 – WEST INDIANS IN PAKISTAN: UMPIRE EXPERIMENT
Qamar Ahmed, 1988

By way of experiment, neutral umpires stood in the Test series, V. K. Ramaswamy and P. D. Reporter of India officiating in the Second and Third matches. The Pakistan authorities were to be congratulated on this decision for, apart from an altercation between Marshall and umpire Reporter in Karachi, there was a welcome absence of bickering over decisions. Marshall was unhappy because he had twice been no-balled and twice refused appeals for lbw against Mohsin Khan early in the first innings.

1987-88 – ENGLAND IN PAKISTAN (FIRST TEST): SOUR GRAPES
1989

At Lahore, November 25, 26, 27, 28, 1987. Pakistan won by an innings and 87 runs. A number of controversial decisions, Broad's refusal to walk when given out, and Gatting's post-match allegations of unfair umpiring all overshadowed a magnificent bowling performance by Abdul Qadir. The Pakistan leg-spinner returned match figures of 13 for 101, having also taken ten wickets against England at The Oval three months earlier. His first-innings analysis of nine for 56 was the best in Test cricket by a Pakistani. Indeed, it was the best by any bowler against England; only H. J. Tayfield and A. A. Mailey had previously taken nine wickets in an England innings.

England had already been upset at several umpiring decisions in the first innings, notably from Shakeel Khan, but worse was to follow. When this same official adjudged Broad caught behind off the left-arm spinner, Iqbal Qasim, on the third afternoon, Broad stood his ground. Almost a minute elapsed before Gooch persuaded him to go. A number of other decisions also angered England, who were eventually dismissed for 130 half an hour after lunch on the fourth day. This equalled their previous-lowest total against Pakistan, made at The Oval in 1954.

Broad was later severely reprimanded by the tour manager, and many observers considered him fortunate to escape a heavy fine. Mr Lush criticised the umpiring at the same time, and after the game Gatting was even more severe in his comments. Mr Stewart, the team manager, was also upset. However, although England undoubtedly received a raw deal, not one of the three appeared to acknowledge that the batting had been woefully substandard. The attendance throughout the match was even more abject, as indeed it was to be for the entire series. When the first ball was bowled, fewer than 200 spectators were at the ground to see it.

England 175 (Abdul Qadir 9-56) **and 130** (Qadir 4-45);
Pakistan 392 (Mudassar Nazar 120, Javed Miandad 65).

1987-88 – PAKISTAN v ENGLAND (SECOND TEST): GATTING v RANA   1989

At Faisalabad, December 7, 8, 9, 11, 12, 1987. Drawn. One of the most acrimonious Test matches in history almost brought about the cancellation of the tour, while the bitter rows that led to the loss of a whole day's play, and half an hour from another, might have cost England their chance of levelling the series.

Gatting won another good toss on a pitch which had again been prepared for the spinners, and this time England also included three slow bowlers. Broad's 421-minute hundred was the cornerstone of an England total well above par for the conditions. Attacking the spinners, Gatting himself made 79 off only 81 deliveries, including 14 fours, a masterly innings apparently sparked by anger at what he considered to be another display of abject umpiring.

The official who most upset him during England's innings was Shakoor Rana, and three deliveries from the end of what had been an absorbing second day, with Pakistan struggling at 106 for five, the two of them became embroiled in an exchange which produced a situation provoking headlines in countries with only the vaguest interest in cricket. The incident occurred when Gatting moved Capel up from deep square leg to prevent a single. He had, he said later, told the batsman, Salim Malik, what he was doing. However, as Hemmings came in to bowl, Gatting signalled to Capel that he had come close enough, whereupon Shakoor Rana, standing at square leg, stopped play to inform Malik of Capel's position. Shakoor claimed that Gatting had been unfairly moving the fielder behind the batsman's back. Gatting informed the umpire that he was, in his opinion, overstepping his bounds. The language employed throughout the discourse was basic.

Shakoor's refusal to play on until he received an apology from Gatting was suspected by some of having more than a little to do with Pakistan's parlous position, and by the time Gatting's enforced apology had restored an uneasy truce, six hours of playing time had been lost. Ironically, a further three and a half hours were then lost to rain and bad light on the fourth day.

England 292 (B. C. Broad 116, M. W. Gatting 79; Iqbal Qasim 5-83, Abdul Qadir 4-105)
and 137-6 dec. (G. A. Gooch 65);
Pakistan 191 (Salim Malik 60; N. A. Foster 4-42) and 51-1.

1989-90 – INDIANS IN PAKISTAN: NEUTRAL UMPIRES   R. Mohan, 1991

Two cricketers made a quiet and yet very effective contribution to the tenth series between India and Pakistan. They were not players. John Hampshire and John Holder, both from England, were the third-country umpires invited to officiate in the four Test matches, and their presence changed the nature of cricket contests between these two Asian neighbours. The frisson was missing. Events on the field were far less contentious, with both teams accepting the umpires, and their rulings, in good faith. The occasional mistakes, some glaring, did not lead to flare-ups, with the result that the atmosphere was refreshingly free of suspicion. Teams had been touring Pakistan for years without any firm belief that they could, or even would be allowed to, win a Test. In this series, the relations between the two sides were cordial and the cricket, if not spectacular, was highly competitive.

Sussex v Gloucestershire. At Hove, July 3, 4, 5, 1963.
A. Buss should have run out Carpenter, but, with the wicket broken, he pulled up a stump with his left hand with the ball in his right. Law 31 provides that a player "may pull up a stump provided always that the ball is held in the hand or hands used".

Little Wonder No. 80

1989-90 – PAKISTAN v INDIA (FIRST TEST): OLD AND YOUNG   1991

At Karachi, November 15, 16, 17, 19, 20, 1989. Drawn. The intrusion of a zealot who became involved in a scuffle with the Indian captain, Srikkanth, provided a contentious moment on the opening day and led to the strengthening of security. This was Kapil Dev's 100th Test, and with his third wicket he became the fourth bowler to take 350 Test wickets. He also became the first bowler to play in 100 Tests, a singular achievement in a career in which he had missed only one match – and that through a controversial disciplinary action by selectors. At the other end of the spectrum, Tendulkar made his debut at the age of 16 years 205 days.

Pakistan 409 (Imran Khan 109*, Javed Miandad 78, Shoaib Mohammad 67; M. Prabhakar 5-104, Kapil Dev 4-69) **and 305-5 dec.** (Salim Malik 102*, Shoaib 95);
India 262 (K. S. More 58*, Kapil Dev 55; Waqar Younis 4-80, Wasim Akram 4-83)
and 303-3 (S. V. Manjrekar 113*, N. S. Sidhu 85).

1991-92 –PAKISTAN v SRI LANKA (THIRD TEST): 14 LBWS   1993

At Faisalabad, January 2, 3, 4, 6, 7. Pakistan won by three wickets. Sri Lanka gave Pakistan a big scare as they almost achieved their first victory on foreign soil and their first series win over Pakistan. They had competed on equal terms right through the five days. The home team started the final day at 95 for four, requiring another 90 runs. Wasim Akram hit a worthy 54 and the winning runs were brought up by wicketkeeper Moin Khan. The Test was also notable for a record 14 lbw decisions, given by two umpires making a comeback. Shakoor Rana had not stood in a Test since his confrontation with Mike Gatting, at the same venue in 1987-88, whereas Khalid Aziz last officiated at Test level in 1979-80.

Sri Lanka 240 (S. T. Jayasuriya 81, R. S. Mahanama 58; Waqar Younis 4-87) **and 165** (Younis 5-65);
Pakistan 221 (Ramiz Raja 63; G. P. Wickremasinghe 5-73)
and 188-7 (Zahid Fazal 78, Wasim Akram 54; K. I. W. Wijegunawardene 4-51).

1994-95 – PAKISTAN v AUSTRALIA (FIRST TEST): GREATEST WIN   1996

At Karachi, September 28, 29, 30, October 1, 2, 1994. Pakistan won by one wicket. Australia's new era, after the end of Allan Border's decade of captaincy, began with an epic encounter. What looked like their first Test victory in Pakistan for 35 years was turned into a home triumph by the bold batting of Inzamam-ul-Haq and Mushtaq Ahmed on a slow, low pitch. Coming together at 258 for nine with the awesome task of averting Pakistan's first-ever defeat at the National Stadium, Inzamam and Mushtaq added 57 on a worn pitch against the redoubtable leg-spin of Warne. To the unrestrained delight of a crowd which steadily grew in number and chanted Allah-O-Akbar (God is great), they accomplished their goal in 8.1 overs, against an attack weakened by the withdrawal of McDermott, with an infected toe, and then by injuries to McGrath and May. In the end, Warne and Angel, in his second Test, were the only frontline bowlers still standing. Pakistan had never scored as much as 314 in a fourth innings to win; coach Intikhab Alam described the victory as the country's finest ever. Observers hoped it might revive interest in Test cricket in Pakistan.

It was especially deflating for Taylor, the first man to score a pair of spectacles in his first Test as captain. He had decided to take the new ball at 229 for seven, when Warne was in full cry. The final result was disappointing for both Warne, who gave another command performance – eight for 150 from 63.1 overs – and Michael Bevan, who announced his arrival in the Test arena with a composed 82. It was especially dispiriting for the vice-captain and wicketkeeper, Healy, who blamed himself for the defeat: Pakistan gained the winning runs from four leg-byes when Inzamam was out of his ground attacking Warne.

Australia 337 (M. G. Bevan 82, S. R. Waugh 73, I. A. Healy 57)
and 232 (D. C. Boon 114*; Wasim Akram 5-63, Waqar Younis 4-69);
Pakistan 256 (Saeed Anwar 85) **and 315-9** (Anwar 77, Inzamam-ul-Haq 58*; S. K. Warne 5-89).

1995-96 – SRI LANKANS IN PAKISTAN: SENSE OF CRISIS   Qamar Ahmed, 1997

Arjuna Ranatunga's Sri Lankans created history by winning a Test series against Pakistan for the first time in six attempts. Their triumph was the more remarkable for the fact that they had lost the First Test by an innings in four days. Over the next fortnight, they came back strongly to level the rubber at Faisalabad and then crush Pakistan at Sialkot. Curiously, they were the third team to come from behind to win a three-Test series in 1995, following South Africa against New Zealand in January, and Pakistan in Zimbabwe a month later; the only previous instance had been England against Australia in 1888. Deservedly, they returned home to a tumultuous welcome, and were driven through the streets of Colombo in a cavalcade. For Pakistan, however, their first home series defeat since 1980-81, when they lost to Clive Lloyd's West Indians, added to a sense of crisis. Their former captain, Salim Malik, had been suspended in March after three Australian players accused him of attempted bribery; investigations were continuing and he was not considered for selection, despite an attempt to secure reinstatement through the law courts.

1996-97 – PAKISTAN v ZIMBABWE (FIRST TEST): AKRAM ASSAULT   1998

At Sheikhupura, October 17, 18, 19, 20, 21, 1996. Drawn. Test cricket's newest venue, the 77th overall and the 16th in Pakistan, had been reconstructed to international standards so recently that it had never even staged a first-class match before this. Now it was graced by a remarkable innings from Wasim Akram. His unbeaten 257, in eight hours ten minutes and 363 balls, was the highest score by a No. 8 in Tests and included 12 sixes, the most in a Test innings, as well as 22 fours. Wally Hammond's record of ten sixes had stood since 1932-33, when he scored 336 not out in Auckland. Wasim broke another record of similar vintage with the help of Saqlain Mushtaq: their stand of 313 in 110 overs was the highest for the eighth wicket in Tests, beating 246 by Les Ames and Gubby Allen, for England against New Zealand in 1931. Wasim and Saqlain combined at 237 for seven, trailing Zimbabwe by 138, but what looked likely to be a sizeable first-innings deficit was transformed into a lead of 178.

Zimbabwe 375 (G. W. Flower 110, P. A. Strang 106*; Shahid Nazir 5-53)
and 241-7 (D. L. Houghton 65; Saqlain Mushtaq 4-75);
Pakistan 553 (Wasim Akram 257*, Saqlain 79, Salim Malik 52, Saeed Anwar 51; P. A. Strang 5-212).

1996-97 – SAHARA CUP: NEW FRONTIERS
R. Mohan, 1998

Canadians hearing the scoreline "Pakistan 3, India 2" in September 1996 may have assumed they were hearing an ice hockey or baseball result. In fact, the Toronto Cricket, Skating & Curling Club had just become the cricket world's latest off-shore venue for official one-day internationals, hosting five games between India and Pakistan. It was not ideal – the playing field was no better than that of a college campus and the local pitch technology was primitive. Moreover, the torrential rains brought by Hurricane Fran washed out the first two scheduled days and gave the pitches no time to recover between matches.

The other unfortunate consequence of the wet weather was that three of the four planned weekend games had to be staged on weekdays, in front of very small crowds. The one match played on a Saturday attracted 5,000, mainly expatriate Indians, Pakistanis and West Indians; a similar number arrived the following day for the series decider but left disappointed. The real target audience, however, was the aspiring middle class of the Indian subcontinent, who could follow the matches on an American television channel beamed out of Singapore. The promoters agreed to a multimillion-dollar five-year deal revolving round the television rights; if the series proved one thing, it was that the clicking turnstile is no longer the index of marketing success.

1998-99 – AUSTRALIANS IN PAKISTAN: HISTORIC VICTORY
Mark Ray, 2000

Australia's visit to Pakistan in October 1998 will always be remembered for Mark Taylor's historic 334 not out in the drawn Second Test at Peshawar, yet the most significant event of a tumultuous tour was their victory in the First Test at Rawalpindi. Taylor's effort, equalling Sir Donald Bradman's record for a Test score by an Australian, was a brilliant individual performance, but an excellent team effort in Rawalpindi was the crux of the series victory – Australia's first in Pakistan since Richie Benaud's team won 2–0 in 1959-60.

1998-99 – PAKISTAN v AUSTRALIA (SECOND TEST): UNBREAKABLE
2000

At Peshawar, October 15, 16, 17, 18, 19, 1998. Drawn. If ever a sound typified a Test then it was the mellow thwack of the ball meeting the middle of Mark Taylor's bat during his undefeated 334 in this game. On a flat, evenly grassed yellow pitch, which hardly changed appearance over five days, Taylor played as well as he ever had in his ten-year Test career. After a less than perfect start against some very fast bowling from Shoaib Akhtar, Taylor made barely an error, hitting the ball with the sweet spot of his bat hour after hour. His pulling was brutal, his cutting precise.

After Shoaib's first spectacular spell, which removed Slater with the score at 16, Taylor and Langer settled into a 279-run stand for the second wicket, asserting a dominance of bat over ball which never faltered. On the second day, Australia added 375 for the loss of three wickets. At stumps, they were 599 for four, with Taylor unbeaten on 334 and level with Bradman's Australian record at Headingley in 1930. He clipped the final ball of the day, from Aamir Sohail, towards square leg, but Ijaz, who had hardly excelled in the field before then, threw down a hand and managed to stop what would have been a record-breaking single.

Taylor had batted for exactly 12 hours and 564 balls, hitting 32 fours and a six. His innings was the seventh-highest score in Test history, the 15th triple-century and the fifth by an Australian. He also became the fourth Australian to pass 7,000 Test runs. Yet more drama followed next morning as the news spread around the ground – and the world – that Taylor had sacrificed the chance of breaking both Bradman's mark and Brian Lara's world-record 375 by declaring. Immediately the theorising and myth-making began. The local experts could not believe that Taylor would deny himself a shot at the record. One explanation which quickly gained currency, though it was later denied by Taylor, was that he had refused to pass the record of Bradman, the greatest batsman the game has produced and a living legend of Australian society. The simplest explanation was the correct one: Taylor thought 599 in two days was more than enough runs, and he wanted to try to win by giving his bowlers a chance at Pakistan's batsmen from the start of the third day. There were a number of team meetings that evening, and several players urged Taylor to bat on and beat Lara. But it was typical of his approach to the game that he should be aware of the record without being obsessed by it.

Australia 599-4 dec. (M. A. Taylor 334*, J. L. Langer 116) **and 289-5** (Taylor 92);
Pakistan 580-9 dec. (Saeed Anwar 126, Ijaz Ahmed 155, Inzamam-ul-Haq 97).

1998-99 –PAKISTAN v ZIMBABWE (First Test): "pathetic"   2000

At Peshawar, November 27, 28, 29, 30, 1998. Zimbabwe won by seven wickets. Zimbabwe completed their first overseas Test win on the fourth morning, after a run-chase led by Goodwin, who hit an unbeaten 73. Like Johnson, who scored a vital first-innings century. Goodwin had returned to his native Zimbabwe after sharpening his skills overseas; he had played in Australia, Johnson in South Africa and England. But the bowlers who set up the victory by skittling Pakistan in their second innings for just 103 were the black pacemen, Olonga and Mbangwa, and their white compatriot Streak, who had all come up through Zimbabwe's ranks. Captain Aamir Sohail was fuming. He called the display pathetic, and wondered if Pakistan had ever batted so badly. But he had set the trend himself, hitting the ball straight back to Olonga in the second over. Sohail also criticised the selectors for giving him the wrong team, and the decision to prepare a green pitch.

Pakistan 296 (Ijaz Ahmed 87, Yousuf Youhana 75; H. H. Streak 4-93)
and 103 (H. K. Olonga 4-42);
Zimbabwe 238 (N. C. Johnson 107; Wasim Akram 5-52)
and 162-3 (M. W. Goodwin 73*).

2000-01 – PAKISTAN v ENGLAND (THIRD TEST): TWILIGHT TRIUMPH

Samiul Hasan, 2002

At Karachi, December 7, 8, 9, 10, 11, 2001. England won by six wickets. The pre-tour scripts proved wrong. The predictions went awry and the critics ate their words when, in near darkness, England achieved an extraordinary victory in a compelling climax to the tour. The win gave them their first Test triumph in Pakistan in 39 years and ended their five-series drought against Pakistan (their last series victory was at home in 1982). For Pakistan, it was their maiden defeat at the National Stadium in 35 Tests, after 17 wins and 17 draws. But it was also their fourth successive home series defeat in three seasons.

With failing light always going to be a factor, Pakistan captain Moin Khan adopted desperate delaying tactics, for which he was fiercely criticised, after his side were bundled out for 158 on the final afternoon, leaving England a target of 176 in a minimum of 44 overs. His bowlers took 40 minutes to send down the first seven of these before tea, and almost three and a half hours to bowl a total of 41.3 intense, nailbiting overs. Moin, who was warned for his go-slow strategy by referee Ranjan Madugalle during the tea interval, made three unsuccessful appeals for bad light to umpire Steve Bucknor as Thorpe and Hussain resolutely stood their ground. With victory in sight, but little else, Thorpe edged the winning runs. Some of the Pakistani players thought he had been bowled, until the ball was spotted by a searching fielder.

"The fielders in the deep just couldn't pick the ball. I have never played in such poor conditions," said Moin later. "Another five minutes and it would have been complete darkness," said Hussain, who praised Hick and Thorpe for their decisive fourth-wicket stand of 91. Thorpe remained undefeated on 64, demonstrating to the end the patience and mental toughness that characterised his series.

Pakistan 405 (Inzamam-ul-Haq 142, Yousuf Youhana 117; A. F. Giles 4-94) and 158;

England 388 (M. A. Atherton 125, N. Hussain 51; Waqar Younis 4-88)

and 176-4 (G. P. Thorpe 64*).

2001-02 – NEW ZEALANDERS IN PAKISTAN: SHATTERED

Qamar Ahmed and Samiul Hasan, 2003

New Zealand were originally due to arrive in Pakistan in September 2001, but called the tour off because of security fears after the terrorist attacks in the USA. Seven months later, they honoured their commitment, travelling to Pakistan for three one-day internationals and two Test matches. Sadly, after all the spadework done by the Pakistan Cricket Board, the tour came to an abrupt and tragic end. A car bomb exploded in front of the Pearl Continental Hotel in Karachi, where both teams were staying, a couple of hours before the start of the Second Test, and killed 14 people, including 11 French engineers who were in Karachi helping the Pakistan Navy to build submarines. None of the players was hurt, though they witnessed some horrific injuries to bystanders, and the New Zealand physiotherapist, Dayle Shackel, was cut by flying glass.

The referee, Mike Procter, swiftly announced the cancellation of the Test, and the tour; the dazed Pakistan officials had no alternative but to agree. But it was depressing news for their board. They had already lost nearly $US20m after India had refused to come to Pakistan for the Asian Test Championship for political reasons, and Sri Lanka and West Indies had also declined to tour after September 11. To fulfil the requirements of the ICC Test Championship, the West Indian series was transferred to Sharjah. Now, the Karachi blast put Test cricket in Pakistan, and the future of the Championship, in jeopardy. The single Test played here did not qualify as a series in the Championship reckoning, and how many times could a tour be rescheduled?

2002-03 – PAKISTAN v AUSTRALIA: ON THE ROAD — Martin Blake, 2004

After months of discontented murmuring from their players, the Australian Cricket Board finally pulled out of their scheduled three-Test tour of Pakistan, citing government advice and security concerns. Confronted with a choice between finding a neutral venue and cancelling the tour, the Pakistani board discussed grounds in Morocco and Bangladesh. But they finally chose Colombo for the First Test and Sharjah for the last two. Steve Waugh wanted a whitewash, and his men delivered.

2002-03 – PAKISTAN v AUSTRALIA (SECOND TEST): 59 AND 53 — 2004

At Sharjah, October 11, 12, 2002. Australia won by an innings and 198 runs. Pakistan arrived in Sharjah comfortable with the familiar conditions and buoyed by their competitive performance in Colombo. But their mood would quickly darken as they slumped to a display that, even allowing for their reputation for spasmodic performances, could only be described as a shocker. In 125 years, Test cricket had produced only 16 two-day defeats; here, on a slow, flat pitch and against an Australian attack weakened by the absence of the injured Gillespie, Pakistan subsided to the 17th.

After Waqar Younis was granted his wish to bat first on one of world cricket's most benign strips, the Pakistanis were rolled over for their lowest-ever score, a pathetic 59, three below their previous-worst at Perth in 1981-82. They had lasted less than 32 overs. Warne caused the damage again, taking four for 11 and bewitching the batsmen with his new "slider". Pushing forward, they found themselves trapped lbw by deliveries that were doing precisely nothing.

Two balls after tea on the first day, the Australians were already in front. With the temperature pushing 50°C in the middle, Hayden likened it to batting in an oven, and wondered whether hell was any hotter. But his sheer hunger for runs came to the fore.

Australia were aiming for 500; although they managed only 310, it proved more than enough. After Nazir simply turned his back on Taufeeq as he charged through for a run in Pakistan's first over, and Razzaq's wrist was broken by Lee in the sixth, their resolve fractured too. Warne once again imposed his authority, taking four for 13, and the quick bowlers mopped up. Pakistan had survived less than 25 overs, and were routed for 53. Their record low had lasted only one day.

Pakistan 59 (S. K. Warne 4-11) **and 53** (Warne 4-13);
Australia 310 (M. L. Hayden 119; Saqlain Mushtaq 4-83).

Glamorgan v Northamptonshire. At Swansea, June 10, 11, 12, 1964. Norman, the Northamptonshire opening batsman, had the unenviable distinction of being dismissed with the first ball of each innings on Wednesday when 23 wickets went down.

Little Wonder No. 81

2003-04 – PAKISTAN v BANGLADESH (THIRD TEST): INZY DOES IT   2004

At Multan, September 3, 4, 5, 6, 2003. Pakistan won by one wicket. Inzamam-ul-Haq played one of the innings of his life to save Pakistan from humiliation and break Bangladeshi hearts. On the third afternoon, Bangladesh's first Test win, so desperately longed for during three years of demoralising defeat, was within touching distance. On a pitch helping seamers, Pakistan were 132 for six – still 129 short of victory.

But Inzamam stood firm for five hours 17 minutes, and his unbeaten 138 guided Pakistan home. It was only the tenth one-wicket win in Test history, and Inzamam had now been at the crease for two of them. While the 1994-95 victory over Mark Taylor's Australians came at Karachi, this triumph was in front of his home crowd, who showered him in rose petals as he left the field.

It was cruel for Bangladesh. They dominated from the word go, and despite Inzamam's heroics might still have won, given a bit more luck. With 49 now needed, eight wickets down and Inzamam farming the strike, the No. 10 Umar Gul survived a run-out despite being beaten by a direct hit. The crestfallen bowler, Mohammad Rafique, had brushed the stumps and dislodged the bails before the ball struck. In the same over, Rafique sportingly chose not to run out Gul when he was backing up too far. By the time Gul was finally run out, after a bad call from Inzamam, they had added 52. Gul's contribution was five.

Four runs were now needed, five balls remained in the over and the No. 11 coming to the striker's end was Yasir Ali – a 17-year-old on first-class debut, with only a handful of junior games and a hurried lunchtime batting lesson from Javed Miandad, the Pakistan coach, behind him. But Yasir kept out three balls and then tickled a single into the leg side. Off the last delivery of the over, Inzamam flicked the winning boundary. Ramiz Raja, the former Test batsman, now chief executive of the PCB, called it "one of the best Test innings of modern times". That might have been a little overblown, but Inzamam's concentration had been steely and his hitting authoritative. Supporters rushed on to the field to hug their local hero.

Bangladesh 281 (Habibul Bashar 72; Umar Gul 4-86) **and 154** (Gul 4-58, Shabbir Ahmed 4-68);
Pakistan 175 (Mohammad Rafique 5-36, Khaled Mahmud 4-37) **and 262-9** (Inzamam-ul-Haq 138*).

2003-04 – INDIANS IN PAKISTAN: BROTHERS, NOT IN ARMS   Rahul Bhattacharya, 2005

India's tour of Pakistan, their first full one in 14 years, was extraordinary even before a ball was bowled. Two years earlier the two countries had appeared on the brink of nuclear war, but the tour gained impetus from what was popularly described as the "wind of brotherhood" blowing at long last between the nations, and also became an agent of change in itself. Sport, far from being an agent of division, turned out to be the centrepiece for something resembling a peace march. For India, there was another dimension. Their rising cricket team shone as never before in Pakistan, winning the Tests 2–1 and the one-day series 3–2. They had never won even a single Test there in 20 previous attempts.

The tour could not have had a more nailbiting, or heart-warming, beginning than it did at Karachi's National Stadium. Never had more runs been scored in a one-day international than the 693 made here, and all results were possible at the last ball, when Moin Khan failed to deposit a full-toss for six. The tension was not restricted to the cricket. The big question was how the crowds at Karachi would respond; indeed, how the peoples of India and Pakistan would respond. Nearly everybody (though the *Times of India* printed the irresponsibly vulgar headline "Karachi Captured") came through shining. Hardened ex-players were amazed and moved to see the national flags flying together through the match. After an initial shocked silence, the Indians left the pitch to a standing ovation. Quietly, the crowds filed out, obeying instructions to avert the type of riots that had occurred at ticket booths five days before.

Thus was the tone set at Karachi: it never let up. The scent of something like love wafted out of the stands. The people-to-people contact was not phenomenal in terms of numbers, but it was in experience. In total, about 11,000 cricket visas were issued, of which almost half were for the two Lahore one-dayers. Pakistani officials believed this to be the heaviest cross-border traffic since the mass migration brought about by Partition in 1947. For many years, obtaining visas for personal visits had been virtually impossible.

The warmth of the tour radiated beyond cricket. The governments decided to tone down the aggressive posturing at the daily closing-of-the-gates ceremony on the Wagah border. Bollywood film-makers suggested that Indian films should stop pushing anti-Pakistan propaganda. About 15 Pakistani musical bands crossed the border between January and May. And the business sector brimmed with optimism at the potential for trade. Of course, it would be presumptuous for cricket to take credit. What is irrefutable, however, is that the tour provided the highest possible profile for friendship, and the strongest metaphorical way of saying "peace over conflict". Personalities as diverse as the actor Peter O'Toole and the American secretary of state Colin Powell praised the series' message.

2003-04 – PAKISTAN v INDIA (First Test): the Sehwag smash   2005

At Multan, March 28, 29, 30, 31, April 1, 2004. India won by an innings and 52 runs. From about 10am on March 28, a regular thud, rather than the roars associated with cricket in the subcontinent, began to emerge. The stadium was virtually desolate, and the thumps, from Virender Sehwag's bat, were to resound for a day and a half as he constructed India's first triple-century in Test cricket. It laid the foundation of a historic victory, India's first in Pakistan in 21 Tests spread over 49 years. It was also, briefly, their most substantial win in a largely wretched 72 years of Tests away from home. Sehwag's 309, and his partnership of 336, an Indian third-wicket record, with Tendulkar, who crafted a meticulous century, carried India to their third-highest total, and second-highest away. Sehwag's glitzy epic was not without luck. He was dropped on 68 and 77 during an opening stand of 160 with Chopra. Later, he offered two chances behind the wicket off Shabbir Ahmed, one ball either side of the four that took him past the Indian record of 281 held by Laxman. None the less, it was an innings of sustained and versatile violence. He thrashed six sixes and 39 fours in 531 minutes and 375 balls; he went from 99 to 105 with a glided six over third man off Shoaib Akhtar, and from 295 to 301 with a roundhouse blast over wide long-on off Saqlain Mushtaq.

India 675-5 dec. (V. Sehwag 309, S. R. Tendulkar 194*);
Pakistan 407 (Yasir Hameed 91, Inzamam-ul-Haq 77; I. K. Pathan 4-100)
and 216 (Yousuf Youhana 112; A. Kumble 6-72).

2006-07 – PAKISTAN v WEST INDIES (Third Test): Yousuf's year   2007

At Karachi, November 27, 28, 29, 30, December 1, 2006. Pakistan won by 199 runs. Mohammad Yousuf's record-breaking year culminated in a comprehensive Pakistan win, even though they had to go an hour into the final session to seal the series 2–0. Yousuf's 102, his fifth century in as many Tests, held together the first innings, in which no one else passed 50. Then his second-innings 124 made Pakistan's position impregnable. It also boosted his aggregate for the calendar year to 1,788, eclipsing the previous record of 1,710 by Viv Richards in 1976. Yousuf also scored an unprecedented nine centuries. A crowd of close to 20,000 turned up on the fourth day to watch Yousuf go for Richards's record. They were not disappointed: he had the rare treat of raising his bat at 48, after a delightful on-driven boundary off Collymore carried him past 1,710. Yousuf, let off at 68 as West Indies' effort flagged, strolled to his second century of the match – his 23rd in Tests, including six in his last five – before he was bowled behind his legs by Sarwan's tempting leg-spin. He was the sixth Pakistani to score twin centuries in a Test.

Pakistan 304 (Mohammad Yousuf 102)
and 399-6 dec. (Yousuf 124, Mohammad Hafeez 104, Inzamam-ul-Haq 58*);
West Indies 260 (D. Ganga 81, D. Ramdin 50; Umar Gul 4-79)
and 244 (S. Chanderpaul 69).

2008-09 – PAKISTAN v SRI LANKA: TRAGEDY STRIKES   Qamar Ahmed, 2010

The fear of terrorist attack, insurgencies and suicide bombers in a politically unstable country had already caused Australia and India to pull out of their scheduled tours of Pakistan. Tragically, it turned out to be fully justified when the Sri Lankan players were attacked by extremists before the start of the third day's play in the Lahore Test.

The tour had been hastily organised after India declined to come. The Sri Lankans had been promised "presidential" security by the interior ministry and the PCB, but in Lahore, Trevor Bayliss, their coach, noticed that the trucks bearing soldiers with fixed machine-guns which had flanked the team bus in Karachi had disappeared. The bus came under attack by terrorists as it approached the ground on the third morning.

It had reached the Liberty Roundabout and was about to turn right for the Gaddafi Stadium when a rocket launcher was fired (luckily, it missed), followed by grenades and then gunfire from every direction. The shocked Sri Lankans immediately dived to the floor of the bus, but even so some of them were hit by shrapnel and bullets. The bus driver, Mehar Mohammed Khalil, had the presence of mind to drive off, and kept his foot on the accelerator until the team reached the safety of the stadium 500m away. He was feted as a hero and later decorated by the PCB, the Pakistani government and the Sri Lankan government, who invited him and his family to a ceremony in Colombo. But his friend Zafar Khan, who was driving the umpires' minibus, was killed instantly as a bullet lodged in his heart. Fourth umpire Ahsan Raza and liaison officer Abdul Sami Khan were wounded, but survived; a policeman managed to drive their bus away as referee Chris Broad attempted to comfort Raza, whose lung and liver had been damaged. Six policemen died, including a traffic warden.

Several Sri Lankan players were injured, most seriously Thilan Samaraweera, who was hit by a bullet in his left side, near the knee joint, and Tharanga Paranavitana, who was struck in the chest. Spinner Ajantha Mendis suffered shrapnel wounds in the head and back: there were also injuries to Mahela Jayawardene, Kumar Sangakkara, Suranga Lakmal, Thilan Thushara Mirando and assistant coach Paul Farbrace. Samaraweera and Paranavitana were rushed to the nearby Services Hospital. Then the entire party was flown back to Colombo overnight in a chartered plane sent by the Sri Lankan president, as the tour was abandoned. All have played again.

Eyewitnesses said there were 12 gunmen involved in the attack; all of them escaped. Suspicion fell on various extremist groups; Pakistanis unwilling to believe that terrorism could be home-grown even accused the Indian intelligence forces. A number of men were later arrested, and three months later the police apprehended a man who claimed he was the head of the gang and a member of the "Punjabi Taliban".

The tour organised to show other nations that Pakistan was a safe place to play cricket thus ended in catastrophe, with the country's future as an international venue in even greater doubt. "It has completely changed the landscape, and not just in the subcontinent. On many occasions we have been told that cricketers would not be targeted in Pakistan. This morning, events have proved that to be incorrect," said ICC president David Morgan.

2011-12 – PAKISTAN v ENGLAND (FIRST TEST): IN A SPIN   Derek Pringle, 2013

At Dubai, January 17, 18, 19, 2012. Pakistan won by ten wickets. A little over two months after three Pakistani players were imprisoned for spot-fixing during their previous Test against England, at Lord's in August 2010, the sides met at the neutral venue of the Dubai Sports City Stadium. But the impressive, if sterile, ground did not preside over neutral cricket – at least not from the Pakistanis, who immediately located top gear to despatch England inside three days. If the meeting of these teams, with their history of volatility, was always likely to be unpredictable, few could have foreseen the drubbing suffered by England in their first Test since officially becoming the world's No. 1 side. To lose by ten wickets was bad enough; to do so after your captain had won the toss, and the pitch offered only moderate assistance to the bowlers, was difficult to credit.

The England attack, it's true, performed manfully, but the haplessness of the batsmen, who – for only the third time in a Test since the 2006-07 Ashes – were dismissed twice for under 200, meant their efforts were wasted. And central to the demise was Saeed Ajmal, whose jerky mix of doosras and off-breaks brought him match figures of ten for 97, the best by a Pakistani against England for over 24 years.

Just in case England had been fussing over their protractors, Ajmal and his captain, Misbah-ul-Haq, also planted the possibility of a new mystery delivery, the teesra – or third one. If it did exist, other than as a deliberate distraction in the build-up to the match, Ajmal didn't need to harness it: only Trott and Prior appeared able to pick even the standard variations in his arsenal. The Decision Review System seemed to make England's batsmen doubly jittery. After they were prevented from using their front pads as a reliable line of defence against spin, their techniques unravelled almost as quickly as their confidence.

England 192 (M. J. Prior 70*; Saeed Ajmal 7-55) **and 160** (Umar Gul 4-63);
Pakistan 338 (Mohammad Hafeez 88, Misbah-ul-Haq 61, Adnan Akmal 61, Taufeeq Umar 58;
G. P. Swann 4-107) **and 15-0.**

SRI LANKA

Ceylon, as Sri Lanka was known until 1972, was a regular stopover for England (or MCC) on tours of Australia as far back as 1882-83. "Fortunately, Ceylon lay on the shipping route between Britain and Australia, and this gave us the golden opportunity of watching world-famed stars in action, if only for a few hours. These 'limb looseners' were raised to Test status by our press, and crowds flocked there. Our cricketers deemed it a great honour to play against the greats," Gerry Vaidyasekera wrote in the 1997 edition, celebrating Sri Lanka's recent World Cup triumph. "They are a welcome addition to the fold," editor John Woodcock wrote in his Notes of 1981 on the granting of Test status to Sri Lanka. It was not until 2000-01 that England conducted a full tour of Sri Lanka, and 2002 before the honour was reciprocated. Despite reaching the World Cup final in 2011, these are trying times for Sri Lankan cricket. Sa'adi Thawfeeq wrote in the 2013 edition: "After seven years of government-appointed interim committees, SLC [*Sri Lanka Cricket*] finally held an annual general meeting in January 2012. The change of attitude followed an ICC resolution that all member boards should be free of political interference."

1981-82 –SRI LANKA v ENGLAND (INAUGURAL TEST): DESERVED ELEVATION
1983

At P. Saravanamuttu Oval, Colombo, February 17, 18, 20, 21, 1982. England won by seven wickets. Although they were beaten five minutes from the end of the fourth day, following a headlong collapse in which seven wickets fell for eight runs, Sri Lanka did enough in their first Test to show they deserved elevation to Full membership of the International Cricket Conference. Apart from the frustration when, in threequarters of an hour, Emburey destroyed their hopes with a spell of five for five, the only disappointment of a long-awaited moment in the island's history was the smallness of the crowds. On only two of the four days was the 25,000-capacity ground even threequarters full, this being variously attributed to high admission prices, television coverage and, disturbingly, the public's preference for one-day cricket. The consequence was a saddening lack of atmosphere, except briefly on the fourth morning when Sri Lanka, 160 ahead with seven wickets standing on a turning pitch, seemed to have the makings of a winning score. Ultimately, both the batting and the spin bowling failed to rise to the occasion, but their overall performance left little doubt that in batsmen Dias, Madugalle and Ranatunga, an 18-year-old left-hander still at school, and opening bowler de Mel, Sri Lanka have a handful of promising young players.

Sri Lanka 218 (R. S. Madugalle 65, A. Ranatunga 54; D. L. Underwood 5-28)
and 175 (R. L. Dias 77; J. E. Emburey 6-33);
England 223 (D. I. Gower 89. A. L. F. de Mel 4-70) and 171-3 (C. J. Tavaré 85).

1985-86 – SRI LANKA v INDIA (SECOND TEST): EARLY SUCCESS   1987

At P. Saravanamuttu Stadium, Colombo, September 6, 7, 8, 10, 11, 1986. Sri Lanka won by 149 runs. Sri Lanka's epochal first Test win, in only their 14th Test match, came despite their own slow batting at the start, but their well-directed seam attack, bowling on and outside off stump, put them well in the hunt by establishing a convincing first-innings lead. Notwithstanding two dubious decisions on the final morning, India, set a target of 348 in 333 minutes plus 20 overs, could have batted out for a draw. However, Ratnayake swung the match for Sri Lanka by running through the middle order. A defiant 78 by Kapil Dev produced moments of anxiety before Ratnayake dived to take a smart return catch to dismiss the Indian captain and seal the victory which led to a nationwide celebration and a public holiday the following day. Silva's century and nine dismissals in the match were an unprecedented feat by a wicketkeeper in a Test match.

Sri Lanka 385 (S. A. R. Silva 111, R. L. Dias 95, R. S. Madugalle 54, L. R. D. Mendis 51; C. Sharma 5-118)
and 206-3 dec. (P. A. de Silva 75, Dias 60*);
India 244 (K. Srikkanth 64, M. Amarnath 60, S. M. Gavaskar 52; R. J. Ratnayake 4-76)
and 198 (Kapil Dev 78; Ratnayake 5-49).

1992-93 – AUSTRALIANS IN SRI LANKA: THEY WAS ROBBED   Mike Coward, 1994

With good fortune on their side, Australia won their first Test series on the Indian subcontinent for 23 years, since Bill Lawry's team beat India 3–1 in 1969-70. Australia won only one of the three Tests, the First, when the Sri Lankans lapsed into old, destructive ways at the very moment they were poised to come of age as a Test country. It must be the greatest heist since the Great Train Robbery, said Border. For Sri Lankan cricket, defeat after four days in the ascendancy was terribly dispiriting.

1992-93 – SRI LANKA v AUSTRALIA (FIRST TEST): YOU HAVE BEEN WARNED
1994

At Sinhalese Sports Club, Colombo, August 17, 18, 19, 21, 22, 1992. Australia won by 16 runs. The carelessness of Aravinda de Silva cost Sri Lanka what would have been their third and most famous victory since entering the Test arena in February 1982. With 54 runs needed from nearly 25 overs, de Silva, who had taken 37 from 32 balls with seven fours, attempted to strike McDermott for the second time over Border at mid-on. Border, at full stretch, ran 25 metres with the flight of the ball and held a magnificent catch over his shoulder.

From that moment Sri Lanka collapsed utterly, losing their last eight wickets for 37 runs. A crowd of 10,000, the biggest of the match, jeered them at the presentation ceremony. In just 17.4 overs they had squandered the impressive gains of the first three days, after Ranatunga had compelled the Australians to bat first on a damp pitch under overcast skies.

Exhorted by Border to show greater guts and determination, Australia scored 367 on the fourth day. A final total of 471 set Sri Lanka 181 in 58 overs and gave the visitors just a little optimism. Then, after de Silva's fateful error, Matthews returned four for 76 and with Warne, who claimed three in 13 balls without conceding a run, he engineered an improbable victory. It was a fine comeback for Matthews, ignored by the Australian selectors for the past year; it was also one of Australia's greatest fightbacks. Only once before had they won a Test after trailing by more than 200 on the first innings.

Australia 256 (I. A. Healy 66*; U. C. Hathurusinghe 4-66)
and 471 (D. C. Boon 68, G. R. J. Matthews 64, D. M. Jones 57, M. E. Waugh 56; S. D. Anurasiri 4-127);
Sri Lanka 547-8 dec. (A. P. Gurusinha 137, R. S. Kaluwitharana 132*,
A. Ranatunga 127, R. S. Mahanama 78) and 164 (Matthews 4-76).

1992-93 – NEW ZEALANDERS IN SRI LANKA: HARSH REALITIES   Sri Krishnamurthi, 1994

What began as a confidence-boosting exercise to develop some of New Zealand's emerging players turned into a tour through a chamber of horrors. After their expected successes in Zimbabwe – whose promotion to Test status New Zealand had enthusiastically supported – Martin Crowe's youthful side arrived in Colombo prepared for stiffer competition in a three-Test series. But 36 hours later Sri Lanka lost all its idyllic enchantment.

On November 16 several players were taking breakfast on the balconies of their hotel in Colombo when, less than 50 metres away, Sri Lanka's naval commander, Vice-Admiral Clancy Fernando, and three other naval personnel were assassinated by a suicide bomber from the Tamil separatist movement. The tourists saw the horrific results at first hand. Dismembered bodies were strewn over the blood-stained street; even the balconies and walls of the hotel were stained with human debris. Many of the players went into shock.

After seeking diplomatic advice, a majority of the tourists voted to leave. But the chairman of New Zealand Cricket, Peter McDermott, having consulted government officials, flew out to insist that the tour should go on. McDermott was concerned about the cost to his board in tour guarantees and compensation to the Sri Lankan board; the government was concerned about trading relations with Sri Lanka, and particularly about a trade exhibition due to start in Colombo two days later. Despite public promises that there would be no pressure and no recriminations, McDermott was forceful in a three-and-a-half-hour meeting with the players, creating division and acrimony within their ranks. Mark Greatbatch was particularly angry at attempts to make him stay, and returned home with Rod Latham, Dipak Patel, Gavin Larsen and Willie Watson. Coach Warren Lees also left, and Crowe took over his duties. Ken Rutherford, one of those who changed their minds and stayed, warned other countries against touring Sri Lanka, though he later withdrew his remarks under pressure from ICC. The departed players were replaced by 38-year-old John Wright, who thought he had played his last Test cricket, Justin Vaughan, Michael Owens and Grant Bradburn. Vaughan, an English-born doctor who played for Gloucestershire in 1992, made himself useful on the flight over by attending a sick woman.

1992-93 – SRI LANKA v ENGLAND (ONLY TEST): "TOO HOT FOR EUROPEANS"   1994

At Sinhalese Sports Club, Colombo, March 13, 14, 15, 17, 18, 1993. Sri Lanka won by five wickets. Sri Lanka comprehensively outplayed England and thoroughly deserved their first win against them in five Tests and their fourth in the 43 they had contested since attaining Test status 11 years previously.

Although there were individual performances of some merit from England, collectively this was another bad display. The tourists once again failed to produce the standard of performance required to compete with technically skilled and highly motivated opposition in a hostile environment. In, Calcutta the climatic peculiarity that had caused so much consternation was smog; here it was the steamy heat. The shirts of the England players were soaked in perspiration throughout the match as temperatures soared into the high 90s and the humidity became quite exhausting. It was hard to disagree with team manager Fletcher's assertion, supported by the fact that England's highest scorers were born in southern Africa, that: "It's very nearly too hot here for Europeans to play cricket."

There were also further murmurings regarding the impartiality of Sri Lankan umpiring and the bowling action of Sri Lankan off-spinners Warnaweera and Muralitharan. But, overall, England had nothing and no one to blame but themselves. The Sri Lankan batting lived up to its high reputation against some of England's best bowling on the entire tour, particularly from Lewis and Tufnell. De Silva and Ranatunga, their two senior batsmen, displayed the determination to build long innings as well as the exquisite wristy strokeplay so widely admired in world cricket.

England 380 (R. A. Smith 128, G. A. Hick 68, A. J. Stewart 63; K. P. J. Warnaweera 4-90,
M. Muralitharan 4-118) **and 228** (J. E. Emburey 59; Warnaweera 4-98);
Sri Lanka 469 (H. P. Tillekeratne 93*, P. A. de Silva 80, A. Ranatunga 64, R. S. Mahanama 64,
U. C. Hathurusinghe 59; C. C. Lewis 4-66) **and 142-5.**

Middlesex v Hampshire. At Lord's, May 30, June 1, 2, 1964. The match hours had been lengthened from 11 until 6.45 on the first two days to permit an early finish on the third day so that preparations could be made for a cocktail party for the Middlesex lady members in the Pavilion on Tuesday evening. As it happened the game was officially called off at one o'clock that day!

Little Wonder No. 82

1997-98 – SRI LANKA v INDIA (FIRST TEST): RECORD TEST TOTAL   1999

At R. Premadasa Stadium, Colombo, August 2, 3, 4, 5, 6, 1997. Drawn. On the fifth and final morning, crowds gathered to see a Sri Lankan assault the peak of Test cricket. West Indian Brian Lara's Test record of 375 was under threat from another left-hander, two months his junior: Sanath Jayasuriya. Jayasuriya began the day on 326 and confidently moved to 340 with three fours and two singles. Then an off-break from Chauhan bounced a little more than he expected; he popped a simple catch to silly point to end his hopes of beating Lara. The disappointment was alleviated to some extent by Sri Lanka establishing two other world records. Jayasuriya and Mahanama put on 576, the highest partnership for any Test wicket and only one run short of the all-time first-class record; and Sri Lanka's total of 952 for six was the highest in Test history.

It was a terrible toss to win. "We should have batted second," said Indian captain Tendulkar. Even so, his team had dominated the first two days of the Test, piling up an apparently impressive 537 for eight – their highest total in Sri Lanka. This remarkable Test produced 1,489 runs for only 14 wickets, with both teams batting only once on a pitch to break bowlers' hearts.

INDIA

†N. R. Mongia c Jayawardene b Pushpakumara	7
N. S. Sidhu c Kaluwitharana b Vaas	111
R. Dravid c and b Jayasuriya	69
*S. R. Tendulkar c Jayawardene b Muralitharan	143
M. Azharuddin c and b Muralitharan	126
S. C. Ganguly c Mahanama b Jayasuriya	0
A. Kumble not out	27
R. K. Chauhan c Vaas b Jayasuriya	23
A. Kuruvilla c Atapattu b Pushpakumara	9
B 10, n-b 12	22

1-36 2-183 3-230 4-451 5-451   (8 wkts dec.) 537
6-479 7-516 8-537

N. M. Kulkarni and B. K. V. Prasad did not bat.

Vaas 23–5–80–1; Pushpakumara 19.3–2–97–2; Jayawardene 2–0–6–0; Muralitharan 65–9–174–2; Silva 39–3–122–0; Jayasuriya 18–3–45–3; Atapattu 1–0–3–0.

SRI LANKA

S. T. Jayasuriya c Ganguly b Chauhan	340
M. S. Atapattu c Mongia b Kulkarni	26
R. S. Mahanama lbw b Kumble	225
P. A. de Silva c Prasad b Ganguly	126
*A. Ranatunga run out	86
D. P. M. D. Jayawardene c Kulkarni b Ganguly	66
†R. S. Kaluwitharana not out	14
W. P. U. J. C. Vaas not out	11
B 28, l-b 9, w 7, n-b 14	58

1-39 2-615 3-615 4-790   (6 wkts dec.) 952
5-921 6-924

K. J. Silva, K. R. Pushpakumara and M. Muralitharan did not bat.

Prasad 24–1–88–0; Kuruvilla 14–2–74–0; Chauhan 78–8–276–1; Kumble 72–7–223–1; Kulkarni 70–12–195–1; Ganguly 9–0–53–2; Tendulkar 2–1–2–0; Dravid 2–0–4–0.

Umpires: K. T. Francis and S. G. Randell.

1999-2000 – SRI LANKA v AUSTRALIA (FIRST TEST): SHOCK HORROR   2001

At Kandy, September 9, 10, 11, 1999. Sri Lanka won by six wickets. The drama of Test cricket rose to new heights as the sound of a helicopter filled Asgiriya Stadium. Reminiscent of a scene from *Apocalypse Now*, the machine had appeared, dark green and menacing, over the adjoining hill, out of tropical vegetation, and play stopped as it swept low over the back of the ground, touched down briefly, then headed towards Colombo. With it went any possible chance Australia might have had of turning round a Test Sri Lanka always deserved to win.

On board were Steve Waugh, with a badly broken nose, and Gillespie, with a broken leg that would keep him out of the national side throughout the Australian season. They had crashed, horrifically, as Waugh ran back from square leg and Gillespie came in from the boundary, both trying to catch the Sri Lankan vice-captain, Jayawardene. The ball always seemed destined to fall between them.

This freak accident represented Australia's lowest point on a rare lowly tour. When it happened on the second morning, Sri Lanka were already 139 for three in reply to Australia's 188, and threatening to bat them out of the match. Jayawardene and de Silva ran two but abandoned a third when they saw the Australians had forgotten the ball and were huddled around their fallen colleagues. Play was held up for six minutes while they received treatment before Gillespie was carried from the field.

Sri Lanka needed just 95 for a historic first Test victory over Australia, but it was no simple affair. They had stumbled to 39 for three but the old firm of Ranatunga and de Silva ensured glory would not drown in a sea of panic. Riding his luck with the cheeky approach that so annoys the Australians, Ranatunga survived a desperately close lbw appeal and a dropped catch before scoring, then broke the game open with a four and six off successive balls from Warne.

Excitement mounted with every delivery, amid rhythmic clapping and wild cheering. The small and picturesque ground was suddenly so full that the crowd spilled out in front of the sightscreen at one end and could not be moved by police. In the end, Sri Lanka scrambled to a six-wicket victory after three days of drama, tension and controversy. It was 14 years to the day since they won their first Test – against India at the Sara Stadium in Colombo. Well as Australia fought, the better team won.

Australia 188 (R. T. Ponting 96; M. Muralitharan 4-63) **and 140** (Ponting 51);
Sri Lanka 234 (P. A. de Silva 78; S. K. Warne 5-52, C. R. Miller 4-62) **and 95-4**.

2000-01 – SRI LANKA v ENGLAND (SECOND TEST): COOL HEADS

Hugh Chevallier, 2002

At Kandy, March 7, 8, 9, 10, 11, 2001. England won by three wickets. This was a bruising, bar-room brawl of a Test, the type that, pre-Fletcher, England would not have won. But with a now-habitual steel, win it they did, squaring the series. In several respects, Kandy was a classic. Thanks to an exemplary pitch that encouraged strokeplay, rewarded seam and took spin – yet never broke up as predicted – the initiative was batted back and forth like a ping-pong ball. And the drama unfolded against a backdrop of hazy blue mountains, fringed with palm and flame trees. Undermining it all, however, was more lamentable umpiring. By some counts there were 15 errors, and tempers inevitably boiled over, coming to a head on the explosive third day – ironically a *poya* day, or "day of peace" for the predominantly Buddhist population. Referee Hanumant Singh issued severe reprimands to Atherton and Sangakkara, as well as fining Jayasuriya 60% of his match fee for dissent and adding a suspended ban of two Tests and two one-day internationals. Both umpires had dreadful games, and most errors favoured England. Home official B. C. Cooray was especially vilified: "BC Bats for England" ran one local headline.

England needed a tricky 161. In his fourth over, Vaas removed Atherton (for the fourth time) and Trescothick, before Hussain and Thorpe put on a nerve-steadying 61. Yet both were gone by stumps, leaving the last day exquisitely poised: 70 runs or six wickets for victory. England probably had the edge if the tail was not exposed to Murali too soon. Stewart went early, handing Hick perhaps a final chance to rekindle the dying embers of a tortured Test career. The flame flickered briefly as a couple of balls sped to the boundary, then quietly, sadly went out. Wickets and runs came at perfect intervals to keep both teams' hopes alive, but Croft, White and then Giles kept admirably cool heads to weather the final storm.

Sri Lanka 297 (D. P. M. D. Jayawardene 101, R. P. Arnold 65; A. R. Caddick 4-55, D. Gough 4-73)

and 250 (K. C. Sangakkara 95, H. D. P. K. Dharmasena 54; Gough 4-50);

England 387 (N. Hussain 109, G. P. Thorpe 59, A. J. Stewart 54; M. Muralitharan 4-127)

and 161-7 (W. P. U. J. C. Vaas 4-39).

2000-01 – SRI LANKA v ENGLAND (THIRD TEST): BRING ON THE AUSSIES
Hugh Chevallier, 2002

At Sinhalese Sports Club, Colombo, March 15, 16, 17, 2001. England won by four wickets. Hard on the heels of Kandy's five-day classic came a three-day thriller at Colombo. On an astounding third day, 22 wickets fell for 229 runs – including ten Sri Lankans for 81 – to give England the series 2–1. True, they made a meal of hitting the required 74, but after losing the First Test by an innings it was a magnificent recovery. It wasn't just the Sri Lankans they overcame; the sun beat down remorselessly, and Thorpe said he had never played in such draining conditions. To widespread relief, the umpiring was of a high standard, and local official Asoka de Silva drew universal praise. With better umpiring came better behaviour, and the referee was invisible. On a wearing pitch, England got into a muddle chasing 74. Atherton finally survived Vaas, only to succumb to Fernando. At 43 for four, Sri Lanka had prised open an escape hatch. Thorpe slammed it shut with an undefeated 32, but not before Hussain, batting at No. 7 with a runner, became the final victim of the St Patrick's Day massacre. He was the eighth and last duck of the day, a record-equalling 11th for the match. "Bring on the Aussies!" sang the Barmy Army.

Sri Lanka 241 (D. P. M. D. Jayawardene 71; R. D. B. Croft 4-56) and 81 (A. F. Giles 4-11);

England 249 (G. P. Thorpe 113*; W. P. U. J. C. Vaas 6-73)

and 74-6 (S. T. Jayasuriya 4-24).

2001-02 – WEST INDIANS IN SRI LANKA: MURALI V LARA   Tony Cozier, 2003

Sri Lanka completed their first clean sweep of a three-Test series after 20 years of trying, but for West Indies the result was dismally familiar. Three crushing defeats – twice by ten wickets, once by 131 runs – extended their overseas record since beating Australia at Perth in February 1997 to a humiliating 21 losses in 25 Tests.

Yet the lasting memory will be of the sublime batting of Brian Lara and especially his duels with the otherwise unstoppable off-spinner, Muttiah Muralitharan, which added fuel to the argument that he was less comfortable bowling to left-handers. Lara had pulled out of West Indies' tour of Zimbabwe in June, and his fitness was still in doubt barely a week before the party flew to Sri Lanka. But he said he was determined to raise his Test average, which had dropped below 48, back above 50. It was a monumental task in a short series, but he coped with Muralitharan so easily that he achieved it during the final Test, when he followed his first-innings 221 with 130, carrying his aggregate to 688 at an average of nearly 115. Before Lara, only Graham Gooch had reached 600 runs in a series of three Tests.

In spite of Lara's eventual mastery over him, Muralitharan posed such problems to the other batsmen with his prodigious turn, teasing flight and clever variations that he took 11 wickets in the First Test at Galle and ten in the Second at his native Kandy. But he was dramatically upstaged at Colombo by Chaminda Vaas, whose controlled, each-way left-arm swing earned him two seven-wicket hauls. Vaas finished with 26 wickets to Muralitharan's 24.

Single Wicket Competition in 1965. Mushtaq Mohammad showed batsmanship of the highest quality in winning the Charrington Single Wicket Competition played over two days at Lord's on July 15 and 16. As a finale he changed in a flash from a right-handed batsman to a left-handed player to deal with a ball pitched well outside what was originally his off stump.

Little Wonder No. 83

2001-02 – SRI LANKA v ZIMBABWE (LG ABANS TRIANGULAR SERIES): VAAS RECORD   2003

At Sinhalese Sports Club, Colombo, December 8, 2001. Sri Lanka won by nine wickets. Vaas became the first bowler to claim eight wickets in a one-day international – five days after taking 14 Test wickets on the same ground against West Indies. As in the Test, his success was based on controlled, each-way swing on a true pitch. He dismissed Ebrahim with his first ball and took Sri Lanka's first limited-overs hat-trick in his sixth over. Vaas was on course for all ten until Muralitharan, who had held the previous one-day record, picked up the last two. Zimbabwe were routed for 38, the lowest total in limited-overs internationals, five less than Pakistan's 43 against

West Indies at Cape Town in 1992-93. That match had also produced the previous-lowest aggregate in a completed one-day international – 88 for 13 wickets – and at 32.2 overs had been the shortest international uninterrupted by bad weather; this game shattered both records. The crowd had witnessed a mere 78 runs for 11 wickets in 20 overs: Sri Lanka needed just 26 balls as they zoomed to victory before noon.

Zimbabwe 38 (15.4 overs) (W. P. U. J. C. Vaas 8–3–19–8); **Sri Lanka 40-1** (4.2 overs).

2003-04 – SRI LANKA v ENGLAND (THIRD TEST): HAPPY HAMMERING

Lawrence Booth, 2004

At Sinhalese Sports Club, Colombo. December 18, 19, 20, 21, 2003. Sri Lanka won by an innings and 215 runs. England arrived in Colombo full of optimism. They left dazed and confused, having suffered their third-heaviest defeat in 127 years of Test cricket and their first series loss under Vaughan's captaincy. After the energy-sapping escape acts of the first two Tests, they played with as much edge as a lump of plasticine.

For Sri Lanka – and not least for their captain, Tillekeratne, whose conservative brand of leadership had roused the critics – it was a delightful surprise. After failing to beat anyone but Bangladesh since March 2002, they pulled off the most crushing win in their history. To beat England in a proper series for the first time was merely a bonus.

There was little sign of the grim fate that awaited Vaughan's men when he won England's first toss in Sri Lanka for ten years, then helped bring up a freewheeling fifty in only the ninth over. In the pre-match build-up, the Sri Lanka coach, John Dyson, had accused England of rekindling a duller, more defensive era of Test cricket. But for the first hour at least, that accusation seemed absurd. Then it all went wrong. Outside the ground there was chaos too, as police prevented a group of Buddhist monks from storming the stadium. The monks were furious that the cricket had not been halted out of respect for a well-known colleague, the Venerable Gangodavila Soma Thera, who had died the previous week.

England's 265 was quickly put into perspective. After two days, Sri Lanka trailed by a single run, and Samaraweera and Jayawardene were doing as they pleased. Even the night-time provided no respite. The hotel management allowed a noisy party to go on till the early hours, infuriating the England players, and on the third morning they duly fielded like insomniacs. The declaration came at 628 for eight, Sri Lanka's second-highest Test score, which left England needing 363 to avoid an innings defeat – or five and a half sessions to survive. They held out for just over two, and when Hussain was given out caught behind to make it 44 for three, Muralitharan became the first bowler to take 100 wickets at a single Test venue. The rest followed like lost sheep. When Kirtley was bowled through the gate to give Muralitharan his 26th wicket of the series, Sri Lanka were home and dry with more than a day to spare. It was no more than they deserved.

England 265 (A. Flintoff 77, M. E. Trescothick 70) **and 148** (M. Muralitharan 4-63);
Sri Lanka 628-8 dec. (T. T. Samaraweera 142, D. P. M. D. Jayawardene 134, S. T. Jayasuriya 85,
T. M. Dilshan 83, U. D. U. Chandana 76).

Colombo century: Sri Lanka's Muttiah Muralitharan during the first Test against England in 2003-04 at the Sinhalese Sports Club when he became the first bowler to take 100 Test wickets at a single venue

2006 –SOUTH AFRICANS IN SRI LANKA: RECORDS AND RECRIMINATIONS

Charlie Austin, 2007

A fascinating tour, full of records and gripping cricket, ended acrimoniously when the South Africans withdrew from the triangular tournament due to follow the Tests because of fears for the players' safety. The decision came in the aftermath of an explosion in Colombo, which was intended to murder a Pakistani diplomat. The Sri Lankan board, faced with the prospect of a $12m loss, was left incensed that its assurance of "presidential-level security", which included armed bodyguards, bullet-proof coaches, three layers of checkpoints around the team hotel and traffic-free roads for all transfers, was not sufficient to allay player concerns and ensure the South Africans' participation. But two separate security firms recommended the pull-out.

Sri Lanka had won both the Tests. That bald scoreline might suggest a comfortable victory, but the second one was fiercely contested to the end, and South Africa almost squared the series. Their failure had almost everything to do with Mahela Jayawardene, Sri Lanka's captain, who followed his successful leadership in England with a quite brilliant performance. Brimming with confidence, Jayawardene started with an epic 374 in the First Test, the fourth-highest score in Test history, and added a masterful 123 in the Second. In the process he also rewrote the record books, sharing an awesome stand of 624 with Kumar Sangakkara – the highest stand in all first-class cricket (see Records, page 966). The tour ought to be best remembered for that.

2010 – SRI LANKA v INDIA (FIRST TEST): 800 DECLARED

2011

At Galle, July 18, 19, 20, 21, 22, 2010. Sri Lanka won by ten wickets. Galle was all agog for Muttiah Muralitharan's farewell Test appearance, with the entire stadium and its neighbourhood decorated with cut-outs depicting him and banners reflecting his performances. Muralitharan came to his final Test requiring eight wickets to become the first to take 800 – he said beforehand that he had given himself one match to make it a challenge. At the start, everything went according to plan: Sangakkara won the toss, chose to bat on a bone-dry pitch and, despite the loss of the second day to rain, Sri Lanka ran up a strong total, leaving India under pressure to bat out the final two days.

The time lost to the weather meant that for Sri Lanka to win – and probably for Muralitharan to make it to 800 – they had to bowl India out twice. They looked on course to do that when the tourists made only 276 in their first innings, with Murali stretching his record number of Test five-fors to 67. India followed on, and the man of the moment made it to 799 by dismissing Yuvraj Singh and Harbhajan Singh as the score lurched to 197 for seven. But India were not going to serve up No. 800 on a platter: Muralitharan had to toil through 23.4 further overs – during which he twice narrowly failed to run out one of the last pair – before Ojha edged him low to slip, where Mahela Jayawardene dived to his left for the catch. It was his 77th catch off Muralitharan's bowling, a Test record for a bowler and non-wicketkeeper, 22 ahead of Anil Kumble and Rahul Dravid.

The entire stadium erupted. Muralitharan was given a 21-gun salute, an honour normally reserved for visiting heads of state. He was carried around the field by his team-mates to the cheers of spectators. It was a momentous occasion for Murali and his family, who were present to witness this unique piece of cricket history.

Sri Lanka 520-8 dec. (N. T. Paranavitana 111, K. C. Sangakkara 103, H. M. R. K. B. Herath 80*;
A. Mithun 4-105) **and 96-0** (T. M. Dilshan 68*);
India 276 (V. Sehwag 109, Yuvraj Singh 52; M. Muralitharan 5-63)
and 336 (S. R. Tendulkar 84, V. V. S. Laxman 69; S. L. Malinga 5-50).

2011 – GOING DOWNHILL FAST   Sa'adi Thawfeeq, 2012

The fortunes of the Sri Lanka Cricket administration and the performances of the national team continued on a downward slide following the 2011 World Cup, in which Sri Lanka were runners-up. The decision by D. S. de Silva's interim committee to build and renovate three stadiums – Hambantota, Pallekele, and the Premadasa in Colombo – in order to host 12 World Cup matches left SLC with a deficit of $US32m. This led to an unprecedented situation in which they could not afford to pay their contracted cricketers, who numbered more than 100, nor around 200 other employees. Matters became so grave that the 2011-12 domestic season came to a standstill, with the 20 Premier Division clubs demanding their annual payments – without which they were unable to play their matches.

ZIMBABWE

Rhodesia first appeared in South Africa's domestic competition, the Currie Cup, in 1905 and competed sporadically until after the Second World War when they became a regular fixture. When independence from Britain was finally achieved in 1980, the new nation of Zimbabwe severed ties with the South African Cricket Union and became an associate member of the ICC. "Zimbabwe-Rhodesia struggled for most of their last season in a South African domestic competition," Peter Sichel wrote in the 1981 edition. "However, their captain D. A. G. Fletcher had a fine season and led the side with distinction." Plenty more would be heard of him, firstly as the man who led Zimbabwe to a shock victory over Australia at their first World Cup in 1983, and later as a successful coach of England. Test status was granted in 1992, by which time they had bagged another high-profile World Cup scalp by beating England – albeit in an inconsequential game – at Albury in the 1992 tournament. Zimbabwe were decently equipped for the Test arena with a core of gritty batsmen, led by another future England coach, Andy Flower. Their bowling was less impressive, though Heath Streak would provide a bullocking presence through the mid-1990s. But by the turn of the millennium Zimbabwe, as a country, was in meltdown and their cricket was part of the collateral damage. The recovery on both counts remains a work in progress.

1992-93 – ZIMBABWE v INDIA (INAUGURAL TEST): HOUGHTON'S HONOUR
1994

At Harare, October 18, 19, 20, 21, 22, 1992. Drawn. Against expectation Zimbabwe held the upper hand for long periods in their inaugural Test match, played in very hot weather on a lifeless pitch. Both attacks were rendered innocuous and much of the batting was also excessively cautious, with a run-rate of barely two an over. Zimbabwe, however, had the satisfaction of gaining a first-innings lead of 149 and, as the ninth Test-playing country, went on to become the first to avoid defeat in their initial Test since Australia in 1876-77, when Test cricket began. Their captain, Houghton, became the first player to score a century on his country's debut since Charles Bannerman, on the same occasion. Houghton shared the individual honours with Manjrekar, who scored a hundred for India, and Traicos, the Zimbabwean off-spinner.

At the age of 45, Traicos became the 14th man to represent two countries at Test level, 22 years and 222 days since playing for South Africa in their last Test before exclusion from international cricket – a record gap between Test appearances. He took five for 86 in 50 overs marked by subtle changes of pace and flight. The game will also be remembered as the first Test to have three appointed umpires. A new sponsorship by the British company National Grid meant that Dickie Bird was flown out from England to stand in his 48th Test and equal the world record set by his compatriot, Frank Chester. Bird stood throughout and the two Zimbabwean umpires on alternate days. Attendances throughout the game were tiny.

Zimbabwe 456 (D. L. Houghton 121, G. W. Flower 82, A. Flower 59) **and 146-4;**
India 307 (S. V. Manjrekar 104, Kapil Dev 60; A. J. Traicos 5-86).

1994-95 – ZIMBABWE v PAKISTAN (FIRST TEST): FRATERNAL FLOURISH   1996

At Harare, January 31, February 1, 2, 4, 1995. Zimbabwe won by an innings and 64 runs. Zimbabwe not only created history with their first victory in their 11th Test, but did it with style by an innings, inside four days. The Flowers took control on the first afternoon in a record-breaking fourth-wicket partnership, and Pakistan never got back into the game. Streak forced them to follow on and they folded in 62 overs on their second attempt.

The match had a farcical start when the referee, Jackie Hendriks, demanded a second toss. Salim Malik had called "Bird", the national symbol on one side of the Zimbabwean coin, instead of "Heads"; Andy Flower congratulated him on winning but Hendriks said he had not heard the call. Flower won at the second attempt and chose to bat. Until lunch, Pakistan seemed to shrug off their frustration. After the interval, Wasim bowled seven maiden overs in succession. But from then on, the Flowers flourished.

Andy, the elder brother, was the dominant partner, reaching his second Test century in three and a half hours. The brothers' stand passed 194, Zimbabwe's all-wicket record set by Campbell and Houghton against Sri Lanka three months earlier. Next day they took it to 269, overtaking the fraternal Test record of 264 shared by Greg and Ian Chappell.

Pakistan lost one wicket on the second evening, to Henry Olonga, the first non-white player to appear for Zimbabwe. His first delivery went for four wides, his second was a bouncer, and Andy Flower caught Saeed Anwar down the leg side off the third. But Olonga's debut ended in disaster next day. As in the previous tour match, he was no-balled for throwing, by umpire Robinson – the first recognised bowler to be called in a Test since Ian Meckiff for Australia against South Africa in Brisbane in 1963-64 – and later retired with a side strain.

Zimbabwe 544-4 dec. (G. W. Flower 201*, A. Flower 156, G. J. Whittall 113*);
Pakistan 322 (Inzamam-ul-Haq 71, Ijaz Ahmed 65, Aamir Sohail 61; H. H. Streak 6-90)
and 158 (Inzamam 65).

Essex v Warwickshire. At Clacton, August 4, 5, 6, 1965. With Webster unable to bowl, A. C. Smith, the wicketkeeper, joined the attack and he performed the hat-trick at the expense of Barker, G. Smith and Fletcher. When disposing of Bailey, Smith had taken four wickets in 34 deliveries without cost.

Little Wonder No. 84

1996-97 – ENGLAND IN ZIMBABWE: AWFUL AMBASSADORS   David Lloyd*, 1998

The English winter began gloomily in Zimbabwe, where the visitors could do no better than draw both Tests, and lost all three one-day internationals rather humiliatingly. Worse still, by the time they left Harare for Auckland in early January, few Zimbabweans were sorry to see the back of the England party. They had accomplished the rare double of failing to win a single match of significance while adopting an approach widely regarded as unfriendly, aloof and, thanks to one crass comment from coach David Lloyd, downright rude. It was hard to think how England could have made a bigger mess of their first senior tour to cricket's ninth and newest Test country.

England spent a dreary Christmas minus their families (another poor decision by the tour planners, unlikely to be repeated), but were set to finish the stronger side in the Second Test before rain washed out the final day. Another moral victory? Maybe. But does any Test team dismissed for 156 in its first innings deserve too much sympathy? Nothing but condemnation followed England's performances during the last two one-day internationals: one they lost from a position of power, the other ended in a rout after an inspired spell of swing bowling from Eddo Brandes, who claimed a hat-trick. Zimbabwe celebrated while England were more than happy to say their goodbyes, having underperformed as a unit throughout and failed in their wider obligations as cricketing tourists. "Lord MacLaurin and I were horrified by what we saw in Zimbabwe," ECB chief executive Tim Lamb confirmed later. "We were not happy with the way the England team presented themselves. Their demeanour was fairly negative and not particularly attractive."

The Press Association reporter, not to be confused with his namesake, the England coach

---

1996-97 – ZIMBABWE v ENGLAND (First Test): "flippin' murdered" 1998

At Bulawayo, December 18, 19, 20, 21, 22, 1996. Drawn. A gently smouldering match suddenly burst into full flame on the last afternoon when England were left to chase 205 from 37 overs. Often up with the rate but never sufficiently ahead to feel comfortable, they eventually needed three from Streak's final delivery. Knight managed two and this inaugural Test between the two countries earned another place in history: it was the first Test to be drawn with the scores level. Such excitement had seemed unlikely during the first four days, on a slow-turning pitch where both runs and wickets needed chiselling out.

Atherton again departed quickly but Knight and, particularly, Stewart, who passed 4,000 Test runs as he scored 73 off 76 balls, gave the run-chase real impetus against increasingly negative bowling and far-flung fields. Stewart's exit, to a miscued pull, when England needed 51 from eight overs, was probably crucial. Three more wickets swiftly followed. Knight, though, brought fresh hope with a glorious square-leg six in Streak's final over, and five runs were wanted from three deliveries. The next ball might have been called as a wide by the Zimbabwe umpire Robinson, whose decision-making was questioned several times. There was no signal, however, and Knight could not find the boundary again. Referee Hanumant Singh busied himself during and after the contest, reprimanding England for the manner of their appealing, investigating but taking no action over coach David Lloyd's "we flippin' murdered them" outburst, and fining Streak 15% of his match fee for implied criticism of the umpires; Streak had said he was lucky not to have been called wide in that last over.

Zimbabwe 376 (A. Flower 112, A. D. R. Campbell 84)
and 234 (G. J. Whittall 56, A. C. Waller 50; P. C. R. Tufnell 4-61);
England 406 (N. Hussain 113, J. P. Crawley 112, N. V. Knight 56; P. A. Strang 5-123)
and 204-6 (Knight 96, A. J. Stewart 73).

2001 – ZIMBABWE v WEST INDIES (Second Test): SCHOOLBOY CENTURY
2002

At Harare, July 27, 28, 29, 30, 31, 2001. Drawn. Eleven days short of his 18th birthday, schoolboy Hamilton Masakadza became the youngest batsman to score a hundred on Test debut, inspiring a remarkable Zimbabwean recovery from a first-innings deficit of 216. It was ironic that their bid for an extraordinary victory should have been spoiled by the first significant rain of the season. Streak's second-innings declaration at 563 for nine, Zimbabwe's highest Test score, left his bowlers a theoretical 114 overs to dismiss West Indies, chasing a target of 348. The performance of Masakadza, the ninth black cricketer to represent his country in Tests, earned significance even beyond its statistical merit. He was cheered on by hundreds of schoolchildren, bussed there in an effort to spread the cricketing gospel to the majority black population. Masakadza, tall, upright and strong on the leg side, benefited from chances at 28 and 101, yet was never unsettled.

Zimbabwe 131 (N. C. McGarrell 4-23) **and 563-9 dec.** (H. Masakadza 119, C. B. Wishart 93,

A. M. Blignaut 92, H. H. Streak 83*, A. D. R. Campbell 65);

West Indies 347 (R. R. Sarwan 86, S. Chanderpaul 74; B. C. Strang 4-83) **and 98-1** (C. H. Gayle 52*).

2003-04 – SRI LANKANS IN ZIMBABWE: A GAME IN MELTDOWN   2005

Sri Lanka's third Test tour of Zimbabwe, through no fault of their own, was a travesty of international cricket from beginning to end. The civil war between Zimbabwe's administrators and cricketers led to the absence of 15 good players in a country desperately short of them. The upshot was a farce in which the Sri Lankans easily won all five one-day internationals and then hammered the team chosen to represent Zimbabwe by record margins in the two Tests.

The International Cricket Council refused to recognise the extent of the crisis until the results of the Test matches meant that they could bury their heads in the sand no longer. They then stepped in to safeguard the Australian tour that followed from similar abuse of international status; the Zimbabwe Cricket Union agreed to postpone those Tests, before they could be stripped of their official standing. But by that time the Sri Lankan series had become a part of cricket history that could not be revoked.

Muttiah Muralitharan's seizure of the title of Test cricket's leading wicket-taker was one record likely to have occurred here whatever the quality of the opposition. It was just sad that he could not have overtaken Courtney Walsh's record of 519 wickets in more salubrious circumstances. It was still a memorable occasion, acclaimed rapturously by his team-mates and all of Sri Lanka.

2006 – TEST CRICKET ON HOLD   2007

The year of 2006 began hopefully for Zimbabwean cricket, but it was swiftly plunged back into the despair that engulfs the country in every area of life. While the International Cricket Council continued to play Pontius Pilate, the game continued to decline under chairman Peter Chingoka and chief executive officer Ozias Bvute.

In late 2005, the details of Zimbabwe Cricket's rule of infamy and incompetence were finally brought to light. Mashonaland Country Districts chairman Charlie Robertson led an investigation into the governing body's affairs, especially its financial dealings, after inadequate and misleading accounts were hurried through the AGM. Several million pounds could not be accounted for, and the group took their case to the Sports Commission and the Reserve Bank of Zimbabwe.

The Reserve Bank decided to prosecute Chingoka and Bvute, and the police took them in for questioning. Then the reality of life in Zimbabwe took over. Chingoka had lengthy meetings with supporters in high places, including the minister for sport and recreation, Aeneas Chigwedere. In January, the Attorney General stepped in to halt the investigations.

Since the initial player revolt in 2004, Zimbabwe had suffered repeated gross humiliations in the Test arena. Even ZC's cricket chiefs realised that, after further defections, they could not continue to play Test cricket with what was, at best, a third eleven. They therefore undertook a voluntary suspension from Test cricket to "rebuild", initially for a year but later extended until November 2007, when they were due to meet West Indies. Few believe they will be ready for anything but further abject defeat.

2011-12 – Bangladeshis In Zimbabwe: papering over the cracks
Neil Manthorp, 2012

The sceptics were ready to pounce, but Zimbabwe's return to Test cricket after an absence of six years was nothing if not carefully organised. New Zealand A had visited to play three four-day games in October 2010, and Zimbabwe's build-up concluded with an intense one-day triangular against A-teams from Australia and South Africa, followed by two four-day matches against an Australia A side packed with Test players. Zimbabwe's Test victory, meanwhile, glossed over comments made 48 hours before the start by former captain Tatenda Taibu, who slammed Zimbabwe Cricket administrators for "struggling to run cricket in the country well". He added: "I don't think much has changed really. Zimbabwe Cricket has just painted a house that's about to fall." Taibu's gripes were that players' match fees had not been paid for almost a year and that central contracts for the national players had still not been finalised. He had a point, but the implication that players were working for nothing was disingenuous. All had received their monthly salaries on time, even if match fees were regarded – questionably, it must be said – as "bonuses" by the players' bosses.

2011-12 – ZIMBABWE v BANGLADESH (Only Test): return to top table
Telford Vice, 2012

At Harare, August 4, 5, 6, 7, 8, 2011. Zimbabwe won by 130 runs. Zimbabwe erased the unhappiness of exile by surging to a convincing victory 15 balls after lunch on the fifth day. Of the team that had last played a Test, against India in September 2005, only Taylor, Masakadza and Taibu remained – though four others had previous Test experience – while Heath Streak was now the bowling coach. Yet each played a crucial role in their country's ninth Test win, their first since February 2004 and their fifth in nine games against Bangladesh. The Zimbabweans celebrated at a local hotel with a rousing *dhindhindi*, the Shona word for party, which roared into the night with the kind of gusto usually reserved for the end of a war.

Hardened into a team by the experience scavenged from 108 one-day internationals during the non-Test years, Zimbabwe – one careless collapse aside – showed discipline and patience with the bat and refreshing energy with the ball, while Taylor earned bonus points for an enterprising declaration that set Bangladesh 375 in four sessions. Taylor also became the seventh player – and the second Zimbabwean, after Dave Houghton – to register his maiden century in his first Test as captain, while Masakadza added a second ten years after his first.

Zimbabwe's previously pedestrian attack was fitted with a pair of jet engines. Brian Vitori, a burly, bustling left-armer, consistently bent the ball back into the right-handers, and Kyle Jarvis (son of former Test seamer Malcolm) bowled with pace. By contrast, Bangladesh's batsmen lacked purpose and belief in their first Test since Old Trafford in June 2010, and their bowlers – even the left-arm spinners, who in the past had flummoxed the Zimbabweans – caused little anxiety.

Zimbabwe 370 (H. Masakadza 104, V. Sibanda 78, B. R. M. Taylor 71)
and 291-5 dec. (Taylor 105*, T. Taibu 59);
Bangladesh 287 (Mohammad Ashraful 73, Shakib Al Hasan 68, Shahriar Nafees 50; B. V. Vitori 4-66)
and 244 (K. M. Jarvis 4-61).

BANGLADESH

As East Pakistan, Bangladesh first hosted Test cricket in 1955 and continued to do so until independence in 1971. "After that," *Wisden* reported in 1998, "cricket took some time to win its place back – the country was ravaged by war, cricket was labelled elitist in certain quarters and there was propaganda against it. But the love of the players overcame this. Club-level competition is the basis of the game's popularity and charm. A match between popular clubs like Abahani and Mohammedan usually draws a crowd above 35.000. In 1993 the ICC chief executive, David Richards, was surprised to see a turnout of about 15,000 for a league match at the Dhaka Stadium between two rather unfancied clubs. He was even more astonished when he was told everyone had had to pay." After a tour by MCC in 1976-77 Bangladesh were granted Associate membership of ICC, and they competed in the ICC Trophy for the first time in 1979. Victory in the 1997 tournament in Kuala Lumpur brought with it qualification for the 1999 World Cup. "Not since independence from Pakistan in 1971 had the country celebrated with such togetherness," said *Wisden*. Test status was achieved in 2000, but it took more than four years and 35 matches before they recorded their first victory. Life in the higher echelons has contained "plenty of the usual heartbreak", as the 2006 *Wisden* described their struggles, and improvement has been barely discernible: Bangladesh won only three of their first 77 Tests.

2000 – TEST STATUS ACHIEVED   Utpal Shuvro, 2001

For the second time in just over a year, Bangladesh turned its gaze towards England, and once again the news coming back to the subcontinent triggered an outpouring of national pride and joy. In 1999, the magical day was May 31, when Bangladesh beat Pakistan against the odds in the World Cup. But June 26, 2000, would become a much more significant date in the nation's cricket heart. It was then that the dream seed, planted as ICC Associate membership in 1977, reached full bloom with the unanimous decision of the ICC annual general meeting at Lord's to welcome Bangladesh into the Test family as its tenth Full member.

2000-01 – INDIANS IN BANGLADESH: NATIONAL CELEBRATION   Richard Hobson, 2002

Saber Chowdhury, the president of the Bangladesh Cricket Board, described his country's elevation to Test status as the third most historic event in their national life, behind independence and the adoption of a United Nations mother-tongue day commemorating the suppression of the Bengali language under Pakistani rule. Certainly, the five days of celebrations leading up to the inaugural Test against India reflected its perceived importance to the national well-being. Events included a ceremonial dinner, a vivid firework display, school activities and the recording of a song written by a local journalist. A near-capacity crowd of around 40,000 watched the first day's play, which began after a simple but poignant opening ceremony in which parachutists carried flags from each of the ten Test-playing countries into the Bangabandhu Stadium.

2000-01 – BANGLADESH v INDIA (INAUGURAL TEST): PROMISING START
                                                         Richard Hobson, 2002

At Dhaka, November 10, 11, 12, 13, 2000. India won by nine wickets. For at least two-thirds of this contest, Bangladesh surpassed all expectations by matching their neighbours, and at times even enjoying the upper hand. Australia, who beat England in 1876-77, and Zimbabwe, who drew with India in 1992-93, remained the only countries to avoid defeat on Test debut.

The quiet pessimism of those who felt Bangladesh would struggle to make India bat twice seemed well founded. They had failed to win any of their previous ten first-class matches, and had just completed a chastening tour of South Africa. Furthermore, their selection process was exposed as chaotic when two of the most experienced players, Enamul Haque and Habibul Bashar, were reinstated in the squad at the personal behest of board president Saber Chowdhury, to the governing body's embarrassment. It was a reflection of how successfully they began that the expected defeat was eventually greeted with widespread disappointment, and heavy newspaper criticism for their second-innings collapse. If the players learned anything, it was that supporters have short memories.

Expectations were raised largely through the performance of Aminul Islam, a familiar figure on English club grounds. His 145 represented the third century for a country playing their inaugural Test, and the highest since Australian Charles Bannerman retired hurt on 165 in 1876-77. Only Dave Houghton of Zimbabwe had achieved the feat in between. Before the end of the game, he was a taka millionaire on donations alone, although an exchange rate of 80 takas to the pound meant this was not quite the fortune it appeared.

Bangladesh 400 (Aminul Islam 145, Habibul Bashar 71; S. B. Joshi 5-142) **and 91**;
India 429 (Joshi 92, S. C. Ganguly 84, S. Ramesh 58; Naimur Rahman 6-132) **and 64-1**.

2002-03 – BANGLADESH v WEST INDIES (First Test): SIX OF THE WORST
Utpal Shuvro, 2004

At Dhaka, December 8, 9, 10, 2002. West Indies won by an innings and 310 runs. Bangladesh hit several new lows on the third day: their lowest innings total, their lowest match aggregate, and the biggest defeat in their 16 Tests. It was all due to Jermaine Lawson, the 20-year-old Jamaican fast bowler, who had made his Test debut at Chennai in October. He propelled himself into the record books with scarcely believable figures of 6.5–4–3–6, the most economical six-wicket haul in Test history. All Lawson's six wickets came in a devastating 15-ball spell, in which he did not concede a single run; in one over, he took three in four deliveries. Bangladesh collapsed from 80 for three, losing their final seven for as many runs as the last five all made ducks.

Bangladesh 139 (Alok Kapali 52; P. T. Collins 5-26, V. C. Drakes 4-61) **and 87** (J. J. C. Lawson 6-3);
West Indies 536 (R. R. Sarwan 119, R. D. Jacobs 91*, M. N. Samuels 91, W. W. Hinds 75, C. H. Gayle 51).

2004-05 – ZIMBABWEANS IN BANGLADESH: WOODEN-SPOON DECIDER
Utpal Shuvro, 2006

This was a title decider of a different kind, the world championship of wooden spoons. But it was never dull. Though these were obviously Test cricket's two weakest nations, the cricket was intense, competitive and sometimes riveting. For Bangladesh, the outcome was historic: their first Test victory led to their first Test-series win, followed by their first win in a one-day series.

2004-05 – BANGLADESH v ZIMBABWE (First Test): MAIDEN VICTORY
2006

At Chittagong, January 6, 7, 8, 9, 10, 2005. Bangladesh won by 226 runs. At 12.53pm on January 10, the moment all Bangladesh had been waiting for arrived. When

Enamul Haque junior had Christopher Mpofu held at silly point, they recorded their maiden victory in their 35th Test. They had been dreaming of this day since gaining Test status in 2000, but first had to endure 31 defeats, three draws and innumerable sleepless nights.

Zimbabwe, fielding three debutants, were the weakest opponents they had ever faced but, from beginning to end, the Test followed Bangladesh's script. After winning the toss in perfect batting conditions, they amassed their highest Test total, took a sizeable first-innings lead, scored quickly in the second innings to earn ample time to dismiss Zimbabwe again, and completed their historic victory shortly after lunch on the final day.

Captain Habibul Bashar called it the best day of his life. They declared for only the second time, leaving Zimbabwe 381 to win.

An inspired new-ball spell from Tapash Baisya reduced Zimbabwe to two for two in their fourth over, and they were three down by the close. But Masakadza, in his first Test since November 2002, and Taylor started the fifth day in brilliant form, adding 66 in 15 overs before the drinks break. Immediately afterwards, however, Taylor was lbw offering no shot to a straight ball from Enamul. That opened the floodgates. Enamul had bowled beautifully in the first innings without reward; this time, luck was on his side, and his flight and turn sent wickets tumbling like ripe mangoes. Dismissing last man Mpofu gave him six for 45, the best Test figures for Bangladesh, before cartwheels and a lap of honour kicked off the national celebrations.

Bangladesh 488 (Habibul Bashar 94, Rajin Saleh 89, Mohammad Rafique 69, Nafis Iqbal 56; C. B. Mpofu 4-109) and 204-9 dec. (Habibul 55; E. Chigumbura 5-54); Zimbabwe 312 (T. Taibu 92, Chigumbura 71; Rafique 5-65) and 154 (H. Masakadza 56; Enamul Haque, jun. 6-45).

2005-06 – BANGLADESH v AUSTRALIA (SECOND TEST): DIZZY HEIGHTS
Nabila Ahmed, 2007

At Chittagong, April 16, 17, 18, 19, 20, 2006. Australia won by an innings and 80 runs. If Australia were taken aback in Fatullah, they were positively shocked in Chittagong. This time, they were not surprised by the opposition, though the Bangladesh tail wagged vigorously at the last. Nor was it the media sit-in, protesting at the alleged police assault of a local photographer, which delayed the match's start by ten minutes and led to an ugly lunchtime brawl between police and press. Nor was it the violent thunderstorms that blew apart the scoreboard on the second day and dismantled the makeshift bamboo shelters in the stands.

No, the most unthinkable sight of all was that of Jason Gillespie tickling a ball down to fine leg and then running back towards the Australian dressing-room, ecstatic and more than a little bemused at the number 201 beside his name. So improbable was his double-century that even he could only shake his head, poke his tongue out and utter astonished expletives. At the Australian High Commission in Dhaka, they named a bar after "Dizzy", and his bat manufacturer announced plans for a "DZ 201" bat. Cast aside after a listless Ashes series, Gillespie, the most threatening of Australia's pace bowlers on this comeback tour, summed up his adventure as a fairytale. "Hansel and Gretel and Dizzy's double-hundred, it's one and the same," he said.

When Ponting asked him to go in as nightwatchman on the opening day, he was focused only on guarding his stumps and staying in as long as possible. Three days later – his 31st birthday, as it happened – his main concern was how to evade an agreement with Hayden and the team masseuse that he must do a nude lap of the ground should he become the first nightwatchman to reach a Test milestone that had eluded the likes of Ian Chappell and Mark Waugh. Gillespie's previous first-class best was 58.

Bangladesh 197 (Rajin Saleh 71)

and 304 (Shahriar Nafees 79, Mohammad Rafique 65; S. K. Warne 5-113, S. C. G. MacGill 4-95);

Australia 581-4 dec. (J. N. Gillespie 201*, M. E. K. Hussey 182, P. A. Jaques 66, R. T. Ponting 52).

2010-11 – BANGLADESH v NEW ZEALAND (ONE-DAY INTERNATIONAL SERIES): BANGLAWASH
Utpal Shuvro, 2011

Bangladesh's team and supporters had become wearily accustomed to the term "whitewash" over the often painful years since they were elevated to Test status. In this series, though, the other side was on the receiving end for a change: Bangladesh won all four completed matches, to send New Zealand home to an embarrassing inquest before their impending tour of India. It was a result few had predicted, and the whole country rejoiced. Bangladesh's leading daily newspaper headlined it "Banglawash". The players were hailed as national heroes, and the prime minister feted them with cash prizes, housing plots and cars. Mark Greatbatch, New Zealand's coach, observed afterwards that his team had "played like dicks". Once the team returned from India, Greatbatch was moved sideways, and John Wright took over as coach.

World Cup

I n the 1968 edition, tucked away in the "Other matches at Lord's" section, was a brief report, with scorecards, of a triangular tournament called the World Cricket Cup. "The Rest of the World team under Sobers carried off the Rothman World Cup with unbelievable ease," *Wisden* said. England and the touring Pakistanis made up the numbers. Eight years later the editor Norman Preston proclaimed: "Surely the season of 1975 will go down in the annals of English cricket as one of the best of all time... the tremendous success of the Prudential World Cup during weeks of glorious sunshine, created new interest and brought back the crowds to the best of all games when the right conditions prevail."

The authorities had been slow on the uptake. A women's World Cup had already taken place in 1973 (see page 847). In his 1975 Notes Preston had been sniffy about this new addition to the summer. "To return to England's problems. Players have to be found to take part in the Prudential (World) Cup." But a monster had been created. The first three tournaments were compact eight-team affairs, held in England and all 60 overs per side. India's shock victory in 1983 transformed that country's relationship with the game and sowed the seeds for the commercial and political power it holds over the game today. The World Cup moved to Asia in 1987 with great success, and returned there in 1996 for a tournament that, according to *Wisden*, "proceeded to frustrate and bewilder". It questioned "the methods and ambitions of those charged with running the tournament". This was first of the heavily commercialised, big-beast World Cups that culminated in the tortuous, over-sanitised and fatally tarnished (literally, with the tragic death of Bob Woolmer) 2007 tournament staged in the Caribbean.

The ICC's response to the debacle was to change the format, reducing the field from 16 teams to 14 and splitting them into two seven-team leagues from which eight quarter-finalists would emerge. It was "a knee-jerk response" according to Sambit Bal's review of the 2011 tournament. "It was designed with the sole purpose of keeping the Indian team, which single-handedly sustains the world cricket economy – unhealthily reliant on the television viewers of just one nation – in contention for as long as possible. The folly of this format was so apparent that, even before a single ball had been bowled, the ICC announced plans for yet another change at the 2015 World Cup in Australia and New Zealand – although those plans were later shelved following outrage among the Associate nations, who would have been excluded. Even so, it was a reflection of the sport's, and the ICC's, indecisiveness and confusion."

Gloucestershire v Yorkshire. At Lydney, July 28, 29, 30, 1965. The home batsmen took no risks and showed no signs of getting out, so Yorkshire eventually employed ten bowlers, including wicketkeeper Binks who bowled two overs in his pads while Trueman went behind the stumps.

Little Wonder No. 85

1975 – ENGLAND v INDIA (GROUP A): GAVASKAR'S GO-SLOW   1976

At Lord's, June 7, 1975. England won by 202 runs. With Amiss in his best form and admirably supported by Fletcher, England ran up the highest score in this country for a 60-over match, although later in the summer it was beaten by Hampshire in the Gillette Cup. India, in turn, gave such a disappointing exhibition that even their own large contingent of supporters showed their disapproval. The culprit was Gavaskar, who sat on the splice throughout the 60 overs for 36 not out. Neither G. S. Ramchand, India's manager, nor the captain, Venkataraghavan, agreed with the way Gavaskar performed. It was said that the pitch was slow and he took the opportunity to have some practice.

England 334-4 (60 overs) (D. L. Amiss 137, K. W. R. Fletcher 68, C. M. Old 51*);
India 132-3 (60 overs).

1975 – AUSTRALIA v WEST INDIES (FINAL): FIRST-CLASS ENTERTAINMENT
Norman Preston, 1976

At Lord's, June 21, 1975. West Indies won by 17 runs. Prince Philip presented the Cup amidst hilarious scenes to West Indies' talented captain, the Man of the Match, Clive Lloyd, just before nine o'clock on a glorious summer's evening. From 11am till 8.43pm the cricketers from the Caribbean had been locked in a succession of thrills with the cricketers from the Southern Cross. It might not be termed first-class cricket, but the game has never produced better entertainment in one day.

Australia gained the initiative when Fredericks hooked a bouncer high over fine leg for six only to lose his balance and tread on his wicket. Greenidge spent 80 minutes crawling to 13, and a rash cut by Kallicharran ended in a flick to the wicketkeeper. Then came Lloyd, and at once he showed himself master of the situation. He hooked Lillee in majestic style, square for six, and then put Walker off the back foot past cover with disdainful ease. Lloyd was at the crease only one hour and 48 minutes while making his scintillating hundred off 82 balls. More powerful hitting came from Boyce and Julien, so that Australia required 292 to lift the Cup.

Although they challenged to the very end and might have won had they shown some discretion when trying to steal precious runs, they contributed to their own

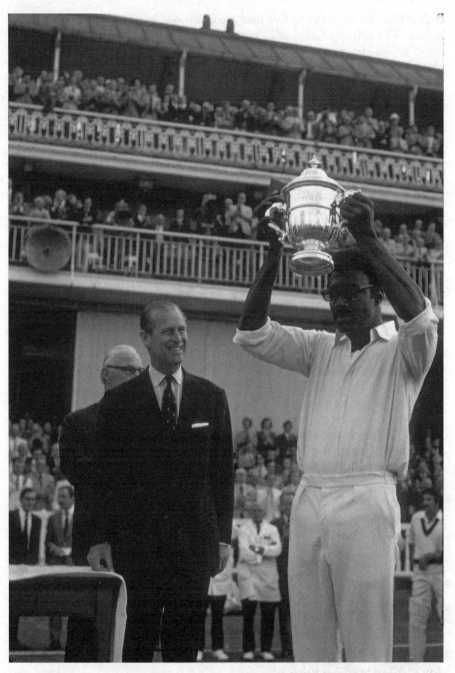

Royal approval: West Indies captain Clive Lloyd receives the World Cup
from the Duke of Edinburgh after the inaugural final at Lord's in 1975

destruction, for as many as five men were run out by the brilliant West Indies fielders. The amazing Kallicharran*, who had begun their troubles with a dazzling slip catch which removed McCosker, threw down the stumps twice from backward square leg, and he also enabled Lloyd to break the wicket at the bowler's end when Ian Chappell hesitated and then set off for the third impossible run. It was the longest day of the year; the longest day in cricket history and one that those who were there and the millions who watched it on television will never forget.

West Indies 291-8 (60 overs) (C. H. Lloyd 102, R. B. Kanhai 55; G. J. Gilmour 5-48);

Australia 274 (58.4 overs) (I. M. Chappell 62, A. Turner 40; K. D. Boyce 4-50).

*This is one of Wisden's more notable mistakes. The following year a correction was published: Errata in Wisden 1976. In fourth paragraph Australia v West Indies read: Richards threw down the stumps twice and was responsible for Ian Chappell being out.

1979 – ENGLAND v WEST INDIES (FINAL): KING OF KINGS

Norman Preston, 1980

At Lord's, June 23, 1979. West Indies won by 92 runs and so retained the Prudential Cup and the title of world champions which they first won in 1975. On another fine day the ground was completely filled by the all-ticket crowd of 25,000, and many would-be spectators were locked out.

Richards, the hero of the day and rightly named Man of the Match, found the right ally in King, who virtually took charge from the moment he arrived and made 86 out of 139 put on the fifth wicket in only 77 minutes. Many of these runs came from England's three fill-in bowlers as King struck three sixes and ten fours in an amazing display. He drove, hooked and pulled with astonishing power and accuracy.

England had the better batting conditions in brilliant sunshine, and Brearley and Boycott gave them a sound start by staying together for two hours ten minutes, although they never managed to take the West Indies' pace bowlers apart. Boycott occupied 17 overs to reach double figures, and when Brearley went England wanted 158 from the last 22 overs. This looked to be out of the question, and so it proved.

West Indies 286-9 (60 overs) (I. V. A. Richards 138*, C. L. King 86);

England 194 (51 overs) (J. M. Brearley 64, G. Boycott 57; J. Garner 5-38).

1983 – INDIA'S SHOCK VICTORY

John Woodcock, Notes by the Editor, 1984

The World Cup was a great success and India's victory a splendid surprise. They brought warmth and excitement in the place of dampness and depression. In the early years of limited-overs cricket no one, themselves included, took India seriously. Their strength lay much more in waging battles of attrition.

At the end of June, when the visiting teams went their separate ways, they were asked to tender, should they wish to, for the next World Cup. First to show an interest were India and Pakistan, who were exploring the idea of staging it jointly.

1983 – AUSTRALIA v ZIMBABWE (GROUP B): THE FIRST UPSET 1984

At Nottingham, June 9, 1983. Zimbabwe won by 13 runs. In their first appearance in the competition, the amateurs of Zimbabwe brought off a bigger surprise than any in the previous two World Cups. The Australian captain described his side as being outplayed. Having been put in, Zimbabwe made no more than a steady start, but from 94 for five their captain, Duncan Fletcher led an acceleration, adding 70 in 15 overs with Curran and 75 in 12 overs with Butchart. Australia missed five catches, bowled moderately and, though Wood and Wessels gave their innings an adequate start, they slipped behind the required rate against Fletcher's four for 42 and some fine fielding and catching.

Zimbabwe 239-6 (60 overs) (D. A. G. Fletcher 69*);
Australia 226-7 (60 overs) (K. C. Wessels 76, R. W. Marsh 50*; Fletcher 4-42).

1983 – INDIA v ZIMBABWE (GROUP B): SMASH AND GRAB 1984

At Tunbridge Wells, June 18, 1983. India won by 31 runs. A remarkable match contained one of the most spectacular innings played in this form of cricket. India, who had chosen to bat on a pitch from which the ball moved a lot, were nine for four – soon to be 17 for five – when their captain, Kapil Dev, came in. No one could foresee then that a week later India would be winning the whole tournament; indeed, qualification for the semi-final was in grave doubt. With Binny and Madan Lal, Kapil Dev took the score to 140 for eight and by then was in full flow. Kirmani provided sensible support in an unbroken ninth-wicket stand of 126 in 16 overs while Kapil Dev, with six sixes and 16 fours in all, reached 175, beating the previous highest for the tournament. The match was still not firmly in India's hands, for Curran, who with Rawson had been responsible for India's early disasters, played a dashing innings of 73, and it was not until he was ninth out at 230 in the 56th over that India were safe.

India 266-8 (60 overs) (Kapil Dev 175*; P. W. E. Rawson 3-47, K. M. Curran 3-65);
Zimbabwe 235 (57 overs) (Curran 73; Madan Lal 3-42).

1983 – INDIA v WEST INDIES (FINAL): DRAMA AND EMOTION
Wilfred Wooller, 1984

At Lord's, June 25, 1983. India defeated on merit the firm favourites, winning a low-scoring match by 43 runs. It was an absorbing game of increasing drama and finally of much emotion. The result, as surprising as, on the day, it was convincing, had much to do with the mental pressures of containment in limited-overs cricket.

Amarnath was named Man of the Match by Mike Brearley for a stabilising innings of 26 against hostile fast bowling after the early loss of Gavaskar, followed by his taking three late West Indian wickets, Dujon's being especially important. Dujon and Marshall had lifted West Indies, needing 184 to win, from 76 for six to 119, a recovery based on the calm application of sound batting principles and one which was threatening to achieve after all the result which everyone had expected.

Lord's, groomed like a high-born lady, bathed in sunshine and packed to capacity, was at its best when Lloyd won the toss and invited India to bat: a distinct advantage, it seemed, for his battery of fast bowlers. There was an explosive start to the match, Garner hurling the ball down, chest-high on the line of the off stump. Roberts, fast but flatter, had Gavaskar caught at the wicket in his third over. To score off such an attack was a problem, but Srikkanth showed how: he hooked Roberts for four, pulled him for six and square-drove him to the Tavern boundary like a pistol shot. India's total of 183 seemed many too few.

West Indies started badly. Greenidge padded up to the deceptive Sandhu and was bowled. Richards, however, swept the total swiftly and effortlessly to 50. Then, when 33, he mistimed a hook and Kapil Dev took a fine catch over his shoulder, running back towards the midwicket boundary. It remained for Amarnath to break the partnership between Dujon and Marshall which, just in time, he did. India were an entertaining and well-drilled team, learning and improving as they progressed towards the final.

India 183 (54.4 overs) (A. M. E. Roberts 3-32);
West Indies 140 (52 overs) (Madan Lal 3-31).

1987 – RELIANCE WORLD CUP: CAPTIVATING   Scyld Berry, 1989

The fourth World Cup was more widely watched, more closely fought, and more colourful than any of its three predecessors held in England. Any doubts about it were dispelled by the opening matches when Pakistan, the favourites, were run close by Sri Lanka; when India, the holders, were beaten by Australia by one run; when England succeeded in scoring 35 off their last three overs to beat West Indies; and when the gallant amateurs of Zimbabwe lost by only three runs to New Zealand.

If the rest of the Reliance Cup, as it was officially known and seldom called, could not quite live up to such a start, the experiment of an oriental World Cup was still acknowledged to have been a great success. The semi-finals in Lahore and Bombay held the subcontinent by the ears and eyes, even if they did not produce the results desired by the tens of millions who were following the matches on radio and television.

Any drawbacks resulted from the geographical enormity of the two host countries and the determination of the Indo–Pakistan Joint Management Committee to spread the games around as many as 21 venues. It was the equivalent of staging a tournament in Europe, barring only the Soviet Union, without quite the same facility of transport and telecommunications.

One especial virtue in staging the World Cup in India and Pakistan was that spin had a full part to play, whereas previous competitions in England had been dominated by repetitive seamers. Not one over of spin was risked in the 1975 final.

1987 – INDIA v ENGLAND (SEMI-FINAL): HOSTS SWEPT ASIDE   1989

At Bombay, November 5, 1987. Kapil Dev put England in, believing that the ball would swing early in the day. In the event it did not. The pitch, slow and providing turn, was more suited to spin bowling, thought to be India's strength but countered masterfully by Gooch and Gatting. Adopting a policy of sweeping and pulling the two slow left-arm bowlers, they put on 117 in 19 overs.

India, with Vengsarkar unable to play because of a stomach upset, suffered an early setback when DeFreitas knocked over Gavaskar's off stump. It was the break England wanted, and they never let India take the initiative. Kapil Dev fell victim to his own impetuosity, caught on the midwicket boundary immediately after Gatting had stationed himself there. For Hemmings, it was the start of a 34-ball spell in which he took four for 21, his next wicket being the important one of Azharuddin. With five wickets and ten overs in hand, India were looking for five runs an over, but with Azharuddin gone, panic and recklessness set in.

England 254-6 (50 overs) (G. A. Gooch 115, M. W. Gatting 56; Maninder Singh 3-54);
India 219 (45.3 overs) (M. Azharuddin 64; N. A. Foster 3-47, E. E. Hemmings 4-52).

Mixed numbers. No fewer than 8,300,000 people dialled UMP to find out the scores in the 1966 Tests between England and West Indies, yet paid county attendances dropped by 146,000 to the dismal figure of 513,578, compared with over two million paying at the turnstiles just after the war. Membership numbers also declined by nearly 5,000.

Little Wonder No. 86

1987 – AUSTRALIA v ENGLAND (FINAL): CRASS GATT   1989

At Calcutta, November 8, 1987. Australia won by seven runs. Batting first suited Australia; and when they took the field to defend a total of 253, it was in the knowledge that no side batting second had scored 254 to win in this World Cup. England, 135 for two after 31 overs, and with Australia beginning to show signs of disarray in the field, were then almost on target. But in a moment too crass to contemplate, Gatting handed back the initiative. To Border's first ball, bowled on the line of his leg stump, the England captain attempted to play a reverse sweep.

Having in the semi-final swept the ball on to his leg stump, he now contrived to hit it on to his shoulder, whence it looped into Dyer's gloves. The Australians' joy was unconcealed.

Australia 253-5 (50 overs) (D. C. Boon 75, M. R. J. Veletta 45*);
England 246-8 (50 overs) (C. W. J. Athey 58, A. J. Lamb 45, M. W. Gatting 41).

1992 – The Benson And Hedges World Cup: expansion   David Frith, 1993

After the manner of the Olympic Games, cricket's World Cup quadrennially grows larger and more spectacular. The event, staged in Australia (25 matches) and New Zealand (14 matches) in 1992, featured, for the first time, all eight Test-playing teams, with aspiring Zimbabwe taking the number of competing sides to an unprecedented nine. The final was the 39th match.

The fifth World Cup was the first to be played in coloured clothing, with a white ball and some games under floodlights. Although it was again 50 overs a side rather than the original 60, it was generally considered to have been the fairest: each side played all the others once before the top four in the qualifying table played off in the semi-finals. Lasting 33 days from first ball to last, it could be faulted seriously only in the matter of the rules governing rain-interrupted matches.

Recognising the imperfection of a straight run-rate calculation when a second innings has to be shortened after rain, and unable to schedule spare days within the time-frame of the tournament, the World Cup committee adopted a scheme whereby the reduction in the target would be commensurate with the lowest-scoring overs of the side which batted first. Against South Africa in Melbourne, England lost nine overs but their target of 237 was reduced by only 11 runs. When the teams next met, in the Sydney semi-final, another rain pause, this time at the climactic moment, led to an uproar which echoed for weeks afterwards.

1992 – AUSTRALIA v ENGLAND: still Beefy   1993

At Sydney, March 5, 1992. England won by eight wickets. The combination of the old enemy, the bright lights and the noisily enthusiastic crowd demanded a show-stopper from Botham, and he provided it. His best bowling figures in limited-overs internationals stopped the Australian innings in its tracks, and he followed up with a confident fifty which made England's victory a formality. The match turned in the 38th over, when Botham bowled Border with the fifth ball. In his next over, Healy drove to Fairbrother at midwicket, Taylor was trapped lbw, and McDermott fell to DeFreitas's running catch. Botham had claimed four wickets for no runs in seven balls, and Australia were 155 for eight. They took only 16 from their last nine overs. Their only hope was to capture some early wickets, and Gooch was repeatedly beaten in McDermott's fiery opening spell. Botham's self-confidence was now complete, however, and he led the way to the hundred partnership in the 23rd over, reaching his first World Cup fifty one ball later.

Australia 171 (49 overs) (T. M. Moody 51; I. T. Botham 4-31);
England 173-2 (40.5 overs) (G. A. Gooch 58, Botham 53).

1992 – ENGLAND v SOUTH AFRICA (Semi-final): IT NEVER RAINS ...   1993

At Sydney, March 22, 1992. England won by 19 runs (revised target). This game's closing minutes buried South Africa's World Cup hopes, and whatever credibility the rain rule had retained. By putting pressure on the team batting second, the rule supposedly created exciting finishes; on this occasion 12 minutes' heavy rain, when South Africa needed 22 from 13 balls, adjusted their target first to 22 from seven, and then to 21 from one. McMillan could only take a single off Lewis. The losers were disconsolate, the winners embarrassed, and the crowd furious. Why, they asked, were the two overs not played out under the floodlights? The majority blamed the World Cup's organising committee, and the inflexibility which prevented a second-day resumption. (The next day was set aside only for a completely new match, to be played if the second team had not faced 25 overs.) Justice was probably done; Wessels chose to field, knowing the rules and the forecast, and his bowlers were fined for going slow and depriving England of five overs' acceleration. But it was not seen to be done, and fine performances on both sides were overshadowed by indignation.

England 252-6 (45 overs) (G. A. Hick 83);
South Africa 232-6 (43 overs) (A. C. Hudson 46, J. N. Rhodes 43).

1992 – ENGLAND v PAKISTAN (Final): CORNERED TIGERS   1993

At Melbourne, March 25, 1992. Pakistan won by 22 runs. Imran Khan's erratically brilliant Pakistanis won their first World Cup final while Gooch and England lost their third, on the broad field of Melbourne with nearly 90,000 in attendance. Afterwards Imran said it was the most fulfilling and satisfying cricket moment of his life. He described the victory as a triumph for his young team's talent over England's experience; he also stressed the role of his aggressive specialist bowlers rather than the stereotyped attack of Gooch's all-rounders. But he enjoyed an all-round triumph himself with the match's highest score and the final wicket.

Imran's role went deeper, however. He had virtually hand-picked the team, and after the disappointment of losing a key player, the pace bowler Waqar Younis, to a stress fracture before leaving Pakistan, and a disastrous start when they won only one in five matches (two of which he missed), he urged them to imitate the action of a cornered tiger before they went on to five successive wins. They reached the giant stadium in peak form, while England looked exhausted. The players who had toured

New Zealand unconquered had gradually weakened in the face of constant travel and frequent injury. As Pakistan had picked up, they had been losing, first to New Zealand and then, most embarrassingly, to Zimbabwe. "It's not the end of the world," said Gooch after the match, "but it is close to it. We got beaten fair and square." England were worn down by the century partnership of veterans Imran and Javed Miandad, which started slowly but gathered force, and the spirit of their batsmen was broken by successive balls from Man of the Match Wasim Akram which dismissed Lamb and Lewis, one swinging in and then straightening again, the next cutting in sharply. Imran dismissed Illingworth to complete his triumph, and pledged the proceeds of his success to the cancer hospital planned in his mother's memory.

Pakistan 249-6 (50 overs) (Imran Khan 72, Javed Miandad 58, Inzamam-ul-Haq 42; D. R. Pringle 3-22); England 227 (49.2 overs) (N. H. Fairbrother 62; Mushtaq Ahmed 3-41, Wasim Akram 3-49).

Victory salute: Imran Khan takes the wicket of England No.11 Richard Illingworth to seal Pakistan's first World Cup title at Melbourne in 1992

1996 – THE WILLS WORLD CUP: PROFIT BUT LOSS — Alan Lee, 1997

There were some good, uplifting aspects to the sixth cricket World Cup, not least the style and smiles of its unsuspected winners, Sri Lanka, but overall this was not a tournament to linger fondly in the memory. Wounded by events beyond its control even before its opening, the competition proceeded to frustrate and bewilder through an interminable and largely irrelevant saga of group games in India, Pakistan and Sri Lanka before hastening frantically through its knockout games in little more than a week.

The logistical chaos of the competition stemmed largely from the decision, laudable in theory but utterly unrealistic, to spread the tournament to virtually every corner of the vast country of India. Travel in India is problematical at best; a few specific alterations were made to airline schedules to oblige the competition organisers, but nowhere near enough to surmount the problem, the size of which became clear during the first, eventful weekend. The teams were all due to gather in Calcutta for a variety of briefing meetings before the much-vaunted opening ceremony.

As it transpired, however, the weekend was dominated by the issue of two teams, Australia and West Indies, adamantly refusing to play their scheduled group games in Colombo. The bomb blast in the city, a fortnight earlier, was the clinching factor, but Australia's players were already uncomfortable about visiting Sri Lanka, with whom they had just played an acrimonious Test series. In truth, they were reluctant to participate in the Cup at all, the backwash of their bribery allegations against Salim Malik having brought threats of an unpleasant nature from a number of fanatics around Pakistan.

1996 – KENYA v WEST INDIES (GROUP A): AMATEUR HOUR   1997

At Pune, February 29, 1996. Kenya won by 73 runs. Kenya's victory was hailed as one of the biggest upsets in cricket history. It was the more extraordinary for being the work of their bowlers, rather than their highly rated batting. Captain Maurice Odumbe thought his team was done for when he lost the toss; once they were all out for 166, he was certain of it. But his amateur attack dismissed West Indies for 93, their lowest World Cup total and their second-worst in any one-day international. West Indies' nightmare began with Richardson being bowled leg stump by Rajab Ali. The collapse became critical when Lara was caught behind by Tariq Iqbal, whose stout figure and village-standard juggling had hitherto caused much mirth. The last wicket went the same way as the first – Cuffy was bowled by Rajab Ali, who fell into his team-mates' arms. As the Kenyans ran an exuberant victory lap, cheered on by local spectators, West Indies realised that, level on points with Kenya and Zimbabwe, they could no longer be certain of reaching the quarter-finals. The future of their captain, Richardson, looked even bleaker.

Kenya 166 (49.3 overs) (R. A. Harper 3-15, C. A. Walsh 3-46);
West Indies 93 (35.2 overs) (M. O. Odumbe 3-15, Rajab Ali 3-17).

1996 – ENGLAND v SRI LANKA (QUARTER-FINAL): LANKAN LASHING   1997

At Faisalabad, March 9, 1996. Sri Lanka won by five wickets. Sri Lanka continued their glorious ascent, while England sank ignominiously; they had never been knocked out before the semi-finals in the five previous World Cups. They were all but dead by the time Jayasuriya departed at 113 for one, virtually halfway to Sri Lanka's target of 236, in their 13th over. Jayasuriya had thumped 82 off 44 balls, with three sixes and 13 fours. He was most savage on the left-arm spin of Illingworth, whom he hit for four successive fours, and the seam of DeFreitas, whose second over went for 22. DeFreitas was withdrawn, having conceded 32 in 12 balls.

England 235-8 (50 overs) (P. A. J. DeFreitas 67);
Sri Lanka 236-5 (40.4 overs) (S. T. Jayasuriya 82, A. P. Gurusinha 45).

1996 – INDIA v SRI LANKA (SEMI-FINAL): ENRAGED AND EMBARRASSED   1997

At Calcutta, March 13, 1996. Sri Lanka won by default after a crowd riot. Sri Lanka played brilliantly after a disastrous first over to achieve an unbeatable advantage. But the headlines were devoted to the riot which ended the match. Enraged by an Indian collapse of seven wickets for 22, some home supporters threw bottles on to the outfield and set fire to the seating. Referee Clive Lloyd took the teams off for 15 minutes, attempted a restart, and then awarded Sri Lanka the game by default. Nobody questioned the result; India needed a near-impossible 132 from 15.5 overs, with only two wickets standing. But the Indian board smarted at the word "default" and asked for Sri Lanka to be declared winners on run-rate. The authorities – and many home fans – were intensely embarrassed by the trouble. Even as the match was abandoned, one Indian raised a banner reading "Congratulation [sic] Sri Lanka – we are sorry". Some took out apologetic advertisements in the Sri Lankan press. But, like the Pakistani fans four days before, others raged against their unsuccessful players, and a guard was put on captain Azharuddin's house. The presentation ceremony went ahead as if nothing untoward had occurred, and, against the smoking backdrop, Tony Greig conducted post-match interviews so normal they were bizarre.

Sri Lanka 251-8 (50 overs) (P. A. de Silva 66, R. S. Mahanama 58 retired hurt; J. Srinath 3-34);
India 120-8 (34.1 overs) (S. R. Tendulkar 65; S. T. Jayasuriya 3-12).

1996 – AUSTRALIA v SRI LANKA (FINAL): DE SILVA LINING   1997

At Lahore, March 17, 1996. Sri Lanka won by seven wickets. Contrary to most expectations, Sri Lanka controlled their first World Cup final after the initial stages. Their batting was a vastly more proficient against spin than Australia's; their catching was flawless whereas the Australians held one chance out of five; their ground-fielding was sure while the Australians frequently fumbled; and their spinners obtained enough turn on what was otherwise a batsmen's pitch to stifle the Australians after their confident start. Only in pace bowling were the Sri Lankans the lesser side on the day, and their two opening bowlers did not feature again after their first 13 overs had cost 72 runs. De Silva went on to score the third hundred in a World Cup final. It was the first time in six attempts that a side batting second had won the World Cup final. While a light-hearted crowd favoured Sri Lanka throughout, no malice was directed towards the Australians, worried though they had been about repercussions from the Salim Malik affair.

> **Australia 241-7** (50 overs) (M. A. Taylor 74, R. T. Ponting 45; P. A. de Silva 3-42);
> **Sri Lanka 245-3** (46.2 overs) (de Silva 107*, A. P. Gurusinha 65).

1999 – FALLER AT THE FIRST
Matthew Engel, Notes by the Editor, 2000

On May 30, 1999, *The Observer* newspaper carried an advert offering readers the chance to win tickets for all England's Super Six games in the World Cup. It is unclear who England will be playing, said the blurb innocently. However, we know they have qualified. At the time the words were written, that was, if not a mathematical fact, then a reasonable assumption. It's just that reasonable assumptions have no place in discussion of the prospects for the England cricket team. A few hours later, they were out of the World Cup.

The script for English cricket now seems to be more like the Book of Job than anything else: the Sabeans have stolen the oxen; the Chaldeans have stolen the camels; and the fire of God has burned up the sheep. Something like that. Anyway, a tournament officially regarded as the English game's make-or-break opportunity to re-establish itself in the public's affection had produced the worst case imaginable: a fall at the first fence.

The miracle, so far as the World Cup was concerned, was that the tournament survived. Local interest remained high. It was as though the British public were able to appreciate everything much better once released from the anguish of following England; and the team's absence enabled the England and Wales Cricket Board to notice the enthusiasm for cricket of Britain's Asians, something which until then had largely escaped them. True, the final was a miserable disappointment, but it was not quite as dreadful as the opening ceremony. And these two let-downs framed much excellent cricket, culminating in the wonderful Edgbaston semi-final and, indeed, the final result: no one could argue with the notion of Australia as world champions.

1999 – INDIA v SOUTH AFRICA (GROUP A): ILLICIT CONTACT
2000

At Hove, May 15, 1999. South Africa won by four wickets. A festive atmosphere and a cracking finish were overshadowed, for the press at least, by the strange case of Cronje's earpiece. South Africa were experimenting with a one-way radio system: Cronje and Donald were wired up to coach Bob Woolmer, who sat in the dressing-room dispensing advice. The referee, Talat Ali, was not impressed, and pounced at the first drinks break. ICC later ruled out remote-control captaincy, at least for the rest of the World Cup. A wonderful match was marred only by a pitch invader who tried to attack Azharuddin and Dravid as they walked off.

> **India 253-5** (50 overs) (S. C. Ganguly 97, R. Dravid 54; L. Klusener 3-66);
> **South Africa 254-6** (47.2 overs) (J. H. Kallis 96).

Leicestershire v Northamptonshire. At Leicester, August 30, 31, September 1, 1967. All ten Northamptonshire wickets in the first innings fell to catches by ten different fieldsmen.

Little Wonder No. 87

1999 – BANGLADESH v PAKISTAN (GROUP B): ODDS ON   2000

At Northampton, May 31, 1999. Bangladesh won by 62 runs. At the last possible moment, a non-Test team felled a giant. Bangladesh had never even come close to beating a major power – while Pakistan were unbeaten in this competition. Since this was a completely dead match, accusations of Pakistani match-fixing grew louder again. English bookmakers had rated Pakistan 33 to 1 on, and there were no reports of unusual betting, but inevitably there were rumours about the subcontinent's illegal bookmakers. Nothing diminished the Bangladeshi fans' euphoria. It was the greatest day in their cricketing history, and perhaps no event since independence had united the country with such delight. Both captains spoke of Bangladesh earning Test cricket soon; with Pakistan unaffected, the only person with reason not to enjoy the result was Gordon Greenidge, sacked as Bangladesh coach just before this game, who quietly left at lunchtime. With nine wickets down, the umpires called for a TV verdict on whether Saqlain had been run out. He was, but the jubilant Bangladeshi fans were already pouring on to the field. The County Ground had never seen anything like it – at least not since the old footballing days there, when Northampton Town knocked Arsenal out of the FA Cup in 1958. The build-up was just as frenzied: Northamptonshire could have sold three times the available tickets.

> **Bangladesh 223-9** (50 overs) (Akram Khan 42; Saqlain Mushtaq 5-35);
> **Pakistan 161** (44.3 overs) (Khaled Mahmud 3-31).

1999 – AUSTRALIA v SOUTH AFRICA (SUPER SIX): THE ICE AGE   2000

At Leeds, June 13, 1999. Australia won by five wickets. This was do or die for Australia. So, in a thriller, they duly did – leapfrogging over South Africa in the process, and loading the dice for the semi-final. South Africa batted first on a bouncy Headingley pitch and rattled up 271, despite the return to form of Warne, who snared his old foe Cullinan and Cronje in one over. At 48 for three in reply, Australia faced meltdown. But no one had told Steve Waugh, that iciest of icemen. He and Ponting, slogging adeptly, added 77 between overs 22 and 29. Then Waugh, on 56, was unfathomably dropped by a prematurely celebrating Gibbs at midwicket.

Waugh reportedly told him: "Hersh, you've just dropped the World Cup." Hindsight suggests he did.

South Africa 271-7 (50 overs) (H. H. Gibbs 101, D. J. Cullinan 50; D. W. Fleming 3-57);
Australia 272-5 (49.4 overs) (S. R. Waugh 120*, R. T. Ponting 69).

1999 – AUSTRALIA v SOUTH AFRICA (Semi-final): UNBEATABLE
Tim de Lisle, 2000

At Birmingham, June 17, 1999. Tied. This was not merely the match of the tournament: it must have been the best one-day international of the 1,483 so far played. The essence of the one-day game is a close finish, and this was by far the most significant to finish in the closest way of all – with both teams all out for the same score. But it was a compressed epic all the way through, and it ended in a savage twist. The tie meant that South Africa, for the third World Cup in a row, failed to reach the final despite making much of the early running. The crucial fact was that Australia finished higher than them in the Super Six table, and that was determined by the obscurity of net run-rate. Many spectators were left baffled.

Klusener's brawn had powered South Africa to the brink of the final but, when he got there, his brain short-circuited. Only he could have smashed and grabbed 31 runs off 14 balls, cutting a daunting target down to a doddle: one needed off four balls, Klusener himself on strike, and a decent, experienced tailender at the other end in Donald. The bowler, Fleming, had only one thing going for him: he had bowled the final over that beat West Indies in the 1996 World Cup semi-final. Having let Klusener pummel consecutive fours to level the scores, he tightened up. Steve Waugh, knowing a tie would be enough, set a field that gave new meaning to the phrase "a ring saving one". Klusener thumped the ball straight, and Donald, backing up too far, would have been run out if Lehmann had hit the stumps. The scare should have been a warning. But Klusener then repeated his straight biff and charged. Donald grounded his bat, dropped it, and finally set off, while the Australians were demonstrating the benefits of a recent visit to a bowling alley: Mark Waugh, at mid-on, flicked the ball to Fleming, who rolled it to Gilchrist, who broke the wicket, and South African hearts.

The game was the last as South Africa's coach for Bob Woolmer, whose blend of science and imagination had produced a 73% success rate in one-day internationals. He deserved better than to go out on a technicality.

Australia 213 (49.2 overs) (M. G. Bevan 65, S. R. Waugh 56; S. M. Pollock 5-36);
South Africa 213 (49.4 overs) (J. H. Kallis 53, J. N. Rhodes 43; S. K. Warne 4-29).

1999 – AUSTRALIA v PAKISTAN (Final): FORGETTABLE   Hugh Chevallier, 2000

At Lord's, June 20, 1999. Australia won by eight wickets. Australia won the seventh World Cup with such single-minded ruthlessness that even an eight-wicket victory failed to do them justice. Pakistan, the most exciting team in the tournament, were totally outplayed and outwitted at the crucial moment. There were barely four and a half hours of cricket, most of it one-sided. For all but the most fervent Australian, it was not a pretty sight.

It was a sight, though, spared many Pakistanis by a controversial ticketing policy. This favoured not the fans of the competing teams but those who had ostensibly proved their loyalty to the game – and the depth of their pocket – by buying a package of tickets long before. So Lord's was awash with disinterested observers, while from outside came the klaxon, whistle and bugle of fanatical Pakistan support. About a hundred fans clambered up a building site overlooking the ground. As the police moved in, a game of cat and mouse ensued, providing an alternative spectacle for the Grand Stand opposite. Eventually, the fans, like their team, were unceremoniously bundled out of St John's Wood.

Pakistan 132 (39 overs) (S. K. Warne 4-33);

Australia 133-2 (20.1 overs) (A. C. Gilchrist 54).

2003 – THE 2003 WORLD CUP: FRAUGHT
Simon Wilde, 2004

The hosts of the eighth World Cup wanted it to be the greatest yet. In financial terms, it was – profits of $US194m represented a huge increase on the $51m made in 1999 – but in other respects, it fell short. Indeed, this traditional organisers' boast rather came back to haunt the South Africans, who headed a pan-African triumvirate also including Zimbabwe and Kenya. A great tournament needs dramatic tension, and the brilliance of the Australians never allowed it.

Shane Warne, their match-winner in the semi-final and final of 1999, had returned home after failing a drugs test taken during the VB Series in Australia the previous month. Warne's "A" sample – later confirmed by the "B" – showed he had taken two banned diuretics, hydrochlorothiazide and amiloride. Warne said he got them from his mum and took them out of vanity, wanting to lose weight before his return to the Australia side after injury. But diuretics can also mask steroids, which could have expedited Warne's swift recovery from a dislocated shoulder. A fortnight into the tournament, he was handed a one-year ban. It was the highest-profile drugs case to afflict cricket and sent shock waves through the game but, as with everything else, the Australians rode them well.

The run-up to the tournament was fraught with problems, with countries courting damages claims from the ICC for failing to fulfil contractual commitments. An intractable dispute between the Indian board and their players, over product endorsement, threatened their participation, while the issue of whether it was safe to play in Zimbabwe and Kenya – and whether it was morally right to do so in Zimbabwe, given the violent and repressive nature of President Robert Mugabe's regime – spilled over into the event itself.

The heat could have been taken out of these disputes had the ICC shown more imagination and willingness to compromise, but Mal Speed, overseeing his first World Cup as ICC chief executive, stuck to the disingenuous line that the ICC were concerned only with cricket-related issues, not politics. Overall, his was the least impressive performance by an Australian at the event.

In the event, New Zealand refused to play in Nairobi, and England in Harare. The ICC appeals committee predictably rejected their cases and awarded "victory" to the hosts – "results" that skewed the tournament off its axis. Had England gone to Harare and avoided defeat they, rather than Zimbabwe, would have reached the second phase.

2003 – ZIMBABWE v NAMIBIA (Pool A): Flower power   2004

At Harare, February 10, 2003. Zimbabwe won by 86 runs (D/L method). In one of the World Cup's most enduring moments, Andy Flower and Henry Olonga issued a powerful statement mourning "the death of democracy in our beloved Zimbabwe", and took the field wearing black armbands in protest at human-rights abuses by the Mugabe regime. Olonga was expelled by his club, Takashinga, and soon left Zimbabwe, while Flower would later be chosen against Australia only after his team-mates revolted against the selectors. By the 26th over, when rain stopped play for the second time, this time for good, Namibia were 104 for five and on the ropes. Zimbabwe breathed a huge sigh of relief: if the game had been abandoned two balls earlier, it would have been declared a draw.

Zimbabwe 340-2 (50 overs) (C. B. Wishart 172*, G. W. Flower 78*);
Namibia 104-5 (25.1 overs).

Immediate registration of overseas players. One of the most vital steps towards improving the standard of county cricket was taken by the Advisory Committee at their autumn meeting on November 29 and 30, 1967, when by a clear two-thirds majority it was decided to permit the immediate registration of one overseas player.

Little Wonder No. 88

2003 – BANGLADESH v SRI LANKA (Pool B): all over in an over   2004

At Pietermaritzburg, February 14, 2003. Sri Lanka won by ten wickets. The classic one-day pattern is for the result to be in doubt until the final over; this was the match in which victory was secured in the first. Vaas, Sri Lanka's nippy left-arm seamer, woke up with a sore back, but the morning damp was just what he needed to soothe the pain. With the first ball of the Bangladesh innings he castled Hannan Sarkar, aiming a wildly ambitious drive. With the second, he clasped a simple return catch off Mohammad Ashraful. And with the third, he forced Ehsanul Haque to edge to second slip. For the first time ever, an international match had begun with a hat-trick. Vaas's celebration was appropriately wild: he looked like an aeroplane piloted by a drunkard. There was more turbulence for Bangladesh when umpire Tiffin gave Sanwar Hossain out leg-before: at five for four after one over, the game was up.

Bangladesh 124 (31.1 overs) (W. P. U. J. C. Vaas 6-25);
Sri Lanka 126-0 (21.1 overs) (M. S. Atapattu 69*).

2003 – AUSTRALIA v ENGLAND (POOL A): ANOTHER CHAPTER · 2004

At Port Elizabeth, March 2, 2003. Australia won by two wickets. As Bichel and Bevan ran off delirious, England stood still. Hussain was on his knees, his head in his hands; Stewart stood with his back to his team-mates: both would later announce their retirement from one-day matches. How had this happened? How had Australia – chasing 205, in terrible trouble at 48 for four, and again at 135 for eight – won with two balls to spare? "Bichel" was the short answer. First, he took seven for 20 on a slow pitch and strangled England's innings; then he struck a granite-willed 34 not out from No. 10 to end their fightback – and, as it turned out, their World Cup. With Australia needing 14 from two overs, Hussain threw the ball not to Caddick (9–2–35–4 at the time) but Anderson (8–0–54–0). It was a hunch he later came to regret: Bichel swung the second ball for six, a four followed, and the game was gone. It was the final twist in a match full of them. Australia had won their 12th successive one-day international – a record – beating West Indies' 11 between June 1984 and February 1985. Defeat was not necessarily disastrous for England – there were tortuous mathematical calculations that suggested it might, in some circumstances, even help their chances of reaching the Super Six. In the event, it did prove their undoing. And it was yet another chapter in the 14-year saga of humiliation against their oldest cricketing enemy.

England 204-8 (50 overs) (A. J. Stewart 46, A. Flintoff 45; A. J. Bichel 7-20);
Australia 208-8 (49.4 overs) (M. G. Bevan 74*; A. R. Caddick 4-35).

2003 – KENYA v SRI LANKA (POOL B): LIONHEARTS · 2004

At Nairobi, February 24, 2003. Kenya won by 53 runs. A World Cup bloated by too many one-sided games needed this like a desert explorer needs a cold beer. Kenya's shock victory was memorable enough, but the style, all wide-grinning, grassy-kneed enthusiasm, was unforgettable: Kenya chased like lion cubs, backed up in gangs and jigged after every wicket. Sri Lanka, by contrast, simply moped. "The worst game of my career," admitted Jayasuriya. Kenya's lap of honour ended up more a half-marathon.

Kenya 210-9 (50 overs) (K. O. Otieno 60; W. P. U. J. C. Vaas 3-41, M. Muralitharan 4-28);
Sri Lanka 157 (45 overs) (P. A. de Silva 41; C. O. Obuya 5-24).

2003 – SOUTH AFRICA v SRI LANKA (POOL B): MISCALCULATION   2004

At Durban, March 3, 2003. Tied (D/L method). Sydney 1992, Edgbaston 1999, and now Durban 2003: South Africa have certainly acquired an unhappy knack of exiting World Cups in bizarre fashion. Late in the South African innings, with rain falling steadily, it had become a question of when – not if – Duckworth/ Lewis would come into play. And so, when Boucher swung the penultimate ball of the 45th – and, as had begun to seem inevitable, final – over for six, he pumped his right fist, believing the job done. The last soggy ball of the match he pushed casually to leg, and stayed put. Crucially, though, the South Africans had misread the fine print: they had needed 229 to tie, when only a win would do. Klusener laboured to a single off eight balls as the rain grew heavier, but had Boucher been given the right information, it might not have mattered. As it was, Sri Lanka progressed – and South Africa's world fell apart. Jayasuriya draped an arm around Pollock's shoulders as they awaited the media inquisition, compassion supplanting his own relief, however briefly.

Sri Lanka 268-9 (50 overs) (M. S. Atapattu 124, P. A. de Silva 73; J. H. Kallis 3-41);
South Africa 229-6 (45 overs) (H. H. Gibbs 73, M. V. Boucher 45*).

2003 – AUSTRALIA v SRI LANKA (SEMI-FINAL): WALK LIKE AN AUSTRALIAN

2004

At Port Elizabeth, March 18, 2003. Australia won by 48 runs (D/L method). This was Gilchrist's match, not for what he did with bat or gloves but for his decision to walk, which astonished everyone unused to such Australian magnanimity. Despite being reprieved by umpire Koertzen, Gilchrist knew he had edged an attempted sweep that was caught off his pad. His departure, swiftly followed by Ponting's, gave Sri Lanka their chance to beat Australia: they blew it.

Australia 212-7 (50 overs) (A. Symonds 91*; W. P. U. J. C. Vaas 3-34);
Sri Lanka 123-7 (38.1 overs).

2003 – AUSTRALIA v INDIA (FINAL): PONTING'S PROCESSION   Chris Ryan, 2003

At Johannesburg, March 23, 2003. Australia won by 125 runs. Australia, after 16 one-day victories in a row, saved their most ruthless, clinical and complete performance for the biggest stage of all. If some of their lesser lights had dominated the earlier games, now the stars came out to play. Ponting, the captain, gave a masterly display of controlled aggression in one of the great one-day innings. Gilchrist set the tone savagely. And then McGrath held a return catch off his fifth ball to secure the critical wicket of Tendulkar. India's only triumph came at the toss, where Ganguly figured his best chance was to let loose his in-form pacemen on a seaming wicket. It was the same flawed logic that Nasser Hussain embraced, to his eternal regret, at Brisbane four months earlier. There was movement, but most of it came after ball hit blade, with Zaheer straying too wide and Srinath too short. Gilchrist and Hayden clumped 15 runs off Zaheer's opening over and 105 in the first 14.

Australia 359-2 (50 overs) (R. T. Ponting 140*, D. R. Martyn 88*, A. C. Gilchrist 57);
India 234 (39.2 overs) (V. Sehwag 82, R. Dravid 47; G. D. McGrath 3-52).

This extract comes from the 2003 edition which carried brief reports of the just-completed World Cup. Others are taken from the 2004 edition.

2007 – THE WORLD CUP: PROTRACTED NIGHTMARE   Tony Cozier, 2008

In securing the World Cup for the third successive time, an unprecedented hat-trick, Australia set standards of power and perfection beyond even West Indies in their supremacy of the tournament's formative years. "They made a lot of good teams look bad" was the simple assessment of Mahela Jayawardene, captain of the admirable runners-up, Sri Lanka.

Such an extraordinary performance would normally have defined any global event. Instead, it was overshadowed by a succession of setbacks, from beginning to end and even beyond, that blighted the first such major extrava-ganza staged in the cricketing Caribbean, an undertaking which cost the nine participating governments a total of $US700m to meet the exacting require-ments of the ICC.

The mantra of Chris Dehring, head of the management company set up by the West Indies Cricket Board, that it would be "the best World Cup ever" was no more than a pipe-dream; it soon turned into a protracted nightmare.

The first disaster came six days into the competition: the death of the widely respected Pakistan coach and former England batsman Bob Woolmer, in his Kingston hotel room, hours after Pakistan were eliminated at the group stage by a shock loss to Ireland.

There were several other hitches, if none quite so dramatic. Some were equally unforeseen, others predictable even before a ball was bowled. Altogether, they explained the general dissatisfaction. The early exits of Pakistan and India (first-round victims of Bangladesh and Sri Lanka) removed two attractive, long-estab-lished teams and several star players, while Bangladesh and Ireland, enthusiastic and deserving but anonymous outsiders, advanced. Such a double blow under-mined the considerable outlay of the main subcontinental sponsors and television networks, and created a flood of cancelled airline, hotel and ticket bookings.

By then, it was obvious from the sprawling emptiness at the impressive – and expensive – new and renovated stadiums that the local organising committees had misjudged the ability of their own people to afford the high ticket prices. In all, the tournament dragged on for 47 days, as long as the last Olympic Games and football World Cup put together.

2007 – IRELAND v PAKISTAN (GROUP D): TRIUMPH AND DESPAIR   2008

At Kingston, March 17, 2007. Ireland won by three wickets (D/L method). Pakistan crashed out of the World Cup at the earliest possible moment, probably the greatest upset in World Cup history. And Ireland's part-timers, cheered on by at least a thousand astonished supporters, did it on St Patrick's Day, too. It was an excellent toss for Trent Johnston to win, with the hard pitch nearly as green as shamrock, and when Mohammad Yousuf slapped an innocuous half-tracker straight to backward point, the first frissons of alarm started to spread through the Pakistani dressing-room. Johnston celebrated with his signature chicken dance, and by the time Andre Botha – who finished with two for five from eight overs of wonderfully controlled medium-pace – removed Inzamam-ul-Haq and Imran Nazir, Pakistan were on the run. Johnston's winning six over midwicket sparked frenetic celebrations, while disconsolate Pakistani fans were left to comfort themselves with news of India's loss, potentially just as calamitous, to Bangladesh in Trinidad. But both triumph and despair would be eclipsed hours later by the saddest news of all: the death of Pakistan's coach Bob Woolmer.

Pakistan 132 (45.4 overs) (W. B. Rankin 3-32);
Ireland 133-7 (41.4 overs) (N. J. O'Brien 72; Mohammad Sami 3-29).

2007 – TRAGEDY AT THE WORLD CUP   Paul Newman, 2008

His mood was sombre as he ordered lasagne and apple pie with ice cream from room service on the evening of March 17. Bob Woolmer sat alone and, according to Deirdre Harvey, the waitress who brought him his last meal, looked desperately sad. "His eyes were red, like somebody who had been crying," she said later.

Woolmer knew all about cricketing disappointment. In his time as coach at Warwickshire, with South Africa through the Hansie Cronje years, and now at Pakistan, the most mercurial team of all, he had seen just about everything. But only South Africa being knocked out by Australia in the 1999 World Cup semi-final compared with losing to Ireland, and with it early elimination for one of the favourites, at the World Cup in 2007.

On the streets of Multan, Inzamam-ul-Haq's home city, they were already burning effigies of him and chanting "Death to Woolmer". At the post-match press conference at Sabina Park in Kingston, Woolmer had been asked: "Are you going to resign?" He replied: "I'd like to sleep on that one." He answered each probing question with his usual courtesy, making sure he praised the ICC development programme – which he himself had pioneered with the very object of bringing Associate Members up to the standard of the Test-playing nations.

Then, in what was to be his last interview, he all but told Alison Mitchell of BBC Radio that he was finished as Pakistan coach. "I asked him if he had made up his mind to go," she said. "He gave me a half-smile and nod, but clearly he wanted to play it by the book. Bob did not look like a man who was unduly stressed. And he didn't appear ill. I remember thinking, 'this man has got the patience of a saint' during the main press conference. He was so helpful to everybody."

Woolmer retreated to his room, number 374, at the end of a musty corridor on the 12th floor of the Pegasus Hotel, a 17-storey skyscraper with 300 rooms in what passes for a luxurious area of Kingston. Next door was Danish Kaneria, Pakistan's spin bowler and, as the only Hindu in a team of Muslims, something of a man apart himself. Across the corridor was the room of Brian Lara, one of the greatest players the game has known, now coming to the end of his West Indian career.

The tired old hotel was alive with the cricketing community, but for Pakistan there was simply despair. The trip back to the hotel had been made in virtual silence – no rows, no recriminations. The only sound that could be heard, according to the bus driver Bertram Carr, came from Woolmer:

"He was coughing all the way back to the hotel," said Carr. After they arrived back at the Pegasus, as the Ireland team decamped to Ocho Rios for the mother and father of all St Patrick's Day celebrations, the Pakistanis went their separate ways, mainly to their rooms. Woolmer had a drink in the bar with Ian Gould, once a county opponent, now an umpire, then retired alone upstairs.

Room 374 was just like hundreds of others Woolmer would have known in his globetrotting career. Functional, in need of a lick of paint, but perfectly comfortable. In it were two bottles of champagne purchased by a Pakistan fan at Heathrow airport en route to Jamaica and given to Woolmer, something of a wine buff, by his assistant coach Mushtaq Ahmed. One bottle was later found empty, the other with the seal unbroken. The lasagne, half-eaten, was found on a tray outside his room. Woolmer, as was his wont, struggled to rest. A large man, he had recently been diagnosed with diabetes. It was later discovered that his heart weighed an abnormally heavy 520 grams, with an enlarged left ventricle and a distinct narrowing of the coronary arteries: threequarters of diabetics die of heart attacks. He also suffered from sleep apnoea, which meant he would stop breathing in his sleep unless he wore a mask attached to a machine that kept his air passages open.

At 8.12pm local time, Woolmer sent an email to his wife Gill, who was home in Cape Town. "Hi darling," it started, "feeling a little depressed currently as you might imagine. I am not sure which is worse, being knocked out in the semi-final at Edgbaston or now in the first round. Our batting performance was abysmal and my worst fears were realised. I could tell the players were for some reason not able to fire themselves up." He went on to say that he was glad he did not have to travel to Guyana, and was looking forward to seeing his family again. "I hope your day was better but I doubt it as you were probably watching. Not much more to add I'm afraid but I still love you lots."

Fourteen hours and 18 minutes after pressing the send button on his computer Woolmer was found dead in that Kingston hotel room, discovered slumped in the bathroom by a maid after being conspicuous by his absence from breakfast the following morning.

2007 – AUSTRALIA v SRI LANKA (Final): GREATNESS OVERSHADOWED 2008

At Bridgetown, April 28, 2007. Australia won by 53 runs (D/L method). The disorganisation which turned the ninth World Cup final into a farce, to be for ever known as The Final Of Two Finishes, should not be allowed to obscure the batting of Adam Gilchrist. His 149 off 104 balls was the highest of the five centuries made in a final, and the first by an opening batsman. It deserved to be ranked as the greatest innings played in a World Cup final.

Rain, which postponed the start from 9.30 to 12.15, prompted the unprecedented disorganisation. The recalculations made it a game of 38 overs a side: although almost three hours had been lost, only 24 overs were to be taken out of the game. This was too ambitious. The rescheduled finish was due to be at 5.45pm, assuming no delays, and sunset was at 6.12, allowing little time for the closing ceremony on a ground without floodlights.

Almost alone, the four umpires and the referee Jeff Crowe believed that 36 overs of Sri Lanka's innings had to be completed for a result. So intent were they on their Duckworth/Lewis calculations that they were oblivious to the fact that a result was going to be achieved on the day the moment 20 overs had been bowled. Crowe, as the person in charge of the "Playing Control Team", admitted afterwards: "It was a mistake on our behalf. I should've known the rules. It was a human error, I guess, at the end of the day." At 6.16 on a damp, dark evening, the players returned to consternation and to bowl three overs of spin, as the captains had agreed, to get the game over.

Australia 281-4 (38 overs) (A. C. Gilchrist 149);
Sri Lanka 215-8 (36 overs) (S. T. Jayasuriya 63, K. C. Sangakkara 54).

2011 – THE WORLD CUP: A BETTER BALANCE
Sambit Bal, 2012

The 2011 edition produced the best run-rate (5.03) in tournament history, and India mounted the highest chase in the final, but the bat did not hold vulgar sway over the ball. In fact, this was as much a bowler's tournament as it was a batsman's. It's true that more 300-plus totals were scored than ever before, but, significantly, none of these came in the knockout matches. New Zealand won a quarter-final after scoring 221, Sri Lanka restricted their quarter-final and semi-final opponents to under 230, and each of India's last three matches was a gripping affair without being high-scoring by modern standards. The bigger picture was more satisfying still. All kinds of bowlers prospered, and among the leading wicket-takers were seriously fast bowlers, canny left-arm exponents of swing and seam, off-spinners and part-time slow left-armers.

2011 – INDIA v ENGLAND (GROUP B): MINI TEST CLASSIC
2012

At Bangalore, February 27, 2011. Tied. This was the match that had everything – except, astonishingly, a winner. Of the 23 previous ties in one-day internationals, only Napier in 2007-08, when New Zealand and England made 340 apiece, had produced more runs. Now, India and England were left with the same mixture of relief and regret, for the last hour contained the ebb and flow of a mini Test classic.

Set 339, more than any team had ever scored batting second in a World Cup match, England were 280 for two after 42 overs when they took the batting powerplay. Zaheer Khan promptly removed Bell, who was suffering from cramp, to end a third-wicket stand of 170 with Strauss, who – having compiled England's largest World Cup innings – was trapped next ball by an unplayable yorker. The powerplay also accounted for Collingwood and Prior, and Yardy soon fell to Patel. England needed an unlikely 29 off two overs. Fifteen came as Swann and Bresnan traded sixes off Chawla, who then bowled Bresnan with his final delivery: 14 needed off the last over, bowled by Patel. Shahzad calmly hit the third ball (the first he had faced in the World Cup) for a straight six, then ran a bye and, when Swann took two off the fifth, England required two to win off the last ball. Swann could manage only a single to mid-off, and the atmosphere at the Chinnaswamy Stadium deflated like a bad soufflé.

India 338 (49.5 overs) (S. R. Tendulkar 120, Yuvraj Singh 58, G. Gambhir 51; T. T. Bresnan 5-48); **England 338-8** (50 overs) (A. J. Strauss 158, I. R. Bell 69; Zaheer Khan 3-64).

Little Wonder No. 89

Wisden 1968. Inspector of pitches: H. C. Lock, former groundsman at The Oval, was appointed a permanent inspector of pitches with adverse reports, and in exceptional circumstances powers were given to the Advisory County Cricket Committee to ban any ground considered unsatisfactory. Umpires and captains could protest at the state of a pitch on the first day of a match. Hardly a single county was free from the accusation that certain pitches were below standard.

2011 – ENGLAND v IRELAND (GROUP B): IN THE PINK   2012

At Bangalore, March 2, 2011. Ireland won by three wickets. The Chinnaswamy Stadium played host to a second thriller in four days as Kevin O'Brien, the chunky all-rounder released by Nottinghamshire in 2009, reduced England's bowlers to mush to give Ireland's cricketers their greatest moment yet. When he walked out to bat – sporting a lurid pink hairdo to support the Irish Cancer Society – his side had slipped to 106 for four in pursuit of 328; moments later, they were 111 for five. But, two days before his 27th birthday, O'Brien threw caution to the wind and the odds out of the window, pummelling fifty in 30 balls and reaching three figures in 50 – easily the fastest World Cup hundred. While he and Cusack were adding 162 in 103 balls, England disintegrated: Broad broke the record for the worst figures for a Test-playing side against an Associate Member only eight days after Anderson had equalled it. And although O'Brien lost his timing, and eventually his wicket – run out attempting a tight second – Mooney provided the finishing touch with five balls to spare, then hurled his bat high into the night sky before he was mobbed by ecstatic team-mates. It was the highest successful run-chase in the World Cup, and Ireland's highest one-day total.

England 327-8 (50 overs) (I. J. L. Trott 92, I. R. Bell 81, K. P. Pietersen 59; J. F. Mooney 4-63);
Ireland 329-7 (49.1 overs) (K. J. O'Brien 113, A. R. Cusack 47; G. P. Swann 3-47).

2011 – INDIA v PAKISTAN (SEMI-FINAL): BOLLYWOOD DRAMA
Dileep Premachandran, 2012

At Mohali, March 30, 2011. India won by 29 runs. Not even a rare diplomatic tête-à-tête between the two countries' political leaders, sitting side by side beyond the boundary, could distract an intense crowd, including a small smattering from across the border, from the action within it. Like most matches between these bitter rivals, this could have been scripted in Bollywood, as jubilant heroes jostled for attention with cartoon-style villains. Sehwag started with a boundary barrage before Wahab Riaz swung one into his pads, but the action quickly centred on his opening partner Tendulkar. First he was reprieved on 23, after umpire Gould initially upheld Saeed Ajmal's convincing shout for leg-before; to gasps from fans on both sides, Hawk-Eye ruled the ball was missing leg stump by the narrowest of margins. Next ball he was almost stumped, then, astonishingly, he was dropped four times – on 27, 45, 70 and 81, all of them catchable, three of them off Shahid Afridi – as Misbah-ul-Haq, Younis Khan and the Akmal brothers tried to outdo each other for comical ineptitude. India fielded almost maniacally, and with Misbah unaccountably leaving the big hitting until the cause was lost, they were comfortable winners for the fifth time out of five in World Cup games against Pakistan.

India 260-9 (50 overs) (S. R. Tendulkar 85; Wahab Riaz 5-46);
Pakistan 231 (49.5 overs) (Misbah-ul-Haq 56, Mohammad Hafeez 43).

2011 – INDIA v SRI LANKA (FINAL): "IT IS TIME WE CARRIED HIM"
Simon Wilde, 2012

At Mumbai, April 2, 2011. India won by six wickets. India, favourites with a battery of pundits and a billion supporters, made light of the expectation to win a seesaw encounter worthy of the occasion. Twice they lost control of the game: first towards the end of Sri Lanka's innings, when Jayawardene swept to a sublime century; then at the beginning of their own, as Malinga silenced a partisan crowd. But, led by an impressively cool innings from Dhoni, they ended up decisive winners, sparking mass celebrations on the streets of Mumbai, across India as a whole and throughout the nation's vast diaspora.

Their previous World Cup triumph, in 1983, had been a surprise. This time, anything but victory would have been a failure, and it was a measure of their progress under Gary Kirsten, their departing coach, that they took so much in their stride. By adding the scalp of Sri Lanka to those of Pakistan in the semi-finals, Australia in the quarters and West Indies in their final group match, they had beaten all the other World Cup winners.

India also became the first team to win a final on home soil, and the outcome was particularly sweet for Tendulkar, playing his sixth World Cup – equalling Javed Miandad's record – and surely his last. The dream scenario entailed a 100th international century to win the game in the city of his birth, but despite an unscripted failure he described the day as one of his most memorable in a career now spanning four decades. Both he and Kirsten were chaired around the outfield. As Kohli, who had just celebrated his first birthday when Tendulkar made his international debut in 1989, put it: "He has carried the burden of the nation for 21 years. It is time we carried him on our shoulders."

Sri Lanka 274-6 (50 overs) (D. P. M. D. Jayawardene 103, K. C. Sangakkara 48);
India 277-4 (48.2 overs) (G. Gambhir 97, M. S. Dhoni 91*).

ICC CHAMPIONS TROPHY

First held in 1998 as the ICC Knock-Out Trophy, the Champions Trophy, for the world's top eight one-day nations, was designed as a quadrennial filler in between World Cup cycles and another way for the ICC to stock its coffers. It was viewed with suspicion and cynicism by many, particularly English cricket writers, and was marginalised by the emergence of Twenty20. The 2013 tournament in England was due to be the final incarnation as, paradoxically, the ICC moved to return the 50-over World Cup to a more manageable, briefer format.

2004 – ENGLAND v WEST INDIES (FINAL): A VICTORY TO SAVOUR   2005

At The Oval, September 25. West Indies won by two wickets. A tournament full of insipid, forgettable moments ended with one of the most memorable finals in recent years, as West Indies scripted a soul-stirring fightback to put paid to England's hopes of winning their first one-day tournament of any significance. For a region devastated by various opponents on the cricket field, and by Hurricanes Ivan and Jeanne off it, this was a victory to savour. The reactions of the players immediately after Bradshaw struck the winning boundary told the story – the entire West Indian party roared on to the field in semi-darkness, hugging, kissing, and screaming, ecstatic yet bewildered by their achievement.

None of those wild celebratory scenes looked even remotely possible when West Indies slumped to 147 for eight in their quest for 218. The top-order batsmen had all perished – Chanderpaul the last of them for a dogged 47 – and England moved in to finish off the formalities as Bradshaw joined Browne. About the only thing in the batsmen's favour was the asking-rate, which was less than four and a half an over.

Browne and Bradshaw – both from Barbados, although Browne was born just round the corner in Lambeth – capitalised on that, initially looking for no more than nudges and pushes. But a stand which started off as nothing more than irritant value for Vaughan slowly assumed more ominous proportions.

England 217 (49.4 overs) (M. E. Trescothick 104; W. W. Hinds 3-24);
West Indies 218-8 (48.5 overs) (S. Chanderpaul 47; A. Flintoff 3-38).

2007-08 – TOURNAMENT ON SPEED   Hugh Chevallier, 2008

This tournament was a dream. It just got things right. In utter contrast to the fiasco of the 50-over World Cup in March and April, this competition, a Twenty20 World Cup in all but name, enjoyed outrageous success. The final typified it: the biggest draw in world cricket, India v Pakistan, went to the last over in a compelling game of shifting fortunes. India eventually triumphed, sending a billion people Twenty20-crazy.

Yet success brought its own problems, even if the ICC was glad to have them. How, for example, should the huge demand for Twenty20 internationals be handled? As the temptation to lift the lid of Pandora's box grew stronger, the ICC stuck to its limit of three home and four away matches for each team. Yet that raised the question of how they could be played in a meaningful context. And in an indication of the strength of the product, even below international level, the ICC announced during the tournament that a Twenty20 version of European football's champions' league would start in 2008. Initially, eight teams from four nations would compete for a winner's purse of $2m (almost £1m). A county's finances would be transformed.

The contest began at Johannesburg when Chris Gayle cut Shaun Pollock's first ball for a whip-crack four. It ended at the same ground 13 days and 26 games later when Misbah-ul-Haq took a risk too many, and his failed scoop-shot gave India glory. In between came, well, pretty much everything. This was a tournament brimming with joie de vivre. Intense, in-your-face, incessant. Most days saw two games, some three; planned as a tournament at speed, sometimes it felt more like a tournament on speed, punctuated by blasts of music and countless dance-sets. Yuvraj Singh epitomised the frenetic pace when he achieved cricketing nirvana by hitting England's Stuart Broad for six sixes in an over. His fifty came from 12 balls: scarcely credible.

2010 – ICC WORLD TWENTY20: CARIBBEAN REDEMPTION   Tony Cozier, 2011

To Paul Collingwood it was "a massive achievement, right up there with last year's Ashes win". To Haroon Lorgat it was "a truly memorable event which showcased the unique culture and passion for cricket in the Caribbean".

Their euphoria following the third ICC World Twenty20 tournament was fully understandable, if generated from different perspectives. Collingwood, England's short-term, short-game captain, had just led his team to their first global trophy after 35 years of failure and frustration in nine World Cups, six editions of the Champions Trophy and two World Twenty20 tournaments.

Lorgat, the ICC's chief executive, was speaking with as much relief as elation; the event did realise one of its aims, to atone for the universally reviled 2007 World Cup, the first major ICC event staged in the region, which smothered "the unique culture and passion for cricket in the Caribbean" with its security-obsessed organisation.

England's triumph, the culmination of a campaign virtually flawless after the qualifying stage, was all the sweeter as the opponents they thoroughly outplayed in the final were their oldest rivals, Australia, who were denied the only global title still eluding them. It was appropriate that it should be at Bridgetown's Kensington Oval, long since the favoured overseas venue for England's supporters, who transformed the stands into a Caribbean Wembley with a sea of St George flags.

It was Afghanistan's inaugural appearance on the world stage. Their enthusiasm and potential were as obvious as their inexperience and their need for more exposure against stronger teams in a variety of conditions.

Little Wonder No. 90

Wisden 1970. The disciplinary sub-committee of the Test and County Cricket Board found that T. W. Graveney had been guilty of "a serious breach of discipline" when he played in a match staged for his benefit, and for which he received £1,000, at Luton the previous Sunday *[the rest day of the First Test against West Indies]*. The committee severely reprimanded Graveney and informed the Test selectors that he should not be considered for the next three Test matches.

Counties

Counties cricket has stood at the heart of the Almanack from the second edition, which carried scorecards for the matches played by Surrey, Kent, Sussex, Middlesex, Nottinghamshire and Yorkshire, as well as Buckinghamshire and Cambridgeshire. Match reports, seasonal summaries, and batting and bowling averages were added from 1870 to produce a format that remains basically unchanged to the present day. Of course, there are now 18 first-class counties, the production is much slicker, scorecards include bowling analyses, and records have been added to the statistics. Moreover, the cricket itself has changed from solely three-day matches to incorporate a plethora of additional limited-overs competitions in the last half-century, starting with the Gillette Cup and, the most recent addition, the Twenty20 Cup. This increase has placed additional demands on the book's space, meaning the compression of one-day reports and scorecards, as well as democratising the game to the extent that all of the current first-class counties have now won silverware; in the purely County Championship era title-winning was largely the preserve of the so-called Big Six: Kent, Lancashire, Middlesex, Nottinghamshire, Surrey, Yorkshire. *Wisden*, too, used to apply a meritocracy in its ordering of the county section: teams' reviews were placed in the order that they had finished in the previous season's Championship. Thank goodness, not least for the sake of the modern researcher, the 1938 redesign changed the order to alphabetical.

Matches between teams bearing county names had begun in the 18th century, but it was not until the middle of the 19th that county clubs were formed. *Wisden* welcomed the birth of a Gloucestershire club, led by W. G. Grace and his brothers, writing in 1872 that the counties "are the real mainstays of the popularity of the game; are productive of the best all-round cricket; are the first to produce to public notice most of the skilled cricketers of the country". This pre-dated regular incoming international tours, but even in 1888, by when the Australians had become regular visitors, the editor Charles Pardon said: "County cricket is now so important, and the spirit of rivalry is so keen, that, interesting as the Australian visit will doubtless be, the competition among the great clubs will lose none of its excitement."

Views about Australian visits have changed somewhat in the intervening 125 years, and debate about the significance of county cricket has continued. In 1931 Stewart Caine expressed concern that, despite the income from Test match proceeds, an annual tour by "a team from some part of the Empire ... will dominate the home season" to the detriment of the Championship "when leading aspirants to first honours have to forgo in a third or more of their engagements the services of some of their best men." The following year some, though not *Wisden*, were arguing in favour of reducing the length of matches on the basis that "everything must be taken at a greater speed than that which satisfied previous generations". Nothing new under the sun, then.

What might Caine have made of central contracts which take players away from their counties for virtually the entire season? The most recent of his successors, Lawrence Booth, was in no doubt in 2012: "The virtual absence of England players has robbed the County Championship of what remained of its glamour, and the days when top-drawer overseas stars returned time and again to the same club have fallen victim to the international treadmill and more lucrative offers elsewhere (this season, the Australian Marcus North was hoping to play for his sixth county)."

It is a far cry from the report in *Wisden* 1956 of the previous season's meeting between Yorkshire and Surrey at Headingley: "This thrilling struggle between the two leading sides in the country drew over 60,000 people and the atmosphere resembled that of a Test match." The gates were closed on the first day when 35,000 were present, which itself was well short of the 38,600 who watched the Roses match at Old Trafford on the August Bank Holiday of 1926, still the biggest single day's attendance at any match in England. That number – and indeed the many thousands who would turn out to see the Victorian phenomenon W. G. Grace when he first appeared at their local ground – might now be unthinkable for a Championship match, but it should not be forgotten that the first Twenty20 Cup match between Middlesex and Surrey at Lord's in 2004 attracted 27,509 spectators, which was the largest crowd to watch a county match, apart from cup finals, since the same sides met there in 1953.

The ideal of fielding only native-born players in a county XI, epitomised (with one or two exceptions) by Yorkshire until 1992, was never practicable for the smaller counties, and from the earliest days they were bolstered by recruits from outside their borders and from overseas. The regulations about county qualification, set out in 1873, prohibited players from appearing for more than one team in a season, and obliged them to serve a qualifying period before they could play for a county other than that of their birth or residence; it was nearly 100 years before the next most fundamental change which, from 1968, allowed the instant regis-tration of overseas players, and meant that much of the leading talent made its way to England. Now, with changes in the UK employment laws and the prolifer-ation of overseas international cricket during the English season, as well as, since 2008, the arrival of the Indian Premier and other Twenty20 leagues, the quality of overseas players in the county game has declined. Their contracts have become shorter and shorter as they head off to play elsewhere, and locums stand in for locums to the bafflement of spectators and team-mates alike. The 2005 *Wisden* carried a list of overseas county players, which totalled 63 for the 18 counties in the previous summer.

Although the press and *Wisden* had previously declared sides to be the champion county – and *Wisden* first carried a Championship table in its 1889 edition – it was only for the 1890 season that the counties had agreed a points system. Each county, however, continued to organise its own fixtures, and remarkably it was not until 1929 that all played the same number of matches (and even that arrangement was initially short-lived); prior to that Yorkshire, say, might play 28 matches, Middlesex 22 and

Somerset only 16. Positions in the table were decided initially by deducting losses from wins, and then on a percentage basis of points acquired in finished games. Indeed, throughout its history there has been frequent tinkering with the format of the County Championship: for example, three-day matches, two-day matches, four-day matches, two divisions (three up, three down; then two up, two down), points for wins (revised many times), points for first-innings lead, bonus points (revised umpteen times), first innings restricted to 65 and 100 overs. Even in 1962 Norman Preston was lamenting that "the game may be killed stone dead if this continuous tampering... does not cease"; by 2000 Matthew Engel deemed that the County Championship was "sunk in wretchedness".

Wisden first ran a list of champion counties in 1907, dating back to 1875 (in 1911 the starting-point was amended to 1873) and even then recording four different methods of reckoning. In the centenary edition (1963) the list was extended back to 1864, following research by the cricket historian Rowland Bowen, only for it to change again in 1997. As it was not until 1890 that the counties had agreed a points system, all champions prior to that date were declared unofficial by *Wisden*, thus depriving – with suitable apologies – Gloucestershire of their only titles and Nottinghamshire of a large number of theirs.

Thus the course of county cricket, so often perceived as a tranquil pursuit, has been far from smooth, and we have set out to reflect those vicissitudes in our selection of reports and often trenchant comments on the counties and the soap operas involving some of their leading figures, matches and events both triumphant and tragic. *Wisden*, through its staff writers or local correspondents, has covered most of those happenings in detail – sometimes too much when a few overs of a rain-affected match were described almost ball by ball in order to fill the allocated page, or once, notably, when the use of a large number of bowlers on each side meant the depth of the scorecard allowed only this as the report of a match that produced 900 runs in four innings and was apparently uninterrupted:

GLOUCESTERSHIRE v SUSSEX

At Bristol, Monday, Tuesday, Wednesday, August 7, 8, 9, 1893. Owing to heavy scoring this game had to be left unfinished.

Unless otherwise stated matches between counties in this chapter and elsewhere in the book were in the County Championship.

DERBYSHIRE

[1953 edition] HISTORY OF DERBYSHIRE CRICKET by W. T. TAYLOR
(county secretary since 1908)

*The history of Derbyshire cricket is that of a gallant struggle against
adversity and financial difficulties. In scarcely one year since the club
was formed has there been a credit balance. In fact, more than once
Derbyshire have carried on only through the generosity of the
cricketing public of the county, who have risen nobly to the club's
many appeals for monetary assistance.*

1879 – DOUBLE JOY
1880

The season will long be remembered by Derbyshire cricketers for two brilliant feats that were accomplished, the double defeat of Yorkshire. Although these were their only successes, the eleven may well congratulate themselves on a performance which no other county were found equal to. Their other four county matches resulted in defeats, three at the hands of Notts and Lancashire. They were also beaten by Marylebone, after a close match, by 15 runs.

1887 – DROPPED CATCHES COST MATCHES
1888

Circumstances generally seemed to conspire against Derbyshire last summer, and for the second year in succession not a single victory rewarded the efforts of the eleven in engagements with their great rivals.

Admitting that Derbyshire experienced an exceptional amount of misfortune, it must not be forgotten that their fielding was probably the worst of any county team in England. At Manchester, in the first of their important engagements, they had an excellent chance of victory over Lancashire, but threw away their prospects of success by their slovenliness at the critical time; while in the return engagement the dropping of eight catches on the opening day might fairly be said to have accounted for Lancashire's victory by 54 runs.

Derbyshire only played six first-class county matches in 1887, abandoning, for financial reasons, the fixtures that had been arranged with Kent; and we may add that in four seasons the county has taken part in 33 first-class county engagements, suffering 29 defeats, and gaining only one victory.

For these various reasons Derbyshire can no longer be regarded as a first-class county. We think the team still quite good enough to do themselves credit in less-powerful company, and we hope after a time to be able to welcome them back among the leading shires.

1895 – ACRIMONY BREEDS CONTEMPT   1896

Where there was so much to praise it is not pleasant to touch upon a disagreeable topic, but we should fail in duty if we did not point out that the acrimonious spirit in which the Derbyshire men occasionally played the game subjected them during the summer to some very sharp criticism. With the strongest belief in keen cricket, we cannot help recognising that, when keenness brings in its train a quarrelsome disposition and a plentiful lack of good humour, it ceases to be desirable.

1896 – STORER MAKES HIS MARK   1897

Far and away in front of everything else that occurred last season in connection with Derbyshire cricket, was the marvellous form displayed by William Storer. The famous professional not only filled his accustomed position behind the wicket in a style fully worthy of his great reputation, but made a vast improvement as a batsman, and frequently succeeded as a change bowler when his more trusted companions had failed. He not only made two separate hundreds against Yorkshire at Derby, but also played a three-figure innings in the return match with that county, and in between the two contests made 142 not out against Leicestershire, thus accomplishing the extraordinary feat of scoring four hundreds in three consecutive matches. He also reached three figures against Lancashire at Old Trafford, and finished up the season with an aggregate of 1,091, his average being just over 57 runs an innings. It seemed a little strange that in all the three representative matches between England and Australia he should have been passed over in favour of Lilley, the Warwickshire professional, but influences other than those of cricket may have swayed the authorities who had the selection of the teams.

1899 – DEATH OF BEST ALL-ROUNDER   1900

GEORGE DAVIDSON. Derbyshire cricket sustained a heavy blow in the death from pneumonia on Wednesday morning, February 8th, of George Davidson. For some years he had been the best all-round man in the team, and, with the exception of William Storer, the county has never produced a player of finer powers. Born on June 29, 1866, he was just in his prime, and but for the illness which – following on influenza – had such a sad termination, he might have assisted Derbyshire for a good many seasons to come. Had he been associated with a stronger county, it is likely that he would have enjoyed a still more brilliant career, the fact of being so often on the beaten side having naturally a somewhat depressing effect on his cricket. A man of barely medium height, Davidson had an appearance that suggested great strength both of muscles and constitution. As a batsman he combined hit and defence in no common degree, and his fast bowling was marked by a really wonderful accuracy of pitch.

1901 – An Unfashionable County

Badly as Derbyshire did in 1899 and 1900, their record for 1901 was even poorer, disaster following disaster throughout the summer in the most depressing manner, with the result that out of 24 matches they were unable to place a victory of any sort to their credit.

Unlike other counties, Derbyshire seldom seem able to gain any promising recruits. Crack cricketers from the Public Schools and Universities appear in the ranks of other sides, but scarcely ever in those of the unfortunate Midlands team, who consequently have to rely on four or five great players who are year by year getting older, and upon a number of youngsters from local clubs who are not able to reach that pitch of excellence necessary for success in first-class cricket.

1902 – West Indian Recruit Makes Promising Start

C. A. Ollivierre, the West Indian batsman, completed his residential qualification late in July, and played county cricket for the first time in the Essex match at Derby. Although he did not do great things at once he speedily proved himself a valuable acquisition, scoring a delightful innings of 167 against Warwickshire. In nine innings he made 363 runs, and averaged over 40, and it is fully expected he will become one of the mainstays of the eleven.

1904 – DERBYSHIRE v ESSEX: Perrin's 343 not enough

At Chesterfield, July 18, 19, 20, 1904. In defeating Essex, Derbyshire accomplished the most phenomenal performance ever recorded in first-class cricket. They went in against a first innings of 597, got within 49, and ultimately won by nine wickets. Such an achievement has no parallel in the history of the game. Two batsmen covered themselves with distinction in the match – P. Perrin whose 343 not out was not only the highest innings of the season, but the fifth-best ever made in a great match, and Ollivierre who scored 321 for once out. Perrin obtained his runs in five hours and threequarters, and hit no fewer than 68 fours.

Essex 597 (Mr P. A. Perrin 343*, Mr F. L. Fane 63) and 97 (A. Warren 4-42);
Derbyshire 548 (Mr C. A. Ollivierre 229, Mr L. G. Wright 68; W. Reeves 5-192)
and 149-1 (Ollivierre 92*).

1910 – Winding-Up Averted

As was the case in 1909, Derbyshire again had the melancholy satisfaction of being last but one. It is small wonder that some of the people who have come forward time after time and helped the county club out of their constantly recurring financial difficulties began to dispair *[sic]*. The loss of matches was not so serious as the lack of public interest. The attendances at Derby were simply deplorable, and even at Chesterfield, where a good crowd used to be procurable, the gates were extremely poor. True it was a wet season, but wet weather or fine made little difference, the public as a rule staying away. Matters came to a crisis, and the Duke of Devonshire, presiding over a meeting in the autumn, made it plain that unless the subscription list was very considerably extended, the club would have to be wound up. Promises of further support, however, were made by the Duke, by Lord Curzon of Kedleston, by Mr S. H. Evershed, and Mr Chas. Wright, among others, and the meeting was adjourned with strong reason to hope that Derbyshire would figure in the Championship during the coming year. At the adjourned meeting on December 2 the committee reported a generous response to their appeal, and at the secretaries' meeting at Lord's the customary fixtures were arranged.

1919 – DERBYSHIRE v AUSTRALIAN IMPERIAL FORCES: NOTABLE WIN
1920

At Derby, July 14, 15, 1919. This match could be described as the surprise of the tour. Derbyshire secured a substantial advantage on the first day, nearly always had a little in hand, and won in the end by 36 runs. It was a notable victory, no other county team managing to beat the Australians. The bowlers had done so well all through the game that when the Australians went in with 169 to get it was felt that the task would be a hard one. Half the side were out for 36, and though Murray made a great effort, 64 runs were still required when Winning, the last man, went to the wicket. In the Australians' first innings Horsley did the hat-trick, getting rid of Murray, Lampard and Stirling with successive balls. Derbyshire won without the help of Bestwick, who had been picked for the Players at Lord's.

Derbyshire 181 and 112 (Mr J. M. Gregory 6-65, Mr H. L. Collins 4-39);
Australians 125 (Mr W. L. Trenerry 69; J. Horsley 6-55, A. Morton 4-66)
and 132 (Mr J. T. Murray 54; Horsley 6-62).

1920 – PLUMBING THE DEPTHS
1921

Derbyshire in 1920 touched an even lower depth than Worcestershire. They had a programme of 18 matches, and of these they lost 17, the other one – against Notts at Chesterfield for Humphries' benefit – having to be abandoned without a ball being bowled. This is perhaps the most dismal record of any county since the Championship came into existence, and going through the games in detail one can find little to excuse the long series of defeats. The chief cause of failure was the lamentable weakness of the batting. No one could get runs, the highest individual score obtained for the county for three months being 61. As regards bowling, Derbyshire had very bad luck, W. Bestwick and Horsley being lured away from the county by the financial attractions of League cricket. Both men reappeared in the eleven before the season was over, but only in isolated matches.

1927 – HITTING NEW HEIGHTS 1928

Fulfilling the promise shown in the latter part of the previous summer, Derbyshire last season enjoyed a greater measure of success than ever before in the history of the club. For a side that only three years earlier, failing to gain a single victory, had been at the bottom of the Championship, their advance in the course of three seasons was truly remarkable. Practically the same players who had appeared for the county in the previous summer, constituted the eleven, yet under the leadership of G. R. Jackson – captain of the team for the sixth year in succession – Derbyshire acquitted themselves so well that they finished fifth in the competition – below four members of the "Big Six," it is true, but ahead of both Surrey and Middlesex.

Such quick and notable improvement can without qualification be attributed to teamwork. Of the 15 men who carried through a programme of 25 matches seven averaged between 28 and 23 runs an innings, and six took between 30 and 70 wickets each.

1936 – PEAK OF ACHIEVEMENT: FIRST CHAMPIONSHIP 1937

Friday, August 28, 1936, must be written down as the greatest day ever in the history of Derbyshire cricket. On that day Derbyshire became, beyond all shadow of doubt, Champion County; Yorkshire's desperate, if belated challenge had failed and there began a new era for the Midlanders.

For the first time since the competition was placed on a sound basis, Derbyshire found themselves at the top. According to accepted records, Derbyshire had some claim to be considered champions in 1874 when the decision rested upon "the smallest number of matches lost", but their doings in those days bore no real comparison with their achievement in 1936. The winning of the Championship was not the sole honour which fell to the county, for Worthington was picked for two of the Test matches with India, and distinguished himself on each occasion, and he and Copson were members of the MCC team which, at the end of the season, toured Australia and New Zealand.

Derbyshire's success in the competition caused no surprise to those who, having studied the county's gradual but steady rise from bottom position in the table 12 years ago to runners-up in 1935, saw the "writing on the wall". Magnificent bowling – they possessed probably the deadliest and best varied attack of any side in the country – teamwork rather than individual brilliance, and a will-to-win spirit no matter the position of the game, were the salient factors which made Derbyshire stand out head and shoulders above most of their rivals.

It must be confessed that the batting frequently revealed striking limitations; but, paradoxically though it may appear, this very weakness influenced Derbyshire's triumph. Had the side put together big totals, their bowlers would never have found the time or opportunity to get rid of opponents for reasonably small scores. Derbyshire's policy of scoring quickly was proved the right one. The county won 13 of their 28 matches and suffered only four defeats. No other team gained so many victories.

While Derbyshire had their share of the good fortune without which no team can hope to carry off premier honours, they met reverses which might easily have upset their expectations. The biggest blow of all was an injury to George Pope, the tall all-rounder who, with his brother Alfred, had played a large part in Derbyshire's rise the previous summer. When bowling at Bristol late in May, Pope so damaged a muscle that he afterwards developed cartilage trouble and for the remainder of the season was *hors de combat*.

Full praise must be given to A. W. Richardson. First leading Derbyshire in 1931, Richardson again captained the eleven with shrewdness and a geniality which brought the best out of the cricketers under him. Unfortunately, he did not strike his real form with the bat until late in the season. For his handling of the bowling, Richardson deserved the highest commendation and undoubtedly his astuteness in "nursing" Copson had a great deal to do with the young fast bowler's striking advance. Unhappily for Derbyshire, Richardson, at the end of the season, was compelled, for business reasons, to resign the captaincy.

A review of the Derbyshire season would not be complete without reference to Sam Cadman, the former Derbyshire player, in charge of the nursery. The fact that most of the players who helped to win the Championship graduated from the nursery forms in itself a tribute to the judgment and perseverance of Cadman and those collaborating with him.

1952 – WORCESTERSHIRE v DERBYSHIRE: 16 FOR GLADWIN   1953

At Stourbridge, July 23, 24, 1952. Derbyshire won by an innings and 57 runs. Gladwin, their inswing bowler, was deadly on a pitch which had not been used for a county match for three years. Aided by brilliant catching in the leg trap and also on the boundary, he took 11 wickets on the last day and returned the remarkable match figures of 16 wickets for 84 runs. His nine for 41 in the second innings was the best analysis of his career. Lobban, Worcestershire's new fast bowler from Jamaica, enjoyed success on the first day when, after taking the new ball with the total 201 for two, he sent back six men – five clean-bowled – in 12 overs. His effectiveness enhanced the value of Elliott's sound innings, which lasted three and threequarter hours, but Worcestershire's hopes were soon dashed by the almost unplayable pace and swing of Gladwin, who took the first five wickets for 25 runs.

Derbyshire 274 (C. S. Elliott 122; K. Lobban 6-52);
Worcestershire 96 (C. Gladwin 7-43) and 121 (Gladwin 9-41).

1965 – DERBYSHIRE v SOUTH AFRICANS: TOURISTS GROUNDED   1966

At Chesterfield, June 26, 28, 29, 1965. Derbyshire won by seven wickets. It was the county's only victory over a South African team since they first met in 1901, and their first over any official touring side since 1937 when they beat the New Zealanders. The match itself was more notable for the no-balling of Rhodes by Buller for throwing in the South Africans' second innings, yet despite his withdrawal from the attack, Derbyshire dismissed them for 119. As Derbyshire had already played for two months, whereas this was the South Africans' first match in strange and difficult conditions for batsmen, the county began with a big advantage. On the first day when van der Merwe won the toss, a strong cross-wind, a softish pitch and slow outfield favoured the bowlers and Rhodes, Jackson and Smith carried all before them. On Monday, with the pitch drier and the weather sunny and warm, the South Africans excelled in the field and, though without P. M. Pollock, gained a lead of six runs. Lack of practice was the main reason for the South Africans failing a second time with the bat and Derbyshire, left to make 126, won comfortably, thanks to a stylish display by Johnson, who appropriately made the winning hit.

South Africans 149 (E. J. Barlow 50; H. J. Rhodes 4-35) **and 119;**
Derbyshire 143 (R. Dumbrill 4-32) **and 126-3**.

1972 – HOPING FOR UPLIFT AFTER UPHEAVAL   1973

After finishing bottom of the County Championship for the second successive season, Derbyshire ended the summer of 1972 with one of the most massive upheavals in their history. Contracts were not offered to four players, J. Harvey, Harvey-Walker, Swarbrook and Russell; two others, Hall and Eyre, had already announced their retirements; and Wilkins decided not to return from South Africa after three successful and colourful years.

In addition, Buxton, captain for three years, relinquished the post, saying that although he had never made excuses for the county's poor performances he could no longer accept the responsibility for them. He will carry on as a player for this season, at least, and Derbyshire were fortunate to secure an immediate replacement when Brian Bolus, the former Yorkshire and England batsman, was released by Nottinghamshire.

Bolus readily accepted the challenge of guiding Derbyshire through the most severe crisis of their post-war years and, with the county's committee at last opening their eyes to the grim situation, the season ended, conversely, on a note of genuine hope and optimism.

1972 – LILLEE DECLINES OFFER

Derbyshire offered Dennis Lillee, the Australian fast bowler, £6,000 for 1973 and the prospects of additional income from other sources, but after much deliberation he declined. The major reason for his decision was that after his long absences from home he felt it better for he and his wife to have six months together before the 1973-74 Australian season. Also the Test selectors wanted to guard against the risk of his burning himself out because of too much cricket.

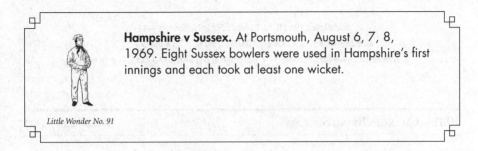

Hampshire v Sussex. At Portsmouth, August 6, 7, 8, 1969. Eight Sussex bowlers were used in Hampshire's first innings and each took at least one wicket.

Little Wonder No. 91

1973 – DERBYSHIRE v YORKSHIRE: WARD SENT OFF   1974

At Chesterfield, June 16, 18, 19, 1973. Drawn. This match produced some splendid cricket, particularly by the Yorkshire batsmen, but everything was overshadowed by the sending from the field of Ward, the Derbyshire fast bowler, by his captain, Bolus, for refusing to bowl on Monday afternoon. (Ward apologised for his behaviour the following day, but two days later announced he was retiring from first-class cricket and his contract was cancelled by mutual agreement.)

Ward's dismissal was only the third known case in the history of first-class cricket. In 1897 Bobby Peel (Yorkshire) was ordered off by Lord Hawke and never played for the county again; in 1922, Jack Newman, of Hampshire, was ordered off by the Hon. Lionel Tennyson.

After Derbyshire had made 311, Ward began by removing Boycott in his first over. Afterwards, although bowling extremely fast he was erratic, bowling nine no-balls, and Hampshire, who was dropped off him before he had scored, took 19 off one over. He conceded 56 runs from nine overs, and when Bolus asked him to bowl again, refused. Bolus, who had previously left the field to talk to the Derbyshire secretary, then made a dismissive gesture and Ward walked off and left the ground before play ended.

Derbyshire 311 (A. J. Borrington 75, M. H. Page 52, J. B. Bolus 52; C. M. Old 4-51) **and 71-2**;
Yorkshire 315 (P. J. Sharpe 110, D. L. Bairstow 53*; I. R. Buxton 4-42).

1979 – DERBYSHIRE v MIDDLESEX: STEELE STALLS   1980

At Derby, June 9, 11, 12, 1979. Drawn. The inexplicable decision of Derbyshire's captain, Steele, not to accept the challenge of making 215 for victory in 177 minutes led to the match ending on a highly acrimonious note. Steele, who made an unbeaten 66 in 49 overs, was jeered from the field by his own members and supporters, and later the club issued a statement in which they said his act was not in accord with their policy of playing purposeful cricket. Steele himself later apologised, explaining that he was upset because of short-pitched bowling at Derbyshire's lower-order batsmen. The incident ruined a final day on which Radley had preceded his sporting declaration with a century, while Butcher's 67 occupied only 57 minutes and included 13 fours.

Middlesex 194 (R. O. Butcher 56; P. N. Kirsten 4-44)
and 289-4 dec (C. T. Radley 103, Butcher 67, G. D. Barlow 55*);
Derbyshire 269-9 inns closed (A. J. Borrington 64) and 107-1 (D. S. Steele 66*).

1981 – CHANGES BRING SUCCESS
Michael Carey, 1982

By becoming the first winners of the NatWest Bank Trophy, Derbyshire achieved their first honour since they were county champions in 1936, and only the second in their entire history. This long-awaited triumph, however, the result of some dedicated team performances under the irrepressible leadership of Barry Wood, was tempered by the departure from the county of two England players in Mike Hendrick and Geoff Miller, and to a lesser extent by further evidence of instability behind the scenes.

Few counties can have experienced so many changes in one season. At one time or another, Derbyshire's chairman, chief executive, captain and even their scorer all resigned. Of these moves, the most important was that of Miller, who handed over the captaincy to Wood only an hour or so before the start of the Championship match against Kent on July 25. Little did anyone sense the historical significance of this at the time. Six weeks later Wood, who had blended the majority of the side into an effective unit with the discipline and ebullience of E. J. Barlow, was holding the NatWest Bank Trophy aloft at Lord's, and the stigma of being one of the only two counties who had not tasted success since the war was wiped away.

1981 – DERBYSHIRE v NORTHAMPTONSHIRE
(NATWEST BANK TROPHY FINAL): FLYING FINISH
1982

At Lord's, September 5, 1981. Derbyshire won by virtue of losing fewer wickets with the scores tied. In deteriorating light, they required seven runs from the 60th over, bowled by Griffiths, but it became apparent that six would suffice for victory if no more than eight Derbyshire wickets had fallen. Miller swatted the first delivery to mid-on for two and took a single to third man off the second, Tunnicliffe pushed the third back to the bowler but ran the next to third man for one, and with Miller getting a single to square leg off the fifth ball, one run was needed off the final delivery. Cook, the Northamptonshire captain, spent two minutes placing his field, but Miller backed up well and his flying finish beat Allan Lamb's throw at the stumps.

Northamptonshire 235-9 (60 overs) (G. Cook 111, W. Larkins 52);
Derbyshire 235-6 (60 overs) (J. G. Wright 76, P. N. Kirsten 63).

1983 – YOUTH TAKES THE HELM
Gerald Mortimer, 1984

For the fifth time in nine years, a change of captaincy was forced upon Derbyshire during a season. Barry Wood, over whose reappointment there had been much debate eight months earlier, stepped down in the first week of May. Geoff Miller, whom Wood had succeeded during the 1981 season, stood in until the committee made the brave decision to appoint Kim Barnett, at 22 the youngest captain in the county's history.

Barnett proved to be an excellent choice and came through the disruption caused by Wood's withdrawal and injuries to John Hampshire, Paul Newman and Miller to lead Derbyshire to seven victories in the Schweppes County Championship, a total bettered only once, under Derek Morgan in 1966, in 20 seasons.

Barnett's batting flourished, especially when he began to open the innings, and he was one of two people who did most to transform moderate expectations into a successful and enjoyable season. The other was Ole Mortensen, a fast bowler from Denmark who took 84 wickets in all competitions. This was an extraordinary story. Mortensen gave up a job in a tax office and came to England to pursue his dream of becoming the first Dane to succeed in county cricket. He arrived as an unknown quantity and soon became an automatic choice, being accurate, hostile and, above all, a bowler of unquenchable spirit.

1984 – STALWARTS BOW OUT
Gerald Mortimer, 1985

Victory over Hampshire in the final match also marked the end of two distinguished careers. John Hampshire spent his last three years with Derbyshire after being with Yorkshire from 1961 to 1981. Hampshire could well have played in more than his eight Tests and like the other leaver, Bob Taylor, combined a love of cricket with a respect for its traditions and courtesies. Taylor, after announcing his retirement, had a royal progress around the counties, the applause which accompanied him indicating the respect and affection in which he was held. Taylor was an artist, acknowledged as one of the greatest wicketkeepers of all time and admired for his consistency whether in front of half-a-dozen spectators or a full house at Lord's. He passed John Murray's world record of dismissals while in Australia in 1982-83, and Hampshire's captain, Mark Nicholas, rated it a rare privilege to be Taylor's 1,646th and final victim. Taylor, whose hair went white in the process of serving Derbyshire for 24 seasons, will continue to be associated with the county as second-team captain.

1989 – HOLDING HOLDS HIS LINE
Gerald Mortimer, 1990

Michael Holding retired and ended a distinguished career by steering Derbyshire to victory over Nottinghamshire by one wicket. It was especially satisfying to Holding, who had refused to retake the field in the earlier meeting at Nottingham. On the second day, the umpires decided that the original Trent Bridge pitch was too dangerous for the match to continue on it and ordered another pitch to be prepared.

Holding, believing that the match had become a farce, declined to take any further part, for which he was severely reprimanded by the county. However, Holding's solitary stand did not diminish his great contribution to world cricket: no fast bowler has had a more hypnotically beautiful action, and his dignified friendliness endeared him to Derbyshire followers.

1990 – DERBYSHIRE v MIDDLESEX: POINTS DEDUCTED   1991

At Derby, August 18, 20, 21, 1990. Derbyshire won by 171 runs. Derbyshire became the first county to beat Middlesex in the 1990 Championship, but it was obvious from the first day that the pitch was unsatisfactory. The umpires reported it and, after inspection by Donald Carr (chairman of the TCCB pitches committee), Tim Lamb (TCCB cricket secretary), Doug Lucas (Northamptonshire) and Old Trafford groundsman Peter Marron, the deputy inspector of pitches, Derbyshire had 25 points deducted. "The pitch was clearly unsuitable for first-class cricket," said the TCCB. There was, however, some interesting cricket. After Morris and O'Gorman batted well for Derbyshire, Gatting compiled a magnificent century from 217 balls, hitting 15 fours in his innings. His display was the more commendable because weekend rain had forced its way under the covers, and Derbyshire's chairman, Chris Middleton, wrote to Middlesex thanking Gatting for his attitude in an embarrassing situation for the home county. Roberts and Miller suggested that sensible application would bring its rewards, but Middlesex, set 271 in a minimum of 54 overs, responded feebly. Base wrecked their innings and bowled well, perhaps too well for Derbyshire's ultimate good.

Derbyshire 249 (J. E. Morris 67, T. J. G. O'Gorman 55; J. E. Emburey 5-32)
and 230-6 dec (P. D. Bowler 56; Emburey 4-71);
Middlesex 209 (M. W. Gatting 119*; O. H. Mortensen 4-29) and 99 (S. J. Base 5-28).

1990 – PUTTING ON THEIR SUNDAY BEST   Gerald Mortimer, 1991

Derbyshire, putting behind them defeat in two days in the County Championship by Essex on the preceding Thursday and Friday, and also the fact that they had not beaten Essex in any competition since 1982, beat them by five wickets at Derby on the last day of the Sunday League season to win the Refuge Assurance Trophy. It was only their third trophy in 120 years, following the County Championship in 1936 and the NatWest Bank Trophy in 1981, and they became the 11th county to win the Sunday title.

1993 – DERBYSHIRE v LANCASHIRE: QUESTIONABLE COLLAPSE   1994

At Derby, June 24, 25, 26, 28, 1993. Lancashire won by 111 runs. No Derbyshire match had ever produced so many runs, the aggregate 1,497 passing the 1,391 between Derbyshire and Essex at Chesterfield in 1904, but the conclusion was startling on the final afternoon, when Morris was 151 and his team 243 for two, then Wasim Akram took six for 11 in 49 deliveries. Although the umpires inspected the ball regularly, Derbyshire were sufficiently concerned about its condition to send it to the TCCB. No action was judged necessary at Lord's but the incident, with its suggestion of tampering, raised the temperature for the Benson and Hedges Cup final a fortnight later. Cork was ordered out of the attack in Lancashire's first innings, for running down the pitch, while Atherton and Wasim scored accomplished centuries. Barnett responded with a fine 161 and then Lancashire's declaration set Derbyshire 379 in 86 overs. While Morris was batting with rare brilliance – he hit 23 fours and a six in 176 balls – they had a chance. But when he became Wasim's first victim of the match, the end was unexpectedly near.

Lancashire 477 (M. A. Atherton 137, Wasim Akram 117, N. J. Speak 74; D. E. Malcolm 5-98)
and 327-8 dec (G. D. Lloyd 80, N. H. Fairbrother 59);
Derbyshire 426 (K. J. Barnett 161, C. J. Adams 74; P. A. J. DeFreitas 5-109)
and 267 (J. E. Morris 151; Akram 6-45, M. Watkinson 4-72).

1997 – THE EVER REVOLVING DOOR
Gerald Mortimer, 1998

As Derbyshire rounded off their season on a lovely September afternoon with a decisive victory over Yorkshire, it was almost possible to believe that all was well. The list of the disappeared at the County Ground told a different story. During an extraordinary four months, Derbyshire contrived to lose their captain, coach, cricket chairman, chairman, secretary and commercial manager. After the season, two of their most gifted players went too.

1999 – DERBYSHIRE v HAMPSHIRE: MIXED SATISFACTION
2000

At Derby, September 15, 16, 17, 18, 1999. Hampshire won by two runs. A controversial match reached a dramatic climax when a skin-of-their-teeth victory ensured that Hampshire joined Derbyshire in the first division in 2000. Such were the complex permutations surrounding the last round of matches that both could have finished in the lower half: realistically, Hampshire needed a win, while Derbyshire had slightly more leeway. The result squeezed Warwickshire out of the top division, and they complained to the ECB about the collusion between the captains. By the third morning, Warwickshire had already won, which left Derbyshire needing two batting points to be safe. They were 231 for eight, still 19 short, when Udal – in charge while Smith was off the field – brought on White, a very occasional legspinner. Runs, and safety for Derbyshire, quickly followed. Cork and Smith maintained that discussions began at lunchtime, *after* Derbyshire had been guaranteed a top-half finish, but some smelled a rat. After rubbish was bowled to speed a third declaration, Smith offered a target, conditioned by an advanced weather forecast, of

285 in four sessions. Members protested at the shenanigans, but the upshot was an enthralling run-chase. Derbyshire recovered from losing three wickets in the sixties, with Cork and DeFreitas batting well. As a home victory neared, Lacey had his right hand broken by McLean. He batted on and, when he had added 104 with DeFreitas, fourth place – and thus £15,000 – were 18 runs away. Then two wickets fell, leaving the last pair to get six. Hartley made amends, juggling a return catch from Lacey. The ECB later ruled that the captains were trying to win, leaving Warwickshire as the game's only losers.

Hampshire 362-8 dec (A. N. Aymes 86, J. S. Laney 67, R. A. Smith 64, A. D. Mascarenhas 51) **and 199-5 dec**; **Derbyshire 277-9 dec** (P. A. J. DeFreitas 54) **and 282** (DeFreitas 61, D. G. Cork 51; N. A. M. McLean 4-87).

2006 – DERBYSHIRE v SOMERSET: HOME COMFORT AT LAST   2007

At Derby, August 8, 9, 10, 11, 2006. Derbyshire won by 80 runs. At last. After 50 months and ten days, and 33 matches, Derbyshire finally won at home in the Championship. They did it the hardest possible way, as Somerset, chasing a ludicrous 579 to win, made the highest losing fourth-innings total ever in England. White – whose unbeaten 260 was the highest fourth-innings score in first-class cricket – single-handedly threatened to deny them, hitting 40 fours and three sixes from 246 balls, in a memorable display that spanned 373 minutes. This was his fifth Championship hundred of the season; Somerset lost every time. He returned to Victoria after this for wrist surgery: he should be useful when fully fit. Durston helped White add 213 in 41 overs, but Derbyshire's bowlers chipped away. They lost a point for a tardy over-rate, but there were extravagant, shirtless, celebrations on the field when Botha's direct hit finally ran out Willoughby.

Derbyshire 316 (S. D. Stubbings 97, T. R. Birt 50) **and 413-8 dec** (M. J. Di Venuto 118, D. J. Pipe 84*, Birt 51); **Somerset 151** (N. J. Edwards 75; P. S. Jones 4-45) **and 498** (C. L. White 260*, W. J. Durston 73; Jones 4-119).

2012 – A RARE TROPHY FOR THE KITCHEN CABINET   Mark Eklid, 2013

Few beyond the boundary ropes of the County Ground in April would have backed Derbyshire, the most success-starved of the first-class counties, to finish on top of the pile in Division Two of the Championship. Galvanised by early victories, they spent most of the season as table leaders, and defied scepticism over their stamina by clinching the title on the final day, at home to Hampshire. They finished level on points with Yorkshire, but above them on the basis of six wins to Yorkshire's five.

This was Derbyshire's first trophy since the Benson and Hedges Cup in 1993, and the first promotion in their history. Their only previous spell in Division One was in 2000, which had been earned by finishing ninth the year before the Championship was split in two. They hold so many wooden spoons – a record 15 – that a kitchen drawer has often seemed more useful than a trophy cabinet.

DURHAM

[1993 edition] In 1992, 71 years after Glamorgan's introduction, Durham join the Britannic Assurance Championship and become the 18th first-class county. Their promotion ends a long association with the Minor Counties Championship, which they left as joint record-holders, with nine titles.

1901 – INAUGURAL AND OFFICIAL CHAMPIONS 1902

For the first time the competition among the Minor Counties had the official recognition of the MCC and was placed on a really proper footing. Seventeen counties – including the second elevens of Surrey and Yorkshire – entered the competition, to qualify for which four out and home matches had to be played. The positions being determined by the same method as in the first-class County Championship, Durham secured first place – which they shared in 1900 with Glamorgan and Northamptonshire.

1959 – MILBURN BURSTS ON THE SCENE Norman Preston, Notes by the Editor, 1960

When the Indians played their last match against Durham at Sunderland, Colin Milburn, 17 years old, of Stanley Grammar School, went in first on his first appearance for the county and hit a sparkling century. In his younger days Milburn attended the Secondary Modern School at Annfield Plain where they did not run a cricket team. He attributes his success to his love of the game and to the help and advice he received at the various Durham indoor schools, and especially from the members of the Burnopfield Cricket Club, where he first began to play at the age of 11. Within three years he was assisting the club's first eleven and at 13 he was chosen for Durham Schoolboys, after which he appeared two years in succession for North of England against the South. He also played for the Durham Public Schools, scoring 285 runs, average 57. In all games last summer he made 1,955 runs, including five centuries, with an average approaching 50. A well-built lad, standing five feet ten inches, he is a fine attacking batsman. He has already assisted Warwickshire Second XI, but whether his future lies with the Midland county may depend on his scholastic studies, for the teaching profession may claim his chief attention.

1973 – YORKSHIRE v DURHAM (GILLETTE CUP): FIRST GIANTKILLING 1974

At Harrogate, June 30, 1973. Durham won by five wickets. It was the first defeat of a first-class county by a junior side since the Minor Counties joined the competition in its second year, ten years earlier. It meant that Yorkshire had not won a Gillette Cup match since they won the Cup in 1969. When Boycott won the toss and had choice of batting or bowling, it seemed that everything was in their favour. Instead, the Durham opening bowlers, Wilkinson and Alan Old (rugby international brother of the Yorkshireman) performed so steadily that only 18 runs came in the first nine overs. At this stage Wilkinson bowled Boycott and this success lifted the Durham bowlers and fieldsmen to unexpected heights. They seldom bowled a bad ball and the fielding was superb. In spite of a good innings by Johnson, Yorkshire were bowled out in 58.4 overs for only 135 runs. The Durham captain, Lander, returned the best bowling figures of his career, and was Man of the Match. Nicholson and Chris Old, with the new ball, often beat the bat in their opening spell, but they could not upset the determination and concentration of the batsmen. With plenty of time in hand, Inglis scored 47 runs in good style. Durham coasted to victory.

Yorkshire 135 (58.4 overs) (C. Johnson 44; B. R. Lander 5-15);
Durham 138-5 (51.3 overs) (R. Inglis 47)

Wisden 1970. The metric pitch: Reassured by the experience of member countries such as Denmark and Holland, the International Cricket Conference saw no problem in converting cricket measurement to the metric system. When Britain went metric, pitches would measure 20.117 metres.

Little Wonder No. 92

1982 – Record Run Comes To An End
1983

Without the services of many key players, defending champions Durham dropped to ninth position in their centenary year, and ended their record of 65 Championship matches without defeat when they succumbed to Staffordshire at Stockton-on-Tees in mid-August.

1992 – Tough At The Top Level
Tim Wellock, 1993

It was the best of times and the worst of times for Durham in their first season in the County Championship. First-class cricket was rapturously received by a membership of over 6,000, and the team made a highly encouraging start. But once the impetus provided by the successful launch was lost they began to struggle, and the early loss of Australian Test batsman Dean Jones plunged them into a depressing slide which left them 36 points adrift at the foot of the table. They finished joint eighth in the Sunday League, while after beating the holders Worcestershire in the Benson and Hedges Cup they failed to reach the quarter-finals because of a disappointing home defeat by Derbyshire. It was a similar story in the NatWest Trophy, in which they surprised Middlesex at Uxbridge in the second round, then lost at Leicester in the quarter-finals.

1992 – GLAMORGAN v DURHAM: PROMISING START   1993

At Cardiff, May 14, 15, 16, 1992. Durham won by an innings and 104 runs. Glamorgan were completely outplayed by Durham, their successors as junior first-class county, who recorded their first Championship win with a day to spare. The home team surrendered the initiative on the first day when, after Morris and Maynard had taken them to 121 for two, they were all out for 224. The 17-year-old seamer Paul Henderson, on his first-class debut, began the collapse in his first over after lunch, claiming Morris and Richards in four balls and later dismissing Maynard. Then Durham ran up their highest total in history – first-class or minor county – as Larkins made his 50th first-class century, Jones narrowly missed his first for Durham, and Parker registered his third in six innings. Resuming 297 behind, Glamorgan's batsmen were immediately in trouble. They took lunch on the third day at 24 for three, after Botham collected two wickets and a catch. Cottey battled for four and a half hours and an unbeaten 112, which kept Durham waiting until the penultimate over of the day. The country's leading wicket-taker, Brown, sealed the win with his 20th victim.

Glamorgan 224 (M. P. Maynard 88) and 193 (P. A. Cottey 112*; S. J. E. Brown 5-66);

Durham 521-9 dec (W. Larkins 143, P. W. G. Parker 124, D. M. Jones 94; R. D. B. Croft 5-105).

1993 – BOTHAM MAKES SUDDEN EXIT   Tim Wellock, 1994

In their second season of first-class cricket, it seemed that every time Durham were edging up the ladder to success, a huge snake was waiting to take them back to base. Five innings defeats exposed their limited resources and they duly retained the Championship's wooden spoon.

Significant progress was made, however, following the sudden retirement of Ian Botham. Even the Durham chairman, Don Robson, did not know of Botham's plans to quit until they were reported in a Sunday newspaper the day before he bowed out, with an unbecoming, flippant performance in the match against the Australians. Botham said he would continue to play on Sundays as long as there was a chance of winning prize money. In the event, it was mutually agreed that one farewell was enough. But the tourist match did mark a bit of a turning point. Durham had played magnificently on the first two days of this game and were the only team all summer to make the Australians follow on. The next game produced their first Championship win in almost 14 months – against an admittedly depleted Essex – and Durham won their last six Sunday League games to finish seventh.

1999 – PROMOTION DESPITE SETBACKS   Tim Wellock, 2000

An amazing season for Durham began with snow, plumbed the depths with a NatWest defeat by Holland, and ended in ecstasy as they secured a place in the first division of the 2000 Championship. The snow robbed them of victory in their opening match against Worcestershire, which was followed by three defeats, with batting as brittle as anything in their darkest days.

2000 – DURHAM v SURREY: 19TH TIME LUCKY   2001

At Chester-le-Street, May 2, 3, 4, 2000. Durham won by 231 runs. Since entering the first-class game in 1992, Durham had played Surrey 18 times in all competitions and lost every match. This first win in nine Championship meetings – and with a day to spare – was achieved on the back of a quite magnificent 98 by Peng, aged 17 years 227 days, the highest score for Durham on Championship debut. He went in at 48 for four, took 15 balls to get off the mark, reached 50 off 104 balls and made his remaining 48 runs off only 41 before being last out. He hit 17 fours. His decision to concentrate on cricket, rather than continue with his A-level studies at Newcastle Royal Grammar School, looked fully justified, and Surrey's captain, Adam Hollioake, described him as "the best young player I've ever seen". Though his birth certificate records him as Nicky Peng Gillender, combining the surnames of his parents (both of whom watched this debut), he asked to be known simply by his mother's name. With moisture just below the surface after the wet April, Durham's seam attack proved better suited to the conditions than Surrey's, and the reigning champions, unbeaten the previous season, twice recorded the lowest Championship total made against Durham. On the second day, they avoided the follow-on figure of 84 through their last pair; on the third, they collapsed from 41 without loss to 85 all out inside the afternoon session.

Durham 234 (N. Peng 98, P. D. Collingwood 66; B. C. Hollioake 4-41)
and 186 (S. M. Katich 65; M. P. Bicknell 5-85);
Surrey 104 and 85.

2003 – THE RICKSHAW AT THE RIVERSIDE   Tim Wellock, 2004

Eleven years after becoming a first-class county, Durham achieved one of their most burning ambitions in 2003 when the Riverside became the eighth English ground to stage a Test match – and the first newcomer to the list in 101 years. The success of the occasion was followed a month later by the shock resignation of the chairman who had done so much to bring it about. In almost four years in charge, Bill Midgley had overseen an improvement in the financial situation and continued the development of the ground to Test standard. It culminated in the installation of 2,000 extra permanent seats, paid for by a private development in the opposite corner of the ground. This new health club had not been part of the original plans, which angered some members, and when Midgley felt complaints had become personal insults, he walked out.

On the field, the highlights were a double over Yorkshire, who had never previously lost to Durham in the Championship, a county-record 273 by the Australian, Martin Love, against Hampshire, and excitement generated for half a season by the world's fastest bowler, Shoaib Akhtar, otherwise known as the "Rawalpindi Express". After his arrival in late June, Shoaib clearly paced himself, prompting one member to call him the "Rawalpindi Rickshaw", but his final statistics were impressive. He took 34 Championship wickets at 17.05.

2007 – SEASON OF FULFILMENT   Tim Wellock, 2008

After 15 seasons of apprenticeship, Durham achieved fulfilment. They won their first prize when they beat Hampshire in the final of the Friends Provident Trophy at Lord's. In the Championship they went top on the penultimate day of the season and remained there for 24 hours until Sussex, whom they had beaten soundly in the previous round, overhauled them by 4.5 points. Durham finished runners-up; their previous-best place was seventh, the year before. As Ottis Gibson, the Professional Cricketers' Association Player of the Year, observed: "It's great to be champions for a day."

If the unforgettable weekend at Lord's was the highlight, Riverside witnessed many moments of high drama. Foremost was Gibson's feat of taking all ten wickets, also against Hampshire, followed by the three-wicket Friends Provident semi-final win against Essex and the victory against Glamorgan which clinched the second division title in the Pro40 League.

2008 – TOP OF THE TREE   Tim Wellock, 2009

Durham's 17th season as a first-class county was the wettest, the longest – and the best. It finally ended on September 27, the most glorious day in every respect for the team and around 200 fans who made the pilgrimage to Canterbury. Only four years after finishing bottom of the pile for the fifth time, Durham were county champions. Their six victories were unmatched in the first division, and four of them came away from home. It was widely acknowledged that they were the best team, not least because they were in the top four in every competition. Semi-finalists in the Friends Provident Trophy and Twenty20 Cup, they achieved third place, their highest finish, in the Pro40, as well as the Championship. They even won the Second Eleven title. In his third season as captain, Dale Benkenstein said they truly believed they could win everything.

At lunchtime on the first day of that final match, however, they must have feared they would be left with nothing. Ten points behind Nottinghamshire at the start, they had taken only two wickets after putting Kent in on a damp pitch, while at Trent Bridge Hampshire were sliding towards 96 for six. But thereafter the transformation in both games was such that, going into the last morning, Durham knew it would take something extraordinary to deny them. They hadn't counted on fog, but by 10.30 clear blue skies presided over the 72 minutes required by Callum Thorp and Steve Harmison to take the five remaining wickets.

The first to reach Harmison after he bowled last man Martin Saggers was his brother Ben; with others in hot pursuit, down they went in a joyous heap. Steve Harmison's left forearm could be seen sticking out protectively, encased in plaster after an attempted gully catch. If ever the pleasure was worth the pain, this was it.

The final triumph was, for Geoff Cook, their director of cricket since 1991, "one of the sweetest moments in my 36 years in the game".

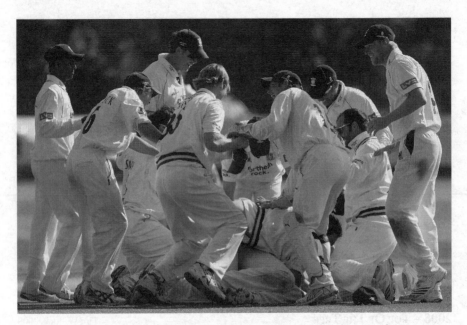

Joyous heap: Durham's players dissolve in delight after their maiden
County Championship title in 2008 is secured by Steve Harmison
taking the wicket of Kent's Martin Saggers at Canterbury

2009 – SECOND TITLE BRINGS UNPRECEDENTED REWARDS   Tim Wellock, 2010

Durham in 2009 were in a class of their own. Their winning margin of 47 points was a record since the advent of two divisions in 2000, even though their last two games were drawn with the title already secured. Durham were unbeaten, won twice as many matches as any other first division side, and conceded a first-innings deficit only once, at Headingley. The £500,000 prizemoney for retaining the title was a five-fold increase, designed to counter the possibility of counties concentrating on chasing Twenty20 riches.

At Chester-le-Street, September 9, 10, 11, 12, 2009. Durham won by an innings and 52 runs. Durham were keen to make sure of retaining the Championship in their final home game, so that this time they could celebrate in front of their own fans: free admission on the last two days brought crowds of 4,000. And they effectively sealed the title on the third afternoon, when Davies had Brown caught behind to gain a second bowling point. They started the match needing 11 points; that gave them seven and, although Durham had to wait until the finish to be officially declared champions, Nottinghamshire had no chance of denying them four for the draw. The visitors had lost Read, their captain and wicketkeeper, with a dislocated thumb on the first morning (though he managed to bat), then in the afternoon Shreck limped off with a knee injury, and Ealham was unfit to bowl after damaging ribs as he completed a run-out. His victim was Coetzer, who had contributed 107 to an opening stand of 314 – one short of Durham's all-wicket Championship record. Di Venuto, who scored 105 between lunch and tea, batted through the day for 219 before edging the first ball of the second day, from Fletcher, to stand-in keeper Shafayat. Chanderpaul advanced to his 50th first-class hundred, while Benkenstein's 15th for Durham made him their leading century-maker. It was the first time Durham had had four hundreds in one innings. They declared after passing their previous-highest total, 645 for six at Lord's in 2002, and showed their determination to push for the win, rather than settling for the draw which would still have made them champions, by making Nottinghamshire follow on. Plunkett bowled with good pace and direction, generally shaping the ball away, to take nine wickets in the match.

Durham 648-5 dec (M. J. Di Venuto 219, S. Chanderpaul 109*, K. J. Coetzer 107, D. M. Benkenstein 105);
Nottinghamshire 384 (C. M. W. Read 65, A. D. Hales 62, A. D. Brown 59, D. J. Pattinson 59;
L. E. Plunkett 6-85, M. Davies 4-87) **and 212** (Hales 78).

ESSEX

[1960 edition] *ESSEX 1876 TO 1960 by Charles Bray (cricket correspondent of the*
London *Daily Herald since 1938, an amateur for Essex from 1928 to 1938,*
sometimes captain):
I played many times at Leyton. There was something
in its dirtiness, its ramshackle pavilion, its "cow-shed" along one side
and those cold, grim, stone terraces which got under your skin.
It was like a dirty urchin – grimy, lovable, but not lovely.

1872 – MCC AND GROUND v THE COUNTY OF ESSEX: STRONG REVIVAL
1873

At Lord's, July 15, 16, 1872. Essex v MCC was first played at Hornchurch so far back as 1791. The next struggle between the club and the county took place in 1793 on old

Lord's ground (Dorset Square). The revival of this ancient match at Lord's, in 1872, brought up an eleven from the old county who defeated the club eleven in a canter. The county team not only included that very clever head-bowler and hard hitter, Mr C. Absolom, but Frank Silcock, and three of the 1872 University Match bowlers – Mr C. K. Francis, Mr Raynor, and Mr Isherwood; in addition to those cricket experts the county played Mr J. Round – a few years back, one of the very best amateur wicket-keepers that ever asked "How's that" – and a very promising batsman in Mr Herbert; in fact, it is doubtful if a stronger Essex eleven ever appeared in the cricket field than this one that defeated MCC and G. in 1872. Alfred Shaw did out and out well for the old club; he scored 87 out of the 230 runs (from the bat) made for MCC in the match, and with his bowling Alfred had five of the 11 Essex wickets down. Wootton was so severely hurt, when batting, as to be unable to finish his first innings, to commence his second, or to bowl more than one over. Silcock made 56 runs for Essex, and had ten MCC wickets – seven bowled. The county beat the club by nine wickets.

MCC and G. 131 (A. Shaw 58*; F. Silcock 6-43) and 116 (Silcock 4-41);
Essex 191 (Silcock 56; Shaw 4-62) and 57-1.

Warwickshire v Nottinghamshire. At Birmingham, August 5, 6, 7, 1970. Warwickshire won by five wickets. The match was marred by the untimely death of the Test umpire J. S. Buller. The former Yorkshire and Worcestershire wicketkeeper collapsed in the pavilion and died during a stoppage for rain on the third day.

Little Wonder No. 93

1886 – ATTRACTIVE NEW GROUND   1887

The Essex club have made considerable progress of late years, and may now fairly rank as one of the best of the second-class counties. Their new county ground at Leyton, which is a very attractive one, was acquired at considerable expense, and will no doubt go a long way to improve their position in the cricket world.

1897 – ABLE TO CHALLENGE THE BEST   1898

Beyond all question the most striking feature of the season of 1897 was the rise of Essex. When the team went into the field at Leyton, on August 12, they were in such a happy position that a victory over Surrey would in all likelihood have given them the Championship. They went down before their great opponents – just then in tremendous form – and thereby lost all chance of coming out first among the counties for the year. Their play on this all-important occasion was a sad disappointment to their supporters, but taking the whole season through they showed splendid cricket and, for the time at least, ranked with Lancashire, Surrey, and Yorkshire. They took part in 16 county matches, of which they won seven, lost only two, and left seven unfinished. The double victory over Yorkshire, the triumph over Lancashire at Leyton in August, and the splendid drawn game with Surrey at The Oval in May were the finest achievements of the eleven, who nearly always showed their best form in the most important matches. No other county in 1897 defeated Yorkshire twice.

It was a great point in favour of Essex that the best players in the county were so regularly available. In the 16 county matches, only 16 men appeared in the team. The one thing lacking in the eleven was a fourth bowler to back up Mr Bull, Mr Kortright, and Walter Mead; Pickett, though always a good worker, is now a little *passé* for county cricket.

Mr Kortright had flashes of greatness, but, emphatically, the bowler of the eleven was young Mr Bull. Like all slow bowlers he came in at times for rather heavy punishment, but it was a splendid performance to take, as he did, 109 wickets in 16 matches. By general consent he was much the best amateur slow bowler of the season.

1905 – ESSEX v AUSTRALIANS: WONDERFUL CATCH   1906

At Leyton, June 22, 23, 24, 1905. A wonderfully exciting game ended early on Saturday in a victory for Essex by 19 runs. The Australians were not at full strength, but there seemed no doubt about their success, when, thanks to Laver, they dismissed Essex for 118. However on a lively wicket Buckenham and Tremlin disposed of the Australians for 100, and before the drawing of stumps Essex lost three batsmen for 31. Next morning, despite much luck enjoyed by McGahey, there were eight wickets down for 110, but Reeves, Douglas and Buckenham batted with such determination that the last two wickets added 93. Wanting 222 to win, the Australians soon lost Duff and Hill, but Darling batted steadily, and Noble and Hopkins added 42 for the fifth wicket. On Saturday with four wickets to fall the Colonials still required 103. Hopkins made a great effort, and, with assistance from McLeod and Laver, the last two wickets added 76. A splendid catch by Fane standing close to the boundary to Buckenham's fast bowling brought the match to an end. Laver swept the ball round almost in a line with the wickets, and Fane, lucky to be standing where he was, held it in very clever fashion.

Essex 118 (F. J. Laver 6-49) and 203 (M. A. Noble 4-66, Laver 4-81);
Australians 100 (C. P. Buckenham 6-45, B. Tremlin 4-54)
and 202 (A. J. Hopkins 67*; Buckenham 6-92, Tremlin 4-81).

1912 – BEST FRIEND SAYS GOODBYE   1913

The financial position being very unfavourable, a special meeting was called in December, at which it was unanimously decided to go on with the Club. At this meeting it was formally announced that Mr C. E. Green – the best friend to Essex cricket from the time the county club was formed – had resigned his position as chairman of the committee, and retired altogether from the management. In a letter to the committee, Mr Green, who resigned in August, said that he was bitterly disappointed at the lack of support accorded to the club, that county cricket as carried on in these days did not appeal to him, and that, speaking frankly, he was tired of the whole thing. In giving up a task to which he had for years devoted much time and money, Mr Green behaved very generously, paying off the club's debts of £400, and so enabling the committee to start in 1913 with a clean sheet.

1921 – FINANCIAL BURDEN OFFLOADED   1922

A still more noteworthy change in the history of the Club for which the season will be remembered was the purchase of the Leyton ground by the Army Sports Control Board. In this way the Essex County Club became relieved of a mortgage of £10,000, while retaining the privilege of using the ground for most of their home matches. From the time it was opened in 1886 the Leyton ground never brought the hoped-for prosperity to Essex cricket, and the officers regard the future as holding out far brighter prospects now that the expenses will be so greatly curtailed.

1926 – ESSEX v SOMERSET: POINTS SHARED   1927

At Chelmsford, June 16, 17, 18, 1926. When Eastman in an attempt to make the winning hit was caught, the umpires removed the bails and although the aggregates were equal declared Somerset entitled to the points for a first-innings lead. As half a minute remained, and the last batsman was hurrying to the wickets, Daniell offered to continue, but Perrin, the not-out batsman, captain of Essex, accepted the umpires' ruling. However, on reference to the MCC, the match was declared a tie, the full points therefore being divided equally. Apart from the exciting finish the first county match played on the new Chelmsford ground did not present any remarkable features.

Somerset 208 (Mr J. C. W. MacBryan 80) **and 107** (Mr L. C. Eastman 6-59, M. S. Nichols 4-45); **Essex 178** (Mr J. C. White 5-57) **and 137-9** (Mr J. J. Bridges 5-33).

See also Essex v Nottinghamshire, page 604

1928 – TOO MUCH CHOPPING AND CHANGING   1929

Essex, falling from eighth to 16th place in the Championship, had a very depressing season in 1928. Their victories were limited to two – over Worcestershire, the team to finish below them, and over Somerset, another of the weaker sides of the year, and their defeats numbered 13. The averages reveal the chief cause of this very poor record. For 30 County Championship engagements no fewer than 38 players were called upon, and 26 of these had a turn with the ball. No more than eight members of the side took part in as many as 20 matches and only three others appeared on ten or more occasions. As an inevitable outcome of the frequent and considerable changes in the eleven lack of teamwork became apparent. The trouble came to a head during the winter when the committee elected as captain H. M. Morris, an Old Reptonian. Morris went up to Cambridge in 1919 but failed to obtain his Blue, and, after doing well for Essex, played little last season. John Douglas, naturally, took exception to this action of the Essex authorities, but declined to make any statement as to his future relations with the county. First appearing in the county eleven in 1901, Douglas became captain of Essex in 1911. As fast bowler and stubborn batsman, possessing unlimited patience and determination, he has done splendid service for the county.

1935 – YORKSHIRE v ESSEX: NICHOLS TRIUMPHANT · 1936

At Huddersfield, July 31, August 1, 1935. This was the match that produced the sensation of the season. Unbeaten up to that point, Yorkshire collapsed twice in two days before the Essex fast bowlers and suffered defeat by an innings and 204 runs. Before half past 12 on the first day, Yorkshire were put out for 31 – their lowest total in an innings for 26 years – and when they went in a second time 303 runs in arrear their batting again broke down completely. Their two innings lasted altogether less than three hours. Nichols, accomplishing fine performances with both ball and bat, enjoyed the greatest triumph of his career. After taking four wickets for 17, he played an innings of 146 and then dismissed seven Yorkshire batsmen for 37 runs. Read's pace was also devastating, and in Yorkshire's first innings six wickets fell for a mere nine runs. Essex lost five wickets for 65, but Nichols and Belle came along with a magnificent partnership of 174 in just over three hours, and Nichols, driving and pulling superbly, hit two sixes and 16 fours. The contrast to what had gone before was amazing. The Essex innings closing on Wednesday, Yorkshire had to bat first thing next morning, and then Nichols and Read again paralysed the batsmen by sheer pace off the ground. Except for three overs by Eastman, those two fast bowlers were on unchanged in each innings.

Yorkshire 31 (Mr H. D. Read 6-11, M. S. Nichols 4-17) **and 99** (Nichols 7-37);
Essex 334 (Nichols 146, Mr B. H. Belle 63).

1947 – SMITHS TO THE FORE · 1948

Financial success was not duplicated on the playing field, the team disappointing a membership which rose beyond the 3,000 mark for the first time in the history of the county by dropping from eighth to 11th place in the Championship. Curiously, Essex were more effective away than at home.

Individuals showed skill deserving of better results. The cousins Smith were notable performers. Each accomplished the double for the first time, and Peter marked his benefit season by taking more wickets than any other Essex bowler has ever done. Their full first-class aggregates were: Ray Smith, 1,386 runs, 125 wickets; Peter Smith, 1,065 runs, 172 wickets. Ray, the younger, again utilised slow off-spin deliveries as a paying variation when conditions did not suit his quick bowling, and Peter puzzled most batsmen with his leg-breaks, googlies and top-spinners. He played the principal part in the overthrow of Middlesex, the ultimate champions, at Colchester by taking 16 wickets. Among several splendid innings by the Smiths, one was really exceptional. This was 163 by Peter when he and Vigar (114 not out) made their great last-wicket stand of 218 against Derbyshire at Chesterfield. There is no record of a player going in No. 11, as Smith did on this occasion, ever scoring as many.

1948 – ESSEX v NOTTINGHAMSHIRE: OUT OF TIME 1949

At Southend, May 19, 20, 21, 1948. Drawn. The last over produced intense excitement. Essex, 325 for six, needed three runs to win. Pearce and Rist each hit a single and made the scores equal, but Pearce was bowled, and Price, after blocking two deliveries, fell to the last ball before time expired. Essex, who at one period were 93 for four, owed much to Pearce and Horsfall, partners in a fifth-wicket stand of 128. Nottinghamshire were well served by Keeton and Simpson in the first innings, when Peter Smith excelled with varied spin in taking nine wickets. In the second Smith split his hand trying to hold a catch. Jepson bowled with pace and accuracy for the visitors, and he ended the first innings by sending back three men in nine balls without cost.

Under the old Laws the result would have been a tie, but the rewritten Laws, which came into force in 1947, ruled that the match was a draw. The Notes referring to Law 22, which governs results, state: "A draw is regarded as a tie when the scores are equal at the conclusion of play, but only if the match has been played out."

Nottinghamshire 371 (R. T. Simpson 123, W. W. Keeton 102; T. P. B. Smith 9-117)
and 217-8 dec (W. A. Sime 63);
Essex 261 (A. V. Avery 77; A. Jepson 6-59) **and 327-8** (T. N. Pearce 127; Jepson 5-121).

1950 – LOSS OF FORM LEADS TEAM TO NEW LOW 1951

An unexpected decline led to Essex finishing bottom of the Championship – for the first time since they entered it in 1895. When Glamorgan and Surrey were beaten in May, normal progress was anticipated, but the good form did not last. Of the remaining 24 Championship games ten were lost and only two won. For the Championship, Essex called on 26 batsmen and 18 bowlers. The desire to give promising players a trial was praiseworthy but in consequence the team never developed a settled outlook.

1957 – ESSEX v HAMPSHIRE: battling Bailey   1958

At Romford, May 25, 27, 28, 1957. Essex won by 46 runs. Bailey dominated the game to a remarkable degree, and earned an ovation from the players of both teams, as well as the spectators, at the finish. Although suffering from a cracked knuckle-bone in the right hand, he scored nearly half his side's runs for once out, took 14 wickets for 81 runs with lively fast-medium bowling, and was on the field for all but one and a half hours of the match. The Hampshire seam bowlers, Shackleton, Cannings and Heath, used a green pitch well, and runs were always hard-earned. Apart from Taylor, Bailey received little batting support in the first innings, but found more solid partners in the second after Essex lost three wickets without a run scored.

Essex 130 (T. E. Bailey 59; M. B. Heath 4-37) and 141 (Bailey 71*; D. Shackleton 5-47);
Hampshire 109 (Bailey 6-32) and 116 (Bailey 8-49).

1962 – Laker Fills A Gap   1963

The acquisition of Laker, the former Surrey off-break bowler, filled a much-needed want in the attack and, with such performances as six wickets for 49 runs against Sussex at Worthing, 13 for 159 in the match with Kent at Dover and six for 52 v Warwickshire at Colchester, he finished at the head of the averages.

1969 – Building For The Future   1970

For the first time since just after the Second World War, Essex were able to report a profit; a more than ordinary cause for satisfaction because, thanks in no small measure to an interest-free loan of £15,000 by the Warwickshire County Cricket Supporters' Association, the county were able to embark upon the erection of a handsome pavilion at their new headquarters at Chelmsford.

The playing success was the more remarkable because to all intents and purposes the programme was carried through with a maximum of 12 men. Happily injuries were far less frequent than in the previous year, and the restricted choice certainly led to a marked enhancement in team spirit under Taylor's go-ahead captaincy. All in all, the summer proved that Essex were amply justified in their policy of placing reliance upon young players, whose standard of fielding was unsurpassed by any side in the country.

1975 – ESSEX v LEICESTERSHIRE: buoyant Boyce   1976

At Chelmsford, May 7, 8, 9, 1975. Drawn. This match will long be remembered for the remarkable all-round ability of Boyce. For after scoring a whirlwind century in only 58 minutes – the fastest Championship hundred for 38 years – he then took 12 wickets for 73. In all, Boyce scored 113 and his innings was all the more sensational from the fact that it was played on a wicket helpful to spin. The West Indian Test star's knock included eight sixes and seven fours, and he scored all his runs during a partnership of 122 with Fletcher for the fourth wicket. Faced with a total of 300, Leicestershire lost their first six wickets for 15, but Illingworth, with a fighting 33, saved them from complete humiliation as Boyce finished with six for 25. Thanks to a resolute and disciplined innings of 101 by Balderstone, Leicestershire managed to force a draw when they followed on. Balderstone eventually fell to Boyce, who finished with six second-innings wickets for 48.

Essex 300 (K. D. Boyce 113, B. R. Hardie 51; J. F. Steele 4-42);
Leicestershire 60 (Boyce 6-25, R. E. East 4-24) **and 207-8** (J. C. Balderstone 101; Boyce 6-48).

1979 – OUT OF THE WILDERNESS
Nigel Fuller, 1980

Promise gave way to fulfilment as Essex, after 103 years of striving, at last emerged from a barren wilderness to make 1979 a year they will treasure. They did so at the double, following up their Benson and Hedges Cup triumph over Surrey by winning the County Championship. Perhaps "winning" is too simple a word to describe their Championship triumph. Their dominance was such that they finished a staggering 77 points clear of the runners-up, making sure of the title when they were still four matches short of completing their programme. They moved to the top of the table shortly after the start of the season and, as the thoroughbreds they are, slowly but relentlessly increased their lead to condemn the rest of the field to also-rans. A total of 13 victories, five of them by an innings, was testimony to their superiority.

The secret of their success was the shrewd tactical brain of skipper Fletcher, allied to magnificent teamwork. Everyone, without exception, played a major role. Loss of form or the absence of key figures was barely detectable, for others would strike a vein of form and provide rewarding compensation.

If they did miss one individual, it was the left-arm paceman Lever, who had the distinction of becoming the first bowler of the season to reach 100 wickets. On eight occasions, Lever finished with five or more wickets in an innings, and during an outstanding June he claimed 53 Championship wickets. Against Leicestershire at Chelmsford he returned his best figures ever of 13 for 117. In the next match, against Warwickshire at Edgbaston, he bettered them with 13 for 87. That performance included eight for 49 in the first innings, which also represented a personal-best.

1985 – FLETCHER COMPLETES THE SET
Nigel Fuller, 1986

The remarkable Essex success story continued in the rain-soaked summer of 1985 with two more titles to take the number in the last seven seasons to eight. In a dramatic end to the season, they not only retained the John Player Sunday League by defeating Yorkshire in the last match, but also emerged with the NatWest Bank Trophy for the first time in a thrilling clash at Lord's when they beat Nottinghamshire by just one run. Keith Fletcher thus became the first captain to lead a county to the game's four major honours.

For good measure, Essex also reached the final of the Benson and Hedges Cup, in which they were forced to admit to second-best against Leicestershire, and they finished fourth in the Britannic Assurance Championship. That may seem like failure, bearing in mind that they had carried off the title in the two previous years; but when one reflects that at the start of the second week of July they were at the foot of the table, with only one victory to their credit, to finish in so lofty a position was in fact a fine achievement.

Once again the county were left owing a great debt of gratitude to Graham Gooch. In all competitions for club and country, he plundered ten centuries and in a total of 57 innings reached 50 on no fewer than 30 occasions. In 1986 Gooch will be skippering the side, following Fletcher's decision to step down after 12 years at the helm.

1985 – ESSEX v NOTTINGHAMSHIRE (NatWest Bank Trophy Final): LAST-GASP WIN
1986

At Lord's, September 7, 1985. Essex won by one run. With 37 still required and only three overs left Essex seemed clear-cut winners. Randall, however, at last began to negotiate most of the strike, improvising to find the gaps, and Pringle bowled the last over to him with 18 needed. To defeat Pringle's leg-stump attack, Randall made room to play on the off side, taking 16 from the first five deliveries so that, remarkably, Nottinghamshire were now only one stroke away from winning. With the last ball, however, Pringle succeeded in tucking Randall up as he again tried to move inside the line, and Prichard plucked down the resulting catch at short midwicket.

Essex 280-2 (60 overs) (B. R. Hardie 110, G. A. Gooch 91, K. S. McEwan 46);
Nottinghamshire 279-5 (60 overs) (R. T. Robinson 80, D. W. Randall 66, B. C. Broad 64).

1988 – SURREY v ESSEX: Gooch doubles up
1989

At The Oval, August 30, 31, September 1, 2, 1988. Drawn. Gooch's somewhat bizarre entry overshadowed Stewart's first century of the summer for Surrey. History of a kind was made on the first day, when Gooch appeared on two scorecards on the same day. He captained England to their first win in 19 attempts in the Test match against Sri Lanka, six miles away at Lord's, and then dashed across the river to take up the place left for him by Essex in the knowledge that the Test was due to finish early that day. Although not unlawful, the practice was seen as questionable in some quarters and was to be considered later by the TCCB. Essex fielded with ten men until Gooch took the field some 45 minutes after lunch, Greig quite rightly not permitting the use of a substitute. Foster and Pringle, also involved at Lord's, remained absentees, which gave Surrey the latitude to gain maximum batting points and build a challenging score. Stewart's 133 lasted 268 minutes and included 21 fours. Gooch masterminded the Essex reply with an unbeaten 78 in the 36 overs batting that the weather allowed Essex on the second day. But their title ambitions received a setback when further rain washed out the third day and permitted only 36 overs on the fourth.

Surrey 362 (A. J. Stewart 133, D. J. Bicknell 50, D. M. Ward 50; I. L. Pont 5-103);
Essex 257-6 dec (G. A. Gooch 123).

Sunday League 1992: Essex were horribly frustrated on August 9 when Gooch and Pringle had to sit out the crucial match against Middlesex at Lord's, even though the Test at The Oval had finished in the morning. This was due to regulations brought in after 1988, when Gooch took part in what was regarded as an unseemly dash in the other direction. Middlesex won by 94 runs.

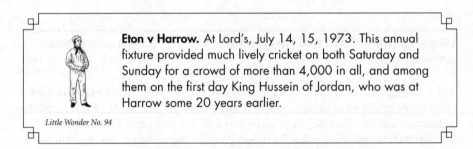

Eton v Harrow. At Lord's, July 14, 15, 1973. This annual fixture provided much lively cricket on both Saturday and Sunday for a crowd of more than 4,000 in all, and among them on the first day King Hussein of Jordan, who was at Harrow some 20 years earlier.

Little Wonder No. 94

1989 – DESTINY TURNS INTO DISCONTENT
Nigel Fuller, 1990

When July dawned with Essex heading the Britannic Assurance Championship and Refuge Assurance League tables, and looking towards the Benson and Hedges Cup final, it appeared that they were destined for a season of glorious achievement. Instead, even allowing for their winning the Refuge Assurance Cup in their final match, it was to be a summer of discontent. Their Benson and Hedges hopes were dashed at Lord's when Hemmings hit John Lever for a last-ball boundary to give Notts victory. And the pain of that defeat was matched only by the bitterness of the players when, after Yorkshire were beaten at Southchurch Park, Southend, ten days later, the TCCB stripped them of 25 Championship points because the pitch was deemed substandard. They felt they were made an example of only because they were the front-runners for the title, and their belief that they had played on worse pitches outside Essex, without their opponents being penalised, compounded their anger and frustration. In the event, Worcestershire went on to retain their title by just six points.

Essex again felt hard done by when, at a crucial stage of their campaign for the Refuge Assurance League, their penultimate match against Lancashire, the eventual champions, was abandoned in controversial circumstances. Victory would have taken Essex back to the top of the table, although Lancashire still had a game in hand. However, with Essex 53 without loss after 10.4 overs and needing another 83 from 17.2 overs, rain halted play. When the rain ceased, the umpires ruled that there was insufficient time for Essex to receive the 20 overs needed to constitute a match. In the Essex camp, suspicion was harboured that the covers were not removed with any great haste, thereby dictating the "no result" outcome.

1992 – FLETCHER'S FINAL BOW

Nigel Fuller, 1993

For the first time in more than 30 years 1993 will be a season when the name Keith Fletcher does not appear on the county payroll. He captained Essex to every major honour in the game after years when they habitually tottered and fell on the very edge of success. For the last four seasons he had devoted himself to bringing players through the Second Eleven but, despite his devotion to the county, he found the invitation to succeed Micky Stewart as England team manager too much of a temptation to resist. Essex owe Fletcher a debt they can never repay, a fact readily acknowledged by Gooch. The standards now set at Essex, which others strive to emulate, stem from his leadership, and England could not have chosen a wiser or more respected character for one of cricket's most arduous jobs.

1997 – GOOCH'S GREAT CAREER ENDS ON LOW NOTE

Nigel Fuller, 1998

Two events dominated Essex cricket in 1997. After five years without any kind of title, and 12 without a one-day trophy, Paul Prichard lifted the NatWest Trophy at Lord's in September, a triumph which redeemed their disastrous performance there a year earlier.

And, for the first time in the club's history, it was a competition won without Graham Gooch. After a miraculous 1996, when he was the leading run-scorer in England, Gooch found it impossible in 1997 to live up to the high standards by which he measured himself. He managed only two half-centuries before announcing in July that he was calling it a day. The only sour note, as far as the county's hierarchy was concerned, was that he chose to tell the *News of the World* before he told them.

Gooch is ninth on the list of all-time century-makers, the tenth-highest run-scorer in the history of first-class cricket, and the greatest run-scorer of all, taking one-day cricket into account.

Essex v Worcestershire. At Chelmsford, July 23, 24, 25, 26. Graham Gooch had chosen this as the final match of his grand career. It began on his 44th birthday, but he failed to sign off in style. The MP for Colchester, Bob Russell, tabled a Commons motion listing Gooch's achievements, and the Chelmsford town crier rang a bell, but Gooch's leg stump was uprooted by the 26th ball he received, bowled by Sheriyar. [He had scored 11].

1997 – ESSEX v GLAMORGAN (NATWEST TROPHY SEMI-FINALS):
PRIME-TIME BOUT   1998

At Chelmsford, August 12, 13, 1997. Essex won by one wicket. A pulsating cricket match achieved notoriety when a live, prime-time BBC audience watched Ilott and Croft start shoving each other during an angry exchange as Ilott appealed against the light. The two players are good friends from tours together with England A, and their wives were watching alongside each other at the time. Next day the men embraced in the morning calm after Essex had come back to eke out victory. Both suffered the consequences: £1,000 fines from their clubs. The umpires agreed it was too dark to continue at 8.10pm, when Essex needed six from seven overs but had only two wickets left, with Waqar Younis bowling. In the morning Essex lost a ninth wicket to Thomas – his fifth victim – but last man Such drove Thomas to the boundary to win.

Glamorgan 301-8 (60 overs) (S. P. James 109, P. A. Cottey 56, A. Dale 45);
Essex 303-9 (55 overs) (S. G. Law 90, D. D. J. Robinson 62, R. C. Irani 51; S. D. Thomas 5-74).

2001 – DEPTHS OF DESPAIR ON AND OFF FIELD   Nigel Fuller, 2002

It might be an exaggeration to describe 2001 as the most turbulent and disastrous season in Essex's history, but the team was certainly the worst this correspondent has seen in more than 30 years reporting on the club's fortunes. It lacked a collective spirit and quality; the inevitability of its plunge into the depths left members in despair. Two Championship victories explained why Essex occupied last place in Division One, 17 points behind Glamorgan, immediately above them. Third-last in the Norwich Union League, and failure to make much progress in the Benson and Hedges Cup and Cheltenham & Gloucester Trophy, contributed further to the summer of discontent.

Off the field, the dressing-room was split asunder as Stuart Law accused team-mates and management of stabbing him in the back. It was no secret that he and some of his colleagues could hardly utter a civil word to each other. And within days of meeting a delegation of angry supporters, seeking answers to the sad decline, chairman David Acfield resigned, citing pressure of business – but that was fooling no one. He was simply fed up with all the flak, and no doubt relieved to hand over to Nigel Hilliard. A month or so later, Graham Gooch, perhaps Essex's favourite son and certainly their most successful player, gave up a blossoming media career to take over as head coach. He succeeded Keith Fletcher, who was to adopt a scouting role, while John Childs moved up from looking after the Second Eleven to become Gooch's assistant.

Predictably, following his verbal blast, Law was not offered a new contract – a sad conclusion to a six-year association, during which he thrilled spectators everywhere with his majestic strokes, while scoring 8,538 first-class runs at 58.88. He was replaced by Zimbabwe's prolific wicketkeeper-batsman, Andy Flower.

Also shown the door was Peter Such, whose 17 Championship wickets in 2001 had cost 65 each. However, his departure, after 12 seasons in which he took 573 first-class wickets for the county and won 11 Test caps, was softened by a substantial benefit cheque.

2004 – ESSEX v GLAMORGAN: DISBELIEF AT DEFEAT

At Chelmsford, September 2, 3, 4, 5, 2004. Glamorgan won by four wickets. After scoring 642 in their first innings Essex had this game under armed guard, not just lock and key. No side had ever lost a first-class match from such a position, but Essex did, making an unwelcome kind of history and, as the game slipped away, losing any realistic chance of promotion. They started imperiously, with three first-innings hundreds: a canny one from Flower, chastened after giving two chances before reaching 30, and more carefree efforts by Irani (also dropped) and Foster, who made 188. Croft conceded 203 in the innings, the first bowling double-century for Glamorgan. Halfway through the second day, Essex were finally all out, on the truest of true pitches, and their expectation of success grew firmer when they had Glamorgan in a mess at 188 for five. But it proved a topsy-turvy innings. Crucially, the linchpin Maynard was missed twice on 46 by Grayson, the first drop so simple that Grayson's team-mates stared in disbelief. Maynard went on to 136, and the last three wickets added 301 as Croft belted 125 from No. 9 and Harrison made a career-best 88 from No. 10. The Essex bowling was wayward but the pace of Glamorgan's scoring (396 came in the first two sessions of day three) meant Essex were batting again, just 55 ahead, on the third evening. By the close they were floundering at 101 for four. Next morning the last six wickets fell before lunch, for the addition of only 64 runs. Essex's rock-solid position had melted away like a mirage, and Glamorgan were left a minimum of 69 overs to make 221. They completed their task comfortably, with 22 balls to spare.

Essex 642 (J. S. Foster 188, R. C. Irani 164, A. Flower 119, A. P. Grayson 57, G. R. Napier 50; S. P. Jones 4-100) **and 165** (M. L. Lewis 4-39, R. D. B. Croft 4-52);

Glamorgan 587 (M. P. Maynard 136, Croft 125, D. S. Harrison 88, D. L. Hemp 67; Danish Kaneria 5-193) **and 223-6** (Hemp 83*).

2008 – ESSEX v SUSSEX (TWENTY20 CUP): NAPIER REWRITES RECORD-BOOK

At Chelmsford, June 24 (floodlit). Essex won by 128 runs. Graham Napier stepped out of the shadows into the floodlights – and smashed a host of records. Earlier in the competition, he had batted as low as No. 9, but now, at No. 3, he found his place as an awesomely destructive batsman. His first 50 came from 29 balls, his second came from 15 and his third an astonishing 13. In all, he faced 58 balls and batted 66 minutes. He hit both Chris Liddle and Dwayne Smith for three consecutive sixes, and finished things off with 29 – including four sixes in five balls – from the final over, bowled by James Kirtley, whose four overs cost 67, the most expensive return in Twenty20 cricket. Napier eclipsed Cameron White's unbeaten 141 for Somerset against Worcestershire in 2006 as the highest score in the Twenty20 Cup, but was one maximum short of Brendon McCullum's 158 not out for Kolkata v Bangalore on the opening night of the Indian Premier League. "It was awesome, fantastic," Napier beamed between innings, "I just started to see the ball better, middle one or two, and then got into a rhythm." That rhythm brought 16 sixes, more than in any other one-day innings (and equalled

Andrew Symonds's first-class record). It also brought 97 runs from the last five overs as Essex sailed past 200 for the first time. It was no surprise that a bruised Sussex capitulated: the margin of 128 runs was the largest in the Twenty20 Cup.

Essex 242-3 (20 overs) (G. R. Napier 152*, J. S. Foster 48);
Sussex 114 (16.4 overs) (M. A. Chambers 3-31, J. D. Middlebrook 3-13).

GLAMORGAN

[1949 edition] *GLAMORGAN'S MARCH OF PROGRESS by J. H. MORGAN*

Cyfarchiad i Morgannwg, y Concwerwyr Cricket Newydd

"Hail Glamorgan! The New Cricket Champions". Cricket, steeped in tradition, has no parallel to compare with Glamorgan's triumph in taking the Championship outside England, cradle of the game, for the first time. It was as spectacular as it was romantic; an achievement beyond the most fantastic dream of a Welsh diehard.

1921 – EARLY PROMISE UNFULFILLED
1922

Glamorgan's promotion to first-class cricket was not justified by results, as against two victories there was a heavy set-off of 14 defeats. The county began with a surprising success, beating Sussex after a tremendous struggle by 23 runs, but this early promise was far indeed from being kept up, the only other win during the season being against Worcestershire at Swansea towards the end of July. The record was, of course, a dismal one, but in some of the matches Glamorgan put up a keen fight, being beaten at various times by the narrow margins of 20 runs, 38 runs, and three wickets. Still, looking at the season's work as a whole, it cannot be said that Glamorgan showed anything better than second-rate form. One would feel more hopeful of improvement in the immediate future if the leading bowlers of the team were not so advanced in years. Nash, who really got on very well, taking 90 wickets for less than 17½ runs each, was born in 1873, and Creber in 1874. Hacker, quite successful on the few occasions he played, has also left his youth far behind him. The difficulty does not apply to bowling alone, as N. V. H. Riches, the captain, and by many degrees the best bat in the eleven, is now in his 39th year.

1924 – GLAMORGAN v LANCASHIRE: RED ROSE TRIMMED
1925

At Swansea, August 13, 14, 15, 1924. This match furnished the sensation of Glamorgan's season, a victory over Lancashire by 38 runs being the biggest thing done for the county since their admission into the Championship. Left to get only 146, Lancashire looked to have the match in their hands when their score stood at 84 with only three men out, but Ryan, on being tried for the second time, proved so unplayable that the last seven wickets went down for 23 runs. There was great enthusiasm at the finish, Ryan being carried off the field shoulder-high. A welcome feature of the match from Glamorgan's point of view was the fine batting of Turnbull, a 17-year-old schoolboy from Downside College.

Glamorgan 153 (R. K. Tyldesley 5-36) **and 143** (C. H. Parkin 5-40);
Lancashire 151 (H. Spencer 6-44, F. P. Ryan 4-69) **and 107** (Ryan 6-40).

1934 – SURREY v GLAMORGAN: FIRST OVAL WIN   1935

At Kennington Oval, May 5, 7, 1934. Glamorgan gained a remarkable victory – their first at The Oval – at half past five on the second day by an innings and 92 runs. The pitch afforded them much assistance, but nevertheless Surrey, apart from Hobbs, gave an inglorious batting display. Rain left the turf lifeless on Saturday, and though Dyson played carefully Glamorgan lost six wickets for 169. Thanks to some vigorous batting by Lavis and Mercer who put on 120 for the last wicket, a fine recovery was effected. On Monday Clay bowled unchanged from the pavilion end until the end of the match, a spell of nearly five hours. Maintaining a steady length and varying his pace, Clay, who had three men close in on the leg side and no slips, bowled cleverly to his field. He took 12 wickets for exactly seven runs apiece, a very fine performance. Emrys Davies also bowled well.

Glamorgan 352 (G. Lavis 83*, A. H. Dyson 72, J. Mercer 72);
Surrey 113 (Mr J. C. Clay 6-33, E. Davies 4-29) **and 147** (J. B. Hobbs 62; Clay 6-51).

Kent v Yorkshire. At Canterbury, August 8, 9, 10, 1973. The Duke and Duchess of Kent, the respective patrons of the Kent and Yorkshire clubs, were introduced to the teams at lunchtime and watched the afternoon's play.

Little Wonder No. 95

1935 – DAVIES THE DOUBLE   1936

Emrys Davies brought distinction to the club by being the first Glamorgan player ever to achieve the double. If he fell off a little with the bat this could not be wondered at, for his bowling improved tremendously. In 1934 only 39 wickets at

30.15 runs apiece rewarded his efforts; last summer he took 93 in Championship matches at an average of 20.77, and altogether 100 for 21.07 runs each.

Unusual circumstances attended his completion of the double. The last day of the match at Worcester, and of Glamorgan's season, had arrived with Davies wanting one more wicket. Warne, of Worcestershire, needed 42 runs for his first 1,000. A wet pitch appeared to have put hope of cricket out of the question, but the players stayed on and a start was made at 20 minutes past five. Glamorgan scored four runs off four balls and lost two wickets before declaring, and then Worcestershire obtained 47 for the loss of Jackson – bowled by Emrys Davies. At that point Warne had completed his four-figure aggregate. But for the issues at stake it is doubtful whether a ball would have been bowled that day.

1954: After 30 seasons with Glamorgan, Emrys Davies at last retired, happy in the knowledge that no player ever rendered the county better service.

1948 – CLAY BUILDS BRICKS OF FIRST CHAMPIONSHIP   1949

On the afternoon of Tuesday, August 24, 1948, Glamorgan set the seal on a wonderful season by winning the County Championship for the first time.

Appropriately, J. C. Clay, a member of the original side which entered the competition in 1921 and whose name has become synonymous with Glamorgan cricket, played a leading part in the victory that day over Hampshire at Bournemouth which ensured for them the honours after an exciting race with Surrey, Yorkshire and Derbyshire. He took nine wickets in the game for 79, and in the preceding fixture against Surrey at Cardiff he claimed a full analysis of ten for 66 – two bowling performances which bear eloquent testimony to the skill and physical fitness of one in his 51st year. On this form it was a pity that Clay could not play more often, but he was frequently engaged on his duties as a Test team selector.

Before the start of the season few people would have prophesied the destination of the 1948 Championship. True, Glamorgan in the two post-war years finished well up in the table, sixth in 1946 and ninth in 1947; yet, apart from the arrival of N. G. Hever and J. Eaglestone from Middlesex, there was nothing to suggest that the county would make such a remarkable advance.

Unlike Middlesex, champion county the previous season, Glamorgan possessed neither abundant batting strength nor experienced reserves. They were fortunate, therefore, in being able to rely on almost the same eleven throughout the season, only 18 players being called upon as against 28 in 1947. While strongly supplied with bowlers – six players took more than 30 wickets each – the batting frequently revealed limitations; but, paradoxical though it may seem, this very weakness influenced Glamorgan's triumph. Had the team made bigger totals, they would not have provided their bowlers with sufficient time to dismiss opponents for reasonably low scores.

Generally speaking, Glamorgan may not have been better equipped in the matter of skill than several of their rivals. Indeed, Wooller himself confessed that he knew of stronger batting and bowling sides. Yet the team displayed a concentration of purpose and an attitude of mind in the field unmistakable to all who watched them. For this the county owed a great deal to Wilfred Wooller, whose leadership developed a splendid spirit among the players. Always alert and active, Wooller set a notable example, and on more than one occasion his remarkable catches close to the bat changed the whole aspect of a game.

1951 – GLAMORGAN v SOUTH AFRICANS: CHAMPAGNE FLOWS   1952

At Swansea, August 4, 6, 1951. Glamorgan won by 64 runs. Welsh enthusiasm for cricket reached its highest pitch of the season when Glamorgan became the only county to defeat the South Africans. Wooller, the captain, was carried shoulder-high from the field, the crowd sang the Welsh national anthem, a collection was made for the winning players, and the toasts of Muncer and McConnon, the architects of victory, were drunk in champagne. The fortunes of the game swayed in dramatic fashion, and the teams even tied on the first innings. Nourse appeared to make the right decision when, after winning the toss, he put in Glamorgan on a rain-affected pitch. Conditions were ideal for Mansell's swing and spin, and Athol Rowan with deceptive off-spinners completed Glamorgan's discomfiture, their last five wickets falling for 19 runs. Muncer made top score for the county, and when the South Africans went in he soon made his presence felt. In a devastating spell of off-spin bowling he took five wickets for nine runs, and at tea seven South Africans were out for 34. Then Athol Rowan batted in resolute fashion, and Mansell helped him add 52 for the eighth wicket. After scoring a century in Glamorgan's previous match, Clift was out for a pair, and apart from Wooller and Pleass no one did much in their second innings. Set 148 for victory, the South Africans seemed to be heading for success at tea, their total standing at 54 without loss. Afterwards a crowd of 25,000 witnessed some amazing cricket, all ten wickets going down in 45 minutes for the addition of 29. McConnon dismissed Cheetham, Melle, and Fullerton with successive deliveries to achieve the only hat-trick against the South Africans, and a deadly final spell brought him six wickets for 11 runs. During the same period Muncer took four for 10, and gained the remarkable match analysis of 11 for 61.

Glamorgan 111 (P. N. F. Mansell 5-37, A. M. B. Rowan 4-45) **and** 147 (Rowan 4-42, Mansell 4-73);
South Africans 111 (B. L. Muncer 7-45) **and** 83 (J. E. McConnon 6-27, Muncer 4-16).

1958 – CAPTAINS PAST AND PRESENT RESIGN   1959

A combination of circumstances brought about a decline in the fortunes of Glamorgan, who dropped from ninth position to 15th in the Championship. This lack of success could, in the main, be attributed to three reasons: (1) a crisis in the committee concerning administration, (2) captaincy of the side, and (3) the weather.

Overshadowing all else was an unfortunate dispute between the committee and Wooller, who from 1947, in addition to being secretary, had led the county so wholeheartedly during some difficult years. Wooller, after declining the offer of a part-time engagement as consultative adviser and representative, resigned from his position as secretary, and this was followed by other resignations from the committee, including Mr J. C. Clay, the former captain and secretary.

Undoubtedly the discord between the leading officials of the club affected the performance of the players as a whole. At times their form was disappointing, to say the least, and Glamorgan went from May 31 to August 12 with only one solitary win over Gloucestershire at Cardiff to offset a string of nine defeats and many drawn matches. In addition, the decision to give a "trial run" as captain to A. C. Burnett, who was considered as a likely successor to Wooller, did not help matters. Burnett, a Cambridge Blue of 1949, played in seven Championship games after coming into the side against the New Zealanders at the beginning of August. The experiment did not prove a success and at the end of the season the committee announced that they were still looking for a new captain.

1964 – GLAMORGAN v AUSTRALIANS: SPINNERS TRIUMPHANT   1965

At Swansea, August 1, 3, 4, 1964. Glamorgan won by 36 runs amid tumultuous scenes by an excited and jubilant Welsh crowd. It was the Australians' first defeat of the tour and the first victory Glamorgan had gained over them in their 43 years as a first-class county. The Glamorgan heroes were Pressdee (left-arm slow) and Shepherd (off-spin). Pressdee was responsible for the initial breakdown when he took four of the first five wickets for only eight runs. Veivers hit six sixes in his daring 51, but despite his assault Pressdee finished the first innings with six wickets for 58 and Shepherd had four for 22 while Glamorgan claimed a valuable lead of 96.

A crowd of 20,000 saw Glamorgan consolidate their advantage in a tense atmosphere one usually associates with a Welsh rugby international. Brisk batting by Lewis and Rees put Glamorgan 200 ahead with six wickets in hand and then Simpson with his skilfully flighted leg-spin rescued his side so that Glamorgan slumped from 126 for four to 172 all out.

The Australians wanted 269 to win with ample time. All went well until at 59 Simpson fell to a catch at silly mid-off, and then Lawry went on the defensive, adding only a single in the last half-hour while he and O'Neill raised the score to 75 for one.

Next day the crowd of 10,000 soon sensed the element of drama when in little more than half an hour the Australians lost three more wickets for the addition of 17. Shepherd made the significant breakthrough by capturing two of these wickets in his first six overs. It was at this critical stage that Lawry took charge.

Then after four hours and 40 minutes for 64 Lawry pulled fiercely, only to fall to a magnificent waist-high catch by Rees at midwicket. Veivers hit his second fifty of the match in 84 minutes, his runs including two sixes and seven fours, but the end of Lawry was virtually the end of the Australians. They lost their last four wickets for 25 runs. In a marathon spell Shepherd, the sole survivor of the Glamorgan team which last defeated a touring side, South Africa in 1951, bowled 52 overs and took five wickets for 51. During the final hour he suffered much pain through cramp, but with Glamorgan on the brink of a great triumph he gallantly maintained his immaculate length and spin. Pressdee finished the match with ten wickets for 123 and Shepherd had nine for 93.

> **Glamorgan 197** (T. R. Veivers 5-85) **and 172** (R. B. Simpson 5-33);
> **Australians 101** (Veivers 51; J. S. Pressdee 6-58, D. J. Shepherd 4-22)
> **and 232** (W. M. Lawry 64, Veivers 54; Shepherd 5-71, Pressdee 4-65).

1966 – GLAMORGAN v SOMERSET: FAREWELL TO ARMS   1967

At Cardiff, August 13, 15, 16, 1966. Somerset won by 71 runs. This was the last County Championship match to be played at Cardiff Arms Park, which had been used as a cricket ground for 100 years, but Glamorgan could not mark the occasion with a win.

1969 – A MEMORABLE TURNAROUND   1970

Watching Glamorgan's last-wicket pair engaged in a tense struggle to avoid defeat in their first match of the season against Yorkshire at Swansea, not even the most optimistic Welshman would have prophesied that Glamorgan would not only win the County Championship but complete a memorable summer unbeaten – a notable double which had not been achieved since Lancashire's record in 1930.

Yorkshire, who had won the title the previous season, looked the better prospect in that match. Yet a complete transformation was to take place. After a not-so-merry-month-of-May when Glamorgan were actually perched perilously at the foot of the table, the team, always potentially strong, found their real strength. They had faith in themselves, and went on to play some glorious cricket with the right touch of adventure in the batting to take full advantage of the bonus points scoring system. Indeed towards the close of the season Glamorgan were playing like real champions, and they finished on a spectacular note with stirring victories in their last three home games against Middlesex, Essex and Worcestershire. Indeed, the thrilling last-over wins against Middlesex and Essex at Swansea will be long remembered as one of the most wonderful weeks in Glamorgan's history.

One of the most vital factors in Glamorgan's supremacy was their batting in depth. While the mercurial Majid, Bryan Davis and the captain Tony Lewis often got their runs quickly to earn bonus points, each player contributed something special at different times to win matches.

Taking the season as a whole Glamorgan made their runs at a faster rate than any other county – averaging 48.98 runs per 100 balls. And as proof positive of their adventurous spirit in pursuit of the title, their scoring tempo increased as their Championship hopes brightened. Indeed in the closing weeks their scoring rate was as high as 52.64 runs per 100 balls. That was why they collected a record number of 67 batting points.

Another phase in which Glamorgan were supreme was their superb close-to-the-wicket fielding. Right through the years Glamorgan have made a speciality of this art, and in Roger Davis, Walker, Bryan Davis and Majid they had worthy successors to such specialists as Watkins, Wooller, Clift, Pressdee, Parkhouse and Muncer. And one must not forget the part played by Eifion Jones, who had the best record of any wicketkeeper in the country.

1972 – GLAMORGAN v SOMERSET: CLOSE ENCOUNTER   1973

At Swansea, June 10, 12, 13, 1972. Somerset won by an innings and 25 runs. In a controversial and unpleasant match in which W. Wooller, the Glamorgan secretary, and D. B. Close, the Somerset captain, were the central figures, Close had the better of the argument. After Somerset had crawled to 113 for two in 72 overs on a short first day's play, Close inspired a revival by completing a fighting century in two and threequarter hours, but acrimony broke out when he delayed his declaration until three o'clock on the second day. This provoked Mr Wooller to announce over the public-address system that any spectator could have his gate-money back on application. Meanwhile, Close relentlessly pursued his set course. Never wavering, Somerset dismissed Glamorgan twice to win by an innings – and have the last laugh. To add to the unpleasantness of the match both umpires, A. E. Fagg and D. L. Evans, felt impelled to report Mr Wooller to Lord's for allegedly criticising them for delaying the start on the opening day. Throughout Close maintained that his only concern was to win the game – and the scoreboard had proved him right. Wooller's defence was that he acted only in the interests of the cricketing public.

Somerset 314-7 dec (D. B. Close 108);
Glamorgan 145 (T. W. Cartwright 5-50) and 144.

1976 – SPARKS FLY AS CAPTAIN DEPARTS   J. H. Morgan, 1977

The long, hot summer brought no joy to Glamorgan. It would be fair to say that some criticism of Majid Khan's captaincy was the spark which was to cause one of the biggest explosions in Welsh sport. Even in 1975 there was talk of dissatisfaction with Majid's leadership amongst people in high places. His attitude to one-day cricket also disturbed some members of the committee. It was a pity that these insinuations were not brought into the open at the time. Instead, in the absence of firm and decisive action, an already unpleasant situation was allowed to drift and, indeed, magnified out of all proportion to the original source of complaint.

First, Majid Khan resigned from the captaincy and later quit the club, alleging interference with his captaincy. The tensions which had been allowed to build became too much for this sensitive and proud, but lonely man, who through his cricketing talents had given many hours of pleasure to the Welsh people. Then certain established first-team players, including Roger Davis, Lawrence Williams and Len Hill, with a sprinkling of juniors, received letters warning them, in effect, that their future with Glamorgan was in jeopardy if their form did not improve.

This led to the resignations of the useful all-rounder, Davis, and Hill. Later Willia. was offered a contract on a match-to-match basis.

1977 – END OF THE WOOLLER ERA
J. H. Morgan, 1978

The year 1977 marked the end of an era in the chequered history of Glamorgan cricket. Only four players remained of the team that won the County Championship ten years previously. Perhaps the biggest wrench was the retirement in November of Wilfred Wooller, who had served the club fearlessly and faithfully for nearly 40 years as player, captain and secretary. With John Clay and Maurice Turnbull, Wilf Wooller was one of the architects of Glamorgan cricket.

In many ways he was a puzzling personality. Sometimes he gave the impression of being too aggressive. He certainly had forthright views and was never afraid to express them, but there was a more gentle and kind-hearted side to his character. If he strolled through the corridors of cricket power with an almost arrogant air, few would question his well-informed background in the game he loved or the rich knowledge he contributed to its well-being. Glamorgan have never had a bonnier fighter. Wilf Wooller would go through fire and water for the county, which in cricket terms was "formed to represent a county and grew to serve a nation".

If 1977 was the end of an era it also opened a new and encouraging chapter. The team, indeed the whole club, under the captaincy of Alan Jones – and the common sense and calm approach of O. S. Wheatley, the new chairman of a stream-lined administration – shook off the troubles which turned the previous season into such a nightmare. Such was the transformation that Glamorgan not only obtained better results in the County Championship but also reached the final of the Gillette Cup to mark a new and important milestone in the life of the club.

1979 – HOBBS UNABLE TO HALT DECLINE
J. B. G. Thomas, 1980

If 1978 was never an easy summer, then 1979 was a disaster for Glamorgan with failure on and off the field. The season, which ended in disappointment and criticism, was the worst in the history of the club. No win was registered in the Schweppes County Championship, and although the county had finished bottom of the table on four previous occasions, it had never failed to win at least one match.

The appointment of a new captain from outside Wales was not a success. Poor R. N. S. Hobbs, called out of retirement and persuaded to take over the job by chairman Wheatley and coach T. W. Cartwright, tried hard enough but found the task beyond him. He did not bowl a great deal, scored very few runs, and the side slipped away. The senior players were getting older, the younger players lost form, and the coach was unable to arrest the decline. The committee became reluctant to share their troubles and the atmosphere lacked the traditional gaiety of Glamorgan cricket. In the later stages of the season few spectators attended matches and interest appeared to be fast fading.

gust 24, 26, 27, 1985. Yorkshire won by 34 runs. Yet another instance of on the final day to overcome the weather saw Yorkshire win in an ix after forfeiting their second innings. Carrick made 92 in 133 minutes with adventurous hitting (three sixes, 11 fours) low in the order and then took seven for 99 to win the match on an old-fashioned St Helen's slow turner. Glamorgan, set to score 272 at a tempting 2.59 runs per over, initially appeared capable of succeeding as Morris and Holmes put on 92 for the second wicket. But then Carrick instituted the collapse, although Maynard played an historic innings. At 19 years, six days, he became the youngest batsman to score a Glamorgan century on debut, taking the record from M. J. Turnbull, who had been 20 years, five months and five days when he scored an unbeaten 106 against Worcestershire at Cardiff Arms Park in 1926. Maynard struck his century in 87 minutes off 98 balls with five sixes and 13 fours, racing from 84 to 102 by hitting three consecutive deliveries from Carrick straight back into the terraces.

Yorkshire 298-9 dec (P. Carrick 92, G. Boycott 64; R. C. Ontong 5-91) **and forfeited second innings**; Glamorgan 27-1 dec and 237 (M. P. Maynard 102, H. Morris 62; Carrick 7-99).

1989 – NATIONAL TORMENT
John Billot, 1990

Glamorgan's disastrous 1989 season caused serious concern throughout Wales. The county represents the nation in first-class cricket and its plight tugged at many consciences. Tony Lewis, the club's chairman, well aware of mounting criticism, said with some bitterness as the season ended: "Everyone who runs Welsh cricket is responsible to Glamorgan. We have no one to recruit. Not one Welsh cricketer has presented himself to us this year."

Finishing bottom of the Britannic Assurance Championship and the Refuge Assurance League daunted many loyal supporters. However, before this position was reached, there were other disappointments, notably the news that I. V. A. Richards, West Indies' captain, was unable to play for the county. He made the journey from Antigua especially to explain at a press conference in Cardiff that after two operations for haemorrhoids, he still needed treatment. He hoped to be able to join Glamorgan for the 1990 season.

Schoolboy holds 14 catches. News comes from Wellington, New Zealand, of a 13-year-old schoolboy, Stephen Lane, snapping up 14 catches at forward short leg on March 16, 1974 while playing for St Patrick's College, Silverstream ninth eleven against St Bernard's. He held seven catches in each innings, but his spectacular efforts were not enough on the day and his team lost.

Little Wonder No. 96

1993 – KENT v GLAMORGAN (AXA EQUITY & LAW LEAGUE): RICHARDS ON TOP
1994

At Canterbury, September 19, 1993. Glamorgan won by six wickets. A crowd of 12,000 which began queuing at four in the morning watched the first season of the revamped Sunday League end in the most dramatic and romantic way imaginable. Fate had brought the top two teams together on the final day of the season; destiny ensured that Vivian Richards would round off his magnificent career by taking Glamorgan to their first trophy since 1969, after 23 seasons of often abject failure. Kent, themselves without a trophy since 1978, began the day as favourites: a washout would have made them champions on run-rate. With Hooper, the League's leading run-scorer, well set after reaching his ninth fifty, Kent had a chance of a good total despite a slow pitch. However, from 168 for four after 41 overs, Kent lost five wickets for 14 and only the last pair's efforts enabled them to scrape to 200. Glamorgan quickly lost James and struggled to get any runs at all against Igglesden and Ealham, before Dale and Morris eventually began to push ahead. The game was far from won when Richards sauntered to the crease in his familiar gunslinger's manner at 98 for three. He was nowhere near his best and was given an especially hard time by the pacy Anglo-Australian Spencer: he was both hit in the chest and caught off a no-ball. Richards prevailed, however, and an unbroken stand of 60 in ten overs with Cottey gave Glamorgan victory. Richards marched off punching the air and a heavy night of Welsh celebration began.

Kent 200-9 (50 overs) (C. L. Hooper 60, M. V. Fleming 44; S. L. Watkin 3-33);
Glamorgan 201-4 (47.4 overs) (H. Morris 67, I. V. A. Richards 46*).

1995 – HOME OWNERS AT LAST
Edward Bevan, 1996

After 74 years as a first-class county, Glamorgan completed negotiations for the purchase of their own ground at Sophia Gardens for £2.5million. Another £4.5million will be spent to provide a headquarters that might serve the club for the next hundred years and eventually provide an arena equipped to stage international cricket.

1997 – SOMERSET v GLAMORGAN: TITLE SECURED
1998

At Taunton, September 18, 19, 20, 1997. Glamorgan won by ten wickets. Batting of rare brilliance from their captain, Maynard, and Morris, his ideal partner, backed up by pointed seam bowling by Waqar Younis and Thomas, carried Glamorgan to victory and their first County Championship since 1969. Leading Kent by only one point as they entered the final round, they had to get the maximum 24 points to make sure of the title. Despite the handicap of rain, they did it in style, with a day to spare. Glamorgan's triumph came with a four to fine leg by James at 6.18 on the Saturday, with four scoreboard lights shining through the September gloom. They were watched by a crowd of almost 4,000, mostly Welsh. The only disappointment was that thousands more were planning to cross the Severn Bridge on the Sunday, the scheduled last day. Six members of the 1969 squad were present: Alan and Eifion Jones, Don Shepherd, Peter Walker, Roger Davis and Kevin Lyons.

In lovely weather, Maynard put Somerset in and Waqar broke through almost at once, dismissing Holloway and Ecclestone for ducks. After going off because of the throat virus which afflicted him throughout the match, he took two more wickets to check the recovery. Bowler steered Somerset towards 252 and Caddick made two early strikes when Glamorgan replied. That brought in Maynard. He and Morris added 117 in 24 overs that evening. Next day, rain prevented any play before 3.50pm, when they resumed in wintry gloom. But Maynard and Morris hardly seemed to notice as they ran up another 118 in 17 overs. Maynard finally fell for 142 from 117 balls, with 28 fours and a six. Morris batted on into the third morning, scoring 165 from 244 balls, with 28 fours. It was his 52nd century for Glamorgan, equalling Alan Jones's county record, and it was to be his last before retiring on being appointed the ECB's technical director a month later. Croft and Shaw contributed attacking fifties and Glamorgan soared to a lead of 275. When Somerset resumed, Waqar was beginning to struggle: he conceded 38 in three overs. But Thomas stepped up to take five wickets, and Glamorgan looked likely to win by an innings when the score was 166 for seven. Rose and Caddick added a defiant 95 in 14 overs to make them bat again. They needed only 11, and did it in eight balls.

Somerset 252 (P. D. Bowler 63, M. N. Lathwell 62; Waqar Younis 4-41)
and 285 (G. D. Rose 67, A. R. Caddick 56*; S. D. Thomas 5-38);
Glamorgan 527 (H. Morris 165, M. P. Maynard 142, R. D. B. Croft 86, A. D. Shaw 53*; Caddick 4-132)
and 11-0.

2000 – GLAMORGAN v SUSSEX: RECORDS GALORE   2001

At Colwyn Bay, August 22, 23, 24, 25, 2000. Glamorgan won by an innings and 60 runs. For the second year in succession, a trip to the Rhos ground brought Glamorgan's biggest total. Their 718 for three, exceeding their previous-best of 648 for four here against Nottinghamshire a year earlier, was the highest Championship score for fewer than four wickets, and the 12th-highest ever. Again, James paved the way, passing Emrys Davies's 61-year-old record of 287 not out, against Gloucestershire at Newport, to become the first batsman to score a triple-hundred for Glamorgan. Put in by Adams on a green pitch, he and Elliott opened with 374 in five hours, eclipsing the county's previous first-wicket record. Elliott's fourth and biggest Championship hundred contained seven sixes and 15 fours; James's fifth double-century for the club beat the record he had shared with Javed Miandad. He had further century stands with Powell and Maynard, and had batted a minute over ten hours, hitting 41 fours – the most by a Glamorgan batsman in an innings – from 491 balls when Maynard declared on the second afternoon. Five Sussex bowlers had conceded more than 100 and, not surprisingly, their early batsmen were swamped by the prospect of making 569 to avoid the follow-on. However Adams and Rashid, scoring his maiden hundred, put on 232 before the last five wickets fell for 24 to Wharf, Watkin and the second new ball. Wharf returned five in an innings for the first time and received his cap. Despite valiant half-centuries from Adams, Martin-Jenkins and Rashid in Sussex's second attempt, Glamorgan banked maximum points just after lunch and jumped from seventh to third in the table.

Glamorgan 718-3 dec (S. P. James 309*, M. T. G. Elliott 177, M. P. Maynard 67, M. J. Powell 64);
Sussex 342 (C. J. Adams 156, U. B. A. Rashid 110; A. G. Wharf 5-68, S. L. Watkin 4-76)
and 316 (R. S. C. Martin-Jenkins 77, Adams 68, Rashid 54; A. Dale 5-46).

New Name, New Test
Edward Bevan, 2009

The Glamorgan chairman, Paul Russell, has promised that when the first ball of the 2009 Ashes is bowled on July 8, the Swalec Stadium (formerly known as Sophia Gardens) will be one of the finest medium-sized Test venues in the world.

2010 – Winter Of Discontent
Edward Bevan, 2011

When Glamorgan failed to win promotion on the final day of the Championship season – they missed out by just five points – there followed a period of turmoil and unrest which lasted throughout the winter. As Matthew Maynard, the director of cricket, and captain Jamie Dalrymple were blanked by a committee member as they climbed the Cardiff pavilion steps on the that last day, it became clear that Dalrymple was likely to be removed following a review of the season conducted by the county's former wicketkeeper Colin Metson – who, it transpired, was soon to be appointed managing director of cricket.

Maynard had earlier warned that if Dalrymple was replaced he would leave too. And when Metson, chairman Paul Russell and chief executive Alan Hamer travelled to Dubai in November to sign the South African batsman Alviro Petersen as captain without Maynard's knowledge, he did, claiming his position was now untenable – although he was later offered the role of first-team coach.

Dalrymple also went and, when the president Peter Walker resigned shortly afterwards, saying he had "serious concerns" about the likely impact of the changes, three prominent officers had left within 48 hours.

Bad behaviour. The TCCB, determined to try to stop bad behaviour on the field, were concerned about bad language and over-aggressive appealing, as well as a habit of batsmen in remaining at the wicket after being given out. Captains were to be told of the board's views at their pre-1976 season meeting.

Little Wonder No. 97

The Grace brothers who were so closely identified with Gloucestershire's early years:
G. F. (back row, left), W. G. (front row, middle), E. M. (front row, right)

GLOUCESTERSHIRE

*[1910 edition] After having held office from the foundation of the county club
Dr E. M. Grace resigned the position of secretary. His retirement marked
the end of an epoch. The Graces made Gloucestershire,
but no member of the family is now associated with the club.*

1871 – New Club Broadens WG's Appeal   1872

The formation in 1871 of a county club for Gloucestershire is a most important addition. That Gloucestershire should be enrolled among the CCCs of the country received an additional welcome from the fact that the Shire's return matches would give opportunities to many of witnessing the great batting abilities of Mr W. G. Grace, who would otherwise perhaps never see him play. Thousands of Nottingham people enjoyed that opportunity in '71, and this year the Yorkshire and Sussex people will have the same chance of witnessing their county cricketers enjoy an outing against the great batsman and his ten amateur confreres.

1872 – A day of Graces   1873

A coincidence worthy of record here is that on the 22nd August all the three brothers Grace scored largely, thus:

At Clifton,	At Clifton,	In Canada,
Dr E. M. GRACE	Mr G. F. GRACE	Mr W. G. GRACE
scored 108	scored 77 not out	scored 81
	(A portion of his innings of 115 runs)	

1876 – GLOUCESTERSHIRE v YORKSHIRE: Highest County Score   1877

At the Cheltenham College Ground, August 17, 18, 19, 1876. A best on record was made by Mr W. G. Grace in this match; that is to say his 318 not out is the largest score ever hit in a county v county contest, made out of the 528 (504 from the bat) runs scored. He was timed to have been about eight hours batting; he ran 524 times between wickets, and the hits he made were 76 singles, 30 twos, 12 threes, 28 fours (112 by fourers), three fives, two sixes, and a seven. One critic described this 318 as "a wonderful innings"; and another as "played in his very best style with only one chance, and that was when he had made 201."

Gloucestershire 528 (Mr W. G. Grace 318*, Mr W. O. Moberley 103);
Yorkshire 127-7.

1877 – Midwinter Breaks Amateur Mould   1878

Hitherto the genuine Gloucestershire team has been wholly composed of amateurs, but in 1877 they played a professional in W. Midwinter from Australia, but who is stated to be Gloucestershire-born. The Shire and the professional are alike to be congratulated, Gloucestershire on gaining an excellent bowler, batsman, and thorough cricketer, and Midwinter on playing so favourable a first season on English grounds, whereon the compiler of this little book has the pleasure of wishing him a long, honourable, and successful career. Midwinter's bowling for Gloucestershire had 31 wickets (10 bowled) for 410 runs; his best success with the ball being against England on The Oval, in which match he had 11 wickets at a cost of a shade over seven runs per wicket. His batting average for the Shire is 21.

1877 – ENGLAND v GLOUCESTERSHIRE: ADMISSION CHARGE DOUBLED 1878

At The Oval, July 26, 27, 1877. This was the novel match of the season, and one which, it was the opinion of many, would have been more appropriately played at Clifton in aid of The Grace Testimonial Fund. The admission charge each day was one shilling, at which increase many a man present exercised his Briton's privilege of grumbling, but for all that the ground was well-attended on the first day, and largely so on the second, when – at 6.25 – the match concluded in favour of Gloucestershire by five wickets, but inasmuch as neither Mr I. D. Walker, Mr A. N. Hornby, Richard Daft, Mr A. J. Webbe, Watson, Barlow, Oscroft, Morley, nor Ulyett played, it can hardly be fairly stated "England" was defeated. Gloucestershire admittedly played full-strength, with the exception of Mr J. A. Bush, whose absence was caused by the dangerous illness of his father, but whose place behind the wickets was ably filled by Captain Kingscote, who, in 1877, kept in a form fit for any match.

"England" 83 (W. E. Midwinter 7-35) and 123 (E. Lockwood 41; Midwinter 4-46, Mr W. G. Grace 4-46);
Gloucestershire 78 (W. Mycroft 6-21, E. D. Barratt 4-33) and 129-5 (Mr F. Townsend 43*).

1878 – Cheltenham Week Inaugurated   1879

Under this title a cricket week in the west has been fairly started at Cheltenham, by the well-known and popular James Lillywhite. The compiler of this book was not favoured with information respecting this week, but he was delighted to read in *Bell's Life* that "for some years past the establishment of a cricket week, at this favourite and charming town, has been the aim of several influential residents in matters connected with the national pastime." We of *Wisden* rejoice at the success of the influential residents in firmly establishing the week, and we hope, with old *Bell's Life*, that "it will continue to live for years and years to come;" for we see no valid reason why there should not be an annual, and successful, week of Wickets in the West, as well as a yearly Canterbury Cricket Week.

1880 – Loss Of G. F. Grace   1881

This notice would indeed be incomplete were mention omitted of the very sad loss the county, and indeed the whole cricketing world, sustained by the death of Mr G. F. Grace. A brilliant field, a splendid batsman, at times a very successful bowler, and one of the most genial and popular men that ever appeared in the cricket field, his early decease will long be deplored, and his memory cherished by all who were acquainted with him, and it will be very difficult to fill the void his death has created.

1882 – Champion Fails   1883

Perhaps the most remarkable circumstance connected with Gloucestershire cricket in 1882 was the failure of the champion [W. G. Grace] to score a three-figure innings for his county; a thing that had not once occurred since the county club was formed.

1887 – Champion Triumphs But County Fails   1888

Gloucestershire cricket in 1887 may be summed up in a phrase – Mr W. G. Grace had a great personal triumph, but the county failed. Out of 14 first-class county matches – home and home [sic] with Surrey, Lancashire, Notts, Middlesex, Yorkshire, Sussex, and Kent – only one, the return with Sussex, resulted in victory. Mr Grace scored 113 against Middlesex at Lord's, 92 and not out 183 against Yorkshire at Gloucester, 97 against Yorkshire at Dewsbury, 113 not out against Notts at Clifton, and 101 and not out 103 against Kent at Clifton – a splendid series of scores indeed. The Kent match formed a worthy climax to the best season Mr Grace had had since 1876, for after an interval of 19 years he repeated his Canterbury feat of scoring two hundreds in one game. No one else in modern days has done this in a first-class match, and the fact of his having twice accomplished a performance so remarkable will stand out among the leading incidents of Mr Grace's career. It was not alone as a batsman that our great cricketer did good work in 1887 for his county. He took 64 wickets at a cost of just under 22 runs each, and badly as this record may compare with what he has done as a bowler in some previous years, it was very good for a man who scored 1,405 runs with an average of 63.19 per innings.

Mr E. M. Grace, who has been playing longer in first-class matches than any other cricketer now before the public – he was the greatest run-getter in England before Alfred Shaw and Emmett were heard of – worked very hard for the side, and made several good scores. Advancing years do not make him more orthodox than he was in his youth, and he still plays his own game – a remarkable game, it is true, but not one that can be pointed to as a model for the beginner.

1892 – Australian Import Disappoints 1893

The repeated failures of the side caused great disappointment among the supporters of the club, and the feeling was all the more intense as a comparatively successful season had been anticipated. This idea was mainly based on the fact that Mr J. J. Ferris acquired his residential qualification in the middle of June, and it was not unnaturally expected that the famous Australian bowler would prove of valuable assistance to the eleven. These hopes, however, were far from being realised, and it must be frankly confessed that for a bowler of such high repute Mr Ferris's first season in English county cricket was singularly unsuccessful. It is true that he took more wickets than anyone else in the team, but he was terribly expensive, each of his 46 wickets costing on an average over 28 runs. How completely Mr Ferris fell below the form he displayed in the seasons of 1888 and 1890, when a member of the Australian band of cricketers, may be gathered from the fact that in no fewer than six innings over 100 runs were hit off his bowling, and that his best achievement was in the return with Yorkshire, when he dismissed four batsman for 64 runs. It is, however, only just to Ferris to point out that he was called upon to do a good deal of bowling, and that he only received poor support.

1893 – Schoolboy Shows His Strength 1894

In the latter part of the summer a remarkable young player was introduced into the eleven in the person of Mr C. L. Townsend, a son of Mr Frank Townsend, one of the old school of Gloucestershire cricketers. Both he and Mr W. G. Grace, jun. – the eldest son of the champion – while still at Clifton College, made their first appearance in county cricket, in the match against Middlesex on their own school ground, and for Mr Townsend there is unquestionably a future as a bowler. In the four games in which he took part he succeeded in taking 21 wickets for just over 23 runs each. For one so young – he is only 17 and looks at least two years younger – he bowls with admirable judgment and is able to make the ball break either way. At first sight this young bowler, with his slight build, gives the impression of being scarcely strong enough to stand the fatigue of a three-days' match, but yet in his first outing in the field he sent down no fewer than 70 overs.

1893 – GLOUCESTERSHIRE v SOMERSET: HATS OFF TO BRAIN 1894

At Cheltenham, August 14, 15, 16, 1893. After a close struggle on the first innings Somerset outplayed the home eleven and won by 127 runs. As the wicket was fiery all through the scoring was rather remarkable, and the achievements of Roe, Lionel Palairet, and De Winton were of great merit, the last-named surpassing all his previous performances for his county. There was a sensational incident on the second afternoon, Townsend finishing off Somerset's second innings with the hat-trick, and all three batsmen being stumped.

Somerset 197 (Mr W. M. Roe 75; F. G. Roberts 4-43, H. W. Murch 4-67)

and 270 (Mr L. C. H. Palairet 72, Mr A. E. Newton st Brain, b Townsend 4,

G. B. Nichols st Brain, b Townsend 0, E. J. Tyler st Brain, b Townsend 0; Mr C. L. Townsend 4-16);

Gloucestershire 166 (Mr G. S. De Winton 80; Tyler 5-39)

and 174 (Tyler 5-71).

1894 – GLOUCESTERSHIRE v SUSSEX: POLICE PROTECTION   1895

At Bristol, August 6, 7, 8, 1894. Owing to unfavourable weather the game could not be commenced on Monday, and an unpleasant episode occurred. Drenching rains on Sunday had left the ground very heavy, there was a further downpour on Monday, and at three o'clock, the umpires declaring the turf quite unfit for cricket, it was decided to postpone the start. In the meantime, however, some two or three thousand spectators had been admitted to the ground, and, on learning the decision, they behaved in a very unsportsmanlike manner. A number of them trampled on the playing portion of the ground, doing considerable damage, and Mr W. G. Grace and Mr Murdoch, the captains, were mobbed and had to be protected by the police. This regrettable incident points to the necessity of gate-money not being taken until play has been definitely decided upon.

Sussex 302 (Mr C. B. Fry 109, H. R. Butt 65; Mr C. L. Townsend 6-125);

Gloucestershire 121 (F. Parris 7-70) and 77 (Parris 8-28).

1897 – JESSOP SEIZES THE STAGE   1898

Next to the captain, the most prominent and attractive figure on the Gloucestershire side was unquestionably Mr G. L. Jessop, who made a great advance in reputation and repeatedly startled the cricket world by remarkable displays of batting. This brilliant young cricketer during 1897 quite rivalled the feats of such great hitters as Mr C. I. Thornton, G. J. Bonnor, H. H. Massie, and J. J. Lyons. Apart from observing that like Hayward of Surrey, and Hirst and Wainwright of Yorkshire, he had the distinction of scoring over 1,000 runs and taking over 100 wickets in first-class cricket, our comments here must be confined entirely to his doings with the Gloucestershire eleven. For the western county Mr Jessop scored 571 runs with an average of 28 while he took 58 wickets at a cost of just over 19 runs each, and was at the head of the bowling table. These bare figures, however, do not convey an adequate idea of his value to the side. His great merit rested in the fact that until he was disposed of no one could say what was likely to happen, as by his fierce and rapid hitting he was able in half an hour to completely change the fortunes of a game. He had many failures, often throwing away his wicket by sheer recklessness; but he had several memorable triumphs. Prior to 1897, Mr Jessop had never played an innings of three figures in first-class cricket, but last summer he exceeded the hundred on four occasions. Three of these big scores were obtained for the county and were – 101 against the Philadelphians, 126 against Warwickshire, and 101 against Yorkshire. The last-named innings was perhaps his most remarkable performance, as he obtained the 101 runs in the astonishingly short time of 40 minutes. As he followed up his great innings by taking nine wickets, he had a big share in the victory over the northern county. Mr Jessop was always a most dependable field, his work at times being quite brilliant.

1899 – W. G. SEVERS HIS CONNECTION

In connection with Gloucestershire cricket in 1899, the most important fact was the secession of Mr W. G. Grace from the eleven. Mr Grace took part in four games in May, his last appearance for the county being against Middlesex at Lord's. It then became known that he had resigned the captaincy and retired from the team. It was understood that his relations with the county committee had been somewhat strained, and there is not much doubt that his acceptance of the position of manager to the new London County Club, organised by the Crystal Palace authorities, was a source of irritation. It would be idle, even if one were in a position to do so, to enter into the merits of the dispute, but the upshot was that Grace withdrew from a post he had held since the formation of the Gloucestershire county club 30 years ago. When interviewed on the subject, Mr Grace said that he had not refused to play for Gloucestershire, but as he was not seen in the eleven after May it may fairly be assumed that his connection with the county has finally ceased. His retirement marked the close of a great and glorious chapter in cricket history.

1903 – SUSSEX v GLOUCESTERSHIRE: JESSOP EXCELS

At Brighton, June 1, 2, 3, 1903. The Whit-Monday match at Brighton was one of heavy scoring, 1,073 runs being obtained in the three days for the loss of 24 wickets. Sussex deserved great credit for saving the game, as they had to play their first innings on a wicket that became difficult after rain. Jessop and Ranjitsinhji were seen at their very best. Jessop on the opening day made the highest score of his life in first-class cricket, and actually obtained 286 runs out of 355 in less than three hours. Even for him on the Brighton ground this was a tremendous pace. His only mistake so far as could be seen was a sharp chance to Marlow at mid-on when he had made 98. He hit 41 fours, and doubled his score in 50 minutes after taking 70 minutes to get his first hundred. Ranjitsinhji played a magnificent innings on the

Wednesday to draw the match. He exercised great restraint so long as any fear of defeat remained, but after that he and Smith put on 139 in an hour and a half and were still together when stumps had to be pulled up.

Gloucestershire 482 (Mr G. L. Jessop 286, J. H. Board 71; E. H. Killick 4-17, G. Cox 4-129);

Sussex 266 (Mr C. B. Fry 83; J. H. Huggins 4-76, Dennett 4-93)

and 325-4 (K. S. Ranjitsinhji 162*, Mr C. L. A. Smith 54*, A. E. Relf 50).

1920 – GLOUCESTERSHIRE v SOMERSET: TABLES TURNED — 1921

At Bristol, July 31, August 2, 3, 1920. This was a remarkable game, as Gloucestershire after being dismissed for 22 – the smallest total of the season in first-class cricket – gained an astonishing victory by four wickets. In declaring when he did – Gloucestershire had plenty of time to get the 274 runs required – Daniell, the Somerset captain, reckoned without Charles Townsend. That famous batsman played a great innings, hitting with such brilliancy that he scored 84 out of 119 in an hour and a quarter. In the circumstances Gloucestershire's victory was one of the events of the year.

Somerset 169 (C. W. L. Parker 4-58, E. G. Dennett 4-68) and 126-7 dec;

Gloucestershire 22 (Mr J. C. White 7-10) and 276-6 (Mr C. L. Townsend 84).

1923 – HAMMOND HAS WORLD AT HIS FEET — 1924

Of far more importance in its bearing on the future was the fine form shown by Hammond – checked in 1922 by the discovery that he was not properly qualified. Here we have in all likelihood one of the best professional batsmen of the future. Irreproachable in style and not yet 21 years of age, Hammond has all the world before him, and there is no telling how far he may go. He led off in wonderful fashion last summer with scores of 110 and 92 against Surrey at Bristol. This exceptional standard he naturally could not keep up in later matches, but he finished with an aggregate of 1,300 runs and an average of 38. Honoured with an invitation to appear for the Players against the Gentlemen at The Oval, he scored 46 and 19, making an excellent impression.

1925 – GLOUCESTERSHIRE v ESSEX: DEADLY PARKER — 1926

At Gloucester, July 25, 27, 28, 1925. Won by Gloucestershire by an innings and 109 runs, the match proved a veritable triumph for Parker, who in the two innings had the astounding record of 17 wickets for 56 runs – a very remarkable performance. He took every wicket that fell to the bowlers when Essex, having been put in after losing the toss, were disposed of soon after lunch on the opening day. So well did

Gloucestershire follow this up that when stumps were drawn they held a lead of five runs with only two men out. There was no play on the Monday so Gloucestershire forced matters on Tuesday and, declaring with a lead of 172 shortly before three o'clock, finished off the match in dramatic fashion. Parker's eight wickets for 12 runs represented deadly bowling. He was almost unplayable on the treacherous pitch.

Essex 115 (C. W. L. Parker 9-44) and 63 (Parker 8-12);
Gloucestershire 287-6 dec (A. E. Dipper 107).

1927 – HAMMOND TOUCHES NEW HEIGHTS
H. E. Roslyn, 1928

Everything in the way of batting was dwarfed by the phenomenal success of Hammond, whose enforced absence from the team had accounted for the disastrous time Gloucestershire experienced in 1926. Happily a winter in South Africa enabled him to throw off all the serious effects of the dangerous illness which followed his visit as a member of the MCC team to the West Indies in the early months of that year. In the opening fixture with Yorkshire he scored 135 in a style which clearly indicated that his long rest, instead of adversely affecting his skill, had materially increased it. Going on to The Oval, he set the seal on his fame by making 128 and 187, and he finished the month with a brilliant display at Southampton, which enabled him to equal W. G. Grace's record of scoring 1,000 runs in May. Subsequently he had a few off-days, yet he wound up with an average of 72 – the highest obtained by any Gloucestershire man since the county has arranged a full programme. The advance made by Hammond is due essentially to the way in which he has strengthened his defence without in any way reducing his forcing powers; indeed, he now possesses a wider range of safe scoring strokes than ever. To mark his great feat in May, the *Bristol Times and Mirror* opened a shilling fund, which enabled them to present him with a cheque for £300, together with a gold watch and chain.

1930 – GLOUCESTERSHIRE v AUSTRALIANS: HISTORIC TIE
1931

At Bristol, August 23, 25, 26, 1930. There was a memorable finish to this match, the Australians, who had been set 118 to make to win, being all dismissed for 117 and the contest thus ending in a tie. Never before in England had a first-class match, in which an Australian team figured, terminated in this way. For a long time after the Australians entered upon their second innings the contest held out no promise of excitement. The pitch was obviously in a condition to assist the bowlers but to begin with Parker proved so erratic that the score reached 50 in 40 minutes. Gradually, however, Parker found not only his length but a worn spot and thenceforward he was deadly in the extreme. Before he sent back McCabe at 59, he twice beat that batsman completely. Goddard, after two unsuccessful appeals for leg-before, disposed of Jackson in that manner and, with Richardson stumped, there were three men out for 67 at the luncheon interval.

The chances of Gloucestershire still appeared remote but on play being resumed the game took a most dramatic turn. Six runs were added and then, with the total at 73, not only did Parker get Kippax leg-before but Sinfield, picking up smartly and getting in a splendid return, threw out Ponsford from mid-on. Roused to tremendous excitement, the spectators cheered everything, and their enthusiasm knew no bounds when at 81 Parker bowled Bradman. They had still further occasion for joy five runs later when a catch in the slips disposed of a'Beckett.

Unhappily for the home side, there came just afterwards a blemish on what up to that point had been a superb display of fielding, Lyon, when Grimmett had made seven, getting his hand to a ball put up by that batsman but failing to effect the catch. As matters turned out, this mistake no doubt robbed Gloucestershire of victory, for Grimmett and Hurwood offered such a determined resistance to Parker and Goddard that they added 22 for the eighth wicket before Hurwood was leg-before. Thus only ten runs were wanted when Hornibrook joined Grimmett. The newcomer surviving two appeals for lbw, the score had been advanced to 115 – three to win – when Parker dismissed Grimmett who had withstood the attack for an hour. Walker followed in and two singles brought the total to 117. With the scores level, there came three maidens in succession and then, on a further appeal against Hornibrook being answered in the bowler's favour, the Australians were all out and the match had ended in a tie.

Gloucestershire 72 (P. M. Hornibrook 4-20) **and 202** (W. R. Hammond 89; Hornibrook 5-49);
Australians 157 (W. H. Ponsford 51; T. W. J. Goddard 5-52) **and 117** (C. W. L. Parker 7-54).

1934 – BACK TURNED ON INJURY   1935

One great misfortune overtook the team. In a last turn in the nets, before the serious work of the season started, Hammond tore a muscle in his back. He managed to play against Middlesex at Lord's and scored 71, but he did so in laborious style. Most unhappily he accentuated the trouble and stood out of the eleven until the middle of June. Then in the next ten innings he made no less than 1,371 runs. Subsequently he was not quite so consistent, but in August against Glamorgan at Bristol he compiled 302 not out, his highest score for the county, and he came out with the phenomenal average of 126.25, his aggregate of 2,020 including seven hundreds. It was appropriate he should surpass all his previous efforts in his benefit year. To dispel all rumours regarding his future Hammond entered into a five-years' agreement with the county.

1936 – SEASON ENDS IN TRAGEDY   1937

Gloucestershire's season closed with a tragedy a few hours after the final match had been played and won. D. A. C. Page was killed when motoring to his home near Cirencester. His sudden passing came at a moment when the fortunes of the county had undergone a remarkable revival, due in a substantial measure to his personal efforts. The lamentable occurrence cast over team, committee and members a gloom from which recovery will be slow. When in 1935 Page was elected captain, in succession to B. H. Lyon, he was only 23 years of age. What he lacked in experience was, to some extent, counter-balanced by keenness. From the outset it was evident that he loved the game, and his enthusiasm made him so popular with his colleagues that they claimed to be the happiest band of cricketers in the country. It is a happy memory that the last thing he did on the field was to make a catch which gave Gloucestershire a decisive victory over Nottinghamshire.

1939 – GLOUCESTERSHIRE v KENT: STAR TURNS — 1940

At Bristol, July 1, 3, 1939. Gloucestershire won by an innings and 40 runs in a match of individual triumphs. Goddard equalled a world's record by taking 17 wickets in a day, a feat previously performed only by the left-handers Verity (Yorkshire) against Essex in 1933 and Blythe (Kent) against Northamptonshire in 1907. Counting the previous match at Bristol, against Yorkshire, Goddard claimed 30 wickets for 205 runs within six days. Even this magnificent achievement did not monopolise the honours, for in the Gloucestershire innings Wright dismissed nine men for little over five runs each, finishing with a hat-trick. Hammond scored more than half the total. After a partnership of 125 with Barnett, he shielded his partners from Wright and took out his bat, having hit a six and 19 fours.

Gloucestershire 284 (Mr W. R. Hammond 153*, C. J. Barnett 66; D. V. P. Wright 9-47);
Kent 120 (T. W. J. Goddard 9-38) **and 124** (Goddard 8-68).

1947 – PIPPED NEAR THE FINISHING-POST — 1948

When, in their opening county fixture, Gloucestershire suffered a crushing reverse from Middlesex at Lord's, they gave no indication that they would participate in one of the closest fights for the Championship for many years. Their fielding was deplorable, the bowling unimpressive, and the loss of the run-getting powers of W. R. Hammond, who retired from first-class cricket upon returning from the MCC Australian tour, appeared likely to prove irremediable.

Thenceforward, until beaten by Lancashire at the beginning of August, their success was such, however, that they avoided further defeat and registered 14 victories. They ran neck-and-neck with Middlesex till in a memorable struggle at Cheltenham they lost a second time to the Metropolitan county, who thus virtually decided the question of the Championship.

Bowling, and after that first wretched display, fielding proved the chief strength of the team. In his 47th year, Goddard took with off-breaks over 200 wickets for the fourth time in a remarkable career, and on July 1 once again won the race for the 100. Among his best performances were: 15 wickets for 81 against Nottinghamshire at Bristol; 15 for 134 v Leicestershire at Leicester; 15 for 156 v Middlesex at Cheltenham; and 12 for 65 v Somerset at Bristol.

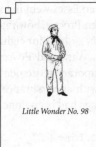

TCCB Summer Meeting 1976. Crowd noise intimidatory: The Test and County Cricket Board spent much of its summer meeting on August 6 discussing noise at Tests, which was considered not only irritating but sometimes intimidatory to players and umpires. West Indies players were among those who found it disconcerting and Clive Lloyd, their captain, was to be asked to co-operate in appealing for relative quiet at the last Test at The Oval. (Appeals by both captains produced the required results.)

Little Wonder No. 98

1953 – GLOUCESTERSHIRE v SURREY: YOUTH TRIUMPHANT   1954

At Bristol, July 25, 27, 28, 1953. Gloucestershire won by 97 runs. The match was notable for a remarkable performance by Allen, a 17-year-old off-spin bowler. Less than four hours' play was possible on the first day because of rain. Young and Crapp put on 98 for Gloucestershire's second wicket, but Loader worried most of the others. Surrey struggled on a difficult pitch, particularly after May left. Gloucestershire, 56 ahead, scored quickly and declared leaving Surrey to get 209 to win. This was far beyond them, for Allen made the most of a drying pitch and was almost unplayable. He finished the match by dismissing Loader with the fourth ball of the final over, and he was carried shoulder-high from the field by boys of Cotham Grammar School, which he left a year previously. Allen was playing in his fourth Championship match.

Gloucestershire 269 (D. M. Young 84, J. F. Crapp 51; P. J. Loader 6-70) **and 152-5 dec;**
Surrey 213 (P. B. H. May 51; C. J. Scott 4-34) **and 111** (D. A. Allen 6-13).

1966 – HAMMOND'S ASHES   1967

The ashes of Walter Hammond, former cricket captain of England and Gloucestershire, who died in July 1965, were scattered on the square of the county ground at Bristol in August 1966. The ceremony took place in the presence of his widows and three children, and four officials of Gloucestershire County Cricket Club. The ashes were brought home from South Africa, where Hammond died.

1972 – ESSEX v GLOUCESTERSHIRE: PROCTER CAUSES DAMAGE   1973

At Westcliff, July 15, 17, 18, 1972. Gloucestershire won by 107 runs. Nearly all the honours of the match went to Procter for a fine all-round feat. Twice he rescued Gloucestershire from impending danger, scoring an aggregate of 153 runs, and he took eight wickets for 73 runs. Most excitement came on the last day when Essex went in to get 245 to win. Any hope they may have possessed disappeared when Procter, bowling round the wicket at a great pace, dismissed the first four batsmen in 27 balls for eight runs. He performed the hat-trick when disposing of Edmeades, Ward and Boyce. Making the ball rear from the hard pitch, Procter caused the temporary retirement through injury of Taylor and Turner. Fletcher alone played him with any assurance. After a rest, Procter did not present the same menace, but the damage had been done.

Gloucestershire 184 (D. R. Shepherd 59, M. J. Procter 51; J. K. Lever 4-39, S. Turner 4-67) **and 238** (Procter 102); **Essex 178** (B. E. A. Edmeades 72; A. S. Brown 4-53) **and 137** (Procter 5-30).

1973 – Success At Last

The highlight of Gloucestershire's performances in 1973 was the winning of the Gillette Cup. It was regarded as the county's first success in top-class cricket of a competitive character for 96 years, since they were [*unofficial*] county champions in 1877. This long interval was almost unbelievable in view of the illustrious crick-eters, including some 25 Test players, the county have possessed.

There were jubilant scenes at Lord's when Sussex were defeated in the exciting final. Several thousands of supporters on the ground showed their delight, and the players themselves could not conceal their joy that they had at last gained a success for Gloucestershire. During the following week, they made triumphant tours of the county in an open-top bus displaying the trophy – and their enthusiasm.

1976 – Zaheer Displays Highest Class

Graham Russell, 1977

The undoubted star was their Pakistani Test player Zaheer Abbas. A slight alteration in his batting technique, whereby he brought his left hand further round the bat, saw him running up big scores nearly everywhere, as in all first-class matches he amassed 2,554 runs.

At The Oval, Zaheer hit a double-century and a century, and he repeated the feat against Kent at Canterbury. Gloucestershire had been waiting a long time for Zaheer to produce regularly the world-class form of which he is capable, but in 1976 he did this and topped the national batting averages.

1977 – New Captain Enhances His Name

Graham Russell, 1978

Procter-shire took on a new meaning in 1977. For several years headline writers have found this term a convenient way of linking the South African Mike Procter with Gloucestershire; a convenience based on individual performance. Now he was in charge as a captain, and while his all-round ability as a player continued to come through he also, importantly, proved himself a leader of men, taking his adopted county into third place in the Championship and to their first success in the Benson and Hedges Cup.

1988 – MODEL OF BAD TIMING

Geoffrey Wheeler, 1989

Near the end of a somewhat disappointing yet far from disastrous season, Gloucestershire shot themselves in the foot when the cricket committee, under the chairmanship of David Allen, voted 4–1 to dismiss David Graveney as captain and replace him with Bill Athey. Unfortunately, the decision was made public as Graveney was engaged in taking 14 wickets against Worcestershire in a Championship match at Bristol. The timing of the announcement and the insensitive way it was handled upset not only Graveney, one of the most popular cricketers in the county game, but also the players and many members.

1994 – WALSH LEADS BY WONDERFUL EXAMPLE

David Foot, 1995

Gloucestershire, who had been desperate to retain the services of Courtney Walsh, logically and astutely gave him the captaincy. Nothing could have been more felicitous. He grew marvellously into the job, full of enthusiasm, surprising energy – ignore that seemingly languid persona – and with a gentle touch of discipline when it was needed.

Although 1994 was hardly a memorable summer for the county, the wise influence of Walsh, allied for the most part to sound tactical judgment, was always apparent. Unlike a number of fellow West Indian Test players, he seldom looked weary. He celebrated his 32nd birthday in October in India, where he took on, in addition, the leadership of his national team. During the 1994 season he often bowled quite magnificently, a tribute to stamina quite apart from the sheer speed or the other penetrative assets that emanate from that lovely, effortless action. He won and nearly won matches for Gloucestershire on his own. But for an injury caused by a car accident and a brief return to the West Indies to discuss his role and responsibilities as Test captain, he would surely have taken 100 wickets. As it was, he took 89, at an average of 17.24. His players listened to his words, and visibly doted on his deeds.

2000 – TRIPLE SUCCESS COMES AT A PRICE

Graham Russell, 2001

A "Trophy" was once a beer that Gloucestershire sold in the club bars, not something they put in the committee-room cabinet. But times have changed at Nevil Road. Two cups in 1999 seemed a feast, but they were simply the hors d'oeuvre for 2000 when, in their best summer ever, the county made a unique clean sweep of the three limited-overs competitions, and missed Championship promotion by two points. Yet even such heady success had a down side. Prizemoney came to £176,400 but, with the players banking record bonuses and revenue affected by the wretched weather, Gloucestershire faced a financial loss. In the circumstances, the club had every reason to be critical of ticket allocation for the showpiece Lord's games, feeling that the participating counties received less than their due.

Getting there was not without scares. They scrambled through the Benson and Hedges Cup qualifying stage after losing the opening tie to Glamorgan, their eventual opponents at Lord's. Eleven days after retaining that title, they looked to have lost their hold on the NatWest Trophy when Worcestershire beat them by three wickets. But a journalist spotted an ineligible player in their neighbours' ranks, the ECB decreed a replay, and Gloucestershire lived again, winning by five runs. Next day, they won against all the odds at Leicester, and marched on to Lord's with home victories over Northamptonshire and Lancashire. Deciding the final on Duckworth/Lewis calculations might have been unsatisfactory for Warwickshire and the neutrals in the crowd; Gloucestershire supporters, brandishing their frozen-chicken talisman, were happy to settle for any method.

The League title came their way ten days later in a hotel lounge in Brighton, where the Gloucestershire players watched Somerset, the only side who could deny them, lose a televised floodlit match at Old Trafford.

2003 – THE BRACEWELL YEARS   2004

Gloucestershire's one-day successes since John Bracewell took over as coach in 1998:

Benson and Hedges Super Cup, 1999   National League, 2000
NatWest Trophy, 1999   National League (Division 2), 2002
Benson and Hedges Cup, 2000   C&G Trophy, 2003
NatWest Trophy, 2000

2004 – GLOUCESTERSHIRE v MIDDLESEX: GRACE AND HOBBS OVERTAKEN
2005

At Gloucester, June 9, 10, 11, 12, 2004. Gloucestershire won by ten wickets. At 2.36pm on the sunny third afternoon, Craig Spearman pushed through midwicket to reach the highest score in Gloucestershire's 135-year first-class history. It was two and a half years after he was lured back to cricket from a planned career in the City, and 498 minutes after his epic innings began. Along the way he eclipsed two towering giants: the previous record-holder was W. G. Grace (318 not out against Yorkshire at Cheltenham in 1876); four balls earlier Spearman had passed Hobbs's record for the biggest first-class innings against Middlesex (316 not out for Surrey at Lord's in 1926). When he finally nibbled a catch behind on 341, he had batted nearly nine hours, faced 390 balls and hit six sixes and 40 fours. Helped when Middlesex lost the sharpness of Hayward, who suffered an early ankle injury, Spearman played an innings of complete control and no chances: he drove, swept and generally mastered a Middlesex attack reduced to going through the motions and waiting for a mistake. He owed much to his opening partner Weston – they put on 227 together – to Taylor who hit his first hundred in nearly two years, and to Gidman, whose aggression eased the burden on Spearman as he approached the record. The final total of 695 was Gloucestershire's highest, and a beaten-down Middlesex failed to bat out the last day to safety.

> Middlesex 383 (L. Klusener 63, P. N. Weekes 50; Shabbir Ahmed 4-96)
> and 358 (O. A. Shah 72, E. C. Joyce 71, Klusener 68*, Weekes 53; I. D. Fisher 4-110);
> Gloucestershire 695-9 dec (C. M. Spearman 341, C. G. Taylor 100, W. P .C. Weston 85,
> A. P. R. Gidman 51; C. T. Peploe 4-199) and 47-0.

2007 – BLOW TO COUNTY'S SOUL
David Foot, 2008

It was almost unthinkable for Gloucestershire cricket to be deprived this past summer of its Cheltenham Festival, the evocative sporting institution which has, after all, been going since 1872. Severe rain, loss of fresh water and electricity problems led to the realistic if reluctant switch to Bristol. But, however efficient the logistics of Nevil Road's rescue act, something had irretrievably gone from the soul of the county's cricket in 2007.

> **Wisden 1979.** Changes in regulations: In the event of a cricketer currently playing in a Championship match being required by England for a Test or a one-day international, it was agreed that the secretary of the TCCB could approve of his substitute being allowed to bat or bowl.

Little Wonder No. 99

HAMPSHIRE

*[1962 edition] Sixty-six years of fruitless striving for the honour terminated
at Bournemouth on September 1 when victory over Derbyshire
put Hampshire beyond reach of Yorkshire, the 1960 champions.*

1874 – HOPE FOR THE FUTURE
1875

There is hope of Hampshire cricket coming to the front again, perhaps in 1875. An earnest practical move to revive the old love for the old game in the old cricketing county was commenced last September, when that genial and generous supporter of the national pastime – Lord Londesborough – liberally arranged for a strong all-round team of Yorkshiremen visiting Hampshire, and there playing a couple of matches on Mr Hargreaves' ground at Lyndhurst. [This is Reginald Hargreaves who later married Alice Liddell, the inspiration for *Alice in Wonderland*.]

1895 – Playing With The Big Boys   1896

Taken as a whole the performances of Hampshire must be considered decidedly satisfactory for a county making its first appearance in the Championship competition, but at the same time the general work of the season must have caused a certain amount of disappointment to the county's supporters. Hampshire had done so well in 1894 that their claim to inclusion among the first-class counties could not be overlooked. Unfortunately, however, after commencing brilliantly with victories over Somerset and Derbyshire, they sustained successive defeats at the hands of Yorkshire, Essex, Somerset, and Surrey. Their final position among the 14 counties was tenth, after they had held quite a prominent place till the last month of the season. Their best performance was, perhaps, the victory by two wickets over Yorkshire at Sheffield.

1897 – Sunstroke Kills Young Batsman   1898

Hampshire's misfortunes were numerous, the most serious being occasioned by the sad death of H. F. Ward. This promising young player had made rapid strides since he first appeared for the county in 1893, and in the opening match of the season scored 40 and 39 against Lancashire. This, as it unhappily proved, was the only game he took part in, as during its progress he contracted an attack of sunstroke, the developments of which caused his death on the eve of the Whit Monday match. Hampshire could ill afford to lose the services of one of their most consistent batsmen.

1898 – Top Guns Missing   1899

Hampshire v Yorkshire, May 1898: With all their Army officers away the Hampshire batting proved lamentably weak.

Hampshire v Surrey, June 1899: Hampshire's middle order – Major R. M. Poore, Captain F. W. D. Quinton, Col. J. Spens, Capt. E. G. Wynyard.

1899 – A Man For One Season   1900

Major Poore and Captain Wynyard had always to be reckoned with when in the eleven, and had they been able to play throughout the summer the county would have undoubtedly held a higher position in the struggle for the Championship. The services of Captain Wynyard were enjoyed fairly regularly after the first three matches and that he was in as good form as ever his average of 49 testifies. Playing consistently well all through, Wynyard enjoyed one great triumph when at Taunton he scored 225. Another brilliant innings was his 108 against Worcestershire. His doings, however, were quite insignificant compared with those of Major Poore whose batting was phenomenal. In the previous summer Poore had proved himself a great acquisition to English cricket and for two months last season he was perhaps the most prominent man playing. Between the 12th of June and the 12th of August he scored 1,399 runs in 16 innings, with an average of 116.58. No one has ever approached such figures as these and it was not only in the matter of average that Major Poore distinguished himself. In his first match – that against Somerset at Portsmouth – he scored 104 and 119 not out, and he followed up this rare feat of making two hundreds in a match with 111 against Lancashire at Southampton, adding his name to the list of those who have scored three consecutive hundreds. Nor did his successes end there. On four other occasions he exceeded the hundred, and surpassed all his other performances by scoring 304 against Somerset in the same game in which Wynyard played his big innings. Moreover Poore never failed, his lowest score being 11 against Essex. Very naturally Poore's superb batting had its reward in his being included in the Gentlemen and Players' matches at The Oval and Lord's. Unfortunately he did not do himself justice on either of the two great London grounds. Had he met with success, he would, no doubt, have had as a concluding triumph the honour of representing England against the Australians.

MOST SENSATIONAL BATSMAN IN THE COUNTRY   Obituary, 1939

POORE, BRIGADIER-GENERAL ROBERT MONTAGU, who during one season was the most prolific scorer in England, died on July 14, 1938, aged 72. He used to relate that he did not take seriously to cricket before going to India as a Lieutenant in the 7th Hussars. Then he studied textbooks on the game while playing in Army matches. From 1892 to 1895 when ADC to Lord Harris, then Governor of Bombay, he averaged 80 for Government House. Going to South Africa, better opportunities came for finding his true ability when facing the formidable bowlers under the command of Lord Hawke. He hit up 112 at Pietermaritzburg, and at Durban, when 15 of Natal were set to get 228, he scored 107, being mainly responsible for the local side winning by five wickets; these were the only hundreds scored against the touring team of 1895-96. He also appeared for South Africa in the three Test matches without distinguishing himself more than did some others in badly beaten elevens.

In the course of a few months in Natal he scored 1,600 runs, including nine separate hundreds, so that when returning to England in 1898 at the age of 32, Major Poore was ready for first-class cricket. On a soft wicket at Lord's he scored 51 and helped appreciably in an innings victory for MCC over Lancashire. He averaged 34 for eleven Hampshire matches and next season he became the most sensational batsman in the country.

Military duty took him back to South Africa before the end of the season, and after occasional appearances his county cricket ceased in 1906, but so well did he retain his form and activity that in 1923, when 57 years old, he hit three consecutive centuries during a tour of MCC in the West Country. His 304 stood as a Hampshire record for 38 years, being surpassed in 1937 by R. H. Moore with 316 against Warwickshire at Bournemouth.

Six feet four inches in height, of massive frame with powerful limbs, Major Poore when at the top of his form used his long reach with great effect in driving, his strokes between the bowler and cover point going with such speed over the turf that fieldsmen, no matter how placed, could not prevent him from scoring freely. Before becoming accustomed to English wickets, he played forward more in defence for smothering the ball than as a hitter, but his drive ripened to one of the most powerful ever known.

A versatile sportsman, Major Poore was one of the finest swordsmen in the Army, taking the highest honours at the Military Tournament. A first-rate polo player, he also twice won the West of India Lawn Tennis Championship, a feat he repeated in Matabeleland, and was in his regimental shooting team. His exceptional physical powers were demonstrated in his wonderful 1899 season; during a fortnight in June he played in the winning team of the Inter-Regimental Polo Tournament, won the best-man-at-arms mounted event at the Royal Naval and Military Tournament, and scored three consecutive centuries for Hampshire.

RICHES FOR POORE'S BOOK

Cricketana, 1996

A 1900 *Wisden*, sent c/o Gen Roberts to Major R. M. Poore, who was engaged in the Boer War, and which recorded his amazing batting for Hampshire, drew a successful bid nearly a century later of £846.

1900 – WAR LEAVES ITS MARK

1901

Never can a county have had to labour under greater disadvantages than beset Hampshire during the season of 1900. The War meant more to them than to any other team. Several counties had representatives at the front, but none suffered to the same extent as Hampshire. Nor was the loss of the majority of the best amateurs the only trouble. With troops constantly embarking or returning, the people of Southampton had more serious matters to think of than cricket. As a consequence the attendance at the county ground – never large – dwindled away, until, with constant reverses occurring, very few people cared to go and see a game. Matters were not much better at Portsmouth, and only at Bournemouth did the public show real interest in the efforts of those who through all this period of ill-luck strove manfully to uphold the traditions of Hampshire cricket.

1912 – HAMPSHIRE v AUSTRALIANS: SWEET VICTORY   1913

At Southampton, July 22, 23, 24, 1912. Playing capital cricket at all points, Hampshire for the first time in the history of the county had the satisfaction of beating an Australian team. To Philip Mead the triumph of the home side by eight wickets was largely due, that batsman scoring 193 runs in the match without being dismissed in either innings. Kennedy, taking 11 wickets, also had a large share in the success of the county. Having, thanks very largely to Mead, who played almost perfect cricket for four hours, put together a total of 371, Hampshire disposed of three Australians for 47, and next day, securing a lead of 174, compelled the Colonials to follow on. This course at first was attended with marked success, four Australian wickets falling for 62, but Gregory and Kelleway saved the visitors from collapse. With better judgment in running those two men might have prevented Hampshire from winning. Set 83 to win, Hampshire hit off the runs in three-quarters of an hour.

Hampshire 371 (C. P. Mead 160*, Rev. W. V. Jephson 55) **and 86-2**;
Australians 197 (W. Bardsley 60, R. B. Minnett 58; A. S. Kennedy 6-90)
and 256 (S. E. Gregory 85; Kennedy 5-91).

1922 – REMARKABLE RECOVERY   1923

Once again Philip Mead was the mainstay of the side in batting. Seeing that during the latter half of the season he so often found himself on a soft wicket, his performance in scoring 2,270 runs with an average of 63 was really wonderful. His success was the more remarkable from the fact that during the winter he was at death's door with pneumonia, being unconscious and given up by the doctors.

1922 – WARWICKSHIRE v HAMPSHIRE: RECOVERY TO BEAT ALL RECOVERIES
1923

At Birmingham, June 14, 15, 16, 1922. This was the sensational match of the whole season, at Birmingham or anywhere else, Hampshire actually winning by 155 runs after being out for a total of 15. That their astounding failure in the first innings was just one of the accidents of cricket, and not due in any way to the condition of the ground, was proved by their getting 521 when they followed on. The victory, taken as a whole, must surely be without precedent in first-class cricket. Hampshire looked in a hopeless position when the sixth wicket in their second innings went down at 186, but Shirley helped Brown to put on 85 runs. and then, with Livsey in after McIntyre had failed, the score was carried to 451. Brown batted splendidly for four hours and threequarters and Livsey made his first hundred without a mistake.

WARWICKSHIRE

	First innings		Second innings	
L. T. A. Bates c Shirley b Newman	3	– c Mead b Kennedy	1
†E. J. Smith c Mead b Newman.	24	– c Shirley b Kennedy	41
Mr F. R. Santall c McIntyre b Boyes	84	– b Newman.	0
W. G. Quaife b Newman	1	– not out	40
*Hon. F. S. G. Calthorpe c Boyes b Kennedy	70	– b Newman.	30
Rev. E. F. Waddy c Mead b Boyes	0	– b Newman.	0
Mr B. W. Quaife b Boyes	0	– c and b Kennedy	7
J. Fox b Kennedy.	4	– b Kennedy.	0
J. A. Smart b Newman	20	– b Newman.	3
C. C. Smart c Mead b Boyes	14	– c and b Boyes	15
H. Howell not out.	1	– c Kennedy b Newman	11
L-b 2	2	B 6, 1-b 4	10
	223		**158**

1-3 2-36 3-44 4-166 5-177 6-184 7-184
8-200 9-219

1-2 2-77 3-85 4-85 5-85 6-89 7-113
8-143 9-147

First Innings – Kennedy 24–7–74–2; Newman 12.3–0–70–4; Boyes 16–5–56–4; Shirley 3–0–21–0;
Second Innings – Kennedy 26–12–47–4; Newman 26.3–12–53–5; Boyes 11–4–34–1; Brown 5–0–14–0.

HAMPSHIRE

	First innings		Second innings	
H. A. W. Bowell b Howell.	0	– c Howell b W. G. Quaife	45
A. S. Kennedy c Smith b Calthorpe	0	– b Calthorpe	7
Mr H. L. V. Day b Calthorpe	0	– c Bates b W. G. Quaife	15
C. P. Mead not out.	6	– b Howell.	24
*Hon. L. H. Tennyson c Calthorpe b Howell.	4	– c C. C. Smart b Calthorpe	45
G. Brown b Howell	0	– b C. C. Smart	172
J. A. Newman c C. C. Smart b Howell	0	– c and b W. G. Quaife	12
Mr W. R. D. Shirley c J. A. Smart b Calthorpe.	1	– lbw b Fox.	30
Mr A. S. McIntyre lbw b Calthorpe	0	– lbw b Howell	5
†W. H. Livsey b Howell.	0	– not out	110
G. S. Boyes lbw b Howell	0	– b Howell.	29
B 4	4	B 14, 1-b 11, w 1, n-b 1.	27
	15		**521**

1-0 2-0 3-0 4-5 5-5 6-9 7-10 8-10 9-15

1-15 2-63 3-81 4-127 5-152 6-177
7-262 8-274 9-451

First Innings – Howell 4.5–2–7–6; Calthorpe 4–3–4–4;
Second Innings – Howell 53–10–156–3; Calthorpe 33–7–97–2; W. G. Quaife 49–8–154–3; Fox 7–0–30–1;
J. Smart 13–2–37–0; Santall 5–0–15–0; C. C. Smart 1–0–5–1.

Umpires: A. J. Atfield and B. Brown.

HAMPSHIRE SHOULD HAVE BEEN ALL OUT FOR SEVEN   Rowland Ryder, 1965

The 1923 edition contains the saga of the Warwickshire–Hampshire match at Edgbaston; surely the most extraordinary game of county cricket ever played. Not long ago I had the good fortune to discuss the match with the late George Brown in his house at Winchester, where, appropriately enough, a framed scorecard of the conflict hung in the hall. He contended that Hampshire should have been out for 7 in their first innings, explaining that "Tiger" Smith, while unsighted, had let a ball go for four byes, and that Lionel Tennyson was missed at mid-on, the ball then travelling to the boundary.

TENNYSON HAS LAST LAUGH

H. L. V. Day, 1962

Lionel Tennyson had no distorted notions that honour or prestige was dependent upon success. He played with the firm conviction that the principal object was to enjoy oneself. It was due to this combination of courage and gaiety that Hampshire won the historic match against Warwickshire at Edgbaston in 1922 after being diddled out for 15 by F. S. G. Calthorpe and Harry Howell in the first innings.

As the match against Leicestershire at Southampton ended early the previous day, Lionel ordered me to accompany him in his car to Edgbaston, which I agreed to do provided he got me there at a reasonable hour. But I reckoned without my Lionel. We made lengthy calls at several country houses and did not get to bed until dawn was breaking. When I tried to remonstrate with him he told me not to worry, he would win the toss. Imagine his disgust when Calthorpe called correctly and, of course, batted. We did well to get rid of Warwickshire for 223, and in I went for a much-needed rest.

Hardly had I settled to a comfortable snooze than Lionel informed me I was to go in first wicket down. I tried to persuade him to put me in lower. A shout announced that one of our opening pair had been removed. It must have been one of the longest two minutes between the outgoing and incoming batsmen.

I eventually reached the crease to be greeted by "Tiger" Smith's enquiry: "Did you have a nice nap, sir?" Little did he guess – I was hardly awake. Calthorpe swung the ball prodigiously that day. He sent me one that seemed to start from mid-on and was destined to finish at third slip. I made no effort to impede it, but there was a rattle of bails. The extraordinary procession continued and only Philip Mead, six not out, looked as if any of us had ever held a bat before.

Before our second innings started Calthorpe suggested that the amateurs should play golf at Stourbridge on the following afternoon, as the match would be over in the morning. This brought forth an immediate flow of good Anglo-Saxon from Lionel, who without a quiver of an eyelid announced that Hampshire would be batting until lunchtime on the third day. Naturally this was greeted with howls of derision, and there were some substantial bets at long odds against us even drawing, let alone winning, in which I was a party.

At the end of the match Lionel gave a passable imitation of a Highland fling under the shower baths, and both teams retired to the Queen's hotel as his guests. What a cricket match! It bore out his whole approach to the game which made it such fun.

1933 – CAPTAINCY AT SIXES AND SEVENS

1934

Considering that five batsmen, Mead, Creese, Pothecary, Brown and Arnold, scored more than 1,000 runs and that Mead enjoyed one of the most successful seasons of his long career, the performances of Hampshire did not furnish happy reading. They won only two matches and dropped from eighth to 14th position.

Several reasons could be advanced to explain the unexpected deterioration that took place. To begin with, illness overtook Lord Tennyson, who played in only three games, and with no other amateur regularly available, Hampshire, during the season, had as many as seven different captains. Generally the leadership fell upon Mead, but at various times the team was led by A. K. Judd, Rev. G. L. O. Jessop, J. P. Parker, Brown and Kennedy. Illness and injury attended other members of the side. Brown fractured a finger; Mead poisoned a foot and sprained a leg muscle; Boyes damaged a finger; Kennedy suffered a leg injury, and Arnold, McCorkell and Pothecary also met with minor mishaps.

1947 – HAMPSHIRE v LANCASHIRE: FIRST TIE 1948

At Bournemouth, August 27, 28, 29, 1947. A tie. For the first time in their history Hampshire took part in a tie. The end was extremely thrilling. With Roberts in hospital because of a broken finger, Lancashire batted only ten men. When Hill began the final over Lancashire needed one run to win with their last pair together. Barlow tried a sharp single, but was run out. On the first day Hampshire batted steadily. Arnold and Rogers opened with 105 and McCorkell and Bailey put on 170 for the fourth wicket. A good display of driving by Cranston, who obtained his first county century, enabled Lancashire to recover from a poor start, and they snatched a first-innings lead of four. Hampshire set their opponents to get 221 in two and a quarter hours. Lancashire accepted the challenge, Washbrook and Place putting up 142 in the first 90 minutes, but Bailey caused a collapse, taking six wickets for 29 runs in six overs; then came the thrilling finish.

Hampshire 363 (J. Bailey 95, N. T. McCorkell 74, N. H. Rogers 71)
and 224-7 dec (Bailey 63, J. Arnold 57);
Lancashire 367-9 dec (K. Cranston 155*, W. Place 66)
and 220 (C. Washbrook 105; Bailey 6-82).

1955 – SOMERSET v HAMPSHIRE: SHACKLETON SUPREME 1956

At Weston-super-Mare, August 17, 18, 1955. Hampshire won by 264 runs. Remarkable bowling by Shackleton gave them their decisive victory. He accomplished one of the best performances in the history of the game in taking eight wickets for four runs in 11.1 overs in the first innings and he followed with six for 25 when Somerset batted again. Rain before the start and during lunch restricted the first day's play, when Hampshire did fairly well until the spin took effect. Then Hilton did the hat-trick for the first time, dismissing Harrison, Shackleton and Burden. The pitch was extremely awkward and the Somerset batsmen were helpless. They were all out in 74 minutes and Hampshire, leading by 117, scored readily. Somerset, needing 363, again failed dismally, only Stephenson offering resistance.

Hampshire 154 (J. Hilton 6-49) **and** 245-7 dec (A. W. H. Rayment 104, H. Horton 59);
Somerset 37 (D. Shackleton 8-4) **and** 98 (H. W. Stephenson 52; Shackleton 6-25).

Sussex v Surrey. At Hove, July 26, 27, 28, 1978.
A hat-trick by Pigott, the Sussex 20-year-old fast bowler, in his first season with the club, suddenly brought drama into a match which was moving peacefully towards a dull draw. What made Pigott's hat-trick all the more exciting was that he had not previously taken a wicket in first-class cricket.

Little Wonder No. 100

1957 – EAGAR GIVES HIS ALL

E. M. Wellings, 1958

Three county captains retired in 1957, and they included E. D. R. Eagar, who had led Hampshire in every post-war season. Figures alone cannot tell the story of Eagar's part in the cricket of that period. He was a Gloucestershire man who gave everything to Hampshire as their captain-secretary. None has done more for that county, and none has made more sacrifice for any county.

In a period when the expression county amateur has concealed many a super-professional, Eagar was too busy working for his adopted county to give thought to himself. He sacrificed any chance of a more financially rewarding career, and also his own batting. In earlier days with Oxford and Gloucestershire Eagar was a bold, attacking batsman. The need in Hampshire was for someone more stubborn, and he did his best to become a solid No. 4. It was, however, off the field that Eagar achieved most. While other counties turned to football pools for revenue, Hampshire existed on the tireless work of their captain. He toiled round the year to popularise the county's cricket, built up the membership to previously unimagined heights, and persuaded more people than ever before to pay at the gates. As secretary he continues at that work.

1961 – FIRST AND UNEXPECTED SUCCESS

1962

Hampshire carried off the County Championship crown for the first time in their history after a long and exciting battle with Yorkshire and Middlesex. Runners-up to Surrey in 1958 – the first season in which Ingleby-Mackenzie captained the side – they dropped to eighth and 12th in the succeeding summers, and many people thought that they would not be serious contenders in 1961. Splendid teamwork and spirit, however, together with the almost complete disappearance of weaknesses in the middle batting and spin bowling, led to their unexpected success.

Ingleby-Mackenzie, who has always been known for his views on "brighter" cricket, revealed a hitherto unknown talent for master strategy. The experimental law which did not allow the follow-on called for intelligent declarations and in this sphere the Hampshire captain excelled. He balanced perfectly the ability of his batsmen – especially Marshall – to score quickly with his bowling strength. It was on this that Hampshire's success was almost entirely based. Had Ingleby-Mackenzie made any serious mistakes, the county might not have been in the running.

The facts speak for themselves. Of Hampshire's 19 victories in the Championship, ten were the direct result of declarations in their third innings. On the six occasions when their opponents declared and Hampshire had to score runs in the fourth innings for victory, they won three times.

1961 – HAMPSHIRE v DERBYSHIRE: TITLE SECURED 1962

At Bournemouth, August 30, 31, September 1, 1961. Hampshire made certain of becoming County Champions when they won by 140 runs. Marshall and Gray gave them a good start on a perfect pitch with an opening partnership of 120. The middle order wasted much of the advantage and half the side were out for 182, but with the last three wickets putting on 76 Hampshire reached 306. Derbyshire replied with spirit. Lee went with only nine scored, but Johnson, in partnerships of 93 with Gibson and 110, in just over an hour, with Oates, put them on top. The West Indian thrashed the Hampshire attack, hitting a six and 19 fours in his 112 made in two and threequarter hours. Derbyshire gained a lead of 12. Then Marshall, Sainsbury and Barnard hit splendidly and enabled Ingleby-Mackenzie to declare, leaving the opposition 252 to win in three hours, ten minutes. Shackleton, although receiving little help from the pitch, broke the back of the Derbyshire batting in a grand spell of controlled pace-bowling. He took the first four wickets and finished with six for 39 in 24 overs, Hampshire winning with just under an hour to spare.

Hampshire 306 (J. R. Gray 78, R. E. Marshall 76)
and 263-8 dec (Marshall 86, P. J. Sainsbury 73, H. M. Barnard 61; E. Smith 4-87);
Derbyshire 318 (H. L. Johnson 112, W. F. Oates 89; A. R. Wassell 5-132)
and 111 (D. Shackleton 6-39).

1968 – RICH HARVEST FOR RICHARDS; SHACKLETON BOWS OUT 1969

Undoubtedly, the batting feats of Richards, the young South African, over-shadowed all else. Although he came to Hampshire with a good reputation, no one could have foreseen that Richards would gather such a rich harvest of runs. His services were obtained after Lloyd, the West Indies Test player, had changed his mind and decided to join Lancashire; the South African's impact on the English game was immediate. To say that he improved Hampshire's batting is an under-statement; he scored 2,000 runs for the county and was also the leading run-getter in the country. Surely, no batsman has ever had a more successful first season in county cricket.

The season also brought to an end the distinguished career of Shackleton, one of the finest exponents of medium-pace bowling in the post-war years. But for his slightly greying hair, one would hardly notice a difference in him from the day he made his debut in 1948. He was still immaculate, sprightly and with a high, economical action; he still swung the ball each way and late, sharp movement off the pitch gained him many of his victims. During the season he was 44 – on his birthday he took five Australian wickets – and, predictably, he reached 100 wickets for the 20th time. Hampshire without Shackleton will be like Blackpool without its tower.

1972 – GREAT ENTERTAINER BIDS FAREWELL   1973

Sadly the 1972 season saw the final appearance of a great Barbadian, Roy Marshall, who for nearly 20 years was, perhaps, the greatest entertainer in county cricket. At the age of 42, he was still a batsman of the highest calibre, and showed this by scoring a magnificent double century against Derbyshire. To say that he will be missed is a gross understatement.

1974 – CHAMPIONSHIP DEFENCE WASHED AWAY   Brian Hayward, 1975

Hampshire's defence of the County Championship, albeit unsuccessful in the end through no fault of their own, was one of the most admirable features of the season. They led the table from early in the season, and were not displaced until the finishing line when rain washed out five days' play in the last three matches, allowing Worcestershire to take the title by two points.

Hampshire were among the first to congratulate the new champions, but there can be no more wretched way to lose than being forced to sit in the pavilion because of rain. Until the skies opened, Hampshire had seemed certain to retain the title and many, in addition to their own supporters, regard them as 1974 champions in everything but name. After all, they had beaten Worcestershire by an innings and 44 runs in two days!

Apart from their obvious strengths in batting and bowling, Hampshire were again a refreshingly happy side, benefiting from the good sense and judgment which attended all Gilliat did as captain. Yet one man, above all others, carved his name indelibly on cricket in 1974 – Roberts, the West Indian fast bowler playing in his first Championship season. No one of his pace had been seen in England since Lillee in 1972, and his impact was both immediate and lasting. He went on to head the national averages with a total of 119 wickets at a cost of 13.62, which was a remarkable achievement for someone who had previously played only one first-class game in this country.

1975 – HAMPSHIRE v SUSSEX: Greenidge leads way   1976

At Southampton. August 30, September 1, 2, 1975. Drawn. Despite their defeats at Bournemouth earlier in the month, Hampshire went into this match still in a position to challenge for the Championship, but they badly missed Roberts, who broke down with a shin injury during his practice run-up, and they neither bowled nor caught well enough. Yet their batting escaped all criticism as they amassed the highest total since the 100-over first innings was introduced.

Without Snow and Greig, playing for England, the Sussex bowlers carried no threat on an easy-paced wicket, and Greenidge led the slaughter with the highest individual innings of the summer and the highest by a Hampshire batsman since the war. Greenidge reached his 50, 100, 150 and 200 with sixes and his 250 with a four, and his major hits in a stay at the crease over five hours were 13 sixes and 24 fours. His 13 sixes set a record for a Championship innings, beating the 11 hit by C. J. Barnett for Gloucestershire against Somerset at Bath in 1934.

Hampshire 501-5 dec (99.5 overs) (C. G. Greenidge 259, D. R. Turner 62, R. M. C. Gilliat 61);
Sussex 259-8 (100 overs) (A. E. W. Parsons 65)
and 524 (M. J. J. Faber 176, J. Spencer 79, J. J. Groome 70, S. J. Hoadley 58, A. W. Mansell 51*).

1978 – Trophy Win Despite Stars' Walkout   Brian Hayward, 1979

The 1978 season set Hampshire a most searching test of character. Barry Richards and Andy Roberts, two international players of great ability, walked out from the county, but the players they left behind overcame the traumas, hardened their resolve, and came through with great credit to win the John Player League for the second time in four years. The Sunday success brought deep satisfaction to Richard Gilliat, the captain, his players, and their supporters. There were still five matches to go when Richards and Roberts departed and, without them, many felt the task would be beyond Hampshire.

The disenchantment shown by Richards and Roberts did not come as a real surprise. Richards had been out of form since 1977, but before then his contribution had been considerable and this should be remembered: Roberts, however, although invaluable particularly in the one-day game, had only one good season: his first.

1988 – Lord's Finalists, And Winners, At Last   1989

In Hampshire, 1988 will be remembered as the year when they at last rid themselves of the tag of being the only county not to have appeared in a Lord's final. Moreover, it was the year in which they won their first knockout trophy, for on their first visit to Lord's they beat Derbyshire handsomely by seven wickets to lift the Benson and Hedges Cup. Their South African opening bowler, Steve Jefferies, had set up the victory with a return of five for 13, the best figures in a Lord's final.

At Lord's, July 9, 1988.
Derbyshire 117 (46.3 overs) (J. E. Morris 42; S. T. Jefferies 5-13);
Hampshire 118-3 (31.5 overs).

1990 – HAMPSHIRE v DERBYSHIRE: MARSHALL RAMPANT 1991

At Portsmouth, July 21, 23, 24, 1990. Hampshire won by 48 runs. Among Malcolm Marshall's many astonishing pieces of fast bowling for Hampshire, few could have bettered that which fashioned this improbable victory. On the opening day, stretched to 7.33pm by Derbyshire's slow over-rate, Hampshire had been dismissed for 307, an innings illuminated by a delightful 45-ball 48 from Gower at his most elegant. Derbyshire had closed at 83 for one, and on Monday Morris's aggressive, unbeaten 157 off 226 deliveries (one six, 28 fours) allowed Barnett to declare at 300 for six after 83.2 overs. As the Derbyshire pace and seam attack dismissed Hampshire for a second time, the only real resistance came from Middleton and Marshall in a fourth-wicket partnership of 94 which Mortensen broke just before the close. The pitch was still playing well on the final day, and when Barnett raced to 63 in under an hour, Derbyshire's target of 235 seemed comfortably attainable. It still seemed so when they lost their second wicket, Bowler, to Marshall at 140, but the great West Indian then gave such a master-class in control and swing that in 16.3 overs Derbyshire lost their remaining wickets for 46 runs. Marshall finished with seven for 47.

Hampshire 307 (C. L. Smith 57) and 227 (M. D. Marshall 60, T. C. Middleton 59);
Derbyshire 300-6 dec (J. E. Morris 157*, P. D. Bowler 58)
and 186 (K. J. Barnett 63, Bowler 56; Marshall 7-47).

Wisden **1980.** The over: During the recent season in Australia the authorities reverted to the six-ball over, which means that only in Pakistan is the eight-ball over now in force. In Australia, the eight-ball over began in 1918. Now the Australians reckon the eight-ball over often slowed down the fast bowlers, and under the present scheme there will be more balls bowled per hour, which will keep the game moving and provide a better spectacle.

Little Wonder No. 101

1996 – HAMPSHIRE v MIDDLESEX: ENTER BOTHAM JUNIOR 1997

At Portsmouth, August 28, 29, 30, 31, 1996. Middlesex won by 188 runs. Liam Botham made a dramatic entrance in the true family tradition, although even his father Ian had failed to start like this. Two days after his 19th birthday, Botham junior was summoned from a Second Eleven match because Stephenson was unfit, wrong-footing journalists, who would have flocked to Portsmouth had the event been well signalled. The game had just begun when he arrived. Coming on second change, he dismissed Gatting with his seventh ball – a leg-side half-volley – and finished with figures of five for 67. His bowling showed the aggression of his father at his best – and his mysterious ability to take wickets with bad balls. Botham scored a commendable 30 to help Hampshire take the lead, but he was not able to bring them victory. For the rest of the match, Fraser took charge. He bowled with controlled hostility on a lively pitch to claim ten for 134.

Middlesex 199 (K. R. Brown 57; L. J. Botham 5-67)
and 426 (J. C. Pooley 111, M. R. Ramprakash 108);
Hampshire 232 (A. R. C. Fraser 5-55)
and 205 (Fraser 5-79, P. C. R. Tufnell 4-39).

2000 – A SEASON OF REVOLUTION
Pat Symes, 2001

Hampshire had not had many seasons, if any, quite as revolutionary or extraordinary as the one they experienced in 2000. From the moment Shane Warne touched down in the dawn of a wet April morning – to unprecedented publicity as the club's overseas player – through to the emotion-charged last day at Northlands Road in the gloom of a September evening, this was a summer never to be forgotten.

On the field, little went right, in spite of Warne's presence and the international-calibre bowling of Alan Mullally, who between them cost Hampshire more than £200,000 in salaries. Hampshire were relegated from Division One, with only three wins to offset nine defeats, and finished second-last in Division Two of the National League. It was somehow typical of their season that, while artefacts were being packed for transportation to the Rose Bowl, and award-winning groundsman Nigel Gray was preparing pitches there, the club should be docked eight points because of a below-standard pitch for their 565th and last first-class match at Northlands Road.

2000 – HAMPSHIRE v NOTTINGHAMSHIRE (NORWICH UNION NATIONAL LEAGUE DIVISION TWO): FAREWELL NORTHLANDS
2001

At Southampton, September 17, 2000. Nottinghamshire won by three runs. A Royal Marines bugler played "Sunset" on the players' balcony as chairman Brian Ford lowered the Hampshire flag at the end of 115 years at Northlands Road. Warne threw his kit to eager hands below, and there were tears among a 2,500 crowd. For Hampshire to celebrate the occasion with a win, Udal had needed to hit the final ball, from Tolley, for four; typical of their season, he missed it.

Nottinghamshire 234-8 (45 overs) (U. Afzaal 95*, P. Johnson 43; A. C. Morris 3-59);
Hampshire 231-8 (45 overs) (W. S. Kendall 63, L. R. Prittipaul 61).

2005 – GLITZ AND GLAMOUR BUT MIXED RESULTS   Pat Symes, 2006

Hampshire continued their metamorphosis from Happy Hampshire into domestic cricket's most fashionable, glamorous, county. They regularly supplied players to international squads, while the Rose Bowl's distinctive architecture became a familiar sight on television. Hampshire may have moved just five miles from Northlands Road, but in other respects they have come a long way in a short time. Even their players' private lives became a staple of the gossip columns.

In the C&G Trophy, Rod Bransgrove, the chairman, at last had tangible reward for his investment in both the stadium and some of the world's best players, not least the inspirational Shane Warne. There were setbacks: Hampshire dropped into the second division of the League, the Twenty20 programme was ruined by three no-results – and Hampshire again came bottom of the MCC Spirit of Cricket behaviour table.

But all would have been long forgotten had Hampshire, newly promoted, won the Championship for the first time since 1973 – and, as September began, they looked as though they might. Then a controversial deal between David Fulton, the Kent captain, and Nottinghamshire's Stephen Fleming took the matter out of Hampshire's hands after Kent lost [*and Notts thus became Champions*]. A furious Warne reacted fiercely, accusing Fulton of bringing the game into disrepute. The ECB was unmoved. It was especially frustrating for Hampshire, who twice beat Nottinghamshire inside three playing days.

KENT

[1946 edition] *The Canterbury and Dover grounds escaped real harm*
although serious bombing took place in both neighbourhoods;
the official report of war-time experiences gave 258 incendiaries as falling
on the Canterbury property – 138 on the playing area, "with negligible
damage; in fact the ingredients appeared good for the grass!"

1869 – CANTERBURY WEEK WITHOUT RIVAL   1870

The week of all weeks in the cricketing season is this, annually held in August on the St Lawrence ground at Canterbury. As a cricket county gathering of all classes, from Peer to Peasant, it never had an equal, and as a cricket week played out by the most eminent Amateurs and Professionals in the country, it is far away beyond rivalry. There have been weeks of finer weather, but otherwise none as successful as the week of 1869. As to the cricket, Fuller Pilch (a good authority) stated he never saw better cricket played on that ground.

1871 – Ladies Enhance The Day 1872

Thursday – the Ladies' Day – was one of those bright, cloudless, hot days, that in August last so frequently gladdened the hearts of farmers, tourists, and pleasure-seekers. When the cricket commenced the company present hardly warranted expectations of an assemblage up to the usual Thursday magnitude, but from noon to 4pm visitors arrived in large numbers. Four-in-hands skilfully tooled, old-fashioned family carriages whisked along in the old-fashioned four-horse postillion form, new-fashioned breaks and waggonettes, dashing dog-carts, tandems, 'busses, and other vehicles, all of them fully, most of them fairly, freighted, rattled up the incline of the fine old ground one after the other in such numbers, that when the rush was over and all were settled in picturesque groups, when the little slope was covered by brightly toileted ladies, when the promenade was thronged by a gay company, and when the ring around the ground was fully formed, it was unanimously acknowledged that the gathering was the gayest, the most numerous and influential ever seen at a cricket match at St Lawrence. Truly was this The Ladies' Day, for of the 7,000 visitors present the better half were ladies, whose presence so very much enhanced the beauty of that charming, animated picture of English summer life.

Team wins without hitting ball. A village cricket team claimed a unique record by winning a match without scoring a run off the bat. Cawood, near York, bowled out their opponents, Dringhouses, for only two runs in a York Senior League match in August 1979. When Peter Wright offered no stroke to the opening ball in the Cawood innings, wicketkeeper Howard Green failed to gather the delivery and it went for four byes.

Little Wonder No. 102

1875 – Harris Lords It Over County's Fortunes 1876

Lord Harris as president, hon. secretary, captain of the county team, greatest aggregate, and highest average scorer for the county, must have been head and hands full of Kent cricket in 1875. It is to be regretted that such influential energy and very fine and successful batting displayed by his lordship should have resulted in so unsuccessful a campaign as six defeats out of nine matches; but it is to be hoped that in 1876 his lordship will go on never minding 1875, and that his last season's experience of who can and will play cricket for the county will enable him to select a team who will work well together and bring off a majority of successes in '76 for old Kent, for if there be one man more than another whose position, influence, earnest devotion to, and practical knowledge of, the glorious old game, can, in due time, work Kent up to its old position among the cricketing counties, that man is Lord Harris.

Lord of Kent: Lord Harris was the county's leading batsman, captain, president
and hon. secretary, as well as an influential figure in the game and beyond

1884 – KENT v AUSTRALIANS: PROUD DOUBLE 1885

At Canterbury, August 4, 5, 6, 1884. Kent won this match by 96 runs, and gained a proud distinction of being the only county which succeeded in lowering the colours of the Australians during their last two visits to England. The victory was the more meritorious inasmuch as Kent won by good all-round cricket after having the worst of the opening day's play. The immediate causes of success were the bowling of Alexander Hearne and the batting of Lord Harris and Frank Hearne. On the first day Kent scored an innings of 169, and the Australians were credited with 136 for the loss of only four wickets, and were thus only 33 runs behind with six wickets to fall.

The next morning those six wickets were captured for the addition of only 41 runs, and the bowling which mainly contributed to this unexpected collapse was of a youth – Alexander Hearne, the youngest of the three brothers who played for Kent in 1884. McDonnell's 80 was a brilliantly-hit innings, and included seven fours, six threes, and five twos. In the second innings of Kent Mackinnon and Kemp scored 42 for the first wicket, and later on Lord Harris and Frank Hearne made a long stand. Lord Harris played fine cricket for 60, and Frank Hearne's 45 was a well-hit innings. The Australians wanted 206 to win when they started their second innings, and at the call of time they had lost six wickets and had 123 runs to make to win. The remaining four wickets fell for 26 runs, and Kent gained a far more brilliant victory than did Notts in 1880.

Kent 169 (G. E. Palmer 4-52)

and 213 (Lord Harris 60; Palmer 7-74);

Australians 177 (P. S. McDonnell 80; A. Hearne 5-36, J. Wootton 4-72) **and 109.**

1898 – NEW CAPTAIN PROVES MORE THAN ADEQUATE REPLACEMENT 1899

There was one notable change in the management of the eleven, Mr J. R. Mason succeeding Mr Marchant as captain. Without in any way disparaging the latter gentleman, who throughout his cricket career has worked most loyally for Kent, we have no hesitation in saying that the change was an improvement. With all his brilliant powers as a player Mr Marchant never struck one as possessing the peculiar qualities needed by the captain of a county eleven, and we think that during the last few years he would have done far better as a batsman if he had played under someone else's leadership. So far as can be judged from the experience of a single season Mr Mason is an excellent captain, and though it would be too much to say that the improved form of the eleven was due to his being at the head of affairs, there can be no doubt that the players worked very keenly under his guidance. He was well in touch with the professionals and was thoroughly successful in earning their goodwill. In captaining Kent he had no easy task, the bowling at his disposal being so ordinary in character that not a single match on the programme could be entered upon without more or less anxiety as to the result.

1906 – Surprise Surrounds First Championship

The season of 1906 was indeed a memorable one in the history of Kent cricket. For the first time in modern days the county came out at the top of the list. The honour was gained by a very narrow margin, a defeat by one run in their return match with Gloucestershire depriving Yorkshire of the Championship, but there was a general consensus of opinion that Kent had the best county side of the year, and showed by far the most brilliant form. The triumph had in it an element of surprise that was quite dramatic. Up to the middle of June there did not seem the least likelihood that Kent would have an exceptional record, and the chance of carrying off the Championship was hardly thought of. The turning point came in the match against Surrey at The Oval.

Kent stood at the top of the list when they entered upon their last week of county cricket. They beat Middlesex at Lord's, but even after that it was necessary that they should avoid defeat at the hands of Hampshire at Bournemouth. In this final match, however, all doubts were soon set at rest, for after getting Hampshire out for 163, Kent scored 610. A draw would have served every purpose, but Kent, though for once their bowling was collared, won the game in the end by an innings and 37 runs.

1906 – Blythe Blooms In Kentish Nursery

Capt. W. McCanlis, 1907

Kent for many years had been essentially an amateur side; doing great things at times, when at full strength in the latter end of the season. For example, Kent has beaten the Australians on five occasions. Occasional brilliancies, however, are not satisfying when a high position is desired in the County Championship competition. A good side in all matches was required. Hence the establishment, in 1897, of the Nursery, with the view of training young professionals so as to render them competent to become members of the county team in due course.

There is an element of luck in discovering likely youngsters. The case of C. Blythe is an instance. Kent was playing a match at Blackheath, and the usual preliminary morning practice was proceeding; I noticed a lad, one of the crowd, bowl a few balls to Walter Wright, and was impressed with his delivery. I arranged for him to come and bowl to me one evening. He came; I was pleased with him and recommended him for a trial at Tonbridge – the result of which was that he was engaged for the Nursery next season. There he improved rapidly, and is now the great, well-known bowler, C. Blythe. There was in this find a considerable amount of luck. Blythe lived at Deptford, a place one would hardly go to in search of cricketers. The lads of this town have only the roughest parts of Blackheath on which to play their occasional cricket. Of course, under such conditions it is quite impossible for a boy to make any headway in the art of batting; but there is always a chance of finding a boy with natural abilities as a bowler, who may be taught to bat and field. Blythe is not half a bad batsman when he goes in with the intention of staying; and yet, when he came to Tonbridge he had no idea whatever of batting.

1907 – NORTHAMPTONSHIRE v KENT: RAIN BEATEN AS WELL 1908

At Northampton, May 30, 31, June 1, 1907. Kent were seen at quite their best in this match, and forced a victory in brilliant style. Rain restricted cricket on the opening day to three hours and prevented anything being done on the Friday, but despite this serious loss of time Kent had won at half-past four on the Saturday afternoon by an innings and 155 runs. This was mainly the work of Blythe who, bowling superbly, took all ten wickets in Northamptonshire's first innings, and had a record for the match of 17 wickets for 48 runs. By consistently good batting, Kent, in the time available on the first afternoon, scored 212 runs for the loss of four wickets, and on the Saturday morning the batsmen hit out in fearless style. Then, on going in, Northamptonshire gave a deplorable display. Against Blythe's bowling seven wickets fell for four runs, two of them extras, but Vials, after being missed, hit pluckily, and the innings extended beyond the luncheon interval. In the end, however, the total only reached 60, and following on 194 behind Northamptonshire were dismissed in an hour and a quarter for 39. Kent only just won in time, for no sooner had the players left the field than rain fell heavily.

Kent 254 (H. T. W. Hardinge 73, Mr K. L. Hutchings 52; W. East 5-77);
Northamptonshire 60 (C. Blythe 10-30) and 39 (Blythe 7-18).

1920 – NOTTINGHAMSHIRE v KENT: SCHOOLBOY'S DEBUT TON 1921

At Nottingham, August 30, 31, September 1, 1920. The last match of the Notts season had to be left drawn, the bat, except during the greater part of Kent's first innings, beating the ball completely. Notts batted finely on the first day, and they looked to have the match in their hands when Kent's eighth wicket fell at 117. J. L. Bryan and Fairservice, however, put on 124 together, and when the side followed on G. J. Bryan and Bickmore opened the second innings with a partnership of 187 for the first wicket. G. J. Bryan, the crack Wellington batsman, will always have pleasant recollections of his first county match. He played splendid cricket. After the tea interval on the third day the light became very bad and with a draw inevitable the match was given up.

Notts 503-8 dec (W. R. D. Payton 138*, J. R. Gunn 105, T. W. Oates 88,
W. W. Whysall 62; A. P. Freeman 4-159);
Kent 255 (Mr J. L. Bryan 86*, W. J. Fairservice 59; F. C. Matthews 5-62, T. L. Richmond 5-127)
and 353-5 (Mr G. J. Bryan 124, Mr A. F. Bickmore 95, H. T. W. Hardinge 50*).

ARMY TOOK PRECEDENCE Obituary, 1992

BRYAN, BRIGADIER GODFREY JAMES, CBE, who died at Canterbury on April 4, 1991, aged 88, was the youngest of three cricketing brothers, all of whom played for Kent. G. J. was possibly the most talented, a tall, strong, dashing left-hander with a fine array of attacking strokes, but he gave himself less chance of reaching the top than his brothers by choosing an Army career.

At Wellington as a 16-year-old in 1919 he made an unbeaten 102 against Westminster, and a year later, scored hundreds against Bradfield, Westminster, Haileybury, Charterhouse and Free Foresters. He played in the Schools Week at Lord's and hit a fifty. This was child's play. Picked for Kent against Nottinghamshire, he hit 124 in the second innings, putting on 187 for the first wicket with A. F. Bickmore. In 1921 he made 179 against Hampshire at Canterbury, with L. P. Hedges adding 208 in only two hours. When the South Africans were over in 1924, he hit 229 against them for the Combined Services. Although his opportunities for county cricket were limited, he returned to Lord's year after year for the Army, and hardly ever failed to give the Navy bowlers a drubbing.

Bryan was 17 years 247 days old when he scored his hundred against Northamptonshire.

1928 – WOOLLEY TOPS 3,000 RUNS
1929

While Hardinge and Ashdown so repeatedly laid the foundation of a big Kent total, they were in personal achievement overshadowed by Woolley who, at the top of his form nearly all the summer, scored for Kent in Championship matches over 1,100 runs more than in 1927, with an average of nearly 59 an innings and on ten occasions – eight times in competition matches – played a three-figure innings. Although not called upon to take any part in the Test matches with West Indies, Woolley enjoyed the satisfaction for the first time in his brilliant career of compiling during the season more than 3,000 runs, whereas his highest total previously had been 2,344 in 1924. In recognition of his splendid services, Woolley, who had had a benefit in 1922 was, for the second time in his career, so honoured in the Kent match against Somerset at Canterbury being awarded to him.

Outstanding among the other features of Kent cricket was the performance of Ames who in his 22nd year not only rose to an aggregate of 1,666, which included a score of 200 against Surrey at Blackheath and four separate hundreds in all, but earned the great distinction of establishing a wicketkeeping record. In the clever work of Freeman, he enjoyed, no doubt, an exceptionally favourable opportunity, but still he made history in disposing in all matches of 121 batsmen – 52 stumped and 69 caught in the course of the season. Despite his youth and comparatively small measure of experience, Ames at the end of the summer was, in view of his ability as batsman as well as wicketkeeper, picked as a member of the team for Australia.

1931 – FREEMAN REWRITES BOWLING RECORDS
1932

For their prominent part in the season's cricket, Kent, as usual in recent years, owed a great deal to Freeman. Their most efficient bowler and outstanding personality as a match-winner, Freeman set up a fresh record in taking 200 wickets for the fourth season in succession. As a matter of fact he disposed of 276 batsmen in all matches, making an aggregate of 1,122 for those years. By taking 304 wickets in 1928 he had beaten Tom Richardson's record for a season, and by getting out the whole Lancashire side at Old Trafford he added to his name the unparalleled achievement, accomplished in the course of three consecutive seasons, of taking all ten wickets in an innings for the third time. Lancashire fell before him at Maidstone in 1929, Essex at Southend a year later, and then Lancashire again at a cost of only 79 runs. Freeman, having already equalled the record made by V. E. Walker in 1865, in taking all ten wickets in an innings for the second time, now stands alone among bowlers with his season's record of 304, an aggregate of 1,122 wickets in four consecutive summers, and the capture three times of all ten wickets in an innings.

1932 – A Foretaste Of Twenty20 Cricket   1933

When Kent were beaten on the Bank Holiday afternoon, Chapman and B. H. Lyon arranged a match, each side to bat for an hour. Gloucestershire occupied nearly their allotted time in scoring 194 but their full innings total was passed by Kent with 201 for the loss of five wickets in 45 minutes. Hammond scored 69 in 25 minutes and Woolley hit up 86 in half an hour. At first some of the large company seemed to expect comic cricket but when the free and powerful hitting brought out brilliant fielding, amusement changed to enthusiasm. A splendid catch at the very start aroused the first cheers, and the earnestness displayed by all the players made the attempt to entertain the holiday crowd a success, upon which the officials received general thanks and congratulations.

Little Wonder No. 103

Test play on Sundays. Subject to the approval of the Australian Cricket Board it was agreed to make arrangements for Sunday play in three of the six Test matches between England and Australia in 1981 – the First, Fourth and Fifth – the hours of play to be from 12 until seven. In these three matches there would be no rest day, play starting on Thursdays and ending on Mondays.

1937 – KENT v GLOUCESTERSHIRE: FASTEST IN HISTORY   1938

At Dover, August 18, 19, 20, 1937. Kent won by eight wickets. Set to get 218 in less than two hours, they actually hit off the runs in 71 minutes. History contains no mention of a faster scoring feat in first-class cricket. Woolley made 44 out of 68 in

25 minutes; Ames hit up 70 out of 100 in 36 minutes and then Watt gave such an amazing display that the last 51 runs came in ten minutes. From the moment that Woolley hit nine runs off the first over that average rate of scoring was maintained. Ashdown played a second admirable innings.

Gloucestershire 434 (Mr G. W. Parker 210, R. A. Sinfield 74*, C. J. Barnett 70; A. E. Watt 6-129)
and 182 (W. R. Hammond 52; Watt 4-69);
Kent 399 (F. E. Woolley 100, Mr T. A. Pearce 59, T. W. Spencer 53; Sinfield 4-83)
and 219-2 (L. E. G. Ames 70, W. H. Ashdown 62).

1938 – ONE OF GAME'S FINEST RETIRES   Hubert Preston, 1939

Elegant and dashing left-handed batsman – best in execution and as an attractive personality whom we have known during 30 years – Woolley announced his decision to retire and on every ground he received a very affectionate farewell, each county team and their supporters clearly demonstrating their appreciation of one of the finest players who have graced the game. Often it was difficult to believe that Woolley became 51 years of age on May 27. Not only did he make 1,386 runs in county matches with 162 his best score, but he took 21 wickets, his performance at Oakham against Leicestershire – 11 wickets for 106 – being surpassed only by Watt with 14 for 90 when Middlesex were trounced at Maidstone. The MCC honoured Woolley by choosing him to captain the Players at Lord's – the scene of some of his finest exploits. A testimonial fund brought a good round sum and Woolley will remain in touch with Kent cricket as coach at King's School, Canterbury.

1939 – KENT v LANCASHIRE: EVANS EMERGES   1940

At Dover, August 26, 28, 29, 1939. [*Godfrey*] Evans, 17 years of age, kept wicket specially well on the first day.

1960 – KENT v WORCESTERSHIRE: OVER IN A DAY   1961

At Tunbridge Wells, June 15, 1960. Kent won by an innings and 101 runs, taking 14 points from the first match to be completed in a day since 1953. The pitch, grassless and soft at first, dried under a hot sun, leaving crusty edges on the indentations made when the ball dug in earlier. No two deliveries behaved alike; many rising sharply, some keeping low and nearly all deviating to an unaccustomed degree. Worcestershire, not the strongest of batting sides, floundered against Brown and Halfyard, both of whom needed to do little more than turn over their arms. The pitch did the rest.

An enterprising innings by Jones, who hit two sixes and nine fours in scoring 73 in one hour 35 minutes, helped Kent to a reasonable total while the pitch was drying out. Worcestershire commenced their first innings at ten to four and, with tea intervening, were all out at 5.25 after batting 75 minutes. Six wickets were down for nine runs, and there never seemed a chance of them hitting the 38 needed to avoid the follow-on. Slade, with two fours off successive balls from Brown, became top scorer with nine, and six extras bolstered the total to 25, the lowest since Hampshire were dismissed by Derbyshire for 23 in August 1958 and only one run better than the lowest in Worcestershire's history.

Brown, six for 12, and Halfyard, four for seven, bowled throughout and continued to demolish Worcestershire when they went in again 162 behind. The second innings stretched ten minutes into the extra half-hour – one hour 35 minutes in all – mainly because of the determination of Broadbent, who stayed for one hour ten minutes, and a bold front by Slade and Booth, whose dismissal was indicative of the pitch, described afterwards by Cowdrey as "disgraceful". The ball flew off one of the many patches on to the top of the bat, struck Booth on the cheekbone and produced a catch.

Kent 187 (P. H. Jones 73; N. Gifford 4-63);
Worcestershire 25 (A. Brown 6-12, D. J. Halfyard 4-7) and 61 (Halfyard 5-20).

1961 – KENT v AUSTRALIANS: COWDREY'S FEAT   1962

At Canterbury, June 17, 19, 20, 1961. Drawn. Cowdrey dominated the match, scoring a century in each innings – the first player to do so against the Australians in England. Kent came within seven runs of beating the Australians for the first time since 1899, but even if the county had been successful their victory would not have detracted from the England captain's magnificent batting. The touring team had shown during the first day that the pitch would give no help to the bowlers, and hundreds by Lawry and O'Neill enabled Harvey to declare at 428 for six. The Kent batsmen found runs as easy to score on the Monday. Cowdrey reached his century in just under three hours and then hit 49 in the next 52 minutes before falling to a catch at fine leg. He closed the innings 88 behind and, after some more attractive batting from the Australians, Harvey left Kent to score 291 in three hours ten minutes to win. The county lost three wickets for 71 and Cowdrey came in with 222 needed in two hours. While he was at the crease anything seemed possible. Harvey manipulated his field well, but Cowdrey always found the gaps with an unending flow of beautifully timed strokes. His century took only 93 minutes and in all he spent an hour and 49 minutes over 121, which included a six and 19 fours. Leary helped his captain add 164 at nearly two a minute, but Kent still needed 13 for victory when the last over began. Jones scored five off four balls, but Misson ended their hopes by bouncing the fifth ball over the batsman's head. Davidson, the Australians' premier fast bowler, did not bowl during the last day after a bad attack of asthma.

Australians 428-6 dec (N. C. O'Neill 104*, W. M. Lawry 100, R. B. Simpson 65)
and 202-5 dec (R. N. Harvey 66);
Kent 340-6 dec (M. C. Cowdrey 149, A. H. Phebey 59, S. E. Leary 51) and 284-6 (Cowdrey 121, Leary 60).

1966 – UNDERWOOD MATCHES COUNTY GREATS 1967

Underwood, although only 21, took over 100 wickets for the third time in four seasons, causing his county officials to rake through past records as he moved from distinction to distinction throughout the summer. Selected for two Tests, he was first in the country to reach 100 wickets and headed the national bowling averages, the first time this had been achieved by a Kent bowler since Colin Blythe did so in 1914. His total of 144 wickets for Kent was the highest since 1935 when "Tich" Freeman topped the 200 mark.

1967 – KENT v YORKSHIRE: SKILL REMAINS 1968

At Canterbury, August 9, 10, 11, 1967. Evans reappeared after retiring for eight years in place of Knott, who was playing for England. Moreover, Evans kept wicket superbly.

1970 – CHAMPIONSHIP CAPS MEMORABLE CENTENARY 1971

All's well that ends well – and for Kent 1970, their centenary year, was a memorable one. After being at the bottom of the County Championship table on July 1 they staged a wonderful recovery and in a thrilling finish to the summer captured the County Championship for the fifth time in their history, and for the first time since 1913. In addition, they were runners-up in the John Player (Sunday) League and the Second Eleven won their championship title for the second successive year. All this in a season when there were demanding Test calls on the county side made it a splendid performance.

Indeed, after the very unsteady start to the season the county's all-round achievement bordered almost on the miraculous. Kent felt that to stand a chance for the Championship title they had to achieve a good start before the Test series began. That was not to be. In those vital first seven Championship matches they recorded only one victory and were fourth from bottom in the table with only 13 batting bonus points.

1972 – KENT v MIDDLESEX (JOHN PLAYER LEAGUE): TWO TOO MANY

1973

At Folkestone, June 11, 1972. Middlesex won by one run. This was surely the most sensational finish ever in the competition. Kent having reached 126 for six in the 37th over, needing two to win, lost their last four wickets at that same score. Nicholls, first to go, had looked certain to guide Kent to victory and Julien, Asif, who got up from his sick bed to bat, and Underwood followed, victory coming to Middlesex off the third ball of the last over. Middlesex had lost half their side for 48 in the 20th over, but a seventh-wicket stand of 54 in nine overs between Murray and Jones retrieved the situation. Kent faltered after a sound start, but Ealham hit 24 out of 33 added for the fourth wicket in six overs to make victory look a certainty. Then came the dramatic finale which proved once again that a game is never lost until it is won.

Middlesex 127 (39.2 overs) (J. T. Murray 40; B. D. Julien 3-20);

Kent 126 (39.3 overs) (D. Nicholls 54; M. W. W. Selvey 3-25, C. J. R. Black 3-30).

1973 – SUSSEX v KENT: MOPPING UP
1974

At Hastings, May 2, 3, 4, 1973. Kent won by an innings and 161 runs. Kent extracted full revenge for their defeat on the same ground the previous July, when they were dismissed for 54, the lowest total by any side in 1972. A wet morning followed by sunshine made just the right conditions for bowlers on Thursday when Graham (five for 13) and Underwood (five for 43) shot out Sussex for 67, and next day heavy thunderstorms preceded some "flashes of lightning" bowling by Underwood as he made the ball turn and lift. While Sussex remained interested onlookers, the Kent players waded barefooted helping the fire brigade to mop up and miraculously play got under way at four o'clock. Twenty overs and one ball later the game was all over, Underwood having taken eight for nine in 10.1 overs as Sussex were demolished for 54. Underwood's figures for the match were 13 for 52. All of which must have been disappointing for Greig in his first Championship match as captain of Sussex.

Kent 282-5 dec (M. H. Denness 106*, B. W. Luckhurst 52);

Sussex 67 (J. N. Graham 5-13, D. L. Underwood 5-43)

and 54 (Underwood 8-9).

1976 – KENT v GLOUCESTERSHIRE (JOHN PLAYER LEAGUE):
SAFE LANDING
1977

At Maidstone, September 5, 1976. Kent won by 123 runs. Kent took the Gloucestershire attack apart right from the start as Woolmer and Tavaré hit 75 in 11 overs. Then Asif raced to 50 off 39 balls and with Denness added 150. Asif reached his century in 82 minutes with three sixes and six fours and Denness reached his 50 in 63 minutes. Gloucestershire began at four an over, needing seven an over, and once Sadiq was third out at 80 the match was over. The interest of Kent and their fans was then centred on the scores from their two main rivals' games and Kent were back in the pavilion in time to see Somerset's pulsating defeat at Cardiff, which made them champions. Soon after the close the helicopter bearing the trophy landed on the square to the delight of most of the 8,000 crowd who had remained to see the presentation.

Kent 278-5 (40 overs) (Asif Iqbal 106, M. H. Denness 56, R. A. Woolmer 46);
Gloucestershire 155-9 (40 overs) (Sadiq Mohammad 42; D. L. Underwood 3-22).

1985 – Injury Forces Knott To Retire
Dudley Moore, 1986

Alan Knott, with little chance to reveal his batting talents, still kept wicket so consistently and well that he was very close to an England recall. Towards the end of the summer, however, his ankle injury manifested itself again, and it was a sad day when, on the penultimate afternoon of the season, he announced his retirement. The club duly acknowledged his "outstanding services to the county and to English cricket", adding that "his ability and professionalism have ranked him among the truly great players in the history of the game".

1998 – KENT v DURHAM (AXA League): SIX IN A ROW
1999

At Canterbury, May 25, 1998. Kent won by 100 runs. Wells and Hooper cut the Durham attack to pieces with a stand of 208 in 24 overs, and Kent raced to their highest-ever 40-over total and the best score in the League all season. Wells achieved a version of one of cricket's most cherished feats by hitting six successive sixes. He drove the last ball of an over from Phillips against the players' balcony. Then, after Hooper took a single from Lewis's first ball, Wells hit the next five over the short boundary by the lime tree. Lewis was immediately taken off, leaving his one over (1-0-31-0) as the most expensive single-over spell in League history. Wells hit eight sixes in all. Meanwhile, Hooper broke the bowlers' hearts and, when 16, the window of a spectator's Volvo. Ealham finished off the innings with an unbeaten 54 off 30 balls. Durham's response was game but unavailing.

Kent 319-4 (40 overs) (A. P. Wells 118, C. L. Hooper 100);
Durham 219 (38.3 overs) (P. D. Collingwood 62; D. W. Headley 4-36, M. V. Fleming 3-37).

2004 – WORCESTERSHIRE v KENT: POISONED ATMOSPHERE
2005

At Worcester, June 9, 10, 11, 12, 2004. Fielding on the second morning, Tredwell and O'Brien had to protect themselves from a swarm of bees. The real venom, though, was in the Kent dressing-room: the opening day saw the start of a row that continued all season. Ed Smith, acting-captain for the injured Fulton, received so little support from his senior team-mates (especially Symonds) that Fulton attempted to take charge as a substitute, until the umpires told him this was against the Laws [2.3: a substitute shall not act as captain]. The internal argument ultimately led to the resignation of cricket committee chairman Mike Denness and Smith's departure to Middlesex.

THE END OF THE LIME Mark Pennell, 2005

In the early hours of January 8, 2005, there were widespread storms across Britain, and summer afternoons at Canterbury felt very distant. But at some time in the darkness, Kent's most regular and durable spectator suddenly gave way. The cause of death was technically the howling gale and *ganoderma*, a heartwood fungus. In truth, it was just old age.

No one was about on such a night, and it was dawn before the body was discovered. "To be honest I'd been out in the middle sweeping the square for about 20 minutes when I looked up and thought 'Something's missing,'" said the head groundsman, Mike Grantham.

It was the lime tree, which had stood guard on the Old Dover Road boundary – at wide midwicket or deep backward point – ever since Kent first used the St Lawrence ground in 1847. It was already semi-mature then. The St Lawrence lime was inside the boundary, and the Laws of Cricket had to be adapted to allow for it, leading to the local rule that hitting the tree is neither six nor out, but four.

2011 – KENT v GLAMORGAN: IN A DIFFERING LIGHT 2012

At Canterbury, September 12, 13, 14, 15, 2011 (day/night). Glamorgan won by eight wickets. With little riding on the match, the ECB decided late on to turn it into a trial of how some believe Test cricket will look in the near future, with afternoon starts, floodlights and – for the first time in first-class cricket in Britain – pink balls. The experiment, which shifted play to between two and nine o'clock, was not a resounding success: spectators generally voted with their feet, so that only a few hundred remained for the final session each day, while some of Kent's players – upset by a lack of consultation beforehand – decried the balls. Jones complained of struggling to see them in the gloaming. "I was glad there wasn't anyone who was seriously quick playing – especially during the twilight period," he said. Stevens claimed fielding was "dangerous". There were other problems. Given so little warning, Tiflex – the official suppliers for the second division – had made only 12 balls, so umpires were instructed not to change them unless essential. The stitching split on the first one, but it was not replaced. For the second innings, Kookaburras – the balls for the MCC v Champion County experiments in Abu Dhabi – were used. MCC's John Stephenson, a leading proponent of pink balls, gave the trial a cautious welcome: "From what I've seen, this form of the game is viable. Four-day cricket under lights, with a pink ball, white clothing – it works."

Kent 237 (J. L. Denly 69; J. C. Glover 4-49)

and 312 (G. O. Jones 79, Azhar Mahmood 70, S. A. Northeast 51; D. A. Cosker 4-106);

Glamorgan 423-9 dec (S. J. Walters 147, M. A. Wallace 57, G. P. Rees 54)

and 129-2 (A. N. Petersen 70*).

666

LANCASHIRE

[1951 edition] *FIFTY YEARS OF LANCASHIRE CRICKET by Neville Cardus:*

It is commonly thought that Lancashire cricket has always expressed North-country dourness and parsimony. This is an error.

1875 – LANCASHIRE v YORKSHIRE: UNBEATEN FEAT — 1876

At Old Trafford, June 24, 25, 26, 1875. Mr A. N. Hornby and Barlow accomplished a big thing in batting in this match. They commenced Lancashire's second innings, their side requiring 146 to win; they made the runs without either losing his wicket, and so Lancashire won by ten wickets. The bowlers against them were Hill, Emmett, Clayton, Ulyett, and Lockwood, but the two batsmen beat the five bowlers so decisively, that they made 148 runs from 72 overs (less two balls), and left their sticks up unconquered, thus accomplishing a batting feat unequalled in the history of county cricket. Mr Hornby's 78 was made by three fours, ten threes, eight twos, and 20 singles; and Barlow's 50 by one five, three fours, four threes, three twos, and 15 singles.

Yorkshire 83 (Mr A. Appleby 5-20)
and 216 (G. Ulyett 50; W. McIntyre 5-96, Appleby 4-73);
Lancashire 154 (A. Hill 4-34)
and 148-0 (Mr A. N. Hornby 78*, R. G. Barlow 50*).

1878 – LANCASHIRE v GLOUCESTERSHIRE: CROWDS OVERFLOW — 1879

At Old Trafford, July 25, 26, 27, 1878. This was the first Lancashire v Gloucestershire match played, and the public interest created in Lancashire by this first visit of the famous West Country team to Old Trafford was so great, that on the third day it resulted in the largest attendance ever seen at a cricket match on the O. T. ground. One who ought to know all about it stated, "Quite 16,000 were present on the Saturday; they were obliged to have four entrances that day, and the people came in such shoals that passing through the turnstiles was difficult; even with the four entrances they could not be admitted fast enough, and it is supposed that quite 2,000 went round, and got over the boards on to the ground without payment." It was estimated that more than 28,000 people witnessed the match.

Lancashire 89 (R. G. Barlow 40; Mr R. F. Miles 7-38)
and 262 (Mr A. N. Hornby 100, Mr W. S. Patterson 50; Miles 5-16);
Gloucestershire 116 (Mr A. G. Steel 5-59, W. McIntyre 4-44)
and 125-5 (Mr W. G. Grace 58*; Steel 4-55).

1881 – LANCASHIRE v CAMBRIDGE UNIVERSITY: LANDMARK OCCASION

1882

At Liverpool, June 13, 14, 1881. This match will be memorable for several reasons. It was the opening match of the splendid new ground of the Liverpool Club at Aigburth. It was the match in which the Lancashire eleven suffered their one defeat in 1881; the only match in 1881 in which they had to follow their innings; and the match in which the lowest number were totalled for an innings by the county team in 1881.

Cambridge University 187 (Mr G. B. Studd 106*; A. Watson 4-56) **and 38-3**;
Lancashire 71 (Mr A. G. Steel 6-22) **and 153** (Steel 5-69).

Little Wonder No. 104

A British Standard cricket ball. In 1981, for the first time, cricket balls used in first-class matches have to meet certain specifications. These have been drawn up with the support of the Cricket Council and the British Sports and Allied Industries Federation, and cover weight, circumference, hardness, height of bounce, width of seam, height of external stitching and resistance to wear. The ball, to be known as the BS 5993, will be in four categories – for use by men, women and juniors, and in first-class cricket (Grade 1).

1883 – SURREY v LANCASHIRE: THROWN INTO CONFUSION

1884

At Kennington Oval, August 23, 24, 25, 1883. This match was productive of some very remarkable cricket, and Crossland's success with the ball in the first innings of Surrey gave rise to another disgraceful exhibition of feeling similar to that displayed in the corresponding match of the previous year. Crossland took seven wickets, all bowled, for only 34 runs. "Well thrown," and "take him off," was shouted from all parts of the ground during the innings, and at its conclusion a large number of the spectators rushed on to the ground, and as Crossland walked quietly to the players' room he was greeted with hissing and hooting, mingled – it is pleasing to record – with a fair amount of cheering. This demonstration nearly resulted in the abandonment of the match, but after an interval of about half an hour Barlow and Mr Taylor appeared to commence the second innings of Lancashire.

Lancashire 75 (Mr C. E. Horner 6-36, E. D. Barratt 4-32)
and 240 (R. G. Barlow 88, Mr F. Taylor 83; Barratt 5-92);
Surrey 82 (J. Crossland 7-34)
and 234-7 (Mr K. J. Key 60*, Mr W. E. Roller 55*; A. Watson 4-44).

1885 – LANCASHIRE v KENT: RETURN DECLINED   1886

At Old Trafford, Manchester, May 28, 29, 30, 1885. The contest may be regarded as marking a chapter in the history of cricket, inasmuch as it was the presence of Crossland and Nash in the Lancashire team that induced Lord Harris, and afterwards the Kent executive, to take the decisive steps on the question of unfair bowling which brought about an estrangement between the counties for the remainder of the season, and induced the Kent County Cricket Club to decline to play the return match arranged to commence on the 20th of August at Tonbridge.

FEARSOME AND CONTROVERSIAL   Obituary, 1904

JOHN CROSSLAND. The death on September 26th of Crossland – at one time the most talked-of bowler in England – recalled a very lively controversy that disturbed the cricket world in the eighties. His pace was tremendous, and even the best batsmen rather dreaded him. Outside Lancashire, however, his delivery was generally condemned, the majority of experts having no hesitation in describing him as a rank thrower. So far as Crossland was concerned the quarrel suddenly came to an end on a different issue altogether, it being ruled by the MCC – after full inquiry – that by living in Notts during the winter he had broken his qualification, and had no longer any right to play for Lancashire. This ended his career in first-class cricket, but he continued to play in small matches, and only gave up the game about four years ago.

1895 – MACLAREN OVERTAKES GRACE   1896

Before anything else which occurred in connection with Lancashire cricket last summer, the season of 1895 will be remembered for the great feat accomplished down at Taunton in the middle of July, when A. C. MacLaren put together his famous innings of 424, and the Lancashire score reached the tremendous total of 801. The county team as a whole played wonderfully well, showing in some respects better form than for several seasons past, but in years to come it will not be the victories over Yorkshire and Surrey, or the dismissal of Notts for 35, that people will recall when the cricket of 1895 is under discussion, but the facts that during the summer Lancashire put together a bigger score than had ever before been made in the history of county cricket, and that A. C. MacLaren succeeded in beating W. G. Grace's far-famed 344, which had stood as the record innings in first-class cricket for 19 years. This personal triumph of the young batsman was especially remarkable, inasmuch as for five weeks in the middle of the season he took no part in first-class matches. Returning from Australia somewhat later than the majority of Mr Stoddart's famous band of cricketers, he did not arrive in time to participate in the first of the Lancashire engagements, and, after he had played against Leicestershire and Yorkshire without particular success, there came the announcement that Mr MacLaren had accepted a mastership in a preparatory school at Harrow, and would be unable to render Lancashire further assistance until the vacation. The three concluding fixtures were especially notable from the fact that Mr MacLaren played an innings of over a hundred in each one of them, the feat being invested with particular merit from the fact that, while at Manchester, against Notts, the wicket was easy, at Lord's, against Middlesex, it was soft, and at the Aylestone Road Ground, against Leicestershire, it was fiery.

1903 – Barnes Best Bowler But Temperament Questionable   1904

[S. F.] Barnes stood out head and shoulders above his colleagues, and was the only bowler in the team who could be described as first-class. He took 131 wickets in county matches for considerably less than 18 runs each, and got through an enormous amount of work, sending down 1,023 overs. He varied a great deal in form, the difference between his best days and his worst being almost immeasurable, but when he was really himself there could be no two opinions as to his quality. Indeed, some good judges went so far as to say that on his good days he was the most difficult right-handed bowler in England. He enjoyed his greatest success against Essex at Leyton, taking in that match 14 wickets with a wonderful average. His strength lay in his quickness off the pitch and his power of making the ball go away abruptly with his arm. Before the summer was over, Barnes's connection with the Lancashire Club came to an end. He declined to sign the usual form promising his services for 1904, and in consequence of this step on his part he was left out of the team in the last match. It was stated that he had accepted an offer from the Church Club, and would return to the Lancashire League cricket which first brought him under the notice of the county authorities. His defection caused quite a sensation, and was commented on in rather bitter terms. It is to be hoped that Lancashire will discover some bowler competent to fill his place, but at present, so far as we know, there is no sign of such a prize. Temperament is a great thing in a cricketer, and in this respect Barnes has always been deficient.

1912 – A Good Season On Balance   1913

Though only fourth in the Championship, Lancashire can look back upon the season of 1912 with considerable satisfaction. They beat the Australians twice; they were the only county to beat the South Africans and, thanks to their share of profits from Test matches, they got through the appallingly wet summer with a balance on the right side.

1912 – LANCASHIRE v AUSTRALIANS: public stay away   1913

At Manchester, June 13, 14, 15, 1912. Winning by 24 runs, Lancashire gained their first victory over an Australian team since the season of 1888. The public, as a

protest against the shilling charge for admission, boycotted the match so severely
that scarcely 300 people witnessed Lancashire's victory.

Lancashire 146 (T. J. Matthews 5-48)
and 188 (H. Makepeace 52);
Australians 177 (C. G. Macartney 80; J. S. Heap 4-41, H. Dean 4-63) **and 133** (Heap 5-26).

1913 – HORNBY DERAILS HARMONY OF CLUB   1914

President: Mr A. N. HORNBY. Captain: Mr A. H. HORNBY.

The most unsuccessful season that Lancashire have had for many years ended in
a domestic storm. While the last match – the return with Essex – was in progress
at Old Trafford, Mr A. H. Hornby, in an interview in the *Manchester Guardian*,
expressed great dissatisfaction at the way in which the affairs of the club were
being conducted, taking particular exception to the proposal, contemplated at
that time, of reducing the fixture list in 1914. The committee did not hesitate to
express their opinion that they thought Mr Hornby might well have consulted
them privately instead of bringing the matter before the public through the
medium of the press, and it certainly struck the outsider that the various questions in dispute might easily have been put right without the outside world
knowing that there had been any friction. Special meetings were held and a
special body appointed to go into the whole question and make such suggestions to the committee as they thought fit for the future guidance of the club.
On the whole it was perhaps best that the facts should have come out. There was
nothing to conceal, and no discredit attached to anyone concerned, the points
raised being only details of management. The air was cleared, and the committee
found their financial position strengthened at once, Lord Derby, Lord Ellesmere,
Mr Edward Hulton and others promising substantial subscriptions for three
years to come.

1925 – LANCASHIRE v YORKSHIRE: GRIM FARE   1926

At Manchester, May 30, June 1, 2, 1925. Tedious cricket marked the Bank Holiday
match at Old Trafford. Yorkshire, after being 33 behind on the first innings, led by
153 with four wickets to fall when the game was left drawn. Cold weather, and a
shower that delayed the start affected the Saturday crowd, but over 35,000 people
watched the play on the Monday, and the full attendance for the three days
reached about 60,000.

Yorkshire 232 (W. Rhodes 59, P. Holmes 51; C. H. Parkin 4-63)
and 186-6 (Rhodes 54);
Lancashire 265 (C. Hallows 111*; R. Kilner 4-67).

1926 – MCDONALD INSPIRES CHAMPIONSHIP SUCCESS   Neville Cardus, 1927

For the first time since 1904 Lancashire are champion county. Their success was popular throughout the country, partly because cricketers felt that the best interests of the game would be served by a change, at long last, in the leadership. Of their last 11 matches Lancashire won nine outright; the other two were won on the first innings, and one of these was against Yorkshire. At Old Trafford, on August Bank Holiday, the biggest crowd that has ever witnessed a single day's cricket in this country [38,600] saw Lancashire make 500 against Yorkshire.

It was McDonald, more than any other one player in the eleven, who won the matches at the season's end, and so took advantage of those chances which came Lancashire's way – partly as a result of the ultra-cautiousness which hindered Yorkshire. McDonald was rarely as fast as he was in 1921. None the less, he was far faster than the average English fast bowler. His temperament seemed to thrive on any situation which gave his side a sporting chance; he won more than one game against time in a manner that did credit both to his imagination and opportunism. He is a bowler of varying moods – and varying paces. But, at a pinch, he can achieve true greatness, both of technique and temperament.

The batting was more reliable all-round than in recent Lancashire sides. Ernest Tyldesley had a wonderful summer. At one stage his consistency recalled the C. B. Fry of 1901. In nine innings from June 26, Tyldesley scored 1,128 runs with an average of 141. He scored seven centuries in consecutive matches – and four in successive innings. He was, at his best, as stylish as he was prolific. A big innings by Tyldesley will exhibit every stroke excepting the cut, all done with infinite grace and mastery. He had bad luck to play in only one of the Test matches.

1934 – CONSISTENT PERFORMERS   Hubert Preston, 1935

After a lapse of three years Lancashire succeeded Yorkshire as champions, just as they did in 1926. Then consistent form enabled them to hold first place for three years, and in 1930 they followed Nottinghamshire as holders of chief honours. So in the course of nine seasons they have secured the premier position five times.

1937 – COMMITTEE CENSURES SLOW PLAY   1938

There were days in 1937 when Lancashire played splendid cricket and were irresistible, but at other times the side sank into inefficiency so that their season provided a series of extraordinary contrasts. Lancashire failed to win any of their first six engagements and the team was so lacking in enterprise that, following total eclipse by Yorkshire in the Whitsuntide match at Old Trafford, the committee issued a reprimand against the policy of stonewalling. This official move made some of the players realise that places in the eleven would be earned not so much by figures in the scoring book as by deeds on the field, and it is to the credit of the men that they changed their methods as was desired.

The committee move had an effect: in the first innings Lancashire scored 106 off 80.5 overs against Yorkshire and in the second 197 off 123.1. A month later they made 495-8 dec off 129 overs against Essex.

1950 – SOMERSET v LANCASHIRE: STATHAM SHINES   1951

At Bath, July 1, 3, 4, 1950. Lancashire won by an innings and 60 runs. A little moisture on the pitch contributed to Somerset's early setback, but this detracted little from the merit of a fine performance by Statham, a 20-year-old pace bowler and newcomer to county cricket. His skill and determination in attacking the stumps brought him the first five wickets for five runs, with Somerset's total only 11. Only Robinson and Stephenson reached double figures. Lancashire passed Somerset's score without loss, and, after splendid batting by Washbrook and Edrich, they finished 198 ahead with five wickets in hand. Rain prevented further play until the third day, when Lancashire declared, and Somerset were easily mastered by Hilton and Tattersall.

Somerset 72 (J. B. Statham 5-18) and 138 (R. Tattersall 4-45, M. J. Hilton 4-50);
Lancashire 270-5 dec (C. Washbrook 91, G. A. Edrich 83).

1960 – LANCASHIRE v YORKSHIRE ROSES DOUBLE AT LAST   1961

At Manchester, July 30, August 1, 2, 1960. Lancashire won by two wickets, taking 12 points and so completed their first Roses double since 1893. They achieved victory in a tense finish when Dyson turned the last ball of the match, sent down by Trueman, to the on boundary. Lancashire were set to make 78 in two hours. Sustained hostility from Trueman and Ryan made the task far from easy, and when Greenhough was bowled by the second ball of Trueman's last over, five runs were still needed. Two singles and two leg-byes led to the dramatic climax. During the three days 74,000 spectators saw the match.

Yorkshire 154 (D. B. Close 63; J. B. Statham 5-43, K. Higgs 4-48) and 149 (Statham 4-23);
Lancashire 226 (A. Wharton 83, R. W. Barber 71; F. S. Trueman 4-65) and 81-8 (M. Ryan 5-50).

1964 – OLD AND NEW GRIEVANCES EMERGE   1965

Hopes that Lancashire would celebrate their centenary year with a better season than the dismal ones of recent summers did not materialise; indeed, to the poor playing record there was added a note of discord, both on and off the field, which resulted in several prominent players not being re-engaged. This action, in turn, was followed by a special meeting of members which, by an overwhelming vote, expressed dissatisfaction at the running of the cricket affairs of the club.

Just for good measure, it seemed, in the centenary match at the end of August, an MCC team beat Lancashire, mainly because of the excellent cricket of former players of the county, Washbrook [aged 49], Ikin [46] and Tattersall [42], who showed all too clearly how Lancashire's standard of play had fallen.

In addition, the county lost the services of their secretary, Mr Geoffrey Howard, who took up a similar post with Surrey. He was succeeded by Mr Jack Wood, the secretary of Wigan Rugby League club.

The decision to dispense with certain players came after the club had called for a survey from the team manager, C. Washbrook, following complaints by other counties of the behaviour of some players, and of the manner in which Lancashire batted in the Gillette Cup semi-final against Warwickshire ["Both sides were heavily barracked by the crowd in the closing stages."]

After announcing their decision, the club issued a statement which said: "The committee have reviewed the performances of the team both on and off the field during the current season in conjunction with a special report which had been called for. A firm decision was taken not to re-engage P. Marner and G. Clayton on the grounds that their retention was not in the best interests of the playing staff or the club. In the case of J. Dyson, he will not be offered re-engagement terms because it is felt he is not now up to the playing standards required." It was also decided to dispense with the services as captain of K. Grieves, who returned to League cricket for 1965.

During the winter Lancashire made strenuous efforts to obtain an experienced new captain, for whom they advertised in *The Times*.

1968 – LANCASHIRE v YORKSHIRE: FAREWELL OVATIONS   1969

At Old Trafford, August 3, 4, 5, 1968. For Statham, who captured six for 34 in the first innings and one for 50 in the second, this was a nostalgic farewell to first-class cricket and on each and every day the big crowds gave him standing ovations as he entered and left the field.

1970 – CROWDS FLOCK TO WATCH DOUBLE-WINNERS   1971

Lancashire's successful defence of their John Player League title and their first success in the Gillette Cup Competition, bracketed with a rise to third place in the County Championship table, illustrated the progress made by Jack Bond and his men in 1970. Few sides could match Lancashire in limited-over matches. Beaten only twice by weather intervention in the John Player League and easy winners over Sussex in the Gillette Cup final, Lancashire justly claimed that they were an attractive team to watch. Crowd figures wherever the side went in the Sunday League proved the point. Over 30,000 crammed into Old Trafford for the final match of the season when Yorkshire were beaten and the Player Trophy retained. The official figures gave the crowd at 27,000, but several more thousands stormed into Old Trafford by devious means just before the gates were closed for the first time since 1948.

1971 – LANCASHIRE v GLOUCESTERSHIRE (GILLETTE CUP SEMI-FINAL):
LONGEST DAY   1972

At Manchester, July 28, 1971. Lancashire won by three wickets. This semi-final attracted a crowd officially returned at 23,520, with receipts of £9,738, and made Gillette Cup history by extending from 11am until 8.50pm, after an hour's delay through rain at lunchtime. Winning the toss, Gloucestershire were given a solid start by Green and Nicholls, who reached 57 before Green was run out. Nicholls played splendidly for 53 until he was second out at 87 when play reopened, and afterwards Procter dominated a well-paced Gloucestershire innings by hitting one six and nine fours in making 65 before being superbly caught behind the wicket.

Gloucestershire contained David Lloyd and Wood so well that Lancashire took 17 overs to raise the first 50 runs. Wood stayed and Pilling built well on a solid foundation, but Lancashire were in trouble when Mortimore dismissed Clive Lloyd and Engineer, and Davey accounted for Sullivan in a mid-innings slump. Play proceeded in gradually worsening light after 7.30pm. Bond and Simmons brought Lancashire back into the picture by adding 40 runs from seven overs for the seventh wicket, after Bond had opted to play on in light that was now murky to say the least.

When Mortimore bowled Simmons at 203, with 27 needed from the last six overs, Hughes joined Bond and put the issue beyond all doubt with a magnificent onslaught against Mortimore. He hit the off-spinner for 24 runs – two sixes, two fours and two twos – in the 56th over to make the scores level and amidst mounting tension, and with lights on in the pavilion Bond got the winning run off the fifth ball of the 57th over. Hughes was given the Man of the Match award and it was well past ten o'clock before the big crowd dispersed.

Gloucestershire 229-6 (60 overs) (M. J. Procter 65, R. B. Nicholls 53);
Lancashire 230-7 (56.5 overs) (B. Wood 50; J. B. Mortimore 3-81).

1972 – LANCASHIRE v WARWICKSHIRE (GILLETTE CUP FINAL):
BANKER LLOYD   1973

At Lord's, September 2, 1972. Lancashire won by four wickets, and so lifted the trophy for the third consecutive year under Jackie Bond's inspiring leadership. No one quarrelled with Basil D'Oliveira when he named Clive Lloyd the Man of the Match. Not only did the talented West Indies cricketer subdue Warwickshire when M. J. K. Smith decided to bat first – he bowled his 12 overs on the trot – but he played one of the finest innings imaginable, hitting his 126 off 42 overs in two and a half hours. Among his many wonderful strokes were three sixes and 14 fours. Few of the 25,000 onlookers, plus the untold number who were glued to their TV sets, will forget Lloyd's sparkling straight-drives which passed the fielders before they could move.

Warwickshire 234-9 (60 overs) (J. Whitehouse 68, A. I. Kallicharran 54, M. J. K. Smith 48);
Lancashire 235-6 (56.4 overs) (C. H. Lloyd 126).

Fielding circles. It was agreed to introduce, in the Benson and Hedges Cup limited-overs competition in 1981, an area inside which, at the moment of delivery and throughout the match, four fielders as well as the wicketkeeper and bowler must be. This was a move against the purely defensive field-placing common in one-day cricket. The area is one "bordered by two half-circles centred on each middle stump, each within a radius of 30 yards and joined by a parallel line on each side of the pitch".

Little Wonder No. 105

1982 – LANCASHIRE v WARWICKSHIRE: CONSTANT ACTION   1983

At Southport, July 28, 29, 30, 1982. Lancashire won by ten wickets. In one of the most remarkable matches in the history of the County Championship, Lancashire won with the utmost ease after Warwickshire had scored 523 for four declared on the opening day. Kallicharran, with his third double-century of the season, and Humpage, with a career-best 254, shared in a stand of 470 in 293 minutes, the biggest for the fourth wicket in English cricket, beating the 448 by Abel and Hayward for Surrey against Yorkshire at The Oval in 1899. It was the highest partnership for any Warwickshire wicket, beating Jameson and Kanhai's 465 against Gloucestershire at Edgbaston in 1974, was the ninth-highest stand ever, and the fourth-best in the Championship. Humpage's 13 sixes were the most by an Englishman in one innings. On the second day of this eventful match, Warwickshire manager David Brown became the first substitute to take a wicket in county cricket when he stood in for Small, who was standing by for England in the morning and was back in the match in the afternoon. Lancashire declared 109 behind after a century in 109 minutes from Fowler, and on the third day McFarlane had a career-best bowling performance to set up an astonishing victory for Lancashire, for whom Fowler hit a second century. Having hurt himself fielding on the opening day, Fowler batted with a runner on the second and third days.

Warwickshire 523-4 dec (G. W. Humpage 254, A. I. Kallicharran 230*) and 111 (L. L. McFarlane 6-59);
Lancashire 414-6 dec (G. Fowler 126, I. Cockbain 98, J. Abrahams 51*)
and 226-0 (Fowler 128*, D. Lloyd 88*).

1987 – LANCASHIRE v YORKSHIRE: FRAUGHT FINISH 1988

At Manchester, June 13, 14, 15, 1987. Drawn. Lancashire set Yorkshire a target of 320 in 79 overs, generous enough in view of the easy-paced pitch, but after Patterson had taken out the heart of the innings with three wickets – all lbw – in 14 balls, only Blakey stood between Lancashire and victory. Blakey, who batted all but the opening over, hit 14 fours, and the last man, Fletcher, stayed with him for 17.5 overs to make it the 11th successive Roses draw. Lancashire claimed that Fletcher had given a bat-pad catch off Simmons's bowling, an appeal turned down by umpire Evans, and Simmons later accused Fletcher of cheating. His public outburst led to a week's suspension imposed by the Lancashire committee.

Lancashire 402-3 dec (G. D. Mendis 155, G. Fowler 77, D. W. Varey 59) and 96-0 dec (Fowler 51*);

Yorkshire 179-1 dec (M. D. Moxon 88*, A. A. Metcalfe 78) and 223-9 (R. J. Blakey 124*)

1996 – SUCCESS DEPENDS ON SUPPORTERS' POINT OF VIEW Brian Bearshaw, 1997

A poll of Lancashire supporters on their impressions of the season would produce a mixed bag. For those who go for the one-day game and its quick cricket, this was a great year, with Lancashire striking the golden double of winning two Lord's finals for the second time. For the out-and-out traditionalist, the abject performance in the County Championship made this a wreck of a summer. In between, there are the loyalists who despair of winning the Championship but draw grudging comfort from the one-day successes. But there are four trophies on offer, and to win two of them – even the two easiest – twice in seven years is something of a triumph. Even the died-in-the-wools would have to admit 1996 was a thrilling, entertaining season.

1996 – LANCASHIRE v YORKSHIRE (BENSON AND HEDGES CUP SEMI-FINALS): ROSES NEW STYLE 1997

At Manchester, June 11, 12, 1996. Lancashire won by one wicket. The draw turned up the most resonant of all county fixtures in the heightened atmosphere of a semi-final, and the contest went to the last ball. It will stand as not only one of the great modern Roses matches but as a contender for any list of best-ever limited-overs matches. Lancashire won through to the final for the fifth time in seven years when their No. 11, Martin, drove the final ball of the 50th over bowled by White for the two runs that were needed. Chapple hit four off the first ball, and there was a wide and a single before Martin missed the fourth and fifth to set up the breathless finale. Martin, who was brought up in Yorkshire, had to beat a throw from Vaughan, born in Manchester. Like many features of this remarkable game, this would not have been possible in an old-fashioned Roses fixture.

Yorkshire 250-5 (50 overs) (M. G. Bevan 95*, R. J. Blakey 80*);

Lancashire 251-9 (50 overs) (W. K. Hegg 81, N. H. Fairbrother 59).

1996 – LANCASHIRE v DERBYSHIRE: TRIPLE-CENTURION LOSES   1997

At Manchester, July 18, 19, 20, 22, 1996. Derbyshire won by two wickets. Jason Gallian finished on the losing side after scoring 312, the highest innings ever played at Old Trafford in its 139 years. Only Percy Perrin of Essex, 92 years earlier, had ever scored a triple-century for a losing side in England – also against Derbyshire. Gallian's innings, the longest in Championship history, occupied 11 hours 10 minutes and 583 balls; he hit 33 fours and four sixes. He beat Bobby Simpson's 311 for Australia in the Old Trafford Test of 1964, and his score was the fourth-highest for Lancashire. It was not an innings that will be remembered for its glittering strokeplay, but Gallian's batting was almost entirely blameless – he gave just one hard chance, when he was past 200 – and he played every ball on its merits right from the start.

Lancashire 587-9 dec (J. E. R. Gallian 312, S. P. Titchard 96, J. P. Crawley 54)
and 174-3 dec (Crawley 97*);
Derbyshire 473-8 dec (C. J. Adams 119, K. M. Krikken 104, D. G. Cork 83*; G. Chapple 4-83)
and 289-8 (D. M. Jones 107, K. J. Barnett 92).

1998 – LANCASHIRE v SURREY: FLINTOFF DEMOLISHES TUDOR   1999

At Manchester, June 18, 19, 20, 21, 1998. Lancashire won by six wickets. This will go down in history as Flintoff's match, or perhaps just Flintoff's over. In a battle between two of English cricket's highest-rated young players, he crashed 34 in an over from his former England Under-19 team-mate Tudor. Since Tudor also bowled two no-balls, the over cost him 38, the most expensive in first-class history – excluding only the bizarre 77-run over at Christchurch in 1989-90, when Robert Vance was bowling deliberate no-balls to try to contrive a finish. It happened as Lancashire closed on their victory target of 250 in 53 overs. Flintoff hit 64444660; the first and fifth deliveries were no-balls. All the hits were on the leg side. Flintoff missed the last ball to lose his chance of passing Garry Sobers and Ravi Shastri's 36 off an over. He was out for 61 off 24 balls with Lancashire just short of victory. Yet Tudor had taken five for 43 in the first innings.

Surrey 146 (Wasim Akram 4-42) and 254-1 dec (N. Shahid 126*, I. J. Ward 81*);
Lancashire 151-7 dec (A. J. Tudor 5-43) and 250-4 (N. T. Wood 80*, J. P. Crawley 78, A. Flintoff 61).

1998 – LANCASHIRE v HAMPSHIRE (AXA LEAGUE): DOUBLE DELIGHT   1999

At Manchester, September 7, 1998. Lancashire won by 16 runs. Wasim Akram lifted a trophy as Lancashire captain for the second day running. Just over 24 hours after his team had romped home in the delayed NatWest final, Lancashire became the last winners of the Sunday League – on a Monday afternoon. It was their fourth title, equalling Kent's record, and they still had hopes of adding the Championship and winning a treble. However, Wasim's week was to take a more sensational turn; two days later, a Pakistani judge was to recommend he should be banned on suspicion of match-fixing. Excluding a washout, it was Lancashire's ninth successive League win at Old Trafford, and their 250th in all since the competition started.

Lancashire 202 (39.4 overs) (A. Flintoff 69; A. D. Mascarenhas 3-24, N. A. M. McLean 3-39);
Hampshire 186-7 (40 overs) (R. A. Smith 44, W. S. Kendall 44; P. J. Martin 3-41).

2007 – SURREY v LANCASHIRE: HEROIC FAILURE   2008

At The Oval, September 19, 20, 21, 22, 2007. Surrey won by 24 runs. In a thrilling end to the season, Lancashire fell just 25 runs short of their first outright Championship for 73 years. As the last round began, they were six points clear, but crucially Sussex, their nearest rivals, had won by the time Lancashire's assault on a mountainous target of 489 neared its climax. Eventually, in fading light just after 6pm, Cork was bowled by off-spinner Murtaza Hussain to send Lancashire into despair and Hove into ecstasy. "I've never seen a changing-room like it in my life," lamented Chilton, the Lancashire captain. "The lads are just broken; we can't believe it." It had been a heroic effort: Newby, the No. 10, was the only batsman dismissed for less than 26. Laxman's run-a-ball 100, a superb 79 from Law and several other solid contributions brought victory tantalisingly close.

Surrey 427-9 dec (M. R. Ramprakash 196, J. G. E. Benning 51; S. I. Mahmood 4-93)
and 295-5 dec (Ramprakash 130*);
Lancashire 234 (V. V. S. Laxman 53) and
464 (Laxman 100, S. G. Law 79; Murtaza Hussain 4-126).

2008 – FINAL RESTING-PLACE   Rev. Malcolm Lorimer, 2009

In August 2008, an unusual ceremony took place on the outfield at Old Trafford. Around 40 former Lancashire cricketers trooped on, and I led a short service of remembrance. It marked the end of an era, as the outfield was to be dug up and a new drainage system installed.

Over the years, many members and former players have requested that their ashes be scattered on the ground; as club chaplain, I started conducting services for their families and friends. I also keep a Book of Remembrance, and have entered over 130 names since 1988, though our former groundsman Peter Marron tells me there were some before.

The first we know of is England cricketer Cec Parkin, whose ashes were spread on the outfield before a Roses match in 1945. More recently Malcolm Hilton and Bob Berry, fellow spinners and close friends, were scattered at either end of the wicket.

There have been funny moments: when we placed the ashes of former groundsman Bert Flack and his wife on the square, Peter remarked: "That's the closest they've been for years!"

I will always remember one lady whose husband had been a member. As we were coming off the field, I said it must be a comfort that he was at a place he loved. "Yes," she said with some feeling. "He spent all his time here when he was alive, and he can spend the rest of it here now he's dead!"

2011 – WONDERLAND RECLAIMED AFTER 77-YEAR WAIT   Andy Wilson, 2012

Lancashire began the 2011 season with their smallest squad for decades, were widely tipped for relegation, and spent an uncomfortable part of an itinerant summer – in which all their home Championship cricket was played on outgrounds to allow the realigned square at Old Trafford to bed in – staring into a financial abyss. They ended it, after four absorbing, fluctuating and unforgettable early autumn days in Taunton, in wonderland: champions for the first time since 1950, when they shared the title with Surrey – but more importantly, outright winners for the first time since 1934. Their success was all the more satisfying as it was achieved by a team dominated by Lancastrians, just as Peter Eckersley's side had been 77 years earlier.

Even at the start of the last day, they were second favourites to Warwickshire, so much so that some long-suffering followers chose to stay at home rather than travel down the M5 to watch yet another near miss; others returned north at the end of day three – not so much fearing that Lancashire would fail to beat Somerset as certain that Warwickshire, ahead on points on the final morning, would steam-roller Hampshire.

But in fact Hampshire's fourth-wicket pair of Neil McKenzie and Michael Carberry batted through the morning session to frustrate Warwickshire at the Rose Bowl. Down in Somerset, though, history was beckoning. Lancashire captain Glen Chapple strapped up the hamstring that had troubled him intermittently throughout the season and flared up again on the first day in Taunton, to take two key victims in one of the quickest spells in his 20 years on the staff.

Hampshire did lose a couple of wickets in the afternoon but, as tea approached, it became clear they had pulled too far ahead for Warwickshire to win. Meanwhile Lancashire were also being seriously frustrated, by a Somerset team with whom their relationship was anything but cordial. Peter Trego scored a stubborn century, and shared a ninth-wicket stand of 95 with Murali Kartik. Within four overs of Trego's fall, however, Gemaal Hussain was run out by 36-year-old Gary Keedy's direct hit from backward point. "I've never done that before," he said.

That left a target of 211 in however few overs Somerset could get away with bowling in two hours and 21 minutes. It sounded tricky, but the force was with Lancashire now as their openers Paul Horton and Stephen Moore rattled up 131 inside 17 overs.

At 5.02pm there were cheers from the few hundred Lancastrians ringing the boundary as news came through from Southampton that Warwickshire had drawn.

Ten minutes or so after that, Steven Croft carved Craig Meschede through backward point for what was deemed the winning four, in forgivably chaotic circumstances. Croft leapt into the arms of Karl Brown, his partner in a third-wicket stand which was a fitting alliance between Blackpool and Atherton; these were two of the low-profile local lads who underpinned the success for which Lancashire had waited so long.

The other players sprinted out to the middle to begin celebrations that continued well into the winter. The previous night at Manchester City's Etihad Stadium, there was an indication of the latent support that remains for cricket in the North-West, as chants of "Lancashire" were heard during the Champions League match against Napoli. There were more at the other Old Trafford during Manchester United's Premier League game against Chelsea a few days later, and the cricketers were invited there to parade the Championship trophy on an official lap of honour before a fixture in October.

2012 – Hangover Follows As Magic Fades	Myles Hodgson, 2013

It was perhaps understandable that Lancashire should succumb to a hangover the season after celebrating their first outright Championship title in 77 years: like Yorkshire in 2002 and Nottinghamshire in 2006, the reigning champions suffered relegation. The blunt truth was that a squad which had delivered beyond the sum of its parts for one glorious summer struggled to recreate the magic. Lancashire had been widely written off before their unexpected triumph, and now their ability to strengthen a squad many regarded as already punching above their weight was compromised by the huge cost of redeveloping Old Trafford, which contributed to a £3.96m loss for 2011.

LEICESTERSHIRE

[1964 edition] *FOLLOWING LEICESTERSHIRE by Brian Chapman:*
If you scan tables, or your fancy is to browse upon title-winning statistics, the county whose badge is the golden running fox may not detain you long. They were always a county of character and characters. Their ups and downs match the rolling landscape of the Quorn, with perhaps more downs than ups.

1878 – Australians Made To Work For Victory	1879

Leicestershire played several matches last season; among them were two that require chronicling in *Wisden*. One was a match v Notts – wherein a bowler (Alfred Shaw) bowled 22 overs (less one ball) for seven runs and seven wickets. The other was a match wherein a batsman (Charles Bannerman) hit the first three-figure innings ever scored by an Australian in Old England; and it was a match wherein two of the

Leicestershire eleven (A. Sankey and John Wheeler) made 113 runs before their first wicket fell. A batting feat this against the Australians that stands alone in its success! The weather was exceptionally favourable, and the attendances extremely large, play on the first day being resumed after luncheon in the presence of about 12,000 spectators, and on the other days the assemblages were also great.

Leicestershire 193 (A. Sankey 70, John Wheeler *(of Lord's)* 60; F. R. Spofforth 5-60, T. W. Garrett 4-30) **and 145** (Wheeler 65; Spofforth 4-26); **Australians 130 and 210-3** (C. Bannerman 133).

1888 – LEICESTERSHIRE v AUSTRALIANS: TABLES TURNED   1889

At Leicester, July 5, 6, 1888. This was one of the sensational matches of the season. The Australians had won 11 and only lost three of their 17 fixtures; but now, with a good deal the worst of a bad wicket, the Colonial eleven came to grief. Warren hit capitally, and the two Leicestershire bowlers, helped by some more rain on the Tuesday night, won a fine match for their county by 20 runs. The Australian bowling was as good as ever, but the batting failed on the wretched ground, and the fielding was faulty. Leicestershire deserved and received a great deal of praise for their achievement, and they certainly played with wonderful spirit all through.

Leicestershire 119 (T. H. Warren 42; C. T. B. Turner 6-44) **and 50** (Turner 5-20, J. J. Ferris 4-27); **Australians 62** (Mr H. T. Arnall-Thompson 6-31, A. D. Pougher 4-31) **and 87** (Pougher 6-40).

1895 – PROFESSIONALS BROUGHT TO BOOK   1896

It was a matter of common knowledge that there was a lack of discipline among the professionals, and it is fair to assume that much of the ill-success attending the later efforts of the eleven can be attributed to this cause. The committee even went to the length of leaving one or two men out of matches. It is to be hoped the punishment, light as it was, will have taught the delinquents the error of their ways before another season opens; otherwise, even more drastic measures may have to be taken to prevent a recurrence of what was really a scandal.

1897 – LEICESTERSHIRE v SURREY: TWICE OUT FOR 35   1898

At Leicester, June 10, 1897. In meeting Surrey on the Aylestone Ground, Leicestershire fared no better than they had done at The Oval, the famous southern eleven winning for the second time in an innings with runs to spare. The match, which was played on a treacherous pitch after rain, was commenced and finished in one day, Leicestershire being out twice and Surrey once in the course of four hours and three quarters. It is not too much to say that while the conditions were equally bad for both, Surrey were able to suit themselves to the difficulties in vastly superior fashion and Leicestershire were simply outplayed. The home side went in first and were got rid of for 35. Against this Surrey made 164, and then, curiously enough, Richardson and Hayward, bowling unchanged as in the first innings dismissed Leicestershire a second time for precisely the same total as before – 35. Hayward bowled finely and took seven wickets for 43 runs, but, exceptional as was his success, it was quite overshadowed by that of Richardson, who sent back five batsmen for six runs in the early part of the day, and seven others for 14 towards the finish, securing in all 12 wickets for 20 runs.

Leicestershire 35 (T. Richardson 5-6, T. W. Hayward 5-23) **and 35** (Richardson 7-14); **Surrey 164** (S. Coe 4-47).

1906 – SPECIAL INVESTIGATION EXPOSES SERIOUS FLAWS IN TEAM   1907

Following upon several years of almost uninterrupted advancement, Leicestershire declined to such an extent that they finished last but one in the competition. The fall to such a humble place among the counties after securing the fifth position during the previous summer caused so much disappointment that a committee of inquiry was appointed. The conclusions which the committee arrived at after a full consideration of the report were – "slackness in the field, a lack of grit and determination on critical occasions, an absence of esprit de corps in the team, and neglect by players in certain instances to travel with the rest of the team overnight."

It was also considered that a second cause of failure was found in unreliable batting and increased weakness in the bowling, together with the limited number of players available for filling up vacancies in the team. The committee considered that a larger number of young players should be engaged upon the ground, and that a local coach should be engaged to supervise and manage the whole of the ground staff. That the ground available for practice should be extended and improved; that a scheme generally on the lines of the Kent Club be drawn up for the management of the groundstaff. Late in the autumn C. E. Richardson, the well-known umpire, was engaged as coach and general superintendent of the ground-staff for 1907.

1911 – LEICESTERSHIRE v YORKSHIRE: A RARE SUCCESS   1912

At Leicester, August 10, 11, 12, 1911. Nothing less likely than a victory for Leicestershire by an innings and 20 runs seemed in prospect when stumps were drawn on the first day, with the home side 16 behind with five wickets in hand. Shipman bowled splendidly, and Wood and Bowden by adding 87 gave their side the upper hand, while the lead obtained on the second morning proved a winning advantage as rain fell in torrents during lunch time, and on the Saturday the pitch was all against the batsmen. Yorkshire lost Rhodes and Denton for 27 on the

Friday evening, but the arrears of 40 did not look serious, and it was thought that the visitors' bowling would win the match on a pitch likely to become more treacherous. As it proved, King allowed the Yorkshiremen no chance of showing their skill in bowling on damaged turf, drying under a hot sun, as he took seven of the remaining eight wickets at a cost of five runs, the last six falling to him while no run was hit from his bowling. In this startling fashion King won the match and made the one break in Leicestershire's disastrous season [this was their only win].

Yorkshire 153 (W. Shipman 7-73) and 47 (J. H. King 8-17);
Leicestershire 220 (Mr C. J. B. Wood 60; M. W. Booth 4-45).

1925 – KING LAYS DOWN HIS CROWN   1926

John King, the oldest man playing county cricket [54], distinguished himself at Brighton by scoring the first hundred of the season, but he could not maintain that successful start. Deciding to retire, he was appointed to the list of umpires after an active career with Leicestershire lasting 30 years. The most efficient left-handed batsman ever to play for Leicestershire, and a slow left-arm bowler capable of dismissing any side cheaply on a damaged pitch, King leaves a vacancy very difficult to fill.

1929 – GLAMORGAN v LEICESTERSHIRE: GEARY CELEBRATES   1930

At Pontypridd, August 14, 15, 1929. An amazing bowling feat by George Geary, who on the day he was selected to play in the Fifth Test match took all ten Glamorgan wickets for 18 runs, enabled Leicestershire to gain a remarkable victory by 15 runs. Glamorgan when they commenced their second innings on Thursday needed only 84 to win, but Geary, making the ball turn sharply, proved almost unplayable, half the side being out for 19. Turnbull and Clay temporarily checked this success by putting on 36, but Geary soon regained the upper hand and dismissed the last four men at the cost of one run.

Leicestershire 102 (F. P. Ryan 5-38, Mr J. C. Clay 4-30) and 141 (Clay 5-63);
Glamorgan 160 (W. E. Bates 70; G. Geary 6-78, W. E. Astill 4-56) and 68 (Geary 10-18).

1933 – STANDING ALONE IN THE DEPTHS   1934

Leicestershire experienced not only their worst season from a playing point of view since the war, but since they were promoted to first-class rank in 1895. In 1898 they were bracketed at the bottom with Somerset, and a similar fate overtook them in

1903, when they shared the unenviable distinction with Hampshire, but never before 1933 did they occupy the last place by themselves. They had to wait until July 21 before they gained their first victory over Glamorgan at Hinckley, and they followed this success three matches later by achieving a remarkable win over Sussex on a bad wicket at Ashby-de-la-Zouch; and in their August Bank holiday fixture with Northamptonshire they won in exciting fashion on the stroke of time. Against these three victories had to be set 15 defeats.

The Leicestershire county club suffered from lack of support at their home matches and, if the truth must be told, this was hardly surprising. For some reason or other the form shown by the Midland eleven entirely lacked distinction. They possessed no cricketer with a personality to exercise a revivifying influence and awaken interest among the general public, by whom their victories were received without any pronounced enthusiasm and their defeats with gloomy indifference. For a county with such traditions this proved a sad state of affairs.

1939 – POINTS IN SHORT SUPPLY
1940

The form of the side in 1938 suggested that Leicestershire, after several lean years, were on the way towards recovering former prestige, but one of the worst years in the history of the club ended with bottom place in the Championship table. For a long time it looked as though Leicestershire would go through the season without securing any points. As it happened they beat the inconsistent Hampshire side late in July, but the only other points obtained were for a lead on the first innings a week later, when Warwickshire won easily.

Sussex v Yorkshire. At Hove, August 28, 29, 30, 1985. Both Imran and Parker employed runners in their seventh-wicket partnership, while S. J. Storey, the Sussex coach, stood at square leg because umpire Cook was ill.

Little Wonder No. 106

1945 – CUT IN POWER LEADS TO UNEASY RETURN
1946

Their enclosure at Aylestone Road being taken over by Leicester Corporation for an extension of the electricity works, Leicestershire were forced to return to their old ground in Grace Road. This was a sad blow to the club, because of poor accommodation at Grace Road. In addition, the ground is now primarily a playing field for secondary schools, and Leicestershire could play there only in the school holidays, with the exception of one game in May.

1953 – CAPTAIN'S INSPIRATION LEADS TEAM TO BEST FINISH 1954

Surpassing even their excellent record of 1952, Leicestershire, under the inspiring captaincy of C. H. Palmer, achieved their highest position in the County Championship since entering the competition in 1895. During August, indeed, they succeeded in heading the table for the first time in their history, and eventually they finished level third with Lancashire, only 28 points behind the champions, Surrey. Palmer gained well-merited recognition by being chosen as manager and player for the MCC side touring West Indies during the winter.

1955 – LEICESTERSHIRE v SURREY: PALMED OFF 1956

At Leicestershire, May 21, 23, 24, 1955. Surrey won by seven wickets. Despite remarkable all-round cricket from Palmer, Surrey, although behind on first innings, won comfortably. On drying turf Leicestershire began well on the first day, but the left-arm spin of Lock brought about a collapse. Then Palmer, bowling medium-pace with great accuracy and bringing the ball back sharply off the seam, so severely troubled the Surrey batsmen that he took eight wickets before conceding a run. He hit the stumps seven times. Alec Bedser and Lock troubled Leicestershire in their second innings, but Tompkin and Palmer resisted strongly. Palmer, defending skilfully, stayed for four hours, but all his efforts went for nought, for in the last innings May, Clark and Constable carried Surrey to victory. Palmer conceded only one run in 13 overs in the second innings.

Leicestershire 114 (G. A. R. Lock 6-37)
and 165 (C. H. Palmer 64, M. Tompkin 50; A. V. Bedser 6-53, Lock 4-41);
Surrey 77 (Palmer 8-7) and 203-3 (P. B. H. May 84).

1955 – GENTLEMEN v PLAYERS: COUNTY DOUBLE 1956

At Lord's, July 13, 14, 15, 1955. Players won by 20 runs with five minutes to spare. Two Leicestershire cricketers, Tompkin and Palmer, carried off the batting honours, each scoring hundreds. Tompkin's hundred was the first by a Leicestershire professional in this fixture at Lord's since J. H. King made 104 and 109 not out in 1904, the only instance of two separate hundreds for the Players. Very sure and driving cleanly, Tompkin hit 16 fours in an attractive display and next day, when the Gentlemen were handicapped through the retirement of Cowdrey at 57, Palmer, with 24 fours, batted neatly and without mistake until near the end of his long and splendid innings.

Players 316 (M. Tompkin 115; J. J. Warr 4-54) and 220 (H. E. Dollery 82; G. Goonesena 6-83);
Gentlemen 336-8 dec (C. H. Palmer 154, D. J. Insole 72)
and 180 (J. P. Fellows-Smith 51).

1959 – LEICESTERSHIRE v GLAMORGAN: Hallam sparkles 1960

At Leicester, May 30, June 1, 2, 1959. Leicestershire won by eight wickets. Hallam, the Leicestershire opening batsman, completely dominated the match by making 367 for once out. He hit his second double-hundred within a fortnight, and then went on to score the fastest century so far this summer when Leicestershire were left just under three hours to get 269 to win. Hallam flayed the bowling to such an extent that he reached three figures in 71 minutes. He hit 27 fours during his first stay of five and a half hours and followed with one six and 12 fours in his fast hundred. Hallam's 210 not out was the highest post-war score by a Leicestershire player. In addition, he became the first Leicestershire batsman to obtain two double-hundreds in a season.

Glamorgan 322-9 dec (A. J. Watkins 132, B. Hedges 53; J. van Geloven 4-82)
and 271-7 dec (Watkins 59, L. N. Devereux 56, W. G. A. Parkhouse 50; van Geloven 4-47);
Leicestershire 325-5 dec (M. R. Hallam 210*)
and 271-2 (Hallam 157, W. Watson 59*).

1960 – Far From Elementary For Watson 1961

After being next to last in 1959, Leicestershire reached rock bottom last summer when only a win in their final match against Kent at Dover saved them from the humiliation of finishing with a smaller number of points than any side since 1939. Once again Watson had a heartbreaking task trying to instil resolution into the batting, but the story was the same throughout the season – matches lost through unreliable batting and far too ordinary bowling. Watson did his best and his efforts did not pass unrewarded, for he was appointed senior professional and vice-captain of the MCC team to visit New Zealand in the winter.

Besides the Dover match, Leicestershire won only one other Championship game, that against Somerset at Leicester in June, when victory by an innings gave the county their first success in 21 Championship fixtures. Leicestershire, who were beaten by an innings on seven occasions and suffered seven of their defeats in two days, reached their lowest ebb against Lancashire in May when they were dismissed for 37, their lowest total since the war. Admittedly, few sides could have done much against Statham on a helpful pitch, but Leicestershire subsequently were twice dismissed by Sussex for under 50.

1962 – Midlands Knock-Out Competition: Cricket's New Turn 1963

This competition, sponsored by Leicestershire at the instigation of Mr Michael Turner, their secretary, proved a success and provided guidance for the official tournament due to be inaugurated in 1963. The winners were Northamptonshire who beat Leicestershire in the final.

LEICESTERSHIRE v DERBYSHIRE

At Leicester, May 2, 1962. Leicestershire won by seven runs. An excellent match showed that one-day knock-out cricket, played in the right spirit and manner, could be most interesting. In this game each bowler was limited to 15 overs and captains had to use their leading men carefully. Leicestershire, put in to bat, began slowly, but steadily increased their scoring rate. Hallam and Wharton added 106 in 75 minutes and hard hitting came from Jayasinghe. Derbyshire started with a flourish, Lee and Carr making 110 in 73 minutes. Everything pointed to a Derbyshire victory at 193 for four, but a collapse followed and Leicestershire just succeeded. In just under seven hours, 493 runs were scored and 15 wickets fell.

Leicestershire 250-5 (65 overs) (M. R. Hallam 86, A. Wharton 50, S. Jayasinghe 49*);

Derbyshire 243 (61.4 overs) (D. B. Carr 62, C. Lee 50, W. F. Oates 46; J. van Geloven 3-60).

1964 – LEICESTERSHIRE v GLAMORGAN: A HORN SYMPHONY   1965

At Leicester, August 26. 27, 28, 1964. Leicestershire won by eight wickets. Their spell of 11 consecutive defeats ended with a decisive victory over Glamorgan, a success signalled by a symphony of car horns and an ovation from the crowd. The match yielded a total of 1.089 runs. Wheatley set Leicestershire to score 187 in two and a quarter hours, and Booth and Inman swept their county to victory with 15 minutes left, having scored 123 together in 77 minutes in an unbroken final stand.

Glamorgan 348-8 dec (A. Jones 147, A. R. Lewis 59, P. M. Walker 54; J. van Geloven 4-100)

and 195-8 dec (B. Hedges 70);

Leicestershire 357-5 dec (B. J. Booth 81, van Geloven 80, S. Jayasinghe 73, J. Birkenshaw 50*)

and 189-2 (C. C. Inman 75*, Booth 68*).

1967 – ONE STEP FROM UNLOCKING DOOR TO TITLE   1968

Whereas so many of Leicestershire's seasons have reached a welcome conclusion with the county having successfully struggled to assert their right to a first-class place, the year of 1967 yielded quite a different climax with an all-out challenge for the Championship. Yorkshire clinched matters in their final match, but Leicestershire finished equal second with Kent, their highest final placing since they entered the Championship in 1894.

The change in Leicestershire's fortunes since Lock took over the captaincy in 1966 has been quite extraordinary. In two seasons under his drive and his brilliance on the field they have ascended from 14th in 1965 to eighth in 1966, and now second. Not only did he take 128 wickets and score 603 in all matches, but he sustained a belief in the capacity to win.

1972 – At last a trophy for the cabinet 1973

For the first time Leicestershire won a major competition when they became the first holders of the new Benson and Hedges League Cup competition by mastering Yorkshire in the final before an almost full house at Lord's on July 22. At one time there was a distinct possibility that they would sweep all before them, but the wheels of fortune turned against them.

Twice Leicestershire failed by the narrow margin of three runs when they were dismissed from the Gillette Cup in the second round by Warwickshire, the eventual runners-up, and by Yorkshire in their last match of the John Player League at Leeds. Victory there would have made them the Sunday League champions, and their fate hung in the balance for a fortnight until Kent disposed of Worcestershire at Canterbury on September 10 and gained the top place which Leicestershire had held from June 18.

In the middle of June, Leicestershire also led the way in the County Championship, but although their colours were lowered in that competition only by Worcestershire and Sussex they had to be content with sixth position.

1975 – Going From Strength To Strength 1976

Leicestershire experienced the best season in their 96-year history. They won the County Championship for the first time in impressive style and displayed their art of the one-day game by lifting the Benson and Hedges Cup for the second time in four years. To add to this aura of success they were also runners-up in the Second Eleven competition and winners of the Under-25 tournament. No wonder that Illingworth, the best captain in the country, described these triumphs as a "magnificent team effort", but there could be no denying that as captain he was supreme, always leading by example.

In his first 15 innings in the County Championship he reached double figures every time, and only in the Gillette Cup did he fail with the bat. He fell three short of 1,000 runs in first-class matches – a milestone no one would have begrudged him, while his off-spin played an increasingly important part in Leicestershire's success as the season wore on. His 48 wickets in the Championship proved vital.

Dedication on the part of the players was an essential facet, and probably the whole summer of success was epitomised by the all-rounder, Balderstone, against Derbyshire.

1975 – DERBYSHIRE v LEICESTERSHIRE: Unique all-rounder 1976

At Chesterfield, September 13, 15, 16, 1975. Leicestershire won by 135 runs. Leicestershire entered this game needing seven points to become County champions for the first time, but success seemed far away on the first day when they were reduced to 77 for six on a pitch where the ball moved about and bounced unevenly. The tail recovered to take two batting points, McKenzie making top score on his last appearance for the county. On the second day Leicestershire took four bowling points, which made them champions. Balderstone, 51 not out overnight, hurried from the ground to play for Doncaster Rovers, the first time, it was thought, that anyone had played county cricket and League football on the same day; the next day he completed a remarkable century, and Leicestershire bowled out Derbyshire with five minutes to spare, having asked them to score 276 in three hours, 20 minutes.

Leicestershire 226 (P. E. Russell 4-51) **and 260-6 dec** (J. C. Balderstone 116, R. W. Tolchard 65*);
Derbyshire 211 (R. Illingworth 4-31, N. M. McVicker 4-56) **and 140** (Balderstone 3-28).

1977 – LEICESTERSHIRE v NORTHAMPTONSHIRE: BEST LEFT TILL LAST
1978

At Leicester, August 27, 29, 30, 1977. Drawn. A last-wicket stand of 228 by Illingworth and Higgs, easily the best for Leicestershire and only seven short of the Championship record, highlighted the match. Illingworth put Northamptonshire in and must have been satisfied by the outcome but disappointed by Leicestershire's reply – at one stage they were 45 for nine. He and Higgs remedied the situation. Both were dropped, but late in their innings, and they took full advantage of a pitch made easier by drying sun. Illingworth hit his only century of the season, but Higgs failed to score his first-ever county hundred, being run out when two short.

Northamptonshire 172 (K. Higgs 5-51) **and 278** (G. Cook 126; J. Birkenshaw 4-55);
Leicestershire 273 (R. Illingworth 119*, Higgs 98; Sarfraz Nawaz 4-27) **and 3-0**.

1986 – GOWER RELIEVED OF CAPTAINCY
Martin Johnson, 1987

Injuries, and a lack of balance in the bowling, produced a somewhat disappointing season for Leicestershire; one which culminated in the removal of David Gower as captain less than three months after his being replaced as England's captain. Gower had just announced that he was to miss the county's last three matches because of "mental and physical exhaustion" when Mr Mike Turner, the secretary-manager, recommended to the committee that he be given a "rest" from the position to which he was appointed at the end of the 1983 season. Gower's absences because of his England commitments had become increasingly detrimental, Turner felt, and there was evidence that he found it difficult to motivate himself adequately on his return to county cricket. In addition, Gower has a benefit in 1987, which could have proved a further distraction to his captaincy. Gower described the decision as "disappointing but understandable".

With Gower playing for England, the vice-captain, Peter Willey, out of domestic cricket until June following surgery on a continuing knee injury, and Nigel Briers suffering a fractured wrist at Hove in the same month, Leicestershire called on Paddy Clift as their fourth captain in July. And when Clift missed the later stages of the season through injury, Chris Balderstone became the fifth player to lead the county.

1987 – DeFreitas's Seasoning Goes From Bad To Worse   James Hunt, 1988

There can hardly have been a time when the county experienced so much media attention and speculation. Unhappily, much of it had little to do with playing performances, which at times were considerable, but with personal and personnel problems.

The most notable of some fine individual performances were the bowling of Jonathan Agnew and the batting of Nigel Briers. Agnew, bowling off a shorter run and with a wicked slower ball added to his armoury, became the first Leicestershire player since Jack Birkenshaw in 1968 to take 100 first-class wickets in a season; Briers, after a poor start in the middle order, moved up to open the innings and scored 806 runs in the final month and a half, totalling 1,257 first-class runs in all.

It was the county's England all-rounder, Phillip DeFreitas, who posed the greatest problem, following his emergence as a player of daunting potential on England's successful tour of Australia the previous winter. Indeed, it may have been his disappointment at failing to live up to the exacting standards set on that tour which led to the many rumours concerning his involvement in dressing-room rifts and conflict with the new captain, Peter Willey. However, the rumours would have remained no more than that but for a notorious incident in which DeFreitas poured a pot of salt over Agnew's lunch on the final day of the Championship match against Sussex late in June. Agnew responded by throwing DeFreitas's kit over the dressing-room balcony, and the all-rounder left the ground for two hours before returning and, in dramatic fashion, helping Leicestershire to their first Championship victory. For DeFreitas, the troubles did not end there. He lost his England place and was then dropped from the county's first team for disciplinary reasons. It was a sorry state of affairs, and in the end it was to prove too much for Willey. During the close season he resigned the captaincy.

Derbyshire v Lancashire. At Buxton, August 9, 11, 12, 1986. The first Championship match to contain Danes, Mortensen and Henriksen, on each side was spoiled by traditional Buxton weather, rain washing out the second day.

Little Wonder No. 107

1994 – LEICESTERSHIRE v NORTHAMPTONSHIRE: Coe outpaced   1995

At Leicester, April 28, 29, 30, 1994. Leicestershire won by ten wickets. Simmons stole the headlines with a sensational innings to mark his arrival as Leicestershire's overseas player. He became the first player to score a double-century on Championship debut and passed not only his own highest score, 202 for Trinidad, but the 80-year-old Leicestershire record, Sam Coe's 252 not out, also against Northamptonshire. Simmons faced 354 balls in seven and a half hours and hit 34 fours and four sixes. His stand of 253 with Nixon, who made an excellent three-hour century, ended nine short of the county's sixth-wicket record.

Leicestershire 482 (P. V. Simmons 261, P. A. Nixon 106, J. J. Whitaker 55) and 9-0;
Northamptonshire 224 (A. J. Lamb 70) and 266 (A. Fordham 102).

1995 – CRONJE INSPIRES YOUNG AND OLD — Chris Goddard, 1996

Hansie Cronje enjoyed his stay so much. After a poor start the South African captain, Parsons's brother-in-law, came good, easily heading the county averages with 1,301 runs at an average of 52.04, including four centuries, one a double against Somerset. Cronje, like Simmons, was a popular figure. His positive attitude and encouragement helped young batsman Ben Smith blossom towards the end of the season, when he received his cap. Even an old hand like Whitaker found inspiration in him.

1996 – LEICESTERSHIRE v MIDDLESEX: PARTY TIME — 1997

At Leicester, September 19, 20, 21, 22, 1996. Leicestershire won by an innings and 74 runs. Leicestershire clinched the second Championship title in their history over a pot of tea and ham sandwiches on the penultimate day of the season. The tea interval had just started when supporters tuning into radios heard that Surrey had forfeited their first innings against Worcestershire, and thus could not get the maximum points they needed to take the title. Within minutes, 3,000 jubilant fans had gathered under the players' balcony to enjoy the tea party to end all tea parties, culminating in Paul Nixon leading a conga of fans on to the field singing "Cricket's coming home".

Middlesex 190 (M. R. Ramprakash 71; A. D. Mullally 4-53) and 248 (Ramprakash 78; D. J. Millns 4-48);
Leicestershire 512 (P. V. Simmons 142*, J. J. Whitaker 89, Mullally 75; R. A. Fay 4-140).

1998 – LEICESTERSHIRE v NORTHAMPTONSHIRE: WHO DARES WINS
1999

At Leicester July 14, 15, 16, 17, 1998. Leicestershire won by four wickets. After Northamptonshire's tail had held out until after tea on the final day, and with the crowd drifting away, Leicestershire embarked on one of the most remarkable run-chases in Championship history. That they attempted to make 204 in 20 overs, even on a good pitch, was daring; that they won by four wickets with five balls to spare was outrageous. Leicestershire were inspired first by Wells, who thrashed 58 off 32 balls, and then by Lewis, whose unbeaten 71 contained four sixes and five fours, and came off 33 deliveries. Opening with Malcolm, and employing a normal field, Curran obviously felt the target was beyond his opponents. But Wells hit Malcolm for 16 – and out of the attack – before taking 18 off the second over from Rose. After three overs, the score was 47, and Northamptonshire had packed the boundary. Lewis maintained the momentum by cracking 27 off seven balls in the 15th and 16th overs; enraged, Rose threatened to run him out as he backed up, only to be restrained by Curran, his captain. Curran himself was later criticised for sticking with his fast bowlers. The outcome was poor reward for Northamptonshire's 19-year-old all-rounder, Swann. He had shown marvellous potential and had seemingly kept his side in the game with innings of 92 and 111, his maiden century, batting No. 8 both times. Smith and Habib gave Leicestershire the original advantage with a fourth-wicket stand of 249. Habib batted almost nine hours and hit 27 fours before being run out two short of a double-century.

Northamptonshire 322 (G. P. Swann 92, M. B. Loye 76; A. D. Mullally 5-62)
and 365 (Swann 111, J. P. Taylor 56; Mullally 4-48);
Leicestershire 484 (A. Habib 198, B. F. Smith 153; F. A. Rose 5-123)
and 204-6 (C. C. Lewis 71*, V. J. Wells 58).

2008 – MIDDLESEX v LEICESTERSHIRE: YOUNG MASTER OF LORD'S   2009

At Lord's, August 20, 21, 22, 23. Drawn. Leicestershire sniffed victory while Ackerman, who batted for 500 minutes, and Josh Cobb (who hit his maiden century in his fifth first-class innings) were putting on 270, just 14 short of Leicestershire's sixth-wicket record – and the highest by any team against Middlesex. Cobb, the son of the former Leicestershire batsman Russell, played the spinners well, and also pulled Murtagh for two sixes. Having celebrated his 18th birthday just three days before the match, he became the youngest batsman to hit a hundred at Lord's, and also Leicestershire's youngest century-maker; he was not long out of Oakham School.

Middlesex 367 (E. C. Joyce 101, A. J. Strauss 71, B. J. M. Scott 58; G. J-P. Kruger 4-95, C. W. Henderson 4-85)
and 185-4 (D. J. Malan 61*; Henderson 4-79);
Leicestershire 533 (H. D. Ackerman 194, J. J. Cobb 148*, M. A. G. Boyce 63; M. Kartik 4-104,
A. Richardson 4-104).

2010 – BITTER IN-FIGHTING AND RECORD DEFICIT   Paul Jones, 2011

Leicestershire was a club in danger of tearing itself apart in 2010. A backdrop of bitter internal unrest diverted attention from a substantial improvement in the Championship, where a young team, under the leadership of Matthew Hoggard for the first time, won seven matches and finished fourth in their division. Leicestershire's limited-overs form was wretched by comparison: they managed just two home wins, both in the CB40, four and a half months apart. It was their poor results in the Friends

Provident T20 which sparked the irrevocable split that led to chief executive David Smith, chairman Neil Davidson and senior coach Tim Boon all leaving the club.

On June 27, Leicestershire won a Twenty20 match at Headingley. But back at Grace Road, the club was heading for turmoil. Smith resigned next morning, citing interference in team selection by the board, an accusation which Davidson strenuously denied.

The crisis came to a head in late August. Boon and Hoggard put their names to a letter calling for Davidson to stand down, and were believed to have the support of all players, groundstaff, and several administrators. Davidson refused to go; he admitted intervening in cricketing matters, but not interfering in selection. He added that the relationship between him and Boon had become "unsustainable". Boon invoked a clause in his contract which allowed him to leave for a development role with the ECB. In October, Davidson did resign, declaring that Hoggard's refusal to withdraw his name from the August letter had made his own position "untenable".

Davidson's departure persuaded the petitioners and directors to reach a compromise and call off an SGM set for November. Three local businessmen were co-opted on to a revamped board, which pledged to put the club's finances back in order. But the true extent of the mess was laid bare in January 2011, when Leicestershire announced a record annual loss of £404,862.

MIDDLESEX

[1966 edition] Because of the new Greater London area, effective from April 1, slight changes would occur in the areas of Middlesex, Surrey and the minor county, Hertfordshire. Although no longer on the map as a county, Middlesex would continue to play under that title.

1869 – CAPITAL SUPPORT REQUIRED FOR CAPITAL'S CLUB   1870

The Middlesex County Club was formed in 1864. The county ground was at the north-east corner of the Islington Cattle Market, but now Middlesex is without a county ground; and unless the many influential admirers of the game resident in the county evince a more active monetary interest than they have of late, Middlesex will, in all probability, ere long be without a county club. If support general and generous was given by the many wealthy admirers of the game in the county, Middlesex would in due time have a ground (as they already have a club and an eleven) worthy of the Metropolitan County of Cricketing England.

1876 – MIDDLESEX v NOTTINGHAMSHIRE: DEATH OF BOX   1877

At Prince's, July 10, 11, 12, 1876. This match will long be remembered with a saddening interest, from its connection with the awfully sudden death of poor Tom

Box, who literally died in harness, the match being in full play on the third day when Box – engaged on his duties at the scoreboard – fell from his seat and died almost instantaneously. As a Sussex county player; as one of The Players of England against The Gentlemen; as a South v North Cricketer; as a member of Clarke's All-England Eleven; as a ground proprietor, and in other capacities, Box had passed a long and honourable lifetime on the cricket grounds of England, taking – and holding, for a long career – front rank as a wicketkeeper and batsman. He continued cricketing until he was an old man, and was playing his part when Death, with such fearful suddenness, cut him down.

1880 – MIDDLESEX v SURREY: UNNECESSARY SACRIFICE   1881

At Lord's, May 27, 28, 1880. When time was called on the second day, and the match declared drawn, expressions of regret were universal that this important and interesting match should be abandoned in order that the Saturday might be devoted to a contest of no interest whatever to cricketers. The object of the match between the Huntsmen and Jockeys, being a charitable one, was to be commended, but it is earnestly to be hoped that it will not be necessary to sacrifice the third day of a first-class match should the fixture find a place in any future programme of the Marylebone Club.

1894 – SUSSEX v MIDDLESEX: DANGEROUS PRACTICE   1895

At Brighton, June 14, 15, 16, 1894. The enjoyment of the match was considerably marred by a painful accident to Mr A. J. Webbe. The Middlesex captain, who on the first evening had scored 46 not out, was practising at the nets on the second morning, and a square-leg hit made by the next batsman passed through an old net, the ball striking him on the side of the face and causing a severe wound. An inch higher, the ball would have struck him on the temple, and there is no knowing what the consequences would have been. Even as it was he had to give up all idea of taking any further part in the match.

Middlesex review: This accident had the effect of drawing the attention of the public to the danger of the present system of practising on cricket grounds, and to the necessity of having longer and higher nets, if men will insist on hitting out to loosen their joints before the game commences. To close followers of the game this danger has been apparent for many years, and it is surprising that there have not been more accidents, not so much to the players as to the public, who will congregate in front of the men who are batting.

1899 – MIDDLESEX v AUSTRALIANS: DEADLY SLOW   1900

At Lord's, August 21, 22, 1899. Invincible at Lord's, the Australians won the match in wonderful style by an innings and 230 runs, the game coming to an end on the second afternoon. On the first day the game was marred by an unseemly demonstration on the part of the spectators, happily without precedent at Lord's ground. Resenting the extreme caution with which Darling and Iredale were batting, a section of the crowd forgot their manners, cheering ironically when a run was obtained, and at one point whistling the "Dead March in Saul". That his play was monotonous may be judged from the fact that Darling took three hours to get his first 88 runs. His explanation of this extreme slowness was that he was suffering from a painfully bruised heel.

Australians 445 (J. Darling 111, F. A. Iredale 111, V. T. Trumper 62; A. E. Trott 4-107);
Middlesex 105 (C. E. McLeod 7-57)
and 110 (E. Jones 7-40).

1903 – CHAMPIONSHIP SECURED IN STYLE

Middlesex, for the first time since the Championship assumed anything like its present proportions, came out at the top of the list. It should be remembered, however, that they stood first in 1866, and again in 1878.

SURREY v MIDDLESEX

At Kennington Oval, August 27, 28, 1903. Middlesex had only to escape defeat in this match – the last on their programme – to be sure of the Championship, but they did much more than that, playing fine cricket all-round and gaining a splendid victory by an innings and 94 runs. Rain on Monday evening placed Surrey at a considerable disadvantage. Their first innings proved a sensational affair, Holland and Hayward raising the score to 33 for the first wicket, and the whole side being out in an hour and a quarter for 57. Trott and Hearne – both in great form – were admirably supported by their colleagues. Trott three times disposed of two batsmen in consecutive overs. Thanks to Bush and Dowson, Surrey in their second innings had 100 on the board with seven wickets in hand, but then Wells carried all before him.

Middlesex 281 (Mr G. W. Beldam 112);
Surrey 57 (A. E. Trott 6-19, J. T. Hearne 4-26)
and 130 (Mr C. M. Wells 5-26).

1907 – MATCH ABANDONED BY HEEL MARK ...

One incident during the season gave rise to a great deal of discussion and not a little ill-feeling, the abandonment on July 23 of the match with Lancashire. A lot of rain fell on the first day and in such time as was available Lancashire scored 57 for one wicket. The following morning play was quite out of the question, and as events turned out it would have been much better if the umpires, who from time to time inspected the pitch, had early in the day declared cricket impracticable. As it was, the people who had paid for admission became very impatient at the long delay, and after stumps had at last been pulled up some of them went so far as to trample on the wicket. A lengthy consultation and discussion by the captains followed, and after six o'clock MacLaren handed the following official statement to the Press:

"Owing to the pitch having been deliberately torn up by the public, I, as captain of the Lancashire eleven, cannot see my way to continue the game, the groundman [sic] bearing me out that the wicket could not again be put right.
A. C. MACLAREN."

Opinion was very much divided as to the action MacLaren took, a letter of indignant protest being addressed to the *Field* by Mr R. D. Walker, the Middlesex president. The actual damage to the pitch did not, it was stated, amount to more than one rather deep heel-mark.

... OR UMBRELLA   E. (Patsy) Hendren, 1938

My first county match was one in which I did not get an innings! That was in 1907 against Lancashire at Lord's, the game being abandoned before lunch on the second day. There were naturally unusual circumstances. After heavy rain, a drizzle set in, but the crowd gathered in front of the Pavilion and clamoured for cricket. In the middle of all the rumpus, somebody got on to the pitch itself and, accidentally or not, stuck the ferrule of an umbrella into the turf. When this was discovered by Mr Archie MacLaren, the Lancashire captain, he refused to play, even if a fresh wicket were cut out. So there was nothing for it but to pack up and go home.

The scorecard, and Middlesex averages, in Wisden *1908 listed Hendren as his brother Denis.*

Little Wonder No. 108

Two places at once. Phil Watson, of the NCI club in Cambridge, played for their first and second teams – on the same afternoon [1986]. The two teams were playing on adjoining pitches on Parker's Piece, Cambridge, which enabled Watson to open the batting for NCI's first team in a Senior League game against Cherry Hinton, and then, when he was out for five after 15 overs, to field for the second team, who were one man short, in their Junior League match against Sotham. He later opened the batting for the second team and scored 46 in 25 overs before returning to field for the first team. Both teams lost.

1907 – MIDDLESEX v SOMERSET: Trott's double hat-trick   1908

At Lord's, May 20, 21, 22, 1907 Albert Trott rendered his benefit match memorable by an extraordinary bowling performance in the second innings of Somerset, dismissing Lewis, Poyntz, Woods, and Robson with successive balls, and later on disposing of Mordaunt, Wickham, and Bailey, also with successive balls. Thus he accomplished the unprecedented feat of performing the hat-trick twice in an innings. Thanks to Trott's bowling, Middlesex won by 166 runs.

Middlesex 286 (F. A. Tarrant 52; A. E. Lewis 4-88)
and 213 (Mr E. S. Litteljohn 52);
Somerset 236 (L. C. Braund 59, Mr P. R. Johnson 57; Tarrant 6-47) and 97 (A. E. Trott 7-20).

The Last Straw   E. (Patsy) Hendren, 1938

At the end of the innings, Albert punched his own head and called himself names for finishing his benefit match early on the third day! Sammy Woods, captain of Somerset, and one of the victims, gave him a straw hat with a hand-painted picture on the band of seven rabbits bolting into the Pavilion. Albert wore it at a good many matches during the rest of the season – to the wonderment of everyone not in the know.

1920 – Warner's Career Crowned With Championship   1921

Never in the history of the County Championship has there been anything so dramatic as the triumph of Middlesex last summer. When on July 27 they lost their return game with Essex by four runs, nothing seemed more unlikely than that they would finish at the head of the list. From that time forward, however, they met with nothing but success, actually winning their last nine matches. Not till the last moment were they secure of their prize, as if they had drawn instead of actually winning their final match with Surrey at Lord's they would, according to the method of scoring points, have finished fractionally below Lancashire. That final match was the event of the year, P. F. Warner, who had previously announced his intention of retiring, winding up his career as Middlesex captain amid a scene of enthusiasm which no one fortunate enough to be present will ever forget. Middlesex had a far better record than any of their rivals. Meeting only the strongest opponents, they won 15 matches, drew three, and lost only two.

1920 – MIDDLESEX v SURREY: unforgettable conclusion   1921

At Lord's, August 28, 30, 31, 1920. Never before has a county match proved such an attraction at Lord's. On the Saturday there must have been nearly 25,000 people on the ground, 20,700 paying for admission at the gates. A great fight was looked forward to, and as it happened all expectations were exceeded. It was a game never to be forgotten, Middlesex in the end winning by 55 runs, and so securing the Championship. Winning the toss, Middlesex had the advantage of batting first on a hard wicket, but nothing could have been less promising than their start. For once Lee and Hearne failed them, and in less than an hour three wickets were down for 35 runs. After these disasters nothing was risked, and-at the end of the afternoon the Middlesex score with eight men out had only reached 253. Warner was blamed in some quarters for over-caution, but he saved his side. In getting 79 he was batting for nearly four hours and a half. On the Monday there was again an enormous attendance, the number paying at the gates this time being 20,021. Owing nearly everything to Sandham, Surrey had the best of the day's cricket. Sandham had some luck but for the most part he played superbly, combining an ever-watchful defence with his clean hitting. For his 167 not out he was batting four hours and 20 minutes, his figures including 17 fours. With the object of getting Middlesex in before the end of the afternoon Fender declared with nine wickets down, but his policy met with no reward, Skeet and Lee batting for 40 minutes and taking the score to 27. For sustained excitement the third day beat everything seen in London last season. Skeet and Lee made victory for Middlesex possible, staying in until after lunch and sending up 208 for the first wicket. Lee was splendid, and Skeet, though not so certain in timing the ball, played better than he had ever played before in a first-class match. Warner declared at 20 minutes to four, leaving Surrey to get 244 in a trifle over three hours. The downfall of Hobbs – caught in the slips at 22 – was discouraging, but Surrey went for the runs and, with Sandham playing even more finely than on the previous day, the 100 was up in an hour and a quarter for two wickets. However, Hendren got rid of Shepherd by means of a wonderful catch in the deep field – just in front of the screen with his hands above his head – this being really the turning-point of the game. Surrey's great hope departed when Sandham – the sixth man out – was caught and bowled from a full pitch. In the end Middlesex won with ten minutes to spare. Warner was carried off the field shoulder-high, and before the crowd dispersed he and Fender had to make speeches.

Middlesex 268 (Mr P. F. Warner 79, Mr G. T. S. Stevens 53; Mr P. G. H. Fender 4-76)

and 316-7 dec (H. W. Lee 108, Mr C. H. L. Skeet 106);

Surrey 341-9 dec (A. Sandham 167*; T. J. Durston 4-97)

and 188 (Sandham 68; Stevens 5-61).

1921 – MIDDLESEX v SURREY: REPEAT PERFORMANCE 1922

At Lord's, August 27, 29, 30, 1921. As in 1920, the Championship hinged on the return match with Surrey. Middlesex entered upon the all-important fixture with a good deal in their favour, as nothing short of an actual victory would have given Surrey the honours in the competition. As things turned out, Middlesex, after more than once looking to be a beaten side, gained a wonderful victory, going in to get 322 in the last innings, and actually hitting off the runs for the loss of four wickets. The match excited enormous interest, 15,945 people paying for admission on the first day, 17,683 on the second, and 14,311 on the third. The third day's cricket was unforgettable. A sterner fight no one could wish to see. The great point in favour of Middlesex was that they were free from anxiety as to the clock. There was always ample time in which to get the runs. Lee was out at 48 and then came the batting that won the match. Hearne joined Twining at five minutes past 12, and not until 20 minutes past five did the second wicket fall, 277 runs being added in four hours and ten minutes of actual play. Surrey fielded untiringly, trying their hardest until at five minutes past six Hendren made the winning hit.

> Surrey 269 (T. F. Shepherd 128*, Mr D. R. Jardine 55; T. J. Durston 4-47)
> and 184 (Mr D. J. Knight 74; Mr N. E. Haig 5-62);
> Middlesex 132 (Mr G. M. Reay 4-44)
> and 322-4 (Mr R. H. Twining 135, J. W. Hearne 106).

1929 – AMATEUR BOWLERS CAPTURE THE LIMELIGHT   1930

Not for many years – if ever – has a county included in its ranks three amateurs who have taken 100 wickets or more in the course of a season. This was the special distinction of Middlesex in 1929, Nigel Haig, R. W. V. Robins and I. A. R. Peebles each accomplishing that notable achievement. With Allen [who took all ten wickets for 40 runs against Lancashire] and Enthoven each enjoying some success, the first five places in the bowling averages were all occupied by amateurs who between them accounted for 367 wickets out of 478 which fell to Middlesex in Championship matches.

1936 – COMPTON ASCENDS THE STAGE   1937

Of perhaps greater importance than the continued excellence of Hendren – because of its bearing on the future – was the leap into prominence of Denis Compton. Last season, at the age of 18, he made his county debut in the Whitsuntide engagement with Sussex at Lord's and, going in last, scored 14. From that point, he never looked back, not only commanding a regular place in the team, but embarking upon a gradual ascent in the batting order. To him fell the distinction of scoring 1,000 runs in his first season in big cricket, a feat he completed in his last match before commencing training with Arsenal Football Club, for whom he is an outside-left of outstanding skill. Mr P. F. Warner, chairman of the Test match selection committee, described him as "the best young batsman since Walter Hammond was a boy".

After being runners-up on five successive occasions, Middlesex deservedly won the Championship for the fifth time since its inception in 1873. The season will be remembered for the feats of Denis Compton and Edrich. Yet, magnificently as they performed for Middlesex as well as England, the Championship came to Middlesex not through any individual brilliance but by the combined efforts in team spirit of a particularly harmonious eleven, intelligently captained by R. W. V. Robins in his final year and backed by good reserves.

By their remarkably rapid scoring the batsmen usually gave the bowlers maximum time to dismiss a side twice, and frequently Middlesex finished the first day with over 400 runs made and three or four wickets taken cheaply. Though statistics give only a slight impression of their power, it is illuminating that Middlesex passed 400 11 times, failed to score 100 only once, and declared in 20 innings, against three opposing totals of 400, six of less than 100, and two declarations both by Kent.

Rarely have the first four batsmen in a side produced combined results comparable with Brown, Robertson, Denis Compton and Edrich. In all matches the four men made 12,193 runs (Compton 3,816, Edrich 3,539, Robertson 2,760, Brown 2,078), 8,213 of these in Championship games, in which they obtained 33 of the county's 37 individual hundreds.

Most Middlesex matches were attended by huge crowds, nearly 30,000 attending on Whit Monday in the Sussex match.

1947 – MIDDLESEX (CHAMPION COUNTY) v REST OF ENGLAND:
ICING ON THE CAKE   1948

At The Oval, September 13, 15, 16, 17, 1947. Middlesex won by nine wickets. For only the third time were the Champion County successful over the Rest of England. Yorkshire were winners in 1905 and 1935, the last occasion on which the game took place. The match provided further personal triumphs for Compton and Edrich, who concluded their remarkable season in superb style. Compton, despite a heavily strapped knee which restricted his freedom, played his highest innings in England. Edrich followed Compton in beating Hayward's record aggregate. Middlesex began by losing three wickets for 53, but Compton and Edrich added 138 before Compton retired through a recurrence of his knee trouble. He resumed on Monday and in all he and Edrich put on 210 and made 426 between them out of the Middlesex total of 543. Compton hit 30 fours, Edrich a six and 21 fours. The Rest lost Washbrook first ball and Place also failed to score. Steady batting by Emmett and a bright display from Evans failed to save the follow-on. Emmett again showed good form, but only Washbrook and Yardley of the others did much and Middlesex were set a simple task.

Middlesex 543-9 dec (D. C. S. Compton 246, W. J. Edrich 180; T. W. J. Goddard 4-179) and 21-1;
Rest of England 246 (G. M. Emmett 89, T. G. Evans 70; L. H. Gray 4-47, Compton 4-57)
and 317 (N. W. D. Yardley 71, C. Washbrook 61).

Golden summer: Bill Edrich, left, and Denis Compton walk out to bat
at The Oval for Middlesex, newly-crowned champions, against Rest of England.
The pair, who scored 7,355 runs between them during the season,
made 426 of Middlesex's first-innings total of 543-9 dec

1949 – SOMERSET v MIDDLESEX: EARLY CONNECTION   1950

At Bath, June 25, 27, 1949. Middlesex won by 36 runs. Test claims severely handicapped Middlesex, who did well to gain victory in two days after a keen struggle. Titmus, at the age of 16, made his first appearance for Middlesex and helped Allen to put on 34 for the eighth wicket.

The team also included Horace Brearley, father of Mike, the future Middlesex and England captain. This was the last of Brearley Senior's five first-class appearances; Titmus went on to play 792 matches including 53 Tests, his last – unexpectedly – for Middlesex in August 1982 under Brearley Junior's captaincy.

Obituaries 2008: BREARLEY, HORACE, who died on August 14, 2007, aged 94, was a batsman who played once for Yorkshire before the war, and twice for Middlesex afterwards: he was Yorkshire's oldest player when he died. Brearley was a teacher, latterly at City of London School, where his pupils included his son Mike, who achieved greater cricketing celebrity. One former pupil told the BBC: "If Mike went in to bat for England during his lesson, he would take us off to the TV room to watch." Mike himself tells the story of his father's only game for Yorkshire, which was against Middlesex: "He batted at No. 5, and faced a side that contained three leg-spinners. Horace had never, or almost never, been confronted by a googly bowler, and here were three all at once. But he was a typical Yorkshireman, and his comment about the occasion was to complain that Len Hutton kept pinching the bowling. One might have thought that this would have suited him fine."

1957 – MIDDLESEX TWINS TAKE THEIR LEAVE   1958

Season 1957 saw the end of an important chapter in the history of Middlesex, the finish of regular cricket for Denis Compton as a professional and the retirement from the captaincy of W. J. Edrich, who had led the side for the past five years.

The season brought special distinction to Murray, the wicketkeeper, who became only the second player in history to score 1,000 runs and claim 100 victims.

1957 – MIDDLESEX v WORCESTERSHIRE: FINAL CURTAIN-CALL   1958

At Lord's, August 28, 29, 30, 1957. Worcestershire won by two wickets, taking 12 points. After a thrilling finish the deciding run came off the fifth ball of the final over. Denis Compton, on his last appearance as a professional for Middlesex, stole the limelight. He scored 191 runs in the match including a sparkling 143 in the first innings. He and Robertson shared a third-wicket stand of 225 when Middlesex batted first on an easy pitch. Compton batted three hours and hit one six and 17 fours.

Middlesex 350-6 dec (D. C. S. Compton 143, J. D. B. Robertson 104) **and 203-7 dec;**
Worcestershire 354-9 dec (D. W. Richardson 113, R. G. Broadbent 56, D. Kenyon 51,
M. J. Horton 51*; R. J. Hurst 4-70) **and 200-8.**

Sussex v Derbyshire. At Horsham, June 4, 6, 7, 1988.
Green had the unusual distinction of being out first ball in
both innings without recording a "king pair"; he was run out
in the second innings, going for a second run.

Little Wonder No. 109

1967 – Failing In Their Responsibility   1968

The county played much substandard and unattractive cricket, particularly at
Lord's. In the quest for points Middlesex failed to fulfil the special responsibility
they have, playing their home matches at the headquarters of the game. The nadir
was reached against Hampshire at the beginning of July.

1967 – MIDDLESEX v HAMPSHIRE: DESERVEDLY CONDEMNED   1968

At Lord's, July 1, 2, 3, 1967. Drawn, no decision, an extraordinary result, for only 12
minutes were lost during the three days, which began with an exciting innings from
Marshall. He hit one six and 18 fours in his 153 out of 210 in only three hours, 23
minutes. On his dismissal Hampshire tossed away a winning position, their
laboured batting on a perfect pitch showing a lack of awareness of their mastery,
and they toiled into the second day. Livingstone, hitting 15 fours, batted four hours,
ten minutes. Facing such an imposing total and with no chance of winning,
Middlesex, too, proved cautious, and when they lost both opening batsmen for only
29, this attitude became deeply rooted. Thus they failed to provide entertaining
batting to mark the first Sunday of county cricket at Lord's. Beginning the last day,
Middlesex still required 148 to save the follow-on. This was achieved during a solid
partnership between Hooker and Radley shortly before tea after seven hours, ten
minutes struggling. More assertive batting threatened briefly to take them in front,
but when Hooker was stumped Titmus deemed it strategic to deny Hampshire
points, though this course also rendered the match fruitless for Middlesex. To the
argument that Middlesex could have discarded their last three wickets, their
secretary replied: "Having been set to score 272 to avoid a follow-on, or 422 for
first-innings lead, and having lost four men for 123, Middlesex were not prepared
to throw away wickets for the sake of gaining two points." The match received
deserved and universal condemnation.

Hampshire 421-7 dec (R. E. Marshall 153, D. A. Livingstone 120);
Middlesex 371-7 (C. T. Radley 100*, R. W. Hooker 66, F. J. Titmus 61).

The teams made amends with an exciting finish at Portsmouth which resulted in the first tie in the Championship for eight years.

1976 – MIDDLESEX v WEST INDIANS: STRENGTH IN ADVERSITY   1977

At Lord's, July 31, August 2, 3, 1976. Middlesex won by four wickets, inflicting on West Indies the first defeat of their tour. The badly understrength Middlesex team performed wonders to hustle West Indies out cheaply. All the batsmen attacked, but only Greenidge, in a cascade of unstoppable, dazzling strokes, succeeded. He hit one six and 20 fours in two and a quarter hours. Middlesex were 160 for three at the close of the first day, Smith having played some crisp, decisive strokes. Edmonds hit power-fully on the second morning and Clark, making his first appearance for the county since 1968, provided a glimpse of past glories. Roberts broke their stand, but Padmore returned his best tour figures to that date in working his way through the rest.

The West Indies batsmen again surged away with fierce, reckless stroke-play, 146 coming in the opening 25 overs. Richards played more calmly than most and Murray and Roberts had to stabilise matters, Roberts eventually driving Titmus for two vast sixes. Middlesex wanted 274 and had almost all the last day to make them. Smith and Brearley recorded their third century partnership in the last four innings and they were halfway there before a wicket fell. Butcher followed the openers' methodical example, but Smith's departure at 240 introduced an abrupt collapse as Middlesex stuttered at the gates of victory. When it came, it was their first over a touring team since the 1936 Indians. A strange feature of the match was that five wicketkeepers were used, Brearley and then Butcher replacing the injured Kinkead-Weekes, and Findlay relieving Murray.

West Indians 222 (C. G. Greenidge 123; F. J. Titmus 5-41, M. W. W. Selvey 4-58)
and 308 (Greenidge 67, A. M. E. Roberts 56*, I. V. A. Richards 53; N. G. Featherstone 4-50);
Middlesex 257 (M. J. Smith 95, P. H. Edmonds 53; A. L. Padmore 6-69)
and 275-6 (Smith 108, J. M. Brearley 62; Padmore 4-78).

1976 – SURREY v MIDDLESEX: SAFELY IN THE BAG   1977

At The Oval, September 1, 2, 3, 1976. Middlesex won by five wickets. Though a century by Edrich, the 99th of his career, was fully appreciated, most of the cheering was delayed until four o'clock on the second day. Then Middlesex, having taken four bonus points altogether, learned that whatever happened subsequently Gloucestershire could not get enough reward from the match against Derbyshire to deny them the County Championship title for the first time since 1949, when they shared it with Yorkshire. Three of the players who were in the side in 1949, W. J.

Edrich, F. G. Mann and H. P. Sharp, now the scorer, were on the ground to see this triumph 27 years later.

> **Surrey 308-8** (100 overs) (J. H. Edrich 100 retired hurt, L. E. Skinner 67; A. A. Jones 5-103)
> **and 172** (N. G. Featherstone 5-58, P. H. Edmonds 5-72);
> **Middlesex 308** (C. T. Radley 70, G. D. Barlow 61, Featherstone 57; P. I. Pocock 5-107)
> **and 176-5** (Edmonds 72*, Featherstone 67*; R. D. Jackman 4-65).

1977 – MIDDLESEX v SOMERSET (Gillette Cup semi-final):
SIXTH TIME LUCKY   1978

At Lord's, August 17, 18, 19, 24, 25, 26, 1977. Middlesex won by six wickets. The appalling weather in London during this period meant that the players spent six days trying to start their game. The original three days were washed out, and a County Championship game between the sides was postponed to try to fit in the tie. A match was finally achieved on the Friday morning as the weather cleared, but it was felt unwise to risk more than 15 overs each.

> **Somerset 59** (14.4 overs) (W. W. Daniel 4-24, M. W. W. Selvey 3-32);
> **Middlesex 61-4** (11.3 overs) (J. Garner 4-27).

1980 – MIDDLESEX v SUSSEX (Benson and Hedges Cup quarter-final):
COMBATIVE CAPTAINS   1981

At Lord's, June 11, 1980. Middlesex won by 29 runs. The match had an extraordinary start and an even more unusual finish. Imran was involved both times. In the morning he swung the ball so extravagantly that he bowled eight wides in his first five overs and 11 of the final count of 19. The extras conceded by Sussex were higher than their margin of defeat. Eight hours later, as Daniel produced some characteristically explosive bowling to clinch Middlesex's win, there was plenty of stuff whistling round the batsman's heads, and Imran protested to umpire van Geloven when Pigott was hit on the arm. (Daniel had broken Wessels's hand with an earlier lifter.) Immediately Brearley came in to give his view and, almost incredibly, he and Imran appeared on the point of grappling. The intervention of van Geloven prevented an unsavoury incident from degenerating. Imran said: "When I bowl bumpers at tailenders, I am warned. Daniel bowled five, so I objected." In his report van Geloven stated that he had never heard such bad language, on or off the field, as Imran's. The TCCB asked each county to inquire and to take action. Over a month later the Board's disciplinary committee stated that the matter was ended, as they were satisfied with the reprimand Sussex delivered to Imran and with Middlesex's expression of regret that Brearley had become involved.

> **Middlesex 195** (54.5 overs) (C. M. Wells 4-21, Imran Khan 3-12);
> **Sussex 166** (53.3 overs) (P. W. G. Parker 59, G. D. Mendis 43; W. W. Daniel 3-21, M. W. Gatting 3-36).

1981 – MIDDLESEX v ESSEX: ALL CAPS

At Lord's, May 6, 7, 8, 1981. For the first time in Championship history a full team of Test players took the field.

Middlesex: J. M. Brearley, P. R. Downton, C. T. Radley, M. W. Gatting, R. O. Butcher, G. D. Barlow, J. E. Emburey, P. H. Edmonds, M. W. W. Selvey (all England), J. R. Thomson (Australia), W. W. Daniel (West Indies).

Despite the talent, Middlesex won no titles and finished only fourth in the Championship.

1982 – WINNING END TO BREARLEY ERA

Terry Cooper, 1983

The Middlesex players were determined that their retirement gift to Mike Brearley should be a trophy – all four if possible. They embarked on their prize-gathering so skilfully, remaining unbeaten until the middle of June, by when they had played 16 matches in three competitions, that the four-timer began to look something less than an impossibility. But this inspired start could not be maintained. Lancashire, in the Benson and Hedges Cup quarter-final, and Surrey, in the NatWest Bank semi-final, both old and successful one-day opponents of Middlesex, ended hopes of a farewell Lord's final for Brearley. A run of three consecutive John Player League defeats also transformed a six-point lead into a six-point deficit, although four wins in the last five games kept Middlesex in second place, their highest in the League's 14 seasons.

There remained the Championship. Middlesex were always winning this most cherished title, even though Leicestershire enlivened the later weeks by reducing the Middlesex lead from 47 points on August 17 to only two on September 5 before Middlesex clinched it at Worcester on September 11. The captain made the winning hit of that final game.

So Brearley departed after a dozen seasons of captaincy, festooned with honours at Test and county level. The Middlesex successes were crammed into his final eight seasons, the necessary spadework having been undertaken in the previous four years. In 1971 he inherited a side disunited and unsuccessful with, at times, an aversion to attacking cricket that was the despair of their dwindling supporters. Brearley restored purposeful cricket to Lord's, while winning four Championships (one shared) and two Gillette Cups. As the best county side of a generation they were a credit also to their coach, Don Bennett.

1987 – NO ROOM FOR PART-TIMER

Terry Cooper, 1988

As the season ended, Edmonds – a lovely, watchable cricketer, but a man who exasperated those in authority – made one unusual demand too many. His wish to play periodically as an amateur could not be granted and so his distinguished 17 years at Lord's concluded with the committee paying due tribute to his part in the triumphs between 1975 and 1986.

1987 – MIDDLESEX v YORKSHIRE: BACK TO SCHOOL   1988

At Lord's, April 25, 26, 27, 1987. Ramprakash [*63 not out*] hit one six and seven fours off 99 balls and made a glowing impression on his first-class debut. Then it was back to school the following day for the 17-year-old.

1993 – MIDDLESEX v AUSTRALIANS: TEMPERS FRAY   1994

At Lord's, May 3, 1993. Australians won by 69 runs. A crowd approaching 10,000 turned out to watch a game in which the cricket seemed to take second place to clashes of temperament. Not that the players directed their hostility towards the opposing team; the first display of temper occurred when Gatting kept a disgruntled Fraser out of the Middlesex attack until the 20th over. Fraser's first four overs cost 35 runs and his obvious annoyance when taken off led to a severe finger-wagging from his captain. But Gatting was even less pleased later in the day when he was run out – sent back, quite justifiably, by Roseberry. Still seething, he put his hand through a glass panel in the dressing-room door and was taken to hospital for stitches. The injury ruled him out of the one-day internationals. His opposite number, Border, also expressed his frustration when bowled by a full toss from Fraser, swiping at the stumps with his bat. As for the game, the Australians had few difficulties.

Australians 243-5 (55 overs) (M. L. Hayden 122, D. R. Martyn 66);
Middlesex 174 (48.1 overs) (M. A. Roseberry 47; Martyn 3-41, C. J. McDermott 3-51).

1997 – CHANGING OF THE GUARD   Norman de Mesquita, 1998

It was a watershed year, which saw a change of captain and the end of Don Bennett's 29 years as coach. Mike Gatting, captain since 1983, already intended to step down in favour of Mark Ramprakash. But at the end of May, with new responsibilities as an England selector, he decided to do it immediately. In contrast with bloody coups at other counties, the handover could not have been smoother. The continuity was emphasised in Ramprakash's first match in charge, against Northamptonshire: both players scored hundreds to set up an innings win.

Bennett's retirement ended nearly half a century's service to Middlesex. He made his debut for them in 1950, retired in 1968, and became coach the following year. His low-key approach was just right for the club, complemented as it was by the positive captaincy of Mike Brearley and Gatting. Perhaps his most important contribution derived from his ability to spot talent, including Gatting himself, Ian Gould and John Emburey.

1998 – HAMPSHIRE v MIDDLESEX: VARIED FORTUNES

At Southampton, August 31, September 1, 2, 3, 1998. Hampshire won by seven wickets. Phil Tufnell will not remember this match fondly. During the course of Hampshire's third successive Championship victory, he discovered he had been ignored by England for the winter tours, and was then stung twice by wasps. Rain then forced Middlesex to surrender a dominant position. Andrew Strauss, South African-born, Durham-educated, marked his first-class debut with a cultured 83 for Middlesex, and Johnson took three wickets in five balls – just too late, after Hampshire had avoided the follow-on. For the third time in 1998, Hampshire increased their record for extras conceded: Middlesex's first innings included 69, despite a £2 club fine for each no-ball. Middlesex were almost as prodigal, and the match total reached 195.

Middlesex 437 (A. J. Strauss 83, M. W. Gatting 77, R. A. Kettleborough 60, K. R. Brown 53) and 173-2 dec (Kettleborough 62*);
Hampshire 311 (G. W. White 106, A. D. Mascarenhas 63; R. L. Johnson 4-75) and 301-3 (J. P. Stephenson 105, W. S. Kendall 78*).

2004 – MIDDLESEX v SURREY (TWENTY20 CUP: SOUTH GROUP):
CROWD-PULLER

At Lord's, July 15, 2004. Surrey won by 37 runs. Attendance: 27,509. Nothing hung on this game – Surrey were already guaranteed a home tie in the next round and Middlesex were out – yet the first Twenty20 game at Lord's produced the biggest crowd to watch a county match, cup finals excepted, since these two sides met here in 1953. Tickets had sold out several days earlier, and the crowd did not quite reach the Lord's capacity of 28,000 only because the pavilion was not full. Ramprakash, a former Middlesex stalwart, was booed occasionally during his measured innings. Hollioake then cut loose with 65 off 41 deliveries. Middlesex were never in the hunt, though the crowd enjoyed Klusener striking 22 from Hollioake's first over. He fell in his second. Westminster Council, which stopped Lord's staging a match in 2003, monitored noise levels to appease anxious residents.

Surrey 183-5 (20 overs) (A. J. Hollioake 65*);
Middlesex 146-7 (20 overs) (L. Klusener 53; N. D. Doshi 3-26).

2008 – SHORT-TERM SUCCESS HIDES LONGER-TERM FAILINGS
Norman de Mesquita, 2009

The 2008 season was a strange and eventful one for Middlesex, on and off the field. They won the Twenty20 Cup – a form of the game where they had previously experienced little success – although one long-suffering supporter said it simply concealed all that was wrong with the county. The sluggish start to the season added to the dissatisfaction that had built up over several undistinguished years, and a members' petition was presented calling for a vote of no confidence in the committee. In the event, a temporary improvement in form meant the vote never took place, although the cumbersome committee structure is to be completely revamped.

2009 – A VISIT FROM THE ROYALS   2010

At Lord's, July 6, 2009 (floodlit). Rajasthan Royals won by 46 runs. This charity match, for the inaugural British Asian Cup, pitted the 2008 English Twenty20 Cup-winners against the first champions of the Indian Premier League. Rajasthan Royals ran up an imposing total on a rainy evening, boosted by a late burst from Dimitri Mascarenhas, who hit 32 from 16 balls before opening the bowling and striking twice to set Middlesex's run-chase on its heels. Sohail Tanvir added the important wickets of Eoin Morgan and Tyron Henderson, and Middlesex never looked like getting the runs after that. Rajasthan's player/coach Shane Warne chimed in with possibly his last wicket at Lord's, when he lured Dawid Malan down the track with a googly and Naman Ojha completed the stumping. Justin Langer, playing his first match for the Royals, was out second ball. Despite a crowd of around 20,000, reports claimed MCC lost around £18,000, after making an agreed £50,000 donation to the British Asian Trust.

> **Rajasthan Royals 162-5** (20 overs) (S. A. Asnodkar 41, M. Kaif 41;
> **Middlesex 116-7** (20 overs) (Sohail Tanvir 3-20).

NORTHAMPTONSHIRE

[1958 edition] *UPS AND DOWNS OF NORTHAMPTONSHIRE by James D. Coldham*

> *Why do Northamptonshire engage so many players from outside*
> *(especially from overseas)? The answer is plain. A small county without*
> *either the population or resources of Yorkshire, Northamptonshire,*
> *nevertheless, possess a public with the palate for good cricket – and cricketers.*
> *Therefore, while talent scouts comb the county and trials are held regularly,*
> *experts from elsewhere are encouraged to become specially registered.*

1898 – TRANSFER SYSTEM FOR PLAYERS REJECTED   1899

Mr Darnell in moving "That this meeting recommends that the [county qualification] committee now appointed do consider the question of monetary compensation being given to the counties transferring a professional," observed that he thought monetary compensation should be given in such cases. His county (Northamptonshire) had suffered through their players leaving, and instanced the case of Bowley, West, Santall, Wood, Thompson, and Mold. First-class counties had plundered and robbed the minor counties. The question of transfer should be considered as well as that of monetary consideration. Mr Darnell's motion, however, was rejected by 13 votes to eight.

Little Wonder No. 110

Sussex v Warwickshire. At Eastbourne, August 4, 6, 7, 1990. A remarkable hat-trick by Paul Smith, wearing odd boots, set up a comfortable victory for Warwickshire. Smith went off to borrow a spare from Munton, which was two sizes too big, after his had split. He returned, promptly bowled Dodemaide, and immediately had Moores caught at short leg and Pigott snapped up by wicketkeeper Piper.

1905 – MAJORITY OF TEAM STRUGGLE AT HIGHER LEVEL 1906

Entering for the first time into the ranks of the leading counties, Northamptonshire had to be content with a very modest measure of success, winning only two of their 12 Championship fixtures and losing eight. Moreover, they suffered a crushing defeat at the hands of the Australians, being beaten by an innings and 329 runs. The merest glance at the averages will show where Northamptonshire were weak. To put the matter bluntly they had only two bowlers – one of them a first-rate all-round man – and only one batsman whose performances rose above the commonplace. The other members of the eleven, whatever their merits in a lower grade of cricket, were a good deal overweighted by their new responsibilities.

1908 – NORTHAMPTONSHIRE v YORKSHIRE: 27 AND 15 ALL OUT 1909

At Northampton, May 7, 8, 1908. In meeting Yorkshire for the first time since promotion to a place among the leading counties Northamptonshire laboured under serious disadvantages, having to take the field without Pool, Driffield, and East. In the circumstances they could hardly be expected to make a fight of it against their powerful rivals, and on the second evening Yorkshire had won by an innings and 314 runs. The cricket on the second day approached the sensational. Rain delayed the resumption until half past two, but by 20 minutes to six the end had been reached. When Newstead and Myers had added 23 more runs Kaye declared the Yorkshire innings closed, and then Northamptonshire cut such an inglorious figure against the bowling of Hirst and Haigh that they were twice dismissed in two hours and a quarter for an aggregate score of 42, of which four were extras. The 15 for which the side were put out in their second innings is the third lowest total ever made in a first-class county match. Owing to an attack of lumbago Thompson could not bat.

Yorkshire 356-8 dec (D. Denton 110; Mr R. W. R. Hawtin 5-78);
Northamptonshire 27 (G. H. Hirst 6-12) and 15 (Hirst 6-7).

1912 – SETTLED TEAM ALMOST REACHES THE SUMMIT   1913

Only less remarkable than the triumph of Warwickshire in 1911 was the advance made by Northamptonshire last summer. From being tenth on the list the youngest of the first-class counties – promoted so recently as 1905 – jumped into second place, only losing the Championship to Yorkshire by a very narrow margin. Out of 18 county matches the team won ten and lost one, their only defeat being suffered at the hands of Warwickshire at Birmingham. These successes against Kent and Surrey naturally dwarfed everything else. As the county had never before beaten Surrey that particular win afforded the keenest satisfaction.

The explanation of Northamptonshire's brilliant season is not far to seek. It is to be found in the possession of very good well-varied bowling, and in the fact that the county put practically the same eleven into the field on all occasions. Taking the players man for man the side could not be compared with many less successful rivals, but constant association gave the eleven a fighting power that was out of all proportion to the individual talent. Except that Thompson has assisted the Players, and S. G. Smith the Gentlemen, not one of the Northamptonshire men has taken any part in representative matches.

1921 – CLUB FACES UP TO UNCERTAIN FUTURE   1922

Northamptonshire had a troubled time in 1921, and after the close of the season the affairs of the club came to a crisis. At a largely-attended and rather stormy meeting on October 10, a drastic change in the management was demanded, all the officials except the president and the trustees being called upon to give up their positions. Mr A. J. Darnell – honorary secretary for 25 years – promptly resigned, as did the committee, and Lord Lilford said that under the altered conditions he could not remain president. At a subsequent meeting – on October 31 – the club was to a certain extent reconstructed, and a little later the engagement of Mr V. W. C. Jupp as paid secretary was officially announced, his name having for weeks before been freely mentioned in connection with the post. Lord Lilford – the good genius of Northamptonshire cricket from the time the county was promoted to the first-class in 1905 – was asked to reconsider his decision, but he declined, stating, however, that he would do all he could to help the club. Mr T. Horton, in accepting the position of president till the end of the financial year, said that as things were going the club might slip out of first-class cricket, but that if the members pulled together things could be put right again. The outlook in the immediate future is, to say the least, dubious, and those in the best position to judge think it will take two or three years to restore the club to its old position. As regards money, adequate support seems assured.

1921 – NORTHAMPTONSHIRE v ESSEX: TIMELY TIMMS   1922

At Northampton, June 11, 13, 14, 1921. Only on one other occasion in the season did Northamptonshire show such batting form, and though overwhelmed on the first day and compelled to follow on against a huge balance of 181, they avoided defeat in splendid style. The honours were divided by Haywood and the young public-school batsman, W. W. Timms. Haywood hit 15 fours in his 132 and, so far as could be seen, gave no chance. Timms, who was taking part in his second county match, had the luck to be missed at backward point at the start of play on the third morning, but apart from this and another chance when 43, he played extraordinarily well. His success delighted the crowd, and at the end of the game he was carried off the field shoulder-high by his fellow schoolboys. He was batting five hours and threequarters. In the Essex innings the second wicket put on 189 runs, the third 152, and the fourth 130. Freeman, never at fault, was batting just seven hours.

> **Essex 604-7 dec** (J. R. Freeman 286, A. C. Russell 108, Mr P. A. Perrin 77; C. N. Woolley 4-90);
> **Northamptonshire 223** (G. J. Thompson 69; P. Toone 4-96)
> **and 445-5** (Mr W. W. Timms 154*, R. A. Haywood 132, Thompson 58, Woolley 50).

TEACHER WHO MADE UP FOR MISSED LESSONS   Obituary, 1987

TIMMS, WILFRID WALTER, who died at Godalming on September 30, 1986, aged 84, was such a modest, self-effacing, unpretentious man that in later years many who knew him as a distinguished teacher of French and Spanish never realised that he had been a well-known cricketer. He made his reputation by a performance which is still unique. In 1921, when captain of Northampton Grammar School, he was given leave by the school to play for the county against Kent in May and then against Essex in June. Two men, I. D. Walker and S. H. Day, had made centuries for their counties the year before leaving school, but no schoolboy before or since has played an innings of that size or length in a county match. Later that season, Timms played for Northamptonshire throughout the summer holidays, on occasion captaining the side.

It was therefore a great disappointment that in four years at Cambridge he failed to get a Blue, but he continued to play for his county until 1932.

After some years as a master at Oundle, he moved in 1930 to Charterhouse, where he ran the cricket from 1932 to 1946. Charterhouse had always been a famous soccer school: the cricket had been neglected. Within a few years of Timms taking over, however, it had become one of the best cricket schools in England.

Peter May acknowledged his debt to him: "He was of great assistance to me in developing the basics of my batting. He was always patient and encouraging: we valued his advice because he had been successful himself in county cricket. He was a very fine player of the cut."

1930 – RAY OF SUNSHINE AMID THE CLOUDS   1931

Depending to a considerable extent upon young players, Northamptonshire failed so completely to realise expectations that the end of the season found them at the bottom of the Championship table – a position they had not occupied since 1923. While they won no more than four matches, they met with a dozen defeats and in only three of the unfinished games did they secure first-innings points. As some compensation for their poor display as competitors for the Championship, the team accomplished a notable performance against the Australians. Indeed to Northamptonshire fell the distinction not only of getting the tourists out for 93 – the lowest score all through the tour – but of making them follow on. This was an achievement of which no county could boast since 1912, when both Essex and Hampshire subjected the Australian team led by S. E. Gregory to that indignity.

1931 – NO END TO JUPP'S BAG OF TRICKS   1932

Jupp once again gave proof of his great abilities, accomplishing the double for the fifth time since he became associated with Northamptonshire, making over 1,000 runs for the seventh time in the course of eight seasons with that county, and on the occasion of the last match on the county programme establishing a world's record in performing the hat-trick for the fifth time.

1936 – TRAGIC FINISH TO SEASON   1937

The season ended in tragic circumstances. On the return journey from Chesterfield, R. P. Northway, the former Somerset amateur, at the end of his first year with Northamptonshire, was killed in a motor accident and Bakewell, a passenger in the car, had a very narrow escape. For some days Bakewell lay in Leicester Royal Infirmary hovering between life and death, but his strong constitution pulled him through and he made a complete recovery.

1938 – FIVE SEASONS IN THE BASEMENT   1939

Led by R. P. Nelson, the Cambridge Blue of 1936, Northamptonshire seemed a better team than in recent years but they could not shake off misfortune and for the fifth season running they occupied the last place in the County Championship. Their record of 17 defeats and seven drawn games shows just one more reverse than those suffered during the previous campaign but they were not so often outplayed completely.

1939 – NORTHAMPTONSHIRE v LEICESTERSHIRE: VICTORY AT LAST 1940

At Northampton, May 27, 29, 1939. Northamptonshire won by an innings and 193 runs. In this emphatic style Northamptonshire gained their first victory in the Championship since May 1935. Partridge and Buswell, with pace from the pitch, began by dismissing five of the visitors for eight runs; Brookes and Davis made 176 together and Timms helped to add 101 by fine hitting. Brookes batted four hours and a quarter and the highest innings of his career included 24 fours; he excelled with drives and cuts. When Nelson declared Merritt did best work with the ball. The whole Leicestershire side fell after tea for 130 runs. In splendid weather over 5,000 people cheered the home team on at last breaking their long spell of misfortune. Their most recent county victory was four years ago at Taunton.

Leicestershire 134 and 183 (W. E. Merritt 6-56);
Northamptonshire 510-8 dec (D. Brookes 187, P. Davis 84, J. E. Timms 55; W. H. Flamson 4-125).

1954 – PROFESSIONALS TO THE FORE 1955

Fears that, without the inspiring leadership of F. R. Brown, Northamptonshire would suffer a setback were fortunately not realised. Under the first regular professional captain [Dennis Brookes] to be appointed since the foundation of the club more than 100 years ago, the form of the team exceeded expectations, and except for that of 1949, when Brown took over the captaincy, the season proved the most successful for several decades. Northamptonshire won nine Championship matches, three more than in 1953, and a total of 136 points enabled them to share seventh place with Middlesex.

The summer brought distinction to several players, with Tribe, the Australian who completed the double for the third successive time, the central figure. A master of flight and spin with left-arm slows, he took 50 more wickets in Championship games than in the previous year, making his total 133, and at much cheaper cost. Livingston, another Australian, not only headed the batting averages, but exceeded 2,000 runs for the first time in a season. Arnold, a New Zealander, showed promising form as an opening batsman.

For the first time in the history of the club two Northamptonshire professionals were selected for the MCC Australian tour, Andrew and Tyson gaining this honour in their first full season of county cricket. Andrew always impressed as a wicketkeeper above the ordinary, a very quick perception enabling him to seize almost every chance. If Tyson, who appeared for England in one Test against Pakistan, never took more than five wickets in an innings, his great pace embarrassed many batsmen, and he became an ideal foil for Tribe.

1956 – NORTHAMPTONSHIRE v YORKSHIRE: LEVEL PEGGING

At Northampton, May 12, 14, 15, 1956. Yorkshire won by six wickets. The match offered a grand opportunity for comparing two of the country's fastest bowlers, Tyson and Trueman. They finished with remarkably similar figures. Sound batting by Reynolds and Tribe, followed by lively hitting from Tyson, helped Northamptonshire to recover from an indifferent start. Yorkshire passed 200 for the loss of four wickets, but excellent bowling by Tyson, who dismissed the last three batsmen for four runs, gave Northamptonshire first-innings lead. Trueman hit back by dismissing Arnold, Brookes and Reynolds in the course of five overs, and on the last day he started another collapse by taking two more wickets. Tribe batted defiantly for nearly three hours. Yorkshire, needing 123 in two hours 35 minutes, fell behind the clock at one stage, but won with five minutes to spare.

Northamptonshire 251 (B. L. Reynolds 61; M. J. Cowan 4-44, F. S. Trueman 1-63)
and 113 (Trueman 5-34);
Yorkshire 242 (F. H. Tyson 5-60)
and 123-4 (Tyson 1-40).

1957 – RECORD RETURNS AS BROOKES REACHES NEW LANDMARKS

Northamptonshire's astute team building and steady improvement over the three previous years were amply rewarded in 1957. They enjoyed the most successful season in their history, finishing second in the County Championship, and although 94 points behind Surrey, were the only side who offered any challenge to the leaders in the last month. Northamptonshire were also runners-up to Yorkshire in 1912, but the achievements of that season were easily surpassed by a team which contained only one regular player born in the county. The 15 Championship victories in 1957 constituted a new record for the county, and they suffered only two defeats – fewer than any other contestant.

It was fitting that Brookes should lead the side to this exalted position in the 20th season since winning his county cap. No player has served the county more loyally; as a batsman he remained a model of correctness and steadiness, even though greater responsibility was thrust upon him by the inconsistency of others. Early in the season he completed 25,000 runs for the county, and his innings of 100 against Surrey at The Oval earned him the distinction of having scored a century against every side in the Championship.

1959 – NORTHAMPTONSHIRE v GLAMORGAN: WON BY THE EIGHT

At Northampton, August 22, 24, 25, 1959. Northamptonshire won by seven wickets, taking 12 points to four by Glamorgan, and this their only win during August was a remarkable performance. Though three players short after the first day, Arnold, Lightfoot and Andrew all receiving finger injuries while fielding, Northamptonshire finished only 22 behind Glamorgan's first-innings total of 345, and when left to score 214 in three hours 20 minutes they hit the runs with eight minutes to spare. The final day belonged to Barrick, whose grand innings of 112 not out in two and threequarter hours included two sixes and 11 fours, but appropriately the winning hit was made by Tribe on his last appearance at Northampton.

Glamorgan 345 (W. G. A. Parkhouse 118, J. S. Pressdee 104; J. S. Manning 5-60)

and 191 (P. M. Walker 54; Manning 4-50);

Northamptonshire 323 (D. Brookes 98, D. W. Barrick 81, M. E. J. C. Norman 77)

and 217-3 (Barrick 112*).

1962 – LEICESTERSHIRE v NORTHAMPTONSHIRE (MIDLANDS KNOCK-OUT CUP FINAL): FIRST WINNERS 1963

At Leicester, May 9, 1962. Northamptonshire won by five wickets and thus became the first holders of the Midlands Knock-Out Cup. Scoring was slower than in the semi-finals, mainly because this time there was no limit on the number of overs allowed a bowler. Consequently slow bowlers were hardly used. Leicestershire, put in to bat, made a slow start, losing Hallam in the first over, and two wickets were down for 17. Wharton and Gardner brought about a recovery, but the last four wickets fell cheaply and 7.4 of the allocated 65 overs were wasted. Norman and Reynolds gave Northamptonshire a solid start and, at the fall of the fourth wicket, 105 runs were needed in 27 overs. These were scored in 20, principally owing to Crump and P. J. Watts. In one day's play, 437 runs were scored, 15 wickets fell and, perhaps most important, there was a result.

Leicestershire 218 (57.2 overs) (L. R. Gardner 56, A. Wharton 53, J. van Geloven 42; J. G. Williamson 5-58, J. D. F. Larter 3-52);

Northamptonshire 219-5 (59.2 overs) (B. L. Reynolds 55, B. S. Crump 52*, P. J. Watts 47, M. E. J. C. Norman 46; D. Kirby 3-42).

1969 – NORTHAMPTONSHIRE v WEST INDIANS: TWO IN A ROW 1970

At Northampton, May 21, 22, 23, 1969. Northamptonshire won by 65 runs and thus repeated their victory of 1966 over the West Indies. The game began with consistent batting by the county. Milburn, Mushtaq and Prideaux all shone with sound play and good strokes. The West Indies came back with an effective bowling spell from Shillingford, who took five for eight in 13 balls. The West Indies lost two wickets in the first over from Durose, and two more in the first over of the second morning. Foster completed fifty in two hours and Butcher batted well. Mushtaq hit an attractive half-century in the second innings against capable bowling by Shillingford,

Holder and Roberts, before Northamptonshire set the tourists to make 300. At one stage the West Indies looked likely to succeed through the batting of Camacho, Butcher, Lloyd and Davis. Then Crump demolished them with a spell of four for nine in 27 balls. Carew could not bat owing to a finger injury, and Sobers suffered from a cold throughout the match.

Northamptonshire 263 (R. M. Prideaux 79; G. C. Shillingford 5-79)

and 182-9 dec (Mushtaq Mohammad 51);

West Indians 146 (M. L. C. Foster 61)

and 234 (G. S. Camacho 87, C. A. Davis 57; B. S. Crump 4-28).

Northamptonshire review: One event that cast a shadow over the season was the serious accident suffered by Colin Milburn on the very night of the triumph over the West Indies. He lost an eye after a car accident and was unable to attempt a comeback during the season.

1972 – NORTHAMPTONSHIRE v AUSTRALIANS: COUNTY FIRST   1973

At Northampton, August 5, 7, 8, 1972. Northamptonshire won by seven wickets after Watts sent in the Australians on a slow pitch. This was their first victory over the Australians and it came just before lunch on the third day when Steele and Mushtaq saw them comfortably on the way to success. The Australians were dismissed cheaply in both innings. The Indian left-arm spinner, Bedi, had them in trouble in the first innings, with good assistance from Willey. Bedi and Dye took cheap wickets in the second innings despite a capable half-century by Watson, the only one in the game by the tourists. Watson also produced a fine bowling performance in the Northamptonshire first innings when a collapse followed some very good batting by Cook and Mushtaq. Bedi excelled and his skilful variations brought him nine wickets at 12 runs apiece. Northamptonshire also fielded brilliantly, bringing off several excellent catches.

Australians 191 (B. S. Bedi 5-57)

and 143 (G. D. Watson 52; Bedi 4-53);

Northamptonshire 210 (Mushtaq Mohammad 88*, G. Cook 62; Watson 5-36)

and 125-3 (D. S. Steele 60*).

Surrey v Essex (NatWest Bank Trophy quarter-final). At The Oval, July 31, 1991. Her Majesty The Queen visited The Oval, after an absence of 36 years, to open the £3million Ken Barrington Sports Centre, and was introduced to the teams between innings.

Little Wonder No. 111

1973 – MILBURN MAKES HOPEFUL RETURN

An interesting feature of the season was the return of Colin Milburn, who had lost his left eye in a car accident four years before and had announced his retirement from the game. When injuries struck at the start Milburn was pressed into service as a middle-order batsman and a medium-pace bowler. He progressed as the season developed and in the last ten innings was back in his old position as opener. In these five games Milburn scored 230 runs, raising hopes for the 1974 season after a winter in Australian cricket.

1974 – MILBURN'S HOPES DASHED

It seems that no more will be seen of Milburn. He never fully recovered from the car accident in which he lost an eye and last summer he averaged only 12.90 in 14 innings in County Championship matches. In all first-class cricket Milburn hit 13,262 runs, average 33.06, and when he was properly fit he had no peer as an entertaining strokemaker. Milburn hit 23 hundreds – all gems.

1976 – SEASON BRINGS INAUGURAL SUCCESS

The season 1976 was Northamptonshire's most successful since they became a first-class county in 1905. They won the Gillette Cup and finished second in the County Championship for the fourth time in their career. The Gillette Cup was the county's first triumph in top cricket, and it was rather appropriate that it should be in this competition, for in recent years when finances had been tight each annual meeting of the club saw officials urging the side to do better in the Gillette Cup where the money lay.

Certainly the season was a triumph for the Pakistan cricketer Mushtaq Mohammad in his first season as captain. He took over a side that had finished eighth in the Championship in 1975 and had made little impact in the one-day competitions, but at once he expressed confidence that they could do better.

1981 – NORTHAMPTONSHIRE v LANCASHIRE (NATWEST BANK TROPHY SEMI-FINALS): UNLIKELY HERO

At Northampton, August 19, 1981. Northamptonshire won by one wicket, with one ball to spare. They needed 13 off eight overs when last man Griffiths joined Man of the Match Tim Lamb. No batsman, Griffiths played 29 balls from Holding, Allott, Reidy and David Lloyd with great determination and, after the winning run came from a bye, he was carried shoulder-high from the field. Lamb began the stand with a two, but the next 11 all came in singles and, with the scores level at the start of the last over, Lamb held up play for five minutes to ascertain that Northamptonshire had been ahead on scoring-rate.

Lancashire 186-9 (60 overs) (G. Fowler 57, D. Lloyd 52; T. M. Lamb 3-28);
Northamptonshire 187-9 (59.5 overs) (R. G. Williams 41; B. W. Reidy 3-22).

1984 – NORTHAMPTONSHIRE v KENT: INITIAL TIE   1985

At Northampton, July 14, 16, 17, 1984. Tied. In a dramatic finish, Walker failed to make contact with the final three balls and Griffiths was run out attempting the bye off the last which would have brought Northamptonshire victory. It was the first tie in 745 Championship games on the Northampton ground.

Kent 250-6 dec and 204-5 dec (N. R. Taylor 86*);
Northamptonshire 124 (T. M. Alderman 5-34, R. M. Ellison 4-22) **and 330** (D. J. Wild 128, G. Cook 59).

1995 – LOWS AND HIGHS DEFY CONVENTION   Andrew Radd, 1996

No one could deny the team's contribution to the season as a whole. Conventional cricketing wisdom was undermined time and again as a burgeoning sense of self-belief helped to secure a string of triumphs that ranged from the unlikely to the almost impossible. Northamptonshire were dismissed for the two lowest totals of the summer – 46 against Essex at Luton and 59 against Surrey at Northampton – but went on to win both matches. They also built up the season's biggest score, 781 for seven declared, to set up an innings victory after Nottinghamshire had made 527.

1995 – NORTHAMPTONSHIRE v NOTTINGHAMSHIRE: NOON
ECLIPSED   1996

At Northampton, August 24, 25, 26, 28, 1995. Northamptonshire won by an innings and 97 runs. Northamptonshire's victory, achieved with 17 balls to spare, went beyond the merely extraordinary into the realms of the apparently impossible. Nottinghamshire scored 527, 61 more than any team in history had ever made in a match they lost by an innings. They were 353 for one after the first day. Lamb decided to go for the jackpot. Northamptonshire raced to the seventh-highest total in Championship history. Four men made hundreds. The third day saw 560 runs in 109.3 overs. Nottinghamshire went in again on the final morning 254 behind, and at 72 for one the match was apparently heading for a draw. Then three wickets fell in eight balls and Northamptonshire picked up the scent of victory. Kumble was again outstanding, with five wickets at barely a run an over. In a final twist Noon, once Northamptonshire's reserve wicketkeeper, threatened to deny them. Overcoming discomfort from a bruised jaw, he held out for a gallant 47 overs before he was dropped by Kumble off Taylor. But Kumble trapped last man Afford next ball.

Nottinghamshire 527 (R. T. Robinson 209, G. F. Archer 158; A. Kumble 4-118) **and 157** (Kumble 5-43); **Northamptonshire 781-7 dec** (R. J. Warren 154, A. Fordham 130, A. J. Lamb 115, D. J. Capel 114*).

1996 – WORCESTERSHIRE v NORTHAMPTONSHIRE: Sales record 1
1997

At Kidderminster, July 24, 25, 26, 27, 1996. Drawn. This otherwise unmemorable high-scoring draw will achieve lasting fame thanks to the performance of 18-year-old David Sales. After a third-ball duck in the first innings, he scored an unbeaten 210, the first double-century ever scored by someone making his first-class debut in a Championship match. Sales became the youngest double-centurion in Britain since W. G. Grace in 1886, and the eighth-youngest worldwide; all 13 players who had previously scored 200 before their 19th birthday went on to play Test cricket. Sales certainly showed the temperament as well as the endurance to advance in the game: he finished the third day on 191, then moved, apparently nervelessly, to his landmark in just five balls next morning. His entire innings only took four and a half hours, and he hit three sixes and 28 fours in 226 balls. It is fair to note that, once the shine was off the ball, batting was easy for just about everyone.

Northamptonshire 328 (D. Ripley 88*; R. K. Illingworth 4-89) **and 446-3 dec** (D. J. Sales 210*, D. J. Capel 103); **Worcestershire 350-7 dec** (T. M. Moody 106, W. P. C. Weston 68, V. S. Solanki 68, T. S. Curtis 65) **and 388-7** (Moody 169, Curtis 107, S. J. Rhodes 53*).

1999 – NORTHAMPTONSHIRE v ESSEX: Sales record 2
2000

At Northampton, July 30, 31, August 1, 1999. Northamptonshire won by an innings and 81 runs. The odds against a Northamptonshire victory when they stood at 58 for six on the opening morning would have been long enough; against them winning by an innings with a day to spare longer still. They owed everything to Sales, who became at 21 years 240 days the youngest English batsmen to record a first-class triple-century. He batted 466 minutes and 355 balls, hitting two sixes and 46 fours. Sales's achievement was all the more astonishing because he had only 229 when the ninth wicket fell. But Davies stayed with him for 20.2 overs and saw him through.

Northamptonshire 579 (D. J. Sales 303*, D. Ripley 94; A. P. Cowan 4-69); **Essex 355** (S. G. Law 117, P. J. Prichard 74; M. K. Davies 5-61) **and 143** (Davies 4-23).

2000 – BATHED IN A SHINING LIGHT
Andrew Radd, 2001

When Northamptonshire celebrated their considerable achievements in 2000 with an end-of-season presentation dinner, the County Championship's Division Two trophy was illuminated throughout the evening by a single spotlight. It could have been the Holy Grail, for it represented the club's first league title since Tom Horton's men were Minor Counties champions in 1904, paving the way for elevation to first-class status the following year.

2002 – NORTHAMPTONSHIRE v ESSEX: 632 A LOSING SCORE
2003

At Northampton, May 31, June 1, 2, 3, 2002. Essex won by four wickets. When Stephenson cut the winning runs on the last afternoon, he created an extraordinary piece of cricketing history: no side had scored more than Northamptonshire's 632 in an innings and gone on to lose. Left 291 to chase in 52 overs, Essex's openers provided a purposeful start but the dramatic final day belonged to Flower. With clouds gathering, the pitch wearing and wickets falling he did the leg-work with a run-a-ball, unbeaten 92. His reverse-sweeping against Brown's off-spin was so devastating that the bowler was at a loss to know what to try next. Flower and Dakin added 111 in only 18 overs, Stephenson rounded off his excellent all-round contribution with 25 from 22 balls and Essex secured an outstanding win with 13 balls to spare. It was an emphatic reversal of the opening day, when Northamptonshire took control on a perfect batting pitch.

Northamptonshire 632 (M. E. K. Hussey 140, J. W. Cook 90, A. S. Rollins 89, R. J. Warren 87,
T. M. B. Bailey 64, R. S. G. Anderson 51, A. L. Penberthy 50; Z. K. Sharif 4-98)
and 155 (J. P. Stephenson 4-25);
Essex 497-7 dec (A. Flower 103*, A. Habib 93, D. D. J. Robinson 68,
J. D. Middlebrook 67, R. C. Irani 54)
and 291-6 (Flower 92*, J. M. Dakin 57).

2004 – "CLUB IN DANGER OF LOSING ITS IDENTITY"
Andrew Radd, 2005

Graeme Swann, a free spirit not always on the same wavelength as Kepler Wessels [first-team manager], turned down a new contract and joined Nottinghamshire. Swann, the club's only senior England player in a decade (and that in a solitary one-day international), wrote in his last regular column for the Northampton *Chronicle & Echo* that Northamptonshire stood "in danger of losing its identity as the county's cricket club, unless there is a conscious effort to rebuild the sense of pride and kinship for the town and people". The fact that Bailey and Powell – like Swann, county-born – were also going, coupled with Wessels's criticisms of locally produced cricketers for not taking their opportunities, caused anger and consternation in some quarters.

Essex v Derbyshire. At Chelmsford, September 3, 4, 5, 6, 1991. Barnett was out one run short of joining the ranks of those with hundreds against all the other first-class counties, just as he was when seeking the same landmark at Southend three years earlier.

Little Wonder No. 112

2005 – FROM LEAGUE OF NATIONS ... TO KOLPAKSHIRE   Andrew Radd, 2006

In the 1950s, Northamptonshire were known – half-derisively, half-affectionately – as "the League of Nations" because of their plethora of imported players. In the 21st century, the jibes came back. In 2006, no county-born player was due to be on the staff for the first time since 1973. Sample teams from 1957 and 2005 (and their birthplaces):

v Sussex at Peterborough, July 20–23, 1957	v Durham at Northampton June 15–18, 2005
Dennis Brookes *Kippax, Yorkshire*	Martin Love *Mundubbera, Queensland*
Peter Arnold *Wellington, NZ*	Bilal Shafayat *Nottingham*
Jock Livingston *Sydney*	Rob White *Chelmsford*
Des Barrick *Fitzwilliam, Yorkshire*	Usman Afzaal *Rawalpindi*
Brian Reynolds* *Kettering*	David Sales *Carshalton*
George Tribe *Melbourne*	Riki Wessels *Nambour, Queensland*
Jon Fellows-Smith *Durban*	Damien Wright *Casino, NSW*
Jack Manning *Adelaide*	Ben Phillips *Lewisham*
Keith Andrew *Oldham*	Johann Louw *Cape Town*
Frank Tyson *Bolton*	Charl Pietersen *Kimberley, South Africa*
Mick Allen *Bedford*	Jason Brown *Newcastle-under-Lyme*

* Reynolds was the only Northamptonshire-born player in either team.

2012 – SORRY END TO COACH'S 33 YEARS WITH CLUB   Andrew Radd, 2013

Rarely since the grim days of the 1930s have the Northamptonshire faithful needed to draw so deeply on their famed reserves of resilience and patience. As if the weather wasn't bad enough – docking more than 1,500 overs (the equivalent of 15 days' play) from the Championship programme – only four matches were won in all competitions, the club's worst tally since the advent of the Sunday League in 1969. Their eighth-place finish in Division Two was in effect their lowest since 1978.

This conspicuous lack of success, particularly in the financially crucial white-ball formats, prompted the mid-season sacking of head coach David Capel. The manner of Capel's departure on July 3 – called in for an early-morning meeting with chief executive David Smith, in his first season at Northampton, and members of the committee ahead of a public announcement – was a sad way for his 33-year involvement with his home county to end.

NOTTINGHAMSHIRE

[1967 edition] *NOTTINGHAMSHIRE'S NOTABLE PART IN THE GROWTH OF CRICKET by R. T. Simpson*
It is the considered opinion of many lovers of cricket that no great cricket ground in these islands has a more charming situation than that of Trent Bridge.

1871 – NOTTINGHAMSHIRE v GLOUCESTERSHIRE: GRACE DELIVERS

1872

At Nottingham, August 21, 22, 23, 1871. This was Mr W. G. Grace's first match on the Trent Bridge ground. His anticipated appearance there had put cricket-loving Nottinghamshire into an extraordinary state of excitement, and the weather being fine the famous old ground was thronged on the Monday and Tuesday to an extent it had never before been thronged at a cricket match. Notwithstanding the attendance on the Wednesday fell far short of either of the preceding days, fully 25,000 visitors must have passed through the entrance gate during the three days. Mr Grace was loudly cheered, and deservedly so, for he made more than half the runs in each innings played by his county. The Notts eleven won by ten wickets.

Notts 364 (T. Bignall 96, R. Daft 84, Mr R. Tolley 54) **and 1-0**;
Gloucestershire 147 (Mr W. G. Grace 79; J. C. Shaw 9-86)
and 217 (Mr. Grace 116; F. Wyld 4-33, Shaw 4-77).

1872 – KEEPING WITHIN THE COUNTY BOUNDARIES

1873

The extra match at Prince's [against Yorkshire] turned out the trump card of the counties' contests in '72, for after a three days' skilful give-and-take struggle the Notts men won by six runs only; the pleasure of witnessing so gallantly contested and even a match being materially enhanced by the fact that there was not one foreigner in either eleven, each team being formed by natives of the Shire whose cricketing honour was so stoutly and ably upheld.

1876 – NORTH v SOUTH (RICHARD DAFT'S COMPLIMENTARY MATCH): DESERVED REWARD
1877

At Nottingham, July 17, 18, 19, 1876. The Nottinghamshire Club's praiseworthy determination to play a match during their 1876 season in compliment to their accomplished batsman, Richard Daft, gratified all classes of cricketers throughout the country; for in the estimation of the whole cricketing community none stand higher for character as a man, or skill as a batsman, than he whose match is here under notice. It was in 1858 or 18 years ago that the compiler of this book first saw Daft play cricket. Since then batsmen have come and batsmen have gone, but Daft has continued playing with a style, grace, and skill that has won him high praise from all classes of cricketers, praise for his batting and esteem for his character growing higher and warmer as season after season was played away and found Daft still the same as batsman and man.

1880 – CHAMPIONS AND VICTORY OVER AUSTRALIANS
1881

Nottinghamshire's splendid record – 12 matches played; eight won, one lost, three drawn – entitle the county to the Championship honours of the year 1880. Two of the victories were one-innings' affairs, and of the three drawn games two were greatly in favour of Notts, and the third an even draw. Notts wound up a brilliant season by defeating the Australians – a task that no other county team had been equal to. This long list of successes was mainly due to the exertions of three men – Shaw, Morley, and Barnes.

1886 – ENGLAND'S FINEST PROFESSIONAL BATSMAN
1887

Arthur Shrewsbury can boast among professional cricketers an absolutely unique record. No other player within our knowledge has ever scored four separate innings of over 200 for his county. He made 207 against Surrey at Kennington Oval in 1882; 209 against Sussex at Brighton in 1884; 224 not out against Middlesex at Lord's in 1885; and 227 not out against Gloucestershire last season. That he is the finest English professional batsman at the present day is indisputable.

1892 – MIDDLESEX v NOTTINGHAMSHIRE: KEEPER TURNS BOWLER
1893

At Lord's, June 20, 21, 22, 1892. The match between Middlesex and Notts will always be remembered for its remarkable finish, the result only being arrived at within four minutes of the call of time on the Wednesday evening, and the great change in the game being brought about by the unexpected success that attended the bowling of Sherwin. The Notts wicketkeeper clean-bowled Webbe at 247, and, with the score unaltered, Stoddart was out leg before wicket. Amidst tremendous excitement Thesiger was bowled at 250, and Rawlin at 252, while at 257 Hearne was caught by the wicketkeeper [Robinson], the ball only being held at the second attempt, and Notts won the match within four minutes of time by an innings and 14 runs.

Notts 466 (A. Shrewsbury 212, Mr J. S. Robinson 72, W. Attewell 59;
J. T. Hearne 4-117, Mr E. A. Nepean 4-133);
Middlesex 195 (Mr Nepean 61, Mr S. W. Scott 55; F. Shacklock 5-103)
and 257 (Mr A. E. Stoddart 130, Mr T. C. O'Brien 57; Attewell 4-38).

1900 – KENT v NOTTINGHAMSHIRE: BEST OF ITS TYPE   1901

At Blackheath, June 28, 29, 30, 1900. So far as it went, the match had one remarkable feature, Arthur Shrewsbury playing an extraordinary innings of 84 not out. He was batting on a very slow wicket for nearly five hours, and so complete was his command over the bowling that, except for a chance at mid-off when he had made 59, he was never at fault. Some of the spectators took exception to his extremely careful methods, but the Kent players were full of admiration for his skill, one prominent member of the team going so far as to describe the innings as, in its way, the best he had ever seen.

Kent 98 (T. G. Wass 4-41) **and 53-3**;
Notts 200-7 dec (A. Shrewsbury 84*).

1907 – UNBEATEN CHAMPIONS EARN EXTRA REWARDS   1908

As the result of first-rate all-round cricket, Notts regained their old position at the head of the counties. It was a great triumph, as 21 years had gone by since they were in front of all their rivals. Like Yorkshire in 1900, and Lancashire in 1904, they carried off the Championship without losing a match, and among the counties they shared with Surrey the honour of beating the South Africans.

As might have been expected, the success of Notts in winning the Championship caused keen delight all over the county. Never in recent times has local feeling in Nottingham reached such a pitch of interest as it did over the closing fixtures. As soon as the Championship had been secured a shilling subscription, with a limit of a guinea a head, was started in Nottingham on behalf of the professional members of the eleven. The response exceeded all expectations, £810 9s. 6d. being subscribed. The money was presented to the players at the Mechanics' Hall on September 18, Hallam and Wass, in recognition of their great bowling, receiving £100 each; Iremonger, John Gunn, George Gunn, Oates, Hardstaff, and Payton £90 each; Alletson £55 9s. 6d.; Stapleton, who kept wicket in place of Oates in two matches, £10; and James £5. Sir Francis Ley, president of the Club, gave a silver cigarette case, suitably inscribed, to every member of the team and a silver rose-bowl as an individual present to Mr A. O. Jones [the captain].

1908 – FIELDING PROBLEMS CAUSE FALL FROM GRACE

Like Kent in the previous year, Notts last season suffered a sudden fall from greatness. They actually lost more county matches than they won, their victories numbering six and their defeats seven.

For the falling off in the team there were several causes, but the chief one could be found in uncertain fielding. A. O. Jones, when discussing the season's play in August, said they had given every batsman opposed to them two innings instead of one. This, of course, was an exaggeration and not meant to be taken literally, but there can be no doubt that inability to hold catches had a disastrous effect. Some of the players took a slightly different view from that of their captain, saying that they seldom happened to be in quite the right places when the chances were given.

1911 – SUSSEX v NOTTINGHAMSHIRE: ALLETSON'S INNINGS

At Brighton, Thursday, Friday, Saturday, May 18, 19, 20, 1911. A phenomenal display of driving on the part of Edward Alletson rendered this match memorable. Alletson went in when Notts in their second innings, with seven men out, were only nine runs ahead. Before lunch, he took 50 minutes to make 47, but on resuming hit away with such extraordinary power and freedom that he added 142 out of 152 for the last wicket in 40 minutes, actually scoring his last 89 runs in 15 minutes. Twice he sent the ball over the stand, and on six other occasions cleared the ring, while in one over from Killick that included two no-balls he hit three sixes and four fours – 34 runs in all. His glorious innings was made up by eight sixes, 23 fours, four threes, ten twos and 17 singles. Sussex, instead of gaining the easy victory which appeared assured before Alletson's tremendous hitting, had 237 to make in three hours and a quarter. Robert Relf and Vine scored 112 in 75 minutes, but six men were out for 148 and the eighth wicket fell ten minutes before time.

Notts **238** (G. Gunn 90, Mr A. O. Jones 57; E. H. Killick 5-14)
and 412 (E. B. Alletson 189, J. Iremonger 83, Gunn 66);
Sussex **414** (Killick 81, J. Vine 77, G. Leach 52) **and 213-8** (R. R. Relf 71, Vine 54; W. Riley 4-82).

1914 – SADLY PREMATURE END TO CAPTAIN'S CAREER

No doubt the unhappy loss of A. O. Jones as captain brought about to a large extent the sort of lassitude that came over the team. Nothing could replace the captain's contagious energy and enthusiasm. Jones started playing at the beginning of the season, but it was plain to all his friends that he would not be able to go on for long. Sadly wasted and looking wretchedly ill, he was a mere shadow of his old self. By sheer pluck he struggled through five matches, his last appearance being against Hampshire at Southampton, in the second week in June. He finished up well, scoring 33 and helping Iremonger to save Notts from a follow-on.

MR ARTHUR OWEN JONES died on December 21, at his brother's house at Dunstable. During the summer he spent some time at a sanatorium in the New Forest, but nothing could be done for him, consumption being too far advanced. He went home, given up as incurable, and the end came as a release from his sufferings. In the winter of 1907-08, when in Australia as captain of the MCC's team, he had a severe illness, from the effects of which he perhaps never wholly recovered. However, he was able to resume his career in England in 1908, and continued to play as much cricket as ever. Early in the season of 1913 he contracted a violent chill, playing on a bitterly cold afternoon at Manchester. This kept him out of the field for more than two months, and no doubt brought on the illness which ended in his premature death.

1921 – NOTTINGHAMSHIRE v AUSTRALIANS: HUMILIATED   1922

At Nottingham, June 25, 27, 1921. In the long history of Notts cricket there has perhaps never been such a deplorable match as this. The county began well when Richmond clean-bowled Bardsley, but for the rest of the game they were hopelessly outplayed, and in the end they suffered defeat by an innings and 517 runs. On the admission of the Notts batsmen themselves nothing in the condition of the ground offered the least excuse for such miserable scores as 58 and 100. Indeed, the pitch was so good that even Gregory could not make the ball get up. Despite Bardsley's failure the Australians on the first day scored 608 for seven wickets. Notts had to pay a terribly high price for one blunder, Macartney being missed in the slips when he had made nine. Never afterwards at fault, he went on to play the highest innings of the season, scoring his 345 in rather less than four hours. He simply did as he liked with the bowling, hitting four sixes and 47 fours. One of the sixes – off John Gunn – went clean out of the ground. Pellew was also very brilliant, getting his 100 in an hour and three quarters. While he was in with Macartney 291 runs were put on. After lunch the Notts bowling was weakened by the absence of Barratt, who had injured his hand. Though batting a man short, Oates having damaged his thumb, Notts ought to have saved the game, but the batting was dreadfully feeble. When they followed on George Gunn shewed good defence for an hour and a quarter, and Carr made a few fine hits, but that was all.

Australians 675 (C. G. Macartney 345, C. E. Pellew 100, H. L. Hendry 51, J. M. Taylor 50; J. Hardstaff 5-133); **Notts 58** (J. M. Gregory 4-23) **and 100** (A. A. Mailey 4-36).

1925 – LARWOOD'S FORM PROMISES BIG FUTURE   1926

Most interesting of all in these new developments was the advent of Larwood who, coming into the team in the middle of June, took 73 wickets for 18 runs apiece.

Although only of moderate height, Larwood is very strong and, with a fine command of pitch, maintains a splendid pace. A useful bat, as well as a fine bowler, he should have a big future in front of him.

1928 – Still Going Great Gunns   1929

George Gunn lives as one of the cricketing marvels of the age. No man has ever made batting look more simple than this veteran, and last season his genius was almost as pronounced as during the earlier stages of his career. He played a wonderful innings to beat Kent at Trent Bridge, and besides that memorable 100 not out he reached three figures upon five other occasions, the graceful ease of his methods being just as striking as it had been 20 years previously.

Barratt scored 1,000 runs and took 100 wickets, and was the first Notts cricketer to accomplish the double feat since John Gunn achieved that distinction in 1906. Larwood, A. Staples, and Voce belonging to the younger generation, and considerable expectations being entertained of F. W. Shipston, W. W. Keeton and G. V. Gunn, the Notts outlook is again distinctly hopeful. The reference to G. V. Gunn recalls the long association of that family with Notts cricket. The late William Gunn first played for the county in 1880, and since then the side has never been representative unless it has included a man bearing that name.

1929 – NOTTINGHAMSHIRE v YORKSHIRE: substandard play   1930

At Nottingham, July 13, 15, 16, 1929. A really appalling game was this return match, no more than 688 runs being registered in the course of three full days' cricket and the average rate of scoring being only 40 an hour. Yorkshire occupied nine hours and three quarters in making 498 and then Notts proceeded to play such purely defensive cricket that at the end of seven hours and a quarter they had registered no more than 190 runs and had lost four wickets. Whatever the motives directing the course pursued, the consequence was cricket of a distressingly wearisome description – play which, whatever the circumstances, should not have been indulged in before spectators who had paid to witness a first-class match.

Yorkshire 498 (P. Holmes 285, W. Rhodes 79; W. Voce 4-99);
Notts 190-4 (G. Gunn 58, W. W. Whysall 58).

1930 – Thousands Mourn Whysall   1931

For the fourth year in succession Whysall headed the batting table. His aggregate in Championship games was not quite so high as in the preceding summer but once again – in all matches – he made more than 2,000 runs and in the course of those contests reached three figures upon eight occasions, among his special triumphs being 248 – the highest individual score of his career – against Northamptonshire. In such wonderful form was he at the height of the season that during one period of less than three weeks he registered 853 runs, among the triumphs of this wonderful spell being four consecutive hundreds – 117 and 101, not out, against Hampshire, 120 against the Australians and 158 against Warwickshire. His splendid success earned him a place in the England eleven for the last Test match but, unhappily, he accomplished nothing on that all-important occasion.

A terribly sad loss befell Notts within two months of the close of the season. Meeting with an injury [to his elbow] through a fall in a dancing hall, Whysall developed blood poisoning of so fatal a description that he died on November 11. In this tragic fashion there passed away the soundest of batsmen who have appeared for Notts since the War. His funeral at Mansfield was attended by a company of several thousand people.

Hampshire v Middlesex. At Bournemouth, August 18, 19, 20, 1992. After the game, Hampshire's final first-class match at Dean Park, a spectator placed a solitary rose on the wicket with a card marked, "Fondest Memories of Hampshire cricket at Bournemouth – Will Ye No Come Back Again?"

Little Wonder No. 113

1938 – RAIN AND INJURIES SPOIL CENTENARY SEASON 1939

Seldom can a county of high renown have experienced so many misfortunes as befell Nottinghamshire during 1938, the season that marked the centenary of the Trent Bridge ground. Three fixtures were abandoned without a first-innings result and to the interference of many home engagements by the weather could be attributed some of the personal mishaps which tended seriously to handicap the eleven. Rain ruined the outdoor ceremonies arranged for centenary day; wet and cold winds spoiled some of the most attractive fixtures.

As if diminished gate receipts were not a sufficient blow, rheumatism attacked Larwood, sciatica incapacitated Staples, appendicitis terminated Butler's activities, synovitis held up Voce, and an injured ankle prevented Woodhead from showing his full possibilities as a fast bowler.

1948 – NOTTINGHAMSHIRE v SURREY: RECORD CROWD 1949

At Nottingham, May 15, 17, 18, 1948. Nottinghamshire won by four wickets. Set to get 266 in 160 minutes, they won with half an hour to spare. A record crowd of

35,000 on Monday saw Keeton and Hardstaff give Nottinghamshire a useful position, but with seven men out 93 were required for the lead. Sime and Butler added 80 in 40 minutes, and Nottinghamshire went ahead with the last man in. Surrey batted brightly before declaring, but splendid hitting by Keeton and Hardstaff, who put on 109 in threequarters of an hour, turned the scale in a splendid game.

Surrey 419 (M. R. Barton 132, L. B. Fishlock 70, A. J. McIntyre 54)

and 266-8 dec (H. S. Squires 110, F. R. Brown 54);

Nottinghamshire 420-9 dec (W. W. Keeton 104, J. Hardstaff 100, W. A. Sime 52*; Squires 4-56)

and 266-6 (Hardstaff 79, Keeton 64).

1951 – DECLINE AND FALL TO NEW LOW POINT   1952

Their steady decline of the post-war years reached a climax in 1951 when Nottinghamshire, for so long among the most powerful of cricket counties, found themselves at the foot of the table for the first time in their long history. How poor was their record can be gauged from the fact that they gained only 40 points from 28 Championship matches – 20 less than any other county – and the summer brought one solitary victory, over Hampshire.

Nottinghamshire broke with tradition in going outside the county for a player when they specially registered Smales, of Yorkshire. He showed promise both as batsman and off-break bowler. The amenities of Trent Bridge were further improved in 1951 by the provision of an electrically operated scoreboard on Australian lines.

1954 – AUSTRALIAN RECRUIT INSPIRES REVIVAL   1955

The revival which began with the acquisition of the Australian, Dooland, the previous summer, continued when the county rose three places in the Championship and finished fifth, their highest position for 18 years. In match after match opposing batsmen fell to his expertly-flighted leg-breaks and googlies in such numbers that, with 196 wickets, he again took more than any other bowler in the country. His pre-eminence among bowlers of his type in England was recognised when MCC chose him to appear for Players against Gentlemen at Lord's.

1968 – SOBERS LEADS FROM THE FRONT   1969

Nottinghamshire county cricket gained a tremendous boost from the introduction of Garfield Sobers, the West Indies captain, to lead the side. From the struggling team of recent seasons they were rejuvenated, and it was no more than they deserved to finish fourth in the County Championship. Sobers, by performance and example, inspired his men and not only were they among the fastest scorers in the Championship but, in addition, they got through their overs quicker than most. Not unexpectedly, Sobers finished top of the batting averages for the county and second in the bowling.

Throughout a hard season, his enthusiasm remained undimmed and he was always ready to gamble to keep a game alive. He played many great innings, but his outstanding feat was the world record of six sixes in an over from Nash, the Glamorgan bowler, at Swansea [see page 969].

1973 – NEW LOOK ACROSS THE BOARD 1974

During the summer, Trent Bridge, Nottinghamshire's well-maintained Test headquarters, began to show the face of change. The former mammoth scoreboard, considered the most comprehensive in the world, disappeared. In full operation it needed five men to work it and was much too costly. It was replaced by a sophisticated streamlined board which is, in the main, electrically operated. Then, too, the Fox and Hound Road stands disappeared and their place will be taken by a big block of flats and offices.

1979 – NOTTINGHAMSHIRE v MIDDLESEX: FINAL FLOURISH 1980

At Nottingham, September 5, 6, 7, 1979. Drawn. Although the game ended early in bad light on the final day, enough cricket was played during the three days for Randall to stamp an historic mark on the proceedings. In what had been a fairly moderate season for him, he signed off with a double-century and a century – the first time the feat had ever been achieved at Trent Bridge.

Nottinghamshire 376-8 (100 overs) (D. W. Randall 209; M. W. W. Selvey 5-109)
and 279-2 dec (Randall 146, M. J. Harris 58*);
Middlesex 362-7 dec (G. D. Barlow 133, W. N. Slack 66, M. W. Gatting 56)
and 101-2 (Barlow 60*).

1980 – NOTTINGHAMSHIRE v AUSTRALIANS: TURN OF THE CENTURY 1981

At Nottingham, August 23, 24, 25, 1980. Nottinghamshire won by an innings and 76 runs. They completed an emphatic victory – the biggest inflicted on the Australians by a county side this century. They began their domination after the Australians slid from 146 for two to 207 all out on the opening day against the inspired bowling of Watson and Hadlee – both overseas players. Then, after losing Todd without a run on the board, Nottinghamshire amassed a huge total at a rate of between five and six runs an over. Surprisingly no century was scored – except in the Australian bowling figures. Had it not been for Lillee, with six for 133, Australia would have been in an even sorrier position. They were 258 behind on first innings and never came to terms with the task of saving the match.

Australians 207 (G. M. Wood 76, A. R. Border 73; W. K. Watson 5-57) **and 182**;
Nottinghamshire 465 (C. E. B. Rice 90, R. J. Hadlee 68, J. D. Birch 57; D. K. Lillee 6-133).

1981 – HADLEE AND RICE REVIVE HAPPY MEMORIES John Lawson, 1982

Not since the days of Harold Larwood and Bill Voce had Trent Bridge hosted such celebratory scenes as those that greeted Nottinghamshire's final victory of the season over Glamorgan. The win – the ninth in their last 11 games of the summer – gave them the County Championship for the first time for 52 years.

It was a title-winning effort that, as in the Nottinghamshire days of old, owed much to the devil and destruction of a formidable new-ball attack. Richard Hadlee and Clive Rice exploited to the full Trent Bridge wickets that were always well-grassed; they capitalised, too, on Rice's remarkable good fortune in winning all but the first toss of the season in home fixtures.

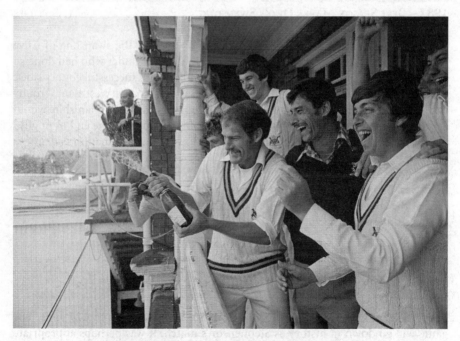

View from the Bridge: Nottinghamshire captain Clive Rice,
with star all-rounder Richard Hadlee at his left shoulder,
celebrates the county's first championship title for 52 years.
Seamer Mike Bore is in the foreground,
wicketkeeper Bruce French visible behind Rice and Hadlee

1984 – LAST MAN'S GAMBLE FALLS JUST SHORT   John Lawson, 1985

They entered the final day of the season against Somerset at Taunton knowing that if they won that match they would pip Essex, who had just overtaken them by accounting for Lancashire in two days. Somerset's declaration was challenging, leaving Nottinghamshire chasing 297 against the clock. With Clive Rice playing a captain's innings, they kept in touch with their target for most of the way, but 27 were needed off the last two overs and 14 off the last. Mike Bore, who has rarely had pretensions to being anything other than a No. 11 batsman, was the unlikely figure Nottinghamshire looked to in this gripping climax to the season, and he looked capable of achieving the unexpected when he reduced the target to four from three balls. Having blocked the first, he gambled all on hitting the penultimate delivery for six, but was caught on the long-off boundary.

As in previous seasons, much emanated from the talents of the New Zealand all-rounder, Richard Hadlee. His remarkable displays, which brought him the coveted double of 1,000 runs and 100 wickets, were a constant source of inspiration to his colleagues. Not since Fred Titmus in 1967 had anyone achieved the double, and there was a lot more first-class cricket in those days.

1987 – BEST SEASON MARKS DUO'S SWANSONG   John Lawson, 1988

A scriptwriter could not have devised anything better for the swansong of Clive Rice and Richard Hadlee, the South African and New Zealander who had done so much to transform Nottinghamshire into one of the most successful county sides. At one time, with the Britannic Assurance Championship, NatWest Bank Trophy and Refuge Assurance League in their sights, it looked as if Nottinghamshire would capture a remarkable treble. Then, for an agonising fortnight at the end of August, all the old doubts and uncertainties returned. However, determination had always been as significant a quality of Rice and Hadlee as their natural talent, and they were determined to capture honours as proof of the best season in the club's history. So it was. First came the NatWest Trophy, then the Championship, and they were denied the treble by Worcestershire's winning the Sunday League, having to settle for the runners-up prizemoney.

1988 – NOTTINGHAMSHIRE v YORKSHIRE: GROUND-BREAKER   1989

At Nottingham, September 14, 15, 16, 17, 1988. Yorkshire won by 127 runs. The game will go down in history as Stephenson's match. It was perhaps appropriate that in the year celebrating the 150th anniversary of Trent Bridge, the final match of the season should produce a feat never before seen on the ground. Only twice before in first-class cricket had a player scored, as Stephenson did against Yorkshire, two hundreds and taken ten wickets in the same match: B. J. T. Bosanquet, Middlesex v Surrey at Lord's in 1905, and G. H. Hirst, Yorkshire v Somerset at

Bath in 1906. At the start of the match, Stephenson required 210 runs to complete the double for the season. Bearing in mind that he had never scored a hundred for Nottinghamshire, the feat appeared beyond him. In the first innings, however, when only Johnson among his colleagues mastered the bowling, he hit 111 in 157 minutes, including a six and 18 fours. In the second innings, his 117 came in 137 minutes with 20 fours and two sixes, and while he chanced his arm, he gave no actual chances.

Yorkshire 380 (P. E. Robinson 98, A. A. Metcalfe 74, M. D. Moxon 68; F. D. Stephenson 4-105)

and 340-7 dec (D. L. Bairstow 94*, Robinson 80; Stephenson 7-117);

Nottinghamshire 296 (Stephenson 111, P. Johnson 59; A. Sidebottom 7-89)

and 297 (Stephenson 117, D. W. Randall 59; S. D. Fletcher 6-74).

1989 – ESSEX v NOTTINGHAMSHIRE (BENSON AND HEDGES CUP FINAL): HAPPY HEMMINGS   1990

At Lord's, July 15, 1989. Nottinghamshire won by three wickets. A match which was often dull began amusingly when Stephenson bowled Hardie with his renowned slower ball in the third over, and ended excitingly with Nottinghamshire requiring nine runs from the last over and four from the final delivery. Had the scores finished level, Essex would have won as they were ahead after 30 overs. The last over was bowled by Lever, whose first eight overs had cost just 15 runs for two wickets; Broad was marvellously caught by Garnham, diving far to his left. Gooch was an age setting the field for Lever's last ball, to Hemmings, and ended up with all but one man on the on side. Hemmings made room, drove, and the ball raced to the backward-point boundary with Hardie in vain pursuit.

Essex 243-7 (55 overs) (A. W. Lilley 95*, G. A. Gooch 48, M. E. Waugh 41);

Nottinghamshire 244-7 (55 overs) (R. T. Robinson 86, P. Johnson 54, D. W. Randall 49).

1993 – NOTTINGHAMSHIRE v WORCESTERSHIRE: PICKED OFF   1994

At Nottingham, April 29, 30, May 1, 2, 1993. Tied. The season began with Nottinghamshire's first-ever tie in first-class cricket and Worcestershire's first since 1939. Pick, suffering from a badly bruised foot, missed the third day's play, on which he became the father of a son. He returned to be at the centre of the drama. He was beaten by Seymour's accurate throw from the square-leg boundary and just failed to complete the second run that would have given Nottinghamshire victory off the last available ball. The last pair had needed five when Newport began the final over.

Worcestershire 203 and 325-8 dec (T. S. Curtis 113; G. W. Mike 5-65);

Nottinghamshire 233 and 295 (D. W. Randall 98, C. L. Cairns 68; P. J. Newport 6-63).

2010 – LANCASHIRE v NOTTINGHAMSHIRE: POINTS MADE 2011

At Manchester, September 13, 14, 15, 16, 2010. Drawn. For Nottinghamshire, three days of frustration and helplessness ended in the exhilaration of a Championship title that had looked wholly improbable during a further delay on the final morning. Only 28 overs had been possible on the previous days. Meanwhile, rival contenders Somerset and Yorkshire were making progress against Durham and Kent, forcing Read to consider contrivance to salvage his side's bid. They decided instead to gamble that a draw plus bonus points would be enough and, in that unwanted extra hour in the pavilion on the last morning, Durham and Kent offered fresh reasons for optimism. Nottinghamshire resumed on 89 for two, needing another 311 from 82, but it was only when Patel joined Voges that the strategy became clear. Patel hit 96 from 91 balls, his best performance of a lean first-class season, and Voges's century was a fine effort considering the pressure he had felt after replacing David Hussey. They added 153 in 28 overs but, after Patel holed out to long-off, Nottinghamshire lost four more wickets. They were still ten short of the magic 400 when last man Pattinson joined Sidebottom. While their team-mates sweated in a silent dressing-room, the tailenders held their nerve, eking out the runs from 31 balls. Provided there were no further sun delays – a possibility on what had become a glorious Manchester evening – that left 18 overs to take three Lancashire wickets for a sixth bonus point, which would put them level on points with Somerset but ahead on matches won. After a single over from the Statham end, Sidebottom switched and had Karl Brown caught low down by Hales at first slip. Adams then had Chilton caught behind off the first ball of the next over and, three deliveries later, Chanderpaul at third slip.

Nottinghamshire 400-9 dec (A. C. Voges 126, S. R. Patel 96; S. C. Kerrigan 5-80);
Lancashire 11-3.

2011 – YORKSHIRE v NOTTINGHAMSHIRE: BEST SINCE BOTHAM

At Leeds, April 20, 21, 22, 2011. Nottinghamshire won by 58 runs. Nottinghamshire staged the biggest turnaround at Headingley since the Botham and Willis Ashes Test almost 30 years earlier, to spark delirium in their dressing-room and despair in Yorkshire's. At the start of the third day, Nottinghamshire trailed by 18 with four wickets remaining. But as the shadows lengthened that evening they ambled off easy winners, having routed Yorkshire, set 145 to win, for their lowest score this century. Bairstow was left stranded and nonplussed: it was the 17th time he had reached a first-class fifty without going on to a hundred, and the ninth in which he was not out. Yorkshire's demise had little to do with the conditions and much to do with their own frailties.

Nottinghamshire 143 (A. D. Hales 85; R. M. Pyrah 5-58, R. J. Sidebottom 4-30)
and 337 (C. M. W. Read 86, Hales 83, S. J. Mullaney 83; Sidebottom 4-67);
Yorkshire 336 (A. W. Gale 145*, A. Lyth 64; L. J. Fletcher 4-97) and 86 (J. M. Bairstow 50*).

SOMERSET

[1895 edition] Somerset cricketers are apparently of a mercurial disposition.
Their history has been a record of brilliant victories and disheartening reverses,
but the variability of their play has made it none the less attractive.

1891 – TABLES TURNED IN BRILLIANT STYLE
1892

The arrangement by Somersetshire at the meeting of county secretaries at Lord's in December, 1890, of an exclusively first-class programme increased the leading counties in 1891 from eight to nine.

Early in the season a crushing defeat [by an innings and 375 runs] was sustained at the hands of Surrey. The return fixture with the champion county was emphatically the match of the season.

Nottinghamshire v Cambridge University. At Nottingham, June 27, 28, 29, 1992. Arscott and Johnson arrived late on the first day because they had been in Cambridge receiving their degrees. The umpires deemed these "exceptional circumstances" and allowed Johnson to bowl at once.

Little Wonder No. 114

1891 – SOMERSET v SURREY: STROKE OF TIME
1892

At Taunton, August 13, 14, 15, 1891. From every point of view this game, so far as Somerset were concerned, was a great success, the home team having the distinction of beating the famous Surrey eleven in the County Championship competition. The attendances were larger than at any previous match on the Taunton ground, fine weather prevailed throughout, and the contest, which was played on a good wicket, produced a remarkable finish, Surrey being only beaten a minute before time. As nearly as possible four hours remained for play when Surrey went in, requiring 372 runs to win, and of course all they had to play for was a draw. At five o'clock only five wickets were down. Then followed some intensely exciting cricket. At 236 Lockwood had his leg stump bowled down, and a run later Mr Key and Brockwell were out to wretched strokes, and Maurice Read was bowled by a fine ball. This last disaster proved fatal to Surrey, for with only one wicket to fall the visitors had still ten minutes to play. Wood and Sharpe played two or three overs, and then Mr Woods, who bowled finely in the last half-hour, got a ball past Sharpe, and the innings closed for 241, Somerset winning almost on the stroke of time by 130 runs. There was a great display of enthusiasm at the finish, and the victorious eleven were warmly congratulated on their brilliant and well deserved triumph.

> **Somersetshire 194** (Mr H. T. Hewett 55; G. A. Lohmann 5-84)
> **and 331-9 dec** (Mr J. B. Challen 89, Mr L. C. H. Palairet 60);
> **Surrey 154** (G. B. Nichols 4-52, Mr S. M. J. Woods 4-70)
> **and 241** (J. M. Read 94, Lohmann 58; Mr Woods 5-103).

1894 – To Lose One Match In One Day Is Unfortunate... 1895

Matches in which the Somerset men are engaged are rarely lacking in points of interest, and some curious ups and downs of fortune were experienced last season. In the first place the eleven assisted in the establishment of a new record in county cricket, the distinction in this instance, however, being far from enviable. As in 1892 the match with Lancashire at Old Trafford was commenced and finished on the second day, and two days later the game with Yorkshire at Huddersfield was concluded in a similarly abrupt manner. On both occasions Somerset, though going in first, were beaten in a single innings, and cricket history contains no previous record of two such disasters overtaking a county in the same week.

1901 – YORKSHIRE v SOMERSET: SENSATIONAL TURNAROUND 1902

At Leeds, July 15, 16, 17, 1901. This was the sensational match of the whole season, and the only county fixture in which Yorkshire suffered defeat. To the wonderful victory gained by Somerset, cricket history can furnish few parallels. They started their second innings on the Tuesday morning against a majority of 238, and yet in the end they won the game by 279 runs. Superb batting turned the scale, L. C. H. Palairet and Braund scoring 222 in two hours and 20 minutes for the first wicket. Thanks to this brilliant partnership, the Yorkshire bowling was quite mastered, and for the rest of the afternoon the hitting went on at such a pace that at the drawing of stumps the total stood at 549 with only five men out. Palairet and Braund of course took the chief honours, but Phillips's play was almost equally fine. Palairet was batting three hours and 40 minutes. The Yorkshiremen thought that Braund was caught at slip by Tunnicliffe when he had 55. Owing to the bowler being in his way, Mycroft could not give a decision, and Walter Wright on being appealed to decided in the batsman's favour. On the third day the Yorkshiremen collapsed very badly.

> **Somerset 87** (W. Rhodes 5-39) **and 630** (Mr L. C. H. Palairet 173, Mr F. A. Phillips 122,
> L. C. Braund 107, Mr S. M. J. Woods 66, Mr V. T. Hill 53; Rhodes 6-145);
> **Yorkshire 325** (S. Haigh 96, G. H. Hirst 61; G. C. Gill 4-105, B. Cranfield 4-113)
> **and 113** (Cranfield 4-35, Braund 4-41).

1903 – BATH WEEK WASHED AWAY 1904

Not a ball could be bowled in the fixture with Hampshire at Bath. On the second day the river Avon, which runs along one side of the Recreation Ground, over-flowed its banks, and before long the enclosure was like a big lake, the water in places being five to six feet deep. The Bath week was utterly ruined, for in the first match cricket was only possible on one day.

1913 – AGE SHALL NOT WEARY HIM ... 1914

The veteran wicketkeeper, A. E. Newton, played in a few matches and showed that his skill had not left him. Born in September, 1862, he is one of the oldest men now taking part in first-class cricket.

1915

In a few matches A. E. Newton showed remarkable form behind the wickets for a man approaching the age of 52.

Obituary, 1953

NEWTON, MR ARTHUR EDWARD, who died at his home at Trull, Somerset on September 15, three days after his 90th birthday, was a famous wicketkeeper who continued his activities in club cricket until the age of 81. When 74, having cycled to the Taunton ground to turn out for Somerset Stragglers, he demon-strated that his ability had not seriously declined by stumping five batsmen. While at Eton in 1880 he began an association with Somerset which lasted for 34 years.

1924 – FOUR GENTLEMEN OF TAUNTON 1925

It was a great compliment to Somerset cricket in 1924 that four members of the eleven – J. C. W. MacBryan, M. D. Lyon, J. C. White, and R. C. Robertson-Glasgow – were given places in the Gentlemen's team against the Players at Lord's, and all strictly on their merits. Three had played in 1923, MacBryan and Robertson-Glasgow now coming in for the first time and T. C. Lowry standing down. That the Gentlemen lost the match is nothing to the point. They had about the best side obtainable, and supporters of Somerset had every reason to be proud that their county was so fully represented.

1931 – FORMER CAPTAIN RETURNS TO PROP UP COUNTY   1932

Mr John Daniell, the old Somerset captain and famous rugby-football forward, undertook to perform the duties of secretary for a year and, at a time of great financial stress, to render the county further help by taking no payment for his services.

1935 – WELLARD ATTRACTS ATTENTION   1936

The oft-repeated assertion that Somerset's cricket in recent years suffered by the absence of a really outstanding personality no longer held good. In Wellard they possessed not only one of the best all-rounders of the year, but a player who achieved such distinction that seldom a day passed without his name figuring prominently in the headlines. Hailed as the modern Jessop – albeit entirely different in style to that great hitter – he owed his popularity to punishing powers that brought him as many as 72 sixes during the season. In the absence of figures to prove otherwise, it would be almost safe to assume that the number of these hits constituted an individual record for first-class cricket in this country. With strong arms and shoulders, Wellard is literally built for driving, and quickness of hand, eye and foot invariably enables him to time his vigorous strokes to perfection. Although he accomplished the cricketers' double for the second time in his career, he did not find a place in England's team, but there is little doubt his claims were closely considered for the Oval Test match. Honoured by an invitation to assist the Rest of England against Yorkshire, he bowled really well in that game.

1935 – SOMERSET v ESSEX: AUDACIOUS GIMBLETT   1936

At Frome, May 18, 20, 21, 1935. A remarkable century by Gimblett, playing in his first match for Somerset, completely overshadowed everything else at Frome, where Essex were beaten by an innings and 49 runs. Full of confidence from the start of his innings, Gimblett, whose previous experience had largely been confined to club cricket at Watchet, reached three figures in 63 minutes – the fastest hundred of the season. He completed his first fifty in 28 minutes, and altogether scored 123 out of 175 in 80 minutes, his principal scoring strokes being three sixes and 17 fours. When Gimblett went in Somerset had lost six wickets for 107 runs; he attacked the bowling like a seasoned player and, ninth out at 282, placed his side in what proved to be a winning position. Possessing a very upright stance, Gimblett cut, drove, pulled and hooked in a manner that set cricket circles talking for weeks of his audacious batting. Without scoring so fast as Gimblett, Andrews also gave a grand display of hard hitting, and with the aid of three sixes and five fours obtained 71 in 50 minutes. Owing to rain, play was impossible on the second day, and on Tuesday Essex, who resumed with half their wickets down for 87, were overwhelmed.

Somerset 337 (H. Gimblett 123, W. H. R. Andrews 71; M. S. Nichols 6-87);
Essex 141 (A. W. Wellard 5-66, J. W. Lee 4-26) and 147 (Lee 5-67).

1936 – SOMERSET v YORKSHIRE: A VERITABLE HAMMERING 1937

At Bath, June 24, 25, 1936. Hunt and Hazell, the last pair, put in some terrific hitting at the expense of Verity. Hazell scored 28 in one over from the left-hander – 666046 – and Hunt hit successive deliveries for two sixes and two fours. Nine overs from Verity yielded 89 runs.

1936 – SOMERSET v DERBYSHIRE: GIVING IT SOME WELLY 1937

At Wells, August 26, 27, 28, 1936. Somerset won by one wicket. In a great finish, they beat Derbyshire for the second time in the season. Needing 271 to win, Somerset lost half their side for 140, but Wellard scored tremendously fast. Missed when one off Armstrong, he drove that bowler for five successive sixes, a feat considered a record. Of the 86 he scored out of 102 in 62 minutes, Wellard made 74 in 15 strokes: seven sixes and eight fours. As he took nine wickets and scored 103 runs, Wellard bore a leading part in the triumph. Despite his batting effort, six runs were wanted when the ninth wicket fell, but Hazell settled matters with two boundaries. McRae, who played a fine defensive innings at a crisis, was carried shoulder-high from the field.

Derbyshire 216 (D. Smith 93; W. H. R. Andrews 5-42, A. W. Wellard 4-52)

and 200 (Mr A. W. Richardson 50; Wellard 5-47);

Somerset 146 (A. V. Pope 5-35)

and 274-9 (Wellard 86; W. H. Copson 6-81).

1937 – MASTER OF SPIN CALLS TIME ON CAREER R. W. Thick, 1938

J. C. White, after taking part in a few matches, announced his retirement from first-class cricket. One of the most distinguished players who ever appeared for Somerset and one of the best slow left-arm bowlers who ever figured in the game, he took 2,358 wickets in first-class cricket. In every season from 1919 to 1932 inclusive he took over 100 wickets, and against Worcestershire at Worcester in 1921 he secured all ten in an innings. He appeared in seven Test matches against Australia.

1938 – SOMERSET v KENT: OWN RECORD BEATEN 1939

At Wells, August 24, 25, 1938. Somerset won by 27 runs. The match provided a personal triumph for Wellard, a Kent-born player, who dismissed 13 batsmen for 115 runs, and gave a magnificent display of hard, clean driving. On a small ground, which favoured forcing tactics, Wellard, in Somerset's first innings, included seven sixes in his 57 made in 37 minutes. So fiercely did he attack one over from Woolley that five sixes and a single obtained through a dropped catch enabled him to surpass his 30 in an over by means of five consecutive sixes off Derbyshire's bowling on the same ground two seasons before.

Somerset 225 (A. W. Wellard 57, Mr M. D. Lyon 50*; C. Lewis 6-76)
and 177 (W. H. R. Andrews 54; N. W. Harding 5-51);
Kent 215 (Mr B. H. Valentine 114, Mr C. H. Knott 65; Wellard 7-65)
and 160 (Wellard 6-50, H. L. Hazell 4-60).

1953 – SOMERSET v LANCASHIRE (H. F. T. Buse's Benefit): HEAVY COST
1954

At Bath, June 6, 1953. Lancashire won by an innings and 24 runs. A newly-laid pitch brought financial disaster for Buse, the match ending before six o'clock on the first day when 30 wickets fell for 292 runs. Tattersall, the England and Lancashire off-spin bowler, carried everything before him, taking 13 for 69. His seven victims in the first innings, when not one Somerset player reached double figures, were all caught. The best stand of the match for the losers came in their second innings, Redman and Langford adding 35 in a plucky final partnership. Ironical as it seemed, Buse proved Somerset's central figure with the ball. Although hit for 18 in one over, he dismissed six batsmen for 41 runs. Lancashire, who lost half their side for 46, were put in a winning position by Marner and Wharton, whose fierce hitting brought 70 for the sixth stand in 25 minutes. Four times Marner cleared the boundary with huge hits for six.

Somerset 55 (R. Tattersall 7-25) and 79 (Tattersall 6-44, J. B. Statham 4-13);
Lancashire 158 (H. F. T. Buse 6-41).

MCC matches in 1994. MCC played a record 220 schools during the season, a pleasing result of their policy of encouraging schools cricket. One of the highlights was the appearance of West Indian umpire Steve Bucknor, who stood in the club's tied game with Wellington College, on a weekend off between Tests in June. He then volunteered to stand in an under-14 six-a-side house match.

Little Wonder No. 115

1954 – SOMERSET v KENT: BONNY LANGFORD
1955

At Bath, June 10, 11, 12, 1954. Somerset won by 153 runs. Their victory proved a great personal triumph for Langford, a 17-year-old off-spin bowler, who took 14 wickets for 156. Making his second appearance for Somerset, he turned the ball to a steady length, and few played him with confidence.

Somerset 123 (J. C. T. Page 5-35, D. V. P. Wright 4-53)

and 416-8 dec (H. Gimblett 146, H. F. T. Buse 102, J. Lawrence 65; Page 4-126);

Kent 178 (B. A. Langford 8-96)

and 208 (A. F. Woollett 73, B. R. Edrich 54; Langford 6-60, Lawrence 4-91).

1955 – Short Of The Required Skill   1956

Once more the Somerset team consisted mostly of players lacking the skill required to form a good match-winning combination and the county finished at the bottom for the fourth consecutive year. Two most depressing experiences occurred during the Weston-super-Mare festival where they were dismissed for 36 by Surrey and 37 by Hampshire, the two lowest totals of the season.

1961 – Veteran Packs A Record Punch   1962

Despite brilliant batting by Alley, Somerset proved a disappointment with much in their favour. The county finished tenth in the Championship compared with 14th in 1960, but had the side shown more application and consistency they might well have ended the summer among the leaders.

Alley deserved every praise. The 42-year-old Australian left-hander was the only batsman in the country to score 3,000 runs during the summer, and his feat was all the more remarkable considering he scored only 807 runs for an average of 23.05 in 1960. Alley rarely wasted time at the crease and preferred to move his score along with boundaries, apparently to conserve his energies. His purple period was in the three matches between June 7 and June 16 when he hit 523 runs in five innings for once out. Two Somerset county records fell to Alley during the game against Essex in August – the highest aggregate in a season, previously held by Wight, who hit 2,316 runs in 1960, and most centuries in a season.

Five Cricketers of the Year: Nothing quite like this had ever been accomplished even for Somerset, a county traditionally famed for their light-hearted approach to the game.

Most players think of retiring at the age that Bill Alley entered county cricket. He was 38 when he joined Somerset in 1957 and he has, during five years with them, proved himself not only a great acquisition on the field, but a splendid man to have in the dressing-room. Nothing daunted him and he breathes a spirit of confidence among his colleagues.

He boasts that he never had a single coaching lesson in his life. At one time, he was a boxer of renown in Australia. As a professional pugilist he won all his 28 contests and had set his sights on the world welterweight title when, of all things, a mishap at cricket compelled him to hang up his gloves. His jaw was broken by a cricket ball. Twenty stitches were necessary and he never boxed again.

1971 – CLOSE ENCOUNTERS OF A DEFIANT KIND

1972

The former Yorkshire and England captain, Close, enjoyed a triumphant year after his previous injury troubles. He did not miss a match, and made five centuries, including one against Yorkshire, as well as one against the eventual champions [*Surrey*] the day after he had suffered a severe facial injury. His death-defying fielding positions brought him many astonishing catches.

1974 – NEWCOMERS MAKE POWERFUL IMPACT

Eric Hill, 1975

Two newcomers were the 22-year-old Vivian Richards, from Antigua, and the 18-year-old Ian Botham, from Yeovil, previously of the Lord's groundstaff. Richards, a wonderful phenomenon, made the biggest impact of any player since Gimblett in 1935. Fresh from club cricket, he glowed with good humour and glorious batting adventure, his broad grin belying the withering force of his exquisitely timed strokes. His happy desire to hit the ball, of course, got him out often when he should have built a big innings. He is a beautiful fielder 30 yards from the bat.

Botham, forced into service by Cartwright's injuries, also showed star quality. His lively right-arm swing bowling, clean flowing driving, and the ability to field magnificently anywhere were soon evident. His successful fight to win the Benson and Hedges quarter-final at Taunton showed technical abilities underlined by courage and temperament of the highest order.

1977 – SOMERSET v AUSTRALIANS: WORTH THE WAIT

1978

At Bath, May 18, 19, 20, 1977. Somerset won by seven wickets off the first ball of the final 20 overs. A splendid match played in superb weather, punctuated with fine cricket throughout brought Somerset their first win over the Australians in 22 fixtures played since 1893. After Garner took a wicket with his fifth ball for Somerset, Chappell, reaching 99 before lunch, and hitting three sixes and 12 fours in a brilliant display of under two and a half hours dominated a third-wicket stand of 120. Then Garner and Burgess caused a collapse as the last eight wickets fell for 55 runs. Thomson bowled 15 no-balls in seven overs as Denning led a fine opening stand of 81. Botham hit three sixes and six fours and Slocombe, missed when three, hit one six and ten fours. All the while Rose batted patiently and steadily, hitting 15 fours while escaping difficult chances at 63 and 96. After the loss of two early wickets with his side still 90 behind, Hookes batted superbly. He reached 100 in 81 balls, eventually making 108 with four sixes and 15 fours. Somerset needed 182 to win in three and threequarter hours. Denning again led a brisk opening of 50 in an hour; Rose played patiently for two hours; Richards hit 11 fours while racing to 53 and then Botham struck boldly to finish this memorable match with an hour to spare.

Australians 232 (G. S. Chappell 113; G. I. Burgess 5-25, J. Garner 4-66)
and 289 (D. W. Hookes 108, C. S. Serjeant 50; I. T. Botham 4-98);
Somerset 340-5 dec (B. C. Rose 110*, Botham 59, P. A. Slocombe 55*)
and 182-3 (I. V. A. Richards 53).

1979 – LATE DOUBLE TRIUMPH HELPS TO ERASE EARLIER SHAME   Eric Hill, 1980

In a year memorable for many reasons, the abiding memories will be of victories in
the Gillette Cup and the John Player League on the last two days of the season
which brought Somerset their first major successes since their foundation in 1875.
In Rose's second year as captain, and following the ignominy of expulsion from the
Benson and Hedges Cup for the well-intentioned but ill-advised declaration at
Worcester, the team really found itself. In precise contrast to 1978, the vital Gillette
and John Player final games were won instead of lost.

1979 – WORCESTERSHIRE v SOMERSET (BENSON AND HEDGES CUP):
UNPRINCIPLED   1980

At Worcester, May 23, 24, 1979. Worcestershire beat Somerset by ten wickets when
the Somerset captain, Rose, sacrificed all known cricketing principles by deliberately losing the game. His declaration after one over from Holder, who bowled a
no-ball to concede the only run, enabled Somerset to maintain their superior
striking-rate in the group.

Rose won the battle of mathematics but lost all the goodwill which Somerset had
gained by playing attractive cricket in the preceding years. Worcestershire, embarrassed if not totally angered, refunded admission money to 100 paying spectators
after Turner had scored two singles to complete their victory in a match which lasted
for 16 deliveries and only 20 minutes, including the ten minutes between the innings.
The TCCB met at Lord's on June 1 and Somerset, for bringing the game into disrepute,
were disqualified from the Benson and Hedges Cup by 17 votes to one (Derbyshire).

Somerset 1-0 dec. (1 over); Worcestershire 2-0 (1.4 overs).

1979 – SOMERSET v NORTHAMPTONSHIRE (GILLETTE CUP FINAL):
CARIBBEAN MAGIC   1980

At Lord's, September 8, 1979. Somerset won by 45 runs, before a capacity crowd of
25,000. While Somerset's triumph was a team effort, two of their West Indies players
achieved outstanding performances. Vivian Richards gave of his best in scoring 117
and, when Northamptonshire faced the enormous task of getting 270, Joel Garner, the
6ft 8in fast bowler, took six wickets for 29. Richards, whom Cyril Washbrook named

Man of the Match, batted superbly from the seventh to the last over; he did not offer a chance. Most of his 11 boundaries came from powerful leg hits and straight drives.

Somerset 269-8 (60 overs) (I. V. A. Richards 117, B. C. Rose 41);

Northamptonshire 224 (56.3 overs) (A. J. Lamb 78, G. Cook 44; J. Garner 6-29).

1979 – NOTTINGHAMSHIRE v SOMERSET (John Player League):
TITLE CLINCHER   1980

At Nottingham, September 9, 1979. Somerset won by 56 runs. With Kent failing at home to Middlesex, Somerset clinched the points needed for victory. Roebuck's first half-century in the competition helped to lift the total to 185, his main assistance coming from Botham, who hoisted sixes off both Cooper and Hemmings before being caught on the boundary edge. Nottinghamshire captain Rice and the talented young Robinson added 68 in 12 overs before Dredge dismissed Rice leg-before, and began a collapse that led to the fall of seven wickets for just 46 runs.

Somerset 185-8 (39 overs) (P. M. Roebuck 50);

Nottinghamshire 129 (33.1 overs) (J. Garner 3-16).

1985 – WARWICKSHIRE v SOMERSET: Botham's blast   1986

At Edgbaston, July 24, 25, 26, 1985. Drawn. Despite a quickfire innings from Richards, the match was dominated by a performance from Botham which ranks alongside any ever seen on the ground. In 67 minutes he faced 65 deliveries and hit an unbeaten 138 out of 169 scored while he was batting. He hit 12 sixes and 13 fours in a whirlwind demonstration of his correct technique, which is backed by a phenomenal strength. Botham's hundred, the fastest of the season, took just 26 scoring strokes – one more than the record – and when he reached three figures off 50 deliveries, 94 runs had come in boundaries.

Somerset 207 (I. V. A. Richards 65; A. M. Ferreira 4-61)

and 418-6 dec (I. T. Botham 138*, P. M. Roebuck 81, N. F. M. Popplewell 70, Richards 53; N. Gifford 4-128);

Warwickshire 338 (R. I. H. B. Dyer 106, P. A. Smith 62; Botham 4-63)

and 74-1 (A. I. Kallicharran 51*).

1986 – Committee Supported Over Richards And Garner Hammer-Blow
Eric Hill, 1987

The season ended with the club in the grip of internal strife. The crux of this was the decision of the committee, in late August, not to renew the contracts of

Vivian Richards and Joel Garner, who had played such a large part in the successful years from 1978 to 1983. The cricketing reasons for this bold move were sound, but they quickly became swamped by the sentimental response of a large number of members. Ian Botham, who had come back from nine weeks' suspension by the TCCB with some thunderous performances, even by his standards, threatened to leave the county if the two West Indian Test players were not reinstated.

In due course, a Special General Meeting was requisitioned, calling for the resignation of the committee – and by inference the re-engagement of Richards and Garner. However, at Shepton Mallet on November 8, a motion of no confidence in the committee was defeated by 1,828 votes to 798, and a motion for the committee to stand down was defeated by 1,863 to 743. The committee had to choose between playing Martin Crowe as their overseas player or retaining Richards and Garner. Looking to the future, they offered Crowe a three-year contract.

1993 – Bitter Memories Overturned

1994

Among the many pleasant memories of the season was one which should have erased any bitter thoughts remaining from the 1986 crisis, when Viv Richards and Joel Garner were sacked and Ian Botham resigned. The county offered – and happily the offer was accepted – honorary life membership to all three.

1991 – Fond Memories Of Cook Provide Silver Lining

Eric Hill, 1992

The year was clouded by the death of the president, Colin Atkinson, by the premature retirement of Peter Roebuck, and by Jimmy Cook's return to South Africa. Each, in his own way, made contributions of great importance to the county. Cook's remarkable three seasons demand expansion. He was 35 years old when he arrived in 1989 and in all his matches for Somerset he compiled 10,639 runs at an average of 62.21, including 7,604 in first-class games at 72.41, with 28 hundreds. He never missed a match, was invariably lively in the field, always put the team's needs first, and established a superb reputation for chivalry and modesty. For all these reasons Jimmy Cook will be fondly remembered by friend and foe, and many were glad on the November day in 1991 when he stepped on to the field at Calcutta to represent South Africa in recognised international competition for the first time.

2001 – Best Season Despite Absence Of Stars

David Foot, 2002

By general agreement, certainly in every parish across the Mendips and the Quantocks, Somerset's season was the best in their variegated history. Perhaps there were more flash, pulsating days when, in 1979 for example, the county picked up two trophies. But 2001 was better, a more balanced triumph from lesser souls. Somerset finished runners-up in the Championship, higher than ever before – at one point, poised at the shoulders of Yorkshire, they actually looked capable of winning the pennant – and, amid much West Country elation, they vanquished Leicestershire in the Cheltenham & Gloucester final at Lord's.

Because of their central contracts, Marcus Trescothick played in just three Championship matches and Andrew Caddick two. They, in theory, represented the best of the batting and bowling, yet such deletions seemed to engender a rallying response from within the dressing-room.

Cambridge University v Glamorgan. At Cambridge, April 17, 18, 19, 1996. The unluckiest participant was Watkin, who had his wallet stolen. He asked a member of the press to cancel his credit cards for him while he was in the field, leading to the unusual shout of "Bowler's mother's maiden name?"

Little Wonder No. 116

2002 – SECRETARY APOLOGIES FOR INEXPLICABLE DESCENT David Foot, 2003

Explanations do not come easily for Somerset's embarrassing decline. By the end of the season they had been relegated in both the Championship and the Norwich Union League. Their chief executive, Peter Anderson, was sufficiently mystified by the team's miserable form to send a letter of apology to each member.

For a reason that was never quite discernible they completely lost backbone and fibre during 2002. Some of the batting was inept and devoid of technical efficiency; the last two Championship matches were lost in two days. In Victorian and Edwardian days, Somerset were hardly renowned for their fielding, and far too many catches were put down again this undulating season.

2007 – SOMERSET v MIDDLESEX: JOY ONLY FOR STATISTICIANS 2008

At Taunton, April 18, 19, 20, 21, 2007. Drawn. This was an extraordinary match, numbingly weighted in favour of batsmen despite a £10,000 investment in revising Taunton's surface to give bowlers more chance. There were eight hundreds, a record in England, and 1,659 runs for the loss of 13 wickets, including 850 for seven by Somerset, their highest total and the fourth-biggest on English soil. Spectators left shaking their heads, no doubt sharing the embarrassment of award-winning groundsman Phil Frost. A few historians and feverishly busy anoraks may have basked in the monumental statistics, and the centuries in their relatively untroubled way were well made. But did a match on an anodyne track with no prospect of a result have any real point? This was Langer's first game as Somerset's captain and only his third for them in the Championship. His previous one, in 2006, had brought a triple-hundred at Guildford; now he simply carried on for another. He batted 573 minutes and hit 38 fours in 412 balls: it was all too easy for this master.

Middlesex 600-4 dec (O. A. Shah 193, B. A. Godleman 113*, D. C. Nash 100*)
and 209-2 (E. T. Smith 103*, Shah 72*);
Somerset 850-7 dec (J. L. Langer 315, P. D. Trego 130, J. C. Hildreth 116, C. L. White 114,
M. E. Trescothick 70; M. Kartik 4-168).

2010 – ALWAYS THE BRIDESMAIDS

Richard Latham, 2011

Few would dispute that Somerset were the outstanding county side in England during 2010. Led for the first time by Marcus Trescothick, they won more matches than any of their rivals and achieved that without abandoning a free spirit and, at times, a cavalier approach to the game which had been a trademark of less successful eras. Yet they lifted not a single trophy, and finished runners-up in all three competitions through a mixture of misfortune, human error, and mental and physical fatigue at the end of a long season.

LV= County Championship: With points equal, Nottinghamshire prevailed over Somerset only by virtue of having claimed one more win.

Friends Provident T20: For once, Twenty20 had a tale to linger long in the memory: the story of a batsman injured in taking two from the penultimate ball, a runner summoned, a scampered leg-bye to tie the scores and then Somerset's glaring ignorance of the laws in not running out the supposedly lame striker who had absent-mindedly advanced to the wrong end.

2010 – HAMPSHIRE v SOMERSET (FRIENDS PROVIDENT T20 FINAL):
IGNORANCE NO DEFENCE

Hugh Chevallier, 2011

At Southampton, August 14, 2010 (floodlit). Hampshire won by virtue of losing fewer wickets. This astonishing match was the consummate riposte to those who claim the shortest form of the game is too fleeting to allow fortunes to ebb and flow.

One from the last ball will tie the scores and win it for Hampshire. But Christian has pulled a hamstring and needs a runner. And it's not just the batsman in trouble: there are no markings on any adjacent pitch. At 10.45, Nigel Gray, the groundsman, rushes out, paint pot in hand. Gray's housekeeping completed, Kieswetter stands up to the stumps for the final ball and, eventually, the match can reach a conclusion. One hell of a conclusion. A run, and Hampshire can celebrate; a wicket, and it's Somerset's triumph.

De Bruyn raps Christian on the pad, there's a huge appeal, and the batsmen – all three of them – run. The ball is heading for somewhere near the edge of leg stump; it is a decent shout, but it does not sway umpire Rob Bailey. Even the hobbling Christian, in the melee forgetting he has a runner, reaches the non-striker's end, sparking an invasion by the delirious Hampshire team. And then they stop.

In the umpteenth example of cricket's magnificent ability to unearth the unexpected, the game is not over. Law 29.2 (e) states that "When a batsman with a runner is striker, his ground is always that at the wicketkeeper's end." The umpires know this, though crucially the players do not. Christian's progress down the pitch keeps the game in play, even when he reaches the non-striker's end – and Somerset have an age in which to break the stumps he has unwisely abandoned. When the umpires see this is not about to happen, the game is at last over, and Hampshire can resume their victory invasion.

2010 – SOMERSET v WARWICKSHIRE (CLYDESDALE BANK 40 FINAL): BELL TAKES TOLL
James Coyne

At Lord's, September 18, 2010 (day/night). Warwickshire won by three wickets. A fatigued Somerset had to defend a mere 199 – uncharted territory for them in the competition, and doubly tough with emotions still raw from seeing the Championship lost just 48 hours earlier. To their credit, Thomas and Phillips circled the wagons for a last hurrah, and when Trott was third out, nibbling behind, Somerset appeared in danger of winning a trophy. Bell abruptly dashed such heady ambitions with a virtually flawless hundred as captain, which single-handedly steered Warwickshire from 20 for two to within one run of victory

Somerset 199 (39 overs) (N. R. D. Compton 60, J. C. Hildreth 44; Imran Tahir 5-41);
Warwickshire 200-7 (39 overs) (I. R. Bell 107; A. C. Thomas 3-33).

2012 – NO CHANGE: ANOTHER YEAR OF NEAR MISSES
Richard Latham, 2013

Somerset came second yet again, this time in their quest for a maiden Championship title, taking their tally of runners-up finishes in domestic competitions to eight in four seasons – and without a single trophy to show for it. This time, however, there was pride rather than frustration in their narrow failure.

In the third Championship match, captain Marcus Trescothick injured his ankle, and required surgery, which ruled him out of the next seven fixtures, as well as the entire Twenty20 group stage and the first six CB40 games. A catalogue of fitness issues meant 24 players featured in the Championship, with only Arul Suppiah, James Hildreth and Peter Trego ever-present. At times, the queue for the treatment room was so long that Somerset – also affected by international call-ups for Craig Kieswetter, Jos Buttler, Nick Compton and George Dockrell – fielded the only 11 available.

SURREY

[1959 edition] The invincible march of Surrey continued in 1958.
On August 29 they became county champions for the seventh year
in succession, and it is difficult to foresee the most redoubtable force
of the future emulating, let alone surpassing, Surrey's record,
which has no parallel in English cricket.

1878 – A Summer Of Note

The Surrey season of 1878 will be memorable in that county's cricket annals, not only for Surrey's victory over the renowned Gloucestershire eleven, but for the facts that the two matches played by the Australians attracted to The Oval larger audiences than were ever seen at a match on that ground, and that the praiseworthily prompt generosity of the Surrey Club enabled a North v South match to be played on the county ground that resulted in the useful sum of £258 swelling the subscriptions so sympathetically raised to alleviate the distressing bereavements brought about by the frightful loss of 700 lives, through the collision, on the Thames, of *The Princess Alice* and *Bywell Castle* steamboats.

1886 – County's Revival In Full Flow

Although they missed the County Championship, the Surrey men had a magnificent season in 1886. In all they played no fewer than 26 matches, and of this number 20 were won, five lost, and only one remained unfinished. The revival of Surrey cricket was talked about and hoped for a long time before it came, but it has come now in full force, and there can be no question that the county occupies a higher position in the cricket world to-day than it has done at any time since the memorable season of 1864, when Tom Humphrey, Jupp, Griffith, H. H. Stephenson, and others were in their prime, and the county went through the whole summer without losing a single 11-a-side match. A double victory was obtained over the Australians, and the second match produced the highest individual score ever hit against Australian bowling in England – Maurice Read's 186 – and up to that time the best total – 501 – ever obtained in this country against the Australians.

1895 – Captain's Career Ends On High Note

A presentation was made to Mr John Shuter in recognition of his long and brilliant services as captain of the Surrey eleven. Only a silver salver was publicly given to Mr Shuter, but the present – valued altogether at £365 – included also a grand piano and a pair of guns. In returning thanks to the Club for the very handsome present they had made him, Mr Shuter said that having been left a free choice by the committee he had selected a piano in order that the occasion might be associated as closely as possible with his wife. His connection with the Surrey Club had given him many of the happiest hours of his life, and while he regretted that business claims had obliged him to retire, he should never lose his interest in the Club.

1899 – SURREY v YORKSHIRE: HEAVY SCORING 1900

At Kennington Oval, August 10, 11, 12, 1899. This was beyond question the most sensational of all the matches played at The Oval during the season, 1,255 runs being scored for the loss of only 17 wickets. The Oval has been the scene of many wonderful things in the way of run-getting, but nothing we fancy quite so startling as this. On each side there was an astonishingly successful partnership, Wainwright and Hirst putting on in three hours and a half 340 runs for Yorkshire's fifth wicket, and Abel and Hayward, with nothing but a draw to play for, staying together for six hours and a half, and in that time adding no fewer than 448 runs for Surrey's fourth wicket. Never before we should think in a first-class match have four such individual scores been made as 228, 186, 193, and 273. The batting, it need hardly be said, was wonderfully good and the wicket perfect. A curious incident occurred on the second afternoon, the Yorkshiremen contending that Hayward was bowled out by a ball from Haigh before he had made 70. The umpire, however, thinking the ball had come back off the wicketkeeper's pads, decided in the batsman's favour. Yorkshire's 704 is the highest total ever hit against Surrey, and Wainwright and Hirst have never scored so heavily in a big match.

Yorkshire 704 (E. Wainwright 228, G. H. Hirst 186, Mr F. Mitchell 87,
J. Tunnicliffe 50; T. Richardson 5-152);
Surrey 551-7 (T. W. Hayward 273, R. Abel 193; Mr F. S. Jackson 4-101).

1900 – LACK OF FITNESS REDUCES RICHARDSON'S THREAT 1901

Richardson improved upon his doings of the previous year, and inasmuch is he took 101 wickets in county matches, was still a useful member of the side. For the most part, he was a very tame edition of the Richardson we saw from 1893 to 1897. We are convinced that he could still bowl very finely if he would only make up his mind to go into real training and get himself into condition. At his present weight he can never have his old stamina. He tires now after doing an amount of work which four years ago he would have got through without turning a hair.

Between 1893 and 1897 Tom Richardson took 1,179 wickets in all matches in England, with a best of 290 in 1895.

1905 – HOBBS CONFIRMS HIGH EXPECTATIONS 1906

A Cambridgeshire man by birth and the best bat for that county in 1904, Hobbs had duly qualified by two years' residence and at the opening of the season it was known that a great deal was hoped of him. His early play exceeded all expectations and by the end of May he had firmly established his reputation, his scoring for three or four weeks being extraordinary. It cannot be said that he kept up his form, but inasmuch as he made 1,004 runs in county matches alone he may fairly be regarded as the best professional batsman Surrey have brought forward in recent seasons. His comparative falling-off as the season advanced may have been due to the strain of having two first-class matches a week nearly the whole summer. He is a cricketer from whom a great deal may be expected, but he should endeavour to brighten up his fielding. Though a safe catch he is not at present very quick on his feet.

1906 – HAYWARD HITS NEW HEIGHTS 1907

Some Cricket Records: Individual aggregates in one season
T. Hayward made 3,518 runs in first-class cricket during 1906. This is the largest aggregate ever obtained by any batsman during a single season.

Surrey review: In batting Hayward stood out by himself as the great player of the year. It was remarkable indeed that in his 14th season for Surrey he should have been a finer batsman than ever. For three months his play was simply beyond criticism. Without sacrificing anything in the way of defence he did the fullest justice to his splendid powers as a hitter, playing with a freedom and brilliancy that except for an occasional innings he has perhaps never equalled. After July, however, a change came over his methods. He may have been influenced by the fetish of record-breaking, and possibly the continuous work in very hot weather made him feel a little stale, but whatever the cause he was not the same man in August that he had been before. He still played finely but his batting lost its electric quality and became by comparison laborious.

His greatest success came in Whitsun week when he scored 144 not out and 100 at Nottingham, and 143 and 125 at Leicester. He thus performed the stupendous feat of getting two separate hundreds in two successive matches. In recognition of this wonderful play he received from Lord Dalmeny the present of a cigarette case on which the four scores were set out in detail and inscribed with the words "With many thanks from his captain".

1906 – SURREY v YORKSHIRE: GREAT ATTRACTION 1907

At Kennington Oval, July 26, 27, 28, 1906. Surrey and Yorkshire having suffered only one defeat each, this match for Lees's benefit was invested with exceptional importance. It was officially estimated that over 80,000 persons attended; 66,923 paid for admission, the numbers being 23,653 on the first day, 21,506 on the second, and 21,764 on the third.

Yorkshire 186 (J. Tunnicliffe 60; W. S. Lees 5-61, Mr N. A. Knox 4-76)
and 297 (G. H. Hirst 87, W. Rhodes 53, Tunnicliffe 53; Knox 6-105);
Surrey 387 (T. W. Hayward 76, E. G. Hayes 53, Mr J. N. Crawford 51) **and 97-1**.

1909 – CRAWFORD HEADS DOWN UNDER AFTER SELECTION DISPUTE   1910

Surrey had trouble with some of their professionals and, as a crowning blow, there came the unhappy quarrel with J. N. Crawford. In the absence of Leveson Gower, Crawford was picked to captain the side in the return match with the Australians, but he refused to act, his reason being that the committee had left out essential players, among others Rushby whose bowling had done so much to win the first match. The committee were much incensed and passed a resolution that Crawford be not again asked to play for the county. At first great secrecy was preserved over the matter, but when the facts came out the correspondence was published and many other letters appeared in the sporting papers. It seemed to outsiders that the quarrel might have been made up very easily, but bitter feeling was aroused, and in October Crawford left England to take up an appointment as an assistant master at St Peter's College, Adelaide. It is sad indeed that at the age of 23 such a player should be lost to Surrey cricket. As to the troubles with the professionals we can say nothing, the committee having kept their own counsel. The fact, however, that the committee took the extreme step of suspending Marshal for a time, at the height of the season, suggests irregularities and insubordi-nation. As the result of the friction with the professionals, Surrey lost Rushby, who at the end of the season signed on for Accrington in the Lancashire League.

Crawford returned to England after the First World War and reappeared for Surrey. Rushby was only absent for one year.

1909 – SURREY v HAMPSHIRE: HUGE MARGIN   1910

At Kennington Oval, May 6, 7, 8, 1909. Scoring 645 in five hours and 20 minutes for the loss of four wickets on Thursday, Surrey, whose innings in all extended over six hours and 20 minutes, put together the highest total of the year and won after an hour's cricket on Saturday by no less than an innings and 468 runs. Strengthened by the assistance of C. B. Fry, Hampshire had hoped to acquit themselves in better form than is usual with that team when opposing Surrey at The Oval, but their bowling was punished with merciless severity and apart from Fry, who played admirably in each innings, their batsmen cut a truly deplorable figure.

Surrey 742 (E. G. Hayes 276, J. B. Hobbs 205, Mr J. N. Crawford 74; C. P. Mead 4-179);
Hampshire 129 (W. S. Lees 5-47) **and 145** (Mr C. B. Fry 60; Lees 4-26).

1914 – WAR BRINGS EARLY END TO SEASON   1915

For the first time since 1899 Surrey came out with the best record among the counties and so won the Championship. A brilliant season had a strange ending. As the military authorities required for about three weeks in August the use of Kennington Oval, the return match with Kent for Hobbs's benefit and the return with Yorkshire on the following days were, by permission of the MCC, transferred to Lord's, and on August 31, public feeling against the continuance of first-class cricket during the War having been worked up to rather a high pitch, the Surrey committee at a special meeting decided unanimously to cancel the two remaining fixtures – with Sussex at Brighton, and Leicestershire at The Oval. It was in some ways a pity that this drastic step should have been found necessary, but in acting as they did the Surrey committee took a wise course. Only two days before the decision was arrived at, Lord Roberts, in a recruiting speech, had made a pointed reference to people who went on playing cricket at such a time.

1919 – SURREY v KENT: VICTORY RUSH   1920

At Kennington Oval, August 18, 19, 1919. Hobbs's benefit match brought county cricket at The Oval to an end for the season, and a glorious end it proved. Nothing quite equal to the cricket at the finish can be recalled. Surrey had 95 to get in less than threequarters of an hour, and in 32 minutes, despite the disadvantage of bad light, Hobbs and Crawford hit off the runs, accomplishing in dazzling style a task that had seemed impossible. Crawford set the pace at first and put his side on good terms with the clock, Hobbs for an over or two being content with a few singles. Once set, however, Hobbs went even faster than his partner and to him fell the honour of making the winning hit. Naturally with such cricket in progress the crowd waited till the end, and when all was over there was a great scene in front of the pavilion.

Kent 218 (E. Humphreys 59, F. E. Woolley 55; J. W. Hitch 4-58) **and 184** (Hitch 4-64);
Surrey 308 (A. Ducat 76, H. S. Harrison 66; W. J. Fairservice 4-96) **and 96-0**.

1922 – FENDER KEEPS HIS EYES ON THE BALL   1923

In scoring 185 against Hampshire in May and 137 against Kent on the last day of July Fender gave the two most astonishing displays of hitting seen at The Oval, or anywhere else, last summer. There has been nothing like his play in these two matches since Jessop was in his prime. Nearly all through the season Fender played in glasses, but as he hit just as well when, now and then, he took them off, there could not have been much amiss with his sight.

Fender's most famous innings – a hundred in 35 minutes at Northampton in 1920 – drew little excitement from Wisden *1921, being described merely as "some of the fiercest [hitting] of the season".*

Durham v Northamptonshire. At Chester-le-Street, May 2, 3, 4, 6, 1996. There was another debutant in the match, besides Collingwood; John Emburey was making his first first-class appearance for Northamptonshire. But it was his 500th first-class game in all. His debut for Middlesex was in 1973, three years before Collingwood was born.

Little Wonder No. 117

1925 – SOMERSET v SURREY: HOBBS'S RECORD

1926

At Taunton, August 15, 17, 18, 1925. This was the match rendered for ever memorable by the triumph of Hobbs who, playing innings of 101 and 101 not out, equalled on the Monday morning W. G. Grace's aggregate of 126 centuries in first-class cricket, and on the Tuesday afternoon beat the Grand Old Man's record. Circumstances generally combined to invest the occasion with exceptional excitement. That the Taunton ground, with its rather short boundaries, might furnish Hobbs with the opportunity he wanted, was very generally expected, and a big crowd gathered in the hope of assisting at his triumph. No such gratification was vouchsafed for those present on the Saturday, but the play was of absorbing interest, Hobbs batting for two hours and 20 minutes and leaving off not out 91. Those spectators who did not hear "no ball" called had an anxious moment when in the first over Hobbs gave a catch to cover point, and there came another thrill shortly afterwards, the famous batsman with his score at seven making on the leg side a stroke which might have brought about his dismissal, had MacBryan moved more smartly. Thenceforward he played masterly cricket, exercising great care when facing White, but making a number of fine drives and leg hits off Bridges and Robertson-Glasgow. Towards the close, however, he was content to score mainly by singles. On Monday morning Hobbs did not keep the large company long in suspense. Three singles, a four off a no-ball and another single brought him to 99, and then, placing a ball from Bridges to square leg for a further single, he attained the object of his great ambition, the total then standing at 167. Tremendous cheering, of course, greeted the accomplishment of the feat; indeed so pronounced was the enthusiasm that the progress of the game was delayed some minutes while at the end of the over all the players in the field shook hands with Hobbs, and the Surrey captain brought out a drink for the hero of the occasion, who raised the glass high and bowed to the crowd before partaking of the refreshment. The memorable innings, put together exactly four weeks after Hobbs's 105 at Blackheath, came to an end shortly afterwards through a catch at the wicket. The total at that point was 177 and Hobbs, batting two hours and 35 minutes, had hit nine fours.

Fortunately for Hobbs, Somerset played up so well at the second attempt that Surrey were set a task substantial enough to furnish that batsman with the chance of making a second hundred. Of that opportunity he duly availed himself, and so less than 30 hours after equalling W. G. Grace's record, he surpassed it. Surrey had 183 to make to win and Hobbs and Sandham obtained that number in two hours and 25 minutes without being separated. Hobbs, who reached three figures with the total at 174. hit 14 fours and gave no chance. As in the first innings he treated White with great respect, but otherwise played a game as bold as it was skilful and attractive. In putting together this further hundred, Hobbs not only beat Grace's record but, bringing his three-figure innings for 1925 up to 14, he created a new record, the previous largest number of centuries in a season having been 13 – made by C. B. Fry in 1901, Tom Hayward in 1906 and Hendren in 1923. On two previous occasions Hobbs had obtained two separate hundreds in the same match.

Somerset 167 (A. Young 58; Mr J. H. Lockton 4-36)
and 374 (Mr J. C. W. MacBryan 109, Young 71, G. E. Hunt 59; Mr P. G. H. Fender 5-120);
Surrey 359 (J. B. Hobbs 101, Fender 59) **and 183 for 0** (Hobbs 101*, A. Sandham 74*).

1934 – NEW CAPTAIN ESPOUSES SPIRIT OF COUNTRY-HOUSE CRICKET — 1935

Their new captain, E. R. T. Holmes, made a welcome return to first-class cricket, which had seen little of him since he came down from Oxford in 1927. He entertained the idea that county cricket generally required some vitalising influence. Modern methods accounted for the loss of much of the real spirit of the game – life and enjoyment. There had crept in a tendency on the part of many leading batsmen to "play for keeps". This view received the support of practically all the Surrey committee, so Holmes, holding strongly to the opinion that county cricket should possess many of the attributes of country-house cricket, applied himself to the task of instilling these precepts into the minds and consequently the play of those under him. Possibly his handling of the bowling and perception of the right time for declaring did not always meet with approval, but he had an eye for the best interests of his team and, as the season progressed, he became more and more efficient.

1935 – RETIREMENT OF HOBBS LEAVES UNFILLABLE GAP — 1936

One great personality was missing from Surrey cricket in 1935. For the first time since 1904, except during the War period, 1915–18, the name of J. B. Hobbs did not appear as a player in any first-class match. The Surrey committee recognised his inestimable services by electing him an honorary life member of the club. In July a farewell dinner, sponsored by Sir Noel Curtis Bennett and organised by *The Star*, was held in London and attended by many notabilities in the sporting world. The retirement of the best professional batsman of all time severed a link in the chain of continuity in great Surrey batsmen. The county, in turn, prospered on the opening partnerships of John Shuter and Abel, Abel and Brockwell, Abel and Hayward, Hayward and Hobbs, then Hobbs and Sandham. The loss of Hobbs proved irreparable; after this succession of five England batsmen, covering a period of nearly 50 years there arose no one good enough to fill the vacancy.

1937 – SANDHAM SLIPS INTO THE SUNSET   1938

Sandham remained a valuable member of the side and on one sunny Saturday at
The Oval he delighted his admirers with a glorious 239 against Glamorgan made
in perfect style. He finished the season by hitting a hundred at Hove and then
without any fuss or bother he allowed the county to announce his retirement.
Associated with Surrey as far back as 1911, Sandham, during his first-class career,
scored 41,165 runs and hit 107 hundreds with an average of 44.99 runs an innings.
For 18 successive seasons he made over 1,000 runs, and eight times he exceeded
the 2,000 mark. Always placing first the interests of his side, Sandham has been the
model professional.

1939 – SURREY v LANCASHIRE: AWAY FROM HOME   1940

At Manchester, August 30, 31, 1939. (No play on third day owing to Crisis.) Drawn.
Owing to the International situation The Oval was not available, and so, for the
second time in the season, Surrey opposed Lancashire at Old Trafford.

1946 – PLAY RESUMES UNDER SEVERAL HANDICAPS   1947

Probably Surrey of all the counties resumed competitive cricket under the most
severe handicaps. The Oval suffered heavy damage during the six years of war; the
playing area, apart from the pitch "table", required complete overhaul, and the
pavilion was knocked about by bombing. Thanks to the wonderful efforts of the
groundstaff a remarkable recovery was effected, yet the easy pace and want of life in
the pitch in most matches usually made batting too simple. The worst trouble was
the difficulty of finding a captain. N. H. Bennett, without previous experience in
first-class cricket, stepped into the breach; but want of knowledge of county cricket
on the field presented an unconquerable hindrance to the satisfactory accomplishment of arduous duties.

"THE COCK-UP"   Obituary, 2009

BENNETT, NIGEL HARVIE, who died on July 26, 2008, aged 95, was an unwitting
entrant into cricket folklore – the man appointed county captain by mistake. Alec
Bedser called it simply "the cock-up", and blamed it on the general muddle everywhere after the Second World War. Events apparently unfolded like this: when
Monty Garland-Wells, Surrey's chosen skipper for the first post-war season of 1946,
had to withdraw after his father died, the committee decided to offer the leadership
to Major Leo Bennett, a well-known and talented club cricketer. While the search
was on for Major Leo, Major Nigel Bennett popped in to renew his membership

after the war. Alf Gover, in his autobiography, wrote that the pavilion clerk took the papers in to the secretary, who happened to have the chairman with him: they offered the captaincy to this Major Bennett, who accepted. He soon revealed his inexperience, twice rolling the new ball back along the ground from the covers for overthrows past a gobsmacked Gover, who had to ask a team-mate to explain the "facts of life over the new ball" and its shine to his captain. Bennett was not a complete duffer, though: he was leading batsman at Stowe School in 1930 and played a few games for Surrey's Second Eleven in the mid-1930s. The players were mostly relaxed about the situation: "I reckon we can cope with him for the summer," one reportedly said. "His wife's a real cracker." Errol Holmes returned as captain in 1947 and, so far as is known, Bennett never returned to The Oval. He moved to the West Country, where he worked for En-Tout-Cas and played club cricket for Taunton.

1950 – SQUIRES SUCCUMBS TO BLOOD VIRUS   1951

There could be no doubt that the skill, particularly in a crisis, of Squires, who died from an obscure complaint during the winter, was sorely missed.
Obituary: SQUIRES, HARRY STANLEY, the Surrey cricketer, died on January 24 in Richmond Royal Hospital as the result of an illness brought about through a virus in the blood. He was in his 41st year.

Throughout his cricket career Squires wore glasses. During the war he served with the RAF, reaching the rank of Flying Officer. After spending two years in the Hebrides he returned to this country wearing contact lenses, which he used for boxing, squash, Rugby and Association football as well as cricket.

1952 – SURRIDGE MOULDS TEAM INTO FIRST PENNANT WINNERS   1953

The appointment of a new captain coincided with a transformation of Surrey cricket, and they won the Championship outright for the first time since 1914 entirely by merit. While most of the credit for their success deservedly went to Surridge, who moulded the team into a winning combination, there was a general all-round improvement by many of the players which went a long way towards making Surrey worthy first holders of the Championship pennant inaugurated by Warwickshire, whom they succeeded as title-holders.

1953 – SURREY v WARWICKSHIRE: ALL IN A DAY   1954

At The Oval, May 16, 1953. Surrey won by an innings and 49 runs. Members rose as one when the triumphant Surrey team walked from the field having begun their Championship programme with victory in a day. The last and only time that a first-class match had been completed in one day at The Oval was in 1857. Special applause was accorded to A. Bedser, who took 12 wickets for 35 runs, and Laker, who performed the hat-trick. Bedser bowled magnificently when play commenced at noon. Unable to obtain a proper foothold on the wet turf, he attacked the leg stump at below normal pace, and, helped by fine catches, he equalled his previous-best analysis of eight for 18. Surrey also found the pitch treacherous, but, chiefly through a sound innings by Constable, they took the lead with only two wickets down. The score then went from 50 for two to 81 for seven, and only the aggressiveness of Surridge, who hit three sixes in four balls from Hollies, Laker and Lock enabled them to gain a substantial lead. Lock became the second-highest scorer before a blow above the right eye led to a visit to hospital and his retirement from the match. Laker was called into the attack for the first time when Warwickshire batted again and he began the final rout by achieving the first hat-trick of the season. Warwickshire, batting for ten minutes of the extra half-hour, were all out in 70 minutes, five minutes less than in their first innings. No Warwickshire batsman was bowled during a day in which 29 wickets fell for 243 runs – a fact that emphasised Surrey's excellent fielding.

Warwickshire 45 (A. V. Bedser 8-18) **and 52** (J. C. Laker 5-29, Bedser 4-17);
Surrey 146 (K. R. Dollery 4-40).

1956 – POWERFUL ATTACK LEADS WAY TO RECORD RUN   1957

Surrey, enthusiastically led by Stuart Surridge, and possessing an attack of international class in the Bedser twins, Loader, Laker and Lock, carried off the Championship for the fifth consecutive year, an achievement without parallel. Moreover, they accomplished another feat when in the middle of May they defeated the Australians at The Oval by ten wickets.

1956 – SURREY v AUSTRALIANS: STAR TURNS   1957

At The Oval, May 16, 17, 18, 1956. Surrey won by ten wickets, so becoming the first county for 44 years to triumph over an Australian team. There could be no doubt about their superiority in a sensational match, and Johnson, in presenting his cap to the Surrey captain, Surridge, admitted it freely.

To Laker belonged the great distinction of taking all ten wickets. Not since 1878, when E. Barratt, another Surrey man, did so for the Players, also at The Oval, had a bowler taken all ten wickets against an Australian side, and Laker was given the ball and a cheque for £50 by the Surrey committee. He and, in the second innings, the left-handed Lock, fully exposed the weakness of the Australian batsmen against the turning ball.

Laker, maintaining a splendid length in a spell of four hours and a quarter broken only by the lunch and tea intervals, exploited off spin on the dry pitch so skilfully that he came out with this analysis: 46–18–88–10.

Surrey gained a lead of 88. For a time matters went well enough with the Australians [in their second innings] and an opening stand of 56 in 95 minutes by Burke and McDonald seemed to have made them reasonably safe from defeat.

Then the course of the game changed completely, for Lock, able by now to make the ball turn quickly and occasionally get up awkwardly from a dusty pitch, caused such a breakdown that in a further 95 minutes the innings was all over for another 51 runs. Lock, who took the first six wickets at a cost of 40 runs, finished with an analysis of seven for 49 – a marked contrast to his 0 for 100 in the first innings! Actually he achieved all his success from the Pavilion end – that from which Laker bowled in the first innings – in a spell of 23.1 overs, six maidens, for 36 runs. He owed something to smart fielding, the catch by which May at slip disposed of Davidson being first-rate.

Surrey required only 20 runs to win, but Lindwall and Crawford bowled so fast and accurately that they took 55 minutes to accomplish the task.

Australians 259 (C. C. McDonald 89, K. R. Miller 57*; J. C. Laker 10-88) **and 107** (G. A. R. Lock 7-49);
Surrey 347 (B. Constable 109, T. H. Clark 58; I. W. Johnson 6-168) **and 20-0**.

Derbyshire v Leicestershire (AXA Equity & Law League).
At Derby, May 5, 1996. At the fall of Barnett's wicket,
a bogus batsman in Derbyshire replica kit made his way to
the crease, along with a startled Adams. The intruder was
allowed to face a joke delivery before being hustled away.

Little Wonder No. 118

1958 – A SEVEN-YEAR WONDER   1959

On August 29 [Surrey] became county champions for the seventh year in succession. Their latest triumph was not all plain sailing. Illness, injury and heavy representative calls presented many difficulties and they needed all their high skill, resource, team spirit and determination to preserve their standing.

The touring New Zealanders were twice beaten by an innings inside two days. In the first match May hit a remarkable 165 on a pitch which was altogether too fast for the other batsmen of either side. This was perhaps the outstanding innings of the season, and an early taste for the tourists of May's exceptional gifts and attacking power. They were to see a lot more. Of May's eight centuries during the season five were hit off the New Zealanders. He also took memorable centuries off Lancashire, Nottinghamshire and Yorkshire.

At the end of the season Herbert Strudwick retired as scorer. Andrew Sandham will be the new scorer and the coaching position he vacated will be filled by McIntyre. So ended for Strudwick 60 glorious years with Surrey. He became scorer when his distinguished career as a wicketkeeper ended in 1928. The playing and administrative staff presented him with a television set.

Seven in a row: Peter May leads out Surrey at The Oval in 1958,
crowned county champions for a record seventh successive time.
To May's right is Eric Bedser, and to his left Ken Barrington and Arthur McIntyre,
the wicketkeeper, who has Jim Laker to his left

1960 – MIDDLESEX v SURREY: BEDSER ACCLAIMED 1961

At Lord's, August 13, 15, 16, 1960. Alec Bedser received a standing ovation from
12,000 people on the first day in recognition of his last appearance as a professional
at Lord's.

1971 – HAMPSHIRE v SURREY: CHAMPAGNE CELEBRATION 1972

At Southampton, September 11, 13, 14, 1971. Hampshire won by four wickets.
Under the September sun and watched by a big crowd, Surrey won the County
Championship by gaining six points, but that was all they got from the match.
Surrey had been in with a chance of picking up the six points they needed in their
first innings when, thanks principally to a century by Edrich, they reached 240 for
three, but they crashed to 269 all out in 83.1 overs, missing a fifth batting point by
six runs. Then followed an anxious weekend and when the game was resumed
Hampshire continued to trouble Surrey. Not until the 58th over did Surrey take the

all-important fourth wicket, Gilliat being caught behind off Intikhab. Stewart's men celebrated by drinking champagne on the pitch.

Surrey 269 (J. H. Edrich 113, M. J. Stewart 54)
and 187 (Edrich 95; C. G. Greenidge 5-49, P. J. Sainsbury 4-28);
Hampshire 295-4 dec (R. E. Marshall 142*, Sainsbury 52*)
and 162-6 (B. A. Richards 95*).

1972 – POCOCK'S SPELL REWRITES RECORD-BOOK   1973

Pocock, always accurate and with good flight though seldom helped by the slow Oval pitches, deservedly headed the bowling averages. He almost enabled Surrey to pull off an extraordinary win over Sussex at Eastbourne in August. With three overs to go Sussex were 187 for one, needing 18 to win, yet finished three short at 202 for nine. In the first of those overs Pocock, beginning with figures of no wickets for 63, dismissed batsmen with his first, third and sixth balls. After Jackman conceded 11 runs in the next over, Pocock began the last with a hat-trick, took another wicket with his fifth ball and the ninth wicket fell to the last ball, a run-out. So five wickets fell in one over, a first-class record, and Pocock had taken six wickets in nine balls and seven wickets in 11 balls, both world records.

Surrey 300-4 dec (M. J. Edwards 81, R. M. Lewis 72) **and 130-5 dec**;
Sussex 226-5 dec (R. M. Prideaux 106*)
and 202-9 (Prideaux 97, G. A. Greenidge 68; P. I. Pocock 7-67).

1977 – MEMBER DEMANDS MONEY BACK AFTER BATTING COLLAPSE
Harold Abel, 1978

One suffering Surrey member, having watched the side disintegrate from 60 for one to 71 for nine against Leicestershire at The Oval, entered the office, put his pass on the counter and asked for his money back. A humorous gesture it was thought at the time. It was only the end of May. But by the end of August others felt like joining him in his protest, and it seemed that a new drive from the management reflected in a better standard in the middle would be necessary before support picked up again.

1983 – ESSEX v SURREY: 14 ALL OUT   1984

At Chelmsford, May 28, 30, 31, 1983. Drawn. On the second afternoon Surrey were skittled out for the lowest score in their history, their first innings lasting a mere 14.3 overs. Phillip and Foster, making the ball swing in the humid atmosphere, were their tormentors and only a boundary from Clarke, the sole one of the innings, spared them the humiliation of recording the lowest-ever first-class score. Five wickets fell with the total on eight. The next day a fine century from Knight, well supported by Clinton, enabled Surrey to win back some self-respect. After a barren opening day because of rain, Fletcher showed that there was nothing wrong with the pitch with a century full of grace and elegance after Knight had gambled on putting the home side in to bat.

Essex 287 (K. W. R. Fletcher 110);
Surrey 14 (N. Phillip 6-4, N. A. Foster 4-10) and 185-2 (R. D. V. Knight 101*, G. S. Clinton 61*).

1990 – SURREY v LANCASHIRE: BATTING PARADISE   1991

At The Oval, May 3, 4, 5, 7, 1990. Drawn. This record-breaking match will long be remembered and chronicled for its quite phenomenal feats of scoring on a pitch exemplifying the tougher standards laid down by the Test and County Cricket Board. Greig, the Surrey captain, drove an extremely hard tactical bargain by amassing 707 for nine declared in the hope that his bowlers could take 20 wickets for an innings victory. However, it presented Lancashire with a *fait accompli*. Needing 558 to avoid the follow-on, and realising that victory for them was out of the question, they settled down to revel in the sumptuous batting conditions. The home bowling was savaged for a colossal 863, the highest Championship total of the century and second only to Yorkshire's 887 against Warwickshire at Birmingham in 1896. Lancashire's dapper left-hander, Fairbrother, was unstoppable in the run-glut, thrashing 366 to pass by two runs the previous-best score at The Oval – 364 by Sir Leonard Hutton in the 1938 Test match against Australia. Greig, who, coming in at No. 7, had made the highest Championship innings by a Surrey player since 1926 and by one on the ground since 1921, could hardly have envisaged his career-best 291 being bettered the next day.

Surrey 707-9 dec (I. A. Greig 291, M. A. Lynch 95, A. J. Stewart 70, R. I. Alikhan 55)
and 80-1 (Stewart 54*);
Lancashire 863 (N. H. Fairbrother 366, M. A. Atherton 191, G. D. Mendis 102).

1991 – WAQAR REAPS A RICH HARVEST   David Field, 1992

It is doubtful whether anyone has bowled faster or straighter in an English season than Waqar Younis did for Surrey in 1991. Contrary to modern practice among quick bowlers, the bouncer had a minimal place in his armoury; stumps were hit and pads thumped regularly to earn the young Pakistani a rich harvest of 151 wickets in all competitions, with an astonishing two-thirds of his victims bowled or lbw. Feet and ankles were constantly in danger of bruising, or worse, from Waqar's wicked full-length deliveries.

1992 – BALL-TAMPERING SWINGS SEASON FROM BAD TO WORSE

David Llewellyn, 1993

Surrey had a disappointing season, which was overshadowed at the end when they were punished by the Test and County Cricket Board for ball-tampering. The county launched their own enquiry and admitted not merely the three offences which had been reported – one in each of the past three seasons – but a fourth as well.

The club were fined £1,000, which was suspended for two years, by the TCCB. They had been reported for breaking both Law 42.5 (changing the condition of the ball) and 42.4 (lifting the seam) against Gloucestershire at Cheltenham in 1990, Yorkshire at Guildford in 1991 and Leicestershire at The Oval in 1992. The fourth occasion was the preceding game at Guildford, against Gloucestershire, in 1991. The upshot was that Surrey undertook that in future the ball would be returned to the umpire at the end of every over and after the fall of a wicket, and they recommended that all other counties adopt a similar procedure.

1993 – SURREY v LANCASHIRE (BENSON AND HEDGES CUP):
THROWN AWAY

1994

At The Oval, May 11, 1993. Lancashire won by six runs. Lancashire achieved one of the most dramatic one-day victories of all time after the Surrey innings went from the sublime to the farcical. They were only 25 runs short of victory, thanks to a 212-run partnership between Stewart and Thorpe; they then contrived to lose nine wickets for just 18 runs – and the match. Only Lynch, who walked for a leg-side catch by Hegg, could claim not to have thrown his wicket away. The TCCB used the game for the first experiment in Britain with a third umpire replaying difficult line decisions on television and communicating with his colleagues on the field by two-way radio. But Allan Jones's only involvement proved that the camera could be as uncertain as the human eye. He was unable to judge whether Wasim should be given run out, and ruled that he should stay. A photograph taken from another angle suggested that Wasim had been lucky.

Lancashire 236 (54.1 overs) (N. H. Fairbrother 87; M. P. Bicknell 3-27);
Surrey 230 (55 overs) (G. P. Thorpe 103, A. J. Stewart 95; I. D. Austin 3-40).

1996 – KERSEY'S DEATH TAKES SHINE OFF SUNDAY SUCCESS

1997

For the first time since 1982, there was a glint of silver in The Oval trophy cupboard, after Surrey won their first Sunday League title. But, as 1997 began, cricketing success was put into perspective by the death – after a car crash in Australia – of wicketkeeper Graham Kersey, the most popular player on the staff. The news left everyone at Surrey stunned.

1997 – SURREY v NOTTINGHAMSHIRE (AXA Life League):
LIGHTS OUT   1998

At The Oval, June 26, 1997 (day/night). No result (abandoned). What was scheduled to be the first day/night match in a major English competition was called off owing to torrential rain over the previous 24 hours. The temporary floodlights had already been positioned around the boundary, however, and the soggy turf was badly cut up as they were driven off in heavy lorries.

2002 – Championship Success A Tribute To Hollioake   David Llewellyn, 2003

The death of Ben Hollioake cast a dark cloud over the start of the season, yet the tragedy had a silver lining. The whole club was drawn closer together, and the collective sense of purpose and spirit played a big hand in Surrey's success – a third Championship title in four years, and promotion in the Norwich Union League

Obituary: HOLLIOAKE, BENJAMIN CAINE, died in Perth, Western Australia, on March 23, 2002 when his Porsche 924 left a freeway exit road, made slippery by light rain, and crashed into a brick wall. He had been driving home from the customary family dinner that preceded his and his brother Adam's return to Surrey for the English season, having spent much of the winter with England's one-day squad in Zimbabwe, India and New Zealand. Ben was just 24 years and 132 days old: no England Test cricketer had died so young.

2002 – SURREY v GLAMORGAN (Cheltenham & Gloucester Trophy
FOURTH ROUND): RECORDS GALORE   2003

At The Oval, June 19, 2002. Surrey won by nine runs. This sensational match left a trail of broken records in its wake. Thanks to a belter of a pitch and a 60-yard boundary under the gasometers, it was a batsman's – and statistician's – delight. At its heart was Ally Brown's brilliant, scarcely credible world-record 268, yet this was no one-man show. Perhaps most astonishing was that Glamorgan, not given a prayer by anyone after conceding 438, so nearly won. Robert Croft, acting-captain while Steve James tended his sick daughter, led a never-say-die fightback with a captain's innings that was also a phenomenal feat of pinch-hitting. He smacked Bicknell's first five balls for four as he sprinted to 50 in 22 balls. His hundred came up in 59 minutes off 56 balls, whereas Brown's first hundred had taken 98 minutes and 80 balls. Hemp, the game's third centurion, got there in 85 balls and kept the run-rate near the required 8.78; off the last ten overs, Glamorgan needed a just-about-feasible 103. Thomas made amends for haemorrhaging 12 runs an over by cracking an unbeaten 71 off only 41 balls. But wickets were falling at the other end, mainly to Hollioake who, with ten runs needed off two balls, bowled Cosker to complete a wonderful contest. The honours, though, went to

Brown. His brutal innings contained 192 in boundaries, including 12 sixes, one short of Ian Botham's world record, and his 268 came off only 160 balls, at a strike-rate of 167. His pulling, especially, was perfection, but he also hit 22 fours and two sixes through or over the covers, driving off the back foot as well as the front.

Surrey 438-5 (50 overs) (A. D. Brown 268, I. J. Ward 97; S. D. Thomas 3-108);
Glamorgan 429 (49.5 overs) (R. D. B. Croft 119, D. L. Hemp 102, Thomas 71*,
A. Dale 49; A. J. Hollioake 5-77).

2007 – RAMPRAKASH DOMINATES TO UNPRECEDENTED DEGREE David Llewellyn, 2008

Mark Ramprakash scored a staggering 30.02% of Surrey's total of runs from the bat, 2,026 out of 6,747 (net of extras). That is a record for all counties, surpassing Graeme Hick's 28.96% for Worcestershire in 1988. The previous-highest percentage for Surrey was Tom Hayward's 23.98 in 1906. For the second summer running, Ramprakash passed 2,000 runs, achieved in his second innings of the final match of the season, coincidentally his 100th first-class appearance for Surrey. In so doing, he became the first player to average more than 100 in consecutive English summers.

2012 – MAYNARD'S DEATH ADDS TO CATALOGUE OF TRAGEDY Richard Spiller, 2013

The death of Tom Maynard cast a pall over Surrey's season. To lose such a talent, seemingly destined for the international stage, devastated his adopted county as well as his old one, Glamorgan. Maynard, 23, was found dead on the line near Wimbledon Park tube station early on June 18. The tragedy provoked intense grief among team-mates and staff at a club shattered by losing a third player in 15 years.

Rory Hamilton-Brown, Maynard's close friend and housemate, was given extended compassionate leave and eventually relinquished the captaincy. He was still badly out of sorts when he returned and, after the season, no objections were raised to his departure for Sussex, from where he had been signed in 2010. The following year, he had led Surrey to promotion in the Championship and success in the CB40.

Maynard had already been disciplined after a late-night incident during the match against Sussex at Horsham – he suffered a mysterious shoulder injury and a black eye – while Oval officials admitted Hamilton-Brown's lifestyle had been causing concern for some time. Both episodes prompted questions about the discipline of a small but influential group within the squad. In the circumstances, avoiding relegation and only narrowly missing out on the CB40 semi-finals were considerable achievements – for which acting-captain Gareth Batty, who welded together a disconsolate squad, deserved immense credit.

SUSSEX

[1954 edition] SUSSEX THROUGH THE YEARS by A. E. R. Gilligan

*Sussex, my own county, have never been champions, but no one will deny
that they have played an historic part in the development of our great game.
Their achievements on the field as a team may have been bettered by many sides,
but individually their famous figures of the past who have seen the county
through the years compare favourably with any.*

1871 – Retreat From The Sea

The Sussex season, '71, was the more interesting from the fact that it was the last the club could play on the old ground by the sea, inasmuch as that eligible plot of land, made so famous by cricketers and cricket, was required for more of those magnificent mansions facing the sea for which the Queen of Watering Places is so celebrated. So we have now seen the last of the uniquely situated and famous run-getting old Brunswick, whereon for the past 28 years the accomplished cricketers of Sussex have bowled, batted, and fielded.

The new Sussex County Ground is a little nearer to Brighton than the old one, and about as far to the north of the Cliftonville road as the other was to the south. Its length from N. to S. is 238 yards, and from E. to W. 181 yards. At the south extremity there is a slip 121 yards by 36 which will be separated from the cricket ground and set apart for archery and croquet. The Tavern will be built outside the ground, at the S.W. corner, and the pavilion will be nearly in the middle of the W. side. The ground is surrounded by a concrete wall seven feet high. Inside this will be planted a double row of trees, and inside these a roadway 20 feet wide runs all round the ground. The whole has been carefully levelled, but more work had to be done than was expected owing to the fact that the fall from N. to S. was found to be 18 feet. Mr Fane Bennett Stanford and the trustees of the estate generously gave the committee of the county club the whole of the turf off the old Brunswick, so that it is hoped that in a couple of years the turf will play nearly as well as it did in its old quarters.

Sussex still play on this ground which is more familiarly known as Hove.

1873 – SUSSEX v NOTTINGHAMSHIRE: 19 ALL OUT

At Brighton, August 14, 15, 1873. 231 overs (less one ball) and 231 runs were all the scorers had to book in this remarkably small county contest. The feature of this little cricket go *[sic]* was an innings of 19 runs played by the ten Sussex men; that innings was commenced at 12.35 and concluded at 1.20, therefore was of exactly threequarters of an hour's duration. One man made nine runs by two threes and three singles; another man took his bat out for 8, made by two twos and four singles; two others scored one run each, but the rest of the crew were ciphered [*including H.*

Phillips, whose scorecard entry read: "had not arrived – missed the train"]. There were just 20 overs and two balls bowled in that small affair.

A singular bit of retributive cricket was played a fortnight later on, when nearly the same Notts eleven, who here got the Sussex men out for 19 runs, were themselves got out by 16 of Derbyshire for an innings of 14 runs!

Sussex 19 (A. Shaw 6-8) **and 96** (Shaw 6-38, F. Morley 4-49);
Nottinghamshire 101 (Jas. Lillywhite 7-56) **and 15-0.**

Little Wonder No. 119

Warwickshire v Hampshire. At Birmingham, May 16, 17, 18, 20, 1996. Hampshire's triumph was overshadowed by the controversy surrounding Reeve's batting tactics on the final afternoon. He decided to counter Maru's left-arm spin from over the wicket by throwing his bat away, to avoid being caught off lifting deliveries. Reeve did this 15 times as he scored 22 from 89 balls, and argued that it was within the Laws. But MCC later ruled that an umpire could "seriously consider" giving a batsman out for obstruction in these circumstances, because the action is likely to impede the close catchers.

1889 – COUNTY SHOULD LOOK OUTSIDE ITS BORDERS – OR SINK   1890

We have thought it well to state clearly and uncompromisingly the unfortunate position of Sussex, and we should say that the best remedy is to import some young professionals from Nottinghamshire or Yorkshire. We do not think that anything will excuse one county club endeavouring to take away from another men who are actually employed and wanted in their own county. Further than that, before importation is resorted to, long and earnest efforts should be made to find native players. Sussex have tried for years, and in the nett result have failed. The courses now open are either to adopt importation as a settled policy or to be content to gradually sink to the position of their neighbour Hampshire. It is notorious that in Nottinghamshire and in Yorkshire there are scores of cricketers who will in all probability never be wanted for their own counties, but who would certainly strengthen less powerful elevens. The strict birth qualification is a beautiful thing in theory, but in practice it goes for very little. County cricket today owes an enormous share of its importance to the wise adoption of the residential law by Surrey, Lancashire, and others, and those who will look at the facts fairly and squarely and free their minds from sentiment and prejudice must admit that residents are quite as loyal and quite as contented as the majority of those men who were born in the counties for which they play. We by no means wish to see English professionals become mere mercenaries, as American baseball players confessedly are, but we do not believe there is any danger of such a condition of things coming about so long as the present restrictions are in force and committees exercise their powers with judgment and good feeling.

1893 – AUSTRALIA CAPTAIN MAKES HIS BOW   1894

It was the first season that Mr W. L. Murdoch [former Australia captain] had become qualified by residence for Sussex, and he quickly made his presence felt, his inclusion in the team being of double value, as not only was his bating of great service, but the duty of leading the eleven was far more congenial to him than it had been in some previous seasons to Mr Newham.

Mr C. A. Smith, having adopted the stage as a profession, did not find much time to play for his county, but on the few occasions he appeared he rendered useful assistance.

HOLLYWOOD'S LEADING MAN   Obituary, 1949

SMITH, Sir CHARLES AUBREY, CBE, famous in the world of cricket before making a name on the stage and becoming a universal favourite on the films in comparatively recent years, died on December 20, aged 85, at Beverly Hills, California. Over six feet tall, he made an unusual run-up to deliver the ball and so became known as "Round The Corner" Smith. Sometimes he started from a deep mid-off position, at others from behind the umpire, and, as described by W. G. Grace, "it is rather startling when he suddenly appears at the bowling crease".

He maintained his love for cricket to the end. Until a few years ago he captained the Hollywood side and visited England for the Test matches, the last time as recently as 1947, when South Africa were here.

He was knighted in 1944 in recognition of his support of Anglo-American friendship.

1893 – SUSSEX v GLOUCESTERSHIRE: LOBSTER'S POT   1894

At Brighton, May 22, 23, 24, 1893. Many contests between Sussex and Gloucestershire have produced very interesting struggles, but none so close and exciting as the one under notice. During the earlier stages of the match Gloucestershire succeeded in obtaining a considerable advantage, but the Sussex men played up in a surprising manner, and, thanks mainly to the brilliant batting of Bean and G. L. Wilson, and the bowling of Humphreys, they gained a remarkable success by the narrow margin of three runs. Humphreys, whose lob bowling turned the scale, was carried shoulder-high to the dressing room.

Sussex 202 (Mr C. A. Smith 70; H. W. Murch 5-50)
and 294 (G. Bean 120, Mr G. L. Wilson 105; F. G. Roberts 5-97);
Gloucestershire 297 (Mr J. J. Ferris 106, Mr S. A. P. Kitcat 52)
and 196 (J. R. Painter 51; W. A. Humphreys 7-30).

1894 – VETERAN SHAW DISPLAYS OLD SKILLS 1895

Sussex had not beaten Notts for 20 years, and it was a very singular coincidence that Alfred Shaw took part in both matches. Of course, in 1874 he assisted Notts, but he was last season included in the ranks of Sussex, having for the first time appeared for the southern county under the residential qualification.

It was thought to be a very risky experiment to ask Alfred Shaw to return to first-class cricket after an absence of seven years, but the famous veteran bowled with a skill and accuracy which proved him by far the best bowler in the Sussex team. It was, we believe, mainly through the influence of Mr Murdoch that the step was taken, and Lord Sheffield, to whom Alfred Shaw has for some years been under an engagement, fell in with the proposal in the most sportsmanlike manner, being, as he always has been, anxious to do the very best on behalf of Sussex cricket. Unfortunately Shaw was not available until the end of July, and he could not play in the last few matches, having arranged to accompany Lord Sheffield on a foreign tour.

1896 – SUSSEX v YORKSHIRE: TWICE IN A DAY 1897

At Brighton, August 20, 21, 22, 1896. Ranjitsinhji, in this engagement, surpassed all his previous performances for the year, scoring two innings of a hundred in the same match. His doings were the more remarkable, as when he went in Sussex looked to be in serious danger of defeat, but his brilliancy and determination enabled the county to escape honourably from their position, the game being left drawn. Ranjitsinhji's batting was more extraordinary than that of the other famous players who have done a similar thing, as his two hundreds were not only made in the same match, but on the same day. As may be supposed, his marvellous exhibition caused the wildest excitement amongst the spectators at Brighton. It is not often that the Yorkshire bowlers have been treated with so little respect. As a matter of record it should be stated that Ranjitsinhji went in on the second day, but had not scored a run when rain caused stumps to be pulled up.

Yorkshire 407 (R. Peel 106, Mr F. S. Jackson 102, J. Tunnicliffe 99);
Sussex 191 (K. S. Ranjitsinhji 100; Mr E. Smith 5-42, G. H. Hirst 4-49)
and 260-2 (Ranjitsinhji 125*, E. H. Killick 53*).

1901 – FRY SCORES SIX CONSECUTIVE HUNDREDS 1902

For the third year in succession the general interest in Sussex cricket centred mainly in the doings of Ranjitsinhji and Fry. Between them they scored 4,449 runs, thus beating their wonderful aggregate of the previous summer. The Sussex captain [Ranjitsinhji], it should be added, became more and more a driving player. Opposing teams endeavoured to cramp his game by putting on additional short legs, but, without abandoning his delightful strokes on that side of the wicket, or his beautifully timed cuts, he probably got the majority of his runs by drives – a notable change, indeed, from his early years as a great cricketer,

To C. B. Fry the season of 1901 brought quite unparalleled honours. On Friday, August 16, at Portsmouth, he commenced the most wonderful series of consecutive hundreds ever recorded in the game of cricket. The wicket afforded the bowlers a lot of assistance, yet Fry in the second innings made 106 out of a total of 212. In the following week he batted twice at Brighton, scoring 209 against the champion county [Yorkshire], and 149 against Middlesex. On the following Monday, Sussex appeared against Surrey at The Oval, and there, on a wicket considerably affected by rain, Fry put together 105, winding up the week and the Sussex season by making 140 against Kent, at Brighton. Following upon this – his fifth successive hundred – he was absent from the cricket field for ten days, and then at Lord's, batting for C. I. Thornton's England Team against Yorkshire, he scored 105, thus accomplishing the truly phenomenal feat of making six consecutive hundreds. Altogether, he played 13 three-figure innings during the season – 11 of them for Sussex, nine in Championship matches. Of the skill and patience displayed in obtaining this remarkable number of big innings it is impossible to speak too highly, for C. B. Fry, with all his greatness, makes nearly all his runs on the on side.

1908 – NOT ALWAYS FOR THE COMMON GOOD — 1909

Playing in some matches and standing out of others, Ranjitsinhji and Fry might be compared to the stars of an opera company. They did brilliant things themselves but they did not help the ensemble.

1908 – SUSSEX v HAMPSHIRE: UNPARDONABLE CONDUCT — 1909

At Chichester, July 16, 17, 18, 1908. Restricted to one day's cricket which naturally led to no definite result, this match was rendered noteworthy by an altogether unpardonable course of conduct on the part of the Sussex team. Continuous rain precluded any possibility of cricket on Thursday but, although the weather continued very wet during the night, the pitch was fit for play at half past 11 next morning. At that hour while the Hampshire men were in attendance only two or three members of the Sussex eleven had made their way to the Priory Park. Fry and Vine arrived some time later but the majority of the side did not put in an appearance until between three and four o'clock in the afternoon. Preparations were then made for a start but the weather, always showery, turned wet again and the game was not entered upon until Saturday. Had the Sussex team arrived at the proper hour comparatively little cricket would have been possible, but that was no excuse for the non-appearance of the men. The only attempt at explanation urged was that as rain fell heavily 20 miles away where the majority of the Sussex team stayed for the night, the cricketers concluded that no play could take place.

Hampshire 173 (Capt. W. N. White 85; G. Cox 6-41);
Sussex 112-6 (H. H. Jam Sahib of Nawanagar [K. S. Ranjitsinhji] 51*).

1923 – OVER AND ABOVE THE CALL OF DUTY   1924

No captain could have worked harder for his side and his county than Arthur
Gilligan. The hottest and most wearying day was not too long for him, and on many
occasions during home matches he would deliver lectures to schoolboys on the
game, its traditions and lessons, before the day's play started.

1925 – TATE SHOWS HIS STAYING-POWER   1926

While, as an eleven, Sussex cut a somewhat inglorious figure, certain members of
the side enjoyed great personal triumphs. Standing out among these players,
Maurice Tate, for the third time in succession, was the first cricketer to take 200
wickets, and get 1,000 runs. In county matches alone he scored 1,662 runs with an
average of nearly 25, being third on the list, and with a record of 194 wickets for less
than 13½ runs apiece he easily headed the bowling figures. As he had gone through
an exacting tour in Australia the previous winter his doings last season were, indeed,
very wonderful. On top of his work as a bowler he played several fine innings.

1930 – SUSSEX v NORTHAMPTONSHIRE: UNCLE OVERTAKEN   1931

At Brighton, May 7, 8, 9, 1930. To Duleepsinhji this match brought the great
distinction of beating the Sussex record made by his uncle, K. S. Ranjitsinhji, at
Taunton in 1901. Going in with one run on the board, Duleepsinhji scored 333 out
of 520 and, when seventh out, was taking many risks. Batting for five hours and a
half, he hit a six and 33 fours, his strokeplay all round the wicket being magnificent.
Three steady partners helped him to master the bowling and then Tate, chiefly by
powerful drives and pulls, hit up 111 out of 255 in an hour and threequarters.
Gilligan having declared first thing on the second morning, Wensley, on a pitch
which, slow and easy on the first day, proved rather treacherous as it became faster,
bowled swingers cleverly. Tate in the follow-on took four of the first five wickets for
22 runs. Bellamy did not concede a bye, and he showed the soundest defence for the
visitors, who in the end had to admit defeat by an innings and 209 runs.

Sussex 521-7 dec (K. S. Duleepsinhji 333, M. W. Tate 111);
Northamptonshire 187 (A. F. Wensley 4-45) and 125 (Tate 7-45).

1936 – FINANCIAL PROBLEMS BRING STAFF AND WAGE CUTS   1937

Wensley, after promising great things with an innings of 106 of out against
Cambridge, could not keep his place in the side. During the winter Sussex decided
to dispense with his services and those of Greenwood, Pearce, and George Cox

(senior), who had charge of the Hove Nursery. The loss of £2,000 last year, increasing their overdraft to £6,000, prompted this action on the part of the county club, whose secretary and assistant secretary voluntarily assented to salary cuts to assist in a financial recovery. The players followed suit in agreeing to a reduction of wages.

1937 – PARKS ACHIEVES UNIQUE DOUBLE   1938

J. H. Parks surpassed anything he had ever done. Not only did he accomplish the double, but he became the first cricketer ever to score 3,000 runs as well as take 100 wickets – a record duly recognised by the Sussex Club in the form of a presentation to Parks. His enterprising methods brought him as many as ten hundreds in Championship engagements and at the same time set a vivid example to his colleagues, who, unfortunately, did not always respond adequately. Not only did Parks lead the way in batting, but, as a bowler, he was more heavily worked than anyone else in the eleven; and yet he shared with James Langridge the distinction of being the foremost all-rounder of the year. Langridge, who also enjoyed the satisfaction of completing the double, more than ever revealed the temperament fitted for the big occasion. Time after time he rescued the side when things were going badly and his steadiness, determination and skill sometimes turned impending defeat into victory.

Tate made only infrequent appearances and at the end of the season Sussex announced that his agreement would not be renewed. The famous England bowler, whose benefit in 1930 yielded nearly £2,000, received an ex gratia grant of £250 from the Club in recognition of his services for over 25 years. Thus a great figure disappeared from the game. The best bowler of his type since pre-war days, Tate accomplished the double in eight successive seasons (1922–1929) and in 1923, 1924 and 1925 took over 200 wickets.

1946 – GRIFFITH RELIEVED OF CAPTAINCY   1947

Finishing last in the County Championship, Sussex experienced their worst season for 50 years. Captained by S. C. Griffith, Cambridge Blue in 1935, the team showed a general decline from the form of 1939 when they occupied tenth position. Except as wicketkeeper, Griffith did not prove anything like the success hoped for. H. T. Bartlett was appointed captain for 1947, the committee feeling that Griffith should devote more time to secretarial duties.

1953 – SHEPPARD LEADS FLOCK TO HIGHER PASTURES   1954

Nothing in the season was more remarkable than the performance of Sussex, who, 13th in the table in 1952, ended last summer as runners-up to Surrey for the Championship. It was their highest position in the competition since 1934. Under

D. S. Sheppard, who, as batsman, fielder close to the wicket and captain, proved a notable success, the side displayed a balance and enterprise missing for a number of years. Generally attractive in method, Sheppard hit seven centuries and scored more runs than any of his colleagues. It was matter for regret from a cricket point of view that his decision to study for Holy Orders meant his resignation from the captaincy after this one highly successful year, though it did not involve his total loss to Sussex.

1962 – SURREY v SUSSEX: Dexter rewarded 1963

At The Oval, July 11, 12, 13, 1962. Sussex won by ten runs. The result was a triumph for Dexter, the Sussex captain, who was the inspiration of his side in every respect. By taking seven wickets for 38, Dexter limited Surrey's first-innings lead to 26. Next, while his own batsmen were labouring for runs – Sheppard spent one and three-quarter hours for 24 – Dexter with glorious strokes made 94 in two and a quarter hours, hitting two sixes and 12 fours. Next day, Surrey needed 227 to win in five hours and with Barrington and May taking part in a stand of 122 they seemed to be romping home. When only 30 more runs were required they had seven wickets left, but with Dexter and Bell sharing the attack four wickets fell in the course of six balls while only a single was scored. First, Barrington was run out; next, Langridge held Willett in the gully off Dexter, and then Storey and Lock left to successive deliveries, both caught in identical fashion off Bell by Dexter at short mid-off. After that debacle. Surrey could not check the landslide and their last six wickets slumped for 19 runs. So Sussex gained a notable victory with 40 minutes to spare, and Dexter was duly rewarded some days later when MCC honoured him with the captaincy of the team to tour Australia.

Sussex 158 and 252 (E. R. Dexter 94; P. J. Loader 5-97);
Surrey 184 (M. J. Stewart 70; Dexter 7-38)
and 216 (K. F. Barrington 89, P. B. H. May 80; Dexter 3-58).

1963 – Kings Of New Knock-Out Competition 1964

The new Knock-Out competition aroused enormous interest. Very large crowds, especially in the later rounds, flocked to the matches and 25,000 spectators watched the final at Lord's where Sussex narrowly defeated Worcestershire by 14 runs in a thoroughly exciting match. It says much for this type of cricket, that tremendous feeling was stirred-up among the spectators as well as the cricketers, with numerous ties being decided in the closest fashion. At Lord's, supporters wore favours and banners were also in evidence, the whole scene resembling an Association Football Cup final more than the game of cricket and many thousands invaded the pitch at the finish to cheer Dexter, the Sussex captain, as he received the Gillette Trophy from the MCC president, Lord Nugent.

Sussex emphasised their superiority in the one-day game when they beat the West Indies by four wickets in a challenge match at Hove on September 12, which attracted a crowd of nearly 15,000.

There were two points which invite criticism. Firstly, the majority of counties were loath to include even one slow bowler in their sides and relied mainly on pace, and secondly the placing of the entire field around the boundary to prevent rapid scoring – Dexter used this tactic in the final – became fairly common. The success of the spinners at Lord's may have exploded the first theory.

There is no doubt that provided the competition is conducted wisely it will attract great support in the future and benefit the game accordingly.

1968 – SUSSEX v GLAMORGAN: DAMAGED IMAGE 1969

At Hove, June 12, 13, 14, 1968. Drawn. It was a pity that the sea fret, so often a nuisance at Hove, could not have done a good turn for a change and blotted out the third day. Glamorgan began at 78 for two and finished at 292 for two, the Jones brothers making little effort to get on with things and Sussex calling on ten men to bowl. Eifion Jones hit one six and 16 fours in reaching a maiden century in three and threequarter hours, facts which reflect his countless moments of inactivity, and his brother spent one period of an hour over two runs. M. A. Buss and Greig bowled ten consecutive maidens. There was no suitable explanation forthcoming for something which served only to irritate the spectators and damage the image of cricket.

Glamorgan at 392-6 dec (P. M. Walker 121*, Majid Khan 101)
and 292-2 (E. W. Jones 146*, A. Jones 84*);
Sussex 375 (K. G. Suttle 103, M. A. Buss 58, J. M. Parks 56, T. B. Racionzer 51*; D. J. Shepherd 4-99).

1971 – SNOW AT CENTRE OF STORMY YEAR 1972

Any recording of the happenings of Sussex cricket in 1971 must have John Snow as its focal point. Adversely criticised by some Australians for his bumpers which helped England to win the Ashes in Australia; kept out of the final onslaught because he dislocated a finger in a Sydney picket fence; dropped by his county for lack of effort; disciplined out of a Test match [after sending Gavaskar sprawling along the ground]; doubts about re-signing for 1972; then off to Australia to play for the Carlton club in Melbourne. All this and still time to finish and have published a first book of poems. Truly cricket's controversial man of the year.

Sussex at the time saw little to please them in the contretemps. All was patched up in the end and if, subsequently, it is found that by his tempestuous 12 months, the best fast bowler in England, if not in the whole world, has got it all out of his system, then the trouble and strife will have been worthwhile.

1972 – SUSSEX v AUSTRALIANS: GRATEFUL RECIPIENTS 1973

At Hove, July 22, 24, 25, 1972. Sussex won by five wickets, so becoming the first county to beat the 1972 touring team. The previous victory for Sussex over the Australians was in 1888. Satisfactory and decisive as was this latest success, it became possible largely because of either a miscalculation or the exceptional generosity of Ian Chappell. He left the county to score 261 in roughly three hours, and on a pitch so perfect this was a very workable proposition, particularly as Lillee, Massie and Gleeson were not in the Australian side. Greenidge did most to see Sussex through successfully by five wickets with 16 balls to spare. He was still there with 125 (14 fours) at the close, having been denied a century in each innings by his own nervousness, and Australia's understandable exploitation of it, when he was on 99 in his first knock.

Australians 294 (I. M. Chappell 58, R. W. Marsh 54; M. A. Buss 5-69)
and 262-2 dec (K. R. Stackpole 154*, A. P. Sheahan 50);
Sussex 296-5 dec (G. A. Greenidge 99, R. M. Prideaux 55) and 261-5 (Greenidge 125*; R. J. Inverarity 4-60).

Little Wonder No. 120

Kent v Derbyshire. At Canterbury, April 23, 24, 25, 26, 1997. The visitors took the field with the wrong side. Kent captain Steve Marsh was under the impression that Matthew Vandrau was in the Derbyshire eleven until the sixth over, when left-arm seamer Dean came on to bowl. Secretary Stuart Anderson walked out on to the pitch, followed by Marsh, and they spent several minutes talking to Derbyshire skipper Jones and the umpires, complaining that Law 1.2 had been broken. In the end it was announced that Derbyshire had made a "genuine error" when they named their team, and Dean was allowed to stay.

1978 – GREIG GRANTED EARLY DEPARTURE Jack Arlidge, 1979

At one time the 1978 season seriously threatened to prove one of the unhappiest and least successful in the long history of Sussex. Snow had gone; Greig left in midseason; there were still various tilts of the committee with Lord's; numerous injuries weakened the playing strength, and generally an air of pessimism prevailed at Hove.

Whatever the rights and wrongs of the Greig affair and his alliance with Kerry Packer, there was an upsurge of spirit and determination later in the summer, culminating in the winning of the Gillette Cup against the formidable Somerset side.

It was on July 11 when Sussex announced that they had "acceded to a request from Tony Greig to be released forthwith from the remainder of his contract, which would have expired in September 1978". The controversial career, which had started back in 1966, was over. It was not until late September, however, that the secret of

Greig being an epileptic, which a few of us had known from an early match with the Second Eleven, was revealed. His association with Packer proved a great blow to the club and the game, but we can still admire the spirit and willpower which enabled him to become so fine a player despite such a handicap.

It was obviously a traumatic season for a new captain, but wicketkeeper Long, so different from Greig in temperament, persevered in cool and admirable fashion, steadily rebuilding the old team spirit and reaping a thrilling reward when he was hoisted on the shoulders of his team-mates, with the Gillette Cup raised aloft, on the balcony at Lord's. It was his experience that had enabled Sussex to restrict the scoring-rate of those brilliant Somerset batsmen, Richards and Botham.

1984 – SUSSEX v KENT: BATTLE ROYAL   1985

At Hastings, June 30, July 2, 3, 1984. Tied. Even disregarding the dramatic result this was a most eventful match, with 21 wickets falling on the first day for 257 runs (Sussex gaining a lead of 51), with Underwood scoring a maiden century in the second innings – in his 22nd season and 618th first-class innings – and with the last four home wickets tumbling for only six runs in four overs when victory looked a formality. Alderman enjoyed both a maiden half-century and his best return for Kent while Colin Wells had a fine all-round game, returning his best-ever figures in Kent's first innings. In the end, though, the first tie in the Championship since 1974 – Sussex and Essex at Hove – seemed the fairest result between the evenly matched neighbours.

Kent 92 (N. R. Taylor 50; C. M. Wells 5-25)
and 243 (D. L. Underwood 111);
Sussex 143 (Wells 51; K. B. S. Jarvis 4-34, T. M. Alderman 4-46)
and 192 (Wells 81; Alderman 5-60).

1989 – SHOPS REPLACE HISTORIC GROUND   Jack Arlidge, 1990

There was a general feeling of great sadness at the loss of the historic Central Ground at Hastings, which staged its last first-class match. The famous ground, created in 1864, has been sold for £19million and will disappear under a massive shopping precinct. Over the years it presented some 230 first-class matches, and no fewer than 625 Test cricketers performed there.

1997 – YEAR OF STRIFE ON AND OFF FIELD   Andy Arlidge, 1998

It was no surprise that 1997 was a struggle for Sussex; six capped players, including Alan Wells, last year's captain, had left amid confusion and bitterness.

It turned out even worse than they feared: one of the most difficult seasons in their 158-year history. The county suffered a dismal double, wooden spoons in both County Championship and Sunday League, lost to the British Universities in the Benson and Hedges Cup, and found solace only in the NatWest Trophy, where two startling wins galvanised the club's supporters and distracted attention from day-to-day reality.

Nothing on the field could quite match the drama that preceded the season, when a members' revolt forced out the old committee at the annual general meeting.

2002 – RASHID'S MEMORY LIVES ON AT HOVE   Andy Arlidge and Bruce Talbot, 2003

The season began in tragedy. Within ten days of the death of Surrey's Ben Hollioake, Sussex lost their gifted all-rounder Umer Rashid, who drowned trying to save his younger brother, Burhan, during the club's pre-season tour to Grenada. The county cap that would have been given to Rashid was presented to his father, Mirza, in a moving ceremony when Sussex played Angus Fraser's XI in a memorial match for the brothers. Adams called Rashid "probably the most naturally gifted player on the staff", and his memory will live on at Hove in the form of a new spin clinic and the refurbished main scoreboard, which has been named after him.

2003 – SUSSEX v LEICESTERSHIRE: LONG WAIT OVER   2004

At Hove, September 17, 18, 19, 2003. Sussex won by an innings and 55 runs. Sussex's long wait for their first Championship finally ended at 1.44 on the second afternoon. Goodwin pulled DeFreitas for four to secure their sixth bonus point, which ensured Lancashire could not catch them. The rest of the squad flooded on to the outfield, and play halted for eight minutes as they did a lap of honour while the county anthem "Sussex by the Sea" echoed around the old ground. It was an unforgettable moment for a near-full house bathed in late summer sunshine. Lengthier celebrations began after Sussex completed their tenth victory, with over a day to spare. There were several outstanding performances. Goodwin amassed an unbeaten 335, beating Duleepsinhji's 333 against Northamptonshire in 1930 as the highest score for Sussex. He batted eight hours nine minutes, striking 52 fours and a six in 390 balls; while the bowling often left a lot to be desired, it was a monumental effort of concentration and a glorious exhibition of back-foot strokeplay. Goodwin added 267 in three hours with Adams, who reached his fourth hundred in six games. And with the last ball before lunch on the opening day, Mushtaq Ahmed had bowled Hodge to become the first bowler since 1998 to reach 100 first-class wickets in a season. That wicket transformed the match. Leicestershire seemed in a mood to delay Sussex on another excellent pitch but, once Mushtaq broke through, they fell in a heap, losing nine for 68. Sussex scored 614 in little over three sessions against demoralised opponents. But Leicestershire's determination revived when the injured Mushtaq rested. Left-hander Sadler equalled his highest score and put on 208 with nightwatchman Masters, who reached a maiden century. Then Lewry, making the old ball swing prodigiously, took five for six in 25 deliveries on his way to a career-best. A few minutes later, Adams was holding the trophy aloft and the party was in full swing.

Leicestershire 179 (D. L. Maddy 55; Mushtaq Ahmed 4-71)
and 380 (J. L. Sadler 145, D. D. Masters 119; J. D. Lewry 8-106);
Sussex 614-4 dec (M. W. Goodwin 335*, C. J. Adams 102, T. R. Ambrose 82, P. A. Cottey 56).

2007 – Winning Becomes A Habit
Andy Arlidge, 2008

It took Sussex 164 years to win their first County Championship, but now they have won three in five seasons. And this was the closest of them: Sussex finished only 4.5 points ahead of Durham, after Lancashire, who had led by six points before the last round, narrowly failed to beat Surrey in an epic run-chase.

WARWICKSHIRE

[1950 edition] *WARWICKSHIRE'S UPS AND DOWNS by M. F. K. Fraser*

There are critics of a policy which has turned the Warwickshire staff into a Cricket League of Nations; but the Birmingham public, nurtured on the liberal transfer system of soccer, will not worry where their cricket favourites come from so long as they play attractively and win matches.

1886 – New Ground Promises New Beginning
1887

Of the counties which are not reckoned as first-class, not one has brighter prospects than Warwickshire, cricket in the county having received a great impetus through the opening of the new ground at Edgbaston, near Birmingham.

1894 – Midlanders Make First-Class Start
1895

Warwickshire arranged a far more ambitious programme than they had ever before attempted, but they thoroughly justified their promotion to the first class, and have every reason to be satisfied with the result of their season's doings. A most remarkable start was made, victories being gained over Notts, Surrey, and Kent, and the Midland team had the unique distinction of being the only county to lower the colours of Surrey on The Oval. The brilliant commencement made by Warwickshire set all the cricket world talking about them.

1911 – FOSTER INSPIRES LEAST-EXPECTED CHAMPIONSHIP WIN   1912

Never since the County Championship became an organised competition has there been a result half so surprising as the triumph in 1911 of Warwickshire. The jump from 14th place in 1910 to the top of the tree was nothing less than astonishing.

Nothing very startling occurred for a couple of months, but from the end of June Warwickshire showed wonderful form. Of their last 12 county matches they won nine outright and won the other three on the first innings, scoring 54 points out of a possible 60.

Their success gave rise to extraordinary enthusiasm. Returning from Northampton immediately after the final match, the eleven had a reception in Birmingham, thousands of people turning out to welcome them. On September 21 a dinner was given at the Grand Hotel, Birmingham, to commemorate Warwickshire's triumph, and also the fact that three members of the eleven – F. R. Foster, Kinneir and Smith – had been given places in the MCC's team for Australia.

Never before has cricket made such an appeal to the Birmingham public as it did last summer. From the moment the team began to win matches people flocked to the Edgbaston ground in such numbers as to relieve the committee of all anxiety about money. Such sudden enthusiasm suggests rather too much the spirit of Association football, and is apt to cause misgivings among old-fashioned crick-eters. One can only hope that the Birmingham public, having at last taken up county cricket in real earnest, will support their eleven in bad seasons as well as in good ones.

Warwickshire's triumph was mainly due to F. R. Foster. Not since W. G. Grace in the early days of the Gloucestershire eleven has so young a captain been such a match-winning force in a county side. Foster [aged 22] was always getting runs, always taking wickets, and over and above all this, he proved himself a truly inspiring leader. No longer could it be said that Warwickshire played a slow or unenterprising game. They went out on all occasions to win, their cricket being keen and energetic to a degree. Foster himself had a splendid record both as batsman and bowler. He came out top of the averages in both tables, scoring 1,383 runs in county matches, with an average of 44, and taking 116 wickets for a little over 19 runs apiece.

Little Wonder No. 121

Yorkshire v Warwickshire (AXA League). At Leeds, September 13, 1998. Dickie Bird's prolonged farewell to umpiring finally reached its conclusion with what was positively his last match after 29 years on the first-class list. The players formed a guard of honour as he took the field. Naturally, there was a Dickie-type incident: he got a bruised knee after being hit by a shot from Parker.

1917 – County's Sons Killed In War

Mr R. V. Ryder [Secretary] writes: "We have suffered a big loss in the death in action of Lieut. H. J. Goodwin, former captain of the club, who was at the time of his death a member of the committee. He was the only son of our honorary treasurer, Mr F. S. Goodwin. It is a lamentable coincidence that three of our principal supporters, Mr G. H. Cartland, Mr Goodwin, and Sir Halliwell Rogers, have lost only sons in the War."

1919 – Play Resumes Without Key Figures

No county last season, except Northamptonshire, took up first-class cricket again under such discouraging conditions as Warwickshire. Mr F. R. Foster – the mainstay of the eleven for several years before the War – had, by reason of a bad accident when motorcycling, resigned the captaincy and given up cricket, and death on the [battle] field had claimed Percy Jeeves, who had given promise in 1914 of developing into one of the best bowlers in England.

1927 – Quaife Still Going Strong At 55

Quaife, at the age of 55, obtained with his leg-breaks 50 wickets – the largest number which fell to any Warwickshire bowler – and in addition, scored 775 runs with an average of 24 – eloquent testimony to the skill and physical fitness of that famous veteran.

Some months after the close of the season an announcement was made that, at the request of the committee, Quaife, in order to make room for the younger players, had retired from the county eleven. A memorable career was that which, it is accordingly to be assumed, has come to an end. Quaife first appeared for Warwickshire in 1893, so his association with the county extended over a period of nearly 35 years. A most skilful and stylish batsman, a clever slow bowler and a brilliant field – especially at cover point – he scored in first-class matches 35,836 runs, played 71 innings of a hundred or more and took 928 wickets – truly a wonderful record for one of the shortest of men who ever figured largely in important cricket.

Quaife did make his mark in one more appearance the following season ...

1928 – WARWICKSHIRE v DERBYSHIRE: FINAL HUNDRED

At Birmingham, August 4, 6, 7, 1928. W. G. Quaife, the famous Warwickshire veteran, could not have wished for a more fitting close to his long career than in playing an innings of 115 on his last appearance for the county. Notwithstanding his 56 years and the fact that it was his first and only county match of the season, he batted with all his old-time steadiness and skill for four hours and 20 minutes, offering no chance and making his runs with nice variety of stroke. His performance coincided with Warwickshire's highest score of the summer.

Warwickshire 564-7 dec (W. G. Quaife 115, J. H. Parsons 114, L. T. A. Bates 90,
Hon. F. S. G. Calthorpe 71*);
Derbyshire 255 (Mr T. W. Durnell 5-63)
and 222-3 (J. Bowden 92, H. Storer 61, G. M. Lee 52*).

1928 – For Parsons Read Parson
1929

Parsons, always a fine forcing batsman, had to yield first place in the averages to Wyatt, but he was very consistent and placed some splendid innings. Unfortunately for Warwickshire, he decided to abandon the pursuit of cricket as a means of livelihood and proceeded to study with the view of entering the clerical profession.

1934 – YORKSHIRE v WARWICKSHIRE: NARROW WIN
1935

At Scarborough, July 18, 19, 20, 1934. After being dismissed for 45, the lowest score of the season, Warwickshire gained a remarkable victory by one wicket. Rain affected the pitch and though the match did not start until 20 minutes to three, 18 wickets fell on Wednesday for 126. Sent in by Parsons, Yorkshire began by losing three men for 12 runs and were all out in two and a half hours, but before stumps were drawn Warwickshire had eight wickets down for 25. On going in again Yorkshire made very slow progress and might have been got rid of quite cheaply had not five chances been missed. The pitch was in better condition than at any previous time in the match when Warwickshire went in to get 216. Parsons rose to the occasion and by superb driving he dominated the cricket to such an extent that in less than two hours he made 94 out of 121, hitting three sixes and 12 fours. Only 12 runs were wanted when he left.

Yorkshire 101 (C. Turner 51; G. A. E. Paine 8-62) and 159 (Paine 4-59);
Warwickshire 45 (H. S. Hargreaves 4-19)
and 216-9 (Rev. J. H. Parsons 94, N. Kilner 58; G. G. Macaulay 4-67).

1937 – Wyatt Usurped As Captain
1938

Once again R. E. S. Wyatt, the captain, stood out above everybody in consistency of run-getting and twice in July he obtained double-hundreds, those being the only occasions he had done so in the course of his career. By scoring eight centuries in a season he also set up a new individual record for the county. In his two big innings he batted for more than seven hours without making an error and the efforts typified the man – remarkable concentration, correct strokeplay and ability to show bowlers that he was their master. He scored more runs in Championship matches than in any season since 1929, and for the sixth successive year he headed the averages.

A sensation was caused at the end of the season when the general committee announced that whilst appreciating the services of Wyatt as captain of the club for eight years it had been unanimously decided to recommend "in the best interests of the club" that a change be made in the captaincy. P. Cranmer accepted the position for 1938.

1944 – Festival Organiser Scores Top Marks For Communication   1945

Ideal weather, cricket at its best, and a happy, intimate atmosphere made the third Birmingham Festival on the Edgbaston ground an unqualified success. Over 42,000 spectators watched the play during the seven days, the attendance on Saturday exceeding 10,000, and the balance sheet revealed a profit of £2,514. Of this, £1,962 went to the Lord Mayor of Birmingham's War Relief Fund and £551 10s. was donated to the RAF Benevolent Fund and other war charities.

Special praise again was due to Councillor R. I. Scorer, who conquered manifold difficulties in inaugurating the Festival week in 1942 when the ground was in a derelict condition, and his effervescing enthusiasm and initiative reaped a just reward in 1944. Besides securing the help of many Test and county players – and entertaining them handsomely – he paid every possible attention to the needs of the public. Each scorecard contained on the reverse a diagram of fielding positions and, over a loudspeaker, Councillor Scorer maintained a constant service of comment and information on the play and players. Music during lunch and tea, news items, and even a Lost Property and Missing People bureau, increased the general enjoyment. The crowds certainly appreciated all this thought, and, as the microphone was used discreetly only between the intervals of actual cricket, the players agreed that it did not affect their concentration on the game.

A large number of schoolboys attended the five games and enjoyed the freedom of the playing area during the intervals – a thing unknown on the ground in peacetime. Although they took full advantage of the privilege, not once was trespass made on the square itself, marked only by small whitewash circles on the turf. A special enclosure for wounded soldiers and the hospitality extended to them also struck a note of comradeship.

1950 – WARWICKSHIRE v WEST INDIANS: Sole success   1951

At Birmingham, August 9, 10, 11, 1950. Warwickshire won by three wickets. The only county side to beat West Indies in 1950, they owed their success mainly to the splendid fast-medium bowling of Grove, who at the age of 38 achieved his best performance in first-class cricket by taking eight wickets for 38. On a greenish pitch

Grove moved the ball either way, and he claimed the first five wickets that fell for 97. Marshall batted stubbornly for two hours and Williams and Jones hit boldly, but Warwickshire fielded splendidly, Spooner, Dollery and Hollies all making fine catches. Taylor, the New Zealander, shaped well in each county innings, but the real mastery was established by Wolton and Spooner, whose stand realised 123. Wolton drove strongly, being specially severe on Valentine. Hollies caused West Indies most trouble in their second innings. Although Warwickshire wanted only 95 they experienced great difficulty in hitting off the runs on a sporting pitch. In 35 minutes before lunch, Gardner and Thompson could score only eight, but their opening stand produced 34. Dollery fell to a magnificent right-hand catch, but Taylor remained firm, and amidst scenes of tremendous enthusiasm Pritchard made the winning hit. Fifty thousand people saw the match. This was the first victory by any county side over a touring team since Worcestershire beat the South Africans in the opening match in 1947.

West Indians 156 (C. W. Grove 8-38) **and** 222 (W. E. Hollies 6-57);
Warwickshire 284 (A. V. Wolton 89, R. T. Spooner 66*; A. L. Valentine 4-57) **and 96-7** (Valentine 4-36).

1951 – PROFESSIONAL EFFORT SECURES SECOND CROWN   1952

Warwickshire, by winning the County Championship after a lapse of 40 years and for only the second time since they entered the competition in 1895, reaped the reward for a good deal of foresight and enterprise since the war.

Back in 1911, Warwickshire set something like a precedent when they elected a 22-year-old captain, F. R. Foster, who led them to victory. Last season Warwickshire established other precedents in English cricket. They were the first county to win the title with a professional captain and an all-professional team. They called on only one amateur, E. B. Lewis, and he appeared in one Championship match.

Another feature of Warwickshire's climb to the top was their number of imported players. Only Grove and Gardner of the regular side were born within the county. The secret of Warwickshire's superiority was their ability to play as a team. There were no stars – no one was chosen for any of the five Tests or the Gentlemen and Players match – but in Dollery they possessed the most skilful of all the county captains. He possessed that rare gift of being a born leader of men both on and off the field. He united his team in a cheerful confidence and behind it all he was a shrewd tactician, particularly in the field, where he exploited the weaknesses of the opposition. Moreover, the runs Dollery scored were often made when the need was greatest.

1951 – WARWICKSHIRE v YORKSHIRE: ALMOST THERE   1952

At Birmingham, July 28, 30, 31, 1951. Warwickshire won by an innings and 16 runs. By beating Yorkshire, their closest challengers, for the second time,

COUNTIES

Warwickshire not only created a county record of 15 Championship victories in a season but made their position at the head of the table virtually unassailable. An aggregate paying attendance of 43,000 spectators, surpassing the record of 32,091 set up in the Lancashire match the previous week, saw Warwickshire complete the double over Yorkshire for the first time for 61 years and become the first county to do so since Gloucestershire in 1947. Nevertheless, Yorkshire were particularly unfortunate to enter this vital match without Hutton, Lowson, Watson and Brennan, all of whom were playing for England. Their absence left the batting immeasurably weaker.

Yorkshire 249 (E. I. Lester 68; W. E. Hollies 4-63) and 97 (Hollies 5-47);
Warwickshire 362 (H. E. Dollery 111, J. S. Ord 67, R. T. Spooner 65; J. H. Wardle 4-106).

1967 – WARWICKSHIRE v ESSEX: ALLAN KEY — 1968

At Birmingham, July 1, 3, 4, 1967. Drawn with the scores level. The match worked up to a tremendous climax, with the scores level at close of play. Allan again played a major part for Warwickshire. His side needed 13 runs to win when the last over came. With Cartwright at the other end, Allan hit Boyce, who had just been recalled, for 4, 4, 2. The pair then took a single and when Cartwright did not connect with the last ball, Allan scampered to the other end for the equalling bye.

Essex 253 (G. E. Barker 124*, K. D. Boyce 56; J. D. Bannister 4-53) and 208-7 dec (G. R. Cass 104*);
Warwickshire 259 (R. E. East 5-61) and 202-8 (R. N. Abberley 50; R. N. S. Hobbs 4-54).

1969 – CARTWRIGHT SPRINGS SURPRISE WITH RESIGNATION — 1970

Yet again Cartwright headed the bowling averages, and the announcement of his resignation from his county in October was a surprising and stunning blow to Warwickshire's hopes for next season. Cartwright is certain of a permanent place in the county records as he is the only player in Warwickshire's history to have scored 10,000 runs and captured 1,000 wickets. He made his debut as a batsman in 1952 and did not take a wicket until his fourth season. In 1962 he became the first Warwickshire player to perform the double since 1926. A magnificent bowler in England, his meticulous accuracy of length and line commanded respect even when conditions offered little help.

1970 – SURREY v WARWICKSHIRE: GOOD BYE — 1971

At The Oval, July 18, 20, 21, 1970. Drawn. Warwickshire came from behind to snatch the major points by levelling the scores with a bye from the final ball. This

786

was run to the wicketkeeper standing back to Jackman and earned Warwickshire five points. They were set 266 in three hours and a half, and an anchor innings by Jameson, 101 in three hours, and brilliant hitting and improvisation by Smith opened the way for the exciting climax.

Surrey 342 (S. J. Storey 106, M. J. Edwards 81; W. Blenkiron 4-85)
and 181 (R. M. Lewis 55; W. N. Tidy 5-36);
Warwickshire 258 (A. Gordon 65, K. Ibadulla 57)
and 265-6 (J. A. Jameson 101, M. J. K. Smith 88).

1972 – Team Toast Title With Champagne And Kippers   1973

Warwickshire, after being beaten on a technicality by Surrey the previous year, won the County Championship for the third time in their history. In addition they reached the final of the Gillette Cup and the semi-final of the new Benson and Hedges League Cup, and only in the John Player League did their performance fall below par. They won by a margin of 36 points, and six of their nine victories were achieved the hard way by bowling the opposition out twice. Their total of victories was two more than any other county, and they were the only unbeaten team – although rain saved them from almost certain defeat by Yorkshire at Sheffield.

Strangely the season began on a very unpropitious note when, in the very first match, the county were defeated by Oxford University. Success was sealed in the penultimate match against Derbyshire, and the captain [A. C. Smith] made true his promise of a champagne and kippers breakfast on the morning of the first day of the final match.

1982 – Kallicharran Shines Amid The Gloom   1983

The season which marked 100 years of Warwickshire cricket came and went with sadly little to celebrate. Instead, there was much heart-searching about a woeful string of results which sent the club carrying two wooden spoons into 1983. For the first time they failed to win a single Championship match; they plunged from third place in 1981 to the foot of the John Player League, winning only three times, and they never emerged from the qualifying stages of the Benson and Hedges Cup. They let some daylight into an otherwise gloomy campaign by battling their way to the final of the NatWest Bank Trophy, although, once there, they were well beaten by Surrey.

The batting did turn up one shining exception to the rule in Alvin Kallicharran, whose scintillating displays did much to chase away the shadows. In the final Championship match at Southampton he became the only player in the country to top 2,000 runs. In all he hit three double-centuries and five singles in equalling the county's record for a season.

Little Wonder No. 122

Central contracts. On May 13, 1999, the First-Class Forum voted by 12–7 that England's leading players should be contracted centrally to the ECB. The initial proposal was that up to 16 Test players and up to eight further one-day players should be given six-month contracts. They would be available to play some matches for their counties, who would be compensated for the loss of these players by an amount yet to be determined.

1984 – WILLIS FORCED TO MAKE EARLY EXIT

Jack Bannister, 1985

A sad note was the retirement of the captain, Bob Willis, whose departure from the first-class game was advanced by six weeks because of a recurrence of the illness which had forced his premature return in March from the England tour of Pakistan. He dropped out of the England side before the Manchester Test, and it was a matter of some regret that his last appearance for his county was in the Benson and Hedges final – not just because his side lost, but because subsequently crowds around the country were denied the opportunity to pay their tribute to such a distinguished cricketer. A combination of Test selection, injuries and illness restricted his appearances for Warwickshire to under half of the possible maximum during his 13-year career at Edgbaston. Nevertheless, his five-year period as club captain, particularly before his appointment to the England captaincy in 1982, was marked by the single-minded approach which characterised so much of his cricket.

1993 – SUSSEX v WARWICKSHIRE (NATWEST BANK TROPHY FINAL):
THRILLING CLIMAX

Paul Weaver, 1994

At Lord's, September 4, 1993. Warwickshire won by five wickets. The 53rd one-day final at Lord's was widely regarded as the greatest ever played. Off the last ball, Warwickshire overhauled the Sussex total of 321 for six, the highest score in a Cup final. The result has to be judged in the context of poor Sussex fielding and some unimaginative captaincy by Wells, but the magnificence of the victory and the thrilling nature of the cricket was beyond dispute.

It was only after tea that Sussex first realised the awful possibility of defeat. Smith, with flowing off-drives, and Asif Din, with wristy improvisation, added 71 in 15 overs. Smith was fourth out at 164 in the 36th over and Asif Din and Reeve were required to score at more than a run a ball. They kept going, but, with 20 needed from two twilit overs Sussex still held a slender advantage. They strengthened their position in the 59th when Giddins conceded just five runs and had Asif Din caught at deep cover. He had scored 104 from 106 balls and added 142 in 23 overs with his captain Reeve. Fifteen were needed from the last over: Reeve scored 13 from the first five deliveries. Twose, facing his first and last ball, sliced it through the close off-side field for two to give Warwickshire their victory; stumps were pulled at both ends before the completion of the second run, and Warwickshire should have been awarded the match through losing fewer wickets. However, it was a day for romance rather than technicalities.

Sussex 321-6 (60 overs) (D. M. Smith 124, N. J. Lenham 58, M. P. Speight 50);
Warwickshire 322-5 (60 overs) (Asif Din 104, D. A. Reeve 81*, P. A. Smith 60).

1994 – TOSS OF COIN PREVENTS UNIQUE CLEAN SWEEP   Jack Bannister, 1995

Warwickshire recorded the most remarkable season by any side in the history of English county cricket. Uniquely, they won three trophies and, arguably, were only denied the fourth by the toss of a coin.

They won their fourth County Championship, their second Sunday League title and their first ever Benson and Hedges Cup. For the ninth successive time, and the 18th in the last 21 years, the NatWest Trophy went to the side batting second in the final; otherwise Warwickshire might have defeated Worcestershire to complete a clean sweep. Arguments about whether they were the best-ever county team are spurious, because conditions and circumstances vary from season to season, but this record is unlikely to be equalled or beaten. The most meritorious achievement was the County Championship, in which they won 11 of their 17 matches, three more than any other county, and finally led by 42 points. Both those margins were unequalled since 1979, when Essex won 13 games to runners-up Worcestershire's seven, to lead by 77 points; but in those days 22 matches were scheduled.

Warwickshire's unforgettable season came from meticulous planning and a stroke of luck in being able to sign Brian Lara when Manoj Prabhakar withdrew because of injury. The publicity surrounding Lara's 375 against England in Antigua started a bandwagon which rolled into Edgbaston 11 days later when he scored 147 against Glamorgan, the first of what were to be six Championship hundreds in seven innings, culminating in his world-record 501 not out (see page 952), and nine in all. By June 6, he had scored 1,176 runs in those seven innings. Of the eight batsmen who have scored 1,000 runs by the end of May, only Bradman did it in seven, and he averaged 170.16 to Lara's 235.20.

Crucial for a good, but not outstanding county attack was Lara's scoring-rate: his 2,066 Championship runs came off 2,262 deliveries, that is five and a half runs per six balls faced. The extra time he created contributed materially to several of the wins, and his presence widened the horizons of his team-mates.

The influence of Bob Woolmer, director of coaching, was incalculable. His fourth season at Edgbaston brought to fruition a rare ability to communicate technical advice and it was no surprise when he was given a similar appointment with the South African Test team just after the triumphant end of the season.

1995 – WARWICKSHIRE v NORTHAMPTONSHIRE: ONE OF THE BEST 1996

At Birmingham, July 27, 28, 29, 31, 1995. Northamptonshire won by seven runs. This nerve-shredding encounter was described by both captains as the best Championship game they had ever played in. It was probably one of the best of all time. Northamptonshire won at 2.45pm on the final day. Had they lost, Warwickshire would have been near-certain champions already; victory reduced the gap between them to two points. A match of dramatic twists was exemplified in the final innings. Chasing 275, Warwickshire slumped to 53 for six against Kumble, recovered to 201 for six thanks to Reeve and Smith, lost their ninth wicket with 47 required and still fell only eight short. There was a succession of heroic performances: from Capel, who scored a crucial fifty, followed up with a career-best seven for 44; from Twose, who batted throughout Warwickshire's first innings and scored 62.5% of their total; from Fordham and Warren, whose determined batting set up the final challenge; but most of all from Donald and Kumble. The South African pace bowler and Indian leg-spinner bowled long spells in exhausting heat and each took ten wickets, Kumble for the second match running. On the first morning, Donald and Munton reduced Northamptonshire to a disastrous 69 for six and, even after Capel's efforts, 152 all out. Capel bounced back with three wickets in four overs, but a patient century from Twose took Warwickshire to a 72-run lead before he was last out, hooking to fine leg. The next-highest scorer was Extras. Back in the field, Warwickshire paid heavily for dropped catches. Fordham reached a century after nearly six hours and Warren struck an aggressive 70. Donald almost bowled himself into the ground for his six wickets. But his role was not over. After Warwickshire had collapsed to a magical spell from Kumble – four for 32 in 16 teasing overs – the application of Reeve and Smith prevented a three-day defeat and then took Warwickshire to within 74 of victory. When Kumble took another three wickets, however, the job was left to Donald and Munton. Combining luck with sensible placement, they scraped together 39 runs before Capel trapped Munton lbw. The players were still drained an hour later. "It was like a little bit of a war out there," said Lamb, "but that's the way county cricket should be played."

> Northamptonshire 152 (D. J. Capel 50; A. A. Donald 4-41, T. A. Munton 4-47)
> and 346 (A. Fordham 101, R. J. Warren 70; Donald 6-95);
> Warwickshire 224 (R. G. Twose 140; Capel 7-44)
> and 267 (N. M. K. Smith 75, D. A. Reeve 74; A. Kumble 7-82).

1997 – DRUG ABUSE CASTS SHADOW OVER CLUB   Jack Bannister, 1998

A less happy feature of the year was the recurrent motif of drug abuse. Former player Paul Smith made lurid revelations about his lifestyle, and the club responded with a surprise test of their present squad. Piper tested positive, and was fined £500 and suspended for one match. Warwickshire were praised for their swift action, but criticised for their arrangements with ex-Sussex fast bowler Ed Giddins. He had signed to join the county in April 1998, after serving a 20-month ban for taking cocaine, and they reportedly paid him to visit Birmingham for practice.

1997 – WARWICKSHIRE v SOMERSET (AXA Life League): {#floodlit-first}

FLOODLIT FIRST   1998

At Birmingham, July 23, 1997 (day/night). Warwickshire won by 35 runs. This was the first Sunday League game to be staged under floodlights, Surrey's earlier attempt having been washed out, and it was a huge success. On perhaps the warmest evening of the year, 15,174 people watched Warwickshire's Wednesday-night win, bringing in about £120,000 – a profit of £70,000, allowing for the cost of the lights. Crowd behaviour was impeccable, and the club were thrilled by their experiment. Smith chose to bat when the match began at 6.10pm and shared an opening stand of 112 with Singh. Though Warwickshire's eventual total was only twice that, Somerset were soon in trouble under the lights. Brown and Small reduced them to 56 for five, which became 99 for seven before Bowler and Kerr put together a stand of 63. Donald ended the match when he bowled Shine at 11.38pm. Kerr was credited with five penalty runs after an incident that occurred in a corner unilluminated by the five pylons. Penney's cap dropped off when he was chasing the ball near the boundary, and the ball struck the cap. Ian Botham, commentating on TV, saw the incident and, after replaying it several times, alerted the third umpire, Barrie Leadbeater, who had the scores amended.

Warwickshire 224-5 (40 overs) (A. Singh 86, N. M. K. Smith 59, D. P. Ostler 42);
Somerset 189 (39.2 overs) (P. D. Bowler 57).

2004 – LOW-KEY VICTORY BRINGS MUTED CELEBRATIONS   Paul Bolton, 2005

The manner in which Warwickshire clinched their sixth County Championship summed up their summer. The title was secured not in the grand manner, with victory on the pitch, but on a day off. They monitored events at Hove, where Middlesex ended Sussex's mathematical hopes of overhauling the leaders, via television and computer scores. The players staged champagne celebrations at a deserted Edgbaston for the sponsors' benefit. And a day later, they were relegated in the totesport League.

Warwickshire spent most of the season talking down their Championship prospects, as if they never quite believed they were good enough, but their understated efficiency paid dividends. They may have completed only five wins, a record low for any Championship-winning side – but they could not be faulted for playing the system. New captain Nick Knight was quick to appreciate that the points were weighted so that not losing was almost as important as winning. He was justifiably proud that Warwickshire were the first county since Surrey in 1999 to survive a season unbeaten.

2004 – WARWICKSHIRE v LANCASHIRE: A WINTRY TALE 2005

At Stratford-upon-Avon, June 18, 19, 20, 21, 2004. Drawn. First-class cricket returned to Stratford after 53 years, but Warwickshire's first Championship game at the pleasant Swan's Nest Lane ground, just across the river from the Royal Shakespeare Theatre, was hit by unseasonably cold, wet weather, and even hail, which blanketed the outfield in white on the third day.

2005 – HOLLAND v WARWICKSHIRE (CHELTENHAM & GLOUCESTER TROPHY FIRST ROUND): LOST AND FOUND 2006

At VOC Club, Rotterdam, May 3, 4, 2005. Warwickshire won by 23 runs. Warwickshire had far more trouble than anticipated: the ground was so new it did not show on the coach driver's satnav system. He drove the players to the old VOC Club, three miles away and now derelict, and they had to wander through the woods in the rain before they were rescued. At the ground, the tent in which they were sheltering was blown from its moorings by the wind. Holland had the best of the conditions in every way, and a sixth-wicket stand of 81 between Daan van Bunge and Billy Stelling gave them hope before Streak returned to finish off the innings.

Warwickshire 237-5 (50 overs) (N. V. Knight 108, T. L. Penney 51*);
Holland 214 (49 overs) (D. L. S. van Bunge 89, W. F. Stelling 45; H. H. Streak 4-27, N. M. Carter 4-34).

2012 – WORCESTERSHIRE v WARWICKSHIRE: NO MISTAKE 2013

At Worcester, September 4, 5, 6, 2012. Warwickshire won by an innings and 202 runs. Warwickshire secured their first Championship title in eight years in the most emphatic manner imaginable, crushing Worcestershire's feeble resistance by 1.35pm on the third day and condemning their local rivals to relegation. There was no repeat of the uncertainty or anguish of a year earlier, when Lancashire had pipped them to the trophy on the final day. Director of cricket Ashley Giles dedicated Warwickshire's seventh Championship pennant to Neal Abberley, who served for five decades as player and coach before his death in August 2011. The outcome was never in doubt once Worcestershire folded on the first morning, on a blameless pitch, for 60 – the lowest total by any county all season, their worst since 1971, and their worst-ever against Warwickshire. It was an abject display, even from a side containing four players with only nine previous Championship appearances between them. Chopra shared his fifth century opening stand of the campaign with Westwood and a third-wicket partnership of 131 with Troughton, and passed 1,000 runs for the second successive summer. Blackwell's quick 84 helped Warwickshire to the fourth batting point that virtually ensured them the title. Worcestershire bowled three seven-ball overs late in the innings, due to mistakes by the umpires. Troughton was able to declare with a lead of 411 as early as tea on the second day. A little over two sessions later, he was celebrating the title with a mixture of joy and relief.

Worcestershire 60 (C. J. C. Wright 5-24, K. H. D. Barker 5-36)
and 209 (M. M. Ali 72; Wright 4-65);
Warwickshire 471-8 dec (V. Chopra 195, I. D. Blackwell 84, I. J. Westwood 54, J. O. Troughton 54).

WORCESTERSHIRE

[1963 edition] *THE RISE OF WORCESTERSHIRE by Noel Stone*

The great batting feats of the Fosters made such an impact upon the public mind that the county won the affectionate title of "Fostershire." Before the Fosters there had been another famous cricketing family in Worcestershire, the Lytteltons of Hagley Hall, who on one historic occasion fielded a full eleven of their own and who have, for over 100 years, provided presidents and chairmen, captains and players for the Worcestershire eleven.

1898 – FROM MINOR TO MAJOR   1899

As in the previous two years, Worcestershire secured first place among the Minor Counties, their position being gained by thoroughly sound cricket at all points of the game. Indeed, so marked was the improvement shown by the members of the eleven that after the meeting of county secretaries at Lord's, in December, application was made to the MCC to give Worcestershire a place among the first-class counties.

1899 – WORCESTERSHIRE v HAMPSHIRE: FRATERNAL FEAT   1900

At Worcester, July 27, 28, 29, 1899. The first of the two engagements with Hampshire had to be left drawn, but it will always take a distinguished place in the history of cricket, for it was marked by a feat quite without precedent, two Worcestershire batsmen playing two innings each of over a hundred. On the first day the honours were easily carried off by W. L. and R. E. Foster, who, between them, put on 161 runs in an hour and a half. W. L. Foster was batting just over three hours and hit 16 fours, while his brother sent the ball 15 times to the boundary during his stay of two hours and three quarters.

Worcestershire 428 (Mr W. L. Foster 140, Mr R. E. Foster 134)
and 308-2 dec (Mr W. L. Foster 172*, Mr R. E. Foster 101*);
Hampshire 353 (Major R. M. Poore 122, V. A. Barton 62; R. D. Burrows 4-73) **and 157-7.**

793

Fraternal foursome: the Foster brothers of Worcestershire.
Back row (from left): G.N. and R.E. Front row: W.L. and H.K.

1907 – Harking Back To The Days Of Grace   1908

Tieing with Yorkshire for second place, Worcestershire did better than in any year since the county was first admitted to the front rank. The record in county matches last season – eight victories, two defeats, and eight drawn games – was more than creditable. The double victory over Yorkshire naturally stood out above all the other successes of the side. In the return Yorkshire were without their three leading bowlers, but, as a set-off, Worcestershire were without R. E. Foster, who, together with Hirst and Rhodes, was kept away by the Test match at The Oval.

The three brothers Foster head the batting, G. N. standing first, R. E. second, and H. K. third, and all three showing an average of over 40. To find a parallel to such batting as this on the part of three brothers in county matches one must go back to the deeds of W. G., E. M. and G. F. Grace in the brightest days of Gloucestershire cricket. G. N. Foster, engaged at Oxford until after the University Match, made no big score, but played so consistently that in 16 innings he was only out three times for less than 20. R. E. Foster, fortunate in having more time to spare for cricket than for some years, did not get into form so quickly as usual, but was quite at his best in two matches, scoring 174 against Kent and 144 against Gloucestershire. Though uneven in his run-getting he was, on his good days, clearly the finest bat in the eleven. H. K. Foster had, owing to lameness, to stand out of one county match, but otherwise he was always at his post. With 1,085 runs he had the best aggregate on the side, and in the averages R. E. Foster only beat him by a fraction.

Little Wonder No. 123

Hampshire v Kent. At Southampton, April 21, 22, 23, 24, 1999. Three Kent players – Fleming, Key and Marsh – plus coach John Wright had their wallets stolen from the dressing-room. They then received a phone call in which "a policeman" asked them to confirm their PIN numbers. This was the thief, who was then able to withdraw large sums from cash machines.

1912 – Bottom Place Follows Persistent Failure   1913

Never since their elevation to a place among the first-class counties have Worcestershire had such a dismal experience as that of last season. Of the 20 county matches in which they took part only one was won outright, this solitary success being gained at Leicester in July. As the result of this persistent failure, Worcestershire finished last in the competition for the County Championship. In one respect, however, the team laboured under a serious disadvantage. For the first time they had to take the field without the regular help of any of the brothers Foster, H. K. Foster, who had done so well in the summer of 1911, making only one appearance in the return match with Yorkshire at Worcester. Better things are hoped for in 1913, H. K. Foster having consented to resume the position of captain.

1913 – CHESTER'S ADVANCE PROMISES INTERNATIONAL FUTURE 1914

Nothing stood out more prominently than the remarkable development of Chester, the youngest professional regularly engaged in first-class cricket. So pronounced was his advance last season that he made 698 runs, playing three innings of over a hundred, and took 43 wickets. Very few players in the history of cricket have shown such form at the age of 17 and a half. It seems only reasonable to expect that when he has filled out and gained more strength he will be an England cricketer.

1917 – WAR WOUND CUTS SHORT PROMISING CAREER 1918

Lord Cobham [formerly The Hon. C. G. Lyttelton], who presided at the annual meeting towards the end of November, said, alluding to Frank Chester's loss of an arm in the War, it was deplorable that his cricket career had been cut short. Probably no cricketer of 18 had shown such promise since the days of W. G. Grace.

1920 – FIRST-CLASS IN NAME ONLY 1921

The Worcestershire authorities were perhaps in too much of a hurry to get back to first-class cricket. It will be remembered that the county took no part in the Championship in 1919. The results last summer were discouraging in the extreme, the team as a set-off against 16 defeats in 18 matches being only able to point to a single victory – gained over Gloucestershire at the beginning of June. In face of such a record it is not unkind to say that only in name could Worcestershire be described as a first-class county.

1925 – ROOT'S FORM NOT THE PROBLEM 1926

While so little in Worcestershire cricket furnished matter for satisfaction, Root showed himself a finer bowler than at any previous period of his career. Indeed, his performance of taking 196 wickets for $17\frac{1}{2}$ runs apiece, stood out – especially considering the moderate nature of the support available – as one of the finest of the year. In match after match he worked his leg theory with striking success, securing 13 wickets against Northamptonshire at Kidderminster, and 12 against Glamorgan at Cardiff and Hampshire at Worcester, while on two occasions 11 wickets fell to his share and on two others ten. Twice he dismissed eight batsmen in an innings and five times he disposed of seven. Some idea of what he has been to Worcestershire may be gathered from the fact that his aggregate number of wickets in Championship matches during the past three seasons has amounted to 508. Last summer, as he obtained 11 wickets against Oxford University, he altogether took 207 wickets for the county. Despite the strain involved in sending down nearly 1,400 overs, he scored over 800 runs.

1933 – WORCESTERSHIRE v WEST INDIANS: Nawab's triumph   1934

At Worcester, May 31, June 1, 2, 1933. In a thrilling finish the county, after being 24 runs behind on the first innings, won by one wicket. The match proved a triumph for the Nawab of Pataudi who, revealing his best form, hit his first hundred for Worcestershire and took out his bat when the match ended. His display was not free from fault, for he was missed when 29 and 51, but apart from these chances he gave a superb exhibition. Batting four hours ten minutes, he made his 162 out of 247. Gibbons helped him to put on 107, and Nichol stayed until lunchtime, when Worcestershire with eight wickets in hand still required 136. Subsequently wickets fell steadily and when Jackson, the last man, went in 16 were needed. These runs the Nawab obtained.

West Indians 239 (E. L. G. Hoad 80*; M. E. White 4-73) and 257 (B. J. Sealy 103);
Worcestershire 215 (R. Howorth 68, H. H. Gibbons 61)
and 284-9 (Nawab of Pataudi 162*).

1934 – Colleagues Hit Hard By Tragedy Of Nichol   1935

Early in the summer the county suffered an almost irreparable blow in the tragic death on May 21 of Nichol, who attained to such high honours the previous year. Naturally, the loss of this fine defensive batsman, in whom the county placed so much reliance, had its effect upon the other players. The frequent absence of C. F. Walters, their captain, playing in the Test matches, and the illness of the Nawab of Pataudi, made the passing of Nichol even more acutely felt.

1939 – Eerie Echo In Bull's Fatal Car Crash   1940

The tragic death of Charles Bull, their opening batsman, robbed Worcestershire of a great deal of the satisfaction they normally would have derived from their second-most-successful season during 40 years in the County Championship. Winning 11 matches, one less than in 1911, they finished five places higher than in 1938. Bull's fatal accident in a car crash at Chelmsford was the second Worcestershire tragedy associated with the annual Whitsuntide match against Essex at Chelmsford. Five years previously, also on Sunday night, Maurice Nichol died while asleep at his hotel. That the Worcestershire players suffered a severe shock by Bull's death and the injury received by Buller in the same accident was only too evident from the indifferent form shown by the side in several subsequent matches, but they gradually regained balance.

1951 – WORCESTERSHIRE v NOTTINGHAMSHIRE: DYNAMIC FINISH 1952

At Worcester, July 25, 26, 27, 1951. Worcestershire won by nine wickets. This match not only produced the best batting performance of the season, but one of the most notable in the whole history of cricket. Worcestershire were set to score 131 in 40 minutes – a task which many county sides would not have considered possible – and they responded with such a dynamic display that they hit off the runs with five minutes to spare. Kenyon struck a challenging note with his first scoring stroke, a hook for six off Farr, and he and Dews scored 54 runs in five overs. At the fall of Kenyon's wicket, Jenkins ran to the crease and in the subsequent assault on the bowlers he overtook Dews, making 47 runs in 15 minutes. When the match had been won excited spectators dashed on to the field to congratulate the batsmen and also to applaud the sporting way in which Simpson, the Nottinghamshire captain, had made sure that no time was wasted in changing the field between overs.

Nottinghamshire 300 (H. R. Cox 64, C. J. Poole 62; R. T. D. Perks 7-111)
and 280 (J. D. Clay 96; R. Howorth 5-42);
Worcestershire 450-9 dec (L. Outschoorn 106, R. E. Bird 80, D. Kenyon 70,
R. O. Jenkins 66; B. H. Farr 5-96) and 131-1.

1955 – FIRST PROFESSIONAL CAPTAIN REMAINS PERKY TO THE LAST 1956

There was a genuine desire in Worcestershire for the county to do well under the captaincy of one of its most faithful servants, R. T. D. Perks, the first professional to lead the side. An auspicious start brought victory over the South Africans, which subsequently proved to be the only defeat of the touring team outside of the Tests, but afterwards there was little of note in the county's performances. Not until the beginning of July did they gain their first victory in the Championship, and with only five wins in all they finished third from bottom in the table.

Towards the end of this disappointing season, Perks announced that after 27 years with the club he would retire at the end of the summer. Even at the age of 43 he remained the most successful and hardworking bowler, and in all matches he took over 100 wickets for the 16th consecutive time. Only A. P. Freeman, of Kent (17 times), exceeded that figure in successive years, and as a slow bowler he was not subjected to the same physical strain. Appropriately, Perks completed this wonderful feat in his last match; and at Bournemouth, where when 16 he embarked on his county career as twelfth man and scorer.

1962 – WORCESTERSHIRE v NOTTINGHAMSHIRE: WET FINISH   1963

At Worcester, September 1, 3, 4, 1962. Worcestershire won by eight wickets, taking 14 points. They needed this victory to put them on top of the table with an advantage of ten points and though in the event Yorkshire won their last game and so supplanted them, this in no way detracted merit from their win or denied them the right to celebrate with champagne at the close of the game. The end came with rain threatening again after thunderstorms twice left pools all over the ground and brought players as well as groundstaff scampering out to manhandle the drying equipment.

Nottinghamshire 193 (A. Gill 61, G. Millman 51*) **and 251** (Millman 63; L. J. Coldwell 5-87);
Worcestershire 253 (D. W. Richardson 56; C. Forbes 4-54, B. D. Wells 4-85)
and 193-2 (D. Kenyon 103*, T. W. Graveney 62*).

1964 – CORKS POP FOR CONCLUSIVE VICTORY   1965

This time they reserved celebrations on a sunny afternoon at Worcester on August 25, and it was two hours after their 16th win in 25 matches had been completed that news came from Southampton of Warwickshire's defeat. Only then did the corks pop again. The Championship had come to Worcestershire after 65 years of trying and a few months before the club became 100 years old.

The title was clinched with three matches to spare, so the triumph was gained with something in hand. Yet supremacy had not been Worcestershire's for long during the summer. Warwickshire, neighbours and rivals all the while, occupied top place for all but two series until August 7, when they were finally knocked off their perch. What happened afterwards left no doubt about Worcestershire's powers to stay the pace better. They won seven of their last eight matches and drew the other whereas Warwickshire won only three, lost three and drew one. Thus the margin by the end of the season widened to a very conclusive 41 points.

Reasons for the success were not difficult to find and it would be apposite to record a splendid team-spirit under solid leadership as the overriding factor. Yet almost invariably superior bowling wins Championships and this was no exception. There is no greater fillip than a successful start in the field; Worcestershire received that through the yeoman efforts of Flavell, assisted mainly by Coldwell and also by Standen, Carter and Brain. Between them, these five seam bowlers took 298 wickets in the competition and 340 altogether. Gifford again proved the more penetrating spin bowler, though Slade combined with him well and justified the use of two left-arm slow men in the side. Gifford took 114 wickets in all, seven in an innings on four occasions, and he, too, earned selection for England in two Tests.

Yet for all the commendation due to the bowlers, their efforts would have been far less telling had they not been ably backed up in the field. Statistics give ample proof of the quality of the work in this important aspect. Richardson and Headley led the country with 51 and 50 catches respectively, and Booth proved the leading wicketkeeper throughout the summer.

Graveney enjoyed a glorious season, with an aggregate of 2,385 runs only 12 short of the best he has known in 16 years of first-class cricket. He played five three-figure innings, the third of which made him the 15th cricketer to hit 100 centuries. In addition, he was twice out for 95 and played 14 other innings of 50 or over. He shared in nine of the side's three-figure partnerships.

1964 – WORCESTERSHIRE v WARWICKSHIRE: COUNTY BEST

At Worcester, June 13, 15, 16, 1964. Drawn. With these two competent sides, who were making the pace in the County Championship, not prepared to yield an inch, the match finished in a dull draw. The aggregate attendance reached 24,500, with the 13,000 on the first day the best for a county match at Worcester and the highest there since the visit of the Australians in 1948.

> **Worcestershire 256** (M. J. Horton 59, R. G. A. Headley 54; J. D. Bannister 4-37)
> **and 241-7 dec.** (D. Kenyon 92, D. W. Richardson 91);
> **Warwickshire 255** (R. W. Barber 51, R. E. Hitchcock 50; L. J. Coldwell 4-51) **and 64-1.**

1965 – GROUND-BREAKING TOUR REWARDS CHAMPIONS   1966

History was made when Worcestershire became not only the first county to undertake an extensive overseas tour, but in their capacity as champion county played matches in countries which had never seen an English county XI, let alone the Championship pennant. Managed by Mr J. Lister and captained by Don Kenyon, the party consisted of 12 players and two members of the club, J. R. Gardiner and R. P. Matkin. The tour covered something like 34,000 miles and visits were made to seven different countries [Kenya, Rhodesia, India, Malaysia, Thailand, Hong Kong, Hawaii].

1965 – CENTENARY CANTER SECURES SECOND PENNANT   1966

Seldom can a county have won the Championship with such a devastating conclusion as did Worcestershire in 1965. As if to make this something extra-special to celebrate their centenary, they finished the season with ten wins in 11 matches, just managing to beat Sussex in the last game to creep over the top of Northamptonshire by four points. All this came after a dismal start in which there seemed almost no prospect of the Championship pennant remaining in their hands for the second year running. There was only one victory in the month of May, another lone win in June and then success over Glamorgan in early July.

The record should have been 11 in 11, for in the odd drawn match, Hampshire, needing 157 to win, were 77 for eight at the close after some unusual lapses by Worcestershire in the field.

1975 – MEMBERS WADE INTO BATTLE BETWEEN PLAYERS AND CLUB 1976

Worcestershire cricket turned into controversy within only a year of the county winning the Championship. The total failure to make a defence of the title won in 1974 was accompanied by increasing unrest in the dressing-room over financial terms, and a most disappointing season finished with extraordinary recriminations off the field.

No fewer than five of the ten home fixtures in the Championship were lost, and the final two-day defeat by Hampshire was followed by a round-robin letter from the players, who expressed "complete lack of confidence" in various leading members of the club's administration. A second bombshell arrived within four days when the committee confirmed that they had not renewed the contracts of Brain, the leading fast bowler, Cass, the wicketkeeper who had scored his best innings of 172 not out when pressed into service as a batsman, Wilkinson, the opener who recorded a maiden century against Kent, Yardley, the slip-fielding specialist and reliable middle-order batsman, and the young pace bowler, Roberts.

The decision to trim the staff had been taken in the light of the county's desire to budget sensibly for 1976 as well as allowing increased opportunity for what is considered to be Worcestershire's most promising crop of Second Eleven players for a decade or more. Understandably, however, the sacking of so many experienced players was not well received by the rank and file of the membership, particularly when it was learned that another pace bowler, Inchmore, had asked for his registration to be cancelled.

With Brain announcing that he had signed a three-year contract to play for Gloucestershire, in addition to the prospect of being without Inchmore and Holder, who may be required for the West Indies tour, an action group of members successfully agitated for an extraordinary meeting of the club.

When the committee faced their critics, the meeting was abandoned in chaos after half an hour owing to the fact that the city's Guildhall could not accommodate an estimated 1,000 members who were unable to gain admission. A second meeting was arranged in Malvern, at which a regrettable public clash between the cricket committee chairman, Dick Howorth, and captain, Norman Gifford, only served to increase the members' concern for the future.

1977 – GLAMORGAN v WORCESTERSHIRE: RECORD PROPORTION 1978

At Swansea, June 29, 30, July 1, 1977. Drawn. This will go down as Turner's match. He scored 141 out of Worcestershire's total of 169 (a world record 83% of an innings total). No other batsman reached double figures. In fact, the other ten batsmen contributed only 14 scoring shots between them. The next-highest scorer was Gifford, with seven, and he stayed with Turner for 50 minutes during which 57 were added for the ninth wicket. This not only enabled Turner to complete a century, but also saved Worcestershire from following on. The only blemish came when he was 93, Ontong missing a slip catch.

Glamorgan 309-4 (100 overs) (M. J. Llewellyn 91*, G. Richards 74*) and 142-7 (R. C. Ontong 56); Worcestershire 169 (G. M. Turner 141*; A. E. Cordle 5-53).

1982 – MATCH-WINNER GOES OUT IN A BLAZE OF HUNDREDS   Chris Moore, 1983

Glenn Turner, who has severed his 17-year association with the county, has been Worcestershire's match-winner on so many occasions in recent years that it will be nigh impossible to replace him. Turner opened up with his 99th century in the first match of the season, scoring an unbeaten 239 against Oxford University. On May 29, against Warwickshire, he completed his 100th hundred with one of the greatest innings of his career. It had to be seen to be believed: 128 out of 181 for none at lunch; 254 out of 389 for one at tea; 300 in 336 minutes, and 311 not out out of 501 for one declared. Two more centuries took him past Don Kenyon's record of 70 hundreds for Worcestershire, and another against Kent at Hereford, in what proved to be his final Championship match, left him with a first-class average of 90.07. An appendix operation at the end of July cut short a season in which he felt he was batting as well as at any time in his career.

1987 – BOTHAM WINS OVER THE DOUBTERS   Chris Moore, 1988

A new era dawned at New Road in 1987 as Worcestershire, inspired almost inevitably by Ian Botham, captured their first trophy for 13 years by becoming the first winners of the Refuge Assurance League. Much of their improvement on the previous season in the Sunday competition, when they finished 16th, could be credited to the England all-rounder. His arrival from Somerset, amid a blaze of publicity, had not met with the approval of all the members, nor with the unanimous backing of the committee. But come the final Sunday of the season, when for the first time since the days of Bradman the County Ground gates were locked behind a capacity crowd, there was no longer any doubting the wisdom of luring Botham to Worcester.

ICC Trophy. Holland v Ireland, at Maple Leaf Ground, July 12, 2001. Journalist James Fitzgerald, by his own admission an average-to-poor club player from Dublin, and in Toronto to report on Ireland's progress, fielded as substitute in this match, and Ireland's next, against Canada, after injuries and disciplinary action had reduced the Irish squad to 11 fit players.

Little Wonder No. 124

1988 – SOMERSET v WORCESTERSHIRE: 405 NOT OUT   1989

At Taunton, May 5, 6, 7, 9, 1988. Worcestershire won by an innings and 214 runs. All else in the match was overshadowed by the immense achievement of the Worcestershire batsman, Hick, who 17 days before his 22nd birthday became one of only seven batsman to score 400 in an innings. W. H. Ponsford performed the feat twice. Hick went in at 78 for one, and having steered his side from the dangers of 132 for five – Rose had taken three for nine in 27 balls – he dominated play until tea on the second day. Worcestershire then declared, with Hick 19 runs short of A. C. MacLaren's highest score in England, made in 1895, also against Somerset at Taunton. The highest score in England this century, and a record for Worcestershire, his unbeaten 405 came from 469 balls and in 555 minutes; he hit 35 fours and 11 sixes. The first hundred came from 126 balls (153 minutes), the second from 151 balls (189 minutes), the third from 134 balls (142 minutes) and the fourth from 58 balls (71 minutes, eight sixes, six fours). On a pitch encouraging movement off the seam, he survived very sharp chances when 67, 101 and 141. Yet there were only two other scores over 50 in the match.

Worcestershire 628-7 dec (G. A. Hick 405*, S. J. Rhodes 56);
Somerset 222 (P. J. Newport 4-59, N. V. Radford 4-77)
and 192 (M. D. Crowe 53; Newport 6-50).

1988 – WORCESTERSHIRE v GLAMORGAN: VANDALS FOILED   1989

At Worcester, September 14, 15, 16, 1988. Worcestershire won by an innings and 76 runs. Not even a vandal's attempt at sabotage could prevent Worcestershire from taking the maximum points needed to clinch their first Championship title for 14 years. Play on the third day was delayed for an hour while a mixture of petroleum jelly and engine oil, spread over the pitch during the night, was cleared with the help of industrial heaters. Then, after Worcestershire had extended their lead to 179, Glamorgan were promptly dismissed for 103 in 36 overs, leaving Worcestershire victors with more than a day to spare.

Glamorgan 244 (M. P. Maynard 69; N. V. Radford 4-84)
and 103 (P. J. Newport 5-23);
Worcestershire 423 (G. A. Hick 197).

1991 – SEVENTH TIME LUCKY IN LORD'S FINAL   Chris Moore, 1992

Victory by 65 runs over Lancashire in the Benson and Hedges Cup finally ended the hoodoo surrounding six defeats in a Lord's final, and the county triumphed again, by seven runs, against the same opponents to win the Refuge Assurance Cup at Old Trafford. The Refuge Assurance Cup final was Ian Botham's farewell appearance for Worcestershire, and it was no coincidence that his five years at New Road were the most successful in the county's history, with two Championships and two Refuge Assurance League titles before 1991. Ironically, Botham left for Durham after re-establishing himself as England's all-rounder in his best season for Worcestershire.

1995 – DEATH OF MIRZA DARKENS CLOSE OF SEASON
John Curtis, 1996

Events in a transitional period at New Road were overshadowed by the sudden death of the 24-year-old fast bowler Parvaz Mirza, less than a week after the season had ended. Mirza had been earmarked to play an important part in Worcestershire's future following his emergence in bolstering an ageing attack. But Mirza's death, by natural causes at his Birmingham home, left a void that will be hard to fill.

2000 – WORCESTERSHIRE v GLOUCESTERSHIRE
(NATWEST TROPHY): RESULT OVERTURNED
2001

At Worcester, June 21, 2000. Worcestershire won by three wickets. The result was subsequently declared void because Worcestershire fielded an ineligible player. Gloucestershire's defence of the trophy looked to have ended at the first hurdle. But they challenged Worcestershire's inclusion of 19-year-old Kabir Ali, pointing out that he had become ineligible by appearing in the first round for the county's Board XI having already played first-team cricket for Worcestershire in 2000 – three games in the Benson and Hedges Cup. While concluding that the mistake had been inadvertent, the ECB ruled that the match be replayed.

Gloucestershire 211-8 (50 overs) (R. C. Russell 84, R. J. Cunliffe 69; R. K. Illingworth 3-43);
Worcestershire 212-7 (48.5 overs) (R. C. Driver 61*, D. A. Leatherdale 53).

At Worcester, July 4, 2000. Gloucestershire won by five runs. It was close-run at the end but Gloucestershire, availing themselves of the ECB's reprieve, lived to defend the NatWest Trophy. A slow, uncertain pitch made most batsmen wary and, even when Worcestershire's last pair needed a just six in two overs, the bowlers dictated terms. Harvey bowled a maiden to McGrath; Rhodes played on to Ball, who had earlier taken two outstanding catches. Worcestershire's day was summed up by the sixth-ball duck that befell Driver, man of the original match.

Gloucestershire 163 (49.3 overs) (G. D. McGrath 4-23);
Worcestershire 158 (49.3 overs) (P. R. Pollard 55, S. J. Rhodes 43; J. M. M. Averis 4-36).

2003 – WORCESTERSHIRE v LANCASHIRE (CHELTENHAM & GLOUCESTER
TROPHY SEMI-FINAL): HALL OF FAME
2004

At Worcester, August 9, 2003. Worcestershire won by six runs. Hall, granted permission to play by the South African tourists, produced one of one-day cricket's unforgettable final overs to pull off a remarkable victory for Worcestershire and condemn Lancashire to their fifth defeat in a semi-final in four years. Lancashire had needed just seven from the final over but, with the centurion Loye watching helplessly from the non-striker's end, Hall bowled Hegg with the first ball, Martin with the third and ran out Wood with the fifth. An exhausted Loye, who faced 154 balls, and hit nine fours and four sixes – three of them with outrageous sweep shots off the quicker bowlers – could not even bring himself to run a single from the final ball. Hall, who had earlier dismissed Hooper and Flintoff cheaply, held a smart slip catch to remove Law and biffed 26 off 20 balls, was carried shoulder-high from the field. Hall received the match award ahead of Loye, who had been on the field all through one of the hottest days of a hot summer. He was so dehydrated – "as dry as a cornflake," said Lancashire manager Mike Watkinson – that he struggled to provide a urine sample for a routine drugs test.

Worcestershire 254-5 (50 overs) (G. A. Hick 97, A. Singh 63);
Lancashire 248-9 (50 overs) (M. B. Loye 116*, G. Chapple 44; A. J. Hall 4-36).

2004 – Captain Quits In Middle Of Match   John Curtis, 2005

County captains come and go in all kinds of mysterious ways. But what happened at Worcester in mid-August was particularly baffling. Ben Smith gave up the job, without notice or logical explanation, in the middle of a match against Northamptonshire. His deputy, 40-year-old Steve Rhodes, had to take charge for the rest of the game and the season, before he retired after 20 years as Worcestershire's first-choice keeper.

2007 – Flood Waters Cause Costly Havoc   John Curtis, 2008

Worcestershire's fluctuating on-field fortunes – relegated in the Championship but Pro40 League winners – were completely overshadowed by the floods which engulfed New Road in midsummer. When Vikram Solanki led his players off at the watery end of the Friends Provident match against Scotland on June 13, he could hardly have known it would be the last time Worcestershire would play at their headquarters in 2007.

The final cost of the damage for a county which aims at an annual profit of around £50,000 was £1.164m. For the first time since May 1969 New Road flooded during the season. The River Severn burst its banks 24 hours before the big-bucks Twenty20 Cup programme was due to start. None of the four group games scheduled for Worcester could go ahead, although three were relocated – two to Kidderminster and one to Himley, in Staffordshire, although that was rained off too.

Another flood, the second-highest in the club's history, meant that the Lancashire match was abandoned too, and the decision to write off any more cricket on the ground was taken early in August. "Home" Pro40 games were relocated to Edgbaston, Taunton and Kidderminster, which also staged the Championship games against Yorkshire and Hampshire.

2008 – WORCESTERSHIRE v MIDDLESEX (NatWest Pro40 League):
HOME FROM HOME 2009

At Kidderminster, September 14, 2008. Middlesex won by 11 runs. Graeme Hick, having announced that this would be his last Worcestershire game before retiring, was given a guard of honour by the Middlesex players, and applauded all the way to and from the wicket by the near-2,000 crowd after scoring 14. As floods had again engulfed New Road, the game was held at Kidderminster, where Hick played in the Birmingham League when he first came to England in 1984.

Middlesex 253-6 (40 overs) (E. C. Joyce 99, B. A. Godleman 48);
Worcestershire 242 (39.4 overs) (B. F. Smith 107, D. K. H. Mitchell 46;
D. P. Nannes 4-38, T. J. Murtagh 3-51).

2011 – THE SECRET LIFE OF ADRIAN SHANKAR
Hugh Chevallier, 2012

"Adrian came to the club's attention during the winter, which he spent playing cricket for Colombo in the Sri Lankan Mercantile League… He was the leading run-scorer in the Twenty20 tournament with an average of over 52 and also scored three successive hundreds in the longer form of the game." So said Worcestershire coach Steve Rhodes in May in support of his decision to offer Adrian Shankar a two-year contract.

In a fortnight, though, Shankar's life was turned upside-down: after he made a duck in a CB40 game and limped out of a Championship match with a cruciate-ligament injury, it transpired that his past had not been quite what it seemed. He was not, as he claimed, 26 years old – young enough for Worcestershire to gain financially by his selection for the first team – but 29. As for those performances in Sri Lanka, they too were shrouded in mystery: there was an unofficial T20 league of that name, but no records could be found. And if those three hundreds existed at all, they certainly weren't first-class.

Once Shankar, a Cambridge University law graduate, was exposed as a Walter Mitty figure, the stories emerged. In November 2008, Lancashire had awarded him a two-year deal, describing him in a press release as one of the finest young players Cambridge had seen since John Crawley. "I phoned Lancashire and made it clear that I'd never said anything of the sort," said the Cambridge coach Chris Scott. "No one at Worcestershire or Lancashire asked my opinion before they signed him."

Luke Sutton, then a colleague at Lancashire, revealed Shankar had made other extravagant claims. "He also told us he had been on the Arsenal Football Academy but we played football every day in warm-ups and he wasn't particularly good. He announced that he had played tennis at a national level, but during pre-season we played against each other and again he was very average." Sutton also bearded him about his age, asking why rumours persisted that he was three years older than stated. His inventive answer was that as a child he had spent three years on a life-support machine and had not grown.

YORKSHIRE

[1936 edition] In 1935 they were again at the top of the tree, occupying the leading position for the fourth time in five years. As A. B. Sellers, their captain, declared towards the end of the season, Yorkshire did not treat cricket as a "picnic" but always played to win, and there can be no doubt that a fine sense of determination in this respect very considerably influenced many of the convincing successes the side achieved.

1871 – MCC AND GROUND v YORKSHIRE: LOSING DOUBLE   1872

At Lord's, May 22, 23, 1871. Yorkshiremen are as good judges and genuine admirers of cricketers and cricket as of racehorses and horse-racing, and this match being set to be played on Monday and Tuesday in the Derby week, it was not surprising to find Lord's ground on those days numerously attended by men from the great Shire to witness their eleven fight the good fight against the very strong eleven of MCC. But fortune was adverse to Yorkshiremen in that memorable week, for at Lord's they lost the valuable bowling aid of Freeman, they lost choice of innings, and they lost the match; and at Epsom the Yorkshire horse – Bothwell – lost the Derby.

MCC and Ground 116 (R. O. Clayton 5-36) and 173 (Mr W. G. Grace 98; Clayton 5-58);
Yorkshire 100 (F. H. Farrands 5-54, G. Wootton 4-17) and 134 (Wootton 5-45, Farrands 5-50).

1872 – TRUE SONS OF THE SHIRE   1873

So many defeats [seven] were not pleasant; but the fact that Yorkshire had no "foreigners" in their ranks, but always fairly fought out their fights with true sons of their Shire, is a credit to them.

1872 – YORKSHIRE v GLOUCESTERSHIRE (ROGER IDDISON'S MATCH): AMAZING GRACE   1873

At the Bramall Lane Ground, Sheffield, July 29, 30, 31, 1872. Yorkshire v Gloucestershire was a judiciously selected match to play in compliment to Roger Iddison, who had served his Shire so long and so ably in the cricket field; for it was the first match ever played by those counties, and it ensured the first appearance of Mr W. G. Grace on the county ground at Sheffield, the centre of as ardent, keen, thorough, and numerous a body of admirers of our national game as any county can boast of, who flocked on to the ground in such numbers that nearly 17,000 were present during Iddison's three days. The thousands that thronged the ground on the Monday went there full of hope of witnessing some big batting by Mr W. G. Grace. Lusty and long was the cheering that greeted the great batsman on his return from the wicket and for many a season to come one of the most prolific sources of cricket gossip among Yorkshiremen will be the 150 made by Mr W. G. Grace at Roger Iddison's benefit match.

Gloucestershire 294 (Mr W. G. Grace 150, Mr T. G. Matthews 85; G. Freeman 5-97);
Yorkshire 66 (Mr Grace 8-33) **and 116** (E. B. Rawlinson 47; Mr Grace 7-46).

Grace also took 15 wickets, although this warranted no mention in the report.

1886 – Too Polite To Run Anyone Out 1887

The fielding left plenty of room for improvement; indeed, the weakness in this respect became so notorious that it was humorously remarked that the Yorkshiremen were far too polite to run a man out.

Cricketana 2002. The infamous ball which Mike Atherton allegedly rubbed in soil from his trouser pocket, and which later became the property of the ICC referee Peter Burge, sold for £1,600.

Little Wonder No. 125

1893 – Welcome End To Surrey's Dominance 1894

After several disappointing seasons, in some of which defeats followed one another with wearisome frequency, whilst in others early success was discounted by subsequent failure, Yorkshire, last summer, achieved the height of their ambition by carrying off the County Championship. The honour was not only thoroughly well deserved but proved generally popular, for in many parts of England there was a feeling of satisfaction that the long-continued supremacy of Surrey had come to an end. The general principle obtained support that the triumph of the same team year after year exercises a baneful effect upon any branch of sport.

1897 – Sorry End To A Brilliant Career 1898

The generally high standard of professional cricket at the present time makes it all the more to be deplored that Peel should have been dismissed from the Yorkshire eleven, through going into the field when not in a fit condition to play. It was a sad finish – if it be the finish – to a brilliant career. Peel complained that he had been harshly treated, but it is inconceivable that Lord Hawke and the Yorkshire committee would without good reason have taken such an extreme measure.

1900 – UNBEATEN SEASON SETS NEW STANDARD   1901

For their doings in 1900 it would not be easy to praise the Yorkshire eleven beyond their deserts. They carried off the Championship in wonderful style without a defeat, winning 16 of the 28 county matches and drawing the other 12. Getting to work on May 7 the Yorkshiremen began by beating Worcestershire in a single afternoon, and it was not until September 5 that they brought their labours to a close in the last match of the Scarborough Festival, winding up as they had commenced with a victory. Such consistency speaks volumes for the stamina of the eleven as well as for their skill, and shows pretty clearly that they were always in first-rate physical condition. Their Championship record is quite unique, no other side having gone through the season unbeaten in county matches since the competition assumed anything like its present dimensions.

1901 – YORKSHIRE v LANCASHIRE: BROWN'S BONANZA   1902

At Leeds, August 5, 6, 7, 1901. The Bank Holiday match with Lancashire had been chosen by J. T. Brown for his benefit, and the results, in a financial sense, exceeded all expectations, the benefit being the best that any professional cricketer has ever enjoyed. On the opening day 30,891 people passed through the turnstiles, and as no adequate provision had been made for dealing with such a crowd, there was a good deal of delay, play after luncheon not being resumed until nearly half past three. Even when the ground had been sufficiently cleared to permit of cricket, the boundaries were decidedly short.

> **Yorkshire 319** (Mr F. Mitchell 106, G. H. Hirst 58, Lord Hawke 55; J. Sharp 5-109)
> **and 175-5** (D. Denton 62, Mitchell 54);
> **Lancashire 413** (Mr A. C. MacLaren 117, A. Ward 100, Mr A. Eccles 59).

1902 – YORKSHIRE v AUSTRALIANS: 23 ALL OUT   1903

At Leeds, June 2, 3, 1902. Apart from the Test games no match last season excited greater or more widespread interest, the attendance on both days being enormous. In winning by five wickets on a very treacherous pitch, after being 24 runs behind on the first innings, Yorkshire accomplished a big performance. They clearly owed their victory to Hirst and Jackson, who got the Australians out in about 70 minutes for 23 – with one exception the lowest total ever obtained by a Colonial team in this country. The score was up to 20 with only four men out, but after that there was a dismal collapse, Jackson finishing off the innings by dismissing Hopkins, Kelly, Jones and Howell in five balls. This was an astonishing piece of bowling, but still finer work was done by Hirst, who got rid of the best batsman, bowling Trumper with one of his deadliest swervers. Noble and Howell bowled splendidly in the last innings, and Yorkshire found it very hard work to get the 48 runs required, but they were tolerably safe when their fifth wicket fell at 41. Washington, who showed fine nerve, finished the match with an on-drive to the boundary.

Australians 131 (Hon. F. S. Jackson 4-30, G. H. Hirst 4-35) **and 23** (Hirst 5-9, Jackson 5-12);
Yorkshire 107 (W. P. Howell 6-53, M. A. Noble 4-30) **and 50-5.**

1904 – YORKSHIRE v LANCASHIRE: RECORD REWARD   1905

At Leeds, August 1, 2, 3, 1904. Given to George Hirst as a reward for his 12 years of splendid service to Yorkshire, the Bank Holiday match at Leeds was happily favoured with fine weather, and during the three days 78,681 people visited the Headingley ground, the proceeds of the benefit [£3,703 2s. 0d.] exceeding all records.

Yorkshire 403 (Mr E. Smith 98, G. H. Hirst 65, J. Tunnicliffe 55, Lord Hawke 54);
Lancashire 173 (Mr A. H. Hornby 59; Hirst 6-42) **and 163-3** (J. T. Tyldesley 108*).

Halcyon days at Headingley:
31,826 people attended the opening day of George Hirst's benefit match in 1904

1906 – HIRST COMPLETES DOUBLE DOUBLE   1907

Hirst set up a record that may possibly never be equalled. In Yorkshire matches alone, including the extra fixtures, he scored over 2,000 runs and took over 200 wickets, a double feat without precedent in first-class cricket. Only a very strong man in perfect health would have been equal to the mere physical labour involved, but Hirst thrives on hard work, and at the end of the season he was so fresh and well that nobody seeing him bat or bowl could have guessed that any extra demands had been made upon him.

1906 – YORKSHIRE v WORCESTERSHIRE: MOMENTARY FAME   1907

At Hull, July 30, 31, 1906. The game, which resulted in a victory for the Yorkshiremen by an innings and ten runs, proved chiefly remarkable for the bowling of Sedgwick, a fast bowler from Littleborough, who, introduced into the Yorkshire team for the first time, accomplished a startling performance. In the first innings he dismissed five batsmen for eight runs, sharing with Hirst the distinction of dismissing Worcestershire for 25 – the lowest score in a county match all through the season – while in the second innings he took four wickets. For the moment Yorkshire seemed to have discovered the fast bowler they so badly required, but Sedgwick failed against Lancashire and was not persevered with. Yorkshire's batting – very successful at first – broke down badly after a tea interval, the last six wickets falling for 46 runs. When Worcestershire followed on Arnold made a great effort for his side, but after the total had reached 207 for six wickets Sedgwick performed the hat-trick.

Yorkshire 271 (D. Denton 65, H. Rudston 50; E. G. Arnold 5-89);
Worcestershire 25 (H. A. Sedgwick 5-8, G. H. Hirst 5-15)
and 236 (Arnold 103*; Sedgwick 4-69).

Sedgwick never played again for Yorkshire after the Lancashire match, but became a stalwart of Staffordshire's minor counties side until 1931.

1919 – NEW OPENING PAIR MAKE THEIR NAMES   1920

In batting Sutcliffe and Holmes stood out by themselves. Their joint success was one of the special features of the season. Holmes was just beginning to assert himself in 1914; Sutcliffe, although known for some time as a young player of exceptional promise, was quite new to first-class cricket. Seldom indeed has a first-season man done such great things. There was little to choose between the two batsmen, but in county matches Sutcliffe was ahead of Holmes both in aggregate of runs and average. As a first-wicket pair they were true successors to Brown and Tunnicliffe. Five times in county matches they sent up 100 for the first wicket, their

253 at Sheffield being a record in Yorkshire's matches with Lancashire. Each batsman made five scores of 100 or more in county fixtures.

1924 – YORKSHIRE v LANCASHIRE: HOLIDAY HORROR   1925

At Leeds, June 7, 9, 10, 1924. The Whitsuntide match furnished the sensation of Yorkshire's season. On Saturday the cricket, twice interrupted by rain, was dreary in the extreme, Lancashire taking three hours and threequarters to hit up a score of 113. Such extremely cautious play naturally flattered the excellent bowling. At the close Yorkshire lost Sutcliffe's wicket for three runs. Yorkshire had much the best of the struggle on Monday, and left off with the game, to all appearance, in their hands, as with all ten wickets to fall they required only 57 runs to win. On Tuesday morning, however, there came, perhaps, the most startling collapse of the year. Bowling on a wicket that gave them a good deal of help, Parkin and Richard Tyldesley proved so irresistible that in 65 minutes they rattled Yorkshire out for 33, Lancashire winning the match by 24 runs.

Lancashire 113 (G. G. Macaulay 6-40) and 74 (R. Kilner 4-13, Macaulay 4-19);
Yorkshire 130 (C. H. Parkin 5-46, R. K. Tyldesley 4-69) and 33 (Tyldesley 6-18).

1924 – YORKSHIRE v MIDDLESEX: IMPROPER SPIRIT   1925

At Sheffield, July 5, 7, 8, 1924. This will always be a match of unhappy memories. It led to no end of ill-feeling, and was one of the chief causes of Middlesex coming to the decision – afterwards revoked – that they would not play Yorkshire in 1925. For some reason the Sheffield crowd, forgetting their old reputation for good sports-manship, barracked more or less persistently all through the game, making the atmosphere almost unbearable. Under such conditions cricket could not be played in a proper spirit. Some fine work was done by both sides, but no one enjoyed the match.

Middlesex 358 (E. H. Hendren 99, Hon. C. N. Bruce 88; E. Robinson 5-59)
and 268 (Mr G. T. S. Stevens 63; R. Kilner 4-73);
Yorkshire 334 (P. Holmes 61, E. Oldroyd 54, M. Leyland 51*; Mr N. E. Haig 6-79) and 43-0.

Notes by the Editor: Butt, the umpire, felt it his duty to report Waddington to Lord's. Waddington duly apologised for his loss of temper and self-control, and there, so far as he was concerned, the matter ended. The trouble in Yorkshire cricket seems to have been confined to a minority of the players – from what I have been told not more than four. In this connection some remarks made by Lord Hawke at the Yorkshire annual meeting were very significant indeed. Speaking of individual doings for the county last summer, he said Macaulay ought to have been in the MCC's team in Australia, and that it was entirely his own fault he was not chosen. To that stern condemnation not a word need be added.

1925 – FOURTH TITLE IN A ROW SETS NEW BENCHMARK 1926

In securing the Championship for the fourth year in succession Yorkshire equalled the record of Notts, who gained that honour in the four seasons beginning in 1883 and ending in 1886, when first place went, regardless of the number of victories, to the county meeting with the fewest defeats. The difference in the nature of the respective performances is emphasised by the fact that Notts during their four seasons of triumph engaged in 48 matches, winning 26, drawing 20, and losing two, whereas Yorkshire in the past four summers have taken part in 124 matches, winning 81, drawing 37, and losing six. Altogether in 1925, Yorkshire, meeting every one of the other 16 counties twice, contested 32 games of which they won 21, lost none and drew 11.

Yorkshire again equal a record of Notts in being unbeaten in three different years, but an honour all their own is the tremendous achievement of having carried off the Championship 14 times in the course of the last 29 seasons.

1927 – SUTCLIFFE DECLINES THE HONOUR 1928

At a meeting of the county club committee, held at Leeds on November 1, Herbert Sutcliffe was elected captain of the Yorkshire eleven, in succession to Sir A. W. Lupton. To this decision considerable exception was taken by some members of the county club on two very different grounds, one of these being the objection to a professional captaining the side, and the other to the passing-over of Rhodes. The trouble which thus threatened was obviated by the action of Sutcliffe who cabled from South Africa a message expressing his thanks for the honour done him, but declining the office, and intimating his readiness to play under any captain. Thereupon the committee decided to ask Captain W. A. Worsley to captain the team in 1928, and that gentleman accepted the invitation. An Old Etonian, playing against Harrow at Lord's in 1908 and 1909, Captain Worsley served in the war with the 2nd Battalion of the Yorkshire Regiment, was wounded, captured by the Germans, and remained a prisoner until the signing of the Armistice.

1931 – YORKSHIRE v WARWICKSHIRE: 10 FOR 36 1932

At Leeds, May 16, 18, 1931. Verity seized upon the occasion to accomplish a memorable bowling performance, the young left-hander in the visitors' second innings taking all ten wickets for 36 runs. Only once previously had a Yorkshire bowler enjoyed so exceptional a measure of success, Drake at Weston-super-Mare in 1914 obtaining all ten wickets in the second innings of Somerset. Up to the time Verity bowled in such deadly form and by so doing finished off the contest on Monday evening in a victory for Yorkshire by an innings and 25 runs, the match had proceeded on somewhat uneventful lines. Subsequent to the tea interval Verity at one point disposed of four batsmen in one over, getting Smart caught at backward point off the first ball and Foster stumped off the second, while Tate was leg-before to the fifth and Paine taken left hand from a return to the bowler off the sixth.

Warwickshire 201 (L. T. A. Bates 54; G. G. Macaulay 4-61) **and 72** (H. Verity 10-36);
Yorkshire 298 (H. Sutcliffe 67, E. Oldroyd 67, P. Holmes 58; J. H. Mayer 6-76).

Verity takes 10 for 10 (see page 967)

1932 – YORKSHIRE v ESSEX: BATTING ASSAULT
1933

At Scarborough, August 10, 11, 12, 1932. Facing a total of 325, Yorkshire hit up 476 runs in five hours and threequarters and directly after lunch on Friday gained a brilliant victory by an innings and eight runs. At such a pace did the Yorkshiremen travel that at one period four overs delivered by Farnes yielded 75 runs, and six successive overs – sent down by Fames, O'Connor and Nichols – produced 102. Leyland helped Sutcliffe to add 149 in 55 minutes. Sutcliffe began by making 51 in 75 minutes, reached his hundred 50 minutes later and then hit away in such wonderful fashion that he increased his score from 100 to 194 in 40 minutes.

Essex 325 (R. H. Taylor 106, M. S. Nichols 105; W. E. Bowes 9-121) **and 143** (Bowes 4-62);
Yorkshire 476-9 dec (H. Sutcliffe 194, A. Mitchell 80).

1935 – YORKSHIRE (CHAMPION COUNTY) v THE REST OF ENGLAND:
GAP BRIDGED 1936

At Kennington Oval, September 14, 16, 17, 1935. After a lapse of 30 years the Champion County beat the Rest of England in the concluding match of the season, Yorkshire – unique in that distinction – having a margin of 149 runs in their favour. In 1905 Yorkshire won by 65 runs under Lord Hawke. Of that victorious side W. Ringrose alone retains an active part with the Yorkshire team; he has been official scorer for several years. On this occasion A. B. Sellers led the county with the close concentration on every detail that has kept Yorkshire in the forefront of our counties for over 50 years. His keenness helped considerably towards the favourable result.

Yorkshire 238 (H. Sutcliffe 59, M. Leyland 58) **and 202-9 dec** (Leyland 133*; Mr F. R. Brown 4-70);
The Rest of England 179 (J. Hardstaff 69; H. Verity 4-24) **and 112** (D. Smith 78; Verity 6-60).

1937 – HUTTON COMES OF AGE
1938

Hutton enjoyed a season of almost unbroken triumph. He reached three-figures on ten occasions, once for England in the second Test match with New Zealand and once for North v South in the Test Trial match at Lord's, and three times in successive innings for Yorkshire he scored a century. Quite sound in defence, he revealed a range of strokes contrasting strongly with his methods of a year before. That Hutton is a batsman of remarkable gifts cannot be disputed. Of the record number of 36 stands of 100 or more made for Yorkshire, he shared in as many as 18, the highest of them – 315, in partnership with Sutcliffe against Leicestershire at Hull – being registered upon his 21st birthday.

1942 – INJURIES GIVE RISE TO FUTURE CONCERN 1943

The discharge from the Army on medical grounds of the two England opening batsmen, Leonard Hutton and Herbert Sutcliffe, during 1942 came as disturbing news to Yorkshire.

Hutton broke his left arm in a gymnasium exercise when fulfilling his duties as sergeant-instructor in 1941, and after undergoing three bone-grafting operations left the Service in June. His first intention was to take up a temporary clerkship with the Ministry of Pensions, but when the opportunity arose of civilian employment as inspector of works and buildings with the Royal Engineers, he preferred to return to his old trade.

Major Sutcliffe, following operations to his nose and shoulder early in the year, gave up in November a military career begun in the last war and resumed on the first day of the present conflict. The nose trouble dated back to the MCC team's tour in Australia in 1932-33. Upon reverting to civilian status Sutcliffe accepted a post with a paper-manufacturing firm.

Late news of Hutton is that his arm is knitting and the opinion is expressed that, providing he has a thorough rest in 1943, he should be able to resume in 1944.

1946 – COMETH THE HOUR... 1947

Most remarkable among the bowlers was Arthur Booth, who was tried in 1931, then went to Northumberland, and now, after some experience in 1945, found a regular place in first-class Championship cricket. Hitherto unwanted because of the incomparable Verity, the slow left-hander took 84 wickets at 11.90 each and gained his county cap. Surely an achievement without parallel at the age of 43.

1951 – SURREY v YORKSHIRE: WORTH THE WAIT 1952

At The Oval, July 14, 16, 17, 1951. Drawn. This match was memorable for the performance of Hutton in completing his century of centuries. After Surrey had broken down when the pitch gave a little help to bowlers, Hutton and Lowson took charge and at the end of the first day their unfinished stand had realised 112. Hutton then wanted 39 for his hundred and on Monday 15,000 people turned up. They were not disappointed, and Hutton achieved his objective with a stroke worthy of the occasion – a superb drive off Wait sped past cover point to the boundary. Yorkshire finally found themselves wanting 43 in 20 minutes. In a hectic scramble for runs, they paid the penalty for hitting recklessly at every ball, and although they raced to and from the pavilion gate the task was beyond them.

Surrey 156 and 317 (L. B. Fishlock 89; E. Leadbeater 4-112);
Yorkshire 431-3 dec (L. Hutton 151, J. V. Wilson 114*, F. A. Lowson 84) and 30-6.

1955 – YORKSHIRE v SURREY: TEST STANDARD   1956

At Leeds, June 18, 20, 21, 1955. Yorkshire won by six wickets. This thrilling struggle between the two leading sides in the country drew over 60,000 people and the atmosphere resembled that of a Test match. Surrey struggled hard to preserve their record, but were beaten for the first time in 16 consecutive games, their previous defeat being in July 1954. The gates were closed on Saturday when 35,000 saw Surrey fight back after losing their first eight wickets for 119. Lock and Loader, who added 96, each made his highest score. Loader and Bedser completed the recovery with a last-wicket stand of 53. Yorkshire found runs hard to get against accurate bowling, but Wilson defended well for nearly three hours and helped to save the follow-on. Then Surrey, leading by 102, broke down completely in the last 100 minutes on Monday, losing seven men for 27 in poor light against the fast bowling of Trueman and Cowan. Next day the last three wickets added 48 and Yorkshire needed 178 to win in three hours ten minutes. Until the last half-hour they were behind the clock, but they obtained the runs with 11 minutes to spare.

Surrey 268 (P. J. Loader 81, G. A. R. Lock 55; J. H. Wardle 4-79)
and 75 (M. J. Cowan 5-15, F. S. Trueman 4-31);
Yorkshire 166 (Lock 4-71)
and 178-4 (F. A. Lowson 52, W. Watson 51*).

1958 – WARDLE LEAVES IMPRINT ON DISMAL SEASON   1959

It is doubtful whether Yorkshire, in their long history, had experienced such a dismal season as in 1958. Apart from the disappointing playing record which led to them falling eight places from third to 11th, a great deal happened off the field which they will hope to forget. At the end of 1957 Yorkshire allowed Watson to leave them to captain Leicestershire. They followed by deciding not to re-engage Appleyard and Lowson for 1959, but an even greater shock was to come when they dispensed with Wardle. So, in the space of a year, four Test cricketers who had been the mainstays of Yorkshire cricket for several seasons left the county.

The circumstances surrounding the departure of Wardle were particularly unfortunate. After Wardle had been told that his services would not be required for 1959 he wrote a series of articles for the *Daily Mail* in which he criticised the running of the county club. The Yorkshire committee thereupon decided that as Wardle had broken his contract with the club by writing these articles he was no longer a Yorkshire player and he did not appear for the county after August 1. Wardle subsequently accepted a position with Nelson in the Lancashire League.

Yorkshire's troubles were far from over, for at the end of the season a fire broke out at the headquarters at Leeds and destroyed the Clock Tower and the press box. Furthermore, in a season when practically every county suffered from the weather, Yorkshire were hit worse than most. Six of their games failed to bring a decision on first innings and in two matches not a ball could be bowled. Altogether Yorkshire were concerned in 24 blank days, 17 within the county.

1959 – SUSSEX v YORKSHIRE: VICTORY RUSH 1960

At Hove, August 29, 31, September 1, 1959. Yorkshire won by five wickets and so became the new county champions. They made sure of the title in one of the most exciting finishes seen on the ground after being left to get 215 in 105 minutes. With their batsmen playing strokes at practically every delivery the winning hit came with seven minutes to spare. Few of the crowd had given Yorkshire much chance of getting the runs, but Stott, the left-hand opening batsman, quickly showed the county's intentions. He hit 13 of the 15 obtained off the first over and the 50 appeared in 20 minutes. Within half an hour 77 were scored; 100 came in 43 minutes; 150 in 63 minutes, 200 in 85 minutes and the winning stroke – a deflection to the fine leg boundary by Bolus – was made at 4.23pm. Stott batted only 86 minutes for 96 and his chief helper, Padgett, stayed just over an hour while 141 were added for the third wicket.

Sussex 210 (Nawab of Pataudi 52; K. Taylor 4-40)
and 311 (J. M. Parks 85, L. J. Lenham 66; R. Illingworth 4-66, D. Wilson 4-78);
Yorkshire 307 (Illingworth 122, Wilson 55; E. R. Dexter 4-63)
and 218-5 (W. B. Stott 96, D. E. V. Padgett 79).

1967 – GAME'S IMAGE BESMIRCHED Notes by the Editor, 1968

Brian Close led England to victory in five of the six Tests and also Yorkshire to the top of the Championship, which they have now won six times in the last nine years. Altogether Yorkshire have won the title outright 30 times, but on this occasion, although their ultimate success was deserved, their deliberate waste of time at Edgbaston in order to prevent Warwickshire winning so that they could take two points, brought upon them and their captain a heap of adverse criticism and the image of cricket was besmirched.

WARWICKSHIRE v YORKSHIRE

1968

At Birmingham, August 16, 17, 18, 1967. Drawn. This was the match with tremendous repercussions. The last hour and 40 minutes, in which Warwickshire had to score 142 to win and failed by nine runs, led to allegations of delaying tactics against Yorkshire and to the eventual censuring of their captain, Close. The last phase was in violent contrast to the urgency of the second day when Warwickshire just wrested the lead by four runs. Yorkshire bowled only 24 overs, and, in the last 15 minutes, during which they left the field to the umpires and the batsmen during a shower, sent down two overs, one from Trueman containing two no-balls and three bouncers. Before the acrimonious end, big hitting by Jameson – who hit a six over the bowler's head – and Amiss had kept Warwickshire up with the clock.

Yorkshire 238 (J. H. Hampshire 102, G. Boycott 57)

and 145 (T. W. Cartwright 4-26, D. R. Cook 4-66);

Warwickshire 242 (D. L. Amiss 53, K. Ibadulla 52; A. G. Nicholson 6-50) **and 133-5**.

Middlesex v Essex. At Southgate, July 18, 19, 20, 21, 2002. A bad-tempered game finally petered out into one of the most boring draws imaginable. Essex had already registered disgust by sitting down in the outfield to eat ice-creams during a pointedly unhurried afternoon drinks break.

Little Wonder No. 126

1968 – TYKES SHOW THEIR TRUE COLOURS

Jack Fingleton, 1969

Yorkshire, under the brilliant captaincy of Fred Trueman – and I saw no better leadership in England during the summer – diddled the Australians completely, an ignominious defeat for a touring side against a county. The Yorkshiremen rubbed it in also, through Ken Taylor, by winning the long-distance throw at the end of the cricket!

Yorkshire, in the field, looked an infinitely better team than the English Test one. And Trueman's captaincy was full of fight, shrewd moves, and colossal Yorkshire bluff. I like the Tykes because they are never false to their nature. When Trueman's team came into the dressing-room, I afterwards learned, they did not indulge themselves in any wild paeans of self-praise. Far from it. They got stuck into a first-class row as to whether individual money prizes – the brass – should go into a communal fund!

Trueman, sadly, will be seen no more on the first-class cricketing field. He was, in very truth, a wonderful character. I met him first when George Duckworth gave the pair of us a lift back to Lymm from Old Trafford. Trueman, then twelfth man for England, talked of himself all the way back. He is Yorkshire to his boot-heels and an unforgettable character on the field. I loved him most at Adelaide one

Australia Day when the artillery on the parade ground opposite the Oval broke out into a salute. Fiery Fred dived to earth immediately and waved his white hanky fiercely in surrender.

1971 – Change Of Captain Leaves County Close To Bottom   1972

Yorkshire had the worst season in their history. A win by 19 points in the last match against Northamptonshire – ending the longest sequence of 17 matches without a victory the county has ever known – lifted them to 13th place in the Championship table. In the John Player League they finished second from the bottom and in the Gillette Cup competition they went out in the first round to Kent.

Unquestionably the loss of such a talented cricketer and knowledgeable captain as Close could not fail to have an adverse influence on the team. Whereas Close had always argued that it was his duty to play the capped players, there now came an urge to encourage the youngsters. Perhaps the senior players felt a sense of insecurity? The new captain, Boycott, responded to his duties in the one way he knew best – he scored more than 2,000 runs for an average of 109.85 for Yorkshire and became the first Englishman to average more than 100 in all matches for the season. But he failed to bring the team along with him.

1973 – SURREY v YORKSHIRE: worst in a century   1974

At The Oval, July 14, 16, 1973. Surrey won by an innings and 165 runs with a day to spare. Yorkshire's double dismissal for an aggregate of 103 was their lowest in a three-day match against another first-class county for 108 years. After Boycott had won the toss, Yorkshire batted feebly and were routed by the lively Jackman, whose seven for 36 was his best performance in the Championship. On Monday, rain prevented play until 2.10pm. In two hours after tea, on a drying pitch, Yorkshire were bowled out for 43. The off-spinner Pocock was the chief destroyer, finishing with six for 11 in 9.2 overs. Lumb held out for an hour and a half and Nicholson was top-scorer with 11. Only three of their players, none of them specialist batsmen, reached double figures in the match.

Yorkshire 60 (R. D. Jackman 7-36) and 43 (P. I. Pocock 6-11);
Surrey 268-9 dec (Younis Ahmed 106, J. H. Edrich 54; A. G. Nicholson 5-57).

1973 – YORKSHIRE v LANCASHIRE: sorry sight   1974

At Sheffield, August 4, 6, 7, 1973. Drawn. This game marked the end of 118 years of cricket at the Bramall Lane ground. Its historic turf had been sold to cricket-lovers, and bulldozers were expected to move in within a week to prepare for the erection of a football stand across the cricket pitch as the Sheffield United club turned completely over to soccer. Unfortunately, the game was ruined by the weather.

There were catcalls in the closing stages as Sharpe and Johnson played very cautiously, and when stumps were pulled up spectators ran on the pitch and dug up pieces of turf for souvenirs. It was a sorry sight; a more pleasing memory had come on the first morning just before the game started. A short service was held by the Bishop of Wakefield in remembrance of Wilfred Rhodes, one of the world's greatest cricketers, who had died a few days earlier aged 95. The Yorkshire and Lancashire teams lined up in the middle of the ground.

Yorkshire 99 (P. G. Lee 6-43)
and 114-2 (P. J. Sharpe 62*);
Lancashire 111-8 dec (A. G. Nicholson 4-40).

1976 – COSTLY FAILURE OF CUP EXAMINATION   John Callaghan, 1977

The biggest sensation of the whole Benson and Hedges competition was the performance of Oxford and Cambridge Universities at Barnsley on May 22, the last day of the group contests, when they outplayed Yorkshire. That [seven-wicket] defeat cost Yorkshire a place in the quarter-finals.

1978 – COMMITTEE SURVIVES ATTACK OVER BOYCOTT   1979

The controversy surrounding the deposing of Geoffrey Boycott as captain of Yorkshire and the appointment of John Hampshire as his successor continued through the autumn. Many Yorkshire members formed a Boycott Reform Group, and they forced a special general meeting at The Royal Hall, Harrogate on December 9 in a battle to regain the captaincy for Boycott, who at the time was with the England team in Australia. The meeting lasted three hours, with the supporters of Boycott losing by 4,826 votes to 2,602, a majority of 2,224. The Reform Group's motion of no confidence in the Yorkshire general committee went closer. It was lost by 4,422 votes to 3,067, a majority of 1,355. The meeting produced the most serious attack on officials of the club in Yorkshire's 115 years' existence.

1981 – DERBYSHIRE v YORKSHIRE (BENSON AND HEDGES CUP):
BATTLING BAIRSTOW   1982

At Derby, May 9, 11, 1981. Yorkshire won by one wicket. A remarkable innings by Gold Award-winner Bairstow, whose unbeaten 103 included nine sixes and three fours, took Yorkshire to a victory that seemed unlikely when they were reduced to 123 for nine. He was joined by Johnson, on his debut, in a tenth-wicket stand of 80

– a new record for the competition. The turning-point came when Bairstow, who made his second 50 off only six overs, took 26 off one over from Steele.

Derbyshire 202-8 (55 overs) (P. N. Kirsten 65, J. G. Wright 47; C. M. Old 3-33);
Yorkshire 203-9 (53.4 overs) (D. L. Bairstow 103*; C. J. Tunnicliffe 5-24).

1982 – Old Failings Remain Despite Captaincy Change   John Callaghan, 1983

In one of the most controversial moves of even Yorkshire's trouble-strewn recent history, Chris Old [the captain] was replaced by the manager, Ray Illingworth, who resumed his playing career at Ilford 15 days after his 50th birthday. Not even Illingworth's experience and tactical skill, however, could compensate for the lack of consistency and, in some cases, application as the side continued to perform some way below expectations.

1986 – Chapter Closes On Opener's Career   John Callaghan, 1987

After a disappointing season, Yorkshire, still with much promise unfulfilled, ended their association with Geoff Boycott. The cricket committee voted 4–1 against offering Boycott another year's contract, and when this recommendation was put before the general committee, an amendment aimed at extending his career failed by 12–9. Boycott, whose final record with Yorkshire in the Championship was 29,485 runs at an average of 58.27, again headed the county's averages, despite missing nine Championship matches with a broken bone in his left wrist. County officials paid due tribute to the 45-year-old opener, while stressing that the committee wanted to give younger talent the chance to develop.

1992 – Tradition Ends But Poor Performance Remains   John Callaghan, 1993

Yorkshire's decision to break with cherished tradition and sign an overseas player brought some commercial success, checking the worrying decline in membership. However, the county enjoyed a disastrous season on the field, emphasising that there are no easy or short-term answers to long-standing problems. They slipped from 14th to 16th in the Championship and from seventh to 15th in the Sunday League, suffering seven successive defeats in the process. They lost interest in the Benson and Hedges Cup at the qualifying stage, while Northamptonshire humiliated them in the second round of the NatWest Trophy.

Australian fast bowler Craig McDermott, the original choice as Yorkshire's first officially recognised "outsider", broke down during the winter and required an operation for groin trouble, so, with little room for manoeuvre, the club turned their attentions at the last minute to Sachin Tendulkar. The 19-year-old Indian's appearance on the scene at least silenced all those who, from a distance, accused Yorkshire of being racist, and he proved extremely popular with the public and fellow players. Tendulkar collected his runs with a good deal of style, scoring quickly in the limited-overs competitions and being prepared to apply himself diligently in the Championship, but he lacked the experience to dominate.

Sussex v Yorkshire. At Arundel, June 26, 27, 28, 29, 2002. Fears that an escapee from the nearby Ford prison had melted into the crowd led to a strong police presence on the second day.

Little Wonder No. 127

1998 – YORKSHIRE v LANCASHIRE: 12 MEN TOO STRONG   1999

At Leeds, August 14, 15, 16, 17, 1998. Lancashire won by 59 runs. A Roses match with the teams in an old-fashioned position – both in the top six – began in a thoroughly untraditional way when Lancashire scored 82 in the first 11 overs and reached 200 immediately after lunch. It was enough to set them on the path to victory. There was another feature that would have been amused old-timers: for the first time in any Championship fixture, 12 different players batted for Lancashire. Austin left the game at lunchtime on the second day when he was called into England's one-day squad instead of the injured Mark Ealham. This meant that Green, who was already on the field as substitute for the injured Wasim Akram, was allowed to play a full part as a replacement for Austin, under ECB regulations. There were precedents for this, but on previous occasions the player replaced had always gone before batting. Austin would have left the ground sooner than he did, but he was selected for a random drugs test and apparently had problems providing a sample.

Lancashire 484 (J. P. Crawley 180, G. D. Lloyd 56)
and 215 (W. K. Hegg 85, Crawley 56; P. M. Hutchison 5-39);
Yorkshire 457-8 dec (D. Byas 101, D. S. Lehmann 71, R. J. Blakey 67*, G. M. Hamilton 56)
and 183 (G. Keedy 5-35, G. Yates 4-69).

2001 – YORKSHIRE v GLAMORGAN: BYAS MAKES HIS POINT   2002

At Scarborough, August 21, 22, 23, 24, 2001. Yorkshire won by an innings and 112 runs. At 12.13 on the final day, Byas took the catch that returned the Championship title to Yorkshire after 33 years. He also contributed one of three centuries to his side's impregnable total, but – not for the first time in the season

– he had refused to be hurried into his declaration by gloomy weather forecasts, preferring to go by his farmer's instincts. Even so, he cut it fine, for heavy rain was setting in as the jubilant winners left the field. When Glamorgan were six down on the third evening, it was decided to fling open the gates on the final morning, although the 5,000 crowd had to watch a spectacular counter-attack by Jones before acclaiming the new champions. Tearing into Lehmann's bowling, he lashed 46 off 14 balls, hitting six sixes and two fours before slicing to backward point where Byas, having dashed from slip, held the catch that sent the champagne corks popping.

Glamorgan 223 (A. Dale 59; R. K. J. Dawson 6-82) **and 245** (S. P. Kirby 4-40);
Yorkshire 580-9 dec (C. White 183, M. J. Wood 124, D. Byas 104, R. J. Blakey 54; D. A. Cosker 4-168).

2002 – HEROES TO ZEROES
David Warner, 2003

In sharp contrast with normal practice, Yorkshire's latest revolution broke out during the season rather than waiting for the winter months. Their fortunes fluctuated wildly both on and off the field. After the long-awaited Championship triumph in 2001 came humble pie: anchored to the bottom of the table from early June, Yorkshire raised their game a little but could not avoid relegation. Some compensation came in the form of a Lord's cup win in the C&G – just like the 2001 Championship, it came after a 33-year gap – but it was the spectacular failure to defend their Championship crown that lingered in the memory.

2004 – YORKSHIRE v WORCESTERSHIRE (TOTESPORT LEAGUE):
HISTORY-MAKER
2005

At Leeds, May 23, 2004. Worcestershire won by 39 runs. This was a historic day for Yorkshire, with the 18-year-old Bradford schoolboy Ajmal Shahzad becoming the first Yorkshire-born Asian to play first-team cricket for the county. Brought in at the last minute because of an injury crisis, Shahzad was thrown the new ball and withstood an early onslaught from Solanki and Peters to concede only 35 runs from six consecutive overs.

Worcestershire 238-6 (45 overs) (V. S. Solanki 68, G. A. Hick 54, K. Ali 51);
Yorkshire 199 (43.3 overs) (M. J. Wood 46; M. N. Malik 3-53).

2005 – AT LAST THEY AGREE ON SOMETHING
David Warner, 2006

Yorkshire rang in the New Year by celebrating ownership of a ground for the first time in their 142-year history. But the £12m deal to buy Headingley was only clinched at the last gasp after lawyers representing Yorkshire and their landlords, Leeds Cricket, Football and Athletic Company, had worked like Bob Cratchits throughout Christmas week to hammer out a final agreement.

The ECB had insisted that Yorkshire must own Headingley by New Year's Day, otherwise they would scrap the 15-year staging agreement to keep international cricket there until 2019. The deal was eventually done on December 30.

Leeds City Council approval came on December 23, just in time for a Yorkshire special general meeting on Christmas Eve to hear about it before voting over-whelmingly for the management board to buy the ground. There were a few dissenters among the proxy voters, but all 206 at the meeting were in favour – the first time ever that Yorkshire members in the same room had been unable to find something to argue about.

Extras

A fter the Test matches, World Cups and counties this section offers a flavour of other parts of the game to which *Wisden* has given prominence down the years.

OTHER MATCHES

In the days before regular Test matches the best players in England were generally to be found in the Gentlemen v Players matches, which took place until the amateur-professional distinction was abolished after 1962, but the biggest crowds at Lord's – albeit attracted by the social occasion as much as the cricket – were to be found at Oxford v Cambridge and Eton v Harrow. Indeed, those two produced matches that have forever been known by the names of the players (Frank Cobden and Robert Fowler) who brought about two of the most remarkable finishes the game has known. Cricket has also spread its wings to some of the extremities of the Earth: Antarctica and Everest.

1870 – RIGHT HANDED v LEFT HANDED OF ENGLAND:
ARRAY OF TALENT 1871

At Lord's, May 9, 10, 1870. This was the opening match of the 84th season of the Marylebone Club. So brilliant an array of the cricketing talent of the country on no prior occasion appeared in an opening match at Lord's, the match being moreover interesting from its not having been played since 1835, and for its being the first match Carpenter, Hayward, and Smith had played in at Lord's since 1866. The weather was bright, but nippingly cold for May. The Left were comparatively weak as batsmen, and were without a professed wicketkeeper, so they were defeated by an innings and eight runs. In less than one hour and a half the first innings of the Left was played out. For the Right, John Smith hit very finely for 45; Mr Grace played well for 35; careful and scientific cricket was played by Carpenter; Hayward was bowled off his thigh and Daft off his pad; Hearne took his bat out for 26, and the innings ended for 185, or 112 on. The second innings of the Left is noteworthy for a superb left-hand c and b (it came back very hot) by Daft, a well-played 21 by

Rylott (a right-hand hitter), and a remarkably good display of effective defence and free, clean, hard hitting by Killick of Sussex, whose 55 (highest innings in the match) won him the hearty applause of the Right eleven; a higher compliment could not well be paid him. At one o'clock on the second day the Right had won in a canter. Howitt's absence on the second day was caused by a domestic bereavement.

The Left 73 (Mr W. G. Grace 6-24) **and 104** (H. Killick 55);
The Right 185 (J. C. Shaw 4-49).

The First Right v Left match was played at (old) Lord's in 1790.

1870 – CAMBRIDGE v OXFORD: COBDEN'S MATCH 1871

At Lord's, June 27, 28, 1870. The large and brilliant attendances, the fine successful stand made for Cambridge at a critical phase of the match by Mr Yardley and Mr Dale, the truly great innings played by Mr Yardley, and the extraordinary finish, stamps the University contest of 1870 as the most remarkable of the 36 yet played. The attendance was one of high class, and numerically estimated at 9,000. On the second day the weather was brilliant, and the attendance (computed at 10,000) one of those rare assemblages of fashion, rank, and eminent men of the country that meet on no other cricket ground but Lord's. Past and present University men mustered strongly; and as the day's extraordinary cricket frequently wavered in favour of Light or Dark Blue, so rang out the old cheering as zealously as ever.

There were five wickets down for 40 runs, Cambridge only 12 runs on. But then it was (at three minutes to one) Mr Yardley went to the wickets; and his brilliant – at times grand – hitting, aided by the careful, scientific play of Mr Dale, put quite another aspect on the match. So effectively did Mr Yardley hit, that at 1.30 the score was increased to 100; at ten minutes past two the 150 was up; at 195 Mr Francis ended Mr Yardley's innings for 100 exact – the highest individual score yet made in these matches, and as fine a display of brilliant hitting as ever witnessed in them. The innings included 14 fours, the leg hitting being especially clean and fine. Earnest applause (in which the Oxford eleven took part) justly complimented Mr Yardley on the completion of his great innings. At ten minutes to four the Cambridge innings was over for 206 runs, leaving the Oxford men 179 to win.

When Mr Ottaway left the innings was at 160 for five wickets, and the time ten past seven; so 20 minutes remained for five wickets to make the 19 runs then required to win. But a catch at slip and an lbw speedily got rid of Mr Townshend and Mr Francis, making seven wickets down for 175 runs, or four to win – an apparently easy task. But then (in an indifferent light for batting) Mr Cobden bowled his now famously effective last over:

From the first ball a single was made (three to win with three wickets to fall).
From the second ball Mr Butler was superbly caught out at mid-off.
The third ball bowled Mr Belcher.
The fourth ball bowled Mr Stewart.

And so, accompanied by excitement unparalleled, did the eighth, ninth, and tenth wickets fall with the score 176, Cambridge after all winning this match of matches by two runs. The sudden break-up of the ring; the wild rush of thousands across the ground to the pavilion; the waving of hats, sunshades, handkerchiefs, fans, and sticks; the loud shouts for Cobden, Yardley, Dale, Ottaway, Fortescue, Francis, and others, to come out and be tossed about by their partisans, formed a fitting climax to a match so excitingly contested and a result so astoundedly unexpected.

Cambridge University 147 (Mr C. K. Francis 5-59, Mr T. H. Belcher 4-52)
and 206 (Mr W. Yardley 100, Mr J. W. Dale 67; Francis 7-102);
Oxford 175 (Mr F. C. Cobden 4-41)
and 176 (Mr C. J. Ottaway 69; Mr E. E. Ward 6-29, Cobden 4-35).

1871 – ETON v HARROW: THE MANHOOD AND BEAUTY OF THE LAND 1872

At Lord's, July 14, 15, 1871. The annually increasing attraction of this match among the upper crust of English Society is something wonderful. So sure as one July succeeds another and the much-talked-of Friday and Saturday arrive, so surely do the attendances at Lord's on these two fashionably important days increase in influence and numbers. In 1870 the attendance during the two days was computed at 20,000, and the admission money estimated at £200 in excess of any previous two days' receipts. The amount of the receipts in 1871 was not made public, but those unerring calculators – the tell-tales – told the following surprising tale as to the number of visitors to the ground in the course of the two days of last July:

ON FRIDAY,
13,494 visitors paid and passed through the turnstiles on to the ground.

ON SATURDAY,
11,132 visitors paid and passed through the turnstiles on to the ground.

Add to this 24,626, the members of MCC, their families and friends, and all who went on to the ground in or on vehicles (600 carriages were estimated as being on the ground), then an idea can be formed of the vast numbers that composed the fashionable crushes up at Lord's. The gatherings were as brilliant in rank as they were unprecedentedly large in numbers. Their Royal Highnesses The Crown Princess of Prussia, Princess Louise Marchioness of Lorne, and Prince Arthur, with the Marquis of Lorne and a large number of the nobility, honoured the match with their presence. The Grand Stand was on each day filled with a fair and fashionable assemblage. The very many drags present were crowded with the manhood and beauty of the land. The pavilion was crammed in front and on roof by MCC members and "Pasts and Presents". The ring was a sight, so compact and pictur-esque was its formation; here and there would be a dull dark spot composed by the accidental gathering together of a score or two of the "lords of creation", but these were charmingly contrasted by the many groups of brilliantly attired ladies, whose varied-hued costumes made the ring as bright and gay as those splendid flower parterres that in season surround the rosary at the Crystal Palace. On the Friday there were showers and sunshine during the cricket, and two sights, greater by contrast, could not well be witnessed on a cricket ground than the sudden upraising of thousands of opened umbrellas all round the ground when the showers fell, and the bright, parti-coloured, brilliant scene afforded when the sunshine beamed on the ground. On Saturday the weather was splendid, the two sights of that day being the extraordinarily extensive scale that "picnicing" was carried on, and the unusual but charming picture the old ground presented when covered by ladies prome-nading during luncheon time.

A total of 38,000 attended the following year, when Wisden *commented on the "wealth of brilliantly attired beauteous women, such as can be seen nowhere out of grumbling but glorious Old England"!*

Manhood and beauty:
Eton v Harrow matches attracted the fashionable elements of Victorian society

1873 – KENT v SUSSEX: ONLY CUP-TIE   1874

At Lord's, June 9, 10, 1873. Prior to the commencement of the 1873 season, the Marylebone Club, with the praiseworthy purpose of increasing the popularity of county cricket, offered a County Champion Cup for annual competition by recog-nised county elevens on the neutral ground at Lord's. Sufficient of the counties agreed to compete to promise these fights for the championship becoming an inter-esting series of struggles, but subsequently several of the counties' authorities declined to contend, and consequently MCC withdrew for that season their offer, and the Cup contests did not come off. However, Kent and Sussex agreed to have their round at Lord's, and on dangerously bad wickets they fought out the old fight, when Kent won by 52 runs.

Kent 122 (James Lillywhite 5-45, R. Fillery 5-70)
and 75 (Lillywhite 6-43, Fillery 4-24);
Sussex 45 (Mr G. E. Coles 6-23, E. Willsher 4-16) **and** 100 (Coles 4-47).

1873 – ETON v HARROW: UNSEEMLY CONDUCT   1874

At Lord's, July 11, 12, 1873. Some disturbance after the conclusion of the match led to the publication of the following letter in *Bell's Life in London* of July 19:

"Mr Editor: The committee regret that notwithstanding all their efforts to prevent a scene of confusion at the termination of the Schools match, their efforts were frustrated by the unseemly conduct of some persons on the ground. Such scenes as those witnessed on Saturday would not occur if the partisans of both schools would assist the authorities in checking the immoderate expression of feeling at the conclusion of the match. The committee appeal to the old and young members of the two schools to assist them in future in preventing a repetition of such disorder which must inevitably end in a discontinuance of the match. By order of the committee, R. A. Fitzgerald, Secretary MCC."

Surrey v Middlesex. At Guildford, July 23, 24, 25, 26, 2003. With Middlesex 163 for one, Ormond dismissed four left-handers in one amazing over. His first ball had Strauss lbw, Hutton offered a leg-side catch off the fourth, Joyce was lbw to the fifth, and Weekes bowled when the sixth dipped in late. It was apparently the first hat-trick composed purely of left-handers in any first-class match in Britain.

Little Wonder No. 128

1878-79 – CRICKET FLOURISHES ON THE ICE   1880

All England will remember, with a shiver and a shudder, the long, sad, and severe winter of 1878-79, commencing, as it did in October '78, and continuing – with more or less severity – up to the middle of May '79; and even then the cold, nipping, bronchitis-creating winds seemed loth [*sic*] to leave the land they had so sorely stricken with distress, disease, and death. But there is no black cloud without its silver lining, and one bright spot in this dark winter was its severity and length enabled more cricket matches on the ice to be played than were ever before played in the course of one winter.

...and under the moonlight

About the time Lord Harris's team were playing one of their matches under the bright and burning sun of an Australian summer, an English team were playing their game in the dear old country at home under the bright and brilliant beams of the new year's full moon.

This match by moonlight came about this wise: The moon was full on January 8, shining with unclouded and truly splendid brightness throughout that evening and night. At the same time a sharp, keen, thoroughly old-fashioned frost was setting the ice in capital form for skating and other icy pastimes. The next day being bright, frosty, and fine, the skating cricketers of the royal borough of Windsor duly announced that "A Cricket Match would be played by Moonlight on the Ice in Windsor Home Park at 7 o'clock that evening."

Consequently several hundred spectators assembled, and the match was played by moonlight. The game (says the chronicler) causing no end of amusement owing to the difficulties encountered by the players while bowling, batting, and fielding.

Mr Bowditch's side (only nine men batted) **15**; **Mr Gage's side** (ten men batted) **17**.

1898 – GENTLEMEN v PLAYERS: GRACE'S HALF-CENTURY   1899

At Lord's, July 18, 19, 20, 1898. When the fixtures for 1898 were being arranged, the committee of the MCC had the happy inspiration to fix their Gentlemen and Players match for July 18 – Mr W. G. Grace's 50th birthday. More than that, they secured at the secretaries' meeting in December a perfectly clear date for the fixture, and thus made themselves certain of getting representative elevens. The match more than fulfilled the most sanguine expectations and was quite the event of the season. Except for an hour's heavy rain on the morning of the second day the weather was always dry, and the support accorded by the public was greater than at any previous Gentlemen and Players match at Lord's Ground. The turnstiles showed that 17,423 people paid for admission on the Monday; 14,633 on the Tuesday; and 9,502 on the Wednesday. Most important of all, the cricket was entirely worthy of the occasion. Feeling no doubt the honour of having been chosen, the cricketers on both sides played quite as keenly as if the match had been between England and Australia. Mr Grace, though handicapped by lameness and a severe blow on the hand, did himself justice, and with Kortright's assistance nearly succeeded in saving the match for the Gentlemen, it wanting only a few minutes to 7pm on the third day when the Players won by 137 runs.

The Gentlemen were left with 296 to get and, as in order to win the game they would have had to score at the rate of 100 an hour for three hours they had nothing to hope for but a draw. Owing to his bruised hand Grace kept himself back. Seven wickets were down at 25 minutes to six for 77. Grace then went in himself, his appearance being greeted with tremendous cheering. He quickly lost Dixon and MacGregor, and with nine wickets down for 80, the match seemed certain to end in the tamest fashion. Kortright, however, stayed with Grace and a superb effort the two batsmen made to save the game. For nearly 70 minutes they stayed together, putting on in that time 78 runs. As seven o'clock drew near it looked as if they would succeed in their object, but Kortright incautiously hit out at a ball from Lockwood and was caught at cover point, the Players winning the match amidst a scene of intense excitement.

Players 335 (W. Gunn 139, W. Storer 59; Mr C. L. Townsend 4-58)
and 263 (Storer 73, Gunn 56; Mr J. R. Mason 4-47);
Gentlemen 303 (Mr A. C. MacLaren 50; J. T. Hearne 5-87, W. H. Lockwood 4-82)
and 158 (Hearne 6-65).

1900 – GENTLEMEN v PLAYERS: Woods gets it in the neck

At Lord's, July 16, 17, 18, 1900. The match was certainly the most remarkable game of the whole season. It presented two points that were quite without precedent in the long series of Gentlemen v Players matches. R. E. Foster followed up his record innings in the University Match by making two separate hundreds, a feat never before performed at Lord's or elsewhere for either Gentlemen or Players, and the Players, though set to make 501 in the last innings, won the game by two wickets. Never before in a match of such importance – and only once indeed in the whole history of first-class class cricket – has a total of over 500 been obtained in the fourth innings. The one previous occasion – also at Lord's – was in 1896, when Cambridge were set to make 507 against the MCC and succeeded in accomplishing the task. The performance of the Players was a magnificent one, but they could consider themselves lucky in having sufficient time left them in which to make such a huge score. On the second afternoon the Gentlemen already held what was on paper an overwhelming advantage, and Mr Woods, their captain, wishing to have the Players in before the close of the afternoon, instructed his side to play a hitting game, and be out by a certain time. His instructions were loyally obeyed, and though the Gentlemen's score stood at 238 for three wickets when Foster left, the innings was all over for 339. From lunchtime till the end of the innings 279 runs were scored in two hours and 20 minutes. No one was disposed to criticise Mr Woods at all severely, some people going so far as to say that if the Gentlemen could not win with a lead of 500 runs they did not deserve to win at all. This was all very well, but the fact remained that there was only one possible way by which the Gentlemen could lose the match, and that their captain adopted it. However, though the Gentlemen suffered a defeat to which they need not have been exposed, the public profited, the cricket on the last day being quite a marvel of sustained interest. Overnight the Players had lost Albert Ward's wicket for 44 runs, so that on Wednesday morning, with nine wickets to go down, they wanted 457 to win. By wonderful batting the task was accomplished, the honours being divided between Brown, Hayward and Abel. Of the three batsmen Abel made the smallest score, but in the opinion of many good judges he played the best cricket.

At Hayward's dismissal the Players wanted 32 to win with three wickets to fall, and the issue remained in doubt. With 16 added John Gunn was bowled, but on

831

Rhodes joining Trott the end soon came. At half past six the score stood at a tie, and on Woods taking the ball Rhodes made the winning hit, a wonderful match ending in favour of the Players by two wickets.

Gentlemen 297 (Mr R. E. Foster 102*, Mr C. B. Fry 68; W. Rhodes 4-93)
and 339 (Foster 136, Fry 72; A. E. Trott 6-142);
Players 136 (Mr J. R. Mason 4-40)
and 502-8 (J. T. Brown 163, T. W. Hayward 111, R. Abel 98).

1910 – ETON v HARROW: Fowler's match 1911

At Lord's, July 8, 9, 1910. Eton and Harrow have been meeting on the cricket field for over 100 years, but they have never played a match quite so remarkable as that of 1910. Indeed in the whole history of cricket there has been nothing more sensational. After following their innings Eton were only four ahead with nine wickets down, and yet in the end they won the game by nine runs. The struggle between the two public schools last season will be known for all time as Fowler's match. Never has a school cricketer risen to the occasion in more astonishing fashion. When Harrow went in with only 55 to get, Fowler took command of the game, secured eight wickets – five of them bowled down – for 23 runs and brought off what might fairly be described as a 40 to one chance.

Until the second afternoon was far advanced the match proved one-sided to a degree. On the first day Harrow going in on a soft, but by no means difficult pitch, ran up a total of 232, and when bad light caused stumps to be drawn, five of Eton's best wickets had fallen for 40 runs. On Saturday morning, Eton's innings was soon finished off for 67, and a follow-on against a balance of 165 was involved. At first things went so badly that half the wickets were down for 65. Despite Fowler's heroic efforts – his 64 was the highest innings in the match – Eton were only four runs ahead with a wicket to fall. Then began the cricket which will for ever make the match memorable. Kaye joined Manners, and so finely and fearlessly did Manners hit that in less than 25 minutes 50 runs were put on, the total being carried from 169 to 219. A remarkable catch in the slips at last brought the innings to an end, Hopley just reaching the ball and turning it to Jameson, who held it a few inches from the ground. In the case of any ordinary match the ground would have been half-empty before the Eton innings closed, but an Eton and Harrow crowd is a law to itself and about 10,000 people watched the cricket. Whatever their feelings, they must have been glad they stayed, as they may never see such a finish again.

Probably Harrow made a mistake in having the heavy roller put on. At any rate Fowler was able at once to bowl his off-break with deadly effect. He bowled Wilson in the first over; at eight he bowled Hopley; and at the same total, Turnbull, the left-handed hitter, was caught in the long field. Earle seemed likely to win the match easily enough for Harrow, but after he had hit up 13 runs, a catch at slip sent him back at 21. Without the addition of a run, Monckton was bowled and Hillyard well caught low down at short mid-on. In this way, as the result of half an hour's cricket, six wickets were down for 21, Fowler having taken them all. Blount was caught and bowled at 26 by Steel, who had just gone on for Kaye, and then Jameson, who had been batting for nearly 40 minutes without getting a run, was so badly hurt that for a few minutes the game had to be delayed. With victory in sight, the Eton team played the keenest possible cricket, nothing being thrown away in the field. A yorker bowled Straker at 29, and, after Graham had hit a three, Jameson was bowled by Fowler. It was not to be expected that Graham and Alexander would get the 23 runs still required, but they made a desperate effort, carrying the score to 45 or only ten to win. Then a catch low down in the slips got rid of Alexander and a wonderful match was over. The scene of enthusiasm at the finish was quite indescribable. From the time he went on at 21, Steel with his leg-breaks gave Fowler excellent support and the Eton fielding all round was magnificent.

Harrow 232 (Mr J. M. Hillyard 62, Mr B. Wilson 53; Mr A. I. Steel 4-69, Mr R. St. L. Fowler 4-90)

and 45 (Fowler 8-23);

Eton 67 and 219 (Fowler 64).

ARMY CLAIMED ETON'S HERO
Obituary, 1926

FOWLER, CAPT. ROBERT ST LEGER, MC, born on April 7, 1891, died at Rahinston, Enfield, County Meath, on June 13, aged 34. Owing to his profession, he was not very well-known to the general cricket public, but he was the hero of a match which may, without exaggeration, he described as the most extraordinary ever played. The story of the Eton and Harrow match in 1910 has been told over and over again, but it can never grow stale. No victory in a match of widespread interest was ever snatched in such a marvellous way. From one point of view it was a pity he went into the Army. In Oxford or Cambridge cricket he would assuredly have played a great part.

When he made 92 not out for Army v MCC at Lord's in 1920 he and Capt. W. V. D. Dickinson (150) put on 237 together for the eighth wicket in 90 minutes, and on the same ground four years later he took seven wickets for 22 runs for Army v Royal Navy. With the Incogniti he toured America in 1920, making 142 v All Philadelphia at Haverford, and with the Free Foresters he visited Germany the same year and Canada in 1923. When it was contemplated sending an MCC team to the West Indies in 1924-25 he was offered, and accepted, the captaincy. In 1924 he appeared in two matches for Hampshire. In the Great War he served as Captain in the 17th Lancers and gained the Military Cross.

1920 – ETON v HARROW: WARNING HEEDED
1921

At Lord's, July 9, 10, 1920. In consequence of the fighting that followed the conclusion of the game in 1919, Hill-Wood, the Eton captain, issued a notice than any repetition of the misconduct would lead to the Eton v Harrow match being taken away from Lord's. The warning had the desired effect, there being nothing in the behaviour of the boys after Eton's victory to which the slightest exception could be taken.

1939 – ETON v HARROW: CROWD INVASION 1940

At Lord's, July 14, 15, 1939. Those who were present will never forget the delirious excitement aroused by Harrow's first victory since 1908 over their great rivals. As Lithgow, the Harrow captain, finished the match with three successive drives to the pavilion boundary, the crowd invaded the field and carried both Lithgow and Crutchley in triumph to the pavilion. Then for 20 minutes an ordered assembly, numbering about 8,000, cheered the heroes. The victorious team, with Hendren, their popular coach, appeared on the balcony; the Harrow school song was sung, and there followed a free fight for top hats.

Lancashire v Middlesex. At Manchester, August 21, 22, 23, 24, 2003. On the last day, Lancashire's manager, Mike Watkinson stood in at square leg until a reserve official arrived, after umpire Hartley broke his wrist: Watkinson immediately rejected an over-exuberant stumping appeal from his players.

Little Wonder No. 129

1950 – ENGLAND v THE REST (TEST TRIAL): LAKER TAKES 8 FOR 2 1951

At Bradford, May 31, June 1, 1950. England won by an innings and 89 runs. One of the most remarkable representative matches on record finished before lunch on the second day. Such was the mastery of the bowlers on drying turf that in seven hours and 50 minutes of playing time 30 wickets fell for 369 runs, of which Hutton made nearly one-quarter. Although the desperate struggle for runs provided keen interest for spectators, the selectors could have learned little not already known to them. Yardley put in The Rest on winning the toss, and the off-breaks of Laker caused so complete a rout that in 110 minutes they were all out for the lowest total in a match of representative class. The previous-smallest score was 30, made by South Africa against England at Port Elizabeth in 1896 and at Edgbaston 1924. On the ground, five miles from his birthplace, on which he had enjoyed many league triumphs for Saltaire, Laker dominated the scene. He took two wickets in his first over and a third before conceding a run; in his fifth over he dismissed four more men before being edged for a second single, and he brilliantly caught and bowled the last man. His full analysis was: 14–12–2–8. He spun the ball skilfully, his length was immaculate and his direction perfect. The young batsmen opposed to Laker did not possess the ripe experience needed to cope with his skill under conditions so suited to his bowling. England obtained a lead of 202, chiefly through superlative batting by Hutton, ably assisted by Edrich, against bowling of moderate quality apart from that of Berry, the left-hander, and Jenkins with leg-spin. Berry did not lose accuracy even when Hutton used every possible means to knock him off his length. Hutton, who made 85 out of 155 in two hours, gave a dazzling display of batsmanship on a difficult pitch. Laker again met with early success in The Rest second innings; but Hollies caused chief damage. He turned the ball sharply and varied flight and pace well. Eric Bedser and Spooner made 42 in the only stand.

The Rest 27 (J. C. Laker 8-2) **and 113** (W. E. Hollies 6-28);
England 229 (L. Hutton 85; R. Berry 5-73).

1954 – ETON v HARROW: ROWDY SCENES 1955

At Lord's, July 9, 10, 1954. Boisterous scenes, degenerating into rowdyism, followed, and water was poured from the Harrow dressing-room balcony on to Eton supporters trying to tear down the colours of the victors. A clergyman had his hat knocked off and kicked about.

1976 – HERTFORDSHIRE v ESSEX (GILLETTE CUP): BRAVE HERTS 1977

At Hitchin, July 14, 1976. Hertfordshire won by 33 runs, becoming the first Minor County to reach the quarter-finals of the competition. They owed their success to a devastating performance by the spin pair, Johns, the Oxford Blue of 1970, and Doshi, the Man of the Match, who had played for Sussex Second Eleven and Nottinghamshire and was professional at Egerton in the Bolton League. The pitch deteriorated badly after lunch, but fine strokeplay by McEwan seemed to make this irrelevant. Then the spinners began finding the edge regularly, the fielders and wicketkeeper held a succession of sharp catches, and by the time Johns and Doshi had finished their overs, Essex were down to their last pair. Hertfordshire based their winning score on two hard-hitting stands, the second wicket contributing 65 and Ambrose and Burridge hitting 45 in nine overs.

Hertfordshire 153 (55.3 overs) (R. E. East 4-28, S. Turner 3-23);
Essex 120 (38 overs) (D. R. Doshi 4-23, R. L. Johns 4-31).

1985 – NO NEED FOR FLOODLIGHTS IN ANTARCTICA 1986

What was almost certainly the most southerly game of cricket ever played, and the coldest, took place in Antarctica, 700 kilometres from the South Pole, on January 11, 1985, between two teams drawn from the 60 scientists, lawyers, environmentalists and administrators engaged in an international workshop being held at the Beardmore South Camp and concerned with the Antarctic Treaty. New Zealand's representative on the Treaty, Christopher Beeby, captained the Gondwanaland Occasionals with players from Australia, New Zealand and South Africa. A British delegate to the Conference, Arthur Watts, captained the Beardmore Casuals, a basically British team. The stumps were improvised, the pitch, such as it was, had been rolled by a Hercules transport aircraft, and the midnight sun allowed play to continue until 11pm. The Occasionals (129) beat the Casuals (102) by 27 runs.

2002 – OXFORD UNIVERSITY v CAMBRIDGE UNIVERSITY:
SHORT BUT SWEET   2003

At Oxford, June 26, 27, 28, 29, 2002. Drawn. The first first-class Varsity Match at Oxford since 1850 belonged to a Cambridge debutant, Stuart Moffat. In what promised to be his only first-class innings – he was about to become a rugby professional – he scored 169 in 193 balls, with 17 fours and five sixes. His *tour de force* carried Cambridge past the fixture's record total, 513 for six by Oxford in 1996; Cambridge's own best had been a mere 432 for nine in 1936.

> **Cambridge 604** (J. S. D. Moffat 169, A. Shankar 143, J. W. R. Parker 86,
> V. H. Kumar 64; J. W. M. Dalrymple 4-152);
> **Oxford 224** (N. Millar 51)
> **and 388-5** (Dalrymple 137, S. J. Hawinkels 78, J. R. S. Redmayne 75*).

Moffat went on to win four rugby caps for Scotland.

2006 – AFGHANS STUN MCC   Andrew Banks, 2007

Despite parts of Afghanistan vying with Iraq as the most dangerous place on Earth, 2006 was the most significant year to date for the country's cricketers. While fighting continued in the south and south-west of the country, most of the important cricketing events took place elsewhere, or indeed abroad. The national team was invited by MCC to play them in Mumbai in March, where Afghanistan scored a stunning 190-run victory over a team led by Mike Gatting. Afghanistan scored 361 runs in 45 overs; MCC were all out for 171. Mohammad Nabi ("the best player I've seen since the young Dexter"– Robin Marlar) made a brilliant 116 from only 44 balls, including 13 sixes; Gatting was out for a duck. After the match, the MCC invited two of the Afghan players, Nabi and Hamid Hassan, to join their Young Cricketers in the summer. And in June, the Afghan national team came to Britain for a seven-match tour, including three matches against county second elevens. They won all but one of the seven: Nabi made two more centuries.

2009 – THE HEIGHT OF FANTASY CRICKET   Lawrence Booth, 2010

To touch the heights is a cliché most sportsmen happily aspire to, yet few can have done so more literally than the Everest Test expedition, which in April 2009 beat the world record for high-altitude sport by playing a game of Twenty20 cricket on the side of the planet's tallest peak. The match, between teams named Hillary and Tensing after the first men to reach the summit in 1953, was the centrepiece of the expedition's money-raising endeavours for the Lord's Taverners and the Himalayan Trust UK, and it took place on the Gorak Shep plateau, 5,165 metres above sea level.

Following a gruelling nine-day hike – during which the teams delivered three bags of Lord's Taverners kit to local schools and led a training session, involving around 70 pupils, at one of them in Khumjung – a non-turf pitch was laid and battle commenced. Team Hillary, who could boast Alastair Cook as its honorary captain, defeated Team Tensing – skippered in spirit by Andrew Strauss – by 36 runs when Glen Lowis bowled his fellow New Zealander Mike Preston, and Charlie Campbell was presented with the match award by the Taverners' Shona Langridge.

MCC

The Marylebone Cricket Club has for long been acknowledged as the most famous in the world, although maybe the 1876 Almanack was overdoing things a little when MCC was allocated more than a third of its 224 pages. A hundred years later it was still going in to bat before the counties, although with a much reduced fixture-list the coverage amounted to little more than nine pages, and now it finds a place nearer the back of the book. MCC watchers will find modern undertones in complaints from the floor at the annual meeting in 1875 and the thousands of names on the waiting-list for membership in 1934.

1869 – MCC AND GROUND v OXFORD UNIVERSITY: WG's DEBUT   1870

At Oxford, May 13, 14, 1869. In this match Mr W. G. Grace not only made a remarkable first appearance as a member of the MCC, but, with his 117 runs, he commenced the most wonderful series of large first-class innings ever played by one man in one season for the old club. The first day's cricket closed with MCC having scored 159 for 6 wickets, Mr W. Grace (in No. 1) then not out 86. Next day, Mr Grace was eighth man out, the score at 203; Mr G.'s 117 being made by two sixes, one five, four fours, 11 threes, &c. This innings was the feature of the match; but there was a splendid catch made by Mr Fortescue, who ran 20 yards to the ball; an equally splendid throw out from cover-point by Capt. F. Watson (Mr Tylecote the victim), and an excellent catch at mid-on by Mr Case. The wickets were good, and weather dry, but rough and cold. The match was over at 5 o'clock on the second day, MCC the winners in one innings by 30 runs. Wootton bowled 63 overs (36 maidens) for 67 runs, one wide, and 12 wickets – eight bowled.

Oxford University 75 (G. Wootton 5-25, Mr W. G. Grace 5-49)
and 124 (Wootton 7-42);
MCC and Ground 229 (Grace 117; Mr B. Pauncefote 5-43).

1875 – MEMBER DECRIES "RUBBISHY" FIXTURE-LIST 1876

Discussion upon the report being invited by the Chair, Mr Willoughby rose to make his annual onslaught on the accounts. The learned gentleman severely criticised the items of expenditure on the Embankment and the Tavern, expressing his belief that the members had not received much additional convenience. After various other strictures, he drew attention to the match list, which he derided as "rubbishy"; the members could play in better matches elsewhere. As to the professional players, it was also easy to explain their reluctance to play at Lord's, where they are worse treated and less liberally paid than on any other ground. He objected strongly to the introduction of the new game of lawn tennis at Lord's Ground, and concluded with a few words of advice to the secretary, that if he wished to persuade the members to take a more active part in the game, a little more politeness on his part would conduce to that desired object.

Mr Heathcote rose to reply with some warmth to the severe strictures passed by Mr Willoughby on the report. As to the introduction of lawn tennis, as he had personally undertaken, with the sub-committee, to revise the rules, he could only say that he considered the game an excellent introduction to and substitute for tennis proper. It was an athletic game, and likely to be popular; and as a kindred game to cricket, as an open-air pursuit, he was strongly in favour of a portion of the ground being set apart for it, on such conditions and restrictions as the committee thought proper.

The secretary declined to reply seriatim to Mr Willoughby, but he could not rest under the imputation of want of courtesy to the members, or of being considered a party to any illiberal treatment of the players. If, in the heat of the day, he had ever offended a member, he was heartily sorry for it; but he at once disclaimed any intention to be uncourteous, and he trusted that the members would believe him to be only actuated by zeal in their behalf.

1877 – PRESIDENT GETS HIS DATES MUDDLED 1878

After the usual loyal toasts the president [Lord Londesborough] proposed "Cricket, and success to the MCC." After stating the pleasure he had experienced during his year of office, and expressing his thanks for the assistance he had received from the committee in the performance of his duties, the noble lord said that he had great satisfaction in proposing the Duke of Beaufort as his successor in office, and that he felt sure that no one would fill the post more worthily than His Grace. He said that he owed an apology to the Duke, who was absent from the dinner through having been misinformed by him as to the day.

1900 – EXPERIMENT RESULTS IN NET LOSS 1901

During the early part of the season of 1900 the MCC tried in their own club matches, as an experiment, a method of enclosing the ground with a net between two and three feet high, the idea being that the game would benefit if batsmen had to run out their hits. The plan agreed upon, however, was a clumsy one and met with no success. It was at first arranged that when the ball went over the netting the batsman should score three, and that when it was stopped by the net two runs should be added to those run. This method of scoring was after a few trials modified, but with no better result, and early in the season the whole notion was abandoned, the net, however, being kept up to mark the ordinary boundary. There was something to be said for the plan of having all the hits run out, and perhaps the experiment would have had a better chance if there had been no allowance of two runs when the ball was stopped by the netting. The plan, as adopted, placed brilliant hitting at a discount, and put such a premium on hits that just reached the ring that it deserved to fail.

HANDSOME MEMORIAL TO GRACE   1922

The committee of MCC, after consideration of several designs, have decided – as authorised by and at the general meeting of May 5, 1920 – that the Memorial of Dr W. G. Grace shall take the form of handsome iron gates at the Members' Entrance to Lord's, and these will be adapted to harmonise with certain improvements at that entrance which the committee feel it necessary to make.

The Gates being thus in public view, the committee feel that it is legitimate to offer to the friends and admirers of the late Dr Grace, and to cricket clubs, the opportunity of being connected with the Memorial by making donations to the extent of one half of the cost of the gates, the Club contributing the balance.

A tender has been accepted amounting to £2,268, and donations of any amount can be sent to the secretary of MCC, Lord's, St. John's Wood.

Should the amount received as above be in excess of one half of the cost, the committee will hand over such excess sum to the Cricketers' Fund Friendly Society.

1929 – ASHES FIND A RESTING-PLACE   1930

The late Earl of Darnley, to whom the urn containing the Ashes was presented, after England, under his captaincy, had defeated the Australians in Australia in 1883, bequeathed the urn to MCC. It is now placed in the large room of the Pavilion and is an interesting addition to the Club's collection of cricketing trophies.

LORD'S PROMOTES WATER CONSERVATION   Sir Francis Lacey, 1931

Changes are frequent in these days but it is doubtful if any place has changed more completely than Lord's Cricket Ground in the last 30 years, or any institution grown more in administration than the MCC which owns it. Taking the physical condition first, the only part remaining of the earliest history of Lord's is the match ground.

Its turf was brought from Dorset Square and North Bank over 100 years ago and, except for a complete system of drainage supplied about 20 years ago, the usual operations of upkeep, the addition of two tanks for conserving rainwater and the work of earthworms, it is the same. The tanks were made on the north and south sides to catch the rainwater falling on the large stands. The value of these additions was soon shown. They provide suitable water for preparing wickets and an opportunity of reducing water rates. It is almost imperative, especially in a large town, to have an independent water supply in case of drought.

1934 – MEMBERSHIP WAITING-LIST REDUCED 1935

The Committee have been considering the position of candidates awaiting election to the Club. In the Candidates' Books there are over 12,000 names, some of which date back to the year 1901. The committee cannot believe that this congestion is in the best interest of the Club. Experience, however, shows that many candidates when reached for election cannot be traced. During last winter it was decided to write to 3,066 candidates entered between the years 1901–1905 inclusive, in order to enable a more accurate estimate to be made. Of this number 1,962 could not be traced, 614 expressed a wish to take up membership when their names were reached, 176 did not desire membership, and 314 were deceased.

1935 – GROUND UNDER ATTACK 1936

The match ground has been attacked by a plague of leather jackets, the larvae of the crane fly, commonly known as Daddy-long-legs. They have destroyed the roots of the grass in places, and bare patches are to be seen especially in the centre of the ground. Every effort is being made to exterminate the grubs.

1940 – CLUB TREASURES MOVED FOR SAFE KEEPING 1941

The valuable collection of paintings in the Long Room has been removed to safer quarters, as also have the library, the drawings of distinguished cricketers in the Writing Room and the photographs of past presidents in the Committee Room.

1941 – ENEMY ACTION CAUSES WIDESPREAD DAMAGE 1942

Considerable damage has been done to Lord's by enemy action. Two bombs have fallen in the playing area, luckily off the centre of the ground, and incendiary bombs have hit the top of the Pavilion and the N. E. corner of the Grand Stand. Thanks to the efforts of our Fire Fighter Squad, helped by the Military and Fire Services, the fires caused by the incendiaries were quickly got under control.

The Secretary's house also was set on fire by incendiaries, and here again the Fire Squad did fine work.

Several houses belonging to the Club suffered seriously. One has been pulled down, and others rendered uninhabitable may have to be rebuilt. Happily there have been no casualties to any of the staff.

1977 – GLOUCESTERSHIRE v KENT (BENSON AND HEDGES CUP FINAL):
DISGRACEFUL BEHAVIOUR   1978

At Lord's, July 16, 1977. In the closing stages play was held up several times as fans invaded the pitch in premature excitement. When the presentation took place in front of the pavilion the fans had to be forced back by squads of police. Helmets went flying and a number of fans and police were injured. The MCC secretary, Mr Jack Bailey, criticised the Gloucestershire supporters. He said: "I thought the behaviour was disgraceful, but it's a problem endemic to society. How can you control a crowd that size? The only way is with fences, and it would be a sad day for cricket if fences ever went up to cage supporters in. The police did well but did not have a chance."

1978 – MCC GIVES WAY TO ENGLAND   1979

England's overseas tour to Pakistan and New Zealand was the first to dispense with MCC's name as its official designation: "During 1977 the Cricket Council accepted a proposal from the Test and County Cricket Board that in future touring teams should be described as 'England'. They felt that, with the present division of duties in English cricket, it might be misleading to retain MCC's name. The Club were gratified, however, to be asked for the agreement – which was freely given – to the retention of MCC's colours by overseas touring parties."

1987 – MCC v REST OF THE WORLD (MCC BICENTENARY MATCH):
SAD END   Graeme Wright, 1988

At Lord's, August 20, 21, 22, 24, 25, 1987. Drawn. Rain washed out the last day's play with the Rest of the World, 13 for one overnight, needing another 340 to win. It was a sad finish to a match which provided many marvellous moments while, off the field, friendships were renewed and nostalgia was indulged in as cricketers, young and old, came together to celebrate the 200th anniversary of MCC. In memory there will be cameos rather than a broad sweep of canvas, for in the modern sporting context this was a game rather than a contest. It may even have been appropriate that neither side won. In their performances and their sportsmanship, the finest players in the world had recognised that cricket should be the winner. Because of the spirit in which the match was played, MCC increased from £25,000 to £30,000 the prize money to be shared by the two teams in the event of a draw. The winners would have received £25,000 and the losers £12,000.

If it is futile to speculate who might have won, it is none the less fascinating to ponder. The pitch was perfect for batting, as it had been from the start. On the fourth day MCC had scored their 318 in 88 overs, indeed having to keep a tight rein on the innings at the end to stop it from bolting. And although the Rest had lost Gavaskar, bowled off stump in Marshall's first over that evening before bad light stopped play, they possessed batsmen of the calibre to challenge such a target. Moreover, Javed Miandad, troubled by a back strain, had been unable to express his unique talent in the first innings. The second would have provided an opportunity.

MCC 455-5 dec (M. W. Gatting 179, G. A. Gooch 117, C. E. B. Rice 59*, C. G. Greenidge 52)
and 318-6 dec (Greenidge 122, Gooch 70);
Rest of the World 421-7 dec (S. M. Gavaskar 188, Imran Khan 82) **and 13-1.**

1991 – INSUFFICIENT VOTES FOR WOMEN
1992

Much attention, particularly in the media, centred on the 204th annual general meeting of MCC, held at Lord's, on May 1, 1991, with the president, Lord Griffiths, in the chair. The reasons for this were two amendments, proposed by T. M. B. Rice and seconded by B. A. Johnston, which if passed would allow women as well as men to be eligible for membership and/or be elected as honorary life members. In the event the members present and those voting by post defeated the first amendment by 4,727 to 2,371. Although the second proposal, that women be eligible for election as honorary life members, received the support of 3,684 members, with 3,365 against, the majority of 319 fell short of the two-thirds majority required by the rules of the Club.

Little Wonder No. 130

Wisden 2004. Frizzell County Championship. There was also widespread alarm at the workings of the liberal rules on overseas player registration, which led to counties shipping cricketers in and out with a frequency that left team-mates and spectators equally bewildered. The situation was compounded by the growing popularity of the "EU player", mostly Australians or South Africans with close enough European ancestry to qualify for a British or other European Union passport, making it legally difficult or impossible for Lord's to restrict their employment.

1992 – LINEKER SCORES ONE AGAINST GERMANY   1993

The match against Germany [at Lord's] was widely reported because the MCC team included the England footballer Gary Lineker, who was out for one and was thus able to say that he always scored one against Germany.

1998 – MOTION PASSED AFTER SECOND MEETING   1999

MCC SPECIAL GENERAL MEETING (1)
On February 24, a resolution that women should be eligible for membership of MCC received 6,969 votes with 5,538 against. But those in favour represented only 55.7% of the members who voted, falling short of the required two-thirds majority.

MCC SPECIAL GENERAL MEETING (2)
On September 28, the resolution was passed by 9,394 to 4,072; 69.8% of the members voting were in favour – sufficient for it to be adopted. It was expected that MCC would name a few honorary female members shortly, with playing members being added in coming seasons; others would join the waiting list of over 9,000.

2005 – NEW SECRETARY BREAKS THE MOULD   Steven Lynch, 2006

For almost 200 years, the credentials to become secretary of MCC were pretty straightforward: public school was obligatory, Oxbridge helped, and a decent rank in the army often sealed the deal. But these days, even at Lord's, things are changing. The successor to the retiring Roger Knight (Dulwich College, Cambridge and various first-class counties) is Keith Bradshaw (New Town High School and the University of Tasmania).

With old-fashioned good-chappery out, MCC's headhunters had two criteria: business experience and a cricket background, and Bradshaw offered both. He is a partner at the accountants Deloittes, and played 25 times for Tasmania in the 1980s, scoring two Sheffield Shield centuries. So on October 1 – the day before his 43rd birthday – he will become only the 14th occupant since 1822 of the office with the best view in the world, overlooking Lord's from high in the pavilion.

Being an Australian turned out to be no bar. It might even have helped, given MCC's determination to look outwards: the search was a global one. But Bradshaw was never mentioned in the general speculation, and he was as surprised as anyone. "A friend of mine works for the recruitment company that handled the process in Australia, and he suggested I apply. At the initial interview, just about my first question was whether they were really serious about appointing someone from overseas, and they said if the best person for the job happened to be from overseas then that's what would happen. I thought that was very encouraging."

Far from being an MCC member, Bradshaw was paying only his second visit to Lord's when he popped in during the final round of interviews. This was not for the interview itself, which was held elsewhere, for secrecy's sake; he discreetly turned up and went on one of the public tours. His previous visit was in 1985: "I was playing in Lancashire, and some of us went down to watch a one-day international against Australia. We didn't have a lot of money, so we grabbed a few hours' sleep in the car before the game. I was in awe of the place. Still am."

2010 – MCC v DURHAM: TRADITION DESERTED
Derek Pringle, 2011

At Abu Dhabi, March 29, 30, 31, April 1, 2010. Durham won by 311 runs. By holding their match against the Champion County under floodlights in Abu Dhabi using a pink cricket ball, MCC shifted three pillars of the first-class game at a stroke. This was only the fifth time a pink ball had been used in first-class cricket (after four matches in the West Indies earlier in the year). It was a cerise Kookaburra, with green stitching, rather than a Dukes of an altogether lighter pink. MCC had borne the cost of development by scientists at Imperial College London of a ball that could be seen clearly by players and spectators (on TV and at the match) for at least 80 overs, and specifically under floodlights. Given the alarming decline in Test crowds in most countries, MCC were keen to see if the trend could be arrested by playing part of the match at night. Their close ties with the Abu Dhabi Cricket Club, owners of the impressive Sheikh Zayed Stadium, provided the perfect laboratory. But if they were hoping for feedback from the public, they were disappointed: no one was there bar a gaggle of about 60 Durham supporters, the parents of a few players and a handful of officials from various cricketing bodies.

The match itself did little to promote this type of pink ball. The first one was used for 90.3 overs, by which point much of the dye had worn off, and the second-division players representing MCC did not put up enough of a fight in their two innings to test subsequent balls rigorously. As in standard one-day "white ball" cricket, the twilight period compromised its visibility. Di Venuto, maker of the season's first hundred, reported problems with seeing the ball's green stitching through the air. "No disrespect to the spinners here, but against the top international spinners, who can turn the ball both ways, if you can't pick up the seam that is going to be pretty hard work," he said. The ICC, based in neighbouring Dubai, sent general manager Dave Richardson, and he too struck a cautious note. "MCC have been great in initiating trials around the world, but before we look at these projects we need to establish, from a scientific point of view, what makes sense," Richardson said. "The [pink] balls that have been developed so far are still a long way off being able to last 80 overs. They just get too dirty. The beauty of the red ball is that it keeps its colour even when it's old."

Durham 459-9 dec (K. J. Coetzer 172, M. J. Di Venuto 131, B. A. Stokes 51; D. J. Malan 4-20)
and 228-6 dec (C. D. Thorp 79*, Coetzer 52*, P. Mustard 50);
MCC 162 (S. G. Borthwick 4-27) **and 214** (T. J. Murtagh 55*; Borthwick 4-57, I. D. Blackwell 4-70).

WOMEN

While *Wisden* waxed lyrical over "brilliantly attired ladies" watching the fashionable matches at Lord's and Canterbury in the 1870s, recorded the abandonment of a Gloucestershire match in 1884 after the death of the Grace brothers' mother, and accorded a brief obituary to WG's wife in 1931, it was another seven years before it reported on women playing the game. Since then women have played at Lord's, beaten the men to staging the first World Cup and Twenty20 international, and played alongside boys in school first elevens, and a woman cricketer has achieved the ultimate personal accolade with Claire Taylor's naming as one of the Five Cricketers of the Year in 2009 (see page 138).

1937 – AUSTRALIA'S RETURN VISIT OPENS NEW CHAPTER   1938

If, ten years ago, anyone had suggested that Test matches between women cricketers would take place in England, and that one day's play in such a game would attract 5,000 spectators, the idea would have been laughed to scorn. Yet this ideal of women cricketers was realised in 1937 when people of the Midlands and elsewhere flocked to Northampton to witness the opening of the first Test match in England between women's teams representing England and Australia.

Pioneers: Hazel Pritchard at the wicket during her innings of 87 for Australia in the First Test at Northampton. The slip fielder offers an unusal pose

Important occasion as was June 12 last summer, the historian must state a date shortly after Christmas in 1934 as the commencement of women's international cricket. On December 28 in that year England met Australia in a women's Test match, the game taking place at Brisbane, Australia, and ending in victory for England by nine wickets. Thus last year's visit of the Australian side completed a chapter in the development of women's cricket.

For the success of this phase of the game, the Women's Cricket Association has been largely responsible. Founded in 1926, the WCA, besides organising the tours, has helped to form clubs and county associations and has set up a complete organisation for the furtherance of women's cricket.

Women play under the MCC Laws of Cricket with the exception of that relating to the ball. For women's cricket in England the weight of the ball varies between $4^{15}/_{16}$ ounces and $5^{1}/_{16}$ ounces, compared with the MCC specification of not less than $5\frac{1}{2}$ ounces and not more than $5\frac{3}{4}$ ounces. In no other respect does the material used for women's cricket differ from that for men. Of course women employ bats, pads and gloves of suitable weight. There is a regulation mode of dress in white.

1969 – SMALL IN STATURE BUT DOUBLY LARGE IN ACHIEVEMENT

Netta Rheinberg, 1970

Women have played a far more important part in the development of cricket than many people realise. W. G. Grace and his brothers learnt the technicalities of the game from their mother, the only woman who has appeared in Wisden's *list of Births and Deaths. Mrs Foster inspired her seven sons at a very early age, and long before most of them played with such distinction for Worcestershire. Here tribute is paid to Enid Bakewell. She achieved the wonderful feat of scoring over 1,000 runs and taking more than 100 wickets for the England Women's team on their 1968-69 tour of Australia and New Zealand.*

Mrs Enid Bakewell (née Turton) cannot remember when she first took up a bat, but the game of cricket attracted her at an early age and in 1950, when she was nine years old, she joined the local boys playing on a small field close to her home as, in her own words, "there were too few girls available". She was the only child of a non-cricketing family, but her parents encouraged her enthusiasm, purchasing and supplying her with all her gear. At her primary school at Newstead, Enid was soon better at cricket than the boys, and when at Brincliffe County Grammar School, Nottingham, the boys used to borrow her gear.

At 14 Enid had already graduated from her club, Notts Casuals WCC, to her county team. In those days she was a quiet, steady, right-hand opening bat, concentrating on staying at the wicket. The lessons of concentration and watchfulness learnt in those early years provided a solid basis for the future, as she found later, when the opportunity arose, that she was not only able to stay at the wicket, but also to score easily.

Enid entered Dartford College of Physical Education, graduating in 1959, the same year in which she was chosen to tour Holland with the WCA team of young and promising players. It was only later that she began to think about her left-arm slow bowling, modelling it on that of Tony Lock, even to the extent of taking the same number of paces in the same run-up round the umpire.

In 1963 Enid's name was among the possibles for Test selection against Australia then touring England. She failed, however, to gain a place, and in 1966 when the New Zealanders toured England she had married and was having a baby. The recent tour, therefore, provided Mrs Bakewell with her first Test appearance and her first opportunity to do battle with Australian and New Zealand cricketers; the rest of the story is one of consistent and amazing success.

Slight of build and small in stature, Enid has been described as diminutive and a tiny blonde. Although she is small, she is athletically built and gives an impression of freshness, alertness and quickwittedness, following many previous cricketers of less than average build in nimbleness of footwork and quick reflex action. Enid's record on the tour of 1,031 runs and 118 wickets is now history. On three occasions, once in Australia and twice in New Zealand, she took eight wickets in an innings, and on nine other occasions five or more. On her first Test appearance against Australia she opened the innings with a maiden century (113), and also as opening batsman scored two consecutive Test centuries against New Zealand in the first innings of the First and Second Tests (124 and 114). She scored six half-centuries on the whole tour, and took ten catches, though ironically enough she dropped an easy chance at a vital stage in the Second Test against Australia. This proved to be the only time the pendulum swung the other way for her.

The consistency of her performances caused her opponents to respect her from the start, and the opposing bowlers and batsmen both suffered from the reputation which she built up. Headlines in the Australian and New Zealand press reflected her prowess. "English girl does a Sobers," stated an Adelaide newspaper reporting her top-score of 59 against Victoria, followed by her skittling of seven batsmen for 28. The Second Test match in New Zealand, won by England by seven wickets, was called Bakewell's match. Her achievements were outstanding. She scored 114 and took four for 68 in the first innings, followed by 66 not out and five for 56 in the second innings. Fittingly, amid much excitement, she also scored the single a bare four minutes before the end to give England their victory, the first win against New Zealand since 1954. After this performance Enid began to be rated as the world's best woman all-rounder.

BATTING

	Played	Inns.	Not Out	Highest Score	Total Runs	Average
Complete Tour	20	29	3	124	1,031	39.6

BOWLING

	Overs	Maidens	Runs	Wickets	Average
Complete Tour	563.7	207	1,153	118	9.7

1973 – ENGLAND WIN CRICKET'S FIRST WORLD CUP
Netta Rheinberg, 1974

In 1777 the Third Duke of Dorset watched the Countess of Derby's XI play a Ladies' Invitation team at The Oaks in Surrey. He wrote afterwards: "What is human life but a game of cricket? And if so, why should not the ladies play it as well as we?" Ever since those days the ladies have been proving his point and certainly, nearly 200 years later, the staging by women cricketers in 1973 of the first-ever World Cup competition has shown beyond a doubt that, thin on the ground as we women cricketers are, we are still not afraid of trying out something new and not lacking in enterprise.

The whole ambitious project of the World Cup competition would not have been possible without the financial generosity and support of our patron, Jack Hayward. The two West Indian teams were government-helped, members of the Australian and New Zealand teams paid their own way to and from this country, and the WCA also footed the bill for a great deal.

One of the most memorable receptions was that given to all the teams by the prime minister at No. 10 Downing Street. Mr Heath, in a short informal speech of welcome, referred to Lady Baldwin, wife of the former prime minister and a cricketer of some repute. She was a member of the White Heather Women's Cricket Club, and she called a committee meeting of the club at No. 10 during the General Strike of 1926.

The final needle match at Edgbaston between England and Australia proved to be of the highest standard and quality, producing some of the best cricket within living memory. England, having won the toss, batted with no sign at all of any tension. Enid Bakewell (118) scored fluently and looked as relaxed as if she had been on the beach. Admittedly she was served a rather tasty diet of all sorts of bowling, which she digested with relish. Her example inspired the team and she received excellent support from Lynne Thomas (40), Rachael Flint (64) and Chris Watmough (32*). Those who watched the morning's performance will not easily forget the sparkle of the game in the excellent setting of Edgbaston and under a cloudless sky. During the afternoon, when the Australians' turn came to bat, Princess Anne arrived to watch and stayed to present the cup at the end. After England's batting, Australia's performance came as something of an anticlimax and they never succeeded in mastering the situation. The fielding of both teams was a joy to watch and especially for England, Jill Cruwys' throwing in from the deep, which would put many county players to shame.

At Edgbaston, July 28:
England 273-3 (E. Bakewell 118, R. Heyhoe-Flint 64, D. L. Thomas 40)
beat Australia 187-9 (J. Potter 57, B. Wilson 41, E. J. Bray 40) by 92 runs.

1976 – LORD'S FINALLY FALLS TO THE LADIES

Netta Rheinberg, 1977

The most memorable event in a Golden Jubilee season packed with cricket as well as social functions was the falling, to women cricketers, of the last stronghold of cricket, Lord's, and with the blessing of the MCC and amidst a considerable flurry from the press, England played Australia on Wednesday, August 4, in a 60-over match and history was made. Fate had also played a certain part as this match, originally scheduled for Sunbury, was moved to Lord's when Middlesex failed to reach the Gillette Cup quarter-final. There was a good crowd which swelled during the day, many spectators coming from a distance to be present at this unique event on a flawless summer day. A centrally pitched wicket was provided and countless press, broadcasting and television personnel took an active interest.

The sight of Australia's opening pair emerging from the pavilion door and of their players sitting on the familiar dressing-room balcony heightened the atmosphere, and tension rose even more when Lorraine Hill, with 1,000 runs and five centuries to her credit on the tour, lost her wicket in the first over. This prompt success on England's part certainly affected the final outcome. Australia seemed overconscious of the fact that they were playing in the hallowed atmosphere of the most famous ground in the world, and their usual batting liveliness was lacking.

England celebrated the day fittingly with an eight-wicket victory, but not before the Australians had staged a partial batting recovery after a shaky start. Sharon Tredrea, their opening bowler, and Wendy Hills entertained an enthusiastic crowd to some lively batting, aided later by Marie Lutschini, their star spin bowler, at No. 10. England, set 161 to get, won in the 56th over. Chris Watmough provided a first-class display and was well partnered by a quieter than usual Rachael Flint, visibly feeling her responsibility as captain. Despite winning this match, England forfeited the St Ivel Jug, Australia having achieved the faster scoring-rate in the combined Canterbury and Lord's limited-over matches.

The scene in the Long Room afterwards was one to be remembered. Many spectators, most of them women, stood there to watch the president of the MCC, Mr C. G. A. Paris, present the trophy to Australia and players of both teams received from the sponsors a specially manufactured blue cricket ball in commemoration of the historic occasion.

Australia Women 161 (59.4 overs) (S. A. Tredrea 54);
England Women 162-2 (56.2 overs) (E. Bakewell 50, C. J. Watmough 50*).

Gloucestershire v Northamptonshire. At Bristol, May 12, 13, 14, 15, 2004. Unsettled by the wet run-ups and their effect on his rhythm, Gloucestershire's new Pakistan pace bowler Shabbir Ahmed first switched ends and then, with four balls of his fifth over left, refused to continue. Following discussions, the umpires decided he was "incapacitated" which, under Law 22.7, allows another bowler to finish the over. No one could recall a similar replacement for reasons other than injury.

Little Wonder No. 131

1977 – SPARKS FLY OVER FLINT'S OMISSION   Netta Rheinberg, 1978

The omission of Rachael Flint from the team [for the second World Cup in India] and her replacement as captain of England by Mary Pilling could be described as the sensation of 1977, and such was the extensive impact of these decisions on both the public and the membership that an extraordinary general meeting of the Women's Cricket Association was called to discuss and vote on the way in which this matter was dealt with. At the end of a well-attended meeting the majority decided that the situation had indeed been mishandled, although it was agreed that, in a democratic association, selectors' decisions must be accepted as final. Furthermore the officers of the WCA had acknowledged the great service that Mrs Flint had given to women's cricket in the last 11 years; and there the matter rests for the time being.

1983 – AUSTRALIAN BASTION BREACHED 1984

Women are to be admitted as full members of the Melbourne Cricket Club. A postal ballot of the 19,800 present members resulted in a 2–1 majority in favour of female admission. With a waiting list already in excess of 50,000, it has been calculated that the first woman is unlikely to become a member for 26 years, without the introduction of some form of associate membership.

1986 – JUBILEE MARKED WITH GAMBLING AND DRINKING Netta Rheinberg, 1987

The Women's Cricket Association celebrated its Diamond Jubilee Year with a Festival match on June 8 which commemorated the first recorded women's cricket match in 1745. Then, at Gosden Common in Surrey, the "maids of Hambleton" beat the "maids of Bramley" by eight notches. The Festival match was played on the same site, by courtesy of the Bramley Cricket Club, and as far as possible in the same atmosphere. Sheep cropped the pitch, a notcher scored, and the game was accompanied by gambling and drinking.

ROEDEAN PROMPT EDITORIAL DILEMMA Preface, 1991

Prompted perhaps by Rachael Heyhoe-Flint's application for membership of MCC, Roedean School submitted their averages for the season, pointing out quite correctly that there was an absence of girls' schools in the section. Their letter arriving two months after the closing date, an editorial dilemma was postponed for a year.

Preface, 1992

Readers will notice a change in the format of the schools section [with] the inclusion of two girls' elevens – Denstone and Roedean.

WOMEN TAKE UP SENIOR POSITIONS
Teresa McLean, 1992

England is the only country where first-class women's games are umpired by women, without payment. Women also umpire a few men's games in the Lancashire League, and in local village matches, as I know from nerve-wracking personal experience. The present, outstanding chairman of the Association of Cricket Umpires is a woman, Sheila Hill.

The last decade has seen the emergence of a new breed of cricket career woman, driven by different motives from Miss Hill, not interested in playing or in working without due payment. Derbyshire, Kent, Sussex and Nottinghamshire county clubs have women physiotherapists, chosen from the big female majority of physio students. Sheila Ball has been the physiotherapist at Trent Bridge since 1985 and has been well treated everywhere, after initial problems gaining entry into the Lord's Pavilion with her team for the 1985 NatWest final. Notts are used to female physios; they started using them back in 1975, and they are proud of the excellent work Sheila does for them.

Women administrators in the upper echelons of men's cricket tend to provoke more and ease. The game's administration is growing into a common cause of assorted secretaries, executives and managers, in which several women now occupy senior positions at several counties. Rose FitzGibbon was made the assistant secretary at Old Trafford in 1978, after starting as the principal private secretary. She is now the cricket secretary, which means, she told me with the weary humour of one who has to survive in this warren of titles, that one of her duties is to "deputise for the chief executive". She says she is accepted by everyone at the club, though it has taken time and she still feels that she, like most women in cricket administration, has been given prominence but not proper recognition.

Lancashire's members have traditionally been a conservative lot, but the debate at the AGM on December 9, 1989, on whether to admit women to full membership, won the club a brief flurry of improbable notoriety. The motion proposing that women be admitted was passed after one of the members, "Mr Keith Hull (otherwise known as Stephanie Lloyd) advised the meeting that by a legal technicality he was the club's first full female Member". He had had a sex-change operation and so the club already had a woman member. After some noble discussion – including Mr John Treveloni's threat to alter his will if women were admitted to membership, and the Rev. Malcolm Lorimer's support for "the preservation of tradition where it was worth preserving… If the Church of England could move towards women priests, if Eastern Europe could make changes as had been seen in recent weeks, then Lancashire CCC could also change" – full membership for women was finally accepted by the necessary two-thirds majority.

1993 – CONNOR BREAKS NEW GROUND AT BRIGHTON
Schools Cricket, 1994

Clare Connor became the first girl to command a regular place in the First XI.

O   M   R   W   Best   Avge
Bowling – Miss C. J. Connor 89–11–304–17–4/33–17.88.

1998 – DISQUIET AS WOMEN JOIN FORCES WITH MEN   1999

Just short of its 72nd birthday, the Women's Cricket Association was disbanded in 1998. At the end of March, an extraordinary general meeting voted to amalgamate with the England and Wales Cricket Board; an executive committee meeting in June signed a sale and purchase agreement to complete the formalities. The move was not unopposed. Members expressed reservations over the speed of events, and complained of a lack of attention to the finer details. Just before the vote, there was further disquiet when a former ECB receptionist, Theresa Harrild, won an undefended and much-publicised case against the Board at an industrial tribunal. Barbara Daniels, the WCA's executive director, described the case and subsequent publicity about the Board's treatment of women staff as "unhelpful".

Daniels and chair Sharon Bayton were the main driving force behind the amalgamation, and in the end they convinced the membership that there was no alternative but to join forces with the men. The Sports Council was not prepared to fund two governing bodies for cricket, and the WCA simply lacked the numbers and the financial clout to advance itself on or off the field.

1998 – FRENCH STAND THEIR GROUND OVER CINDY   Cricket Round the World, 1999

In July, 15-year-old leg-spinner Cindy Paquin was picked in the French squad for the European Colts Championship. Despite the much-publicised UK example of Laura Harper (who turned down a place in the West of England boys' team to play in the women's County Championship instead) and the absence of any rules concerning gender, the European Cricket Council told France that, because of the risk of physical injury, female players would not be welcome. After referring the matter to the sports minister, France refused to alter their squad, and were barred from the tournament.

2004 – SIXTH AND BEST FOR BALUCH   2005

At Karachi, March 15, 16, 17, 18, 2004. Drawn. This was Pakistan's first Test since they visited Ireland in 2000, and West Indies' first since they toured England in 1979. Kiran Baluch's 242 was the sixth and highest double-hundred in women's Tests; it lasted 584 minutes and 488 balls and included 38 fours, and she put on 241 for the first wicket with 16-year-old Sajjida Shah. Pakistan captain and leg-spinner Shaiza Khan took a first-innings hat-trick, only the second in women's Test cricket after Betty Wilson for Australia v England in 1957-58, to help enforce the follow-on. She finished with 13 wickets, beating the previous women's record of 11 in a Test. Nadine George scored West Indies' first Test century.

Pakistan 426-7 dec (Kiran Baluch 242, Sajjida Shah 98; F. Cummings 4-54) and 58-2;
West Indies 147 (Shaiza Khan 7-59)
and 440 (N. A. J. George 118, J. Robinson 57, S. J. Power 57, V. M. Felicien 55; Shaiza Khan 6-167).

2004 – Innovators Fail To Attract Crowds   Sarah Potter, 2005

Hove, with its striped deckchairs and whirling seagulls, is an incongruous outpost for anything radical. That does not explain truthfully why only 500 spectators turned out to watch the world's first Twenty20 international, however: it was because it was played by women. England and New Zealand were rightly proud to have made history. Nail-biters did not have to chew their quicks as the tourists won by nine runs, but it was an innovative start to the tour.

New Zealand Women 131-8 (20 overs) (R. J. Rolls 39; R. A. Birch 4-27);
England Women 122-7 (20 overs) (S. C. Taylor 43, C. M. Edwards 34; A. L. Mason 3-27).

2005 – History-Makers Join The Bus Tour   Sarah Potter, 2006

England's women had waited even longer than the men to beat Australia in a Test series. Mary Duggan had led them to their last series win at The Oval in July 1963, when the country was more interested in the Profumo Affair. Of the 22 Tests since then, they had won just one, at Adelaide in December 1984 – Australia's last Test defeat by any side. But in 2005, England held out to save the First Test at Hove and then overturned the odds to beat Australia at Worcester.

Their triumph was celebrated alongside the men's: Clare Connor and her side were presented with the Ashes – the first time England had ever held the trophy, which was created only during the 1998 series – during the men's final Test, and given a lap of honour round The Oval. A few days later, they rode in their own open-top bus right behind Michael Vaughan's men, cheered on by the crowds filling every vantage point en route to the rally in Trafalgar Square. In the New Year's honours, Connor, like Vaughan, was awarded the OBE.

There was drama aplenty in the two Tests. Holly Colvin became England's youngest-ever Test player, a month short of her 16th birthday, and took two wickets with successive balls at Hove, where Arran Brindle saved the team with a last-day hundred. And at Worcester, 20-year-old Katherine Brunt scored a maiden fifty and took nine wickets to humble Australia. At the start of the summer, Brunt said her role model was Darren Gough, whose older brother, Adrian, has captained her in Barnsley's Second XI. By the end of August, clutching her Player of the Series award, her allegiance was torn: "I want to be a baby Freddie Flintoff now," she said.

SCHOOLS CRICKET

Under the pre-1938 arrangement of the Almanack into two parts, schools cricket received a prominent place, with a review in the first part (which one year ran to 30 pages) and reports, scores and averages in the second (88 pages in that same edition). Even in 2013 it commanded almost 40 pages, but around a third of county cricketers were products of independent schools. One of the small joys of the schools section is to find the names of players who have gone on to achieve greater things in cricket or other fields and there is now even a *Wisden* Schools Cricketer of the Year award, inaugurated in 2007, the first three winners of which had all played for England by 2011.

LET DOWN BY FRY

Sydney Pardon (Editor), 1895

I had been promised to again have Mr C. B. Fry's estimate of the public school cricket of the season. However, that famous athlete failed me, and it was too late to get a substitute for him.

1897 – HIGHBURY PARK SCHOOL v ISLINGTON HIGH SCHOOL 1898

At Muswell Hill, June 12, 1897. The score of this match is published as a curiosity, the losers being dismissed without getting a run and second innings for five, a total of 21 proving sufficient to win the game by an innings and 16 runs. Wiggins took 11 wickets for two runs.

Highbury Park School 21; Islington High School 0 and 5.

England v Australia (NatWest Series)**.** At Chester-le-Street, June 23, 2005. Gough taunted Watson with ghost impressions after reports that alleged ghostly sightings at the Lumley Castle Hotel had scared Watson so badly that he moved into Lee's room.

Little Wonder No. 132

EARLY AND CONVENIENT PLEASE!

W. J. Ford, 1899

School secretaries have some highly original notions as the way purely clerical work should be done: hence, with a view to future *Wisdens*, I am going to preach a mild homily to those hard-worked officials. First of all, please be prompt! Please try to make the requested "earliest convenience" something under three weeks! This year, no less that ten schools (out of 35) have extended "earliest convenience" to this period, leaving my moral system in a state of profane disrupture. Secondly, when forms are sent you to be filled up, please fill them up, and don't paste clippings from school magazines all over them at various angles; it takes less time, believe me, to copy out the names and figures required than to hunt up scissors and paste; further, scissors and paste are essentially the panoply of the hapless men who edit weekly "comics". Thirdly, please keep your scorebooks! I know the malignant way in which a scorebook will secrete itself; it will hide among fair copies of Greek Prose, or stale impositions. It loves the bottoms and backs of cupboards, and the dusty tops of bookshelves; hence it must be treated as copies of the Bible were treated in the brave days of old, and be chained fast to a fixture. In some well-regulated schools the old scorebooks are regarded as important archives and have a shelf to themselves in the school library, and as this is an excellent plan, from both a sentimental and a practical point of view, I commend it with much heartiness to all schools with who secretaries I have dealt, am dealing, or may in the dusky future have to deal.

Thank You For Taking Notice
W. J. Ford, 1900

I must thank the school secretaries and captains for the promptitude with which my circular was, as a general rule, answered. To only one school had I to write a third application, to only five a second; only one captain filled up his paper in pencil, while scorebooks seem to have been so readily accessible that my homily in last year's *Wisden* must have been read, marked, learned and inwardly digested.

1904 – A Summer Filled With Records
Capt. W. J. Seton, 1905

The season of 1904 was undoubtedly the season of records for public school cricket. For a schoolboy to take part in county cricket throughout August, and head the first-class bowling analyses with a genuine analysis for nearly 50 wickets, as J. N. Crawford did, is a record that will probably stand even longer than Sir Emilius Bayley-Laurie's score for the Eton and Harrow match, now deprived of its pride of place after a reign of 63 years. Then the record number of runs made by a player in public school cricket no longer stands to the credit of Raphael, but is placed against the name of Tebbutt of Leys School, as is also a list of eight centuries in one season, a number that will probably not be exceeded until the squaring of the circle is accomplished, or an equally improbable event occurs – the advent of a second WG.

1921 – ETON v WINCHESTER: Guise's 278
1922

At Eton, June 24, 25, 1921. The wonderful batting of J. L. Guise, who, when Winchester were in an almost hopeless position, played an innings of 278 – the highest individual score ever made in this series of matches – dwarfed everything else in the game. That Winchester would make such a splendid recovery, after being dismissed in their first innings in 65 minutes for the paltry score of 57 and going in against a balance of 198, did not seem possible, but Guise played like a veteran. Nursing the bowling very cleverly, he hit finely all round the wicket, his figures including 45 fours. His play on the on side was especially good. Thanks to his brilliant effort Winchester set Eton 184 to get to win. Eton, however, made light of this task, obtaining the runs for the loss of only two men, and winning by eight wickets. R. Aird batted superbly, receiving useful assistance from P. E. Lawrie, who also played fine cricket in Eton's first innings.

PRESSING NEED FOR MORE MODERATE REPORTING
H. S. Altham, 1924

There is a growing feeling in a good many quarters that school cricket, and indeed school athletics generally, is suffering from an excess of publicity. On the principle that the reading public really determine the contents of any paper, this publicity is perhaps surprising, but it is none the less a fact. Eton and Harrow, and to a less degree Winchester and such schools as appear at Lord's, have been more or less accustomed to having their prospects discussed, their performances criticised and their personalities described: but of recent years the process has extended to practically every school of athletic standing: few school cricketers of outstanding performance escape altogether the ever-widening arc of its limelight, and close-ups, whether by camera or pen, seem to meet a growing demand in not merely the purely sporting papers.

Cricket fields for the most part have no doors, and moreover most schools are perfectly ready, and indeed anxious to have the scores of their matches recorded, and on big occasions at least the play and players described, for the sake of a widely scattered, but still intensely interested, circle of old boys. No amount of publishing of scoresheets can do much harm: figures, more or less, tell cricket truth, and the elation of seeing three of them opposite one's name in print generally provokes Nemesis to provide a salutary and effective antidote. The crux lies in the match reports, and in the periodical reviews of contemporary school performances which are becoming increasingly common in the London press. I am not suggesting for a moment that the writers – many of them players of distinguished experience – have not the best interests of the game, and of amateur cricket in particular, at heart: it is their occasional methods that seem open to question. A school cricketer, worth his salt, should be able to stand both praise and criticism, but it is very important that both should be judicious, and based upon unmistakable evidence, and there does seem to be a growing tendency to write up school cricketers into a class to which they do not yet belong, to use superlatives when positives are adequate, to compare a boy to some great cricketer on the strength of a single innings or even of one or two strokes. As for the criticism, it will, I think, be generally agreed that except for slackness or breaches of the spirit of the game, this should be temperate and should err on the side of generosity, but what is more important is that the critic should be very chary indeed of advocating change in method unless he is quite sure of his ground.

1944 – LORD'S XI v PUBLIC SCHOOLS: BOYS' BRAVERY APPLAUDED
1945

At Lord's, August 11, 12, 1944. During the first innings a flying bomb exploded less than 200 yards from Lord's. Pieces of soil fell on the pitch, but the players, particularly the boys, most of whom had never experienced such an attack, stopped only while the bomb was seen hurtling down. The break in the game lasted little more than half a minute, and the spectators, some of whom had thrown themselves flat under seats for protection, showed their appreciation of the boys' pluck with hearty handclaps.

1946 – MAY DROPPED BECAUSE OF HIS FIELDING
E. M. Wellings, 1947

Good, too, was May, of Charterhouse. At the age of 15 the previous year he played for the Public School team. In 1946 he was left out, although he made top score for the Southern Schools. The reason is easily found. His batting had not gone back, but his fielding was anything but up to the standard of his batting, and he was in effect made an example to all school players, who need to learn that cricket consists of more than batting and bowling.

Surrey in 1950: Besides fielding with marked ability, P. B. H. May, the Cambridge Blue, lent strength to the batting from mid-July onwards.

1957 – CLIFTON v TONBRIDGE: IVORY TOWERS
1958

At Lord's, July 29, 30, 1957. Clifton Batting: (1st innings) J. M. Cleese not out 13, (2nd innings) not out 13. Clifton Bowling: (2nd innings) Cleese 9-2-28-0.

1960 – BOYS CAN TEACH SENIORS A LESSON
E. M. Wellings, 1961

After watching so much first-class cricket, in which the object of far too many players seemed to be the expenditure of time by devious devices and without commensurate expenditure of energy, I found the cricket of the boys at Lord's exhilarating. The standard of play was good, but the lingering memory is of young players who got on with the game and so gave proof that they had been brought up in the right way by their games masters and coaches. It was a tonic to see bowlers moving briskly back to their mark in advance of the ball's return from the field. It was strange, and wonderfully refreshing, to see no bowler loitering in the middle of the pitch, frittering away valuable playing time, while the ball was being relayed exasperatingly from fielder to fielder. These boys have obviously been taught that a man's playing life is not long enough to allow him to waste time on the field, and I hope they will carry that lesson into higher realms of the game. Senior cricket badly needs to be taught the same lesson.

1967 – OVER-RATES SHOW WORRYING DECLINE — E. M. Wellings, 1968

Criticism is valid when applied to the over-rate of the boys. At Lord's in 1967 we had a match lasting the full day and producing 116.1 overs. Forty years earlier I played in a Lord's Schools v The Rest match reduced by rain on the first day to a single day. The overs bowled numbered 144.4 – 171 balls more than in 1967. The game has in fact slowed down by 4½ overs an hour, a drop of almost 20%, and it has virtually all happened in the past 15 years.

A brisk over-rate is the essential core of a cricket match. Even when we expected 22 overs an hour in Test cricket – England at Lord's in 1930 averaged 23 while Australia were scoring 729 for six, of which Bradman made 251 – cricket was described as a slow game. Now, when we are lucky to get 18 an hour, it has become too slow to maintain sufficient spectator interest to keep the first-class game financially prosperous.

1991 – FAILURE RATE OF 78 PER CENT — Graeme Wright (Editor), 1992

Much has been written in recent years about the decline of cricket in schools. This does not necessarily mean that the game is losing interested young players, however, for the responsibility for the development has moved to other areas, such as local clubs and the county associations. There are good young cricketers in England, and it was encouraging to see how well the England Under-19 players fought back to level the series against their Australian counterparts, after being drubbed in the first "Test" at Leicester.

In some ways I am less concerned about the state of cricket in schools than I am about the state of education there, if the replies for the Almanack's schools section is any indication. Some 78% of schools last year were unable to fill in the form correctly; in 32% of the forms returned, there were numerical errors; almost 7% of the schools made mistakes in spelling the names of their opponents. In some instances, what passed for handwriting was beyond even the skill of our typesetter. This is not a new phenomenon, but that should be a worry more than a consolation. Given the restriction on space in the Almanack, I am tempted to include only those schools whose forms are 100% correct. This may smack of elitism, but as most of the schools are of the fee-paying variety, such a charge will carry little weight.

1993 – SCHOOLS PUT TEST MATCH IN SHADE — Christopher Martin-Jenkins, 1994

The really big cricket match in Colombo on March 13, 1993, attracted a crowd of 15,000. There was radio commentary all day long; most of the back-page space in Colombo's two newspapers was devoted to it. The build-up to the great event had been going on all week. President Premadasa was there on the first day, not so much because he was a cricket enthusiast as because this was the place for a politician to be seen. The match was staged on Sri Lanka's most famous ground, where Test cricket was first played. But this was not a Test match: it was the annual game between two of Colombo's largest schools, Royal College and St Thomas's. The final day of three in the 114th match between the two clashed with the opening day of the Test between Sri Lanka and England and, though cricket followers in other lands may find it hard to believe, it completely put the Test into the shade.

Tickets were more expensive, and in far greater demand, than those for a Test which ought to have been a rare treat for such a cricket-loving island, only the second Sri Lanka had ever played at home against England. I was told that all five Sri Lankan radio channels were carrying cricket commentaries on March 13, only one of them on the Test.

1997 – FAIR PLAY GIVES WAY TO FOUL   Andrew Longmore, 1998

Now that Eton v Harrow is no longer the great social occasion of an English summer, cricket between English public schools rarely gets much space in the national press. The 1997 match between Marlborough and Radley was different.

On a rain-hit day, Marlborough, who were put in to bat, spent 68.3 overs scoring 170, leaving Radley a mere 18 overs in reply. The Marlborough innings was marred by verbal abuse of the batsmen and a number of deliberate no-balls, while on the boundary tempers flared among the spectators. The Warden of Radley admitted that the match "was not played in an attractive atmosphere", and fixtures in major sports between these two historic schools were cancelled for the fore-seeable future.

This was not the only instance of bad sportsmanship to emerge from schools. In an Under-17 match in Kent, a boy spat at the wicketkeeper after being bowled and had to be forced into the opposition dressing-room at the end of play to apologise.

A match between two crack cricketing schools, Tonbridge of Kent and Grey High School from Port Elizabeth, South Africa, with both sides protecting unbeaten records, quickly degenerated from competitiveness into verbal intimi-dation, and highlighted a clash of prevailing sporting cultures. Tonbridge won, but only after an unpleasant afternoon. One of the umpires deemed the South Africans 80% responsible.

"Most schools will now play two or three overseas sides a season," Paul Taylor, the Tonbridge cricket master, said. "That has an influence on the boys. Grey were competitive to a degree our players had not seen before and one of our boys was drawn into that."

1997 – LORD WANDSWORTH COLLEGE: ALL-ROUNDER JONNY   1998

In an experienced side, boosted by a successful winter tour to South Africa, Jonny Wilkinson continued his outstanding form, although his rugby commitments with England Under-18 and Newcastle prevented him from playing in more than seven games. He left the school with 85 wickets to his name.

1999 – BEDFORD SCHOOL: COOK IN THE BOOKS   2000

Alastair Cook, aged 14, won a place in the side after scoring an undefeated 102 *against* the school; MCC had been a player short.

2004 – UPPINGHAM SCHOOL: FLYING HIGHER   2005

Harry Judd, who scored 252 runs last season, left Uppingham to become a full-time drummer in the pop group McFly. The summer ended well for the side, with four wins in the last five matches, but even better for Harry Judd: McFly topped the UK singles chart twice, with "Five Colours In Her Hair" and "Obviously".

Bangladesh v Australia 2005-06. The nastiest shock was reserved for security manager Reg Dickason during the First Test. There had been months of planning and checks, guarantees and pledges, assurances and reassurances from the Bangladesh board and government about the players' safety. Then Dickason spotted, on closed-circuit TV, a gunman in a black bandanna in the Fatullah crowd. He rushed towards him, heart in mouth, only to find that the man was a member of the government's Rapid Action Brigade, employed to protect the Australians. A keen cricket-lover, he was using the telescopic sight on his rifle to get a better view.

Little Wonder No. 133

2005 – A QUAINT SENSE OF CHIVALRY   Douglas Henderson, 2006

Shortly after the 2005 season ended, Robin Marlar, the new MCC president, caused a furore when he suggested that girls should not play with or against boys. His comments came barely three weeks after England's Ashes win had apparently brought cricket to a new generation with attitudes far removed from those long associated with the Lord's pavilion.

"It looks today as if MCC stands for Misogynists' Cricket Club," said a leader in *The Times*. "It is an unfortunate end to a scintillating summer of cricket."

Marlar's comments were given added topicality by the fact that Holly Colvin, who had already played for the once all-male Brighton College first team, had just broken into the England women's team, aged only 15.

Brighton College has often been an innovator in this field: Clare Connor was believed to have been the first girl to appear in a leading boys' team, in 1994. In 2005, Brighton played two girls against Wellington College: Colvin and wicketkeeper Sarah Taylor. Other schools picked girls too. Susie Rowe at Colfe's was second in their averages with 31.00, and Sophie Le Marchand was also second at King's, Worcester, with a very healthy 411 runs at 34.25. The success of these two is proof that girls are more than able to thrive in predominantly male first-team cricket.

Marlar's comments were apparently motivated by chivalry and a concern that a blow from a cricket ball on the chest could possibly lead to breast cancer. If so, this should mean that chest-protection becomes mandatory. John Spencer, the cricket master at Brighton (who started his first-class career at Sussex in 1969, the year after Marlar's ended), commended Marlar for "sensibly showing concern about girls being injured". But he insisted these risks were not a matter of gender: "I would never pick anyone who I feel may be set back or put at risk by an opposition's fast bowler, whether male or female," Spencer said. "In all cases the most important thing is to have the parents' permission. Robin has a rather quaint sense of chivalry which I don't think many girls would regard as necessary – both Taylor and Colvin are a lot tougher than many boys who have played for me."

2007 – Ripping Yarn Of Bad Losers
Douglas Henderson, 2008

Some masters also worry that a culture of bad behaviour is seeping down from the higher reaches of the game, though one, explaining why his Surrey school could not supply any averages, did not blame the professionals: "Our scorebook was ripped up by some unsporting opposition, after being beaten."

Obituaries

he cover of the 1867 Almanack flagged up a "Calendar of the Births and Deaths of nearly all the celebrated Players". At the back of the book was a seven-page listing arranged alphabetically. From these small beginnings it grew in the 1920s into a mighty section: on each page there were two columns of names and it still ran to more than 100 pages. As subsequent editors sought to reduce demands on space, it was steadily reduced; but "Births and Deaths" has remained a feature right through to the 150th edition, albeit recently merged with the register of Test cricketers.

Written obituaries took a little longer to appear. A panel with a heavy black border headed Deaths of Cricketers in the previous year was first published in 1870, but it contained only names, teams and date of death. There was the occasional written notice about some notable such as the proprietor himself, John Wisden (whom we have put in to bat first, at the head of an otherwise alphabetical arrangement) in 1885; but it was not until 1892 that the mere announcements came to be "supplemented by a short biographical notice". Short became longer for major figures in the game, and they might also receive special additional tributes. The term obituary was not adopted until the 1938 revamp.

Wisden has covered the passing of just about every notable and not so notable cricketer, even in 1994 publishing a section of supplementary obituaries which covered those who might have missed out – and even obituarising some players more than once. It has also written about those who had only a marginal contact with cricket but made their mark in other fields. Two of the oft-recorded examples of this type, Rupert Brooke (1916) and Samuel Beckett (1990), will be found here, together with many leading Test and county players and a host of other characters, some seemingly larger than life, who have been associated with the game – as well as a cat and some kings. The style of writing has, of course, changed over the years: no greater contrast can be found than by comparing the treatment of Edward Pooley in 1908 – "Of the faults of private character that marred Pooley's career... there is no need now to speak" – with the warts and all account of the flawed talent who was Peter Roebuck in 2012.

"THE LITTLE WONDER"   1885

JOHN WISDEN

Born at Brighton, September 5, 1826. Died April 5, 1884.

A splendid all-round cricketer in his day: a good bat, a fine field, and as a bowler unsurpassed. A quiet, unassuming, and thoroughly upright man.

A fast friend and a generous employer. Beloved by his intimates and employees, and respected by all with whom he came in contact.

As a given man in the North v South match of 1850, John Wisden performed the unrivalled feat in a first-class contest of clean-bowling the whole of his opponents in their second innings. As an instructor of our national game he was most successful, and during the time he was cricket tutor at Harrow the school team were never beaten by Eton.

In 1852, in conjunction with James Dean, he formed the United All-England Eleven, and in 1859, with George Parr, took a team of cricketers to Canada and the United States, and thus inaugurated a movement which has had a most important bearing on the prosperity of the game.

In 1855, in partnership with Frederick Lillywhite, he established the cricket outfitting business which for so many years was conducted by him personally, and which is now carried on by those who managed it for many years and enjoyed his fullest confidence. In 1857 he was appointed secretary to the Cricketers' Fund Friendly Society, and continued to act in that capacity until his death.

In 1864 he issued the first number of the *Cricketers' Almanack*, a very primitive production consisting of scores only, but which, thanks to the enthusiasm of subsequent editors, has now been accorded the title of "the most accurate and authentic record of the game" published.

John Wisden was one of the smallest of men who have become famous as cricketers, his height being but 5ft 4½in, and his weight in his prime being only seven stone. Owing to his diminutive size, and prowess as a cricketer, he earned the soubriquet of "the little wonder".

ORIGINATOR OF THE CHINAMAN   1987

ACHONG, ELLIS EDGAR ("PUSS"), died in Port-of-Spain, Trinidad, on August 29, 1986, aged 82. A left-arm spin bowler, he was the first cricketer of Chinese extraction to play Test cricket, appearing for West Indies in six matches against England and taking eight wickets at 47.25. Chosen to tour England in 1933, he played in all three Tests but with limited success, and in all first-class matches that season took 71 wickets. Essentially an orthodox slow left-armer, at Manchester he had Robins stumped by a ball which, bowled with a wrist-spinner's action, turned into the right-hander from the off and gave rise to the use in England of the word "chinaman" to describe such a delivery.

FORCEFUL HALF-CENTURY IN THE CORRIDORS OF POWER   1990

ALLEN, SIR GEORGE OSWALD BROWNING (GUBBY), CBE, TD, who died on November 29, 1989, aged 87, had a stronger influence on the welfare and development of cricket than anyone since Lord Harris over a period of more than 50 years. For his services to the game he was made CBE in 1974 and knighted in 1986. Sir George ("Gubby", as he was universally known) was born in Sydney on July 31, 1902. His father, believing firmly in the value of an English education, brought the family to England when he was six. A mere 27 years later he was elected to the committee of MCC.

By impressing his seniors with his strong views and a general interest in the game, he had quickly been recognised as good committee material, and by 1933 he was treading the corridors of power, familiarising himself with the inner workings of Lord's. He was ten years younger than the next-youngest member of the committee. He had been elected to the Middlesex committee in 1931.

After service in the Second World War, early on in an anti-aircraft battery and later as an intelligence officer, rising to the rank of lieutenant-colonel, Allen returned to Lord's fully aware that cricket needed revitalising. With the help of other like-minded spirits he was soon disturbing the peace. In 1949 Allen launched his campaign for action by proposing the election of famous retired professionals to honorary life membership of MCC – an imaginative and popular move. He became the driving force behind the formation of the MCC Youth Cricket Association and its related coaching scheme.

By now he was ready to assume the chairmanship of the Test selection committee, a post he held for seven momentous years from 1955 to 1961. Most of the selectors' deliberations in this period had a successful outcome. Some of their choices were inspired, notably Washbrook, Sheppard and Compton in the last three Tests in 1956 against Australia. The loss of the Ashes in 1958-59 and the failure to regain them in 1961 were major disappointments, but winning home series at the expense of West Indies, India, South Africa and New Zealand was ample compensation. Allen laid down one principle for selection: class before averages.

He was president of MCC in 1963-64, and in 1964 he became treasurer, holding this influential post for 12 years. As treasurer he had much to do with the setting up of the Cricket Council with its subordinate executive bodies, the Test and County Cricket Board and the National Cricket Association. During all this time he was England's representative on ICC.

Allen's deep knowledge and unique ability to advise on any aspect of cricket was based on his playing experience at the highest level, although he could never find the time to make either 1,000 runs or take 100 wickets in a season.

By 1921, his third year in the [Eton] XI, he was a genuinely quick bowler who could make useful runs, and he was chosen to play for Middlesex in two matches before going up to Cambridge. Going down after his second year, Allen remained a true amateur and played first-class cricket only when his work in the City permitted. He took trouble to keep himself fit by playing squash regularly and playing good-quality club cricket at weekends. That he was able to step up a gear and invariably make his mark was a tribute to his natural ability and dedication. He had a superb action with a rhythmical run-up and full follow-through, and it needed only a little fine tuning to be running smoothly.

In 1925 he made the first of his 11 first-class centuries, for the Gentlemen at The Oval. Selection for the Test Trial followed in 1926, but the sudden emergence of Larwood was to delay his first taste of Test cricket. In June 1929 he achieved his most spectacular analysis, ten for 40 at Lord's against the reigning champions, Lancashire, having been brought on as first change because he did not take the field until almost midday. He had been working earlier in the day. All but one of his ten wickets were taken after lunch, and his achievement remains unique in a county match at Lord's.

In 1930 his chance finally came against Australia at Lord's, but, with Australia amassing more than 700 on the plumbest of pitches, he conceded 115 runs, failed to take a wicket and did not play again in the series. He did, however, score 57 in the second innings, and the following year, going in at No. 9, he made 122 against New Zealand at Lord's, putting on 246 with Ames (137) for the eighth wicket.

Five for 14 in New Zealand's first innings at The Oval in the Second Test emphasised his potential as a Test player. Even so, Allen's selection for the 1932-33 tour of Australia was widely criticised, yet by normal, orthodox methods he played a leading part in regaining the Ashes, claiming 21 wickets at 28.23 apiece and more than once making useful runs.

The 1936 series against India saw him captain England to a 2–0 victory in the three Tests, his personal contribution being 20 wickets for an average of 16.50, and thus the greatest prize in cricket was his: the captaincy of MCC in Australia. England lost the 1936-37 series 2–3 after leading 2–0 against all the odds. Bad luck with the weather and Bradman's wonderful batting tipped the scales against Allen, and yet, by his efforts on and off the field, the proper relationship between the old antagonists was restored and goodwill abounded once again. At Brisbane in the First Test, and before his exertions had drained his reserves of energy, he took eight wickets for 107 and made 103 runs.

After the war, at the age of 45, he undertook to lead MCC in the West Indies in 1947-48. Though he was never fully fit and the opposition were too strong, he again proved to be the ideal touring captain. Nothing was too much trouble for him in seeing to the need of his men. At home he confined himself to a few games for Middlesex and an annual return to Fenner's for the Free Foresters, when as often as not he made a century.

With his death cricket lost one of its most devoted and dedicated servants. Active almost to the end, he returned to his home from hospital to die only a pitch's length from the Pavilion at Lord's and the stand next door now named after him.

PATRIARCH OF INDIAN CRICKET   2001

AMARNATH, NANIK BHARDWAJ, died on August 5, 2000, aged 88. "Lala" Amarnath scored India's first Test century and went on to become Indian cricket's patriarchal figure: as selector, manager, coach and broadcaster, as well as in a literal sense – his three sons became first-class cricketers and two played in Tests. Amarnath, a Punjabi, was also the first to kick against the stifling domination of Indian cricket by the local princes and their imperial backers. It severely damaged his career. Amarnath's figures in his 24 Tests are nothing special, but they do no justice to either his spasmodic brilliance or his enduring influence.

From a poor background in Lahore, when it was still part of India, he rose to prominence by scoring 109 for Southern Punjab against MCC in 1933-34, and a few weeks later became a star with a century on his Test debut, India's first Test at home, at the genteel old Gymkhana ground in Bombay. With India facing an innings defeat, he took on the England attack and played, so he said later, "as if possessed by a mysterious power". According to Mihir Bose: "Amarnath was engulfed with spectators, garlanded and congratulated while the band played 'God Save the King'… As the day's play ended, women tore off their jewellery to present it to him, Maharajahs made gifts of money, and India hailed a hero." England's eventual easy win was almost forgotten in the hysteria.

Though he did little in the remaining two Tests of that series, Amarnath was by far the best player – with bat and ball – in the early stages of the unhappy Indian tour of 1936, captained by the Maharajkumar of Vizianagram ("Vizzy"). Having waited, padded up, during an unusually big partnership in the match against Minor Counties at Lord's, he was infuriated to be told that other batsmen would be promoted ahead of him. He swore at the captain and tour treasurer, and was sensationally sent home. The team's subsequent failures, a commission of inquiry, and history as written by people with a more egalitarian world view than Vizzy have all combined to exonerate him. But it meant a 12-year gap between his third Test and his fourth.

Then cricket politics again turned against him. There were arguments about money and second-class treatment (the visitors were treated royally; Indian players were dumped in second-class hotels). Amarnath fell foul of the powerful board secretary, Anthony de Mello, who was furious with the man he had dragged "out of the gutter and made captain of India" and had him suspended for "continuous misbehaviour and breach of discipline".

He was restored, though reduced to the ranks, in 1951-52 and took part when India at last won a Test, against England in Madras; passed over for the humiliating 1952 tour of England; and then given back the captaincy against Pakistan in 1952-53, apparently at the insistence of – of all people – Vizzy. Although India won their first series, Amarnath's contributions as a player were minor, and yet more internal machinations meant he left the job in anger. However, the wheel keeps spinning in Indian cricket, and Amarnath's reputation grew with the years. He became chairman of selectors, most famously insisting on the inclusion of off-spinner Jasu Patel at Kanpur in 1959-60, which led to a historic win over Australia. He was a well-informed and humorous commentator, and in old age he acquired widespread affection as the nation's leading source of cricket anecdotes. But he never lost his habit of speaking his mind. The Indian prime minister, A. B. Vajpayee, called him an icon.

A True Man Of Kent
1991

AMES, LESLIE ETHELBERT GEORGE, CBE, who died suddenly at his home in Canterbury on February 26, 1990, aged 84, was without a doubt the greatest wicketkeeper-batsman the game has so far produced; and yet, at the time he was playing, it used to be said there were better wicketkeepers than Ames, and that he was in the England team because of his batting. If this was so, would Jardine, for example, have preferred him to Duckworth in Australia in 1932-33? Surely not.

When fully fit, Ames was England's first-choice wicketkeeper from 1931 to 1939, when he virtually gave up the job. For Kent, he was an integral part of their Championship side from 1927 to the first match of 1951, when a sharp recurrence of back trouble, which had dogged him for so long, brought his career to an end while he was actually at the crease.

By this time he had amassed 37,248 runs, average 43.51, made 102 hundreds, including nine double-centuries, and passed 1,000 runs in a season 17 times, going on to 3,000 once and 2,000 on five occasions. He had had a direct interest in 1,121 dismissals, of which more than 1,000 were effected when he was keeping wicket. His total of 418 stumpings is easily a record.

In 1928 Ames, making 122 dismissals and 1,919 runs, achieved the wicket-keeper's double for the first time.

A year later he repeated what had been a unique achievement, but with a record 128 dismissals, and in 1932, when he was in superlative all-round form, he scored 2,482 runs, including nine centuries, at 57.72 to finish third in the national averages and made a record 64 stumpings in a total of 104 dismissals. In 1933, a batsman's year, he enjoyed an annus mirabilis. Far from feeling stale after a gruelling tour of Australia, he discovered an even greater appetite for runs, scoring 3,058 including three double-hundreds and six other three-figure innings. He also made the highest score of his career, 295 against Gloucestershire at Folkestone.

Ames represented England in 47 Tests, making 2,434 runs, including eight hundreds, and 97 dismissals (74 catches and 23 stumpings). On the Bodyline tour he took the thunderbolts of Larwood and Voce with quiet efficiency. His style was unobtrusive; there were no flamboyant gestures. He saw the ball so early that he was invariably in the right position without having to throw himself about. His glovework was neat and economical, his stumpings almost apologetic.

Well versed in man-management and administrative skills from his war service, he was given charge of three MCC tours – the 1966-67 Under-25 team to Pakistan, and the senior sides to the West Indies in 1967-68 and Ceylon and Pakistan in 1968-69 – and he was a selector from 1950 to 1956 and again in 1958, the first professional to be appointed as such. From 1960–74 he was secretary/manager of Kent, a post he filled with conspicuous success, commanding the respect of the players by his sense of discipline and absolute fairness. From years of failure Kent improved steadily until they won the Championship in 1970.

If ever there was a true Man of Kent it was he. The attendance of a thousand people at his memorial service in Canterbury Cathedral was a worthy tribute to him.

"THE HAND THAT BOWLED BRADMAN" 1990

ANDREWS, WILLIAM HARRY RUSSELL (BILL), who died on January 9, 1989, aged 80, welcomed strangers with the cheery greeting, "Shake the hand that bowled Bradman", after he performed the feat at Taunton in 1938. Andrews was always honest enough to record that this happened only after the Australian captain had helped himself to 202 against Somerset. He was in the true tradition of county all-rounders – a tall, right-handed fast-medium bowler, who kept a good length and moved the ball sharply, and a dangerous late-order bat. But in the extra tradition of the slightly rebellious or eccentric characters in which Somerset cricket has specialised, Andrews led a chequered career, almost proud of the fact that he had been sacked four times by the county: twice as player and twice as coach. In his autobiography, *The Hand that Bowled Bradman*, published in 1973, he declared generously that he bore the county no grudge. He recorded a first-class career running from 1930 to 1947 before returning to Somerset as coach, as well as playing with Devon.

Hampshire v Lancashire. At Southampton, September 20, 21, 22, 23, 2006. Once it became clear Lancashire were batting on, the circus really began: Warne bowled bouncers off a 20-yard run-up one moment, lobs that threatened to go into orbit the next, while Benham revealed his ambidexterity by bowling right- and left-arm spin.

Little Wonder No. 134

CAPTAIN WHO THREW HIS WEIGHT AROUND
1948

ARMSTRONG, MR WARWICK WINDRIDGE, one of the most famous Australian cricketers, died on July 13, 1947, aged 68. While a great all-round player, he remains in one's memory chiefly for his unequalled triumph in leading Australia to victory in eight consecutive Tests with England. During this period the England touring team, led by J. W. H. T. Douglas, lost all five matches, and the following summer [1921] Armstrong commanded Australia, who won the first three Tests and drew the other two. In that superb manner Armstrong terminated a remarkable career. Of colossal build at 42, Armstrong then weighed about 22 stone and bore himself in a way likely to cause offence, but he invariably carried his desires over all opposition and sometimes with good reason.

At The Oval Armstrong acted in an extraordinary manner by way of emphasising his opinion that all Test matches should be played to a finish irrespective of time. When a draw was certain he rested his regular bowlers, went into the long field himself, an unknown position for him, and actually picked up and read a fully extended newspaper that was blown from the crowd!

Armstrong established a record by playing in 42 Test matches against England – one more than Clem Hill. In these games he scored 2,172 runs, average 35.03, and took 74 wickets at an average cost of 30.91. He made four Test centuries against England – all in Australia.

Very tall and slim when first coming to England, Armstrong was of quite different build 19 years later, and his massive frame made him a dominating personality as captain. Like many cricketers, after retiring from active participation in the game, Armstrong wrote for the press, and his caustic Test criticisms created ill-feeling of a kind which should not be associated with cricket.

CAREER SPANNED TWO WORLD WARS 1980

ASHDOWN, WILLIAM HENRY, died at his home at Rugby on September 15, 1979, aged 80. For Kent between 1920 and 1937 he scored 22,218 runs with an average of 30.35 and took 597 wickets at 32.25. He made 40 centuries and twice scored over 300, being one of the very few who have accomplished this rare feat more than once in county cricket. His 332 against Essex at Brentwood, which took only six and a quarter hours, is still a Kent record; a year later he made 305 not out against Derbyshire at Dover.

In 1914, at the age of 15, he had played for G. J. V. Weigall's XI against Oxford University, and in 1947, after ten years' absence from first-class cricket, he appeared in a festival match at Harrogate in which he scored 42 and 40 and took five for 73. He was thus the only man to take part in first-class cricket in England both before the Great War and after the Second.

FIRST FEMALE SCORER AT LORD'S 1998

ASHMORE, FAVELL MAY, died on April 30, 1997, aged 79. Fay Ashmore worked for MCC for 40 years up to 1986, first as personal assistant to the secretary, Colonel R. S. Rait Kerr, then in the museum. Her late husband, Bill, played twice for Middlesex. She is believed to have been the first woman to act as scorer at Lord's, in 1944.

FLYER IN THE FACE OF ADVERSITY 1983

BADER, GROUP CAPTAIN SIR DOUGLAS, CBE, DSO, DFC, the famous airman, who died on September 5, 1982, aged 72, was captain of St Edward's School, Oxford, in 1928. A good attacking bat and a useful fast-medium bowler, he later played for the RAF and in 1931 made 65, the top score, for them against the Army, a fixture which in those days had first-class status. He gained greater distinction at rugger, and at the time of the accident the following winter which cost him his legs he was in the running for an England cap.

MOST POPULAR MAN IN YORKSHIRE 1998

BAIRSTOW, DAVID LESLIE, was found hanged at his home on January 5, 1998. He was 46. Reports said he had been suffering from depression: his wife was ill, he had financial troubles, he faced a drink-driving charge and was in pain from his own injuries. The news stunned cricket, especially as Bairstow had always seemed the most indomitable and least introspective of men, and led to much comment on the problems faced by retired sportsmen.

David "Bluey" Bairstow was not merely the Yorkshire wicketkeeper but almost the embodiment of the county's cricket throughout the 1970s and 1980s. He arrived in county cricket amid a blaze of publicity when he was drafted from grammar school in Bradford into the Yorkshire side as an 18-year-old on the day he sat an English Literature A-level. He was allowed to sit the exam at 7am, then went out and caught five Gloucestershire batsmen over the next three days. From then on, he was a regular, and while Yorkshire's affairs swirled turbulently around him, Bairstow was always there: loud, combative, combustible. "He wasn't a great wicketkeeper and he wasn't a great batsman," said his team-mate Phil Carrick, "but he was a great cricketer."

His fighting qualities overrode any technical deficiencies, and he did equal a world record by taking 11 catches against Derbyshire at Scarborough in 1981. But he was at his best when batting in one-day games when victory was improbable but just short of impossible: in the Benson and Hedges Cup at Derby in 1981, he was joined by Mark Johnson, the No. 11 and a debutant, with Yorkshire 80 short of victory. Bairstow hit nine sixes in an innings that left everyone on the ground aghast; Yorkshire won with Bairstow on 103, and Johnson four. He was picked for the Oval Test against India in 1979, made a brisk 59 in the second innings, and went to Australia for the post-Packer tour that winter. Though Bob Taylor played in the Tests, Bairstow was a regular in the one-day games, and played a succession of small but vital innings. Most famously, Graham Stevenson walked out to join him at the SCG with 35 wanted from six overs. "Evening, lad," said Bairstow. "We can piss this." Which they duly did.

In 1984, he became captain of Yorkshire, after Geoff Boycott's supporters had seized control of the club. With the rest of Yorkshire torn asunder, depending on whether they worshipped Boycott or loathed him, Bairstow seemed the last man to believe he was still leading a normal cricket team, but Bairstow's sheer willpower saved Yorkshire from utter collapse; indeed, having been bottom of the Championship the year before he took over, they improved slightly in each of his seasons in charge.

He was perhaps the only unequivocally popular man in Yorkshire. Bairstow believed he could intimidate the bowling simply by announcing that he was going to whack the ball back over the bowler's head, and often enough he kept his promise.

His thoughts never seemed private, and he was a firm believer that there was no dispute that could not be settled by a shouting-match over a pint or six. Even after he died, people wrote of David Bairstow's "unquenchable spirit". But in the end, the stress of life outside cricket meant his spirit was quenched, and crushed.

GREEK WHO FOUND CRICKET A DRUG 1995

BALASKAS, XENOPHON CONSTANTINE, died at his home in Johannesburg on May 12, 1994, aged 83. "Bally" Balaskas was the leg-spinner who bowled South Africa to their first victory in England, at Lord's in 1935. It was his only Test of the tour and the only one that produced a result. The pitch, ravaged by leather-jackets, turned from an early stage; Bruce Mitchell and Jock Cameron batted far better than anyone on the England team and Balaskas, bowling tirelessly and with great accuracy from the Pavilion end, had figures of 32–8–49–5 in England's first innings and 27–8–54–4 in the second.

Balaskas was not merely one of the most improbably named of all Test players, he had one of the most improbable backgrounds. His parents were Greek migrants who owned the first restaurant in the diamond town of Kimberley. Pre-war South African cricketers usually came from a narrow, English social background but De Beers, the diamond company that controlled Kimberley, always ensured the two local high schools had big-name coaches, and Charlie Hallows taught Balaskas. He played first-class cricket for Griqualand West when he was 15, and in 1929-30 was both leading run-scorer and wicket-taker in the Currie Cup, with 644 – including 206 against Rhodesia – and 39.

Balaskas made his Test debut at 20 the following year: he made little impact with bat or ball in two Tests at home to England, and never made the Test team when South Africa travelled to Australia in 1931-32, though he scored 122 not out against New Zealand in the Second Test at Wellington.

He played for five different provincial teams, moving round partly for cricketing reasons, partly because of his work as a pharmacist. Apart from his century, his batting was never a success in Test cricket: he scored 174 runs at 14.50 and took 22 wickets at 36.63; his first-class figures were 2,696 runs at 28.68 and 276 wickets at 24.11.

He settled in Johannesburg, bought a lovely house very cheaply and laid out a concrete pitch with a net in his garden; many players would go there for advice and he would always try to get them to play his way: vigorous body action when bowling, and forward defence à la Hallows, planting the foot forward first and keeping the bat close to the pad. "He was always discovering some new theory about his bowling," said Bruce Mitchell. He was a cheerful, twinkling man in old age and he still loved cricketing theory.

OPENING BAT (AND NOBEL LAUREATE) 1990

BECKETT, SAMUEL BARCLAY, who died in Paris on December 22, 1989, aged 83, had two first-class games for Dublin University against Northamptonshire in 1925 and 1926, scoring 35 runs in his four innings and conceding 64 runs without taking a wicket. A left-hand opening batsman. possessing what he himself called a gritty defence, and a useful left-arm medium-pace bowler, he had enjoyed a distinguished all-round sporting as well as academic record at Portora Royal School, near Enniskillen, and maintained his interest in games while at Trinity College, Dublin. Indeed, Beckett, whose novels and plays established him as one of the important literary figures of the 20th century, bringing him the Nobel Prize for Literature in 1969, never lost his affection for and interest in cricket.

DIFFICULT TASK BECAME IMPOSSIBLE 2009

BLACKLEDGE, JOSEPH FREDERICK, died on March 19, 2008, aged 79. Joe Blackledge was the last of the long line of amateurs plucked from club cricket to preside over a bunch of combative county professionals. He was chosen to captain Lancashire in 1962, the last season before the amateur/professional distinction was abolished. Blackledge had captained the Second Eleven and been a high-scoring batsman for Chorley – only Rohan Kanhai scored more in the Northern League in 1961. But he was neither good enough, fit enough nor strong enough for the task in hand. It was hard to imagine who might have been. He inherited an unusually high number of gifted but difficult pros plus his just-sacked predecessor, Bob Barber, and it would have taken a great deal to earn their respect. But after he made 68 in the opening match at Cardiff – his first-class debut, aged 34 – his batting form collapsed, along with any hope of winning over the dressing-room. A team that should have been contending for the Championship finished second-bottom, and Blackledge averaged 15. When the season ended, he returned to the family textile business which is now headed by his nephew, the former England rugby captain Bill Beaumont, whose middle name is Blackledge. Blackledge's reputation at Old Trafford grew with the years through a long stint on the committee; he was heavily involved in the rebuilding projects of the 1990s, and became Lancashire's president in 2001-02.

GREAT SPIN BOWLER WITH REMARKABLE POWERS Sydney H. Pardon, 1918

BLYTHE, SERGT. COLIN (Kent Fortress Engineers, attd. K.O.Y.L.I.), born at Deptford May 30, 1879; killed in November, 1917. Went to Australia 1901-02 and 1907-08; to South Africa 1905-06 and 1909-10; to America (with the Kent team) 1903.

The news that Blythe had been killed in France was received everywhere with the keenest regret. The loss is the most serious that cricket has sustained during the war. It is true Blythe had announced his intention of playing no more in first-class matches, but quite possibly this decision was not final. He had certainly no need to think of retiring at the age of 38. That Blythe was a great bowler is beyond question. He had no warmer admirers than the many famous batsmen who had the satisfaction of making big scores against him. So far as I know they were unanimous in paying tribute to his remarkable powers. He was one of five left-handed slow bowlers of the first rank produced by England in the last 40 years, the other four being Peate, Peel, Briggs and Rhodes.

Blythe had all the good gifts that pertain to the first-rate slow bowler, and a certain imaginative quality that was peculiarly his own. Very rarely did he get to the end of his resources. To see him bowl to a brilliant hitter was a sheer delight. So far from being disturbed by a drive to the ring he would, instead of shortening his length to escape punishment, send up the next ball to be hit, striving of course to put on, if possible, a little extra spin. Blythe's spin was something quite out of the ordinary. On a sticky wicket or on a dry pitch ever so little crumbled he came off the ground in a way that beat the strongest defence. He had, too, far more pace than most people supposed. The ball that went with his arm often approached the speed of a fast bowler and had of course the advantage of being unsuspected.

He was 20 years of age when he first played for Kent, and in 1900 – his second season – he took 114 wickets in county matches alone. Illness during the winter affected his bowling in 1901, but after his visit to Australia with the team captained by A. C. MacLaren in 1901-02 he never looked back. His best season was 1909, when he took in first-class matches 215 wickets, at a cost of 14½ runs each. A list of Blythe's feats with the ball for Kent would fill a column. Against Northamptonshire, at Northampton, in 1907, he obtained 17 wickets in one day, taking all ten in the first innings for 30 runs, and seven in the second for 18. Test matches, owing to his tendency to epileptic fits, were very trying to him, and after having had a big share in England's victory over Australia at Birmingham in 1909 he was practically forbidden to play at Lord's. Still he was, out by himself, England's best bowler in the three matches with the famous South African team of 1907, taking 26 wickets for less than 10½ runs apiece. Blythe's reputation will rest on his doings in England. His two visits to Australia scarcely added to his fame, and when he went to South Africa in 1905-06 and again in 1909-10, he did not find the matting wickets altogether to his liking. He will live in cricket history as the greatest Kent bowler of modern days. Nearly all his finest work was done for his county. It is pleasant to know that the Kent committee have decided to put up a suitable memorial to him.

Yorkshire v Sussex. At Leeds, May 3, 4, 5, 6, 2006. Yorkshire's first innings included two five-run penalties: first when a helmet was hit, then when Prior flung down his wicketkeeper's glove to chase a leg-side bye. Adams put it on, and caught the return, contravening Law 41.2.

Little Wonder No. 135

PROFESSOR OF FAST-MEDIUM BOWLING
1988

BOWES, WILLIAM ERIC (BILL), who died in hospital on September 5, 1987, aged 79, was one of the great bowlers of his day. He is often, for convenience, loosely classed as fast, but Robertson-Glasgow, writing in the early days of the war, described him, correctly, as the most difficult fast-medium bowler in England. Like most of the great, he came off the pitch faster than the batsman expected.

No man has ever worked harder at his art. He was constantly practising, constantly experimenting, but throughout he remained content with the ten yards to which that great coach, Walter Brearley, had cut his run. He concentrated on control of length and direction and on moving the ball. He could always bowl a late inswinger, but Brearley told him that he would never reach the top class unless he could make the ball run away as well.

Yet by the middle of 1931, after three years of trying, Bowes was no nearer to discovering how to produce this ball. Meanwhile he was already on the fringe of the England side. He went on trying, and finally found the required hint in an obscure coaching manual, which told him it was all in the position of the feet at the moment of delivery. Within a week or two he was bowling awayswingers as easily as inswingers, with a barely perceptible change of action. Thenceforward the batsman who had successfully cut two or three inswingers, and tried to repeat the stroke, was liable to find that he had picked the wrong ball and to chop it into his stumps.

Now that he was a recognised member of the Yorkshire side, he was taken in hand by the senior professionals and taught his trade with a thoroughness which does much to explain why for so many years the county was by and large the most formidable in the Championship. Night after night he and Verity, who started at the same time, were taken up to a hotel bedroom and the day's cricket was discussed, the field set out on the bed with toothbrushes, shaving tackle and the like, and praise and blame administered impartially as required. At one of the first of these sessions Verity, who had accomplished his biggest performance to date, seven for 26 against Hampshire, was greeted with, "Seven for 26 and it ought to have been seven for 22! I never saw such bowling. Whatever wast thou doing to give A. K. Judd that four?"

There has probably never been a great cricketer who looked less like one than Bowes. Standing 6ft 4in, he was clumsily built and a poor mover. Wearing strong spectacles, he looked far more like a university professor, and indeed batted and fielded like one. He was stationed at mid-on and, if the ball came to him, he was to catch it or stop it as the case might be. But if it passed him, he was not to move; it was someone else's duty to chase it and throw it in.

Getting a commission in the war, Bowes was captured at Tobruk in 1942 and spent three years as a prisoner. By the time he returned home, he had lost four and a half stone and was not really fit to stand the rigours of first-class cricket. Moreover, at 38 he had reached an age at which a bowler of his type is sure to have lost some of his fire. His troubles were compounded by a severe strain to the muscles of his side and back.

In 1947 his benefit brought him £8,000, at that time a record, and he decided to retire, though Yorkshire were anxious to retain him even if he could bowl only off-spinners. Fortunately he had still 40 years of service to cricket in front of him. To the day of his death he wrote regularly on cricket for the papers, and with his profound knowledge of the game every word he wrote was worth reading. His autobiography, *Express Deliveries*, published in 1949, is probably the best book on cricket ever written by a professional.

In his first-class career of 372 games, Bowes took 1,639 wickets at 16.76: as he made only 1,530 runs, his wickets outnumber his runs. In 15 Tests, his figures were 68 wickets at 22.33.

A POET OF SOME REPUTE   1916

BROOKE, SUB-LIEUT. RUPERT C. (Royal Naval Division), born at Rugby on August 3, 1887, died at Lemnos of sunstroke on April 23, 1915. In 1906 he was in the Rugby eleven, and although he was unsuccessful in the Marlborough match he headed the school's bowling averages with a record of 19 wickets for 14.05 runs each. He had gained considerable reputation as a poet.

REJUVENATOR OF ENGLISH FORTUNES

BROWN, FREDERICK RICHARD, CBE, who died on July 24, 1991, aged 80, was an all-rounder of exceptional skill and achievement who will always be remembered for the courage and determination of his leadership of England in the 1950-51 Test series in Australia. Few visiting captains have been received with so much acclaim by the crowds of Melbourne and Sydney. Although England lost the series by four matches to one, it was soon appreciated that the 40-year-old Brown had almost single-handedly, and against every forecast, done a huge amount to revitalise English cricket, which had been humbled in turn by Australian speed and West Indian spin.

What is in many ways a romantic story started when Brown was offered the captaincy of Northamptonshire early in 1949. He called his new charges back for three weeks' training before the season began and went on to lead them to sixth place in the Championship – after two years at the bottom of the table. In addition, he was invited to captain England in the last two Tests against New Zealand and, crucially, a year later, the Gentlemen at Lord's.

A sudden first-innings collapse, the presence of the selectors, and his sense of the occasion put Brown on his mettle. In a wonderful innings of 122, made in 110 minutes, he hit a six and 16 fours, scoring all but nine of the runs put on while he was at the wicket. The selectors had no need to look further for the man they wanted in Australia, and he was recalled to lead England at The Oval in the last Test against West Indies.

Brown's career fell into two distinct halves. When he took over at Northampton in 1949 he had had virtually no first-class cricket for nine years, but by 1953, when he finally called it a day in county cricket, he had made 4,331 runs for them and taken 391 wickets. Before the war, he played for Surrey from 1931 to 1939, and although available for less than half their matches he delighted Oval regulars with his refreshing energy and enthusiasm. He greatly enjoyed the captaincy and the company of Percy Fender, Errol Holmes and Monty Garland-Wells in those years, and from Fender he learned that there was pace enough in the pre-war Oval pitches to reward top-class leg-spin.

Freddie Brown was born at Lima, Peru, where his father, no mean cricketer himself, was in business. The boy's left-handedness at everything met with paternal disapproval, and he was forced to change over, fortunately with no damage to his natural co-ordination.

It is estimated that he scored at 64 runs per hour in his longer innings, usually with shirt billowing and with a white handkerchief ever present. In a career stretching from 1930 to 1961, he made 13,325 runs at 27.36, including 22 hundreds, took 1,221 wickets at 26.21 apiece, and held 212 catches. He performed the double again in 1949, and in 1952 he missed a third by a single wicket.

In his 22 Tests, 15 as captain, Brown made 734 runs for an average of 25.31 and took 45 wickets at 31.06. He was chairman of selectors in 1953, and later in the decade he managed the MCC sides in South Africa and Australia. He was president of MCC in 1971-72 and also of the NCA and ESCA.

FORTY-YEAR WAIT REWARDED 1990

CAKOBAU, RATU SIR GEORGE KADAVULEVU, GCMG, GCVO, who died in Suva on November 23, 1989, aged 77, was the first Fijian to be Governor-General of the then Commonwealth state, and a keen games player who was vice-captain of P. A. Snow's 1947-48 Fiji side in New Zealand. In 1987, ICC approved first-class status for the five major provincial matches, giving 75-year-old Sir George great satisfaction at gaining such confirmation of his cricket quality and making him the oldest cricketer to be graded so. He had missed the last four matches of the tour after having a toe broken while batting at Napier against Hawke's Bay – the only such injury sustained by the several members of the team who played barefoot.

THE LORD'S PROWLER 1965

CAT, PETER, whose ninth life ended on November 5, 1964, was a well-known cricket-watcher at Lord's, where he spent 12 of his 14 years. He preferred a close-up view of the proceedings and his sleek, black form could often be seen prowling on the field of play when the crowds were biggest. He frequently appeared on the television screen. Mr S. C. Griffith, secretary of MCC, said of him: "He was a cat of great character and loved publicity."

MISSING, EVENTUALLY FOUND 1990

CHALK, FREDERICK GERALD HUDSON, DFC, who was a strokeplaying right-hand batsman, first with Oxford and then Kent, was shot down over the English Channel on February 17, 1943, while serving with the RAF as a flight lieutenant. He was posted missing, presumed dead, and it was not until early in 1989 that his body was found, still in the cockpit of his Spitfire, when excavations were made 12 miles inland from Calais. His obituary appeared in *Wisden 1945*.

1945

CHALK, FLIGHT LIEUT. FREDERICK GERALD HUDSON, DFC, missing from February 1943, was in January officially "presumed killed". His tragic and uncertain death at the age of 32 was deplored by all who knew him and everyone interested in cricket. For Uppingham, Oxford and Kent he batted and fielded so brilliantly that he became an attractive figure whenever he played.

CHARMING AND PERSUASIVE LEADER   1962

CHAPMAN, MR ARTHUR PERCY FRANK, who died in Alton Hospital, Hampshire, on September 16, 1961, aged 61, will always be remembered as a player who brought to cricket a light-hearted air seldom encountered in these days, and as an England captain of great personal charm who got the best out of the men under him. As a tall, polished left-handed batsman who, excelling in the off-drive and leg-side strokes, was generally willing and able to attack the bowling, he scored 16,309 runs, average 31.97, in a first-class career dating from 1920 to 1939.

In 1921 he took part in that famous match at Eastbourne where an England XI defeated Warwick Armstrong's hitherto unbeaten Australians by 28 runs, justifying the assertion of A. C. MacLaren, maintained throughout the summer, that he could pick a side good enough to overcome the touring team.

Chapman played with distinction for Berkshire before qualifying for Kent in 1924, and he became one of the few players to appear for England while taking part in Minor Counties' cricket. He turned out for England 26 times in all, 17 of them as captain, in which role he was only twice on the losing side. Twice he went to Australia, under A. E. R. Gilligan in 1924-25 and as leader of the 1928-29 side who, regarded as probably the best in fielding ever sent out, won the Test rubber by four wins to one.

Though he played several good innings for his country, sharing stands of 116 with E. Hendren in 1926 and 125 with G. O. Allen in 1930, both at Lord's against Australia, he only once scored a century in a Test match. Then, in hitting 121 against Australia at Lord's in 1930, he achieved a triple performance never before accomplished, for on the same ground he had previously reached three figures in both the University and – in 1922 – the Gentlemen v Players match, a fixture in which he figured 19 times. He captained Kent from 1931 to 1936.

Tributes included:
G. Duckworth, former Lancashire and England wicketkeeper: "He was a most delightful gentleman and an ideal captain. He had such a persuasive charm as a leader that you could not help trying your utmost for him."

GREATEST UMPIRE OF HIS TIME   1958

CHESTER, FRANK, who died at his home at Bushey, Hertfordshire, on April 8, 1957, aged 61, will be remembered as the man who raised umpiring to a higher level than had ever been known in the history of cricket. For some years he had suffered from stomach ulcers. Often he stood as umpire when in considerable pain, which unfortunately caused him to become somewhat irascible at times, and at the end of the 1955 season he retired, terminating a career in which he officiated in over 1,000 first-class fixtures, including 48 Test matches.

The First World War cut short his ambitions as an all-rounder for Worcestershire. In the course of service with the Army in Salonika, he lost his right arm just below the elbow. That, of course, meant no more cricket as a player for Chester; but in 1922 he became a first-class umpire and, with the advantage of youth when the majority of his colleagues were men who had retired as cricketers on the score of *Anno Domini*, he swiftly gained a big reputation. His lack of years caused him difficulty on one occasion at Northampton, for a gateman refused him admission, declining to believe that one so young could be an umpire, and suggested that he should try the ground of a neighbouring works team!

From the very beginning of his career as an umpire, he gave his decisions without fear or favour. Chester began the custom, now prevalent among umpires, of bending low over the wicket when the bowler delivered the ball, and his decisions were both prompt and rarely questioned. Yet the ruling which probably caused most discussion was one in which Chester was wrong. This occurred during the England v West Indies Test match at Trent Bridge in 1950, when S. Ramadhin bowled D. J. Insole off his pads. Chester contended that the batsman was leg before wicket, because he (Chester) gave his decision in the brief time before the ball hit the stumps, and as "lbw" Insole remained in the score. Soon after this, MCC added a Note to Law 34 which made it clear beyond dispute that, where a batsman is dismissed in such circumstances, he is out "bowled."

Chester had some brushes with Australian touring players, whose demonstrative methods of appealing annoyed him, but nevertheless Sir Donald Bradman termed him "the greatest umpire under whom I played". Chester, for his part, rated Bradman "the greatest run-making machine I have ever known," and considered Sir John Hobbs the greatest batsman of all time on all pitches.

Throughout his long spell as an umpire Chester used, for counting the balls per over, six small pebbles which he picked up from his mother's garden at Bushey before he stood in his first match.

Natural Wicketkeeper But Railwayman At Heart 1996

CLARK, ARTHUR HENRY SEYMOUR, who died on March 17, 1995, aged 92, was an engine driver from Weston-super-Mare and one of the most improbable of all county cricketers. Seymour Clark never played the game at all before he was 25, when he was drafted in to keep wicket for a makeshift railwaymen's side. He turned out to be a brilliant natural wicketkeeper, with fantastic reflexes, and quickly became first choice for the Weston town club. Three years later, when the regular Somerset keeper Wally Luckes was ill, Clark was brought in and, though he had trouble getting time off from the railway, played five matches in 1930. He kept magnificently; however, he is mainly remembered for his batting, which was hopeless. Clark thought his highest score in club cricket was three, and two of them came from overthrows. He bought a new bat when he was picked for the county, but hardly ever made contact, failing to score a run in nine innings (though twice at Kettering his partner got out before he could). Peter Smith of Essex tried to give him one off the mark, and produced a ball that bounced twice before it reached him; Clark still got bowled. He was offered a contract for 1931 but thought the Great Western Railway offered more secure employment. "I got a tremendous kick out of playing for Somerset," he said later, "but it seemed sensible to go back to the locos."

PREFERRED PULLING TEETH   2008

CRANSTON, KENNETH, died on January 8, 2007, aged 89. Ken Cranston's first-class career was brief – less than 18 months as a regular player – but he packed a remarkable amount into it. He played his first Test less than two months after his first-class debut, took four wickets in an over in his second Test, captained on his fourth appearance, and won eight caps in all. Cranston had been a fine player at Liverpool College – Lancashire's coach, the former England batsman Harry Makepeace, thought he was the most gifted boy he ever came across – and hit 289 in a club game while still at school. He scored a century for Lancashire's Second Eleven against Yorkshire in 1938, and would in all probability have made the full county side sooner had war not intervened. Instead he served in the Navy, and was 29 when, out of the blue, he received an invitation to captain Lancashire as an amateur in 1947. His father agreed to keep their dental practice ticking over for a while, as he had done during the war, and Cranston stepped into county cricket. A natural athlete who was also a fine hockey player, he had immediate success as a hard-hitting batsman and a handy change bowler, making 79 in his first match, against Oxford University, and taking five for 32 against Kent in his second. A few weeks later Cranston was a surprising choice for the Third Test against South Africa at Old Trafford. Some tight bowling kept him in the side for Headingley, where he polished off the second innings with a quadruple-wicket maiden (W0W0WW), which probably saved his place for the final Test. He finished the season not far short of the double – 1,228 runs and 84 wickets – and Lancashire came third in the Championship. His style had its critics: "He had no pretensions to leadership", wrote local reporter John Kay, while others felt he did not consult enough. The Lord's hierarchy was impressed, though, and Cranston was named as vice-captain for the winter tour of the West Indies. He led the team in the First Test when 45-year-old Gubby Allen was unfit. Cranston's tour figures were unspectacular, although *Wisden* said he was "by far" England's best all-rounder. His response was to decide he had fulfilled himself in cricket. In 1948 he again threatened to get the double – 1,063 runs and 79 wickets this time – and returned to the England side for the Fourth Test at Headingley, being one of the suffering bowlers as Don Bradman's "Invincibles" famously scored 404 on the final day to win. (Bradman reputedly asked him for advice about his teeth.) And, at the end of the season, Cranston did indeed retire. He continued playing for his club, Neston, and occasionally turned out at the Scarborough Festival, clattering 156 not out in his first match back, for MCC against Yorkshire in 1949, going in at No. 8. Cranston carried on his dental practice, in the Aigburth house in which he was born, until 1990, and was Lancashire's president in 1993 and 1994. At the time of his death he was the oldest England Test cricketer.

CRISP, ROBERT JAMES, DSO, MC, who died in Essex on March 3, 1994, aged 82, was one of the most extraordinary men ever to play Test cricket. His cricket, which is only a fraction of the story, was explosive enough: he is the only bowler to have taken four wickets in four balls twice. Born in Calcutta, he was educated in Rhodesia and, after taking nine for 64 for Western Province against Natal in 1933-34, which included his second set of four in four, was chosen for the South Africans' 1935 tour of England. He took 107 wickets on the tour at a brisk fast-medium, including five for 99 in the Old Trafford Test. Crisp played four further Tests against Australia in 1935-36, and appeared eight times for Worcestershire in 1938 without ever achieving a huge amount.

But it is astonishing that he ever found a moment for such a time-consuming game as cricket. He was essentially an adventurer – he had just climbed Kilimanjaro when he got news that he was wanted for the 1935 tour – with something of an attention-span problem. Like other such characters, his defining moment came in the Second World War when he was an outstanding but turbulent tank commander, fighting his own personal war against better-armoured Germans in Greece and North Africa. He had six tanks blasted from under him in a month but carried on fighting and was awarded the DSO "for outstanding ability and great gallantry". However, he annoyed authority so much that General Montgomery intervened personally and prevented him being given a Bar a year later; his second honour was downgraded to an MC. Crisp was mentioned in despatches four times before being invalided out in Normandy. The King asked if his bowling would be affected. "No, sire," he is alleged to have replied. "I was hit in the head."

Crisp never did play again, and found that the tedium of peacetime presented him with a problem far harder than anything offered by the Germans. He was briefly a journalist for a succession of newspapers, and went back to South Africa where he founded the now firmly established paper for blacks, *Drum*. But he wanted a magazine about tribal matters rather than something appealing to urban blacks, and rapidly fell out with his proprietor. He returned to England, tried mink farming and, for an unusually long time by Crisp standards, worked as a leader-writer on the *East Anglian Daily Times*. While there he wrote two accounts of his war exploits, *Brazen Chariots* (1957) and *The Gods Were Neutral* (1960). Then he suddenly left and lived in a Greek hut for a year. Told he had incurable cancer, he spent a year walking round Crete, selling accounts to the *Sunday Express*. He died with a copy of the *Sporting Life* on his lap, reportedly having just lost a £20 bet, a risk-taker to the last. Crisp's 276 career wickets came at an average of only 19.88, but statistics are absurd for such a man.

DARNLEY, THE 8TH EARL OF (IVO FRANCIS WALTER BLIGH), born in Bruton Street, London, on March 13, 1859, died peacefully in his sleep of heart failure at Puckle Hill, Cobham, Kent, on April 10, 1927, aged 68. It was in October, 1900, that he had succeeded to the Earldom. Naturally, he developed his cricket considerably whilst at Eton, and in his four matches against Harrow and Winchester – in 1876 and 1877 – made 106 runs with an average of 26.50, his highest innings being 73 against the latter side in 1876. A feature of Mr Bligh's batting was his driving – he was 6ft 3in in height – and, until ill-health handicapped him, he was a capital long field and point. At Cambridge he gained his Blue as a Freshman, and in his four games with Oxford he was on the winning side three times.

His association with the Kent eleven, owing to ill-health, extended only from 1877 to 1883, during which period he played in 47 matches, scoring 1,490 runs with an average of 18.86 and occasionally, during the absence of Lord Harris, leading the side. There can be little doubt that, had he remained in full vigour, he would have developed into a really great batsman, for he was only 21 when his breakdown occurred.

The most interesting episode of his short career was his visit to Australia in 1882-83 as captain of a team in an endeavour to regain for England the laurels lost in the historic Test at The Oval the previous summer. The Australians, under W. L. Murdoch's captaincy, had then, it will be remembered, won, after a thrilling finish, by seven runs – a result which led to the term The Ashes being coined. The said Ashes were supposed to have been taken to Australia, and hopes ran high that Mr Bligh's team would recover them. As it happened, Mr Bligh was successful in his quest, for, meeting Murdoch's men in three matches the Englishmen, after losing the first by nine wickets, won the second by an innings and 27 runs and the third by 69 runs.

Mr Bligh's interest in cricket remained as great as ever after he had dropped out of first-class matches, and he was president of the MCC in 1900 and of Kent in 1892 and 1902. He played a fair amount of golf, but his great love was always cricket – the game with which his family had been associated for nearly 150 years. Lord Darnley was one of the most genial and kind-hearted of men.

Little Wonder No. 136

Cheltenham & Gloucester Trophy 2006. The C&G was chosen for an innovative experiment in pitch preparation. Too often, one-day pitches had started to disintegrate late in the game, favouring the side bowling second. In an attempt to make the surface last throughout (and so lessen the importance of the toss), some pitches were sprayed with dilute PVA glue. Far from creating a sticky wicket, it gave the surface a durable gloss – and so test bed became featherbed.

GETTING HIS DUCKS IN A ROW — 1993

DAVIES, JACK GALE WILMOT, OBE, who died at Cambridge on November 5, 1992, aged 81, was a remarkable man who achieved many distinctions both within cricket and outside it. He had many of the Renaissance Man qualities of C. B. Fry; but he was a shy person and often those who knew him well in one field were quite unaware of his achievements elsewhere. Perhaps his greatest cricketing feat was to cause the dismissals of both Hutton and Bradman for ducks in one week when playing for Cambridge University in May 1934. Against Yorkshire he ran out the young Hutton, who was making his first-class debut and had pushed a ball to cover expecting to score his first run. The significance of this only became apparent with the years. But six days later he caused a sensation by clean-bowling Bradman for his first-ever nought in England with a ball that went straight on and hit off stump. A large crowd at Fenner's was not entirely pleased with Davies.

The rest of his playing career, though a little anticlimactic, was still very successful, but conducted in an old-fashioned amateur way. He was a stylish and dashing right-hand batsman, mostly in the middle order (though he had a notably successful period as an opener for Kent in 1946), a slow off-break bowler capable of running through an innings and a brilliant cover point.

He also found time to take a first-class honours degree in classics – an unusual achievement for a cricket Blue, especially in that era – play rugby for Blackheath and Kent, and win the Cyriax Cup, the Rugby fives singles championship, three times.

In 1939 Davies took a degree at the National Institute of Industrial Psychology and he became Chief Psychologist, Directorate for the Selection of Personnel, at the War Office. He later served at the United Nations. In 1952 he was appointed secretary of the Cambridge University Appointments Board, and thereafter he became a father figure to generations of Cambridge cricketers. He was also treasurer (1976–80) and president (1985-86) of MCC and was made an honorary vice-president in 1988. From 1969 to 1976 he was an executive director of the Bank of England. As late as 1990, he reported a couple of cricket matches from Fenner's for the *Daily Telegraph*. The sharpness of his mind was obvious to anyone who worked with him in committee, whatever the subject. His engaging laugh prevented his intelligence becoming too intimidating.

BATSMAN KEPT IN THE RUNNING   Supplementary Obituary, 1994

DENTON, ARTHUR DONALD, died on January 23, 1961, aged 64. Don Denton was a middle-order batsman for Northamptonshire who showed great promise in four matches in 1914 but lost part of a leg during the First World War. He also played three matches after the war, batting with a runner. The Lancashire captain, approached for special permission, wrote: "If any fellow has been to the war and has had his leg off and wants to play, he is good enough for me and can have 20 runners." His two elder brothers, the twins Jack and Billy Denton, also played for the county either side of the war.

ENGLAND CAPTAIN AND OLYMPIC GOLD MEDALLIST   1931

DOUGLAS, MR JOHN WILLIAM HENRY TYLER, born at Clapton, Middlesex on September 3, 1882, was drowned on December 19, 1930, in a collision which occurred in the Cattegat between the steamships *Oberon* and *Arcturus*. Together with his father, Mr J. H. Douglas, Mr Douglas, when the accident occurred, was a passenger on the *Oberon* returning to England from a business trip.

Johnny Douglas had a remarkable career. He was not only a fine cricketer but an even greater boxer, and he attained some fame at Association football, appearing for the Corinthians and the Casuals and gaining an amateur international cap. He came to the front as a boxer when still at Felsted by his doings in the Public Schools' Championship. Later on, as he developed physically, he reached the highest class as a middleweight and in 1905 won the Amateur Championship, while in 1908 he carried off the Olympic middleweight Championship by beating in a memorable encounter the Australian Snowy Baker.

Douglas first appeared for Essex in 1901 – the year he left school – and had a most disheartening experience in his opening match, being bowled in each innings by George Hirst's swerver without making a run either time. He became captain of Essex in 1911 and continued to hold that post until the close of the season of 1928.

Heavy responsibility was soon thrust upon his shoulders, for with P. F. Warner, who had been appointed captain of the team which went out to Australia in 1911-12, falling ill after the opening contest, the duties of leadership devolved upon Douglas. The First Test match was lost but, the side enjoying the services of those exceptionally fine bowlers, S. F. Barnes and F. R. Foster, the other four were won and so Douglas returned home with his reputation as a captain established.

After the War, in the course of which, getting a commission in the Bedfordshire Regiment, he reached the rank of Lieutenant-Colonel, Douglas was appointed captain of the MCC side that visited Australia in 1920-21 and lost all five Test matches. He played against Australia in the five Test contests of 1921 – in the first two as captain and in the remainder under the leadership of Tennyson. Finally he accompanied to Australia the team sent out under A. E. R. Gilligan in 1924-25, but played a very small part in that tour.

Possessed of exceptional defensive skill and inexhaustible patience, Douglas was a batsman very hard to dismiss. Sometimes, so intent was he upon keeping up his wicket, that he carried caution to excess and became tiresome to watch. As a bowler he was a much more interesting figure. Distinctly above medium-pace, he could keep at work for hours without losing either speed or length, and to a new ball he imparted, late in its flight, a very awkward swerve to leg. Always extremely fit, Douglas, even at the end of the hottest and longest day, scarcely knew what fatigue was. To balance any lack of restraint in expressing his views about a blunder, he possessed that saving grace of humour which enjoyed tales against himself. How thoroughly he realised his limitations was shown by his remark "An optimist is a man who, batting with Johnny Douglas, backs up for a run."

LADY WHO RULED OVER LORD'S LUNCHES   2006

DOYLE, ANNIE GERTRUDE, died on July 4, 2005, aged 76. Nancy Doyle was the *châtelaine* of the players' dining-room at Lord's for many years until her retirement in 1996. Her lavish lunches – Mike Brearley once asked, unsuccessfully, if she could limit the number of courses to five – were legendary around a county circuit on which the staple diet in most places at the time was salad, and she was popular with generations of players. Nancy, who first worked at Lord's as a waitress in 1961, was small yet volcanic, and some colleagues found her quick tongue hard to take. Steadfastly Irish to the end, she was awarded an honorary MBE in 1994.

THE ADVENTURE OF THE ILLUSTRIOUS VICTIM · 1931

DOYLE, SIR ARTHUR CONAN, MD, the well-known author, born at Edinburgh on May 22, 1859, died at Crowborough, Sussex, on July 7, 1930, aged 71. Although never a famous cricketer, he could hit hard and bowl slows with a puzzling flight. For MCC v. Cambridgeshire at Lord's, in 1899, he took seven wickets for 61 runs, and on the same ground two years later carried out his bat for 32 against Leicestershire, who had Woodcock, Geeson and King to bowl for them. In *The Times* of October 27, 1915, he was the author of an article on "The Greatest of Cricketers. An Appreciation of Dr Grace". (It is said that Shacklock, the former Nottinghamshire player, inspired him with the Christian name of his famous character, Sherlock Holmes, and that of the latter's brother Mycroft was suggested by the Derbyshire cricketers.)

Conan Doyle's slows claimed one first-class wicket – W. G. Grace – when MCC played London County at Crystal Palace in 1900. Grace had scored 110 and Conan Doyle was the fifth bowler tried, but he was not too abashed to compose a 19-verse poem about how he "captured that glorious wicket, The greatest, the grandest of all".

FAITH, AND CRICKET, KEY TO LONG LIFE · 1997

DOYLE, SISTER MARY PETER, who died in Upper Hutt, New Zealand, on April 17, 1996, aged 109, attributed her longevity to her faith in God and her interest in cricket. She was believed to be the oldest Sister of Mercy in the world.

DEATH AT THE WICKET · Hubert Preston, 1943

The sudden death at Lord's, on July 23, 1942, of ANDREW DUCAT, Surrey batsman of high talent and effective execution, England international Association footballer, captain of a cup-winning Aston Villa team, and in recent years cricket coach at Eton, came as a shock to countless friends and admirers.

That Ducat should collapse and die, bat in hand, was the last thing anyone would have expected of such a well set-up, vigorous, healthy looking and careful-living man. Evidence of those in the field proved clearly that he expired directly after playing a stroke and as he prepared to receive another ball, for he was dead when carried to the pavilion. The medical report gave the cause of death – failure of a heart that showed signs of definite weakness.

The loss of Ducat in this way may be attributed to the war, but for which there would not have been the Home Guard for him to join. His Surrey Unit were playing their Sussex brothers-in-arms, and Ducat was not out at lunchtime. On resuming, he raised his score from 12 to 29 before the catastrophe occurred.

Born on February 16, 1886, at Brixton, in South London, Ducat died at the age of 56.

Good batting for the Surrey Second Eleven soon took him to the first-class rank, in which he stood out conspicuously from 1909 to 1931. Altogether he put together 52 three-figure innings, all for Surrey, the highest being 306 not out against Oxford University at The Oval in 1919. That season he scored 1,695 runs, entirely for Surrey, and his 52.96 placed him sixth in the batting averages for the whole country.

He was picked for the Leeds Test match against Australia in 1921, when J. M. Gregory and E. A. McDonald struck terror into the hearts of many batsmen. Speed and sure hands in deep fielding also influenced his selection. Honoured with the distinguished place of No. 4, Ducat still found himself dogged by ill luck, for, in playing McDonald, the shoulder of his bat was broken and the ball went to the slips, where Gregory held the catch, while the splinter of wood fell on the stumps, shaking off a bail. So Ducat was doubly out. Carter, the Australian wicketkeeper, handed to Ducat the piece of wood; and he stumped Ducat in the second innings!

When incapacitated in 1924, Ducat became manager of the Fulham football club, and was not always available for Surrey, but he invariably resumed full of runs. In 1928 Ducat, although not playing in every engagement, made 994 runs in less than six weeks. Altogether in first-class cricket he scored 23,373 runs at an average of 38.31.

The match was abandoned and Ducat recorded as "not out 29" in the scorecard.

A Supreme Run-Smith

DULEEPSINHJI, KUMAR SHRI, who died from a heart attack in Bombay on December 5, 1959, aged 54, was among the best batsmen ever to represent England and certainly one of the most popular. Ill-health limited his first-class career to eight seasons, but in that time he scored 15,537 runs, including 49 centuries, at an average of 50.11. A remarkably good slip fieldsman, he brought off 243 catches. "Duleep", or "Mr Smith", as he was affectionately known in cricket circles, was in the Cheltenham XI from 1921 to 1923, and in 1925 he went up to Cambridge. He got his Blue as a Freshman, scoring 75 in the University Match, and also played against Oxford in 1926 and 1928. Illness kept him out of the side for most of the 1927 season.

His career with Sussex, whom he captained in 1932, began in 1926, and he headed the county averages in every season until 1932, when doctors advised him not to take further part in cricket. In 1930 he hit 333 in five and a half hours against Northamptonshire at Hove, which still stands as the highest individual innings played for Sussex and beat the biggest put together by his famous uncle, K. S. Ranjitsinhji – 285 not out against Somerset at Taunton in 1901; three times he reached three figures in each innings of a match, and in 1931 he registered 12 centuries, four of them in successive innings.

He made 12 appearances for England, and in his first against Australia at Lord's in 1930 he obtained 173. Of this display a story is told that, when Prince Duleepsinhji was at last caught in the long field from a rash stroke, his uncle remarked: "He always was a careless lad." His one tour abroad was with the MCC team in New Zealand and Australia in 1929-30, when he scored more runs than any other member of the side. A. H. H. Gilligan, the captain, rated him the best player of slow bowling on a wet pitch that he ever saw. "Duleep" had to withdraw from the team for D. R. Jardine's "body-line" tour of 1932-33. He joined the Indian foreign service in 1949 and became High Commissioner for India in Australia and New Zealand. Upon returning to India in 1953 he was appointed chairman of the public service commission in the State of Saurashtra.

PRESSED NOTTS INTO DECLARATION — 1996

EASTERBROOK, BASIL VIVIAN, who died on December 15, 1995, aged 75, was cricket and football writer for Kemsley (later Thomson Regional) Newspapers from 1950 to 1983, and thus covered all the major domestic matches for many of Britain's largest regional papers. Easterbrook was a much-loved member of the press corps with a puckish humour. He claimed that while covering a match from the old Lord's press box, he leaned out of the window to throw away his pencil shavings and the Nottinghamshire batsmen walked in, thinking it was the signal to declare.

Middlesex v Hampshire (Twenty20 Cup). At Southgate, June 25, 2007. The game was overshadowed by two off-field events: stones were thrown at the windows of the Hampshire team coach from outside the ground, and valuables were stolen from the Middlesex dressing-room.

Little Wonder No. 137

PLAYED POLITICS AND CRICKET — 1941

ECKERSLEY, LIEUTENANT PETER THORP, RNVR, MP, died on August 13, 1940, at the age of 36 as the outcome of an accident when flying. Known as the cricketer-airman, he often flew his own plane to matches. In 1928, when prospective candidate for the Newton division of Lancashire, he announced the compulsion of deciding between politics and cricket, and he chose cricket. Experience at Rugby and Cambridge University, where he did not get his Blue, equipped Eckersley so well in batting and fielding that after one season in the eleven he was appointed captain of

Lancashire when only 24. This difficult position, with little amateur companionship, he held with honour for six years, and led his side to the Championship in 1934.

In the seasons 1923 to 1936 Eckersley often played well when his side were badly placed, and he scored 5,730 runs, including a very good century against Gloucestershire at Bristol. A first-rate fieldsman, he set his team a splendid example, notably at times when some slackness was apparent. Still, he retained a liking for politics and, reversing his previous decision, he contested the Leigh division in 1931 before he achieved his ambition by becoming Unionist Member of Parliament for the Exchange Division of Manchester in 1935. He consequently resigned the captaincy of Lancashire, but his restless nature, known so well to intimate friends, influenced him to join the Air Arm of the RNVR when war broke out. Despite indifferent health he was always keen for duty until his strength became overtaxed.

DOUGHTY PERFORMER WHO RODE THE BLOWS   1987

EDRICH, WILLIAM JOHN (BILL), DFC, who died at Chesham as the result of an accident on April 23, 1986, aged 70, was a cricketer who would have been the answer to prayer in the troubled England sides of today and especially in the West Indies in 1985-86. Endlessly cheerful, always optimistic and physically courageous, he was a splendid hitter of short-pitched fast bowling and took the blows he received as a part of the game. When he made 16 in an hour and threequarters on a hideous wicket at Brisbane in the first innings of the first Test in 1946-47, an innings which *Wisden*'s correspondent described as "one of the most skilful batting displays I have ever seen", it was reckoned that he was hit ten times by Lindwall, Miller and Toshack.

So far from being demoralised by this experience, he scored in the series 462 runs with an average of 46.20, and that for a side which lost three Tests, two of them by an innings, and drew the other two. Moreover, his cricket did not end with his batting. Though he stood only 5ft 6in tall, and had a low, slinging action, he could off a run of 11 strides bowl genuinely fast for a few overs.

He came of a Norfolk farming family, which sometimes produced its own XI. Three of his brothers played with some success in first-class cricket and his cousin, John, later had a distinguished Test match career. Bill Edrich first appeared for Norfolk in 1932 at the age of 16, and by 1935 had begun to qualify for Middlesex. In his first full season of first-class cricket [1937], he scored 2,154 runs with an average of 44.87, heading the batting, and was picked for Lord Tennyson's side in India. In 1938 he started by making 1,000 runs before the end of May. During the war Edrich joined the RAF and had a distinguished career, winning the DFC as a bomber pilot. Up to the war he had played as a professional; after it he became an amateur.

In England in 1947 came his *annus mirabilis*. Scoring in all 3,539 runs with an average of 80.43 he beat Hayward's 41-year-old aggregate of 3,518: however, Compton beat it by even more. In the Tests in 1947 against South Africa he made 552 runs with an average of 110.40. At Manchester he made 191, adding 228 with Compton for the third wicket in 196 minutes. At Lord's in the previous Test, also for the third wicket, they had added 370. Edrich made 189.

It was a great surprise when he was omitted from the team for Australia at the end of the [1950] season. No reasons were given at the time for his omission, but in fact an ill-advised late-night party during the First Test against West Indies, followed by his calamitous showing in the Second, had convinced the selectors, and not least the captain-elect, that the team would be better without him. By a generous gesture Edrich himself was at the station to see the team off and to wish them well.

In first-class cricket he scored 36,965 runs, with an average of 42.39, and made 86 hundreds, nine of them double-centuries: he took 479 wickets at 33.31 and held 526 catches. His highest score was 267 not out for Middlesex against Northamptonshire at Northampton in 1947. In Tests he made 2,440 runs with an average of 40, including six hundreds: he also took 41 wickets at 41.29 and held 39 catches.

MAJESTIC SUPPORTER OF THE GAME   1911

EDWARD VII, HM KING, died at Buckingham Palace on May 6, 1910. As a small boy he received tuition at Windsor from F. Bell, of Cambridge, but it cannot be said that he ever showed much aptitude for the game. He played occasionally during his Oxford days, however, and, while he was staying at Madingley Hall, a special wicket was reserved for his use at Fenner's. He showed his interest in the game in many ways. When funds were being collected to pay off the pavilion debt at Fenner's, he contributed ten pounds, at the same time promising to make up any amount required at the end of the term, and during one of the critical moments in the history of the MCC was the largest contributor to the fund raised to pay for the freehold of Lord's. Furthermore, as Duke of Cornwall his late Majesty was for many years landlord of The Oval, and in several ways he showed his interest in the Surrey County Club. His Majesty was born at Buckingham Palace on November 9, 1841, and was therefore in his 69th year at the time of his death.

REPORT OF DEATH WAS AN EXAGGERATION   Supplementary Obituary, 1994

FARGUS, Rev. ARCHIBALD HUGH CONWAY, who died on October 6, 1963, aged 84, has been obituarised before in *Wisden*. However, this was 48 years before his death. The 1915 edition said Fargus had gone down with the *Monmouth*, the ship on which he was acting-chaplain, in action in the Pacific. But he had missed a train and failed to rejoin the ship. Fargus, whose father Hugh Conway was a well-known Victorian author, won a Cambridge Blue in 1900 and 1901 and played 15 games for Gloucestershire. His actual death was not reported in the Almanack.

GIANT WHO SENT THE STUMPS FLYING   1942

FARNES, PILOT OFFICER KENNETH, RAF, the Cambridge, Essex and England fast bowler, was killed during the night of October 20, 1941, when the plane in which he was pilot crashed. His death at the age of 30 came as a great shock to countless friends and the whole world of cricket. After training in Canada he desired to become a night-flying pilot, and within four weeks of his return to England he met his disastrous end. [Wisden 1979: *"He misjudged his landing and died in the blazing wreckage of his crashed aeroplane."*]

Discovered when 19 years of age by Mr Percy Perrin in an Essex Club and Ground match against Gidea Park in 1930, Kenneth Farnes took five Kent wickets for 36 runs in his second county match and was welcome in the Essex team whenever available. After three years in the Cambridge eleven, he went as a master to Worksop College, and consequently his appearances in first-class cricket were limited. In 1933 his work for Cambridge showed 41 wickets at 17.39 runs apiece, and he was by far the most effective amateur bowler in the country with a record of 113 wickets at 18.38 each. His best performance that season – 11 wickets for 114 runs, 7 for 21 in the second innings – enabled Essex to beat Surrey by 345 runs at Southend, their first success against these opponents since 1914. This form brought him the honour of representing England in the First Test against Australia in 1934. Despite his fine performance – ten wickets for 179 runs – England lost by 238 runs. Strangely enough, when England won by an innings and 38 runs at Lord's, Farnes did not meet with any reward, Verity taking the honours. Farnes was not called upon again in that series, but in 1938 he took most wickets in Tests against Australia – 17 at 34.17 each.

In 1934 he was largely responsible for the first victory of Essex over Yorkshire since 1911 by taking 11 wickets for 131, Southend again proving a favourable ground for him. After a tour in West Indies knee trouble prevented Farnes from playing in 1935, but next season, for the Gentlemen at Lord's, he created a sensation by bowling Gimblett, Hammond and Hardstaff in quick succession, a stump being sent flying in each case [Wisden 1937: *"head high to drop at the feet of Levett, who stood back more than a dozen yards"*]. This fine work influenced the choice of Farnes to tour Australia with the team captained by G. O. Allen in the winter of 1936. Never did he bowl better than in the last Test, when he took six wickets for 96 runs in a total of 604.

Nearly 6ft 5in tall, Farnes, taking a comparatively short and easy run, brought the ball down from a great height with the inevitable effect of sharp lift, which made him extremely difficult to time when retaining a good length. Altogether in first-class cricket Farnes took 720 wickets at an average of 20.55 each.

A very good field near the wicket, Farnes reached many catches that would have been impossible for a man of medium height. He had no pretension as a batsman, but in 1936, at Taunton, hit up 97 not out in two hours, Wade helping to add 149 for the last wicket. He laughed at just failing to get a century.

Farnes wrote a very interesting book – *Tours and Tests*, published in 1940; among his hobbies were painting and music.

THE LONGEST RECORDED HITTER 1903

FELLOWS, The REV. WALTER who was born at Rickmansworth, in Hertfordshire, on February 23, 1834, died at Toorak Parsonage, near Melbourne, July 23, 1902. He was educated at Westminster and Oxford, and is described in *Scores and Biographies* as "a hard slashing hitter, and a tremendous fast round-armed bowler". Whilst at practice on the Christ Church Ground at Oxford in 1856, Mr Fellows hit a ball, bowled by Rogers, a distance of 175 yards from hit to pitch, the length of the drive being carefully measured by E. Martin, the ground-keeper. In 1863 he emigrated to Australia, and joined the Melbourne Club the following year. Height, 5ft 11in, and playing weight as much as 17st 4lb.

LASTING MEMORIAL IN CAMBRIDGE   1897

F. P. FENNER'S death, on May 22, 1896, destroyed one of the few remaining links between the cricket of the present day and the generation of Mynn and Fuller Pilch. Born at Cambridge on March 1, 1811, Mr Fenner had reached a ripe old age. In his day he was a capital cricketer, taking his part with no little distinction in big matches, but his fame rests not so much upon what he did in the field, as on the fact that he laid out the beautiful ground at Cambridge, which, though now the property of the University, is nearly always spoken of by old cricketers as Fenner's. The ground was opened in 1846, and is still, after 50 years' play, one of the best in the world.

KILLED BY MEDICAL ERROR   1994

FOLLEY, IAN, the former Lancashire left-arm spin bowler, died in hospital on August 30, 1993, aged 30. He had been struck under the eye trying to hook a short ball, while captaining Whitehaven in a North Lancashire League match against Workington. He jogged off the field and it was assumed he would only need a few stitches but, while under anaesthetic, apparently suffered a heart attack. Folley played for Lancashire from 1982 until 1990, and was regarded as a promising medium-pace bowler before the manager Jack Bond encouraged him to switch to spin. At first the change worked magnificently, and he took 68 Championship wickets in 1987, including seven for 15 against Warwickshire at Southport. He took 57 wickets in 1988 but then began to suffer the yips and found bowling almost impossible. In 1991 Folley moved to Derbyshire, but played in only four matches. In 140 first-class games he took 287 wickets. At the time of his death he was managing a nightclub.

Cricket and the Law, 2000

Jack Folley, four-year-old son of Ian Folley, was awarded £51,155 compensation against West Cumberland Infirmary by the High Court in Newcastle-upon-Tyne on January 19 for the medical error that killed his father. A tube which should have fed air into his lungs was found leading to his stomach, and the anaesthetist,

Dr Murali Krishnan, admitted he had neglected to fit a carbon-dioxide analyser which would have indicated the problem. The hospital denied liability until a week before the case, brought by Jill Barwise, Folley's girlfriend.

ENTRANCED BY THE GAME   2006

FOWLES, JOHN ROBERT, who died on November 5, 2005, aged 79, was a novelist whose work included *The Magus* and *The French Lieutenant's Woman*. Cricket remained a lifelong interest from the time Fowles learnt the game from the Essex captain, Denys Wilcox, at Alleyn Court prep school in Westcliff-on-Sea. He and Trevor Bailey used to cycle there together. As a fast bowler, Fowles took plenty of wickets for Bedford School, which he captained in 1944, and had a trial for Essex. His off-cutter remained a source of pride – though demonstrations of how he achieved this were lost on American film directors. While watching England nervily bat to victory over West Indies at Lord's in 2000, he was joined in his living-room in Lyme Regis by a stranger asking the score. When Fowles told him, his visitor sat down and watched with him until Dominic Cork had hit the winning runs. Only when he subsequently asked how much Fowles charged for bed and breakfast did both men realise that the stranger had walked uninvited into the wrong house.

LIFE LIVED IN THE FAST LANE   1946

GANDAR-DOWER, MR KENNETH CECIL, was lost at sea through Japanese action in February 1944 at the age of 36. At Cambridge he did well in the Freshmen's Match and was a Crusader, but his time was mainly given up to tennis, at which he captained the University team. One of the most versatile players of games of any period, he was amateur squash champion in 1938, won amateur championships at fives, and played lawn tennis for Great Britain. In all, he represented Cambridge at six forms of sport: tennis, lawn tennis, Rugby fives, Eton fives, squash rackets and billiards. In fact, time hardly sufficed for their rival calls. He probably created a record when he played simultaneously in the Freshmen's Match and Freshmen's Tournament, with the connivance of the tennis but not the cricket authorities; he disappeared to play off a round during the early part of his side's innings, with relays of cyclist friends to keep him informed as to the fall of wickets! He flew a private aeroplane to India. In spite of other demands he continued to find time for cricket, making some ten appearances for the Frogs each season almost to the outbreak of war, and got many runs and wickets.

Famous as a big-game shot, and extensive traveller, he introduced a team of cheetahs from Kenya jungle to London and on greyhound tracks they set up speed records. A writer of articles and books, he acted as a war correspondent in various theatres of operations up to the time of his death.

A RIGHT ROYAL HAT-TRICK 1953

GEORGE VI, HM KING, died at Sandringham on February 6, 1952. He was Patron of the Marylebone, Surrey and Lancashire clubs. When Prince Albert, he performed the hat-trick on the private ground on the slopes below Windsor Castle, where the sons and grandsons of Edward VII used to play regularly. A left-handed batsman and bowler, the King bowled King Edward VII, King George V and the present Duke of Windsor in three consecutive balls, thus proving himself the best Royal cricketer since Frederick, Prince of Wales, in 1751, took a keen interest in the game. The ball is now mounted in the mess-room of the Royal Naval College, Dartmouth.

King George VI, like his father, often went to Lord's when Commonwealth teams were playing there, and invariably the players and umpires were presented to His Majesty in front of the pavilion. He entertained the 1948 Australian team at Balmoral, and in his 1949 New Year's Honours Donald Bradman, the captain, received a Knighthood.

BENEFACTOR WHO LIVED OUT HIS ENGLISH IDYLL 2004

GETTY, Sir JOHN PAUL, KBE, who died on April 17, 2003, aged 70, described himself in *Who's Who* as simply a "philanthropist". Paul Getty inherited a fortune from the family oil business but, unlike his tycoon father, had little interest in adding to it. Instead, he settled in Britain and gave away huge chunks of his money to a vast array of beneficiaries, most of them institutions representing what he saw as the country's threatened heritage, including cathedrals, art galleries, the British Film Institute's archive and the Conservative Party. Cricket was close to the top of the list.

Born at sea off Italy and originally called Eugene Paul, he came to the game by an unbelievably circuitous route after an unhappy American childhood, a tumultuous youth and reclusive middle years. For nine years he worked for the Italian subsidiary of Getty Oil before being seduced by the distractions of the 1960s, divorcing his first wife, Gail, and marrying a Dutch beauty, Talitha, who died of a heroin overdose in Italy in 1971. He moved to London and lived as a recluse in Chelsea, subject to depression and his own drug dependence, a period that included the terrible kidnap of his eldest son Paul. During this period Mick Jagger, a friend since the 1960s, visited him, insisted on switching the TV over to the cricket and explained what was going on. Getty got the bug. Gubby Allen, éminence grise of MCC and at one time a fellow patient at the London Clinic, described by Getty as being "like a father", encouraged him into the cricketing community. Men like Brian Johnston and Denis Compton became friends, and he took delight in the game's history, traditions and etiquette, which were at one with the concept of Englishness that he embraced.

So he sprinkled cricket with some of the stardust that his wealth made possible. He gave an estimated £1.6m to build the Mound Stand at Lord's, but this was the tip of an iceberg of donations: to every county, to countless clubs, to individuals fallen on hard times and to organisations like the Arundel Cricket Foundation, back.

which received £750,000 from him to help disadvantaged youngsters play cricket. Even his pleasures were inclusive ones. At Wormsley, his estate nestling in the Chilterns, he created his own private cricketing Eden Project: a square like a billiard table with a thatched pavilion. Getty built his field of dreams, and they really did come: the Queen Mother and the Prime Minister, John Major, attended Wormsley's inaugural match in 1992; touring teams made it a regular stopover; and cricketers ranging from the great to the gormless delighted in playing there or simply sharing the idyll. There was a touch of Scott Fitzgerald's West Egg about the place, but that was not inappropriate for a ground where the most coveted side-trip was to the library to see the host's rare first editions. The Getty box at Lord's also became a London salon where celebrities, cricketing and otherwise, rubbed shoulders.

His ownership of *Wisden*, sealed in 1993, brought together the two great passions: cricket and books. In 1994 Getty sealed his own personal happiness by marrying Victoria, who had nursed him through the bad years, and four years later tied the knot with the country he had come to love, becoming a British citizen, which allowed him to use the knighthood that had been bestowed on him for his charitable services 12 years earlier. His presidency of Surrey, in 1996, was another honour he cherished. Those who knew him valued him as a generous spirit, a quality that has nothing to do with money. And cricket repaid him a little by giving him a sense of his own self-worth as a man, not just as a benefactor.

Second Eleven Championship 2009. Somerset's Kolpak player, Omari Banks, was seen scoring the ball with his thumbnails and fingernails during the game against Essex. The umpires promptly awarded five penalty runs to Essex and reported the incident to the ECB. Banks was banned for three matches for ball-tampering, while Somerset were deducted all their points from the game and fined £500, plus another £500 in costs. Banks admitted the offence, saying he acted out of boredom.

Little Wonder No. 138

FASTEST BOWLER BRADMAN FACED   1979

GILBERT, EDWARD, who was the best-remembered aboriginal cricketer to play first-class cricket in Australia, had been long absent from the scene of his some-times sensational fast-bowling feats of the 1930s and in ill health for many years before his death in the Wolston Park Hospital near Brisbane on January 9, 1978, aged 69. Nevertheless, this notably quiet but well-spoken product of Queensland's Cherbourg Aboriginal Settlement has remained a legend down through the years. After successfully graduating through the Queensland Colts XI in 1930, Eddie Gilbert quickly reached the headlines in the 1931 Sheffield Shield match against NSW in Brisbane by his first-over dismissals, of Wendell Bill and Bradman without scoring. Both were caught by wicketkeeper Len Waterman within seven deliveries, but not before one ball rising from a greentop had flicked off Sir Donald's cap and another knocked the bat from his hands! Sir Donald has since recalled that the six deliveries he faced on this occasion were the fastest experienced during his career.

Lightly built and only a little over 5ft 7in in height, Gilbert possessed exceptionally long arms and could bowl at great pace off a run sometimes no longer than four paces. It was this, allied with a somewhat whippy forearm action, which led to suggestions that his right arm bent on occasions during a pronounced arc action which finished with his hand almost touching the ground and his head at knee level. Strong advocacy for Gilbert's Test selection was nullified by the suspect action, a view several times shared and acted on by senior umpires. Nevertheless, the same officials completely accepted his delivery on most other occasions. Several films were taken without conclusive decision, and controversy continued throughout Gilbert's career which was undoubtedly affected by the publicity. He faded out of the game in 1936 after showing fine form while taking six wickets in his final match – against Victoria at the Brisbane Cricket Ground in 1936. In 19 Shield matches, he took 73 wickets at an average of 29.75, while a further 14 wickets were gained in Queensland matches against touring MCC, West Indies and South African sides.

CHANGE OF STYLE HAD DRAMATIC EFFECT   1967

GODDARD, THOMAS WILLIAM JOHN, who died at his home in Gloucester on May 22, 1966, aged 65, was one of the greatest off-break bowlers the game has known. A big man, standing 6ft 3in, with massive hands, he spun the ball to a remarkable degree and on a helpful pitch was almost unplayable. The Gloucestershire combination of Goddard and the slow left-hander, Charlie Parker, was probably the most feared in Championship cricket.

The early days of Goddard's career gave no hint of the success he was later to achieve. Born on October 1, 1900, he first played for Gloucestershire in 1922 as a fast bowler. Despite his strong physique he made little progress and in six years took only 153 wickets at a cost of 34 runs each.

At the end of the 1927 season he left the county and joined the MCC ground-staff at Lord's. There he decided to experiment with off-breaks; his long, strong fingers were ideally suited to this type of bowling. Beverley Lyon, the Gloucestershire captain, saw him in the nets at Lord's and, immediately struck by Goddard's new-found ability, persuaded Gloucestershire to re-engage him. The effect was immediate and dramatic. In 1929 Goddard took 184 wickets at 16 runs apiece and he never looked back.

When he finally retired in 1952, at the age of 51, Goddard had taken 2,979 wickets, average 19.84, and in a period when off-break bowlers were not fashionable in Test cricket, he played eight times for England. He finished with six hat-tricks, the same number as his colleague, Parker, and only one less than the all-time record of seven, by D. V. P. Wright of Kent.

One of the hat-tricks came in a Test match, against South Africa on Boxing Day, 1938, still the only hat-trick achieved in Test cricket in Johannesburg.

On 16 occasions Goddard took 100 or more wickets in a season, four times reaching 200. His most successful year was 1937 when he claimed 248 victims. His final tally of wickets places him fifth in the order of bowlers the game has known. Umpires over the years got to know Goddard's frequent and loud appeals.

W<small>IFE'S</small> T<small>ALES</small> E<small>VOKE</small> H<small>APPY</small> M<small>EMORIES</small>   1931

GRACE, MRS AGNES NICHOLLS, widow of W. G., died at Hawkhurst, Kent, on March 23, 1930, aged 76. Mrs Grace possessed a rare fund of reminiscences of the game. Her memory will be cherished by many cricketers.

C<small>HAMPION'S</small> L<small>AST</small> S<small>ON</small> D<small>IES</small> D<small>URING</small> M<small>ATCH</small>   1939

GRACE, MR CHARLES BUTLER, the last surviving son of W. G. Grace, died while playing in a cricket match at Hawkhurst, on June 6, 1938, aged 56.

L<small>IVING</small> I<small>N</small> H<small>IS</small> B<small>ROTHER'S</small> S<small>HADOW</small>   1912

GRACE, MR EDWARD MILLS died on May 20, 1911, after a long illness, at his residence, Park House, Thornbury, Gloucestershire. But for the accident that his own brother proved greater than himself, E. M. Grace would have lived in cricket history as perhaps the most remarkable player the game has produced. Barring WG, it would be hard indeed to name a man who was a stronger force on a side or a more remarkable match-winner. Primarily, he was a batsman, but his value in an eleven went far beyond his power of getting runs. As a fieldsman at point – at a time when that position was far more important than it is in modern cricket – he never had an equal, and, though he did not pretend to be a first-rate bowler, he took during his career thousands of wickets. In his young days he bowled in the orthodox roundarm style, but his success in club cricket was gained by means of old-fashioned lobs. Fame came to him early in life. Born on November 28, 1841, he made his first appearance at Lord's in 1861, and a year later he was beyond question the most dangerous bat in England. It was in the Canterbury Week in 1862 that, playing as an emergency for the MCC against the Gentlemen of Kent, he scored 192 not out, and took all ten wickets in one innings. This was a 12-a-side game, but one man was absent in the second innings when he got the ten wickets. He reached his highest point as a batsman in 1863, scoring in all matches that year over 3,000 runs.

E. M. Grace continued to play for Gloucestershire for many years, dropping out of the eleven after the season of 1894. Thenceforward his energies were devoted to club cricket, chiefly in connection with his own team at Thornbury. Lameness gradually robbed him of his old skill as a run-getter, but even in 1909, 119 wickets fell to his lobs. As a batsman E. M. Grace was unorthodox. Partly, it is thought, through using a full-sized bat while still a small boy, he never played with anything like WG's perfect straightness, but his wonderful eye and no less wonderful nerve enabled him to rise superior to this grave disadvantage. He was perhaps the first right-handed batsman of any celebrity who habitually used the pull. In his young days batting was a very strict science, but he cared little for rules. If an open place in the field suggested runs the ball soon found its way in that direction. Personally, EM was the cheeriest of cricketers – the life and soul of the game wherever he played.

MEMBER OF AUSTRALIA'S PRIME CRICKET FAMILY   1930

GREGORY, MR SYDNEY EDWARD, born on the site of the present cricket ground at Sydney, on April 14, 1870, died at Randwick, Sydney, on August 1, 1929, aged 59. It is given to few men to enjoy such a long and successful career in international cricket as that which fell to his lot, but he had cricket in his blood, for what the Graces and the Walkers were to the game in England, the Gregory family, it could be urged, was to that in Australia. Twelve years after his uncle Dave had come to England, as captain of the pioneer side of 1878, S. E. Gregory paid his first visit here as a member of the 1890 team under W. L. Murdoch, and he was chosen for every side up to and including that of 1912.

Altogether he played in 52 Test matches for Australia, a larger number than any other Australian cricketer. In the course of these he made four three-figure scores and obtained 2,193 runs with an average of 25.80. He captained the Australian team of 1912 – the year of the Triangular Tournament – but had a somewhat thankless task in filling that office. Dissatisfied with the financial terms offered, several of the leading Australian cricketers refused to make the trip and the side, as finally constituted, included, in the regrettable circumstances, several players who had little claim to figure as representatives of the best in Australian cricket.

Pronounced and numerous as were his triumphs in batting, Sydney Gregory will probably be remembered more for what he accomplished as a fieldsman for, while several men have equalled and some have beaten his achievements as a run-getter, the cricket field has seen no more brilliant cover point. Clever in anticipation and quick to move, he got to and stopped the hardest of hits, gathered the ball cleanly and returned it with deadly accuracy. His work, indeed, was always an inspiration to his colleagues and a joy to the spectators. Small of stature – he was little more than five feet in height – Gregory overcame this disadvantage in a batsman by splendid footwork.

RECORD-BREAKER CAST ASIDE LIKE AN OLD BOOT   W. J. [Bill] O'Reilly, 1981

Born in Dunedin in the South Island of New Zealand on Christmas Day, 1891, CLARENCE VICTOR GRIMMETT must have been the best Christmas present Australia ever received from that country. Going to Australia in 1914, on a "short working holiday" which lasted for 66 years, he died in Adelaide on May 2, 1980.

It was after his visit to Sydney with Victoria, for the first Shield match after the Great War, that I managed to see him for the first time. The Victorian team, on its way home to Melbourne, played an up-country match in the mountain city of Goulburn. The attention of a 13-year-old boy named O'Reilly was riveted on a wiry little leg-spinner whose name on the local scoreboard was "Grummett". To me, from that day onward, "Grummett" he remained, and my own endearing name for him throughout our later long association was "Grum".

We played together for the first time in an Australian team at Adelaide against Jock Cameron's South Africans in 1931, and for the last time in the Durban Test of 1936 when Vic Richardson's Australian side became the first ever to go through a tour undefeated. On that tour, "Grum" set an Australian record for a Test series with 44 wickets, yet he came home to be dropped forever from the Australian side. He was shoved aside like a worn-out boot for each of the five Tests against Gubby Allen's English team in Australia in 1936-37, and he failed to gain a place in the 1938 team to England.

He was 47, it is true, when the touring side was chosen, yet two years later, at the age of 49, he established an Australian record of 73 wickets for a domestic first-class season. Which raises, rather pointedly, the question of "why the hell was he dropped?" By now Don Bradman was Grimmett's captain for South Australia, and also Australia's captain. As such he was an Australian selector, and Bradman, it seemed, had become inordinately impressed with the spin ability of Frank Ward, a former clubmate of his in Sydney. It was Ward who was chosen for the first three Tests against Allen's side in 1936-37, and who caught the boat for England in 1938. Bradman, it seemed had lost faith in the best spin bowler the world has seen. "Grum's" diagnostic type of probing spin buttressed my own methods to such a degree that my reaction to his dismissal was one of infinite loss and loneliness.

Grimmett never insisted on spin as his chief means of destruction. To him it was no more than an important adjunct to unerring length and tantalising direction. Bowling a long-hop was anathema to Grimmett, who believed that a bowler should bowl as well as he possibly could every time he turned his arm over. And Grimmett was perhaps the best and most consistently active cricket thinker I ever met.

He loved to tell his listeners that it was he who taught Stan McCabe how to use his left hand correctly on the bat handle – and I never heard Stan deny it. The "flipper" was originated by "Grum" during that Babylonian Captivity of his, and he used it to good effect in his record-breaking last season before the Second World War. He seldom bowled the wrong'un, because he preferred not to toss the ball high. He never let a batsman off the hook; once you were under his spell you were there to stay.

Grimmett joined South Australia from Victoria in 1923, just in time to bowl his way into the final Test in Sydney against Arthur Gilligan's 1924-25 England team. In his baptismal effort he took 11 wickets. In 79 Sheffield Shield games he tallied 513 wickets, an Australian record that will probably last for ever. The most successful Shield spinner in modern times, Richie Benaud, totalled 266 wickets in 73 matches. Of Grimmett's 106 Test wickets against England, nearly 70 were collected on English pitches in a land where savants say leg-spinners are ineffective.

Social life meant little to "Grum". Not until late in his career did he discover that it was not a bad idea to relax between matches. In England in 1934 I bought him a beer in the Star Hotel in Worcester to celebrate his first ten wickets of the tour. It took him so long to sink it that I decided to wait for his return gesture till some other time on the tour. Later he told me, with obvious regret, that on previous tours he had been keeping the wrong company and had never really enjoyed a touring trip. With "Grum" at the other end, prepared to pick me up and dust me down, I feared no batsman. Our association must have been one of cricket's greatest success stories of the 20th century.

ONE-MATCH WONDER   2002

HAMMOND-CHAMBERS-BORGNIS, RICHARD PETER, who played his one first-class game as R. P. Borgnis, died in France on May 28, 2001, aged 90. Few can have enjoyed a sole first-class appearance of such dreamlike quality. A relative of Sir H. D. G. Leveson Gower, Peter Borgnis was a Royal Navy lieutenant when, in 1937, he played for the Combined Services at Portsmouth against the New Zealand tourists. He entered the fray with the score 18 for four and, in two and a half hours, struck a bold 101 out of 180. He then opened the bowling and took three for 38 in the visitors' first innings. The New Zealanders won easily by nine wickets, and that, as far as his first-class cricket was concerned, was that.

TESTING THE 30-MILE LIMIT   1956

HARGREAVES, MR TOM KNIGHT, who died in hospital at Rotherham on November 19, 1955, aged 61, was a prominent all-rounder in Yorkshire Council cricket from 1921 till 1951. He played for Wath till he was 57, scoring many runs and proving successful as a slow bowler. He brought off one of the biggest hits in cricket on one occasion when playing at the Wath Athletic Ground. A mighty six sent the ball soaring out of the ground and into a wagon of a goods train on the nearby railway line. The ball was carried on to Scunthorpe.

The distance is roughly 30 miles.

DOMINANT FIGURE OF THE GAME   Stewart Caine, 1933

A great batsman and a brilliant field in his younger days, and all his life a commanding figure in the world of cricket, LORD HARRIS, who died on March 24, 1932, was born at St Anne's, Trinidad, on February 3, 1851, and so at the time of his death had entered upon his 82nd year.

Prior to his career with Oxford there had commenced that close association with Kent which during the rest of his life commanded so much of Lord Harris's energy and enthusiasm. Indeed, so far back as 1870 he played for Kent, and was elected to the committee of the county club – his father at that time being president

– and in 1874 he succeeded to the honorary secretaryship which for 25 years previously had been held by W. de Chair Baker.

Twelve months later, he became captain of the eleven and so continued for 15 seasons, resigning after the summer of 1889 on his appointment to the Governorship of Bombay, which kept him out of England from 1890 to 1895. Even after the five years in India, he, when in the middle forties, played occasionally for Kent in 1896 and 1897. He was president of that county so far back as 1875 when he also officiated as secretary and captain. During the latter years of his life, he was not only a trustee but also chairman of the county club.

Almost as close as the connection with Kent was that of Lord Harris with the Marylebone Club. First elected to the committee in 1875, he was president in 1895, and was chosen in 1906 as one of the trustees, a position he resigned ten years later when, on the death of the Hon. Sir Spencer Ponsonby-Fane, he became treasurer.

In the autumn of 1878 he took a team out to Australia. In the second game with New South Wales, there occurred over an umpire's decision a disturbance of so disgraceful a nature that the Australians, on the occasion of their second visit to England in 1880, could secure scarcely any fixtures with first-class sides. Whatever the dominating cause of this cold reception, the fact remains that at the end of August the Australians had taken part in only five 11-a-side games. Such wonderful work with the ball against local eighteens, however, stood to the credit of Spofforth, Boyle and Palmer that public opinion demanded the tourists should be given a real trial of strength. Accordingly – Sussex agreeing to the postponement of a fixture – Lord Harris got up a team and there was decided at The Oval, in the early days of September, the first real Test match. Lord Harris captained not only the side victorious on that occasion but four years later, when for the first time in this country the number of Test matches was increased to three, led England at Lord's and at The Oval.

While his work for Kent cricket, into the improvement of which he threw himself heart and soul – he had his reward in seeing that county carry off the Championship on four occasions – was his great monument, Lord Harris will always be remembered for the splendid stand he made against unfair bowling. Thanks largely to his efforts, cricket today is practically free from that evil, but in the early eighties the practice of throwing obtained to no inconsiderable extent in first-class cricket and threatened to become more and more pronounced.

Lord Harris in 1887 was mainly responsible for the establishment of the County Cricket Council. This was a body of considerable possibilities but very jealously regarded by some of the older brigade of cricketers, and when Lord Harris left England for Bombay, the Council, passing a resolution to adjourn *sine die*, voted itself out of existence. In these days the work which, no doubt, would have gradually fallen into the hands of the Council is performed by the Advisory County Cricket Committee of the MCC, which was formed in 1904.

A batsman of very high class, possessed of an excellent style and great punishing powers, and full of pluck, Lord Harris was never afraid of a rough wicket – he played, when suffering from a damaged or broken finger, an heroic innings against Derbyshire on a vile pitch at Derby in 1884. In 1882 and in each of the following years he had a batting average of over 30 – no small achievement in those days – that of 1884 being 33 with an aggregate of 1,417.

Lord Harris's highest innings for Kent was 176 against Sussex in 1882, when he and Lord Throwley made 208 for the first wicket. Altogether, he scored 7,806 runs for Kent with an average of 30 – a figure he exceeded in nine different seasons – and for that county played nine separate innings of 100 or more.

A great figure at the Canterbury Week over a period of 60 years, Lord Harris first participated in the Festival in 1870. Always keenly interested in the Cricketers' Fund Friendly Society, he had been president of that body for many years to the time of his death. Lord Harris was the author of three books – *A History of Kent County Cricket*, *A Few Short Runs*, and (in conjunction with Mr F. S. Ashley Cooper) *Lord's and the MCC*.

Little Wonder No. 139

Warwickshire v Leicestershire (Friends Provident T20). At Birmingham, June 23, 2010. Matt Boyce's remarkable contribution as twelfth man, running out Carter, Troughton and Tim Ambrose, secured him the match award. Boyce was pressed into service after Will Jefferson, who made 50 from 31 balls, jabbed a ball on to his ankle.

RUNS IN THE FAMILY   1939

HAYWARD, THOMAS WALTER, who died on July 19, 1938, aged 68, at his Cambridge home, was one of the greatest batsmen of all time. He afforded a notable instance of hereditary talent. A son of Daniel Hayward, a player of some repute, he was a nephew of Thomas Hayward, who in the 1860s was by common consent the leading professional batsman in England.

Born at Cambridge on March 29, 1871, he belonged to a family which lived for many generations at Mitcham; both his father and grandfather appeared in the Surrey XI. Like his famous uncle he played in beautiful style. It may be questioned whether anyone ever surpassed him in making the off-drive, the stroke being executed delightfully and so admirably timed that the ball was rarely lifted. Of good height and build, Hayward had remarkable powers of endurance. He first appeared for Surrey in a county match in 1893, and in 1898 played his greatest innings – 315 not out against Lancashire at The Oval.

Equal in merit was his 130 for England when badly needed in the fourth match against Australia at Old Trafford in 1899. At The Oval that season Hayward and F. S. Jackson, the best batsmen in the earlier Tests, were chosen by A. C. MacLaren to open the England innings and they made 185, the amateur's share being 118. England put together 576, so beating the 551 by Australia on the Surrey ground in 1884. Hayward altogether played in 29 Tests against Australia, which he visited three times, and he also played in six matches against South Africa. An automatic choice for the Players, Hayward, in 29 matches against the Gentlemen at Lord's and The Oval, scored 2,374 runs with an average over 47.

For 20 years in succession, 1895–1914, he scored over 1,000 runs each season in first-class cricket. In 1904 he made 3,170, and in 1906 3,518, which still stands as the record aggregate in first-class cricket*. Hayward, 273, and Abel, 193, made a world record for the fourth wicket, 448 against Yorkshire at The Oval in 1899. Before the war – 1905 to 1914 – Hayward and Hobbs, also born at Cambridge, became the most notable opening pair in the game. They put up 100 or more for the first wicket on 40 occasions. In 1907 they accomplished a performance without parallel in first-class cricket by making 100 for Surrey's first wicket four times in one week: 106 and 125 against Cambridge University at The Oval; 147 and 105 against Middlesex at Lord's.

Hayward was the first batsman after W. G. Grace to complete the hundred centuries, and altogether he reached three figures on 104 occasions, 58 times at The Oval and 88 for Surrey. In three matches he scored a hundred in each innings, excelling in 1906 by doing this twice in six days – 144 not out and 100 at Trent Bridge off the Nottinghamshire bowlers, 143 and 125 at Leicester. He carried his bat through the first innings for 225 at Nottingham, the next-best score being 32. That season Hayward made 13 centuries, equalling the record set up by C. B. Fry in 1901. Eight times he carried his bat through an innings; he achieved the double event in 1897 with 1,368 runs and 114 wickets, and another distinction he enjoyed was scoring 1,000 runs before the end of May in 1900.

Putting on weight, he became rather slow in the field, though playing to the end of season 1914; 43 years of age when the war broke out, he did not attempt to return to active participation in the game when cricket was resumed in 1919.

Altogether in first-class cricket Tom Hayward scored 43,409 runs with an average of 41.69 and took 481 wickets at a cost of 22.94 each.

* *Hayward's record was beaten by Denis Compton and Bill Edrich in 1947.*

ONE OF THE VERY BEST   1945

HEARNE, JOHN THOMAS, one of the finest bowlers the game has ever known, who played for Middlesex and England, died on April 17, 1944, after a long illness, at Chalfont St Giles in Buckinghamshire, the place of his birth on May 3, 1867. From 1891 to 1914 he held a prominent place among the very best bowlers, and finished his career with a record of 3,060 wickets, an aggregate surpassed only by W. Rhodes, 4,187, A. P. Freeman, 3,775, and C. W. L. Parker, 3,274.

Right-hand medium-pace, he took a fairly long run-up to the wicket, and it would be difficult to recall a bowler with a more beautiful delivery. On a bowler's wicket he could dismiss the strongest sides, and on one of the crumbling pitches which occasionally bothered batsmen 40 years ago he was simply unplayable.

Jack Hearne came of famous cricket stock. A nephew of old Tom Hearne and of George Hearne, both of whom played for Bucks and Middlesex before the latter went to Catford Bridge, he was a cousin of G. G. Hearne, Frank Hearne and Alec Hearne, all distinguished professionals for Kent. His brother, Walter Hearne, also a good Kent bowler, broke down through knee trouble when he looked to have many years of success before him.

In 1891 at Lord's he took 14 Yorkshire wickets for less than five runs apiece, and in 14 matches the capture of 118 wickets for ten runs each put him top of the first-class averages. From that proof of ability he went steadily ahead, and his aggregate rose to 257 wickets at 14.72 each in 1896. In fact, that was Hearne's greatest year. With 56 wickets at 13.17 runs apiece he far surpassed the work of any other bowler during the summer against the [Australian] touring team. In the three Test matches he took 15 wickets at 14.1 each, dividing the honours with Tom Richardson, whose 24 wickets cost 18.7 each. At The Oval, where Australia scored only 119 and 44, he took six wickets for 41 and four for 19 – ten in all for six runs apiece, so having a large share in winning the rubber match by 66 runs.

In the winter of 1897 he went to Australia with A. E. Stoddart, and his nine wickets for 141 in the First Test at Sydney helped materially in England's only win in the rubber of five matches, which all told yielded him no more than 20 victims. He took part in three Test matches in 1899 – the first experience of a rubber of five in England – and at Leeds set up a record that still stands by doing the only hat-trick against Australia in a Test match in England.

In 15 different seasons Jack Hearne took over 100 wickets; three times more than 200.

TOO LATE IN THE DAY
Supplementary Obituary, 1994

HEARNE, THOMAS JOHN, who died on May 25, 1947, aged 59, was called late to take part in his only first-class match, for Middlesex against the Gentlemen of Philadelphia at Lord's in 1908, as a replacement for his cousin J. T. Hearne. However, the game was played on a treacherous pitch and finished in a day; Hearne, arriving late afternoon, never took the field. Many of his relatives were better-known cricketers; he did play usefully for Berkshire.

LIFE AND SOUL OF THE PARTY
1963

HENDREN, ELIAS HENRY, who died in a London hospital on October 4, 1962, aged 73, was one of the most famous batsmen to play for Middlesex and England. Only one cricketer, Sir John Hobbs, in the whole history of the first-class game hit more centuries than Hendren's 170; only two, Hobbs and F. E. Woolley, exceeded his aggregate of runs, 57,610 scored at an average of 50.80 per innings.

"Patsy", as, because of his Irish ancestry, he was affectionately known the world over, joined the Lord's groundstaff in 1905, and from his first appearance for Middlesex in 1909 he played regularly till 1937. Not always orthodox in style, this short, stockily built batsman was celebrated for the power with which he invested his driving, for his cutting and for his courage in hooking fast bowlers. On pitches helpful to bowlers, he used his feet with consummate skill. His ability as a deep fieldsman is illustrated to some extent by the number of catches he brought off, 725, but the number of runs he saved cannot be gauged.

Apart from his achievements, "Patsy" was a "character" of a type sadly lacking in modern cricket. No game in which he was engaged could be altogether dull. If it looked like becoming so, Hendren could be relied upon at one time or another to produce some antic which would bring an appreciative chuckle from the onlookers. Furthermore, he was a first-rate mimic and wit, qualities which made him an admirable member of teams on tours, of which he took part in six – three in Australia, one in South Africa and two in the West Indies. Altogether he played in 51 Test matches, 28 of them against Australia, scoring 3,525 runs.

Of his seven centuries in Tests the highest was 205 not out against the West Indies at Port-of-Spain in 1930. His highest innings in first-class cricket was 301 not out from the Worcestershire bowling at Dudley in 1933; and he reached three figures for Middlesex against every other first-class county. His best season was that of 1928 when he hit 3,311 runs, including 13 centuries, at an average of 70.44. In three summers he exceeded 3,000 runs; in 12 he made more than 2,000 and in ten over 1,000. Among many big partnerships with his great friend and county colleague, J. W. Hearne, that of 375 against Hampshire at Southampton in 1923 was at the time a world's record for the third wicket.

In 1933 Hendren caused something of a sensation at Lord's when he batted against the West Indies fast bowlers wearing a special cap. Fashioned by his wife, this cap had three peaks, two of which covered the ears and temples, and was lined with sponge rubber. Hendren explained that he needed protection after being struck on the head two years earlier by the new-fashioned persistent short-pitched bouncers.

Following his retirement from the field, he succeeded Wilfred Rhodes as coach at Harrow School, and for four years held a similar post with Sussex. He was elected a life member of MCC in 1949 and also served on the Middlesex committee. In 1952 he became scorer for Middlesex, continuing till ill-health compelled him to give up in 1960. In his younger days he was a fine Association football wing forward, playing in turn for Brentford, Queen's Park Rangers, Manchester City and Coventry City, and he appeared in a "Victory" international for England in 1919.

PERSONIFICATION OF WOMEN'S CRICKET   1996

HIDE, MARY EDITH, died in hospital on September 10, 1995, aged 81. Molly Hide was a farmer's daughter from Surrey (though she was born in Shanghai) who became one of the great pioneers of women's cricket in England. She played in the first-ever women's Test, in Brisbane in December 1934, and was England captain for 17 years. Tall and lithe, she could drive the ball beautifully, but her batting had a strength as well as a style that astonished sceptical male spectators, many of whom in her era thought women's cricket was like a dog on its hind legs. Her first great triumph came after the 1934-35 tour moved on to New Zealand, when she scored a century in the Christchurch Test, putting on 235 with Betty Snowball. England declared at 503 for five – New Zealand had been bowled out for 44, and lost by an innings and 337. She became captain for the home series against Australia two years later and held the post until her retirement in 1954. She would have missed the 1939-40 tour of Australia, because her parents persuaded her to stay on the farm and not go gallivanting. But the tour was cancelled anyway, and when it finally took place nine years later she scored five centuries, including 124 not out at the Sydney Cricket Ground, and her portrait was hung in the pavilion. In 15 Tests she scored 872 runs at 36.33, and took 36 wickets at 15.25, with the slowish off cutters that she bowled only reluctantly. Her captaincy was firm, even stern, and she remained in touch with the game, as a selector and, in 1973, president of the Women's Cricket Association. Molly Hide also played lacrosse for England. As Netta Rheinberg said, "she was the personification of women's cricket", doing an immense amount to give the game credibility.

UNHINDERED CLIMB TO THE TOP   1946

HILL, MR CLEMENT, the Australian left-handed batsman, ranked among the finest cricketers in the world during a long period, died on September 5, 1945, aged 68. Born at Adelaide on March 18, 1877, the son of H. J. Hill, who scored the first century on Adelaide Oval, Clem Hill excelled his brothers – all good at the game – and when 16 he put together the remarkable score of 360 in an inter-college match at Adelaide. This was the highest innings hit in Australia at that time, 1893, and young Clem Hill gave clear indication of the skill which matured without a check.

From 1896 to 1912 he played in 49 Test matches, 41 against England, eight against South Africa; he captained Australia when South Africa were the visitors in 1910, and in the following season against the England touring side, led by J. W. H. T. Douglas.

As a rule Clem Hill, going in first wicket down, was at his best on the important occasion and in Test matches he scored 3,412 runs; average 39. He hit seven centuries against South Africa and four against England, besides 96, 99, 98 and 97.

A specially brilliant batsman on hard pitches, Clem Hill scored 6,274 runs, average 52.28 in Sheffield Shield matches – a record until beaten by Don Bradman. His highest innings was 365 not out for South Australia against New South Wales at Adelaide in December 1900, his average that season being 103.33.

A splendid field particularly in the deep, Clem Hill brought off one catch that will never be forgotten by the spectators at the Third Test match at Old Trafford in 1902. When England wanted eight runs for victory with two wickets in hand, Dick Lilley made a square-leg hit which looked like carrying the pavilion rails, but as Hill ran from long-on the wind seemed to check the force of the hit. The ball fell almost straight and Hill, racing across its flight, with outstretched hands, held it, so accepting a chance that few fieldsmen would have thought worth attempting. Australia won by three runs, and the victory, following success at Sheffield, where Hill scored 119, by far the highest innings in the match, gave them the rubber.

NATIONAL LEADER, NOT LEADING CRICKETER   1996

HOME OF THE HIRSEL, The Baron, KT, PC, who died at his home on October 9, 1995, aged 92, was the only British prime minister to have played first-class cricket. As Lord Dunglass, he was a useful member of the Eton XI. In the rain-affected

Eton–Harrow match of 1922 he scored 66, despite being hindered by a saturated outfield, and then took four for 37 with his medium-paced outswingers. He played ten first-class matches for six different teams: Middlesex, Oxford University, H. D. G. Leveson Gower's XI, MCC (with whom he toured South America under Pelham Warner), Free Foresters and Harlequins. His two games for Middlesex were in 1924 and 1925, both against Oxford University while he was actually an Oxford under-graduate; he did not represent the university until the following year. His cricket was gradually overtaken by politics, and he entered the Commons in 1931. After he succeeded to his father's title and became the 14th Earl of Home, he rose to be foreign secretary and then prime minister, when he emerged as a totally unexpected compromise choice as Harold Macmillan's successor. After renouncing his title (and becoming Sir Alec Douglas-Home until he returned to the Lords as a life peer) he remained in Downing Street for a year until the 1964 election. Despite all his honours, Alec Home never made an enemy and was much valued, in cricket as in politics, for his quiet charm and sagacity. He was president of MCC in 1966 and an important behind-the-scenes influence whenever the game was in difficulties. From 1977 to 1989 Lord Home was Governor of I Zingari. The general opinion is that, even if he had devoted himself to the game, he would not have been a regular county player, but then no one expected him to rise so high in politics either.

GIVEN A HARD TIME BY THE PRESS CORPS 2006

HUGHES, MARGARET PATRICIA, who died on January 30, 2005, aged 85, was believed to be the first woman ever to report an Ashes tour for a daily newspaper. She went out to Australia in 1954-55 and persuaded Sir Frank Packer (Kerry's father) to let her report the Tests for his Sydney tabloid, the *Daily Telegraph*. It is thought no one emulated her until Chloe Saltau covered the 2005 series for *The Age*. Hughes published a discursive tour diary, *The Long Hop*, a follow-up to her earlier cricket book, *All on a Summer's Day*. John Arlott praised her eye for detail and character. But she was spurned by most of the cricket writers ("I have been treated as a freak, rather like the fat lady at the circus," she wrote), perhaps due in part to gossip about the exact nature of her relationship with her mentor, Neville Cardus, who was 30 years older. When Cardus died, Hughes became his literary executor and edited the successful collections of his work. She was a regular at Lord's until just before she died.

WINE, WOMEN AND SONG – BUT NOT MUCH SINGING 2007

INGLEBY-MACKENZIE, ALEXANDER COLIN DAVID, OBE, died of cancer on March 9, 2006, aged 72. Colin Ingleby-Mackenzie was one of the most extraor-dinary, and best-loved, men ever to play cricket. He gave the impression that his life was a party that lasted 72 years, which was not that far from the truth. Nonetheless, he was a successful captain – leading Hampshire to their first County Championship – and a radical president of MCC.

Colin's father was Surgeon Vice-Admiral Sir Alexander Ingleby-Mackenzie, who had been with the Hampshire president, Harry Altham, at Repton. Altham saw Colin, aged 12, execute a perfect on-drive in the nets, and marked him down as a future Hampshire captain – which says something about both the attitudes of the era, and Altham's prescience. In 1956 he began to score runs, finally impressing the old pros with an unbeaten 130 against Worcestershire at Cowes. It was an appropriate place for him to make his name, since he was to bring to Hampshire the air of a regatta: complete with a breezy freshness, a sense of style and pretty girls.

In 1957, the long-standing captain Desmond Eagar occasionally stood aside to let Ingleby take charge, which he did full-time in 1958. Still only 24, he led Hampshire to second place in the Championship, their highest-ever position. In early August, they had looked like being champions before falling away. But the template for his captaincy had been set: a spirit of enterprise sometimes bordering on what sterner minds called recklessness. It was exemplified by his own batting – Ingleby scored two centuries in 1958: one took 98 minutes, the other 61. He would score 1,000 each year from 1957 to 1962 (except 1960, when he missed by two), and averaged 26, but that really was an average, not a benchmark.

But the next two seasons Hampshire drifted. They finished eighth and 12th: a lot of catches were dropped; the captain's concentration wavered under the pressure of six-day-a-week cricket; and it was noted that his injuries appeared to coincide with the fashionable race meetings. In January 1961, however, the admiral died, and the effect on his son was profound: Prince Hal turned into Henry V.

With fearsome batting – led by the brilliant Roy Marshall – and an attack spearheaded by Butch White and Derek Shackleton, he had the side to back him up. Hampshire won a succession of breathless and improbable victories to stay in contention. In July he broke his thumb (for Goodwood, this time) and the team again got nervy. But he came back, with renewed vigour, and Hampshire won five successive matches. They sealed their first title on a glorious afternoon at Bournemouth against Derbyshire after another exquisitely timed declaration.

The aura round this triumph still glows, and the legend grows. What exactly was Hampshire's famous training regime? There have been various versions of the story but, at the memorial service (venue: St Paul's; attendance: 1,600), Mark Nicholas traced it back to an interview with a po-faced reporter from BBC *Sportsview*, with Ingleby in full mickey-taking mode. "To what do you attribute your success?" "Oh, wine, women and song, I should say, though in truth there wasn't so much singing." "But don't you have certain rules, discipline, helpful hints for younger viewers?" "Well, everyone in bed by breakfast, I suppose." "Yes, thank you, now might we take a look in the dressing-room?" "Certainly, as long as you don't mind me wandering around in the nude."

It was on one of E. W. Swanton's tours to the Caribbean that Jim is supposed to have suggested the players all went to bed by 11 and drawn the reply from Ingleby: "Well, that's pretty silly. The game starts at half past." It certainly wasn't all legend. The 61-minute hundred evidently came after a day at Ascot and a mad all-nighter. Contemporaries swear the captain really did turn up at games in his dinner jacket.

Hampshire faded after 1961: the fielding declined, and the next four seasons comprised a long anticlimax. Ingleby gave up cricket, aged 31, and went into insurance. When he retired from business, he enlivened the Country Gentlemen's

Association by becoming its chairman, and MCC, by taking on the presidency from 1996 to 1998. He set out to achieve the long-resisted admission of women, failing narrowly to get the required two-thirds majority the first time; the walls finally tumbled two days before he handed over to his successor, Tony Lewis. But Ingleby couldn't help being Ingleby: when Lewis presented the membership cards to the first ten women, who had all been waiting a long time, his predecessor whispered: "Perhaps we should have inspected the merchandise first."

Little Wonder No. 140

Australia v Pakistan (Fifth One-Day International). At Perth, January 31, 2010. In the closing overs Shahid Afridi – captain for the day after Mohammad Yusuf pulled out pleading knee trouble – was captured on television biting the ball as if it were an apple. The umpires immediately replaced the ball, and Afridi was subsequently banned for two Twenty20 internationals for ball-tampering. His initial explanation was, "I tried to smell it, how it's feeling. There was something on it so I tried to move it." Later he added: "There is no team in the world that doesn't tamper with the ball."

EPITOME OF THE PROFESSIONAL AMATEUR

2006

KEIGHLEY, WILLIAM GEOFFREY, OAM, died in Australia on June 14, 2005, aged 80. Apart from Lord Hawke, Geoffrey Keighley was perhaps the most significant exception ever allowed to the "county-born only" rule at Yorkshire before it collapsed in 1991. Born in Nice, he played 35 matches as an amateur between 1947 and 1951, apparently without comment or complaint. His father was a well-known Bradford industrialist; and Keighley was an Eton and Oxford-educated opening bat with a classical style, seen as a potential captain. In only his second first-class appearance, he made a "faultless" 105 for the university against the 1947 South Africans, and scored 99 in the Varsity Match, being bowled by Trevor Bailey to end a stand with Tony Pawson of 226. Pawson thought Keighley had imbibed so much Yorkshire influence about playing correctly, it inhibited his talent and thirst for runs: "After getting out for seven or something, he'd say 'Yorkshire would be pleased with that.'" But in the end he was too restless to be constrained by county cricket. He married, moved to Australia, took on a 1,000-acre sheep farm, and confined his cricket to captaining Stockinbingal and Cootamundra, but in other respects became the epitome, as one obituarist put it, of the professional amateur. He became an idiosyncratic Country Party member of the New South Wales Legislative Council (advocating the decriminalisation of both abortion and marijuana), represented Australia at international agricultural negotiations, learned to fly and paint, filled his house with art treasures, and ran a classical-music radio station.

LINDWALL, RAYMOND RUSSELL, MBE, died on June 23, 1996, aged 74. Ray Lindwall was undeniably one of the great fast bowlers, arguably the greatest of all the Australian practitioners, and perhaps the man who established fast bowling's role in the modern game. In the 1930s the game had been dominated by batsmen, with the brief, unacceptable, interlude of Bodyline. Lindwall began a new era in which bat and ball were more evenly matched, when the bouncer (or "bumper" as it was then called) was an accepted weapon, provided it was not overused. He bowled the bumper sparingly but brilliantly, and the mere possibility of it made batsmen uneasy. He thus paved the way for all the other great fast bowlers of the post-war era, from Trueman to Ambrose. But in fact more than two-fifths of Lindwall's 228 Test victims were bowled.

Ray was a Sydney boy and watched Larwood during the Bodyline series. He played with other kids on patches of green and in the streets, choosing – it is said – the street down which the great leg-spinner Bill O'Reilly walked home in the hope of catching his eye.

Halfway through the home 1946-47 series against England, he and Keith Miller emerged as the undisputed leaders of Australia's attack; on top of that Lindwall actually beat Miller to a Test century, scoring 100 at the MCG in the New Year Test of 1947, batting at No. 9. At Sydney two months later, Lindwall took seven for 63 and, after getting seven for 38 against India in 1947-48, came to England in 1948 an established star.

On that tour, he rose to even greater fame as the leader of the attack in Australia's 4–0 triumph. And though Bradman used him carefully, his very presence dictated the terms. Lindwall was injured during the First Test, but in three of the subsequent four he was devastating, reaching his peak at The Oval when he took six for 20 as England were bowled out for 52. He had a clever slower ball (which would have stood him in good stead in modern one-day cricket) and, though his arm was too low to satisfy the sternest purists, he was close to being the complete fast bowler. The low arm meant his bowling had a skidding effect, which made the bouncers all the more fearsome.

Lindwall never quite reached such a peak after 1948, but he was opening Australia's attack as late as January 1960, when he was 38, and played the last of his 61 Tests a few weeks later. Lindwall simply would not go away. Inevitably, his shock effect had declined by then but, like his eventual heir Dennis Lillee, he compensated by his canniness, mastery of technique – he began to use the inswinger far more – and utter determination. He captained Australia once and, for several seasons, Queensland, having moved from New South Wales, before finishing with 228 Test wickets at 23.03 and 794 first-class wickets at 21.35.

He was a much-liked man but not a flamboyant character like Miller. He was a phenomenal all-round sportsman: had he not played cricket, Lindwall could easily have been a rugby league international, and he ran 100 yards in 10.6 seconds. But when he retired he ran a flower shop with his wife in the centre of Brisbane. If anyone in Australia ever imagined floristry was unmanly, his presence in the shop provided an answer, though he concentrated on the figures, and his assistant claimed he could not tell a rose from a dandelion.

While still playing for New South Wales, he once saw the young Alan Davidson bowl a bouncer at an opposing No. 8. "You've just insulted all fast bowlers," Lindwall told him. "You've admitted No. 8 can bat better than you can bowl. Get into the nets and learn how to bowl." And he took him there, and taught him.

LOST AND FOUND KEY TO SPIN BOWLING 1996

LOCK, GRAHAM ANTHONY RICHARD, died on March 29, 1995, aged 65, in Perth, Western Australia, where, in the 1960s, he enjoyed a career as rewarding as that pursued throughout the previous decade for Surrey and England. Tony Lock was an aggressive, attacking left-arm spinner, who complemented ideally the subtleties of Jim Laker's off-spin when Surrey were winning the County Championship every year from 1952 to 1958 and England regained, then retained, the Ashes; their names were twinned in cricket lore in a way usually associated with opening batsmen and fast bowlers. The final phase of his playing days saw him as a more orthodox slow bowler, relying on guile and flight as much as spin, and as a driving captain of Western Australia and Leicestershire.

Recommended to Surrey by H. D. G. Leveson Gower, Lock made his Championship debut in 1946, a week after his 17th birthday, against Kent at The Oval, and marked it with a hot catch at backward short leg off Alf Gover – the first of 830 in his career. In 1951 he took 100 wickets for the first time. But the 1952 *Wisden* said he would struggle to gain higher honours "unless he imparts more spin to his leg-break". After two winters working at an indoor school in Croydon, he emerged with a lower trajectory that produced vicious spin at around medium-pace. Now the ball spat from leg stump to hit the top of the off, or spun devilishly and jumped shoulder-high. Gone were his original high-arm action and the classical spin bowler's loop, victims, it was said, of a low beam in those Croydon nets that had forced him to drop his arm. His new method was far more effective but produced mutterings about its legitimacy. In 1952 he was called up for the Old Trafford Test against India, and took four for 36 in the second innings. But a week later, when Surrey played the tourists at The Oval, he was no-balled three times in two overs for throwing his quicker ball. Raising the beam at the Croydon nets helped restore something of Lock's original action, but he was again called for throwing in the West Indies in 1953-54 and for a time he refrained from bowling his faster ball.

Although picked for the First Test against Australia in 1953, he wore his spinning finger raw the day after selection and played in only the last two Tests. At The Oval his return of 21-9-45-5 on the third afternoon, along with Laker's four for 75, was instrumental in Australia's dismissal for 162. Next day, England regained the Ashes for the first time since 1932-33. It was a different story at Old Trafford in 1956, when Laker took 19 Australian wickets while Lock had to be content with the leftover, and economical match figures of one for 106 from 69 overs.

When he was omitted from the side for Australia in 1962-63, he went instead to play for Western Australia, where he immediately became a fixture. In 1966-67, he was the first post-war bowler to take 50 or more Shield wickets in a season. He assumed the captaincy in 1967-68 and led Western Australia to only their second Shield. Meanwhile, he had been recruited by Leicestershire for midweek games in 1965, and captained them in the next two seasons with such infectious enthusiasm that they rose from 14th in 1965 to second in 1967, then their highest position in the Championship.

There was an unexpected twist to this phase of his career when he was called to the Caribbean to replace the injured Fred Titmus in 1967-68 and played in the last two Tests. In the final one, at Georgetown, his belligerent 89 in England's first innings surpassed his previous-highest first-class score, and put England on course for the draw that gave them the series.

Lock continued as a coach in Perth, and from 1987 to 1991 was cricket professional at Mill Hill School in north London. His final years were overshadowed by two allegations of sexual abuse involving young girls, the second only months before his death from cancer. Cleared of both charges, he was nevertheless forced to sell some of his cricket memorabilia to meet his legal costs, and while the second court case was pending his wife died of a heart attack. He said bitterly just before he died that he would be remembered only for the charges and not for his cricket, but he will be proved wrong.

Only W. G. Grace and Frank Woolley have taken more catches. Lock is also ninth in the list of all-time wicket-takers with 2,844 at 19.23; 174 of those came in his 49 Tests, at 25.58. He was a volatile, vulnerable man but he was an astonishingly durable cricketer and the memory of that will endure too.

Airtel Champions League Twenty20 2010-11. Wayamba v Central Districts. At Port Elizabeth, September 22, 2010. With consecutive deliveries left-arm medium-pacer Isuru Udana had Brad Patton caught behind and Mathew Sinclair stumped off a wide, and bowled George Worker to complete a hat-trick from two legal balls (believed to be unique in senior cricket).

Little Wonder No. 141

Free Thinker Ahead Of His Time   1971

LYON, BEVERLEY HAMILTON, who died on June 22, 1970, aged 68, was one of the most astute captains of his era. In 1921, Lyon began his association with Gloucestershire. He became captain in 1929, a position which he filled for four seasons, and under his inspiring influence the county enjoyed greater success than for many years. Lyon also played his part as a hard-hitting batsman.

Lyon, known as an apostle of brighter cricket, was revolutionary in his cricket outlook. He was the originator in 1931 of the scheme by which a declaration by each side with only four byes scored in the first innings enabled maximum points to be available to the winning county after the loss of the opening two days of a Championship match through rain. This caused the Advisory County Cricket Committee to revise the regulations.

In all first-class cricket, Lyon made 10,615 runs for an average of 25.15, four times exceeding 1,000 runs in a season. He was also an excellent fieldsman, either at short leg or in the slips.

He was the first to suggest first-class county games on Sundays, an idea which it took 36 years for the authorities to adopt. He also advanced the scheme for a knockout competition, which came into being over 30 years afterwards.

There was no funeral for Beverley Lyon, for he bequeathed his body to the Royal College of Surgeons.

MASTER AND COMMANDER OF BOWLERS
1959

MACARTNEY, MR CHARLES GEORGE, who died in Sydney on September 9, 1958, aged 72, was one of the most brilliant and attractive right-handed batsmen in the history of Australian cricket. Daring and confident, he possessed a quickness of eye, hand and foot, a perfection of timing which made him a menace to the best of bowlers.

Of medium height and stocky build, "The Governor-General," as Macartney came to be known, was specially good in cutting and hitting to leg, though there was no stroke, orthodox or unorthodox, of which he did not show himself master. Intolerant of batsmen who did not treat bowling upon its merits, he was quoted as giving, not long before his death, as the reason why he had ceased to be a regular cricket spectator: "I can't bear watching luscious half-volleys being nudged gently back to bowlers." Yet in regard to his own achievements this man with the Napoleonic features could not have been more modest; he had no regard at all for records or averages, nor was he ever known to complain about an umpire's decision.

How punishing a batsman he could be was never more fully demonstrated than in 1921 when, at Trent Bridge, he took such full advantage of a missed chance when nine that he reached 345 from the Nottinghamshire bowling in less than four hours, with four sixes and 47 fours among his figures. This still stands as the highest innings put together by an Australian in England and, furthermore, no other batsman in first-class cricket has scored as many runs in a single day. It was also the third of four centuries in following innings, the others being 105 v. Hampshire at Southampton, 193 v. Northamptonshire at Northampton and 115 v. England at Leeds, where he performed the rare feat of getting to three figures before lunch.

From the time that he made his first appearance for Australia in 1907 till he ended his Test career in 1926, Macartney represented his country 35 times, scoring 2,132 runs, including seven centuries, average 41.80. His highest Test innings was 170 against England at Sydney in 1920-21. He headed the Australia averages with 86.66 that season and also figured at the top in England in 1926 when, with the aid of innings of 151, 133 not out and 109, his average was 94.60. In all cricket his runs numbered 15,003, average 45.87, and he hit 48 hundreds.

INNINGS THAT MADE BRADMAN PROUD
1969

McCABE, STANLEY JOSEPH, who died on August 25, 1968, aged 58, following a fall from a cliff at his home in Sydney, was one of Australia's greatest and most enterprising batsmen. In 62 Test innings between 1930 and 1938 he scored 2,748 runs, including six centuries, for an average of 48.21. During a first-class career lasting from 1928 to 1942, he obtained 11,951 runs, average 49.39, reaching three figures on 29 occasions. Short and stockily built, with strong arms, flexible wrists and excellent footwork, he was at his best when facing bowlers of pace.

Against D. R. Jardine's team in 1932-33 McCabe distinguished himself by hitting 385 runs in the five Tests, average nearly 43. His 187 not out in the first match of the series at Sydney was a remarkable exhibition of both craftsmanship and courage. He made his runs out of 278 in less than four and threequarter hours, after his earlier colleagues failed. His hooking of short-pitched deliveries by H. Larwood and W. Voce was something which will forever hold a place in Australian cricket history.

In England again in 1934, he put together eight centuries – more than any of his team-mates – including 240, the highest of his career, against Surrey at The Oval and 137 in the Third Test at Old Trafford. Perhaps McCabe's most famous innings was his 232 not out in the opening Test against England at Trent Bridge in 1938 which, scored at the rate of one a minute, prompted Sir Donald Bradman, his captain, to greet him on his return to the pavilion with the words: "If I could play an innings like that, I'd be a proud man, Stan."

KEY MEMBER OF AUSTRALIA'S POST-WAR FORCE · 1938

McDONALD, EDGAR ARTHUR, famous with Australia and Lancashire, was killed on the road near Bolton after being concerned in a motor-car collision early in the morning of July 22, 1937.

Born in Tasmania on January 6, 1892, McDonald went to Melbourne in his youth and became a good fast bowler in pennant matches. He played once for Victoria against the MCC team captained by P. F. Warner in February 1912, but not until 1919 did he become prominent by taking eight wickets, six bowled, for 42 runs at Sydney under conditions favourable to batsmen, in the first innings of New South Wales.

McDonald did Australia splendid service in Test matches. He played in three against the MCC team that went to Australia in the winter of 1920 with J. W. H. T. Douglas as captain. Mailey, Gregory and Kelleway were the bowlers mainly responsible for the five defeats then inflicted on England. McDonald's six wickets cost 65 runs apiece, but he was picked for the ensuing visit to England and in the Tests he took 27 wickets for 24 runs apiece.

In the Test at Nottingham McDonald took eight wickets for 74, and at Lord's and Leeds he was mainly responsible for the fall of England's first three wickets so cheaply that defeat became inevitable. The Australians thus won the rubber and so beat England eight times in consecutive engagements.

At the end of the tour McDonald decided to accept an engagement as professional with the Nelson club, and in due course became qualified for Lancashire. Naturally enough, a bowler capable of such devastating work against the flower of England's batting accomplished remarkable things in county cricket and from 1924, when he was available only in midweek matches, until 1931, when his ability suddenly declined, he took 1,040 wickets for Lancashire. In his best season, 1925, he dismissed in all matches 205 batsmen at an average cost of 18.67. During this period Lancashire won the County Championship four times. One of his best performances was at Dover in 1926 when Kent, wanting 426 to win, got within 65 of victory for the loss of five wickets. McDonald then performed the hat-trick and Lancashire triumphed by 33 runs. In the match he took 12 wickets for 187 runs.

Of good height and loosely built, McDonald ran with easy grace to the crease and his rhythmical action, with accurate length and off-break, surprised every batsman when first facing him and often afterwards. In these particulars he was very different from Gregory with a longer, faster run and leaping delivery; but in Australian cricket the names of these two fast bowlers must be coupled as the terrific force which humiliated England in the first years of Test cricket after the War. Ordinarily of small account as a batsman, McDonald hit up a not-out century in 100 minutes against Middlesex at Old Trafford in 1926. His benefit match with Middlesex at Old Trafford in 1929 brought him nearly £2,000.

After giving up county cricket, McDonald returned to the Lancashire League with the Bacup club as successor to Arthur Richardson, another Australian. McDonald played for Victoria at both rugby and Association football.

GROUND-BREAKER WHO DEMANDED ATTENTION   1994

MACLAGAN, MYRTLE ETHEL, MBE, who died at Farnham on March 11, 1993, aged 81, was one of the best-known women cricketers of her day. She was in the cricket team at the Royal School, Bath, for six years and, having been coached by Tich Freeman, took five wickets in five balls with her off-breaks against Cheltenham Ladies College. She became a national personality after being chosen for the pioneering tour of Australia in 1934-35. In the first Test at Brisbane she made 72 and took seven for ten; in the second game at Sydney she made 119, the first hundred in a women's Test. England's men had just lost the Ashes but soon Maclagan's opening partnership with Betty Snowball was being compared to Hobbs and Sutcliffe, and the *Morning Post* published the following quatrain:

> What matter that we lost, mere nervy men
> Since England's women now play England's game,
> Wherefore Immortal *Wisden*, take your pen
> And write MACLAGAN on the scroll of fame.

MacLagan made another century against Australia in 1937, toured again in 1948-49, and captained England in two Tests at home in 1951. She was an officer in the ATS during the war and rejoined the Army in 1951, becoming Inspector, PT for the WRAC. Her last major match was against the Australian touring team for the Combined Services in 1963, when she scored 81 not out. She was 52.

In 1966 she was appointed MBE. At various times in her life she won prizes for squash, tennis, badminton and knitting. It was reported that so many people turned up for her 80th birthday she had to make a speech from the top of a stepladder and got attention by a blast on her whistle.

Honorary Killer With 624,000 Victims

MILLAR, MR CHARLES CHRISTIAN HOYER, founder and for 55 years president of Rosslyn Park rugby football club, who died on November 22, 1942, aged 81, deserved mention in *Wisden* for a very special and unique reason. He undertook on his own initiative to weed Lord's turf, and Sir Francis Lacey, secretary of MCC, signed a deed of appointment making him Honorary Weedkiller to GHQ Cricket. From 1919 to 1931 he kept up his task, being particularly busy on summer evenings after stumps were drawn, and his zeal often received comment from pressmen walking to the exit when their duties were done. Mr Millar, according to his own reckoning, accounted for 624,000 victims, having spent 956 hours in his war against plantains and other unwanted vegetation.

Last Of A Special Line

MILTON, CLEMENT ARTHUR died on April 25, 2007, aged 79. Arthur Milton was the 12th and last man to represent England at both cricket and soccer. There will never be another. And it seems unlikely there will be anyone else who quite so readily represents the schoolboy ideal of sporting excellence, in his looks, athleticism, grace and modesty.

Milton was at Cotham Grammar School in Bristol when Arsenal recruited him; he was in their reserve team before being called up in 1946. Over the next three years his sport was inevitably limited, though he was able to play his first two games for Gloucestershire in 1948, making an unbeaten 58 in the second match, against Combined Services. Soon Milton was a regular run-getter, though it would be 1951 before he made a century himself.

By then he was Arsenal's first-choice right-winger, and that autumn – after only a dozen first division matches – his team-mate Jimmy Logie wandered over at a training session to tell him Tom Finney was injured and that he was playing for England against Austria at Wembley. Milton took his boots, caught the bus and went to the team hotel. It was a strange experience, he said later, playing in front of 98,000 people, in stiff new socks. It was his only soccer international, and soon he even lost his Arsenal place and was left out for the FA Cup final. He won a League Championship medal in 1953, before being transferred to Bristol City in 1954-55, and winding down his football to concentrate on cricket. In 1952, he was Gloucestershire's leading batsman, and in 1953 his outstanding close catching was obvious enough for him to be used as a reserve fielder in the Ashes Tests.

Milton improved steadily (until he missed much of 1957 through injury), developing into an opener at the urging of his Gloucestershire mentors, George Emmett and Jack Crapp, who suggested it offered his best chance of a Test place. They were right, and in 1958 he got his chance at Headingley. In contrast to Wembley, he grabbed it – against an admittedly poor New Zealand side he became the first Gloucestershire player since W. G. Grace to score a century on his England debut. He performed respectably at The Oval, made another hundred on his debut for the Players, and won his place in the Ashes party. As a predominantly back-foot player, he might have been expected to succeed in Australia. But, after a promising start, he broke a finger twice and failed in both the Brisbane and Sydney Tests. He was picked to open with Ken Taylor of Yorkshire in the first two matches against India in 1959, but missed out again. After seven low scores in a row, he was dropped. Milton actually had his best season yet that hot summer, finishing 16 short of his 2,000.

Throughout the 1960s he remained one of the most admired and best-loved of cricketers. In 1967, aged 39, he did reach 2,000, almost carrying a weak team as he continued to open, though he insisted he would rather bat at No. 5. The following year he was finally made captain, but it had come too late, and he soon resigned. Milton carried on playing for another six seasons, until he was 46, and even then he was good enough to score a farewell 76 on a fiery pitch at Worcester. Still in love with the open air, he became coach at Oxford University and then a postman in Bristol, and when he reached retirement age he took on a paper round over the same route, cycling seven miles a day for £30 a week. He said that, riding over the Downs with his postbag in the early-morning sun, he felt like a millionaire.

Lucky To Bowl For So Long Without Being No-Balled Sydney Pardon, 1922

MOLD, ARTHUR, died, after a long illness, on April 29, 1921, at Middleton Cheney, near Banbury, his native village, where he had resided since his retirement. Arthur Mold had been out of first-class cricket for nearly 20 years, but he remained fresh in the memory of all who follow the game at all closely. He was one of the deadliest fast bowlers of his day, but right through his career the fairness of his delivery formed the subject of lively discussion. This may be said without doing him the smallest injustice. Born in Northamptonshire on May 30, 1865, he came out for his native county, but quickly qualified for Lancashire by residence. He gained a place in the Lancashire eleven in 1889, and remained associated with the team till he gave up public play. Season after season he met with brilliant success, keeping at his best till 1895 or 1896. After that he began to decline, but he was still a bowler to be feared. Even while he was at the height of his fame his delivery was, in private, spoken of in strong terms by many famous batsmen, but nothing happened till 1900, when in the Notts and Lancashire match at Trent Bridge he was no-balled by James Phillips, and sent down only one over in the whole game.

A little later the county captains took up the question of unfair bowling, and at their famous meeting Mold's delivery was condemned by 11 votes to one. The climax came when at Manchester in July, 1901, in the Lancashire and Somerset match, Mold was no-balled by James Phillips 16 times in ten overs. Mold played for England against Australia at Lord's, The Oval, and Manchester in 1893, but he was never picked for a tour in Australia. It has been urged in some quarters that Mold was an ill-used man, and that there was no ground for the severe criticisms passed upon him. I should say, on the other hand, that he was extremely lucky to bowl for so many seasons before being no-balled. To pretend that a perfectly fair bowler could have been condemned as he was is absurd. I happen to know that a famous batsman who played against him in his Northamptonshire days said: "If he is fair he is the best bowler in England, but I think he is a worse thrower than ever Crossland was." This opinion – expressed before Mold had been seen in a first-class match – and the vote of the county captains towards the close of his career, surely dispose of the notion that Mold was unjustly attacked. He did wonders for Lancashire, but personally I always thought he was in a false position.

INVETERATE AUTOGRAPH-HUNTER 2010

Baron MOORE of WOLVERCOTE, GCB, GCVO, CMG, QSO, PC, who died on April 7, 2009, the day after his 88th birthday, was the Queen's private secretary between 1977 and 1986. Philip Moore was an outstanding sportsman in his youth, playing rugby for England and cricket for Oxfordshire. He was top of both the batting and bowling averages at Cheltenham College in 1940 and, on being ennobled, he chose to include cricket and rugby balls in his coat of arms. In 1930 Moore had been one of a bunch of schoolboys who asked Don Bradman for his autograph during the Australians' match at Canterbury, only to be brusquely turned down just after The Don had been dismissed for 18 by Tich Freeman. At a lunch in Adelaide in 1986, Moore – accompanying the Queen on a Royal Tour – asked Bradman if he remembered the incident. Typically, he did: "I was very angry, I really was. He diddled me with that top-spinner ... I'm awfully sorry. I must make amends." And he promptly signed the menu.

THE FIRST BLACK TEST PLAYER Supplementary Obituary, 1994

MORRIS, SAMUEL, who died on September 20, 1931, aged 76, was the first black Test cricketer and the only one to play for Australia. He was born in Tasmania, according to some reports the son of West Indian parents attracted by the gold-rush, became recognised as a wicketkeeper there and moved into first-class cricket as a batsman and medium-paced bowler after being appointed curator at the St Kilda ground in Melbourne. He played his only Test, at Melbourne in 1884-85, after the entire team from the previous Test had pulled out after a row about their share of the gate money. The team was predictably beaten, but Morris dismissed two of England's top three and opened the batting in the first innings, when he was out for four. He remained a regular player for Victoria for the next eight years. He was curator at South Melbourne for 30 years from 1887, giving up only when he lost his sight.

INDIA'S FIRST SUPERSTAR 2006

MUSHTAQ ALI, SYED, died on June 18, 2005, aged 90. Tall and debonair, often with a kerchief knotted jauntily round his neck, Mushtaq Ali – the son of an Indore police inspector – was a prototype for India's modern cricket heroes. In his foreword to Mushtaq's autobiography, *Cricket Delightful*, Keith Miller called him "the Errol

Flynn of cricket – dashing, flamboyant, swashbuckling and immensely popular wherever he played". He was the first Indian to score a Test century overseas, with 112 at Old Trafford in 1936, when he beat Vijay Merchant to the mark during an opening stand of 203. He reached his hundred inside the final session on the second day, entrancing Neville Cardus, who enthused: "He transforms the bat into a conjuror's wand." There was one other Test century, 106 against West Indies at Calcutta in 1948-49. Mushtaq had a long career, starting in 1930 and continuing until 1963-64 when, aged 48, he scored 41 off several Test bowlers in a Defence Fund match. In between there were numerous Ranji Trophy finals for Holkar, but just 11 Test appearances. These were spread over almost 20 years and finished with India's first victory, by an innings, over England at Madras in 1951-52. Mushtaq's contribution was 22 in a useful opening stand of 53 with Pankaj Roy. He should have played more Test cricket, but the authorities were suspicious of him: there was an early mix-up when a selection letter apparently went astray, and later the Calcutta crowd chanted "No Mushtaq, no Test" when he was originally left out of a representative match against the Australian Services shortly after the war. He pulled out of the 1947-48 trip to Australia after one of his brothers died, and was not selected for the disastrous England tour of 1952. Even at 37 he might have been useful because, unlike most who toured that year, he relished fast bowling. Later, he was a slim, graceful, elder statesman at many of the multifarious awards nights that punctuate India's cricket seasons. Mushtaq's son, Gulrez Ali, and his grandson, Abbas Ali, both played first-class cricket.

Little Wonder No. 142

New Zealand v South Africa (World Cup). At Mirpur, March 25, 2011. New Zealand twelfth man Kyle Mills – who had just arrived in the middle carrying drinks – made physical contact with the nervy du Plessis following his part in the run-out of de Villiers. Mills was later fined 60% of his match fee on two counts of misconduct – a total of 120% – while du Plessis and Vettori, who was also involved in the argy-bargy, were both fined 50%.

INTIMIDATING SPIN-BOWLER TOUCHED WITH GREATNESS   1993

O'REILLY, WILLIAM JOSEPH, OBE, who died in a Sydney hospital on October 6, 1992, aged 86, was probably the greatest spin bowler the game has ever produced. Bill "Tiger" O'Reilly was unquestionably one of cricket's great figures: as a player, as a character and later as a writer on the game. His cricket was proof that spin bowling was not necessarily a gentle art. He was 6ft 2in tall, gripped the ball in his enormous right hand and released it at a pace that could be almost fast-medium. It would then bounce ferociously on the hard pitches of his time and, on occasion, knock wicketkeepers off their feet. He bowled leg-breaks and, especially, top-spinners and googlies, backed up by an intimidating manner. Off the field, his gruffness was mitigated by his intelligence, erudition, wit and twinkling eyes.

He played 27 Test matches and took 144 wickets – 102 of them Englishmen and the vital wicket of Walter Hammond ten times – averaging 22.59. But his figures have to be judged by the fact that all but one of his Tests came in the 1930s, when other bowlers were dominated by batsmen to an unprecedented extent. No one ever dominated O'Reilly. Even when England made 903 at The Oval in 1938, he bowled 85 overs and finished with figures of three for 178. And before that, he had secured the Ashes by taking five for 66 and five for 56 at Headingley.

O'Reilly was born in White Cliffs in the New South Wales bush into a large Irish family on December 20, 1905. His father was a small-town schoolmaster, and young Bill was above average at several sports, including tennis, athletics and rugby. In 1917 the family moved to Wingello. When he played his first match for Wingello Juniors, the team walked to the opposition's ground seven miles away in Tallong.

In the summer of 1925-26, the young O'Reilly, by now an undergraduate at the teachers' college in Sydney University, met the man whose destiny was to be linked with his for ever. O'Reilly's own account of this remains a classic. He was passing through Bowral Station on his way home to Wingello for his summer holiday when he heard his name being called down the platform. He put his head out of the carriage window and was told to get out at once: Wingello were playing at Bowral and needed him.

"How was I to know that I was about to cross swords with the greatest cricketer that ever set foot on a cricket field? He didn't have it all his own way, let me tell you. Well, not for the first couple of overs, anyway." By the close of play, 17-year-old Don Bradman was 234 not out. The match resumed a week later, according to the local custom. "The sun shone, the birds sang sweetly and the flowers bloomed as never before. I bowled him first ball with a leg-break which came from the leg stump to hit the off bail. Suddenly cricket was the best game in the whole wide world."

In 1926-27 O'Reilly was chosen for the New South Wales state practice squad on the strength of one match for North Sydney. A year later he made his first-class debut against the New Zealanders. But teachers in New South Wales work for the state rather than an individual school and the newly qualified O'Reilly was despatched to three different bush towns. He was transferred back to Sydney in time for the 1931-32 season, and after four more matches made his debut for Australia. He performed quietly in a match in which Bradman scored 299 not out and Grimmett took 14 wickets, but he had arrived. In the 1932-33 Bodyline series he took 27 wickets, without anyone noticing much, given what else was happening. In the series in England in 1934 he took 28 wickets, including seven in an innings twice.

He went back to Australia and suddenly announced his retirement. He had married in 1933, had a daughter and was anxious about his teaching career. However, Sydney Grammar School offered him a job that enabled him to play on. He toured South Africa in 1935-36 and took 27 wickets again, 25 in the great series against England in 1936-37 and 22 back in England in 1938, despite the unforgiving wickets of Trent Bridge and The Oval.

O'Reilly wrote on cricket for the *Sydney Morning Herald* with a muscular, very Australian prose style flavoured with wit and imagery. Until he finally retired in 1988, he was as revered in Australian press-boxes as he had been on the field. He was hot-blooded and humorous, which perhaps explains why his relationship with the cooler Bradman is believed to have been based on intense mutual respect rather than the profoundest form of Australian mateship. While Sir Donald walked the corridors of cricketing power O'Reilly was the rumbustious backbencher.

In his career he took 774 wickets at 16.60 and was successful at every level: playing for North Sydney and St George, he topped the Sydney Grade averages 12 times and took 962 wickets at 9.44. He took a wicket every 49 balls in his first-class career, and it was said he never bowled a wide.

When O'Reilly died, Bradman said he was the greatest bowler he had ever faced or watched.

FAR FROM A TRADITIONAL JAZZ-HATTER 2013

PARR, FRANCIS DAVID, died on May 8, 2012, aged 83. There were some sound judges, Herbert Strudwick among them, who saw Frank Parr keep wicket for Lancashire in the early 1950s and concluded that a rival might be emerging for Godfrey Evans's England place. Instead, Parr's career ended after 49 matches when he became victim of the martinet Cyril Washbrook's promotion to the Lancashire captaincy. Washbrook took vigorous exception to Parr's immersion in jazz music, a world that could hardly have been more different from his captain's view of county cricket.

Parr employed the hands that were so dextrous in the wicketkeeper's gloves to play the trombone and, if his cricket career did not reach the predicted heights, his life as a musician proved more fulfilling. In the late '50s, he was a member of the highly regarded Mick Mulligan Band, with George Melly as lead singer, and also played on stage with Louis Armstrong. Parr was a scruffy bohemian with a relaxed approach to personal hygiene and a penchant for cigarettes and whisky. According to Brian Statham, he "looked what he was: a spare-time musician"; Melly felt he "concealed a formidable, well-read intelligence behind a stylised oafishness".

He was born in Wallasey, on the Wirral, and made his Lancashire debut at Fenner's in 1951. The following summer, in only his second Championship appearance, he caught the attention of Strudwick at The Oval. And while his keeping to the spinners was a work in progress, he was acrobatic by the standards of the time, especially for a tall man. He was selected for MCC against Yorkshire at Lord's in 1953, and asked whether he might be available to tour the West Indies that winter. But he was not selected, and by July 1954 his first-class career was over.

The reason was simple: the intransigent Washbrook had taken over as captain from the easy-going Nigel Howard. He was enraged when Parr arrived for a House of Commons reception wearing a blue shirt and, when Parr produced an untidy performance at Bristol, it was just the excuse he'd been looking for. As the team prepared to head to Edgbaston, Washbrook told him: "Frank, you're going home." Exiled to the Seconds, Parr began to play better than ever, leading to discussions about a move to Worcestershire. He might have thrived in the relaxed atmosphere of New Road, but Washbrook put paid to those ambitions with a letter to Worcestershire calling him a "grave social risk". Parr was devastated. "It's probably when I took up serious drinking," he said.

He moved to London and joined the Mick Mulligan Band, whose chaotic years on the road are detailed in Melly's book *Owning Up*, which devotes six pages to Parr. He continued to play cricket with a wandering team of jazz musicians called The Ravers, keeping wicket immaculately beyond the age of 60. In his final years, he lived in a council flat not far from Lord's, where the writer Stephen Chalke was a visitor: "He was a good man, intelligent and sensitive, who lived in a state of complete and utter squalor, existing on coffee, whisky and the odd sausage." Parr was a regular at ex-players' evenings at Old Trafford, where Jim Cumbes, the former Lancashire chief executive, recalled: "He used to walk in without fuss, very unobtrusively, looking for the bar. He'd order a large scotch, however early it was. He was always good company."

DISTINCTIVE CAREER DOGGED BY ILL-HEALTH   1953

PATAUDI, NAWAB IFTIKHAR ALI OF, who died after a heart attack while playing polo at New Delhi on January 5, 1952, at the age of 41, will always be associated with Ranjitsinhji and Duleepsinhji as three great Indian batsmen who became leading figures in English cricket. Pataudi, known as "Pat" throughout the world, achieved the rare distinction of representing England and India in Test cricket.

Born at Pataudi in the Punjab on March 16, 1910, he went to Chiefs' College, Lahore, and received cricket coaching from M. G. Salter, the Oxford Blue. Going to England in 1926, he obtained further guidance from Frank Woolley, the Kent and England left-hander. In October 1927 Pataudi went to Oxford, but had to wait until 1929 before gaining his Blue. That season he accomplished little with the bat until the University Match, when his innings of 106 and 84 went a long way towards saving the game.

On his third appearance in 1931 he reached the height of his powers. In form from the start of the season, he scored 1,307 runs in 16 innings and finished top of the Oxford batting with the splendid average of 93. In successive innings he made 183 not out against The Army at Folkestone, 165 and 100 against Surrey at The Oval and 138 and 68 against H. D. G. Leveson Gower's XI at Eastbourne. Even this he overshadowed with a remarkable 238 not out against Cambridge at Lord's, the highest individual score ever made in the University Match. The innings caused him so much physical and nervous strain that he collapsed on his return to the pavilion.

His health was never strong, and he was not always fit when touring Australia with D. R. Jardine's team in 1932-33. Nevertheless, he added another great triumph to his name by scoring a century in his first Test match and helping England to victory by ten wickets at Sydney. He played in the next Test but did little, and was left out for the remaining three games.

On returning to England he was again in fine form for Worcestershire, his adopted county. In 1934 he was once more chosen for England against Australia, but scored only 12 and 10 at Nottingham in the First Test, and ill-health handicapped him afterwards. Although making occasional appearances for Worcestershire, he virtually dropped out of the game, but surprised everyone by returning to England as captain of the Indian touring team in 1946. He showed glimpses of his class, notably when becoming one of four batsmen to score a hundred in the same innings against Sussex at Hove, and finished third in the averages, but he was again handicapped by ill-health and he failed in the three Test matches.

A quick-footed batsman with a splendid eye, Pataudi possessed a wide variety of strokes, but did not have the fluency of Ranjitsinhji and Duleepsinhji. He was also a fine hockey and billiards player and an accomplished speaker, although some considered his wit to be sharp and cynical. After the Partition of India and Pakistan, Pataudi, a Moslem, found himself without a state to rule, but preserved his ruling status and was employed in the Indian Foreign Office in New Delhi. He left three daughters besides an 11-year-old son, who has shown promise of developing into a good cricketer.

Man Who Shone In A Crisis   1980

PAYNTER, EDWARD, who died at Keighley on February 5, 1979, aged 77, was a left-handed batsman who averaged 84.42 for his seven Tests against Australia, a figure which no other Englishman can approach. This in itself would entitle him to a place among the great, but his figures become even more remarkable if his innings are analysed. In three of these matches he came to the rescue at a grave crisis. On the first occasion, the Third Test in 1932-33, he came in at 186 for five, not a good score by the standards of Tests in Australia in those days, and made 77, adding 96 with Verity for the eighth wicket.

In the Fourth Test at Brisbane, he was taken to hospital with tonsillitis and, had all gone well with England, would doubtless not have batted. But all did not go well, and at 216 for six he emerged from the pavilion, refused Woodfull's offer of a runner, was still there at the close, and returned to bed in hospital. Next morning, he was not out until he had scored 83 in nearly four hours. On this occasion he and Verity put on 92 for the ninth wicket.

He had conserved energy by waiting for opportunities to hit the ball to leg, preferably to the boundary. Few innings in history have so captivated the imagination of the public. Moreover, Paynter insisted on fielding for a couple of hours before retiring and then, as if to show that he was none the worse, in a brief second innings he finished the match with a six.

In 1938 at Lord's, he came in at 31 for three and helped Hammond in a stand of 222, of which his own share was 99. In the previous Test at Nottingham he had broken the record for England against Australia in this country with an innings of 216 not out. In all Tests, Paynter's average was 59.23. In the series in South Africa in 1938-39 he averaged 81.62, scoring a hundred in each innings of the First Test, and 243 in the Third. Yet Paynter was 24 when he first made a hundred for Lancashire seconds, and between 1926 and 1929 he appeared only 11 times for the first team without any success.

It was not until 1931, when he was 30, that he made his first century against Warwickshire at Old Trafford, gained a regular place, and reached his thousand runs.

It was four years after the 1932-33 tour before Paynter played for England again. Meanwhile, he had made plenty of runs for Lancashire, and in 1936 actually scored 964 runs in August; unfortunately the side for Australia had already been picked. In 1937, however, he could be denied no longer. He scored 2,904 runs with an average of 53.77, including 322 in five hours against Sussex at Hove, and 266 against Essex at Old Trafford, and played in two Tests against New Zealand, missing the Third because of injury.

He was one of the great outfields of his day and almost equally good at cover – a beautiful thrower with a safe pair of hands. This was the more remarkable as early in life he had lost the top joints of two fingers in an accident. At Lord's in 1938, when Ames had broken a finger, Paynter kept wicket through the Australian second innings of 204, and though he had little or no experience of wicketkeeping conceded only five byes and held a catch. A wonderful cricketer.

CRICKET DEMANDED AS MUCH CARE AS HIS PLAYS   2009

PINTER, HAROLD, CH, CBE, who died on December 24, 2008, aged 78, was regarded as one of the 20th century's greatest playwrights and won the Nobel Prize for Literature in 2005. A previous winner, Samuel Beckett, had played first-class cricket, but Pinter easily surpassed him for devotion to the game. He took over an old theatrical team, Gaieties, which became a sort of personal fiefdom. No athlete, he became a fair club cricketer; and, although he never passed 39, each game was a matter of importance to him. "He was so magnificently unapologetic about it," said the writer and Gaieties player Robert Winder. "He always insisted that you take cricket as seriously as you take *The Caretaker* or *No Man's Land*, and he didn't care who knew it." In later life, he umpired with the same seriousness, though rumours that he would insert his trademark dramatic pause before raising the finger were false. Sometimes his attitude could head towards slightly risible self-importance. He allowed the publication of an expensively produced booklet which consisted entirely of an interview giving a description of a catch he had once taken, but wrote little himself about cricket except a much-admired vignette about his friend Arthur Wellard. A month before he died, and very ill, he recited Francis Thompson's *At Lord's* to a gathering of friends, as he was wont to do. The circumstances lent the poem ("… the field is full of shades as I near the shadowy coast") the same sense of grim portent he habitually brought to the stage. His biographer Michael Billington said that only Beckett could match Pinter as an influence on the modern theatre, and added: "I often thought he was as proud of the Gaieties as of almost all his literary accomplishments."

LOVEABLE ROGUE "BORN TO KEEP WICKET"   1908

POOLEY, EDWARD, the once famous Surrey wicketkeeper, died in Lambeth Infirmary on July 18, 1907. He had for a long time been in very poor circumstances and was often compelled to seek the shelter of the workhouse. Born on February 13, 1838, he was in his 70th year. All through his cricket career it was generally supposed that he was born in 1843, and the real date of his birth was only made known by himself in his interview in *Old English Cricketers*. It seems that when he determined to take up cricket professionally his father thought that he would have a better chance if he knocked a few years off his age.

The story of how he came to succeed Tom Lockyer is graphically told by himself in *Old English Cricketers*. He said "My introduction to wicketkeeping would be about the year 1863. Old Tom Lockyer's hands were bad, and the ground being fiery he could not take his usual place behind the sticks. Mr F. P. Miller, the Surrey captain, was in a quandary as to who should relieve him, so I, saucy-like, as usual, went up to him and said 'Mr Miller, let me have a try.' 'You? What do you know about wicketkeeping? Have you ever kept wicket at all?' was Mr Miller's remark. 'No, never, but I should like to try,' I replied. 'Nonsense' said he, and when just at that moment H. H. Stephenson came up and remarked 'Let the young'un have a go, sir,' Mr Miller thereupon relented. I donned the gloves, quickly got two or three wickets, and seemed so much at home that Tom Lockyer was delighted, and said I was born to keep wicket and would have to be his successor in the Surrey team. What he said came true."

Of the faults of private character that marred Pooley's career and were the cause of the poverty in which he spent the later years of his life there is no need now to speak. He was in many ways his own enemy, but even to the last he had a geniality and sense of humour that to a certain extent condoned his weaknesses.

ARRESTED IN NEW ZEALAND
Gordon Ross, 1976

Not many historians could tell you off the cuff the results of any of the matches in New Zealand [in 1877], but all of them will mention – as if it were a legend – the story of Pooley, and the trouble he got into. A number of versions have been given of the incident, but we must take note of what Alfred Shaw said; after all, he was there.

"We were playing at Christchurch against Eighteen of Canterbury. In a discussion as to the prospects of the match that occurred in an hotel bar at night, Pooley offered to take £1 to one shilling that he named the individual score of every member of the local team. It is a trick familiar to cricketers, and in the old days of matches against local eighteens and twenty-twos it not infrequently worked off against the unwary. The bet being accepted Pooley named a duck as the score of each batsman on the local side. A fair proportion of ducks was recorded, and Pooley claimed £1 each for them, while prepared to pay a shilling for the other scores. The man with whom the bet had been made said it was a catch bet on Pooley's part, and he declined to pay. The man's name was Ralph Donkin. His refusal to pay led to a scene of disorder, and brought Pooley's services with the team to an unpleasant end.

"We had to go next to Otago, and at the close of the match there Pooley was arrested on a charge of 'having at Christchurch maliciously injured property above the value of £5, and also of assaulting Donkin'. For the assault he had £5 and costs to pay. In the other charge he had as partner in trouble Alf Bramall, a supernumerary attached to our team. The two were committed for trial. We never saw Pooley again during the tour. He and his companion were tried before the Supreme

Court at Christchurch on April 6, and found not guilty. The local public thought he had been hardly used in having been taken away from the team. They subscribed £50 for division between Pooley and Bramall, and in addition they presented Pooley with a gold ring. The old Surrey wicketkeeper had to make the journey back to England alone."

THE HARROW BOY — 1978

RATTIGAN, SIR TERENCE MERVYN, CBE, the famous playwriter, who died in Bermuda on November 30, 1977, aged 66, was, like his father and his uncle, in the Harrow XI. He won his place in 1929 as an opening bat, but next year though he played in the XI was not in the side at Lord's. He was an elegant strokeplayer, but unsound.

Yorkshire v Sussex. At Scarborough, August 17, 18, 19, 20, 2011. Fred Bernard, 75, an umpire in the local Beckett League, twice answered an SOS on the second day to stand at square leg when Trevor Jesty had to leave the field ill, having initially been replaced by Yorkshire assistant coach

Little Wonder No. 143 and former England all-rounder Craig White. "I have waited 63 years for such an opportunity," Bernard said. *The Guardian* paid tribute in an editorial.

PLAYER – AND GENTLEMAN OF THE PRESS — 1966

ROBERTSON-GLASGOW, RAYMOND CHARLES, who died suddenly on March 4, 1965, aged 63, was both a distinguished player and a celebrated cricket writer. He appeared for Somerset with varying frequency from 1920 till 1937 and played five times for Gentlemen v Players between 1924 and 1935.

In all first-class cricket he scored 2,083 runs, average 12.93, dismissed 464 batsmen at a cost of 25.74 runs each and held 79 catches.

He was known to his host of friends as "Crusoe", a nickname which came to him as the outcome of a match between Somerset and Essex. C. P. McGahey, the Essex and England amateur, was in and out so rapidly that the next batsman, who had not been watching the play at the time, asked what had happened. "First ball," explained McGahey, "from a chap named Robinson Crusoe."

Of considerable personal charm, an infectious laugh, and possessing an infallible sense of humour which found its way into his writings when he became cricket correspondent in 1933 for *The Morning Post*, "Crusoe" was popular wherever he went. He later wrote for *The Daily Telegraph*, *The Observer* and *The Sunday Times*, contributed a number of articles to *Wisden* and was the author of many books.

His stories regarding the game he loved were many and various, but never ill-natured. One against him concerned the occasion when he was in the Pavilion at Lord's during the match following the University game of 1922. A friend introduced him to a certain celebrated pressman who, as was his wont, paid little attention to his name. When the friend left them, the pressman, endeavouring to make conversation, enquired: "Did you see Chapman's wonderful innings in the Varsity Match?" For once "Crusoe" was speechless. A. P. F. Chapman had hit a brilliant 102 for Cambridge, a big proportion of his runs coming at the expense of Robertson-Glasgow, who sent down 43.1 overs for 97 runs and did not take a wicket!

From Prodigy To Paranoia   2012

ROEBUCK, PETER MICHAEL, was found dead outside a Cape Town hotel on November 12, 2011. He was 55. Police said he had jumped from the window of his sixth-floor room after officers arrived to question him about an alleged sexual assault on a 26-year-old Zimbabwean man. Even in a game with a penchant for producing improbable characters, Roebuck was among the most fascinating. A brilliant student who got a first in law at Cambridge, he arrived in the Somerset dressing-room on April Fools' Day 1974, alongside Viv Richards, Ian Botham and Vic Marks. Sophocles might have struggled to script the drama that followed.

Not an obvious athlete, Roebuck was still a cricketing prodigy. He arrived for interview at Millfield School in 1969 to be thrown an orange as he headed diffidently into the headmaster's study. He caught it. The orange came from the ever-unpredictable R. J. O. "Boss" Meyer, who offered him an assisted place and also employed his parents. He became Roebuck's idol and role model.

Before the summer was out Roebuck, then 13, got a game for Somerset Second Eleven as a leg-spinner. He was enough of a player to make the Somerset staff and enough of a scholar to get into Cambridge, where he flourished, hitting 158 in the 1975 University Match, including a six off Imran Khan into the Lord's Pavilion.

As Somerset progressed and began to win trophies, Roebuck was a vital part of the mix. He would say, only half-jokingly, that his job was to stop Richards and Botham batting together, which was a recipe for disaster. His scores were self-effacing too – he made only four centuries for Somerset in the first ten years – but he was a perpetual irritant to opposing bowlers, including some of the quickest. His nuisance value was enhanced by his owlish specs, his strange stance and what some saw as an air of disdain.

He soon made his mark off the field too, writing pieces in *The Cricketer* that were collected into a well-received debut book, *Slices of Cricket*, in 1982. Two years later came *It Never Rains…*, a diary of the 1983 season. It was exceptional – full of wit, insight, self-deprecation but, tellingly, a great deal of despair. Roebuck was by now spending his winters teaching at Cranbrook School in Sydney.

Yet within the Somerset dressing-room he remained largely one of the boys, if an unusual one. Richards called him "the professor"; Botham "Pete lad". They respected both his brain and his cricket. In 1984, the fifties turned into hundreds and he scored 1,702 runs. However, after five one-day trophies in five years,

Somerset's success dried up, and the dressing-room egos grew dangerously large. In 1985, the county finished bottom, and Roebuck became increasingly angered by the captaincy of Botham. That winter Roebuck took over.

Relations did not collapse immediately. But the new leadership began to chafe the galacticos. The team improved only from 17th to 16th and, between the committee and the new captain, a plan emerged – to replace the overseas players, the increasingly distracted Richards and the now-wearying Joel Garner, with the New Zealander Martin Crowe. The upshot was disaster: the news came as a bombshell and Botham stormed out in protest. For Roebuck, it marked the descent towards paranoia: for the rest of his life he imagined Botham-inspired plots.

In the short term, Roebuck thrived. He gave up his Australian teaching to report the 1986-87 Ashes tour, was anointed Bill O'Reilly's improbable Pommie heir as columnist for both the *Sydney Morning Herald* and *The Age* in Melbourne, and wrote a fine tour book, *Ashes to Ashes*. He had a wonderful summer with the bat in 1987, despite suffering one of his many broken fingers, and was named one of *Wisden*'s Five the next spring.

He had given up the Somerset captaincy and, in 1991, he retired and increasingly gravitated towards Australia. But he had a decade of unlikely English summers captaining Devon to four successive Minor Counties championships, turning into a purveyor of brisk off-cutters, a middle-order thumper and a studiedly eccentric leader.

His Australian portfolio soon included a place on the ABC commentary team. In the 1990s, he also discovered southern Africa, and began to support orphans in Zimbabwe. When he was in England, he shied away from "hostile" Taunton, and filled his home with African and Australian school-leavers. He coached them, mentored them, and sometimes, if he thought them unfit, caned them.

At Taunton Crown Court in 2001, Judge Graham Hume Jones gave Roebuck a suspended sentence after he admitted three charges of common assault. Roebuck's defence was feeble (his word): "I had not grasped that pleading guilty meant accepting everything in the statements made by the complainants." This from a man with a first-class law degree.

The case completed his disillusionment with England: he returned only to cover the 2005 and 2009 Ashes. When the Ashes story changed after 2005, his work recaptured much of its old incision. And on radio he was superb, his insight and humour spoiled only by an accent that now wandered from Oxbridge to Bondi depending on his mood. Sometimes it even veered towards Natal, where he set up a home for the deprived boys he called his "sons".

Some of those sons have added to the allegations about Roebuck's sexual behaviour, but these remained unproven. He was palpably a lonely man: even those who knew him well had no knowledge of anything approaching a normal adult relationship, straight or gay. He was distant, though not estranged, from his family. He sensed enemies where there were only well-wishers. Though a great talker, he was a shocking listener. He preferred disciples – Devonians or African boys or young cricket writers – to equals. The Meyer influence never faded: he liked being the Boss, the genial and beloved master who would always be the one to decide when enough was enough. Indeed, it seems as though that was his final decision.

NOBLEMAN WHO COULD SPOT A WINNER 1975

ROSEBERY, SIXTH EARL OF, who died on May 30, 1974, aged 92, was a cricketer, soldier, politician and administrator of distinction. When Lord Dalmeny, he was in the Eton XI of 1900, scoring 52 against Harrow and 55 against Winchester. In 1901 he turned out for Buckinghamshire, took part in two matches for Middlesex the following season and began playing for Surrey in 1903. He took over the Surrey captaincy in 1905 and held the post till 1907. Both his centuries for the county were made at The Oval in 1905, against Leicestershire and Warwickshire. While hitting the first, he drove fiercely during a stand for the sixth wicket of 260 with J. N. Crawford. That season was the first for Surrey of J. B. Hobbs, and Lord Dalmeny was always proud of the fact that he awarded that great batsman his cap after two games.

He succeeded to the title of Lord Rosebery when his father, a former prime minister, died in 1929, and became president of Surrey from 1947 to 1949. It was thanks to his approach to the Prince of Wales in 1905 that the county club adopted the Prince of Wales's feathers as their crest. For many years Lord Rosebery was a celebrated figure in the world of horse racing.

In 164 innings in first-class cricket he scored 3,551 runs, average 23.05.

He left £9,650,986 net.

VICTOR OF WIDER FIELDS 1991

ROTHSCHILD, THE THIRD LORD, GBE, GM, FRS (NATHANIEL MAYER VICTOR), who died in London on March 20, 1990, aged 79, was one of the most versatile and gifted men of his time, and a cricketer of considerable talent. In 1929, his last year at Harrow, made his mark in all departments of the game: he was one of three boys to score more than 500 runs in schools matches, he took 20 wickets at 25 apiece, and he was a high-class performer in the slips. At Lord's against Eton, opening with Terence Rattigan, he made a dashing 43 out of 68 to launch Harrow's reply to a total of 347, to which his bizarre mixture of pace and spin had made much too generous a contribution. He made runs for the Lord's Schools against the Rest, and towards the end of August he was given a run by Northamptonshire, making an auspicious start in first-class cricket with scores of 27, 31, 11, 16 not out, 36, 5 and 28. His 36 was made against Larwood, Barratt and Voce after five wickets had gone down for 39. In 1930 he played in the Freshmen's match at Cambridge, and in a further trial he drove finely in making 112 for the Perambulators against the Etceteras. This innings and his highest first-class score of 63 against Kent at Peterborough (st Ames b Freeman) earned him a game for the University against Sussex. However, he found Maurice Tate too much of a handful in both innings. He was looked upon as a possible captain of Northamptonshire on the retirement of V. W. C. Jupp, but the job was given to W. C. Brown and Rothschild went on to conquer wider fields. In his 11 first-class matches he made 282 runs for an average of 15.66 and held eight catches.

UMPIRE WHO CONFRONTED TEST CAPTAINS   2002

SHAKOOR RANA, who found his few minutes of fame in an unedifying spat with Mike Gatting in the 1987-88 Faisalabad Test, died of a heart attack in Lahore on April 9, 2001, aged 65. As much as threequarters of his press obituaries were consumed by the squabble after he halted play because, Shakoor Rana alleged, Gatting had moved a fielder without the batsman's knowledge. Umpire and England captain had a toe-to-toe, finger-jabbing confrontation, there were reciprocal charges of cheating and swearing, and the third day's play was lost, helping Pakistan escape with a draw. The match did not resume until an apology was forthcoming from the English camp.

A right-hand batsman and medium-fast bowler in his playing days, Shakoor Rana made his first-class debut for Punjab in 1957-58, and between then and 1972-73 he also played for Lahore, Khairpur and Pakistan Railways, with whom he held a post as a sports officer. In 11 first-class games, he scored 226 runs, took a dozen wickets and held 11 catches. Burly of frame and jocose by nature, he stood in 18 Tests and 22 one-day internationals from 1974-75 to 1996-97, and was reckoned to be upright and bold in his decision-making. It seems he could be self-important, too. In the 1984-85 Test at Karachi, he quarrelled with the New Zealand captain, Jeremy Coney, when he ignored an appeal for a catch at the wicket against Javed Miandad, and the outraged New Zealander threatened to lead his team from the arena. But former Sussex captain John Barclay remembered a much friendlier character from the 1981 summer, when Shakoor Rana was umpiring in England. Barclay had been told by an Indian taxi-driver to ask "Where's Allah?" (rather than the customary "Howzat?") when appealing; the response would be a finger pointing to the sky. Shakoor Rana was having none of it. "Not that silly trick again," he said sotto voce as Barclay walked back to his mark.

MUCH-DECORATED DOUBLE INTERNATIONAL   1939

SHARP, JOHN, who died on January 27, 1938, enjoyed an unparalleled career in cricket and football. As a professional with Everton, he took part in two final ties for the Football Association Cup and was on the winning side in 1906. He helped England beat Ireland in 1903, in 1905 was in the eleven victorious over Scotland and he became a director of the Everton club. When still in his football prime as an outside-right, he played in three cricket Tests against the Australian team of 1909, scoring 105 at The Oval, the only century for England in that series. From 1899 to 1914 Sharp was a regular member of the Lancashire eleven and played in all the matches of 1904 when the Championship was won without defeat being suffered. After the War he appeared as an amateur and captained the side from 1923 to 1925 when he retired. In 1924 he was on the England Test selection committee with H. D. G. Leveson Gower and John Daniell – so completing a unique set of honours.

Born at Hereford on February 15, 1878, John Sharp showed exceptional batting ability when 14 years of age by scoring 208 not out against Ledbury, but for Lancashire he did best as a bowler for some time. Short and thick-set, he put a lot of power behind the ball and, if not very fast, he kept up a good pace with off-break and lift. In 1901 he took 112 wickets at 22.43 each, and with 883 runs, average 25.22, he was the one notable all-rounder in his county eleven. Altogether for Lancashire Sharp took 448 wickets at 26.22 runs apiece. His batting figures are much more impressive – 20,829 runs for the county and 22,715 all told, average nearly 32 in each case, while his first-class centuries numbered 38, the highest being 211 against Leicestershire at Old Trafford in 1912.

Brilliant fielding, usually at cover point, completed John Sharp's cricket equipment, and a bright cheerful disposition helped him as captain; yet an error in judging a catch influenced his retirement from first-class cricket. This happened when Cecil Parkin was taking his benefit at Old Trafford in 1925. Middlesex won the toss and John Sharp, fielding at short leg, missed H. W. Lee off the first ball. An opening partnership of 121 between Lee and J. W. Hearne ensued, and Middlesex won decisively. Sharp was greatly upset by the attitude of some of the crowd over the dropped catch, and he threatened never again to play at Old Trafford. The Lancashire committee persuaded him to change his decision, but at the end of the season Sharp sent in his resignation.

BEST SLOW BOWLER IN ENGLAND 1908

SHAW, ALFRED, after a long illness, died at his home, Gedling, near Nottingham, on January 16, 1907. In him there passed away one of the greatest figures in modern cricket. His connection with the game lasted more than 40 years, only ending in 1905, when, despite shattered health, he managed somehow to get through his duties as one of the umpires in county matches. Born at Burton Joyce on August 29, 1842, Alfred Shaw played his first match at Lord's in 1864 for the Colts of England against the MCC and Ground. The Colts were beaten by ten runs, but Shaw did great things, taking 13 wickets. He was at once given a place in the Notts eleven, and in the following year had the distinction of being picked for Players against Gentlemen, both at Lord's and The Oval. In this early part of his career Shaw's bowling was faster than in later years, and he was essentially an all-round man. Indeed, so good was his batting that in the Gentlemen and Players' match at The Oval in 1866 he made a score of 70. From 1872 to 1880 he was, beyond all question, the best slow bowler in England. After his first trip to Australia he was laid aside in the season of 1877 by a severe attack of bronchitis, but otherwise his success was uninterrupted. After being on the MCC's groundstaff from 1865 to 1867, inclusive, he had a year with the All-England Eleven, but in 1870 he returned to Lord's, and for the MCC and Notts most of his best work was done.

Of all his feats, perhaps the most remarkable was accomplished in a match at Lord's in 1875, between Notts and the MCC. In the MCC's second innings he sent down 41 overs and two balls for seven runs and seven wickets, bowling out, among other batsmen, W. G. Grace, A. W. Ridley, C. F. Buller, and Lord Harris. On May 27, 1878, he played for the MCC at Lord's in the sensational match against the first Australian Eleven, and it was no fault of his that the Club suffered a nine-wickets' defeat, he and the late Fred Morley getting the Australians out for a total of 41. A little over two years later Shaw appeared for England against Australia at The Oval in the first Test match ever played in this country. After 1880 his bowling began to show some falling-off, and in the great match at The Oval in 1882 England's slow bowler was Peate. In the meantime the only regrettable incident of Shaw's career had occurred, he being one of the prime movers in the strike of the Notts professionals in 1881. The quarrel was made up before the end of the season, but it left some feeling of soreness behind. Shaw continued to play for Notts for some years longer, dropping out of the eleven in 1887. That the veteran had a good deal of cricket left in him was proved when he afterwards played, under the residential qualification, for Sussex. Time had robbed him of much of his spin, but his bowling was still wonderfully steady. However, he soon found the strain of county cricket too much for him at his age, and without any formal farewell, he retired from the active pursuit of the game, and in due course took up umpiring.

In Shaw's great days scores were by no means so big as they are now, and as compared with the doings of even the best of his successors his figures seem very wonderful. To give only one example, he took in 1880 177 wickets in first-class matches for less than nine runs apiece.

Zimbabwe v Pakistan (Second One-Day International). At Harare, September 11, 2011. Pakistan won by ten wickets. A crestfallen Brendan Taylor will never be allowed to forget saying "bat" when he meant "bowl" on winning the toss. Asked by Alistair Campbell – presiding over the toss for television, but also Zimbabwe's convenor of selectors – why he had chosen to bat, Taylor was speechless for a moment, before mumbling: "Er, can I change my mind?" Campbell replied: "No. So, why did you bat?" Taylor later said: "God knows what possessed me – the wrong word came out."

Little Wonder No. 144

SUSPECTED BOLIVIAN SPY, GENUINE ESSEX WICKETKEEPER   1998

SHEFFIELD, JAMES ROY, died in New Zealand on November 16, 1997, aged 90. Roy Sheffield was probably the only Essex wicketkeeper ever to be arrested on suspicion of being a Bolivian spy. He was a small, agile man who kept wicket in 177 games for Essex between 1929 and 1936. Though he was an efficient keeper, Sheffield's batting shone only intermittently – he scored 85 not out on his debut against Warwickshire, and made a century at Hove in his last season, but did little in between. Sheffield was more notable for his off-season adventures. In 1932-33, while England's most famous cricketers were involved in the Bodyline series, he was working as a cowboy in South America and trying to canoe down the River Paraguay. There was a war going on between Paraguay and Bolivia, and the Paraguayans arrested Sheffield and locked him up until a British businessman intervened. He later wrote a novel based on the incident, entitled *Bolivian Spy?* A year later he spent two months walking through the Drakensberg Mountains and Basutoland. Essex did not retain him after 1936 and he left for New Zealand, meeting his future wife on the boat, and never returned to England. He played three games for Wellington in 1938-39, but later concentrated on his canoeing. He competed in the 50-mile Waikato River Marathon when he was well into his eighties; the Essex secretary Peter Edwards visited him in 1992 and described him as astonishingly fit. He died a few days after his daughter, a BBC producer who had been visiting him, was knocked off her bike and killed.

CALLED BY CRICKET AND THE CHURCH   2006

Baron SHEPPARD OF LIVERPOOL (Rt Rev. David Stuart Sheppard) died on March 5, 2005, the day before his 76th birthday. Rev. David Sheppard, as he was known for most of his playing career, was one of the most remarkable men ever to play cricket to a high level. His involvement was intermittent but always eventful. He captained England in two Tests in 1954. Had he devoted himself to cricket, Sheppard would have captained more often, and could easily have scored a hundred hundreds. Instead he devoted himself to the Church, where he rose to become a long-serving, distinctive and, by most reckonings, outstanding Bishop of Liverpool. Politics cost him his chance of becoming an archbishop.

Unlike his exact contemporary, Peter May, Sheppard was no schoolboy prodigy. He was 17 before he broke into the team at Sherborne. But, under the tutelage of Micky Walford and Len Creese, he blossomed as a batsman as he grew from a shrimp into a strong young man, good enough to get three games for Sussex just after he left school, and 204, 147 and 130 in 11 days for them as a 20-year-old late in 1949. The next year, when Sheppard and May arrived at Cambridge together after National Service, it was Sheppard who was first to sparkle, when he shared an opening stand of 343 with John Dewes, and went on to a chanceless 227, against the mighty 1950 West Indians. That helped catapult Sheppard into the Test team at The Oval and both men on to the tour of Australia. Brisbane in December being far more than half a world away from Fenner's in May, they were palpably unready.

He scored heavily for Cambridge and Sussex in 1951, though now May was ahead of him in the selectors' minds, and Sheppard did not return to the Test team until 1952, when he took a century off the weak Indian team at The Oval without looking in touch. By now, after hearing an American Presbyterian preach in Cambridge, he had turned to an intense form of evangelical Christianity, and the two poles of his life were starting to pull him in contrary directions. He agreed, after some hesitation, to captain Sussex in 1953, leading them from 13th to a near-miss second. "We always said he was the best captain we ever had," said Alan Oakman. "He led by example and he supported everyone."

Now he did put the church first, and studied for the priesthood at Ridley Hall, Cambridge. But his success at Sussex had given him a national reputation as a potential captain and, in 1954, when Len Hutton was ill, England asked Sheppard to take charge at Trent Bridge and Old Trafford against the infant Pakistan team.

Now, with the 1954-55 Ashes tour looming, came one of those great captaincy controversies that so often convulse English cricket. To the discomfort of both men, the arguments raged between the claims of the gritty northern pro and the genteel southern amateur. It was resolved in Hutton's favour because he returned to cricket, and form, in the nick of time, which enabled him to beat the old-fashioned class prejudice that might have defeated him.

Sheppard was ordained in 1955 and became curate of St Mary's in Islington. But still he could not wholly resist the call of cricket, and the selectors could not resist him. Despite minimal match practice, he was recalled for the 1956 Old Trafford Ashes Test made immortal by Jim Laker's 19 wickets. It is largely forgotten that England's position was set up by centuries from Peter Richardson and Sheppard – chanceless and showing no signs of rust. He made another 62 at The Oval, and 68 against West Indies the next year.

But that really did seem like his last hurrah. Gradually, the church took over. Sheppard opted for the sharp end, being appointed warden of the Mayflower Family Settlement in the East End, working, alongside his wife Grace, with the poor and the new migrants who were starting to pour in. Still, cricket pulled him back. And in 1962 he went on sabbatical, returned to the England team for the last two Tests, scored two half-centuries, and sailed to Australia.

In Melbourne, he got a first-innings duck, dropped two catches, was dropped on a pair in the second innings – then went on to stroke a match-winning century. On Sundays, he would preach in the local cathedrals. "He drew bigger crowds than we did," noted Tom Graveney. After the tour, he returned to the East End and never played seriously again.

In 1969, Sheppard became Suffragan Bishop of Woolwich, and in 1975 Bishop of Liverpool, where for 22 years he became almost synonymous with the city and its troubles. He was vice-chairman of the committee that produced a much-discussed report on urban poverty, Faith in the City, in 1985, and had to defend it at a lunch with Mrs Thatcher, who kept interrupting him. Sheppard said his mouth went dry, just as it had done when he faced Lindwall and Miller. When Archbishop Runcie retired six years later, Sheppard had no chance, even though normal Anglican politics dictated that the evangelical wing should provide Runcie's successor, and Sheppard was an outstanding figure. He retired in 1997 and became a life peer, alongside Colin Cowdrey, but was soon diagnosed with cancer, and his last years were difficult, although cricket was a great solace.

His memorial service took place at a packed Liverpool Cathedral, with a bat placed on a table alongside his ordination Bible.

SMART "ALEC" ENHANCED THE ENTERTAINMENT   1961

SKELDING, ALEXANDER, who died at Leicester on April 17, 1960, aged 73, stood as a first-class umpire from 1931 to 1958. He began his cricket career as a very fast bowler with Leicestershire in 1905, but, because he wore spectacles, was not re-engaged at the end of the season. He then joined Kidderminster in the Birmingham League and achieved such success that in 1912 the county re-signed him and he continued with them till 1929. His best season was that of 1927, when he took 102 wickets, average 20.81. Altogether he dismissed 593 batsmen at a cost of less than 25 runs each. One of the most popular personalities in the game, he always wore white boots when umpiring and he was celebrated for his sense of humour. It was his custom at the close of play to remove the bails with an exaggerated flourish and announce: "And that concludes the entertainment for the day, gentlemen."

"Alec" was the central figure in many amusing incidents. Once in response to an appeal for run-out, he stated: "That was a 'photo-finish' and as there isn't time to develop the plate, I shall say not out." In another match a batsman who had been celebrating a special event the previous evening was rapped on the pad by a ball. At once the bowler asked: "How is he?" Said Alec, shaking his head sadly: "He's not at all well, and he was even worse last night." Occasionally the joke went against Alec. In a game in 1948 he turned down a strong appeal by the Australian touring team. A little later a dog ran on to the field, and one of the Australians captured it, carried it to Skelding and said: "Here you are. All you want now is a white stick!"

BURIED IN HIS ENGLAND BLAZER   1990

SLACK, WILFRED NORRIS, the Middlesex and England left-handed opener, collapsed and died while batting in Banjul, capital of The Gambia, on January 15, 1989, at the age of 34. He had suffered four blackouts on the field or in the nets in the two previous years, but exhaustive tests had failed to identify the cause. Born in St Vincent, Slack came to England at the age of 11 and learned his cricket at High Wycombe.

Quiet, even reserved, Slack was often Middlesex's leading scorer. In addition to his three Tests, Slack played twice in one-day internationals, and while he never made the climb from domestic cricket, he tried hard, kept cool and was regarded with warm affection, especially by Middlesex crowds. He held nearly 200 catches – many in the demanding bat-pad position – and was always eager to bowl medium-pace, especially in limited-overs matches. He was particularly popular among fellow cricketers, who spoke feelingly of their respect and sorrow when he died. He was mourned, too, in New Zealand, where he coached in five English winters. Slack was buried in his prized England blazer, bat at his side, and as the funeral cortege drove past Lord's, the Grace Gates bore a sign reading "Farewell Wilf".

CUT DOWN IN HIS PRIME   1960

SMITH, O'NEILL GORDON, who died in hospital at Stoke-on-Trent on September 9, 1959, aged 26, following injuries received in a motor-car accident in which two other West Indies players, G. Sobers and T. Dewdney, were also involved, took part in 26 Test matches between 1955 and 1959, scoring 1,331 runs, including four centuries, average 31.69. His death came as a heavy blow to the West Indies, for much had been hoped from him against P. B. H. May's MCC team last winter.

In 1955 he first appeared for Jamaica. This was against the visiting Australians, and he gave full evidence of his quality by playing an innings of 169. That performance earned him a place in the opening Test match and, by hitting 104 in the second innings, he joined the list of men who obtained a century on Test debut.

He learned to curb his natural desire to hit at practically every ball, though he never lost his punishing powers, and in England in 1957 he scored 161 in the Edgbaston Test, becoming the only batsman to register a century on first appearance against both Australia and England. In the third meeting with England at Trent Bridge he made his highest Test score, 168, doing much to rescue the West Indies from what had seemed a hopeless position.

His body was taken to Jamaica where it was estimated that about 60,000 people attended the funeral.

THE DEMON	Recollections of MR F. R. SPOFFORTH, by The Earl of Darnley, 1927

I well remember the first time that I encountered the Demon bowler – in the Cambridge v Australian match, at Lord's, in 1878. We had all been warned by our captain, the Hon. Edward Lyttelton, who had, I think, recently made a big score against the Australians, to watch Spofforth's bowling hand as he came to the wicket. If the wrist was bent, one was to expect a slower ball with break-back; if the wrist was straight, a very fast ball, and not improbably a "yorker".

In some of the accounts recently published of Spofforth's bowling it was said that he was never a really fast bowler. I believe this statement to be quite incorrect. If my memory does not deceive me, there were two very distinct stages in his bowling. When he first came to England in 1878, his bowling was very fast indeed, almost as fast as the fastest we have seen, with occasional very well-disguised slower ones, which were very deceiving to the batsman and caused many a premature forward stroke and retirement of the batsman – caught and bowled.

After 1878 he greatly moderated his pace, and relied more on the fast-medium ball of wonderfully good length and considerable break-back, with the occasional variation of the very fast one, including a particularly deadly "yorker".

I should imagine that the nickname of "Demon" arose from the terrifying aspect of his final bound at the wicket when delivering the ball – long lean arms whirling through the air from a commanding height, and a long stride coming down with great force and damaging effect on a very awkward spot for a breaking-back ball bowled from the other end. The long arms seemed to be whirling round at much the same speed whether the ball was coming fast or slow, and he had practised these disguises of pace to great perfection.

Some of his bowling success may be traced to certain physical attributes of an unusual character – very tall, 6ft 3in, broad-shouldered, but unusually lean and sinewy and carrying very little weight. A year or two ago, he told me that at his best he only weighed 11st 7lb. His early life on horseback in the Australian bush gave to him the lasting power which made him incomparably the best stayer of any fast or medium-pace bowler that I can remember. Though of so comparatively light build, he was exceptionally strong, and one of his feats was to support Bonnor, weighing over 16st, on the calf of his leg, held horizontally backwards at right angles to the upright leg – no mean feat. He and Bonnor were the two fastest 100-yards runners in the Australian elevens of those days, one weighing some 5st more than the other.

In addition to these physical features, no bowler that I ever saw had a more graceful, spacious sweep of the arm, and his delivery gave a most satisfactory sensation of perfection of pace and power combined. Unlike most of the modern fast bowlers, his run-up to the wicket was only of average length, and his pace and power owed nothing to the impetus of an abnormally long run.

One of the very best bowlers that the last 50 years have seen, unquestionably; possibly the best of all. A cheery and amusing companion, withal, amongst his fellow cricketers. Fond of a good story, and, like many of his compatriots, not inclined to understatement. His old cricketing friends will cherish a very kindly recollection of his unique personality.

SECOND ONLY TO GRACE   A Tribute by the Hon. R. H. Lyttelton, 1915

The death of MR ALLAN GIBSON STEEL came with the most painful suddenness. Few, if any, knew that he was ill, and as he was only in his 56th year there was every reason to expect many more years of life for him, but he died after only a few hours' illness at his house in London on June 15, 1914. Mr Steel was captain of the Cambridge eleven in 1880, president of the MCC in 1902, and for several years was a barrister with a good practice in Liverpool, and Recorder of Oldham from 1904 till his death.

His first season in first-class cricket was as a member of the celebrated Cambridge eleven of 1878. They played eight matches, including one against the Australians, and won them all. He headed the batting averages with an average of 37, and his bowling took 75 wickets in 282 overs at an average of seven runs a wicket. In the whole season he was actually at the head of the bowling averages for All England, taking 164 wickets for an average of nine runs per wicket.

A. G. Steel was essentially a tricky bowler, and it is easy to imagine him as developing this side of cricket by a considerable amount of painstaking practice, but as a batsman it is impossible to conceive him as anything but a purely natural cricketer, wanting little practice, and quite capable of playing a fine innings after standing out of first-class or any cricket for weeks. In 1886 he only played 12 innings the whole season, but in the three matches he played for Lancashire his innings were 83, 55, 80 not out and 14, and it was sad for cricket that after seven seasons, from 1878 to 1884, he could only make casual appearances.

It was said that on one occasion the famous Tom Emmett, when he found that Steel was playing for Lancashire against Yorkshire at Old Trafford, said to the Yorkshire eleven, "Let's go home, lads, Steel's playing, and Yorkshire's beat!"

For England against Australia, A. G. Steel played in 13 matches, and twice he scored centuries. Taken altogether in his prime as an all-round cricketer he had good claims to be considered the best in England, always excepting W. G. Grace.

STODDART, ANDREW ERNEST, one of the greatest of batsmen, died by his own hand on Saturday, April 3, 1915, shooting himself through the head. A brilliant career thus came to the saddest of ends. Mr Stoddart was born at South Shields on March 11, 1863, and had thus completed his 52nd year. Curiously enough, considering the great fame he won, he did not take to cricket seriously until 22 years of age, when he became associated with the Hampstead club, and showed such form, scoring no fewer than five separate hundreds for that team, that before the end of the season of 1885 he had been tried for Middlesex.

From 1886 to 1898 Mr Stoddart proved a tower of strength to Middlesex in batting, keeping up his skill so well that in 1898 – his last full season in county cricket – he averaged 52. He soon became a popular idol at Lord's, his batting, in conjunction with that of T. C. O'Brien, making the Middlesex matches far more attractive than they had ever been before his day.

He turned out only once for Middlesex in 1899, and twice in the following year, but in his last match for the county – against Somerset at Lord's – he put together a score of 221, the highest of his career in first-class cricket. Among his most famous innings were 215 not out against Lancashire at Manchester in 1891 and 151 for England against the MCC at Lord's in 1887, when he and Arthur Shrewsbury raised the total to 266 for the first wicket. In 1886, for Hampstead against the Stoics, he played an innings of 485 – at that time the highest individual score on record.

On four occasions Mr Stoddart paid visits to Australia, first in 1887, as a member of G. F. Vernon's team, when he averaged 32. Four years later he formed one of the side taken out by Lord Sheffield, his average then amounting to 37. In 1894-95, and again in 1897-98, he himself took a team out to Australia. The first of these undertakings resulted in England winning the rubber after two victories had been gained by each country, but the second proved a big disappointment, no fewer than four of the five Test matches ending in favour of Australia. Still, in the two tours associated with his leadership, Mr Stoddart came out well with averages of 51 and 34. As a Test match player in this country, Mr Stoddart achieved no special distinction. He took no part in those games in 1890, and although he played in all three matches three years later, making 83 at The Oval, his only other appearances for England at home were at Lord's and Manchester in 1896.

Mr Stoddart was one of the very few men who have represented their country at rugby football as well as at cricket. Between 1886 and 1893 he took part in ten international rugby matches. A splendid runner, with plenty of pace and dodging ability, and not above jumping over an opponent on occasion, he was a great three-quarter – possessed of a very fine pair of hands – a brilliant kick, and a player full of resource.

SURRIDGE, WALTER STUART, the famous Surrey captain of the 1950s, died suddenly on April 13, 1992, while visiting his company's factory at Glossop. He was

74. Stuart Surridge was the most successful leader in the history of the County Championship. In 1952 he took control of a side which was rich in talent but needed to feel the smack of firm government to do itself real justice. According to Alec Bedser, Surridge had the nerve to write in his diary after being confirmed as captain: "Surrey will win the Championship for the next five years." The correct figure was seven, the first five under Surridge.

Surridge possessed enormous enthusiasm and irrepressible energy, coupled with a strong streak of aggression. He combined something of the qualities of two of his predecessors as Surrey captain, the imaginative Percy Fender and the combative Douglas Jardine. As Sir Neville Cardus put it in a different context, "invisible arrows of antagonism darted across the field" when Surrey were playing, and some opponents let it be known that they thought things had gone a bit far. It was significant that Surridge was never chosen to captain the Gentlemen against the Players. Indeed, Surridge fought to avoid losing his players for what he regarded as an irrelevant fixture.

He was never an autocrat, preferring at all times to share his ideas with his players. Before he became captain he had established a long-standing and informal relationship with the younger professionals, some of whom he would pack into his father's substantial Buick when they set off to play in club and ground matches. When captain, he abolished the antiquated accommodation and travel distinctions which then prevailed between amateurs and professionals – in spite of rumblings from the committee.

The name Stuart Surridge was famous in cricket long before he began playing. Surridge's grandfather was a batmaker (he also made violins) who set up his own business in the 1870s; Stuart Surridge bats were used by such players as Herbert Sutcliffe and Duleepsinhji.

When his playing days were over, Surridge served for many years on Surrey's cricket committee and was president in 1982. His familiar presence round The Oval and the family business will be greatly missed. The company is now in the hands of Surridge's son, also called Stuart.

YORKSHIREMAN AT HOME BEYOND ITS BOUNDARIES   J. M. Kilburn, 1979

Born at Summerbridge, near Harrogate, November 24, 1894; died at Crosshills, January 22, 1978.

HERBERT SUTCLIFFE was one of the great cricketers, and he brought to cricket as to all his undertakings an assurance and capacity for concentration that positively commanded success. His technical talent matched his character, and his achievements were therefore on the highest plane.

In a career extending from 1919 to 1939 Herbert Sutcliffe scored more than 50,000 runs and averaged 52. He never knew a season of failure, except by the standard of his own astonishing peaks, and at the zenith of his career he scored 16,255 runs in five years as a measure of mastery in all conditions and over the world's best bowling of the time.

The First World War delayed his entry into county cricket until he was 24 years old when, after demobilisation from a commission in the Green Howards, he was given a place in the Yorkshire side. His quality was never in doubt and by the end of the 1919 season he had scored five centuries in an aggregate of 1,839 runs. He had also established a first-wicket partnership with Percy Holmes. For 14 years these two batsmen opened the innings for Yorkshire, representing a partnership of unparalleled success in which they put up the hundred on 74 occasions. Equally happy was Sutcliffe's Test match association with J. B. Hobbs, for this became the most accomplished of all opening partnerships. Sutcliffe's good fortune, however, was only in the presentation of opportunity. Seizure of it was his own merit, and with one partner or another he constructed 145 first-wicket century stands.

His artistry and efficiency in difficult conditions became legendary in his lifetime, with his hundreds against Australia at The Oval in 1926 and at Melbourne in 1929 as historic examples. Matches against Lancashire stirred him to nine centuries. His defensive patience and skill became a byword, yet at need his hitting was brilliant in the extreme. Against Northamptonshire at Kettering he met spin on the sticky wicket with an innings of 113 which included ten sixes. At Scarborough against the fast bowling of Farnes and Nichols, Sutcliffe took his personal score from 100 to 194 in 40 minutes. His 100th first-class century was the 132 he hit in less than two hours at Bradford when Yorkshire were hurrying to defeat Gloucestershire.

During his playing days he founded and developed a sports-outfitting business, now directed by his elder son. After his retirement form the field he took a managerial appointment in the paper trade. He showed himself as successful in commerce as in cricket and for the same reasons of application and reliability. His repayment to the game which had given him so much was service on the Yorkshire committee, as an England selector, and as sponsor for many good causes in cricket.

Though he was born in Summerbridge, Sutcliffe was a Pudsey native in cricket association. There, as a schoolboy, he began league cricket, and from there he advanced to the county, but neither Pudsey nor any other nursery could have claimed Herbert Sutcliffe as a typical product. He was a Yorkshireman in his loyalty and training, but he was cosmopolitan in approach and outlook. His manner fitted Lord's as expressively as it fitted Leeds.

Immaculate, alert, brisk of movement, serene in repose, he carried his character with a clear label wherever he appeared. His off-drive wore a silk hat and his hook was a ready response to the aggressive intent of any bumper. His defensive play was the reduction of risk to the minimum and his self-confidence was unshakeable.

In his first-class career he scored 149 centuries. He shared with Holmes a partnership of 555 for Yorkshire, and with Hobbs a partnership of 283 for England against Australia.

Second in the nominal batting order, Herbert Sutcliffe was second to none in steadfastness on all occasions. He was esteemed for accomplishment, he was acclaimed for his unfailing resolution. His name will always stay in the headlines.

Sri Lanka v India (First One-Day International). At Hambantota, July 21, 2012. There was a mix-up when Kohli signalled to the dressing-room for a cap, and the umpires thought he was asking for the batting powerplay. He and Sehwag didn't change their approach, and later asked for the powerplay – only to be told they had already had it: luckily, the confusion made no difference to the result.

Little Wonder No. 145

FAR MORE THAN A CARTOON CHARACTER   1957

TATE, MAURICE WILLIAM, "Chubby" to his many friends and admirers, died at his home at Wadhurst, Sussex, on May 18, 1956, aged 61. Only three weeks earlier he had umpired the opening match of the Australians' tour against the Duke of Norfolk's XI at Arundel.

Maurice Tate was the son of Fred Tate, the Sussex and England cricketer whose name will ever be associated with the 1902 Test at Old Trafford, which England lost by three runs. Fred Tate missed a vital catch and was last out when England wanted only four runs to win. In his reminiscences, published in 1934, Maurice Tate wrote that his father's greatest ambition was to see his son playing for England and retrieving his own tragic blunder. How well the son atoned for the father's misfortune! Maurice Tate began as a slow off-break bowler and had been playing some years before he developed his fast-medium action which gave him a deceptive swerve and tremendous pace off the pitch. He was probably the first bowler deliberately to use the seam, and many of the best batsmen of the day regarded him as the most dangerous bowler they had ever played against.

He will be remembered as one of the greatest-hearted bowlers in the game – and one of cricket's most lovable and colourful personalities. He was an inveterate fun-maker and wherever he went he found new friends. He could go on bowling for hours, keeping an immaculate length and seeming to enjoy every moment of the game. A large and amiable man, with many of the characteristics of the true rustic, his broad grin and large feet were a gift to contemporary cartoonists.

Between 1912 and 1937, when he retired from the game, Tate took 2,784 wickets at an average cost of 18.12 runs.

Maurice was a member of the 1924-25 MCC team to Australia and on this tour he beat Arthur Mailey's record of 36 wickets in a Test series by taking 38. He bowled Mailey out to gain his 37th success! Besides being a great bowler, Maurice was a hard-hitting batsman with a wealth of strokes. He scored 17,518 runs (average 24.19) for the county and took 2,223 wickets (average 16.34).

Tate played in 20 consecutive Test matches against Australia and represented England in a further 19 Tests against South Africa, India and the West Indies. In all he took 155 Test wickets – a feat excelled only by A. V. Bedser and S. F. Barnes.

Tate was so consistently successful as a bowler that the quality of his batting is now often overlooked. Yet he was one of the best all-rounders of his generation. He scored 100 not out against South Africa in the Lord's Test in 1929. Eight times he completed the cricketers' double of 1,000 runs and 100 wickets in a season – and in 1923, 1924 and 1925 his bag of wickets topped 200. Fourteen times he took over 100 wickets in a season. As a batsman, his best season was 1927, when he scored 1,713 runs, including five centuries.

Tate was the first professional ever to captain Sussex and after his retirement he was elected an honorary life member of the county club. He was also one of the former professionals similarly honoured by MCC in 1949.

When he retired from first-class cricket, Tate took over the licences of several Sussex inns and for a number of years coached the boys of Tonbridge School.

SPUN HIS WEB DOWN THE YEARS
2012

TITMUS, FREDERICK JOHN, MBE, died on March 23, 2011, aged 78. Fred Titmus began his first-class career when Clement Attlee was in office and ended it during the premiership of Margaret Thatcher; his career outlasted seven other prime ministers in between. To play in five decades was remarkable enough; to finish his first-class career with 2,830 wickets and 21,588 runs – on 16 occasions he claimed more than 100 wickets in a summer, and he performed the double eight times – even more so. As an all-rounder in county cricket, he breathed the same air as the very best, while in 53 Tests he was never less than tough and resourceful.

Although a good enough batsman to open against Australia in an emergency, it was as an off-spinner that Titmus made his reputation for Middlesex and England. He began as a seam bowler, which is perhaps why he was feared not for extravagant turn but for his mastery of flight and drift and the subtlety of his variations. He loved to immerse himself in a long spell, building pressure and patiently awaiting his moment. Titmus was quick-witted, opinionated, sometimes caustic and never lost for a word. There was romance in his Middlesex debut, against Somerset in 1949, and in his improbable finale in 1982, when he was press-ganged into playing Surrey while on a social visit to Lord's.

Titmus was born in Somers Town, St Pancras, the son of a railwayman. In early 1949 he wrote to Lord's asking for a trial, and bowled only 12 balls before being offered the chance to join the groundstaff. He was supposed to sell scorecards at the Test when, with Middlesex shorn of five regulars on international duty, he was selected to play at Bath. His whites were in the wash, so kit had to be borrowed. An inauspicious debut it may have been, but he became the county's youngest player, at 16 years 213 days.

After National Service, he returned to Middlesex and enjoyed the first of his 100-wicket seasons in 1953. His first Test call came against South Africa in 1955 but, after taking one for 50 at Lord's and none for 51 at Old Trafford, and making 39 runs in four innings, he was discarded. But his self-confidence was not dented, and 1955 was his most successful year: 191 wickets and 1,235 runs. He also profited enormously from a conversation with Jim Laker, who had spotted that his delivery stride was still that of a seam bowler, and therefore too long.

There was a clutch of talented off-spinners waiting to succeed Laker – David Allen and John Mortimore at Gloucestershire and Ray Illingworth at Yorkshire. "All were fine practitioners, but I always believed Fred Titmus had the edge," Laker said. Titmus played in two Tests against Pakistan in 1962, and 136 wickets that summer persuaded the selectors to take him to Australia. He showed particular relish for Sydney: seven for 79 in the Third Test, and five for 103 when the sides returned for the Fifth. He was England's leading wicket-taker in the series with 21 at 29, and contributed 182 runs.

In India the following winter, he took 27 Test wickets as well as making his highest Test score, 84 not out. And in South Africa in 1964-65, he and Allen bowled England to victory at Durban in the only decisive result of the series. Titmus was frequently more successful overseas but, against New Zealand at Headingley in 1965, he took four wickets without conceding a run in his 21st over. He was an automatic selection for a second Ashes tour in 1965-66, and once again he starred at Sydney, sharing eight wickets with Allen in the second innings.

He was vice-captain in the West Indies in 1967-68, but his trip ended abruptly when he was one of a group enjoying a day on the beach in Barbados. Several players were hanging on the side of a motorboat. Unaware that the propeller was in the middle, Titmus allowed his legs to rise towards the hull. Two toes were sliced off and two left dangling, but he had the good fortune to be treated by Dr Homer Rogers, a Canadian surgeon with experience of foot injuries suffered by ice-hockey players. Rogers reassured Titmus that, because his big toe had been spared, he would be able to play again. He was back in action little more than two months later; initially bowling in crepe-soled shoes, he took 111 wickets that summer. He was Middlesex captain – the first professional to do the job full-time – from 1965 to 1968, but his tactical appreciation was not matched by his man-management. As vice-captain under Mike Brearley from 1971, he remained an essential component of the side.

Few would have forecast a return to international duty, but he was included in the squad to defend the Ashes in 1974-75. He took only seven wickets in four Tests, but there was an unexpected batting triumph against Lillee and Thomson at Perth, where he made 61, England's highest score in the match. His Test career ended with 153 wickets at 32.22 and 1,449 runs at 22.29.

In his final full season, in 1976, he was sometimes kept out of the team by the emerging John Emburey, but he returned in August to play a key part in a charge that earned Middlesex their first outright Championship since 1947. Titmus became coach of Surrey (and played one match for them in 1978), but did not enjoy the pressures and after two years retired to run a post office in Hertfordshire.

He had a spell as a Test selector in the 1990s, but he was more content at home in Potten End, rising at 4am to pick up the newspapers and often delivering them himself. Once he was knocked off his bike by a post-office van and, writhing in mock agony, ripped off his sock. Pointing to his disfigured foot, he shouted at the ashen-faced driver: "Look what you've done!"

IGNOBLE END FOR ONLY MAN TO CLEAR LORD'S PAVILION   1915

TROTT, ALBERT EDWIN, shot himself at his lodgings, Denbigh Road, Willesden Green, on July 30, 1914. He had been very ill for some time without hope of recovery and, finding the monotony of life in hospital intolerable, he thought a pistol shot the best way out. His death, in his 42nd year, was indeed a tragedy. At his best, Albert Trott was one of the greatest all-round men of his time. The misfortune was that he declined in skill so soon after reaching his highest point. There is nothing unkind in the statement that he ought to have had a much longer career.

Born in Melbourne on February 6, 1873, he sprang into fame by reason of his splendid cricket against Mr Stoddart's England eleven in the winter of 1894-95. At that time he was the most promising young cricketer in Australia. His greatest success was gained in the Test match at Adelaide in which he scored 38 and 72, both times not out, and took in the last innings of the game eight wickets for 43 runs.

It was taken for granted in this country that Albert Trott would come to England with the team captained by his brother in 1896 but, for some reason which has never been properly explained, he was not selected. Having been thus passed over by his own people, he came to England on his own account and qualified in due course for Middlesex.

In first-class matches in 1899 he scored 1,175 runs and took 239 wickets, and in 1900 his figures came out at 1,337 runs and 211 wickets. Thanks to his bowling, his hard hitting and brilliant fielding, and also his strong personality, he became for the time more popular at Lord's than any other professional. In 1901, though he took 176 wickets, he was not quite the man he had been, and from that time he steadily declined. Becoming heavy and musclebound, he could no longer bowl the extra-fast ball that had been so deadly, and batsmen ceased to fear him.

In his benefit match against Somerset at Lord's on Whit Monday, 1907, he came out with a last flash of greatness, taking four wickets in four balls, and finishing the game by doing the hat-trick a second time in the same innings. This was a feat without precedent in first-class cricket. Trott played for Middlesex for the last time in 1910. His active career as a cricketer over, he became one of the county umpires, giving up the work early last season. His health was then so bad that he could go on no longer. One fact in Trott's career must not be forgotten. He was the only batsman who ever hit a ball over the present Pavilion at Lord's. The great hit was made off Noble's bowling in a match between the MCC and the Australians in 1899.

BEST CAPTAIN ENGLAND NEVER HAD
J. C. Clay, 1945

TURNBULL, MAJOR MAURICE JOSEPH, Welsh Guards, was killed in action near Montchamp in Normandy on August 5, 1944. He was 38. During an attack his company got cut off, and while making a reconnaissance he was shot through the head by a sniper and killed instantaneously.

"Maurice was such a grand person. So often have I seen him go into action and never have I seen him rattled. He was always the same: quiet, confident, thinking always of his men and disregarding all danger to himself. A really great person." This extract from a letter written from France is a straightforward appreciation of him as a soldier; there are other and sometimes more fulsome tributes paid to him. But I choose this one because it also exactly describes his leadership of Glamorgan in the days of peace, and shows that in his greatest Test of all he did not alter his style but played his own game to the end.

Maurice Turnbull played cricket for England and rugby football and hockey for Wales; he also held the South Wales squash rackets championship. He captained Cambridge at cricket, was a member of the Test match selection committee, and had been captain and secretary of the Glamorgan club since 1930.

A great player he may have been, but an astute brain made him an even greater captain – the best of his generation who never captained England – and there is little doubt that he would have become one of the game's foremost administrators.

Glamorgan lacked a regular captain, and by the close of the 1929 season, during which the side had no less than seven leaders, it resembled a bedraggled flock without a shepherd. At this unpropitious moment Maurice took charge, comforted perhaps by the knowledge that any change he could bring about was almost bound to be for the better. And change there was, not only in the playing results but in the whole atmosphere: and this better spirit enabled the club to overcome the financial disaster which was shortly to face it. By 1939 he converted a shambling, shamefaced, bankrupt into a worthy and respected member of society with a bank balance of £1,000.

For a batsman who appeared in nine Tests and held for many years what amounted to a standing invitation for the Gentlemen v Players, an average of 30 is moderate enough: honest toilers with no great gifts have attained better figures. The reason is that Maurice never made runs unnecessarily; an innings by him invariably had some definite effect on the game, and he was at his best when others were failing or when runs were required at a pace to beat the clock.

Needless to say, the professionals thought the world of him; and well they might, for nobody kept their interests more at heart or gave them sounder advice. The result was that he always got the best out of what was really a moderate side and did not have to contend seriously with those petty grievances and squabbles which may arise.

The example he set in the field, of course, accounted largely for his beneficial influence. He could field anywhere, but short leg was his real position: the risks he ran and the catches he caught there had to be seen to be believed. Sometimes he literally picked the ball off the defensively held bat and at others he would hang on to red-hot drives although standing but a few yards away from the batsman.

BOWLER WHO TERRORISED ENGLAND
Hubert Preston, 1945

TURNER, MR CHARLES THOMAS BIASS, a bowler ranking with the best ever produced by Australia, and by many who played against him considered without superior, died on New Year's Day 1944 in Sydney, aged 81. Records that stand to his name tell of his work with the ball, but it is remarkable that in the first set of photographs that appeared in *Wisden* [1889] he is holding a bat and wearing pads in company with his colleague J. J. Ferris, grasping a ball in his left hand. The two members of the team captained by P. S. McDonnell fully deserved the honour, for they practically dominated every match in which they played on this their first visit to England. In a season when bowlers accomplished wonderful things, almost beyond belief in these days, Turner took 314 wickets at 11.12 runs apiece and Ferris 224 at 14.10 – G. H. S. Trott coming next with 48 at 23.41. In nine matches against specially chosen sides, three representing England, 70 wickets fell to Turner and 41 to Ferris, seven others claiming only 23 between them.

To have seen these masters of the art at The Oval is a pleasant recollection, and not one of them creates a happier memory than Turner in his rather long rhythmic run and beautiful right-arm action without any effort to make the most of his medium height – 5ft 9in. He delivered the ball almost facing square down the pitch, and, added to his off-break with slightly varied pace about fast-medium, was ability to turn the ball from leg, send down a fast yorker, and, above all, to get quick lift from the turf.

Altogether in 17 Test matches – all against England – Turner took 101 wickets at 16.53 runs apiece in the course of ten years. This average far surpasses the next-best Australian record, 141 at 20.88 by Hugh Trumble in 32 Tests.

Northamptonshire v Derbyshire. At Northampton, August 21, 22, 23, 24, 2012. David Willey had to apologise for calling his home town a "dive" on Twitter. "I popped into Northampton town centre to get barged by one guy who didn't apologise, held the door open for a family who didn't say 'thank you', and flashed a car at a junction and didn't get a thank you," he later explained.

Little Wonder No. 146

BODYLINE PROTAGONIST ALSO EXCELLED ON NEXT TOUR   1985

VOCE, WILLIAM (BILL), who died at Nottingham on June 6, 1984, aged 74, is largely thought of in these days as the junior in one of the great bowling partnerships, Larwood and Voce, and for the contribution that he made to the Bodyline attack in Australia in 1932-33. Although he was somewhat slower than Larwood, his line, from left arm over the wicket, and the steeper bounce that he obtained from his height, made him formidable enough, and the batsmen got no relief when facing him.

His job in that 1932-33 series was to maintain the pressure and he did it nobly, taking, besides, 15 wickets in four matches: he missed the Fourth Test owing to injury. The controversy which this tour excited and the amount that has been written since has diverted attention from his performances in the first two Tests in 1936-37. No English side in this century had had such a bad press before the tour started: it was popularly regarded as having no chance whatever. Its captain, G. O. Allen, the third fast bowler on the previous trip, had been irredeemably opposed to Bodyline and had refused to bowl it. So before the selection of the team was completed the chairman arranged a meeting between Allen and Voce, at which Allen insisted on an undertaking being given that Bodyline tactics would not be employed. Voce demurred at first, but finally agreed to fall in with his captain's wishes and throughout the tour bowled over the wicket to an off-side field. In the First Test he took six for 41 and four for 16: Australia lost by 322 runs and the critics were confounded.

The Second Test was even more sensational. Allen declared at 426 for six in order to get Australia in on a wet wicket, and with the seventh ball of the first over Voce had O'Brien, a left-hander, caught at slip: from the next ball Bradman was caught at short leg. A maiden followed, and off the second ball of his next over McCabe was caught. Australia were three wickets down for one run and Voce had taken them all in four balls. The side was out for 80 and, though they got 324 in their second innings, they lost by an innings, Voce's figures being four for 10 and three for 66.

During this tour a close and lifelong friendship had arisen between Voce and his captain. Years later he told Allen that he now reckoned that Bodyline had been wrong, but that, from loyalty to his old friend Larwood, he was not prepared to say anything on the subject to the press. This sidelight on his character helps to explain why he was so widely respected when, after his playing days were over, he coached first at Trent Bridge and later for many years for MCC at Lord's and elsewhere.

His cricket by no means ended with his bowling. A tall, very strong man, he could hit immensely hard and soon became a dangerous batsman, who made four hundreds in first-class cricket and in 1933 scored over 1,000 runs. Against Glamorgan at Trent Bridge in 1931 he made 129 in 75 minutes, having reached his 100 in 45 minutes. He was also a splendid field and a fine thrower with a very loose arm. In all first-class matches he scored 7,583 runs with an average of 19.19 and took 1,558 wickets at 23.08 apiece. In 27 Tests his figures were 98 wickets at 27.88.

UNHAPPY END TO FIRST-CLASS CAREER   1986

WARDLE, JOHN HENRY, died at Hatfield, near Doncaster, on July 23, 1985, after a long illness, aged 62. For some ten years he was one of England's leading bowlers: he played in 28 Tests, and would have played in many more had he not been a contemporary of Tony Lock. Both were slow left-armers and in England the orthodox methods of Lock were usually preferred; abroad Wardle's ability to bowl chinamen and googlies made him the more dangerous of the two. He was in fact the first top-class English slow left-arm bowler to employ this style, if one excepts an occasional chinaman from Roy Kilner: otherwise it had been confined to change bowlers like Leyland and Compton.

In 1948 he headed the Yorkshire averages with 129 wickets at 17.62. Thenceforward he never looked back. Each year he took his 100 wickets, and in Tests his record was 102 wickets at 20.39 and 653 runs with an average of 19.78. In England his chief bowling performance in these matches was seven for 56 against Pakistan at The Oval in 1954, but in 1953 at Old Trafford Australia in their second innings were 35 for eight when the match ended, and of these Wardle had taken four for seven. In 1956-57 in South Africa he enjoyed a triumph, heading the averages in first-class matches with 90 wickets at 12.25 (in all matches he took 105 wickets) and, though kept out of one Test by injury, taking in the other four 26 wickets at 13.80: in the Second Test he took 12 for 89 in a memorable piece of bowling. He was also a fine, fearless left-handed hitter in the lower part of the order, never deterred by any bowler's reputation from hitting him hard, high and often, and frequently suggesting by his success that some of the earlier batsmen might have done better had they adopted more aggressive tactics.

His first-class career came to an unhappy end in 1958. On July 27 he received the expected invitation to go with MCC to Australia, but three days later the Yorkshire committee announced that they would not be employing him after the end of the year. Thereupon Wardle requested that he should stand down from the team for the Bank Holiday match with Lancashire because of comments he intended to make about his colleagues in a newspaper article to be published while the match was in progress. His request was granted and the article appeared in the *Daily Mail*. The Yorkshire committee, meeting on August 11, terminated Wardle's engagement immediately. They explained that their original decision, which was unanimous, had been taken because on several occasions in the past he had been warned that "his general behaviour on the field and in the dressing-rooms left much to he desired" and he had paid no attention whatever. Now, by writing the articles without obtaining permission, he had in addition broken his contract. On August 19 the MCC committee, having interviewed him, withdrew the invitation for the Australian tour. It was no coincidence that Peter May's side suffered a heavy defeat. Wardle was still a beautiful bowler and he was an incalculable loss.

In 1970 Yorkshire elected him an honorary life member and recently they had appointed him bowling consultant to the county. He was also elected an honorary member of MCC. In all first-class cricket he made 7,318 runs with an average of 16.11 and took 1,842 wickets at 18.95.

RENOWNED AT THE CENTRE OF TWO SPORTS 1952

WILLIAMS, MR WILLIAM, who died at his home at Hampton Wick on April 14, 1951, aged 90, was a fine all-round sportsman. Born on April 12, 1860, he was a member of MCC from 1900. In the seasons of 1885 and 1886 he appeared as wicketkeeper for Middlesex, and after an absence of 14 years returned to the county side as a bowler of leg-breaks, playing occasionally till 1905. He often assisted MCC, and was credited with taking 100 or more wickets a season in all matches for 55 years. In his last summer as a player, he turned out at the age of 74 for MCC against the House of Lords and, after dismissing Lord Dalkeith, Lord Tennyson and Major L. George for 16 runs, was presented by the Marylebone Club with the ball.

Apart from his cricket, "Billy" Williams, as he was known to everyone for many years, was celebrated as the man who, in the early part of the century, ended a long search for a suitable site for a national rugby union ground by discovering a cabbage field of ten acres which has since developed into the famous Twickenham enclosure. For a long time the ground, later extended by 18 acres, was known to rugby football followers as "Billy Williams's cabbage patch".

NEVER AFRAID TO EXPRESS HIMSELF 1958

WILSON, MR EVELYN ROCKLEY, who died at Winchester on July 21, 1957, aged 78, was one of the best amateur slow right-arm bowlers of his time. He made a brief appearance for Yorkshire in 1899, but when, on going down from Cambridge, he became a master at Winchester, a position he held for 40 years, he preferred to engage in club cricket during the school holidays, his stated reason being that he preferred to play in three matches a week rather than two.

A suggestion that Wilson might use his residential qualification for Hampshire led to him being pressed into service once again by Yorkshire when over 40 years of age, but, whatever the reason, there could be no doubt as to his immense value to the county during the closing weeks of each season. In 1913 he made his only century for Yorkshire, 104 not out against Essex at Bradford, in the course of which he claimed to have hit the only six obtained by skying a ball directly over the wicketkeeper's head, but it was as a bowler that he achieved his best work. He met with such success in 1920 that he took 64 wickets for 13.84 runs apiece, being fourth in the English averages. This brought him a place in J. W. H. T. Douglas's MCC team who, the following winter, toured Australia. Wilson played in his only Test match during that tour, of which *Wisden* of the time reported: "A good deal of friction was caused by cable messages sent home to the *Daily Express* by Mr E. R. Wilson. This led to a resolution passed at the annual meeting of the Marylebone Club in May deprecating the reporting of matches by players concerned in them."

Immaculate length and cleverly disguised variation of pace made Wilson difficult to punish. His own explanation of his success was typically whimsical. "I have always been a lucky bowler," he said, "as my best ball has been the ball which broke from the off when I meant to break from leg. I bowled far more of these as a man of 40 than as a young man." Another example of this slightly built, diffident cricketer's sense of humour was provided at the nets at Winchester when to a somewhat inept boy batsman he said: "My dear boy, you must hit one ball in the middle of your bat before you meet your Maker."

GODFATHER OF MIRTH   1976

WODEHOUSE, SIR PELHAM GRENVILLE, the famous novelist, who died in hospital on Long Island on February 14, 1975, at the age of 93, had been a member of the Dulwich College XI in 1899 and 1900. He was godfather of M. G. Griffith, the late captain of Sussex.

Wodehouse also appeared six times at Lord's, where his first captain was Sir Arthur Conan Doyle.

Records

Records are part and parcel of cricket, from the basic book-keeping of the scorecard to the eye-catching accomplishment of previously unattained feats. *Wisden* first published a dedicated section, Some Cricket Records, in the 1889 edition; it ran to two pages and was little more than a listing of the highest individual scores, innings totals and partnerships, with a single final paragraph detailing nine bowlers who had taken all ten wickets in an innings. By 2013 the index to the records alone ran to six pages and the whole section to 150 – and an even more comprehensive, and regularly updated, version could be found at www.wisdenrecords.com.

We have chosen to represent the records by concentrating on what might be called the ultimates – the highest individual innings; the highest, and lowest, innings total; the highest wicket partnership; and a few others – and seeing how *Wisden* has reported on them as the mark has progressed down the years. We have concentrated on first-class cricket, with a few significant examples from minor matches added; Test match records have been left to the chapters on international cricket.

Batting is easy, bowling less easily definable. Cricket does not have the equivalent of baseball's perfect game in which a pitcher allows no batter even to reach first base. Brian Langford, of Somerset, once bowled his spell of eight overs in a limited-overs match without conceding a run, but he didn't actually dismiss any of his opponents. A better comparison is a bowler who takes all ten wickets in an innings or, still better, all 20 wickets in a match. Of the many who have taken all ten in an innings one instance stands out numerically: Verity's ten for ten, followed as an achievement by Hollies's single-handed dismantling of Nottinghamshire (John Wisden himself, playing for North at Lord's in 1850, bowled ten South batsmen in an innings, but he was more than a decade too early for the feat to be recorded in the Almanack that bears his name). All 20 remains in the realms of fantasy: Jim Laker's 19 for 90 for England against Australia has came nearest in first-class cricket, but a brief item headed "All the 20 Wickets" three pages from the end of the 1873 edition gives an instance in a minor match that comes close to this cricketing nirvana.

The closest to batting perfection comes, perhaps, from hitting every ball in an over for six. The two who have achieved that are here, together with a selection of other landmarks including a table of the all-time record runmakers (first-class and one-day matches combined) and one record that has remained unchallenged since 1884: throwing the cricket ball.

THE HIGHEST INDIVIDUAL SCORE
FIRST-CLASS CRICKET

1876 – THE COUNTY OF KENT v THE GENTLEMEN OF MCC: GRACE 344
1877

At Canterbury, August 10, 11, 12, 1876. A marvellous run-getting match, which – like its predecessor – three days of splendid cricketing weather was insufficient to play out.

With the large lot of 329 runs to hit off ere they could make a start from Kent's first innings, the MCC men commenced their follow-on at five minutes to five with Mr W. Grace and Mr Lucas. With the score at seven only Mr Lucas was out, and the previously seeming hopeless task appeared still more hopeless; but then Mr Grace started his wonderful hitting in such form, that he made 20 runs from two successive overs of Hearne's, had brought the score to 100 in 25 minutes; and when the stumps were drawn at 6.45 he (by hitting almost unexampled in its brilliant severity) had in 110 minutes raised the score to 217 for four wickets.

Saturday was the last day of "the Week", and Mr Grace's day; for on that day he completed the largest innings ever played for MCC, made three-fifths of the runs in the largest innings ever scored on the Canterbury ground, and had – according to *The Kent Herald* – "completely settled the Kentish Twelve".

The day was intensely hot, and so was the hitting of the MCC two – Mr W. Grace and Mr Crutchley – who resumed their innings at noon, and were not parted until late in the afternoon when they had increased the score by 227 runs! – as Mr Crutchley went to wickets with the score at 203, and was out for 84 with it at 430. There were then five wickets down at an average of 86 runs per wicket, and Mr Grace as full of fine hitting as he had been at any phase of this great display, and he kept on hitting, scoring, and fagging the field until near the end, for he was not out until 546 runs had been scored, and play finally ceased when the score was at 557, nine wickets having then fallen.

Mr W. Grace commenced MCC's second innings; he was six hours and 20 minutes at wickets, and had scored 344 runs out of the 546 booked, when he was caught out at mid-off, *Bell's Life* stating: "He scored those 344 runs without positively giving a chance." His hits consisted of 76 singles, 20 twos, eight threes, and 51 fours (204 runs by fourers in one innings!).

Kent 473 (Lord Harris 154, G. Hearne, jun. 57; Mr W. G. Grace 4-116);

MCC 144 (Capt. J. Fellowes 5-50)

and 557-9 (Grace 344, Mr P. E. Crutchley 84; Lord Harris 4-59).

1895 – SOMERSET v LANCASHIRE: MACLAREN 424
1896

At Taunton, July 15, 16, 17, 1895. Severe as had been their beating in the previous match, Somerset fared even worse in this engagement, Lancashire defeating them by an innings and 452 runs – one of the most decisive wins on record. The match was made memorable for all time by the wonderful innings of 424 by A. C. MacLaren, who thus surpassed all previous individual scores in first-class matches. The previous-highest was, of course, W. G. Grace's 344 in 1876. Only once has MacLaren's score been beaten in any kind of cricket, A. E. Stoddart making 485 for the Hampstead Club in 1886. MacLaren, who went in first and was seventh out at 792, was batting for seven hours and 50 minutes, and only gave two chances, the first at 262. His score comprised one six, 62 fours, 11 threes, 37 twos, and 63 singles. Paul, who played a fine innings of 177, assisted MacLaren to put on 363 runs in three hours and ten minutes for the second wicket – a partnership which has only been surpassed in first-class cricket by the 398 by Shrewsbury and Gunn for Notts against Sussex in 1890. Lancashire's innings only lasted eight hours, the total of 801 being the highest ever obtained in a county match.

Lancashire 801 (Mr A. C. MacLaren 424, A. G. Paul 177, A. Ward 64; Mr L. C. H. Palairet 4-133); **Somerset 143** (J. Briggs 4-59, A. W. Mold 4-75) **and 206** (Mr S. M. J. Woods 55; Mold 3-76, Briggs 5-78).

Little Wonder No. 147

Afghanistan v Australia (One-Day International). At Sharjah, August 25, 2012. Javed Ahmadi was playing in this match the day after captaining Afghanistan in the plate final of the Under-19 World Cup in Brisbane; not surprisingly, perhaps, he and his Under-19 team-mate Najibullah Zadran both made ducks (Najibullah was out first ball, so was dismissed by successive deliveries on successive days roughly 7,500 miles apart).

1923 – VICTORIA v TASMANIA: Ponsford 429   1924

GREAT INDIVIDUAL SCORES – FIRST-CLASS MATCHES.

429 W. H. Ponsford, Victoria v Tasmania, at Melbourne 1922-23

Because the match was not part of the Sheffield Shield competition Wisden *did not carry a report, although the feat was listed in the Records section.*

1927 – VICTORIA v QUEENSLAND: Ponsford 437   1928

At Melbourne, December 16, 17, 19, 20, 1927. This match, which Victoria won by an innings and 197 runs, was the most noteworthy of the series. O'Connor, the Queensland captain, won the toss and sent Victoria in, but at the end of the first day's play only two men were out with 400 runs on the board, and ultimately

Victoria completed their innings for the huge total of 793. Scoring 437, Ponsford established a new world's record, beating his 429 against Tasmania in 1922, the previous record for an individual innings in first-class cricket. At the crease for ten hours and 21 minutes, Ponsford gave two chances – both difficult ones. He might have been caught off a return to Bensted when 162, and offered a chance of stumping with his score 239. Using a bat weighing 2lb 10oz, he placed his shots with rare judgment, and was practically always master of the situation throughout his long stay.

Victoria 793 (W. H. Ponsford 437, H. L. Hendry 129, J. Ryder 70; G. S. Amos 5-148);

Queensland 189 (O. E. Nothling 66; D. D. Blackie 6-46)

and 407 (F. C. Thompson 118, L. P. D. O'Connor 66, F. J. Gough 54; H. Ironmonger 5-88).

1930 – NEW SOUTH WALES v QUEENSLAND: BRADMAN 452 NOT OUT 1931

At Sydney, January 3, 4, 6, 7, 1930. Everything else in this game paled before the phenomenal performance of Bradman who, in scoring 452 not out – a feat that occupied him 415 minutes – played the highest individual innings recorded in first-class cricket. That splendid exhibition led the way to a victory for New South Wales by 685 runs. Displaying a wider range of strokes than usual, Bradman batted without a trace of error during his long stay and hit no fewer than 49 fours. His prolific scoring followed upon comparatively low totals in the first innings of each side.

New South Wales 235 (W. C. Andrews 56; A. Hurwood 4-57, H. M. Thurlow 4-83)

and 761-8 dec (D. G. Bradman 452*, A. F. Kippax 115, A. H. Allsopp 66,

S. J. McCabe 60; Hurwood 6-179);

Queensland 227 (V. H. V. Goodwin 67, E. C. Bensted 51; McCabe 5-36) **and 84** (C. S. Everett 6-23).

1959 – KARACHI v BAHAWALPUR: HANIF 499   1959

Hanif Mohammad, Pakistan's 24-year-old opening batsman, made 499, the world's highest individual score in first-class cricket, for Karachi against Bahawalpur in the semi-final of the Quaid-e-Azam Trophy at the Karachi Parsi Institute ground on January 8, 9, 11, 12, 1959. This beat the 452 not out by Sir Donald Bradman for New South Wales against Queensland at Sydney in 1929-30.

On a coir matting pitch, Hanif scored 25 in 40 minutes on the first evening, 230 in five hours on the second day, and 244 in four hours 55 minutes on the third. He was run out when going for his 500 off the last ball of the day. Altogether he batted ten hours 35 minutes and hit 64 fours. Hanif played superbly, rarely putting the ball in the air, he did not offer a chance and was beaten only once, and then off the pitch. Hanif shared a stand of 259 with Wallis Mathias for the second wicket.

Hanif is one of four brothers all playing in first-class cricket. Three appeared for Karachi in this match; Wazir was captain and the other was Mushtaq.

Bahawalpur 185 (Mohammad Ramzan 64; Ikram Elahi 4-48) **and 108**;
Karachi 772-7 dec (Hanif Mohammad 499, Wallis Mathias 103).

In the final, a few days later, Abdul Aziz, the Karachi wicketkeeper [*aged 17*], died while batting against Combined Services. He was struck on the heart by a slow off-break from Dildar Awan and fell. He died 15 minutes later on the way to hospital. Play was postponed for a day.

Hanif's achievement received special treatment with inclusion advanced to the same year's Almanack, although it occurred in January.

1994 – WARWICKSHIRE v DURHAM: LARA 501 NOT OUT   1995

At Birmingham, June 2, 3, 4, 6, 1994. Drawn. The astonishing record-strewn Monday, including Lara's 501 not out – the highest score in the history of first-class cricket – that concluded this game was possible only because the third day was lost to rain. Having narrowly missed joining Bradman, Fry and Procter in scoring six successive first-class hundreds, Lara became the first man to score seven in eight innings. When he ran off, the first man ever to have scored 500 runs in an innings, with one ball of the day to spare, Lara had set a string of other records. As with his five previous hundreds for Warwickshire, it was his run-rate, as well as the volume of runs, which set him apart. His 501 took six minutes under eight hours, in which he faced only 427 balls and hit 308 in boundaries – 62 fours and ten sixes. He took his staggering County Championship record to 1,176 runs from 1,175 balls in seven innings – at 235.20. Lara shared two partnerships over 300, with Penney scoring 44 out of 314, and Piper making a career-best 116 not out from 322 – the highest stand for Warwickshire's fifth wicket. The circumstances that allowed his assault on the record derived from Durham's own total, 556 for eight declared, injuries to two of their bowlers, Graveney and Saxelby, and a playing surface which was reported to Lord's by the umpires as too heavily in favour of batting. Bainbridge would not risk setting Warwickshire a target. By the end of the second day, Lara had announced himself with an unbeaten 111 off 143 balls, although he made an uncertain start – bowled by a Cummins no-ball on 12 and dropped behind the wicket on 18 off Brown. Once Durham decided, after the loss of the third day, to play only for bonus points, Lara was given an open cheque to bat. He scored more boundaries before lunch than Penney managed runs – 25 fours and seven sixes to 27 runs – and his 174 runs in the 135-minute session were six short of the Championship record, 180 by K. S. Ranjitsinhji in 150 minutes for Sussex against Surrey in 1902. His first 100 had come from 138 balls; the second came from 82, the third from 58, the fourth from 72 and the fifth from 77. Between lunch and tea he scored 133, which left him needing 82 for the record. But Lara was unaware of the playing conditions by which the game had to end half an hour early, because there could be no result. Only when

Piper informed him, four balls into the last over, that he had only two balls left, did he blaze his final four to pass Hanif Mohammad's 499 at Karachi in 1958-59. The innings took Warwickshire to a club-record 810 for four, and Lara's calendar year aggregate to 2,689 from 24 innings. His 501 came seven weeks to the day after his 375 in Antigua. No one had held both individual records, Test and first-class, since Bradman more than 60 years before.

Durham 556-8 dec (J. E. Morris 204, P. Bainbridge 67, D. A. Graveney 65*,
A. C. Cummins 62, S. Hutton 61);
Warwickshire 810-4 dec (B. C. Lara 501*, K. J. Piper 116*, R. G. Twose 51).

MINOR CRICKET

1899 – CLIFTON COLLEGE: CLARKE'S v NORTH TOWN: COLLINS **628** NOT OUT

A junior house match at Clifton College, begun on Thursday, June 22 and completed on the following Wednesday, is noteworthy for having produced the greatest score known to have been made by a single player in a game of any description. The hero of the occasion, A. E. J. Collins, was batting for six hours and 50 minutes, his innings being continued in unequal instalments during five days. His hits included a six, four fives, 31 fours, 33 threes, and 146 twos. The previous-best score was that of A. E. Stoddart, who made 485 for the Hampstead Club against the Stoics in 1886. It is remarkable that it was in a Clifton College game that E. F. S. Tylecote made his score of 404 in 1868.

Clarke's 836 (Collins 628*, Whittey 42);
North Town 87 and 61.

KILLED IN ACTION

COLLINS, LIEUT. ARTHUR EDWARD JEUNE, of the Royal Engineers, who was killed in action on November 11, 1914, came suddenly into note by scoring 628 not out when only 13 years old. Collins also obtained 11 wickets in the match, seven in the first innings and four in the second, and in partnership with Redfern (13) put on as many as 183 for the last wicket. In 1901 and 1902 he was in the College XI, in the former year scoring 342 runs with an average of 38.00, his highest innings being 112 against Old Cliftonians. He was a free-hitting batsman, but his military duties prevented him from taking cricket seriously: still he made many good scores in Army matches, and for Old Cliftonians v Trojans at Southampton in August, 1913, he and F. G Robinson made 141 without being parted for the first wicket in 38 minutes, Collins scoring 63 and his partner 77. His best performance at Lord's was to make 58 and 36 for Royal Engineers v Royal Artillery in 1913. He was born in India in 1885, gazetted Second Lieutenant in 1904 and promoted Lieutenant in 1907.

EBERLE, VICTOR FULLER, who died in Bristol in 1974 aged about 90, claimed fame as the man who in 1899 dropped A. E. J. Collins when he had scored 20. It was in the house match at Clifton College in which Collins went on to score 628 not out!

THE HIGHEST TOTAL:
FIRST-CLASS CRICKET

1887 – SMOKERS v NON-SMOKERS: 803   1888

At Melbourne, on the East Melbourne Ground, March 17, 18, 19, 21, 1887. This game did not count in the averages of the Englishmen, but it was remarkable for producing the highest total ever obtained in a first-class match, the Non-Smokers going in first, and scoring 803. The previous best was 775 by New South Wales against Victoria at Sydney in 1882. Though the East Melbourne Ground is small, the performance was an extraordinary one, Shrewsbury, Bruce, and Gunn batting splendidly. After four days' cricket the result was a draw.

[this is how the scorecard appeared originally in *Wisden*]

Non-Smokers first innings
*A. Shrewsbury c Duffy b Briggs	236
W. Bruce lbw b Palmer	131
W. Bates b Palmer	4
W. Gunn b Boyle	150
R. G. Barlow b Palmer	29
R. S. Houston c and b Briggs	57
H. A. Musgrove st Lewis b Briggs	62
J. Worrall b Read	78
W. H. Cooper c and b Briggs	46
†M. Sherwin not out	5
W. Barnes absent hurt	
Extras (b 3, lb 1, w 1)	5

Total   (all out) 803

Fall of wickets: 1-196, 2-204, 3-514, 4-524, 5-575, 6-656, 7-686, 8-788, 9-803.

Smokers bowling
	Overs	Mdns	Runs	Wkts
Briggs	55.1	11	141	4
Palmer	54	10	189	3
Boyle	31	14	60	1
Lohmann	48	18	113	0
Flowers	38	12	93	0
Scotton	26	4	82	0
Duffy	15	2	52	0
Read	26	10	43	1
Walters	9	4	25	0

1893 – AUSTRALIANS v OXFORD AND CAMBRIDGE PAST AND PRESENT: 843

At Portsmouth, July 31, August 1, 2, 1893. When this match opened there was every reason to expect that it would prove one of the least interesting of the whole tour, for the team of past and present University players which C. W. Wright had got together was so far from representative that over a dozen cricketers might be mentioned, any one of whom had better qualifications than those who took the field against the Colonials. The extreme weakness, however, of the Englishmen served to render the match memorable, for so completely did the Australians master the bowling of their opponents that, one after another, records which had stood for several years were all broken.

While Trumble and Bruce were together the previous record of an Australian eleven in England – 643 by the 1882 team against Sussex at Brighton – was headed, and two more records were broken during the partnership of Turner and Walter Giffen, the 703 made by Cambridge against Sussex at Brighton in 1890, which had stood as the best score made in a big match in England, and the world's record of 803 obtained by the Non-Smokers against the Smokers at Melbourne in March 1887.

The innings, which lasted ten hours, closed for 843.

Australians first innings
J. J. Lyons b Bainbridge 51
*A. C. Bannerman c Forster b Hornsby 133
G. Giffen c Arkwright b Bainbridge 43
G. H. S. Trott c Wilson b Arkwright 61
S. E. Gregory c Hornsby b Wilson 11
H. Graham c Wilson b Forster 83
W. Bruce st Gay b Forster 191
H. Trumble b Bainbridge 105
C. T. B. Turner c Forster b Arkwright 66
W. F. Giffen b Berkeley 62
†A. H. Jarvis not out 6
Extras (b 20, lb 8, w 3) 31

Total   (all out) 843

Fall of wickets: 1-72, 2-133, 3-221, 4-236, 5-372, 6-469, 7-701, 8-701, 9-822, 10-843.

Oxford and Cambridge Universities Past and Present bowling

	Overs	Mdns	Runs	Wkts
Wilson	35	5	126	1
Berkeley	60.2	15	165	1
Forster	51	9	162	2
Bainbridge	29	5	122	3
Arkwright	29	7	62	2
Hornsby	17	1	84	1
Roe	13	1	48	0
Ranjitsinhji	6	0	27	0
Lindley	3	0	9	0
Wright	1	0	7	0

1896 – WARWICKSHIRE v YORKSHIRE: 887

At Birmingham, May 7, 8, 9, 1896. A match that will always be remembered from the fact that Yorkshire scored the huge total of 887 and put into the shade all previous records in first-class cricket. By making so many runs Yorkshire robbed themselves of the chance of victory, but, of course, it was a great thing to have accomplished such a memorable performance. As may be supposed the wicket was in almost perfect condition, but for all that the Yorkshiremen deserve the highest praise for the manner in which they seized their opportunity. Yorkshire had the honour of lowering another record, this being the first time in an important match that four separate scores of over a hundred had been obtained in the same innings. Jackson played splendid cricket, while the Warwickshire bowling was at its best, and late in the innings Lord Hawke and Peel put on 240 runs during their partnership. Every member of the Warwickshire team, with the exception of Law, went on to bowl. Yorkshire's innings occupied the whole of the two first days.

Yorkshire first innings
Hon. F. S. Jackson c Law b Ward	117
J. Tunnicliffe c Pallett b Glover	28
J. T. Brown c Hill b Pallett	23
D. Denton c W. G. Quaife b Santall	6
R. Moorhouse b Ward	72
E. Wainwright run out	126
R. Peel not out	210
F. W. Milligan b Pallett	34
*Lord Hawke b Pallett	166
G. H. Hirst c Glover b Santall	85
†D. Hunter b Pallett	5
Extras (b 5, lb 6, w 4)	15
Total (all out)	887

Fall of wickets: 1-43, 2-124, 3-141, 4-211, 5-339, 6-405, 7-448, 8-740, 9-876, 10-887.

Warwickshire bowling
	Overs	Mdns	Runs	Wkts
Santall	65	9	223	2
Ward	62	11	175	2
Glover	30	1	154	1
Pallett	75.3	14	184	4
W. G. Quaife	8	1	33	0
Bainbridge	6	1	17	0
Hill	3	0	14	0
Lilley	6	1	13	0
W. Quaife	9	1	18	0
Diver	10	1	41	0

1901 – NEW SOUTH WALES v SOUTH AUSTRALIA: 918

At Sydney, January 5, 7, 8, 9, 1901. In this match New South Wales set up a new record in first-class cricket, their total beating the 887 obtained by Yorkshire against

Warwickshire in May 1896. In another particular their innings was unique, five individual scores of over 100 being obtained. Perhaps the feature of the batting was the success gained by Poidevin in his first big match. The huge score of 918 was obtained very rapidly, the innings only lasting nine hours and 20 minutes. New South Wales had the game in their hands all the way through and won by an innings and 605 runs – one of the most overwhelming victories in the history of cricket.

New South Wales first innings

V. T. Trumper b A. Jarvis	70
F. A. Iredale c A. H. Jarvis b Travers	118
M. A. Noble c Giffen b Matthews	153
A. J. Y. Hopkins c A. H. Jarvis b Travers	27
*S. E. Gregory b A. Jarvis	168
R. A. Duff st A. H. Jarvis b Travers	119
L. O. S. Poidevin not out	140
T. H. Howard c Bailey b Matthews	64
†J. J. Kelly c Hill b Hack	34
A. McBeath c Walkley b Bailey	7
J. Marsh lbw b Travers	1
Extras (b 9, lb 8)	17
Total (all out)	918

Fall of wickets: 1-148, 2-238, 3-306, 4-414, 5-628, 6-679, 7-784, 8-900, 9-911, 10-918.

South Australia bowling

	Overs	Mdns	Runs	Wkts
Travers	69	15	197	4
Matthews	27	2	162	2
Giffen	23	0	119	0
A. Jarvis	49	7	225	2
Reedman	17	1	70	0
Walkley	6	0	43	0
Hack	10	1	44	1
Hill	1	0	18	0
Bailey	6	1	23	1

1923 – VICTORIA v TASMANIA: 1059   1924

GREAT AGGREGATE SCORES – FIRST-CLASS MATCHES.

1059 Victoria v Tasmania, at Melbourne 1922-23

Because the match was not part of the Sheffield Shield competition Wisden *did not carry a report, although the feat was listed in the Records section.*

1926 – VICTORIA v NEW SOUTH WALES: 1107 1928

At Melbourne, December 24, 27, 28, 29, 1926. In this match Victoria set up a new record in first-class cricket, their total of 1,107 beating that of 1,059 obtained by the same State against Tasmania in the 1922-23 season. Throughout the innings which lasted ten hours and a half, runs came at a great pace. A brilliant opening partnership between Ponsford and Woodfull produced 375 runs in three hours and threequarters, then Ponsford and Hendry added a further 219 for the second wicket in just under two hours. Ponsford hit 36 fours in a memorable display. The brightest of some wonderful batting was that of Ryder, who, by powerful driving, obtained six sixes and 33 fours and scored 295 out of 449 in rather more than four hours. New South Wales, with a weak team, were outplayed from the start and suffered defeat by an innings and 656 runs.

Victoria first innings
*W. M. Woodfull c Ratcliffe b Andrews	133
W. H. Ponsford b Morgan	352
H. S. T. L. Hendry c Morgan b Mailey	100
J. Ryder c Kippax b Andrews	295
H. S. B. Love st Ratcliffe b Mailey	6
S. P. King st Ratcliffe b Mailey	7
A. E. V. Hartkopf c McGuirk b Mailey	61
A. E. Liddicut b McGuirk	36
†J. L. Ellis run out	63
F. L. Morton run out	0
D. D. Blackie not out	27
Extras (b 17, lb 8, nb 2)	27

Total   (all out) 1107

Fall of wickets: 1-375, 2-594, 3-614, 4-631, 5-657, 6-834, 7-915, 8-1043, 9-1046, 10-1107.

New South Wales bowling
	Overs	Mdns	Runs	Wkts
McNamee	24	2	124	0
McGuirk	26	1	130	1
Mailey	64	0	362	4
Campbell	11	0	89	0
Phillips	11.7	0	64	0
Morgan	26	0	137	1
Andrews	21	2	148	2
Kippax	7	0	26	0

THE LOWEST TOTAL

1872 – MCC AND GROUND v THE COUNTY OF SURREY: 16 1873

At Lord's, May 14, 1872. This was the most remarkable match of the MCC season. Seven MCC wickets, including the crack's [W. G. Grace], being got rid of before a run was scored. Eight 0s were booked in that innings of MCC's, whose eleven were out in threequarters of an hour for a total of 16 runs. 19 was the highest score made in the match, which was commenced at ten past 12, and concluded at 20 minutes to seven; the whole number of runs made in the match being 175, and that, too, notwithstanding such batsmen as Mr W. Grace, Jupp, John Smith, Richard Humphrey, Pooley, T. Hearne, T. Humphrey, and Mr L. S. Howell had played their two innings.

Incessant rain from dawn to dusk on May 13 (the day set to commence the match) necessitated a postponement until the following day, when on dead, deceitful playing wickets, and in a queer light for batting, Mr W. Grace and John Smith commenced (!) MCC's marvellous little innings of 16 runs, wherein seven of the wickets (including the crack's) went down before a run was scored in this form. To the fourth ball delivered Mr Grace was lbw; from the sixth ball Smith was caught out by long-stop; the 15th ball shot down Mr Coote's wicket, and the 22nd bowled Shaw. From the 23rd ball Mr Onslow was smartly had at mid-off; the 35th thoroughly beat and bowled Mr Brune, and the very next ball slick bowled Hearne; seven wickets – and good ones too – in this way falling in 25 minutes before a run was scored.

Captain Becher then made a two from the first ball of Marten's fifth over, but in Southerton's sixth over (another maiden) a clever catch by Pooley got rid of Biddulph; then Captain Becher made his score eight, when a truly splendid left-hand catch – low down – by Marten settled him; Captain Becher (ninth man out) having made all the runs (eight) then scored for the Club. When Rylott and Hewitt had doubled the score Marten bowled Howitt, and so, in exactly 45 minutes, were the MCC eleven out for an innings of 16 runs.

Marylebone Cricket Club first innings

W. G. Grace lbw b Southerton	0
J. Smith c Jupp b Marten	0
C. P. Coote b Marten	0
C. J. Brune b Southerton	0
A. Shaw b Marten	0
D. R. Onslow c Strachan b Marten	0
A. W. R. Becher c and b Marten	8
T. Hearne b Southerton	0
†S. Biddulph c Pooley b Southerton	0
A. Rylott not out	6
G. Howitt b Marten	2
Extras	0
Total (all out)	16

Fall of wickets: 1-0, 2-0, 3-0, 4-0, 5-0, 6-0, 7-0, 8-2, 9-8, 10-16.

Surrey bowling

	Overs	Mdns	Runs	Wkts
Southerton	9	6	5	4
Marten	9	5	11	6

Sussex v Somerset. At Hove, September 4, 5, 6, 7, 2012. Abdur Rehman arrived before lunch on the first day, replaced Jack Leach at 2pm, then knocked over Somerset's tail, having flown through the night from Dubai to Gatwick after Pakistan's one-day international against Australia, which finished at 2.09am Sharjah time. He was believed to be the first professional cricketer to play in two matches in two different continents on the same day.

Little Wonder No. 148

1877 – MCC AND GROUND v OXFORD UNIVERSITY: 12　　1878

At Cowley Marsh, Oxford, May 24, 1877. This match was played out in one day, and, notwithstanding only 171 runs were made in the match, MCC won by an innings and 77 runs. The match was played in the memorable wet season, and the wickets were of bad form; one end playing very badly. In the first innings, the Oxford men played without their captain's aid, and could not get into their form on such wickets; in fact they were got out for two surprisingly small totals of 12 and 35. But that little innings of a dozen runs was made from 174 balls bowled, and took them near upon two hours to play, so the runs scored must have been greatly out of proportion to the cricket played.

The only hits made were one three, three twos, and three singles.

Oxford University first innings
H. G. Tylecote b Rylott	0
H. R. Webbe b Morley	1
E. T. Hirst b Morley	0
E. W. Wallington not out	7
†H. Fowler b Morley	4
A. G. Pearson b Morley	0
H. J. B. Hollings b Morley	0
J. H. Savory b Morley	0
C. E. Horner c Walker b Morley	0
F. G. G. Jellicoe b Rylott	0
*A. J. Webbe absent hurt	
Extras	0
Total　　(all out)	12

Fall of wickets: 1-1, 2-1, 3-1, 4-8, 5-8, 6-8, 7-8, 8-12, 9-12.

Marylebone Cricket Club bowling
	Overs	Mdns	Runs	Wkts
Morley	22	18	6	7
Rylott	21.2	18	6	2

1907 – GLOUCESTERSHIRE v NORTHAMPTONSHIRE: 12   1908

At Gloucester, June 10, 11, 12, 1907. In this game a fresh record was made by Dennett and Jessop in dismissing Northamptonshire for 12 runs. This is the smallest total for a first-class inter-county match, the previous-lowest being 13 by Notts against Yorkshire at Trent Bridge in 1901. Play on the first day was restricted to 50 minutes, Gloucestershire losing four wickets for 20 runs, and, despite some hitting by Jessop, being all out next day for 60. The first innings of Northamptonshire only lasted 40 minutes, Dennett, who made the ball turn in a remarkable manner, being practically unplayable. Dennett accomplished the hat-trick, in dismissing Hawtin, Beasley, and Buswell with successive balls, and should have had four wickets in as many balls, Wrathall dropping a catch offered by East. In Gloucestershire's second innings Jessop and Mackenzie were the only batsmen to overcome the difficulties of the wicket, but Northamptonshire were set 136 to get to win. At their second attempt the visitors again failed before Dennett, who in the course of the day took 15 wickets for 21 runs. Northamptonshire finished up on the second day in practically a hopeless position, wanting 97 runs to win with only three wickets left, but rain came to their rescue. Not a ball could be bowled on the Wednesday, the game having to be abandoned as a draw.

Northamptonshire first innings

*E. M. Crosse c Board b Dennett	4
M. Cox lbw b Dennett	2
C. J. T. Pool c Spry b Dennett	4
†W. A. Buswell st Board b Dennett	1
L. T. Driffield b Dennett	0
G. J. Thompson b Dennett	0
R. W. R. Hawtin lbw b Dennett	0
W. East st Board b Dennett	0
R. N. Beasley b Jessop	1
S. King not out	0
W. Wells c Parker b Jessop	0
Extras	0
Total (all out)	12

Fall of wickets: 1-6, 2-10, 3-11, 4-11, 5-11, 6-11, 7-11, 8-12, 9-12, 10-12.

Gloucestershire bowling

	Overs	Mdns	Runs	Wkts
Dennett	6	1	9	8
Jessop	5.3	4	3	2

1959 – BORDER v NATAL (CURRIE CUP, SECTION A): 16 AND 18   1961

At East London, December 19, 21, 22, 1959. Natal 90 (S. Knott 5-40, A. F. Hagemann 5-49) and 294-8 dec (M. K. Elgie 162*; E. F. Schreiber 6-126); Border 16 (T. L. Goddard 6-3, J. M. Cole 4-13) and 18 (G. M. Griffin 7-11). Natal won by 350 runs.

Note: Border's match total of 34 for two completed innings constituted a record for first-class cricket.

HIGHEST PARTNERSHIPS

1898 – DERBYSHIRE v YORKSHIRE: 554 1899

At Chesterfield, August 18, 19, 20, 1898. This game will live long in the memories of those who were fortunate enough to witness it, for Brown and Tunnicliffe, commencing Yorkshire's innings on the Thursday, were not parted for five hours and five minutes, their stand lasting until Friday and producing the unprecedented number of 554. Needless to say this remarkable achievement completely eclipsed all previous records in important cricket, not only for the first, but for any wicket. Tunnicliffe was out first and Brown, having reached his 300, knocked his wicket down. Subsequently the other batsmen threw away their wickets in the most sports-manlike fashion in order to give their side time to win, and the innings realised 662.

Yorkshire 662 (J. T. Brown 300, J. Tunnicliffe 243; Mr G. G. Walker 4-199);
Derbyshire 118 (Mr F. S. Jackson 4-52) **and 157** (W. Chatterton 54).

1932 – ESSEX v YORKSHIRE: 555 1933

At Leyton, June 15, 16, 17, 1932. Holmes and Sutcliffe, Yorkshire's famous opening batsmen, made this match memorable by creating a world's record first wicket stand of 555. They surpassed an achievement that had stood unequalled for 84 years – that of two other Yorkshiremen, J. T. Brown and John Tunnicliffe, who scored 554 together for the first wicket against Derbyshire at Chesterfield in 1898. The partnership between Holmes and Sutcliffe was the 70th of three figures in which those two men had participated, and their 65th for Yorkshire.

While every credit can be given to the two batsmen for their performance, the fact must not be overlooked that Holmes, almost directly he went in, experienced a great piece of luck. He had indeed scored merely three runs when he was missed behind the wicket, low down on the off side where Sheffield got both hands to the ball but failed to hold it. That fault apart, the batting during the big partnership proved wonderfully sound and confident. Rather unusually, Holmes scored more slowly than his colleague, but the pair put 100 runs on the board in an hour and threequarters and proceeded to maintain their mastery over the bowling for nearly seven hours and a half. The following times indicate the progress of the batsmen:

100 in an hour and 45 minutes.
200 in three hours 20 minutes.
300 in four hours 35 minutes.
400 in five hours 25 minutes.
500 in six hours 55 minutes.
555 in seven hours 25 minutes.

A curious incident occurred immediately after the new record had been made. Sutcliffe – very naturally, since it was obviously Yorkshire's policy to declare as soon

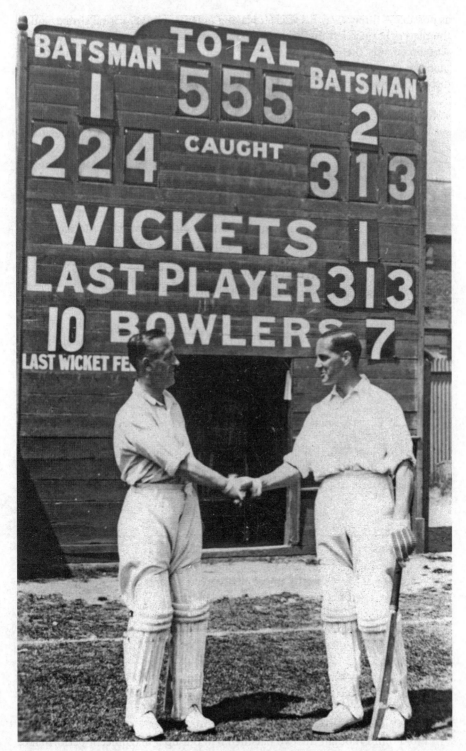

One that nearly got away: Percy Holmes and Herbert Sutcliffe
pose in front of the scoreboard after their record opening partnership

as possible – threw away his wicket, playing on with a rather casual stroke, and all the players at once left the field. Then, to everyone's amazement, the total on the scoreboard was altered to read 554. For the moment there seemed reason to fear that the chance of beating the record had been missed, but eventually it was discovered that a no-ball had not been counted in the total.

Holmes and Sutcliffe, on a perfect Leyton wicket, made their runs in admirable style. They ran singles skilfully and, if neither man took many risks, runs came at an average rate of scoring. Playing the highest innings of his career, Sutcliffe cut, drove and hit to leg with sound judgment. His straight-drives, perfectly timed, were particularly good to watch. Holmes, too, showed a lot of skill when off-driving and cutting, but in this innings did not properly reveal his strength on the leg side. He hit 19 fours while Sutcliffe among his figures had a six and 33 fours. The partnership was a magnificent feat in every way, and especially in endurance.

The contrast of the Yorkshiremen's batting with that which followed proved truly remarkable. Bowes, with pace off the pitch, and Verity, by cleverly flighted bowling, developed such a mastery that inside two hours Essex were all out for 78. A fourth-wicket stand of 29 between O'Connor and Nichols represented the best of the innings. The last five wickets fell for 19 runs, Verity having the striking figures of five wickets in seven overs for eight runs.

From this pronounced collapse, Essex did not recover, and shortly after one o'clock on Friday Yorkshire emerged from an historic match winners by an innings and 313 runs.

Yorkshire 555-1 dec. (H. Sutcliffe 313, P. Holmes 224*);

Essex 78 (H. Verity 5-8, W. E. Bowes 4-38)

and 164 (M. S. Nichols 59*; Verity 5-45, Bowes 5-47).

Yorkshire review: Whether the record was or was not beaten, there can be no question that the batsmen, had they not felt assured they had beaten it, could have put on heaps more runs.

HAPPY SCORER   Charles Bray (captain of Essex in the match), 1960

The scorers used to sit directly under the scoreboard and consequently could not see when it went wrong. It erred on that fateful morning. With the total 555 Sutcliffe, with the new record achieved, took a terrific swipe at a ball from Laurie Eastman and was clean bowled. The two batsmen posed under the scoreboard for the press photographers and then the balloon went up. The scorers declared the total to be 554 and not 555.

A very worried Charles McGahey, then Essex scorer, came to me in the dressing-room. Would I agree to the total being changed? The umpires (what accommodating people they are) said a no-ball had not been recorded. There was no doubt in Charles's mind an extra run was being "found".

I told him I thought the two batsmen had put up a magnificent performance and it would be cruel luck if they were to be deprived of the honour of breaking the record because our scoreboard had gone wrong. If the umpires said a no-ball had not been recorded it was OK with me. Charles went away happy.

1946 – TRINIDAD v BARBADOS: 574

At Port of Spain, February 2, 4, 5, 6, 7, 1946. Drawn. The first match played by Trinidad and Barbados being drawn, it was agreed that the second and concluding game should last five days, and though this, too, remained undecided, records were set up in a match of remarkable cricket. Barbados, leading by 52, lost three second-innings wickets for 45 before 20-year-old Clyde Walcott and Frank Worrell, coming together early on the third day, by merciless hitting gained complete ascendancy. Walcott established a record individual score for the ground before the close, when the total stood at 461 – Walcott 233 and Worrell 179. Next day the world fourth-wicket record of 502 (held by Worrell and Goddard) was smashed, and with a great drive to the boundary Walcott took the partnership to 559, breaking the 555 record for any wicket made by Yorkshire's Sutcliffe and Holmes in 1932. Barbados declared at 619 for three wickets – a new ground record – Walcott 314 not out, Worrell 255 not out. Walcott, surviving chances at 108, 232 and 286, hit five sixes and 25 fours in 348 minutes, while Worrell's best strokes produced a five and 18 fours in seven minutes less time.

Barbados 246 (C. L. Pouchet 6-52) **and 619-3 dec** (C. L. Walcott 314*, F. M. M. Worrell 255*);
Trinidad 194 (E. A. V. Williams 4-56)
and 576-8 (G. E. Gomez 213*, K. B. Trestrail 151, A. G. Ganteaume 85).

1947 – BARODA v HOLKAR: 577

At Baroda, March 7, 8, 9, 10, 11, 1947. Baroda won by an innings and 409 runs. A new world-record partnership of 577 for the Baroda fourth wicket by Gul Mahomed and Vijay Hazare, in the final of the Ranji Trophy tournament, exceeded every other performance in Indian cricket. Holkar were beaten in the match by an innings and 409 runs. Baroda lost three men for 91 in reply to Holkar's first-innings total of 202 before Gul Mahomed and Hazare joined forces. They punished nine bowlers freely and took the score to 668, surpassing the previous-highest first-class partnership of 574 by F. M. Worrell and C. L. Walcott in the West Indies in February 1946. Gul Mahomed hit 319 and Hazare 288 in a stand lasting 533 minutes. The more patient Hazare batted ten and a half hours.

Holkar 202 (C. T. Sarwate 94*, V. S. Hazare 6-85)
and 173 (B. B. Nimbalkar 87, Amir Elahi 6-62);
Baroda 784 (Gul Mahomed 319, V. S. Hazare 288).

2006 – SRI LANKA v SOUTH AFRICA (First Test): 624   2007

At Sinhalese Sports Club, Colombo, July 27, 28, 29, 30, 31, 2006. Sri Lanka won by an innings and 153 runs. This match will forever be remembered for the batting of Sri Lanka's captain, Mahela Jayawardene, and Kumar Sangakkara, who destroyed 143 years of *Wisden* records with a quite devastating stand. They put on 624 for the third wicket, beating by 47 the largest partnership for any wicket in first-class cricket, anywhere, ever. Jayawardene made 374, the fourth-highest score in all Tests (and the highest by a right-hander), and Sangakkara fell just short of his own triple-century. There was still time for Muttiah Muralitharan to winkle out the South Africans, who batted much better in their second innings than their first – but not quite well enough for long enough.

South Africa 169 (A. B. de Villiers 65; C. R. D. Fernando 4-48)
and 434 (J. A. Rudolph 90, M. V. Boucher 85, A. J. Hall 64, A. G. Prince 61; M. Muralitharan 6-131);
Sri Lanka 756-5 dec (D. P. M. D. Jayawardene 374, K. C. Sangakkara 287).

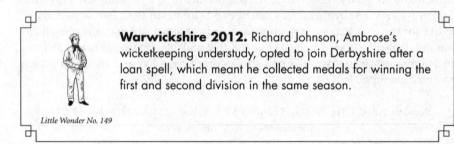

Warwickshire 2012. Richard Johnson, Ambrose's wicketkeeping understudy, opted to join Derbyshire after a loan spell, which meant he collected medals for winning the first and second division in the same season.

Little Wonder No. 149

MINOR CRICKET

2006 – ST PETER'S v ST PHILIP'S: 721   2008

When India set a new world record, it came from two Under-13 cricketers who shared a stand of 721 in a school match. Turning out for St Peter's against St Philip's in Secunderabad, Manoj Kumar scored 320 and Mohammed Shaibaz Tumbi 324 as they downed the famous Tendulkar–Kambli stand of 664, also in schools cricket. St Philip's, playing their very first game, lost by 700 runs – bowled out for 21 in seven overs – but their punishment could have been even greater: the umpires lopped ten overs off the slated 50, because it was taking the fielders so long to fetch the ball from beyond the boundary.

BEST BOWLING ANALYSIS

1932 – YORKSHIRE v NOTTINGHAMSHIRE: 10 for 10   1933

At Leeds, July 9, 11, 12, 1932. Verity in this match took – for the second time in his career – all ten wickets in an innings. Prior to lunch on the last day Notts scored 38 without loss but, on resuming, their ten wickets went down for 29 runs. Verity not only performed the hat-trick in sending back Walker, Harris and Gunn, but got rid of Arthur Staples and Larwood with the last two balls of his next over and then, disposing of Voce and Sam Staples with the third and fourth balls of his following over, brought the innings to a close. This splendid bowling feat Sutcliffe and Holmes followed up by hitting off in about an hour and a half the 139 runs required for victory. Thus, Yorkshire gained a glorious win by ten wickets although, when on Monday afternoon a thunderstorm burst over the ground, they had stood 71 behind with only one wicket to fall.

Notts 234 (M. Leyland 4-14) **and 67** (H. Verity 10-10);
Yorkshire 163-9 (P. Holmes 65; H. Larwood 5-73) **and 139-0** (Holmes 77*, H. Sutcliffe 54*).

Nottinghamshire second innings

W. W. Keeton c Macaulay b Verity	21
F. W. Shipston c Wood b Verity	21
W. Walker c Macaulay b Verity	11
*A. W. Carr c Barber b Verity	0
A. Staples c Macaulay b Verity	7
C. B. Harris c Holmes b Verity	0
G. V. Gunn lbw b Verity	0
†B. Lilley not out	3
H. Larwood c Sutcliffe b Verity	0
W. Voce c Holmes b Verity	0
S. J. Staples st Wood b Verity	0
Extras (b 3, nb 1)	4
Total (all out)	67

Fall of wickets: 1-44, 2-47, 3-51, 4-63, 5-63, 6-63, 7-64, 8-64, 9-67, 10-67.

Yorkshire bowling

	Overs	Mdns	Runs	Wkts
Bowes	5	0	19	0
Macaulay	23	9	34	0
Verity	19.4	16	10	10

Yorkshire review: Not only did Verity secure all ten wickets – seven for three runs with the last 16 balls he sent down – but he obtained the whole ten wickets at a cost of only ten runs. In so doing Verity accomplished what was probably an unprecedented achievement for no case, since bowling analyses have been kept, can be found of all ten wickets being obtained at such a low cost.

1946 – WARWICKSHIRE v NOTTINGHAMSHIRE: ALL HIS OWN WORK 1947

At Birmingham, July 24, 25, 1946. Nottinghamshire won by seven wickets. The match was made memorable by a brilliant bowling performance, Hollies taking all ten wickets very cheaply in the Nottinghamshire first innings. Keeton and Harris opened with a stand of 47; then Hollies, changing ends, was unplayable. He did not receive any help from his colleagues, seven batsmen being bowled and the other three lbw. Warwickshire again failed and Nottinghamshire, thanks to a good stand between Harris and Hardstaff, easily obtained the 149 required to win, although Hollies in 31 overs bowled 20 maidens.

Warwickshire 170 (W. E. Fantham 51; H. J. Butler 4-49) and 113 (A. Jepson 4-43);
Notts 135 (W. E. Hollies 10-49) and 150-3 (C. B. Harris 80*).

Nottinghamshire First Innings

W. W. Keeton b Hollies	40
C. B. Harris b Hollies	10
R. T. Simpson lbw b Hollies.	14
J. Hardstaff lbw b Hollies	0
T. B. Reddick b Hollies	1
*G. F. H. Heane lbw b Hollies.	4
F. W. Stocks not out	37
A. Jepson b Hollies	7
H. J. Butler b Hollies	8
†E. A. Meads b Hollies	0
F. G. Woodhead b Hollies.	8
Extras (b 4, lb 2)	6
Total (all out)	135

Fall of wickets: 1-47, 2-52, 3-54, 4-58, 5-62, 6-89, 7-109, 8-125, 9-125, 10-135.

Warwickshire bowling

	Overs	Mdns	Runs	Wkts
Mitchell	6	2	19	0
Maudsley	7	3	19	0
Hollies	20.4	4	49	10
Fantham	20	3	42	0

The report on Jim Laker's 19 for 90 v Australia at Old Trafford in 1956 will be found in the England section, p. 249.

1872 – ALL THE 20 WICKETS 1873

Mr C. Absolon – an old and liberal supporter of Metropolitan cricket and cricketers – was the grey-haired hero of this very successful bowling feat, i.e. having a hand in the downfall of all the 20 wickets; he bowled ten, two hit wicket, six were caught from his bowling, and he caught out the remaining two. The match made famous by this bowling of Mr Absolon's was Wood Green v United Willesden, played at Wood Green, July 21, 1872. Wood Green won by an innings and 45 runs.

United Willesden

Morley b Absolon	1	–	b Absolon		6
Williams b Absolon	0	–	c Absolon b Fluker		7
Skipper hit wkt b Absolon	0	–	b Absolon		2
Parfitt c Thomas b Absolon	0	–	b Absolon		7
Bickwell c Thomas b Absolon	9	–	b Absolon		1
Bishop c Absolon b Wheeler	5	–	c Chamberlain b Absolon		0
Digby b Absolon	6	–	c Ringrose b Absolon		1
Lawrence not out	0	–	b Absolon		0
Howard b Absolon	0	–	b Absolon		2
Morris hit wkt b Absolon	2	–	not out		1
Emerson c Fluker b Absolon	0	–	c Wheeler b Absolon		0
Extra	1	–	Extras		4
	24				31

Charles Absolon was aged 55 at the time of this match and died in January 1908 at the age of 90. Although a club cricketer – "the most prominent figure in local cricket in and around London" who often took part in two matches on the same day – he was honoured by Wisden *with an obituary in the same year that he died, as well as a further two pages the following year, devoted to the extraordinary feats and some statistics of his career: between the ages of 50 and 80 he took 8,500 wickets with his lob bowling and scored 26,000 runs.*

SIX SIXES IN AN OVER

1968 – GLAMORGAN v NOTTINGHAMSHIRE: INCREDIBLE SOBERS 1969

At Swansea, August 31, September 1, 2, 1968. Nottinghamshire won by 166 runs. This was the history-making match in which the incredible Garfield Sobers created a new world record by hitting six sixes in a six-ball over. Somehow one sensed that something extraordinary was going to happen when Sobers sauntered to the wicket. With over 300 runs on the board for the loss of only five wickets, he had the right sort of platform from which to launch a spectacular assault, and the manner in which he immediately settled down to score at a fast rate was ominous.

Then came the history-making over by the 23-year-old Malcolm Nash. First crouched like a black panther eager to pounce, Sobers with lightning footwork got into position for a vicious straight-drive or pull. As Tony Lewis, Glamorgan's captain said afterwards, "It was not sheer slogging through strength, but scientific hitting with every movement working in harmony." Twice the ball was slashed out of the ground, and when the last six landed in the street outside it was not recovered until the next day. Then it was presented to Sobers and will have a permanent place in the Trent Bridge Cricket Museum.

Nottinghamshire 394-5 dec (J. B. Bolus 140, G. S. Sobers 76*, R. A. White 73, G. Frost 50;
M. A. Nash 4-100) **and 139-6 dec** (Sobers 72);
Glamorgan 254 (P. M. Walker 104*)
and 113 (A. R. Lewis 52; M. N. S. Taylor 5-47, White 4-9).

1985 – BOMBAY v BARODA: SPEEDY SHASTRI   1986

At Bombay, January 8, 9, 10, 1985. Drawn. Ravi Shastri reached 200 in 113 minutes off 123 balls to record the fastest-ever double-century and in doing so he hit six sixes in one over from G. Tilak Raj, equalling the record of G. S. Sobers. In all, Shastri hit 13 sixes.

> **Bombay 371-4 dec** (G. A. Parkar 170 ret hurt, S. S. Hattangadi 83, L. S. Rajput 66)
> **and 457-5 dec** (R. J. Shastri 200*, Rajput 136);
> **Baroda 330-8 dec** (S. Keshwala 100*, M. Amarnath 88, G. Tilak Raj 55)
> **and 81-7** (B. S. Sandhu 4-43).

1990 – CRICKET IN NEW ZEALAND: A SHAMEFUL FOOTNOTE   C. R. Buttery, 1991

Unfortunately for Wellington, the season will be remembered for their farcical tactics at the end of the third day of their return match against Canterbury. In order to narrow the 94-run gap between the two sides, in the hope of then buying the last two wickets to win the game, Wellington captain Ervin McSweeney incurred the wrath of cricket purists by instructing his bowlers to toss up a series of deliberate no-balls. In the penultimate over, comprising 22 balls, Robert Vance conceded a record 77 runs (1444664614114116666600401), 69 coming from the bat of the Canterbury wicket-keeper Lee Germon. In the circumstances the question of whether Germon's feat should go in the record books is debatable. As it turned out, McSweeney's tactics almost cost him the game, which ended in a draw with the scores level.

UNIQUE ACHIEVEMENT

1938 – ESSEX v KENT: DOUBLE-HUNDRED DOUBLE   1939

At Colchester, July 13, 14, 15, 1938. Drawn. The match was notable for the world-record feat achieved by Fagg, of Kent, in scoring two double-hundreds. Essex were without their regular bowlers, engaged in the Gentlemen and Players game at Lord's, but Fagg's performance, nevertheless, was extraordinary. In the first innings he made 244 out of 386 in five hours, and in the second innings batted two hours and 50 minutes for 202 not out, before Chalk declared. Vigorous on-drives and powerful strokes to leg were his chief means of scoring, and he hit 31 fours in the first innings and 27 in the other. Play on the last morning was rendered memorable by the completion of Fagg's exploit, and spectators and players alike applauded him all the way to the pavilion. Essex, needing 393 to win, started badly, but rain intervened and prevented a finish.

> **Kent 429** (A. E. Fagg 244*, Mr F. G. H. Chalk 61; R. M. Taylor 4-41)
> **and 313-1 dec** (Fagg 202*, P. R. Sunnucks 82);
> **Essex 350** (Mr T. N. Pearce 137*, J. O'Connor 63; D. V. P. Wright 7-107) **and 8-2.**

MISCELLANEOUS

1925 – BURROWS IS TALK OF THE TOWN 1926

Just as the Almanack is going to press comes a letter from Hobart, stating that in a match there between New Town and North-West Hobart A Grade on November 21 last, A. O. Burrows of New Town bowled one of his opponents with a ball which sent the bail 83 yards 1ft 9in. The statement is vouched for by no fewer than half a dozen different men associated with one club or the other, among these being Joe Darling, the famous left-handed batsman who captained Australia in this country in 1899, 1902 and 1905, and who is now president of the New Town Club. Previously the record was 70½ yards by A. F. Morcom for Bedfordshire against Suffolk at Luton in 1908.

1946 – CLIFTON v TONBRIDGE: LORD'S TYRO 1947

At Lord's, July 29, 30, 1946. Tonbridge won by two runs. Reputed to be the youngest player to appear in a match at Lord's, 13-year-old Michael Cowdrey, in his first match for Tonbridge, contributed largely to the success of his side. When Tonbridge were sent in to bat on a drying pitch, Cowdrey scored one more than the runs made by his colleagues and in the second innings raised his aggregate to 119. A right-arm spin bowler, mainly with leg-break, he proved deadly in the Clifton second innings and with Kirch, medium, supported by smart fielding, dismissed the last five Clifton batsmen for 33 runs, so snatching a victory. Exton, with length and spin, excelled as a bowler, taking 14 wickets for 125.

Tonbridge 156 (M. C. Cowdrey 75; R. N. Exton 6-64) **and 175** (D. K. Horton 51; Exton 8-61);
Clifton 214 (P. M. Crawford 57, M. L. Green 56; P. N. Kirch 4-20) **and 115** (Cowdrey 5-59).

Pakistan v Australia in the UAE 2012-13. Because of the 6pm starts, the one-day internationals ended well past 1am, so that they were, technically, two-day games. The match in Abu Dhabi even spanned two months, starting in August and finishing in September.

Little Wonder No. 150

THROWING THE CRICKET BALL – PERCIVAL'S RECORD 1977

As some doubt has been cast about the Cricket Ball Throwing Record of R. Percival which has appeared in our records for many years the following extract from *Scores and Biographies*, Vol. 14, page 1076, provides verification:

The following letter appeared in the *Sportsman* of March 27, 1889:

Sir, I have been greatly interested by the remarks you have lately published on the subject of throwing the cricket ball, and would have begged a little space from you earlier only that I have been (as far as I am able) testing the real value of my information.

I think R. Percival, one of the professional staff of the New Brighton CC, can claim the record. On Easter Monday, 1884, he threw a cricket ball 140 yards, 2 feet (*with the wind, of course*) on the Durham Sands Racecourse, at an athletic meeting promoted by the race committee. He was complimented on all sides, and informed that that was the record. The account of the throw was published in the *Auckland Times and Herald* of the following Saturday, and again alluded to as part of a special article on Percival's career, published in the September or October following.

The throw was measured by the committee. Percival has competed at over 20 athletic meetings and never yet has he been beaten at throwing the cricket ball. Some of the prizes were gained at Byers Green (2), West Auckland (2), Woodlands (2), Hyghton, Aycliffe, Darlington, Weimer Castle, Spennymoor, Durham, Mickleton, Willington, Bishop Auckland and, I think, at Barnard Castle he was debarred from competing.

Subsequently, he slightly injured his arm and cannot throw so well now; but in 1885, at Liverpool, he threw a cricket ball, on the Stoneycroft Ground, 127 yards, 1 foot. He bowls and throws with his left arm.

Yours, &c., T. E. Edwards,
New Brighton, Cheshire, March 22.

N.B. *Wisden* has usually given Percival's Christian name as Richard, but apparently it was Robert.

THE FIFTY THOUSAND CLUB

Philip Bailey, 2007

| | | First-class matches | | One-day matches | | |
	Total runs	Runs	Average	Runs	Average	Career span
1 G. A. Gooch	67,057	44,846	49.01	22,211	40.16	1973–2000
2 G. A. Hick	63,171	41,112	52.23	22,059	41.30	1983-84–2008
3 J. B. Hobbs	61,237	61,237	50.65	–	–	1905–1934
4 F. E. Woolley	58,969	58,969	40.75	–	–	1906–1938
5 G. Boycott	58,521	48,426	56.83	10,095	39.12	1962–1986
6 E. H. Hendren	57,611	57,611	50.80	–	–	1907–1938
7 D. L. Amiss	55,942	43,423	42.86	12,519	35.06	1960–1987
8 C. P. Mead	55,061	55,061	47.67	–	–	1905–1936
9 W. G. Grace	54,896	54,896	39.55	–	–	1865–1908
10 C. G. Greenidge	53,703	37,354	45.88	16,349	40.56	1970–1992
11 I. V. A. Richards	53,207	36,212	49.40	16,995	41.96	1971-72–1993
12 M. W. Gatting	51,025	36,549	49.52	14,476	33.74	1975–1998
13 W. R. Hammond	50,551	50,551	56.10	–	–	1920–1951
14 H. Sutcliffe	50,138	50,138	51.95	–	–	1919–1945

Figures updated to the end of Hick's career

2009 – RAWALPINDI v QUETTA (QUAID-E-AZAM TROPHY):
SHORTEST FIRST-CLASS MATCH   2010

At Marghzar Cricket Ground, Islamabad, February 13, 14, 15, 2009. Rawalpindi won by nine wickets. The entire game lasted only 20.1 overs, the shortest completed match in first-class cricket; 85 was the lowest aggregate. After the first two days were washed out, both sides forfeited their first innings; Quetta were bowled out in 13.3 overs, and Rawalpindi knocked off a target of 42 in 40 balls, losing only one wicket in the match.

Quetta forfeited first innings and 41 (Mohammad Rameez 6-17);
Rawalpindi forfeited first innings and 44-1.

2011 – DURHAM MCCU v YORKSHIRE: YOUNGEST YET   2012

At Durham, April 27, 28, 29, 2011. Yorkshire won by ten wickets. After 144 years, Charles Young lost his record as the youngest player in English first-class cricket to a schoolboy from Pudsey. Barney Gibson replaced him, keeping wicket for Yorkshire aged 15 years 27 days – 104 days younger than Young had been in 1867 when he first appeared as a left-arm seamer for Hampshire. Right from the start, Gibson was keeping to a genuinely quick bowler, Shahzad, and in the tenth over he held the first of six catches in the match – a very good one by any measure, diving one-handed towards the leg side – to dismiss Luc Durandt off Hannon-Dalby. A Year 10 pupil at Crawshaw School, Gibson had to be given special dispensation to skip classes. "It was probably a good day to avoid," he said. "I was supposed to have triple science, double maths and RE. They have sent me up here with some homework to do, though." Gibson had time to face one ball, which he prodded into the off side. The last wicketkeeper in England to bat at No. 11 (excluding injury or the use of a nightwatchman) was Tim Edwards of Worcestershire, against Yorkshire at New Road in 1994.

Durham MCCU 196 (C. R. Jones 69; D. J. Wainwright 6-40)
and 287 (T. Westley 127; A. Shahzad 5-61);
Yorkshire 355 (J. J. Sayers 139, G. S. Ballance 72, Wainwright 62; N. A. T. Watkins 5-88)
and 129-0 (Ballance 73*, Sayers 53*).

Unusual Occurrences

Aﬀter all the serious stuff we offer some fun, not made up and written for laughs but actual and unusual events on or around the cricket field. Briefly in the 1930s *Wisden* ran a page headed Miscellany, where such happenings were chronicled, and since 1996 an Index of Unusual Occurrences has helpfully provided a steer for the reader; but actually these nuggets have been present throughout the Almanack's history. Much of their joy is that they emerge from the depths of a match report and are related in *Wisden's* authoritatively deadpan style.

Our selection dates back to 1864, when the English touring team found time on their hands after a match against Otago finished early and they engaged in a series of running races: E. M. Grace was beaten over distances ranging from 100 to 600 yards, but upheld the family's honour by throwing the cricket ball the greatest distance.

Almost all of these gems come from first-class cricket; all, we hope, will raise a smile or an eyebrow.

BIRDS OF THE AIR AND BEASTS OF THE FIELD

DID ANYONE SEE THE SPARROW FALL?
A sparrow was killed by a ball bowled by Jahangir Khan in the MCC and Cambridge University match at Lord's [in 1936]. T. N. Pearce, the batsmen, managed to play the ball and the bird fell against the stumps without dislodging the bails.

Obituary 1988: JAHANGIR KHAN, DR MOHAMMAD. He was bowling to T. N. Pearce, who had just played a defensive push when it was noticed that the bails had been dislodged. It was then that a dead sparrow was found beside the stumps. The unfortunate bird was stuffed and subsequently displayed in the Memorial Gallery at Lord's; but while legend has it that the sparrow was struck by the ball in flight, it is thought no one actually saw this happen.

BATH v LONDON COUNTIES
At Bath, July 28, 1945. Gimblett, in his only innings of the season for London Counties, hit 101 in 110 minutes, including four sixes and nine fours. Once he sent the ball soaring over a ring of tall trees and the road outside the ground into the judging ring at the local Dog Show, scattering people and animals. Directly after reaching his century Gimblett broke his bat. The blade flew yards, leaving Gimblett standing with only the handle in his hand.

SNAKE ON THE PITCH

A schoolboy batsman quickly changed his stance when he saw a 3ft 6in poisonous snake slithering up the pitch during cricket practice at Cowell, South Australia in October 1967.

The boy, Tony Wiseman, let pass a ball which had just been bowled, stepped from his crease and hit the snake, killing it. Then he looked behind to see if he had been stumped, but the wicketkeeper had vanished.

DUCK SAVED BY SWALLOW

A freak accident saved Western Australia's John Inverarity from a duck in a Sheffield Shield match against South Australia in Adelaide on November 22, 1969. He was bowled by Greg Chappell, but the ball had been deflected on to the wicket by a swallow, which was killed by the delivery. Inverarity was called back by the umpire and went on to make 89.

PIGEON AND RABBIT MAKE COPYCAT APPEARANCES

During the John Player League match between Warwickshire and Kent at Edgbaston on June 6, 1982, a fox – a stray Leicestershire supporter perhaps – ran around the ground behind the arm of the bowler, Derek Underwood, before disappearing into the crowd.

A week later, at The Oval where Surrey were playing Gloucestershire, a pigeon crept up behind the Surrey batsmen Monte Lynch into the closest of short-leg positions, causing him to move away from the crease just as the bowler was about to deliver the ball.

As has happened with animals of the human variety, word of these invasions of the field of play spread quickly around the kingdom. At Trent Bridge in August, a rabbit ran on to the pitch, where it was apprehended by the Derbyshire captain Barry Wood.

ESSEX v NORTHAMPTONSHIRE

At Chelmsford, June 13, 14, 15, 17, 1996. On the second day, spectators were briefly diverted when a muntjac fawn appeared from under the parked covers, jumped into the members' enclosure and then into the river. It was found later, safe but scared, in a nearby churchyard.

AUSTRALIA v INDIA (World Cup)

At The Oval, June 4, 1999. Two pigeons met untimely deaths during India's innings. The first was shot down in mid-flight by Reiffel when he drilled the ball back from the outfield; the second, picking the ground at short third man, was walloped by a thick edge from Jadeja's bat, leading to speculation that pigeons also had problems seeing the white ball in the evening gloom.

TAMIL NADU v PUNJAB (Ranji Trophy quarter-final)

At M. A. Chidambaram Stadium, Chennai, March 30, 31, April 1, 2, 3, 2000. Play was delayed for several minutes on the opening morning by a snake in the outfield, and for 20 minutes on the final morning by a swarm of bees, which stung spectators and caused the players to throw themselves to the ground, until the umpires decided to take an early lunch.

HAMPSHIRE v LEICESTERSHIRE
At Southampton, April 24, 25, 26, 27, 2002. Play was briefly halted in mid-afternoon when a swarm of bees invaded the Rose Bowl: as players dived for cover and seats were evacuated, a Hampshire member, known as "the Honeyman", was called from the stands and, with the help of council workers, he removed the culprits.

SURREY v YORKSHIRE
At Guildford, July 24, 25, 26, 27, 2002. Yorkshire might have put more pressure on Surrey had it not been for a bizarre interlude when Blakey swept a four into the press tent. After the ball was fetched, Hollioake noticed some toothmarks; the culprit, it transpired, was Bumper, a labrador who belonged to Geoffrey Dean from *The Times*. The damage prompted Hollioake to take the new ball – 21 overs after it had become available – and Surrey's seamers quickly despatched the Yorkshire tail.

GLAMORGAN v SOMERSET
At Cardiff, July 9, 10, 11, 12, 2003. Croft remained unruffled when about 200 seagulls, looking for their own tea after the players had taken theirs, stopped play for several minutes.

SUSSEX v YORKSHIRE (totesport League)
At Arundel, June 27, 2004. Yorkshire won with 18.1 overs spare. They did so in dark blue kit, after Wood went out to toss in their intended yellow away shirt and was attacked by a swarm of insects.

DERBYSHIRE v WORCESTERSHIRE
At Chesterfield, July 26, 27, 28, 29, 2006. Specially trained collies were on standby during the match in case there was a pitch invasion from geese on the boating lake, but there was no need to deploy them.

ENGLAND LIONS v AUSTRALIANS
At Canterbury, August 15, 16, 2009. Lee dismissed both openers and bowled Liam Plunkett, whereupon a seagull swooped down and stole one of the bails. Lee pursued the bird across the outfield but failed to recover the bail, which had to be replaced for the remaining nine balls.

YORKSHIRE v LANCASHIRE (Twenty20 Cup)
At Leeds, May 29, 2009. Jacques Rudolph got the bird when his throw from near the boundary killed a pigeon flying across the outfield.

BROKEN WINDOWS
AND OTHER FAULTY GOODS

YORKSHIRE v DERBYSHIRE
At Dewsbury, June 8, 9, 10, 1899. During Friday night the Derbyshire professionals' dressing-room was flooded, and they all had to turn out next morning in ordinary

clothes and boots. Higson and Wright escaped the misfortune, and these two acted as the Derbyshire bowlers.

SOMERSET v LANCASHIRE

At Taunton, July 21, 22, 23, 1926. Earle hit up 54 out of 58 in 35 minutes, one drive breaking a window in the scorebox. Ernest Tyldesley obtained his seventh 100 in consecutive matches. Curiously enough one drive he made sent the ball through the same pane of glass that Earle had broken in the morning.

LANCASHIRE v HAMPSHIRE

At Manchester, June 20, 21, 22, 1934. Between the innings on the first day the motor roller broke down and had to be hauled away from the middle of the ground. Also a sightscreen was blown down and broken.

MIDDLESEX 1934

Smith, the former Wiltshire professional, played several dashing innings, and huge sixes from him were no rare occurrences. Once at Lord's he drove a ball with such force that it pitched in the Pavilion and shattered a committee-room window.

SOMERSET v WORCESTERSHIRE

At Wells, July 17, 18, 1935. In the first county match to be played at the old cathedral city of Wells, Worcestershire triumphed by an innings and 105 runs. The game was played under novel conditions; there were no sightscreens, and the match details were broadcast from the scorers' box by means of a microphone and loudspeakers.

MISCELLANY 1938

Playing for Notts against Northamptonshire at Trent Bridge on June 22, J. Knowles cracked two bats and borrowed another from Keeton before he scored the first of the eight runs he made during 55 minutes at the wickets.

MIDDLESEX v DERBYSHIRE

At Lord's, August 24, 25, 26, 1949. The equanimity of the Lord's Pavilion was disturbed when Gladwin, after being run out by his partner, accidentally put his bat through the dressing-room window.

ESSEX v WORCESTERSHIRE

At Leyton, August 3, 5, 6, 1963. There was an unusual incident before the match began. The umpires discovered that the wickets were eight and a half inches in width instead of nine, and the start was delayed while the stumps were pulled up and replaced in new holes. A pitch-marker out of alignment caused the trouble.

NORTHAMPTONSHIRE v ESSEX

At Peterborough, June 18, 20, 21, 1966. When Bear hit Scott out of the ground for six on the first morning it went through a house window. The housewife refused to return the ball until the window was repaired at a cost of 25 shillings [£1.25].

MIDDLESEX v LEICESTERSHIRE
At Lord's, July 12, 13, 14, 1978. The prelude to the match was possibly unique. Following the poor state of the pitch for Middlesex's game against the New Zealanders the day before, MCC intended to stage this match on a pitch near the Tavern end of the square instead of one closer to the middle. But Illingworth rejected the new pitch, saying that it was only 45 yards from the boundary and therefore infringed the regulations.

WORCESTERSHIRE v SOMERSET
At Worcester, May 2, 3, 4, 1979. Of all the reasons for a hold-up during the bitterly cold weather – rain, sleet, and hail caused various interruptions – the most unusual was an accident during the groundstaff's final preparations. The starting handle from the heavy roller was crushed into the pitch by the machine, and the pitch had to be moved across by two yards before play could begin on the first afternoon.

NOTTINGHAMSHIRE v WARWICKSHIRE
At Nottingham, July 8, 10, 11, 1989. Lloyd, who had borrowed a bat from Broad after thieves stole nine bats from the Warwickshire dressing-room, hit 12 fours and batted 185 minutes for his first hundred of the season.

GLAMORGAN v LEICESTERSHIRE
At Cardiff, July 26, 27, 28, 1989. On the final day, with Leicestershire requiring only 100 runs for victory when they began their second innings, there was a remarkable occurrence as the pavilion clock went into reverse.

BOLAND v BORDER (Castle Cup)
At Paarl, February 3, 4, 5, 6, 1995. It was reported that fried calamari stopped play when Cullinan hit a six off R. Telemachus into a frying pan. It was about ten minutes before the ball was cool enough for the umpires to remove the grease. Even then, Telemachus was unable to grip the ball and it had to be replaced.

LANCASHIRE v YORKSHIRE (NatWest Trophy semi-final)
At Manchester, August 13, 1996. Bevan could look back on one moment of light relief, when a ball he struck flew into two pieces; its leather cover, ripped by a fielder's boot, fell off as he hit it, prompting speculation about what might have happened had either section been caught.

PAKISTAN v NEW ZEALAND (Second Test Match)
At Rawalpindi, November 28, 29, 30, December 1, 1996. Play was delayed 20 minutes because the Pakistani Cricket Board had forgotten to supply balls. The match eventually got under way using a ball bought from a local sports shop.

SUSSEX v ESSEX
At Hove, June 12, 13, 14, 1997. At the end of the second day, umpire Bird was locked in his dressing-room; he was rescued after yelling for help.

GLAMORGAN v NORTHAMPTONSHIRE
At Abergavenny, August 20, 21, 22, 23, 1997. The umpires led the players from the field after just two overs of play. They had noticed that the stumps were four inches out of line, and 27 minutes were added at the end of the day to make up for the time spent re-aligning the creases.

LANCASHIRE v YORKSHIRE (CGU National League)
At Manchester, August 17, 1999. Lancashire completed a competition double over Yorkshire, despite a floodlight failure which interrupted their run-chase. Lancashire needed 19 from 51 balls when one of the four banks of lights went out at 10.05pm. Three overs were lost, and a straightforward target became even easier: seven required from 33 balls.

HAMPSHIRE v GLOUCESTERSHIRE
At Southampton, June 27, 28, 29, 30, 2003. Umpire Allan Jones was locked in the Rose Bowl overnight on the second evening after sharing fish and chips in a camper van belonging to his colleague Alan Whitehead.

SURREY v NOTTINGHAMSHIRE
At Whitgift School, August 13, 14, 15, 2003. The facilities were as uneven as the cricket: Surrey commandeered the pleasant school pavilion while the Nottinghamshire dressing-room comprised a set of Portakabins in which the players' showers, before the third day, were as visible to the spectators as the actual game.

MIDDLESEX v NOTTINGHAMSHIRE
At Lord's, September 10, 11, 12, 13, 2003. When Nash became the tenth Middlesex bowler (it would have been 11, but Bloomfield was injured) his figures were omitted on the scoreboard, with a note at the top reading: "Sorry Nashy – no more room."

ZIMBABWE v WEST INDIES (First Test Match)
At Harare, November 4, 5, 6, 7, 8, 2003. A freak incident delayed the start on the third day. As the pitch was being rolled, players were practising on the outfield; Gripper hit a ball right under the roller which left a deep indentation just short of a fast bowler's length to a left-hander. An auger was borrowed from the neighbouring golf club to replace the turf, play started one and a half hours late, and referee Gundappa Viswanath postponed lunch to allow a two-hour session.

MIDDLESEX v SURREY
At Lord's, April 21, 22, 23, 24, 2004. Koenig, out for 62, was so annoyed he hurled his helmet at a dressing-room chair, only for it to bounce and shatter a window. The seats below were showered with broken glass, but fortunately their occupants had decided to go for lunch early.

NEW ZEALAND v SRI LANKA (First Test Match)
At Napier, April 4, 5, 6, 7, 8, 2005. The secret of Malinga's success – or so the New Zealanders claimed – lay in the umpires' trousers. "We can't see him when it's a bit overcast and late in the evening," complained Fleming on the last day. "We asked the

umpires to change the colour of their trousers." The umpires drew the line at changing their clothing because of Malinga's low, roundarm action and delivery from near the stumps, but on the first day they did agree to take off their dark ties and, on the last, umpire Bucknor tied a sweater round his waist as a sort of personal sightscreen.

YORKSHIRE v LANCASHIRE
At Leeds, June 8, 9, 10, 11, 2005. Chilton, who was out to the first ball of the match, atoned in the second innings with 112 before becoming one of three victims for Hoggard in the space of 14 deliveries with three different balls – the first two came apart at the seam.

YORKSHIRE v WARWICKSHIRE
At Scarborough, July 19, 20, 21, 2006. Sea mist and a distant foghorn provided an eerie atmosphere at the start, and a bizarre fault on the PA system meant spectators were given commentary on a nearby bowls match.

WORCESTERSHIRE v NORTHAMPTONSHIRE (Twenty20 Cup)
At Kidderminster, June 29, 2007. The game was transferred to Kidderminster at 72 hours' notice. Spectators were asked to bring their own seats – and the visitors the stumps, as Worcestershire's were trapped in flooded buildings at New Road.

MIDDLESEX v GLAMORGAN
At Lord's, April 22, 23, 24, 25, 2009. Play was late starting on the third day because of a lack of bails. To compound matters, the groundstaff were on their mid-morning break, and it was some time before umpire Garratt found them and the missing woodwork.

YORKSHIRE v NOTTINGHAMSHIRE
At Scarborough, July 21, 22, 23, 24, 2009. Coverage of a nearby funeral service was somehow picked up by the Scarborough club's public-address system, and some readings were broadcast during the first morning's play.

SOMERSET v GLAMORGAN (Clydesdale Bank 40)
At Taunton, May 2, 2011. Nearing his hundred, Peter Trego launched Robert Croft up towards the commentary box on top of the old pavilion, where Edward Bevan, Wisden's Glamorgan correspondent and the BBC Wales commentator, was sitting. The ball smashed through the window and hit Bevan on the back, causing a small bruise. "We all thought the screen was Perspex. It was just ordinary glass and it went everywhere," said Bevan. "And in probably the worst commentary box in the country as well." Twice before he had been sitting in the Cardiff commentary box when its window was broken by a six.

ENGLAND v SRI LANKA (Second npower Test) — James Coyne
At Lord's, June 3, 4, 5, 6, 7, 2011. Bell and Prior had a mix-up familiar to every cricketer when the hit is on and silly runs are attempted. Prior stomped back to the dressing-room, where somehow he broke a window pane, sending glass six metres on to MCC members below. A 22-year-old medical student, Emma Baker, suffered a small cut above her ankle. Prior was visibly upset and apologised alongside his captain when England took the field. Baker planned to keep a shard as a souvenir,

which was less surprising once it emerged that, in March 2005, her brother Daniel had been standing dangerously close by when Adam Gilchrist smashed the window of a function room at Wellington's Basin Reserve with a six.

LANCASHIRE v WARWICKSHIRE
At Liverpool, April 19, 20, 21, 22, 2012. On the first day, the umpires had to turn off the walkie-talkies they used to speak to the scorers, because they kept hearing messages from a local taxi firm.

CALL-UPS AND COMEBACKS

AUSTRALIANS v CAMBRIDGE UNIVERSITY
At Cambridge, June 9, 10, 1902. So greatly were the Australians weakened by illness that they had to complete their side by playing Dr R. J. Pope, a cricketer who, it will be remembered, appeared several times for H. J. H. Scott's eleven in 1886. Dr Pope came over from Australia for a holiday mainly to see the cricket, and was a sort of general medical adviser to the eleven.
Pope batted at No. 9, scoring 2 not out, and did not bowl.

GENTLEMEN v PLAYERS
At Kennington Oval, July 7, 8, 9, 1904. One point in connection with the match gave rise to a good deal of discussion. G. W. Beldam and P. F. Warner appeared for the Gentlemen on the opening day, Beldam bowling 14 overs, but on the Friday, owing to illness, they retired from the game, Murdoch and L. V. Harper taking their places. Appealed to privately to give a ruling on the legality of allowing a substitute to take the place of a man who had bowled in a match, the committee of the MCC issued the following notice: "Allowing a substitute to take the place of Mr G. W. Beldam, after he had bowled, was an infringement of Law 37. Having regard, however, to the fact that similar cases have occurred in the past upon which the MCC have not been asked to give a ruling, no retrospective action will be taken."

Law 37 reads: "A substitute shall be allowed to field or run between wickets for any player who may during the match be incapacitated by illness or injury, but for no other reason, except with the consent of the opposite side."

OLDEST CHAMPIONSHIP DEBUTANT   E. L. Peake, 1972
Unique is the case of the Rev. R. H. Moss. Born on February 24, 1868, his first and only Championship appearance was for Worcestershire v Gloucestershire on May 23–26, 1925. He was thus over 57 years old at the time; the greatest age at which any cricketer has played in a Championship match.
In his younger days Moss had played for Oxford University and MCC.

DERBYSHIRE v NOTTINGHAMSHIRE
At Ilkeston, July 19, 21, 22, 1947. H. Elliott, Derbyshire's pre-war wicketkeeper, reappeared at the age of 51.

Obituary 1976: ELLIOTT, HARRY. In 1946 he became an umpire, but retired when he was appointed coach for 1947, reappearing to keep wicket in four matches at the age of almost 56, though it was not until 1967, at the reunion of the Championship-winning side of 1936, that he disclosed that he had been born in 1891.

NOTTINGHAMSHIRE v SUSSEX
At Nottingham, August 8, 9, 10, 1951. Voce, the former England left-arm bowler, now Nottinghamshire coach, enjoyed a triumph when recalled to the side on his 42nd birthday because of injuries to the regular bowlers. Bowling with much of his old skill and fire and supported by fine fielding, Voce troubled most of the batsmen. With the pitch difficult on the final day Voce (three sixes and three fours) ensured first-innings points for Nottinghamshire by hitting 45 in half an hour, although, because of a swollen knee, he batted with a runner.

MIDDLESEX v NORFOLK (Gillette Cup)
At Lord's, April 28, 1970. [*Bill*] Edrich, returning to Lord's at the age of 54, 33 years after first playing there, ended his hour's batting with a flourish of 22 in six balls – 2, 4, 6, 4, 0, 6 – against Jones, before the next ball bowled him.

DERBYSHIRE v SURREY
At Derby, August 3, 5, 6, 1985. Jesty was taken ill before the start so Surrey summoned Ward, who had been due to play for his club, Banstead. Ward arrived at lunch when Surrey, who had been put in, were 115 for four but he, Richards and Doughty flayed some poor bowling. Ward, whose previous-best was 35, hit a six and 21 fours in his 143, an exciting, unblemished maiden century.

KENT v AUSTRALIANS
At Canterbury, August 24, 25, 26, 27, 1985. Luckhurst, Kent's 46-year-old manager, called out of retirement because of illness and injury to his team, remained unbeaten after 62 minutes.

LEICESTERSHIRE v YORKSHIRE
At Leicester, August 6, 7, 8, 1986. Higgs, the former England fast bowler, 49 years of age and Leicestershire's coach, made a romantic return to first-class cricket after a four-year absence, taking five wickets in an innings for the 50th time with model line-and-length bowling on an uneven pitch. Called up because of injuries in the county's ranks, he undermined Yorkshire's first innings with a spell of three for one in 28 balls.

NOTTINGHAMSHIRE v MIDDLESEX
At Nottingham, June 2, 3, 4, 1992. The game's principal excitement was the dramatic return to first-class cricket of 41-year-old left-arm spinner Phil Edmonds, who arrived by Rolls-Royce to come out of retirement after five years for this one game, while Tufnell recovered from an operation on his appendix. Edmonds bowled as if he had never been away, splitting eight wickets with his old partner Emburey on a helpful pitch as a bamboozled Notts conceded a lead of 190 runs, and followed on.

LEICESTERSHIRE v ESSEX (NatWest Bank Trophy semi-final)
At Leicester, August 12, 13, 1992. Hit by injuries to Millns and Wells, Leicestershire recalled Jonathan Agnew, the 32-year-old former England fast bowler, who retired in 1990 and was now BBC cricket correspondent. He performed admirably, gaining one wicket for just 31 runs, with no boundaries, in an unbroken spell. He confessed later that he felt "absolutely exhausted". His return led to the entry c Nixon b Agnew in the scorebook, for the benefit of students of American history.

SURREY v DERBYSHIRE
At The Oval, August 6, 7, 8, 1998. Surrey, hit by injuries, Test calls and their decision to suspend Ratcliffe for one match for disciplinary reasons, called on 44-year-old Alan Butcher, now the Second Eleven coach, to play his first game for the club for 12 years. Butcher contributed 22 and 12 to Surrey's victory, and began his first innings while son Mark was on his way to a maiden Test hundred at Headingley. Greeted by a doff of the panama from umpire Kitchen, he drove his first ball through the covers for four.

MCC v NEW ZEALAND A
At Oxford, July 18, 19, 20, 21, 2000. Photographers and camera crews descended on The Parks for Graham Gooch's return to first-class cricket, a week short of his 47th birthday. Three years out of county cricket, he said he had accepted MCC's invitation thinking it was for a one-day game. His dismissal, lbw on the back foot to Tuffey to the second ball of the match, made it a wasted journey for the media latecomers.

MINOR COUNTIES 2007
Herefordshire finished bottom and winless for the second consecutive season. It was not a summer most players would care to remember – except for wicketkeeper Tim Riley, who hit a hundred on Minor County debut, aged 47, and then promptly announced his retirement.

CONFUSING CONCLUSIONS

YORKSHIRE v KENT
At Harrogate, July 7, 8, 1904. In this match there occurred the unprecedented instance of a game being declared void in consequence of an infringement of Law 9. It was noticed in the course of Thursday's play that the pitch at one end had broken in several places, but when on Friday morning the players turned into the field to proceed with the contest these holes had all disappeared. That the ground had been tampered with after the drawing of stumps on Thursday was agreed by the players as well as the umpires, and, exercising the powers entrusted to them, the latter ruled that the game could not stand.

SOMERSET v SUSSEX
At Taunton, May 21, 22, 1919. An extraordinary and in some respects very regrettable incident marked the first of the Taunton matches last season. On the second

afternoon Sussex, with the score at a tie, had a wicket to fall, the remaining batsmen being Heygate who was crippled by rheumatism. It was understood when the innings began that he would not be able to bat, and as there was some doubt as to whether he would come in, one of the Somerset players – not J. C. White, the acting captain – appealed to Street, the umpire, on the ground that the limit of two minutes had been exceeded. Street pulled up the stumps and the match was officially recorded as a tie. The matter gave rise to much discussion and the MCC committee, when the question was referred to them, upheld the umpire's decision. Whether or not Heygate would have been able to crawl to the wicket, it was very unsportsmanlike that such a point should have been raised when there remained ample time to finish the match.

THE SECOND-CLASS COUNTIES

An unfortunate oversight in the notification of the result of the match between Yorkshire Second Eleven and Staffordshire in the Minor Counties' Competition of 1933 led to a serious blunder coming to light. As originally made up, the final table of results showed that Norfolk, with a percentage of 72.00, and Yorkshire Second Eleven, with 71.66, finished first and second in the Competition. Exercising their right to participate in a Challenge Match with the leaders, Yorkshire Second Eleven duly met Norfolk and defeated them. Some seven weeks later, when the table was being checked for insertion in *Wisden*, it was discovered that certain of the columns of figures did not agree.

Mistakes had occurred in calculating the points of the Yorkshire Second Eleven v Staffordshire match at Sheffield in July, when cricket did not take place on the second day. Yorkshire had been credited with points for a win in a one-day match instead of points for a win on the first innings. This revelation meant that Yorkshire's percentage was reduced from 71.66 to 68.33, and that in consequence, their position in the table was third, Wiltshire being second with a percentage of 70.00.

An extraordinary situation was thus created. Yorkshire had played Norfolk in the Challenge Match when actually they possessed no right to an honour which should have fallen to Wiltshire but, the cricket season being closed (it was then towards the end of October), no opportunity presented itself, should Wiltshire have claimed to play the leaders, for a meeting between Norfolk and Wiltshire. It was agreed to regard the Championship of 1933 as "not decided".

GLAMORGAN v MIDDLESEX

At Cardiff, July 27, 28, 29, 1955. Middlesex won by one wicket. The match had an amazing finish, for the teams had to turn out on the last morning for what proved to be less than one minute's cricket. The remarkable situation was created the previous evening. Middlesex needed 145 to win with ample time to finish the game in two days, but when the extra half-hour was claimed they still required 19 with three wickets to fall. They lost two more men and the last over came with six runs wanted, but Young could get only two twos and a single. Five hundred spectators, admitted free next morning, saw Young win the match by driving the third ball from Watkins to the boundary. Play lasted 52 seconds. The players were properly attired and all the usual procedure was observed. Moss, Young's partner, whose arm had swollen through an insect bite, had an injection to relieve pain before he went in, and on returning to London spent the next night in hospital.

GLOUCESTERSHIRE v YORKSHIRE

At Bristol, June 21, 22, 23, 1961. The game had to go to a third day because Gloucestershire, after claiming the extra half-hour and disposing of Yorkshire's last wicket, could only score 23, out of the 26 they needed to win, in the remaining 18 minutes. The last day's play consisted of one ball. All the players changed into flannels for the rather farcical closing stage. Bainbridge bowled the one delivery needed and Bernard, whose name had been drawn out of a hat to accompany Nicholls to the wicket, off-drove it to the boundary.

DERBYSHIRE v WORCESTERSHIRE

At Derby, August 18, 20, 21, 1979. This game ended on an unfortunate and probably unique note of controversy. Worcestershire started their second innings at 5.50pm on the last day under the impression that they had four overs in which to make 25 to win. According to the Worcestershire captain, Gifford, this information had been imparted to them by the umpires, but as the innings started a telephone call to Lord's established that the officials had apparently misinterpreted the regulations. The game was left drawn, and so Worcestershire missed the opportunity to stay in the Championship race by acquiring an extra 12 points. Gifford himself protested to Lord's and asked that the final ten minutes be replayed, a request that was turned down.

NATIONAL VILLAGE CHAMPIONSHIP 2002

The North Yorkshire South final between neighbours Folkton & Flixton and Staxton had a strange conclusion. Staxton's tenth-wicket pair needed three from the last ball; the keeper appealed unsuccessfully for a stumping, then started to celebrate, assuming the ball was dead. The batsmen ran three byes, and the umpires, agreeing play was still in progress, awarded them the match.

MIDDLESEX v SOMERSET (Friends Provident Trophy)

At Lord's, May 17, 2009. Somerset won by five wickets (D/L method). Somerset benefited from three extra powerplay overs due to a miscalculation by umpires Peter Willey and Michael Gough, which led to a complaint from Middlesex. However, the ECB "decided to uphold the precedent that umpire errors cannot form the basis to declare a match null and void". The official statement added: "ECB has great sympathy for the position in which Middlesex CCC has been placed but a replay cannot be ordered in these circumstances."

ENGLAND UNDER-19 v SRI LANKA UNDER-19 (Fifth one-day international)

At Canterbury, August 13, 2010. Sri Lanka were set a revised target of 177 from 41 overs. They blazed another 82 in 14 before being bowled out [for 125] at 6.54pm. England celebrated levelling the series, but the post-tour report by Sri Lanka's team manager Muttaiah Devaraj, leaked to a Sri Lankan newspaper, appeared to explain the tourists' pell-mell batting – and cast doubt on the real value of England's achievement. Having been assured by his board that the return flight with Oman Air would wait at Heathrow for up to two hours, Devaraj learned during the match that it would leave on schedule, at 10.35pm. Faced with a rush-hour coach journey on the M25, Devaraj said he asked his batsmen to hit out or get out. They made the flight.

ESSEX v KENT (Friends Life t20)

At Chelmsford, June 20, 2012. There was controversy in the 19th over, when Matt Coles was dropped at midwicket and ran two. But the scorers entered a dot-ball instead, apparently distracted by dealing with a six-run penalty for Essex's slow over-rate which the umpires had just levied. Coles was out soon afterwards for six, and insisted he had actually scored eight. However, the ECB ruled the scores as recorded had to stand, and Essex edged home when Mark Davies, needing a four from Graham Napier's last delivery, was bowled.

CONSPICUOUS BY THEIR ABSENCE

GLOUCESTERSHIRE v YORKSHIRE

At Bristol, June 25, 26, 27, 1891. Mr Townsend was caught at cover point, and before another man could come in Mr Cranston, to the consternation of the players and spectators, was seized with a fit and had to be carried off the ground.

YORKSHIRE v AN ENGLAND ELEVEN

At Scarborough, September 5, 6, 1895. Owing to the state of the ground a start could not be made at the ordinary time on the first day, and a section of the crowd indulged in a most unseemly demonstration, such insulting remarks being addressed to Mr H. T. Hewett that that gentleman – who was to have captained the England team – retired from the match after fielding till the luncheon interval. We think he acted unwisely, but he was much provoked.

OXFORD v CAMBRIDGE

At Lord's, July 8, 9, 10, 1912. G. E. V. Crutchley scored 99 not out for Oxford on the first day, but at the end of his innings he was found to be suffering from an attack of measles. He could, of course, take no further part in the match. He was very unwell before the game began, but naturally had no idea what was the matter with him. It was stated that while he was scoring his 99 not out his temperature went up two degrees.

NOTTINGHAMSHIRE v HAMPSHIRE

At Nottingham, August 6, 7, 8, 1914. B. G. Melle started playing for Hampshire, but when the game had been a little time in progress he received orders to join his Regiment. In the special circumstances Stone was allowed to take his place.

WARWICKSHIRE v SURREY

At Birmingham, June 23, 24, 1919. There was a painful incident on the second afternoon. Brown, one of the umpires, had an epileptic seizure, and had to be carried off the field, Santall officiating in his absence.

MIDDLESEX v NOTTINGHAMSHIRE

At Lord's, August 15, 17, 18, 1925. Middlesex lost the services of Allen, through that player being badly stung by a mosquito, and also those of Durston who was called away after lunch owing to the death of his mother. The third day robbed Notts of nearly all the honours, for, with the Middlesex attack short not only of Allen and Durston but also of Haig who, as the result of a blow on the thigh, was too lame to turn out, the visitors had only Hearne and North to face and yet, set only 105 to win, they lost seven wickets.

WARWICKSHIRE v NOTTINGHAMSHIRE
At Birmingham, July 7, 9, 10, 1934. Notts, who won easily by ten wickets, suffered two big blows during the course of the game. A. W. Carr, taken ill while motoring over the weekend, could not play again during the season, and Larwood broke down early in Warwickshire's second innings.
Carr had suffered a heart attack.

RUGBY SCHOOL v MCC (Tom Brown Centenary Match), June 17, 1941.
Picture caption. Absent from group: L. G. H. Hingley (who arrived late after bombing German factories up to 5am).

MIDDLESEX AND ESSEX v KENT AND SURREY
At Lord's, August 28, 1943. Steady rain lasting many hours suggested a wet day, but after an early lunch the downfall ceased and the precaution of covering the pitch entirely enabled a start at half past two. Meanwhile, when everyone present regarded cricket as impossible, the Arsenal club obtained permission for the brothers Compton to play at Charlton in the opening match of the football season. An injury to A. V. Avery of Essex, who tripped over his bag when leaving home for Lord's, further weakened what could be called the home team, and Arthur Fagg spent the day looking for his bag mislaid on the railway.

MIDDLESEX v NOTTINGHAMSHIRE
At Lord's, May 4, 6, 7, 1957. Nottinghamshire were unfortunate to lose Walker, who returned home suffering from mumps, after he had caused Middlesex trouble by taking seven wickets for 56 runs, the best performance of his career.

LANCASHIRE v DERBYSHIRE
At Liverpool, June 15, 17, 18, 1963. Howard forfeited his innings on Monday morning when, as a not-out batsman, he arrived late.
Scorecard: K. Howard retired out 1.

ESSEX v YORKSHIRE
At Westcliff, July 24, 25, 26, 1968. A note of drama was provided on the first day when, with the players on the field and the first ball about to be bowled in the Yorkshire innings, there came a telephone call from the selectors requesting Sharpe to travel to Leeds to join the England party for the Fourth Test. Sharpe was thereupon replaced by Leadbeater, the twelfth man.

SURREY v SUSSEX
At The Oval, August 15, 16, 17, 1979. Long, the former Surrey player, declined to allow Butcher to resume batting at the fall of the fifth wicket after he had retired ill with the score 26 for nought. He reasoned that Butcher, having been ill before the

match began, should not have been playing at all. But the action rebounded on Long. Intikhab, who came in when Butcher was "sent off", hit a quick fifty, and when Long agreed to Butcher returning on the fall of the seventh wicket, the opening batsman, with that little extra time to recover, looked a vastly different player to the one who scratched around during a good opening spell from Imran Khan. He hit three sixes, going on to score 71 not out.

SUSSEX 1983
Ian Greig was first on the casualty list when he fell from his flat window, trying to gain entrance there after snapping his key in the lock.

NORTHAMPTONSHIRE v ESSEX
At Northampton, August 8, 10, 11, 1987. Lamb, who was at a local hospital where his wife was about to give birth to their first child, was recalled to the County Ground as wickets fell and hit 40 quick runs before resuming bedside duties.

NORTHAMPTONSHIRE v GLAMORGAN
At Wellingborough School, August 20, 22, 23, 1988. Glamorgan were handicapped by the absence of Ontong and Barwick, who were both badly shaken in a road accident near Colchester the evening before the match.

ESSEX v DERBYSHIRE
At Chelmsford, August 29, 30, 31, September 1, 1995. Barnett pulled out on the morning of the match because of a stomach bug; DeFreitas responded to the sudden challenge of captaincy with five wickets and a dashing 91 – but, after two days, had to rush to his five-year-old daughter's hospital bedside after she was scalded in the bath.

NORTHAMPTONSHIRE v MIDDLESEX
At Northampton, July 18, 19, 20, 22, 1996. John Emburey also played a key role – chiefly through his absence. He was called to the High Court on the first day to give evidence for Ian Botham and ex-Northamptonshire captain Allan Lamb in their libel case against Imran Khan, then returned in time to take two wickets and batted at No. 3 rather than risk missing his turn while back in court next day.

GLAMORGAN v YORKSHIRE (NatWest Trophy quarter-final)
At Cardiff, July 29, 1997. Glamorgan won by one wicket. The Glamorgan captain Maynard was not able to play a full part in the celebrations: he was suffering from chicken-pox and, though he played [and scored 62], was isolated in a separate dressing-room.

GLAMORGAN v NOTTINGHAMSHIRE
At Colwyn Bay, July 31, August 1, 2, 4, 1997. Philip North, the left-arm spinner who captains the Wales Minor Counties team, was called up by Glamorgan for the first time in eight years, but he was dropped again after arriving at the ground late. He said his wake-up call had not come through.

ENGLAND v SRI LANKA (NatWest Series)
At Manchester, July 7, 2002. Umpire Dave Orchard missed the first four overs of the match after turning up late because he thought it was a day/nighter. The third umpire, Jeremy Lloyds, stepped in.

SOUTH AFRICA v WEST INDIES (Fourth Test Match)
At Centurion, January 16, 17, 18, 19, 20, 2004. Andre Nel must have been relieved when play – extended because of the shortened first day – was ended again by bad light. He just had time to be whisked off by helicopter to his wedding, arranged long before, at nearby Benoni. Nel was back next morning.

DELHI v UTTAR PRADESH (Ranji Trophy)
At Feroz Shah Kotla, Delhi, December 1, 2, 3, 4, 2006. Referee Sambaran Banerjee and umpire Sameer Bandrekar were suspended for the rest of the season after leaving the ground when bad light stopped play, and missing a subsequent inspection.

GUYANA v WINDWARD ISLANDS (Carib Beer Cup)
At Providence Stadium, Guyana, March 29, 30, 31, April 1, 2008. Drawn. The match began a day late as Windward Islands were awaiting their kit. Then Shivnarine Chanderpaul, who ended the first day on 78 not out, flew to Trinidad for the West Indies' Players Association awards (where he was named Test Cricketer, One-day International Cricketer and International Cricketer of the Year), not returning until the third afternoon. He was deemed "retired out" and Windwards refused to allow Guyana a substitute fielder; "This is not a curry goat match," said their coach, Lockhart Sebastien.

SOUTH AFRICA v AUSTRALIA (First Test Match)
At Cape Town, November 9, 10, 11, 2011. South Africa reached lunch at a relatively serene 49 for one. Gary Kirsten, South Africa's coach, took that as his cue to go home and spend a few hours with his wife, Deborah, and their newborn daughter. When Kirsten returned to the ground for the last hour he struggled to believe a scoreboard that alleged South Africa were 72 for one. "Has it been raining?" he asked when he reached the dressing-room. "Um, no, coach," was the gentle reply. "We're in the second innings." *South Africa were bowled out for 96 in the first innings, Australia for 47.*

LANCASHIRE v NETHERLANDS (Clydesdale Bank 40)
At Manchester, August 12, 2012. Already missing four injured or unavailable players, the Netherlands were then denied visas for two more by the UK Border Agency. Werner Coetsee was drafted in from Lancashire League side Enfield at the last minute.

DEATH AND BATTLE OF BRITAIN (AMONG OTHER THINGS) STOP PLAY

OXFORD UNIVERSITY v GENTLEMEN OF ENGLAND
On the New Parks Ground, Oxford, June 2, 3, 4, 1882. A commencement was made on the Christ Church ground in order that a charge might be made for

admission – an arrangement not permitted by the Dons on the New Parks Ground – but when 40 runs had been scored for the Gentlemen of England for the loss of three wickets, Mr Webbe was severely injured in the face by a ball from Mr Peake, owing to the hard and lumpy state of the ground, and it was decided after a consultation between the captains to leave the dangerous spot and recommence the match on the New Parks ground.

LANCASHIRE v GLOUCESTERSHIRE
At Manchester, July 24, 25, 1884. Gloucestershire went in for the second time 22 runs to the bad. They had 12 minutes' batting before luncheon, and upon resuming Dr E. M. Grace was splendidly caught at mid-off, and his brother had just succeeded him when a telegram was received announcing the death of Mrs Grace, the mother of Drs E. M. and W. G. Grace. A short consultation was held, and it was decided to at once abandon the match.

SURREY v DERBYSHIRE
At Kennington Oval, May 5, 6, 1910. Owing to the death of King Edward this match was abandoned on the Saturday morning.

LANCASHIRE v KENT
At Manchester, May 19, 21, 1910. Owing to the funeral of King Edward no play took place on the Friday of this match, and a few weeks later it was decided by the MCC that, as an item in the County Championship programme, the contest, in common with all others arranged for the same days, should be ignored.

LANCASHIRE v ESSEX
At Manchester, August 21, 22, 1911. Originally fixed for Blackpool, this match was afterwards arranged to be played at Liverpool but owing to the serious labour troubles prevailing in that city it was further transferred to Manchester.

SURREY v NOTTINGHAMSHIRE
At Kennington Oval, August 1, 3, 4, 1925. A curious thing happened when the players came out after a shower at the end of the afternoon, such numberless pieces of newspaper being blown across the ground as to put further cricket out of the question. An enormous crowd watched the game on the Bank Holiday. Much to the disadvantage of the Notts team, the big attendance involved a serious curtailment of the playing area.

SURREY v YORKSHIRE
At Kennington Oval, August 22, 24, 25, 1931. A curious occurrence marked the opening stage of this contest, the players after cricket had been in progress for about ten minutes leaving the field and nothing further being done until 80 minutes later. It transpired that when Greenwood having won the toss decided to bat, Fender, without having inspected the conditions, accepted the situation but found when play began – Greenwood meanwhile having had the heavy roller put over the pitch – that his bowlers could not obtain a satisfactory footing. The umpires being appealed to at once removed the bails and, but for pressure brought upon them, the resumption might have been further delayed than it was.

BUCCANEERS v BRITISH EMPIRE XI

At Lord's, August 31, 1940. The Battle of Britain interfered with the match, causing late arrivals, which necessitated an altered batting order and bringing about an early cessation when the Buccaneers seemed within sight of victory.

SURREY v YORKSHIRE

At The Oval, July 5, 7, 8, 1952. Yorkshire concentrated on defence, much to the annoyance of a section of the crowd, who indulged in so much barracking when Leadbeater was defying Surrey – he stayed an hour – that umpire Price sat and lay on the grass until the noise subsided.

Obituary 1969: PRICE, WILLIAM FREDERICK FRANK: "I did so because three times there were catcalls just as the batsman was about to play the ball. That is not my idea of British sportsmanship and under the Laws of 'fair and unfair play', I will not tolerate such things on any ground, Lord's included, when I am umpiring."

NOTTINGHAMSHIRE v AUSTRALIANS

At Nottingham, May 30, June 1, 1953. Although reduced to two days in order to permit the Australians to watch the Coronation procession on the Tuesday, the game was subsequently pronounced first-class.

SOMERSET v HAMPSHIRE (NatWest Bank Trophy quarter-final)

At Taunton, August 7, 8, 1985. A low sun reflecting off an adjacent building at 7.45pm ended play [on the first day] to considerable agitation from a capacity crowd of 8,500.

CRICKET ROUND THE WORLD 1995

ASCENSION ISLAND: The barren, volcanic rock of Ascension Island in the South Atlantic is believed to be the only place where "wedding stopped play" – to be resumed 40 minutes later as the last of the congregation left for the reception. The little Church of St Mary the Virgin is inside the boundary.

MCC MATCHES 1996

MCC's Over-40s side visited The Netherlands as part of CTC de Flamingo's 75th anniversary celebrations. They and their opponents returned from tea to discover that the local groundsman, thinking the game over, had rolled up the mat and stored it away.

WORCESTERSHIRE v SRI LANKA A

At Worcester, August 10, 11, 12, 13, 1999. In this match, "non-arrival of kit stopped play" – and then the solar eclipse did. The kit disaster cost the whole first day. The Sri Lankans had flown back from Copenhagen a day earlier. However, their original flight had been forced to turn back because of technical trouble and, although the players caught a later flight, their bags did not. A courier was supposed to be bringing them to Worcester next morning, but he got caught in pre-eclipse traffic and did not arrive until 5pm, an hour after play was called off. The match finally began at 11.45 next morning, after the solar eclipse, which darkened all Britain; it was only partial over Worcester, but cricket was clearly going to be impossible.

ORISSA v MADHYA PRADESH (Ranji Trophy quarter-final)
At Captain Roop Singh Stadium, Gwalior, March 22, 23, 24, 25, 26, 2001. Play was held up for 38 minutes on the fourth day after journalists invaded the pitch to demand an apology from Hirwani and Yadav who, they claimed, had manhandled one of their colleagues.

KENT v YORKSHIRE (Norwich Union League)
At Canterbury, May 19, 2002. Yorkshire's reply was delayed by a Gurkha pipe band, who disregarded the end of the interval and continued marching at long-on, oblivious to the bewildered players and umpires.

SURREY v DERBYSHIRE (Second Eleven Championship)
At The Oval, August 13, 14, 15, 2003. This historic match will be remembered for broken records and a bizarre stoppage. Surrey openers Scott Newman and Nadeem Shahid hammered their way past 500, in 74 overs. At this point, New Zealand Test umpire Billy Bowden, renowned for the originality of his hand signals, added to his aura of eccentricity by producing a camera. He halted play to snap the grinning batsmen in front of the scoreboard, which showed 501 for nought. Bowden, getting his eye in before standing in the Fourth Test, took more photos at the close of play, by which time 547 had been plundered in just over two sessions. His sense of occasion was justified: the partnership of 552 was the best in the history of the Second Eleven Championship. Newman finally made 284 off 292 balls, with three sixes and 49 fours, Shahid 266 from 271 balls, with three sixes and 41 fours.

WORCESTERSHIRE v LEICESTERSHIRE
At Worcester, August 30, 31, September 1, 2, 2005. Play was stopped for 25 minutes because of glare from the makeshift sightscreen of plastic sheeting over the Basil D'Oliveira Stand. Two portable screens were borrowed from the nearby King's School playing fields, but the regulations did not allow for the seven overs lost to be made up.

BANGLADESH v AUSTRALIA (Second Test Match)
At Chittagong Divisional Stadium, Chittagong, April 16, 17, 18, 19, 20, 2006. A media sit-in, protesting at the alleged police assault of a local photographer, delayed the match's start by ten minutes and led to an ugly lunchtime brawl between police and press. Violent thunderstorms blew apart the scoreboard on the second day and dismantled the makeshift bamboo shelters in the stands.

LANCASHIRE v WARWICKSHIRE
At Blackpool, August 30, 31, September 1, 2, 2006. Play was halted twice by water bombs catapulted on to the pitch from outside the ground, but it was common-place Blackpool rain that ensured a draw. Lancashire's innings was interrupted briefly by the first water bomb, which was dismissed as an accident until another landed two days later. The water-filled balloons (or maybe condoms) were catapulted on to the pitch itself with an accuracy some of the bowlers might have envied. However, the second landed alarmingly near Kartik, who had just had a bat-pad appeal turned down, and Loye quickly scaled the wall dividing the ground from the rest of Stanley Park, trying to spot the culprits, while a team of stewards

scanned the Italian gardens: they reported four teenagers cycling towards Blackpool Zoo, perhaps to be devoured by the lion. Meanwhile, the groundsman dried the pitch with a bar towel.

SURREY v BRADFORD/LEEDS UCCE
At The Oval, April 14, 15, 16, 2007. Play was held up when a man dressed as a cigarette walked behind the bowler's arm, forcing the announcer to ask "Would the cigarette please sit down?" The miscreant had been engaged to promote Surrey's smoking ban.

LANCASHIRE v KENT
At Manchester, June 15, 16, 17, 18, 2007. The pavilion was evacuated, forcing a halt: two fire engines arrived, to find the alarms had been set off by smoke rising from gravy in the kitchens.

DERBYSHIRE v NORTHAMPTONSHIRE
At Derby, September 19, 20, 21, 22, 2007. There was an unusual delay of 30 minutes on the first day as a sightscreen was towed from one end to the other because batsmen had difficulty seeing the ball in front of the Gateway Centre.

SCOTLAND v WARWICKSHIRE (Friends Provident Trophy)
At Edinburgh, May 16, 2009. Scotland's run-chase was bizarrely interrupted by a visiting supporter who came on to the field of play, helped himself to a bail, and legged it over the perimeter wall and into the Edinburgh afternoon. Scotland skipper Gavin Hamilton called the thief an "idiot" who upset the momentum of their chase when they were going strongly.

"HOW'S ABOUT THAT?"
SOME UNUSUAL DISMISSALS

NORTH v SOUTH (The Thames Calamity Fund match)
At The Oval, September 17, 18, 19, 1878. A very remarkable catch by Shrewsbury got out Mr Thornton in the second innings. Shrewsbury was fielding deep long-on in front of the people by the tavern; Mr Thornton let out powerfully at one from Morley; Shrewsbury ran to the front of the pavilion, and there, with back hard up against the paling, he caught the ball and tumbled over – head first, heels in the air– into the lap of some old member, cosily enjoying the cricket on a front seat; but Shrewsbury held the ball all the while, and came up smiling and tossing the ball up in the usual neat form that Shrewsbury displays in all his cricket.

MIDDLESEX v SUSSEX
At Lord's, July 6, 7, 8, 1893. An extraordinary incident marked the first day of the match, Foley, on an appeal by the bowler, being given out by Henty for picking up one of the bails and replacing it while the ball was in play. The decision was so preposterous that Murdoch, the Sussex captain, went into the pavilion and succeeded in persuading Foley to resume his innings.

LANCASHIRE v DERBYSHIRE

At Manchester, June 12, 13, 14, 1899. Ward was out curiously, part of the shoulder of his bat coming off and breaking the wicket.

HAMPSHIRE v GLOUCESTERSHIRE

At Southampton, June 27, 28, 1919. On the second day, just at the close of Hampshire's first innings, Pothecary played a ball into the top of his pad and shook it out into the hands of Smith, the wicketkeeper. He was given out "caught" contrary to Law 33b, which states "if the ball, whether struck by the bat or not, lodges in the batsman's clothing, the ball shall become 'dead.'"

SUSSEX v LANCASHIRE

At Hastings, August 18, 19, 1919. A curious thing happened, Gilligan walking away under the impression that he was bowled when Boddington knocked the bails off. At the close of the innings Blake, the square-leg umpire, said that Gilligan was not stumped as the scorers had supposed, so as a matter of fact the batsman was not out at all. *The scorebook never lies: "Mr A. H. H. Gilligan st Boddington b R. Tyldesley 2"*

MISCELLANY 1938

During the match between The Army and the Australians at Aldershot on August 17, J. H. Fingleton, fielding at mid-on, tried to run out one of the Army batsmen. His throw-in proved so accurate that the ball removed the bails at the bowler's end and went on to hit the wicket at the other end. Despite this wonderful piece of work, neither batsman was out.

KENT v DERBYSHIRE

At Tonbridge, June 11, 13, 1938. Cole was dismissed in an unusual way. Levett drove a no-ball on to the opposite stumps. Cole was backing up and before he could regain his crease Mitchell, with ball in hand, ran and pulled up a stump.

SURREY v DERBYSHIRE

At The Oval, June 3, 4, 1953. The game was notable for the curious hit-wicket dismissal of Revill. As Revill shaped to play the ball it rose sharply and struck his hand. Still moving in his attempted defensive stroke, the batsman drew back his hand in pain and shook off his glove, which fell against the stumps and dislodged a bail.

WARWICKSHIRE v YORKSHIRE

At Birmingham, July 23, 25, 26, 1955. Wilson was given "run out" when 54 but as he returned to the pavilion spectators protested that the ball struck a boundary flag and was therefore "dead" when Horner threw in. After consulting the fieldsman and Pothecary, his fellow umpire, Spencer signalled a boundary hit and Wilson was recalled to resume his innings.

GLAMORGAN v ESSEX

At Cardiff, July 14, 16, 17, 1956. Barker, the visitors' opening batsman, was dismissed in unusual fashion in the first innings. Backing up as Wooller ran up to bowl, he was run out by the Glamorgan captain, who had warned Barker three times previously for leaving his crease.

SURREY v GLAMORGAN

At The Oval, May 11, 13, 1957. May's run-out caused much controversy. The Surrey captain thought Hedges had held the ball when he dived towards the stumps from mid-on, but the ball was under Hedges as he lay on the ground. Hedges signalled no catch, but May had arrived at the pavilion end where Barrington had not moved. Wooller, the Glamorgan captain, broke the stumps at the vacant end.

SOMERSET v HAMPSHIRE

At Bath, June 15, 17, 1957. Following a run-out, Horton returned to the pavilion, but was recalled when the new batsman, Rayment, was already at the wicket. Following a consultation, it was decided Gray was the man run out, and Horton resumed. Later Horton was run out, this time conclusively.

NORTHAMPTONSHIRE v WORCESTERSHIRE

At Northampton, July 26, 28, 1958. Kenyon saved a complete rout in the second innings. He hit 56, including nine fours, out of 71 before dislodging a bail with his trousers when pulling Tribe.

YORKSHIRE v MCC

At Scarborough, September 1, 3, 4, 1962. A little later rain began, and when play was resumed with only ten minutes left Illingworth, under the impression that the game had been called off, had left for home. He was recorded as "retired out".

SUSSEX v NOTTINGHAMSHIRE

At Hove, July 1, 3, 4, 1967. A bold bid for victory by Sussex was thwarted by Stead and Forbes in a thrilling finish. They played out the last three balls after Swetman had been dismissed hit wicket when his cap fell on to the stumps.

HAMPSHIRE v NOTTINGHAMSHIRE

At Portsmouth, August 28, 29, 30, 1968. Brilliant batting by Richards [206] overshadowed all else in this match, but he would have been out when 29 but for a tremendous slice of luck. A snick sent the ball on to a stump, but the bail, instead of falling to the ground, became deeply embedded into the groove and the umpires called for new stumps.

LANCASHIRE v GLAMORGAN (Benson and Hedges Cup quarter-finals)

At Manchester, June 13, 1973. Majid fell to a remarkable catch when he hit his rival captain full on the head at short leg in pulling Lever, only to see Pilling make the catch running in from mid-on. David Lloyd was taken to hospital with concussion, but returned and watched.

DERBYSHIRE v GLAMORGAN

At Chesterfield, June 10, 12, 1978. History was made just before the end of this game when Russell, fielding at short leg, was struck by a fierce blow from Nash, the ball temporarily lodging in the visor of his protective helmet. Despite this protection,

Russell suffered a fractured cheekbone. The umpires had to decide whether a catch had technically been made. In the event, they ruled "dead ball", a decision subsequently approved by the TCCB.

ESSEX v MIDDLESEX

At Southend, July 21, 22, 23, 1982. In the Middlesex first innings, Downton, batting with Tomlins as his runner, was given run out while standing at the bowler's end. When Downton played the ball into the covers, both he and Tomlins raced through for a single, so contravening the Law, which states that a batsman who has a runner may not himself run.

LEICESTERSHIRE v DERBYSHIRE

At Leicester, July 1, 2, 3, 1987. Mortensen was dismissed in unusual circumstances. Batting with a runner, he set off for a single, forgetting that he should not leave his crease. Willey, alert to Law 2.7, instructed the wicketkeeper to remove the bails and Mortensen, by now at the bowler's end with his runner, was run out.

GLAMORGAN v DERBYSHIRE (Benson and Hedges Cup semi-finals)

At Swansea, June 8, 9, 10, 1988. Maynard had struck four boundaries in his 22 when, as he twisted to play a delivery from Holding, his shoulder knocked his helmet off and it fell on to his wicket. "I had not been wearing my chinstrap and nobody let me forget it for weeks," he recalled.

KENT v ESSEX

At Canterbury, August 4, 5, 6, 7, 1999. A tense game took a controversial twist when Irani, stranded outside his crease as Marsh removed the bails, was given not out. He was on 106 when Marsh, who until then had been standing back, came up to the stumps as Ealham ran in to bowl. A pre-arranged leg-side delivery beat the bat, and Marsh claimed a stumping. But umpire Harris ruled that this had broken Law 42, on unfair play. However, he forgot to call "dead ball", later admitting that in all his time on the circuit he had never encountered such an incident.

LANCASHIRE v YORKSHIRE

At Manchester, August 19, 20, 21, 1999. Chapple played on to Vaughan, dislodging the end of one bail. It remained precariously balanced, even when the fielders stamped on the ground trying to displace it.

BORDER v FREE STATE (SuperSport Series)

At East London, September 27, 28, 29, 2002. Vasbert Drakes was recorded as timed out in Border's first innings: he had not even reached the ground, having been delayed on a flight from Colombo, where he had been with the West Indian squad. He did arrive in time to bowl.

NOTTINGHAMSHIRE v DURHAM UCCE

At Nottingham, April 12, 13, 14, 2003. The most remarkable incident was only the third case of a player being timed out in first-class cricket. Nottinghamshire were delaying the declaration for Read's century, but No. 10 Charlie Shreck lasted just three balls on first-class debut. Harris, nursing a groin strain, had not expected to bat and, by the time he had strapped on his pads, and raced part-way down the pavilion steps, the fielders were heading his way – he had already exceeded the three minutes now allowed for players to arrive at the crease under Law 31.

SRI LANKA v PAKISTAN (Bank Alfalah Cup)
At Dambulla, May 10, 2003. Lokuarachchi survived a run-out appeal at one end only to be given out at the other as he attempted an extra run in the confusion. Both decisions had to be referred to the third umpire.

NORTHAMPTONSHIRE v MIDDLESEX
At Northampton, August 18, 19, 20, 21, 2004. The talking point of the match came on the second afternoon, when Cook could have been out in three different ways off the same delivery from Louw. It struck the pad and, evidently, something else, then flew to Swann in the slips. Umpire Constant initially turned down an enquiry for lbw, while Swann threw down the stumps, with Cook possibly out of his ground. Then the captain, Sales, appealed for a catch, which was upheld after the umpires conferred.

NEW ZEALAND v SRI LANKA (First Test Match)
At Christchurch, December 7, 8, 9, 2006. As Murali completed the easy single that brought up Sangakkara's century – out of just 170 – some of the nearby fielders moved towards the middle of the pitch to observe the courtesies. After touching down for the single, Murali also strolled back to add his good wishes. But Martin rifled in a long throw from the deep, keeper McCullum broke the wicket, and umpire Brian Jerling, already moving in from square leg (and apparently giving a small hand signal which the batsman did not see), gave Muralitharan out.

WARWICKSHIRE v SUSSEX
At Birmingham, July 7, 8, 9, 10, 2009. Trott pocketed – quite literally – a catch at short leg when the ball lodged in his right trouser pocket as he jumped to take evasive action from Joyce's full-blooded sweep off Botha.

SURREY v NORTHAMPTONSHIRE
At The Oval, April 8, 9, 10, 11, 2011. Palpably leg-before to his first Championship delivery since 2009, Michael Brown found himself walking off with the scoreboard clock still reading 10.59 – a minute before the season's official start time.

ENGLAND v INDIA (Third npower Test)
At Birmingham, August 10, 11, 12, 13, 2011. Gambhir fell to Anderson's first delivery of the day, before Dravid was undone by his eighth, failing to review a caught-behind decision which was based, replays showed, on the sound of bat on aglet, the plastic tip of his fatally floppy shoelace.

BANGLADESH v PAKISTAN (Asia Cup)
At Mirpur, March 11, 2012. Shahid Afridi poked his first ball back towards the bowler, Shakib, who juggled it, palmed it on to the chest of Misbah-ul-Haq, the non-striker, then somehow pocketed the rebound.

IT'S A DANGEROUS GAME

MCC AND GROUND v NOTTINGHAMSHIRE

At Lord's, June 13, 14, 15, 1870. A lamentable celebrity will ever attach to this match, through the fatal accident to Summers, whose death resulted from a ball bowled by Platts in the second innings of Notts. The wickets were excellent, and the sad mishap universally regretted.

The scorecard reads:

G. Summers hurt (not out)   0

Hubert Preston, 1943: Summers received so severe a blow on the head that he died from the effects of the accident a few days afterwards. Pitches at Lord's at that time were notoriously bad, and, as the outcome of this accident, far more attention was paid to the care of the turf. Over the grave of George Summers at Nottingham the MCC erected a memorial tablet "testifying their sense of his qualities as a cricketer and regret at the untimely accident on Lord's ground".

KENT 1890

Kent's season was, in a sense, very unlucky, as two of the most prominent cricketers met with accidents in the course of the summer. When playing in the match against Gloucestershire at Gloucester Mr C. J. M. Fox, in endeavouring to stop a hard cut at point, dislocated his shoulder so badly that he had to be put under chloroform, and the injury prevented him from again assisting his county for very nearly a month. A more serious thing than this was the unfortunate blow that Walter Wright received on his thumb in the last match against Surrey at The Oval, and which caused him to remain an inmate of St Thomas' Hospital for just over five weeks. There has seldom been a more painful sensation created in an important match. Wright had the thumb of his bowling hand knocked right out of its socket, and as the result of a surgical examination it was found that the dislocation was a compound one.

GLOUCESTERSHIRE v MIDDLESEX

At Cheltenham, August 20, 21, 22, 1891. Mr W. R. Moon, the famous Association football player, kept wicket for Middlesex, and was unlucky enough to meet with two accidents, having his chin cut open on Thursday and his hand badly injured on Friday.

KENT v NOTTINGHAMSHIRE

At Gravesend, May 25, 26, 1905. The wicket was very fiery and while Notts were scoring 337 – a splendid total in the circumstances – A. O. Jones, John Gunn, and George Gunn were all rather badly hurt. Jones received such a severe blow on the elbow that he had to retire for a long time, and George Gunn, who was hit over the heart, took no part in the game after the completion of his innings. Fielder did the mischief, his bowling getting up a great deal.

LEICESTERSHIRE v SURREY

At Leicester, June 9, 10, 1920. The match was remarkable for the fact that five men were unable to play on the Thursday. Salmon, Mounteney, and Benskin were injured by severe blows when batting on the previous day; Rushby strained his side when bowling, and Fender, called away on urgent business, did not return until the match was over.

MIDDLESEX v YORKSHIRE
At Lord's, June 8, 9, 10, 1921. After the game was over a sad mishap befell Yorkshire, Dolphin slipping off a chair in the dressing-room and fracturing his wrist. He played no more first-class cricket last summer.

LANCASHIRE v YORKSHIRE
At Manchester, July 31, August 2, 3, 1926. Oldroyd, struck on the head by a ball from McDonald, had to be conveyed to the infirmary, and played no more last season.

GLOUCESTERSHIRE v YORKSHIRE
At Gloucester, May 7, 9, 10, 1927. Parry, an umpire whose leg had been amputated below the knee, fell in getting out of the way of a ball, and fractured the maimed limb.

LEICESTERSHIRE v GLOUCESTERSHIRE
At Leicester, July 14, 16, 17, 1928. No doubt the course of the game was materially affected [Gloucestershire lost by six wickets] by an accident to Hammond, who injured his fingers in a deckchair, and in addition to being unable to field, went in sixth wicket in the second innings.

LEICESTERSHIRE v LANCASHIRE
At Leicester, July 8, 10, 11, 1933. An unfortunate accident to Corrall occurred just before half past six on the opening day. Washbrook swung his bat at a high ball from Astill and struck the wicketkeeper on the left ear. He was removed to hospital in a semi-unconscious condition.
Obituary 1995: Fracturing his skull, Corrall was on the danger list for several weeks, but not only did he pull through, he returned next season better than ever and played in every Championship match.

MIDDLESEX v KENT
At Lord's, July 22, 23, 1953. A spectator in the Mound Stand, struck over the eye when Bennett hit a boundary, was taken to hospital, where the injury was stitched. He returned and saw the finish.

NOTTINGHAMSHIRE v WARWICKSHIRE
At Nottingham, August 11, 13, 14, 1956. Soon after a start was possible at 3.30, Walker slipped in delivering the ball, which pitched short and struck Gardner, who was taken to hospital with a fractured left elbow.

WORCESTERSHIRE v YORKSHIRE
At Worcester, June 3, 5, 6, 1961. Yorkshire won by one wicket. Spectators at this casualty-stricken match will long remember the plucky effort of Don Wilson. Nine wickets tumbled to a combination of pace and spin with 36 runs still required. Then Wilson, with his left arm in plaster from the elbow to the knuckles because of a fractured thumb, joined Platt with 25 minutes to play. Though the pain quickly

prompted him to bat one-handed, Wilson swept Gifford twice for four, and when Flavell took the new ball five minutes from the end with 22 runs still needed, he immediately struck three boundaries and a two with one-handed drives. This over also brought four byes. Then Platt took a single off Coldwell and the crowd rose to cheer when Wilson straight-drove to the boundary to complete a thrilling finish. He hit 29 in a last-wicket stand of 37.

Worcestershire had their casualties, too. Kenyon went for an X-ray after being struck on the left wrist by a ball from Trueman, and Broadbent was reduced to a hobble by a pulled hamstring.

YORKSHIRE v. MIDDLESEX

At Bradford, July 10, 12, 13, 1976. Yorkshire won by one run. A late collapse brought the injured Radley [who broke a finger fielding in the slips] to the wicket with his arm in a sling. His brave effort to help in making the vital last five runs was in vain, however, Bairstow stumping him at 235.

GLOUCESTERSHIRE v GLAMORGAN

At Bristol, June 25, 27, 28, 1977. Shackleton, who wears contact lenses, went to hospital after being struck in the face, and Graveney needed six stitches after splitting the webbing of his bowling hand. Davey batted in the second innings with a runner after suffering a recurrence of trouble to an Achilles tendon.

WORCESTERSHIRE v GLAMORGAN

At Worcester, June 3, 5, 6, 1989. The cricket was overshadowed by the injury to Botham just three days before his scheduled return to Test cricket. Batting without a helmet, he suffered a fractured right cheekbone when he top-edged the ball into his face trying to hook a short delivery from Barwick.

NORTHAMPTONSHIRE v ESSEX

At Northampton, August 24, 25, 26, 28, 1989. Shahid was taken to hospital with a broken nose during Northampton's second innings after misjudging a catch in the deep, offered by Larkins.

HAMPSHIRE v MIDDLESEX

At Basingstoke, June 10, 1990. Downton, keeping wicket for Middlesex, was hit in the left eye by a bail when Emburey bowled Wood, and was later admitted to hospital. **Middlesex in 1991:** The saddest note of a sorry season was struck by Paul Downton's sudden retirement, brought about by the after-effects of his eye injury in 1990. It robbed the county of not only a fine wicketkeeper but also an ideal No. 6 batsman and team man.

KENT v MIDDLESEX

At Canterbury, August 28, 29, 30, 31, 1991. Gatting, who on the first day had broken the little finger on his left hand, also suffered a scalded chest. The second injury occurred at lunch on the third day, when a waitress spilled a pot of tea over him.

INDIAN CRICKET'S MOST SHAMEFUL MOMENT 1990-91

In the final of the nation's premier tournament, the Duleep Trophy, the violent action, senseless yet far from unprovoked, of Rashid Patel of West Zone, who went after Raman Lamba of North Zone, stump in hand, will be remembered as the most shameful moment in the history of Indian cricket. It occurred on the final afternoon of the five-day match in Jamshedpur, after Patel had come down the pitch to aim a head-high full toss at the batsman, Lamba. Patel and Lamba were banned for 13 and ten months respectively. The sequel to the violence on the pitch was a riot in the crowd, which resulted in the covers and anything else suitable being set alight, bringing the match to a premature conclusion.

SUSSEX v GLAMORGAN

Eastbourne, August 4, 5, 6, 1992. Glamorgan's visit to the Saffrons will be remembered mainly by umpire John Harris and a 74-year-old spectator, both of whom were hit on the head by the ball. Harris was struck by a throw from Maynard on the first day and took no further part in the match; Sussex's assistant secretary, Michael Charman, stood in until Roy Palmer arrived from a Second Eleven game at Hove. Then, on the final day, Moores crashed a six over long-on so hard that Tony Hone of Farnborough required stitches.

ESSEX v LEICESTERSHIRE

At Chelmsford, April 27, 28, 29, 30, 1995. A painful accident brought Whitticase's 114-run partnership with Millns to an abrupt end. In poor light, he lost sight of a ball from Williams and had seven teeth knocked out. Jack Birkenshaw, Leicestershire's cricket manager, said the umpires should have offered the light to the batsmen, and Whitticase was later reported to be seeking legal advice to recover the cost of his treatment [£2,000].

SUSSEX v GLOUCESTERSHIRE

At Hove, June 1, 2, 3, 5, 1995. During his first-innings 83, shots from Symonds twice hit the same spectator, a woman from Bristol. Having been struck in the face by a four, she returned from treatment only to be hit on the leg by a six.

MINOR COUNTIES 1995

Cornwall's season was marred by a horrific accident to their captain, Godfrey Furse, and his girlfriend, Valerie Stow, who were both badly burned when one of Furse's hot-dog vans exploded as they were clearing up the day after the NatWest Trophy tie with Middlesex at St Austell.

NOTTINGHAMSHIRE v LANCASHIRE

At Nottingham, May 16, 17, 18, 20, 1996. Gallian, his right arm in plaster after he broke a finger trying to take a catch, blocked out the final four deliveries from Afford as the fielders crowded round the bat. The real last man, Keedy, survived ten overs before that; had he gone sooner, Gallian would not have been risked and Notts would have won.

SURREY v DERBYSHIRE

At The Oval, May 30, 31, June 1, 3, 1996. Wells, requiring a runner after a severe foot injury, was too badly hurt to hobble back to the pavilion at tea on the final day, so groundstaff took a deckchair and a cup of tea to the middle for him, and Cork stayed to keep him company.

DERBYSHIRE 1997
Australian-born Matthew Cassar, in his first year after qualifying residentially, was unfortunate to damage ankle ligaments in April while practising with his wife Jane, the England women's team wicketkeeper. Not until late August was he fit enough to confirm his potential.

DERBYSHIRE v SOMERSET
At Derby, August 27, 28, 29, 30, 1997. Rollins involuntarily moved his left pad with his bat as he played forward to Shine and the ball struck his unprotected kneecap. The resulting fracture ended his season, although he did return in this innings to bat with a runner.

EUROPEAN NATIONS CUP 1997
France retained the Nations Cup at Zuoz, Switzerland, in astonishing circumstances. They beat Germany by one run in a pulsating 50-over final. The unwitting hero was France's last man, David Bordes, who was hit on the forehead, and staggered through for a single at the end of the French innings before collapsing with a fractured skull. He had to spend the next two weeks in hospital, and was ill for some time but, happily, was able to resume playing indoor cricket before Christmas. Bordes normally bats with a helmet but did not bother this time because he had only the one ball to face.

KENT 2003
A week before the opening game, the captain, David Fulton, was hit on the right eye by a 90mph delivery from a bowling machine. The blow scarred his retina and threatened his career – but he returned by the end of May, having regained half his sight in the damaged eye.

DERBYSHIRE 2005
Graeme Welch was, as ever, a model professional. Not much keeps him out of action, but he suffered the season's oddest injury when his son, practising John Travolta-style disco dancing, jabbed him in the eye.

SOMERSET v SURREY (totesport League)
At Taunton, May 2, 2005. Ramprakash, after dislocating his toe on the pavilion steps fetching a cup of tea, batted at No. 7 and scored 11.

KENT v GLAMORGAN
At Canterbury, August 3, 4, 5, 2005. Stevens hit one six, which sent pints flying in the CAMRA real-ale tent. Kemp, meanwhile, launched a six into the president's marquee, felling waitress Danielle Weston-Webb; he presented her with the autographed ball next day.

SURREY v KENT

At Guildford, July 20, 21, 22, 23, 2005. Defeat so angered Jimmy Ormond that he punched the home dressing-room door and fractured his right hand, which kept him out of the next four matches.

ENGLAND LIONS v NEW ZEALANDERS

At Southampton, May 8, 9, 10, 11, 2008. The match's third hundred came from Carberry, who was stretchered off with severe cramp after celebrating the landmark with a leap in the air.

SOMERSET v NORTHAMPTONSHIRE (Twenty20 Cup)

At Taunton, June 11, 2008. Ben Phillips, after suffering concussion when part of a bowling machine fell on his head, was unavailable.

DERBYSHIRE 2010

Tom Lungley's campaign – and, it later transpired, his 11-season career with his home county – came to an end when his arm was broken by his batting partner Steffan Jones as they tried to win the match against Surrey at Chesterfield at the beginning of July.

LANCASHIRE v WARWICKSHIRE (Clydesdale Bank 40 semi-final)

At Manchester, September 1, 2012. Troughton snapped up four catches, and his only frustration was losing Ambrose to a bizarre thigh strain, picked up when – from the comfort of his chair as he waited to bat – he extended his leg on the dressing-room balcony.

KEEPING IT IN THE FAMILY

SURREY v NOTTINGHAMSHIRE

At Kennington Oval, August 3, 4, 5, 1891. In Arthur Shrewsbury's absence a place was given to the veteran batsman, Richard Daft, who had not been seen in the Nottinghamshire eleven since the season of 1881, but was at this time nearly 56 years old. As H. B. Daft was also playing for Notts the remarkable spectacle was presented of father and son appearing in the same county team. Such a thing, to the best of our knowledge, has not been seen in first-class cricket since old William Lillywhite and his son John played together.

SOMERSET v SUSSEX

At Taunton, August 6, 7, 8, 1896. Some extremely fine batting was witnessed on the part of the brothers Palairet, who were partners for two hours and threequarters, and put on 249 runs. Lionel Palairet's 154 was a faultless display, including 26 fours, but Richard Palairet's 156 was marred by two or three sharp chances. Against Middlesex in the previous season, both brothers in the same innings made over 100 runs.

OBITUARIES 1980
DENTON, WILLIAM HERBERT, the last survivor of three brothers who played together for Northamptonshire, died on April 23, 1979, aged 88. He and his identical twin, J. S., who between them caused endless confusion to spectators and scorers, first appeared in 1909. By 1912, when the county, calling upon only 12 players in the Championship, came second, they had become essential members of the side. In 1913 both exceeded 1,000 runs and, from August that year until cricket was stopped by the War, they formed the regular opening pair. Both were taken prisoner in the closing months of the War and J. S. played little county cricket afterwards, but W. H., after a few appearances between 1919 and 1923, resumed a regular place for the season of 1924. When Northamptonshire played Somerset in 1914, the Denton twins opened for Northamptonshire and the Rippon twins, A. D. E. and A. E. S., for Somerset – an occurrence unique in first-class cricket.

DERBYSHIRE v WARWICKSHIRE
At Derby, June 3, 5, 1922. At one time the two Quaifes were opposed by the two Bestwicks. For father and son to be batting against bowlers similarly related was a remarkable incident.

Obituary 1985: BESTWICK, ROBERT SAXTON, who died in Jersey on July 3, 1980, aged 80, will be remembered for an incident which one can safely say is unique in first-class cricket. For some ten minutes he bowled at one end while his father, the much better-known Bill Bestwick, bowled at the other, against W. G. Quaife and his son, B. W.

OBITUARIES 1957
GUNN, GEORGE VERNON, who died in hospital at Shrewsbury on October 15, 1957, aged 52, as the result of injuries received in a motor-cycle accident, played for Nottinghamshire from 1928 to 1939, scoring in that time just over 10,000 runs and taking close upon 300 wickets. In 1931 he scored 100 not out – his first century – against Warwickshire at Edgbaston and in the same innings his father, George Gunn, then 53, hit 183. This, it is believed, is the only instance of a father and son each reaching three figures in the same first-class match.

SURREY v OXFORD UNIVERSITY
At Kennington Oval, June 21, 22, 23, 1939. For Surrey, the Bedser twins made their first appearance in a first-class match. Eric created a fine impression while staying nearly an hour, but the pitch afforded Alec no chance of proving his ability as a bowler. These two tall, dark boys resembled each other so closely that it was impossible to distinguish them, especially when they fielded together in the slips!

SURREY v SOMERSET
At The Oval, May 18, 20, 21, 1946. Surrey did not gain the upper hand until Tuesday morning, when the Bedser twins, Eric wearing a cap to distinguish him from Alec, enjoyed their first partnership.

LANCASHIRE v MIDDLESEX
At Liverpool, July 13, 14, 15, 1955. G. A. Edrich, hitting two sixes and 11 fours, celebrated his birthday by helping Lancashire to recover from an indifferent start, but he owed much to his brother, W. J. Edrich, who dropped him when seven and 70.

DERBYSHIRE v NOTTINGHAMSHIRE
At Ilkeston, July 26, 28, 29, 1958. Derbyshire always held the initiative in this match, in which A. E. G. Rhodes stood as umpire while his son, H. J., played for Derbyshire.

NORTHAMPTONSHIRE v LEICESTERSHIRE
At Northampton, August 22, 23, 24, 1973. In two high-scoring first-innings, good centuries were hit by the Steele brothers, John of Leicestershire and David of Northamptonshire.

SURREY v ESSEX (Benson and Hedges Cup quarter-final)
At The Oval, June 9, 1976. John Edrich received the Gold Award, judged by his cousin, Bill Edrich.

YORKSHIRE v NOTTINGHAMSHIRE
At Bradford, August 7, 9, 10, 1976. When Smedley and Stead were together in Nottinghamshire's second innings all 15 men on the field were Yorkshiremen, both umpires [H. D. Bird and R. Aspinall] being former Yorkshire players.

OXFORD UNIVERSITY v CAMBRIDGE UNIVERSITY
At Lord's, June 26, 28, 29, 1982. John Varey, bowling for Oxford, gave the 1982 match another place in history by taking the wicket of his twin brother, David.

DERBYSHIRE 1992
In the final match, at Cardiff, Alastair Richardson created history as the third generation to represent Derbyshire. His grandfather, Arthur, led them to the 1936 Championship and his father, William, played from 1959 to 1965.

OBITUARIES 1998
TOWNSEND, DAVID CHARLES HUMPHERY, who died on January 27, 1997, aged 84, was the last man to play cricket for England without ever playing for a first-class county. Townsend was picked for the 1934-35 tour of the West Indies on the strength of his form for Oxford University. He played, opening each time with Bob Wyatt, in the last three Tests of the series, and top-scored with 36 in the second innings of his debut when England were all out for 107. But his highest score otherwise was 16. The Townsends were a cricketing dynasty: six members of the family have played first-class cricket, including David's grandfather Frank, his father Charles, and his son Jonathan; Charles Townsend also played two Tests, in 1899. No other family is known to have produced four generations of first-class cricketers. Thereafter, he went back to Norton-on-Tees, County Durham, where he was born and died, and took over the family law firm in Stockton. He practised as a solicitor for more than 50 years and played for the Norton club and Durham, whom he captained from 1937 to 1947.

CRICKET PEOPLE 2003: Wedded to the game

For the second year running, the official scorers for the Oval Test were a married couple – Keith Booth, the regular Surrey scorer, and his wife Jennifer, who is actually the senior scorer of the two. She met Keith at Reading University in the 1960s, when he played for the university team and she kept the scorecards.

LANCASHIRE v NORTHAMPTONSHIRE (totesport League)

At Manchester, June 25, 2004. Graeme Swann was caught by his elder brother Alec to complete a pair of symmetrical dismissals: Alec had earlier been caught by Graeme.

NEW ZEALAND v AUSTRALIA (Third Test Match)

At Auckland, March 26, 27, 28, 29, 2005. Although they drafted in a batsman for his Test debut, there was no new face in the New Zealand side: in came James Marshall, near enough indistinguishable from his brother, Hamish. The Marshalls were Test cricket's second set of twins after the Waugh brothers, but the first identical pair. It also had the potential advantage of confusing the Australians; even the twins' father said he had problems telling them apart dressed in whites, so it was understandable when, before the Test, Ponting admitted he had no idea how his bowlers would distinguish one from the other should the Marshalls bat together. That moment arrived inside the first 30 minutes after Gillespie removed Cumming. In fact, the brothers did their bit to aid the Australians by just one of them (James) using a forearm guard, and, on a funereal first day, twin-spotting was about as exciting as it got.

IRELAND v ENGLAND (One-Day International)

At Stormont, Belfast, June 13, 2006. The happiest of a delirious full house of 7,000 appeared to be James Joyce – not the author of *Ulysses* but the father of Dublin-born Ed, who made his debut for England, and Ireland's Dominick, who opened the batting for their respective sides.

KENYA v BANGLADESH (Second one-day international)

At Nairobi Gymkhana, August 13, 2006. Kenya's Hitesh Modi was given out lbw by his father, umpire Subhash Modi, who proudly admitted afterwards: "Yes, I gave my son out – and I gave him out in the first match too, caught bat and pad."

ESSEX v NEW ZEALANDERS

At Chelmsford, May 2, 3, 4, 5, 2008. On the opening day, James Marshall scored an entertaining 128 while, 140 miles away in Bristol, his twin Hamish was striking 105 for Gloucestershire.

REED v WOODHOUSE GRANGE (Yorkshire Tea Village Cup final)

At Lord's, September 9, 2012. The match included six pairs of brothers – three on each side.

Woodhouse Grange: A. J. Bilton, C. R. Bilton, M. N. Burdett, S. D. Burdett, C. J. Suddaby, D. A. Suddaby.

Reed: J. A. Heslam, W. J. Heslam, K. J. Ward, K. L. Ward, J. P. Tidey, S. W. Tidey.

NUMBER CRUNCHING

LEICESTERSHIRE v NOTTINGHAMSHIRE
At Leicester, July 16, 18, 19, 1927. All ten Leicestershire wickets were clean-bowled at the same end by the fast bowlers [Larwood and Barratt] who had identical averages [5 wickets for 20 runs].

WARWICKSHIRE v NORTHAMPTONSHIRE
At Birmingham, July 14, 16, 17, 1934. This match, which Warwickshire won by nine wickets, was rendered noteworthy by two opening three-figure stands in one day for the same county. Bakewell and Snowden for Northamptonshire on Monday morning scored 119 together before the next nine wickets went down for 45 runs, and later in the day the two men took part in a partnership which produced 121.

WORCESTERSHIRE v AUSTRALIANS
At Worcester, April 30, May 2, 3, 1938. McCormick, the fast bowler, repeatedly went over the crease and during his first three overs was no-balled 19 times by umpire Baldwin. His first over actually comprised 14 balls and the second over 15. In the match, McCormick was no-balled 35 times.

SUSSEX v KENT
At Hastings, August 10, 12, 13, 1946. The two matches at Hastings – the County Week – realised a net profit of £1066 after paying all expenses and entertainment tax. The coincidence of the figure and the date of the Battle of Hastings inspired some humorous comment!

WORCESTERSHIRE v WARWICKSHIRE
At Dudley, May 4, 6, 7, 1957. The end became an anticlimax. Horton hit a boundary in the final over for the only scoring stroke during the last hour, when 24 successive maidens were sent down.

OXFORD UNIVERSITY v DERBYSHIRE
At Oxford, May 30, 31, June 1, 1962. Though Derbyshire won easily enough, the highlight of the match occurred when Manasseh became the first Oxford bowler to hit the stumps in 1962. Manasseh ended an unhappy sequence when he bowled Oates with the 3,992nd ball sent down by 15 Oxford bowlers.

HAMPSHIRE v KENT
At Portsmouth, June 10, 11, 12, 1970. The Kent first-innings total was boosted considerably by 40 extras, to which Holder was the major contributor with 12 wides and 19 no-balls. He bowled one over of 12 balls, which, incredibly, was a maiden. In the match overall he bowled 16 wides and 22 no-balls.

KENT v LEICESTERSHIRE (John Player League)
At Folkestone, July 18, 1971. McKenzie was no-balled eight times in an over, which contained 14 deliveries, under the front-foot rule by Alley, the Australian-born

umpire. Denness struck six fours and a two, five of the no-balls registered, and the total had jumped dramatically by 31 runs at the end of the over.

SURREY v SUSSEX
At The Oval, May 7, 8, 9, 1980. At the start of the second day, Imran Khan gave Surrey a boost. Their first 20 runs came from 13 byes, six wides and one no ball, all but one of them accountable to the Pakistani fast bowler as he found lots of pace but little length or direction.

TWO TIMES TEN
Andy Langston, an opening bowler for the Alexandra Park club in North London, performed a remarkable double feat inside one week in June 1988. On June 18, playing for Buckingham Palace, his former employer, he took all ten wickets for 59 in 20.3 overs against the Royal Household at Windsor Great Park. Five days later, on June 23, playing for Alexandra Park in a match celebrating their centenary, he took all ten wickets for 77 in 25.1 overs against a Club Cricket Conference President's XI.

NOTTINGHAMSHIRE v WARWICKSHIRE
At Nottingham, September 16, 17, 18, 20, 1993. Ratcliffe suffered a double misfortune. He was run out backing up when Moles's drive was deflected on to the stumps at the non-striker's end, leaving him one short of 1,000 first-class runs for the season.

SOMERSET v LANCASHIRE
At Taunton, July 27, 28, 29, 1995. Lancashire reached their six-run target when Gallian hit Bowler's first delivery, a no-ball, for four, to give him a baffling bowling analysis [0–0–6–0].

KENT v LANCASHIRE
At Canterbury, May 2, 3, 4, 6, 1996. Wooden-spoon holders Kent produced an unexpected victory shortly after five o'clock on a gorgeous bank-holiday afternoon. It was their first Championship win for 11 months and the first time in 23 seasons they had won their opening game.

WORCESTERSHIRE v SUSSEX (AXA League)
At Worcester, May 19, 1998. A stirring, if confusing, performance by brothers Keith and Mark Newell took Sussex to a comfortable win. They added 181 for the second wicket, but Keith had his century snatched away after it had been applauded. First, he lost two runs because an umpire's signal was amended from six to four, and then three more after a mix-up was sorted out and a scoring stroke was switched to brother Mark. But it was Keith's day, hundred or no hundred. Bowling third change, he took five for 33 as Worcestershire collapsed.

DURHAM v SUSSEX
At Chester-le-Street, July 18, 19, 20, 21, 2001. In Durham's first innings, it took three bowlers to deliver one over: Lewry was injured after two balls, Robinson was removed for running down the pitch and Adams completed it.

SUSSEX v NOTTINGHAMSHIRE

At Horsham, May 21, 22, 23, 24, 2003. History was made at Cricketfield Road when Innes became the first twelfth man in first-class cricket to score a century. Under new ECB regulations, Kirtley, released from England's squad, could replace a nominated player. But before Kirtley could arrive from Lord's, his replacement, Innes, was needed at the crease. He made a thoroughly deserved maiden hundred as Sussex piled up 619 on the second morning. Kirtley was there in time to see his alter ego reach 100. The situation was so unusual that the ECB computers – and at least one daily paper – credited the runs to Kirtley, who did take over in the field.

YORKSHIRE v GLAMORGAN (National League)

At Leeds, May 25, 2003. Sidebottom ended the match with figures of 0.1–0–11–0: after bowling two wides, one short ball hooked for six, and three more leg-side wides, he retired with a tight hamstring.

MIDDLESEX v LEICESTERSHIRE

At Southgate, July 9, 10, 11, 12, 2003. Only two members of the Middlesex team, Nash and Weekes, were born in the UK, a statistic repeated in two further Championship games in 2003.

GLAMORGAN v KENT (totesport League)

At Cardiff, August 29, 2004. Kent won an amazing victory when Ian Butler hit the last ball for six, the only shot that would do. It was a disaster for one poor (or maybe greedy) punter. After they lost their ninth wicket, a Kent win was being traded at odds of 999-1 on the betting exchange Betfair. Several happy punters collected, but one customer is known to have been on the wrong end, and lost £49,950 trying to win £50.

KENT v NOTTINGHAMSHIRE

At Canterbury, September 14, 15, 16, 17, 2005. Gallian dominated the innings until, pressing for quick runs, he risked a fourth to the lime-tree boundary. For the second time in the season, he ran himself out for 199. This made him not merely the only player in history to be run out twice on 199, but the only one with two 199s in a career.

WARWICKSHIRE v MIDDLESEX

At Birmingham, April 27, 28, 29, 30, 2005. Styris scored a remarkable 53, comprising 13 fours and one single. No previous case of someone reaching a first-class fifty with 13 fours has yet been found.

CRICKET IN NEW ZEALAND 2006-07

Auckland pulled off a Houdini-class escape in the Twenty20 league: to beat Northern Districts, they needed 12 from the final ball. Their chances looked a shade thin – but Aldridge's sixth delivery was a chest-high full toss, costing two for a no-ball plus four as it ran to the boundary. Andre Adams blithely hit the next ball for six.

OXFORD UCCE v MIDDLESEX

At Oxford, April 14, 15, 16, 2007. Nash completed his eighth first-class century for Middlesex – his first for nearly three years – in unusual circumstances. The scoreboard showed him as out for 98, but Nash strode over to the scorers and told them they had missed a swept four off Nick Woods. The umpires agreed, and Nash got his hundred.

DERBYSHIRE v LEICESTERSHIRE

At Derby, May 9, 10, 11, 12, 2007. Derbyshire included eight left-handed batsmen, Taylor, Pipe and Wagg being the exceptions.

The left-handers were S. D. Stubbings, W. P. C. Weston, S. M. Katich, T. R. Birt, A. G. Botha, T. Lungley, K. J. Dean, W. B. Rankin.

DERBYSHIRE v GLOUCESTERSHIRE: HALF A MILLION TO ONE

At Derby, June 5, 6, 7, 8, 2007. When Simon Katich called correctly on the morning of June 5, Derbyshire won the toss for the 19th game in succession. (This includes all senior games stretching back to September 2006: County Championship, Pro40, Twenty20 Floodlit Cup and the Friends Provident Trophy.) The sequence ended in their next game, against Lancashire on June 10. The odds against winning 19 successive tosses are more than half a million to one against (524,288–1, to be precise). Until the second half of the 20th century, the result of the toss was not always reliably recorded, but Derbyshire's run of fortune is believed to be a record, beating the 15 successive correct calls by the Bangladeshi side, Khulna, in the 2005-06 season. The longest sequence of losing the toss is believed to be 14, by Sussex from 1899 to 1900, though this includes three occasions when the result of the toss is conjecture.

SURREY v GLAMORGAN

At The Oval, May 24, 25, 26, 27, 2011. The Surrey fielders were wayward, with over-throws contributing a five and seven to Petersen's 210 (he also hit 24 fours and a six, eventually recording every scoring shot from one to seven).

ZIMBABWE v NEW ZEALAND (Third One-Day International)

At Bulawayo, October 25, 2011. Williamson followed his captain to three figures, despite being on 93 as the debutant Njabulo Ncube prepared to bowl the final delivery of the innings. It proved to be a high full-toss – and thus a no-ball – which Williamson top-edged over short third man for four. With Ncube now removed from the attack as he had bowled another beamer earlier, Williamson hit Chigumbura over mid-off and scampered back for three.

SUSSEX v GLOUCESTERSHIRE (Friends Provident t20)

At Hove, July 24, 2012. The first delivery of the 18th over, from James Fuller, was a beamer that sped to the fence for six no-balls; the second a front-foot no-ball that Styris belted for four; and the third – a free hit – he lofted for six. One legitimate ball had yielded 18 runs. The remaining five (including a dot) produced another 20, making it the most expensive over in Twenty20 history.

TRANSPORTS OF FRUSTRATION

KENT v SURREY
At Mote Park, August 22, 23, 24, 1872. The Surrey eleven travelled from Brighton to Maidstone on the morning of the commencement of this match; railway delays caused them to arrive late at Mote Park, where they commenced the batting so disastrously that they lost their first four wickets for five runs.

KENT, with Mr W. G. Grace and Mr A. W. Ridley, v ENGLAND
At Canterbury, August 6, 7, 8, 1877. Bank-holiday emergencies prevented the Railway men coming up to time at Canterbury that morning, and when at 12.25 Kent began the batting, Mr W. Grace, Watson, and others had not arrived.

GLOUCESTERSHIRE v NORTHAMPTONSHIRE
At Cheltenham, August 21, 22, 23, 1911. Owing to the railway strike the Northampton cricketers journeyed to Cheltenham by motor cars.

SOMERSET v YORKSHIRE
At Taunton, September 1, 3, 4, 1923. It was not possible to start play on Tuesday until 20 minutes past 12. Holmes and Sutcliffe sent up 62 together, and the end was soon reached. Owing to a motor accident, Bridges did not arrive on the ground till the match was over.

WARWICKSHIRE v HAMPSHIRE
At Birmingham, May 8, 10, 11, 1926. Consequent upon the troubles arising from the General Strike, Hampshire, when the time arrived for the commencement of their match with Warwickshire, found themselves with only eight men. They won the toss and, as the players present included all their bowlers, the captain, with the possibility existing of his side having to bat three short, decided to give Warwickshire first innings. At that moment it was not certain who would complete the visiting team. These proved to be Bowell, Kneller, and Gibbons. It was in the irony of things that, after being sent especially to Birmingham to fill the vacancies, they took no part in the match. They did not arrive in time for play on Saturday, and rain prevented any cricket on Monday and Tuesday.

MISCELLANY 1938
Leicestershire players were delayed on a train journey to Northampton on August Bank Holiday and three of the home eleven fielded as substitutes.

KENT v YORKSHIRE
At Dover, August 20, 22, 23, 1949. After spending ten hours in trains and not reaching their Folkestone headquarters until nearly four in the morning, Yorkshire shaped like a tired side on the opening day.

KENT v MIDDLESEX
At Tunbridge Wells, June 15, 17, 18, 1963. The late arrival on Monday morning of nine of the Middlesex team, including Drybrough, the captain, provided a situation

without parallel in the history of first-class cricket. At the close on Saturday, Middlesex, having dismissed Kent for 150, were 121 for three wickets with White 43 not out, Hooker 13 not out. The team had stayed at a local hotel on Friday night and arranged to do the same on Monday night, but they returned to their London homes at the weekend.

Three players arrived at the ground with plenty of time to spare. They were White and S. E. Russell, who had already been dismissed, and Clark, the twelfth man. White put on his pads and gloves and waited on the boundary, hoping his partner would be in time while the umpires and the Kent players went to the middle. After a wait of a liberal two minutes, the umpires led the players off the field and it was officially stated that the umpires had closed the Middlesex innings.

It was decided that Kent should begin their second innings within ten minutes, and Cowdrey agreed that Clark could keep wicket while if necessary White and S. E. Russell shared the bowling, Kent providing sufficient substitute fielders to make up 11 in the field for Middlesex. Actually, Underwood, Catt, Prodger, Brown and Dye assisted their opponents, but within three overs the whole Middlesex side were present and fielding.

SURREY v KENT
At The Oval, June 12, 13, 14, 2002. As play should have been resuming on the second day, Kent had two players at The Oval and ten stuck in traffic: a burst water-main in Buckingham Palace Road, roadworks and an accident had conspired to cause gridlock. The umpires spoke to Alan Fordham, the ECB cricket operations manager, and decided to delay the start and make up lost time later. Play began 90 minutes late, with Kent forced to field a twelfth man until 1.30, when Patel, whose BMW had overheated, finally arrived.

HAMPSHIRE v YORKSHIRE (Cheltenham & Gloucester Trophy semi-final)
At Southampton, August 20, 2005. Yorkshire had been playing an enervating Roses match in Manchester, which finished late the previous evening and prevented them from reaching their Southampton hotel until after midnight. And next morning, with the team assembled for an 8.30 departure to the Rose Bowl, the coach driver was unable to leave for another hour because health and safety regulations made it mandatory for him to have a nine-hour break between stints at the wheel. Finding a long backlog of vehicles on the only road to the ground, the players then had to walk the last mile among 9,000 spectators. Some hitched lifts; captain Craig White jogged and, on arrival, had to ask the umpires to delay the start by 15 minutes.

LANCASHIRE v MIDDLESEX (Clydesdale Bank 40)
At Manchester, July 16, 2012. Middlesex were denied the services of Eoin Morgan, who chose to travel separately by train and got caught in severe delays on the London–Manchester line. He found an alternative route via York, and arrived at the ground shortly after the scheduled 4.40pm start – but by then he had missed the toss and been replaced in the side by Ollie Rayner. Middlesex did not discipline him.

UNUSUAL FIXTURES

TWENTY-TWO OF OTAGO v THE ENGLAND ELEVEN
At Dunedin, February 16, 17, and 18, 1864. The Eleven winning in one innings and 51 runs.

Having time on hand at Otago, the following foot races were run.

	Distance Run	Winners
Jackson v Tinley	100 yards	Jackson, by a yard
Caffyn v Caesar	100 yards	Caesar, won easily
Mr Grace v Holmes	¼ mile	Holmes won as he liked
Hayward v Mr Wills	100 yards	Hayward, by a yard
Mr Grace v Tarrant	600 yards	Tarrant, by six yards
Anderson v Jones	100 yards	Two dead heats
English Eleven Handicap	120 yards	Caffyn (9 yards start)
Caffyn v Jackson	100 yards	Caffyn
Hurdle Race	about 620 yards	Tarrant
Mr Wardill v Mr Grace	100 yards	Mr Wardill

Throwing the Cricket Ball – Mr Grace won; distance thrown, 101 yards.

Time on their hands: the England touring team to Australia and New Zealand 1863-64.
Back row (from left): J. Caesar, A. Clarke, G. Tarrant, G. Parr, E.M. Grace, R. Carpenter, G. Anderson, W. Caffyn. Front row: R. C. Tinley, T. Lockyer, T. Hayward, J. Jackson

GOVERNMENT v OPPOSITION
At Lord's, Saturday, July 29, 1893. A match between Members of Parliament representing respectively the Government and Opposition was played, but did not prove the attraction expected. However, the weather was most unfavourable. The Opposition, which included several well-known cricketers, won very easily, declaring their innings at an end when three wickets had fallen for 243 runs.

YORKSHIRE v NOTTINGHAMSHIRE (Time-limit match)
At Leeds, May 2, 3, 4, 1904. This was a match arranged to try a time-limit scheme, the chief conditions of which were that each innings should be limited to four hours and a quarter, with the qualification that time lost on innings one and two was to be equally deducted from innings three and four; time saved on the first two innings being added to the third and fourth innings. The result was to be determined by the runs scored irrespective of the number of wickets lost. Unfortunately, the course of the play prevented the special regulations being really tested, the match ending early on the third morning, in a victory for Yorkshire by 71 runs. The game, the main object of which was, of course, to render play more attractive, quite failed from that point of view, the attendance proving meagre to a degree.

SURREY v OXFORD UNIVERSITY
At Reigate, June 21, 22, 21, 1909. Arranging to meet Oxford on the same days that they were playing Lancashire, Surrey, of course, could only place a second eleven in the field at Reigate, and the team, led by John Shuter, the famous Surrey captain of the 1880s, suffered defeat by an innings and 98 runs.

REFLECTIONS by E. (Patsy) Hendren   1938
A funny thing once happened to me when on an MCC tour in Australia. Between fixtures, I was journeying into the Bush by motor-car with a colleague when we stopped to watch a cricket match. One of the players, unaware of our identity, approached and asked if, as his team was a man short, one of us would play. I had already been in the field for two and a half days, but I yielded to persuasion and, rigged out in borrowed gear, was put in the deep field at the bottom of a pronounced slope, from where I could see nothing at all of the cricket. For hour after hour I fielded there, throwing the ball back at intervals until, at long last, I caught one. I ran to the top of the hill and announced with some satisfaction that I had made a catch. To my consternation, I was informed that the other team's innings had closed and that I had caught one of my own side!

MIDDLESEX v NOTTINGHAMSHIRE
At Kennington Oval, July 15, 17, 18, 1939. Surrey lent The Oval because Lord's was engaged by Eton and Harrow on the Saturday.

SURREY v HAMPSHIRE
At Guildford, June 26, 27, 1957. The match was over by three o'clock on the second afternoon. Afterwards the teams staged an exhibition game, the last half-hour of which was watched by the Queen and the Duke of Edinburgh. They were visiting Guildford as part of the town's celebrations of the 700th anniversary of the granting

of its first known charter by King Henry III. During a break in play the teams and officials were presented to the Royal visitors.

YORKSHIRE v CAMBRIDGESHIRE (Gillette Cup)
At Castleford, May 25, 1967. Yorkshire won by six wickets. The match became a desperate improvisation reduced to ten overs for each side after play had been impossible on any of the three days originally allocated. Assembling at Headingley on the new date range, the teams found the ground under water, and when they moved to Castleford, some 12 miles away, they met further frustration through a thunderstorm. Honouring the agreement that a result would be obtained whatever the conditions, Cambridgeshire fielded in drenching rain and the cricket verged on the farcical, though some notable catches were held.

Cambridgeshire 43-8 (10 overs) (A. G. Nicholson 3-11);
Yorkshire 46-4 (6.5 overs).

24-HOUR MARATHON AT CAMBRIDGE
Something unique for cricket took place on June 14–15 1973 at Parker's Piece, Cambridge. At 5pm on June 14 two sides comprised of members of the Cambridge University Cricket Society took the field, and at 5pm the following day the same 22 players left the field having played cricket continuously, except for a "lunch" break, to MCC Laws for 24 hours. As well as creating a new world record for continuous cricket the effort raised over £170 for charity.

Each side had five innings in the match and a total of 1,395 runs were scored off 367 overs. During the hours of darkness gas lights illuminated the playing area, and light-coloured cricket balls, specially prepared by Alfred Reader, were used.

In the period of darkness between 1am and 4am Roger Coates scored the only century of the match. Though the light was adequate the captains, Peter Such and David Langley, agreed to suspend fast bowling during the night on the grounds of safety.
The players included A. S. I. [Scyld] Berry, editor of Wisden *2008–11.*

MIDDLESEX v COMBINED UNIVERSITIES (Benson and Hedges Cup)
At Lord's, May 14, 15, 1987. This fixture was unique in a knockout competition, for the teams began three matches yet could not finish. The first day was lost. A 54-over-a-side game achieved only 14 overs in which Combined Universities scored 31 for two. In the afternoon a 25 overs-a-side game managed 17 overs with Middlesex, put in, making 113 for one (Slack 57 not out). The last resort was the minimum ten-overs dash, but rain arrived again in the fifth over.

GLAMORGAN v GLOUCESTERSHIRE
At Swansea, July 4, 5, 7, 1987. The first two days were played on Saturday and Sunday and the third on Tuesday. Monday featured a match between the counties under Sunday League regulations, watched by the Prince of Wales (patron of Glamorgan) and Princess (patron of Gloucestershire) to launch Glamorgan's centenary celebrations.

LANCASHIRE v HAMPSHIRE (Benson and Hedges Cup)
At Manchester, May 8, 9, 1990. No result. After rain and bad light had interrupted Hampshire's reply to Lancashire's 352 for six on the second day, the umpires ruled that there was not sufficient time to complete the match under the playing conditions and another of 18 overs a side was started. However, torrential rain and bad light again intervened and at 7.15pm this game, too, was called off. In the original match, which was subsequently declared void, Lancashire's total would have been a record for the competition and a county record in limited-overs cricket.

HERTFORDSHIRE v DERBYSHIRE (NatWest Bank Trophy first round)
At Bishop's Stortford, June 26, 27, 1991. Hertfordshire won 2–1 in a bowling contest, after the match was abandoned. At 4.15pm on the second day the "bowl-out" was used for the first time in this competition to achieve a result. Five players from each team were required to bowl two deliveries each at a wicket (three stumps) on the Hertfordshire pitch. Derbyshire bowled first, and Goldsmith scored the only hit, with their ninth delivery; Hertfordshire's former Middlesex players, Needham and Merry, then won the match for the Minor County with four deliveries to spare.

EARL OF CARNARVON'S XI v SOUTH AFRICANS
At Highclere, June 23, 1994. The South Africans played their first official match in England for 29 years amid the curiously old-fashioned atmosphere of country-house cricket. The Queen attended the exclusive gathering at Highclere Castle and 2,000 other spectators paid £25 a head, raising £30,000 for the National Playing Fields Association, with South African township cricket among the beneficiaries. However, the emphasis was on corporate hospitality, and there were complaints that the public had found it difficult to get tickets. The tourists also had problems: they arrived late because of traffic jams.
Highclere found later fame as the setting for the popular television drama Downton Abbey.

HIMACHAL PRADESH v TRIPURA (Ranji Trophy, Plate Group A)
At HPCA Stadium, Dharmasala, December 1, 2, 3, 4, 2005. Abandoned. Two Himachal Pradesh teams, selected by rival factions of the HPCA, attempted to take the field; the referee decided to recognise the side representing the Pawar-supporting faction, but the match was called off after their officials claimed the Dalmiya supporters had damaged the pitch.
Sharad Pawar had just replaced Jagmohan Dalimya as president of the Board of Control for Cricket in India.

AIR FORCE v SEEDUWA RADDOLUWA (Sri Lanka Premier League Tier B)
At Air Force Ground, Colombo, January 2, 17, 18, 2009. A bomb explosion near the ground on January 3 injured one Seeduwa player and damaged the eardrums of three others; there was a two-week delay before the match was resumed.

WEATHER WATCH

PHEW, WHAT A SCORCHER!
Notwithstanding those three days of July 1878 included "St Swithin", the weather throughout was magnificent for cricket, being dry, bright, and so hot, that on Tuesday (the 16th) the sun bubbled up the quicksilver to 130, and on the Wednesday the public papers recorded the heat indicator at Wimbledon having reached 144. P-h-e-w! It almost makes one perspire to think of those baking hot days.

KENT v WORCESTERSHIRE
At Tonbridge, June 12, 14, 1920. An astonishing thunderstorm, lasting only ten minutes but followed by heavy rain, cut play short at 3 o'clock on the Saturday. Kent had made 169 for five wickets when the storm broke with hurricane force, stripping the canvas off a stand and soaking the spectators, the ground being enveloped in the deluge.

YORKSHIRE v MIDDLESEX
At Bradford, May, 12, 14, 15, 1923. The weather was very ungenial, snow-showers curtailing Saturday's play by about 50 minutes.

NOTTINGHAMSHIRE v DERBYSHIRE
At Nottingham, August 6, 8, 9, 1927. There was a remarkable occurrence on Monday when, with the ground practically flooded at noon, it was officially announced at one o'clock that all idea of play had been abandoned. The Derbyshire captain, as it happened, had not been consulted on the matter, and the weather clearing after lunch, he requested the umpires to wait. Those officials, late in the afternoon, pronounced the pitch fit for cricket, and the Notts players having been gathered together again, nearly an hour's play took place.

WORCESTERSHIRE v WARWICKSHIRE
At Worcester, August 15, 17, 18, 1931. Warwickshire resumed under strange conditions on Monday, a belt of floodwater covering part of the playing field which had to be curtailed in this particular direction by some 25 yards.

LEICESTERSHIRE v HAMPSHIRE
At Leicester, August 16, 17, 18, 1933. Clouds of dust caused much discomfort to the batsmen, and the game was frequently interrupted owing to the bails falling off the stumps. After tea, much time having been wasted in trying to keep the bails in position, the umpires agreed to do without them. Consequently when the ball appeared to touch the stumps both Dawson and Shipman got the benefit of the doubt. Dawson, however, obviously playing on, a united appeal was upheld.

NOTTINGHAMSHIRE v GLOUCESTERSHIRE
At Nottingham, May 11, 13, 14, 1935. After a snowstorm had interrupted play, rain before five o'clock prevented further cricket and the match was left drawn. Cold weather always handicapped the players.

ESSEX v SURREY
At Chelmsford, May 19, 20, 21, 1937. Nothing could be done on the last day when the swollen River Chelmer flooded the ground.

GLAMORGAN v HAMPSHIRE
At Swansea, July 10, 11, 12, 1946. On the second day cricket was held up by heat haze which enshrouded the ground.

YORKSHIRE v GLOUCESTERSHIRE
At Sheffield, July 8, 9, 10, 1953. At the start of the last day an astonishing phenomenon occurred, strips of ice four or five inches long falling near the players, who had to protect their heads with their hands.

ESSEX v GLAMORGAN
At Colchester, July 24, 26, 27, 1954. Rain and wind, which upset the sightscreen, blew numbers off the scoreboard and whipped off bails, interrupted the last day's play.

ESSEX v WORCESTERSHIRE
At Leyton, August 5, 7, 8, 1961. During the last day's play a high wind, which had wrecked tents, blew off the bails every few minutes, but the cricket was not seriously affected.

KENT v YORKSHIRE
At Gravesend, May 29, 30, 31, 1963. The weather during the game went from extreme to extreme. On the first day hot drinks were brought out to warm the players and on the second cold drinks were provided to cool them!

DERBYSHIRE v LANCASHIRE
At Buxton, May 31, June 2, 3, 1975. This was one of the heaviest defeats in County Championship history [Derbyshire lost by an innings and 348 runs] and certainly one of the most remarkable games. No play was possible on June 2 because of snow which covered the ground to a depth of an inch.

MIDDLESEX v YORKSHIRE
At Lord's, August 13, 14, 15, 1975. The character of the match was altered dramatically by a thunderstorm of almost unparalleled violence which ended play 70 minutes early [on the second day] and did not permit a resumption until 2.30 on the final day.

CAMBRIDGE UNIVERSITY v ESSEX
At Cambridge, April 22, 23, 24, 1981. After an hour and a quarter on the third morning, the umpires called a halt, considering it unreasonable and dangerous to continue because of the extreme cold.

MIDDLESEX v SOMERSET
At Lord's, August 20, 22, 23, 1983. An electric storm on the second afternoon transformed what until then had been an unremarkable encounter. Lashed by almost cyclonic winds, the rain fell with such intensity that in 20 minutes it not only flooded the ground but the Long Room also.

SOMERSET v HAMPSHIRE
At Taunton, August 31, September 1, 2, 1983. On the final day, gale-force winds led to the abandonment of the bails, and the large sightscreen at the River end was blown down and rendered useless.

DERBYSHIRE v NORTHAMPTONSHIRE
At Derby, April 27, 29, 30, 1985. Finney was awarded his county cap during an interruption because of snow on a bleak opening day after taking five of the first six Northamptonshire wickets to fall. Sleet and rain penetrated the covers, cutting out four hours of the second day.

WORCESTERSHIRE v SUSSEX (NatWest Bank Trophy semi-finals)
At Worcester, August 13, 14, 15, 1986. Worcestershire on the first day used a helicopter to help dry out their ground, under water earlier in the week.

SUSSEX v WARWICKSHIRE
At Hove, August 17, 18, 19, 1988. Asif Din retired ill with heatstroke, but after his return added 74 with Tedstone and dominated a stand of 55 in eight overs with Small.

BEDFORDSHIRE v WORCESTERSHIRE (NatWest Bank Trophy first round)
At Bedford, June 26, 1991. Play did not begin until 5.15pm, after an RAF helicopter had been hired to fan the pitch and Worcestershire had sent for more conventional drying aids from New Road.

DERBYSHIRE v LEICESTERSHIRE
At Ilkeston, August 4, 5, 6, 1992. At the Rutland ground, which was staging its first Championship match since 1980, second-placed Leicestershire went down to their second heavy defeat of the week. A sightscreen, which looked of pre-1980 vintage, blew down to end the opening session early.

LANCASHIRE v LEICESTERSHIRE
At Manchester, September 15, 16, 17, 19, 1994. For the second time in four weeks, play ended early because the sun sinking behind the bowler's arm at the Stretford end was shining into the batsmen's eyes. Old Trafford is unusual among first-class grounds in having wickets pitched roughly east to west, but experienced players and members could not remember such a problem occurring until this season.

TRANSVAAL v WESTERN PROVINCE (Castle Cup)
At Wanderers Stadium, Johannesburg, January 27, 28, 29, 30, 1995. Lightning stopped play after a bolt hit close to the stadium, causing players to dive to the ground during E. O. Simons's run-up.

NOTTINGHAMSHIRE v LANCASHIRE
At Nottingham, May 16, 17, 18, 20, 1996. On a chilly opening day, umpire Hampshire protected himself against the cold by wearing gloves and a tea-cosy.

DURHAM v WORCESTERSHIRE
At Chester-le-Street, April 13, 14, 15, 16, 1999. Durham, as usual, had asked to play their first match away from the chilly north-east. However, their first three were all at home, and the opening day was greeted by an inch of snow. Boon began his final season tossing up a snowball for the cameras.

A DIFFERENT KIND OF CENTURY   Philip Eden
Kent were not playing on Sunday August 10, 2003, the day when a new UK temperature record of 38.5°C (101.3°F) was established at Faversham, just ten miles from their Canterbury headquarters. Not that far away, though, Middlesex were entertaining Durham in a National League match at Lord's, and just after two o'clock in the afternoon the nearest weather-reporting stations at Clerkenwell and Hampstead recorded shade temperatures of 37.6°C (99.7°F) and 37.4°C (99.4°F) respectively. The temperature inside the ground at Lord's was probably fractionally higher, partly because it is more enclosed, and this may well have been the first time county cricketers in England have played in a ground where the shade temperature was over 100°F.

DERBYSHIRE v LANCASHIRE (Twenty20 Cup)
At Derby, June 27, 2006. Lord's refused to sanction a request from Derbyshire that – if the setting sun caused problems – bowlers would temporarily abandon the Scoreboard (western) end. Considerately, the sun did not appear.

MCC v NOTTINGHAMSHIRE
At Abu Dhabi, March 27, 28, 29, 2011. As Fletcher ran in to bowl on a windy second day, he was forced to pull up, eyes burning, when a mini-sandstorm blew directly into his path from the surrounding desert.

SUSSEX v WARWICKSHIRE
At Hove, April 26, 27, 28, 29, 2012. The Sussex groundstaff spent much of the abandoned fourth day repairing the Sea end sightscreen, which blew over when the steel rope and three of the six posts tethering it to the ground were uprooted during overnight gale-force winds. On the third day the ground was flooded, and the flattened sightscreen was being pecked by sodden seagulls.

YORKSHIRE v LEICESTERSHIRE
At Scarborough, May 2, 3, 4, 5, 2012. North Marine Road is probably the only ground in the world that could attract daily four-figure crowds in temperatures hovering around 6°C. In cruel wind, two spectators of indeterminate gender even watched from their sleeping bags.

SUSSEX v SURREY
At Horsham, June 6, 7, 8, 9, 2012. At one point on the gusty third day, an advertising hoarding blew 40 yards into the middle, causing a terrified Dernbach to run for cover.

WHAT'S IN A NAME?

MCC AND GROUND v YORKSHIRE

At Lord's, May 14, 15, 16, 1900. The credit of the triumph – the solitary defeat sustained by the Yorkshiremen throughout the season – was due in the first place to Carpenter, Warner and C. O. H. Sewell (playing under the assumed name of "C. L. Lewes").

GREAT-GRANDSON OF AN IRISH CHIEFTAIN

JOHN ELICIUS BENEDICT BERNARD PLACID QUIRK CARRINGTON DWYER – always referred to as E. B. Dwyer – died on October 19, 1912, at Crewe, where he had been engaged during the season. He was born on May 3, 1876, at Sydney (New South Wales), where all his early cricket was played. On P. F. Warner's suggestion he came to England in the spring of 1904, and early that year, whilst engaged temporarily at Lord's, came under the notice of C. B. Fry, who persuaded him to qualify for Sussex. Although having good pace, he was an unequal bowler, but deadly on his day. In 1906 he took nine wickets in an innings for 35 runs against Derbyshire, at Brighton, and 16 for 100 – the first time for 80 years so many had been obtained by a bowler for Sussex in a match – v Notts. on the same ground.

Dwyer was a great-grandson of Michael Dwyer, the Wicklow chieftain, who was one of the boldest leaders in the Irish insurrection of 1798. He held out for five years in the Wicklow mountains and was exiled in 1804 to Australia, where he died in 1826.

LANCASHIRE 1923

President — Mr O. P. Lancashire.

SUSSEX 1936

President — Mr A. F. Somerset, DL, JP.

WARWICKSHIRE v SUSSEX

At Birmingham, May 17, 19, 20, 1924.
SUSSEX BOWLING (Second Innings)
Watson 1–0–4–0
Holmes 0.1–0–2–0

MIDDLESEX v SOMERSET

At Lord's, June 14, 15, 16, 1933.
MIDDLESEX (First Innings)
H. W. Lee c F. S. Lee b J. W. Lee 82
All three were brothers!

OBITUARY 1943

So much doubt has prevailed as to the relationship of the six Tyldesleys who played for Lancashire that it is opportune to emphasise that the brothers John Thomas, who died in 1930, and Ernest, both famous batsmen and England Test players, belonged to a Worsley family and were not related to the four Westhoughton professionals; these were:

William K. Tyldesley, a batsman. Killed in 1918 during the last war while a lieutenant in the North Lancashire Regiment. Obituary 1919 *Wisden*.

James Darbyshire Tyldesley, a fast bowler and good batsman; played first for Lancashire in 1910, died in 1923. Obituary 1924 *Wisden*.

Harry Tyldesley, died in 1935. Played first for the county in 1914, at Derby on July 11, when two pairs of Tyldesley brothers figured in the Lancashire eleven; that season the Lancashire averages included five Tyldesleys. Harry toured with A. C. MacLaren's team in the winter of 1922 and headed the bowling averages both in Australia and New Zealand. Obituary 1936 *Wisden*.

Richard Tyldesley, the youngest, the subject of this obituary.

NORTHAMPTONSHIRE 1947

C. B. Clarke, the West Indies Test leg-break and googly exponent, excelled when he took seven Yorkshire first-innings wickets at Northampton.

The end of the summer brought the announcement that E. W. Clark intended to retire. Late in the summer R. W. Clarke, also left-arm fast, showed promise as a likely successor.

Childs-Clarke, the captain, played several characteristically gallant innings when situations were most awkward.

This led to such "Clerical" scorecard entries as:

Leicestershire
J. E. Walsh c Childs-Clarke b C. B. Clarke 15
P. Corrall c R. Clarke b C. B. Clarke 2

Nottinghamshire
R. T. Simpson c R. W. Clarke b C. B. Clarke 8
J. Hardstaff c Childs-Clarke b R. W. Clarke 47

AUSTRALIA v ENGLAND (First Test Match)
At Perth, December 14, 15, 16, 18, 19, 1979.
Australia – Second Innings
D. K. Lillee c Willey b Dilley 19

OBITUARIES 1993
GARLAND-WELLS, HERBERT MONTANDON. In the war his name was informally used as a code word in North Africa: Garland-Wells = Monty = Montgomery. This was more impenetrable to the Germans than the most complicated cipher.

WARWICKSHIRE v GLAMORGAN
At Birmingham, July 30, 31, August 1, 2, 1998. Both sides fielded a Michael J. Powell.

SOMERSET v YORKSHIRE
At Bath, June 13, 14, 15, 16, 2001. It was an auspicious game for players named Matthew James Wood: Somerset's – a 20-year-old Devonian making his debut – had every reason to be pleased with 71, while Yorkshire's hit his first century in over a year.

MIDDLESEX 2002
Nick Compton scored a stylish and entertaining 86 not out against Lancashire at the Denis Compton Oval, Shenley – the ground named after his illustrious grandfather. With Hutton – the grandson of Len – already on the staff, Middlesex added another big name when they signed Mali Richards, son of Sir Viv, on a part-time contract.

RANJITH TO HIS FRIENDS   Matthew Engel, Notes by the Editor, 2004
It is possible that not every *Wisden* reader will make it through to page 1415, the Sri Lankan domestic scores. This seems a pity, because you might be missing the following:

At FTZ Sports Complex, Katunayake, February 14, 15.
Kurunegala Youth won by an innings and four runs. Toss: Kurunegala Youth.
Antonians 100 (A. R. R. A. P. W. R. R. K. B. Amunugama 4-39) **and 121** (A. R. R. A. P. W. R. R. K. B. Amunugama 4-34, A. W. Ekanayake 4-18); **Kurunegala Youth 225** (K. G. S. Sirisoma 5-40).

The successful bowler in this game, as we all know, is Amunugama Rajapakse Rajakaruna Abeykoon Panditha Wasalamudiyanse Ralahamilage Ranjith Krishantha Bandara Amunugama – Ranjith to his friends, apparently. With ten initials, he has now established a commanding lead over his nearest rival, A. K. T. D. G. L. A. S. de Silva and the leading international player W. P. U. J. C. Vaas. This is an area where England used to fancy it could hold its own with any other cricketing country, but such stars of yesteryear as J. W. H. T. Douglas, M. E. J. C. Norman and R. I. H. B. Dyer have long been eclipsed by these ex-colonial upstarts. Only the Essex newcomer A. G. A. M. McCoubrey carries on the tradition – and he's Irish.

Amunugama is not a newcomer. As far back as 1990-91 *Wisden* reported him taking match figures of 12 for 91 for Tamil Union against Sebastianites. But in those days he was plain old R. K. B. Amunugama.

AUCKLAND v HAMPSHIRE (Champions League)
At Centurion, October 10, 2012. Both sides fielded a Michael David Bates, but the Hampshire wicketkeeper – down at No. 11 – did not get a chance to face the New Zealand left-arm seamer.

Index

Page numbers in **bold** refer to illustrations.

First-class cricketers are listed by surname and initials.

2004 578, 709, 979;
v Northamptonshire, 2011 997;
v Nottinghamshire, 1887 42;
v Nottinghamshire, 1891 1003;
v Nottinghamshire, 1925 990;
v Nottinghamshire, 1948 730–1;
v Nottinghamshire, 1957 723;
v Nottinghamshire, 1997 766;
v Nottinghamshire, 2003 979; v Old
England, 1947 276; v Oxford
University, 1909 1014; v Oxford
University, 1939 1004; v Somerset,
1891 737–8; v Somerset, 1925 756–7;
v Sussex, 1972 763; v Sussex, 1978
647; v Sussex, 1979 987–8; v Sussex,
1980 1008; v Sussex, 2005 1002;
v Sussex, 2012 1020; v Warwickshire,
1919 986; v Warwickshire, 1953
759–60; v Warwickshire, 1970 786–7;
v Yorkshire, 1899 752; v Yorkshire,
1906 753–4; v Yorkshire, 1931 990;
v Yorkshire, 1951 815–6; v Yorkshire,
1952 991; v Yorkshire, 1955 379, 816;
v Yorkshire, 1956 578; v Yorkshire,
1973 819; v Yorkshire, 2002 976
Surridge, W. S. 186, 759, 760,
936–7
Sussex County Cricket Club 768; 1889
season 769; 1893 season 770; 1894
season 771; 1901 season 771–2; 1908
season 772; 1923 season 773; 1925
season 773; 1936 season president
1021; 1937 season 774; 1946 season
774; 1953 season 774–5; 1963 Gillette
Cup 775–6; 1971 season 776; 1978
season 777–8; 1979 season 778–9;
1983 season 988; 2002 season 779;
2007 season 780; Central Ground 778;
County Ground 768; financial
position, 1936 773–4; v Australia,
1972 777; v Derbyshire, 1988 704;
v Durham, 2001 1008; v Essex, 1991
718; v Essex, 1997 978; v Essex, 2008
611–2; v Glamorgan, 1957 430;
v Glamorgan, 1968 776; v Glamorgan,
1992 1001; v Glamorgan, 2000 622–3;
v Gloucestershire, 1893 579, 770;
v Gloucestershire, 1894 629;

v Gloucestershire, 1903 630–1;
v Gloucestershire, 1963 515;
v Gloucestershire, 1995 1001;
v Gloucestershire, 2012 1010;
v Hampshire, 1908 772; v Hampshire,
1969 587; v Hampshire, 1975 650;
v Kent, 1873 828–9; v Kent, 1882 23;
v Kent, 1946 1007; v Kent, 1973 664;
v Kent, 1984 778; v Lancashire, 1919
994; v Leicestershire, 1962 483;
v Middlesex, 1893 993; v Middlesex,
1894 695; v Middlesex, 1963 509;
v Northamptonshire, 1930 773;
v Nottinghamshire, 1873 768–9;
v Nottinghamshire, 1911 727;
v Nottinghamshire, 1951 982;
v Nottinghamshire, 1967 995;
v Nottinghamshire, 2003 1009;
v Somerset, 1896 1003; v Somerset,
1919 983–4; v Somerset, 1930 179;
v Somerset, 2012 960; v Surrey, 1962
775; v Surrey, 1972 763; v Surrey,
1978 647; v Surrey, 1979 987–8;
v Surrey, 1980 1008; v Surrey, 2012
1020; v Warwickshire, 1924 1021;
v Warwickshire, 1988 1019;
v Warwickshire, 1990 711;
v Warwickshire, 1993 788–9;
v Warwickshire, 2009 997;
v Warwickshire, 2012 1020;
v Worcestershire, 1986 1019;
v Worcestershire, 1998 1008;
v Yorkshire, 1896 771; v Yorkshire,
1957 425; v Yorkshire, 1959 817;
v Yorkshire, 1985 685; v Yorkshire,
2002 822; v Yorkshire, 2004 976;
v Yorkshire, 2006 873; v Yorkshire,
2011 924
Susskind, M. J. 218
Sutcliffe, B. 240, 260
Sutcliffe, H. 70, 109, 166–7, 187, 218,
219, 222, 361–2, 364, 364–5, 366,
811–2, 813, 814, 815, 937–8, 962, **963**,
964–5, 967, 972
Sutcliffe, I. J. 140
Suttle, K. G. 776
Sutton, L. D. 806
Swann, A.J. 1005